THE NORTON SHAKESPEARE

BASED ON THE OXFORD EDITION

Tragedies

*The original Oxford Text on which this
edition is based was prepared by*

Stanley Wells
Gary Taylor
General Editors

John Jowett
William Montgomery

THE NORTON SHAKESPEARE

BASED ON THE OXFORD EDITION

Tragedies

Stephen Greenblatt, *General Editor*
HARVARD UNIVERSITY

Walter Cohen
CORNELL UNIVERSITY

Jean E. Howard
COLUMBIA UNIVERSITY

Katharine Eisaman Maus
UNIVERSITY OF VIRGINIA

With an essay on the Shakespearean stage
by Andrew Gurr

W · W · NORTON & COMPANY · NEW YORK · LONDON

The text of this book is composed in Electra with the display set in Centaur.
Composition by Binghamton Valley Composition.
Manufacturing by R. R. Donnelley & Sons.
Book design by Antonina Krass.

The Library of Congress has cataloged the one-volume edition as follows:
Shakespeare, William, 1564–1616.
The Norton Shakespeare / Stephen Greenblatt, general editor ;
Walter Cohen, Jean E. Howard, Katharine Eisaman Maus [editors] ;
with an essay on the Shakespearean stage by Andrew Gurr.
p.   cm.
"Based on the Oxford edition."
Includes bibliographical references and index.

ISBN 0-393-97087-6. — ISBN 0-393-04107-7

I. Greenblatt, Stephen Jay.   II. Cohen, Walter, 1949–   .
III. Howard, Jean E. (Jean Elizabeth), 1948–   .   IV. Maus,
Katharine Eisaman, 1955–   .   V. Title.
PR2754.G74   1997
822.3'3—DC21

97-7083
CIP
Rev.

Tragedies: ISBN 0-393-97672-6 (pbk.)

W. W. Norton & Company, Inc., 500 Fifth Avenue, New York, N.Y. 10110
www.wwnorton.com

W. W. Norton & Company Ltd., 10 Coptic Street, London WC1A 1PU

1 2 3 4 5 6 7 8 9 0

Contents

General Introduction

STEPHEN GREENBLATT

Tragedies

Appendices

Preface

Since Shakespeare's principal medium, the drama, was thoroughly collaborative, it seems appropriate that this edition of his works is itself the result of a sustained collaboration. Two lists of editors' names on the title-page spread hint at the collaboration that has brought to fruition *The Norton Shakespeare*. But the title page does not tell the full history of this project. The text on which *The Norton Shakespeare* is based was published in both modern-spelling and original-spelling versions by Oxford University Press, in 1986. Under the general editorship of Stanley Wells and Gary Taylor, the Oxford text was a thorough rethinking of the entire body of Shakespeare's works, the most far-reaching and innovative revision of the traditional canon in centuries. When many classroom instructors who wanted to introduce their students to the works of Shakespeare through a modern text expressed a need for the pedagogical apparatus they have come to expect in an edition oriented toward students, Norton negotiated with Oxford to assemble an editorial team of its own to prepare the necessary teaching materials around the existing Oxford text. Hence ensued a collaboration of two publishers and two editorial teams.

To what extent is this the *Norton Shakespeare* and to what extent the Oxford text? Since the Norton contributions appear here for the first time, the many pages that follow will provide the answer to the first part of the question. Introductions (both the General Introduction and those to individual plays and poems), footnotes, glosses, bibliographies, genealogies, annals, documents, and illustrations have all been the responsibility of the Norton team. We also asked Andrew Gurr of the University of Reading to contribute to this edition an essay on the London theater in Shakespeare's time, and we asked Donald W. Foster of Vassar College to introduce, edit, and gloss *A Funeral Elegy*, a poem, included here in an appendix, that raises important questions about the attribution of works to Shakespeare.

   The textual notes and variants derive for the most part from the work of the Oxford team, especially as represented in *William Shakespeare: A Textual Companion* (Oxford University Press, 1987), a remarkably comprehensive explanation of editorial decisions that is herewith strongly recommended to instructors as a valuable companion to this volume. Some of the annotations spring from the never-published commentaries of the Oxford team, who have graciously allowed the Norton editors full use of them.

   The Oxford text is widely available and already well-known to scholars. A few words here may help clarify the extent of our fidelity to that text and the nature of the collaboration that has brought about this volume. The Oxford editors have profited from the massive and sustained attention accorded their edition by Shakespeare scholars across the globe, and of course they have continued to participate actively in the ongoing scholarly discussion about the nature of Shakespeare's text. In the reprintings of the Oxford volumes and in various articles over the past years, the Oxford editors have made a number of refinements of the edition they originally published. Such changes have been incorporated silently here. A small number of other changes made by the Norton team, however, were not part of the Oxford editors' design and were only accepted by them after we reached, through lengthy consultation, a mutual understanding about the nature, purpose, and intended audience of this volume. In all such changes, our main concern was for the classroom; we wished to make fully and clearly available the scholarly innovation and freshness of the Oxford text, while at the same time making certain that this was a superbly useful teaching text. It is a pleasure here to record, on behalf of the Norton team, our gratitude for the personal and professional generosity of the Oxford editors in offering advice and entertaining arguments in our common goal of providing the best student Shakespeare for our times. The Norton changes to the Oxford text are various, but in only a few instances are they major. The following brief notes are sufficient to summarize all of these changes, which are also indicated in appropriate play introductions, footnotes, or textual notes.

1. The Oxford editors, along with other scholars, have strenuously argued—in both the Oxford text and elsewhere—that the now-familiar text of *King Lear*, so nearly omnipresent in our classrooms as to seem unquestionably authoritative but in reality dating from the work of Alexander Pope (1723) and Lewis Theobald (1733), represents a wrong-headed conflation of two distinct versions of the play: Shakespeare's original creation as printed in the 1608 Quarto and his substantial revision as printed in the First Folio (1623). The Oxford text, therefore, prints both *The History of King Lear* and *The Tragedy of King Lear*. Norton follows suit, but where Oxford presents these two texts sequentially, we print them on facing pages. While each version may be read independently, and to ensure this we have provided glosses and footnotes for each, the substantial points of difference between the two are immediately apparent and available for comparison. But even many who agree with the scholarly argument for the two texts of *Lear* nevertheless favor making available a conflated text, the text on which innumerable performances of the play have been based and on which a huge body of literary criticism has been written. With the reluctant acquiescence, therefore, of the Oxford editors, we have included a conflated *Lear*, a text that has no part in the Oxford canon and that has been edited by Barbara K. Lewalski of Harvard University rather than by Gary Taylor, the editor of the Oxford *Lears*.

The Norton Shakespeare, then, includes three separate texts of *King Lear*. The reader can compare them, understand the role of editors in constructing the texts we now call Shakespeare's, explore in considerable detail the kinds of decisions that playwrights, editors, and printers make and remake, witness first-hand the historical transformation of what might at first glance seem fixed and unchanging. *The Norton Shakespeare* offers extraordinary access to this supremely brilliant, difficult, compelling play.

2. *Hamlet* (along with several other plays, including *Richard II*, *Troilus and Cressida*, and *Othello*) offers similar grounds for objections to the traditional conflation, but both the economics of publishing and the realities of bookbinding—not to mention our recognition of the limited time in the typical undergraduate syllabus—preclude our offering three (or even four) *Hamlets* to match three *Lears*.

The Oxford text of *Hamlet* was based upon the Folio text, with an appended list of Additional Passages from the Second Quarto (Q2). These additional readings total more than two hundred lines, a significant number, among which are lines that have come to seem very much part of the play as widely received, even if we may doubt that they belong with all the others in any single one of Shakespeare's *Hamlets*. The Norton team, while following the Oxford text, has moved the Q2 passages from the appendix to the body of the play. But in doing so, we have not wanted once again to produce a conflated text. We have therefore indented the Q2 passages, printed them in a different typeface, and numbered them in such a way as to make clear their provenance. Those who wish to read the Folio version of *Hamlet* can thus simply skip over the indented Q2 passages, while at the same time it is possible for readers to see clearly the place that the Q2 passages occupy. We have adopted a similar strategy with several other plays: passages printed in Oxford in appendices are generally printed here in the play texts, though clearly demarcated and not conflated. In the case of *The Taming of the Shrew* and the related quarto text, *The Taming of a Shrew*, however, we have followed Oxford's procedure and left the quarto passages in an appendix, since we believe the texts reflect two distinct plays rather than a revision of one. We have similarly reproduced Oxford's brief appendices to A *Midsummer Night's Dream* and *Henry V*, enabling readers to consider alternative revisions of certain passages.

3. For reasons understood by every Shakespearean (and rehearsed at some length in this volume), the Oxford editors chose to restore the name "Sir John Oldcastle" to the character much better known as Falstaff in *1 Henry IV*. (They made comparable changes in the names of the characters known as Bardolph and Peto.) But for reasons understood by everyone who has presented this play to undergraduates or sampled the centuries of enthusiastic criticism, the Norton editors, with the Oxford editors' gracious agreement, have for this classroom edition opted for the familiar name "Falstaff " (and those of his boon companions), properly noting the change and its significance in the play's introduction.

4. The Oxford editors chose not to differentiate between those stage directions that appeared in the early editions up to and including the Folio and those that have been added by subsequent editors. Instead, in *A Textual Companion* they include separate lists of the original stage directions. These lists are not readily available to readers of the Norton text, whose editors opted instead to bracket all stage directions that derive from editions published after the Folio. Readers can thus easily see which stage directions derive from texts that may bear at least some relation to performances in Shakespeare's time, if not to Shakespeare's own authorship. The Norton policy is more fully explained in the General Introduction.

It has long been the dream of the publisher, W.W. Norton, to bring out a Shakespeare edition. The task proved to be a complex one, with many players. The initial efforts of the late John Benedict at Norton were followed, with the crucial encouragement of the firm's chairman, Donald S. Lamm, by the efforts of Barry Wade, who brought together with patience, tact, and goodwill the scholars who eventually carried the project to fruition. To our deep sadness and regret, Barry Wade did not live to see the completion of the work to which he devoted so much energy. He was succeeded in overseeing the project by Julia Reidhead, whose calm intelligence, common sense, and steady focus have been essential in enabling us to reach the end of the long road. We were blessed with the exceptionally thoughtful and scrupulous developmental editing of Marian Johnson and with the assistance of an extraordinary group of Norton staffers: head manuscript editor Susan Gaustad, who was assisted by copyeditor Alice Falk and project editor Kurt Wildermuth; editorial assistant Tara Parmiter, who, among many other things, coordinated the art program; production manager Diane O'Connor; in-house editor of the *Norton Shakespeare Workshop CD-ROM* Anna Karvellas; and proofreaders Carol Walker and Rich Rivellese.

The *Norton Shakespeare* editors have, in addition, had the valuable, indeed indispensable support of a host of undergraduate and graduate research assistants, colleagues, friends, and family. Even a partial listing of those to whom we owe our heartfelt thanks is very long, but we are all fortunate enough to live in congenial and supportive environments, and the edition has been part of our lives for a long time. We owe special thanks for sustained dedication and learning to our principal research assistants: Pat Cahill, Jody Greene, Nate Johnson, Jesse Liu, Joseph Nugent, Beth Quitslund, Henry Turner, and Michael Witmore. Particular thanks are due to Noah Heringman for his work on the texts assembled in the documents section and for the prefatory notes and comments on those texts; to Philip Schwyzer for preparing the genealogies and the glossary and for conceiving and preparing the Shakespearean Chronicle; and to Young Jean Lee for a variety of complex editorial tasks. In addition, we are deeply grateful to Jim, Kate, and Caleb Baker, Gen Beckman, Aimée Boutin, Dan Brayton, Laura Brown, Francesca Coppelli, Adam Feldman, Margaret Ferguson, William Flesch, Elizabeth Gardner, Ellen Greenblatt, Josh and Aaron Greenblatt, Mark Hazard, David Kastan, Dennis Kezar, Shawn Kirschner, Jeffrey Knapp, Baty Landis, Wendy Lesser, Laurie Maguire, Fred Everett Maus, Stephen

Orgel, Phyllis Rackin, James Shapiro, Debora Shuger, Melissa Wiley Stickney, Ramie Targoff, Elda Tsou, and the staff of the Wissenschaftskolleg zu Berlin. All of these companions, and many more besides, have helped us find in this long collective enterprise what the Dedicatory Epistle to the First Folio promises to its readers: delight. We make the same promise to the readers of our edition and invite them to continue the great Shakespearean collaboration.

Stephen Greenblatt
Walter Cohen
Jean E. Howard
Katharine Eisaman Maus

Acknowledgments

Among our many critics, advisers, and friends, the following were of special help in providing critiques of particular plays or of the project as a whole: Barry Adams (Cornell University), Richard Adams (California State University, Sacramento), Denise Albanes (George Mason University), Mark Anderson (SUNY Brockport), Herman Asarnow (University of Portland), John H. Astington (Erindale, University of Toronto), Jonathan Baldo (University of Rochester), Jonathan Bate, Leonard Barkan (New York University), John Baxter (Dalhousie University), D. A. Beecher (Carleton University), S. Berg (University of Alberta), Paula Berggren (CUNY), Edward Berry (University of Victoria), Walter Blanco (Lehman, CUNY), Thomas L. Blanton (Central Washington University), Al Braunmuller (UCLA), Stephen Brown (Trent University), Douglas Bruster (University of Chicago), Kate Buckley (Pontifical College, Josephinum), Joseph Candido (University of Arkansas), William Carroll (Boston University), Thomas Cartelli (Muhlenberg College), Sheila Cavanaugh (Emory University), Susan Cerasano (Colgate University), Gerald N. Chapman (University of Denver), Lois Chapman (South Suburban College), Maurice Charney (Rutgers University), Thomas Clayton (University of Minnesota), Peter J. Connelly (Grinnell College), Barbara Correll (Cornell University), Jonathan Crewe (Dartmouth College), Earl Dachslager (University of Houston), Roger Deakins (New York University), Kenneth L. Deal (Huntingdon College), Margreta de Grazia (University of Pennsylvania), H. Delisle (Bridgewater State University), Alan Dessen (University of North Carolina, Chapel Hill), Nirmal Singh Dhesi (Sonoma State University), William R. Drennan (University of Wisconsin, Center Baraboo), Heather Dubrow (University of Wisconsin), Sara Eaton (North Central College), Katherine Eggert (University of Colorado), Charles R. Forker (Indiana University), Donald Foster (Vassar College), Michael Frachmann (California State University, Bakersfield), Lisa Freinkel (University of Oregon), Charles Frey (University of Washington), Lloyd G. Gibbs (University of South Carolina), Dominique Goy-Blanquet (University of Amiens), Hugh Grady (Beaver College), Anthony Graham-White (University of Illinois, Chicago), Peter Greenfield (University of Puget Sound), R. Chris Hassel Jr. (Vanderbilt University), David Haley (University of Minnesota), Jay Halio (University of Delaware), Richard Helgerson (University of California, Santa Barbara), Richard Hillman (York University), Barbara Hodgdon (Drake University), Peter Holland (Cambridge University), Trevor Howard-Hill (University of South Carolina), Clark Hulse (University of Illinois, Chicago), Gabriele Bernhard Jackson (Temple University), Henry D. Janzen (University of Windsor), Barbara Kachur (University of Missouri, St. Louis), Coppelia Kahn (Brown University), Michael H. Keefer (Université Sainte Anne), Robert Knapp (Reed College), Mary Kramer (University of Lowell), James Lake (Louisiana State University, Shreveport), Ian Lancashire (New College, University of Toronto), Judiana Lawrence (St. John Fisher College), Alexander Leggatt (University College, University of Toronto), Ted Leinwand (University of Maryland, College Park), Carol Leventen (Adrian College), Murray J. Levith (Skidmore College), Barbara Lewalski (Harvard University), Cynthia Lewis (Davidson College), Arthur Little (UCLA), M. Loyola (University of Saskatchewan), J. M. Lyon (University of Bristol), Joyce MacDonald (University of Kentucky), Irene R. Makaryk (University of Ottawa), Eric Mallin (University of Texas, Austin), Leah Marcus (University of Texas, Austin), Arthur Marotti (Wayne State University), Cynthia Marshall (Rhodes College), Steven Marx (Cal Poly State University, San Luis Obispo), Margaret Maurer (Colgate University), M. A. McDonald (Belmont College), Nan Morrison (College of Charleston), Richard E. Morton (McMaster University), Steven Mullaney (University of Michigan), Ronnie Mulryne (University of Warwick), Carol Thomas Neely

(University of Illinois), Malcolm A. Nelson (SUNY Fredonia), Karen Newman (Brown University), M. Noble (Defiance College), John O'Connor (George Mason University), Gail Paster (George Washington University), Donald Peet (Indiana University), Lois Potter (University of Delaware), Phyllis Rackin (University of Pennsylvania), Constance Relihan (Auburn University), Neil Rhodes (University of St. Andrews), Jeremy Richard (University of Connecticut, Stamford), Gilbert Robinson (San Francisco State University), D. S. Rodes (UCLA), Mark Rose (University of California, Santa Barbara), David Rosen (University of Maine, Machias), Kiernan Ryan (Cambridge University), Peter Saccio (Dartmouth College), Nadine S. St. Louis (University of Wisconsin, Eau Claire), Naheeb Shaheen (Memphis State University), J. W. Shaw (University of Massachusetts), William P. Shaw (LeMoyne College), John W. Sider (Westmont College), Jim Siemon (Boston University), W. W. E. Slights (University of Saskatchewan), Molly Smith (Aberdeen University), Edward V. Stackpoole (University of San Francisco), Lisa Starks (East Texas State University), Michael J. Taylor (University of New Brunswick), Richard C. Tobias (University of Pittsburgh), Robert K. Turner (University of Wisconsin), Virginia Mason Vaughan (Clark University), Wendy Wall (Northwestern University), Robert N. Watson (UCLA), Valerie Wayne (University of Hawaii, Manoa), Herbert S. Weil, Jr. (University of Manitoba), Barry Weller (University of Utah), Paul Werstine (King's College), R. L. Widmann (University of Colorado, Boulder), Inga Wiehl (Yakina Valley Community College), Douglas B. Wilson (University of Denver).

Mr. WILLIAM
SHAKESPEARES
COMEDIES,
HISTORIES, &
TRAGEDIES.

Published according to the True Originall Copies.

Martin Droeshout sculpsit London.

LONDON
Printed by Isaac Iaggard, and Ed. Blount. 1623.

Engraving of Shakespeare by Martin Droeshout. Title page of the 1623 First Folio. (The Documents appendix, below, reproduces the front matter to the Folio, including Ben Jonson's poem "To the Reader.")

General Introduction
by
STEPHEN GREENBLATT

"He was not of an age, but for all time!"

The celebration of Shakespeare's genius, eloquently initiated by his friend and rival Ben Jonson, has over the centuries become an institutionalized rite of civility. The person who does not love Shakespeare has made, the rite implies, an incomplete adjustment not simply to a particular culture—English culture of the late sixteenth and early seventeenth centuries—but to "culture" as a whole, the dense network of constraints and entitlements, dreams and practices that links us to nature. Indeed, so absolute is Shakespeare's achievement that he has himself come to seem like great creating nature: the common bond of humankind, the principle of hope, the symbol of the imagination's power to transcend time-bound beliefs and assumptions, peculiar historical circumstances, and specific artistic conventions.

The near-worship Shakespeare inspires is one of the salient facts about his art. But we must at the same time acknowledge that this art is the product of peculiar historical circumstances and specific conventions, four centuries distant from our own. The acknowledgment is important because Shakespeare the working dramatist did not typically lay claim to the transcendent, visionary truths attributed to him by his most fervent admirers; his characters more modestly say, in the words of the magician Prospero, that their project was "to please" (*The Tempest*, Epilogue, line 13). The starting point, and perhaps the ending point as well, in any encounter with Shakespeare is simply to enjoy him, to savor his imaginative richness, to take pleasure in his infinite delight in language.

"If then you do not like him," Shakespeare's first editors wrote in 1623, "surely you are in some manifest danger not to understand him." Over the years, accommodations have been devised to make liking Shakespeare easier for everyone. When the stage sank to melodrama and light opera, Shakespeare—in suitably revised texts—was there. When the populace had a craving for hippodrama, plays performed entirely on horseback, *Hamlet* was dutifully rewritten and mounted. When audiences went mad for realism, live frogs croaked in productions of *A Midsummer Night's Dream*. When the stage was stripped bare and given over to stark exhibitions of sadistic cruelty, Shakespeare was our contemporary. And when the theater itself had lost some of its cultural centrality, Shakespeare moved effortlessly to Hollywood and the sound stages of the BBC.

This virtually universal appeal is one of the most astonishing features of the Shakespeare phenomenon: plays that were performed before glittering courts thrive in junior high school auditoriums; enemies set on destroying one another laugh at the same jokes and weep at the same catastrophes; some of the richest and most complex English verse ever written migrates with spectacular success into German and Italian, Hindi, Swahili, and Japanese. Is there a single, stable, continuous object that underlies all of these migrations and metamorphoses? Certainly not. The fantastic diffusion and long life of Shakespeare's works depends on their extraordinary malleability, their protean capacity to elude definition and escape secure possession. At the same time, they are not without identifiable shared features: across centuries and continents, family resemblances link many of the wildly diverse manifestations of plays such as *Romeo and Juliet*, *Hamlet*, and *Twelfth Night*. And if there is no clear limit or end point, there is a reasonably clear beginning, the

1

England of the late sixteenth and early seventeenth centuries, when the plays and poems collected in this volume made their first appearance.

An art virtually without end or limit but with an identifiable, localized, historical origin: Shakespeare's achievement defies the facile opposition between transcendent and time-bound. It is not necessary to choose between an account of Shakespeare as the scion of a particular culture and an account of him as a universal genius who created works that continually renew themselves across national and generational boundaries. On the contrary: crucial clues to understanding his art's remarkable power to soar beyond its originary time and place lie in the very soil from which that art sprang.

Shakespeare's World

Life and Death

Life expectation at birth in early modern England was exceedingly low by our standards: under thirty years old, compared with over seventy today. Infant mortality rates were extraordinarily high, and it is estimated that in the poorer parishes of London only about half the children survived to the age of fifteen, while the children of aristocrats fared only a little better. In such circumstances, some parents must have developed a certain detachment—one of Shakespeare's contemporaries writes of losing "some three or four children"—but there are many expressions of intense grief, so that we cannot assume that the frequency of death hardened people to loss or made it routine.

Still, the spectacle of death, along with that other great threshold experience, birth, must have been far more familiar to Shakespeare and his contemporaries than to ourselves. There was no equivalent in early modern England to our hospitals, and most births and deaths occurred at home. Physical means for the alleviation of pain and suffering were extremely limited—alcohol might dull the terror, but it was hardly an effective anesthetic—and medical treatment was generally both expensive and worthless, more likely to intensify suffering than to lead to a cure. This was a world without a concept of antiseptics, with little actual understanding of disease, with few effective ways of treating earaches or venereal disease, let alone the more terrible instances of what Shakespeare calls "the thousand natural shocks that flesh is heir to."

The worst of these shocks was the bubonic plague, which repeatedly ravaged England, and particularly English towns, until the third quarter of the seventeenth century. The plague was terrifyingly sudden in its onset, rapid in its spread, and almost invariably lethal. Physicians were helpless in the face of the epidemic, though they prescribed amulets, preservatives, and sweet-smelling substances (on the theory that the plague was carried by

Bill recording plague deaths in London, 1609.

noxious vapors). In the plague-ridden year of 1564, the year of Shakespeare's birth, some 254 people died in Stratford-upon-Avon, out of a total population of 800. The year before, some 20,000 Londoners are thought to have died; in 1593, almost 15,000; in 1603, 36,000, or over a sixth of the city's inhabitants. The social effects of these horrible visitations were severe: looting, violence, and despair, along with an intensification of the age's perennial poverty, unemployment, and food shortages. The London plague regulations of 1583, reissued with modifications in later epidemics, ordered that the infected and their households should be locked in their homes for a month; that the streets should be kept clean; that vagrants should be expelled; and that funerals and plays should be restricted or banned entirely.

The plague, then, had a direct and immediate impact on Shakespeare's own profession. City officials kept records of the weekly number of plague deaths; when these surpassed a certain number, the theaters were peremptorily closed. The basic idea was not only to prevent contagion but also to avoid making an angry God still angrier with the spectacle of idleness. While restricting public assemblies may in fact have slowed the epidemic, other public policies in times of plague, such as killing the cats and dogs, may have made matters worse (since the disease was spread not by these animals but by the fleas that bred on the black rats that infested the poorer neighborhoods). Moreover, the playing companies, driven out of London by the closing of the theaters, may have carried plague to the provincial towns.

Even in good times, when the plague was dormant and the weather favorable for farming, the food supply in England was precarious. A few successive bad harvests, such as occurred in the mid-1590s, could cause serious hardship, even starvation. Not surprisingly, the poor bore the brunt of the burden: inflation, low wages, and rent increases left large numbers of people with very little cushion against disaster. Further, at its best, the diet of most people seems to have been seriously deficient. The lower classes then, as throughout most of history, subsisted on one or two foodstuffs, usually low in protein. The upper classes disdained green vegetables and milk and gorged themselves on meat. Illnesses that we now trace to vitamin deficiencies were rampant. Some but not much relief from pain was provided by the beer that Elizabethans, including children, drank almost incessantly. (Home brewing aside, enough beer was sold in England for every man, woman, and child to have consumed forty gallons a year.)

Wealth

Despite rampant disease, the population of England in Shakespeare's lifetime was steadily growing, from approximately 3,060,000 in 1564 to 4,060,000 in 1600 and 4,510,000 in 1616. Though the death rate was more than twice what it is in England today, the birthrate was almost three times the current figure. London's population in particular soared, from 60,000 in 1520 to 120,000 in 1550, 200,000 in 1600, and 375,000 a half-century later, making it the largest and fastest-growing city not only in England but in all of Europe. Every year in the first half of the seventeenth century, about 10,000 people migrated to London from other parts of England—wages in London tended to be around 50 percent higher than in the rest of the country—and it is estimated that one in eight English people lived in London at some point in their lives. The economic viability of Shakespeare's profession was closely linked to this extraordinary demographic boom: between 1567 and 1642, a theater historian has calculated, the London playhouses were paid close to 50 million visits.

As these visits to the theater indicate, in the capital city and elsewhere a substantial number of English men and women, despite hardships that were never very distant, had money to spend. After the disorder and dynastic wars of the fifteenth century, England in the sixteenth and early seventeenth centuries was for the most part a nation at peace, and with peace came a measure of enterprise and prosperity: the landowning classes busied themselves building great houses, planting orchards and hop gardens, draining marshlands, bringing untilled "wastes" under cultivation. The artisans and laborers who actually accomplished these tasks, though they were generally paid very little, often managed to accumulate something, as did the small freeholding farmers, the yeomen, who are repeatedly celebrated in the period as the backbone of English national independence and well-being. William Harrison's *Description of Britaine* (1577) lovingly itemizes the yeoman's precious possessions: "fair garnish of pewter on his cupboard, with so much more odd vessel going about the house, three or four featherbeds, so many coverlets and carpets of tapestry, a silver salt[cellar], a bowl for wine (if not a whole nest) and a dozen of spoons." There are comparable accounts of the hard-earned acquisitions of the city dwellers — masters and apprentices in small workshops, shipbuilders, wool merchants, cloth makers, chandlers, tradesmen, shopkeepers, along with lawyers, apothecaries, schoolteachers, scriveners, and the like — whose pennies from time to time enriched the coffers of the players.

The chief source of England's wealth in the sixteenth century was its textile industry, an industry that depended on a steady supply of wool. In *The Winter's Tale*, Shakespeare provides a richly comic portrayal of a rural sheepshearing festival, but the increasingly intensive production of wool had in reality its grim side. When a character in Thomas More's *Utopia* (1516) complains that "the sheep are eating the people," he is referring to the practice of enclosure: throughout the sixteenth and early seventeenth centuries, many acres of croplands once farmed in common by rural communities were enclosed with fences by wealthy landowners and turned into pasturage. The ensuing misery, displacement, and food shortages led to repeated riots, some of them violent and bloody, along with a series of government proclamations, but the process of enclosure was not reversed.

The economic stakes were high, and not only for the domestic market. In 1565, woolen cloth alone made up more than three-fourths of England's exports. (The remainder consisted mostly of other textiles and raw wool, with some trade in lead, tin, grain, and skins.) The Merchant Adventurers Company carried cloth to distant ports on the Baltic and Mediterranean, establishing links with Russia and Morocco (each took about 2 percent of London's cloth in 1597–98). English lead and tin, as well as fabrics, were sold in Tuscany and Turkey, and merchants found a market for Newcastle coal on the island of Malta. In the latter half of the century, London, which handled more than 85 percent of all exports, regularly shipped abroad more than 100,000 woolen cloths a year, at a value of at least £750,000. This figure does not include the increasingly important and profitable trade in so-called New Draperies, including textiles that went by such exotic names as bombazines, callamancoes, damazellas, damizes, mockadoes, and virgenatoes. When the Earl of Kent in *King Lear* insults Oswald as a "filthy worsted-stocking knave" (2.2.14–15) or when the aristocratic Biron in *Love's Labour's Lost* declares that he will give up "taffeta phrases, silken terms precise, / Three-piled hyperboles" and woo henceforth "in russet yeas, and honest kersey noes" (5.2.406–07, 413), Shakespeare is assuming that a substantial portion of his audience will be alert to the social significance of fabric.

There is amusing confirmation of this alertness from an unexpected source: the report of a visit made to the Fortune playhouse in London in 1614 by a foreigner, Father Orazio Busino, the chaplain of the Venetian embassy. Father Busino neglected to mention the name of the play he saw, but like many foreigners, he was powerfully struck by the presence of gorgeously dressed women in the audience. In Venice, there was a special gallery for courtesans, but socially respectable women would not have been permitted to attend plays, as they could in England. In London, not only could middle- and upper-class women go to the theater, but they could also wear masks and mingle freely with male spectators and women of ill repute. The bemused cleric was uncertain about the ambiguous social situation in which he found himself:

> These theatres are frequented by a number of respectable and handsome ladies, who come freely and seat themselves among the men without the slightest hesitation. On the evening in question his Excellency and the Secretary were pleased to play me a trick by placing me amongst a bevy of young women. Scarcely was I seated ere a very elegant dame, but in a mask, came and placed herself beside me. . . . She asked me for my address both in French and English; and, on my turning a deaf ear, she determined

to honour me by showing me some fine diamonds on her fingers, repeatedly taking off not fewer than three gloves, which were worn one over the other. . . . This lady's bodice was of yellow satin richly embroidered, her petticoat of gold tissue with stripes, her robe of red velvet with a raised pile, lined with yellow muslin with broad stripes of pure gold. She wore an apron of point lace of various patterns: her head-tire was highly perfumed, and the collar of white satin beneath the delicately-wrought ruff struck me as extremely pretty.

Father Busino may have turned a deaf ear on this "elegant dame" but not a blind eye: his description of her dress is worthy of a fashion designer and conveys something of the virtual clothes cult that prevailed in England in the late sixteenth and early seventeenth centuries, a cult whose major shrine, outside the royal court, was the theater.

Imports, Patents, and Monopolies

England produced some luxury goods, but the clothing on the backs of the most fashionable theatergoers was likely to have come from abroad. By the late sixteenth century, the English were importing substantial quantities of silks, satins, velvets, embroidery, gold and silver lace, and other costly items to satisfy the extravagant tastes of the elite and of those who aspired to dress like the elite. The government tried to put a check on the sartorial ambitions of the upwardly mobile by passing sumptuary laws—that is, laws restricting to the ranks of the aristocracy the right to wear certain of the most precious fabrics. But the very existence of these laws, in practice almost impossible to enforce, only reveals the scope and significance of the perceived problem.

Sumptuary laws were in part a conservative attempt to protect the existing social order from upstarts. Social mobility was not widely viewed as a positive virtue, and moralists repeatedly urged people to stay in their place. Conspicuous consumption that was tolerated, even admired, in the aristocratic elite was denounced as sinful and monstrous in less exalted social circles. English authorities were also deeply concerned throughout the period about the effects of a taste for luxury goods on the balance of trade. One of the principal English imports was wine: the "sherris" whose virtues Falstaff extols in 2 Henry IV came from Xeres in Spain; the malmsey in which poor Clarence is drowned in Richard III was probably made in Greece or in the Canary Islands (from whence came Sir Toby Belch's "cup of canary" in Twelfth Night); and the "flagon of rhenish" that Yorick in Hamlet had once poured on the Gravedigger's head came from the Rhine region of Germany. Other imports included canvas, linen, fish, olive oil, sugar, molasses, dates, oranges and lemons, figs, raisins, almonds, capers, indigo, ostrich feathers, and that increasingly popular drug tobacco.

Joint stock companies were established to import goods for the burgeoning English market. The Merchant Venturers of the City of Bristol (established in 1552) handled great shipments of Spanish sack, the light, dry wine that largely displaced the vintages of Bordeaux and Burgundy when trade with France was disrupted by war. The Muscovy Company (established in 1555) traded English cloth and manufactured goods for Russian furs, oil, and beeswax. The Venice Company and the Turkey Company—uniting in 1593 to form the wealthy Levant Company—brought silk and spices home from Aleppo and carpets from Constantinople. The East India Company (founded in 1600), with its agent at Bantam in Java, brought pepper, cloves, nutmeg, and other spices from east Asia, along with indigo, cotton textiles, sugar, and saltpeter from India. English privateers "imported" American products, especially sugar, fish, and hides, in huge quantities, along with more precious cargoes. In 1592, a privateering expedition principally funded by Sir Walter Ralegh captured a huge Portuguese carrack (sailing ship), the Madre de Dios, in the Azores and brought it back to Dartmouth. The ship, the largest that had ever entered any English port, held 536 tons of pepper, cloves, cinnamon, cochineal, mace, civet, musk, ambergris, and nutmeg, as well as jewels, gold, ebony, carpets, and silks. Before order could be established, the English seamen began to pillage this immensely rich prize, and witnesses said

Cannoneer. From *Edward Webbe, His Travailes* (1590).

they could smell the spices on all the streets around the harbor. Such piratical expeditions were rarely officially sanctioned by the state, but the queen had in fact privately invested £1,800, for which she received about £80,000.

In the years of war with Spain, 1586–1604, the goods captured by the privateers annually amounted to 10–15 percent of the total value of England's imports. But organized theft alone could not solve England's balance-of-trade problems. Statesmen were particularly worried that the nation's natural wealth was slipping away in exchange for unnecessary things. In his *Discourse of the Commonweal* (1549), the prominent humanist Sir Thomas Smith exclaims against the importation of such trifles as mirrors, paper, laces, gloves, pins, inkhorns, tennis balls, puppets, and playing cards. And more than a century later, the same fear that England was trading its riches for trifles and wasting away in idleness was expressed by the Bristol merchant John Cary. The solution, Cary argues in "An Essay on the State of England in Relation to Its Trade" (1695), is to expand productive domestic employment. "People are or may be the Wealth of a Nation," he writes, "yet it must be where you find Employment for them, else they are a Burden to it, as the Idle Drone is maintained by the Industry of the laborious Bee, so are all those who live by their Dependence on others, as Players, Ale-House Keepers, Common Fiddlers, and such like, but more particularly Beggars, who never set themselves to work."

Stage players, all too typically associated here with vagabonds and other idle drones, could have replied in their defense that they not only labored in their vocation but also exported their skills abroad: English acting companies routinely traveled overseas and performed as far away as Bohemia. But their labor was not regarded as a productive contribution to the national wealth, and plays were in truth no solution to the trade imbalances that worried authorities.

The government attempted to stem the flow of gold overseas by establishing a patent system initially designed to encourage skilled foreigners to settle in England by granting them exclusive rights to produce particular wares by a patented method. Patents were granted for such things as the making of hard white soap (1561), ovens and furnaces (1563), window glass (1567), sailcloths (1574), drinking glasses (1574), sulphur, brimstone, and oil (1577), armor and horse harness (1587), starch (1588), white writing paper made from rags (1589), aqua vitae and vinegar (1594), playing cards (1598), and mathematical instruments (1598).

Although their ostensible purpose was to increase the wealth of England, encourage technical innovation, and provide employment for the poor, the effect of patents was often the enrichment of a few and the hounding of poor competitors by wealthy monopolists, a group that soon extended well beyond foreign-born entrepreneurs to the favorites of the monarch who vied for the huge profits to be made. "If I had a monopoly out" on folly, the Fool in *King Lear* protests, glancing at the "lords and great men" around him, "they would have part on't." The passage appears only in the quarto version of the play (*History of King Lear* 4.135–36); it may have been cut for political reasons from the Folio. For the issue of monopolies provoked bitter criticism and parliamentary debate for decades. In 1601, Elizabeth was prevailed upon to revoke a number of the most hated monopolies, including aqua vitae and vinegar, bottles, brushes, fish livers, the coarse sailcloth known as poldavis and mildernix, pots, salt, and starch. The whole system was revoked during the reign of James I by an act of Parliament.

Haves and Have-Nots

When in the 1560s Elizabeth's ambassador to France, the humanist Sir Thomas Smith, wrote a description of England, he saw the commonwealth as divided into four sorts of people: "gentlemen, citizens, yeomen artificers, and laborers." At the forefront of the class of gentlemen was the monarch, followed by a very small group of nobles—dukes, marquesses, earls, viscounts, and barons—who either inherited their exalted titles, as the eldest male heirs of their families, or were granted them by the monarch. Under Elizabeth, this aristocratic peerage numbered between 50 and 60 individuals; James's promotions increased the number to nearer 130. Strictly speaking, Smith notes, the younger sons of the nobility were only entitled to be called "esquires," but in common speech they were also called "lords."

Below this tiny cadre of aristocrats in the social hierarchy of gentry were the knights, a title of honor conferred by the monarch, and below them were the "simple gentlemen." Who was a gentleman? According to Smith, "whoever studieth the laws of the realm, who studieth in the universities, who professeth liberal sciences, and to be short, who can live idly and without manual labor, and will bear the port, charge and countenance of a gentleman, he shall be called master . . . and shall be taken for a gentleman." To "live idly and without manual labor": where in Spain, for example, the crucial mark of a gentleman was "blood," in England it was "idleness," in the sense of sufficient income to afford an education and to maintain a social position without having to work with one's hands.

For Smith, the class of gentlemen was far and away the most important in the kingdom. Below were two groups that had at least some social standing and claim to authority: the citizens, or burgesses, those who held positions of importance and responsibility in their cities, and yeomen, farmers with land and a measure of economic independence. At the bottom of the social order was what Smith calls "the fourth sort of men which do not rule." The great mass of ordinary people have, Smith writes, "no voice nor authority in our commonwealth, and no account is made of them but only to be ruled." Still, even they can bear some responsibility, he notes, since they serve on juries and are named to such positions as churchwarden and constable.

In everyday practice, as modern social historians have observed, the English tended to divide the population not into four distinct classes but into two: a very small empowered group—the "richer" or "wiser" or "better" sort—and all the rest who were without much social standing or power, the "poorer" or "ruder" or "meaner" sort. References to the "middle sort of people" remain relatively rare until after Shakespeare's lifetime; these people are absorbed into the rulers or the ruled, depending on speaker and context.

The source of wealth for most of the ruling class, and the essential measure of social status, was land ownership, and changes to the social structure in the sixteenth and seventeenth centuries were largely driven by the land market. The property that passed into private hands as the Tudors and early Stuarts sold off confiscated monastic estates and then their own crown lands for ready cash amounted to nearly a quarter of all the land in England. At the same time, the buying and selling of private estates was on the rise throughout the period. Land was bought up not only by established landowners seeking to enlarge their estates but by successful merchants, manufacturers, and urban professionals; even if the taint of vulgar moneymaking lingered around such figures, their heirs would be taken for true gentlemen. The rate of turnover in land ownership was great; in many counties, well over half the gentle families in 1640 had appeared since the end of the fifteenth century. The class that Smith called "simple gentlemen" was expanding rapidly: in the fifteenth century, they had held no more than a quarter of the land in the country, but by the later seventeenth, they controlled almost half. Over the same period, the land held by the great aristocratic magnates held steady at 15–20 percent of the total.

Riot and Disorder

London was a violent place in the first half of Shakespeare's career. There were thirty-five riots in the city in the years 1581–1602, twelve of them in the volatile month of June

1595. These included protests against the deeply unpopular lord mayor Sir John Spencer, attempts to release prisoners, anti-alien riots, and incidents of "popular market regulation." There is an unforgettable depiction of a popular uprising in *Coriolanus*, along with many other glimpses in Shakespeare's works, including John Cade's grotesque rebellion in *The First Part of the Contention (2 Henry VI)*, the plebeian violence in *Julius Caesar*, and Laertes' "riotous head" in *Hamlet*.

The London rioters were mostly drawn from the large mass of poor and discontented apprentices who typically chose as their scapegoats foreigners, prostitutes, and gentlemen's servingmen. Theaters were very often the site of the social confrontations that sparked disorder. For two days running in June 1584, disputes between apprentices and gentlemen triggered riots outside the Curtain Theatre involving up to a thousand participants. On one occasion, a gentleman was said to have exclaimed that "the apprentice was but a rascal, and some there were little better than rogues that took upon them the name of gentlemen, and said the prentices were but the scum of the world." These occasions culminated in attacks by the apprentices on London's law schools, the Inns of Court.

The most notorious and predictable incidents of disorder came on Shrove Tuesday (the Tuesday before the beginning of Lent), a traditional day of misrule when apprentices ran riot. Shrove Tuesday disturbances involved attacks by mobs of young men on the brothels of the South Bank, in the vicinity of the Globe and other public theaters. The city authorities took precautions to keep these disturbances from getting completely out of control, but evidently did not regard them as serious threats to public order.

Of much greater concern throughout the Tudor and early Stuart years were the frequent incidents of rural rioting against the enclosure of commons and waste land by local landlords (and, in the royal forests, by the crown). This form of popular protest was at its height during Shakespeare's career: in the years 1590–1610, the frequency of anti-enclosure rioting doubled from what it had been earlier in Elizabeth's reign.

Although they often became violent, anti-enclosure riots were usually directed not against individuals but against property. Villagers—sometimes several hundred, often fewer than a dozen—gathered to tear down newly planted hedges. The event often took place in a carnival atmosphere, with songs and drinking, that did not prevent the participants from acting with a good deal of political canniness and forethought. Especially in the Jacobean period, it was common for participants to establish a common fund for legal defense before commencing their assault on the hedges. Women were frequently involved, and on a number of occasions wives alone participated in the destruction of the enclosure,

"The Peddler." From Jost Amman, *The Book of Trades* (1568).

since there was a widespread, though erroneous, belief that married women acting without the knowledge of their husbands were immune from prosecution. In fact, the powerful Court of Star Chamber consistently ruled that both the wives and their husbands should be punished.

Although Stratford was never the scene of serious rioting, enclosure controversies turned violent more than once in Shakespeare's lifetime. In January 1601, Shakespeare's friend Richard Quiney and others leveled the hedges of Sir Edward Greville, lord of Stratford manor. Quiney was elected bailiff of Stratford in September of that year but did not live to enjoy the office for long. He died from a blow to the head struck by one of Greville's men in a tavern brawl. Greville, responsible for the administration of justice, neglected to punish the murderer.

There was further violence in January 1615,

when William Combe's men threw to the ground two local aldermen who were filling in a ditch by which Combe was enclosing common fields near Stratford. The task of filling in the offending ditch was completed the next day by the women and children of Stratford. Combe's enclosure scheme was eventually stopped in the courts. Though he owned land whose value would have been affected by this controversy, Shakespeare took no active role in it, since he had previously come to a private settlement with the enclosers insuring him against personal loss.

Most incidents of rural rioting were small, localized affairs, and with good reason: when confined to the village community, riot was a misdemeanor; when it spread outward to include multiple communities, it became treason. The greatest of the anti-enclosure riots, those in which hundreds of individuals from a large area participated, commonly took place on the eve of full-scale regional rebellions. The largest of these disturbances, Kett's Rebellion, involved some 16,000 peasants, artisans, and townspeople who rose up in 1549 under the leadership of a Norfolk tanner and landowner, Robert Kett, to protest economic exploitation. The agrarian revolts in Shakespeare's lifetime were on a much smaller scale. In the abortive Oxfordshire Rebellion of 1596, a carpenter named Bartholomew Steere attempted to organize a rising against enclosing gentlemen. The optimistic Steere promised his followers that "it was but a month's work to overrun England" and informed them "that the commons long since in Spain did rise and kill all gentlemen . . . and since that time have lived merrily there." Steere expected several hundred men to join him on Enslow Hill on November 21, 1596, for the start of the rising; no more than twenty showed up. They were captured, imprisoned, and tortured. Several were executed, but Steere apparently died in prison.

Rebellions, most often triggered by hunger and oppression, continued into the reign of James I. The Midland Revolt of 1607, which may be reflected in *Coriolanus*, consisted of a string of agrarian risings in the counties of Northamptonshire, Warwickshire, and Leicestershire, involving assemblies of up to five thousand rebels in various places. The best-known of their leaders was John Reynolds, called "Captain Powch" because of the pouch he wore, whose magical contents were supposed to defend the rebels from harm. (According to the chronicler Edmund Howes, when Reynolds was captured and the pouch opened, it contained "only a piece of green cheese.") The rebels, who were called by themselves and others both "Levelers" and "Diggers," insisted that they had no quarrel with the king but only sought an end to injurious enclosures. But Robert Wilkinson, who preached a sermon against the leaders at their trial, credited them with the intention to "level all states as they leveled banks and ditches." Most of the rebels got off relatively lightly, but, along with other ringleaders, Captain Powch was executed.

The Legal Status of Women

Though England was ruled for over forty years by a powerful woman, the great majority of women in the kingdom had very restricted social, economic, and legal standing. To be sure, a tiny number of influential aristocratic women, such as the formidable Countess of Shrewsbury, Bess of Hardwick, wielded considerable power. But, these rare exceptions aside, women were denied any rightful claim to institutional authority or personal autonomy. When Sir Thomas Smith thinks of how he should describe his country's social order, he declares that "we do reject women, as those whom nature hath made to keep home and to nourish their family and children, and not to meddle with matters abroad, nor to bear office in a city or commonwealth." Then, with a kind of glance over his shoulder, he makes an exception of those few for whom "the blood is respected, not the age nor the sex": for example, the queen.

English women were not under the full range of crushing constraints that afflicted women in some countries in Europe. Foreign visitors were struck by their relative freedom, as shown, for example, by the fact that respectable women could venture unchaperoned into the streets and attend the theater. Single women, whether widowed or unmarried, could, if they were of full age, inherit and administer land, make a will, sign a contract, possess property, sue and be sued, without a male guardian or proxy. But married women had no such rights under the common law.

Early modern writings about women and the family constantly return to a political model of domination and submission, in which the father justly rules over wife and children as the monarch rules over the state. This conception of a woman's role conveniently ignores the fact that a *majority* of the adult women at any time in Shakespeare's England were not married. They were either widows or spinsters (a term that was not yet pejorative), and thus for the most part managing their own affairs. Even within marriage, women typically had more control over certain spheres than moralizing writers on the family cared to admit. For example, village wives oversaw the production of eggs, cheese, and beer, and sold these goods in the market.

Women were not in practice as bereft of economic power and property as, according to English common law, they should have been. Demographic studies indicate that the inheritance system called primogeniture, the orderly transmission of property from father to eldest male heir, was more often an unfulfilled wish than a reality. Some 40 percent of marriages failed to produce a son, and in such circumstances fathers often left their land to their daughters, rather than to brothers, nephews, or male cousins. In many families, the father died before his male heir was old enough to inherit property, leaving the land, at least temporarily, in the hands of the mother. And while they were less likely than their brothers to inherit land ("real property"), daughters normally inherited a substantial share of their father's personal property (cash and movables).

In fact, the legal restrictions upon women, though severe in Shakespeare's time, actually worsened in subsequent decades. The English common law, the system of law based on court decisions rather than on codified written laws, was significantly less egalitarian in its approach to wives and daughters than were alternative legal codes (manorial, civil, and ecclesiastical) still in place in the late sixteenth century. The eventual triumph of common law stripped women of many traditional rights, slowly driving them out of economically productive trades and businesses.

Limited though it was, the economic freedom of Elizabethan and Jacobean women far exceeded their political and social freedom—the opportunity to receive a grammar school or university education, to hold office in church or state, to have a voice in public debates, or even simply to speak their mind fully and openly in ordinary conversation. Women who asserted their views too vigorously risked being perceived as shrewish and labeled "scolds." Both urban and rural communities had a horror of scolds. In the Elizabethan period, such women came to be regarded as a threat to public order, to be dealt with by the local authorities. The preferred methods of correction included public humiliation—of the sort Katherine endures in *The Taming of the Shrew*—and such physical abuse as slapping, bridling, and soaking by means of a contraption called the "cucking stool" (or "ducking stool"). This latter punishment originated in the Middle Ages, but its use spread in the sixteenth century, when it became almost exclusively a punishment for women. From 1560 onward, cucking stools were built or renovated in many English provincial towns; between 1560 and 1600, the contraptions were installed by rivers or ponds in Norwich, Bridport, Shrewsbury, Kingston-upon-Thames, Marlborough, Devizes, Clitheroe, Thornbury, and Great Yarmouth.

Such punishment was usually intensified by a procession through the town to the sound of "rough music," the banging together of pots and pans. The same cruel festivity accompanied the "carting" or "riding" of those accused of being whores. In some parts of the country, villagers also took the law into their own hands, publicly shaming women who married men much younger than themselves or who beat or otherwise domineered over their husbands. One characteristic form of these charivaris, or rituals of shaming, was known in the West Country as the Skimmington Ride. Villagers would rouse the offending couple from bed with rough music and stage a raucous pageant in which a man, holding a distaff, would ride backward on a donkey, while his "wife" (another man dressed as a woman) struck him with a ladle. In these cases, the collective ridicule and indignation was evidently directed at least as much at the henpecked husband as at his transgressive wife.

Women and Print

Books published for a female audience surged in popularity in the late sixteenth century, reflecting an increase in female literacy. (It is striking how many of Shakespeare's women are shown reading.) This increase is probably linked to a Protestant longing for direct access to the Scriptures, and the new books marketed specifically for women included devotional manuals and works of religious instruction. But there were also practical guides to such subjects as female education (for example, Giovanni Bruto's *Necessary, Fit, and Convenient Education of a Young Gentlewoman*, 1598), midwifery (James Guillemeau's *Child-birth; or, the Happy Delivery of Women*, 1612), needlework (Federico di Vinciolo's *New and Singular Patterns and Works of Linen*, 1591), cooking (Thomas Dawson's *The Good Housewife's Jewel*, 1587), gardening (Pierre Erondelle, *The French Garden*, 1605), and married life (Patrick Hanney's *A Happy Husband; or, Directions for a Maid to Choose Her Mate*, 1619). As the authors' names suggest, many of these works were translations, and almost all were written by men.

Starting in the 1570s, writers and their publishers increasingly addressed works of recreational literature (romance, fiction, and poetry) partially or even exclusively to women. Some books, such as Robert Greene's *Mamillia, a Mirror or Looking-Glass for the Ladies of England* (1583), directly specified in the title their desired audience. Others, such as Sir Philip Sidney's influential and popular romance *Arcadia* (1590–93), solicited female readership in their dedicatory epistles. The ranks of Sidney's followers eventually included his own niece, Mary Wroth, whose romance *Urania* was published in 1621.

In the literature of Shakespeare's time, women readers were not only wooed but also frequently railed at, in a continuation of a popular polemical genre that had long inspired heated charges and countercharges. Both sides in the polemic generally agreed that it was the duty of women to be chaste, dutiful, shamefast, and silent; the argument was whether women fulfilled or fell short of this proper role. Ironically, then, a modern reader is more likely to find inspiring accounts of courageous women not in the books written in defense of female virtue but in attacks on those who refused to be silent and obedient.

The most famous English skirmish in this controversy took place in a rash of pamphlets at the end of Shakespeare's life. Joseph Swetnam's crude *Arraignment of Lewd, Idle, Froward, and Unconstant Women* (1615) provoked three fierce responses attributed to women: Rachel Speght's *A Muzzle for Melastomus*, Esther Sowernam's *Esther Hath Hang'd Haman*, and Constantia Munda's *Worming of a Mad Dog*, all 1617. There was also an anonymous play, *Swetnam the Woman-hater Arraigned by Women* (1618), in which Swetnam, depicted as a braggart and a lecher, is put on trial by women and made to recant his misogynistic lies.

Prior to the Swetnam controversy, only one English woman, "Jane Anger," had published a defense of women (*Jane Anger Her Protection for Women*, 1589). Learned women writers in the sixteenth century tended not to become involved in public debate but rather to undertake a project to which it was difficult for even obdurately chauvinistic males to object: the translation of devotional literature into English. Thomas More's daughter Margaret More Roper translated Erasmus (*A Devout Treatise upon the Pater Noster*, 1524); Francis Bacon's mother, Anne Cooke Bacon, translated Bishop John Jewel (*An Apology or Answer in Defence of the Church of England*, 1564); Anne Locke Prowse, a friend of John Knox, translated the *Sermons of John Calvin* in 1560; and Mary Sidney, the Countess of Pembroke, completed the metrical version of the Psalms that her brother Sir Philip Sidney had begun. Elizabeth Tudor (the future queen) herself translated, at the age of eleven, Marguerite de Navarre's *Le Miroir de l'âme pécheresse* (*The Glass of the Sinful Soul*, 1544). The translation was dedicated to her stepmother, Katherine Parr, herself the author of a frequently reprinted book of prayers.

There was in the sixteenth and early seventeenth centuries a social stigma attached to print. Far from celebrating publication, authors, and particularly female authors, often apologized for exposing themselves to the public gaze. Nonetheless, a number of women ventured beyond pious translations. Some, including Elizabeth Tyrwhitt, Anne Dowriche,

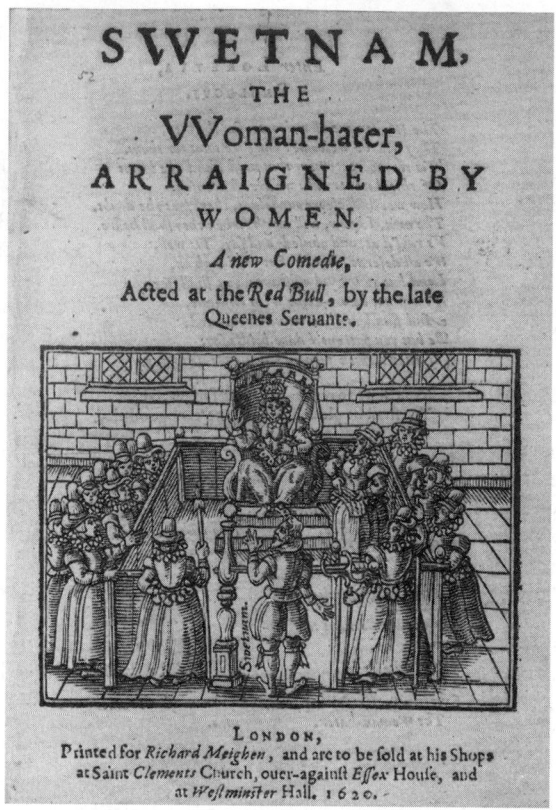

SWETNAM,
THE
VVoman-hater,
ARRAIGNED BY
WOMEN.

A new Comedie,
Acted at the *Red Bull*, by the late
Queenes Seruants.

LONDON,
Printed for *Richard Meighen*, and are to be fold at his Shops
at Saint *Clements* Church, ouer-againft *Effex* Houfe, and
at *Weftminfter* Hall. 1 6 2 0.

Title page of *Swetnam the Woman-Hater Arraigned by Women*
(1620), a play written in response to Joseph Swetnam's *The
Arraignment of Lewd, Idle, Froward and Unconstant Women*
(1615); the woodcut depicts the trial of Swetnam in Act 4.

Isabella Whitney, Mary Sidney, and Aemilia Lanyer, composed and published their own
poems. Aemilia Lanyer's *Salve Deus Rex Judaeorum*, published in 1611, is a poem in praise
of virtuous women, from Eve and the Virgin Mary to her noble patron, the Countess of
Cumberland. "A Description of Cookeham," appended to the poem, may be the first
English country house poem.

The first Tudor woman to translate a play was the learned Jane Lumley, who composed an English version of Euripides' *Iphigenia at Aulis* (c. 1550). The first known original play in English by a woman was by Elizabeth Cary, Viscountess Falkland, whose
Tragedy of Mariam, the Fair Queen of Jewry was published in 1613. This remarkable play,
which was not intended to be performed, includes speeches in defense of women's equality, though the most powerful of these is spoken by the villainous Salome, who schemes to
divorce her husband and marry her lover. Cary, who bore eleven children, herself had a
deeply troubled marriage, which effectively came to an end in 1625 when, defying her
husband's staunchly Protestant family, she openly converted to Catholicism. Her biography was written by one of her four daughters, all of whom became nuns.

Henry VIII and the English Reformation

There had long been serious ideological and institutional tensions in the religious life
of England, but officially, at least, England in the early sixteenth century had a single
religion, Catholicism, whose acknowledged head was the pope in Rome. In 1517, drawing

upon long-standing currents of dissent, Martin Luther, an Augustinian monk and professor of theology at the University of Wittenberg, challenged the authority of the pope and attacked several key doctrines of the Catholic Church. According to Luther, the Church, with its elaborate hierarchical structure centered in Rome, its rich monasteries and convents, and its enormous political influence, had become hopelessly corrupt, a conspiracy of venal priests who manipulated popular superstitions to enrich themselves and amass worldly power. Luther began by vehemently attacking the sale of indulgences—certificates promising the remission of punishments to be suffered in the afterlife by souls sent to purgatory to expiate their sins. These indulgences were a fraud, he argued; purgatory itself had no foundation in the Bible, which in his view was the only legitimate source of religious truth. Christians would be saved not by scrupulously following the ritual practices fostered by the Catholic Church—observing fast days, reciting the ancient Latin prayers, endowing chantries to say prayers for the dead, and so on—but by faith and faith alone.

This challenge, which came to be known as the Reformation, spread and gathered force, especially in northern Europe, where major leaders like the Swiss pastor Ulrich Zwingli and the French theologian John Calvin established institutional structures and elaborated various and sometimes conflicting doctrinal principles. Calvin, whose thought came to be particularly influential in England, emphasized the obligation of governments to implement God's will in the world. He advanced too the doctrine of predestination, by which, as he put it, "God adopts some to hope of life and sentences others to eternal death." God's "secret election" of the saved made Calvin uncomfortable, but his study of the Scriptures had led him to conclude that "only a small number, out of an incalculable multitude, should obtain salvation." It might seem that such a conclusion would lead to passivity or even despair, but for Calvin predestination was a mystery bound up with faith, confidence, and an active engagement in the fashioning of a Christian community.

The Reformation had a direct and powerful impact on those territories, especially in northern Europe, where it gained control. Monasteries were sacked, their possessions seized by princes or sold off to the highest bidder; the monks and nuns, expelled from their cloisters, were encouraged to break their vows of chastity and find spouses, as Luther and his wife, a former nun, had done. In the great cathedrals and in hundreds of smaller churches and chapels, the elaborate altarpieces, bejeweled crucifixes, crystal reliquaries holding the bones of saints, and venerated statues and paintings were attacked as "idols" and often defaced or destroyed. Protestant congregations continued, for the most part, to celebrate the most sacred Christian ritual, the Eucharist, or Lord's Supper, but they did so in a profoundly different spirit from that of the Catholic Church—more as commemoration than as miracle—and they now prayed not in the old liturgical Latin but in the vernacular.

The Reformation was at first vigorously resisted in England. Indeed, with the support of his ardently Catholic chancellor, Thomas More, Henry VIII personally wrote (or at least lent his name to) a vehement, often scatological attack on Luther's character and views, an attack for which the pope granted him the honorific title "Defender of the Faith." Protestant writings, including translations of the Scriptures into English, were seized by officials of the church and state and burned. Protestants who made their views known were persecuted, driven to flee the country, or arrested, put on trial, and burned at the stake. But the situation changed drastically and decisively when in 1527 Henry decided to seek a divorce from his first wife, Catherine of Aragon, in order to marry Anne Boleyn.

Catherine had given birth to six children, but since only a daughter, Mary, survived infancy, Henry did not have the son he craved. Then as now, the Catholic Church did not ordinarily grant divorce, but Henry's lawyers argued on technical grounds that the marriage was invalid (and therefore, by extension, that Mary was illegitimate and hence unable to inherit the throne). Matters of this kind were far less doctrinal than diplomatic: Catherine, the daughter of Ferdinand of Aragon and Isabella of Castile, had powerful allies in Rome, and the pope ruled against Henry's petition for a divorce. A series of momentous events followed, as England lurched away from the Church of Rome. In 1531, Henry charged the entire clergy of England with having usurped royal authority in the

"The Pope as Antichrist riding the Beast of the Apocalypse." From *Fierie Tryall of God's Saints* (1611; author unknown).

administration of canon law (the ecclesiastical law that governed faith, discipline, and morals, including such matters as divorce). Under extreme pressure, including the threat of mass confiscations and imprisonment, the Convocation of the Clergy begged for pardon, made a donation to the royal coffers of over £100,000, and admitted that the king was "supreme head of the English Church and clergy" (modified by the rider "as far as the law of Christ allows"). On May 15 of the next year, the convocation submitted to the demand that the king be the final arbiter of canon law; on the next day, Thomas More resigned his post.

In 1533, Henry's marriage to Catherine was officially declared null and void, and on June 1 Anne Boleyn was crowned queen (a coronation Shakespeare depicts in *All Is True*). The king was promptly excommunicated by the pope, Clement VII. In the following year, the parliamentary Act of Succession confirmed the effects of the divorce and required an oath from all adult male subjects confirming the new dynastic settlement. Thomas More and John Fisher, the Bishop of Rochester, were among the small number who refused. The Act of Supremacy, passed later in the year, formally declared the king to be "Supreme Head of the Church in England" and again required an oath to this effect. In 1535 and 1536, further acts made it treasonous to refuse the oath of royal supremacy or, as More had tried to do, to remain silent. The first victims were three Carthusian monks who rejected the oath—"How could the king, a layman," said one of them, "be Head of the Church of England?"—and in May 1535, they were duly hanged, drawn, and quartered. A few weeks later, Fisher and More were convicted and beheaded. Between 1536 and 1539, the monasteries were suppressed and their vast wealth seized by the crown.

Royal defiance of the authority of Rome was a key element in the Reformation but did not by itself constitute the establishment of Protestantism in England. On the contrary, in the same year that Fisher and More were martyred for their adherence to Roman Catholicism, twenty-five Protestants, members of a sect known as Anabaptists, were burned for heresy on a single day. Through most of his reign, Henry remained an equal-opportunity persecutor, ruthless to Catholics loyal to Rome and hostile to many of those who espoused Reformation ideas, though many of these ideas gradually established themselves on English soil.

Even when Henry was eager to do so, it proved impossible to eradicate Protestantism, as it would later prove impossible for his successors to eradicate Catholicism. In large part this tenacity arose from the passionate, often suicidal heroism of men and women who felt that their souls' salvation depended on the precise character of their Christianity. It arose too from a mid-fifteenth-century technological innovation that made it almost impossible to suppress unwelcome ideas: the printing press. Early Protestants quickly grasped that with a few clandestine presses they could defy the Catholic authorities and flood the country with their texts. "How many printing presses there be in the world," wrote the Protestant polemicist John Foxe, "so many blockhouses there be against the high castle" of the pope in Rome, "so that either the pope must abolish knowledge and printing or printing at length will root him out." By the century's end, it was the Catholics who were using the clandestine press to propagate their beliefs in the face of Protestant persecution.

The greatest insurrection of the Tudor age was not over food, taxation, or land but over religion. On Sunday October 1, 1536, stirred up by their vicar, the traditionalist parishioners of Louth in Lincolnshire, in the north of England, rose up in defiance of the ecclesiastical visitation sent to enforce royal supremacy. The rapidly spreading rebellion, which became known as the Pilgrimage of Grace, was led by the lawyer Robert Aske. The city of Lincoln fell to the rebels on October 6, and though it was soon retaken by royal forces, the rebels seized cities and fortifications throughout Yorkshire, Durham, Northumberland, Cumberland, Westmoreland, and northern Lancashire. Carlisle, Newcastle, and a few castles were all that were left to the king in the north. The Pilgrims soon numbered 40,000, led by some of the region's leading noblemen. The Duke of Norfolk, representing the crown, was forced to negotiate a truce, with a promise to support the rebels' demands that the king restore the monasteries, shore up the regional economy, suppress heresy, and dismiss his evil advisers.

The Pilgrims kept the peace for the rest of 1536, on the naive assumption that their demands would be met. But Henry moved suddenly early in 1537 to impose order and capture the ringleaders; 130 people, including lords, knights, heads of religious houses, and, of course, Robert Aske, were executed.

In 1549, two years after the death of Henry VIII, the west and the north of England were the sites of further unsuccessful risings for the restoration of Catholicism. The Western Rising is striking for its blend of Catholic universalism and intense regionalism among people who did not yet regard themselves as English. One of the rebels' articles, protesting against the imposition of the English Bible and religious service, declares, "We the Cornish men (whereof certain of us understand no English) utterly refuse this new English." The rebels besieged but failed to take the city of Exeter. As with almost all Tudor rebellions, the number of those executed in the aftermath of the failed rising was far greater than those killed in actual hostilities.

Henry VIII's Children: Edward, Mary, and Elizabeth

Upon Henry's death in 1547, his ten-year-old son, Edward VI, came to the throne, with his maternal uncle Edward Seymour named as Lord Protector and Duke of Somerset. Both Edward and his uncle were staunch Protestants, and reformers hastened to transform the English church accordingly. During Edward's reign, Archbishop Thomas Cranmer formulated the forty-two articles of religion that became the core of Anglican orthodoxy and wrote the first *Book of Common Prayer*, which was officially adopted in 1549 as the basis of English worship services.

Somerset fell from power in 1549 and was replaced as Lord Protector by John Dudley, later Duke of Northumberland. When Edward fell seriously ill, probably of tuberculosis, Northumberland persuaded him to sign a will depriving his half-sisters, Mary (the daughter of Catherine of Aragon) and Elizabeth (the daughter of Anne Boleyn), of their claim to royal succession. The Lord Protector was scheming to have his daughter-in-law the Protestant Lady Jane Grey, a granddaughter of Henry VII, ascend to the throne. But when Edward died in 1553, Mary marshaled support, quickly secured the crown from Lady Jane (who had been titular queen for nine days), and had Lady Jane executed, along with her husband and Northumberland.

Queen Mary immediately took steps to return her kingdom to Roman Catholicism. Though she was unable to get Parliament to agree to restore church lands seized under

The Family of Henry VIII: An Allegory of the Tudor Succession. By Lucas de Heere (c. 1572).
Henry, in the middle, is flanked by Mary to his right, and Edward and Elizabeth to his left.

Henry VIII, she restored the Catholic Mass, once again affirmed the authority of the pope,
and put down a rebellion that sought to depose her. Seconded by her ardently Catholic
husband, Philip II, King of Spain, she initiated a series of religious persecutions that earned
her (from her enemies) the name "Bloody Mary." Hundreds of Protestants took refuge
abroad in cities such as Calvin's Geneva; almost three hundred less fortunate Protestants
were condemned as heretics and burned at the stake.

Mary died childless in 1558, and her younger half-sister Elizabeth became queen.
Elizabeth's succession had been by no means assured. For if Protestants regarded Henry
VIII's marriage to Catherine as invalid and hence deemed Mary illegitimate, so Catholics
regarded his marriage to Anne Boleyn as invalid and deemed Elizabeth illegitimate. Henry
VIII himself seemed to support both views, since only three years after divorcing Catherine, he beheaded Anne Boleyn on charges of treason and adultery and urged Parliament
to invalidate the marriage. Moreover, though during her sister's reign Elizabeth outwardly
complied with the official Catholic religious observance, Mary and her advisers were
deeply suspicious, and the young princess's life was in grave danger. Poised and circum-
spect, Elizabeth warily evaded the traps that were set for her. As she ascended the throne,
her actions were scrutinized for some indication of the country's future course. During her
coronation procession, when a girl in an allegorical pageant presented her with a Bible in
English translation—banned under Mary's reign—Elizabeth kissed the book, held it up
reverently, and laid it to her breast; when the abbot and monks of Westminster Abbey
came to greet her in broad daylight with candles (a symbol of Catholic devotion) in their
hands, she briskly dismissed them with the telling words "Away with those torches! we can
see well enough." England had returned to the Reformation.

Many English men and women, of all classes, remained loyal to the old Catholic faith,
but English authorities under Elizabeth moved steadily, if cautiously, toward ensuring at
least an outward conformity to the official Protestant settlement. Recusants, those who
refused to attend regular Sunday services in their parish churches, were fined heavily.

Anyone who wished to receive a university degree, to be ordained as a priest in the Church of England, or to be named as an officer of the state had to swear an oath to the royal supremacy. Commissioners were sent throughout the land to confirm that religious services were following the officially approved liturgy and to investigate any reported backsliding into Catholic practice or, alternatively, any attempts to introduce more radical reforms than the queen and her bishops had chosen to embrace. For the Protestant exiles who streamed back were eager not only to undo the damage Mary had done but to carry the Reformation much further. They sought to dismantle the church hierarchy, to purge the calendar of folk customs deemed pagan and the church service of ritual practices deemed superstitious, to dress the clergy in simple garb, and, at the extreme edge, to smash "idolatrous" statues, crucifixes, and altarpieces. Throughout her long reign, however, Elizabeth herself remained cautiously conservative and determined to hold in check religious zealotry.

In the space of a single lifetime, England had gone officially from Roman Catholicism, to Catholicism under the supreme headship of the English king, to a guarded Protestantism, to a more radical Protestantism, to a renewed and aggressive Roman Catholicism, and finally to Protestantism again. Each of these shifts was accompanied by danger, persecution, and death. It was enough to make some people wary. Or skeptical. Or extremely agile.

The English Bible

Luther had undertaken a fundamental critique of the Catholic Church's sacramental system, a critique founded on the twin principles of salvation by faith alone *(sola fide)* and the absolute primacy of the Bible *(sola scriptura)*. *Sola fide* contrasted faith with "works," by which was meant primarily the whole elaborate system of rituals sanctified, conducted, or directed by the priests. Protestants proposed to modify or reinterpret many of these rituals or, as with the rituals associated with purgatory, to abolish them altogether. *Sola scriptura* required direct lay access to the Bible, which meant in practice the widespread availability of vernacular translations. The Roman Catholic Church had not always and everywhere opposed such translations, but it generally preferred that the populace encounter the Scriptures through the interpretations of the priests, trained to read the Latin translation known as the Vulgate. In times of great conflict, this preference for clerical mediation hardened into outright prohibition of vernacular translation and into persecution and book burning.

Zealous Protestants set out, in the teeth of fierce opposition, to put the Bible into the hands of the laity. A remarkable translation of the New Testament, by an English Lutheran named William Tyndale, was printed on the continent and smuggled into England in 1525; Tyndale's translation of the Pentateuch, the first five books of the Hebrew Bible, followed in 1530. Many copies of these translations were seized and burned, as was the translator himself, but the printing press made it extremely difficult for authorities to eradicate books for which there was a passionate demand. The English Bible was a force that could not be suppressed, and it became, in its various forms, the single most important book of the sixteenth century.

Tyndale's translation was completed by an associate, Miles Coverdale, whose rendering of the Psalms proved to be particularly influential. Their joint labor was the basis for the Great Bible (1539), the first authorized version of the Bible in English, a copy of which was ordered to be placed in every church in the kingdom. With the accession of Edward VI, many editions of the Bible followed, but the process was sharply reversed when Mary came to the throne in 1553. Along with people condemned as heretics, English Bibles were burned in great bonfires.

Marian persecution was indirectly responsible for what would become the most popular as well as most scholarly English Bible, the translation known as the Geneva Bible, prepared, with extensive, learned, and often fiercely polemical marginal notes, by English exiles in Calvin's Geneva and widely diffused in England after Elizabeth came to the throne. In addition, Elizabethan church authorities ordered a careful revision of the Great Bible, and this version, known as the Bishops' Bible, was the one read in the churches. The success of the Geneva Bible in particular prompted those Elizabethan Catholics who now in turn found themselves in exile to bring out a vernacular translation of their own in order to counter the Protestant readings and glosses. This Catholic translation, known as the Rheims Bible, may have been known to Shakespeare, but he seems to have been far better acquainted with the Geneva Bible, and he would also have repeatedly heard the Bishops' Bible read aloud. Scholars have identified over three hundred references to the Bible in Shakespeare's work; in one version or another, the Scriptures had a powerful impact on his imagination.

A Female Monarch in a Male World

In the last year of Mary's reign, 1558, the Scottish Calvinist minister John Knox thundered against what he called "the monstrous regiment of women." When the Protestant Elizabeth came to the throne the following year, Knox and his religious brethren were less inclined to denounce female rulers, but in England as elsewhere in Europe there remained a widespread conviction that women were unsuited to wield power over men. Many men seem to have regarded the capacity for rational thought as exclusively male; women, they assumed, were led only by their passions. While gentlemen mastered the arts of rhetoric and warfare, gentlewomen were expected to display the virtues of silence and good housekeeping. Among upper-class males, the will to dominate others was acceptable and indeed admired; the same will in women was condemned as a grotesque and dangerous aberration.

Apologists for the queen countered these prejudices by appealing to historical prece-

The Armada portrait: note Elizabeth's hand on the globe.

dent and legal theory. History offered inspiring examples of just female rulers, notably Deborah, the biblical prophetess who judged Israel. In the legal sphere, crown lawyers advanced the theory of "the king's two bodies." As England's crowned head, Elizabeth's person was mystically divided between her mortal "body natural" and the immortal "body politic." While the queen's natural body was inevitably subject to the failings of human flesh, the body politic was timeless and perfect. In political terms, therefore, Elizabeth's sex was a matter of no consequence, a thing indifferent.

Elizabeth, who had received a fine humanist education and an extended, dangerous lesson in the art of survival, made it immediately clear that she intended to rule in more than name only. She assembled a group of trustworthy advisers, foremost among them William Cecil (later named Lord Burghley), but she insisted on making many of the crucial decisions herself. Like many Renaissance monarchs, Elizabeth was drawn to the idea of royal absolutism, the theory that ultimate power was properly concentrated in her person and indeed that God had appointed her to be His deputy in the kingdom. Opposition to her rule, in this view, was not only a political act but also a kind of impiety, a blasphemous grudging against the will of God. Apologists for absolutism contended that God commands obedience even to manifestly wicked rulers whom He has sent to punish the sinfulness of humankind. Such arguments were routinely made in speeches and political tracts and from the pulpits of churches, where they were incorporated into the *Book of Homilies*, which clergymen were required to read out to their congregations.

In reality, Elizabeth's power was not absolute. The government had a network of spies, informers, and *agents provocateurs*, but it lacked a standing army, a national police force, an efficient system of communication, and an extensive bureaucracy. Above all, the queen had limited financial resources and needed to turn periodically to an independent and often recalcitrant Parliament, which by long tradition had the sole right to levy taxes and to grant subsidies. Members of the House of Commons were elected from their boroughs, not appointed by the monarch, and though the queen had considerable influence over their decisions, she could by no means dictate policy. Under these constraints, Elizabeth ruled through a combination of adroit political maneuvering and imperious command, all the while enhancing her authority in the eyes of both court and country by means of an extraordinary cult of love.

"We all loved her," Elizabeth's godson Sir John Harington wrote, with just a touch of irony, a few years after the queen's death, "for she said she loved us." Ambassadors, courtiers, and parliamentarians all submitted to Elizabeth's cult of love, in which the queen's gender was transformed from a potential liability into a significant asset. Those who approached her generally did so on their knees and were expected to address her with extravagant compliments fashioned from the period's most passionate love poetry; she in turn spoke, when it suited her to do so, in the language of love poetry. The court moved in an atmosphere of romance, with music, dancing, plays, and the elaborate, fancy-dress entertainments called masques. The queen adorned herself in gorgeous clothes and rich jewels. When she went on one of her summer "progresses," ceremonial journeys through her land, she looked like an exotic, sacred image in a religious cult of love, and her noble hosts virtually bankrupted themselves to lavish upon her the costliest pleasures. England's leading artists, such as the poet Edmund Spenser and the painter Nicholas Hilliard, enlisted themselves in the celebration of Elizabeth's mystery, likening her to the goddesses and queens of mythology: Diana, Astraea, Gloriana. Her cult drew its power from cultural discourses that ranged from the secular (her courtiers could pine for her as a cruel Petrarchan mistress) to the sacred (the veneration that under Catholicism had been due to the Virgin Mary could now be directed toward England's semidivine queen).

There was a sober, even grim aspect to these poetical fantasies: Elizabeth was brilliant at playing one dangerous faction off against another, now turning her gracious smiles on one favorite, now honoring his hated rival, now suddenly looking elsewhere and raising an obscure upstart to royal favor. And when she was disobeyed or when she felt that her prerogatives had been challenged, she was capable of an anger that, as Harington put it, "left no doubtings whose daughter she was." Thus when Sir Walter Ralegh, one of the queen's glittering favorites, married without her knowledge or consent, he found himself promptly imprisoned in the Tower of London. And when the Protestant polemicist John Stubbs ventured to publish a pamphlet stridently denouncing the queen's proposed marriage to the French Catholic Duke of Alençon, Stubbs and his publisher were arrested and had their right hands chopped off. (After receiving the blow, the now prudent Stubbs lifted his hat with his remaining hand and cried, "God save the Queen!")

The queen's marriage negotiations were a particularly fraught issue. When she came to the throne at twenty-five years old, speculation about a suitable match, already widespread, intensified and remained for decades at a fever pitch, for the stakes were high. If Elizabeth died childless, the Tudor line would come to an end. The nearest heir was her cousin Mary, Queen of Scots, a Catholic whose claim was supported by France and by the papacy and whose penchant for sexual and political intrigue confirmed the worst fears of English Protestants. The obvious way to avert the nightmare was for Elizabeth to marry and produce an heir, and the pressure upon her to do so was intense.

More than the royal succession hinged on the question of the queen's marriage; Elizabeth's perceived eligibility was a vital factor in the complex machinations of international diplomacy. A dynastic marriage between the Queen of England and a foreign ruler would forge an alliance powerful enough to alter the balance of power in Europe. The English court hosted a steady stream of ambassadors from kings and princes eager to win the hand of the royal maiden, and Elizabeth, who prided herself on speaking fluent French and Italian (and on reading Latin and Greek), played her romantic part with exemplary skill, sighing and spinning the negotiations out for months and even years. Most probably, she never meant to marry any of her numerous foreign (and domestic) suitors. Such a decisive act would have meant the end of her independence, as well as the end of the marriage game by which she played one power off against another. One day she would seem to be on the verge of accepting a proposal; the next, she would vow never to forsake her virginity. "She is a Princess," the French ambassador remarked, "who can act any part she pleases."

The Kingdom in Danger

Beset by Catholic and Protestant extremists, Elizabeth contrived to forge a moderate compromise that enabled her realm to avert the massacres and civil wars that poisoned France and other countries on the Continent. But menace was never far off, and there were constant fears of conspiracy, rebellion, and assassination. Many of the fears swirled around Mary, Queen of Scots, who had been driven from her own kingdom in 1568 by a powerful faction of rebellious nobles and had taken refuge in England. Her presence, under a kind of house arrest, was the source of intense anxiety and helped generate continual rumors of plots. Some of these plots were real enough, others imaginary, still others traps set in motion by the secret agents of the government's intelligence service under the direction of Sir Francis Walsingham. The situation worsened greatly after the St. Bartholomew's Day Massacre of Protestants (Huguenots) in France (1572), after Spanish imperial armies invaded the Netherlands in order to stamp out Protestant rebels, and after the assassination there of Europe's other major Protestant leader, William of Orange (1584).

The queen's life seemed to be in even greater danger after Pope Gregory XIII's proclamation in 1580 that the assassination of the great heretic Elizabeth (who had been excommunicated a decade before) would not constitute a mortal sin. The immediate effect of the proclamation was to make existence more difficult for English Catholics, most of whom were loyal to the queen but who fell under grave suspicion. Suspicion was intensified by the clandestine presence of English Jesuits, trained at seminaries abroad and smuggled back into England to serve the Roman Catholic cause. When Elizabeth's spymaster Walsingham unearthed an assassination plot in the correspondence between the Queen of Scots and the Catholic Anthony Babington, the wretched Mary's fate was sealed. After vacillating, a very reluctant Elizabeth signed the death warrant in February 1587, and her cousin was beheaded.

The long-anticipated military confrontation with Catholic Spain was now unavoidable.

Elizabeth learned that Philip II, her former brother-in-law and onetime suitor, was preparing to send an enormous fleet against her island realm. It was to sail to the Netherlands, where a Spanish army would be waiting to embark and invade England. Barring its way was England's small fleet of well-armed and highly maneuverable fighting vessels, backed up by ships from the merchant navy. The Invincible Armada reached English waters in July 1588, only to be routed in one of the most famous and decisive naval battles in European history. Then, in what many viewed as an act of God on behalf of Protestant England, the Spanish fleet was dispersed and all but destroyed by violent storms.

As England braced itself to withstand the invasion that never came, Elizabeth appeared in person to review a detachment of soldiers assembled at Tilbury. Dressed in a white gown and a silver breastplate, she declared that though some among her councillors had urged her not to appear before a large crowd of armed men, she would never fail to trust the loyalty of her faithful and loving subjects. Nor did she fear the Spanish armies. "I know I have the body of a weak and feeble woman," Elizabeth declared, "but I have the heart and stomach of a king, and of England too." In this celebrated speech, Elizabeth displayed many of her most memorable qualities: her self-consciously histrionic command of grand public occasion, her subtle blending of magniloquent rhetoric and the language of love, her strategic appropriation of traditionally masculine qualities, and her great personal courage. "We princes," she once remarked, "are set on stages in the sight and view of all the world."

The English and Otherness

Shakespeare's London had a large population of resident aliens, mainly artisans and merchants and their families, from Portugal, Italy, Spain, Germany, and above all France and the Netherlands. Many of these people were Protestant refugees, and they were accorded some legal and economic protection by the government. But they were not always welcome by the local populace. Throughout the sixteenth century, London was the site of repeated demonstrations and, on occasion, bloody riots against the communities of foreign artisans, who were accused of taking jobs away from Englishmen. There was widespread hostility as well toward the Welsh, the Scots, and especially the Irish, whom the English had for centuries been struggling unsuccessfully to subdue. The kings of England claimed to be rulers of Ireland, but in reality they effectively controlled only a small area known as the Pale, extending north from Dublin. The great majority of the Irish people remained stubbornly Catholic and, despite endlessly reiterated English repression, burning of villages, destruction of crops, and massacres, incorrigibly independent.

Shakespeare's *Henry V* (1598–99) seems to invite the audience to celebrate the conjoined heroism of English, Welsh, Scots, and Irish soldiers all fighting together as a "band of brothers" against the French. But such a way of imagining the national community must be set against the tensions and conflicting interests that often set these brothers at each other's throats. As Shakespeare's King Henry realizes, a feared or hated foreign enemy helps at least to mask these tensions, and indeed, in the face of the Spanish Armada, even the bitter gulf between Catholic and Protestant Englishmen seemed to narrow significantly. But the patriotic alliance was only temporary.

Another way of partially masking the sharp differences in language, belief, and custom among the peoples of the British Isles was to group these people together in contrast to the Jews. Medieval England's Jewish population, the recurrent object of persecution, extortion, and massacre, had been officially expelled by King Edward I in 1290, but Elizabethan England harbored a tiny number of Jews or Jewish converts to Christianity who were treated with suspicion and hostility. One of these was Elizabeth's own physician, Roderigo Lopez, who was tried in 1594 for an alleged plot to poison the queen. Convicted and condemned to the hideous execution reserved for traitors, Lopez went to his death, in the words of the Elizabethan historian William Camden, "affirming that he loved the Queen as well as he loved Jesus Christ; which coming from a man of the Jewish profession moved

A Jewish man depicted poisoning a well. From Pierre Boaistuau, *Certaine Secrete Wonders of Nature* (1569).

no small laughter in the standers-by." It is difficult to gauge the meaning here of the phrase "the Jewish profession," used to describe a man who never as far as we know professed Judaism, just as it is difficult to gauge the meaning of the crowd's cruel laughter.

Elizabethans appear to have been fascinated by Jews and Judaism but quite uncertain whether the terms referred to a people, a foreign nation, a set of strange practices, a living faith, a defunct religion, a villainous conspiracy, or a messianic inheritance. Protestant Reformers brooded deeply on the Hebraic origins of Christianity; government officials ordered the arrest of those "suspected to be Jews"; villagers paid pennies to itinerant fortune-tellers who claimed to be descended from Abraham or masters of cabalistic mysteries; and London playgoers, perhaps including some who laughed at Lopez on the scaffold, enjoyed the spectacle of the downfall of the wicked Barabas in Christopher Marlowe's *Jew of Malta* (c. 1592) and the forced conversion of Shylock in Shakespeare's *Merchant of Venice* (1596–97). Few if any of Shakespeare's contemporaries would have encountered on English soil Jews who openly practiced their religion, though England probably harbored a small number of so-called Marranos, Spanish or Portuguese Jews who had officially converted to Christianity but secretly continued to observe Jewish practices. Jews were not officially permitted to resettle in England until the middle of the seventeenth century, and even then their legal status was ambiguous.

Shakespeare's England also had a small African population whose skin color was the subject of pseudo-scientific speculation and theological debate. Some Elizabethans believed that Africans' blackness resulted from the climate of the regions in which they lived, where, as one traveler put it, they were "so scorched and vexed with the heat of the sun, that in many places they curse it when it riseth." Others held that blackness was a curse inherited from their forefather Chus, the son of Ham, who had, according to Genesis, wickedly exposed the nakedness of the drunken Noah. George Best, a proponent of this theory of inherited skin color, reported that "I myself have seen an Ethiopian as black as coal brought into England, who taking a fair English woman to wife, begat a son in all respects as black as the father was, although England were his native country, and an English woman his mother: whereby it seemeth this blackness proceedeth rather of some natural infection of that man."

As the word "infection" suggests, Elizabethans frequently regarded blackness as a physical defect, though the blacks who lived in England and Scotland throughout the sixteenth century were also treated as exotic curiosities. At his marriage to Anne of Denmark, James I entertained his bride and her family by commanding four naked black youths to dance before him in the snow. (The youths died of exposure shortly afterward.) In 1594, in the festivities celebrating the baptism of James's son, a "Black-Moor" entered pulling an elaborately decorated chariot that was, in the original plan, supposed to be drawn in by a lion. There was a black trumpeter in the courts of Henry VII and Henry VIII, while Elizabeth had at least two black servants, one an entertainer and the other a page. Africans became increasingly popular as servants in aristocratic and gentle households in the last decades of the sixteenth century.

Some of these Africans were almost certainly slaves, though the legal status of slavery in England was ambiguous. In Cartwright's Case (1569), the court ruled "that England was too Pure an Air for Slaves to breathe in," but there is evidence that black slaves were owned in Elizabethan and Jacobean England. Moreover, by the mid-sixteenth century, the English had become involved in the profitable trade that carried African slaves to the New World. In 1562, John Hawkins embarked on his first slaving voyage, transporting some three hundred blacks from the Guinea coast to Hispaniola, where they were sold for £10,000. Elizabeth is reported to have said of this venture that it was "detestable, and would call down the Vengeance of Heaven upon the Undertakers." Nevertheless, she invested in Hawkins's subsequent voyages and loaned him ships.

English men and women of the sixteenth century experienced an

Man with head beneath his shoulders. From a Spanish edition of Mandeville's *Travels*. See *Othello* 1.3.144–45: "and men whose heads / Do grow beneath their shoulders." Such men were occasionally reported by medieval travelers to the East.

unprecedented increase in knowledge of the world beyond their island, for a number of reasons. Religious persecution compelled both Catholics and Protestants to live abroad; wealthy gentlemen (and, in at least a few cases, ladies) traveled in France and Italy to view the famous cultural monuments; merchants published accounts of distant lands such as Turkey, Morocco, and Russia; and military and trading ventures took English ships to still more distant shores. In 1496, a Venetian tradesman living in Bristol, John Cabot, was granted a license by Henry VII to sail on a voyage of exploration; with his son Sebastian, he discovered Newfoundland and Nova Scotia. Remarkable feats of seamanship and reconnaissance soon followed: on his ship the *Golden Hind*, Sir Francis Drake circumnavigated the globe in 1579 and laid claim to California on behalf of the queen; a few years later, a ship commanded by Thomas Cavendish also completed a circumnavigation. Sir Martin Frobisher explored bleak Baffin Island in search of a Northwest Passage to the Orient; Sir John Davis explored the west coast of Greenland and discovered the Falkland Islands off the coast of Argentina; Sir Walter Ralegh ventured up the Orinoco Delta, in what is now Venezuela, in search of the mythical land of El Dorado. Accounts of these and other exploits were collected by a clergyman and promoter of empire, Richard Hakluyt, and published as *The Principal Navigations* (1589; expanded edition 1599).

"To seek new worlds for gold, for praise, for glory," as Ralegh characterized such enterprises, was not for the faint of heart: Drake, Cavendish, Frobisher, and Hawkins all died at sea, as did huge numbers of those who sailed under their command. Elizabethans sensible enough to stay at home could do more than read written accounts of their fellow countrymen's far-reaching voyages. Expeditions brought back native plants (including, most famously, tobacco), animals, cultural artifacts, and, on occasion, samples of the native

An Indian dance. From Thomas Hariot, A *Briefe and True Report of the New Found Land of Virginia* (1590).

peoples themselves, most often seized against their will. There were exhibitions in London of a kidnapped Eskimo with his kayak and of Virginians with their canoes. Most of these miserable captives, violently uprooted and vulnerable to European diseases, quickly perished, but even in death they were evidently valuable property: when the English will not give one small coin "to relieve a lame beggar," one of the characters in *The Tempest* wryly remarks, "they will lay out ten to see a dead Indian" (2.2.30–31).

Perhaps most nations learn to define what they are by defining what they are not. This negative self-definition is, in any case, what Elizabethans seemed constantly to be doing, in travel books, sermons, political speeches, civic pageants, public exhibitions, and theatrical spectacles of otherness. The extraordinary variety of these exercises (which include public executions and urban riots, as well as more benign forms of curiosity) suggests that the boundaries of national identity were by no means clear and unequivocal. Even peoples whom English writers routinely, viciously stigmatize as irreducibly alien—Italians, Indians, Turks, and Jews—have a surprising instability in the Elizabethan imagination and may appear for brief, intense moments as powerful models to be admired and emulated before they resume their place as emblems of despised otherness.

James I and the Union of the Crowns

Though under great pressure to do so, the aging Elizabeth steadfastly refused to name her successor. It became increasingly apparent, however, that it would be James Stuart, the son of Mary, Queen of Scots, and by the time Elizabeth's health began to fail, several of her principal advisers, including her chief minister, Robert Cecil, had been for several years in secret correspondence with him in Edinburgh. Crowned King James VI of Scotland in 1567 when he was but one year old, Mary's son had been raised as a Protestant by his powerful guardians, and in 1589 he married a Protestant princess, Anne of Denmark. When Elizabeth died on March 24, 1603, English officials reported that on her deathbed the queen had named James to succeed her.

Upon his accession, James—now styled James VI of Scotland and James I of England—made plain his intention to unite his two kingdoms. As he told Parliament in 1604, "What God hath conjoined then, let no man separate. I am the husband, and all of the whole isle is my lawful wife; I am the head and it is my body; I am the shepherd and it is my flock." But the flock was less perfectly united than James optimistically envisioned: English and Scottish were sharply distinct identities, as were Welsh and Cornish and other peoples who were incorporated, with varying degrees of willingness, into the realm.

Fearing that to change the name of the kingdom would invalidate all laws and institutions established under the name of England, a fear that was partly real and partly a cover for anti-Scots prejudice, Parliament balked at James's desire to be called "King of Great Britain" and resisted the unionist legislation that would have made Great Britain a legal reality. Though the English initially rejoiced at the peaceful transition from Elizabeth to her successor, there was a rising tide of resentment against James's advancement of Scots friends and his creation of new knighthoods. Lower down the social ladder, English and Scots occasionally clashed violently on the streets: in July 1603, James issued a proclamation against Scottish "insolencies," and in April 1604, he ordered the arrest of "swaggerers" waylaying Scots in London. The ensuing years did not bring the amity and docile obedience for which James hoped, and, though the navy now flew the Union Jack, combining the Scottish cross of St. Andrew and the English cross of St. George, the unification of the kingdoms remained throughout his reign an unfulfilled ambition.

Funeral procession of Queen Elizabeth. From a watercolor sketch by an unknown artist (1603).

The Jacobean Court

With James as with Elizabeth, the royal court was the center of diplomacy, ambition, intrigue, and an intense jockeying for social position. As always in monarchies, proximity to the king's person was a central mark of favor, so that access to the royal bedchamber was one of the highest aims of the powerful, scheming lords who followed James from his sprawling London palace at Whitehall to the hunting lodges and country estates to which he loved to retreat. A coveted office, in the Jacobean as in the Tudor court, was the Groom of the Stool, the person who supervised the disposal of the king's wastes. The officeholder was close to the king at one of his most exposed and vulnerable moments and enjoyed the further privilege of sleeping on a pallet at the foot of the royal bed and putting on the royal undershirt. Another, slightly less privileged official, the Gentleman of the Robes, dressed the king in his doublet and outer garments.

The royal life-style was increasingly expensive. Unlike Elizabeth, James had to maintain separate households for his queen and for the heir apparent, Prince Henry. (Upon Henry's death at the age of eighteen in 1612, his younger brother, Prince Charles, became heir, eventually succeeding his father in 1625.) James was also extremely generous to his friends, amassing his own huge debts in the course of paying off theirs. As early as 1605, he told his principal adviser that "it is a horror to me to think of the height of my place, the greatness of my debts, and the smallness of my means." This smallness notwithstanding, James continued to lavish gifts upon handsome favorites such as the Earl of Somerset, Robert Carr, and the Duke of Buckingham, George Villiers.

The attachment James formed for these favorites was highly romantic. "God so love me," the king wrote to Buckingham, "as I desire only to live in the world for your sake,

and that I had rather live banished in any part of the earth with you than live a sorrowful widow's life without you." Such sentiments, not surprisingly, gave rise to widespread rumors of homosexual activities at court. The rumors are certainly plausible, though the surviving evidence of same-sex relationships, at court or elsewhere, is extremely difficult to interpret. A statute of 1533 made "the detestable and abominable vice of buggery committed with mankind or beast" a felony punishable by death. (English law declined to recognize or criminalize lesbian acts.) The effect of the draconian laws against buggery and sodomy seems to have been to reduce actual prosecutions to the barest minimum: for the next hundred years, there are no known cases of trials resulting in a death sentence for homosexual activity alone. If the legal record is therefore unreliable as an index of the extent of homosexual relations, the literary record (including, most famously, the majority of Shakespeare's sonnets) is equally opaque. Any poetic avowal of male-male love may simply be a formal expression of affection based on clas-

James I. By Marc Gheeraerts II, court painter.

Two Young Men. By Crispin van den Broeck.

sical models, or, alternatively, it may be an expression of passionate physical and spiritual love. The interpretive difficulty is compounded by the absence in the period of any clear reference to a homosexual "identity," though there are many references to same-sex acts and feelings. What is clear is that male friendships at the court of James and elsewhere were suffused with a potential eroticism, at once delightful and threatening, that subsequent periods policed more anxiously.

In addition to the extravagant expenditures on his favorites, James was also the patron of ever more elaborate feasts and masques. Shakespeare's work provides a small glimpse of these in *The Tempest,* with its exotic banquet and its "majestic vision" of mythological goddesses and dancing nymphs and reapers, but the actual Jacobean court masques, designed by the great architect, painter, and engineer Inigo Jones, were spectacular, fantastic, technically ingenious, and staggeringly costly celebrations of regal magnificence. With their exquisite costumes and their elegant blend of music, dancing, and poetry, the masques, generally performed by the noble lords and ladies of the court, were deliberately ephemeral exercises in conspicuous expenditure and consumption: by tradition, at the end of the performance, the private audience would rush forward and tear to pieces the gorgeous scenery. And though masques were enormously sophisticated entertainments, often on rather esoteric allegorical themes, they could on occasion collapse into grotesque excess. In a letter of 1606, Sir John Harington describes a masque in honor of the visiting Danish king in which the participants, no doubt toasting their royal majesties, had had too much to drink. A lady playing the part of the Queen of Sheba attempted to present precious gifts, "but, forgetting the steps arising to the canopy, overset her caskets into his Danish Majesty's lap. . . . His Majesty then got up and would dance with the Queen of Sheba; but he fell down and humbled himself before her, and was carried to an inner chamber and laid on a bed." Meanwhile, Harington writes, the masque continued with a pageant of Faith, Hope, and Charity, but Charity could barely keep her balance, while Hope and Faith "were both sick and spewing in the lower hall." This was, we can hope, not a typical occasion.

While the English seem initially to have welcomed James's free-spending ways as a change from the parsimoniousness of Queen Elizabeth, they were dismayed by its consequences. Elizabeth had died owing £400,000. In 1608, the royal debt had risen to

£1,400,000 and was increasing by £140,000 a year. The money to pay off this debt, or at least to keep it under control, was raised by various means. These included customs farming (leasing the right to collect customs duties to private individuals); the highly unpopular impositions (duties on the import of nonnecessities, such as spices, silks, and currants); the sale of crown lands; the sale of baronetcies; and appeals to an increasingly grudging and recalcitrant Parliament. In 1614, Parliament demanded an end to impositions before it would relieve the king and was angrily dissolved without completing its business.

James's Religious Policy and the Persecution of Witches

Before his accession to the English throne, the king had made known his view of Puritans, the general name for a variety of Protestant sects that were agitating for a radical reform of the church, the overthrow of its conservative hierarchy of bishops, and the rejection of a large number of traditional rituals and practices. In a book he wrote, *Basilikon Doron* (1599), James denounced "brainsick and heady preachers" who were prepared "to let King, people, law and all be trod underfoot." Yet he was not entirely unwilling to consider religious reforms. In religion, as in foreign policy, he was above all concerned to maintain peace.

On his way south to claim the throne of England in 1603, James was presented with the Millenary Petition (signed by one thousand ministers), which urged him as "our physician" to heal the disease of lingering "popish" ceremonies. He responded by calling a conference on the ceremonies of the Church of England, which duly took place at Hampton Court Palace in January 1604. The delegates who spoke for reform were moderates, and there was little in the outcome to satisfy Puritans. Nevertheless, while the Church of England continued to cling to such remnants of the Catholic past as wedding rings, square caps, bishops, and Christmas, the conference did produce some reform in the area of

The "swimming" of a suspected witch.

ecclesiastical discipline. It also authorized a new English translation of the Bible, known as the King James Bible, which was printed in 1611, too late to have been extensively used by Shakespeare. Along with Shakespeare's works, the King James Bible has probably had the profoundest influence on the subsequent history of English literature.

Having arranged this compromise, James saw his main task as ensuring conformity. He promulgated the 1604 Canons (the first definitive code of canon law since the Reformation), which required all ministers to subscribe to three articles. The first affirmed royal supremacy; the second confirmed that there was nothing in the Book of Common Prayer "contrary to the Word of God" and required ministers to use only the authorized services; the third asserted that the central tenets of the Church of England were "agreeable to the Word of God." There were strong objections to the second and third articles from those of Puritan leanings inside and outside the House of Commons. In the end, many ministers refused to conform or subscribe to the articles, but only about ninety of them, or 1 percent of the clergy, were deprived of their livings. In its theology and composition, the Church of England was little changed from what it had been under Elizabeth. In hindsight, what is most striking are the ominous signs of growing religious divisions that would by the 1640s burst forth in civil war and the execution of James's son Charles.

James seems to have taken seriously the official claims to the sacredness of kingship, and he certainly took seriously his own theories of religion and politics, which he had printed for the edification of his people. He was convinced that Satan, perpetually warring against God and His representatives on earth, was continually plotting against him. James thought moreover that he possessed special insight into Satan's wicked agents, the witches, and in 1597, while King of Scotland, he published his *Demonology*, a learned exposition of their malign threat to his godly rule. Hundreds of witches, he believed, were involved in a 1590 conspiracy to kill him by raising storms at sea when he was sailing home from Denmark with his new bride.

In the 1590s, Scotland embarked on a virulent witch craze of the kind that had since the fifteenth century repeatedly afflicted France, Switzerland, and Germany, where many thousands of women (and a much smaller number of men) were caught in a nightmarish web of wild accusations. Tortured into lurid confessions of infant cannibalism, night flying, and sexual intercourse with the devil at huge, orgiastic "witches' Sabbaths," the victims had little chance to defend themselves and were routinely burned at the stake.

In England too there were witchcraft prosecutions, though on a much smaller scale and with significant differences in the nature of the accusations and the judicial procedures. Witch trials began in England in the 1540s; statutes against witchcraft were enacted in 1542, 1563, and 1604. English law did not allow judicial torture, stipulated lesser punishments in cases of "white magic," and mandated jury trials. Juries acquitted more than half of the defendants in witchcraft trials; in Essex, where the judicial records are particularly extensive, some 24 percent of those accused were executed, while the remainder of those convicted were pilloried and imprisoned or sentenced and reprieved. The accused were generally charged with *maleficium*, an evil deed—usually harming neighbors, causing destructive storms, or killing farm animals—but not with worshipping Satan.

After 1603, when James came to the English throne, he somewhat moderated his enthusiasm for the judicial murder of witches, for the most part defenseless, poor women resented by their neighbors. Though he did nothing to mitigate the ferocity of the ongoing witch-hunts in his native Scotland, he did not try to institute Scottish-style persecutions and trials in his new realm. This relative waning of persecutorial eagerness principally reflects the differences between England and Scotland, but it may also bespeak some small, nascent skepticism on James's part about the quality of evidence brought against the accused and about the reliability of the "confessions" extracted from them. It is sobering to reflect that plays like Shakespeare's *Macbeth* (1606), Thomas Middleton's *Witch* (before 1616), and Thomas Dekker, John Ford, and William Rowley's *Witch of Edmonton* (1621) seem to be less the allies of skepticism than the exploiters of fear.

The Playing Field

Cosmic Spectacles

The first permanent, freestanding public theaters in England date only from Shakespeare's own lifetime: a London playhouse, the Red Lion, is mentioned in 1567, and James Burbage's playhouse, The Theatre, was built in 1576. (The innovative use of these new stages, crucial to a full understanding of Shakespeare's achievement, is the subject of a separate essay in this volume, by the theater historian Andrew Gurr.) But it is quite misleading to identify English drama exclusively with these specially constructed playhouses, for in fact there was a rich and vital theatrical tradition in England stretching back for centuries. Many towns in late medieval England were the sites of annual festivals that mounted elaborate cycles of plays depicting the great biblical stories, from the creation of the world to Christ's Passion and its miraculous aftermath. Most of these plays have been lost, but the surviving cycles, such as those from York, are magnificent and complex works of art. They are sometimes called "mystery plays," either because they were performed by the guilds of various crafts (known as "mysteries") or, more likely, because they represented the mysteries of the faith. The cycles were most often performed on the annual feast day instituted in the early fourteenth century in honor of the Corpus Christi, the sacrament of the Lord's Supper, which is perhaps the greatest of these religious mysteries.

The feast of Corpus Christi, celebrated on the Thursday following Trinity Sunday, helped give the play cycles their extraordinary cultural resonance, but it also contributed to their downfall. For along with the specifically liturgical plays traditionally performed by religious confraternities and the "saints' plays, which depicted miraculous events in the lives of individual holy men and women, the mystery cycles were closely identified with the Catholic Church. Protestant authorities in the sixteenth century, eager to eradicate all remnants of popular Catholic piety, moved to suppress the annual procession of the Host, with its gorgeous banners, pageant carts, and cycle of visionary plays. In 1548, the Feast of Corpus Christi was abolished. Towns that continued to perform the mysteries were under increasing pressure to abandon them. It is sometimes said that the cycles were already dying out from neglect, but recent research has shown that many towns and their guilds were extremely reluctant to give them up. Desperate offers to strip away any traces of Catholic doctrine and to submit the play scripts to the authorities for their approval met with unbending opposition from the government. In 1576, the courts gave York permission to perform its cycle but only if

> in the said play no pageant be used or set forth wherein the Majesty of God the Father, God the Son, or God the Holy Ghost or the administration of either the Sacraments of baptism or of the Lord's Supper be counterfeited or represented, or anything played which tend to the maintenance of superstition and idolatry or which be contrary to the laws of God . . . or of the realm.

Such "permission" was tantamount to an outright ban. The local officials in the city of Norwich, proud of their St. George and the Dragon play, asked if they could at least parade the dragon costume through the streets, but even this modest request was refused. It is likely that as a young man Shakespeare had seen some of these plays: when Hamlet says of a noisy, strutting theatrical performance that it "out-Herods Herod," he is alluding to the famously bombastic role of Herod of Jewry in the mystery plays. But by the century's end, the cycles were no longer performed.

Early English theater was by no means restricted to these civic and religious festivals. Payments to professional and amateur performers appear in early records of towns and aristocratic households, though the terms—"ministralli," "histriones," "mimi," "lusores," and so forth—are not used with great consistency and make it difficult to distinguish among minstrels, jugglers, stage players, and other entertainers. Performers acted in town halls and the halls of guilds and aristocratic mansions, on scaffolds erected in town squares

Panorama of London, showing two theaters, both round and both flying flags: a flying flag indicated that a performance was in progress. The Globe is in the foreground, and the Beargarden or Hope is to the left.

and marketplaces, on pageant wagons in the streets, and in inn yards. By the fifteenth century, and probably earlier, there were organized companies of players traveling under noble patronage. Such companies earned a living providing amusement, while enhancing the prestige of the patron.

A description of a provincial performance in the late sixteenth century, written by one R. Willis, provides a glimpse of what seems to have been the usual procedure:

> In the City of Gloucester the manner is (as I think it is in other like corporations) that when the Players of Interludes come to town, they first attend the Mayor to inform him what nobleman's servant they are, and so to get licence for their public playing; and if the Mayor like the Actors, or would show respect to their Lord and Master, he appoints them to play their first play before himself and the Aldermen and common Council of the City and that is called the Mayor's play, where everyone that will come in without money, the Mayor giving the players a reward as he thinks fit to show respect unto them.

In addition to their take from this "first play," the players would almost certainly have supplemented their income by performing in halls and inn yards, where they could pass the hat after the performance or even on some occasions charge an admission fee. It was no doubt a precarious existence.

The "Interludes" mentioned in Willis's description of the Gloucester performances are likely plays that were, in effect, staged dialogues on religious, moral, and political themes. Such works could, like the mysteries, be associated with Catholicism, but they were also used in the sixteenth century to convey polemical Protestant messages, and they reached outside the religious sphere to address secular concerns as well. Henry Medwall's *Fulgens and Lucrece* (c. 1490–1501), for example, pits a wealthy but dissolute nobleman against a virtuous public servant of humble origins, while John Heywood's *Play of the Weather* (c. 1525–33) stages a debate among social rivals, including a gentleman, a merchant, a forest ranger, and two millers. The structure of such plays reflects the training in argumentation that students received in Tudor schools and, in particular, the sustained practice in examining all sides of a difficult question. Some of Shakespeare's amazing ability to look at critical issues from multiple perspectives may be traced back to this practice and the dramatic interludes it helped to inspire.

Another major form of theater that flourished in England in the fifteenth century and continued on into the sixteenth was the morality play. Like the mysteries, moralities addressed questions of the ultimate fate of the soul. They did so, however, not by rehearsing scriptural stories but by dramatizing allegories of spiritual struggle. Typically, a person named Human or Mankind or Youth is faced with a choice between a pious life in the company of such associates as Mercy, Discretion, and Good Deeds and a dissolute life among riotous companions like Lust or Mischief. Plays like *Mankind* (c. 1465–70) and *Everyman* (c. 1495) show how powerful these unpromising-sounding dramas could be, in part because of the extraordinary comic vitality of the evil character, or Vice, and in part because of the poignancy and terror of an individual's encounter with death. Shakespeare clearly grasped this power. The hunchbacked Duke of Gloucester in *Richard III* gleefully likens himself to "the formal Vice, Iniquity." And when Othello wavers between Desdemona and Iago (himself a Vice figure), his anguished dilemma echoes the fateful choice repeatedly faced by the troubled, vulnerable protagonists of the moralities.

If such plays sound a bit like sermons, it is because they were. Clerics and actors shared some of the same rhetorical skills. It would be misleading to regard churchgoing and playgoing as comparable entertainments, but in attacking the stage, ministers often seemed to regard the professional players as dangerous rivals. The players themselves were generally too discreet to rise to the challenge; it would have been foolhardy to present the theater as the church's direct competitor. Yet in its moral intensity and its command of impassioned language, the stage frequently emulates and outdoes the pulpit.

Music and Dance

Playacting took its place alongside other forms of public expression and entertainment as well. Perhaps the most important, from the perspective of the theater, were music and dance, since these were directly and repeatedly incorporated into plays. Many plays, comedies and tragedies alike, include occasions that call upon the characters to dance: hence Beatrice and Benedick join the other masked guests at the dance in *Much Ado About Nothing*; in *Twelfth Night*, the befuddled Sir Andrew, at the instigation of the drunken Sir Toby Belch, displays his skill, such as it is, in capering; Romeo and Juliet first see each other at the Capulet ball; the witches dance in a ring around the hideous caldron and perform an "antic round" to cheer Macbeth's spirits; and, in one of Shakespeare's strangest and most wonderful scenes, the drunken Antony in *Antony and Cleopatra* joins hands with Caesar, Enobarbus, Pompey, and others to dance "the Egyptian Bacchanals."

Moreover, virtually all plays in the period, including Shakespeare's, apparently ended with a dance. Brushing off the theatrical gore and changing their expressions from woe to pleasure, the actors in plays like *Hamlet* and *King Lear* would presumably have received the audience's applause and then bid for a second round of applause by performing a stately pavane or a lively jig. Indeed, jigs, with their comical leaping dance steps often accompanied by scurrilous ballads, became so popular that they drew not only large crowds but also official disapproval. A court order of 1612 complained about the "cut-purses and other lewd and ill-disposed persons" who flocked to the theater at the end of every play to be entertained by "lewd jigs, songs, and dances." The players were warned to suppress these disreputable entertainments on pain of imprisonment.

The displays of dancing onstage clearly reflected a widespread popular interest in dancing outside the walls of the playhouse as well. Renaissance intellectuals conjured up visions of the universe as a great cosmic dance, poets figured relations between men and women in terms of popular dance steps, stern moralists denounced dancing as an incitement to filthy lewdness, and, perhaps as significant, men of all classes evidently spent a great deal of time worrying about how shapely their legs looked in tights and how gracefully they could leap. Shakespeare assumes that his audience will be quite familiar with a variety of dances. "For, hear me, Hero," Beatrice tells her friend, "wooing, wedding, and repenting is as a Scotch jig, a measure, and a cinquepace" (2.1.60–61). Her speech dwells on the comparison a bit, teasing out its implications, but it still does not make much sense if you do not already know something about the dances and perhaps occasionally venture to perform them yourself.

Closely linked to dancing and even more central to the stage was music, both instrumental and vocal. In the early sixteenth century, the Reformation had been disastrous for sacred music: many church organs were destroyed, choir schools were closed, the glorious polyphonal liturgies sung in the monasteries were suppressed. But by the latter part of the century, new perspectives were reinvigorating English music. Latin masses were reset in English, and tunes were written for newly translated, metrical psalms. More important for the theater, styles of secular music were developed that emphasized music's link to humanist eloquence, its ability to heighten and to rival rhetorically powerful texts.

This link is particularly evident in vocal music, at which Elizabethan composers excelled. Renowned composers William Byrd, Thomas Morley, John Dowland, and others wrote a rich profusion of madrigals (part songs for two to eight voices unaccompanied) and ayres (songs for solo voice, generally accompanied by the lute). These works, along with hymns, popular ballads, rounds, catches, and other forms of song, enjoyed immense popularity, not only in the royal court, where musical skill was regarded as an important accomplishment, and in aristocratic households, where professional musicians were employed as entertainers, but also in less

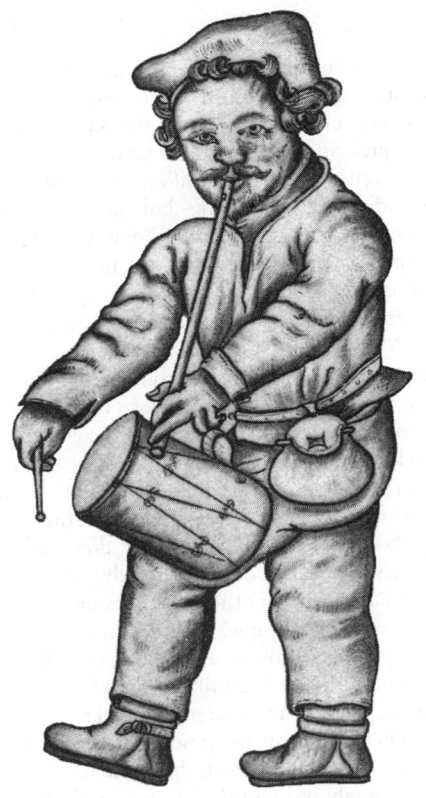

Richard Tarlton. Tarlton was the lead comedian of the Queen's Company from 1583, the year of its founding, until 1588, when he died.

exalted social circles. In his *Plain and Easy Introduction to Practical Music* (1597), Morley tells a story of social humiliation at a failure to perform that suggests that a well-educated Elizabethan was expected to be able to sing at sight. Even if this is an exaggeration in the interest of book sales, there is evidence of impressively widespread musical literacy, reflected in a splendid array of music for the lute, viol, recorder, harp, and virginal, as well as the marvelous vocal music.

Whether it is the aristocratic Orsino luxuriating in the dying fall of an exquisite melody or bully Bottom craving "the tongs and the bones," Shakespeare's characters frequently call for music. They also repeatedly give voice to the age's conviction that there was a deep relation between musical harmony and the harmonies of the well-ordered individual and state. "The man that hath no music in himself," warns Lorenzo in *The Merchant of Venice*, "nor is not moved with concord of sweet sounds, / Is fit for treasons, stratagems, and spoils" (5.1.82–84). This conviction in turn reflects a still deeper link between musical harmony and the divinely created harmony of the cosmos. When Ulysses in *Troilus and Cressida* wishes to convey the image of universal chaos, he speaks of the untuning of a string (1.3.109).

The playing companies must have regularly employed trained musicians, and many actors (like the actor who in playing Pandarus in *Troilus and Cressida* is supposed to accompany himself on the lute) must have possessed musical skill. Unfortunately, we possess the original settings for very few of Shakespeare's songs, possibly because many of them may have been set to popular tunes of the time that everyone knew and no one bothered to write down.

Alternative Entertainments

Plays, music, and dancing were by no means the only shows in town. There were jousts, tournaments, royal entries, religious processions, pageants in honor of newly installed civic officials or ambassadors arriving from abroad; wedding masques, court masques, and costumed entertainments known as "disguisings" or "mummings"; juggling acts, fortune-tellers, exhibitions of swordsmanship, mountebanks, folk healers, storytellers, magic shows; bearbaiting, bullbaiting, cockfighting, and other blood sports; folk festivals such as Maying, the Feast of Fools, Carnival, and Whitsun Ales. For several years, Elizabethan Londoners were delighted by a trained animal—Banks's Horse—that could, it was thought, do arithmetic and answer questions. And there was always the grim but compelling spectacle of public shaming, mutilation, and execution.

Most English towns had stocks and whipping posts. Drunks, fraudulent merchants, adulterers, and quarrelers could be placed in carts or mounted backward on asses and paraded through the streets for crowds to jeer and throw refuse at. Women accused of being scolds could be publicly muzzled by an iron device called a "brank" or tied to a cucking stool and dunked in the river. Convicted criminals could have their ears cut off, their noses slit, their foreheads branded. Public beheadings (generally reserved for the elite) and hangings were common. In the worst cases, felons were sentenced to be "hanged by the neck, and being alive cut down, and your privy members to be cut off, and your bowels to be taken out of your belly and there burned, you being alive."

Shakespeare occasionally takes note of these alternative entertainments: at the end of *Macbeth*, for example, with his enemies closing in on him, the doomed tyrant declares, "They have tied me to a stake. I cannot fly, / But bear-like I must fight the course" (5.7.1–2). The audience is reminded then that it is witnessing the human equivalent of a popular spectacle—a bear chained to a stake and attacked by fierce dogs—that they could have paid to watch at an arena near the Globe. And when, a few moments later, Macduff enters carrying Macbeth's head, the audience is seeing the theatrical equivalent of the execution of criminals and traitors that they could have also watched in the flesh, as it were, nearby. In a different key, the audiences who paid to see *A Midsummer Night's Dream* or *The Winter's Tale* got to enjoy the comic spectacle of a Maying and a Whitsun Pastoral, while

An Elizabethan hanging.

the spectators of *The Tempest* could gawk at what the Folio list of characters calls a "salvage and deformed slave" and to enjoy an aristocratic magician's wedding masque in honor of his daughter.

The Enemies of the Stage

In 1624, a touring company of players arrived in Norwich and requested permission to perform. Permission was denied, but the municipal authorities, "in regard of the honorable respect which this City beareth to the right honorable the Lord Chamberlain," gave the players twenty shillings to get out of town. Throughout the sixteenth and early seventeenth centuries, there are many similar records of civic officials prohibiting performances and then, to appease a powerful patron, paying the actors to take their skills elsewhere. As early as the 1570s, there is evidence that the London authorities, while mindful of the players' influential protectors, were energetically trying to drive the theater out of the city.

Why should what we now regard as one of the undisputed glories of the age have aroused so much hostility? One answer, curiously enough, is traffic: plays drew large audiences—the public theaters could accommodate thousands—and residents objected to the crowds, the noise, and the crush of carriages. Other, more serious concerns were public health and crime. It was thought that numerous diseases, including the dreaded bubonic plague, were spread by noxious odors, and the packed playhouses were obvious breeding grounds for infection. (Patrons often tried to protect themselves by sniffing nosegays or stuffing cloves into their nostrils.) The large crowds drew pickpockets, cutpurses, and other scoundrels. On one memorable afternoon, a pickpocket was caught in the act and tied for the duration of the play to one of the posts that held up the canopy above the stage. The theater was, moreover, a well-known haunt of prostitutes, and, it was alleged, a place where innocent maids were seduced and respectable matrons corrupted. It was darkly rumored that "chambers and secret places" adjoined the theater galleries, and in any case, taverns, disreputable inns, and whorehouses were close at hand.

There were other charges as well. Plays were performed in the afternoon and therefore drew people, especially the young, away from their work. They were schools of idleness, luring apprentices from their trades, law students from their studies, housewives from their kitchens, and potentially pious souls from the sober meditations to which they might otherwise devote themselves. Wasting their time and money on disreputable shows, citizens exposed themselves to sexual provocation and outright political sedition. Even when the content of plays was morally exemplary—and, of course, few plays were so gratify-

Syphilis victim in tub. Frontispiece to the play *Cornelianum Dolium* (1638), possibly authored by Thomas Randolph. The tub inscription translates as "I sit on the throne of love, I suffer in the tub"; and the banner as "Farewell O sexual pleasures and lusts."

ingly high-minded—the theater itself, in the eyes of most mayors and aldermen, was inherently disorderly.

The attack on the stage by civic officials was echoed and intensified by many of the age's moralists and religious leaders, especially those associated with Puritanism. While English Protestants earlier in the sixteenth century had attempted to counter the Catholic mystery cycles and saints' plays by mounting their own doctrinally correct dramas, by the century's end a fairly widespread consensus, even among those mildly sympathetic toward the theater, held that the stage and the pulpit were in tension with one another. After 1591, a ban on Sunday performances was strictly enforced, and in 1606, Parliament passed an act imposing a fine of £10 on any person who shall "in any stage-play, interlude, show, May-game, or pageant, jestingly or profanely speak or use the holy name of God, or of Christ Jesus, or of the Holy Ghost, or of the Trinity (which are not to be spoken but with fear and reverence)." If changes in the printed texts are a reliable indication, the players seem to have complied at least to some degree with the ruling. The Folio (1623) text of *Richard III*, for example, omits the quarto's (1597) four uses of "zounds" (for "God's wounds"), along with a mention of "Christ's dear blood shed for our grievous sins"; "God's my judge" in *The Merchant of Venice* becomes "well I know"; "By Jesu" in *Henry V* becomes a very proper "I say"; and in all the plays, "God" is from time to time metamorphosed to "Jove."

But for some of the theater's more extreme critics, these modest expurgations were tiny bandages on a gaping wound. In his huge book *Histriomastix* (1633), William Prynne regurgitates a half-century of frenzied attacks on the "sinful, heathenish, lewd, ungodly Spectacles." In the eyes of Prynne and his fellow antitheatricalists, stage plays were part of a demonic tangle of obscene practices proliferating like a cancer in the body of society. It is "manifest to all men's judgments," he writes, that

> effeminate mixed dancing, dicing, stage-plays, lascivious pictures, wanton fashions, face-painting, health-drinking, long hair, love-locks, periwigs, women's curling, powdering and cutting of their hair, bonfires, New-year's gifts, May-games, amorous pastorals, lascivious effeminate music, excessive laughter, luxurious disorderly Christmas-keeping, mummeries . . . [are] wicked, unchristian pastimes.

Given the anxious emphasis on effeminacy, it is not surprising that denunciations of this kind obsessively focused on the use of boy actors to play the female parts. The enemies of the stage charged that theatrical transvestism excited illicit sexual desires, both heterosexual and homosexual.

Since cross-dressing violated a biblical prohibition (Deuteronomy 22:5), religious antitheatricalists attacked it as wicked regardless of its erotic charge; indeed, they often seemed to consider any act of impersonation as inherently wicked. In their view, the theater itself was Satan's domain. Thus a Cambridge scholar, John Greene, reports the sad fate of "a Christian woman" who went to the theater to see a play: "She entered in well and sound, but she returned and came forth possessed of the devil. Whereupon certain godly brethren demanded Satan how he durst be so bold, as to enter into her a Christian. Whereto he answered, that *he found her in his own house*, and therefore took possession of her as his own" (italic in original). When the "godly brethren" came to power in the mid-seventeenth century, with the overthrow of Charles I, they saw to it that the playhouses, temporarily shut down in 1642 at the onset of the Civil War, remained closed. The theater did not resume until the restoration of the monarchy in 1660.

Faced with enemies among civic officials and religious leaders, Elizabethan and Jacobean playing companies relied on the protection of their powerful patrons. As the liveried servants of aristocrats or of the monarch, the players could refute the charge that they were mere vagabonds, and they claimed, as a convenient legal fiction, that their public performances were necessary rehearsals in anticipation of those occasions when they would be called upon to entertain their noble masters. But harassment by the mayor and aldermen continued unabated, and the players were forced to build their theaters outside the immediate jurisdiction of the city authorities, either in the suburbs or in the areas known as the "liberties." A liberty was a piece of land within the City of London itself that was not directly subject to the authority of the lord mayor. The most significant of these from the point of view of the theater was the area near St. Paul's Cathedral called "the Blackfriars," where, until the dissolution of the monasteries in 1538, there had been a Dominican monastery. It was here that in 1608 Shakespeare's company, then called the King's Men, built the indoor playhouse in which they performed during the winter months, reserving the open-air Globe in the suburb of Southwark for their summer performances.

Censorship and Regulation

In addition to those authorities who campaigned to shut down the theater, there were others whose task was to oversee, regulate, and censor it. Given the outright hostility of the former, the latter may have seemed to the London players equivocal allies rather than enemies. After all, plays that passed the censor were at least licensed to be performed and hence conceded to have some limited legitimacy. In April 1559, at the very start of her reign, Queen Elizabeth drafted a proposal that for the first time envisaged a system for the prior review and regulation of plays throughout her kingdom:

> The Queen's Majesty doth straightly forbid all manner interludes to be played either openly or privately, except the same be notified beforehand, and licensed within any city or town corporate, by the mayor or other chief officers of the same, and within any shire, by such as shall be lieutenants for the Queen's Majesty in the same shire, or by two of the Justices of Peace inhabiting within that part of the shire where any shall be played. . . . And for instruction to every of the said officers, her Majesty doth likewise charge every of them, as they will answer: that they permit none to be played wherein either matters of religion or of the governance of the estate of the commonweal shall be handled or treated upon, but by men of authority, learning and wisdom, nor to be handled before any audience, but of grave and discreet persons.

This proposal, which may not have been formally enacted, makes an important distinction between those who are entitled to address sensitive issues of religion and politics—authors "of authority, learning and wisdom" addressing audiences "of grave and discreet persons"—and those who are forbidden to do so.

The London public theater, with its playwrights who were the sons of glovers, shoemakers, and bricklayers and its audiences in which the privileged classes mingled with rowdy apprentices, masked women, and servants, was clearly not a place to which the government wished to grant freedom of expression. In 1581, the Master of the Revels, an official in the lord chamberlain's department whose role had hitherto been to provide entertainment at court, was given an expanded commission. Sir Edmund Tilney, the functionary who held the office, was authorized

> to warn, command, and appoint in all places within this our Realm of England, as well within franchises and liberties as without, all and every player or players with their playmakers, either belonging to any nobleman or otherwise . . . to appear before him with all such plays, tragedies, comedies, or shows as they shall in readiness or mean to set forth, and them to recite before our said Servant or his sufficient deputy, whom we ordain, appoint, and authorize by these presents of all such shows, plays, players, and playmakers, together with their playing places, to order and reform, authorize and put down, as shall be thought meet or unmeet unto himself or his said deputy in that behalf.

What emerged from this commission was in effect a national system of regulation and censorship. One of its consequences was to restrict virtually all licensed theater to the handful of authorized London-based playing companies. These companies would have to submit their plays for official scrutiny, but in return they received implicit, and on occasion explicit, protection against the continued fierce opposition of the local authorities. Plays reviewed and allowed by the Master of the Revels had been deemed fit to be performed before the monarch; how could mere aldermen legitimately claim that such plays should be banned as seditious?

The key question, of course, is how carefully the Master of the Revels scrutinized the plays brought before him either to hear or, more often from the 1590s onward, to peruse. What was Tilney, who served in the office until his death in 1610, or his successor, Sir George Buc, who served from 1610 to 1621, looking for? What did they insist be cut before they would release what was known as the "allowed copy," the only version licensed for performance? Unfortunately, the office books of the Master of the Revels in Shakespeare's time have been lost; what survives is a handful of scripts on which Tilney, Buc, and their assistants jotted their instructions. These suggest that the readings were rather painstaking, with careful attention paid to possible religious, political, and diplomatic repercussions. References, directly or strongly implied, to any living Christian prince or any important English nobleman, gentleman, or government official were particularly sensitive and likely to be struck. Renaissance political life was highly personalized; people in power were exceptionally alert to insult and zealously patrolled the boundaries of their prestige and reputation.

Moreover, the censors knew that audiences and readers were quite adept at applying theatrical representations distanced in time and space to their own world. At a time of riots against resident foreigners, Tilney read *Sir Thomas More*, a play in which Shakespeare probably had a hand, and instructed the players to cut scenes that, though set in 1517, might have had an uncomfortable contemporary resonance. "Leave out the insurrection wholly," Tilney's note reads, "and the cause thereof and begin with Sir Thomas More at the Mayor's sessions, with a report afterwards of his good service done being sheriff of London upon a mutiny against the Lombards only by a short report and not otherwise at your own perils. E. Tilney." Of course, as Tilney knew perfectly well, most plays succeed precisely by mirroring, if only obliquely, their own times, but this particular reflection evidently seemed to him too dangerous or provocative.

The topical significance of a play depends in large measure on the particular moment in which it is performed, and on certain features of the performance—for example, a striking resemblance between one of the characters and a well-known public figure—that the script itself will not necessarily disclose to us at this great distance or even to the censor at the time. Hence the Master of the Revels noted angrily of one play performed in 1632 that "there were diverse personated so naturally, both of lords and others of the court, that I took it ill." Hence too a play that was deemed allowable when it was first written and performed could return, like a nightmare, to haunt a different place and time. The most famous instance of such a return involves Shakespeare, for on the day before the Earl of Essex's attempted coup against Queen Elizabeth in 1601, someone paid the Lord Chamberlain's Men (the name of Shakespeare's company at the time) forty shillings to revive their old play about the deposition and murder of Richard II. "I am Richard II," the queen declared. "Know ye not that?" However distressed she was by this performance, the queen significantly did not take out her wrath on the players: neither the playwright nor his company was punished, nor was the Master of the Revels criticized for allowing the play in the first place. It was Essex and several of his key supporters who lost their heads.

Evidence suggests that the Master of the Revels often regarded himself not as the strict censor of the theater but as its friendly guardian, charged with averting catastrophes. He was a bureaucrat concerned less with subversive ideas per se than with potential trouble. That is, there is no record of a dramatist being called to account for his heterodox beliefs; rather, plays were censored if they risked offending influential people, including important foreign allies, or if they threatened to cause public disorder by exacerbating religious or other controversies. The distinction is not a stable one, but it helps to explain the intellectual boldness, power, and freedom of a censored theater in a society in which the perceived enemies of the state were treated mercilessly. Shakespeare could have Lear articulate a searing indictment of social injustice—

Robes and furred gowns hide all. Plate sin with gold,
And the strong lance of justice hurtless breaks;
Arm it in rags, a pygmy's straw does pierce it.
(4.5.155–57)

—and evidently neither the Master of the Revels nor the courtiers in their robes and furred gowns protested. But when the Spanish ambassador complained about Thomas Middleton's anti-Spanish allegory *A Game at Chess*, performed at the Globe in 1624, the whole theater was shut down, the players were arrested, and the king professed to be furious at his official for licensing the play in the first place and allowing it to be performed for nine consecutive days.

In addition to the system for the licensing of plays for performance, there was also a system for the licensing of plays for publication. At the start of Shakespeare's career, such press licensing was the responsibility of the Court of High Commission, headed by the Archbishop of Canterbury and the Bishop of London. Their deputies, a panel of junior clerics, were supposed to review the manuscripts, granting licenses to those worthy of publication and rejecting any they deemed "heretical, seditious, or unseemly for Christian ears." Without a license, the Stationers' Company, the guild of the book trade, was not supposed to register a manuscript for publication. In practice, as various complaints and attempts to close loopholes attest, some playbooks were printed without a license. In 1607, the system was significantly revised when Sir George Buc began to license plays for the press. When Buc succeeded to the post of Master of the Revels in 1610, the powers to license plays for the stage and the page were vested in one man.

Theatrical Innovations

The theater continued to flourish under this system of regulation after Shakespeare's death; by the 1630s, as many as five playhouses were operating daily in London. When the theater reemerged after the eighteen-year hiatus imposed by Puritan rule, it quickly resumed its cultural importance, but not without a number of significant changes. Major innovations in staging resulted principally from continental influences on the English artists who accompanied the court of Charles II into exile in France, where they supplied it with masques and other theatrical entertainments.

The institutional conditions and business practices of the two companies chartered by Charles after the Restoration in 1660 also differed from those of Shakespeare's theater. In place of the more collective practice of Shakespeare's company, the Restoration theaters were controlled by celebrated actor-managers who not only assigned themselves starring roles, in both comedy and tragedy, but also assumed sole responsibility for many business decisions, including the setting of their colleagues' salaries. At the same time, the power of the actor-manager, great as it was, was limited by the new importance of outside capital. No longer was the theater, with all of its properties from script to costumes, owned by the "sharers," that is, by those actors who held shares in the joint-stock company. Instead, entrepreneurs would raise capital for increasingly fantastic sets and stage machinery that could cost as much as £3,000, an astronomical sum, for a single production. This investment in turn not only influenced the kinds of new plays written for the theater but helped to transform old plays that were revived, including Shakespeare's.

In his diary entry for August 24, 1661, Samuel Pepys notes that he has been "to the Opera, and there saw Hamlet, Prince of Denmark, done with scenes very well, but above all, Betterton did the prince's part beyond imagination." This is Thomas Betterton's first review, as it were, and it is typical of the enthusiasm he would inspire throughout his fifty-year career on the London stage. Pepys's brief and scattered remarks on the plays he voraciously attended in the 1660s are precious because they are among the few records from the period of concrete and immediate responses to theatrical performances. Modern readers might miss the significance of Pepys's phrase "done with scenes": this production of *Hamlet* was only the third play to use the movable sets first introduced to England by its producer, William Davenant. The central historical fact that makes the productions of this period so exciting is that public theater had been banned altogether for eighteen years until the Restoration of Charles II.

A brief discussion of theatrical developments in the Restoration period will enable us at least to glance longingly at a vast subject that lies outside the scope of this introduction: the rich performance history that extends from Shakespeare's time to our own, involving tens of thousands of productions and adaptations for theater, opera, Broadway musicals, and of course films. The scale of this history is vast in space as well as time: as early as 1607, there is a record of a *Hamlet* performed on board an English ship, HMS *Dragon*, off the coast of Sierra Leone, and troupes of English actors performed in the late sixteenth and early seventeenth centuries as far afield as Poland and Bohemia.

William Davenant, who claimed to be Shakespeare's bastard son, had become an expert on stage scenery while producing masques at the court of Charles I, and when the theaters reopened, he set to work on converting an indoor tennis court into a new kind of theater. He designed a broad open platform like that of the Elizabethan stage, but he replaced the relatively shallow space for "discoveries" (tableaux set up in an opening at the center of the stage, revealed by drawing back a curtain) and the "tiring-house" (the players' dressing room) behind this space with one expanded interior, framed by a proscenium arch, in which scenes could be displayed. These elaborately painted scenes could be moved on and off, using grooves on the floor. The perspectival effect for a spectator of one central painted panel with two "wings" on either side was that of three sides of a room. This effect anticipated that of the familiar "picture frame" stage, developed fully in the nineteenth century, and began a subtle shift in theater away from the elaborate verbal descriptions that are so central to Shakespeare and toward the evocative visual poetry of the set designer's art.

Another convention of Shakespeare's stage, the use of boy actors for female roles, gave way to the more complete illusion of women playing women's parts. The king issued a decree in 1662 forcefully permitting, if not requiring, the use of actresses. The royal decree is couched in the language of social and moral reform: the introduction of actresses will require the "reformation" of scurrilous and profane passages in plays, and this in turn will help forestall some of the objections that shut the theaters down in 1642. In reality, male theater audiences, composed of a narrower range of courtiers and aristocrats than in Shakespeare's time, met this intended reform with the assumption that the new actresses were fair game sexually; most actresses (with the partial exception of those who married male members of their troupes) were regarded as, or actually became, whores. But despite the social stigma, and the fact that their salaries were predictably lower than those of their male counterparts, the stage saw some formidable female stars by the 1680s.

The first recorded appearance of an actress was that of a Desdemona in December 1660. Betterton's Ophelia in 1661 was Mary Saunderson (c. 1637–1712), who became Mrs. Betterton a year later. The most famous Ophelia of the period was Susanna Mountfort, who appeared in that role for the first time at the age of fifteen in 1705. The performance by Mountfort that became legendary occurred in 1720, after a disappointment in love, or so it was said, had driven her mad. Hearing that *Hamlet* was being performed, Mountfort escaped from her keepers and reached the theater, where she concealed herself until the scene in which Ophelia enters in her state of insanity. At this point, Mountfort rushed onto the stage and, in the words of a contemporary, "was in truth Ophelia herself, to the amazement of the performers and the astonishment of the audience."

That the character Ophelia became increasingly and decisively identified with the mad scene owes something to this occurrence, but it is also a consequence of the text used for Restoration performances of *Hamlet*. Having received the performance rights to a good number of Shakespeare's plays, Davenant altered them for the stage in the 1660s, and many of these acting versions remained in use for generations. In the case of *Hamlet*, neither Davenant nor his successors did what they so often did with other plays by Shakespeare, that is, alter the plot radically and interpolate other material. But many of the lines were cut or "improved." The cuts included most of Ophelia's sane speeches, such as her spirited retort to Laertes' moralizing; what remained made her part almost entirely an emblem of "female love melancholy."

Thomas Betterton (1635–1710), the prototype of the actor-manager, who would be the dominant figure in Shakespeare interpretation and in the theater generally through the nineteenth century, made Hamlet his premier role. A contemporary who saw his last performance in the part (at the age of seventy-four, a rather old Prince of Denmark) wrote that to *read* Shakespeare's play was to encounter "dry, incoherent, & broken sentences," but that to see Betterton was to "prove" that the play was written "correctly." Spectators especially admired his reaction to the Ghost's appearance in the Queen's bedchamber: "his Countenance . . . thro' the violent and sudden Emotions of Amazement and Horror, turn[ed] instantly on the Sight of his fathers Spirit, as pale as his Neckcloath, when every Article of his Body seem's affected with a Tremor inexpressible."

The Spanish Tragedie:
OR,
Hieronimo is mad againe.

Containing the lamentable end of *Don Horatio*, and *Belimperia*; with the pittifull death of *Hieronimo*.

Newly corrected, amended, and enlarged with new Additions of the *Painters* part, and others, as it hath of late been diuers times acted.

LONDON,
Printed by W. White, for I. White and T. Langley, and are to be fold at their Shop ouer againft the Sarazens head without New-gate. 1615.

Title page of Thomas Kyd's *Spanish Tragedy* (1615). The first known edition dates from 1592.

A piece of stage business in this scene, Betterton's upsetting his chair on the Ghost's entrance, became so thoroughly identified with the part that later productions were censured if the actor left it out. This business could very well have been handed down from Richard Burbage, the star of Shakespeare's original production, for Davenant, who had coached Betterton in the role, had known the performances of Joseph Taylor, who had succeeded Burbage in it. It is strangely gratifying to notice that Hamlets on stage and screen still occasionally upset their chairs.

Shakespeare's Life and Art

Playwrights, even hugely successful playwrights, were not ordinarily the objects of popular curiosity in early modern England, and few personal documents survive from Shakespeare's life of the kind that usually give the biographies of artists their appeal: no diary, no letters, private or public, no accounts of his childhood, almost no contemporary gossip, no scandals. Shakespeare's exact contemporary the great playwright Christopher Marlowe, lived a mere twenty-nine years—he was murdered in 1593—but he left behind tantalizing glimpses of himself in police documents, the memos of high-ranking government officials, and detailed denunciations by sinister double agents. Ben Jonson recorded his opinions and his reading in a remarkable published notebook, *Timber; or, Discoveries made upon men and matter,* and he also shared his views of the world (including some criticisms of his fellow playwright Shakespeare) with a Scottish poet, William Drummond of Hawthornden, who had the wit to jot them down for posterity. From Shakespeare, there is nothing comparable, not even a book with his name scribbled on the cover and a few marginal notes such as we have for Jonson, let alone working notebooks.

Yet Elizabethan England was a record-keeping society, and centuries of archival labor have turned up a substantial number of traces of its greatest playwright and his family. By themselves the traces would have relatively little interest, but in the light of Shakespeare's plays and poems, they have come to seem like precious relics and manage to achieve a considerable resonance.

Shakespeare's Family

William Shakespeare's grandfather Richard farmed land by the village of Snitterfield, near the small, pleasant market town of Stratford-upon-Avon, about ninety-six miles northwest of London. The playwright's father, John, moved in the mid-sixteenth century to Stratford, where he became a successful glover, landowner, moneylender, and dealer in wool and other agricultural goods. In or about 1557, he married Mary Arden, the daughter of a prosperous and well-connected farmer from the same area, Robert Arden of Wilmcote.

John Shakespeare was evidently highly esteemed by his fellow townspeople, for he held a series of important posts in local government. In 1556, he was appointed ale taster, an office reserved for "able persons and discreet," in 1558 was sworn in as a constable, and in 1561 was elected as one of the town's fourteen burgesses. As burgess, John served as one of the two chamberlains, responsible for administering borough property and revenues. In 1567, he was elected bailiff, Stratford's highest elective office and the equivalent of mayor. Though John Shakespeare signed all official documents with a cross or other sign, it is likely, though not certain, that he knew how to read and write. Mary, who also signed documents only with her mark, is less likely to have been literate.

According to the parish registers, which recorded baptisms and burials, the Shakespeares had eight children, four daughters and four sons, beginning with a daughter Joan born in 1558. A second daughter, Margaret, was born in December 1562 and died a few months later. William Shakespeare ("Gulielmus, filius Johannes Shakespeare"), their first son, was baptized on April 26, 1564. Since there was usually a few days' lapse between birth and baptism, it is conventional to celebrate Shakespeare's birthday on April 23, which happens to coincide with the feast of St. George, England's patron saint, and with the day of Shakespeare's death fifty-two years later.

William Shakespeare had three younger brothers, Gilbert, Richard, and Edmund, and

"Southeast Prospect of Stratford-upon-Avon, 1746." From *The Gentleman's Magazine* (December 1792).

two younger sisters, Joan and Anne. (It was often the custom to recycle a name, so the first-born Joan must have died before the birth in 1569 of another daughter christened Joan, the only one of the girls to survive childhood.) Gilbert, who died in his forty-fifth year in 1612, is described in legal records as a Stratford haberdasher; Edmund followed William to London and became a professional actor, though evidently of no particular repute. He was only twenty-eight when he died in 1607 and was given an expensive funeral, perhaps paid for by his successful older brother.

At the high point of his public career, John Shakespeare, the father of this substantial family, applied to the Herald's College for a coat of arms, which would have marked his (and his family's) elevation from the ranks of substantial middle-class citizenry to that of the gentry. But the application went nowhere, for soon after he initiated what would have been a costly petitioning process, John apparently fell on hard times. The decline must have begun when William was still living at home, a boy of twelve or thirteen. From 1576 onward, John Shakespeare stopped attending council meetings. He became caught up in costly lawsuits, started mortgaging his land, and incurred substantial debts. In 1586, he was finally replaced on the council; in 1592, he was one of nine Stratford men listed as absenting themselves from church out of fear of being arrested for debt.

The reason for the reversal in John Shakespeare's fortunes is unknown. Some have speculated that it may have stemmed from adherence to Catholicism, since those who remained loyal to the old faith were subject to increasingly vigorous and costly discrimination. But if John Shakespeare was a Catholic, as seems quite possible, it would not necessarily explain his decline, since other Catholics (and Puritans) in Elizabethan Stratford and elsewhere managed to hold on to their offices. In any case, his fall from prosperity and local power, whatever its cause, was not absolute. In 1601, the last year of his life, his name was included among those qualified to speak on behalf of Stratford's rights. And he was by that time entitled to bear a coat of arms, for in 1596, some twenty years after the application to the Herald's office had been initiated, it was successfully renewed. There is no record of who paid for the bureaucratic procedures that made the grant possible, but it is likely to have been John's oldest son William, by that time a highly successful London playwright.

Education

Stratford was a small provincial town, but it had long been the site of an excellent free school, originally established by the church in the thirteenth century. The main purpose of such schools in the Middle Ages had been to train prospective clerics; since many aristocrats could neither read nor write, literacy by itself conferred no special distinction and was not routinely viewed as desirable. But the situation began to change markedly in the sixteenth century. Protestantism placed a far greater emphasis upon lay literacy: for the sake of salvation, it was crucially important to be intimately acquainted with the Holy Book, and printing made that book readily available. Schools became less strictly bound up with training for the church and more linked to the general acquisition of "literature," in the sense both of literacy and of cultural knowledge. In keeping with this new emphasis on reading and with humanist educational reform, the school was reorganized during the reign of Edward VI (1547–53). School records from the period have not survived, but it is almost certain that William Shakespeare attended the King's New School, as it was renamed in Edward's honor.

Scholars have painstakingly reconstructed the curriculum of schools of this kind and have even turned up the names and rather impressive credentials of the schoolmasters who taught there when Shakespeare was a student. (Shakespeare's principal teacher was Thomas Jenkins, an Oxford graduate, who received £20 a year and a rent-free house.) A child's education in Elizabethan England began at age four or five with two years at what was called the "petty school," attached to the main grammar school. The little scholars carried a "hornbook," a sheet of paper or parchment framed in wood and covered, for protection, with a transparent layer of horn. On the paper was written the alphabet and the Lord's Prayer, which were reproduced as well in the slightly more advanced *ABC with the Catechism*, a combination primer and rudimentary religious guide.

The Cholmondeley sisters, c. 1600–1610. This striking image brings to mind Shakespeare's fascination with twinship, both identical (notably in *The Comedy of Errors*) and fraternal (in *Twelfth Night*).

After students demonstrated some ability to read, the boys could go on, at about age seven, to the grammar school. Shakespeare's images of the experience are not particularly cheerful. In his famous account of the Seven Ages of Man, Jaques in *As You Like It* describes

> the whining schoolboy with his satchel
> And shining morning face, creeping like snail
> Unwillingly to school.
>
> (2.7.144–46)

The schoolboy would have crept quite early: the day began at 6:00 A.M. in summer and 7:00 A.M. in winter and continued until 5:00 P.M., with very few breaks or holidays.

At the core of the curriculum was the study of Latin, the mastery of which was in effect a prolonged male puberty rite involving much discipline and pain as well as pleasure. A late sixteenth-century Dutchman (whose name fittingly was Batty) proposed that God had created the human buttocks so that they could be severely beaten without risking permanent injury. Such thoughts dominated the pedagogy of the age, so that even an able young scholar, as we might imagine Shakespeare to have been, could scarcely have escaped recurrent flogging.

Shakespeare evidently reaped some rewards for the miseries he probably endured: his works are laced with echoes of many of the great Latin texts taught in grammar schools. One of his earliest comedies, *The Comedy of Errors*, is a brilliant variation on a theme by the Roman playwright Plautus, whom Elizabethan schoolchildren often performed as well as read; and one of his earliest tragedies, *Titus Andronicus*, is heavily indebted to Seneca. These are among the most visible of the classical influences that are often more subtly and pervasively interfused in Shakespeare's works. He seems to have had a particular fondness for *Aesop's Fables*, Apuleius's *Golden Ass*, and above all Ovid's *Metamorphoses*. His learned contemporary Ben Jonson remarked that Shakespeare had "small Latin and less Greek," but from this distance what is striking is not the limits of Shakespeare's learning but rather the unpretentious ease, intelligence, and gusto with which he draws upon what he must have first encountered as laborious study.

Traces of a Life

In November 1582, William Shakespeare, at the age of eighteen, married twenty-six-year-old Anne Hathaway, who came from the village of Shottery near Stratford. Their first daughter, Susanna, was baptized six months later. This circumstance, along with the fact that Anne was eight years Will's senior, has given rise to a mountain of speculation, all the more lurid precisely because there is no further evidence. Shakespeare depicts in several plays situations in which marriage is precipitated by a pregnancy, but he also registers, in *Measure for Measure* (1.2.125ff.), the Elizabethan belief that a "true contract" of marriage could be legitimately made and then consummated simply by the mutual vows of the couple in the presence of witnesses.

On February 2, 1585, the twins Hamnet and Judith Shakespeare were baptized in Stratford. Hamnet died at the age of eleven, when his father was already living for much of the year in London as a successful playwright. These are Shakespeare's only known children, though the playwright and impressario William Davenant in the mid-seventeenth century claimed to be his bastard son. Since people did not ordinarily advertise their illegitimacy, the claim, though impossible to verify, at least suggests the unusual strength of the Shakespeare's posthumous reputation.

William Shakespeare's father, John, died in 1601; his mother died seven years later. They would have had the satisfaction of witnessing their eldest son's prosperity, and not only from a distance, for in 1597 William purchased New Place, the second largest house in Stratford. In 1607, the playwright's daughter Susanna married a successful and well-known physician, John Hall. The next year, the Halls had a daughter, Elizabeth, Shakespeare's first grandchild. In 1616, the year of Shakespeare's death, his daughter Judith married a vintner, Thomas Quiney, with whom she had three children. Shakespeare's widow, Anne, died in 1623, at the age of sixty-seven. His first-born, Susanna, died at the age of sixty-six in 1649, the year that King Charles I was beheaded by the parliamentary army. Judith lived through Cromwell's Protectorate and on to the Restoration of the monarchy; she died in February 1662, at the age of seventy-seven. By the end of the century, the line of Shakespeare's direct heirs was extinct.

Patient digging in the archives has turned up other traces of Shakespeare's life as a family man and a man of means: assessments, small fines, real estate deeds, minor actions in court to collect debts. In addition to his fine Stratford house and a large garden and cottage facing it, Shakespeare bought substantial parcels of land in the vicinity. When in *The Tempest* the wedding celebration conjures up a vision of "barns and garners never empty," Shakespeare could have been glancing at what the legal documents record as his own "tithes of corn, grain, blade, and hay" in the fields near Stratford. At some point after 1610, Shakespeare seems to have begun to shift his attention from the London stage to his Stratford properties, though the term "retirement" implies a more decisive and definitive break than appears to have been the case. By 1613, when the Globe Theatre burned down during a performance of *All Is True (Henry VIII)*, Shakespeare was probably residing for the most part in Stratford, but he retained his financial interest in the rebuilt playhouse and probably continued to have some links to his theatrical colleagues. Still, by this point, his career as a playwright was substantially over. Legal documents from his last years show him concerned to protect his real estate interests in Stratford.

A half-century after Shakespeare's death, a Stratford vicar and physician, John Ward, noted in his diary that Shakespeare and his fellow poets Michael Drayton and Ben Jonson "had a merry meeting, and it seems drank too hard, for Shakespeare died of a fever there contracted." It is not inconceivable that Shakespeare's last illness was somehow linked, if only coincidentally, to the festivities on the occasion of the wedding in February 1616 of his daughter Judith (who was still alive when Ward made his diary entry). In any case, on March 25, 1616, Shakespeare revised his will, and on April 23 he died. Two days later, he was buried in the chancel of Holy Trinity Church beneath a stone bearing an epitaph he is said to have devised:

> Good friend for Jesus' sake forbear,
> To dig the dust enclosed here:
> Blest be the man that spares these stones,
> And curst be he that moves my bones.

The verses are hardly among Shakespeare's finest, but they seem to have been effective: though bones were routinely dug up to make room for others—a fate imagined with unforgettable intensity in the graveyard scene in *Hamlet*—his own remains were undisturbed. Like other vestiges of sixteenth- and early seventeenth-century Stratford, Shakespeare's grave has for centuries now been the object of a tourist industry that borders on a religious cult.

Shakespeare's will has been examined with an intensity befitting this cult; every provision and formulaic phrase, no matter how minor or conventional, has borne a heavy weight of interpretation, none more so than the bequest to his wife, Anne, of only "my second-best bed." Scholars have pointed out that Anne would in any case have been provided for by custom and that the terms are not necessarily a deliberate slight, but the absence of the customary words "my loving wife" or "my well-beloved wife" is difficult to ignore.

Portrait of the Playwright as Young Provincial

The great problem with the surviving traces of Shakespeare's life is not that they are few but that they are a bit dull. Christopher Marlowe was a double or triple agent, accused of brawling, sodomy, and atheism. Ben Jonson, who somehow clambered up from bricklayer's apprentice to classical scholar, served in the army in Flanders, killed a fellow actor in a duel, converted to Catholicism in prison in 1598, and returned to the Church of England in 1610. Provincial real estate investments and the second-best bed cannot compete with such adventurous lives. Indeed, the relative ordinariness of Shakespeare's social background and life has contributed to a persistent current of speculation that the glover's son from Stratford-upon-Avon was not in fact the author of the plays attributed to him.

The anti-Stratfordians, as those who deny Shakespeare's authorship are sometimes called, almost always propose as the real author someone who came from a higher social class and received a more prestigious education. Francis Bacon, the Earl of Oxford, the Earl of Southampton, even Queen Elizabeth, have been advanced, among many others, as glamorous candidates for the role of clandestine playwright. Several famous people, including Mark Twain and Sigmund Freud, have espoused these theories, though very few scholars have joined them. Since Shakespeare was quite well-known in his own time as the author of the plays that bear his name, there would need to have been an extraordinary conspiracy to conceal the identity of the real master who (the theory goes) disdained to appear in the vulgarity of print or on the public stage. Like many conspiracy theories, the extreme implausibility of this one only seems to increase the fervent conviction of its advocates.

To the charge that a middle-class author from a small town could not have imagined the lives of kings and nobles, one can respond by citing the exceptional qualities that Ben Jonson praised in Shakespeare: "excellent *Phantsie*; brave notions, and gentle expressions." Even in ordinary mortals, the human imagination is a strange faculty; in Shakespeare, it seems to have been uncannily powerful, working its mysterious, transforming effects on everything he encountered. It is possible to study this power in his reworking of books by Raphael Holinshed, Plutarch, Ovid, Plautus, Seneca, and others. But books were clearly not the only objects of Shakespeare's attention; like most artists, he drew upon the whole range of his life experiences.

To integrate some of the probable circumstances of Shakespeare's early years with the particular shape of the theatrical imagination associated with his name, let us indulge briefly in the biographical daydreams that modern scholarship is supposed to have rendered forever obsolete. The vignettes that follow are conjectural, but they may suggest ways in which his life as we know it found its way into his art.

1. THE GOWN OF OFFICE

Shakespeare was a very young boy—not quite four years old—when his father was chosen by the Stratford council as the town bailiff. The bailiff of an Elizabethan town was a significant position; he served the borough as a justice of the peace and performed a variety of other functions, including coroner and clerk of the market. He dealt routinely with an unusually wide spectrum of local society, for on the one hand he distributed alms and on the other he negotiated with the lord of the manor. More to the point, for our purposes, the office was attended with considerable ceremony. The bailiff and his deputy were entitled to appear in public in furred gowns, attended by sergeants bearing maces before them. On Rogation Days (three days of prayer for the harvest, before Ascension Day), they would solemnly pace out the parish boundaries, and they would similarly walk in processions on market and fair days. On Sundays, the sergeants would accompany the bailiff to church, where he would sit with his wife in a front pew, and he would have a comparable seat of honor at sermons in the Guild Chapel. On special occasions, there would also be plays in the Guildhall, at which the bailiff would be seated in the front row.

On a precocious child (or even, for that matter, on an ordinary child), the effect of this ceremony would be at least threefold. First, the ceremony would convey irresistibly the power of clothes (the ceremonial gown of office) and of symbols (the mace) to transform identity as if by magic. Second, it would invest the father with immense power, distinction, and importance, awakening what we may call a lifelong dream of high station. And third, pulling slightly against this dream, it would provoke an odd feeling that the father's clothes do not fit, a perception that the office is not the same as the man, and an intimate, first-hand knowledge that when the robes are put off, their wearer is inevitably glimpsed in a far different, less exalted light.

2. PROGRESSES AND ELECTIONS

This second biographical fantasy, slightly less plausible than the first but still quite likely, involves a somewhat older child witnessing two characteristic forms of Elizabethan political ceremony, both of which were well-known in the provinces. Queen Elizabeth was fond of going on what were known as "Progresses," triumphant ceremonial journeys around her kingdom. Let us imagine that the young Shakespeare—say, in 1574, when he was ten years old—went with his kinsfolk or friends to Warwick, some eight miles distant, to witness a Progress. He would thus have participated as a spectator in an elaborate cele-bration of charismatic power: the courtiers in their gorgeous clothes, the nervous local officials bedecked in velvets and silks, and at the center, carried in a special litter like a painted idol, the bejeweled queen. Let us imagine further that in addition to being struck by the overwhelming force of this charisma, the boy was struck too by the way this force depended paradoxically on a sense that the queen was after all quite human. Elizabeth was in fact fond of calling attention to this peculiar tension between near-divinization and human ordinariness. For example, on this occasion at Warwick (and what follows really happened), after the trembling Recorder, presumably a local civil official of high standing, had made his official welcoming speech, Elizabeth offered her hand to him to be kissed: "Come hither, little Recorder," she said. "It was told me that you would be afraid to look upon me or to speak boldly; but you were not so afraid of me as I was of you; and I now thank you for putting me in mind of my duty." Of course, the charm of this royal "confes-sion" of nervousness depends on its manifest implausibility: it is, in effect, a theatrical performance of humility by someone with immense confidence in her own histrionic power.

A royal Progress was not the only form of spectacular political activity that Shakespeare might well have seen in the 1570s; it is still more likely that he would have witnessed parliamentary elections, particularly since his father was qualified to vote. In 1571, 1572, 1575, and 1578, there were shire elections conducted in nearby Warwick, elections that would certainly have attracted well over a thousand voters. These were often memorable events: large crowds came together; there was usually heavy drinking and carnivalesque festivity; and at the same time, there was enacted, in a very different register from that of the monarchy, a ritual of empowerment. The people, those entitled to vote by virtue of meeting the property and residence requirements, chose their own representatives by giv-ing their votes—their voices—to candidates for office. Here, legislative sovereignty was conferred not by God but by the consent of the community, a consent marked by shouts and applause.

Recent cultural historians have been so fascinated by the evident links between the spectacles of the absolutist monarchy and the theater that they have largely ignored the significance of this alternative public arena, one that generated intense excitement throughout the country. A child who was a spectator at a parliamentary election in the 1570s might well have found the occasion enormously compelling. It is striking, in any case, how often the adult Shakespeare returns to scenes of acclamation and mass consent, and striking too how much the theater depends on the soliciting of popular voices.

3. EXORCISMS

A third and final Shakespearean fantasy is even more speculative than the second and involves a controversial discovery. It is a fact that in April 1757, the owner of Shakespeare's birthplace in Stratford decided to retile the roof. One of the workmen, described as of "very honest, sober, industrious character," found an old document between the rafters and the tiling. The document, six leaves stitched together, was a profession of faith in fourteen articles, conspicuously Catholic in form; it was, if genuine (for the original has disappeared), by John Shakespeare. The clear implication of this find, that the playwright was probably brought up in a Roman Catholic household in a time of official suspicion and persecution of recusancy, has found support in a recent biographical study by E. A. J. Honigmann. Honigmann has turned up a network of interlinked Catholic families in Lancashire with whom one "William Shakeshafte," possibly a young schoolmaster or player, was connected in the late 1570s or early 1580s.

Accepting for the moment that William Shakespeare was raised in the recusant faith of his father, let us imagine that one day in the early 1580s the young man attended a strange and extraordinary event: an exorcism conducted in secret in the house of a member of the Catholic gentry. These events, though illegal and potentially dangerous, were fairly common in the period and are known to have drawn substantial crowds. The rituals were generally conducted by Jesuits, living in hiding and under constant threat of torture and execution, and centered on the spectacular struggle between the sacred authority of the church and the obscene, blasphemous, and tenacious demons lodged deep within the demoniacs' tortured bodies. Elizabethan authorities were alarmed by the compelling power of exorcisms, which they regarded, not without some justification, as highly self-conscious Catholic propaganda. (The demons, speaking from within the possessed, had the disquieting habit of declaring their admiration for Martin Luther and John Calvin.) Official spokesmen repeatedly stigmatized the rituals as a form of illicit theater: a "play of sacred miracles," a "wonderful pageant," a "devil Theater."

Exorcism: Nicole Aubry, in the Cathedral at Laon, 1566.

The young Shakespeare, whether

true believer or skeptic or something in between ("So have I heard, and do in part believe it," says Hamlet's friend Horatio [1.1.146]), might have carried away from such an occasion several impressions: an awareness that strange, alien voices may speak from within ordinary, familiar bodies; a sense of the irresistible power of illusion; an intimation of immense, cosmic forces that may impinge upon human life; a belief in the possibility of making contact with these forces and compelling them to speak.

These imaginary portraits of the playwright as a young provincial introduce us to several of the root conditions of the Elizabethan theater. Biographical fantasies, though entirely speculative and playful, are useful in part because some people have found it difficult to conceive how Shakespeare, with his provincial roots and his restricted range of experience, could have so rapidly and completely mastered the central imaginative themes of his times. Moreover, it is sometimes difficult to grasp how seeming abstractions such as market society, monarchical state, and theological doctrine were actually experienced directly by peculiar, distinct individuals. Shakespeare's plays were social and collective events, but they also bore the stamp of a particular artist, one endowed with a remarkable capacity to craft lifelike illusions (what Jonson called "excellent *Phantsie*"), a daring willingness to articulate an original vision ("brave notions"), and a loving command, at once precise and generous, of language ("gentle expressions"). These plays are stitched together from shared cultural experiences, inherited dramatic devices, and the pungent vernacular of the day, but we should not lose sight of the extent to which they articulate an intensely personal vision, a bold shaping of the available materials. Four centuries of feverish biographical speculation, much of it foolish, bears witness to a basic intuition: the richness of these plays, their inexhaustible openness, is the consequence not only of the auspicious collective conditions of the culture but also of someone's exceptional skill, inventiveness, and courage at taking those conditions and making of them something rich and strange.

The Theater of the Nation

What precisely are the collective conditions highlighted by these vignettes? First, the growth of Stratford-upon-Avon, the bustling market town of which John Shakespeare was bailiff, is a small version of a momentous sixteenth-century development that made Shakespeare's career possible: the making of an urban "public." That development obviously depended on adequate numbers; the period experienced a rapid and still unexplained growth in population. With it came an expansion and elaboration of market relations: markets became less periodic, more continuous, and more abstract—centered, that is, not on the familiar materiality of goods but on the liquidity of capital and goods. In practical terms, this meant that it was possible to conceive of the theater not only as festive entertainment for special events—lord mayor's pageants, visiting princes, seasonal festivals, and the like—but as a permanent, year-round business venture. The venture relied on ticket sales—it was an innovation of this period to have money advanced in the expectation of pleasure rather than offered to servants afterward as a reward—and counted on habitual playgoing with a concomitant demand for new plays from competing theater companies: "But that's all one, our play is done," sings Feste at the end of *Twelfth Night* and adds a glance toward the next afternoon's proceeds: "And we'll strive to please you every day" (5.1.394–95.

Second, the royal Progress is an instance of what the anthropologist Clifford Geertz has called the Theater State, a state that manifests its power and meaning in exemplary public performances. Professional companies of players, like the one Shakespeare belonged to, understood well that they existed in relation to this Theater State and would, if they were fortunate, be called upon to serve it. Unlike Ben Jonson, Shakespeare did not, as far as we know, write royal entertainments on commission, but his plays were frequently performed before Queen Elizabeth and then before King James and Queen Anne, along with their courtiers and privileged guests. There are many fascinating glimpses of these performances, including a letter from Walter Cope to Robert Cecil, early in James's reign. "Burbage is come," Cope writes, referring to the leading actor of Shakespeare's company, "and says there is no new play that the queen hath not seen, but they have revived an old one, called *Love's Labours Lost*, which for wit and mirth he says will please her exceedingly. And this is appointed to be played tomorrow night at my Lord of Southampton's." Not only would such theatrical performances have given great pleasure—evidently, the queen had already exhausted the company's new offerings—but they conferred prestige upon those who commanded them and those in whose honor they were mounted.

Monarchical power in the period was deeply allied to spectacular manifestations of the ruler's glory and disciplinary authority. The symbology of power depended on regal magnificence, reward, punishment, and pardon, all of which were heavily theatricalized. Indeed, the conspicuous public display does not simply serve the interests of power; on many occasions in the period, power seemed to exist in order to make pageantry possible, as if the nation's identity were only fully realized in theatrical performance. It would be easy to exaggerate this perception: the subjects of Queen Elizabeth and King James were acutely aware of the distinction between shadow and substance. But they were fascinated by the political magic through which shadows could be taken for substantial realities, and the ruling elite was largely complicit in the formation and celebration of a charismatic absolutism. At the same time, the claims of the monarch who professes herself or himself to be not the representative of the nation but its embodiment were set against the counterclaims of the House of Commons. And this institution too, as we have glimpsed, had its own theatrical rituals, centered on the crowd whose shouts of approval, in heavily stage-managed elections, chose the individuals who would stand for the polity and participate in deliberations held in a hall whose resemblance to a theater did not escape contemporary notice.

Third, illicit exorcism points both to the theatricality of much religious ritual in the late Middle Ages and the Renaissance and to the heightened possibility of secularization. English Protestant authorities banned the medieval mystery plays, along with pilgrimages and other rituals associated with holy shrines and sacred images, but playing companies could satisfy at least some of the popular longings and appropriate aspects of the social energy no longer allowed a theological outlet. That is, official attacks on certain Catholic practices made it more possible for the public theater to appropriate and exploit their allure. Hence, for example, the plays that celebrated the solemn miracle of the Catholic Mass were banned, along with the most elaborate church vestments, but in *The Winter's Tale* Dion can speak in awe of what he witnessed at Apollo's temple:

> I shall report,
> For most it caught me, the celestial habits—
> Methinks I so should term them—and the reverence
> Of the grave wearers. O, the sacrifice—
> How ceremonious, solemn, and unearthly
> It was i'th' off'ring!
>
> (3.1.3–8)

And at the play's end, the statue of the innocent mother breathes, comes to life, and embraces her child.

The theater in Shakespeare's time, then, is intimately bound up with all three crucial cultural formations: the market society, the theater state, and the church. But it is important to note that the institution is not *identified* with any of them. The theater may be a market phenomenon, but it is repeatedly and bitterly attacked as the enemy of diligent, sober, productive economic activity. Civic authorities generally regarded the theater as a pestilential nuisance, a parasite on the body of the commonwealth, a temptation to students, apprentices, housewives, even respectable merchants to leave their serious business and lapse into idleness and waste. That waste, it might be argued, could be partially recuperated if it went for the glorification of a guild or the entertainment of an important dignitary, but the only group regularly profiting from the theater were the players and their disreputable associates.

For his part, Shakespeare made a handsome profit from the commodification of theatrical entertainment, but he seems never to have written "city comedy"—plays set in London and more or less explicitly concerned with market relations—and his characters express deep reservations about the power of money and commerce: "That smooth-faced gentleman, tickling commodity," Philip the Bastard observes in *King John*, "wins of all, / Of kings, of beggars, old men, young men, maids" (2.1.570–74). We could argue that the smooth-faced gentleman is none other than Shakespeare himself, for his drama famously mingles kings and clowns, princesses and panderers. But the mingling is set against a romantic current of social conservatism: in *Twelfth Night*, the aristocratic heiress Olivia falls in love with someone who appears far beneath her in wealth and social station, but it is revealed that he (and his sister Viola) are of noble blood; in *The Winter's Tale*, Leontes' daughter Perdita is raised as a shepherdess, but her noble nature shines through her humble upbringing, and she marries the Prince of Bohemia; the strange island maiden with whom Ferdinand, son of the King of Naples, falls madly in love in *The Tempest* turns out to be the daughter of the rightful Duke of Milan. Shakespeare pushes against this conservative logic in *All's Well That Ends Well*, but the noble young Bertram violently resists the unequal match thrust upon him by the King, and the play's mood is notoriously uneasy.

Similarly, Shakespeare's theater may have been patronized and protected by the monarchy—after 1603, his company received a royal patent and was known as the King's Men—but it was by no means identical in its interests or its ethos. To be sure, *Richard III* and *Macbeth* incorporate aspects of royal propaganda, but given the realities of censorship, Shakespeare's plays, and the period's drama as a whole, are surprisingly independent and complex in their political vision. There is, in any case, a certain inherent tension between kings and player kings: Elizabeth and James may both have likened themselves to actors onstage, but they were loath to admit their dependence on the applause and money, freely given or freely withheld, of the audience. The charismatic monarch insists that the sacredness of authority resides in the body of the ruler, not in a costume that may be worn and then discarded by an actor. Kings are not *representations* of power—or do not admit that they are—but claim to be the thing itself. The government institution that was actually based on the idea of representation, Parliament, had theatrical elements, as we have seen, but it significantly excluded any audience from its deliberations. And Shakespeare's oblique portraits of parliamentary representatives, the tribunes Sicinius Velutus and Junius Brutus in *Coriolanus*, are anything but flattering.

Finally, the theater drew significant energy from the liturgy and rituals of the late medieval church, but as Shakespeare's contemporaries widely remarked, the playhouse and the church were scarcely natural allies. Not only did the theater represent a potential competitor to worship services, and not only did ministers rail against prostitution and other vices associated with playgoing, but theatrical representation itself, even when ostensibly pious, seemed to many to empty out whatever it presented, turning substance into mere show. The theater could and did use the period's deep currents of religious feeling, but it had to do so carefully and with an awareness of conflicting interests.

Shakespeare Comes to London

How did Shakespeare decide to turn his prodigious talents to the stage? When did he make his way to London? How did he get his start? To these and similar questions we have a mountain of speculation but no secure answers. There is not a single surviving record of Shakespeare's existence from 1585, when his twins were baptized in Stratford church, until 1592, when a rival London playwright made an envious remark about him. In the late seventeenth century, the delightfully eccentric collector of gossip John Aubrey was informed that prior to moving to London the young Shakespeare had been a schoolteacher in the country. Aubrey also recorded a story that Shakespeare had been a rather unusual apprentice butcher: "When he killed a calf, he would do it in a high style, and make a speech."

These and other legends, including one that has Shakespeare whipped for poaching game, fill the void until the unmistakable reference in Robert Greene's *Groats-worth of Wit Bought with a Million of Repentaunce* (1592). An inspired hack writer with a university education, a penchant for self-dramatization, a taste for wild living, and a strong streak of resentment, Greene, in his early thirties, was dying in poverty when he penned his last farewell, piously urging his fellow dramatists Christopher Marlowe, Thomas Nashe, and George Peele to abandon the wicked stage before they were brought low, as he had been, by a new arrival: "For there is an upstart crow, beautified with our feathers, that with his 'Tiger's heart wrapped in player's hide' supposes he is as well able to bombast out a blank verse as the best of you, and, being an absolute *Johannes Factotum*, is in his own conceit the only Shake-scene in a country." If "Shake-scene" is not enough to identify the object of his attack, Greene parodies a line from Shakespeare's early play *Richard Duke of York (3 Henry VI)*: "O tiger's heart wrapped in a woman's hide!" (1.4.138). Greene is accusing Shakespeare of being an upstart, a plagiarist, an egomaniacal jack-of-all-trades—and, above all perhaps, a popular success.

By 1592, then, Shakespeare had already arrived on the highly competitive London theatrical scene. He was successful enough to be attacked by Greene and, a few months later, defended by Henry Chettle, another hack writer who had seen Greene's manuscript through the press (or, some scholars speculate, had written the attack himself and passed it off as the dying Greene's). Chettle expresses his regret that he did not suppress Greene's diatribe and spare Shakespeare "because myself have seen his demeanor no less civil than he excellent in the quality he professes." Besides, Chettle adds, "divers of worship have reported his uprightness of dealing, which argues his honesty and his facetious [polished] grace in writing that approves his art." "Divers of worship": not only was Shakespeare established as an accomplished writer and actor, but he evidently had aroused the attention and the approbation of several socially prominent people. In Elizabethan England, aristocratic patronage, with the money, protection, and prestige it alone could provide, was probably a professional writer's most important asset.

This patronage, or at least Shakespeare's quest for it, is most visible in the dedications in 1593 and 1594 of his narrative poems *Venus and Adonis* and *The Rape of Lucrece* to the young nobleman Henry Wriothesley, Earl of Southampton. It may be glimpsed as well, perhaps, in the sonnets, with their extraordinary adoration of the fair youth, though the identity of that youth has never been determined. What return Shakespeare got for his exquisite offerings is likewise unknown. We do know that among wits and gallants, the narrative poems won Shakespeare a fine reputation as an immensely stylish and accomplished poet. An amateur play performed at Cambridge University at the end of the sixteenth century, *The Return from Parnassus*, makes fun of this vogue, as a foolish character effusively declares, "I'll worship sweet Mr. Shakespeare, and to honour him will lay his *Venus and Adonis* under my pillow." Many readers at the time may have done so: the poem went through sixteen editions before 1640, more than any other work by Shakespeare.

Patronage was crucially important not only for individual artists but also for the actors, playwrights, and investors who pooled their resources to form professional theater companies. The public playhouses had enemies, especially among civic and religious authorities, who wished greatly to curb performances or to ban them altogether. An act of 1572 included players among those classified as vagabonds, threatening them therefore with the horrible punishments meted out to those regarded as economic parasites. The players' escape route was to be nominally enrolled as the servants of high-ranking noblemen. The legal fiction was that their public performances were a kind of rehearsal for the command performances before the patron or the monarch.

When Shakespeare came to London, presumably in the late 1580s, there were more than a dozen of these companies operating under the patronage of various aristocrats. We do not know for which of these companies, several of which had toured in Stratford, he originally worked, nor whether he began, as legend has it, as a prompter's assistant and then graduated to acting and playwriting. Shakespeare is listed among the actors in Ben Jonson's *Every Man in His Humour* (performed in 1598) and *Sejanus* (performed in 1603), but we do not know for certain what roles he played, nor are there records of any of his other performances. Tradition has it that he played Adam in *As You Like It* and the Ghost in *Hamlet*, but he was clearly not one of the leading actors of the day.

By the 1590s, the number of playing companies in London had been considerably reduced, in part through competition and in part through legislative restriction. (In 1572, knights and gentry lost the privilege of patronizing a troupe of actors; in 1598, justices of the peace lost the power to authorize performances.) By the early years of the seventeenth century, there were usually only three companies competing against one another in any season, along with two children's companies, which were often successful at drawing audiences away from the public playhouses. Shakespeare may initially have been associated with the Earl of Leicester's company or with the company of Ferdinando Stanley, Lord Strange; both groups included actors with whom Shakespeare was later linked. Or he may have belonged to the Earl of Pembroke's Men, since there is evidence that they performed *The Taming of a Shrew* and a version of *Richard Duke of York (3 Henry VI)*. At any event,

by 1594, Shakespeare was a member of the Lord Chamberlain's Men, for his name, along with those of Will Kempe and Richard Burbage, appears on a record of those "servants to the Lord Chamberlain" paid for performance at the royal palace at Greenwich on December 26 and 28. Shakespeare stayed with this company, which during the reign of King James received royal patronage and became the King's Men, for the rest of his career.

Many playwrights in Shakespeare's time worked freelance, moving from company to company as opportunities arose, collaborating on projects, adding scenes to old plays, scrambling from one enterprise to another. But certain playwrights, among them the most successful, wrote for a single company, often agreeing contractually to give that company exclusive rights to their theatrical works. Shakespeare seems to have followed such a pattern. For the Lord Chamberlain's Men, he wrote an average of two plays per year. His company initially performed in The Theatre, a playhouse built in 1576 by an entrepreneurial carpenter, James Burbage, the father of the actor Richard, who was to perform many of Shakespeare's greatest roles. When in 1597 their lease on this playhouse expired, the Lord Chamberlain's Men passed through a difficult and

Edward Alleyn (1566–1626). Artist unknown. Alleyn was the great tragic actor of the Lord Admiral's Men (the principal rival to Shakespeare's company). He was famous especially for playing the great Marlovian heroes.

legally perilous time, but they formed a joint-stock company, raising sufficient capital to lease a site and put up a splendid new playhouse in the suburb of Southwark, on the south bank of the Thames. This playhouse, the Globe, opened in 1599. Shakespeare is listed in the legal agreement as one of the principal investors, and when the company began to use Blackfriars as their indoor playhouse around 1609, he was a major shareholder in that theater as well. The Lord Chamberlain's Men, later the King's Men, dominated the theater scene, and the shares were quite valuable. Then as now, the theater was an extremely risky enterprise—most of those who wrote plays and performed in them made pathetically little money—but Shakespeare was a notable exception. The fine house in Stratford and the coat of arms he succeeded in acquiring were among the fruits of his multiple mastery, as actor, playwright, and investor of the London stage.

The Shakespearean Trajectory

Though Shakespeare's England was in many ways a record-keeping society, no reliable record survives that details the performances, year by year, in the London theaters. Every play had to be licensed by a government official, the Master of the Revels, but the records kept by the relevant officials from 1579 to 1621, Sir Edmund Tilney and Sir George Buc, have not survived. A major theatrical entrepreneur, Philip Henslowe, kept a careful account of his expenditures, including what he paid for the scripts he commissioned, but unfortunately Henslowe's main business was with the Rose and the Fortune theaters and not with the playhouses at which Shakespeare's company performed. A comparable ledger must have been kept by the shareholders of the Lord Chamberlain's Men, but it has not survived. Shakespeare himself apparently had no interest in preserving for posterity the sum of his writings, let alone in clarifying the chronology of his works or in specifying which plays he wrote alone and which with collaborators.

The principal source for Shakespeare's works is the 1623 Folio volume of *Mr. William Shakespeares Comedies, Histories, & Tragedies*. Most scholars believe that the editors were careful to include only those plays for which they knew Shakespeare to be the main author. Their edition does not, however, include any of Shakespeare's nondramatic poems, and it omits two plays in which Shakespeare is now thought to have had a significant hand, *Pericles, Prince of Tyre* and *The Two Noble Kinsmen*, along with his probable contribution to the multi-authored *Sir Thomas More*. (A number of other plays were attributed to Shakespeare, both before and after his death, but scholars have not generally accepted any of these into the established canon.) Moreover, the Folio edition does not print the plays in chronological order, nor does it attempt to establish a chronology. We do not know how much time would normally have

IF YOV KNOW NOT ME,
You know no body.
OR,
The troubles of Queene ELIZABETH.

LONDON.
Printed by B.A. and T.F. for *Nathanaell Butter*. 1632.

Title page of *If You Know Not Me, You Know No Body; or, the Troubles of Queene Elizabeth* (1632).

elapsed between the writing of a play and its first performance, nor, with a few exceptions, do we know with any certainty the month or even the year of the first performance of any of Shakespeare's plays. The quarto editions of those plays that were published during Shakespeare's lifetime obviously establish a date by which we know a given play had been written, but they give us little more than an end point, because there was likely to be a substantial though indeterminate gap between the first performance of a play and its publication.

With enormous patience and ingenuity, however, scholars have gradually assembled a considerable archive of evidence, both external and internal, for dating the composition of the plays. Besides actual publication, the external evidence includes explicit reference to a play, a record of its performance, or (as in the case of Greene's attack on the "upstart crow") the quoting of a line, though all of these can be maddeningly ambiguous. The most important single piece of external evidence appears in 1598 in *Palladis Tamia*, a long book of jumbled reflections by Francis Meres that includes a survey of the contemporary literary scene. Meres finds that "the sweet, witty soul of Ovid lives in mellifluous and honey-tongued Shakespeare, witness his *Venus and Adonis*, his *Lucrece*, his sugered Sonnets among his private friends, etc." Meres goes on to list Shakespeare's accomplishments as a playwright as well:

> As Plautus and Seneca are accounted the best for Comedy and Tragedy among the Latins: so Shakespeare among the English is the most excellent in both kinds for the stage; for Comedy, witness his *Gentlemen of Verona*, his *Errors*, his *Love labors lost*, his *Love labours won*, his *Midsummers night dream*, & his *Merchant of Venice*: for Tragedy his *Richard the 2*, *Richard the 3*, *Henry the 4*, *King John*, *Titus Andronicus* and his *Romeo and Juliet*.

Meres thus provides a date by which twelve of Shakespeare's plays had definitely appeared (including one, *Love's Labour's Won*, that appears to have been lost). Unfortunately, Meres provides no clues about the order of appearance of these plays, and there are no other comparable lists.

Faced with the limitations of the external evidence, scholars have turned to a bewildering array of internal evidence, ranging from datable sources and topical allusions on the one hand to evolving stylistic features (ratio of verse to prose, percentage of rhyme to blank verse, colloquialisms, use of extended similes, and the like) on the other. Thus, for example, a cluster of plays with a high percentage of rhymed verse may follow closely upon Shakespeare's writing of the rhymed poems *Venus and Adonis* and *The Rape of Lucrece* and therefore be datable to 1594–95. Similarly, vocabulary overlap probably indicates proximity in composition, so if four or five plays share relatively "rare" vocabulary, it is likely that they were written in roughly the same period. Again, there seems to be a pattern in Shakespeare's use of colloquialisms, with a steady increase from *As You Like It* (1599–1600) to *Coriolanus* (1608), followed in the late romances by a retreat from the colloquial.

More sophisticated computer analysis should provide further guidance in the future, though the precise order of the plays, still very much in dispute, is never likely to be settled to universal satisfaction. Still, certain broad patterns are now widely accepted. These patterns can be readily grasped in the *Norton Shakespeare*, which presents the plays in the chronological order proposed by the Oxford editors.

Shakespeare began his career, probably in the early 1590s, by writing both comedies and history plays. The attack by Greene suggests that he made his mark with the series of theatrically vital but rather crude plays based on the foreign and domestic broils that erupted during the unhappy reign of the Lancastrian Henry VI. Modern readers and audiences are more likely to find the first sustained evidence of unusual power in *Richard III* (c. 1592), a play that combines a brilliantly conceived central character, a dazzling command of histrionic rhetoric, and an overarching moral vision of English history.

At virtually the same time that he was setting his stamp on the genre of the history play, Shakespeare was writing his first—or first surviving—comedies. Here, there are even fewer signs than in the histories of an apprenticeship: *The Comedy of Errors*, one of his early efforts in this genre, already displays a rare command of the resources of comedy: mistaken identity, madcap confusion, and the threat of disaster, giving way in the end to reconciliation, recovery, and love. Shakespeare's other comedies from the early 1590s, *The Taming of the Shrew*, *The Two Gentlemen of Verona*, and *Love's Labour's Lost*, are no less remarkable for their sophisticated variations on familiar comic themes, their inexhaustible rhetorical inventiveness, and their poignant intimation, in the midst of festive celebration, of loss.

Successful as are these early histories and comedies, and indicative of an extraordinary theatrical talent, Shakespeare's achievement in the later 1590s would still have been all but impossible to foresee. Starting with *A Midsummer Night's Dream* (c. 1595), Shakespeare wrote an unprecedented series of romantic comedies—*The Merchant of Venice*, *The Merry Wives of Windsor*, *Much Ado About Nothing*, *As You Like It*, and *Twelfth Night* (c. 1602)—whose poetic richness and emotional complexity remain unmatched. In the same period, he wrote a sequence of profoundly searching and ambitious history plays— *Richard II*, *1* and *2 Henry IV*, and *Henry V*—which together explore the death throes of feudal England and the birth of the modern nation-state ruled by a charismatic monarch. Both the comedies and histories of this period are marked by their capaciousness, their ability to absorb characters who press up against the outermost boundaries of the genre: the comedy *Merchant of Venice* somehow contains the figure, at once nightmarish and poignant, of Shylock, while the *Henry IV* plays, with their somber vision of crisis in the family and the state, bring to the stage one of England's greatest comic characters, Falstaff.

If in the mid to late 1590s Shakespeare reached the summit of his art in two major genres, he also manifested a lively interest in a third. As early as 1593, he wrote the crudely violent tragedy *Titus Andronicus*, the first of several plays on themes from Roman history, and a year or two later, in *Richard II*, he created in the protagonist a figure who achieves by the play's close the stature of a tragic hero. In the same year that Shakespeare wrote the wonderfully farcical "Pyramus and Thisbe" scene in *A Midsummer Night's Dream*, he probably also wrote the deeply tragic realization of the same story in *Romeo and Juliet*. But once again, the lyric anguish of *Romeo and Juliet* and the tormented self-revelation of *Richard II*, extraordinary as they are, could not have led anyone to predict the next phase of Shakespeare's career, the great tragic dramas that poured forth in the early years of the seventeenth century: *Hamlet*, *Othello*, *King Lear*, *Macbeth*, *Antony and Cleopatra*, and *Coriolanus*. These plays, written from 1601 to 1607, seem to mark a major shift in sensibility, an existential and metaphysical darkening that many readers think must have originated in a deep personal anguish, perhaps caused by the death of Shakespeare's father, John, in 1601.

Whatever the truth of these speculations—and we have no direct, personal testimony either to support or to undermine them—there appears to have occurred in the same period a shift as well in Shakespeare's comic sensibility. The comedies written between 1601 and 1604, *Troilus and Cressida*, *All's Well That Ends Well*, and *Measure for Measure*, are sufficiently different from the earlier comedies—more biting in tone, more uneasy with comic conventions, more ruthlessly questioning of the values of the characters and the resolutions of the plots—to have led many twentieth-century scholars to classify them as "problem plays" or "dark comedies." This category has recently begun to fall out of favor, since Shakespeare criticism is perfectly happy to demonstrate that *all* of the plays are "problem plays." But there is another group of plays, among the last Shakespeare wrote, that continue to constitute a distinct category. *Pericles*, *Cymbeline*, *The Winter's Tale*, and *The Tempest*, written between 1608 and 1611, when the playwright had developed a remarkably fluid, dreamlike sense of plot and a poetic style that could veer, apparently effortlessly, from the tortured to the ineffably sweet, are known as the "romances." These plays share an interest in the moral and emotional life less of the adolescents who dominate the earlier comedies than of their parents. The romances are deeply concerned with patterns of loss and recovery, suffering and redemption, despair and renewal. They have seemed to many critics to constitute a deliberate conclusion to a career that began in histories and comedies and passed through the dark and tormented tragedies.

One effect of the practice of printing Shakespeare's plays in a reconstructed chronological order, as this edition does, is to produce a kind of authorial plot, a progress from youthful exuberance and a heroic grappling with history, through psychological anguish and radical doubt, to a mature serenity built upon an understanding of loss. The ordering of Shakespeare's "complete works" in this way reconstitutes the figure of the author as the beloved hero of his own, lived romance. There are numerous reasons to treat this romance with considerable skepticism: the precise order of the plays remains in dispute, the obsessions of the earliest plays crisscross with those of the last, the drama is a collaborative art form, and the relation between authorial consciousness and theatrical representation is murky. Yet a longing to identify Shakespeare's personal trajectory, to chart his psychic and spiritual as well as professional progress, is all but irresistible.

The Fetishism of Dress

Whatever the personal resonance of Shakespeare's own life, his art is deeply enmeshed in the collective hopes, fears, and fantasies of his time. For example, throughout his plays, Shakespeare draws heavily upon his culture's investment in costume, symbols of authority, visible signs of status—the fetishism of dress he must have witnessed from early childhood. Disguise in his drama is often assumed to be incredibly effective: when Henry V borrows a cloak, when Portia dresses in a jurist's robes, when Viola puts on a young man's suit, it is as if each has become unrecognizable, as if identity resided in clothing. At the end of *Twelfth Night*, even though Viola's true identity has been disclosed, Orsino continues to call her Cesario; he will do so, he says, until she resumes her maid's garments, for only then will she be transformed into a woman:

> Cesario, come—
> For so you shall be while you are a man;
> But when in other habits you are seen,
> Orsino's mistress, and his fancy's queen.
> (5.1.372–75)

The pinnacle of this fetishism of costume is the royal crown, for whose identity-conferring power men are willing to die, but the principle is everywhere from the filthy blanket that transforms Edgar into Poor Tom to the coxcomb that is the badge of the licensed fool. Antonio, wishing to express his utter contempt, spits on Shylocks' "Jewish gaberdine," as if the clothing were the essence of the man; Kent, pouring insults on the loathsome Oswald, calls him a "filthy worsted-stocking knave"; and innocent Innogen, learning that her husband has ordered her murder, thinks of herself as an expensive cast-off dress, destined to be ripped at the seams:

> Poor I am stale, a garment out of fashion,
> And for I am richer than to hang by th' walls
> I must be ripped. To pieces with me!
> (*Cymbeline* 3.4.50–52)

What can be said, thought, felt, in this culture seems deeply dependent on the clothes one wears—clothes that one is, in effect, *permitted* or *compelled* to wear, since there is little freedom in dress. Shakespearean drama occasionally represents something like such freedom: after all, Viola in *Twelfth Night* chooses to put off her "maiden weeds," as does Rosalind, who declares, "We'll have a swashing and a martial outside" (*As You Like It* 1.3.114). But these choices are characteristically made under the pressure of desperate circumstances, here shipwreck and exile. Part of the charm of Shakespeare's heroines is their ability to transform distress into an opportunity for self-fashioning, but the plays often suggest that there is less autonomy than meets the eye. What looks like an escape from cultural determinism may be only a deeper form of constraint. We may take, as an allegorical emblem of this constraint, the transformation of the beggar Christopher Sly in the playful Induction to *The Taming of the Shrew* into a nobleman. The transformation seems to suggest that you are free to make of yourself whatever you choose to be—the play begins with the drunken Sly indignantly claiming the dignity of his pedigree ("Look in the Chronicles" [Induction 1.3–4])—but in fact he is only the subject of the mischievous lord's experiment, designed to demonstrate the interwovenness of clothing and identity. "What think you," the lord asks his huntsman,

> if he were conveyed to bed,
> Wrapped in sweet clothes, rings put upon his fingers,
> A most delicious banquet by his bed,
> And brave attendants near him when he wakes—
> Would not the beggar then forget himself?

To which the huntsman replies, in words that underscore the powerlessness of the drunken beggar, "Believe me, lord, I think he cannot choose" (Induction 1.33–38).

Petruccio's taming of Katherine is similarly constructed around an imposition of identity, an imposition closely bound up with the right to wear certain articles of clothing. When the haberdasher arrives with a fashionable lady's hat, Petruccio refuses it over his wife's vehement objections: "This doth fit the time, / And gentlewomen wear such caps as these." "When you are gentle," Petruccio replies, "you shall have one, too, / And not till then" (4.3.69–72). At the play's close, Petruccio demonstrates his authority by commanding his tamed wife to throw down her cap: "Off with that bauble, throw it underfoot" (5.2.126). Here as elsewhere in Shakespeare, acts of robing and disrobing are intensely charged, a charge that culminates in the trappings of monarchy. When Richard II, in a scene that was probably censored during the reign of Elizabeth from the stage as well as the printed text, is divested of his crown and scepter, he experiences the loss as the eradication of his name, the symbolic melting away of his identity:

> Alack the heavy day,
> That I have worn so many winters out
> And know not now what name to call myself!
> O, that I were a mockery king of snow,
> Standing before the sun of Bolingbroke
> To melt myself away in water-drops!
> (4.1.255–60)

When Lear tears off his regal "lendings" in order to reduce himself to the nakedness of the Bedlam beggar, he is expressing not only his radical loss of social identity but the breakdown of his psychic order as well, expressing therefore his reduction to the condition of the "poor bare forked animal" that is the primal condition of undifferentiated existence. And when Cleopatra determines to kill herself in order to escape public humiliation in Rome, she magnificently affirms her essential being by arraying herself as she had once done to encounter Antony:

> Show me, my women, like a queen. Go fetch
> My best attires. I am again for Cydnus
> To meet Mark Antony.
> (5.2.223–25)

Such scenes are a remarkable intensification of the everyday symbolic practice of Renaissance English culture, its characteristically deep and knowing commitment to illusion: "I know perfectly well that the woman in her crown and jewels and gorgeous gown is an aging, irascible, and fallible mortal—she herself virtually admits as much—yet I profess that she is the virgin queen, timelessly beautiful, wise, and just." Shakespeare understood how close this willed illusion was to the spirit of the theater, to the actors' ability to work on what the chorus in *Henry V* calls the "imaginary forces" of the audience.

But there is throughout Shakespeare's works a counterintuition that, while it does not exactly overturn this illusion, renders it poignant, vulnerable, fraught. The "masculine usurp'd attire" that is donned by Viola, Rosalind, Portia, Jessica, and other Shakespeare heroines alters what they can say and do, reveals important aspects of their character, and changes their destiny, but it is, all the same, not theirs and not all of who they are. They have, the plays insist, natures that are neither transformed nor altogether concealed by their dress: "Pray God defend me," exclaims the frightened Viola. "A little thing would make me tell them how much I lack of a man" (*Twelfth Night* 3.4.268–69).

The Paradoxes of Identity

The gap between costume and identity is not simply a matter of what women supposedly lack; virtually all of Shakespeare's major characters, men and women, convey the sense of both a *self-division* and an *inward expansion*. The belief in a complex inward realm beyond costumes and status is a striking inversion of the clothes cult: we know perfectly well that the characters have no inner lives apart from what we see on the stage, and yet we believe that they continue to exist when we do not see them, that they exist apart from their represented words and actions, that they have hidden dimensions. How is this conviction aroused and sustained? In part, it is the effect of what the characters themselves say: "My grief lies all within," Richard II tells Bolingbroke,

> And these external manner of laments
> Are merely shadows to the unseen grief
> That swells with silence in the tortured soul.
> (4.1.294–96)

Similarly, Hamlet, dismissing the significance of his outward garments, declares, "I have that within which passeth show— / These but the trappings and the suits of woe" (1.2.85–86). And the distinction between inward and outward is reinforced throughout this play and elsewhere by an unprecedented use of the aside and the soliloquy.

The soliloquy is a continual reminder in Shakespeare that the inner life is by no means transparent to one's surrounding world. Prince Hal seems open and easy with his mates in Eastcheap, but he has a hidden reservoir of disgust:

> I know you all, and will a while uphold
> The unyoked humour of your idleness.
> Yet herein will I imitate the sun,
> Who doth permit the base contagious clouds
> To smother up his beauty from the world,
> That when he please again to be himself,
> Being wanted he may be more wondered at
> By breaking through the foul and ugly mists
> Of vapours that did seem to strangle him.
> (*I Henry IV* 1.2.173–81)

"When he please again to be himself": the line implies that identity is a matter of free choice—you decide how much of yourself you wish to disclose—but Shakespeare employs other devices that suggest more elusive and intractable layers of inwardness. There is a peculiar, recurrent lack of fit between costume and character, in fools as in princes, that is not simply a matter of disguise and disclosure. If Hal's true identity is partially "smothered" in the tavern, it is not completely revealed either in his soldier's armor or in his royal robes, nor do his asides reach the bedrock of unimpeachable self-understanding.

Identity in Shakespeare repeatedly slips away from the characters themselves, as it does from Richard II after the deposition scene and from Lear after he has given away his land and from Macbeth after he has gained the crown. The slippage does not mean that they retreat into silence; rather, they embark on an experimental, difficult fashioning of themselves and the world, most often through role-playing. "I cannot do it," says the deposed and imprisoned Richard II. "Yet I'll hammer it out" (5.5.5). This could serve as the motto for many Shakespearean characters: Viola becomes Cesario, Rosalind calls herself Ganymede, Kent becomes Caius, Edgar presents himself as Poor Tom, Hamlet plays the madman that he has partly become, Hal pretends that he is his father and a highwayman and Hotspur and even himself. Even in comedy, these ventures into alternate identities are rarely matters of choice; in tragedy, they are always undertaken under pressure and compulsion. And often enough it is not a matter of role-playing at all, but of a drastic transformation whose extreme emblem is the harrowing madness of Lear and of Leontes.

There is a moment in *Richard II* in which the deposed King asks for a mirror and then, after musing on his reflection, throws it to the ground. The shattering of the glass serves to remind us not only of the fragility of identity in Shakespeare but of its characteristic appearance in fragmentary mirror images. The plays continually generate alternative reflections, identities that intersect with, underscore, echo, or otherwise set off that of the principal character. Hence, Desdemona and Iago are not only important figures in Othello's world, they also seem to embody partially realized aspects of himself; Falstaff and Hotspur play a comparable role in relation to Prince Hal, Fortinbras and Horatio in relation to Hamlet, Gloucester and the Fool in relation to Lear, and so forth. In many of these plays, the complementary and contrasting characters figure in subplots, subtly interwoven with the play's main plot and illuminating its concerns. The note so conspicuously sounded by Fortinbras at the close of *Hamlet*—what the hero might have been, "had he been put on"—is heard repeatedly in Shakespeare and contributes to the overwhelming intensity, poignancy, and complexity of the characters. This is a world in which outward appearance is everything and nothing, in which individuation is at once sharply etched and continually blurred, in which the victims of fate are haunted by the ghosts of the possible, in which everything is simultaneously as it must be and as it need not have been.

Are these antinomies signs of a struggle between contradictory and irreconcilable perspectives in Shakespeare? In certain plays—notably, *Measure for Measure, All's Well That Ends Well, Coriolanus,* and *Troilus and Cressida*—the tension seems both high and entirely unresolved. But Shakespearean contradictions are more often reminiscent of the capacious spirit of Montaigne, who refused any systematic order that would betray his sense of reality. Thus, individual characters are immensely important in Shakespeare—he is justly celebrated for his unmatched skill in the invention of particular dramatic identities, marked with distinct speech patterns, manifested in social status, and confirmed by costume and gesture—but the principle of individuation is not the rock on which his theatrical art is founded. After the masks are stripped away, the pretenses exposed, the claims of the ego shattered, there is a mysterious remainder; as the shamed but irrepressible Paroles declares in *All's Well That Ends Well,* "Simply the thing I am / Shall make me live" (4.3.309–10). Again and again the audience is made to sense a deeper energy, a source of power that at once discharges itself in individual characters and seems to sweep right through them.

The Poet of Nature

In *The Birth of Tragedy,* Nietzsche called a comparable source of energy that he found in Greek tragedy "Dionysos." But the god's name, conjuring up Bacchic frenzy, does not seem appropriate to Shakespeare. In the late seventeenth and eighteenth centuries, it was more plausibly called Nature: "The world must be peopled," says the delightful Benedick in *Much Ado About Nothing* (2.3.213–14), and there are frequent invocations elsewhere of the happy, generative power that brings couples together—

> Jack shall have Jill,
> Naught shall go ill,
> the man shall have his mare again, and all shall be well.
> (*A Midsummer Night's Dream* 3.3.45–47)

—and the melancholy, destructive power that brings all living things to the grave: "Golden lads and girls all must, / As chimney-sweepers, come to dust" (*Cymbeline* 4.2.263–64).

But the celebration of Shakespeare as a poet of nature—often coupled with an inane celebration of his supposedly "natural" (that is, untutored) genius—has its distinct limitations. For Shakespearean art brilliantly interrogates the "natural," refusing to take for granted precisely what the celebrants think is most secure. His comedies are endlessly inventive in showing that love is not simply natural: the playful hint of bestiality in the line quoted above, "the man shall have his mare again," (from a play in which the Queen of the Fairies falls in love with an ass-headed laborer), lightly unsettles the boundaries between the natural and the perverse. These boundaries are called into question throughout Shakespeare's work, from the cross-dressing and erotic crosscurrents that deliciously complicate the lives of the characters in *Twelfth Night* and *As You Like It* to the terrifying violence that wells up from the heart of the family in *King Lear* or from the sweet intimacy of sexual desire in *Othello*. Even the boundary between life and death is not secure, as the ghosts in *Julius Caesar*, *Hamlet*, and *Macbeth* attest, while the principle of natural death (given its most eloquent articulation by old Hamlet's murderer, Claudius!) is repeatedly tainted and disrupted.

Disrupted too is the idea of order that constantly makes its claim, most insistently in the history plays. Scholars have observed the presence in Shakespeare's works of the so-called Tudor myth—the ideological justification of the ruling dynasty as a restoration of national order after a cycle of tragic violence. The violence, Tudor apologists claimed, was divine punishment unleashed after the deposition of the anointed king, Richard II, for God will not tolerate violations of the sanctified order. Traces of this propaganda certainly exist in the histories—Shakespeare may, for all we know, have personally subscribed to its premises—but a closer scrutiny of his plays has disclosed so many ironic reservations and qualifications and subversions as to call into question any straightforward adherence to a political line. The plays manifest a profound fascination with the monarchy and with the ambitions of the aristocracy, but the fascination is never simply endorsement. There is always at least the hint of a slippage between the great figures, whether admirable or monstrous, who stand at the pinnacle of authority and the vast, miscellaneous mass of soldiers, scriveners, ostlers, poets, whores, gardeners, thieves, weavers, shepherds, country gentlemen, sturdy beggars, and the like who make up the commonwealth. And the idea of order, though eloquently articulated (most memorably by Ulysses in *Troilus and Cressida*), is always shadowed by a relentless spirit of irony.

The Play of Language

If neither the individual nor nature nor order will serve, can we find a single comprehensive name for the underlying force in Shakespeare's work? Certainly not. The work is too protean and capacious. But much of the energy that surges through this astonishing body of plays and poems is closely linked to the power of language. Shakespeare was the supreme product of a rhetorical culture, a culture steeped in the arts of persuasion and verbal expressiveness. In 1512, the great Dutch humanist Erasmus published a work called *De copia* that taught its readers how to cultivate "copiousness," verbal richness, in discourse. (Erasmus obligingly provides, as a sample, a list of 144 different ways of saying "Thank you for your letter.") Recommended modes of variation include putting the subject of an argument into fictional form, as well as the use of synonym, substitution, paraphrase, metaphor, metonymy, synecdoche, hyperbole, diminution, and a host of other figures of speech. To change emotional tone, he suggests trying *ironia, interrogatio, admiratio, dubitatio, abominatio*—the possibilities seem infinite.

In Renaissance England, certain syntactic forms or patterns of words known as "figures" (also called "schemes") were shaped and repeated in order to confer beauty or heighten expressive power. Figures were usually known by their Greek and Latin names, though in an Elizabethan rhetorical manual, *The Arte of English Poesie*, George Puttenham made a valiant if short-lived attempt to give them English equivalents, such as "*Hyperbole*, or the

Overreacher," "*Ironia*, or the Dry Mock," and "*Ploce*, or the Doubler." Those who received a grammar school education throughout Europe at almost any point between the Roman Empire and the eighteenth century probably knew by heart the names of up to one hundred such figures, just as they knew by heart their multiplication tables. According to one scholar's count, Shakespeare knew and made use of about two hundred.

As certain grotesquely inflated Renaissance texts attest, lessons from *De copia* and similar rhetorical guides could encourage mere prolixity and verbal self-display. But though he shared his culture's delight in rhetorical complexity, Shakespeare always understood how to swoop from baroque sophistication to breathtaking simplicity. Moreover, he grasped early in his career how to use figures of speech, tone, and rhythm not only to provide emphasis and elegant variety but also to articulate the inner lives of his characters. Take, for example, these lines from *Othello*, where, as scholars have noted, Shakespeare deftly combines four common rhetorical figures—*anaphora, parison, isocolon*, and *epistrophe*—to depict with painful vividness Othello's psychological torment:

> By the world,
> I think my wife be honest, and think she is not.
> I think that thou art just, and think thou art not.
> I'll have some proof.
>
> (3.3.388–91)

Anaphora is simply the repetition of a word at the beginning of a sequence of sentences or clauses ("I/I"). *Parison* is the correspondence of word to word within adjacent sentences or clauses, either by direct repetition ("think/think") or by the matching of noun with noun, verb with verb ("wife/thou"; "be/art"). *Isocolon* gives exactly the same length to corresponding clauses ("and think she is not/and think thou art not"), and *epistrophe* is the mirror image of *anaphora*, in that it is the repetition of a word at the end of a sequence of sentences or clauses ("not/not"). Do we need to know the Greek names for these figures in order to grasp the effectiveness of Othello's lines? Of course not. But Shakespeare and his contemporaries, convinced that rhetoric provided the most natural and powerful means by which feelings could be conveyed to readers and listeners, were trained in an analytical language that helped at once to promote and to account for this effectiveness. In his 1593 edition of *The Garden of Eloquence*, Henry Peacham remarks that *epistrophe* "serveth to leave a word of importance in the end of a sentence, that it may the longer hold the sound in the mind of the hearer," and in *Directions for Speech and Style* (c. 1599), John Hoskins notes that *anaphora* "beats upon one thing to cause the quicker feeling in the audience."

Shakespeare also shared with his contemporaries a keen understanding of the ways that rhetorical devices could be used not only to express powerful feelings but to hide them: after all, the artist who created Othello also created Iago, Richard III, and Lady Macbeth. He could deftly skewer the rhetorical affectations of Polonius in *Hamlet* or the pedant Holophernes in *Love's Labour's Lost*. He could deploy stylistic variations to mark the boundaries not of different individuals but of different social realms; in *A Midsummer Night's Dream*, for example, the blank verse of Duke Theseus is played off against the rhymed couplets of the well-born young lovers, and both in turn contrast with the prose spoken by the artisans. At the same time that he thus marks boundaries between both individuals and groups, Shakespeare shows a remarkable ability to establish unifying patterns of imagery that knit together the diverse strands of his plot and suggest subtle links among characters who may be scarcely aware of how much they share with one another.

One of the hidden links in Shakespeare's own works is the frequent use he makes of a somewhat unusual rhetorical figure called *hendiadys*. An example from the Roman poet Virgil is the phrase *pateris libamus et auro*, "we drink from cups and gold" (*Georgics* 2.192). Rather than serving as an adjective or a dependent noun, as in "golden cups" or "cups of gold," the word "gold" serves as a substantive joined to another substantive, "cups," by a conjunction, "and." Shakespeare uses the figure over three hundred times in all, and since it does not appear in ancient or medieval lists of tropes and schemes and is treated only briefly by English rhetoricians, he may have come upon it directly in Virgil. *Hendiadys* literally means "one through two," though Shakespeare's versions often make us quickly, perhaps only subliminally, aware of the complexity of what ordinarily passes for straightforward perceptions. When Othello, in his suicide speech, invokes the memory of "a malignant and a turbaned Turk," the figure of speech at once associates enmity with cultural difference and keeps them slightly apart. And when Macbeth speaks of his "strange and self-abuse," the *hendiadys* seems briefly to hold both "strange" and "self" up for scrutiny. It would be foolish to make too much of any single feature in Shakespeare's varied and diverse creative achievement, and yet this curious rhetorical scheme has something of the quality of a fingerprint.

But all of his immense rhetorical gifts, though rich, beautiful, and supremely useful, do not adequately convey Shakespeare's relation to language, which is less strictly functional than a total immersion in the arts of persuasion may imply. An Erasmian admiration for copiousness cannot fully explain Shakespeare's astonishing vocabulary of some 25,000 words. (His closest rival among the great English poets of the period was John Milton, with about 12,000 words, and most major writers, let alone ordinary people, have much smaller vocabularies.) This immense word hoard, it is worth noting, was not the result of scanning a dictionary; in the late sixteenth century, there were no English dictionaries of the kind to which we are now accustomed. Shakespeare seems to have absorbed new words from virtually every discursive realm he ever encountered, and he experimented boldly and tirelessly with them. These experiments were facilitated by the very fact that dictionaries as we know them did not exist and by a flexibility in grammar, orthography, and diction that the more orderly, regularized English of the later seventeenth and eighteenth centuries suppressed.

Owing in part to the number of dialects in London, pronunciation was variable, and there were many opportunities for phonetic association between words: the words "bear," "barn," "bier," "bourne," "born," and "barne" could all sound like one another. Homonyms were given greater scope by the fact that the same word could be spelled so many different ways—Christopher Marlowe's name appears in the records as Marlowe, Marloe, Marlen, Marlyne, Merlin, Marley, Marlye, Morley, and Morle—and by the fact that a word's grammatical function could easily shift, from noun to verb, verb to adjective, and so forth. Since grammar and punctuation did not insist on relations of coordination and subordination, loose, nonsyntactic sentences were common, and etymologies were used to forge surprising or playful relations between distant words.

It would seem inherently risky for a popular playwright to employ a vocabulary so far in excess of what most mortals could possibly possess, but Shakespeare evidently counted on his audience's linguistic curiosity and adventurousness, just as he counted on its general and broad-based rhetorical competence. He was also usually careful to provide a context that in effect explained or translated his more arcane terms. For example, when Macbeth reflects with horror on his murderous hands, he shudderingly imagines that even the sea could not wash away the blood; on the contrary, his bloodstained hand, he says, "will rather / The multitudinous seas incarnadine." The meaning of the unfamiliar word "incarnadine" is explained by the next line: "Making the green one red" (2.2.59–61).

What is most striking is not the abstruseness or novelty of Shakespeare's language but its extraordinary vitality, a quality that the playwright seemed to pursue with a kind of passionate recklessness. Perhaps Samuel Johnson was looking in the right direction when he complained that the "quibble," or pun, was "the fatal Cleopatra for which [Shakespeare] lost the world, and was content to lose it." For the power that continually discharges itself throughout the plays, at once constituting and unsettling everything it touches, is the polymorphous power of language, language that seems both costume and that which lies beneath the costume, personal identity and that which challenges the merely personal, nature and that which enables us to name nature and thereby distance ourselves from it.

Shakespeare's language has an overpowering exuberance and generosity that often resembles the experience of love. Consider, for example, Oberon's description in *A Mid-*

summer Night's Dream of the moment when he saw Cupid shoot his arrow at the fair vestal: "Thou rememb'rest," he asks Puck,

> Since once I sat upon a promontory
> And heard a mermaid on a dolphin's back
> Uttering such dulcet and harmonious breath
> That the rude sea grew civil at her song
> And certain stars shot madly from their spheres
> To hear the sea-maid's music?
>
> (2.1.149–54)

Here, Oberon's composition of place, lightly alluding to a classical emblem, is infused with a fantastically lush verbal brilliance. This brilliance, the result of masterful alliterative and rhythmical technique, seems gratuitous; that is, it does not advance the plot, but rather exhibits a capacity for display and self-delight that extends from the fairies to the playwright who has created them. The rich music of Oberon's words imitates the "dulcet and harmonious breath" he is intent on recalling, breath that has, in his account, an oddly contradictory effect: it is at once a principle of order, so that the rude sea is becalmed like a lower-class mob made civil by a skilled orator, and a principle of disorder, so that celestial bodies in their fixed spheres are thrown into mad confusion. And this contradictory effect, so intimately bound up with an inexplicable, supererogatory, and intensely erotic verbal magic, is the key to *A Midsummer Night's Dream*, with its exquisite blend of confusion and discipline, lunacy and hierarchical ceremony.

The fairies in this comedy seem to embody a pervasive sense found throughout Shakespeare's work that there is something uncanny about language, something that is not quite human, at least in the conventional and circumscribed sense of the human that dominates waking experience. In the comedies, this intuition is alarming but ultimately benign: Oberon and his followers trip through the great house at the play's close, blessing the bridebeds and warding off the nightmares that lurk in marriage and parenthood. But there is in Shakespeare an alternative, darker vision of the uncanniness of language, a vision also embodied in creatures that test the limits of the human—not the fairies of *A Midsummer Night's Dream* but the weird sisters of *Macbeth*. When in the tragedy's opening scene the witches chant, "Fair is foul, and foul is fair," they unsettle through the simplest and most radical act of linguistic equation (x is y) the fundamental antinomies through which a moral order is established. And when Macbeth appears onstage a few minutes later, his first words unconsciously echo what we have just heard from the witches' mouths: "So foul and fair a day I have not seen" (1.3.36). What is the meaning of this linguistic "unconscious"? On the face of things, Macbeth presumably means only that the day of fair victory is also a day of foul weather, but the fact that he echoes the witches (something that we hear but that he cannot know) intimates an occult link between them, even before their direct encounter. It is difficult, perhaps impossible, to specify exactly what this link signifies—generations of emboldened critics have tried without notable success—but we can at least affirm that its secret lair is in the play's language, like a half-buried pun whose full articulation will entail the murder of Duncan, the ravaging of his kingdom, and Macbeth's own destruction.

Macbeth is haunted by half-buried puns, equivocations, and ambiguous grammatical constructions known as amphibologies. They manifest themselves most obviously in the words of the witches, from the opening exchanges to the fraudulent assurances that deceive Macbeth at the close, but they are also present in his most intimate and private reflections, as in his tortured broodings about his proposed act of treason:

> If it were done when 'tis done, then 'twere well
> It were done quickly. If th'assassination
> Could trammel up the consequence, and catch
> With his surcease success: that but this blow

Might be the be-all and the end-all, here,
But here upon this bank and shoal of time,
We'd jump the life to come.

(1.7.1–7)

The dream is to reach a secure and decisive end, to catch as in a net (hence "trammel up") all of the slippery, unforeseen, and uncontrollable consequences of regicide, to hobble time as one might hobble a horse (another sense of "trammel up"), to stop the flow ("success") of events, to be, as Macbeth later puts it, "settled." But Macbeth's words themselves slip away from the closure he seeks; they slide into one another, trip over themselves, twist and double back and swerve into precisely the sickening uncertainties their speaker most wishes to avoid. And if we sense a barely discernible note of comedy in Macbeth's tortured language, a discordant playing with the senses of the word "done" and the hint of a childish tongue twister in the phrase "catch / With his surcease success," we are in touch with a dark pleasure to which Shakespeare was all his life addicted.

Look again at the couplet from *Cymbeline*: "Golden lads and girls all must, / As chimney-sweepers, come to dust."

The playwright who insinuated a pun into the solemn dirge is the same playwright whose tragic heroine in *Antony and Cleopatra*, pulling the bleeding body of her dying lover into the pyramid, says, "Our strength is all gone into heaviness" (4.16.34). He is the playwright whose Juliet, finding herself alone on the stage, says, "My dismal scene I needs must act alone" (*Romeo and Juliet* 4.3.19), and the playwright who can follow the long, wrenching periodic sentence that Othello speaks, just before he stabs himself, with the remark "O bloody period!" (5.2.366). The point is not merely the presence of puns in the midst of tragedy (as there are stabs of pain in the midst of Shakespearean comedy); it is rather the streak of wildness that they so deliberately disclose, the sublimely indecorous linguistic energy of which Shakespeare was at once the towering master and the most obedient, worshipful servant.

The Dream of the Master Text

Shakespeare and the Printed Book

Ben Jonson's famous tribute to Shakespeare—"He was not of an age, but for all time!"—comes in one of the dedicatory poems to the 1623 First Folio of *Mr. William Shakespeares Comedies, Histories, & Tragedies*. This large, handsome volume, the first collection of Shakespeare's plays, was not, as far as we know, the product of the playwright's own design. We do not even know if he would have approved of the Folio's division of each play into five acts or its organization of the plays into three loose generic categories, comedies, histories, and tragedies (to which modern editors have often added a fourth, the romances, to group together *Cymbeline, Pericles, The Winter's Tale,* and *The Tempest*). Published seven years after the playwright's death, the Folio was printed by the London printers William and Isaac Jaggard, who were joined in this expensive venture by Edward Blount, John Smethwicke, and William Apsley. It was edited by two of Shakespeare's old friends and fellow actors, John Heminges and Henry Condell, who claimed to be using "True Originall Copies" in the author's own hand. (None of these copies has survived, or, more cautiously, none has to date been found.) Eighteen plays included in the First Folio had already appeared individually in print in the small-format and relatively inexpensive texts called "quartos" (or, in one case, the still smaller format called "octavo"); to these, Heminges and Condell added eighteen others never before published: *All's Well That Ends Well, Antony and Cleopatra, As You Like It, The Comedy of Errors, Coriolanus, Cymbeline, All Is True (Henry VIII), Julius Caesar, King John, Macbeth, Measure for Measure, The Taming of the Shrew, The Tempest, Timon of Athens, Twelfth Night, The Two*

Sixteenth-century printing shop. Engraving by Jan van der Straet. From *Nova Reperta* (1580).

Gentlemen of Verona, The Winter's Tale, and *1 Henry VI.** None of the plays included in the Folio has dropped out of the generally accepted canon of Shakespeare's works, and only two plays not included in the volume *(Pericles* and *The Two Noble Kinsmen)* have been allowed to join this select company, along with the nondramatic poems. Of the latter, *Venus and Adonis* (1593) and *The Rape of Lucrece* (1594) first appeared during Shakespeare's lifetime in quartos with dedications from the author to the Earl of Southampton. *Shakespeare's Sonnets* (1609) were apparently printed without his authorization, as were his poems in a collection called *The Passionate Pilgrim* (1599).

The plays were the property of the theatrical company in which Shakespeare was a shareholder. It was not normally in the interest of such companies to have their scripts circulating in print, at least while the plays were actively in repertory: players evidently feared competition from rival companies and thought that reading might dampen playgoing. Plays were generally sold only when the theaters were temporarily closed by plague, or when the company was in need of capital (four of Shakespeare's plays were published in 1600, presumably to raise money to pay the debts incurred in building the new Globe), or when a play had grown too old to revive profitably. There is no evidence that Shakespeare himself disagreed with this professional caution, no sign that he wished to see his plays in print. Unlike Ben Jonson, who took the radical step of rewriting his own plays for

*This sketch simplifies several complex questions such as the status of the 1594 Quarto called *The Taming of a Shrew,* sufficiently distinct from the similarly titled Folio text as to constitute for many editors a different play.

publication in the 1616 folio of his *Works*, Shakespeare evidently was not interested in constituting his plays as a canon. If in the sonnets he imagines his verse achieving a symbolic immortality, this dream apparently did not extend to his plays, at least through the medium of print.

Moreover, there is no evidence that Shakespeare had an interest in asserting authorial rights over his scripts, or that he or any other working English playwright had a public "standing," legal or otherwise, from which to do so. (Jonson was ridiculed for his presumption.) There is no indication whatever that he could, for example, veto changes in his scripts or block interpolated scenes or withdraw a play from production if a particular interpretation, addition, or revision did not please him. To be sure, in his advice to the players, Hamlet urges that those who play the clowns "speak no more than is set down for them," but—apart from the question of whether the Prince speaks for the playwright—the play-within-the-play in *Hamlet* is precisely an instance of a script altered to suit a particular occasion. It seems likely that Shakespeare would have routinely accepted the possibility of such alterations. Moreover, he would of necessity have routinely accepted the possibility, and in certain cases the virtual inevitability, of cuts in order to stage his plays in the two to two and one-half hours that was the normal performing time. There is an imaginative generosity in many of Shakespeare's scripts, as if he were deliberately offering his fellow actors more than they could use on any one occasion and hence giving them abundant materials with which to reconceive and revivify each play again and again, as they or their audiences liked it. The Elizabethan theater, like most theater in our own time, was a collaborative enterprise, and the collaboration almost certainly extended to decisions about selection, trimming, shifts of emphasis, and minor or major revision.

For many years, it was thought that Shakespeare himself did little or no revising. Some recent editors—above all the editors of the *Oxford Shakespeare*, whose texts the *Norton* presents—have argued persuasively that there are many signs of authorial revision, even wholesale rewriting. But there is no sign that Shakespeare sought through such revision to bring each of his plays to its "perfect," "final" form. On the contrary, many of the revisions seem to indicate that the scripts remained open texts, that the playwright and his company expected to add, cut, and rewrite as the occasion demanded.

Ralph Waldo Emerson once compared Shakespeare and his contemporary Francis Bacon in terms of the relative "finish" of their work. All of Bacon's work, wrote Emerson, "lies along the ground, a vast unfinished city." Each of Shakespeare's dramas, by contrast, "is perfect, hath an immortal integrity. To make Bacon's work complete, he must live to the end of the world." Recent scholarship suggests that Shakespeare was more like Bacon than Emerson thought. Neither the Folio nor the quarto texts of Shakespeare's plays bear the seal of final authorial intention, the mark of decisive closure that has served, at least ideally, as the guarantee of textual authenticity. We want to believe, as we read the text, "This is the play as Shakespeare himself wanted it read," but there is no license for such a reassuring sentiment. To be "not of an age, but for all time" means in Shakespeare's case not that the plays have achieved a static perfection, but that they are creatively, inexhaustibly unfinished.

That we have been so eager to link certain admired scripts to a single known playwright is closely related to changes in the status of artists in the Renaissance, changes that led to a heightened interest in the hand of the individual creator. Like medieval painting, medieval drama gives us few clues as to the particular individuals who fashioned the objects we admire. We know something about the places in which these objects were made, the circumstances that enabled their creation, the spaces in which they were placed, but relatively little about the particular artists themselves. It is easy to imagine a wealthy patron or a civic authority in the late Middle Ages commissioning a play on a particular subject (appropriate, for example, to a seasonal ritual, a religious observance, or a political festivity) and specifying the date, place, and length of the performance, the number of actors, even the costumes to be used, but it is more difficult to imagine him specifying a particular playwright and still less insisting that the entire play be written by this dramatist alone. Only with the Renaissance do we find a growing insistence on the name of the maker, the signature that heightens the value and even the meaning of the work by implying that it is the emanation of a single, distinct shaping consciousness.

In the case of Renaissance painting, we know that this signature does not necessarily mean that every stroke was made by the master. Some of the work, possibly the greater part of it, may have been done by assistants, with only the faces and a few finishing touches from the hand of the illustrious artist to whom the work is confidently attributed. As the skill of individual masters became more explicitly valued, contracts began to specify how much was to come from the brush of the principal painter. Consider, for example, the Italian painter Luca Signorelli's contract of 1499 for frescoes in Orvieto Cathedral:

> The said master Luca is bound and promises to paint [1] all the figures to be done on the said vault, and [2] especially the faces and all the parts of the figures from the middle of each figure upwards, and [3] that no painting should be done on it without Luca himself being present. . . . And it is agreed [4] that all the mixing of colours should be done by the said master Luca himself.

Such a contract at once reflects a serious cash interest in the characteristic achievement of a particular artist and a conviction that this achievement is compatible with the presence of other hands, provided those hands are subordinate, in the finished work. For paintings on a smaller scale, it was more possible to commission an exclusive performance. Thus the contract for a small altarpiece by Signorelli's great teacher, Piero della Francesca, specifies that "no painter may put his hand to the brush other than Piero himself."

There is no record of any comparable concern for exclusivity in the English theater. Unfortunately, the contracts that Shakespeare and his fellow dramatists almost certainly signed have not, with one significant exception, survived. But plays written for the professional theater are by their nature an even more explicitly collective art form than paintings; they depend for their full realization on the collaboration of others, and that collaboration may well extend to the fashioning of the script. It seems that some authors may simply have been responsible for providing plots that others then dramatized; still others were hired to "mend" old plays or to supply prologues, epilogues, or songs. A particular playwright's name came to be attached to a certain identifiable style—a characteristic set of plot devices, a marked rhetorical range, a tonality of character—but this name may refer in effect more to a certain product associated with a particular playing company than to the individual artist who may or may not have written most of the script. The one contract whose details do survive, that entered into by Richard Brome and the actors and owners of the Salisbury Court Theatre in 1635, does not stipulate that Brome's plays must be written by him alone or even that he must be responsible for a certain specifiable proportion of each script. Rather, it specifies that the playwright "should not nor would write any play or any part of a play to any other players or playhouse, but apply all his study and endeavors therein for the benefit of the said company of the said playhouse." The Salisbury Court players want rights to everything Brome writes for the stage; the issue is not that the plays associated with his name be exclusively *his* but rather that he be exclusively *theirs*.

Recent textual scholarship, then, has been moving steadily away from a conception of Shakespeare's plays as direct, unmediated emanations from the mind of the author and toward a conception of them as working scripts, composed and continually reshaped as part of a collaborative commercial enterprise in competition with other, similar enterprises. One consequence has been the progressive weakening of the idea of the solitary, inspired genius, in the sense fashioned by Romanticism and figured splendidly in the statue of Shakespeare in the public gardens in Germany's Weimar, the city of Goethe and Schiller: the poet, with his sensitive, expressive face and high domed forehead sitting alone and brooding, a skull at his feet, a long-stemmed rose in his crotch. In place of this projection of German Romanticism, we have now a playwright and sometime actor who is also (to his considerable financial advantage) a major shareholder in the company—the Lord Chamberlain's Men, later the King's Men—to which he loyally supplies for most of his career an average of two plays per year.

These developments are salutary insofar as they direct attention to the actual conditions in which the textual traces that the Folio calls Shakespeare's "Comedies, Histories, & Tragedies" came to be produced, reproduced, consumed, revised, and transmitted to future generations. They highlight elements that Shakespeare shared with his contemporaries, and they insistently remind us that we are encountering scripts written primarily for the stage and not for the study. They make us more attentive to such matters as business cycles, plague rolls, the cost of costumes, government censorship, and urban topography and less concerned with the elusive and enigmatic details of the poet's biography—his supposed youthful escapades and erotic yearnings and psychological crises.

All well and good. But the fact remains that in 1623, seven years after the playwright's death, Heminges and Condell thought they could sell copies of their expensive collection of Shakespeare's plays—"What euer you do," they urge their readers, "buy"—by insisting that their texts were "as he conceiued them." This means that potential readers in the early seventeenth century were already interested in Shakespeare's "conceits"—his "wit," his imagination, and his creative power—and were willing to assign a high value to the products of his particular, identifiable skill, one distinguishable from that of his company and of his rival playwrights. After all, Jonson's tribute praises Shakespeare not as the playwright of the incomparable King's Men but as the equal of Aeschylus, Sophocles, and Euripides. And if we now see Shakespeare's dramaturgy in the context of his contemporaries and of a collective artistic practice, readers continue to have little difficulty recognizing that most of the plays attached to his name tower over those of his rivals.

From Foul to Fair: The Making of the Printed Play

What exactly is a printed play by Shakespeare? Is it like a novel or a poem? Is it like the libretto or the score of an opera? Is it the trace of an absent event? Is it the blueprint of an imaginary structure that will never be completed? Is it a record of what transpired in the mind of a man long dead? We might say cautiously that it is a mechanically reproduced version of what Shakespeare wrote, but unfortunately, with the possible (and disputed) exception of a small fragment from a collaboratively written play called *Sir Thomas More*, virtually nothing Shakespeare actually wrote in his own hand survives. We might propose that it is a printed version of the script that an Elizabethan actor would have held in his hands during rehearsals, but here too no such script of a Shakespeare play survives; and besides, Elizabethan actors were evidently not given the whole play to read. To reduce the expense of copying and the risk of unauthorized reproduction, each actor received only his own part, along with the cue lines. (Shakespeare uses this fact to delicious comic effect in *A Midsummer Night's Dream* 3.1.80–88.) Nonetheless, the play certainly existed as a whole, either in the author's original manuscript or in the copy prepared for the government censor or for the company's prompter or stage manager, so we might imagine the text we hold in our hands as a printed copy of one of these manuscripts. But since no contemporary manuscript survives of any of Shakespeare's plays, we cannot verify this hypothesis. And even if we could, we would not have resolved the question of the precise relation of the printed text either to the playwright's imagination or to the theatrical performance by the company to which he belonged.

All of Shakespeare's plays must have begun their textual careers in the form of "foul papers," drafts presumably covered with revisions, crossings-out, and general "blotting." To be sure, Heminges and Condell remark that so great was the playwright's facility that they "have scarce received from him a blot in his papers." This was, however, a routine and conventional compliment in the period. The same claim, made for the playwright John Fletcher in an edition published in 1647, is clearly contradicted by the survival of Fletcher's far-from-unblotted manuscripts. It is safe to assume that, as Shakespeare was human, his manuscripts contained their share of second and third thoughts scribbled in the margins and between the lines. Once complete, this authorial draft would usually have to be written out again, either by the playwright or by a professional scribe employed by the theater company, as "fair copy."

In the hands of the theater company, the fair copy (or sometimes, it seems, the foul papers themselves) would be annotated and transformed into "the book of the play" or the "playbook" (what we would now call a "promptbook"). Shakespeare's authorial draft presumably contained a certain number of stage directions, though these may have been sketchy and inconsistent. The promptbook clarified these and added others, noted theatrical properties and sound effects, and on occasion cut the full text to meet the necessities of performance. The promptbook was presented to the Master of the Revels for licensing, and it incorporated any changes upon which the master insisted. As the editors of the Oxford Shakespeare put it, the difference between foul papers and promptbook is the difference between "the text in an as yet individual, private form" and "a socialized text."

But the fact remains that for Shakespeare's plays, we have neither foul papers nor fair copies nor promptbooks. We have only the earliest printed editions of these texts in numerous individual quartos and in the First Folio. (Quartos are so called because each sheet of paper was folded twice, making four leaves or eight pages front and back; folio sheets were folded once, making two leaves or four pages front and back.) From clues embedded in these "substantive" texts—substantive because (with the exception of *The Two Noble Kinsmen*) they date from Shakespeare's own lifetime or from the collected works edited by his associates using, or claiming to use, his own manuscripts—editors attempt to reconstruct each play's journey from manuscript to print. Different plays took very different journeys.

Of the thirty-six plays included in the First Folio, eighteen had previously appeared in quarto editions, some of these in more than one printing. Generations of editors have distinguished between "good quartos," presumably prepared from the author's own draft or from a scribal transcript of the play (fair copy), and "bad quartos." The latter category, first formulated as such by A. W. Pollard in 1909, includes, by widespread though not universal agreement, the 1594 version of *The First Part of the Contention (2 Henry VI)*, the 1595 *Richard Duke of York (3 Henry VI)*, the 1597 *Richard III*, the 1597 *Romeo and Juliet*, the 1600 *Henry V*, the 1602 *Merry Wives of Windsor*, the 1603 *Hamlet*, and *Pericles* (1609). Some editors also regard the 1591 *Troublesome Reign of King John*, the 1594 *Taming of a Shrew*, and the 1608 *King Lear* as bad quartos, but others have strenuously argued that these are distinct rather than faulty texts, and the whole concept of the bad quarto has come under increasingly critical scrutiny. The criteria for distinguishing between "good" and "bad" texts are imprecise, and the evaluative terms seem to raise as many questions as they answer. Nevertheless, the striking mistakes, omissions, repetitions, and anomalies in a number of the quartos require some explanation beyond the ordinary fallibility of scribes and printers.

The explanation most often proposed for suspect quartos is that they are the products of "memorial reconstruction." The hypothesis, first advanced in 1910 by W. W. Greg, is that a series of features found in what seem to be particularly flawed texts may be traced to the derivation of the copy from the memory of one or more of the actors. Elizabethan actors, Greg observed, often found themselves away from the London theaters, for example on tour in the provinces during plague periods, and may not on those occasions have had access to the promptbooks they would ordinarily have used. In such circumstances, those in the company who remembered a play may have written down or dictated the text, as best they could, perhaps adapting it for provincial performance. Moreover, unscrupulous actors may have sold such texts to enterprising printers eager to turn a quick profit.

Memorially reconstructed texts tend to be much shorter than those prepared from foul papers or fair copy; they frequently paraphrase or garble lines, drop or misplace speeches and whole scenes, and on occasion fill in the gaps with scraps from other plays. In several cases, scholars think they can detect which roles the rogue actors played, since these parts (and the scenes in which they appear) are reproduced with greater accuracy than the rest of the play. Typically, these roles are minor ones, since the leading parts would be played by actors with a greater stake in the overall financial interest of the company and hence less inclination to violate its policy. Thus, for example, editors speculate that the bad quarto of *Hamlet* (Q1) was provided by the actor playing Marcellus (and doubling as Lucianus). What is often impossible to determine is whether particular differences between a bad quarto and a good quarto or Folio text result from the actor's faulty memory or from changes introduced in performance, possibly with the playwright's own consent, or from both. Shakespearean bad quartos ceased to appear after 1609, perhaps as a result of greater scrutiny by the Master of the Revels, who after 1606 was responsible for licensing plays for publication as well as performance.

The syndicate that prepared the Folio had access to the manuscripts of the King's Men. In addition to the previously published editions of eighteen plays, they made use of scribal transcripts (fair copies), promptbooks, and (more rarely) foul papers. The indefatigable labors of generations of bibliographers, antiquaries, and textual scholars have recovered an extraordinary fund of information about the personnel, finances, organizational structure, and material practices of Elizabethan and Jacobean printing houses, including the names and idiosyncrasies of particular compositors who calculated the page length, set the type, and printed the sheets of the Folio. This impressive scholarship has for the most part intensified respect for the seriousness with which the Folio was prepared and printed, and where the Folio is defective, it has provided plausible readings from the quartos or proposed emendations to approximate what Shakespeare is likely to have written. But it has not succeeded, despite all its heroic efforts, in transforming the Folio, or any other text, into an unobstructed, clear window into Shakespeare's mind.

The dream of the master text is a dream of transparency. The words on the page should ideally give the reader unmediated access to the astonishing forge of imaginative power that was the mind of the dramatist. Those words welled up from the genius of the great artist, and if the world were not an imperfect place, they would have been set down exactly as he conceived them and transmitted to each of us as a precious inheritance. Such is the vision—at its core closely related to the preservation of the holy text in the great scriptural religions—that has driven many of the great editors who have for centuries produced successive editions of Shakespeare's works. The vision was not yet fully formed in the First Folio, for Heminges and Condell still felt obliged to apologize to their noble patrons for dedicating to them a collection of mere "trifles." But by the eighteenth century, there were no longer any ritual apologies for Shakespeare; instead, there was a growing recognition not only of the supreme artistic importance of his works but also of the uncertain, conflicting, and in some cases corrupt state of the surviving texts. Every conceivable step, it was thought, must be undertaken to correct mistakes, strip away corruptions, return the texts to their pure and unsullied form, and make this form perfectly accessible to readers.

Paradoxically, this feverishly renewed, demanding, and passionate editorial project has produced the very opposite of the transparency that was the dream of the master text. The careful weighing of alternative readings, the production of a textual apparatus, the writing of notes and glosses, the modernizing and regularizing of spelling and punctuation, the insertion of scene divisions, the complex calculation of the process of textual transmission from foul papers to print, the equally complex calculation of the effects that censorship, government regulation, and, above all, theatrical performance had on the surviving documents all make inescapably apparent the fact that we do not have and never will have any direct, unmediated access to Shakespeare's imagination. Every Shakespeare text, from the first that was published to the most recent, has been edited: it has come into print by means of a tangled social process and inevitably exists at some remove from the author.

Heminges and Condell, who knew the author and had access to at least some of his manuscripts, lament the fact that Shakespeare did not live "to have set forth and overseen his own writings." And even had he done so—or, alternatively, even if a cache of his manuscripts were discovered in a Warwickshire attic tomorrow—all of the editorial problems would not be solved, nor would all of the levels of mediation be swept away. Certainly the entire textual landscape would change. But the written word has strange powers: it seems to hold on to something of the very life of the person who has written it, but it also seems to pry that life loose from the writer, exposing it to vagaries of history and chance quite independent of those to which the writer was personally subject. Moreover, with the passing of centuries, the language itself and the whole frame of reference within which language and symbols are understood have decisively changed. The most learned modern scholar still lives at a huge experiential remove from Shakespeare's world and, even holding a precious copy of the First Folio in hand, cannot escape having to read across a vast chasm of time what is, after all, an edited text. The rest of us cannot so much as indulge in the fantasy of direct access: our eyes inevitably wander to the glosses and the explanatory notes.

The Oxford Shakespeare

The shattering of the dream of the master text is no cause for despair, nor should it lead us to throw our hands up and declare that one text is as good as another. What it does is to encourage the reader to be actively interested in the editorial principles that underlie the particular edition that he or she is using. It is said that the great artist Brueghel once told a nosy connoisseur who had come to his studio, "Keep your nose out of my paintings; the smell of the paint will poison you." In the case of Shakespeare, it is increasingly important to bring one's nose close to the page, as it were, and sniff the ink. More precisely, it is important to understand the rationale for the choices that the editors have made.

The text of the *Norton Shakespeare* is, with very few changes, that published in 1988 by the Oxford University Press. The *Oxford Shakespeare* was the extraordinary achievement of a team of editors, Stanley Wells, Gary Taylor, John Jowett, and William Montgomery, with Wells and Taylor serving as the general editors. The Oxford editors approached their task with a clear understanding that, as we have seen, all previous texts have been mediated by agents other than Shakespeare, but they regard this mediation not as a melancholy obstacle intervening between the reader and the "true" Shakespearean text but rather as a constitutive element of this text. The art of the playwright is thoroughly dependent on the craft of go-betweens.

Shakespeare's plays were not written to be circulated in manuscript or printed form among readers. They were written to be performed by the players and, as the preface to the quarto *Troilus and Cressida* indelicately puts it, "clapper-clawed with the palms of the vulgar." The public was thus never meant to be in a direct relationship with the author but in a "triangular relationship" in which the players gave voice and gesture to the author's words. As we have seen, Shakespeare was the master of the unfinished, the perpetually open. And even if we narrow our gaze and try to find only what Shakespeare himself might have regarded as a textual resting point, a place to stop and go on to another play, we have, the Oxford editors point out, a complex task. For whatever Shakespeare wrote was meant from the start to be supplemented by an invisible "para-text" consisting of words spoken by Shakespeare to the actors and by the actors to each other, concerning emphasis, stage business, tone, pacing, possible cuts, and so forth. To the extent that this para-text was ever written down, it was recorded in the promptbook. Therefore, in contrast to standard editorial practice, the Oxford editors prefer, when there is a choice, copy based on the promptbook to copy based on the author's own draft. They choose the text immersed in history, that is, in the theatrical embodiment for which it was intended by its author, over the text unstained by the messy, collaborative demands of the playhouse. The closest we can get to Shakespeare's "final" version of a play—understanding that for him as for us there is no true "finality" in a theatrical text—is the latest version of that play performed by his company during his professional life, that is, during the time in which he could still oversee and participate in any cuts and revisions.

This choice does not mean that the Oxford editors are turning away from the very idea of Shakespeare as author. On the contrary, Wells and Taylor are deeply committed to establishing a text that comes as close as possible to the plays as Shakespeare wrote them, but they are profoundly attentive to the fact that he wrote them as a member of a company of players, a company in which he was a shareholder and an actor as well as a writer. "Writing" for the theater, at least for Shakespeare, is not simply a matter of setting words to paper and letting the pages drift away; it is a social process as well as individual act. The Oxford editors acknowledge that some aspects of this social process may have been frustrating to Shakespeare: he may, for example, have been forced on occasion to cut lines and even whole scenes to which he was attached, or his fellow players may have insisted that they could not successfully perform what he had written, compelling him to make changes he did not welcome. But compromise and collaboration are part of what it means to be in the theater, and Wells and Taylor return again and again to the recognition that Shakespeare was, supremely, a man of the theater.

Is there a tension between the Oxford editors' preference for the performed, fully socialized text and their continued commitment to recovering the text as Shakespeare himself intended it? Yes. The tension is most visible in their determination to strip away textual changes arising from circumstances, such as government censorship, over which Shakespeare had no control. ("We have, wherever possible," they write, put "profanities back in Shakespeare's mouth.") It can be glimpsed as well in the editors' belief, almost a leap of faith, that there was little revision of Shakespeare's plays in his company's revivals between the time of his death and the publication of the Folio. But the tension is mainly a creative one, for it forces them (and therefore us) to attend to the playwright's unique imaginative power as well as his social and historical entanglements.

The Oxford editors took a radical stance on a second major issue: the question of authorial revision. Previous editors had generally accepted the fact that Shakespeare practiced revision within individual manuscripts, that is, while he was still in the act of writing a particular play, but they generally rejected the notion that he undertook substantial revisions from one version of a play to another (and hence from one manuscript to another). Wells and Taylor point out that six major works *(Hamlet, Othello, 2 Henry IV, King Lear, Richard II,* and *Troilus and Cressida)* survive in two independent substantive sources, both apparently authoritative, with hundreds of significant variant readings. Previous editors have generally sought to deny authority to one edition or another ("faced with two sheep," the Oxford editors observe wryly, "it is all too easy to insist that one *must* be a goat") or have conflated the two versions into a single text in an attempt to reconstruct the ideal, definitive, complete, and perfect version that they imagine Shakespeare must have reached for each of his plays. But if one doubts that Shakespeare ever conceived of his plays as closed, finished entities, if one recalls that he wrote them for the living repertory of the commercial playing company to which he belonged, then the whole concept of the single, authoritative text of each play loses its force. In a startling departure from the editorial tradition, the *Oxford Shakespeare* printed two distinct versions of *King Lear,* quarto and Folio, and the editors glanced longingly at the impractical but alluring possibility of including two texts of *Hamlet, Othello,* and *Troilus.*

The *Oxford Shakespeare* was published in both old-spelling and modern-spelling editions. The former, the first of its kind ever published, raised some reviewers' eyebrows because the project, a critical edition rather than a facsimile, required the modern editors to invent plausible Elizabethan spellings for their emendations and to add stage directions. The modern-spelling edition, which is the basis for Norton's text, is noteworthy for taking the principles of modernization further than they had generally been taken. Gone are such words as "murther," "mushrump," "vild," and "porpentine," which confer on many modern-spelling editions a certain cozy, Olde-English quaintness; Oxford replaces them with "murder," "mushroom," "vile," and "porcupine."

The inclusion of two texts of *King Lear* aroused considerable controversy when the *Oxford Shakespeare* first appeared, though by now the arguments for doing so have received widespread, though not unanimous, scholarly support. Other features remain controversial: "Ancients" Pistol and Iago have been modernized to "Ensigns"; *Henry VIII* has reverted to its performance title *All Is True;* demonic spirits in *Macbeth* sing lyrics written by Thomas Middleton. The inclusion of a poem not usually considered part of Shakespeare's canon, "Shall I die?" provoked an enormous wave of charge and countercharge. The white-hot intensity of the debates triggered by the *Oxford Shakespeare*'s editorial choices casts an interesting light on the place of Shakespeare not only in the culture at large but in the psyches of millions of individuals: any alteration, however minor, in a deeply familiar and beloved text, even an alteration based on thoughtful and highly plausible scholarly principles, arouses genuine anxiety. The anxiety in this case was intensified not only by the boldness of certain crucial emendations but also by the fact that the editors' explanations, arguments, and justifications for all their decisions were printed in a separate, massive volume, *William Shakespeare: A Textual Companion*. This formidable, dense volume is an astonishing monument to the seriousness, scholarly rigor, and immense labor of the Oxford editors. Anyone who is interested in pursuing why Shakespeare's words appear as they do in the current edition, anyone who wishes insight into the editors' detailed reasons for making the thousands of decisions required by a project of this kind, should consult the *Textual Companion*.

The Norton Shakespeare

The primary task that the editors of the *Norton Shakespeare* set themselves was to present the modern-spelling Oxford *Complete Works* in a way that would make the text more accessible to modern readers. The *Oxford Shakespeare* prints little more than the text itself: along with one-page introductions to the individual works, it contains a short general introduction, a list of contemporary allusions to Shakespeare, and a brief glossary. But while it is possible to enjoy a Shakespeare play on stage or screen without any assistance beyond the actors' own art, many readers at least since the eighteenth century have found it far more difficult to understand and to savor the texts without some more substantial commentary.

In addition to writing introductions, textual notes, and brief bibliographies for each of the works, the Norton editors provide glosses and footnotes designed to facilitate comprehension. Such is the staggering richness of Shakespeare's language that it is tempting to gloss everything, but there is a law of diminishing returns: too much explanatory whispering at the margins makes it difficult to enjoy what the reader has come for in the first place. Our general policy is to gloss only those words that cannot be found in an ordinary dictionary or whose meanings have altered out of recognition. The glosses attempt to be simple and straightforward, giving multiple meanings for words only when the meanings are essential for making sense of the passages in which they appear. We try not to gloss the same word over and over—it becomes distracting to be told three times on a single page that "an" means "if"—but we also assume that the reader does not have a perfect memory, so after an interval we will gloss the same word again.

Marginal glosses generally refer to a single word or a short phrase. The footnotes paraphrase longer units or provide other kinds of information, such as complex plays on words, significant allusions, textual cruxes, historical and cultural contexts. Here too, however, we have tried to check the impulse to annotate so heavily that the reader is distracted from the pleasure of the text, and we have avoided notes that provide interpretation, as distinct from information.

Following each of the works, the Norton editors have provided lists of textual variants. These are variants from the control text only; that is, they do not record all of the variants in all of the substantive texts, nor do they record all of the myriad shifts of meaning that may arise from modernization of spelling and repunctuation. Readers who wish to pursue these interesting, if complex, topics are encouraged to consult the *Textual Companion*, along with the old-spelling *Oxford Shakespeare*, the Norton facsimile of the First Folio, and the quarto facsimiles published by the University of California Press. The *Norton Shakespeare* does provide a convenient list for each play of the different ways the same characters are designated in the speech prefixes in the substantive texts. These variants (for example, Lady Capulet in *Romeo and Juliet* is called, variously, "Lady, "Mother," "Wife," "Old Woman," etc.) often cast an interesting light on the ways a particular character is conceived. Variants as they appear in this edition, as well as their line numbers, are printed in boldface; each is followed by the corresponding reading in the control text, and sometimes the source from which the variant is taken. Further information on readings in substantive texts is given in brackets.

Stage directions pose a complex set of problems for the editors of a one-volume Shakespeare. The printing conventions for the stage directions in sixteenth- and seventeenth-century plays were different from those of our own time. Often all of the entrances for a particular scene are grouped together at the beginning, even though some of the characters clearly do not enter until later; placement in any case seems at times haphazard or simply incorrect. There are moments when the stage directions seem to provide stunning insight into the staging of the plays in Shakespeare's time, other moments when they are absent or misleading. It is difficult to gauge how much the stage directions in the substantive editions reflect Shakespeare's own words or at least decisions. It would seem that he was often relatively careless about them, understanding perhaps that these decisions in any precise sense would be the first to be made and unmade by different productions.

The Oxford editors, like virtually all modern editors, necessarily altered and supplemented the stage directions in their control texts. They decided to mark certain of the stage directions with a special sign to indicate a dubious action or placement, but they did not distinguish between the stage directions that came from the substantive texts and those added in later texts, from the seventeenth century to the present. They referred readers instead to the *Textual Companion*, which provides lists of the exact wording of the stage directions in the substantive texts.

The editors of the *Norton Shakespeare* share a sense of the limitations of the early stage directions and share as well some skepticism about how many of these should be attributed even indirectly to Shakespeare. Hence we do not routinely differentiate between quarto and Folio stage directions; we do so only when we think it is a significant point. But there is, it seems to us, a real interest in knowing which stage directions come from those editions of the plays published up to the 1623 Folio (and including *The Two Noble Kinsmen*, published shortly thereafter) and which were added when the editors were no longer in contact with Shakespeare's presence or his manuscripts. Therefore, we have placed brackets around all stage directions that were added after the First Folio. Unbracketed stage directions, then, all derive from editions up through the Folio.

The *Norton Shakespeare* has made several other significant departures from the Oxford text. The Oxford editors note that when *I Henry IV* was first performed, probably in 1596, the character we know as Sir John Falstaff was called Sir John Oldcastle. But in the wake of protests from Oldcastle's descendants, one of whom, William Brooke, Seventh Lord Cobham, was Elizabeth I's lord chamberlain, Shakespeare changed the name to "Falstaff" (and probably for similar reasons changed the names of Falstaff's companions, Russell and Harvey, to "Bardolph" and "Peto"). Consistent with their decision not to honor changes that Shakespeare was *compelled* to make by censorship or other forms of pressure, the Oxford editors changed the names back to their initial form. But this decision is a problem for several reasons. It draws perhaps too sharp a distinction between those things that Shakespeare did under social pressure and those he did of his own accord. More seriously, it pulls against the principle of a text that represents the latest performance version of a play during Shakespeare's lifetime: after all, even the earliest quarto title page advertises "the humorous conceits of Sir John Falstaff." And, of course, it asks the reader to ignore completely and radically centuries of response—elaboration, fascination, and love—all focused passionately on Sir John Falstaff. The response is not a modern phenomenon: it began with Shakespeare, who developed the character as Sir John Falstaff in *2 Henry IV* and *The Merry Wives of Windsor*. Norton thus restores the more familiar names.

Another major departure from the Oxford text is Norton's printing of the so-called Additional Passages, especially in *Hamlet*. Consistent with their decision not to conflate quarto and Folio texts, the Oxford editors adhere to their control text for *Hamlet*, the Folio, and print those passages that appear only in the Second Quarto in an appendix at the end of the play. As explained at length in the Textual Note to the play, the Norton editors decided not to follow this course, but instead chose a different way of demarcating the quarto and Folio texts (inserting the quarto passages, indented, in the body of the text), one that makes it easier to see how the quarto passages functioned in a version of the play that Shakespeare also authored.

The *Norton Shakespeare* follows Oxford in printing separate quarto and Folio texts of *King Lear*. But we have departed from Oxford in printing these on facing pages, so that their differences can be readily weighed, and we have added a conflated version of *King*

Lear, so that readers will have the opportunity to assess for themselves the effects of the traditional editorial practice.

Finally, the *Norton Shakespeare* includes, among its appendices, a poem called "A Funeral Elegy," edited by Donald Foster, who has recently made a case for Shakespeare's authorship. An introduction presents some of the arguments for and against this attribution. We should add that there are several other texts that have been with some plausibility attributed at least in part to Shakespeare—among the most interesting, a play entitled *Edward III*—and that more may be found in the years to come. This should surprise no one who has read this General Introduction: with Shakespeare, the boundaries are and must remain forever open.

TRAGEDIES

TRAGEDIES

Titus Andronicus

Human sacrifice. Gang rape. Mutilation. Ritual butchery. Mother-son cannibalism. *Titus Andronicus* delighted audiences of the 1590s, but several centuries of critics since then have deplored the play's gratuitous violence and its generally "un-Shakespearean" character. The late-seventeenth-century playwright Edward Ravenscroft considered *Titus Andronicus* "a heap of rubbish"; the twentieth-century poet and critic T. S. Eliot called it "one of the stupidest and most uninspired plays ever written." Some have even claimed that Shakespeare could not have written *Titus Andronicus*, although contemporaries testify to his authorship, and although it inaugurates themes that will interest him again: he returns to the Machiavellian villain in *Richard III*, to the urgency of revenge in *Hamlet*, to the old man unwisely relinquishing power in *Lear*, to questions of race and intermarriage in *Othello* and *The Tempest*, to important moments in Roman history in *The Rape of Lucrece*, *Julius Caesar*, *Coriolanus*, and *Antony and Cleopatra*.

Of course, Shakespeare himself, writing his first tragedy in 1592, could not have anticipated the reasons for which he would eventually be canonized. Moreover, the distinction between "high art" and "low entertainment" that often underlies complaints about *Titus Andronicus* would have been unfamiliar to Shakespeare and to his audience: the contrast between popular and elite culture was drawn differently in early modern England than it has been in later centuries. Even by the standards of Shakespeare's contemporaries, however, *Titus Andronicus* is an extravagantly bloody play, often deliberately shocking or grotesque. It seems worth asking how it fits into an oeuvre in which many have been reluctant to grant it a place.

Generically speaking, *Titus Andronicus* is a tragedy of revenge, a very old form that originated in ancient Greece, flourished in ancient Rome, and was revived in the 1580s in England by Shakespeare's predecessor Thomas Kyd. English Renaissance revenge tragedies typically feature a man whose family members have been raped or murdered by a king, duke, or emperor. Because the administration of justice rests in the hands of the very person who has committed the outrage, no redress is obtainable through established institutions. As a result, the hero takes matters into his own hands. Ironically, as he struggles to impose a just order upon his world, he loses his own moral bearings and even his sanity: the commonsensical standards of "justice" upon which he has initially relied often come to seem either flawed or unreachable. In the final scenes, the revenger wreaks some appalling vengeance upon his enemies and then is killed, or commits suicide, himself. By staging the spectacle of a subject exterminating his "betters," Renaissance revenge tragedy taps into frustrations and ambivalences that must have accumulated in the hierarchical, deliberately inequitable social arrangements of early modern England. Spectators could experience a vicarious thrill of sympathy with the revenger, even while, at the end of the play, acknowledging the moral unacceptability of revenge and the necessity for the revenger's death.

Titus Andronicus differs from roughly contemporary revenge tragedies in degree rather than in kind. Revengers typically begin as conscientious, law-abiding types: otherwise their eventual descent into illegality would furnish little dramatic interest. In Titus's case, these traits are highly exaggerated: when offered the imperial diadem, his sense of propriety induces him to defer to Saturninus, the eldest son of the last emperor, even though in Rome the office of emperor was not necessarily an inherited one. Of course, the obligation that Saturninus thus incurs makes Titus's later suffering at the hands of the imperial family seem all the more galling. At the same time, Shakespeare complicates the action by giving Saturninus's wife, Tamora, an excellent reason for hating Titus: in the first scene, he has ignored her desperate pleas and sacrificed her eldest son. So in fact, Titus's revenge is a response to Tamora's own vengeance. The doubling of reprisals in *Titus Andronicus* gives some pretext for the play's relentless bloodiness; but it is worth remembering too that bloodiness is an earmark of revenge tragedy, then and now. One modern corollary to a play like *Titus Andronicus* is the movie thriller in which a rogue cop or ex-military officer brutally retaliates against those who have murdered his partners or loved ones: the kind of film, in other words, that is likely to attract a vast audience even while provoking condemnation of "media violence."

Some aspects of *Titus*, then, seem less grotesque when it is compared with other plays of its kind rather than, say, with *Romeo and Juliet*. In its elaborately detailed antique setting, however, *Titus Andronicus* differs strikingly from most Renaissance revenge tragedies. The play is an early manifestation of Shakespeare's enduring interest in classical culture, a "Roman" play akin to *Julius Caesar, Coriolanus*, and *Antony and Cleopatra*. But in contrast to the later Roman plays, which are based on history and biography, the plot of *Titus Andronicus* is pure fiction. Unfettered by fact, Shakespeare is free to fabricate an extravagant nightmare universe that presses against the frontiers of plausibility. At the same time, he puts a great deal of emphasis on the play's "Roman-ness," making constant reference to classical myths, to legendary and historical figures, to imperial institutions, to the places and customs of ancient Rome.

Shakespeare creates what might be called a "Rome effect" by an eclectic process of extracting and combining motifs from a wide variety of classical stories. Titus as he appears in the opening scene, for instance—in his austere patriotism, his intolerance of dissent, his acute sense of personal and family honor, his traditional piety, and his ferocious commitment to patriarchal hierarchy—is a recurrent Roman personality type. Shakespeare could have found historical precedents for these traits in several figures: Horatius, who after a victory in battle killed his sister for lamenting her betrothed, a man of the enemy nation whom he himself had slain in combat; Gaius Mucius Scaevola, who deliberately burned off his right hand in the presence of an enemy king to demonstrate the resolution of the Romans; Titus Manlius Torquatus, a general so severe that he had his own son executed for eagerly anticipating an order to engage the enemy; Marcus Portius Cato, whose contempt for "softness" made him both an extraordinary military leader and an eloquent misogynist; Appius Claudius, who killed his daughter after her sexual honor was compromised. Most likely, Shakespeare had all these exemplary figures in mind, and probably more. Likewise the career of Titus's son Lucius, a soldier who defends Rome bravely against external enemies but who finds himself persecuted by his own countrymen, recalls the experience of several historic figures: the brothers Publius Scipio Africanus and Lucius Scipio Asiaticus, who subdued much of North Africa and Asia only to be falsely accused of embezzlement; or Caius Marcius Coriolanus, who after his exile joined Rome's enemies and marched on his native city.

Similarly, Lavinia has a number of classical precursors. The story of her rape and mutilation is loosely based on a story that, as retold in Ovid's *Metamorphoses*, was commonly assigned to Elizabethan boys in school. In this ancient legend, King Tereus rapes his sister-in-law Philomela and cuts out her tongue in order to prevent her from revealing his identity. Philomela, however, imparts the truth to her sister Progne (or Procne), Tereus's wife, by weaving a tapestry that illustrates the crime. In revenge, Progne butchers her own son by Tereus and serves him to her husband as part of a feast. The similarities between Lavinia's plight and Philomela's are often noted in *Titus Andronicus*, and Lavinia herself reveals the truth about the crime when she gets her stumps on a copy of the *Metamorphoses*.

But Philomela is not the only model for Lavinia. Shakespeare draws upon the story of the rape of Lucretia, an ancient Roman matron violated by Tarquin, the king's son; she committed suicide after revealing the crime to her male relatives. She was revenged by a group of men who, like Lucius in *Titus Andronicus*, used the outrage as a pretext for overthrowing tyrannical power and setting up a new government. Shakespeare also incorporates into *Titus Andronicus* some features of the story of Appius and Virginia, to which I have already briefly referred. Virginia was a young Roman woman who was sexually threat-

Progne serving Itys to Tereus. From Antonio Tempesta, Ovid's "Metamorphoses" (1606).

ened by a powerful judge and killed by her father to prevent her rape; like Lucretia, she became the pretext for a revolutionary uprising. Lavinia's story, then, is an amalgam of classical rape narratives. Her terribly mutilated body condenses a long history of sporadic violence against women into a single, intensely imagined brutalization. Like Titus, Lavinia seems to sum up a whole tradition, one highly prestigious in an age that venerated the classics, and at the same time deeply disturbing.

This particular way of imagining "Rome," as an anthology of stories, reflects Shakespeare's education in Renaissance England. England had, of course, been a Roman territory, and marks of the Roman occupation persisted. Romans had built the road system still in use in Shakespeare's time; the remains of their fortifications were (and are) still visible in many locations. But England had been a remote outpost of the empire, not a place where the treasures of antiquity were commonly to be found. While Renaissance Italians could ground their knowledge of antiquity upon great architecture and statuary all around them, the English, few of whom traveled to Italy in the sixteenth century, imbibed the classical past through books, through a grammar school curriculum that emphasized a firm grounding in Latin literature and history. For Shakespeare and his compatriots, in other words, the Roman past had less to do with places or artifacts than with texts.

The influence of these texts echoes through *Titus Andronicus*: Ovid's *Metamorphoses*, a fantastic compilation of pagan myths; Virgil's *Aeneid*, which recounts the epic voyage of the Trojan prince Aeneas to Carthage and then Italy; the gory legends of vengeance dramatized by the tragedian Seneca; the histories of the Roman Republic and Empire, written by Livy, Plutarch, Tacitus, Sallust, and Suetonius. In *Titus Andronicus*, the sign of Rome's dominion often seems less a moral or political superiority than a kind of narrative ascendancy. Shakespeare's Goths and Africans apparently have no history, no myths, of their own: instead, they invoke and mimic examples provided by their conquerors, just as Renaissance Europeans revived the classical literary inheritance, testifying to its importance in the very acts of reading and imitating it.

In *Titus Andronicus*, all the characters in the play are acutely conscious of the glorious Roman past as it is enshrined in narrative. Their dependence on old stories means that their lives have a curiously derivative quality. The characters not only model their behavior on these stories, but they consistently exceed the prototype. Whereas in the *Metamorphoses* one man rapes Philomela and cuts out her tongue afterward, in *Titus Andronicus* two men rape Lavinia, and they cut off her hands as well. Whereas Progne cooks one child, Titus bakes two. "For worse than Philomel you used my daughter," Titus declares, "And worse than Progne I will be revenged" (5.2.193–94). He both invokes and goes beyond his original example, intensifying the original crime in a way characteristic of revengers ancient and modern: "An act is not revenged," writes the ancient tragedian Seneca, "unless it is surpassed." Thus there is an interesting corollary between the spiraling ferocity typical of the revenge plot and the competitive way in which the characters in Shakespeare's revenge play fit themselves into a Roman tradition by exceeding its paradigms, enacting its stories "with a vengeance," as one says.

Of course, the oppressive weight of the past is a problem not merely for the characters of *Titus Andronicus* but also for its playwright. Like his characters, Shakespeare recycles the old stories with a difference, "surpassing" them just as the revenger surpasses the original crime. From our point of view, Shakespeare seems the world's preeminent dramatist, secure in the greatness that was already beginning to be accorded him at the time of his death. But in the early years of his career, Shakespeare might well have wondered whether and how it was possible to use, even while surpassing, the examples earlier writers had set for him. The notorious excesses of *Titus Andronicus* are one way of employing, even while going beyond, the examples he inherited.

If, in fact, Shakespeare worried about how he would measure up against his predecessors, and about whether the present and future would be able to compete with the past, it is interesting that he sets *Titus Andronicus* in the late fourth century A.D. At this point in history, Rome had dominated Europe, North Africa, and the Middle East for almost five hundred years: in both extent and duration, its empire was historically unprecedented

Triumphal arch and its collapse. From Jan van der Noot, *A Theatre for Worldlings* (1569).

and has never been achieved again. The Roman ritual that embodies and celebrates that rule is the "triumph" with which *Titus Andronicus* begins: a victory procession accorded, from time immemorial, to conquering Roman generals when they returned from the perimeters of the empire with barbarian chieftains in tow. By the fourth century, however, the long Roman dominion was drawing to a close. Shakespeare's sixteenth-century audience knows that although Titus may still be winning battles against the Goths, the time is near when the boundaries of the empire will crumble and invaders will sweep down from the north, annihilating Rome's power and bringing the era of classical civilization to an end.

In *Titus Andronicus*, then, Shakespeare portrays a society teetering on the verge of obsolescence: a place with a long, long history but not much of a future. The signs of decadence, corruption, and loss of cultural confidence are everywhere. For instance, the difference between Roman and barbarian initially seems clearly, even absolutely, marked: Tamora and her sons are in chains, Titus and his sons conquering heroes. "Thou art a Roman, be not barbarous," Marcus advises Titus, as if the two terms were necessarily incompatible. Even in the first scene, however, the Roman sense of superiority seems unwarranted. The quarrel over the imperial throne precedes Titus's victory celebration, suggesting the institutional instability that will ultimately subvert Rome from within even as uncouth armies threaten to overwhelm it from without. Moreover, the climax of Titus's victory celebration is his insistence on sacrificing Alarbus despite Tamora's maternal pleas: a case in which the traditional forms of piety that underlie Roman civilization seem to require the barbaric practice of human sacrifice. If Rome's conviction of racial and cultural supremacy—of *deserving* to rule the world—was once a workable notion, it is so no longer. The obsession with the past that pervades *Titus Andronicus* thus seems oddly empty. Even as inherited stories provide the only paradigms for action, they fail to nourish a fertile sense of tradition that might help Rome renew itself.

As traditional distinctions lose their prestige and their plausibility, the social procedures that depend on such distinctions likewise begin to collapse. The play's first scene neatly exemplifies the problem. The brothers Saturninus and Bassianus quarrel first over the possession of the imperial throne and then over the possession of Lavinia, whom both wish to marry. In Shakespeare's England, the first dispute would have been settled according to the principle of "primogeniture," which gave priority to the elder brother; the second would have been settled in favor of the younger brother, on the grounds of his preexisting betrothal to Lavinia. In Rome, however, it seems impossible to settle competing claims in an orderly way. In fact, Saturninus does eventually get the throne and Bassianus the woman, but not without a good deal of confusion and some lethal violence. The suggestion is that established methods of allocating property or privilege to one or another person may be quite arbitrary, but that the alternative to such methods is chaos.

In case the point is not sufficiently clear, Shakespeare immediately follows the quarrel between the two Roman brothers with another scene of sibling rivalry, this time between Tamora's sons, once again over sexual access to Lavinia. Unlike their Roman counterparts, these men are seeking not marriage but an adulterous relationship, and their villainous confidant Aaron has little difficulty massaging their illicit ambitions into plans for a rape. Adultery and rape seem the "opposites" of the marriage desired by the Roman men; and certainly the ferocity of the Gothic brothers' attack on Lavinia makes abundantly clear why such behavior is intolerable. At the same time, Shakespeare's juxtaposition of scenes suggests, subversively, the *similarities* between Roman marriage and rape. In neither case is Lavinia's consent at issue: she becomes the property of whoever happens to carry her off by force. Once again the distinction between legitimate and illegitimate behavior seems indispensable and at the same time remarkably indistinct.

The characters apparently best equipped to function in this world of collapsing distinctions are Aaron and Tamora, whose interracial adultery is perceived as particularly scandalous by both Romans and Goths. Their relationship is perhaps the most obvious example of the play's tendency to juxtapose opposites that turn out to have a great deal in common. Both Tamora and Aaron are outsiders who recognize from the outset the artificiality of the precepts by which Rome pretends to govern itself and the world. Neither character has much to gain by endorsing Rome's view of itself, which has relegated them to positions of servitude and powerlessness. In a world in which women are treated as the sexual property of their male relatives, "good" women like Lavinia seem destined for passivity and victimization. One acquires power in such circumstances by refusing to play by the rules. In a few lines, Tamora—manipulative, ruthless, and cunning—transfers herself from the extreme of subjugation, as Titus's captive, to the apex of power as empress of Rome.

Aaron is Tamora's natural counterpart. He is a stage descendant of the "black men" of the medieval morality plays, which conflated traditional depictions of the devil with racist conceptions of "Moors" and "Africans." But at the same time that Shakespeare exploits to the full Aaron's capacity for gleeful villainy, he makes Aaron's point of view comprehensible, even at some points attractive, to the audience. Roman hierarchies would consign Aaron permanently to a subordinate position, for racial rather than sexual reasons; and like Tamora, he sees no reason to accept the validity of that assignment. Why should he collaborate in his own oppression? It is no coincidence that Shakespeare's verse seems at its best in this play when Aaron is delivering a soliloquy. His view of the world is very close to what the play as a whole seems to endorse: that the assumptions upon which ethical behavior and social institutions depend represent fictions rather than facts.

For the dramatic technique of *Titus Andronicus*, like its villains, seems to insist that the "normal" or the "proper" is a mere construct, that apparently vivid distinctions are not as clear-cut as they seem, that moral opposites have a way of turning into one another. We have already seen Shakespeare setting the behavior of Bassianus and Saturninus beside the behavior of Chiron and Demetrius, as well as associating his white empress with his black slave. Such juxtapositions seem to be designed to induce a sort of evaluative vertigo, an effect that becomes most intense, perhaps, in the figure of the unnamed infant who results from Tamora's adultery with Aaron. In the view of most of the play's characters, this child physically embodies, and thus serves as both proof and symbol of, its parents' utter depravity. At the same time, Aaron's unexpectedly fierce solicitude for the child—which contrasts attractively with Titus's casual willingness to slaughter his own son—prevents the audience from taking at face value the rhetoric of disgust and fear discharged upon the little unfortunate from everyone else in the play. This is, after all, a baby. Every time it is brought onstage, the function it seems designed to serve in the play's symbolic economy powerfully conflicts with its intrinsic infant appeal.

In other cases, Shakespeare produces jarringly appropriate incongruities not by juxtaposing characters but by evoking apparently inappropriate dramatic genres. For instance, when Quintus and Martius find Bassianus's body, the audience knows they are being framed for murder, and one might expect a playwright to exploit the pathos of the situation, encouraging the audience to pity and sympathize with the innocent characters. Instead, the scene

Ethiopian soldier. From Cesare Vecellio, *De gli habiti antichi et moderni* (1590).

is played for laughs, as Titus's sons struggle farcically to pull one another out of a hole. Another jarring technique in *Titus Andronicus* is the deliberately awful play on words: "Mark, Marcus, mark" (3.1.143), cries Titus as they behold the ravished and mutilated Lavinia. In such cases, Shakespeare's humor shatters the norms of dramatic and moral suitability, implying the artificiality of what is conventionally considered "normal" or "proper."

If the moral and social problem of *Titus* is that eventually nothing is taboo, the aesthetic problem of the play is that literary convention too comes to seem entirely artificial. Shakespeare's deliberate rule breaking in *Titus Andronicus* risks looking like, or simply being the equivalent of, tasteless incompetence. This is especially true when terrible suffering is at stake. Marcus's long, garishly metaphorical speech at the sight of his niece's bleeding body, for instance, seems grossly beside the point. Is Shakespeare merely being inept here—is he as out of control as Marcus seems to be? Or is he deliberately exploring the limits of his medium by unexpectedly violating its usual rules, in the manner of modern surrealists, absurdists, or postmodernists? The critical debate about *Titus Andronicus* has largely involved quarrels between those who would claim the former and those who would claim the latter.

Even if Shakespeare sometimes seems to share the heartlessness of Aaron and Tamora, he does not represent the Goth and the African as admirable characters. Rebelling against the principles of "civilization" puts them outside any moral community. At the end of the play, Lucius orders Aaron starved to death and Tamora's body thrown over the city walls, as if it were mere garbage. Their treatment indicates his conviction that their behavior has put themselves outside the classification of the human, so that when they are starving, no one has an obligation to relieve them, and when they are dead, no one need respect their remains. The final scene reasserts the difference between human society and what Titus calls "a wilderness of tigers," a difference that the revenge plot has come close to erasing. And despite the abundant evidence that Roman social organization is fundamentally flawed and soon to be toppled, it is not surprising that both Goths and Romans should greet Lucius's restoration of order at the end of the play with profound relief.

Titus Andronicus, then, suggests that the principles of Roman order are patently false and often arbitrarily oppressive; but it also suggests that acknowledging this arbitrariness, or rebelling against this falsity and oppression, will have disastrous consequences. What produces Roman "virtue" seems to be a delusion; but being undeluded, as Tamora and Aaron are and Titus becomes, is even more terrible. In Shakespeare's later tragedies, the alternative to normality is often a visionary possibility that seems, if only it could be lived out, to improve upon the status quo: the loves of Romeo and Juliet, Antony and Cleopatra, Othello and Desdemona, are examples of such "constructive rulebreaking." In *Titus Andronicus*, however, traditional taboos, however cruel, brittle, or despotic they seem, are the sole guarantors of order. Once they are shattered, nothing can take their place, and sheer chaos ensues.

The pessimism, even nihilism, of this vision, combined with Shakespeare's almost playful emphasis on what most writers prefer to skirt or play down, is doubtless what has made *Titus* seem merely bad to so many readers since the late seventeenth century. From another point of view, however, *Titus Andronicus* is a daring experiment: one that Shakespeare did not repeat, but that nonetheless provides fascinating insight into his development as a dramatist.

KATHARINE EISAMAN MAUS

TEXTUAL NOTE

There are three extant quarto editions of *Titus Andronicus*. The First Quarto (Q1) was printed in 1594 and seems to derive directly from Shakespeare's manuscript. Only one copy of Q1 now survives. Q2, published in 1600, was prepared from a copy of Q1 whose last few pages had been damaged; the printer invented several lines to fill in text missing from the final scene of the play. In most cases, Q2's deviations from Q1 have no authority, but in several instances, it seems to have preserved corrected readings not found in the single copy of Q1 now extant. (Since proofreading in Elizabethan times was done while the text was in the process of being printed instead of beforehand, it is often the case that copies printed late in a press run will rectify errors present in earlier copies.) The most notable of Q2's corrections is the omission of three and a half lines from 1.1. These lines seem inappropriate to their context: they suggest that Alarbus has already been sacrificed, an act portrayed later in the scene. Q3 reprints Q2 with some minor corrections and corruptions.

The First Folio of 1623 (F) was prepared from Q3, apparently a copy annotated by comparison with the playhouse promptbook. It includes one entire scene missing from the quartos, the "fly-killing scene" at the end of Act 3, probably written by Shakespeare for a revival of the play in 1594. It also includes more stage directions than the quarto texts, as well as one complete and one fragmentary line that are probably authentic.

In general, Q1 is the most authoritative text, but the Oxford editors accept eight substantive readings from Q2 and resort to F for the fly-killing scene and some stage directions. The three and a half lines omitted from 1.1 and two other passages from Q1 probably intended for deletion are to be found, indented, after 1.1.35, 1.1.283, and 4.3.92, respectively.

SELECTED BIBLIOGRAPHY

Barker, Francis. "A Wilderness of Tigers: *Titus Andronicus*, Anthropology, and the Occlusion of Violence." *The Culture of Violence: Essays on Tragedy and History*. Chicago: University of Chicago Press, 1993. 143–206.

Bartels, Emily. "Making More of the Moor: Aaron, Othello, and Renaissance Refashionings of Race." *Shakespeare Quarterly* 41 (1990): 433–54.

James, Heather. "Cultural Disintegration in *Titus Andronicus*: Mutilating Titus, Vergil, and Rome." *Violence in Drama*. Ed. James Redmond. Cambridge: Cambridge University Press, 1991. 123–40.

Palmer, D. J. "The Unspeakable in Pursuit of the Uneatable: Language and Action in *Titus Andronicus*." *Critical Quarterly* 14 (1972): 320–39.

Tricomi, Albert. "The Aesthetics of Mutilation in *Titus Andronicus*." *Shakespeare Survey* 27 (1974): 11–19.

Waith, Eugene. "The Metamorphosis of Violence in *Titus Andronicus*." *Shakespeare Survey* 10 (1957): 39–59.

Willbern, David. "Rape and Revenge in *Titus Andronicus*." *English Literary Renaissance* 8 (1978): 159–82.

The Most Lamentable Tragedy of
Titus Andronicus

THE PERSONS OF THE PLAY

SATURNINUS, eldest son of the late Emperor of Rome; later Emperor
BASSIANUS, his brother
TITUS ANDRONICUS, a Roman nobleman, general against the Goths
LUCIUS
QUINTUS
MARTIUS } sons of Titus
MUTIUS
LAVINIA, daughter of Titus
YOUNG LUCIUS, a boy, son of Lucius
MARCUS ANDRONICUS, a tribune of the people, Titus' brother
PUBLIUS, his son
SEMPRONIUS
CAIUS } kinsmen of Titus
VALENTINE
A CAPTAIN
AEMILIUS
TAMORA, Queen of the Goths, later wife of Saturninus
ALARBUS
DEMETRIUS } her sons
CHIRON
AARON, a Moor, her lover
A NURSE
A CLOWN
Senators, tribunes, Romans, Goths, soldiers, and attendants

1.1

*Flourish. Enter the Tribunes and Senators[1] aloft, and
then enter [below]* SATURNINUS *and his followers at one
door and* BASSIANUS *and his followers at the other, with
drum° and colours°*   drummer / standard-bearer

SATURNINUS   Noble patricians, patrons° of my right,   supporters
  Defend the justice of my cause with arms.
  And countrymen, my loving followers,
  Plead my successive title° with your swords.   right to succeed
5 I am his first-born son that was the last
  That ware° the imperial diadem of Rome.   wore
  Then let my father's honours live in me,
  Nor wrong mine age° with this indignity.   seniority
BASSIANUS   Romans, friends, followers, favourers of my right,
10 If ever Bassianus, Caesar's[2] son,
  Were gracious° in the eyes of royal Rome,   Found favor

1.1 Location: Before the Roman Capitol, represented by
the upper stage ("aloft"). The tomb of the Andronicus
family, a stage structure or a trapdoor, is accessible onstage.

1. Respectively the representatives of the common people (plebeians) and the upper classes (patricians).
2. The previous emperor (Bassianus is Saturninus's
younger brother).

Keep° then this passage° to the Capitol,   *Defend / path*
And suffer not dishonour to approach
The imperial seat, to virtue consecrate,°   *consecrated*
15   To justice, continence, and nobility;
But let desert[3] in pure election[4] shine,
And, Romans, fight for freedom in your choice.
       Enter MARCUS ANDRONICUS *aloft with the crown*
MARCUS   Princes that strive by factions and by friends
Ambitiously for rule and empery,°   *imperial rule*
20   Know that the people of Rome, for whom we stand
A special party,[5] have by common voice
In election for the Roman empery
Chosen Andronicus, surnamèd *Pius*[6]
For many good and great deserts to Rome.
25   A nobler man, a braver warrior,
Lives not this day within the city walls.
He by the Senate is accited° home   *summoned*
From weary wars against the barbarous Goths,
That with his sons, a terror to our foes,
30   Hath yoked° a nation strong, trained up in arms.   *subdued*
Ten years are spent since first he undertook
This cause of Rome, and chastisèd with arms
Our enemies' pride. Five times he hath returned
Bleeding to Rome, bearing his valiant sons
35   In coffins from the field;[7]
35.1   *and at this day*
         To the monument of the Andronici
         Done sacrifice of expiation,
         And slain the noblest prisoner of the Goths.
And now at last, laden with honour's spoils,
Returns the good Andronicus to Rome,
Renownèd Titus, flourishing in arms.
Let us entreat by honour of his° name   *(the late emperor's)*
40   Whom worthily you would have now succeeded,[8]
And in the Capitol and Senate's right,[9]
Whom you pretend° to honour and adore,   *claim*
That you withdraw you and abate your strength,
Dismiss your followers, and, as suitors should,
45   Plead your deserts in peace and humbleness.
SATURNINUS   How fair the Tribune speaks to calm my thoughts.
BASSIANUS   Marcus Andronicus, so I do affy°   *trust*
In thy uprightness and integrity,
And so I love and honour thee and thine,
50   Thy noble brother Titus and his sons,
And her to whom my thoughts are humbled all,
Gracious Lavinia, Rome's rich ornament,
That I will here dismiss my loving friends
And to my fortunes and the people's favour

---

3. Merit (as opposed to birth order).
4. Free choice of the citizens.
5. A representative elected for a particular purpose.
6. He has been given the honorary title of "Dutiful."
7. The following indented passage (lines 35.1–35.4), found in Q1 following a comma after "field" but not

included in Q2 or Q3 or F, conflicts with the subsequent action and presumably should have been deleted. (In the second line, Q1 reads "of that" for "of the.")
8. Whose place you want a worthy candidate to fill.
9. To choose a new emperor, traditionally an elected and not an inherited office.

55   Commit my cause in balance to be weighed.

Exeunt [his] soldiers [and followers]

SATURNINUS   Friends that have been thus forward in my right,
    I thank you all, and here dismiss you all,
    And to the love and favour of my country
    Commit myself, my person, and the cause.

[Exeunt his soldiers and followers]
[To the Tribunes and Senators]

60   Rome, be as just and gracious unto me
    As I am confident° and kind to thee.   *trusting*
    Open the gates and let me in.

BASSIANUS   Tribunes, and me, a poor competitor.°   *co-petitioner*

Flourish.° They go up into the Senate House.   *Trumpet fanfare*
Enter a CAPTAIN

CAPTAIN   Romans, make way. The good Andronicus,
65   Patron° of virtue, Rome's best champion,   *Representative; pattern*
    Successful in the battles that he fights,
    With honour and with fortune is returned
    From where he circumscribèd° with his sword   *restrained*
    And brought to yoke the enemies of Rome.

*Sound drums and trumpets, and then enter [*MARTIUS
and MUTIUS,] *two of Titus' sons, and then men bearing*
*coffin[s] covered with black, then [*LUCIUS *and* QUINTUS,]
two other sons; then TITUS ANDRONICUS *[in his chariot],*
and then TAMORA *the Queen of Goths and her sons*
*[*ALARBUS,] CHIRON, *and* DEMETRIUS, *with* AARON *the*
Moor[1] and others as many as can be. Then set down the
coffin[s], and TITUS *speaks*

70 TITUS   Hail, Rome, victorious in thy mourning weeds!°   *garments*
    Lo, as the bark° that hath discharged his° freight   *ship / its*
    Returns with precious lading° to the bay   *cargo*
    From whence at first she weighed her anchorage,°   *anchor*
    Cometh Andronicus, bound with laurel bows,[2]
75   To re-salute his country with his tears,
    Tears of true joy for his return to Rome.
    Thou great defender[3] of this Capitol,
    Stand gracious to the rites that we intend.
    Romans, of five-and-twenty valiant sons,
80   Half of the number that King Priam[4] had,
    Behold the poor remains, alive and dead.
    These that survive let Rome reward with love;
    These that I bring unto their latest° home,   *last*
    With burial amongst their ancestors.
85   Here Goths have given me leave[5] to sheathe my sword.
    Titus unkind,[6] and careless of thine own,
    Why suffer'st thou thy sons unburied yet
    To hover on the dreadful shore of Styx?[7]
    Make way to lay them by their brethren.

---

1. "Moor" in classical times referred to an inhabitant of Mauretania, in northwest Africa; the term was later applied to Islamic Africans of Arab descent who conquered Spain in the Middle Ages. In Renaissance England, the word often was used of any black-skinned African.
2. Laurel wreath, symbol of victory.
3. Jupiter Capitolinus, king of the Roman gods, to whose shrine on the Capitol victorious generals brought their spoils.
4. King of Troy during the Trojan War.
5. Allowed me (ironic, since the Goths were defeated in battle).
6. Devoid of natural feeling; undutiful.
7. River surrounding the underworld; the dead could not cross it until they had been properly buried.

They open the tomb

90   There greet in silence as the dead are wont,
And sleep in peace, slain in your country's wars.
O sacred receptacle of my joys,
Sweet cell of virtue and nobility,
How many sons hast thou of mine in store
95   That thou wilt never render° to me more!°   *return / again*
LUCIUS   Give us the proudest prisoner of the Goths,
That we may hew his limbs and on a pile
Ad manes fratrum° sacrifice his flesh   *To our brothers' shades*
Before this earthy prison of their bones,
100   That so the shadows° be not unappeased,   *spirits*
Nor we disturbed with prodigies° on earth.   *evil happenings*
TITUS   I give him you, the noblest that survives,
The eldest son of this distressèd Queen.
TAMORA [*kneeling*]   Stay, Roman brethren! Gracious conqueror,
105   Victorious Titus, rue° the tears I shed—   *pity*
A mother's tears in passion° for her son—   *grief*
And if thy sons were ever dear to thee,
O, think my son to be as dear to me!
Sufficeth not that we are brought to Rome
110   To beautify thy triumphs,° and return   *triumphal processions*
Captive to thee and to thy Roman yoke;
But must my sons be slaughtered in the streets
For valiant doings in their country's cause?
O, if to fight for king and commonweal
115   Were piety in thine,° it is in these.°   *(your sons) / (my sons)*
Andronicus, stain not thy tomb with blood.
Wilt thou draw near the nature of the gods?
Draw near them then in being merciful.
Sweet mercy is nobility's true badge.
120   Thrice-noble Titus, spare my first-born son.
TITUS   Patient° yourself, madam, and pardon me.   *Calm*
These are their brethren whom your Goths beheld
Alive and dead, and for their brethren slain
Religiously° they ask a sacrifice.   *On religious grounds*
125   To this your son is marked, and die he must
T'appease their groaning shadows that are gone.
LUCIUS   Away with him, and make a fire straight,°   *immediately*
And with our swords upon a pile of wood
Let's hew his limbs till they be clean consumed.
                     Exeunt Titus' sons with ALARBUS
130 TAMORA [*rising*]   O cruel irreligious piety!
CHIRON   Was never Scythia[8] half so barbarous.
DEMETRIUS   Oppose not Scythia to ambitious Rome.
Alarbus goes to rest, and we survive
To tremble under Titus' threat'ning look.
135   Then, madam, stand resolved; but hope withal
The selfsame gods that armed the Queen of Troy[9]
With opportunity of sharp revenge
Upon the Thracian tyrant in his tent

---

8. Uncivilized region north of the Black Sea.
9. In Ovid's *Metamorphoses* 13, Queen Hecuba, enslaved by the Greeks after the defeat of Troy, avenged her son Polydorus by killing the sons of his murderer, Polymnestor, tyrant of Thrace.

May favour Tamora, the Queen of Goths—
140 When Goths were Goths and Tamora was queen—
To quit° her bloody wrongs upon her foes.   *revenge*

Enter [QUINTUS, MARCUS, MUTIUS, and LUCIUS,] the sons
of Andronicus, again, with bloody swords

LUCIUS   See, lord and father, how we have performed
Our Roman rites. Alarbus' limbs are lopped
And entrails feed the sacrificing fire,
145 Whose smoke like incense doth perfume the sky.
Remaineth naught but to inter our brethren
And with loud 'larums° welcome them to Rome.   *trumpet calls*
TITUS   Let it be so, and let Andronicus
Make this his latest° farewell to their souls.   *last*

Flourish. Then sound trumpets and lay the coffins in the
tomb

150 In peace and honour rest you here, my sons;
Rome's readiest champions, repose you here in rest,
Secure from worldly chances and mishaps.
Here lurks no treason, here no envy° swells,   *malice*
Here grow no damnèd drugs,° here are no storms,   *poisons*
155 No noise, but silence and eternal sleep.
In peace and honour rest you here, my sons.

Enter LAVINIA

LAVINIA   In peace and honour live Lord Titus long,
My noble lord and father, live in fame.
Lo, at this tomb my tributary° tears   *tribute-bearing*
160 I render for my brethren's obsequies,°   *funeral rites*
[*Kneeling*] And at thy feet I kneel with tears of joy
Shed on this earth for thy return to Rome.
O, bless me here with thy victorious hand,
Whose fortunes Rome's best citizens applaud.
165 TITUS   Kind Rome, that hast thus lovingly reserved
The cordial° of mine age to glad my heart!   *comfort*
Lavinia, live; outlive thy father's days
And fame's eternal date, for virtue's praise.[1]

[*LAVINIA rises*]

MARCUS [*aloft*]   Long live Lord Titus, my belovèd brother,
170 Gracious triumpher in the eyes of Rome!
TITUS   Thanks, gentle Tribune, noble brother Marcus.
MARCUS   And welcome, nephews, from successful wars,
You that survive and you that sleep in fame.
Fair lords, your fortunes are alike in all,
175 That in your country's service drew your swords,
But safer triumph is this funeral pomp
That hath aspired to Solon's happiness[2]
And triumphs over chance in honour's bed.
Titus Andronicus, the people of Rome,
180 Whose friend in justice thou hast ever been,
Send thee by me, their tribune and their trust,
This palliament[3] of white and spotless hue,
And name thee in election for the empire

1. And may the praise of your virtue outlive eternity.
2. Solon, a Greek statesman, said, "Call no man happy
until he is dead."
3. Ceremonial garment worn by aspirants to public
office.

With these our late-deceasèd emperor's sons.
185 Be *candidatus*⁴ then, and put it on,
And help to set a head on headless Rome.
TITUS   A better head her glorious body fits
Than his that shakes for age and feebleness.
What should I don this robe and trouble you?—
190 Be chosen with proclamations today,
Tomorrow yield up rule, resign my life,
And set abroad new business for you all.°   *make you busy once again*
Rome, I have been thy soldier forty years,
And led my country's strength successfully,
195 And buried one-and-twenty valiant sons
Knighted in field, slain manfully in arms
In right° and service of their noble country.   *the just cause*
Give me a staff of honour for mine age,
But not a sceptre to control the world.
200 Upright he held it, lords, that held it last.
MARCUS   Titus, thou shalt obtain and ask° the empery.   *simply by asking*
SATURNINUS   Proud and ambitious Tribune, canst thou tell?°   *how do you know*
TITUS   Patience, Prince Saturninus.
SATURNINUS   Romans, do me right.
Patricians, draw your swords, and sheathe them not
205 Till Saturninus be Rome's emperor.
Andronicus, would thou were shipped to hell
Rather than rob me of the people's hearts!
LUCIUS   Proud Saturnine, interrupter of the good
That noble-minded Titus means to thee.
210 TITUS   Content thee, Prince. I will restore to thee
The people's hearts, and wean them from themselves.
BASSIANUS   Andronicus, I do not flatter thee
But honour thee, and will do till I die.
My faction if thou strengthen with thy friends
215 I will most thankful be; and thanks to men
Of noble minds is honourable meed.°   *reward*
TITUS   People of Rome, and people's tribunes here,
I ask your voices and your suffrages.°   *votes*
Will ye bestow them friendly on Andronicus?
220 TRIBUNES   To gratify the good Andronicus
And gratulate° his safe return to Rome   *salute*
The people will accept whom he admits.°   *allows into office*
TITUS   Tribunes, I thank you, and this suit I make:
That you create° our emperor's eldest son   *elect*
225 Lord Saturnine, whose virtues will, I hope,
Reflect on Rome as Titan's° rays on earth,   *the sun god*
And ripen justice in this commonweal.°   *community*
Then if you will elect by my advice,
Crown him and say, 'Long live our Emperor!'
230 MARCUS   With voices and applause of every sort,
Patricians and plebeians, we create
Lord Saturninus Rome's great emperor,
And say, 'Long live our Emperor Saturnine!'
                    A long flourish [while MARCUS *and the other Tribunes,*
                    with SATURNINUS *and* BASSIANUS], *come down*

---

4. Candidate (literally, "one wearing the white toga").

[MARCUS *invests°* SATURNINUS *in the white palliament*   *dresses*
      and hands him a sceptre]

SATURNINUS   Titus Andronicus, for thy favours done
235   To us in our election this day
    I give thee thanks in part of thy deserts,[5]
    And will with deeds requite thy gentleness.°   *pay back your kindness*
    And for an onset, Titus, to advance
    Thy name and honourable family,
240   Lavinia will I make my empress,
    Rome's royal mistress, mistress of my heart,
    And in the sacred Pantheon[6] her espouse.
    Tell me, Andronicus, doth this motion please thee?
TITUS   It doth, my worthy lord, and in this match
245   I hold me highly honoured of your grace,
    And here in sight of Rome to Saturnine,
    King and commander of our commonweal,
    The wide world's emperor, do I consecrate
    My sword, my chariot, and my prisoners—
250   Presents well worthy Rome's imperious° lord.   *imperial*
    Receive them, then, the tribute that I owe,
    Mine honour's ensigns° humbled at thy feet.   *symbols*
SATURNINUS   Thanks, noble Titus, father of my life.
    How proud I am of thee and of thy gifts
255   Rome shall record; and when I do forget
    The least of these unspeakable° deserts,   *inexpressible*
    Romans, forget your fealty° to me.   *duty*
TITUS [*to* TAMORA]   Now, madam, are you prisoner to an emperor,
    To him that for your honour and your state°   *royal dignity*
260   Will use you nobly, and your followers.
SATURNINUS   A goodly lady, trust me, of the hue°   *appearance; color*
    That I would choose were I to choose anew.[7]
    Clear up, fair queen, that cloudy countenance.
    Though chance of war hath wrought this change of cheer,°   *expression*
265   Thou com'st not to be made a scorn in Rome.
    Princely shall be thy usage every way.
    Rest° on my word, and let not discontent   *Rely*
    Daunt all your hopes. Madam, he comforts you
    Can° make you greater than the Queen of Goths.   *Who can*
270   Lavinia, you are not displeased with this?
LAVINIA   Not I, my lord, sith° true nobility   *since*
    Warrants° these words in princely courtesy.   *Justifies*
SATURNINUS   Thanks, sweet Lavinia. Romans, let us go.
    Ransomless here we set our prisoners free.
275   Proclaim our honours, lords, with trump° and drum.   *trumpet*
                [*Flourish. Exeunt* SATURNINUS, TAMORA,
                DEMETRIUS, CHIRON, *and* AARON *the Moor*]
BASSIANUS   Lord Titus, by your leave, this maid° is mine.   *(Lavinia)*
TITUS   How, sir, are you in earnest then, my lord?
BASSIANUS   Ay, noble Titus, and resolved withal
    To do myself this reason and this right.
280 MARCUS   *Suum cuique°* is our Roman justice.   *To each his own*
    This prince in justice seizeth but his own.

5. *in . . . deserts*: as part of what you deserve.   7. *A goodly . . . anew*: these two lines may be spoken as
6. Roman temple dedicated to all the gods.   an aside.

LUCIUS And that he will and shall, if Lucius live.
TITUS Traitors, avaunt!° Where is the Emperor's guard?[8] *be off*
283.1   TITUS *Treason, my lord! Lavinia is surprised.*
SATURNINUS *Surprised, by whom?*
BASSIANUS   *By him that justly may*
Bear his betrothed from all the world away.
MUTIUS Brothers, help to convey her hence away,
285   And with my sword I'll keep this door safe.
                    [*Exeunt* BASSIANUS, MARCUS, QUINTUS, *and*
                                    MARTIUS, *with* LAVINIA]
[*To* TITUS] My lord, you pass not here.
TITUS   What, villain boy,
Barr'st me my way in Rome?
        [*He attacks* MUTIUS]
MUTIUS   Help, Lucius, help!
        [TITUS] *kills him*
LUCIUS [*to* TITUS] My lord, you are unjust; and more than so,
In wrongful quarrel you have slain your son.
290   TITUS Nor thou nor he are any sons of mine.
My sons would never so dishonour me.
Traitor, restore Lavinia to the Emperor.
LUCIUS Dead, if you will, but not to be his wife
That is another's lawful promised love.
                        [*Exit with Mutius' body*]
        Enter aloft [SATURNINUS] *the Emperor with* TAMORA *and*
        [CHIRON *and* DEMETRIUS,] *her two sons, and* AARON *the*
        Moor
295   TITUS Follow, my lord, and I'll soon bring her back.
SATURNINUS No, Titus, no. The Emperor needs her not,
Nor° her, nor thee, nor any of thy stock. *Neither*
I'll trust by leisure° him that mocks me once, *I'm in no hurry to trust*
Thee never, nor thy traitorous haughty sons,
300   Confederates all thus to dishonour me.
Was none in Rome to make a stale° *laughingstock*
But Saturnine? Full well, Andronicus,
Agree these deeds with that proud brag of thine
That saidst I begged the empire at thy hands.
305   TITUS O monstrous, what reproachful words are these?
SATURNINUS But go thy ways, go give that changing piece° *fickle wench*
To him that flourished for her with his sword.[9]
A valiant son-in-law thou shalt enjoy,
One fit to bandy° with thy lawless sons, *brawl*
310   To ruffle° in the commonwealth of Rome. *swagger*
TITUS These words are razors to my wounded heart.
SATURNINUS And therefore, lovely Tamora, Queen of Goths,
That like the stately Phoebe° 'mongst her nymphs *Diana (the moon)*
Dost overshine the gallant'st dames of Rome,
315   If thou be pleased with this my sudden choice,
Behold, I choose thee, Tamora, for my bride,
And will create thee Empress of Rome.

---

8. The following indented passage (lines 283.1–283.3), found in the quartos and F, is difficult to reconcile with the apparent need for Saturninus and his party to leave the stage at line 275 stage direction before entering "aloft" at line 294 stage direction. The Oxford editors believe that Shakespeare intended it to be deleted after adding the episode of Mutius's killing to his original draft, and that the printers of Q1 included it by accident.
9. To him who brandished his sword to win her.

Speak, Queen of Goths, dost thou applaud my choice?
And here I swear by all the Roman gods,
320 Sith priest and holy water are so near,
And tapers burn so bright, and everything
In readiness for Hymenaeus° stand,   *god of marriage*
I will not re-salute the streets of Rome,
Or climb° my palace, till from forth this place   *ascend to*
325 I lead espoused my bride along with me.
TAMORA   And here, in sight of heaven, to Rome I swear
If Saturnine advance the Queen of Goths
She will a handmaid be to his desires,
A loving nurse, a mother to his youth.°   *youthfulness*
330 SATURNINUS   Ascend, fair Queen, Pantheon. Lords, accompany
Your noble emperor and his lovely bride,
Sent by the heavens for Prince Saturnine,
Whose wisdom[1] hath her fortune conquerèd.
There shall we consummate our spousal rites.
                            Exeunt [all but TITUS]
335 TITUS   I am not bid° to wait upon this bride.   *invited*
Titus, when wert thou wont to walk alone,
Dishonoured thus and challengèd° of wrongs?   *accused*
              Enter MARCUS *and Titus' sons* [LUCIUS, QUINTUS, *and*
              MARTIUS, *carrying Mutius' body*]
MARCUS   O Titus, see, O see what thou hast done—
In a bad quarrel slain a virtuous son.
340 TITUS   No, foolish Tribune, no; no son of mine,
Nor thou, nor these, confederates in the deed
That hath dishonoured all our family;
Unworthy brother and unworthy sons!
LUCIUS   But let us give him burial as becomes,°   *as is proper*
345 Give Mutius burial with our brethren.
TITUS   Traitors, away, he rests not in this tomb.
This monument five hundred years hath stood,
Which I have sumptuously re-edified.°   *rebuilt*
Here none but soldiers and Rome's servitors°   *defenders*
350 Repose in fame, none basely slain in brawls.
Bury him where you can; he comes not here.
MARCUS   My lord, this is impiety in you.
My nephew Mutius' deeds do plead for him.
He must be buried with his brethren.
355 QUINTUS *and* MARTIUS   And shall, or him we will accompany.
TITUS   'And shall'? What villain was it spake that word?
QUINTUS   He that would vouch it° in any place but here. *back it up*
TITUS   What, would you bury him in my despite?°   *in defiance of me*
MARCUS   No, noble Titus, but entreat of thee
360 To pardon Mutius and to bury him.
TITUS   Marcus, even thou hast struck upon my crest,
And with these boys mine honour thou hast wounded.
My foes I do repute° you every one,   *consider*
So trouble me no more, but get you gone.
365 MARTIUS   He is not with° himself, let us withdraw.   *is beside*
QUINTUS   Not I, till Mutius' bones be burièd.

---

1. Wise consent to my proposal.

            [MARCUS, LUCIUS, QUINTUS, *and* MARTIUS] *kneel*
MARCUS   Brother, for in that name doth nature plead—
QUINTUS   Father, and in that name doth nature speak—
TITUS   Speak thou no more, if all the rest will speed.[2]
370 MARCUS   Renownèd Titus, more than half my soul—
LUCIUS   Dear father, soul and substance of us all—
MARCUS   Suffer thy brother Marcus to inter
    His noble nephew here in virtue's nest,
    That died in honour and Lavinia's cause.
375   Thou art a Roman; be not barbarous.
    The Greeks upon advice° did bury Ajax,[3]   *deliberation*
    That slew himself; and wise Laertes' son
    Did graciously plead for his funerals.
    Let not young Mutius then, that was thy joy,
    Be barred his entrance here.
380 TITUS   Rise, Marcus, rise.
    The dismall'st day is this that e'er I saw,
    To be dishonoured by my sons in Rome.
    Well, bury him, and bury me the next.
    They put [MUTIUS] *in the tomb*
LUCIUS   There lie thy bones, sweet Mutius, with thy friends',
385   Till we with trophies° do adorn thy tomb.   *memorial tributes*
ALL BUT TITUS [*kneeling*]   No man shed tears for noble Mutius;
    He lives in fame, that died in virtue's cause.
                Exeunt [*all but* MARCUS *and* TITUS]
MARCUS   My lord—to step out of these dreary dumps°—   *melancholy*
    How comes it that the subtle° Queen of Goths   *cunning*
390   Is of a sudden thus advanced in Rome?
TITUS   I know not, Marcus, but I know it is—
    Whether by device° or no, the heavens can tell.   *scheming*
    Is she not then beholden to the man
    That brought her for this high good turn[4] so far?
395 MARCUS   Yes, and will nobly him remunerate.
    Flourish. Enter the Emperor [SATURNINUS], TAMORA,
    and her two sons [CHIRON *and* DEMETRIUS], *with*
    [AARON] *the Moor at one door.*
    Enter at the other door BASSIANUS *and* LAVINIA *with*
    [LUCIUS, QUINTUS, *and* MARTIUS]
SATURNINUS   So, Bassianus, you have played your prize.°   *won your bout*
    God give you joy, sir, of your gallant bride.
BASSIANUS   And you of yours, my lord. I say no more,
    Nor wish no less; and so I take my leave.
400 SATURNINUS   Traitor, if Rome have law or we have power,
    Thou and thy faction shall repent this rape.°   *abduction*
BASSIANUS   'Rape' call you it, my lord, to seize my own—
    My true betrothèd love, and now my wife?
    But let the laws of Rome determine all;
405   Meanwhile am I possessed of that° is mine.   *what*
SATURNINUS   'Tis good, sir; you are very short with us.
    But if we live we'll be as sharp with you.
BASSIANUS   My lord, what I have done, as best I may

---

2. If the rest of you wish to meet with good fortune (that is, escape my anger).
3. In the Trojan War, after the Greek hero Ajax committed suicide, Odysseus ("wise Laertes' son") convinced Agamemnon, leader of the Greeks, to grant him honorable burial.
4. Recompense; "turn" was also slang for the sexual act. "Remunerate" (line 395) continues the sexual innuendo.

Answer I must, and shall do with my life.
410 Only thus much I give your grace to know:
By all the duties that I owe to Rome,
This noble gentleman, Lord Titus here,
Is in opinion° and in honour wronged,   *reputation*
That, in the rescue of Lavinia,
415 With his own hand did slay his youngest son
In zeal to you, and highly moved to wrath
To be controlled° in that he frankly gave.⁵   *opposed*
Receive him then to favour, Saturnine,
That hath expressed himself in all his deeds
420 A father and a friend to thee and Rome.
TITUS   Prince Bassianus, leave to plead° my deeds.   *stop defending*
'Tis thou and those that have dishonoured me.
        [*He kneels*]
Rome and the righteous heavens be my judge
How I have loved and honoured Saturnine!
425 TAMORA [*to* SATURNINUS]   My worthy lord, if ever Tamora
Were gracious in those princely eyes of thine,
Then hear me speak indifferently° for all;   *impartially*
And at my suit, sweet, pardon what is past.
SATURNINUS   What, madam—be dishonoured openly
430 And basely put it up° without revenge?   *ignobly submit*
TAMORA   Not so, my lord. The gods of Rome forfend°   *forbid*
I should be author to dishonour⁶ you.
But on mine honour dare I undertake°   *vouch*
For good lord Titus' innocence in all,
435 Whose fury not dissembled speaks his griefs.
Then at my suit look graciously on him.
Lose not so noble a friend on vain suppose,°   *idle conjecture*
Nor with sour looks afflict his gentle heart.
[*Aside to* SATURNINUS] My lord, be ruled by me, be won at last,
440 Dissemble all your griefs and discontents.
You are but newly planted in your throne;
Lest then the people, and patricians too,
Upon a just survey° take Titus' part,   *examination*
And so supplant you for ingratitude,
445 Which Rome reputes to be a heinous sin,
Yield at entreats;° and then let me alone: *to entreaty*
I'll find a day to massacre them all,
And raze their faction and their family,
The cruel father and his traitorous sons
450 To whom I suèd for my dear son's life,
And make them know what 'tis to let a queen
Kneel in the streets and beg for grace in vain.
[*Aloud*] Come, come, sweet Emperor; come, Andronicus,°   *(Marcus)*
Take up° this good old man, and cheer the heart   *Raise to his feet*
455 That dies in tempest of thy angry frown.
SATURNINUS   Rise, Titus, rise; my empress hath prevailed.
TITUS [*rising*]   I thank your majesty and her, my lord,
These words, these looks, infuse new life in me.
TAMORA   Titus, I am incorporate in° Rome,   *made a part of*

---

5. Freely bestowed (Lavinia upon Saturninus).   6. I should be responsible for dishonoring.

460 A Roman now adopted happily,
And must advise the Emperor for his good.
This day all quarrels die, Andronicus;
And let it be mine honour, good my lord,
That I have reconciled your friends and you.
465 For you, Prince Bassianus, I have passed
My word and promise to the Emperor
That you will be more mild and tractable.
And fear not, lords, and you, Lavinia;
By my advice, all humbled on your knees,
470 You shall ask pardon of his majesty.
    [BASSIANUS, LAVINIA, LUCIUS, QUINTUS, *and* MARTIUS
    kneel]
LUCIUS   We do, and vow to heaven and to his highness
That what we did was mildly as we might,°   *possible*
Tend'ring° our sister's honour and our own.   *Having regard for*
MARCUS [*kneeling*]   That on mine honour here do I protest.°   *solemnly declare*
475 SATURNINUS   Away, and talk not, trouble us no more.
TAMORA   Nay, nay, sweet Emperor, we must all be friends.
The Tribune and his nephews kneel for grace.
I will not be denied; sweetheart, look back.
SATURNINUS   Marcus, for thy sake and thy brother's here,
480 And at my lovely Tamora's entreats,
I do remit° these young men's heinous faults.   *forgive*
Stand up!
    [MARCUS, BASSIANUS, LAVINIA, *and Titus' sons stand*]
           Lavinia, though you left me like a churl,°   *boorishly*
I found a friend, and sure as death I swore
I would not part° a bachelor from the priest.   *depart*
485 Come, if the Emperor's court can feast two brides
You are my guest, Lavinia, and your friends.
This day shall be a love-day,[7] Tamora.
TITUS   Tomorrow an° it please your majesty   *if*
To hunt the panther and the hart with me,
490 With horn and hound we'll give your grace *bonjour*.°   *good day*
SATURNINUS   Be it so, Titus, and gramercy,° too.   *thank you*
                              Exeunt. Flourish

2.1

    [*Enter* AARON *alone*]
AARON   Now climbeth Tamora Olympus' top,[1]
Safe out of fortune's shot,° and sits aloft,   *range*
Secure of° thunder's crack or lightning flash,   *from*
Advanced above pale envy's° threat'ning reach.   *malice's*
5 As when the golden sun salutes the morn
And, having gilt the ocean with his beams,
Gallops° the zodiac in his glistering coach   *Gallops through*
And overlooks the highest-peering hills,
So Tamora.
10 Upon her wit° doth earthly honour wait,°   *intelligence / attend*
And virtue stoops and trembles at her frown.
Then, Aaron, arm thy heart and fit thy thoughts

---

7. Day for love; day appointed to settle disputes amicably.   1. Mountain home of the Greek gods.
2.1 Scene continues, but the tomb is no longer needed.

To mount aloft with thy imperial mistress,
And mount her pitch[2] whom thou in triumph long
15   Hast prisoner held fettered in amorous chains,
And faster bound to Aaron's charming eyes
Than is Prometheus tied to Caucasus.[3]
Away with slavish weeds° and servile thoughts!   *clothes*
I will be bright, and shine in pearl and gold
20   To wait upon this new-made empress.
To wait, said I?—to wanton° with this queen,   *play amorously*
This goddess, this Semiramis,[4] this nymph,
This siren[5] that will charm Rome's Saturnine
And see his shipwreck and his commonweal's.
25   Hollo, what storm is this?
          Enter CHIRON *and* DEMETRIUS, *braving*°   *defying each other*
DEMETRIUS   Chiron, thy years wants° wit, thy wits wants edge°   *lack / sharpness*
And manners to intrude where I am graced°   *favored*
And may, for aught thou knowest, affected° be.   *loved*
CHIRON   Demetrius, thou dost overween° in all,   *behave presumptuously*
30   And so in this, to bear me down with braves.°   *threats*
'Tis not the difference of a year or two
Makes me less gracious, or thee more fortunate.
I am as able and as fit as thou
To serve, and to deserve my mistress' grace,
35   And that my sword upon thee shall approve,°   *prove*
And plead my passions for Lavinia's love.
AARON [*aside*]   Clubs, clubs![6] These lovers will not keep the peace.
DEMETRIUS   Why, boy, although our mother, unadvised,°   *rashly*
Gave you a dancing-rapier° by your side,   *an ornamental sword*
40   Are you so desperate grown to threat° your friends?   *threaten*
Go to, have your lath[7] glued within your sheath
Till you know better how to handle it.
CHIRON   Meanwhile, sir, with the little skill I have
Full well shalt thou perceive how much I dare.
DEMETRIUS   Ay, boy, grow ye so brave?
          They draw
45   AARON   Why, how now, lords?
So near the Emperor's palace dare ye draw
And maintain such a quarrel openly?[8]
Full well I wot° the ground of all this grudge.°   *know / quarrel*
I would not for a million of gold
50   The cause were known to them it most concerns,
Nor would your noble mother for much more
Be so dishonoured in the court of Rome.
For shame, put up.°   *sheathe your swords*
DEMETRIUS   Not I, till I have sheathed
My rapier in his bosom, and withal
55   Thrust those reproachful speeches down his throat
That he hath breathed in my dishonour here.

---

2. Rise to her height, a hawking term (sexually suggestive).
3. In Greek mythology, Zeus punished Prometheus by
chaining him to a rock in the Caucasus Mountains; a
vulture fed on his liver daily.
4. In Mesopotamian mythology, the Assyrian queen who
founded and ruled Babylon, and who also had attributes
of Ishtar, goddess associated with sexual lust.

5. In Greek mythology, sirens were female creatures that
lured sailors to destruction.
6. Here's a brawl (a cry among London apprentices to
join or quell a fight).
7. Wooden sword used in theatrical productions.
8. In the Renaissance, it was illegal to draw a sword in
the presence of the sovereign or at court.

CHIRON   For that I am prepared and full resolved,
   Foul-spoken coward, that thund'rest with thy tongue,
   And with thy weapon nothing dar'st perform.
60 AARON   Away, I say.
   Now, by the gods that warlike Goths adore,
   This petty brabble° will undo us all.   *quarrel*
   Why, lords, and think you not how dangerous
   It is to jet° upon a prince's right?   *encroach*
65   What, is Lavinia then become so loose,
   Or Bassianus so degenerate,
   That for her love such quarrels may be broached°   *begun*
   Without controlment,° justice, or revenge?   *restraint*
   Young lords, beware; and should the Empress know
70   This discord's ground,[9] the music would not please.
   CHIRON   I care not, I, knew she° and all the world,   *if she knew*
   I love Lavinia more than all the world.
   DEMETRIUS   Youngling, learn thou to make some meaner° *lesser*
     choice.
   Lavinia is thine elder brother's hope.
75 AARON   Why, are ye mad? Or know ye not in Rome
   How furious and impatient they be,
   And cannot brook° competitors in love?   *endure*
   I tell you, lords, you do but plot your deaths
   By this device.
   CHIRON   Aaron, a thousand deaths
80   Would I propose° to achieve her whom I love.   *face*
   AARON   To achieve her how?
   DEMETRIUS   Why makes thou it so strange?
   She is a woman, therefore may be wooed;
   She is a woman, therefore may be won;
   She is Lavinia, therefore must be loved.
85   What, man, more water glideth by the mill
   Than wots the miller of, and easy it is
   Of a cut loaf to steal a shive,° we know.   *slice*
   Though Bassianus be the Emperor's brother,
   Better than he have worn Vulcan's badge.[1]
90 AARON [*aside*]   Ay, and as good as Saturninus may.
   DEMETRIUS   Then why should he despair that knows to court it° *carry on a courtship*
   With words, fair looks, and liberality?°   *generosity*
   What, hast not thou full often struck° a doe   *struck dead*
   And borne her cleanly° by the keeper's nose?   *deftly and unnoticed*
95 AARON   Why then, it seems some certain snatch[2] or so
   Would serve your turns.
   CHIRON   Ay, so the turn were served.°   *(with sexual innuendo)*
   DEMETRIUS   Aaron, thou hast hit it.
   AARON   Would you had hit it[3] too,
   Then should not we be tired with this ado.
   Why, hark ye, hark ye, and are you such fools
100   To square° for this? Would it offend you then   *quarrel*
   That both should speed?°   *succeed*
   CHIRON   Faith, not me.

---

9. Basis; in music, the bass line.
1. *worn Vulcan's badge*: been cuckolded, as the god Vulcan was by Venus, the goddess of love.

2. Bite (with sexual innuendo).
3. Hit the nail on the head; "scored" sexually.

DEMETRIUS   Nor me, so° I were one.   *provided that*
AARON   For shame, be friends, and join for that you jar.[4]
105   'Tis policy° and stratagem must do   *cunning*
      That° you affect,° and so must you resolve   *What / desire*
      That what you cannot as you would achieve,
      You must perforce accomplish as you may.
      Take this of me: Lucrece[5] was not more chaste
110   Than this Lavinia, Bassianus' love.
      A speedier course than ling'ring languishment°   *lovesickness*
      Must we pursue, and I have found the path.
      My lords, a solemn° hunting is in hand;   *ceremonial*
      There will the lovely Roman ladies troop.°   *walk together*
115   The forest walks are wide and spacious,
      And many unfrequented plots° there are,   *places*
      Fitted by kind° for rape and villainy.   *nature*
      Single° you thither then this dainty doe,   *Isolate*
      And strike her home by force, if not by words,
120   This way or not at all stand you in hope.
      Come, come; our Empress, with her sacred wit
      To villainy and vengeance consecrate,
      Will we acquaint with all what we intend,
      And she shall file our engines° with advice   *sharpen our wits*
125   That will not suffer you to square yourselves,°   *be at odds*
      But to your wishes' height advance you both.
      The Emperor's court is like the house of Fame,[6]
      The palace full of tongues, of eyes and ears,
      The woods are ruthless, dreadful, deaf, and dull.°   *insensible*
130   There speak and strike, brave boys, and take your turns.
      There serve your lust, shadowed from heaven's eye,
      And revel in Lavinia's treasury.
CHIRON   Thy counsel, lad, smells of no cowardice.
DEMETRIUS   *Sit fas aut nefas,*° till I find the stream   *Be it right or wrong*
135   To cool this heat, a charm to calm these fits,
      Per Styga, per manes vehor.[7]   *Exeunt*

2.2

Enter TITUS ANDRONICUS *and his three sons* [QUINTUS,
LUCIUS, *and* MARTIUS], *and* MARCUS, *making a noise
with hounds and horns*

TITUS   The hunt is up, the morn is bright and grey,°   *(used of dawn light)*
      The fields are fragrant and the woods are green.
      Uncouple[1] here, and let us make a bay°   *deep barking*
      And wake the Emperor and his lovely bride,
5   And rouse the Prince, and ring° a hunter's peal,   *sound*
      That all the court may echo with the noise.
      Sons, let it be your charge, as it is ours,
      To attend the Emperor's person carefully.
      I have been troubled in my sleep this night,
10   But dawning day new comfort hath inspired.

4. And join to get what you fight over.
5. Virtuous Roman matron raped by Tarquin, a member of the Roman royal family; after her suicide, her kin avenged her by overthrowing the king and establishing the Roman Republic. Shakespeare retells the story in *The Rape of Lucrece*.
6. Rumor; the House of Fame is described by Ovid in

Metamorphoses 12 and by Chaucer in *The House of Fame*.
7. I am carried through the underworld, through the spirits (that is, I am in hell). Adapted from Seneca's *Hippolytus*.
2.2 Location: A forest near the Emperor's palace.
1. Unleash the hounds.

Here a cry of hounds, and wind° horns in a peal; then   blow
enter SATURNINUS, TAMORA, BASSIANUS, LAVINIA,
CHIRON, DEMETRIUS, *and their attendants*
Many good-morrows to your majesty.
Madam, to you as many, and as good.
I promisèd your grace a hunter's peal.
SATURNINUS And you have rung it lustily,° my lords,   *heartily*
15 Somewhat too early for new-married ladies.
BASSIANUS Lavinia, how say you?
LAVINIA   I say no.
I have been broad awake two hours and more.
SATURNINUS Come on then, horse and chariots let us have,
And to our sport. [*To* TAMORA] Madam, now shall ye see
Our Roman hunting.
20 MARCUS   I have dogs, my lord,
Will rouse the proudest panther in the chase,°   *hunting ground*
And climb the highest promontory top.
TITUS And I have horse will follow where the game
Makes way, and run like swallows o'er the plain.
25 DEMETRIUS [*aside*] Chiron, we hunt not, we, with horse nor hound,
But hope to pluck a dainty doe to ground.   *Exeunt*

2.3

Enter AARON *alone* [*with gold*]
AARON He that had wit would think that I had none,
To bury so much gold under a tree
And never after to inherit° it.   *possess*
Let him that thinks of me so abjectly
5 Know that this gold must coin a stratagem
Which, cunningly effected, will beget
A very excellent piece of villainy.
And so repose, sweet gold, for their unrest
That have their alms out of the Empress' chest.[1]
[*He hides the gold*]
Enter TAMORA *alone to the Moor*
10 TAMORA My lovely Aaron, wherefore look'st thou sad
When everything doth make a gleeful boast?°   *display*
The birds chant melody on every bush,
The snakes lies rollèd in the cheerful sun,
The green leaves quiver with the cooling wind
15 And make a chequered shadow on the ground.
Under their sweet shade, Aaron, let us sit,
And whilst the babbling echo mocks the hounds,
Replying shrilly to the well-tuned horns,
As if a double hunt were heard at once,
20 Let us sit down and mark their yellowing° noise,   *bellowing*
And after conflict such as was supposed
The wand'ring prince and Dido once enjoyed[2]
When with a happy storm they were surprised,
And curtained with a counsel-keeping° cave,   *secret-keeping*
25 We may, each wreathèd in the other's arms,

2.3 Location: The forest.
1. *That . . . chest:* Who get this gold, which comes from the Empress's treasury.

2. In Virgil's *Aeneid* 4, the Carthaginian queen Dido and Aeneas, later founder of Rome, make love in a cave where they have taken refuge.

Our pastimes done, possess a golden slumber
Whiles hounds and horns and sweet melodious birds
Be unto us as is a nurse's song
Of lullaby to bring her babe asleep.

30 AARON   Madam, though Venus govern your desires,
Saturn is dominator over mine.[3]
What signifies my deadly-standing° eye,   *murderously glaring*
My silence, and my cloudy° melancholy,   *gloomy*
My fleece of woolly hair that now uncurls
35 Even as an adder when she doth unroll
To do some fatal execution?
No, madam, these are no venereal[4] signs.
Vengeance is in my heart, death in my hand,
Blood and revenge are hammering in my head.
40 Hark, Tamora, the empress of my soul,
Which never hopes more heaven than rests in thee,
This is the day of doom for Bassianus.
His Philomel[5] must lose her tongue today,
Thy sons make pillage of her chastity
45 And wash their hands in Bassianus' blood.
Seest thou this letter? [*Giving a letter*] Take it up, I pray thee,
And give the King this fatal-plotted scroll.
Now question me no more. We are espied.
Here comes a parcel° of our hopeful° booty,   *part / hoped-for*
50 Which dreads not yet their lives' destruction.
    Enter BASSIANUS *and* LAVINIA
TAMORA [*aside to* AARON]   Ah, my sweet Moor, sweeter to me than life!
AARON [*aside to* TAMORA]   No more, great Empress; Bassianus comes.
Be cross with him, and I'll go fetch thy sons
To back thy quarrels, whatsoe'er they be.   *Exit*
55 BASSIANUS   Who have we here? Rome's royal empress
Unfurnished of her well-beseeming troop?[6]
Or is it Dian,[7] habited° like her   *dressed*
Who hath abandonèd her holy groves
To see the general hunting in this forest?
60 TAMORA   Saucy controller° of my private steps,   *Insolent observer*
Had I the power that some say Dian had,
Thy temples should be planted presently°   *immediately*
With horns, as was Actaeon's, and the hounds
Should drive° upon thy new-transformèd limbs,   *rush*
65 Unmannerly intruder as thou art![8]
LAVINIA   Under your patience, gentle Empress,
'Tis thought you have a goodly gift in horning,[9]
And to be doubted° that your Moor and you   *suspected*
Are singled forth° to try experiments.   *drawn apart*
70 Jove shield your husband from his hounds today—
'Tis pity they should take him for a stag.

---

3. Those born when the planet Venus was ascendant were supposed to be amorous; Saturn produced a colder, gloomier temperament.
4. Sexual; derived from Venus.
5. In Greek mythology, an Athenian princess raped by her brother-in-law Tereus; he cut out her tongue, but she wove a tapestry incriminating him (see Introduction and Ovid, *Metamorphoses* 6).

6. *Unfurnished . . . troop:* Not accompanied by an appropriate escort.
7. Diana, chaste goddess of the hunt (sarcastic).
8. In Greek mythology, the hunter Actaeon came upon Diana naked; she turned him into a stag, and his own hounds tore him apart (see Ovid, *Metamorphoses* 3).
9. The husbands of unfaithful women were supposed to grow staglike horns.

BASSIANUS   Believe me, Queen, your swart° Cimmerian[1]   *swarthy*
  Doth make your honour of his body's hue,
  Spotted, detested, and abominable.
75 Why are you sequestered from all your train,
  Dismounted from your snow-white goodly steed,
  And wandered hither to an obscure plot,
  Accompanied but with a barbarous Moor,
  If foul desire had not conducted you?
80 LAVINIA   And being intercepted in your sport,
  Great reason that my noble lord be rated°   *scolded*
  For sauciness. [*To* BASSIANUS] I pray you, let us hence,
  And let her joy° her raven-coloured love.   *enjoy*
  This valley fits the purpose passing well.
85 BASSIANUS   The King my brother shall have note of this.
  LAVINIA   Ay, for these slips have made him noted° long.   *notorious*
  Good King, to be so mightily abused!°   *deceived*
  TAMORA   Why have I patience to endure all this?
   Enter CHIRON *and* DEMETRIUS
  DEMETRIUS   How now, dear sovereign and our gracious mother,
90 Why doth your highness look so pale and wan?
  TAMORA   Have I not reason, think you, to look pale?
  These two have 'ticed° me hither to this place.   *enticed*
  A barren detested vale you see it is;
  The trees, though summer, yet forlorn and lean,
95 Overcome° with moss and baleful[2] mistletoe.   *Overgrown*
  Here never shines the sun, here nothing breeds
  Unless the nightly owl or fatal° raven,   *ominous*
  And when they showed me this abhorrèd pit
  They told me here at dead time of the night
100 A thousand fiends, a thousand hissing snakes,
  Ten thousand swelling toads, as many urchins°   *goblins*
  Would make such fearful and confusèd cries
  As any mortal body hearing it
  Should straight fall mad or else die suddenly.
105 No sooner had they told this hellish tale
  But straight they told me they would bind me here
  Unto the body of a dismal yew[3]
  And leave me to this miserable death.
  And then they called me foul adulteress,
110 Lascivious Goth,[4] and all the bitterest terms
  That ever ear did hear to such effect.
  And had you not by wondrous fortune come,
  This vengeance on me had they executed.
  Revenge it as you love your mother's life,
115 Or be ye not henceforward called my children.
  DEMETRIUS   This is a witness that I am thy son.
   [*He*] *stab*[*s* BASSIANUS]
  CHIRON   And this for me, struck home to show my strength.
   [*He stabs* BASSIANUS, *who dies.*
   TAMORA *turns to* LAVINIA]

---

1. The Cimmerians were a legendary people upon whom the sun never shone.
2. Harmful (mistletoe is parasitic).
3. The yew tree is associated with sadness.
4. Punning on "goat," a proverbially lustful animal.

LAVINIA Ay, come, Semiramis[5]—nay, barbarous Tamora,
For no name fits thy nature but thy own.

120 TAMORA [to CHIRON] Give me the poniard. You shall know, my boys,
Your mother's hand shall right your mother's wrong.

DEMETRIUS Stay, madam, here is more belongs to her.
First thresh the corn, then after burn the straw.
This minion stood° upon her chastity,   *hussy prided herself*

125 Upon her nuptial vow, her loyalty,
And with that quaint° hope braves° your mightiness.   *fine / defies*
And shall she carry this unto her grave?

CHIRON An if° she do I would I were an eunuch.   *An if = If*
Drag hence her husband to some secret hole,

130 And make his dead trunk pillow to our lust.

TAMORA But when ye have the honey ye desire
Let not this wasp outlive, us both to sting.

CHIRON I warrant you, madam, we will make that sure.
Come, mistress, now perforce we will enjoy

135 That nice-preservèd honesty[6] of yours.

LAVINIA O Tamora, thou bearest a woman's face—

TAMORA I will not hear her speak. Away with her!

LAVINIA Sweet lords, entreat her hear me but a word.

DEMETRIUS [to TAMORA] Listen, fair madam, let it be your glory

140 To see her tears, but be your heart to them
As unrelenting flint to drops of rain.

LAVINIA When did the tiger's young ones teach the dam?°   *mother*
O, do not learn her wrath! She taught it thee.
The milk thou sucked'st from her did turn to marble,

145 Even at thy teat thou hadst° thy tyranny.   *took in*
Yet every mother breeds not sons alike.
[To CHIRON] Do thou entreat her show a woman's pity.

CHIRON What, wouldst thou have me prove myself a bastard?

LAVINIA 'Tis true, the raven doth not hatch a lark.

150 Yet have I heard—O, could I find it now!—
The lion, moved with pity, did endure
To have his princely paws° pared all away.   *claws*
Some say that ravens foster forlorn children°   *abandoned baby birds*
The whilst their own birds famish in their nests.

155 O, be to me, though thy hard heart say no,
Nothing so kind, but something pitiful.[7]

TAMORA I know not what it means. Away with her!

LAVINIA O, let me teach thee for my father's sake,
That gave thee life when well he might have slain thee.

160 Be not obdurate, open thy deaf ears.

TAMORA Hadst thou in person ne'er offended me
Even for his sake am I pitiless.
Remember, boys, I poured forth tears in vain
To save your brother from the sacrifice,

165 But fierce Andronicus would not relent.
Therefore away with her, and use her as you will—
The worse to her, the better loved of me.

LAVINIA O Tamora, be called a gentle queen,
And with thine own hands kill me in this place;

170 For 'tis not life that I have begged so long;
Poor I was slain when Bassianus died.
TAMORA What begg'st thou then, fond° woman? Let me go.   *foolish*
LAVINIA 'Tis present° death I beg, and one thing more   *immediate*
That womanhood denies° my tongue to tell.   *forbids*
175 O, keep me from their worse-than-killing lust,
And tumble me into some loathsome pit
Where never man's eye may behold my body.
Do this, and be a charitable murderer.
TAMORA So should I rob my sweet sons of their fee.
180 No, let them satisfy their lust on thee.
DEMETRIUS [*to* LAVINIA] Away, for thou hast stayed us here
too long.
LAVINIA No grace, no womanhood—ah, beastly creature,
The blot and enemy to our general name,°   *the reputation of women*
Confusion° fall—   *Destruction*
CHIRON Nay then, I'll stop your mouth. [*To* DEMETRIUS]
185 Bring thou her husband.
This is the hole where Aaron bid us hide him.
[DEMETRIUS *and* CHIRON *cast Bassianus' body into the*
pit and cover the mouth of it with branches, then exeunt
dragging LAVINIA]
TAMORA Farewell, my sons. See that you make her sure.[8]
Ne'er let my heart know merry cheer indeed
Till all the Andronici[9] be made away.°   *murdered*
190 Now will I hence to seek my lovely Moor,
And let my spleenful° sons this trull° deflower.   *Exit*   *lustful / whore*
Enter AARON *with* [QUINTUS *and* MARTIUS,] *two of*
Titus' sons
AARON Come on, my lords, the better foot before.
Straight will I bring you to the loathsome pit
Where I espied the panther fast asleep.
195 QUINTUS My sight is very dull, whate'er it bodes.[1]
MARTIUS And mine, I promise you. Were it not for shame,
Well could I leave our sport to sleep awhile.
[*He falls into the pit*]
QUINTUS What, art thou fallen? What subtle° hole is this,   *treacherous*
Whose mouth is covered with rude-growing briers
200 Upon whose leaves are drops of new-shed blood
As fresh as morning dew distilled on flowers?
A very fatal° place it seems to me.   *ill-omened*
Speak, brother. Hast thou hurt thee with the fall?
MARTIUS O brother, with the dismall'st object hurt
205 That ever eye with sight made heart lament.
AARON [*aside*] Now will I fetch the King to find them here,
That he thereby may have a likely guess
How these were they that made away his brother.   *Exit*
MARTIUS Why dost not comfort me and help me out
210 From this unhallowed and bloodstainèd hole?
QUINTUS I am surprisèd with an uncouth° fear.   *uncanny*
A chilling sweat o'erruns my trembling joints;
My heart suspects more than mine eye can see.

---

8. Make sure of her, keep her from doing harm; kill her.   1. Sleepiness was a bad omen.
9. Family of Andronicus.

MARTIUS   To prove thou hast a true-divining heart,
215   Aaron and thou look down into this den,
         And see a fearful sight of blood and death.
QUINTUS   Aaron is gone, and my compassionate heart
         Will not permit mine eyes once to behold
         The thing whereat it trembles by surmise.°   *merely by imagining it*
220   O, tell me who it is, for ne'er till now
         Was I a child to fear I know not what.
MARTIUS   Lord Bassianus lies berayed° in blood   *defiled*
         All on a heap, like to a slaughtered lamb,
         In this detested, dark, blood-drinking pit.
225 QUINTUS   If it be dark how dost thou know 'tis he?
MARTIUS   Upon his bloody finger he doth wear
         A precious ring² that lightens all this hole,
         Which like a taper° in some monument   *candle*
         Doth shine upon the dead man's earthy° cheeks   *clay-colored*
230   And shows the ragged entrails° of this pit.   *rough interior*
         So pale did shine the moon on Pyramus³
         When he by night lay bathed in maiden° blood.   *innocent*
         O brother, help me with thy fainting hand—
         If fear hath made thee faint, as me it hath—
235   Out of this fell° devouring receptacle,   *dreadful*
         As hateful as Cocytus'° misty mouth.   *a river of hell*
QUINTUS   Reach me thy hand, that I may help thee out,
         Or, wanting° strength to do thee so much good,   *lacking*
         I may be plucked into the swallowing womb
240   Of this deep pit, poor Bassianus' grave.
         I have no strength to pluck thee to the brink,
MARTIUS   Nor I no strength to climb without thy help.
QUINTUS   Thy hand once more, I will not loose again
         Till thou art here aloft or I below.
245   Thou canst not come to me; I come to thee.
                    [*He*] *fall*[*s into the pit*]
                    Enter [SATURNINUS] *the Emperor* [*with attendants*], *and*
                    AARON *the Moor*
SATURNINUS   Along with me! I'll see what hole is here,
         And what he is that now is leapt into it.
                    [*He speaks into the pit*]
         Say, who art thou that lately didst descend
         Into this gaping hollow of the earth?
250 MARTIUS   The unhappy sons of old Andronicus,
         Brought hither in a most unlucky hour
         To find thy brother Bassianus dead.
SATURNINUS   My brother dead! I know thou dost but jest.
         He and his lady both are at the lodge
255   Upon the north side of this pleasant chase.°   *hunting ground*
         'Tis not an hour since I left them there.
MARTIUS   We know not where you left them all alive,
         But, out° alas, here have we found him dead!   *(emphatic)*
                    Enter TAMORA, TITUS ANDRONICUS, *and* LUCIUS
TAMORA   Where is my lord the King?

2. Perhaps a carbuncle, thought to emit light.
3. In Ovid's version of a classical legend (*Metamorphoses*
4), Pyramus thinks his beloved Thisbe dead and kills himself; this is the subject of the mechanicals' play in *A Midsummer Night's Dream*.

260 SATURNINUS   Here, Tamora, though gripped with killing grief.
TAMORA   Where is thy brother Bassianus?
SATURNINUS   Now to the bottom dost thou search° my wound.   probe
      Poor Bassianus here lies murderèd.
TAMORA   Then all too late I bring this fatal writ,°   document
265   The complot° of this timeless° tragedy,   plot / untimely
      And wonder greatly that man's face can fold
      In pleasing smiles such murderous tyranny.
            She giveth SATURNINE *a letter*
SATURNINUS [*reads*]   'An if we miss to meet him handsomely,°   conveniently
      Sweet huntsman—Bassianus 'tis we mean—
270   Do thou so much as dig the grave for him.
      Thou know'st our meaning. Look for thy reward
      Among the nettles at the elder tree
      Which overshades the mouth of that same pit
      Where we decreed to bury Bassianus.
275   Do this, and purchase us thy lasting friends.'
      O Tamora, was ever heard the like!
      This is the pit, and this the elder tree.
      Look, sirs, if you can find the huntsman out
      That should° have murdered Bassianus here.   was to
280 AARON   My gracious lord, here is the bag of gold.
SATURNINUS [*to* TITUS]   Two of thy whelps, fell curs of bloody
            kind,°   nature; breed
      Have here bereft my brother of his life.
      Sirs, drag them from the pit unto the prison.
      There let them bide until we have devised
285   Some never-heard-of torturing pain for them.
TAMORA   What, are they in this pit? O wondrous thing!
      How easily murder is discoverèd!°   revealed
            [*Attendants drag* QUINTUS, MARTIUS, *and Bassianus'*
            body from the pit]
TITUS [*kneeling*]   High Emperor, upon my feeble knee
      I beg this boon with tears not lightly shed:
290   That this fell fault of my accursèd sons—
      Accursèd if the fault be proved in them—
SATURNINUS   If it be proved? You see it is apparent.°   obvious
      Who found this letter? Tamora, was it you?
TAMORA   Andronicus himself did take it up.
295 TITUS   I did, my lord, yet let me be their bail,
      For by my father's reverend tomb I vow
      They shall be ready at your highness' will
      To answer their suspicion[4] with their lives.
SATURNINUS   Thou shalt not bail them. See thou follow me.
300   Some bring the murdered body, some the murderers.
      Let them not speak a word—the guilt is plain;
      For by my soul, were there worse end than death
      That end upon them should be executed.   [*Exit*]
TAMORA   Andronicus, I will entreat the King.
305   Fear not° thy sons, they shall do well enough.   Fear not for
TITUS [*rising*]   Come, Lucius, come, stay not to talk with
            them.°   *Exeunt*   (Quintus and Marcus)

---

4. The suspicion they are under.

2.4

*Enter the Empress' sons, [*CHIRON *and* DEMETRIUS,] *with*
LAVINIA, *her hands cut off and her tongue cut out, and*
ravished

DEMETRIUS   So, now go tell, an if thy tongue can speak,
  Who 'twas that cut thy tongue and ravished thee.

CHIRON   Write down thy mind, bewray° thy meaning so,   *reveal*
  An if thy stumps will let thee play the scribe.

5 DEMETRIUS   See how with signs and tokens she can scrawl.

CHIRON [*to* LAVINIA]   Go home, call for sweet° water, wash thy   *perfumed*
  hands.

DEMETRIUS   She hath no tongue to call nor hands to wash,
  And so let's leave her to her silent walks.

CHIRON   An 'twere my cause[1] I should go hang myself.

10 DEMETRIUS   If thou hadst hands to help thee knit° the cord.   *knot*

                Exeunt [CHIRON *and* DEMETRIUS]

        Wind° *horns. Enter* MARCUS *from hunting to* LAVINIA   *Blow*

MARCUS   Who is this—my niece that flies away so fast?
  Cousin,° a word. Where is your husband?   *Kinswoman*
  If I do dream, would all my wealth would wake me.[2]
  If I do wake, some planet strike me down

15 That I may slumber an eternal sleep.
  Speak, gentle niece, what stern ungentle hands
  Hath lopped and hewed and made thy body bare
  Of her two branches, those sweet ornaments
  Whose circling shadows kings have sought to sleep in,

20 And might not gain so great a happiness
  As half thy love. Why dost not speak to me?
  Alas, a crimson river of warm blood,
  Like to a bubbling fountain stirred with wind,
  Doth rise and fall between thy rosèd lips,

25 Coming and going with thy honey breath.
  But sure some Tereus[3] hath deflowered thee
  And, lest thou shouldst detect° him, cut thy tongue.   *expose*
  Ah, now thou turn'st away thy face for shame,
  And notwithstanding all this loss of blood,

30 As from a conduit with three issuing spouts,
  Yet do thy cheeks look red as Titan's face°   *(the sun)*
  Blushing to be encountered with a cloud.
  Shall I speak for thee? Shall I say 'tis so?
  O that I knew thy heart,° and knew the beast,   *what is in thy heart*

35 That I might rail at him to ease my mind!
  Sorrow concealèd, like an oven stopped,°   *stopped up*
  Doth burn the heart to cinders where it is.
  Fair Philomel, why she but lost her tongue
  And in a tedious sampler° sewed her mind.   *laborious tapestry*

40 But, lovely niece, that mean° is cut from thee.   *method*
  A craftier Tereus, cousin, hast thou met,
  And he hath cut those pretty fingers off
  That could have better sewed than Philomel.
  O, had the monster seen those lily hands

2.4 Location: Scene continues.   2. *would all . . . me:* I would give all I had to wake up.
1. If I were in her position.   3. See note to 2.3.43.

45   Tremble like aspen leaves upon a lute
And make the silken strings delight to kiss them,
He would not then have touched them for his life.
Or had he heard the heavenly harmony
Which that sweet tongue hath made,
50   He would have dropped his knife and fell asleep,
As Cerberus at the Thracian poet's feet.[4]
Come, let us go and make thy father blind,
For such a sight will blind a father's eye.
One hour's storm will drown the fragrant meads:°   *meadows*
55   What will whole months of tears thy father's eyes?
Do not draw back, for we will mourn with thee.
O, could our mourning ease thy misery!   *Exeunt*

3.1

Enter the Judges, [Tribunes,][1] and Senators with Titus'
*two sons, [*MARTIUS *and* QUINTUS,] *bound, passing [over]*
the stage to the place of execution, and TITUS *going*
before, pleading

TITUS   Hear me, grave fathers; noble Tribunes, stay.
For pity of mine age, whose youth was spent
In dangerous wars whilst you securely slept;
For all my blood in Rome's great quarrel shed;
5   For all the frosty nights that I have watched,
And for these bitter tears which now you see
Filling the agèd wrinkles in my cheeks,
Be pitiful to my condemnèd sons,
Whose souls is not corrupted as 'tis thought.
10   For two-and-twenty sons I never wept,
Because they died in honour's lofty bed.
      ANDRONICUS *lieth down, and the Judges pass by him*
For these two, Tribunes, in the dust I write
My heart's deep languor° and my soul's sad tears.   *grief*
Let my tears stanch° the earth's dry appetite;   *satisfy*
15   My sons' sweet blood will make it shame° and blush.   *feel shame*
                           Exeunt [all but TITUS]
O earth, I will befriend thee more with rain
That shall distil from these two ancient ruins°   *(his eyes)*
Than youthful April shall with all his showers.
In summer's drought I'll drop upon thee still.
20   In winter with warm tears I'll melt the snow
And keep eternal springtime on thy face,
So° thou refuse to drink my dear sons' blood.   *Provided that*
      Enter LUCIUS *with his weapon drawn*
O reverend Tribunes, O gentle, agèd men,
Unbind my sons, reverse the doom of death,
25   And let me say, that never wept before,
My tears are now prevailing° orators!   *persuasive*
LUCIUS   O noble father, you lament in vain.

---

4. The Thracian poet Orpheus, attempting to rescue his
dead wife, Eurydice, used his music to lull to sleep Cerberus, the watchdog of the underworld.

3.1 Location: A Roman street.
1. Not including Marcus, who enters at line 58.

The Tribunes hear you not. No man is by,
And you recount your sorrows to a stone.
30   TITUS   Ah Lucius, for thy brothers let me plead.
Grave Tribunes, once more I entreat of you—
LUCIUS   My gracious lord, no tribune hears you speak.
TITUS   Why, 'tis no matter, man. If they did hear,
They would not mark° me; if they did mark,   *attend to*
35   They would not pity me; yet plead I must.
Therefore I tell my sorrows to the stones,
Who, though they cannot answer my distress,
Yet in some sort they are better than the Tribunes
For that they will not intercept° my tale.   *interrupt*
40   When I do weep they humbly at my feet
Receive my tears and seem to weep with me,
And were they but attirèd in grave weeds°   *sober garments*
Rome could afford° no tribunes like to these.   *provide*
A stone is soft as wax, tribunes more hard than stones.
45   A stone is silent and offendeth not,
And tribunes with their tongues doom men to death.
But wherefore stand'st thou with thy weapon drawn?
LUCIUS   To rescue my two brothers from their death,
For which attempt the Judges have pronounced
50   My everlasting doom of banishment.
TITUS [*rising*]   O happy man, they have befriended thee!
Why, foolish Lucius, dost thou not perceive
That Rome is but a wilderness of tigers?
Tigers must prey, and Rome affords no prey
55   But me and mine. How happy art thou then
From these devourers to be banishèd!
But who comes with our brother Marcus here?
        Enter MARCUS *with* LAVINIA
MARCUS   Titus, prepare thy agèd eyes to weep,
Or if not so, thy noble heart to break.
60   I bring consuming sorrow to thine age.
TITUS   Will it consume me? Let me see it then.
MARCUS   This was thy daughter.
TITUS   Why, Marcus, so she is.
LUCIUS [*falling on his knees*]   Ay me, this object° kills me.   *spectacle*
65   TITUS   Faint-hearted boy, arise and look upon her.
        [LUCIUS *rises*]
Speak, Lavinia, what accursèd hand
Hath made thee handless in thy father's sight?
What fool hath added water to the sea,
Or brought a faggot° to bright-burning Troy?[2]   *piece of firewood*
70   My grief was at the height before thou cam'st,
And now like Nilus it disdaineth bounds.[3]
Give me a sword, I'll chop off my hands too,
For they have fought for Rome, and all in vain;
And they have nursed this woe in feeding life;[4]
75   In bootless° prayer have they been held up,   *useless*
And they have served me to effectless° use.   *fruitless*
Now all the service I require of them

2. Troy was torched by the Greeks after their victory.   4. And by defending Rome, they have induced this
3. Before it was dammed, the river Nile flooded annually.   misery.

Is that the one will help to cut the other.
'Tis well, Lavinia, that thou hast no hands,
80   For hands to do Rome service is but vain.
LUCIUS   Speak, gentle sister, who hath martyred° thee.   *mutilated*
MARCUS   O, that delightful engine° of her thoughts,   *instrument*
That blabbed° them with such pleasing eloquence,   *uttered*
Is torn from forth that pretty hollow cage
85   Where, like a sweet melodious bird, it sung
Sweet varied notes, enchanting every ear.
LUCIUS   O, say thou for her, who hath done this deed?
MARCUS   O, thus I found her, straying in the park,
Seeking to hide herself, as doth the deer
90   That hath received some unrecuring° wound.   *incurable*
TITUS   It was my dear, and he that wounded her
Hath hurt me more than had he killed me dead;
For now I stand as one upon a rock
Environed° with a wilderness of sea,   *Surrounded*
95   Who marks the waxing tide grow wave by wave,
Expecting° ever when some envious° surge   *Awaiting / malignant*
Will in his° brinish bowels swallow him.   *its*
This way to death my wretched sons are gone.
Here stands my other son, a banished man,
100   And here my brother, weeping at my woes.
But that which gives my soul the greatest spurn°   *contemptuous blow*
Is dear Lavinia, dearer than my soul.
Had I but seen thy picture in this plight
It would have madded me.° What shall I do   *made me insane*
105   Now I behold thy lively° body so?   *living*
Thou hast no hands to wipe away thy tears,
Nor tongue to tell me who hath martyred thee.
Thy husband he is dead, and for his death
Thy brothers are condemned and dead by this.°   *this time*
110   Look, Marcus, ah, son Lucius, look on her!
When I did name her brothers, then fresh tears
Stood on her cheeks, as doth the honey-dew
Upon a gathered lily almost witherèd.
MARCUS   Perchance she weeps because they killed her husband;
115   Perchance because she knows them innocent.
TITUS   If they did kill thy husband, then be joyful,
Because the law hath ta'en revenge on them.
No, no, they would not do so foul a deed;
Witness the sorrow that their sister makes.
120   Gentle Lavinia, let me kiss thy lips;
Or make some sign how I may do thee ease.
Shall thy good uncle, and thy brother Lucius,
And thou, and I, sit round about some fountain,
Looking all downwards to behold our cheeks
125   How they are stained, like meadows yet not dry
With miry slime left on them by a flood?
And in the fountain shall we gaze so long
Till the fresh taste be taken from that clearness,
And made a brine pit with our bitter tears?
130   Or shall we cut away our hands like thine?
Or shall we bite our tongues, and in dumb shows
Pass the remainder of our hateful days?

What shall we do? Let us that have our tongues
Plot some device° of further misery,   *contrivance*
135 To make us wondered at in time to come.
LUCIUS Sweet father, cease your tears, for at your grief
 See how my wretched sister sobs and weeps.
MARCUS Patience, dear niece. Good Titus, dry thine eyes.
TITUS Ah, Marcus, Marcus, brother, well I wot°   *know*
140 Thy napkin° cannot drink a tear of mine,   *handkerchief*
 For thou, poor man, hast drowned it with thine own.
LUCIUS Ah, my Lavinia, I will wipe thy cheeks.
TITUS Mark, Marcus, mark. I understand her signs.
 Had she a tongue to speak, now would she say
145 That to her brother which I said to thee.
 His napkin with his true tears all bewet
 Can do no service on her sorrowful cheeks.
 O, what a sympathy° of woe is this—   *consensus*
 As far from help as limbo[5] is from bliss.
    Enter AARON *the Moor, alone*
150 AARON Titus Andronicus, my lord the Emperor
 Sends thee this word: that, if thou love thy sons,
 Let Marcus, Lucius or thyself, old Titus,
 Or any one of you, chop off your hand
 And send it to the King. He for the same
155 Will send thee hither both thy sons alive,
 And that shall be the ransom for their fault.
TITUS O gracious Emperor! O gentle Aaron,
 Did ever raven sing so like a lark
 That gives sweet tidings of the sun's uprise?
160 With all my heart I'll send the Emperor my hand.
 Good Aaron, wilt thou help to chop it off?
LUCIUS Stay, father, for that noble hand of thine,
 That hath thrown down so many enemies,
 Shall not be sent. My hand will serve the turn.
165 My youth can better spare my blood than you,
 And therefore mine shall save my brothers' lives.
MARCUS Which of your hands hath not defended Rome
 And reared aloft the bloody battleaxe,
 Writing destruction on the enemy's castle?
170 O, none of both but are of high desert.
 My hand hath been but idle; let it serve
 To ransom my two nephews from their death,
 Then have I kept it to a worthy end.
AARON Nay, come, agree whose hand shall go along,
175 For fear they die before their pardon come.
MARCUS My hand shall go.
LUCIUS   By heaven it shall not go.
TITUS Sirs, strive no more. Such withered herbs as these
 Are meet° for plucking up, and therefore mine.   *proper*
LUCIUS Sweet father, if I shall be thought thy son,
180 Let me redeem my brothers both from death.
MARCUS And for our father's sake and mother's care,
 Now let me show a brother's love to thee.

---

5. Region in hell dedicated to those denied entrance to heaven ("bliss") through no fault of their own: for instance, unbaptized infants, or virtuous people who lived before the advent of Christianity.

TITUS   Agree between you. I will spare my hand.
LUCIUS   Then I'll go fetch an axe.
MARCUS   But I will use the axe.
                      Exeunt [LUCIUS *and* MARCUS]
185   TITUS   Come hither, Aaron. I'll deceive them both.
    Lend me thy hand, and I will give thee mine.
  AARON [*aside*]   If that be called deceit, I will be honest
    And never whilst I live deceive men so.
    But I'll deceive you in another sort,°   *way*
190   And that you'll say ere half an hour pass.
             He cuts off Titus' hand.
             Enter LUCIUS *and* MARCUS *again*
  TITUS   Now stay your strife. What shall be is dispatched.
    Good Aaron, give his majesty my hand.
    Tell him it was a hand that warded° him   *defended*
    From thousand dangers; bid him bury it.
195   More hath it merited; that° let it have.   *(burial)*
    As for my sons, say I account of them
    As jewels purchased at an easy price,
    And yet dear too, because I bought mine own.
  AARON   I go, Andronicus; and for thy hand
200   Look by and by to have thy sons with thee.
    [*Aside*] Their heads, I mean. O, how this villainy
    Doth fat° me with the very thoughts of it!   *feast*
    Let fools do good, and fair men call for grace:
    Aaron will have his soul black like his face.   *Exit*
205   TITUS   O, here I lift this one hand up to heaven
    And bow this feeble ruin to the earth.
          [*He kneels*]
    If any power pities wretched tears,
    To that I call. [*To* LAVINIA, *who kneels*] What, wouldst thou
          kneel with me?
    Do then, dear heart; for heaven shall hear our prayers,
210   Or with our sighs we'll breathe the welkin dim°   *make the heavens misty*
    And stain the sun with fog, as sometime° clouds   *sometimes do*
    When they do hug him in their melting° bosoms.   *(with rain)*
  MARCUS   O brother, speak with possibility,°   *what is possible*
    And do not break into these deep extremes.
215   TITUS   Is not my sorrows deep, having no bottom?
    Then be my passions° bottomless with them.   *expression of suffering*
  MARCUS   But yet let reason govern thy lament.
  TITUS   If there were reason for these miseries,
    Then into limits could I bind my woes.
220   When heaven doth weep, doth not the earth o'erflow?
    If the winds rage, doth not the sea wax mad,
    Threat'ning the welkin with his big-swoll'n face?
    And wilt thou have a reason for this coil?°   *turmoil*
    I am the sea. Hark how her sighs doth blow.
225   She is the weeping welkin, I the earth.
    Then must my sea be movèd with° her sighs,   *by*
    Then must my earth with her continual tears
    Become a deluge overflowed and drowned,
    Forwhy° my bowels[6] cannot hide her woes,   *Because*

---

6. The bowels were thought to be the seat of compassion.

230 But like a drunkard must I vomit them.
Then give me leave, for losers will have leave
To ease their stomachs[7] with their bitter tongues.
        Enter a MESSENGER *with two heads and a hand*
MESSENGER   Worthy Andronicus, ill art thou repaid
For that good hand thou sent'st the Emperor.
235 Here are the heads of thy two noble sons,
And here's thy hand in scorn to thee sent back—
Thy grief their sports, thy resolution mocked,
That° woe is me to think upon thy woes   *So that*
More than remembrance of my father's death.
        [*He sets down the heads and hand*]   *Exit*
240 MARCUS   Now let hot Etna° cool in Sicily,   *volcano in Sicily*
And be my heart an ever-burning hell.
These miseries are more than may be borne.
To weep with them that weep doth ease some deal,°   *somewhat*
But sorrow flouted° at is double death.   *mocked*
245 LUCIUS   Ah, that this sight should make so deep a wound
And yet detested life not shrink thereat—
That ever death should let life bear his name°   *be called life*
Where life hath no more interest but to breathe!⁸
        [LAVINIA *kisses* TITUS]
MARCUS   Alas, poor heart, that kiss is comfortless
250 As frozen water to a starvèd° snake.   *numb with cold*
TITUS   When will this fearful slumber° have an end?   *nightmare*
MARCUS   Now farewell, flatt'ry;° die, Andronicus.   *pleasing delusion*
Thou dost not slumber. See thy two sons' heads,
Thy warlike hand, thy mangled daughter here,
255 Thy other banished son with this dear sight
Struck pale and bloodless, and thy brother, I,
Even like a stony image, cold and numb.
Ah, now no more will I control° thy griefs.   *try to restrain*
Rend off thy silver hair, thy other hand
260 Gnawing with thy teeth, and be this dismal sight
The closing up° of our most wretched eyes.   *(in death)*
Now is a time to storm. Why art thou still?
TITUS   Ha, ha, ha!
MARCUS   Why dost thou laugh? It fits not with this hour.
265 TITUS   Why, I have not another tear to shed.
Besides, this sorrow is an enemy,
And would usurp upon my wat'ry eyes
And make them blind with tributary⁹ tears.
Then which way shall I find Revenge's cave?—
270 For these two heads do seem to speak to me
And threat me I shall never come to bliss
Till all these mischiefs° be returned° again   *calamities / turned back*
Even in their throats that hath committed them.
Come, let me see what task I have to do.
        [*He and* LAVINIA *rise*]
275 You heavy° people, circle me about,   *sad*
That I may turn me to each one of you

---

7. Resentments (with play on "vomit").   9. Paying tribute (to sorrow, the enemy).
8. Where nothing is left of life but breathing.

And swear unto my soul to right your wrongs.
     [MARCUS, LUCIUS, *and* LAVINIA *circle* TITUS. *He pledges them*]
The vow is made. Come, brother, take a head,
And in this hand the other will I bear.
280 And Lavinia, thou shalt be employed.
Bear thou my hand, sweet wench, between thine arms.
As for thee, boy, go get thee from my sight.
Thou art an exile and thou must not stay.
Hie° to the Goths, and raise an army there,   *Hurry*
285 And if ye love me, as I think you do,
Let's kiss and part, for we have much to do.
     [*They kiss.*] *Exeunt* [*all but* LUCIUS]
LUCIUS   Farewell, Andronicus, my noble father,
The woefull'st man that ever lived in Rome.
Farewell, proud Rome, till Lucius come again;
290 He loves his pledges[1] dearer than his life.
Farewell, Lavinia, my noble sister:
O, would thou wert as thou tofore° hast been!   *formerly*
But now nor° Lucius nor Lavinia lives   *neither*
But in oblivion and hateful griefs.
295 If Lucius live he will requite your wrongs
And make proud Saturnine and his empress
Beg at the gates like Tarquin and his queen.[2]
Now will I to the Goths and raise a power,°   *an army*
To be revenged on Rome and Saturnine.   *Exit*

3.2

     A banquet.° Enter ANDRONICUS, MARCUS, LAVINIA, *and*   *light meal*
     the boy [YOUNG LUCIUS]
TITUS   So, so, now sit, and look you eat no more
Than will preserve just so much strength in us
As will revenge these bitter woes of ours.
     [*They sit*]
Marcus, unknit° that sorrow-wreathen knot.   *unfold (your arms)*
5 Thy niece and I, poor creatures, want° our hands,   *lack*
And cannot passionate° our tenfold grief   *feelingly express*
With folded arms. This poor right hand of mine
Is left to tyrannize° upon my breast,   *(by beating)*
Who,° when my heart, all mad with misery,   *Which*
10 Beats in this hollow prison of my flesh,
Then thus I thump it down.
     [*He beats his breast*]
[*To* LAVINIA] Thou map° of woe, that thus dost talk in signs,   *image*
When thy poor heart beats with outrageous beating
Thou canst not strike it thus to make it still!
15 Wound it with sighing,[1] girl; kill it with groans,
Or get some little knife between thy teeth
And just against° thy heart make thou a hole,   *next to*
That all the tears that thy poor eyes let fall
May run into that sink° and, soaking in,   *receptacle*
20 Drown the lamenting fool[2] in sea-salt tears.

---

1. Vows; hostages (family members left behind in Rome).
2. Tarquin and his family were banished from Rome after the rape of Lucrece; see note to 2.1.109.

3.2 Location: In Titus's house.
1. Sighs were thought to draw blood from the heart.
2. Often a term of endearment.

MARCUS   Fie, brother, fie! Teach her not thus to lay
　　Such violent hands upon her tender life.
TITUS   How now! Has sorrow made thee dote° already?　　　　　*insane*
　　Why, Marcus, no man should be mad but I.
25　What violent hands can she lay on her life?
　　Ah, wherefore dost thou urge the name of hands
　　To bid Aeneas tell the tale twice o'er
　　How Troy was burnt and he made miserable?[3]
　　O, handle not the theme, to talk of hands,
30　Lest we remember still that we have none.
　　Fie, fie, how franticly I square° my talk,　　　　　*regulate*
　　As if we should forget we had no hands
　　If Marcus did not name the word of hands!
　　Come, let's fall to; and, gentle girl, eat this.
35　Here is no drink! Hark, Marcus, what she says.
　　I can interpret all her martyred signs.
　　She says she drinks no other drink but tears,
　　Brewed with her sorrow, mashed[4] upon her cheeks.
　　Speechless complainer, I will learn thy thought.
40　In thy dumb action° will I be as perfect°　　　　　*gesture / expert*
　　As begging hermits in their holy prayers.
　　Thou shalt not sigh, nor hold thy stumps to heaven,
　　Nor wink, nor nod, nor kneel, nor make a sign,
　　But I of these will wrest an alphabet,
45　And by still° practice learn to know thy meaning.　　　　　*continual*
YOUNG LUCIUS   Good grandsire, leave these bitter deep laments.
　　Make my aunt merry with some pleasing tale.
MARCUS   Alas, the tender boy in passion° moved　　　　　*sorrow*
　　Doth weep to see his grandsire's heaviness.
50　TITUS   Peace, tender sapling, thou art made of tears,°　　　　　*(i.e., still soft)*
　　And tears will quickly melt thy life away.
　　　　　MARCUS *strikes the dish with a knife*
　　What dost thou strike at, Marcus, with thy knife?
MARCUS   At that that I have killed, my lord—a fly.
TITUS   Out on thee, murderer! Thou kill'st my heart.
55　Mine eyes are cloyed with view of tyranny.
　　A deed of death done on the innocent
　　Becomes not Titus' brother. Get thee gone.
　　I see thou art not for my company.
MARCUS   Alas, my lord, I have but killed a fly.
60　TITUS   'But'? How if that fly had a father, brother?
　　How would he° hang his slender gilded wings　　　　　*(the father)*
　　And buzz lamenting dirges in the air!
　　Poor harmless fly,
　　That with his pretty buzzing melody
65　Came here to make us merry—and thou hast killed him!
MARCUS   Pardon me, sir, it was a black ill-favoured° fly,　　　　　*ugly*
　　Like to the Empress' Moor. Therefore I killed him.
TITUS   O, O, O!
　　Then pardon me for reprehending thee,
70　For thou hast done a charitable deed.
　　Give me thy knife. I will insult on° him,　　　　　*triumph over*

3. In Virgil's *Aeneid* 2, Aeneas tells Dido the story of　　4. Mixed with water, like beer for brewing.
Troy's fall.

Flattering myself as if[5] it were the Moor
Come hither purposely to poison me.
            [*He takes a knife, and strikes*]
There's for thyself, and that's for Tamora. Ah, sirrah!
75 Yet I think we are not brought so low
But that between us we can kill a fly
That comes in likeness of a coal-black Moor.
MARCUS Alas, poor man! Grief has so wrought on him
He takes false shadows for true substances.
80 TITUS Come, take away.° Lavinia, go with me.   (*the meal*)
I'll to thy closet° and go read with thee   *private room*
Sad stories chancèd° in the times of old.   *that happened*
Come, boy, and go with me. Thy sight is young,
And thou shalt read when mine begin to dazzle.°   *Exeunt*   *my eyes grow dim*

<h2 style="text-align:center">4.1</h2>

Enter Lucius' son and LAVINIA *running after him, and
the boy flies from her with his books under his arm.
Enter* TITUS *and* MARCUS
YOUNG LUCIUS Help, grandsire, help! My aunt Lavinia
Follows me everywhere, I know not why.
Good uncle Marcus, see how swift she comes.
Alas, sweet aunt, I know not what you mean.
            [*He drops his books*]
5 MARCUS Stand by me, Lucius. Do not fear thine aunt.
TITUS She loves thee, boy, too well to do thee harm.
YOUNG LUCIUS Ay, when my father was in Rome[1] she did.
MARCUS What means my niece Lavinia by these signs?
TITUS Fear her not, Lucius; somewhat° doth she mean.   *something*
10 MARCUS See, Lucius, see how much she makes of thee.
Somewhither° would she have thee go with her.   *Somewhere*
Ah, boy, Cornelia[2] never with more care
Read to her sons than she hath read to thee
Sweet poetry and Tully's[3] *Orator*.
15 Canst thou not guess wherefore she plies° thee thus?   *importunes*
YOUNG LUCIUS My lord, I know not, I, nor can I guess,
Unless some fit or frenzy do possess her;
For I have heard my grandsire say full oft
Extremity of griefs would make men mad,
20 And I have read that Hecuba of Troy[4]
Ran mad for sorrow. That made me to fear,
Although, my lord, I know my noble aunt
Loves me as dear as e'er my mother did,
And would not but in fury° fright my youth,   *except in madness*
25 Which made me down to throw my books and fly,
Causeless, perhaps. But pardon me, sweet aunt;
And, madam, if my uncle Marcus go°   *go with us*
I will most willingly attend your ladyship.
MARCUS Lucius, I will.
            [LAVINIA *turns the books over with her stumps*]

---

5. Pleasing myself with the thought that.
4.1 Location: Titus's garden.
1. That is, here to protect me.
2. Mother of the two Gracchi, famous tribunes; Cornelia
was viewed as the ideal Roman mother because of her

devotion to their education.
3. Cicero's; his *Orator* and *De Oratore*, treatises on rhetoric written c. 50 B.C., were both standard texts in Renaissance grammar schools.
4. See 1.1.136 and note.

30   TITUS   How now, Lavinia? Marcus, what means this?
      Some book there is that she desires to see.
      Which is it, girl, of these?—Open them, boy.
      [*To* LAVINIA] But thou art deeper read and better skilled.[5]
      Come and take choice of all my library,
35   And so beguile thy sorrow till the heavens
      Reveal the damned contriver of this deed.—
      Why lifts she up her arms in sequence° thus?   *one after the other*
  MARCUS   I think she means that there were more than one
      Confederate in the fact.° Ay, more there was,   *crime*
40   Or else to heaven she heaves them for revenge.
  TITUS   Lucius, what book is that she tosseth[6] so?
  YOUNG LUCIUS   Grandsire, 'tis Ovid's *Metamorphoses*.
      My mother gave it me.
  MARCUS   For love of her that's gone,
      Perhaps, she culled° it from among the rest.   *picked*
45   TITUS   Soft, so busily she turns the leaves.
      Help her. What would she find? Lavinia, shall I read?
      This is the tragic tale of Philomel,
      And treats of Tereus' treason and his rape,[7]
      And rape, I fear, was root of thy annoy.°   *injury*
50   MARCUS   See, brother, see. Note how she quotes° the leaves.   *examines*
  TITUS   Lavinia, wert *thou* thus surprised, sweet girl,
      Ravished and wronged as Philomela was,
      Forced in the ruthless, vast, and gloomy woods?
      See, see. Ay, such a place there is where we did hunt—
55   O, had we never, never hunted there!—
      Patterned by° that the poet here describes,   *On the pattern of*
      By nature made for murders and for rapes.
  MARCUS   O, why should nature build so foul a den,
      Unless the gods delight in tragedies?
60   TITUS   Give signs, sweet girl, for here are none but friends,
      What Roman lord it was durst do the deed.
      Or slunk not Saturnine,[8] as Tarquin erst,°   *once*
      That left the camp to sin in Lucrece' bed?[9]
  MARCUS   Sit down, sweet niece. Brother, sit down by me.
        [*They sit*]
65   Apollo, Pallas, Jove, or Mercury[1]
      Inspire me, that I may this treason find.°   *discover the truth of*
      My lord, look here. Look here, Lavinia.
      This sandy plot is plain.° Guide if thou canst   *flat*
      This after me.
        He writes his name with his staff, and guides it with feet
        and mouth
            I here have writ my name
70   Without the help of any hand at all.
      Cursed be that heart that forced us to this shift!°   *contrivance*
      Write thou, good niece, and here display at last
      What God will have discovered° for revenge.   *revealed*
      Heaven guide thy pen to print thy sorrows plain,

---

5. Than to read schoolbooks.
6. Clumsily turns the pages.
7. See note to 2.3.43.
8. Was it Saturninus who slunk.
9. See note to 2.1.109.

1. Roman gods: Apollo was the god of prophecy, Pallas (Minerva) of wisdom, Mercury of hidden knowledge. Jove (Jupiter), the king of the gods, was often imagined as all-knowing.

75   That we may know the traitors and the truth.
        She takes the staff in her mouth, and guides it with her
        stumps, and writes[2]
    O, do ye read, my lord, what she hath writ?
TITUS '*Stuprum*°—Chiron—Demetrius.'   *Defilement*
MARCUS What, what!—The lustful sons of Tamora
    Performers of this heinous bloody deed?
80 TITUS *Magni dominator poli,*
    Tam lentus audis scelera, tam lentus vides?[3]
MARCUS   O, calm thee, gentle lord, although I know
    There is enough written upon this earth
    To stir a mutiny in the mildest thoughts,
85   And arm the minds of infants to exclaims.°   *exclamations*
    My lord, kneel down with me; Lavinia, kneel;
    And kneel, sweet boy, the Roman Hector's[4] hope,
        [*All kneel*]
    And swear with me—as, with the woeful fere°   *husband*
    And father of that chaste dishonoured dame
90   Lord Junius Brutus[5] sware for Lucrece' rape—
    That we will prosecute by good advice°   *after careful planning*
    Mortal revenge upon these traitorous Goths,
    And see their blood, or die with this reproach.°   *dishonor*
        [*They rise*]
TITUS 'Tis sure enough an° you knew how,   *if*
95   But if you hunt these bear-whelps, then beware.
    The dam° will wake, and if she wind° ye once   *mother / scent*
    She's with the lion deeply still in league,
    And lulls him whilst she playeth on her back,
    And when he sleeps will she do what she list.°   *pleases*
100   You are a young huntsman, Marcus. Let alone,
    And come, I will go get a leaf° of brass   *sheet*
    And with a gad° of steel will write these words,   *spike*
    And lay it by. The angry northern wind
    Will blow these sands like Sibyl's leaves abroad,[6]
105   And where's our lesson then? Boy, what say you?
YOUNG LUCIUS I say, my lord, that if I were a man
    Their mother's bedchamber should not be safe
    For these base bondmen to the yoke of Rome.
MARCUS Ay, that's my boy! Thy father hath full oft
110   For his ungrateful country done the like.[7]
YOUNG LUCIUS And, uncle, so will I, an if I live.
TITUS Come go with me into mine armoury.
    Lucius, I'll fit° thee; and withal,° my boy,   *equip / in addition*
    Shall carry from me to the Empress' sons
115   Presents that I intend to send them both.
    Come, come, thou'lt do my message, wilt thou not?
YOUNG LUCIUS Ay, with my dagger in their bosoms, grandsire.
TITUS No, boy, not so. I'll teach thee another course.
    Lavinia, come. Marcus, look to my house.

---

2. This action recalls Io in Ovid's *Metamorphoses* 1, who after her rape by Jove was turned into a heifer by Jove's jealous wife, Juno; she revealed her identity to her family by writing her story in the dust with her hoof.
3. Ruler of the great heavens, are you so slow to hear and see crimes? (adapted from Seneca's *Hippolytus*).
4. Lucius the elder, champion of Rome as Hector was of Troy.
5. Leader of those who drove the Tarquins from Rome.
6. The Sybil of Cumae (in Italy) wrote prophecies on leaves and placed them outside her cave; they sometimes blew away before they could be read.
7. That is, fought against the Goths.

120 Lucius and I'll go brave it° at the court.   *cut a fine figure*
    Ay, marry, will we, sir, and we'll be waited on.
                                        Exeunt [all but MARCUS]
    MARCUS O heavens, can you hear a good man groan
       And not relent, or not compassion° him?   *pity*
       Marcus, attend him in his ecstasy,°   *madness*
125   That hath more scars of sorrow in his heart
       Than foemen's marks upon his battered shield,
       But yet so just that he will not revenge.
       Revenge the heavens[8] for old Andronicus!   *Exit*

4.2

Enter AARON, CHIRON, *and* DEMETRIUS *at one door, and*
at the other door YOUNG LUCIUS *and another with a*
bundle of weapons, and verses writ upon them
    CHIRON Demetrius, here's the son of Lucius.
       He hath some message to deliver us.
    AARON Ay, some mad message from his mad grandfather.
    YOUNG LUCIUS My lords, with all the humbleness I may
5   I greet your honours from Andronicus
       [*Aside*] And pray the Roman gods confound° you both.   *destroy*
    DEMETRIUS Gramercy,° lovely Lucius. What's the news?   *Thank you*
    YOUNG LUCIUS [*aside*] That you are both deciphered,° that's the   *detected*
          news,
       For villains marked with rape. [*Aloud*] May it please you,
10   My grandsire, well advised, hath sent by me
       The goodliest weapons of his armoury
       To gratify° your honourable youth,   *grace*
       The hope of Rome, for so he bid me say;
          [*His attendant gives the weapons*]
       And so I do, and with his gifts present
15   Your lordships that, whenever you have need,
       You may be armèd and appointed° well;   *equipped*
       And so I leave you both [*aside*] like bloody villains.
                                        Exit [with attendant]
    DEMETRIUS What's here—a scroll, and written round about?
       Let's see.
20   'Integer vitae, scelerisque purus,
       Non eget Mauri iaculis, nec arcu.'[1]
    CHIRON O, 'tis a verse in Horace, I know it well.
       I read it in the grammar long ago.
    AARON Ay, just,° a verse in Horace; right, you have it.   *exactly*
25   [*Aside*] Now what a thing it is to be an ass!
       Here's no sound° jest. The old man hath found their guilt,   *wholesome*
       And sends them weapons wrapped about with lines
       That wound beyond their feeling to the quick.[2]
       But were our witty° Empress well afoot°   *clever / up and about*
30   She would applaud Andronicus' conceit.°   *device*
       But let her rest in her unrest[3] a while.

8. May the heavens take revenge.
4.2 Location: The imperial palace.
1. "The man upright in life and free from crime needs
neither the Moorish javelin nor the bow" (Horace, *Odes*
1.22.1–2); quoted in William Lily's Latin grammar, standard in Elizabethan schools.
2. That pierce them deeply though they are too dull to
feel it.
3. Remain in her distress (Tamora is in childbirth).

[*To* CHIRON *and* DEMETRIUS] And now, young lords, was't not a
    happy star
Led us to Rome, strangers and, more than so,
Captives, to be advancèd to this height?
35   It did me good before the palace gate
To brave[4] the Tribune in his brother's hearing.
DEMETRIUS But me more good to see so great a lord
    Basely insinuate° and send us gifts.   *curry favor*
AARON Had he not reason, Lord Demetrius?
40   Did you not use his daughter very friendly?
DEMETRIUS I would we had a thousand Roman dames
    At such a bay,° by turn to serve our lust.   *Cornered like that*
CHIRON A charitable wish, and full of love.
AARON Here lacks but your mother for to say amen.
45 CHIRON And that would she, for twenty thousand more.
DEMETRIUS Come, let us go and pray to all the gods
    For our belovèd mother in her pains.°   *(labor pains)*
AARON Pray to the devils; the gods have given us over.
        Trumpets sound
DEMETRIUS Why do the Emperor's trumpets flourish thus?
50 CHIRON Belike° for joy the Emperor hath a son.   *Probably*
DEMETRIUS Soft, who comes here?
        Enter NURSE *with a blackamoor child*
NURSE   Good morrow, lords.
    O tell me, did you see Aaron the Moor?
AARON Well, more° or less, or ne'er a whit at all,   *(punning on "Moor")*
    Here Aaron is; and what with Aaron now?
55 NURSE O gentle Aaron, we are all undone.
    Now help, or woe betide thee evermore!
AARON Why, what a caterwauling dost thou keep!
    What dost thou wrap and fumble° in thy arms?   *bundle up*
NURSE O, that which I would hide from heaven's eye,
60   Our Empress' shame and stately Rome's disgrace.
    She is delivered, lords, she is delivered.
AARON To whom?
NURSE   I mean she is brought abed.°   *delivered of a child*
AARON Well, God give her good rest. What hath he sent her?
NURSE A devil.[5]
AARON   Why then, she is the devil's dam.
65   A joyful issue!°   *outcome; child*
NURSE A joyless, dismal, black, and sorrowful issue.
    Here is the babe, as loathsome as a toad
    Amongst the fair-faced breeders of our clime.
    The Empress sends it thee, thy stamp, thy seal,[6]
70   And bids thee christen it with thy dagger's point.
AARON Zounds,° ye whore, is black so base a hue?   *God's wounds*
    Sweet blowze,° you are a beauteous blossom, sure.   *red-cheeked wench*
DEMETRIUS Villain, what hast thou done?
AARON That which thou canst not undo.
75 CHIRON Thou hast undone our mother.
AARON Villain, I have done° thy mother.   *used sexually*
DEMETRIUS And therein, hellish dog, thou hast undone her.

---

4. To defy (not shown in the play).   devils.
5. The devil was often imagined as black, and Africans as   6. *thy stamp, thy seal:* bearing your imprint.

Woe to her chance, and damned her loathèd choice,
Accursed the offspring of so foul a fiend.
CHIRON It shall not live.
80 AARON   It shall not die.
NURSE Aaron, it must; the mother wills it so.
AARON What, must it, nurse? Then let no man but I
Do execution on my flesh and blood.
DEMETRIUS I'll broach° the tadpole on my rapier's point.   *impale*
85 Nurse, give it me. My sword shall soon dispatch it.
AARON Sooner this sword shall plough thy bowels up.
[He takes the child and draws his sword]
Stay, murderous villains, will you kill your brother?
Now, by the burning tapers of the sky
That shone so brightly when this boy was got,°   *conceived*
90 He dies upon my scimitar's sharp point
That touches this, my first-born son and heir.
I tell you, younglings, not Enceladus[7]
With all his threat'ning band of Typhon's° brood,   *father of the Titans*
Nor great Alcides,[8] nor the god of war
95 Shall seize this prey out of his father's hands.
What, what, ye sanguine,[9] shallow-hearted boys,
Ye whitelimed° walls, ye alehouse painted signs,[1]   *whitewashed*
Coal-black is better than another hue
In that it scorns to bear another hue;
100 For all the water in the ocean
Can never turn the swan's black legs to white,
Although she lave° them hourly in the flood.[2]   *bathe*
Tell the Empress from me I am of age
To keep mine own, excuse it how she can.
105 DEMETRIUS Wilt thou betray thy noble mistress thus?
AARON My mistress is my mistress, this myself,
The figure° and the picture of my youth.   *image*
This before all the world do I prefer;
This maugre° all the world will I keep safe,   *in spite of*
110 Or some of you shall smoke° for it in Rome.   *suffer*
DEMETRIUS By this our mother is for ever shamed.
CHIRON Rome will despise her for this foul escape.°   *escapade*
NURSE The Emperor in his rage will doom° her death.   *decree*
CHIRON I blush to think upon this ignomy.°   *ignominy*
115 AARON Why, there's the privilege your beauty bears.
Fie, treacherous hue, that will betray with blushing
The close enacts° and counsels of thy heart.   *secret purposes*
Here's a young lad framed of another leer.°   *complexion*
Look how the black slave smiles upon the father,
120 As who should say 'Old lad, I am thine own.'
He is your brother, lords, sensibly° fed   *manifestly*
Of that self° blood that first gave life to you,   *same*
And from that womb where you imprisoned were
He is enfranchisèd° and come to light.   *freed*
125 Nay, he is your brother by the surer side,°   *(the mother's)*
Although my seal be stampèd in his face.

7. In Greek mythology, a Titan who warred against the
gods.
8. Hercules (literally, descendant of Alcaeus).
9. Ruddy (as opposed to black).

1. Cheap, garish images of men.
2. Stream; alluding to the proverb "One cannot wash an
Ethiop white."

NURSE   Aaron, what shall I say unto the Empress?
DEMETRIUS   Advise thee,° Aaron, what is to be done,   *Consider*
   And we will all subscribe to° thy advice.   *follow*
130   Save thou the child, so° we may all be safe.   *provided that*
AARON   Then sit we down, and let us all consult.
   My son and I will have the wind of you.[3]
   Keep there; now talk at pleasure of your safety.
   [*They sit*]
DEMETRIUS [*to the* NURSE]   How many women saw this child of his?
135 AARON   Why, so, brave lords, when we do join in league
   I am a lamb; but if you brave the Moor,
   The chafèd° boar, the mountain lioness,   *enraged*
   The ocean swells not so as Aaron storms.
   [*To the* NURSE] But say again, how many saw the child?
140 NURSE   Cornelia the midwife, and myself,
   And no one else but the delivered Empress.
AARON   The Empress, the midwife, and yourself.
   Two may keep counsel when the third's away.
   Go to the Empress, tell her this I said.
    He kills her
145   'Wheak, wheak'[4]—so cries a pig preparèd to the spit.
DEMETRIUS   What mean'st thou, Aaron? Wherefore didst thou this?
AARON   O Lord, sir, 'tis a deed of policy.°   *prudence*
   Shall she live to betray this guilt of ours—
   A long-tongued, babbling gossip? No, lords, no.
150   And now be it known to you my full intent.
   Not far, one Muliteus my countryman
   His wife[5] but yesternight was brought to bed.
   His child is like to° her, fair as you are.   *resembles*
   Go pack° with him, and give the mother gold,   *conspire*
155   And tell them both the circumstance of all,°   *the full details*
   And how by this their child shall be advanced
   And be receivèd for the Emperor's heir,
   And substituted in the place of mine,
   To calm this tempest whirling in the court;
160   And let the Emperor dandle him for his own.
   Hark ye, lords, you see I have given her physic,°   *medicine*
   And you must needs bestow her funeral.
   The fields are near, and you are gallant grooms.°   *fellows*
   This done, see that you take no longer days,°   *waste no time*
165   But send the midwife presently to me.
   The midwife and the nurse well made away,
   Then let the ladies tattle what they please.
CHIRON   Aaron, I see thou wilt not trust the air
   With secrets.
DEMETRIUS   For this care of Tamora,
170   Herself and hers are highly bound to thee.
    Exeunt [CHIRON *and* DEMETRIUS *with the Nurse's body*]
AARON   Now to the Goths, as swift as swallow flies,
   There to dispose° this treasure in mine arms   *bestow*
   And secretly to greet the Empress' friends.

---

3. Will keep downwind (as a wary hunter does when stalking game).
4. Aaron imitates her death cry.
5. one . . . wife: the wife of a certain Muliteus, my countryman.

Come on, you thick-lipped slave, I'll bear you hence,
175 For it is you that puts us to our shifts.°   *force us to scheme*
I'll make you feed on berries and on roots,
And fat on curds and whey, and suck the goat,
And cabin in a cave, and bring you up
To be a warrior and command a camp.° *Exit [with the child]*   *an army*

4.3

Enter TITUS, *old* MARCUS, [*his son* PUBLIUS,] YOUNG
LUCIUS, *and other gentlemen* [SEMPRONIUS, CAIUS] *with
bows; and* TITUS *bears the arrows with letters on the ends
of them*

TITUS Come, Marcus, come; kinsmen, this is the way.
Sir boy, let me see your archery.
Look ye draw home° enough, and 'tis there straight.°   *fully / immediately*
Terras Astraea reliquit.[1]
5   Be you remembered,° Marcus: she's gone, she's fled.   *Remember*
Sirs, take you to your tools. You, cousins, shall
Go sound the ocean and cast your nets.
Happily° you may catch her in the sea;   *Perhaps*
Yet there's as little justice as at land.
10   No, Publius and Sempronius, you must do it.
'Tis you must dig with mattock and with spade
And pierce the inmost centre of the earth.
Then, when you come to Pluto's region,[2]
I pray you deliver him this petition.
15   Tell him it is for justice and for aid,
And that it comes from old Andronicus,
Shaken with sorrows in ungrateful Rome.
Ah, Rome! Well, well, I made thee miserable
What time° I threw the people's suffrages°   *When / votes*
20   On him that thus doth tyrannize o'er me.
Go, get you gone, and pray be careful all,
And leave you not a man-of-war unsearched.
This wicked Emperor may have shipped her[3] hence,
And, kinsmen, then we may go pipe[4] for justice.
25   MARCUS O, Publius, is not this a heavy case,°   *sad situation*
To see thy noble uncle thus distraught?
PUBLIUS Therefore, my lords, it highly us concerns
By day and night t'attend him carefully
And feed his humour° kindly as we may,   *humor him*
30   Till time beget some careful° remedy.   *solicitous; laborious*
MARCUS Kinsmen, his sorrows are past remedy,
But [   ][5]
Join with the Goths, and with revengeful war
Take wreak on Rome for this ingratitude,
35   And vengeance on the traitor Saturnine.
TITUS Publius, how now? How now, my masters?
What, have you met with her?
PUBLIUS No, my good lord, but Pluto sends you word
If you will have Revenge from hell, you shall.

4.3 Location: Outside the Emperor's palace.
1. "Astraea [goddess of justice] has abandoned the earth"
(Ovid, *Metamorphoses* 1.150).
2. The underworld, ruled by Pluto.
3. Astraea, whom the mad Titus imagines being smuggled out of Rome in a war boat.
4. Whistle (that is, seek in vain).
5. A line may be missing here; see Textual Variants.

40   Marry, for° Justice, she is now employed,   *as for*
        He thinks, with Jove, in heaven or somewhere else,
        So that perforce you must needs stay a time.[6]
    TITUS   He doth me wrong to feed me with delays.
        I'll dive into the burning lake[7] below
45   And pull her out of Acheron° by the heels.   *river of the underworld*
        Marcus, we are but shrubs, no cedars we,
        No big-boned men framed of the Cyclops'[8] size,
        But metal, Marcus, steel to the very back,
        Yet wrung with wrongs more than our backs can bear;
50   And sith° there's no justice in earth nor hell,   *since*
        We will solicit heaven and move the gods
        To send down Justice for to wreak° our wrongs.   *revenge*
        Come, to this gear.° You are a good archer, Marcus.   *business*
            He gives them the arrows
        'Ad Iovem', that's for you. Here, 'ad Apollinem'.
55   'Ad Martem',[9] that's for myself.
        Here, boy, 'to Pallas'.° Here 'to Mercury'.   *Minerva*
        'To Saturn',° Caius—not 'to Saturnine'!   *father of Jove*
        You were as good to° shoot against the wind.   *might as well*
        To it, boy! Marcus, loose° when I bid.   *(the arrows)*
60   Of° my word, I have written to effect.   *On*
        There's not a god left unsolicited.
    MARCUS   Kinsmen, shoot all your shafts into the court.
        We will afflict the Emperor in his pride.
    TITUS   Now, masters, draw.
            [They shoot]
                    O, well said,° Lucius!   *done*
65   Good boy, in Virgo's[1] lap! Give it Pallas.
    MARCUS   My lord, I aim a mile beyond the moon.[2]
        Your letter is with Jupiter by this.
    TITUS   Ha, ha! Publius, Publius, what hast thou done?
        See, see, thou hast shot off one of Taurus'[3] horns.
70   MARCUS   This was the sport, my lord. When Publius shot,
        The Bull, being galled,° gave Aries[4] such a knock   *angered*
        That down fell both the Ram's horns in the court,
        And who should find them but the Empress' villain!°   *servant; scoundrel*
        She laughed, and told the Moor he should not choose
75   But give them[5] to his master for a present.
    TITUS   Why, there it goes. God give his lordship joy.
          Enter the CLOWN° *with a basket and two pigeons in it*   *rustic*
        News, news from heaven; Marcus, the post is come.
        Sirrah, what tidings? Have you any letters?
        Shall I have justice? What says Jupiter?
80   CLOWN   Ho, the gibbet-maker?[6] He says that he hath taken them
        down again, for the man must not be hanged till the next week.
    TITUS   But what says Jupiter, I ask thee?
    CLOWN   Alas, sir, I know not 'Jupiter'. I never drank with him in
        all my life.

6. So that by necessity ("preface") you must wait a while.
7. Phlegethon, river of fire of the underworld.
8. One-eyed giants of Greek legend.
9. "To Jove," "to Apollo," "to Mars"; Mars was the god of war.
1. Constellation identified with Astraea after her flight from earth.

2. Marcus, humoring Titus, expects him to take the words literally; but they also mean "talk wildly, make extravagant claims."
3. Constellation of the bull.
4. Constellation of the ram.
5. The horns, as the sign of the cuckold.
6. The Clown hears "gibbetter" for "Jupiter."

85   TITUS   Why, villain, art not thou the carrier?

    CLOWN   Ay, of my pigeons, sir; nothing else.

    TITUS   Why, didst thou not come from heaven?

    CLOWN   From heaven? Alas, sir, I never came there. God forbid
I should be so bold to press to heaven in my young days. Why,
90   I am going with my pigeons to the tribunal plebs⁷ to take up a
matter of brawl betwixt my uncle and one of the Emperal's°   *(for "Emperor")*
men.⁸

92.1   MARCUS [*to* TITUS]   *Why, sir, that is as fit as can be to serve*
for your oration, and let him deliver the pigeons to the
Emperor from you.

      TITUS [*to the* CLOWN]   *Tell me, can you deliver an oration*
92.5   *to the Emperor with a grace?*

      CLOWN   *Nay, truly, sir, I could never say grace in all my*
life.

    TITUS   Sirrah, come hither. Make no more ado,
But give your pigeons to the Emperor.
95   By me thou shalt have justice at his hands.
Hold, hold—[*giving money*] meanwhile, here's money for thy
    charges.
Give me pen and ink. Sirrah, can you with a grace
Deliver up a supplication?

    CLOWN   Ay, sir.

100   TITUS [*writing and giving the* CLOWN *a paper*]   Then here is a
supplication for you, and when you come to him, at the first
approach you must kneel, then kiss his foot, then deliver up
your pigeons, and then look for your reward. I'll be at hand, sir;
see you do it bravely.°   *handsomely*
105   CLOWN   I warrant you, sir. Let me alone.°   *Leave it to me*

    TITUS   Sirrah, hast thou a knife? Come, let me see it.
Here, Marcus, fold it in the oration,
For thou hast made it like an humble suppliant.
And when thou hast given it to the Emperor,
110   Knock at my door and tell me what he says.

    CLOWN   God be with you, sir. I will.   *Exit*

    TITUS   Come, Marcus, let us go. Publius, follow me.   *Exeunt*

4.4

Enter [SATURNINUS,] *the Emperor, and* [TAMORA,] *the*
Empress, and [CHIRON *and* DEMETRIUS,] *her two sons,*
and others. The Emperor brings the arrows in his hand
that TITUS *shot at him*

    SATURNINUS   Why, lords, what wrongs are these! Was ever seen
An emperor in Rome thus overborne,°   *insolently treated*
Troubled, confronted thus, and for the extent
Of egall justice¹ used in such contempt?
5   My lords, you know, as know the mightful gods,
However these disturbers of our peace
Buzz in the people's ears, there naught hath passed
But even with° law against the wilful sons   *according to*
Of old Andronicus. And what an if

---

7. *Tribunus plebis*, tribune of the common people.
8. The following indented passage (lines 92.1–92.7), found in the early texts, appear to be a draft of the subsequent six lines.
4.4. Location: The Emperor's Palace.
1. *for . . . justice:* in return for exercising impartial justice.

His sorrows have so overwhelmed his wits?
Shall we be thus afflicted in his wreaks,°   *vindictive deeds*
His fits, his frenzy, and his bitterness?
And now he writes to heaven for his redress.
See, here's 'to Jove' and this 'to Mercury',
This 'to Apollo', this 'to the god of war' —
Sweet scrolls to fly about the streets of Rome!
What's this but libelling against the Senate
And blazoning° our unjustice everywhere?   *proclaiming*
A goodly humour,° is it not, my lords? —   *whim*
As who would° say, in Rome no justice were.   *As if one were to*
But, if I live, his feignèd ecstasies°   *pretended insanity*
Shall be no shelter to these outrages,
But he and his shall know that justice lives
In Saturninus' health, whom if he sleep
He'll so awake[2] as he in fury shall
Cut off the proud'st conspirator that lives.

TAMORA   My gracious lord, my lovely Saturnine,
Lord of my life, commander of my thoughts,
Calm thee, and bear the faults of Titus' age,
Th'effects of sorrow for his valiant sons
Whose loss hath pierced him deep and scarred his heart;
And rather comfort his distressèd plight
Than prosecute the meanest or the best[3]
For these contempts. *(Aside)* Why, thus it shall become
High-witted° Tamora to gloze° with all.   *Intelligent / delude*
But, Titus, I have touched thee to the quick.
Thy life blood out if Aaron now be wise,
Then is all safe, the anchor in the port.
      Enter CLOWN
How now, good fellow, wouldst thou speak with us?

CLOWN   Yea, forsooth, an° your mistress-ship be Emperial.   *if*

TAMORA   Empress I am, but yonder sits the Emperor.

CLOWN   'Tis he. God and Saint Stephen give you good-e'en.° I   *good evening*
have brought you a letter and a couple of pigeons here.
      [SATURNINUS] *reads the letter*

SATURNINUS *[to an attendant]*   Go, take him away, and hang
      him presently.°   *instantly*

CLOWN   How much money must I° have?   *am I to*

TAMORA   Come, sirrah, you must be hanged.

CLOWN   Hanged, by' Lady?[4] Then I have brought up a neck to a
      fair end.   *Exit [with attendant]*

SATURNINUS   Despiteful and intolerable wrongs!
Shall I endure this monstrous villainy?
I know from whence this same device proceeds.
May this be borne? — As if his traitorous sons,
That died by law for murder of our brother,
Have by my means been butchered wrongfully!
Go, drag the villain hither by the hair.
Nor° age nor honour shall shape privilege.°   *Neither / afford immunity*

---

2. *whom . . . awake:* A confusing passage. If the first "he" (in line 24) refers to Titus, then the meaning is "If Titus impairs Saturninus's health (tries to 'put him to sleep'), then Saturninus will rouse himself angrily." If the first "he" refers to Saturninus, then "Although Saturninus seems not to respond now, he will awaken." Some editors change the first and third (line 25) "he"s to "she"s, making the phrase refer to justice.
3. Lowest or highest ranking.
4. By our Lady (the Virgin Mary).

For this proud mock I'll be thy slaughterman,
Sly frantic wretch, that holp'st° to make me great   *helped*
In hope thyself should govern Rome and me.
       Enter AEMILIUS [*a messenger*]
60 SATURNINUS   What news with thee, Aemilius?
AEMILIUS   Arm, my lords! Rome never had more cause.
   The Goths have gathered head,° and with a power   *an army*
   Of high-resolvèd men bent to the spoil°   *eager to plunder*
   They hither march amain° under conduct°   *swiftly / command*
65   Of Lucius, son to old Andronicus,
   Who threats in course of this revenge to do
   As much as ever Coriolanus[5] did.
SATURNINUS   Is warlike Lucius general of the Goths?
   These tidings nip me, and I hang the head,
70   As flowers with frost, or grass beat down with storms.
   Ay, now begins our sorrows to approach.
   'Tis he the common people love so much.
   Myself hath often heard them say,
   When I have walkèd like a private man,[6]
75   That Lucius' banishment was wrongfully,°   *wrongfully imposed*
   And they have wished that Lucius were their emperor.
TAMORA   Why should you fear? Is not your city strong?
SATURNINUS   Ay, but the citizens favour Lucius,
   And will revolt from me to succour him.
80 TAMORA   King, be thy thoughts imperious like thy name.
   Is the sun dimmed, that° gnats do fly in it?   *because*
   The eagle suffers little birds to sing,
   And is not careful° what they mean thereby,   *troubled*
   Knowing that with the shadow of his wings
85   He can at pleasure stint° their melody.   *stop*
   Even so mayst thou the giddy° men of Rome.   *fickle*
   Then cheer thy spirit; for know thou, Emperor,
   I will enchant the old Andronicus
   With words more sweet and yet more dangerous
90   Than baits to fish or honey-stalks[7] to sheep
   Whenas° the one is wounded with the bait,   *When*
   The other rotted[8] with delicious feed.
SATURNINUS   But he will not entreat his son for us.
TAMORA   If Tamora entreat him, then he will,
95   For I can smooth° and fill his agèd ears   *flatter*
   With golden promises that, were his heart
   Almost impregnable, his old ears deaf,
   Yet should both ear and heart obey my tongue.
   [*To* AEMILIUS] Go thou before to be our ambassador.
100   Say that the Emperor requests a parley
   Of warlike Lucius, and appoint the meeting
   Even at his father's house, the old Andronicus.
SATURNINUS   Aemilius, do this message honourably,
   And if he stand on hostage[9] for his safety,
105   Bid him demand what pledge will please him best.
AEMILIUS   Your bidding shall I do effectually.   *Exit*

---

5. Early Roman warrior who, after he was banished, joined his former enemies and led an army against Rome; the subject of Shakespeare's *Coriolanus*.
6. Disguised as an ordinary man.
7. Clover (large quantities make sheep ill).
8. Afflicted by the rot, a liver disease in sheep.
9. If he demand a hostage (to be killed if Titus is threatened).

TAMORA   Now will I to that old Andronicus,
 And temper° him with all the art I have   *work on*
 To pluck proud Lucius from the warlike Goths.
110 And now, sweet Emperor, be blithe again,
 And bury all thy fear in my devices.
SATURNINUS   Then go incessantly,° and plead to him.   *immediately*
          Exeunt [*severally*]°   *separately*

5.1

Flourish. Enter LUCIUS *with an army of Goths with*
drums° and soldiers   *drummers*
LUCIUS   Approvèd° warriors and my faithful friends, *Proven*
 I have receivèd letters from great Rome
 Which signifies what hate they bear their emperor
 And how desirous of our sight they are.
5 Therefore, great lords, be as your titles witness,
 Imperious, and impatient of your wrongs,
 And wherein Rome hath done you any scath°   *harm*
 Let him make treble satisfaction.
A GOTH   Brave slip° sprung from the great Andronicus, *offspring*
10 Whose name was once our terror, now our comfort,
 Whose high exploits and honourable deeds
 Ingrateful Rome requites with foul contempt,
 Be bold° in us. We'll follow where thou lead'st, *confident*
 Like stinging bees in hottest summer's day
15 Led by their master[1] to the flowered fields,
 And be avenged on cursèd Tamora.
GOTHS   And as he saith, so say we all with him.
LUCIUS   I humbly thank him, and I thank you all.
 But who comes here, led by a lusty Goth?
   Enter a GOTH, *leading of* AARON *with his child in his arms*
20 GOTH   Renownèd Lucius, from our troops I strayed
 To gaze upon a ruinous monastery,
 And as I earnestly did fix mine eye
 Upon the wasted° building, suddenly   *ruined*
 I heard a child cry underneath a wall.
25 I made unto the noise, when soon I heard
 The crying babe controlled° with this discourse: *calmed*
 'Peace, tawny slave,[2] half me and half thy dam!
 Did not thy hue bewray° whose brat thou art,   *show*
 Had nature lent thee but thy mother's look,
30 Villain, thou mightst have been an emperor.
 But where the bull and cow are both milk-white
 They never do beget a coal-black calf.
 Peace, villain, peace!'—even thus he rates° the babe— *scolds*
 'For I must bear thee to a trusty Goth
35 Who, when he knows thou art the Empress' babe,
 Will hold thee dearly for thy mother's sake.'
 With this, my weapon drawn, I rushed upon him,
 Surprised him suddenly, and brought him hither
 To use as you think needful of° the man.   *appropriate to*
40 LUCIUS   O worthy Goth, this is the incarnate devil

5.1 Location: Outside Rome.   2. Used affectionately, like "brat," and "villain" below.
1. The queen bee was thought to be male.

That robbed Andronicus of his good hand.
This is the pearl that pleased your Empress' eye,
And here's the base fruit of her burning lust.
[*To* AARON] Say, wall-eyed slave, whither wouldst thou convey
45 This growing image of thy fiendlike face?
Why dost not speak? What, deaf? What, not a word?
A halter, soldiers! Hang him on this tree,
And by his side his fruit of bastardy.
AARON   Touch not the boy; he is of royal blood.
50 LUCIUS   Too like the sire for ever being° good.   *ever to be*
First hang the child, that he may see it sprawl°—   *twitch convulsively*
A sight to vex the father's soul withal.
Get me a ladder.
          [A GOTH *brings a ladder, which* AARON *climbs*]
AARON   Lucius, save the child,
And bear it from me to the Empress.
55 If thou do this, I'll show thee wondrous things
That highly may advantage thee to hear.
If thou wilt not, befall what may befall,
I'll speak no more but 'Vengeance rot you all!'
LUCIUS   Say on, and if it please me which thou speak'st
60 Thy child shall live, and I will see it nourished.
AARON   And if it please thee? Why, assure thee, Lucius,
'Twill vex thy soul to hear what I shall speak;
For I must talk of murders, rapes, and massacres,
Acts of black night, abominable deeds,
65 Complots° of mischief, treason, villainies   *Conspiracies*
Ruthful° to hear yet piteously[3] performed,   *Lamentable*
And this shall all be buried in my death
Unless thou swear to me my child shall live.
LUCIUS   Tell on thy mind. I say thy child shall live.
70 AARON   Swear that he shall, and then I will begin.
LUCIUS   Who should I swear by? Thou believest no god.
That granted, how canst thou believe an oath?
AARON   What if I do not?—as indeed I do not—
Yet for I know thou art religious
75 And hast a thing within thee callèd conscience,
With twenty popish tricks and ceremonies
Which I have seen thee careful to observe,
Therefore I urge° thy oath; for that I know   *insist on*
An idiot holds his bauble° for a god,   *jester's stick*
80 And keeps the oath which by that god he swears,
To that I'll urge him, therefore thou shalt vow
By that same god, what god soe'er it be,
That thou adorest and hast in reverence,
To save my boy, to nurse and bring him up,
85 Or else I will discover naught to thee.
LUCIUS   Even by my god I swear to thee I will.
AARON   First know thou I begot him on the Empress.
LUCIUS   O most insatiate and luxurious° woman!   *lascivious*
AARON   Tut, Lucius, this was but a deed of charity
90 To° that which thou shalt hear of me anon.   *Compared to*
'Twas her two sons that murdered Bassianus.

3. In a way that would excite pity.

They cut thy sister's tongue, and ravished her,
And cut her hands, and trimmed her as thou sawest.
LUCIUS   O detestable villain! Call'st thou that trimming?
95   AARON   Why, she was washed and cut and trimmed, and 'twas
Trim° sport for them which had the doing of it.   *Fine*
LUCIUS   O barbarous beastly villains, like thyself!
AARON   Indeed, I was their tutor to instruct them.
That codding° spirit had they from their mother,   *lustful*
100   As sure a card as ever won the set.°   *game*
That bloody mind I think they learned of me,
As true a dog as ever fought at head.[4]
Well, let my deeds be witness of my worth.
I trained° thy brethren to that guileful hole   *lured*
105   Where the dead corpse of Bassianus lay.
I wrote the letter that thy father found,
And hid the gold within that letter mentioned,
Confederate with the Queen and her two sons;
And what not done that thou hast cause to rue
110   Wherein I had no stroke of mischief in it?
I played the cheater[5] for thy father's hand,
And when I had it drew myself apart,°   *went off alone*
And almost broke my heart° with extreme laughter.   *died*
I pried me° through the crevice of a wall   *I peered*
115   When for his hand he had his two sons' heads,
Beheld his tears, and laughed so heartily
That both mine eyes were rainy like to his;
And when I told the Empress of this sport
She swoonèd almost at my pleasing tale,
120   And for my tidings gave me twenty kisses.
A GOTH   What, canst thou say all this and never blush?
AARON   Ay, like a black dog, as the saying is.
LUCIUS   Art thou not sorry for these heinous deeds?
AARON   Ay, that I had not done a thousand more.
125   Even now I curse the day—and yet I think
Few come within the compass of my curse—
Wherein I did not some notorious ill,
As kill a man, or else devise his death;
Ravish a maid, or plot the way to do it;
130   Accuse some innocent and forswear myself;
Set deadly enmity between two friends;
Make poor men's cattle break their necks;
Set fire on barns and haystacks in the night,
And bid the owners quench them with their tears.
135   Oft have I digged up dead men from their graves
And set them upright at their dear friends' door,
Even when their sorrows almost was forgot,
And on their skins, as on the bark of trees,
Have with my knife carvèd in Roman letters
140   'Let not your sorrow die though I am dead.'
But I have done a thousand dreadful things
As willingly as one would kill a fly,

---

4. As ever went for the bull's head (in the sport of bull-baiting).

5. Swindler; escheator, an officer appointed to look after property forfeited to the crown.

And nothing grieves me heartily indeed
But that I cannot do ten thousand more.
145 LUCIUS Bring down the devil, for he must not die
So sweet a death as hanging presently.°   *immediately*
[*Goths bring* AARON *down the ladder*]
AARON If there be devils, would I were a devil,
To live and burn in everlasting fire,
So I might have your company in hell
150 But to torment you with my bitter tongue.
LUCIUS Sirs, stop his mouth, and let him speak no more.
[*Goths gag* AARON]
Enter AEMILIUS
A GOTH My lord, there is a messenger from Rome
Desires to be admitted to your presence.
LUCIUS Let him come near.
155 Welcome, Aemilius. What's the news from Rome?
AEMILIUS Lord Lucius, and you princes of the Goths,
The Roman Emperor greets you all by me,
And for he understands you are in arms,
He craves a parley at your father's house,
160 Willing you to demand your hostages,
And they shall be immediately delivered.
A GOTH What says our general?
LUCIUS Aemilius, let the Emperor give his pledges
Unto my father and my uncle Marcus,
165 And we will come. Away!   *Flourish. Exeunt* [*marching*]

5.2

Enter TAMORA *and* [CHIRON *and* DEMETRIUS,] *her two*
sons, disguised
TAMORA Thus, in this strange and sad habiliment,°   *somber costume*
I will encounter with Andronicus
And say I am Revenge, sent from below
To join with him and right his heinous wrongs.
5 Knock at his study, where they say he keeps°   *stays*
To ruminate strange plots of dire revenge.
Tell him Revenge is come to join with him
And work confusion on his enemies.
They knock, and TITUS [*aloft*] *opens his study door*
TITUS Who doth molest my contemplation?
10 Is it your trick to make me ope the door,
That so my sad decrees° may fly away   *solemn resolutions*
And all my study be to no effect?
You are deceived; for what I mean to do,
See here, in bloody lines I have set down,
15 And what is written shall be executed.
TAMORA Titus, I am come to talk with thee.
TITUS No, not a word. How can I grace my talk,
Wanting° a hand to give it action?°   *Lacking / gesture*
Thou hast the odds° of me, therefore no more.   *advantage*
20 TAMORA If thou didst know me thou wouldst talk with me.
TITUS I am not mad, I know thee well enough;

5.2 Location: Titus's courtyard.

Witness this wretched stump, witness these crimson lines,
Witness these trenches° made by grief and care,   *wrinkles*
Witness the tiring day and heavy night,
25   Witness all sorrow that I know thee well
For our proud empress, mighty Tamora.
Is not thy coming for my other hand?
TAMORA   Know, thou sad man, I am not Tamora.
She is thy enemy, and I thy friend.
30   I am Revenge, sent from th'infernal kingdom
To ease the gnawing vulture[1] of thy mind
By working wreakful° vengeance on thy foes.   *vindictive*
Come down, and welcome me to this world's light.
Confer with me of murder and of death.
35   There's not a hollow cave or lurking-place,
No vast obscurity° or misty vale   *dark wasteland*
Where bloody murder or detested rape
Can couch° for fear, but I will find them out,   *hide*
And in their ears tell them my dreadful name,
40   Revenge, which makes the foul offender quake.
TITUS   Art thou Revenge, and art thou sent to me
To be a torment to mine enemies?
TAMORA   I am; therefore come down, and welcome me.
TITUS   Do me some service ere I come to thee.
45   Lo by thy side where Rape and Murder stands.
Now give some surance° that thou art Revenge,   *proof*
Stab them, or tear them on thy chariot wheels,
And then I'll come and be thy wagoner,
And whirl along with thee about the globe,
50   Provide two proper palfreys,° black as jet,   *handsome horses*
To hale° thy vengeful wagon swift away   *draw*
And find out murderers in their guilty caves.
And when thy car is loaden with their heads
I will dismount, and by thy wagon wheel
55   Trot like a servile footman all day long,
Even from Hyperion's° rising in the east   *the sun god*
Until his very downfall in the sea;
And day by day I'll do this heavy task,
So° thou destroy Rapine and Murder there.   *Provided that*
60 TAMORA   These are my ministers, and come with me.
TITUS   Are they thy ministers? What are they called?
TAMORA   Rape and Murder, therefore callèd so
'Cause they take vengeance of such kind of men.
TITUS   Good Lord, how like the Empress' sons they are,
65   And you the Empress! But we worldly° men   *mortal*
Have miserable, mad, mistaking eyes.
O sweet Revenge, now do I come to thee,
And if one arm's embracement will content thee,
I will embrace thee in it by and by.   *[Exit aloft]*
70 TAMORA   This closing° with him fits his lunacy.   *agreeing*
Whate'er I forge° to feed his brainsick humours   *invent*
Do you uphold and maintain in your speeches,
For now he firmly takes me for Revenge,
And being credulous in this mad thought

---

1. Alluding to the story of Prometheus; see note to 2.1.17.

75 I'll make him send for Lucius his son,
 And whilst I at a banquet hold him sure
 I'll find some cunning practice out of hand²
 To scatter and disperse the giddy Goths,
 Or at the least make them his enemies.
80 See, here he comes, and I must ply my theme.°   *keep up the act*
    [*Enter* TITUS, *below*]
  TITUS Long have I been forlorn, and all for thee.
 Welcome, dread Fury, to my woeful house.
 Rapine and Murder, you are welcome, too.
 How like the Empress and her sons you are!
85 Well are you fitted, had you but a Moor.
 Could not all hell afford you such a devil?—
 For well I wot° the Empress never wags°   *know / stirs*
 But in her company there is a Moor,
 And would you represent our Queen aright
90 It were convenient° you had such a devil.   *fitting*
 But welcome as you are. What shall we do?
  TAMORA What wouldst thou have us do, Andronicus?
  DEMETRIUS Show me a murderer, I'll deal with him.
  CHIRON Show me a villain that hath done a rape,
95 And I am sent to be revenged on him.
  TAMORA Show me a thousand that hath done thee wrong,
 And I will be revengèd on them all.
  TITUS [*to* DEMETRIUS] Look round about the wicked streets of Rome,
 And when thou find'st a man that's like thyself,
100 Good Murder, stab him; he's a murderer.
 [*To* CHIRON] Go thou with him, and when it is thy hap°   *chance*
 To find another that is like to thee,
 Good Rapine, stab him; he is a ravisher.
 [*To* TAMORA] Go thou with them, and in the Emperor's court
105 There is a queen attended by a Moor.
 Well shalt thou know her by thine own proportion,
 For up and down° she doth resemble thee.   *top to toe*
 I pray thee, do on them some violent death;
 They have been violent to me and mine.
110 TAMORA Well hast thou lessoned us. This shall we do;
 But would it please thee, good Andronicus,
 To send for Lucius, thy thrice-valiant son,
 Who leads towards Rome a band of warlike Goths,
 And bid him come and banquet at thy house—
115 When he is here, even at thy solemn° feast,   *ceremonious*
 I will bring in the Empress and her sons,
 The Emperor himself, and all thy foes,
 And at thy mercy shall they stoop and kneel,
 And on them shalt thou ease thy angry heart.
120 What says Andronicus to this device?
  TITUS Marcus, my brother! 'Tis sad Titus calls.
    Enter MARCUS
 Go, gentle Marcus, to thy nephew Lucius.
 Thou shalt enquire him out among the Goths.
 Bid him repair° to me, and bring with him   *come*
125 Some of the chiefest princes of the Goths.

2. I'll find some scheme on the spur of the moment.

Bid him encamp his soldiers where they are.
Tell him the Emperor and the Empress too
Feast at my house, and he shall feast with them.
This do thou for my love, and so let him,
130   As he regards his agèd father's life.
MARCUS   This will I do, and soon return again.   [*Exit*]
TAMORA   Now will I hence about thy business,
And take my ministers along with me.
TITUS   Nay, nay, let Rape and Murder stay with me,
135   Or else I'll call my brother back again,
And cleave to no revenge but Lucius.[3]
TAMORA [*aside to her sons*]   What say you, boys, will you abide
    with him
Whiles I go tell my lord the Emperor
How I have governed our determined jest?[4]
140   Yield to his humour, smooth and speak him fair,°   *flatter and humor him*
And tarry with him till I turn° again.   *return*
TITUS [*aside*]   I knew them all, though they supposed me mad,
And will o'erreach them in their own devices—
A pair of cursèd hell-hounds and their dam.
145 DEMETRIUS   Madam, depart at pleasure. Leave us here.
TAMORA   Farewell, Andronicus. Revenge now goes
To lay a complot to betray thy foes.
TITUS   I know thou dost, and sweet Revenge, farewell.
                                         [*Exit* TAMORA]
CHIRON   Tell us, old man, how shall we be employed?
150 TITUS   Tut, I have work enough for you to do.
Publius, come hither; Caius and Valentine.
       [*Enter* PUBLIUS, CAIUS, *and* VALENTINE]
PUBLIUS   What is your will?
TITUS   Know you these two?
PUBLIUS   The Empress' sons I take them°—Chiron, Demetrius.   *take them to be*
TITUS   Fie, Publius, fie! Thou art too much deceived.
155   The one is Murder, and Rape is the other's name.
And therefore bind them, gentle Publius;
Caius and Valentine, lay hands on them.
Oft have you heard me wish for such an hour,
And now I find it. Therefore bind them sure,
160   And stop their mouths if they begin to cry.   [*Exit*]
CHIRON   Villains, forbear! We are the Empress' sons.
PUBLIUS   And therefore do we what we are commanded.
       [PUBLIUS, CAIUS, *and* VALENTINE *bind and gag* CHIRON
       and DEMETRIUS]
Stop close their mouths. Let them not speak a word.
Is he sure° bound? Look that you bind them fast.   *securely*
      Enter TITUS ANDRONICUS *with a knife, and* LAVINIA *with
      a basin*
165 TITUS   Come, come, Lavinia. Look, thy foes are bound.
Sirs, stop their mouths. Let them not speak to me,
But let them hear what fearful words I utter.
O villains, Chiron and Demetrius!
Here stands the spring whom you have stained with mud,
170   This goodly summer with your winter mixed.

---

3. That is, depend on Lucius's invading army for revenge.   4. How have I managed the jest we planned?

You killed her husband, and for that vile fault
Two of her brothers were condemned to death,
My hand cut off and made a merry jest,
Both her sweet hands, her tongue, and that more dear
175 Than hands or tongue, her spotless chastity,
Inhuman traitors, you constrained and forced.
What would you say if I should let you speak?
Villains, for shame. You could not beg for grace.°   *mercy*
Hark, wretches, how I mean to martyr you.
180 This one hand yet is left to cut your throats,
Whiles that Lavinia 'tween her stumps doth hold
The basin that receives your guilty blood.
You know your mother means to feast with me,
And calls herself Revenge, and thinks me mad.
185 Hark, villains, I will grind your bones to dust,
And with your blood and it I'll make a paste,°   *dough*
And of the paste a coffin° I will rear,   *piecrust (with wordplay)*
And make two pasties of your shameful heads,
And bid that strumpet, your unhallowed dam,
190 Like to the earth swallow her own increase.°   *progeny*
This is the feast that I have bid her to,
And this the banquet she shall surfeit on;
For worse than Philomel you used my daughter,
And worse than Progne I will be revenged.[5]
195 And now, prepare your throats. Lavinia, come.
Receive the blood, and when that they are dead
Let me go grind their bones to powder small,
And with this hateful liquor temper° it,   *mix*
And in that paste let their vile heads be baked.
200 Come, come, be everyone officious°   *busy*
To make this banquet, which I wish may prove
More stern and bloody than the Centaurs' feast.[6]
       He cuts their throats
So, now bring them in, for I'll play the cook
And see them ready against° their mother comes.   *by the time*
       Exeunt [carrying the bodies]

5.3

       Enter LUCIUS, MARCUS, *and the Goths [with* AARON, *pris-*
       oner, and an attendant with his child]
LUCIUS Uncle Marcus, since 'tis my father's mind
    That I repair to Rome, I am content.
A GOTH   And ours with thine,[1] befall what fortune will.
LUCIUS Good uncle, take you in this barbarous Moor,
5   This ravenous tiger, this accursèd devil.
    Let him receive no sust'nance, fetter him
    Till he be brought unto the Empress' face
    For testimony of her foul proceedings,
    And see the ambush° of our friends be strong.   *troops lying in wait*
10   I fear the Emperor means no good to us.

---

5. Philomela's sister, Progne, revenged herself on her rapist husband, Tereus, by killing their son Itys and serving his flesh in a meal (see Introduction).
6. In Greek legend, the wedding feast of Hippodamia ended in a bloody battle when the Centaurs tried to carry off the bride and other women (see Ovid, *Metamorphoses* 12).
5.3 Location: Titus's courtyard.
1. Our minds accord with yours.

AARON   Some devil whisper curses in my ear
And prompt me, that my tongue may utter forth
The venomous malice of my swelling heart.
LUCIUS   Away, inhuman dog, unhallowed slave!
15   Sirs, help our uncle to convey him in.
                        [*Exeunt Goths with* AARON *and his child*]
            Flourish
The trumpets show the Emperor is at hand.
            Enter [SATURNINUS] *the Emperor, and* [TAMORA] *the*
            Empress, with [AEMILIUS,] *Tribunes,* [*Senators,*] *and*
            others
SATURNINUS   What, hath the firmament more suns than one?
LUCIUS   What boots° it thee to call thyself a sun?   *avails*
MARCUS   Rome's emperor and nephew, break the parle.°   *stop the dispute*
20   These quarrels must be quietly debated.
The feast is ready which the careful° Titus   *assiduous; troubled*
Hath ordained to an honourable end,
For peace, for love, for league, and good to Rome.
Please you therefore draw nigh, and take your places.
25   SATURNINUS   Marcus, we will.
            Hautboys.[2] *A table brought in.* [*They sit.*]
            Enter TITUS *like a cook, placing the dishes, and* LAVINIA
            with a veil over her face; [YOUNG LUCIUS, *and others*]
TITUS   Welcome, my gracious lord; welcome, dread Queen;
Welcome, ye warlike Goths; welcome, Lucius;
And welcome, all. Although the cheer° be poor,   *refreshments*
'Twill fill your stomachs. Please you, eat of it.
30   SATURNINUS   Why art thou thus attired, Andronicus?
TITUS   Because I would be sure to have all well
To entertain your highness and your Empress.
TAMORA   We are beholden to you, good Andronicus.
TITUS   An if your highness knew my heart, you were.
35   My lord the Emperor, resolve me this:
Was it well done of rash Virginius[3]
To slay his daughter with his own right hand
Because she was enforced, stained, and deflowered?
SATURNINUS   It was, Andronicus.
TITUS   Your reason, mighty lord?
40   SATURNINUS   Because the girl should not survive her shame,
And by her presence still renew his sorrows.
TITUS   A reason mighty, strong, effectual;
A pattern, precedent, and lively warrant
For me, most wretched, to perform the like.
45   Die, die, Lavinia, and thy shame with thee,
And with thy shame thy father's sorrow die.
            He kills her
SATURNINUS   What hast thou done, unnatural and unkind?
TITUS   Killed her for whom my tears have made me blind.
I am as woeful as Virginius was,
50   And have a thousand times more cause than he
To do this outrage, and it now is done.

---

2. Oboes, used to provide music for ceremonial occasions.
3. A Roman centurion who in some versions of the story

killed his daughter to prevent her rape; in other versions,
he acted as Titus describes.

SATURNINUS   What, was she ravished? Tell who did the deed.
TITUS   Will't please you eat? Will't please your highness feed?
TAMORA   Why hast thou slain thine only daughter thus?
55   TITUS   Not I, 'twas Chiron and Demetrius.
They ravished her, and cut away her tongue,
And they, 'twas they, that did her all this wrong.
SATURNINUS   Go, fetch them hither to us presently.°   at once
TITUS [revealing the heads]   Why, there they are, both bakèd in
this pie,
60   Whereof their mother daintily hath fed,
Eating the flesh that she herself hath bred.
'Tis true, 'tis true, witness my knife's sharp point.°   (with pun on "period")
He stabs the Empress
SATURNINUS   Die, frantic° wretch, for this accursèd deed.   deranged
[He kills TITUS]
LUCIUS   Can the son's eye behold his father bleed?
65   There's meed for meed,° death for a deadly deed.   measure for measure
[He kills SATURNINUS. Confusion follows.
Enter Goths. LUCIUS, MARCUS, and others go aloft]
MARCUS   You sad-faced men, people and sons of Rome,
By uproars severed, as a flight of fowl
Scattered by winds and high tempestuous gusts,
O, let me teach you how to knit again
70   This scattered corn° into one mutual° sheaf,   grain / unified
These broken limbs again into one body.
A ROMAN LORD   Let Rome herself be bane° unto herself,   destroyer
And she whom mighty kingdoms curtsy to,
Like a forlorn and desperate castaway,
75   Do shameful execution on herself
But if my frosty signs and chaps° of age,   white hair and wrinkles
Grave witnesses of true experience,
Cannot induce you to attend my words.
[To LUCIUS] Speak, Rome's dear friend, as erst° our ancestor[4]   once
80   When with his solemn tongue he did discourse
To lovesick Dido's sad-attending° ear   seriously listening
The story of that baleful-burning night
When subtle Greeks surprised King Priam's Troy.
Tell us what Sinon[5] hath bewitched our ears,
85   Or who hath brought the fatal engine[6] in
That gives our Troy, our Rome, the civil° wound.   incurred in civil war
My heart is not compact° of flint nor steel,   composed
Nor can I utter all our bitter grief,
But floods of tears will drown my oratory
90   And break° my utt'rance even in the time   interrupt
When it should move ye to attend me most,
And force you to commiseration.
Here's Rome's young captain. Let him tell the tale,
While I stand by and weep to hear him speak.
95   LUCIUS   Then, gracious auditory,° be it known to you   audience
That Chiron and the damned Demetrius
Were they that murderèd our Emperor's brother,
And they it were that ravishèd our sister.

4. Aeneas, Trojan ancestor of the Roman people.   wooden horse full of soldiers.
5. The Greek who persuaded the Trojans to admit the   6. Instrument (the wooden horse).

For their fell° faults our brothers were beheaded,   *cruel*
100   Our father's tears despised, and basely cozened°   *cheated*
Of that true hand that fought Rome's quarrel out°   *to the finish*
And sent her enemies unto the grave.
Lastly myself, unkindly° banishèd,   *unnaturally*
The gates shut on me, and turned weeping out
105   To beg relief among Rome's enemies,
Who drowned their enmity in my true tears
And oped their arms to embrace me as a friend.
I am the turned-forth, be it known to you,
That have preserved her° welfare in my blood,   *(Rome's)*
110   And from her bosom took the enemy's point,
Sheathing the steel in my advent'rous body.
Alas, you know I am no vaunter,° I.   *boaster*
My scars can witness, dumb although they are,
That my report is just and full of truth.
115   But soft, methinks I do digress too much,
Citing my worthless praise. O, pardon me,
For when no friends are by, men praise themselves.
MARCUS   Now is my turn to speak. Behold the child.
Of this was Tamora deliverèd,
120   The issue of an irreligious Moor,
Chief architect and plotter of these woes.
The villain is alive in Titus' house,
And as he is to witness, this is true.
Now judge what cause had Titus to revenge
125   These wrongs unspeakable, past patience,°   *endurance*
Or more than any living man could bear.
Now have you heard the truth. What say you, Romans?
Have we° done aught amiss, show us wherein,   *If we have*
And from the place where you behold us pleading
130   The poor remainder of Andronici
Will hand in hand all headlong hurl ourselves[7]
And on the ragged stones beat forth our souls
And make a mutual closure° of our house.°   *end / family*
Speak, Romans, speak, and if you say we shall,
135   Lo, hand in hand Lucius and I will fall.
AEMILIUS   Come, come, thou reverend man of Rome,
And bring our emperor gently in thy hand,
Lucius, our emperor—for well I know
The common voice do cry it shall be so.
140   ROMANS   Lucius, all hail, Rome's royal emperor!
MARCUS [*to attendants*]   Go, go into old Titus' sorrowful house
And hither hale that misbelieving Moor
To be adjudged some direful slaught'ring death
As punishment for his most wicked life.   [*Exeunt some*]
    [LUCIUS, MARCUS, *and the others come down*]
145   ROMANS   Lucius, all hail, Rome's gracious governor!
LUCIUS   Thanks, gentle Romans. May I govern so
To heal Rome's harms and wipe away her woe.
But, gentle people, give me aim° awhile,   *encourage me*
For nature puts me to° a heavy task.   *sets me*
150   Stand all aloof, but, uncle, draw you near

---

7. Traditionally, traitors were thrown from the Tarpeian Rock on the Capitoline Hill.

To shed obsequious° tears upon this trunk. *mournful*
[*Kissing* TITUS] O, take this warm kiss on thy pale cold lips,
These sorrowful drops upon thy bloodstained face,
The last true duties of thy noble son.
155 MARCUS [*kissing* TITUS]   Tear for tear, and loving kiss for kiss,
Thy brother Marcus tenders on thy lips.
O, were the sum of these that I should pay
Countless and infinite, yet would I pay them.
LUCIUS [*to* YOUNG LUCIUS]   Come hither, boy, come, come, and
learn of us
160 To melt in showers. Thy grandsire loved thee well.
Many a time he danced thee on his knee,
Sung thee asleep, his loving breast thy pillow.
Many a story hath he told to thee,
And bid thee bear his pretty tales in mind,
165 And talk of them when he was dead and gone.
MARCUS   How many thousand times hath these poor lips,
When they were living, warmed themselves on thine!
O now, sweet boy, give them their latest° kiss. *last*
Bid him farewell. Commit him to the grave.
170 Do them° that kindness, and take leave of them. *(his lips)*
YOUNG LUCIUS [*kissing* TITUS]   O grandsire, grandsire, ev'n with
all my heart
Would I were dead, so° you did live again. *provided that*
O Lord, I cannot speak to him for weeping.
My tears will choke me if I ope my mouth.
[*Enter some with* AARON]
175 A ROMAN   You sad Andronici, have done with woes.
Give sentence on this execrable wretch
That hath been breeder of these dire events.
LUCIUS   Set him breast-deep in earth and famish him.
There let him stand, and rave, and cry for food.
180 If anyone relieves or pities him,
For the offence he dies. This is our doom.° *judgment*
Some stay to see him fastened in the earth.
AARON   Ah, why should wrath be mute and fury dumb?
I am no baby, I, that with base prayers
185 I should repent the evils I have done.
Ten thousand worse than ever yet I did
Would I perform if I might have my will.
If one good deed in all my life I did
I do repent it from my very soul.
190 LUCIUS   Some loving friends convey the Emperor hence,
And give him burial in his father's grave.° *ancestral tomb*
My father and Lavinia shall forthwith
Be closèd in our household's monument.
As for that ravenous tiger, Tamora,
195 No funeral rite nor man in mourning weed,° *garments*
No mournful bell shall ring her burial;
But throw her forth to beasts and birds to prey.° *prey upon*
Her life was beastly and devoid of pity,
And being dead, let birds on her take pity.
Exeunt [*with the bodies*]

TEXTUAL VARIANTS

Control text: Q1, with additional material from F

F: The Folio of 1623
Q1: The Quarto of 1594
Q2: The Quarto of 1600
Q3: The Quarto of 1611

s.p. SATURNINUS [Q1's use of *Saturnine, King,* and *Emperour* has been standardized throughout.]
s.p. AARON [Q1's use of *Moore* and *Aron* has been standardized throughout.]
s.p. YOUNG LUCIUS [*Puer* in Q1; standardized throughout.]

1.1.18 s.p. MARCUS [not in Q1] **35 field;** [Four lines follow in Q1, indented in this edition.] **35.2 the** that **40 succeeded** succeede **64 s.p. Captain** [not in Q1] **98** *manes manus* **141 quit her** quit the **157 s.p. LAVINIA** [not in Q1] **226 Titan's** [Q2] Tytus **242 Pantheon** Pathan **264 chance** [Q2] change **280** *cuique cuiqum* **283 guard?** [Q1 and F have four lines following, indented in this edition.] **295 Follow . . . back** [In Q1, this line follows 1.1.285.] **313 Phoebe** Thebe **355 s.p. QUINTUS and MARTIUS** Titus two sonnes speakes. **357 s.p. QUINTUS** Titus sonne speakes. **365 s.p. MARTIUS** 3. Sonne. **366 s.p. QUINTUS** 2. Sonne. **395 s.p. MARCUS** Yes . . . **remunerate** [The line does not occur in Q1; it does appear in F, but without the attribution to Marcus.] **471 s.p. LUCIUS** [not in Q1] All. [Q3] Son. [F]
2.1.110 than this
2.2.1 morn [Q3] Moone **24 run** runs
2.3.33 and ann **72 swart** [F] swartie **85 note** notice **88 have I** I have **115 henceforward** hence forth **126 quaint** painted **131 ye desire** we desire **153 Some** [Q2] So me **192 s.p. AARON** [not in Q1] **210 unhallowed** [F] vnhollow **222 berayed** bereaud **231 Pyramus** Priamus **236 Cocytus** Ocitus **260 gripped** griude **268 s.p. SATURNINUS** [s.p. *"King."* printed after the text of the letter, at line 276.]
2.4.11 s.p. MARCUS [not in Q1] **27 him** them **30 three** their **38 Philomel** Philomela
3.1.12 two [not in Q1] **35 must** must, / and bootlesse vnto them **146 with his** with her **215 sorrows** sorrow **224 blow** flow **280–81 And Lavinia, thou shalt be employed. / Bear thou my hand, sweet wench, between thine arms.** And *Lauinia* thou shalt be imployde in these Armes, / Beare thou my hand sweet wench betweene thy teethe:
3.2 [This scene appears first in F. There is no Q1 counterpart.] **13 with outrageous** without ragious **39 complainer** complaynet **52 thy** [not in F] **53 fly** Flys **55 are** [not in F] **60 father, brother?** father and mother? **62 dirges** doings **72 myself** my selfes
4.1.10 s.p. MARCUS [In Q1, speech continued to Titus.] **69 here** [not in Q1] **77 s.p. TITUS** [not in Q1] **90 sware** sweare
4.2.15 that [not in Q1] **123 that** [Q3] your **135 do join** joine **177 fat** feede
4.3.32 But [Catchword in Q1 but not reproduced on the following page, presumably because a line was accidentally omitted.] **40 now** so **54 Apollinem** Apollonem **57 'To Saturn', Caius** To Saturnine, to Caius **77** [Speech continued to Titus in Q2 is attributed to the Clown in Q1.] **92** [After this line, Q1 and F print a short exchange, indented in this edition.]
4.4.5 as know [not in Q1] **92 feed** [Q3] seede **104 on** in **112 incessantly** sucessantly
5.1.17 s.p. GOTHS [not in Q1] **46 What, deaf? What, not a word?** what deafe, not a word? **53 Get me a ladder** [attributed to Aaron in Q1] **133 haystacks** haystalks **165 come. Away!** come, march away
5.2.18 it action F that accord **49 globe** Globes **50 two** thee two **52 murderers** murder **52 caves** cares **56 Hyperion's** Epeons **61 they thy** them thy
5.3.26 gracious [Q2–3, F, not in Q1] **42 effectual** and effectuall **124 cause** course **140 s.p. ROMANS** Marcus. **141 s.p. MARCUS** [not in Q1] **143 adjudged** [Q3] adiudge **145 s. p.ROMANS** [not on Q1] **153 bloodstained** blood slaine

Romeo and Juliet

Plato's great dialogue *The Symposium* recounts a memorable dinner party where the guests spent a long night in impassioned, brilliant philosophical conversation about love. By daybreak, most of the guests had fallen asleep, but Socrates, who had spoken with particularly luminous intelligence, was still awake, trying to prove that a single playwright was capable of writing both comedy and tragedy. As he clinched his case, his weary interlocutors nodded off to sleep. Thus we never learn the argument that Socrates was making for the convergence of the tragic and comic visions in one dramatist, and neither the ancient Greek nor the Roman world has left us an instance of that convergence. But we have its supreme embodiment in Shakespeare. The achievement is particularly striking in two plays probably written around 1595. Scholars have been unable to determine with certainty whether *Romeo and Juliet* was written before or after *A Midsummer Night's Dream*; one of Shakespeare's most delightful comedies and one of his most beloved tragedies appear to have been written at virtually the same time and out of some very similar materials.

In the entertainment performed for the newlyweds at the close of *A Midsummer Night's Dream*, the young lovers, Pyramus and Thisbe, are separated by a "vile wall." They attempt to elope together, but Pyramus, mistakenly thinking that Thisbe has been killed, rashly commits suicide, whereupon Thisbe in despair stabs herself. A strange way, it would seem, to celebrate festive nuptials, but Shakespeare's comedy continually triumphs over fears of rashness, mutability, and death by staging and laughing at them. The inept amateur actors call attention so crudely to the tragedy's artificiality and contrivance that it provokes derisive laughter: "This is the silliest stuff that ever I heard" (5.1.207).

In *Romeo and Juliet*, whose climax closely resembles that of Pyramus and Thisbe, Shakespeare does not shy away from artifice and contrivance. His tragedy is unusually dependent on coincidence, mischance, and accident to produce what the Chorus, in the sonnet that serves as the prologue, calls the lovers' "misadventured piteous overthrows." Nor does he forswear the note of witty, wicked parody that transformed the woes of Pyramus and Thisbe into an occasion for mirth. Romeo's friend Mercutio gives voice to an irrepressible spirit of mockery, a spirit that seems to challenge the very possibility of romantic love or tragic destiny. (There is a seventeenth-century report—it doesn't date from the playwright's own lifetime—that Shakespeare remarked that he was forced to kill Mercutio in the third act to prevent being killed by him.) But Shakespeare manages to make the story of his reckless, star-crossed lovers immensely moving, resistant at once to corrosive irony and to moralizing disapproval. He does so principally through his mastery of what the bumbling performers in *A Midsummer Night's Dream* conspicuously lack: the power of language to make and unmake the world.

It is this poetic power—"poetic" derives from the Greek word for "making"—that provides Shakespeare with the key to resolving the paradox addressed by Socrates in *The Symposium* and that enables him to transform his rather shopworn source materials into something rich and strange. The story of the ill-fated lovers from bitterly feuding families had been told many times in the sixteenth century by Italian and French writers and had already appeared more than once in English. Shakespeare's direct source is Arthur Brooke's *Tragical History of Romeus and Juliet* (1562), a long, leaden English poem based on a French prose version by Pierre Boiastuau (1559), who was in turn adapting an Italian version by Bandello (1554), who in turn based his narrative on Luigi da Porto's version (1525) of a tale by Masuccio Salernitano (1476). Shakespeare follows the main outline of Brooke's narrative, though he makes many changes in the interests of theatrical compression and intensification. Hence the events that in Brooke take nine months are telescoped into a few days. The figure of Mercutio is brilliantly developed, as is the vulgar, meddling, earthy Nurse. Juliet, eighteen years old in Bandello's version and sixteen in Brooke's, is depicted as only thirteen, a young girl suddenly awakening to passionate desires that set her against the will of her family.

But it is principally by means of the incandescent brilliance of its language that *Romeo and Juliet* has earned its place as one of the greatest love stories in world literature. Shakespeare makes linguistic power actually figure thematically in the play by insisting on the crucial importance of naming and, more generally, by repeatedly calling attention to the force of verbal actions. This was by no means the playwright's private obsession. His play is the product of a rhetorical culture, a culture steeped in an awareness—in the philosopher J. L. Austin's phrase—of "how to do things with words." What are some of the things that characters do with words? For a start, they insult each other, a dangerous pastime of both servants and masters. They also invite one another (Capulet's favorite pastime); they confess (formally, to a priest; informally, to friends); they conjure; they curse; they make contracts; they vow; and, if they have the power of the prince, they banish. And through all of these verbal actions, no matter how serious or even deadly they may be, they constantly play with language.

Romeo and Juliet is saturated with language games: paradoxes, oxymorons, double entendres, rhyming tricks, verbal echoings, multiple puns. The obvious question is, why? One possible answer, proposed as early as the eighteenth century, is that Shakespeare could not resist: verbal wit was an addiction, an obsession, the object of an irrational passion. He could indulge this passion because a display of wit would appeal to those segments of the audience most attuned to rhetorical acrobatics. Another answer is that puns are a clarifying challenge, an assault on sentiments to test whether they are genuine or merely forced and empty. Hence Mercutio attempts to mock Romeo's passion with a set of ribald jests, jests that are reiterated unconsciously by the Nurse in such exclamations

Two gallants fight a duel in the street. From George Wither, A *Collection of Emblemes* (1635)

as "Stand up, stand up, stand an you be a man" (3.3.88). To survive the corrosive effect of such mockery is a measure of true love and a sign of authenticity: "He jests at scars that never felt a wound" (2.1.43).

But this explanation for the tragedy's pervasive wordplay is not wholly adequate, since at the height of both their love and their despair, Romeo and Juliet also pun. Romeo on the verge of suicide plays with the word "engrossing" (death as wholesaler; monopolist; lawyer); Juliet plays with the word "restorative" (the kiss as medicine; poison; death; resurrection); and both play with the Elizabethan "die" as a term for "orgasm." Here wordplay functions not to deflate but to cram into brief utterances more meanings than language would ordinarily hold and to force us to confront both unresolvable contradictions and hidden connections. That is, puns work to juxtapose or hold open possibilities that normally are viewed as mutually exclusive. Thus they may be said to reach both a psychological and a thematic level at which oppositions—pain and joy, loss and restoration, love and death, comedy and tragedy—are canceled.

Wordplay would be impossible in a language in which words were strictly bound to things in a perfect correspondence between naming and nature. Punning is possible only if there is some slippage in sound and meaning, so that one sign can refer to two or more objects or, as Mercutio wittily demonstrates in his Queen Mab speech, to nothing at all. Yet wordplay can also suggest surprising linkages and secret realities. Hence, for example, the punning in Romeo and Juliet's initial exchange at the Capulet ball derives its power from the lovers' conviction that there really is an essential relation between the touching of their hands and lips and a religious experience. This relation, invisible to the ordinary social world around them, is disclosed in the language game they spontaneously play, a game that takes the form of a shared sonnet.

Even to speak of this first exchange as a game is to risk diminishing its intense seriousness. For Mercutio, words are fantastic trifles in a world fit only for satire, sexual teasing, and make-believe. He is a young man in love with masks; indeed, as he readies himself for the masked ball, he seems to regard his own face as a mask: "Give me a case to put my visage in, / A visor for a visor" (1.4.29–30). The moment Romeo and Juliet meet, all masks seem to fall away, all prior emotions fade into nothingness, and all games become earnest. "Did my heart love till now?" asks Romeo, and Juliet, sending the Nurse to find out Romeo's name, declares, "If he be marrièd, / My grave is like to be my wedding bed" (1.5.131–32).

At some moments in Romeo and Juliet, then, wordplay reveals the arbitrariness of language; at other moments, it seems to reveal a hidden reality, even a sacred truth. These contradictory revelations are explored in the famous balcony scene in Act 2. Mercutio's mockery gives way, after Romeo's abrupt, one-line dismissal, to incantatory language so intense as to create a new heaven and a new earth. A bare, day-lit stage (as it would have been in the Elizabethan playhouse) becomes a dark garden above which Juliet appears like the sun. Visibility is canceled and then restored, by means of metaphor, to the "white upturnèd wond'ring eyes / Of mortals" (2.1.71–72). Romeo's ecstatic words are the poetic record of a revelation, a vision of a creature unique, perfect, and infinitely beautiful.

The visionary moment turns into a moment of auditory revelation as well, as Romeo, in an intense, eroticized version of what audiences routinely do, overhears Juliet's soliloquy. He has entered into her most intimate thoughts and longings and has an overpowering proof of their authenticity, since she speaks with no awareness of his presence. The inner world his lyrical utterance has conjured up is miraculously united with her own. But her words at once offer a complete fulfillment of this union and a shattering of fulfillment: "O Romeo, Romeo, wherefore art thou Romeo?" (2.1.75). Only if Romeo's name is an arbitrary sign, to be stripped away, discarded, and replaced, can her love be realized. But in a world in which words are divorced from reality, what would be the status of a love made by language? In a world in which names are mere empty signs, how could language create a new reality?

If words are arbitrary, then Romeo and Juliet's love, woven of words, is wedded to nothingness. If they are not arbitrary, if they cannot float free of the body and society, then

"Then I defy you, stars!" (5.1.24). *Imagines Constellationum.* From Ptolemy, *Almagest* (1541), after Dürer.

their love will be destroyed by the rage of feuding parents—the parents who have bestowed proper names on their offspring—and by the whole daylight world of social exchange that gives ordinary language its normal meanings. Against the magical, passionate, transformative language of Romeo and Juliet is set not only Mercutio's mockery but the Nurse's garrulous evocation of the inescapable life cycle: birth, weaning, sexual maturity, and death.

In the Nurse's view, all lives seem to have a certain interchangeability. Juliet's value can be measured—"I tell you, he that can lay hold of her / Shall have the chinks" (1.5.114–15)—and an exiled husband can be replaced: Paris is "a lovely gentleman," she tells the grieving Juliet, "Romeo's a dishclout to him" (3.5.218–19). Romeo and Juliet insist by contrast on the absolute singularity of their love, on the stilling of cyclical time, and on the cancellation of the social network of form and compliment. For a moment on her balcony, Juliet regrets that Romeo has heard her declare her "true-love passion," but then she bids farewell to conventional restraint and boldly steps forward into the magical realm of reciprocal desire. This realm is not without its own solemn order: their love must be formally confirmed in honorable vows of holy matrimony spoken before the friar. But first in the garden, away from church and family and friends, the fullness of the lovers' matched longings finds expression in words that seem to possess mythic power, power to transform darkness into intense light and at the same time to block out the harsh, unforgiving light of the everyday.

The everyday has its own powerful resources, however, and forces its way back into the world that love has transformed. It does so through the ability of names like "Capulet" and "Montague" to conjure up bitter social rivalries. For, as *Romeo and Juliet* repeatedly discloses, words as we ordinarily use them are rarely wholly arbitrary, as in Mercutio's wild fantasies, or wholly mythic, as in the lovers' ecstatic passion. They are social constructions, communal creations that are neither complete unto themselves nor empty and hence malleable by individuals. Both language as mythic and language as arbitrary are radical attempts to challenge this notion of words as shared creations carrying with them the tensions and resolutions present in communities, but the community in effect kills off the challenge—whether it comes from Mercutio, who tries to turn social hatred and love alike into an arbitrary game about "nothing," or from Romeo and Juliet, who try to escape through darkness, subterfuge, and the language of love into a realm apart.

How does the communitarian spirit of language, and with it a sense of the inescapability of the social, manifest itself in *Romeo and Juliet?* It does so, first of all, through a series of characters such as those we glimpse in the opening moments of the play, when the Capulet servants, Samson and Gregory, provoke the absurd quarrel with the Montague servants, Abraham and Balthasar. The point is not only the foolishness of the social codes— "Do you bite your thumb at us, sir?" "I do bite my thumb, sir" (1.1.39–40)—but also their pervasiveness. In a tragedy memorable for its dreams of the most intense privacy—Juliet longs for Romeo to leap to her arms "untalked of and unseen" (3.2.7)—the bustling world makes its presence felt as insistently as the Nurse's voice calling again and again to Juliet as she stands at her window. Shakespeare is wonderfully resourceful in conveying this presence. There is, for example, the nameless servant whose inability to read the list of those invited to the Capulets' ball leads him to turn for assistance to Romeo and Benvolio, who chance at that moment to be walking by. The list itself deftly conjures up the social elite of Verona, with its network of kinship bonds:

> Signor Placentio and his lovely nieces,
> Mercutio and his brother Valentine,
> Mine uncle Capulet, his wife and daughters,

and so on through the whole "fair assembly" (1.2.63ff). At the ball itself, Shakespeare is careful to include a glimpse of the servants, hurrying to clear the dishes but finding time to put aside a piece of marzipan for themselves or arranging for a private party with Susan Grindstone and Nell. And, in the midst of the horror and lamenting when Juliet's cold and stiff body is discovered on the morning she was to be married to Paris, Shakespeare turns our attention to the musicians who had been hired to entertain the wedding guests and who now stand around cracking lame jokes and hoping for a bit of dinner (as if—to invert a celebrated line from *Hamlet*—the marriage-baked meats will coldly furnish forth the funeral table).

There are, besides the servants, other social units that carry the glacial weight of the collective norms and ordinary interests against which Romeo and Juliet struggle. The exclusiveness and intensity of their love is clearly in tension with the bond that links Romeo to his male friends. "Now art thou sociable," says Mercutio with evident relief, when Romeo briefly resumes the old mocking repartee; "now art thou Romeo" (2.3.77). But neither Romeo nor Juliet is any longer the same person, and the passionate love that divides Romeo from his friends sets both lovers still more decisively against the values of their powerful families. Those values involve a complex intertwining of honor, dignity, love, will, and property, a blend that can manifest itself as gracious hospitality or as murderous feuding, as gentle nostalgia or as cold calculation, as a father's indulgent affection for his daughter or as blind rage when she attempts to thwart his will. Romeo and Juliet's love and clandestine marriage can find no place in this familial order of things, just as its absoluteness is incompatible with the familial sense of cyclical time.

Beyond the structure of the family in the society of Verona, though linked to that structure by ties of kinship, lies the state, embodied in the figure of Prince Escalus. For-

The city of Verona. From John Speed, *Prospect of the Most Famous Parts of the World* (1676).

mally, *Romeo and Juliet* is built around the well-meaning ruler's attempt to stop the "civil brawls" (1.1.82) at the play's beginning, his banishment of Romeo at its midpoint, and his final inquiry, to "clear these ambiguities" (5.3.216), at its close. But this necessary principle of civic order, though it has important consequences, seems almost beside the point, as inadequate and uncomprehending as the statues in pure gold that the grieving fathers propose to erect.

A much deeper social principle is figured in Friar Laurence, who embodies the collective wisdom and sanctity of the community. Though set apart, the friar is not a hermit or a recluse; he is an active agent in the community's affairs. His attempt to use Romeo and Juliet's love as a means to resolve the feud between the Montagues and the Capulets disastrously backfires, and with his sleeping potions, his elaborate plots, and, at the close, his fatal cowardice, he has some of the qualities of the stereotypical meddling friar of anticlerical satire. But Friar Laurence is a more complex figure, with a subtle grasp of the doubleness—both poison and medicine—of the natural world and a thoughtful advocacy of moderation. This advocacy draws on an ancient and powerful critique of extremes in passion, which the play's tragic outcome would seem to endorse.

Yet few readers or spectators come away from *Romeo and Juliet* with the conviction that it would be better to love moderately. The intensity of the lovers' passion seems to have its own compelling, self-justifying force, which quietly brushes away all social obstacles and moralizing warnings: "Think true love acted simple modesty" (3.2.16). And the play's incantatory language of love—braiding together the wildly fanciful and the exquisitely simple—has after four hundred years an unforgettable freshness:

> Come, gentle night; come, loving, black-browed night,
> Give me my Romeo, and when I shall die
> Take him and cut him out in little stars,
> And he will make the face of heaven so fine
> That all the world will be in love with night
> And pay no worship to the garish sun.   (3.2.20–25)

If the society of the play will not tolerate such ecstatic desire, if the contingencies of the ordinary world manage to destroy it, *Romeo and Juliet* offers us the consoling realization that the lovers themselves have all along been in love with night.

Stephen Greenblatt

TEXTUAL NOTE

Romeo and Juliet was first published in quarto in 1597 (Q1). A second edition (Q2), advertised on the title page as "newly corrected, augmented, and amended," was published two years later. Q2 provided copy for a third quarto published in 1609 (Q3), from which in turn was printed another quarto (Q4) and the First Folio (F) text (both in 1623). Since Q3 and Q4, along with the Folio version of the play, all depend on Q2, the complex textual problems posed by *Romeo and Juliet* are focused on the precise nature of Q2 and its relation to the substantially different versions of the play, Q1.

Scholars generally agree that Q1 is a so-called bad quarto, a defective text that derives not from the author's manuscript but from the recollection of actors. Since Elizabethan playing companies usually tried to keep the plays out of print, Q1 would in all likelihood have been an unauthorized and illicit transcript; modern analysis has directed suspicion on the actors who played Romeo and Paris. The title page identifies neither author nor publisher, and the text was evidently not licensed in the Stationers' Register.

Q2 is a fuller, more authoritative text. Certain of its features—inconsistent speech prefixes, "permissive" stage directions (e.g., "Enter three or four Citizens," 1.1.66 stage direction), and the preservation of lines that Shakespeare evidently meant to cross out after revision—indicate that Q2 was set from the author's own rough draft, or "foul papers." The draft appears to have posed difficulties for the printing house, for the compositors seem on a number of occasions to have had difficulty making sense of the manuscript. Moreover, perhaps because a page of the manuscript was missing, one passage in Q2— from 1.2.51 to 1.3.36—is taken directly from Q1. With the exception of this passage, for which Q1 serves as the control text, the text of *Romeo and Juliet* is based on Q2.

SELECTED BIBLIOGRAPHY

Andrews, John F., ed. *"Romeo and Juliet": Critical Essays*. New York: Garland, 1993.

Cartwright, Kent. "Theater and Narrative in *Romeo and Juliet*." *Shakespearean Tragedy and Its Double: The Rhythms of Audience Response*. University Park, Pa.: Pennsylvania State University Press, 1991. 43–88.

Kahn, Coppélia. "Coming of Age in Verona." *The Woman's Part: Feminist Criticism of Shakespeare*. Ed. Carolyn Ruth Swift Lenz, Gayle Greene, and Carol Thomas Neely. Urbana, Ill.: University of Illinois Press, 1983. 171–93.

Kristeva, Julia. "*Romeo and Juliet*: Love-Hatred in the Couple." *Shakespearean Tragedy*. Ed. John Drakakis. Harlow, Essex: Longman Group Limited, 1992. 296–315.

Levenson, Jill L. *Shakespeare in Performance: "Romeo and Juliet."* Manchester: Manchester University Press, 1987.

Levin, Harry. "Form and Formality in *Romeo and Juliet*." *Shakespeare and the Revolution of the Times*. Oxford: Oxford University Press, 1976. 103–20.

Nevo, Ruth. "Tragic Form in *Romeo and Juliet*." *Studies in English Literature* 9 (1969): 241–58.

Porter, Joseph. *Shakespeare's Mercutio: His History and Drama*. Chapel Hill, N.C.: University of North Carolina Press, 1983.

Snow, Edward. "Language and Sexual Difference in *Romeo and Juliet*." *Shakespeare's "Rough Magic": Essays in Honor of C. L. Barber*. Ed. Peter Erickson and Coppélia Kahn. Newark: University of Delaware Press, 1985. 168–92.

Snyder, Susan. "*Romeo and Juliet*: Comedy into Tragedy." *Essays in Criticism* 20 (1970): 391–402.

The Most Excellent and Lamentable Tragedy of Romeo and Juliet

THE PERSONS OF THE PLAY

CHORUS
ROMEO
MONTAGUE, his father
MONTAGUE'S WIFE
BENVOLIO, Montague's nephew
ABRAHAM, Montague's servingman
BALTHASAR, Romeo's man
JULIET
CAPULET, her father
CAPULET'S WIFE
TYBALT, her nephew
His page
PETRUCCIO
CAPULET'S COUSIN
Juliet's NURSE
PETER ⎫
SAMSON ⎬ servingmen of the Capulets
GREGORY ⎭
Other SERVINGMEN
MUSICIANS
Escalus, PRINCE of Verona
MERCUTIO ⎫ his kinsmen
County PARIS ⎭
PAGE to Paris
FRIAR LAURENCE
FRIAR JOHN
An APOTHECARY
CHIEF WATCHMAN
Other CITIZENS OF THE WATCH
Masquers, guests, gentlewomen, followers of the Montague and Capulet factions

Prologue

[*Enter*] CHORUS

CHORUS   Two households, both alike in dignity°   *status*
    In fair Verona, where we lay our scene,
    From ancient grudge break to new mutiny,°   *wrangling*
    Where civil blood makes civil hands unclean.[1]
5   From forth the fatal° loins of these two foes   *ill-fated*
    A pair of star-crossed[2] lovers take their life,
    Whose misadventured° piteous overthrows   *unfortunate*
    Doth with their death bury their parents' strife.

Prologue
1. Where citizens' hands are stained with the blood of their fellow citizens.

2. Thwarted by the adverse influence of the stars appearing at the time of their birth, which controlled their destinies.

The fearful passage of their death-marked love
10   And the continuance of their parents' rage—
Which but their children's end, naught could remove—
Is now the two-hours' traffic° of our stage;   business; movement
The which if you with patient ears attend,
What here shall miss, our toil shall strive to mend.³   [*Exit*]

1.1

Enter SAMSON *and* GREGORY, *of the house of Capulet,*
with swords and bucklers°   small round shields
SAMSON   Gregory, on my word, we'll not carry coals.¹
GREGORY   No, for then we should be colliers.²
SAMSON   I mean an° we be in choler,° we'll draw.°   if / anger / draw swords
GREGORY   Ay, while you live, draw your neck out of collar.°   a noose
5   SAMSON   I strike quickly,° being moved.³   vigorously
GREGORY   But thou art not quickly° moved to strike.   speedily
SAMSON   A dog of the house of Montague moves me.
GREGORY   To move is to stir, and to be valiant is to stand,⁴ there-
fore if thou art moved, thou runn'st away.
10   SAMSON   A dog of that house shall move me to stand. I will take
the wall of⁵ any man or maid of Montague's.
GREGORY   That shows thee a weak slave, for the weakest goes to
the wall.⁶
SAMSON   'Tis true, and therefore women, being the weaker ves-
15   sels,⁷ are ever thrust to the wall;° therefore I will push Mon-   ravished
tague's men from the wall, and thrust his maids to the wall.
GREGORY   The quarrel is between our masters and us their men.
SAMSON   'Tis all one.° I will show myself a tyrant: when I have   the same
fought with the men I will be civil with the maids—I will cut
20   off their heads.
GREGORY   The heads of the maids?
SAMSON   Ay, the heads of the maids, or their maidenheads, take
it in what sense thou wilt.
GREGORY   They must take it in sense° that feel it.   through sensation
25   SAMSON   Me they shall feel while I am able to stand, and 'tis
known I am a pretty piece of flesh.⁸
GREGORY   'Tis well thou art not fish. If thou hadst, thou hadst
been poor-john.⁹
Enter [ABRAHAM *and another servingman*] *of the Mon-*
tagues
Draw thy tool.¹ Here comes of the house of Montagues.
30   SAMSON   My naked weapon is out. Quarrel, I will back thee.
GREGORY   How—turn thy back and run?
SAMSON   Fear me not.²
GREGORY   No, marry³—I fear thee!
SAMSON   Let us take the law of our side. Let them begin.

---

3. *What . . . mind*: The actors will try to rectify whatever
is missing or ill told in the Prologue.
1.1 Location: A street or public place in Verona.
1. We'll not suffer humiliation.
2. Professional coal porters, proverbially sneaky.
3. Being roused to anger.
4. Stand firm against assault. Playing, as with "strike" and
"stir," on sexual arousal.
5. I will assert superiority over. The sidewalk nearest the
wall was cleaner than that nearer the street.
6. Proverbial: The weakest are always pushed aside.

7. Paul's description of women in 1 Peter 3:7.
8. An attractive fellow possessed of an impressive
member.
9. Dried salted hake, appropriate as a taunt because shriv-
eled and cheap. "Neither fish nor flesh" was proverbial
for an uncategorizable oddity.
1. Weapon (and continuing the bawdy wordplay).
2. Do not doubt my fortitude; in the next line, Gregory
takes it in the modern sense of "Do not be afraid of me."
3. By the Virgin Mary, a mild oath with a meaning similar to "indeed."

35   GREGORY I will frown as I pass by, and let them take it as they
list.°   *like*

SAMSON Nay, as they dare. I will bite my thumb at them,[4] which
is disgrace to them if they bear it.
              [*He bites his thumb*]

ABRAHAM Do you bite your thumb at us, sir?

40   SAMSON I do bite my thumb, sir.

ABRAHAM Do you bite your thumb at us, sir?

SAMSON [*to* GREGORY] Is the law of our side if I say 'Ay'?

GREGORY No.

SAMSON [*to* ABRAHAM] No, sir, I do not bite my thumb at you,
45   sir, but I bite my thumb, sir.

GREGORY [*to* ABRAHAM] Do you quarrel, sir?

ABRAHAM Quarrel, sir? No, sir.

SAMSON But if you do, sir, I am for you.[5] I serve as good a man
as you.

50   ABRAHAM No better.

SAMSON Well, sir.
             Enter BENVOLIO

GREGORY Say 'better'. Here comes one of my master's kinsmen.

SAMSON [*to* ABRAHAM] Yes, better, sir.

ABRAHAM You lie.

55   SAMSON Draw, if you be men. Gregory, remember thy washing°   *slashing; violent*
blow.
             They [*draw and*] *fight*

BENVOLIO [*drawing*] Part, fools. Put up your swords. You know
not what you do.
             Enter TYBALT

TYBALT [*drawing*] What, art thou drawn among these heartless
hinds?[6]

60   Turn thee, Benvolio. Look upon thy death.

BENVOLIO I do but keep the peace. Put up thy sword,
Or manage° it to part these men with me.   *wield*

TYBALT What, drawn and talk of peace? I hate the word
As I hate hell, all Montagues, and thee.

65   Have at thee, coward.
             They fight. Enter three or four CITIZENS [OF THE
             WATCH], *with clubs or partisans*°   *broad-tipped spears*

CITIZENS OF THE WATCH Clubs, bills° and partisans! Strike! Beat   *axe-bladed spears*
them down!
Down with the Capulets. Down with the Montagues.
            Enter old CAPULET *in his gown, and his* WIFE

CAPULET What noise is this? Give me my long sword, ho!

CAPULET'S WIFE A crutch, a crutch—why call you for a sword?
            Enter old MONTAGUE [*with his sword drawn*], *and his*
            WIFE

70   CAPULET My sword, I say. Old Montague is come,
And flourishes his blade in spite° of me.   *defiance*

MONTAGUE Thou villain Capulet!
            [*His* WIFE *holds him back*]
                     Hold me not, let me go.

---

4. Flick the thumbnail from behind the upper teeth, an
insulting gesture.
5. I accept your invitation to fight.

6. These cowardly servants, punning on female deer
("hinds") unprotected by a stag ("hart/heart").

MONTAGUE'S WIFE   Thou shalt not stir one foot to seek a foe.

    [*The* CITIZENS OF THE WATCH *attempt to*] *part them.*
    Enter PRINCE *Escalus with his train*

PRINCE   Rebellious subjects, enemies to peace,

75   Profaners of this neighbour-stainèd steel[7] —

    Will they not hear? What ho, you men, you beasts,

    That quench the fire of your pernicious rage

    With purple° fountains issuing from your veins: *crimson*

    On pain of torture, from those bloody hands

80   Throw your mistempered[8] weapons to the ground,

    And hear the sentence of your movèd° Prince.   *furious*

        [MONTAGUE, CAPULET, *and their followers throw*
        down their weapons]

    Three civil brawls bred of an airy° word   *unsubstantial*

    By thee, old Capulet, and Montague,

    Have thrice disturbed the quiet of our streets

85   And made Verona's ancient° citizens   *elderly*

    Cast by° their grave-beseeming ornaments[9]   *Cast away*

    To wield old partisans in hands as old,

    Cankered° with peace, to part your cankered° hate.   *Rusty / malignant*

    If ever you disturb our streets again

90   Your lives shall pay the forfeit° of the peace.   *ransom*

    For this time all the rest depart away.

    You, Capulet, shall go along with me;

    And Montague, come you this afternoon

    To know our farther pleasure in this case

95   To old Freetown,[1] our common judgement-place.

    Once more, on pain of death, all men depart.

        Exeunt [*all but* MONTAGUE,
        his WIFE, *and* BENVOLIO]

MONTAGUE   Who set this ancient quarrel new abroach?°   *open*

    Speak, nephew: were you by when it began?

BENVOLIO   Here were the servants of your adversary

100   And yours, close fighting ere I did approach.

    I drew to part them. In the instant came

    The fiery Tybalt with his sword prepared,

    Which, as he breathed° defiance to my ears,   *uttered*

    He swung about his head and cut the winds

105   Who, nothing hurt withal,° hissed him in scorn.   *by that*

    While we were interchanging thrusts and blows,

    Came more and more, and fought on part and part[2]

    Till the Prince came, who parted either part.

MONTAGUE'S WIFE   O where is Romeo — saw you him today?

110   Right glad I am he was not at this fray.

BENVOLIO   Madam, an hour before the worshipped sun

    Peered forth° the golden window of the east,   *out from*

    A troubled mind drive° me to walk abroad,   *drove*

    Where, underneath the grove of sycamore[3]

115   That westward rooteth° from this city side,   *grows out*

---

7. You who defile weapons with the stains of your neighbors' blood.
8. Badly shaped and hardened, as well as unnecessarily
wrathful by disposition.
9. Attire and symbolic staffs appropriate to grave old age.
Possibly playing on the old men's proximity to the grave.

1. In Brooke's translation from the Italian source, the
Capulet house is called Villa Franca.
2. Fought for one side and the other.
3. Associated with melancholy lovers, who are "sick-
amour."

So early walking did I see your son.
Towards him I made, but he was ware° of me,   *wary*
And stole into the covert° of the wood.   *covering*
I, measuring his affections° by my own—   *inclination*
120 Which then most sought where most might not be found,[4]
Being one too many by my weary self—
Pursued my humour° not pursuing his,   *mood*
And gladly shunned who gladly fled from me.
MONTAGUE Many a morning hath he there been seen,
125 With tears augmenting the fresh morning's dew,
Adding to clouds more clouds with his deep sighs.
But all so soon as the all-cheering sun
Should in the farthest east begin to draw
The shady curtains from Aurora's[5] bed,
130 Away from light steals home my heavy° son,   *melancholy*
And private in his chamber pens himself,
Shuts up his windows, locks fair daylight out,
And makes himself an artificial night.
Black and portentous° must this humour[6] prove,   *ominous (of illness)*
135 Unless good counsel may the cause remove.
BENVOLIO My noble uncle, do you know the cause?
MONTAGUE I neither know it nor can learn of him.
BENVOLIO Have you importuned him by any° means?   *all*
MONTAGUE Both by myself and many other friends,
140 But he, his own affection's counsellor,°   *confidant*
Is to himself—I will not say how true,[7]
But to himself so secret and so close,°   *discreet*
So far from sounding and discovery,°   *fathoming and revelation*
As is the bud bit with an envious worm°   *a spiteful grub (larva)*
145 Ere he can spread his sweet leaves° to the air   *petals*
Or dedicate his beauty to the sun.
Could we but learn from whence his sorrows grow
We would as willingly give cure as know.
    Enter ROMEO
BENVOLIO See where he comes. So please you° step aside, *please you = please*
150 I'll know his grievance or be much denied.
MONTAGUE I would° thou wert so happy° by thy stay   *wish / fortunate*
To hear true shrift.° Come, madam, let's away.   *confession*
     Exeunt [MONTAGUE *and his* WIFE]
BENVOLIO Good morrow, cousin.
ROMEO   Is the day so young?
BENVOLIO But new° struck nine.   *only just*
ROMEO   Ay me, sad hours seem long.
155 Was that my father that went hence so fast?
BENVOLIO It was. What sadness lengthens Romeo's hours?
ROMEO Not having that which, having, makes them short.
BENVOLIO In love.
ROMEO Out.
160 BENVOLIO Of love?
ROMEO Out of her favour where I am in love.

---

4. *where . . . found*: in a place where I was unlikely to have company.
5. Goddess of the dawn in classical legend.
6. "Humors," essential bodily fluids, were considered the basis of human beings' physical and psychological constitution. Too much black bile caused melancholy and a host of illnesses and derangements.
7. Loyal, but also playing on the proverbial wisdom that only one who is "true to him- or herself" can be upstanding in dealing with others.

BENVOLIO   Alas that love, so gentle in his view,°   *appearance*
    Should be so tyrannous and rough in proof.°   *experience*
ROMEO   Alas that love, whose view is muffled still,[8]
165   Should without eyes see pathways to his will.°   *intention; lust*
    Where shall we dine? [*Seeing blood*] O me! What fray was here?
    Yet tell me not, for I have heard it all.
    Here's much to do with hate, but more with love.
    Why then, O brawling love, O loving hate,
170   O anything of nothing first create;[9]
    O heavy lightness, serious vanity,
    Misshapen chaos of well-seeming forms,
    Feather of lead, bright smoke, cold fire, sick health,
    Still-waking° sleep, that is not what it is!   *Always awake*
175   This love feel I, that feel no love in this.
    Dost thou not laugh?
BENVOLIO   No, coz,° I rather weep.   *cousin*
ROMEO   Good heart, at what?
BENVOLIO   At thy good heart's oppression.°   *affliction*
ROMEO   Why, such is love's transgression.
    Griefs of mine own lie heavy in my breast,
180   Which thou wilt propagate° to have it pressed[1]   *multiply*
    With more of thine. This love that thou hast shown
    Doth add more grief to too much of mine own.
    Love is a smoke made with the fume of sighs,
    Being purged,° a fire sparkling in lovers' eyes,   *clarified*
185   Being vexed,° a sea nourished with lovers' tears.   *stirred up*
    What is it else? A madness most discreet,°   *wise*
    A choking gall and a preserving sweet.
    Farewell, my coz.
BENVOLIO   Soft,° I will go along;   *Wait*
    An if° you leave me so, you do me wrong.   *An if = if*
190 ROMEO   Tut, I have lost myself. I am not here.
    This is not Romeo; he's some other where.
BENVOLIO   Tell me in sadness,[2] who is that you love?
ROMEO   What, shall I groan and tell thee?
BENVOLIO   Groan? Why no; but sadly tell me who.
195 ROMEO   Bid a sick man in sadness make his will,
    A word ill urged to one that is so ill.
    In sadness, cousin, I do love a woman.
BENVOLIO   I aimed so near when I supposed you loved.
ROMEO   A right good markman; and she's fair I love.
200 BENVOLIO   A right fair mark,° fair coz, is soonest hit.   *target; vulva*
ROMEO   Well, in that hit you miss. She'll not be hit
    With Cupid's arrow; she hath Dian's wit,[3]
    And, in strong proof° of chastity well armed,° *tested armor / covered*
    From love's weak childish bow she lives unharmed.
205   She will not stay° the siege of loving terms,   *undergo*
    Nor bide th'encounter of assailing eyes,[4]

---

8. Who cannot see. Cupid was often depicted as blind.
9. Inverting the proverb "Nothing can come of nothing" and also recalling the doctrine that God made the world out of nothing. Romeo catalogues the "miraculous" paradoxes of love.
1. Burdened; embraced.

2. Seriousness, although Romeo plays on the sense "melancholy."
3. The scruples and cleverness of Diana, the classical goddess of hunting and chastity.
4. *th'encounter of assailing eyes*: military metaphors for courtship conventionally used in Petrarchan love poetry.

Nor ope her lap to saint-seducing gold.⁵

O, she is rich in beauty, only poor

That when she dies, with beauty dies her store.°   *wealth*

210 BENVOLIO   Then she hath sworn that she will still° live chaste?   *always*

ROMEO   She hath, and in that sparing° makes huge waste;   *refraining; thrift*

For beauty starved with her severity

Cuts beauty off from all posterity.⁶

She is too fair, too wise, wisely too fair,°   *just*

215 To merit bliss° by making me despair.⁷   *heaven's blessing*

She hath forsworn to love, and in that vow

Do I live dead, that live to tell it now.

BENVOLIO   Be ruled by me; forget to think of her.

ROMEO   O, teach me how I should forget to think!

220 BENVOLIO   By giving liberty unto thine eyes.

Examine other beauties.

ROMEO   'Tis the way

To call hers, exquisite, in question more.⁸

These happy masks that kiss fair ladies' brows,

Being black, puts us in mind they hide the fair.

225 He that is strucken blind cannot forget

The precious treasure of his eyesight lost.

Show me a mistress that is passing° fair,   *surpassingly*

What doth her beauty serve but as a note

Where I may read who passed that passing fair?

230 Farewell, thou canst not teach me to forget.

BENVOLIO   I'll pay° that doctrine, or else die in debt.⁹   *Exeunt*   *impart*

1.2

Enter old CAPULET, *County* PARIS, *and the Clown*

[PETER, *a servingman*]

CAPULET   But Montague is bound° as well as I,   *under oath*

In penalty alike, and 'tis not hard, I think,

For men so old as we to keep the peace.

PARIS   Of honourable reckoning¹ are you both,

5 And pity 'tis you lived at odds so long.

But now, my lord: what say you to my suit?

CAPULET   But saying o'er what I have said before.

My child is yet a stranger in the world;

She hath not seen the change of fourteen years.

10 Let two more summers wither in their pride

Ere we may think her ripe to be a bride.

PARIS   Younger than she are happy mothers made.

CAPULET   And too soon marred are those so early made.²

But woo her, gentle Paris, get her heart;

15 My will to her consent is but a part,

And, she agreed, within her scope of choice

Lies my consent and fair-according voice.

This night I hold an old-accustomed feast

---

5. To golden gifts that are irresistibly persuasive. Also, in classical legend, Jupiter descended upon Danae as a shower of gold.
6. *For . . . posterity*: Since she will not have children, her beauty will die with her. *starved*: killed.
7. Despair of salvation, a grave sin.
8. *in question more*: more intensely to mind.
9. Die whatever the cost to me; die still owing you the doctrine of forgetfulness.
1.2 Location: A street or plaza in Verona.
1. Repute, with a play on "accounting."
2. Q2 includes two more lines following line 13, probably rejected by Shakespeare in the writing process: "Earth hath swallowed all my hopes but she, / She's the hopeful Lady of my earth" (*earth*: body).

Whereto I have invited many a guest
20   Such as I love, and you among the store,
One more most welcome, makes my number more.
At my poor house look to behold this night
Earth-treading stars that make dark heaven light.
Such comfort as do lusty young men feel
25   When well-apparelled April on the heel
Of limping winter treads—even such delight
Among fresh female buds shall you this night
Inherit° at my house; hear all, all see,   *Enjoy*
And like her most whose merit most shall be,
30   Which on more view of many, mine, being one,
May stand in number, though in reck'ning none.[3]
Come, go with me. [*Giving* PETER *a paper*] Go, sirrah,° trudge   *(address to an inferior)*
    about;
Through fair Verona find those persons out
Whose names are written there, and to them say
35   My house and welcome on their pleasure stay.°   *wait*
                Exeunt [CAPULET *and* PARIS]
PETER   Find them out whose names are written here? It is writ-
    ten that the shoemaker should meddle with his yard° and the   *yardstick*
    tailor with his last,° the fisher with his pencil° and the painter   *shoe form / paintbrush*
    with his nets; but I am sent to find those persons whose names
40   are here writ, and can never find° what names the writing per-   *figure out*
    son hath here writ. I must to the learned.
           Enter BENVOLIO *and* ROMEO
    In good time.
BENVOLIO [*to* ROMEO]   Tut, man, one fire burns out another's burning,
    One pain is lessened by another's anguish.
45   Turn giddy,° and be holp° by backward turning.   *Turn until dizzy / helped*
    One desperate grief cures with another's languish.[4]
Take thou some new infection[5] to thy eye,
And the rank poison of the old will die.
ROMEO   Your plantain leaf[6] is excellent for that.
50   BENVOLIO   For what, I pray thee?
ROMEO   For your broken° shin.   *gashed*
BENVOLIO   Why, Romeo, art thou mad?
ROMEO   Not mad, but bound more than a madman is;
    Shut up in prison, kept without my food,
    Whipped and tormented and— [*to* PETER] Good e'en,° good   *evening (afternoon)*
55   fellow.
PETER   God gi'good e'en. I pray, sir, can you read?
ROMEO   Ay, mine own fortune in my misery.[7]
PETER   Perhaps you have learned it without book.[8] But I pray,
    can you read anything you see?
60   ROMEO   Ay, if I know the letters and the language.
PETER   Ye say honestly. Rest you merry.[9]
ROMEO   Stay, fellow, I can read.
        He reads the letter

3. *Which . . . none:* Which may make a part of the gorgeous display, but be of no account by herself. "One" was
proverbially "no number."
4. Is displaced by the languishing pain of a new grief.
5. New object of passion, which causes a distortion of
sight in the lover.
6. The ordinary plaintain leaf, used to dress wounds or

bruises and thought to have curative powers.
7. Romeo takes "read" to mean "understand."
8. *without book:* from memory or by ear, as well as
through experience rather than education.
9. A farewell. Peter takes Romeo to mean "If only I knew
the letters and the language."

'Signor Martino and his wife and daughters,
County° Anselme and his beauteous sisters,   *Count*
65 The lady widow of Vitruvio,
Signor Placentio and his lovely nieces,
Mercutio and his brother Valentine,
Mine uncle Capulet, his wife and daughters,
My fair niece Rosaline and Livia,
70 Signor Valentio and his cousin Tybalt,
Lucio and the lively Helena.'
A fair assembly. Whither should they come?
PETER   Up.[1]
ROMEO   Whither?
75 PETER   To supper to our house.
ROMEO   Whose house?
PETER   My master's.
ROMEO   Indeed, I should have asked thee that before.
PETER   Now I'll tell you without asking. My master is the great
80 rich Capulet, and if you be not of the house of Montagues, I
pray come and crush° a cup of wine. Rest you merry.   *Exit*   *drink*
BENVOLIO   At this same ancient° feast of Capulet's   *traditional*
Sups the fair Rosaline, whom thou so loves,
With all the admirèd beauties of Verona.
85 Go thither, and with unattainted° eye   *innocent*
Compare her face with some that I shall show,
And I will make thee think thy swan a crow.
ROMEO   When the devout religion° of mine eye   *pious belief*
Maintains such falsehood, then turn tears to fires;
90 And these° who, often drowned, could never die,   *these eyes*
Transparent° heretics, be burnt for liars.   *Obvious; self-evident*
One fairer than my love!—the all-seeing sun
Ne'er saw her match since first the world begun.
BENVOLIO   Tut, you saw her fair, none else being by,
95 Herself poised° with herself in either eye;   *balanced against*
But in that crystal scales let there be weighed
Your lady's love against some other maid
That I will show you shining at this feast,
And she shall scant show well that now seems best.
100 ROMEO   I'll go along, no such sight to be shown,
But to rejoice in splendour of mine own.   *[Exeunt]*

1.3

Enter CAPULET'S WIFE *and* NURSE
CAPULET'S WIFE   Nurse, where's my daughter? Call her forth to me.
NURSE   Now, by my maidenhead at twelve year old,[1]
I bade her come. What,[2] lamb, what, ladybird—
God forbid[3]—where is this girl? What, Juliet!
Enter JULIET
5 JULIET   How now, who calls?
NURSE   Your mother.
JULIET   Madam, I am here. What is your will?

---

1. "Come up" is a phrase expressing scorn.
1.3 Location: Capulet's house.
1. Presumably the latest date that the Nurse could swear by her virginity.

2. An expression of impatience.
3. Either an apology for the promiscuous connotation of "ladybird" or fearing something amiss in Juliet's absence.

CAPULET'S WIFE This is the matter.—Nurse, give leave° a while.   *excuse us*
    We must talk in secret.—Nurse, come back again.
10 I have remembered me, thou's° hear our counsel.°   *you shall / secrets*
    Thou knowest my daughter's of a pretty age.
NURSE Faith, I can tell her age unto an hour.
CAPULET'S WIFE She's not fourteen.
NURSE I'll lay fourteen of my teeth—and yet, to my teen° be it   *sorrow*
15 spoken, I have but four—she's not fourteen. How long is it now
    to Lammastide?[4]
CAPULET'S WIFE A fortnight and odd days.
NURSE Even or odd, of all days in the year
    Come Lammas Eve at night shall she be fourteen.
20 Susan[5] and she—God rest all Christian souls!—
    Were of an age. Well, Susan is with God;
    She was too good for me. But, as I said,
    On Lammas Eve at night shall she be fourteen,
    That shall she, marry, I remember it well.
25 'Tis since the earthquake now eleven years,
    And she was weaned—I never shall forget it—
    Of all the days of the year upon that day,
    For I had then laid wormwood[6] to my dug,°   *on my breast*
    Sitting in the sun under the dovehouse wall.
30 My lord and you were then at Mantua.
    Nay, I do bear a brain!° But, as I said,   *memory*
    When it did taste the wormwood on the nipple
    Of my dug and felt it bitter, pretty fool,°   *(an endearment)*
    To see it tetchy° and fall out wi'th' dug!   *peevish*
35 'Shake', quoth the dove-house![7] 'Twas no need, I trow,
    To bid me trudge;°   *remove myself*
    And since that time it is eleven years,
    For then she could stand high-lone.° Nay, by th' rood,°   *upright alone / cross*
    She could have run and waddled all about,
40 For even the day before, she broke her brow,°   *cut her forehead*
    And then my husband—God be with his soul,
    A° was a merry man!—took up the child.   *He*
    'Yea,' quoth he, 'dost thou fall upon thy face?
    Thou wilt fall backward when thou hast more wit,°   *knowledge*
45 Wilt thou not, Jule?' And, by my halidom,°   *holiness; holy relic*
    The pretty wretch left° crying and said 'Ay'.   *stopped*
    To see now how a jest shall come about!°   *come true*
    I warrant an° I should live a thousand years   *if*
    I never should forget it. 'Wilt thou not, Jule?' quoth he,
50 And, pretty fool, it stinted° and said 'Ay'.   *she ceased*
CAPULET'S WIFE Enough of this. I pray thee hold thy peace.
NURSE Yes, madam. Yet I cannot choose but laugh
    To think it should leave crying and say 'Ay'.
    And yet, I warrant,° it had upon it° brow   *assure you / its*
55 A bump as big as a young cock'rel's stone.°   *rooster's testicle*
    A perilous knock, and it cried bitterly.
    'Yea,' quoth my husband, 'fall'st upon thy face?

---

4. August 1, originally celebrated by the church as a harvest festival.
5. The Nurse evidently suckled Juliet after her own daughter died.
6. A proverbially bitter plant extract.
7. The dove house shook with the earthquake.

Thou wilt fall backward when thou com'st to age,
Wilt thou not, Jule?' It stinted and said 'Ay'.
60 JULIET And stint thou too, I pray thee, Nurse, say I.
NURSE Peace, I have done. God mark° thee to his grace,   elect
Thou wast the prettiest babe that e'er I nursed.
An I might live to see thee married once,°   one day
I have my wish.
65 CAPULET'S WIFE Marry, that 'marry' is the very theme
I came to talk of. Tell me, daughter Juliet,
How stands your dispositions to be married?
JULIET It is an honour that I dream not of.
NURSE 'An honour'! Were not I thine only nurse,
70 I would say thou hadst sucked wisdom from thy teat.⁸
CAPULET'S WIFE Well, think of marriage now. Younger than you
Here in Verona, ladies of esteem,
Are made already mothers. By my count
I was your mother much upon these years
75 That you are now a maid. Thus then, in brief:
The valiant Paris seeks you for his love.
NURSE A man, young lady, lady, such a man
As all the world—why, he's a man of wax.⁹
CAPULET'S WIFE Verona's summer hath not such a flower.
80 NURSE Nay, he's a flower, in faith, a very flower.
CAPULET'S WIFE [to JULIET] What say you? Can you love the gentleman?
This night you shall behold him at our feast.
Read o'er the volume of young Paris' face,
And find delight writ there with beauty's pen.
85 Examine every married lineament,¹
And see how one° another lends content;²   one to
And what obscured in this fair volume lies
Find written in the margin³ of his eyes.
This precious book of love, this unbound° lover,   single; unrestrained
90 To beautify him only lacks a cover.
The fish lives in the sea, and 'tis much pride
For fair without the fair within to hide.⁴
That book in many's eyes doth share the glory
That in gold clasps locks in the golden story.⁵
95 So shall you share all that he doth possess
By having him, making yourself no less.
NURSE No less, nay, bigger. Women grow° by men.   swell with child
CAPULET'S WIFE [to JULIET] Speak briefly: can you like of Paris' love?
JULIET I'll look° to like, if looking liking move;   expect; examine
100 But no more deep will I endart⁶ mine eye
Than your consent gives strength to make it fly.
          Enter a servingman [PETER]
PETER Madam, the guests are come, supper served up, you
    called, my young lady asked for, the Nurse cursed in the pantry,
    and everything in extremity.° I must hence to wait.° I beseech   a terrible state / serve
105 you follow straight.°   immediately

8. From the teat that nourished you.
9. Model of perfection, as if sculpted rather than born.
1. Harmoniously composed feature; a joined line of flowing handwriting.
2. Completion; meaning.
3. Glosses to difficult passages of text were set in the margin.

4. For a lovely setting (Juliet) to frame and enrich the fair Paris.
5. *That book . . . story:* Many judge the book by the cover and fittings, such as the clasps that fasten a large volume. The speech thoroughly confuses who is covering whom.
6. Sink itself like an arrow into its target; shoot glances that, like Cupid's arrows, inflame his passions.

CAPULET'S WIFE　We follow thee.　　*Exit a servingman* [PETER]
　　　　　　　　Juliet, the County stays.°　　　　　　*the Count awaits*
NURSE　Go, girl; seek happy nights to° happy days.　　*Exeunt*　　*at the end of*

1.4

Enter ROMEO, MERCUTIO, *and* BENVOLIO, [*as masquers,*]
with five or six other masquers[1] [*bearing a drum and
torches*]

ROMEO　What, shall this speech° be spoke for our excuse,　　*prologue*
　　　Or shall we on without apology?
BENVOLIO　The date is out of° such prolixity.　　　　　*past for*
　　　We'll have no Cupid hoodwinked[2] with a scarf,
5　　Bearing a Tartar's painted bow of lath,[3]
　　　Scaring the ladies like a crowkeeper,°　　　　　*scarecrow*
　　　Nor no without-book° Prologue faintly spoke　　　*memorized*
　　　After° the prompter for our entrance.　　　　　　*Repeating after*
　　　But let them measure° us by what they will,　　　*judge*
10　　We'll measure° them a measure,° and be gone.　　*apportion / dance*
ROMEO　Give me a torch. I am not for this ambling;°　　*dancing*
　　　Being but heavy,° I will bear the light.　　　　*melancholy*
MERCUTIO　Nay, gentle° Romeo, we must have you dance.　*noble; softhearted*
ROMEO　Not I, believe me. You have dancing shoes
15　　With nimble soles; I have a soul of lead
　　　So stakes me to the ground I cannot move.
MERCUTIO　You are a lover; borrow Cupid's wings,
　　　And soar with them above a common bound.[4]
ROMEO　I am too sore° empiercèd with his shaft　　　　*deeply*
20　　To soar with his light° feathers, and so bound　　*cheery; agile; wanton*
　　　I cannot bound a pitch[5] above dull woe;
　　　Under love's heavy burden do I sink.
MERCUTIO　And to sink in it should you burden love—
　　　Too great oppression for a tender thing.[6]
25　ROMEO　Is love a tender thing? It is too rough,
　　　Too rude, too boist'rous, and it pricks like thorn.
MERCUTIO　If love be rough with you, be rough with love.
　　　Prick° love for pricking, and you beat love down.[7]　　*Stab; sexually penetrate*
　　　Give me a case[8] to put my visage in,
30　　A visor for a visor.[9] What care I
　　　What curious eye doth quote° deformity?　　　　*notice*
　　　Here are the beetle brows° shall blush for me.　　*protruding eyebrows*
　　　　[*They put on visors*]
BENVOLIO　Come, knock and enter, and no sooner in
　　　But every man betake him to his legs.°　　　　*to dancing; to flight*
35　ROMEO　A torch for me. Let wantons light of heart
　　　Tickle the sense-less rushes° with their heels,　　*floor matting*
　　　For I am proverbed with a grandsire° phrase.　　*an ancient*

1.4 Location: Before Capulet's house.
1. Performers or participants in an aristocratic masked entertainment, consisting of dances and sometimes dumb shows and set speeches.
2. Blindfolded and foolish Cupid, a typical costume for the presenter of the masque's theme.
3. Short bow shaped like the upper lip, made of the thin wood used for theatrical properties.
4. A normal limit; an average dancer's leap; possibly, a constrained plebian.

5. Height from which a hawk stoops to kill.
6. Suggesting a pudendum. "Love" can also be taken as "lover."
7. *Prick . . . down:* Playing on the sense "satiate desire by fulfilling it."
8. Literally, "mask," but also slang for the vagina. The bawdy joke turns into a different play on words in this line.
9. Mask for an ugly face. Proverbial. "A well-favored visor to hide an ill-favored face."

I'll be a candle-holder and look on.[1]
The game was ne'er so fair, and I am done.[2]
                    [*He takes a torch*]

40   MERCUTIO   Tut, dun's the mouse,[3] the constable's own word.°   *phrase*
        If thou art dun we'll draw thee from the mire[4]
        Of—save your reverence[5]—love, wherein thou stickest
        Up to the ears. Come, we burn daylight,° ho!   *waste time*
      ROMEO   Nay, that's not so.
      MERCUTIO   I mean, sir, in delay
45   We waste our lights in vain, like lights by day.
        Take our good meaning, for our judgement sits
        Five times in that ere once in our five wits.[6]
      ROMEO   And we mean° well in going to this masque,   *intend*
        But 'tis no wit° to go.   *intelligence*
      MERCUTIO   Why, may one ask?
      ROMEO   I dreamt a dream tonight.°   *last night*
50   MERCUTIO   And so did I.
      ROMEO   Well, what was yours?
      MERCUTIO   That dreamers often lie.
      ROMEO   In bed asleep while they do dream things true.
      MERCUTIO   O, then I see Queen Mab[7] hath been with you.
      BENVOLIO   Queen Mab, what's she?
55   MERCUTIO   She is the fairies' midwife, and she comes
        In shape no bigger than an agate stone[8]
        On the forefinger of an alderman,
        Drawn with a team of little atomi°   *dust motes*
        Athwart men's noses as they lie asleep.
60   Her wagon spokes made of long spinners'° legs;   *spiders'*
        The cover, of the wings of grasshoppers;
        Her traces, of the moonshine's wat'ry beams;
        Her collars, of the smallest spider web;
        Her whip, of cricket's bone, the lash of film;°   *spider's-web thread*
65   Her wagoner,° a small grey-coated gnat   *driver*
        Not half so big as a round little worm
        Pricked from the lazy finger of a maid.[9]
        Her chariot is an empty hazelnut
        Made by the joiner° squirrel or old grub,[1]   *carpenter*
70   Time out o' mind the fairies' coachmakers.
        And in this state° she gallops night by night   *regal finery*
        Through lovers' brains, and then they dream of love;
        O'er courtiers' knees, that dream on curtsies straight;[2]
        O'er ladies' lips, who straight on kisses dream,
75   Which oft the angry Mab with blisters plagues
        Because their breaths with sweetmeats° tainted are.   *candies*
        Sometime she gallops o'er a lawyer's lip,

1. Proverbial: "A good candleholder proves a good game-ster. A spectator loses nothing."
2. Proverbial: "When play is best, it is time to leave."
3. Keep silent and unseen.
4. In the Christmas game "Dun is in the mire," players pantomimed drawing a log representing a horse out of a boggy road. Mercutio is suggesting that Romeo is a stick-in-the-mud.
5. An apology for crude language, here used mockingly.
6. *Take . . . wits:* Understand my intended good meaning using your common sense ("judgement") rather than excessive wit or the five senses.

7. Possibly Celtic, but probably Shakespeare's invention. "Quean" meant "whore," and "Mab" was a stereotypical name for prostitutes.
8. A small human figure was often carved on agate stones set in seal rings.
9. According to popular belief, worms generated in idle girls' fingers.
1. Grubs bore holes. Lines 68–70, from Q1, do not appear in Q2 at all; numerous other changes in the order and wording of his speech suggest that Q1 incorporated revisions that Q2 and later revisions did not.
2. Dream of respectful bows immediately.

And then dreams he of smelling out a suit;[3]
And sometime comes she with a tithe-pig's[4] tail
80 Tickling a parson's nose as a° lies asleep;   *he*
Then dreams he of another benefice.
Sometime she driveth o'er a soldier's neck,
And then dreams he of cutting foreign throats,
Of breaches, ambuscados, Spanish blades,[5]
85 Of healths five fathom deep;[6] and then anon°   *soon*
Drums in his ear, at which he starts and wakes,
And being thus frighted, swears a prayer or two,
And sleeps again. This is that very Mab
That plaits° the manes of horses in the night,   *entangles*
90 And bakes the elf-locks[7] in foul sluttish° hairs,   *dirty*
Which once untangled much misfortune bodes.
This is the hag, when maids lie on their backs,
That presses them[8] and learns° them first to bear,   *teaches*
Making them women of good carriage.[9]
This is she —
95 ROMEO   Peace, peace, Mercutio, peace!
Thou talk'st of nothing.°   *imaginings; a vagina*
MERCUTIO   True. I talk of dreams,
Which are the children of an idle brain,
Begot of nothing but vain fantasy,°   *empty imagination*
Which is as thin of substance as the air,
100 And more inconstant than the wind, who woos
Even now the frozen bosom of the north,
And, being angered, puffs away from thence,
Turning his face to the dew-dropping south.
BENVOLIO   This wind you talk of blows us from ourselves.
105 Supper is done, and we shall come too late.
ROMEO   I fear too early, for my mind misgives°   *fears*
Some consequence yet hanging in the stars
Shall bitterly begin his fearful date°   *period*
With this night's revels, and expire° the term   *finish*
110 Of a despisèd life, closed in my breast,
By some vile forfeit of untimely death.[1]
But he° that hath the steerage of my course   *(God)*
Direct my sail! On, lusty gentlemen.
BENVOLIO   Strike, drum.
They march about the stage and [exeunt]

1.5

[PETER and other SERVINGMEN] come forth with napkins
PETER Where's Potpan, that he helps not to take away? He shift
a trencher,° he scrape a trencher!   *wooden plate*
FIRST SERVINGMAN When good manners shall lie all in one or
two men's hands, and they unwashed too, 'tis a foul° thing.   *bad; dirty*

3. A petition at court, which the lawyer could facilitate for a fee.
4. Pig paid as a tithe to the parish for the support of the priest.
5. *breaches:* burst fortifications. *ambuscados:* ambushes. *Spanish blades:* swords made in Toledo were famous for their quality.
6. Fantastically deep cups of liquor.
7. And hardens the tangles. According to folk legend, unknotting them would anger the malicious elves.
8. Evil spirits were supposed to be responsible for erotic dreams, taking the form of an illusory sexual partner.
9. Excellent deportment; the capacity for carrying the weight of a lover; childbearing.
1. As fate prematurely foreclosing on a mortgaged life.
1.5 Location: Capulet's house.

5 PETER   Away with the joint-stools,[1] remove the court-cupboard,°   *sideboard*
look to the plate.° Good thou, save me a piece of marzipan,   *silverware*
and, as thou loves me, let the porter let in Susan Grindstone
and Nell. Anthony and Potpan!
SECOND SERVINGMAN   Ay, boy, ready.
10 PETER   You are looked for and called for, asked for and sought
for, in the great chamber.
FIRST SERVINGMAN   We cannot be here and there too. Cheerly,
boys! Be brisk a while, and the longest liver take all.[2]
        [*They come and go, setting forth tables and chairs*]
        Enter old CAPULET [*and family and*] *all the guests and*
        gentlewomen to the masquers
CAPULET [*to the masquers*]   Welcome, gentlemen. Ladies that
        have their toes
15 Unplagued with corns will walk a bout° with you.   *dance a turn*
Aha, my mistresses, which of you all
Will now deny to dance? She that makes dainty,°   *coyly demurs*
She, I'll swear, hath corns. Am I come near ye now?[3]
Welcome, gentlemen. I have seen the day
20 That I have worn a visor, and could tell
A whispering tale in a fair lady's ear
Such as would please. 'Tis gone, 'tis gone, 'tis gone.
You are welcome, gentlemen. Come, musicians, play.
        Music plays, and they dance. [ROMEO *stands apart*]
A hall,[4] a hall! Give room, and foot it, girls.
25 [*To* SERVINGMEN] More light, you knaves, and turn the tables up,[5]
And quench the fire, the room is grown too hot.
[*To his* COUSIN] Ah sirrah, this unlooked-for° sport comes well.   *unexpected*
Nay, sit, nay, sit, good cousin° Capulet,   *kinsman*
For you and I are past our dancing days.
        [CAPULET *and his* COUSIN *sit*]
30 How long is't now since last yourself and I
Were in a masque?
CAPULET'S COUSIN   By'r Lady, thirty years.
CAPULET   What, man, 'tis not so much, 'tis not so much.
'Tis since the nuptial of Lucentio,
Come Pentecost[6] as quickly as it will,
35 Some five-and-twenty years; and then we masqued.
CAPULET'S COUSIN   'Tis more, 'tis more. His son is elder, sir.
His son is thirty.
CAPULET   Will you tell me that?
His son was but a ward[7] two years ago.
ROMEO [*to a* SERVINGMAN]   What lady's that which doth enrich the hand
Of yonder knight?
40 SERVINGMAN   I know not, sir.
ROMEO   O, she doth teach the torches to burn bright!
It seems she hangs upon the cheek of night
As a rich jewel in an Ethiope's ear—
Beauty too rich for use, for earth too dear.[8]

---

1. Stools made by a furniture maker, commonly used for
seating at large banquets.
2. Proverbial, meaning "Life is short."
3. Does that strike home?
4. Make space in the hall.
5. Dismantle and stack the trestle tables.

6. The seventh Sunday after Easter, a standard reference
point in the medieval and Renaissance calendar.
7. Subject to a guardian; a minor.
8. Too precious for this world; too valuable to die and be
buried in earth.

45 So shows a snowy dove trooping° with crows   *flocking*
    As yonder lady o'er her fellows shows.
    The measure° done, I'll watch her place of stand,°   *dance / standing*
    And, touching hers, make blessèd my rude hand.
    Did my heart love till now? Forswear it, sight,
50 For I ne'er saw true beauty till this night.
  TYBALT   This, by his voice, should be a Montague.
    Fetch me my rapier, boy.   [*Exit page*]
                   What, dares the slave
    Come hither, covered with an antic face,[9]
    To fleer° and scorn at our solemnity?°   *sneer / festivity*
55 Now, by the stock and honour of my kin,
    To strike him dead I hold it not a sin.
  CAPULET [*standing*]   Why, how now, kinsman? Wherefore storm you so?
  TYBALT   Uncle, this is a Montague, our foe,
    A villain° that is hither come in spite   *An ill-doer; a slave*
60 To scorn at our solemnity this night.
  CAPULET   Young Romeo, is it?
  TYBALT   'Tis he, that villain Romeo.
  CAPULET   Content° thee, gentle coz, let him alone.   *Calm*
    A bears him like a portly° gentleman,   *dignified*
    And, to say truth, Verona brags of him
65 To be a virtuous and well-governed° youth.   *upstanding*
    I would not for the wealth of all this town
    Here in my house do him disparagement.
    Therefore be patient, take no note of him.
    It is my will, the which if thou respect,
70 Show a fair presence° and put off these frowns,   *demeanor*
    An ill-beseeming semblance° for a feast.   *expression*
  TYBALT   It fits when such a villain is a guest.
    I'll not endure him.
  CAPULET   He shall be endured.
    What, goodman[1] boy, I say he shall. Go to,[2]
75 Am I the master here or you? Go to—
    You'll not endure him! God shall mend my soul.
    You'll make a mutiny° among my guests,   *brawl*
    You will set cock-a-hoop![3] You'll be the man!
  TYBALT   Why, uncle, 'tis a shame.
  CAPULET   Go to, go to,
80 You are a saucy boy. Is't so, indeed?
    This trick° may chance to scathe° you. I know what,[4]   *stupidity / harm*
    You must contrary me. Marry, 'tis time[5]—
        [*A dance ends.* JULIET *retires to her place of stand, where*
        ROMEO *awaits her*]
    [*To the guests*] Well said,° my hearts! [*To* TYBALT] You are a   *done*
       princox,° go.   *cheeky boy*
    Be quiet, or— [*to* SERVINGMEN] more light, more light!— [*to*
       TYBALT] for shame,
85 I'll make you quiet. [*To the guests*] What, cheerly, my hearts!
       [*The music plays again, and the guests dance*]

---

9. A grotesque mask; a playful mask.
1. Courtesy title applied to a commoner (and thus an insult to the noble Tybalt).
2. An expression of impatience.
3. You will abandon restraint, like a drinker who removes the tap ("cock") from the barrel or like a boastfully crowing rooster.
4. Know what I'll do; mean what I say.
5. Time to teach you a lesson; time that you became obedient.

TYBALT Patience perforce° with wilful choler° meeting   *enforced / rash anger*
    Makes my flesh tremble in their different° greeting.   *hostile*
    I will withdraw, but this intrusion shall,
    Now seeming sweet, convert to bitt'rest gall.   *Exit*
90 ROMEO *[to* JULIET, *touching her hand]*   If I profane with my unworthiest hand[6]
    This holy shrine, the gentler sin is this:
    My lips, two blushing pilgrims,[7] ready stand
    To smooth that rough touch with a tender kiss.
    JULIET   Good pilgrim, you do wrong your hand too much,
95   Which mannerly° devotion shows in this.   *seemly*
    For saints[8] have hands that pilgrims' hands do touch,
    And palm to palm is holy palmers'° kiss.   *pilgrims'*
    ROMEO   Have not saints lips, and holy palmers, too?
    JULIET   Ay, pilgrim, lips that they must use in prayer.
100 ROMEO   O then, dear saint, let lips do what hands do:
    They pray; grant thou, lest faith turn to despair.
    JULIET   Saints do not move, though grant for prayers' sake.[9]
    ROMEO   Then move not while my prayer's effect I take.
    [He kisses her]
    Thus from my lips, by thine my sin is purged.
105 JULIET   Then have my lips the sin that they have took.
    ROMEO   Sin from my lips? O trespass sweetly urged![1]
    Give me my sin again.°   *back*
    [He kisses her]
    JULIET   You kiss by th' book.[2]
    NURSE   Madam, your mother craves a word with you.
    *[*JULIET *departs to her mother]*
    ROMEO   What is her mother?
    NURSE   Marry, bachelor,°   *young man*
110   Her mother is the lady of the house,
    And a good lady, and a wise and virtuous.
    I nursed her daughter that you talked withal.°   *with*
    I tell you, he that can lay hold of her
    Shall have the chinks.°   *plenty of coins*
    ROMEO *[aside]*   Is she a Capulet?
115   O dear account!° My life is my foe's debt.[3]   *costly reckoning*
    BENVOLIO   Away, be gone, the sport is at the best.
    ROMEO   Ay, so I fear, the more is my unrest.
    CAPULET   Nay, gentlemen, prepare not to be gone.
    We have a trifling foolish banquet towards.[4]
    [They whisper in his ear]
120   Is it e'en so? Why then, I thank you all.
    I thank you, honest gentlemen. Good night.
    More torches here! Come on then, let's to bed.
    [To his COUSIN*]* Ah, sirrah, by my fay,° it waxes late.   *faith*
    I'll to my rest.

---

6. Romeo and Juliet here address each other in the form of a sonnet.
7. Florio's *World of Words* (1598) translates the Italian word *romeo* as "wanderer" or "palmer" (pilgrim to the Holy Land).
8. Statues or pictures of saints, which attracted Catholic pilgrims. The Elizabethan Anglican church held that the worship of such images was blasphemy; in English terms, therefore, Romeo is describing his love as a kind of idolatry.

9. Again identifying the saint with her image. As a statue she does not move, but as a saint in heaven she can intercede with God on behalf of the worshipper.
1. Sweetly argued that the first kiss was a transgression, and sweetly advocated that the transgression of a second kiss is needed to take the sin of the first away.
2. According to the rules; implies "proficiently," "politely," or "with poetic flatteries."
3. A debt owing to my foe; in the power of my foe.
4. A trifling, paltry dessert coming.

Exeunt [CAPULET, *his* WIFE, *and his* COUSIN. *The*
guests, gentlewomen, masquers, musicians, and
servingmen begin to leave]

125 JULIET Come hither, Nurse. What is yon gentleman?
NURSE The son and heir of old Tiberio.
JULIET What's he that now is going out of door?
NURSE Marry, that, I think, be young Petruccio.
JULIET What's he that follows here, that would not dance?
130 NURSE I know not.
JULIET Go ask his name.
[NURSE *goes*]
If he be marrièd,
My grave is like° to be my wedding bed.   *likely*
NURSE [*returning*]   His name is Romeo, and a Montague,
The only son of your great enemy.
135 JULIET [*aside*]   My only love sprung from my only hate!
Too early seen unknown, and known too late!
Prodigious° birth of love it is to me   *Monstrous; ominous*
That I must love a loathèd enemy.
NURSE What's tis?° what's tis?   *this*
JULIET   A rhyme I learnt even now
Of one I danced withal.
One calls within 'Juliet!'
140 NURSE   Anon,° anon.   *Right away*
Come, let's away. The strangers all are gone.   *Exeunt*

2.0

[*Enter*] CHORUS
CHORUS   Now old° desire doth in his deathbed lie,   *Romeo's former*
And young affection gapes° to be his heir.   *longs*
That fair for which love groaned for and would die,
With tender Juliet matched,° is now not fair.   *compared*
5   Now Romeo is beloved and loves again,°   *in return; once more*
Alike bewitchèd by the charm of looks;[1]
But to his foe supposed° he must complain,[2]   *presumed*
And she steal love's sweet bait from fearful° hooks.   *fearsome*
Being held a foe, he may not have access
10   To breathe such vows as lovers use° to swear,   *are accustomed*
And she as much in love, her means much less
To meet her new belovèd anywhere.
But passion lends them power, time means, to meet,
Temp'ring extremities° with extreme sweet.   [*Exit*]   *Modifying dangers*

2.1

Enter ROMEO *alone*[1]
ROMEO   Can I go forward when my heart is here?
Turn back, dull earth,[2] and find thy centre[3] out.
[*He turns back and withdraws.*]
Enter BENVOLIO *with* MERCUTIO

2.0
1. Appearances; desirous glances.
2. Conventionally, make lovesick speeches.
2.1 Location: Outside Capulet's house.
1. The main stage represents the area outside the wall of
Capulet's orchard and then the inside of the orchard
below the window of Juliet's room. Romeo is imagined to

leap over the garden wall when he withdraws at line 2.
2. Romeo's flesh, drawing on two traditional views of the
human body: animated dust or clay, and a "microcosm,"
or little world, which mirrors the order of the universe.
Earth was the most sluggish and immobile element.
3. The point in the earth toward which everything falls;
or Romeo's heart (metaphorically, Juliet).

BENVOLIO [*calling*]   Romeo, my cousin Romeo, Romeo!

MERCUTIO   He is wise, and, on my life, hath stol'n him° home to bed.   *himself*

5   BENVOLIO   He ran this way, and leapt this orchard wall.
Call, good Mercutio.

MERCUTIO   Nay, I'll conjure° too.   *summon as a spirit*
Romeo! Humours![4] Madman! Passion! Lover!
Appear thou in the likeness of a sigh.
Speak but one rhyme and I am satisfied.

10   Cry but 'Ay me!' Pronounce but 'love' and 'dove'.
Speak to my gossip° Venus one fair word,   *crony*
One nickname for her purblind° son and heir,   *dim-sighted*
Young Adam[5] Cupid, he that shot so trim
When King Cophetua loved the beggar maid.[6]—

15   He heareth not, he stirreth not, he moveth not.
The ape[7] is dead, and I must conjure him.—
I conjure thee by Rosaline's bright eyes,
By her high forehead and her scarlet lip,
By her fine foot, straight leg, and quivering thigh,

20   And the demesnes° that there adjacent lie,   *estates*
That in thy likeness thou appear to us.

BENVOLIO   An if he hear thee, thou wilt anger him.

MERCUTIO   This cannot anger him. 'Twould anger him
To raise a spirit[8] in his mistress' circle

25   Of some strange° nature, letting it there stand   *other's*
Till she had laid it and conjured it down.
That were some spite. My invocation
Is fair and honest. In his mistress' name,
I conjure only but to raise up him.

30   BENVOLIO   Come, he hath hid himself among these trees
To be consorted° with the humorous[9] night.   *in company*
Blind is his love, and best befits the dark.

MERCUTIO   If love be blind, love cannot hit the mark.°   *target; vulva*
Now will he sit under a medlar[1] tree

35   And wish his mistress were that kind of fruit
As maids call medlars when they laugh alone.
O Romeo, that she were, O that she were
An open-arse,° and thou a popp'rin' pear.[2]   *medlar*
Romeo, good night. I'll to my truckle-bed.[3]

40   This field-bed[4] is too cold for me to sleep.
Come, shall we go?

BENVOLIO   Go then, for 'tis in vain
To seek him here that means not to be found.

                    Exeunt [BENVOLIO *and* MERCUTIO]

ROMEO [*coming forward*]   He jests at scars that never felt a wound.[5]
But soft,° what light through yonder window breaks?   *wait*

---

4. Pure moods, not mixed together to form an even "temper."
5. Probably alluding to Adam Bell, a famously accurate sixteenth-century archer.
6. The story of a king who falls in love with a beggar and makes her his queen was the subject of a popular ballad.
7. Foolish creature (a disrespectful endearment), or alluding to a magician's trick of "reviving" an ape that had been trained to play dead.
8. A word for "semen"; the entire speech is filled with obscene wordplay.
9. Dumpy; melancholy.

1. A fruit thought to resemble the female sex organs, with a play on "meddle" in the sense "have sexual intercourse with."
2. A pear from Poperinghe in Flanders, punning on "popper-in" or "pop her in."
3. Small bed, often for a child, which was stored under a larger one.
4. A lying place in the open, and a soldier's portable bed.
5. Rhymes with "found." This line precedes a scene change in most editions, although the location remains the same if both the inside and the outside of the orchard are supposed to be visible onstage.

45 It is the east, and Juliet is the sun.
Arise, fair sun, and kill the envious moon,[6]
Who is already sick and pale with grief
That thou, her maid, art far more fair than she.
Be not her maid, since she is envious.
50 Her vestal° livery is but sick and green,[7]   *virginal*
And none but fools do wear it; cast it off.
      [*Enter* JULIET *aloft*]
It is my lady, O, it is my love.
O that she knew she were!
She speaks, yet she says nothing. What of that?
55 Her eye discourses; I will answer it.
I am too bold. 'Tis not to me she speaks.
Two of the fairest stars in all the heaven,
Having some business, do entreat her eyes
To twinkle in their spheres[8] till they return.
60 What if her eyes were there, they in her head?—
The brightness of her cheek would shame those stars
As daylight doth a lamp; her eye in heaven
Would through the airy region° stream so bright   *ethereal sky*
That birds would sing and think it were not night.
65 See how she leans her cheek upon her hand.
O, that I were a glove upon that hand,
That I might touch that cheek!
JULIET   Ay me.
ROMEO [*aside*]   She speaks.
O, speak again, bright angel; for thou art
As glorious to this night, being o'er my head,
70 As is a wingèd messenger° of heaven   *angel*
Unto the white upturnèd[9] wond'ring eyes
Of mortals that fall back to gaze[1] on him
When he bestrides the lazy-passing clouds
And sails upon the bosom of the air.
JULIET [*not knowing* ROMEO *hears her*]   O Romeo, Romeo,
75   wherefore° art thou Romeo?   *why*
Deny thy father and refuse thy name,
Or if thou wilt not, be but sworn my love,
And I'll no longer be a Capulet.
ROMEO [*aside*]   Shall I hear more, or shall I speak at this?
80 JULIET   'Tis but thy name that is my enemy.
Thou art thyself, though° not a Montague.   *even if*
What's Montague? It is nor hand, nor foot,
Nor arm, nor face, nor any other part
Belonging to a man. O, be some other name!
85 What's in a name? That which we call a rose
By any other word would smell as sweet.
So Romeo would, were he not Romeo called,
Retain that dear perfection which he owes°   *owns*
Without that title. Romeo, doff° thy name,   *shed*
90 And for thy name—which is no part of thee—
Take all myself.

---

6. Emblem of Diana, goddess of chastity.
7. Unfulfilled sexual desire was thought to cause green sickness (anemia) in adolescent girls; also alluding to the moon's pallor.

8. Crystalline spheres around the earth that carried the heavenly bodies in their rotations.
9. Turned up, revealing the whites at the bottoms.
1. Fall backward in gazing.

ROMEO [*to* JULIET] I take thee at thy word.[2]
    Call me but love and I'll be new baptized.[3]
    Henceforth I never will be Romeo.
JULIET   What man art thou that, thus bescreened in night,
    So stumblest on my counsel?°   *private thoughts*
95   ROMEO   By a name
    I know not how to tell thee who I am.
    My name, dear saint, is hateful to myself
    Because it is an enemy to thee.
    Had I it written, I would tear the word.
100 JULIET   My ears have yet not drunk a hundred words
    Of thy tongue's uttering, yet I know the sound.
    Art thou not Romeo, and a Montague?
    ROMEO   Neither, fair maid, if either thee dislike.°   *displeases you*
    JULIET   How cam'st thou hither, tell me, and wherefore?
105   The orchard walls are high and hard to climb,
    And the place death, considering who thou art,
    If any of my kinsmen find thee here.
    ROMEO   With love's light wings did I o'erperch° these walls,   *fly over*
    For stony limits cannot hold love out,
110   And what love can do, that dares love attempt.
    Therefore thy kinsmen are no stop° to me.   *obstacle*
    JULIET   If they do see thee, they will murder thee.
    ROMEO   Alack, there lies more peril in thine eye
    Than twenty of their swords. Look thou but sweet,
115   And I am proof° against their enmity.   *armed*
    JULIET   I would not for the world they saw thee here.
    ROMEO   I have night's cloak to hide me from their eyes,
    And but° thou love me, let them find me here.   *unless*
    My life were better ended by their hate
120   Than death proroguèd,° wanting of° thy love.   *deferred / lacking*
    JULIET   By whose direction found'st thou out this place?
    ROMEO   By love, that first did prompt me to enquire.
    He lent me counsel,° and I lent him eyes.   *advice*
    I am no pilot, yet wert thou as far
125   As that vast shore washed with the farthest sea,
    I should adventure° for such merchandise.   *voyage*
    JULIET   Thou knowest the mask of night is on my face,
    Else would a maiden blush bepaint my cheek
    For that which thou hast heard me speak tonight.
130   Fain° would I dwell on form,° fain, fain deny   *Gladly / propriety*
    What I have spoke; but farewell, compliment.°   *polite convention*
    Dost thou love me? I know thou wilt say 'Ay',
    And I will take thy word. Yet if thou swear'st
    Thou mayst prove false. At lovers' perjuries,
135   They say, Jove laughs. O gentle Romeo,
    If thou dost love, pronounce° it faithfully;   *utter*
    Or if thou think'st I am too quickly won,
    I'll frown, and be perverse,° and say thee nay,   *contrary*
    So thou wilt woo; but else,° not for the world.   *otherwise*
140   In truth, fair Montague, I am too fond,°   *infatuated*
    And therefore thou mayst think my 'haviour light.° *licentious; capricious*

---

2. At face value; as you have asked me to.   3. Given a new name; born into a new persona.

But trust me, gentleman, I'll prove more true
Than those that have more cunning to be strange.°   *distant*
I should have been more strange, I must confess,
145 But that thou overheard'st, ere I was ware,°   *aware*
My true-love passion. Therefore pardon me,
And not° impute this yielding to light love,   *do not*
Which the dark night hath so discoverèd.°   *revealed*
ROMEO   Lady, by yonder blessèd moon I vow,
150 That tips with silver all these fruit-tree tops—
JULIET   O swear not by the moon, th'inconstant moon
That monthly changes in her circled orb,°   *orbital sphere*
Lest that thy love prove likewise variable.
ROMEO   What shall I swear by?
JULIET   Do not swear at all,
155 Or if thou wilt, swear by thy gracious self,
Which is the god of my idolatry,[4]
And I'll believe thee.
ROMEO   If my heart's dear love—
JULIET   Well, do not swear. Although I joy in thee,
I have no joy of this contract° tonight.   *exchange of vows*
160 It is too rash, too unadvised,° too sudden,   *undeliberated*
Too like the lightning which doth cease to be
Ere one can say it lightens. Sweet, good night.
This bud of love by summer's ripening breath
May prove a beauteous flower when next we meet.
165 Good night, good night. As sweet repose and rest
Come to thy heart as that within my breast.
ROMEO   O, wilt thou leave me so unsatisfied?
JULIET   What satisfaction canst thou have tonight?
ROMEO   Th'exchange of thy love's faithful vow for mine.
170 JULIET   I gave thee mine before thou didst request it,
And yet I would it were° to give again.   *were available*
ROMEO   Wouldst thou withdraw it? For what purpose, love?
JULIET   But to be frank° and give it thee again.   *generous; honest*
And yet I wish but for the thing I have.
175 My bounty is as boundless as the sea,
My love as deep. The more I give to thee
The more I have, for both are infinite.
         [NURSE] *calls within*
I hear some noise within. Dear love, adieu.—
Anon,° good Nurse!—Sweet Montague, be true.   *One moment*
180 Stay but a little; I will come again.   [*Exit*]
ROMEO   O blessèd, blessèd night! I am afeard,
Being in night, all this is but a dream,
Too flattering-sweet to be substantial.
         [*Enter* JULIET *aloft*]
JULIET   Three words, dear Romeo, and good night indeed.
185 If that thy bent of love be honourable,
Thy purpose marriage, send me word tomorrow,
By one that I'll procure to come to thee,
Where and what time thou wilt perform the rite,
And all my fortunes at thy foot I'll lay,
190 And follow thee, my lord, throughout the world.

---

4. Not only was loving a man more than God idolatrous, but so was swearing oaths by anything other than God.

NURSE (*within*)   Madam!
JULIET   I come, anon. [*To* ROMEO] But if thou mean'st not well,°   *honorably*
  I do beseech thee—
NURSE (*within*)   Madam!
195 JULIET   By and by I come.—
  To cease thy strife° and leave me to my grief.   *striving*
  Tomorrow will I send.
ROMEO   So thrive my soul⁵—
JULIET   A thousand times good night.   *Exit*
200 ROMEO   A thousand times the worse to want° thy light.   *lack*
  Love goes toward love as schoolboys from their books,
  But love from love, toward school with heavy looks.
      [*He is going*]
      Enter JULIET [*aloft*] *again*
JULIET   Hist,° Romeo! Hist! O for a falconer's voice   *(falconer's call)*
  To lure this tassel-gentle⁶ back again.
205 Bondage⁷ is hoarse, and may not speak aloud,
  Else would I tear° the cave where Echo⁸ lies,   *split with cries*
  And make her airy tongue more hoarse than mine
  With repetition of my Romeo's name. Romeo!
ROMEO   It is my soul that calls upon my name.
210 How silver-sweet sound lovers' tongues by night,
  Like softest music to attending ears!
JULIET   Romeo!
ROMEO   My nyas?°   *young hawk*
JULIET   What o'clock tomorrow
  Shall I send to thee?
ROMEO   By the hour of nine.
JULIET   I will not fail; 'tis twenty year till then.
215 I have forgot why I did call thee back.
ROMEO   Let me stand here till thou remember it.
JULIET   I shall forget, to have thee still° stand there,   *always*
  Rememb'ring how I love thy company.
ROMEO   And I'll still stay, to have thee still forget,
220 Forgetting any other home but this.
JULIET   'Tis almost morning. I would have thee gone—
  And yet no farther than a wanton's° bird,   *spoiled child's*
  That lets it hop a little from his hand,
  Like a poor prisoner in his twisted gyves,°   *fetters*
225 And with a silk thread plucks it back again,
  So loving-jealous of his liberty.
ROMEO   I would° I were thy bird.   *wish*
JULIET   Sweet, so would I.
  Yet I should kill thee with much cherishing.
  Good night, good night. Parting is such sweet sorrow
230 That I shall say good night till it be morrow.
ROMEO   Sleep dwell upon thine eyes, peace in thy breast.
                              [*Exit* JULIET]
  Would I were sleep and peace, so sweet to rest.
  Hence will I to my ghostly° sire's close° cell,   *spiritual / small; private*
  His help to crave, and my dear hap° to tell.   *Exit*   *fortune*

5. On peril of damnation.   family.
6. Tercel-gentle, a male peregrine falcon. Literally, a   8. In classical legend, a woman who, scorned by Narcis-
noble ("gentle") hawk.   sus, wasted away with grief until only a voice remained to
7. Confinement within her family's home; duty owed her   haunt empty caves.

2.2

Enter FRIAR [LAURENCE] *alone, with a basket*

FRIAR LAURENCE   The grey°-eyed morn smiles on the frowning night,   *pale blue*
    Chequ'ring the eastern clouds with streaks of light,
    And fleckled° darkness like a drunkard reels   *dappled*
    From forth° day's path and Titan's[1] fiery wheels.   *out of*
5   Now, ere the sun advance° his burning eye   *bring up*
    The day to cheer and night's dank dew to dry,
    I must up-fill this osier cage° of ours   *willow basket*
    With baleful weeds and precious-juicèd flowers.
    The earth, that's nature's mother, is her tomb.
10   What is her burying grave, that is her womb,
    And from her womb children of divers° kind   *several; varied*
    We sucking on her natural bosom find,
    Many for many virtues° excellent,   *healthful properties*
    None but for some,[2] and yet all different.
15   O mickle° is the powerful grace° that lies   *great / divine beneficence*
    In plants, herbs, stones, and their true qualities,
    For naught° so vile that on the earth doth live   *nothing is*
    But to the earth some special good doth give;
    Nor aught so good but, strained° from that fair use,   *twisted*
20   Revolts from true birth, stumbling on abuse.[3]
    Virtue itself turns vice being misapplied,
    And vice sometime's by action dignified.

    Enter ROMEO

    Within the infant rind of this weak flower
    Poison hath residence, and medicine power,
25   For this, being smelt, with that part° cheers each part;°   *act / bodily member*
    Being tasted, slays all senses with the heart.
    Two such opposèd kings encamp them still°   *always*
    In man as well as herbs—grace and rude will;
    And where the worser is predominant,
30   Full soon the canker° death eats up that plant.   *grub; cancer*
ROMEO   Good morrow, father.
FRIAR LAURENCE   *Benedicite.*°   *God bless you*
    What early tongue so sweet saluteth me?
    Young son, it argues a distempered head
    So soon to bid good morrow to thy bed.
35   Care keeps his watch in every old man's eye,
    And where care lodges, sleep will never lie,
    But where unbruisèd° youth with unstuffed° brain   *fresh / unanxious*
    Doth couch his limbs, there golden sleep doth reign.
    Therefore thy earliness doth me assure
40   Thou art uproused with some distemp'rature;
    Or if not so, then here I hit it right:
    Our Romeo hath not been in bed tonight.
ROMEO   That last is true; the sweeter rest was mine.
FRIAR LAURENCE   God pardon sin!—Wast thou with Rosaline?
45 ROMEO   With Rosaline, my ghostly father? No,
    I have forgot that name and that name's woe.
FRIAR LAURENCE   That's my good son; but where hast thou been then?

2.2 Location: A street in Verona.
1. Helios, a classical sun god, was descended from the Titans. He traveled across the sky in a chariot.
2. None that is not excellent for some use.
3. Turns from its intended benefits if it happens to be misused.

ROMEO   I'll tell thee ere thou ask it me again.
　　　I have been feasting with mine enemy,
50　　Where on a sudden one hath wounded me
　　　That's by me wounded. Both our remedies
　　　Within thy help and holy physic° lies.　　　　　　　　　　　　　*medicine*
　　　I bear no hatred, blessèd man, for lo,
　　　My intercession° likewise steads° my foe.　　　　　*request / benefits*
55 FRIAR LAURENCE   Be plain, good son, and homely° in thy drift.　　*direct*
　　　Riddling confession finds but riddling shrift.°　　　　　　*absolution*
ROMEO   Then plainly know my heart's dear love is set
　　　On the fair daughter of rich Capulet.
　　　As mine on hers, so hers is set on mine,
60　　And all combined save what thou must combine
　　　By holy marriage. When and where and how
　　　We met, we wooed, and made exchange of vow
　　　I'll tell thee as we pass; but this I pray,
　　　That thou consent to marry us today.
65 FRIAR LAURENCE   Holy Saint Francis, what a change is here!
　　　Is Rosaline, that thou didst love so dear,
　　　So soon forsaken? Young men's love then lies
　　　Not truly in their hearts, but in their eyes.
　　　Jesu Maria, what a deal of brine
70　　Hath washed thy sallow° cheeks for Rosaline!　　　　　　　*yellowed*
　　　How much salt water thrown away in waste
　　　To season° love, that of it doth not taste!　　　　　*preserve; flavor*
　　　The sun not yet thy sighs[4] from heaven clears.
　　　Thy old° groans yet ring in mine ancient ears.　　　　　　　*former*
75　　Lo, here upon thy cheek the stain doth sit
　　　Of an old tear that is not washed off yet.
　　　If e'er thou wast thyself, and these woes thine,
　　　Thou and these woes were all for Rosaline.
　　　And art thou changed? Pronounce this sentence° then:　　*maxim; verdict*
80　　Women may° fall when there's no strength in men.　　　　*might well*
ROMEO   Thou chidd'st me oft for loving Rosaline.
FRIAR LAURENCE   For doting, not for loving, pupil mine.
ROMEO   And bad'st me bury love.
FRIAR LAURENCE　　　　　　　　　Not in a grave
　　　To lay one in, another out to have.
85 ROMEO   I pray thee, chide me not. Her I love now
　　　Doth grace for grace and love for love allow.
　　　The other did not so.
FRIAR LAURENCE　　　　　O, she knew well
　　　Thy love did read by rote, that could not spell.[5]
　　　But come, young waverer, come, go with me.
90　　In one respect I'll thy assistant be;
　　　For this alliance may so happy prove
　　　To turn your households' rancour to pure love.
ROMEO   O, let us hence! I stand° on sudden haste.　　　　　　　*depend*
FRIAR LAURENCE   Wisely and slow. They stumble that run fast.
　　　　　　　　　　　　　　　　　　　　Exeunt

4. The mist Romeo's exhalations produced.　　　out understanding or meaning them.
5. Did recite the memorized phrases of love poetry, with-

2.3

Enter BENVOLIO *and* MERCUTIO

MERCUTIO Where the devil should this Romeo be? Came he
  not home tonight?°   *last night*

BENVOLIO Not to his father's. I spoke with his man.

MERCUTIO Why, that same pale° hard-hearted wench, that   *fair-skinned; frigid*
  Rosaline,

5 Torments him so that he will sure run mad.

BENVOLIO Tybalt, the kinsman to old Capulet,
  Hath sent a letter to his father's house.

MERCUTIO A challenge, on my life.

BENVOLIO   Romeo will answer° it.   *accept*

MERCUTIO Any man that can write may answer a letter.

10 BENVOLIO Nay, he will answer the letter's master, how he dares,
  being dared.

MERCUTIO Alas, poor Romeo, he is already dead—stabbed with
  a white wench's black eye, run through the ear with a love
  song, the very pin[1] of his heart cleft with the blind bow-boy's

15 butt-shaft;[2] and is he a man to encounter Tybalt?

BENVOLIO Why, what is Tybalt?

MERCUTIO More than Prince of Cats.[3] O, he's the courageous
  captain of compliments.° He fights as you sing pricksong:[4]   *formalities of dueling*
  keeps time, distance,[5] and proportion.° He rests his minim   *harmony; form*

20 rests:[6] one, two, and the third in your bosom; the very butcher
  of a silk button.[7] A duellist, a duellist; a gentleman of the very
  first house of the first and second cause.[8] Ah, the immortal
  passado, the *punto reverso*, the *hai*.[9]

BENVOLIO The what?

25 MERCUTIO The pox of° such antic,° lisping, affecting° phantas-   *on / grotesque / affected*
  ims,° these new tuners of accent![1] 'By Jesu, a very good blade, *bizarrely mannered men*
  a very tall° man, a very good whore.' Why° is not this a lamenta- *valiant / Why, now*
  ble thing, grandsire, that we should be thus afflicted with these
  strange[2] flies,° these fashionmongers, these 'pardon-me's',[3] *gaudy buzzers*

30 who stand so much on the new form that they cannot sit at
  ease on the old bench?[4] O, their bones, their bones![5]

Enter ROMEO

BENVOLIO Here comes Romeo, here comes Romeo!

MERCUTIO Without his roe, like a dried herring.[6] O flesh, flesh,

---

2.3 Location: Scene continues.
1. Peg in the center of an archery target.
2. Blunt practice arrow, fit for children and hence for Cupid.
3. Called Tybalt or Tibert in medieval stories of Reynard the fox. "Catso," from the Italian word for "penis," was also a slang term for a rogue.
4. Sung from sheet music and thus more precise and invariable than extempore or remembered music.
5. Musical intervals between notes; also, a set space to be kept between combatants.
6. Short musical rests, referring to the brief strategic pauses in a duel.
7. Alluding to the boast of an Italian fencing master in London that he could "hit any Englishman with a thrust upon a button."
8. *gentleman . . . cause*: superior practitioner of taking up quarrels as duels. *first house*: the best fencing school. *cause*: a reason that according to the etiquette of fencing would require an honorable gentleman to seek a duel.

9. Italian fencing terms for a lunging sword thrust, back-handed thrust, and thrust that reaches through.
1. These faddishly novel speakers, such as those importing foreign phrases. A typical Renaissance English satire, here seemingly unaffected by the fact that Italian is the native tongue of Verona.
2. Newfangled; foreign.
3. *pardon-me's*: the fastidiously mannered, affecting the French *pardonnez-moi*.
4. *who . . . bench*: as if both Mercutio and Benvolio were elderly, viewing the decline of the young. *stand*: insist. *form*: etiquette; fashion; bench.
5. *O . . . bones*: Aching on the austere furniture of their predecessors; infected with the "bone disease," syphilis. Mercutio may also be satirizing the courtly habit of crying "Bon! Bon!" (French for "good") as a kind of inane flattery.
6. Emaciated, since the roe is removed in curing. This leaves Romeo's name a mournful wail, "Me, O." He is also missing his roe deer (female, named Rosaline).

how art thou fishified![7] Now is he for the numbers° that
35 Petrarch[8] flowed in. Laura to° his lady was a kitchen wench—
marry, she had a better love to berhyme her—Dido[9] a dowdy,
Cleopatra a gypsy,[1] Helen and Hero[2] hildings° and harlots,
Thisbe[3] a grey° eye or so, but not to the purpose.° Signor
Romeo, *bonjour*. There's a French salutation to your French
40 slop.° You gave us the counterfeit fairly last night.

ROMEO Good morrow to you both. What counterfeit did I give
you?

MERCUTIO The slip,[4] sir, the slip. Can you not conceive?°

ROMEO Pardon, good Mercutio. My business was great, and in
45 such a case as mine a man may strain° courtesy.

MERCUTIO That's as much as to say such a case as yours constrains a man to bow in the hams.[5]

ROMEO Meaning to curtsy.[6]

MERCUTIO Thou hast most kindly hit[7] it.

50 ROMEO A most courteous exposition.

MERCUTIO Nay, I am the very pink° of courtesy.

ROMEO Pink for flower.°

MERCUTIO Right.

ROMEO Why, then is my pump° well flowered.[8]

55 MERCUTIO Sure wit, follow me° this jest now till thou hast worn
out thy pump, that when the single° sole of it is worn, the jest
may remain, after the wearing, solely singular.°

ROMEO O single-soled° jest, solely° singular for the singleness!°

MERCUTIO Come between us, good Benvolio. My wits faints.[9]

60 ROMEO Switch and spurs,[1] switch and spurs, or I'll cry a match.°

MERCUTIO Nay, if our wits run the wild-goose chase,[2] I am done,
for thou hast more of the wild goose° in one of thy wits than I
am sure I have in my whole five. Was I with° you there for the
goose?

65 ROMEO Thou wast never with me for anything when thou wast
not there for the goose.[3]

MERCUTIO I will bite thee by the ear[4] for that jest.

ROMEO Nay, good goose, bite not.[5]

MERCUTIO Thy wit is very bitter sweeting,° it is a most sharp
70 sauce.°

ROMEO And is it not then well served in to a sweet goose?

MERCUTIO O, here's a wit of cheveril,° that stretches from an
inch narrow to an ell broad.[6]

verses	
compared to	
hussies	
blue / of consequence	
loose breeches	
understand	
nearly abandon	
nonpareil; dianthus bloom	
dianthus; vulva	
shoe; penis	
chase; respond to	
thin	
utterly unique	
shoddy / only / foolishness	
claim a victory	
folly	
even with	
apple	
mockery	
kid leather	

7. Gone pale and limp, turned into a herring. Fish, thought weak and relatively unnourishing, was the substitute for "flesh" (meat) during fasts.
8. Petrarch's sonnets addressed to Laura were the model for an English love sonnet craze.
9. The beautiful queen of Carthage who fell in love with Aeneas but was deserted by him in Virgil's *Aeneid*.
1. A term of abuse. Gypsies were supposed to have come from Egypt, where Cleopatra was queen and lover of Julius Caesar and Mark Antony.
2. Helen's abduction by Paris initiated the Trojan War. Hero was Leander's lover in a tragic legend.
3. Beloved of Pyramus in a classical legend that parallels *Romeo and Juliet*. The young lovers, coming from hostile families, die as a result of a missed meeting and misinterpreted evidence.
4. Counterfeit coin.

5. Further playing on "business" as "sexual intercourse" and "case" as "vagina." Mercutio suggests that Romeo needs to flex his buttocks or he may wind up with a leg-weakening venereal disease.
6. Pronounced the same as "courtesy."
7. Most truly guessed it; most truly sexually penetrated it.
8. Pinked, or decoratively perforated.
9. Treating the exchange of wit as a duel.
1. Flog your wits to a full gallop; continue.
2. A cross-country horse race in which the leader chose the course and the rest had to follow.
3. Silliness; whore's company.
4. Usually suggesting affectionate nibbling.
5. A proverbial cry for mercy, here used ironically.
6. That spreads itself very thin (an ell was forty-five inches).

ROMEO   I stretch it out for that word 'broad', which, added to the
75   goose, proves thee far and wide a broad goose.[7]
MERCUTIO   Why, is not this better now than groaning for love?
        Now art thou sociable, now art thou Romeo, now art thou what
        thou art by art° as well as by nature, for this drivelling love is   *learning*
        like a great natural° that runs lolling up and down to hide his   *idiot*
80   bauble[8] in a hole.
BENVOLIO   Stop there, stop there.
MERCUTIO   Thou desirest me to stop in[9] my tale° against the   *story; penis*
        hair.[1]
BENVOLIO   Thou wouldst else have made thy tale large.
85 MERCUTIO   O, thou art deceived, I would have made it short, for
        I was come to the whole depth of my tale, and meant indeed
        to occupy the argument° no longer.   *topic*
            Enter NURSE, *and her man* [PETER]
ROMEO   Here's goodly gear.[2]
BENVOLIO   A sail, a sail![3]
90 MERCUTIO   Two, two—a shirt° and a smock.°   *man / woman*
NURSE   Peter.
PETER   Anon.°   *At your service*
NURSE   My fan, Peter.
MERCUTIO   Good Peter, to hide her face, for her fan's the fairer
95   face.
NURSE   God ye° good morrow,° gentlemen.   *give you / morning*
MERCUTIO   God ye good e'en,° fair gentlewoman.   *afternoon*
NURSE   Is it good e'en?
MERCUTIO   'Tis no less, I tell ye: for the bawdy hand of the dial
100   is now upon the prick° of noon.   *mark; penis*
NURSE   Out upon you,[4] what° a man are you!   *what sort of*
ROMEO   One, gentlewoman, that God hath made for himself to
        mar.[5]
NURSE   By my troth, it is well said. 'For himself to mar', quoth
105   a?° Gentlemen, can any of you tell me where I may find the   *he*
        young Romeo?
ROMEO   I can tell you, but young Romeo will be older when you
        have found him than he was when you sought him. I am the
        youngest of that name, for fault° of a worse.   *lack*
110 NURSE   You say well.
MERCUTIO   Yea, is the worst well? Very well took, i'faith, wisely,
        wisely.
NURSE [*to* ROMEO]   If you be he, sir, I desire some confidence
        with you.
115 BENVOLIO   She will endite[6] him to some supper.
MERCUTIO   A bawd, a bawd, a bawd. So ho![7]
ROMEO   What hast thou found?°   *spotted; figured out*

---

7. A gross idiot; a licentious fellow; a goose fattened for
the table.
8. *that . . . bauble:* who runs with his tongue hanging out
to cover up a Jester's wand, at one end either grotesquely
carved or adorned with an inflated pig's bladder; penis.
9. Cease; stuff in.
1. Against the grain; in an unnatural place.
2. Spoken ironically of Mercutio's witticisms or the
Nurse's voluminous appearance.
3. A sailor's cry upon sighting another ship.

4. An expression of indignation.
5. *One . . . mar:* combines two proverbial expressions. "It
is his to make or mar" suggests that Mercutio has the free
will to determine his own character. "He is a man of
God's making" places the blame for Mercutio's character
on God.
6. Deliberately substituted for "invite," to mock the
Nurse's erroneous use of "confidence" for "conference"
in the line above.
7. The cry of a hunter who has spotted his quarry.

MERCUTIO No hare,° sir, unless a hare, sir, in a lenten pie,[8] that   *prostitute*
is something stale and hoar ere it be spent.[9]
        He walks by them and sings
120   An old hare hoar
               And an old hare hoar
                  Is very good meat in Lent.
               But a hare that is hoar
                  Is too much for a score[1]
125   When it hoars ere it be spent.
      Romeo, will you come to your father's? We'll to dinner thither.
MERCUTIO I will follow you.
MERCUTIO Farewell, ancient lady. Farewell, [*sings*] 'lady, lady,
      lady'.[2]   *Exeunt* MERCUTIO [*and*] BENVOLIO
130 NURSE I pray you, sir, what saucy merchant° was this that was so   *commoner*
full of his ropery?°   *knavery*
ROMEO A gentleman, Nurse, that loves to hear himself talk, and
will speak more in a minute than he will stand to° in a month.   *perform*
NURSE An a° speak anything against me, I'll take him down° an   *If he / humble him*
135 a were lustier[3] than he is, and twenty such jacks;° an if I cannot,   *scoundrels*
I'll find those that shall. Scurvy knave! I am none of his flirt-
jills,° I am none of his skeans-mates.[4] [*To* PETER] And thou   *loose women*
must stand by, too, and suffer every knave to use me at his
pleasure.
140 PETER I saw no man use you at his pleasure. If I had, my weapon
should quickly have been out; I warrant you, I dare draw as
soon as another man if I see occasion in a good quarrel, and
the law on my side.
NURSE Now, afore God, I am so vexed that every part about me
145 quivers. Scurvy knave! [*To* ROMEO] Pray you, sir, a word; and,
as I told you, my young lady bid me enquire you out. What she
bid me say I will keep to myself, but first let me tell ye if ye
should lead her in a fool's paradise, as they say, it were a very
gross° kind of behaviour, as they say, for the gentlewoman is   *outrageous*
150 young; and therefore if you should deal double° with her, truly   *falsely; forcefully*
it were an ill thing to be offered to any gentlewoman, and very
weak° dealing.   *poor*
ROMEO Nurse, commend me to thy lady and mistress. I protest°   *swear*
unto thee—
155 NURSE Good heart, and i'faith I will tell her as much. Lord,
Lord, she will be a joyful woman.
ROMEO What wilt thou tell her, Nurse? Thou dost not mark°   *pay attention to*
me.
NURSE I will tell her, sir, that you do protest;[5] which as I take it
160 is a gentlemanlike offer.
ROMEO Bid her devise
      Some means to come to shrift this afternoon,
      And there she shall at Friar Laurence' cell
      Be shrived and married. [*Offering money*] Here is for thy pains.
165 NURSE No, truly, sir, not a penny.

---

8. Meat illicitly eaten during Lent by disguising it in a pie, just as the Nurse's unattractiveness hides whatever promiscuity she may practice.
9. Somewhat stale and moldy by the time the last of the rationed luxury is consumed.
1. Is too much to pay for.

2. Refrain to a ballad about a perfectly chaste woman, intended derisively.
3. Stronger; hornier.
4. Knife-wielding rogues.
5. The Nurse takes this as a marriage offer, probably confusing "protest" with "propose."

ROMEO Go to, I say, you shall.
NURSE [*taking the money*] This afternoon, sir. Well, she shall be there.
ROMEO And stay, good Nurse, behind the abbey wall.
  Within this hour my man shall be with thee
170 And bring thee cords made like a tackled stair,°   *a knotted ladder*
  Which to the high topgallant[6] of my joy
  Must be my convoy° in the secret night.   *means of conveyance*
  Farewell. Be trusty, and I'll quit° thy pains.   *repay*
  Farewell. Commend me to thy mistress.
175 NURSE Now God in heaven bless thee! Hark you, sir.
ROMEO What sayst thou, my dear Nurse?
NURSE Is your man secret?° Did you ne'er hear say   *discreet*
  'Two may keep counsel, putting one away'?
ROMEO I warrant thee my man's as true as steel.
180 NURSE Well, sir, my mistress is the sweetest lady.
  Lord, Lord, when 'twas a little prating thing—
  O, there is a nobleman in town, one Paris,
  That would fain lay knife aboard;[7] but she, good soul,
  Had as lief° see a toad, a very toad,   *gladly*
185 As see him. I anger her sometimes,
  And tell her that Paris is the properer° man;   *more handsome*
  But I'll warrant you, when I say so she looks
  As pale as any clout° in the versal° world.   *sheet / entire*
  Doth not rosemary[8] and Romeo begin
190 Both with a° letter?   *the same*
ROMEO Ay, Nurse, what of that? Both with an 'R'.
NURSE Ah, mocker—that's the dog's name. 'R' is for the—no, I
  know it begins with some other letter, and she hath the prettiest
  sententious[9] of it, of you and rosemary, that it would do you
195 good to hear it.
ROMEO Commend me to thy lady.
NURSE Ay, a thousand times. Peter!
PETER Anon.
NURSE [*giving* PETER *her fan*] Before,° and apace.°   *Lead / quickly*
     Exeunt [PETER *and* NURSE *at one door,*
        ROMEO *at another door*]

2.4

 Enter JULIET
JULIET The clock struck nine when I did send the Nurse.
  In half an hour she promised to return.
  Perchance she cannot meet him. That's not so.
  O, she is lame! Love's heralds should be thoughts,
5 Which ten times faster glides than the sun's beams
  Driving back shadows over louring° hills.   *dark; threatening*
  Therefore do nimble-pinioned doves draw Love,°   *Venus*
  And therefore hath the wind-swift Cupid wings.
  Now is the sun upon the highmost hill°   *zenith*
10 Of this day's journey, and from nine till twelve
  Is three long hours, yet she is not come.
  Had she affections° and warm youthful blood   *passions*

6. The highest platform on a mast, from which the topgallant sail was handled.
7. One claimed a place at dinner by laying one's personal
knife on the table ("board").
8. A token of remembrance, between lovers and also of
the dead.
9. Blunder for "sentences"; sayings.
2.4 Location: Capulet's orchard.

She would be as swift in motion as a ball.
My words would bandy° her to my sweet love,   *volley (as in tennis)*
15   And his to me.
But old folks, many feign° as they were dead—   *act*
Unwieldy, slow, heavy, and pale as lead.
       Enter NURSE [*and* PETER]
O God, she comes! O honey Nurse, what news?
Hast thou met with him? Send thy man away.
20   NURSE   Peter, stay° at the gate.   [*Exit* PETER]   *wait*
JULIET   Now, good sweet Nurse—O Lord, why look'st thou sad?
Though news be sad, yet tell them merrily;
If good, thou sham'st the music of sweet news
By playing it to me with so sour a face.
25   NURSE   I am a-weary. Give me leave° a while.   *Let me alone*
Fie, how my bones ache. What a jaunce° have I!   *trotting about*
JULIET   I would thou hadst my bones and I thy news.
Nay, come, I pray thee speak, good, good Nurse, speak.
NURSE   Jesu, what haste! Can you not stay a while?
30   Do you not see that I am out of breath?
JULIET   How art thou out of breath when thou hast breath
To say to me that thou art out of breath?
The excuse that thou dost make in this delay
Is longer than the tale thou dost excuse.
35   Is thy news good or bad? Answer to that.
Say either, and I'll stay° the circumstance.°   *wait for / full details*
Let me be satisfied: is't good or bad?
NURSE   Well, you have made a simple° choice. You know not   *foolish*
how to choose a man. Romeo? No, not he; though his face be
40   better than any man's, yet his leg excels all men's, and for a
hand and a foot and a body, though they be not to be talked
on,° yet they are past compare. He is not the flower of courtesy,   *worth mentioning*
but, I'll warrant him, as gentle as a lamb. Go thy ways,[1] wench.
Serve God. What, have you dined at home?
45   JULIET   No, no. But all this did I know before.
What says he of our marriage—what of that?
NURSE   Lord, how my head aches! What a head have I!
It beats as it would fall in twenty pieces.
My back—
       [JULIET *rubs her back*]
          a' t'other side—ah, my back, my back!
50   Beshrew° your heart for sending me about   *Curse*
To catch my death with jauncing up and down.
JULIET   I'faith, I am sorry that thou art not well.
Sweet, sweet, sweet Nurse, tell me, what says my love?
NURSE   Your love says, like an honest° gentleman, and a courte-   *honorable*
55   ous, and a kind,° and a handsome, and, I warrant, a virtuous—   *true*
where is your mother?
JULIET   Where is my mother? Why, she is within.
Where should she be? How oddly thou repliest!
'Your love says like an honest gentleman
"Where is your mother?" '
60   NURSE   O, God's Lady° dear!   *Mary, Mother of God*
Are you so hot?° Marry come up, I trow.[2]   *impatient; aroused*

---

1. Off you go; do as you will do.   2. *I trow*: an expression of reproof.

Is this the poultice for my aching bones?
Henceforward do your messages yourself.
JULIET   Here's such a coil!° Come, what says Romeo?   *to-do*
65   NURSE   Have you got leave to go to shrift today?
JULIET   I have.
NURSE   Then hie° you hence to Friar Laurence' cell.   *hurry*
There stays a husband to make you a wife.
Now comes the wanton° blood up in your cheeks.   *fickle; lustful*
70   They'll be in scarlet straight° at any news.   *immediately*
Hie you to church. I must another way,
To fetch a ladder by the which your love
Must climb a bird's nest soon, when it is dark.
I am the drudge, and toil in your delight,
75   But you shall bear the burden³ soon at night.
Go, I'll to dinner. Hie you to the cell.
JULIET   Hie to high fortune! Honest Nurse, farewell.
                             Exeunt [severally]°   *separately*

2.5

Enter FRIAR [LAURENCE] *and* ROMEO
FRIAR LAURENCE   So smile the heavens upon this holy act
That after-hours with sorrow chide us not!
ROMEO   Amen, amen. But come what sorrow can,
It cannot countervail the exchange° of joy   *profit*
5   That one short minute gives me in her sight.
Do thou but close° our hands with holy words,   *join*
Then love-devouring death do what he dare—
It is enough I may but call her mine.
FRIAR LAURENCE   These violent° delights have violent ends,   *sudden; intense*
10   And in their triumph° die like fire and powder,   *victory; celebration*
Which as they kiss consume. The sweetest honey
Is loathsome in his own deliciousness,
And in the taste confounds the appetite.¹
Therefore love moderately. Long love doth so.
15   Too swift arrives as tardy as too slow.
      Enter JULIET *somewhat fast, and embraceth* ROMEO
Here comes the lady. O, so light² a foot
Will ne'er wear out the everlasting flint.³
A lover may bestride the gossamers°   *spiders' threads*
That idles in the wanton° summer air,   *playful*
20   And yet not fall, so light is vanity.⁴
JULIET   Good even° to my ghostly° confessor.   *evening / spiritual*
FRIAR LAURENCE   Romeo shall thank thee, daughter, for us both.
JULIET   As much to him,⁵ else is his thanks too much.
ROMEO   Ah, Juliet, if the measure° of thy joy   *measuring vessel*
25   Be heaped like mine, and that thy skill be more
To blazon° it, then sweeten with thy breath°   *describe; trumpet / speech*
This neighbour air, and let rich music's tongue
Unfold the imagined° happiness that both   *unexpressed ideas of*
Receive in either by this dear encounter.

---

3. Do the work; carry a lover; sing the theme of a duet, alluding to the sounds of lovemaking.
2.5 Location: Friar Laurence's cell.
1. *The sweetest . . . appetite:* from the proverb "Too much honey cloys the stomach." *his:* its. *confounds:* over-

whelms.
2. Swift; dainty; free of care; sexually open.
3. Will never endure or subdue the hard road of life.
4. Temporary worldly pleasure.
5. An equal amount. Both greetings consist of a kiss.

30 JULIET   Conceit,° more rich in matter than in words,   *Imagination*
      Brags of his substance,[6] not of ornament.°   *rhetoric; form*
      They are but beggars that can count their worth,
      But my true love is grown to such excess
      I cannot sum up some of half my wealth.[7]
35 FRIAR LAURENCE   Come, come with me, and we will make short work,
      For, by your leaves, you shall not stay alone
      Till Holy Church incorporate two in one.[8]   *Exeunt*

3.1

Enter MERCUTIO [*with his page*], BENVOLIO, *and men*

BENVOLIO   I pray thee, good Mercutio, let's retire.
      The day is hot, the Capels are abroad,
      And if we meet we shall not scape a brawl,
      For now, these hot days, is the mad blood stirring.
5 MERCUTIO   Thou art like one of these fellows that, when he
      enters the confines of a tavern, claps me° his sword upon the   *claps me = claps*
      table and says 'God send me no need of thee', and by the opera-
      tion° of the second cup, draws him on the drawer[1] when   *effect*
      indeed there is no need.
10 BENVOLIO   Am I like such a fellow?
MERCUTIO   Come, come, thou art as hot a jack° in thy mood as   *rogue*
      any in Italy, and as soon moved° to be moody,° and as soon   *provoked / angry*
      moody to be° moved.   *at being*
BENVOLIO   And what to?
15 MERCUTIO   Nay, an there were two such, we should have none
      shortly, for one would kill the other. Thou—why, thou wilt
      quarrel with a man that hath a hair more or a hair less in his
      beard than thou hast. Thou wilt quarrel with a man for crack-
      ing nuts, having no other reason but because thou hast hazel
20   eyes. What eye but such an eye would spy out such a quarrel?
      Thy head is as full of quarrels as an egg is full of meat,° and yet   *foodstuff*
      thy head hath been beaten as addle° as an egg for quarrelling.   *rotten; confused*
      Thou hast quarrelled with a man for coughing in the street
      because he hath wakened thy dog that hath lain asleep in the
25   sun. Didst thou not fall out with a tailor for wearing his new
      doublet before Easter;[2] with another for tying his new shoes
      with old ribbon? And yet thou wilt tutor me from quarrelling!
BENVOLIO   An I were so apt to quarrel as thou art, any man
      should buy the fee-simple[3] of my life for an hour and a quarter.
30 MERCUTIO   The fee simple? O, simple!°   *foolish*
                Enter TYBALT, PETRUCCIO, *and others*
BENVOLIO   By my head, here comes the Capulets.
MERCUTIO   By my heel, I care not.
TYBALT [*to* PETRUCCIO *and the others*]   Follow me close, for I
      will speak to them.
      [*To the Montagues*] Gentlemen, good e'en. A word with one
      of you.

6. Wealth; content.
7. *I . . . wealth:* The amount is too large to be understood
precisely.
8. Literally, put two into one body. Marriage mystically
united man and woman in "one flesh" (Genesis 2:2).
3.1 Location: A street in Verona.

1. Draws his sword on the server.
2. New fashions came out at Easter, after the austere penitence of Lent.
3. Outright possession of land, usually an inherited right;
here, the whole value of Benvolio's life.

35 MERCUTIO   And but one word with one of us? Couple it with
        something: make it a word and a blow.
    TYBALT   You shall find me apt enough to that, sir, an you will
        give me occasion.
    MERCUTIO   Could you not take some occasion without giving?
40 TYBALT   Mercutio, thou consort'st° with Romeo.   *associate*
    MERCUTIO   'Consort'?° What, dost thou make us minstrels? An   *Play in a band*
        thou make minstrels of us, look to hear nothing but discords.
        [*Touching his rapier*] Here's my fiddlestick; here's that shall
        make you dance. Zounds°—'Consort'!   *By God's wounds*
45 BENVOLIO   We talk here in the public haunt° of men.   *gathering place*
        Either withdraw unto some private place,
        Or reason coldly° of your grievances,   *dispassionately*
        Or else depart.° Here all eyes gaze on us.   *separate*
    MERCUTIO   Men's eyes were made to look, and let them gaze.
50   I will not budge for no man's pleasure, I.
            Enter ROMEO
    TYBALT   Well, peace be with you, sir. Here comes my man.
    MERCUTIO   But I'll be hanged, sir, if he wear your livery.[4]
        Marry, go before to field, he'll be your follower.°   *servant; pursuer*
        Your worship in that sense may call him 'man'.
55 TYBALT   Romeo, the love I bear thee can afford
        No better term than this: thou art a villain.°   *base commoner; rogue*
    ROMEO   Tybalt, the reason that I have to love thee
        Doth much excuse the appertaining rage
        To[5] such a greeting. Villain am I none.
60   Therefore, farewell. I see thou knowest me not.
    TYBALT   Boy, this shall not excuse the injuries
        That thou hast done me. Therefore turn and draw.
    ROMEO   I do protest I never injured thee,
        But love thee better than thou canst devise°   *imagine*
65   Till thou shalt know the reason of my love.
        And so, good Capulet—which name I tender°   *regard; love*
        As dearly as mine own—be satisfied.
    MERCUTIO [*drawing*]   O calm, dishonourable, vile submission!
        Alla stoccado carries it away.[6]
70   Tybalt, you ratcatcher, come, will you walk?°   *withdraw to fight*
    TYBALT   What wouldst thou have with me?
    MERCUTIO   Good King of Cats, nothing but one of your nine
        lives. That I mean to make bold withal,° and, as you shall use   *be so bold as to take*
        me hereafter,[7] dry-beat° the rest of the eight. Will you pluck   *soundly thrash*
75   your sword out of his pilcher° by the ears? Make haste, lest   *leather garment*
        mine be about your ears ere it be out.
    TYBALT [*drawing*]   I am for you.
    ROMEO   Gentle Mercutio, put thy rapier up.
    MERCUTIO [*to* TYBALT]   Come, sir, your *passado*.°   *forward thrust*
            [*They fight*]
80 ROMEO [*drawing*]   Draw, Benvolio. Beat down their weapons.
        Gentlemen, for shame forbear this outrage.°   *disgraceful tumult*
        Tybalt, Mercutio, the Prince expressly hath
        Forbid this bandying° in Verona streets.   *strife*

---

4. Mercutio obnoxiously mistakes Tybalt's "my man" for
"personal servant."
5. *Doth . . . / To:* Permits me to put aside my otherwise
appropriate anger at.
6. The rapier thrust wins the day.
7. And, according to how you subsequently treat me.

Hold, Tybalt, good Mercutio.
[ROMEO *beats down their points and rushes between*
them.] TYBALT *under Romeo's arm thrusts* MERCUTIO *in*
85 PETRUCCIO   Away, Tybalt!
             Exeunt TYBALT [PETRUCCIO, *and their followers*]
MERCUTIO   I am hurt.
  A plague o' both your houses. I am sped.°   *finished*
  Is he gone, and hath nothing?
BENVOLIO   What, art thou hurt?
MERCUTIO   Ay, ay, a scratch, a scratch; marry, 'tis enough.
90   Where is my page? Go, villain. Fetch a surgeon.
                                  [*Exit page*]
ROMEO   Courage, man. The hurt cannot be much.
MERCUTIO   No, 'tis not so deep as a well, nor so wide as a church
  door, but 'tis enough. 'Twill serve. Ask for me tomorrow, and
  you shall find me a grave man. I am peppered,° I warrant, for   *done for*
95   this world. A plague o' both your houses! Zounds, a dog, a rat,
  a mouse, a cat, to scratch a man to death! A braggart, a rogue,
  a villain, that fights by the book of arithmetic!⁸ Why the devil
  came you between us? I was hurt under your arm.
ROMEO   I thought all for the best.
100 MERCUTIO   Help me into some house, Benvolio,
  Or I shall faint. A plague o' both your houses.
  They have made worms' meat of me.
  I have it, and soundly, too. Your houses!
                      Exeunt [*all but* ROMEO]
ROMEO   This gentleman, the Prince's near ally,°   *relative*
105   My very° friend, hath got this mortal hurt   *true*
  In my behalf, my reputation stained
  With Tybalt's slander—Tybalt, that an hour
  Hath been my cousin! O sweet Juliet,
  Thy beauty hath made me effeminate,
110   And in my temper⁹ softened valour's steel.
    Enter BENVOLIO
BENVOLIO   O Romeo, Romeo, brave Mercutio is dead!
  That gallant spirit hath aspired° the clouds,   *ascended to*
  Which too untimely here did scorn the earth.
ROMEO   This day's black fate on more days doth depend.°   *hang over*
115   This but begins the woe others must end.
    Enter TYBALT
BENVOLIO   Here comes the furious Tybalt back again.
ROMEO   He gad in triumph, and Mercutio slain?
  Away to heaven, respective lenity,°   *respectful lenience*
  And fire-eyed fury be my conduct° now.   *guide*
120   Now, Tybalt, take the 'villain' back again
  That late thou gav'st me, for Mercutio's soul
  Is but a little way above our heads,
  Staying for thine to keep him company.
  Either thou, or I, or both must go with him.
125 TYBALT   Thou, wretched boy, that didst consort° him here, *accompany*
  Shalt with him hence.

---

8. By the numbers; according to a fencing manual.
9. Emotional makeup, here suggesting the hardened
character of a fighting man. It was believed that too much
time with or passion for women would cause a man to
become effeminate.

ROMEO   This shall determine that.
    They fight. TYBALT *falls [and dies]*
BENVOLIO   Romeo, away, be gone.
  The citizens are up,° and Tybalt slain.   *up in arms*
  Stand not amazed.° The Prince will doom° thee death   *stupefied / sentence*
130 If thou art taken. Hence, be gone, away.
ROMEO   O, I am fortune's fool!°   *dupe*
BENVOLIO   Why dost thou stay?
                                          Exit ROMEO
    Enter CITIZENS [OF THE WATCH]
CITIZEN OF THE WATCH   Which way ran he that killed Mercutio?
  Tybalt, that murderer, which way ran he?
BENVOLIO   There lies that Tybalt.
CITIZEN OF THE WATCH [*to* TYBALT] Up, sir, go with me.
135 I charge thee in the Prince's name, obey.
    Enter PRINCE, *old* MONTAGUE, CAPULET, *their* WIVES,
    and all
PRINCE   Where are the vile beginners of this fray?
BENVOLIO   O noble Prince, I can discover° all   *reveal*
  The unlucky manage° of this fatal brawl.   *handling*
  There lies the man, slain by young Romeo,
140 That slew thy kinsman, brave Mercutio.
CAPULET'S WIFE   Tybalt, my cousin, O, my brother's child!
  O Prince, O cousin, husband! O, the blood is spilled
  Of my dear kinsman! Prince, as thou art true,
  For blood of ours shed blood of Montague!
  O cousin, cousin!
145 PRINCE   Benvolio, who began this fray?
BENVOLIO   Tybalt, here slain, whom Romeo's hand did slay.
  Romeo, that spoke him° fair,° bid him bethink   *to him / courteously*
  How nice° the quarrel was, and urged withal°   *trivial / also*
  Your high displeasure. All this—utterèd
150 With gentle breath, calm look, knees humbly bowed—
  Could not take° truce with the unruly spleen°   *arrange / bitter mood*
  Of Tybalt deaf to peace, but that he tilts
  With piercing steel at bold Mercutio's breast,
  Who, all as hot, turns deadly point to point,
155 And, with a martial scorn, with one hand beats
  Cold death aside,[1] and with the other sends
  It back to Tybalt, whose dexterity
  Retorts° it. Romeo, he cries aloud,   *Returns*
  'Hold, friends, friends, part!' and swifter than his tongue
160 His agent° arm beats down their fatal points,   *effective*
  And 'twixt them rushes, underneath whose arm
  An envious° thrust from Tybalt hit the life   *A malicious*
  Of stout° Mercutio, and then Tybalt fled,   *courageous*
  But by and by comes back to Romeo,
165 Who had but newly entertained° revenge,   *considered*
  And to't they go like lightning; for ere I
  Could draw to part them was stout Tybalt slain,
  And as he fell did Romeo turn and fly.
  This is the truth, or let Benvolio die.

---

1. *with . . . aside:* the two would have been fighting either with daggers in or cloaks rolled about their second hand to ward off the other's weapon.

170 CAPULET'S WIFE   He is a kinsman to the Montague.
     Affection makes him false; he speaks not true.
     Some twenty of them fought in this black strife,
     And all those twenty could but kill one life.
     I beg for justice, which thou, Prince, must give.
175 Romeo slew Tybalt; Romeo must not live.
     PRINCE   Romeo slew him, he slew Mercutio.
     Who now the price of his° dear blood doth owe?   (Mercutio's)
     MONTAGUE   Not Romeo, Prince. He was Mercutio's friend.
     His fault° concludes but what the law should end,   offense
     The life of Tybalt.
180 PRINCE   And for that offence
     Immediately we do exile him hence.
     I have an interest in your hate's proceeding;
     My blood° for your rude brawls doth lie a-bleeding.   kinsman
     But I'll amerce° you with so strong a fine   penalize
185 That you shall all repent the loss of mine.
     I will be deaf to pleading and excuses.
     Nor tears nor prayers shall purchase out° abuses.   compensate for
     Therefore use none. Let Romeo hence in haste,
     Else, when he is found, that hour is his last.
190 Bear hence this body, and attend our will.
     Mercy but murders, pardoning those that kill.
                              Exeunt [with the body]

                         3.2

           Enter JULIET *alone*
     JULIET   Gallop apace,° you fiery-footed steeds,   quickly
     Towards Phoebus' lodging.¹ Such a waggoner°   charioteer
     As Phaëton² would whip you to the west
     And bring in cloudy night immediately.
5   Spread thy close° curtain, love-performing night,   covering
     That runaways'³ eyes may wink,° and Romeo   close
     Leap to these arms untalked of and unseen.
     Lovers can see to do their amorous rites
     By their own beauties; or, if love be blind,
10   It best agrees with night. Come, civil° night,   solemn
     Thou sober-suited matron all in black,
     And learn me how to lose a winning match⁴
     Played for a pair of stainless maidenhoods.
     Hood my unmanned° blood, bating⁵ in my cheeks,   untamed; virgin
15   With thy black mantle till strange° love grown bold   shy
     Think true love acted simple° modesty.   mere; innocent
     Come night, come Romeo; come, thou day in night,
     For thou wilt lie upon the wings of night
     Whiter than new snow on a raven's back.
20   Come, gentle night; come, loving, black-browed night,
     Give me my Romeo, and when I shall die

3.2 Location: Capulet's house.
1. Under the world to the west, where the sun god Phoebus Apollo was imagined to rest with his fiery chariot at
night.
2. The son of Apollo, who rashly attempted to steer his
father's chariot across the sky. To save the earth from
scorching, Jupiter struck him down with a lightning bolt.

3. Either the runaway horses of the sun or roving and
curious vagabonds.
4. A competition, marriage, or husband. All are won by
surrendering.
5. Fluttering like a restless falcon before its eyes are covered with a "hood" to calm it.

Take him and cut him out in little stars,[6]
And he will make the face of heaven so fine
That all the world will be in love with night
25 And pay no worship to the garish sun.
O, I have bought the mansion of a love
But not possessed it, and though I am sold,[7]
Not yet enjoyed. So tedious is this day
As is the night before some festival
30 To an impatient child that hath new robes
And may not wear them.

> *Enter* NURSE, [*wringing her hands,*] *with the ladder of*
> *cords in her lap*°   bodice fold

                    O, here comes my Nurse,
And she brings news, and every tongue that speaks
But Romeo's name speaks heavenly eloquence.
Now, Nurse, what news? What, hast thou there
The cords that Romeo bid thee fetch?
35 NURSE [*putting down the cords*]   Ay, ay, the cords.
JULIET   Ay me, what news? Why dost thou wring thy hands?
NURSE   Ah, welladay!° He's dead, he's dead, he's dead!   alas
   We are undone, lady, we are undone.
   Alack the day, he's gone, he's killed, he's dead!
JULIET   Can heaven be so envious?°   spiteful; jealous
40 NURSE   Romeo can,
   Though heaven cannot. O Romeo, Romeo,
   Who ever would have thought it Romeo?
JULIET   What devil art thou that dost torment me thus?
   This torture should be roared in dismal hell.
45 Hath Romeo slain himself? Say thou but 'Ay',
   And that bare vowel 'I' shall poison more
   Than the death-darting eye of cockatrice.[8]
   I am not I if there be such an 'Ay',
   Or those eyes shut that makes thee answer 'Ay'.
50 If he be slain, say 'Ay'; or if not, 'No'.
   Brief sounds determine of my weal° or woe.   welfare
NURSE   I saw the wound, I saw it with mine eyes,
   God save the mark,[9] here on his manly breast—
   A piteous corpse, a bloody, piteous corpse—
55 Pale, pale as ashes, all bedaubed in blood,
   All in gore° blood; I swoonèd at the sight.   clotted
JULIET   O, break, my heart, poor bankrupt,[1] break at once!
   To prison, eyes; ne'er look on liberty.
   Vile earth,[2] to earth resign; end motion° here,   movement; emotion
60 And thou and Romeo press[3] one heavy° bier!   weighty; sad
NURSE   O Tybalt, Tybalt, the best friend I had!
   O courteous Tybalt, honest° gentleman,   honorable
   That ever I should live to see thee dead!
JULIET   What storm is this that blows so contrary?
65 Is Romeo slaughtered, and is Tybalt dead?

---

6. *Take . . . stars:* an imagined tranformation, based on
those in Ovid's *Metamorphoses*, whereby Romeo also dies
and is immortalized. Q4's reading of "he" for "I" (line 21)
makes more immediate sense and is often accepted. Also,
"die" could mean "have an orgasm."
7. *O . . . sold:* the image is symmetrical: first Juliet buys
the mansion, and then she becomes the "sold" house.

8. A mythical serpent that kills by merely looking.
9. An apology for mentioning something unpleasant, but
also emphasizing the fatal "mark" of the rapier.
1. Bankruptcy was punishable by imprisonment.
2. The despised body, echoing Ecclesiastes 12:7. "Then
shall the dust return to the earth as it was."
3. Burden; embrace.

My dearest cousin and my dearer lord?
Then, dreadful trumpet, sound the general doom,[4]
For who is living if those two are gone?
NURSE   Tybalt is gone and Romeo banishèd.
70   Romeo that killed him—he is banishèd.
JULIET   O God, did Romeo's hand shed Tybalt's blood?
NURSE   It did, it did, alas the day, it did.
JULIET   O serpent heart hid with° a flow'ring° face!   *by / lovely; benign*
Did ever dragon keep° so fair a cave?   *guard*
75   Beautiful tyrant, fiend angelical!
Dove-feathered raven, wolvish-ravening lamb!
Despisèd substance of divinest show!°   *appearance*
Just opposite to what thou justly° seem'st—   *precisely; rightfully*
A damnèd saint, an honourable villain.
80   O nature, what hadst thou to do[5] in hell
When thou didst bower[6] the spirit of a fiend
In mortal paradise of such sweet flesh?
Was ever book containing such vile matter
So fairly bound? O, that deceit should dwell
85   In such a gorgeous palace!
NURSE   There's no trust, no faith, no honesty in men;
All perjured, all forsworn, all naught,° dissemblers all.   *wicked*
Ah, where's my man? Give me some aqua vitae.°   *brandy*
These griefs, these woes, these sorrows make me old.
Shame come to Romeo!
90   JULIET   Blistered be thy tongue
For such a wish! He was not born to shame.
Upon his brow shame is ashamed to sit,
For 'tis a throne where honour may be crowned
Sole monarch of the universal earth.
95   O, what a beast was I to chide at him!
NURSE   Will you speak well of him that killed your cousin?
JULIET   Shall I speak ill of him that is my husband?
Ah, poor my° lord, what tongue shall smooth° thy name   *my poor / praise*
When I, thy three-hours wife, have mangled it?
100   But wherefore, villain, didst thou kill my cousin?
That villain cousin would have killed my husband.
Back, foolish tears, back to your native spring!
Your tributary[7] drops belong to woe,
Which you, mistaking, offer up to joy.[8]
105   My husband lives, that Tybalt would have slain;
And Tybalt's dead, that would have slain my husband.
All this is comfort. Wherefore° weep I then?   *Why*
Some word there was, worser than Tybalt's death,
That murdered me. I would forget it fain,°   *gladly*
110   But O, it presses to my memory
Like damnèd guilty deeds to sinners' minds!
'Tybalt is dead, and Romeo banishèd.'
That 'banishèd', that one word 'banishèd'
Hath slain ten thousand Tybalts. Tybalt's death
115   Was woe enough, if it had ended there;

4. The Last Judgment announced with angel's trumpets.
5. What were you doing.
6. Lodge or enclose, suggesting a surrounding garden.
7. Tribute-paying; in-flowing.
8. Offer up to a joyful (and thus inappropriate) occasion.

Or, if sour woe delights in fellowship
And needly° will be ranked with⁹ other griefs,   *necessarily*
Why followed not, when she said 'Tybalt's dead',
'Thy father', or 'thy mother', nay, or both,
120 Which modern° lamentation might have moved?°   *ordinary / produced*
But with a rearward following Tybalt's death,
'Romeo is banishèd'—to speak that word
Is father, mother, Tybalt, Romeo, Juliet,
All slain, all dead. 'Romeo is banishèd'—
125 There is no end, no limit, measure, bound,
In that word's death. No words can that woe sound.°   *utter; fathom*
Where is my father and my mother, Nurse?
NURSE Weeping and wailing over Tybalt's corpse.
Will you go to them? I will bring you thither.
130 JULIET Wash they his wounds with tears; mine shall be spent
When theirs are dry, for Romeo's banishment.
Take up those cords. Poor ropes, you are beguiled,°   *cheated*
Both you and I, for Romeo is exiled.
He made you for a highway to my bed,
135 But I, a maid, die maiden-widowèd.
Come, cords; come, Nurse; I'll to my wedding bed,
And death, not Romeo, take my maidenhead!
NURSE [*taking up the cords*] Hie to your chamber. I'll find Romeo
To comfort you. I wot° well where he is.   *know*
140 Hark ye, your Romeo will be here at night.
I'll to him. He is hid at Laurence' cell.
JULIET [*giving her a ring*] O, find him! Give this ring to my true knight,
And bid him come to take his last farewell.   *Exeunt [severally]*

3.3
Enter FRIAR [LAURENCE]
FRIAR LAURENCE Romeo, come forth, come forth, thou fear-full man.
Affliction is enamoured of thy parts,°   *qualities*
And thou art wedded to calamity.
Enter ROMEO
ROMEO Father, what news? What is the Prince's doom?°   *sentence*
5 What sorrow craves acquaintance at my hand
That I yet know not?
FRIAR LAURENCE   Too familiar
Is my dear son with such sour company.
I bring thee tidings of the Prince's doom.
ROMEO What less than doomsday is the Prince's doom?
10 FRIAR LAURENCE A gentler judgement vanished° from his lips: *escaped*
Not body's death, but body's banishment.
ROMEO Ha, banishment? Be merciful, say 'death',
For exile hath more terror in his look,
Much more than death. Do not say 'banishment'.
15 FRIAR LAURENCE Hence from Verona art thou banishèd.
Be patient,° for the world is broad and wide.   *able to endure*
ROMEO There is no world without° Verona walls   *outside*
But purgatory, torture, hell itself.
Hence banishèd is banished from the world,
20 And world's exile is death. Then 'banishèd'

9. Will be accompanied by.   **3.3** Location: Friar Laurence's cell.

Is death mistermed. Calling death 'banishèd'
Thou cutt'st my head off with a golden axe,
And smil'st upon° the stroke that murders me.   *at*
FRIAR LAURENCE   O deadly° sin, O rude unthankfulness!   *damnable*
25   Thy fault our law calls death,° but the kind Prince,   *a capital offense*
    Taking thy part, hath rushed° aside the law   *forced*
    And turned that black word 'death' to banishment.
    This is dear mercy, and thou seest it not.
ROMEO   'Tis torture, and not mercy. Heaven is here
30   Where Juliet lives, and every cat and dog
    And little mouse, every unworthy thing,
    Live here in heaven and may look on her,
    But Romeo may not. More validity,°   *health*
    More honourable state, more courtship° lives   *courtly state; wooing*
35   In carrion flies than Romeo. They may seize
    On the white wonder of dear Juliet's hand,
    And steal immortal blessing from her lips,
    Who, even in pure and vestal° modesty,   *virginal*
    Still° blush, as thinking their own kisses[1] sin.   *Always*
40   But Romeo may not, he is banishèd.
    Flies may do this, but I from this must fly.
    They are free men, but I am banishèd.
    And sayst thou yet that exile is not death?
    Hadst thou no poison mixed, no sharp-ground knife,
45   No sudden mean° of death, though ne'er so mean,°   *method / ignoble*
    But 'banishèd' to kill me — 'banishèd'?
    O friar, the damnèd use that word in hell.[2]
    Howling attends it. How hast thou the heart,
    Being a divine, a ghostly confessor,
50   A sin-absolver and my friend professed,
    To mangle me with that word 'banishèd'?
FRIAR LAURENCE   Thou fond° mad man, hear me a little speak.   *foolish; infatuated*
ROMEO   O, thou wilt speak again of banishment.
FRIAR LAURENCE   I'll give thee armour to keep off that word —
55   Adversity's sweet milk, philosophy,
    To comfort thee though thou art banishèd.
ROMEO   Yet 'banishèd'? Hang up° philosophy!   *Hang up = Hang*
    Unless philosophy can make a Juliet,
    Displant° a town, reverse a prince's doom,   *Uproot*
60   It helps not, it prevails not. Talk no more.
FRIAR LAURENCE   O, then I see that madmen have no ears.
ROMEO   How should they, when that wise men have no eyes?
FRIAR LAURENCE   Let me dispute° with thee of thy estate.°   *discuss / position*
ROMEO   Thou canst not speak of that thou dost not feel.
65   Wert thou as young as I, Juliet thy love,
    An hour but° married, Tybalt murderèd,   *only*
    Doting like me, and like me banishèd,
    Then mightst thou speak, then mightst thou tear thy hair,
    And fall upon the ground, as I do now,
        [*He falls upon the ground*]
70   Taking the measure of an unmade grave.
        Knock [*within*]
FRIAR LAURENCE   Arise, one knocks. Good Romeo, hide thyself.

1. Their touching each other in closing.   2. Because they are banished from heaven.

ROMEO   Not I, unless the breath of heartsick groans
   Mist-like enfold me from the search of eyes.
       Knock [within]
FRIAR LAURENCE   Hark, how they knock!—Who's there?—
   Romeo, arise.
75   Thou wilt be taken.—Stay a while.—Stand up.
       [Still] knock [within]
   Run to my study.—By and by!—God's will,°   *By providence*
   What simpleness° is this?   *stupidity*
       Knock [within]
                 I come, I come.
   Who knocks so hard? Whence come you? What's your will?
NURSE *[within]*[3]   Let me come in, and you shall know my errand.
   I come from Lady Juliet.
80 FRIAR LAURENCE *[opening the door]* Welcome then.
       Enter NURSE
NURSE   O holy friar, O tell me, holy friar,
   Where is my lady's lord? Where's Romeo?
FRIAR LAURENCE   There on the ground, with his own tears
       made drunk.
NURSE   O, he is even° in my mistress' case,°   *exactly / condition; vagina*
85   Just in her case! O woeful sympathy,
   Piteous predicament! Even so lies she,
   Blubb'ring and weeping, weeping and blubb'ring.
   [To ROMEO] Stand up, stand up, stand an° you be a man,   *if*
   For Juliet's sake, for her sake, rise and stand.
90   Why should you fall into so deep an O?°   *a groaning*
ROMEO *[rises]*   Nurse.
NURSE   Ah sir, ah sir, death's the end of all.[4]
ROMEO   Spak'st thou of Juliet? How is it with her?
   Doth not she think me an old° murderer,   *a practiced*
   Now I have stained the childhood of our joy
95   With blood removed but little from her own?
   Where is she, and how doth she, and what says
   My concealed lady° to our cancelled° love?   *secret wife / invalidated*
NURSE   O, she says nothing, sir, but weeps and weeps,
   And now falls on her bed, and then starts up,
100   And 'Tybalt' calls, and then on Romeo cries,
   And then down falls again.
ROMEO   As if that name
   Shot from the deadly level° of a gun   *aim*
   Did murder her as that name's cursèd hand
   Murdered her kinsman. O tell me, friar, tell me,
105   In what vile part of this anatomy
   Doth my name lodge? Tell me, that I may sack
   The hateful mansion.
       He offers to stab himself, and NURSE *snatches the dagger*
       away
FRIAR LAURENCE   Hold° thy desperate hand.   *Restrain*
   Art thou a man? Thy form cries out thou art.
   Thy tears are womanish, thy wild acts denote
110   The unreasonable° fury of a beast.   *incapable of reason*

---

3. Behind one of the doors at the back of the stage, repre-   4. A proverbial "consolation."
senting the door of the cell.

Unseemly° woman in a seeming man,   *Inappropriate; immodest*
And ill-beseeming beast in seeming both!⁵
Thou hast amazed° me. By my holy order,   *flabbergasted*
I thought thy disposition better tempered.
115 Hast thou slain Tybalt? Wilt thou slay thyself,
And slay thy lady that in thy life lives
By doing damnèd° hate upon thyself?   *sinful*
Why rail'st thou on thy birth, the heaven, and earth,
Since birth° and heaven° and earth,° all three, do meet   *nobility / soul / body*
120 In thee at once, which thou at once wouldst lose?
Fie, fie, thou sham'st thy shape, thy love, thy wit,
Which like a usurer abound'st in all,
And usest none in that true use indeed
Which should bedeck thy shape, thy love, thy wit.⁶
125 Thy noble shape is but a form° of wax,   *figure*
Digressing° from the valour of a man;   *If it deviates*
Thy dear love sworn but hollow perjury,
Killing that love which thou hast vowed to cherish;
Thy wit, that ornament° to shape and love,   *necessary accessory*
130 Misshapen° in the conduct° of them both,   *Inept / management*
Like powder in a skilless soldier's flask
Is set afire by thine own ignorance,
And thou dismembered° with thine own defence.°   *blown apart / weapon*
What, rouse thee, man! Thy Juliet is alive,
135 For whose dear sake thou wast but lately dead:
There art thou happy. Tybalt would kill thee,
But thou slewest Tybalt: there art thou happy.
The law that threatened death becomes thy friend,
And turns it to exile: there art thou happy.
140 A pack of blessings light upon thy back,
Happiness courts thee in her best array,
But, like a mishavèd° and sullen wench,   *misbehaved*
Thou pout'st upon thy fortune and thy love.
Take heed, take heed, for such die miserable.
145 Go, get thee to thy love, as was decreed.
Ascend her chamber; hence and comfort her.
But look thou stay not till the watch be set,⁷
For then thou canst not pass to Mantua,
Where thou shalt live till we can find a time
150 To blaze° your marriage, reconcile your friends,°   *make public / kin*
Beg pardon of the Prince, and call thee back
With twenty hundred thousand times more joy
Than thou went'st forth in lamentation.
Go before, Nurse. Commend me to thy lady,
155 And bid her hasten all the house to bed,
Which heavy sorrow makes them apt unto.
Romeo is coming.
NURSE   O Lord, I could have stayed here all the night
To hear good counsel! O, what learning is!
160 My lord, I'll tell my lady you will come.
ROMEO   Do so, and bid my sweet prepare to chide.

---

5. An unnatural beast in seeming both man and unreasoning animal.
6. *thou sham'st . . . wit:* you abound in looks, love, and intelligence ("wit"), but you do not use them judiciously

and are therefore like a usurer who acquires money for its own sake, without putting it to good use.
7. Until the guards take up their positions (at the city gates).

NURSE *offers to go in, and turns again*
NURSE [*giving the ring*]   Here, sir, a ring she bid me give you, sir.
    Hie you,° make haste, for it grows very late.   *Hurry*
ROMEO   How well my comfort° is revived by this.   *Exit* NURSE   *happiness*
FRIAR LAURENCE   Go hence, good night, and here stands° all   *and on this depends*
165   your state.
    Either be gone before the watch be set,
    Or by the break of day disguised from hence.
    Sojourn in Mantua. I'll find out your man,
    And he shall signify from time to time
170   Every good hap° to you that chances here.   *event*
    Give me thy hand. 'Tis late. Farewell. Good night.
ROMEO   But that a joy past joy calls out on me,
    It were a grief so brief° to part with thee.   *hastily*
    Farewell.   *Exeunt* [*severally*]

3.4

Enter old CAPULET, *his* WIFE, *and* PARIS
CAPULET   Things have fall'n out, sir, so unluckily
    That we have had no time to move° our daughter.   *persuade*
    Look you, she loved her kinsman Tybalt dearly,
    And so did I. Well, we were born to die.
5   'Tis very late. She'll not come down tonight.
    I promise you, but for your company
    I would have been abed an hour ago.
PARIS   These times of woe afford no times to woo.
    Madam, good night. Commend me to your daughter.
10 CAPULET'S WIFE   I will, and know her mind early tomorrow.
    Tonight she's mewed up to¹ her heaviness.°   *sadness*
           PARIS *offers to go in, and* CAPULET *calls him again*
CAPULET   Sir Paris, I will make a desperate tender°   *a reckless offer*
    Of my child's love. I think she will be ruled
    In all respects by me. Nay, more, I doubt it not.
15   Wife, go you to her ere you go to bed.
    Acquaint her here of my son Paris' love,
    And bid her—mark you me?—on Wednesday next—
    But soft—what day is this?
PARIS   Monday, my lord.
CAPULET   Monday. Ha, ha! Well, Wednesday is too soon.
20   O' Thursday let it be. O' Thursday, tell her,
    She shall be married to this noble earl.
    Will you be ready? Do you like this haste?
    We'll keep° no great ado—a friend or two.   *celebrate with*
    For hark you, Tybalt being slain so late,°   *recently*
25   It may be thought we held° him carelessly,°   *regarded / indifferently*
    Being our kinsman, if we revel much.
    Therefore we'll have some half a dozen friends,
    And there an end. But what say you to Thursday?
PARIS   My lord, I would° that Thursday were tomorrow.   *wish*
30 CAPULET   Well, get you gone. O' Thursday be it, then.
    [*To his* WIFE] Go you to Juliet ere you go to bed.
    Prepare her, wife, against° this wedding day.—   *for*

3.4 Location: Capulet's house.   1. Shut in with. The "mews" are hawks' housing.

Farewell, my lord.—Light to my chamber, ho!—
Afore me,° it is so very late that we   *By my life*
35   May call it early by and by. Good night.

Exeunt [CAPULET *and his* WIFE *at*
one door, PARIS *at another door*]

3.5

Enter ROMEO *and* JULIET *aloft* [*with the ladder of cords*]

JULIET   Wilt thou be gone? It is not yet near day.
It was the nightingale, and not the lark,
That pierced the fear-full hollow of thine ear.
Nightly she sings on yon pom'granate tree.
5   Believe me, love, it was the nightingale.
ROMEO   It was the lark, the herald of the morn,
No nightingale. Look, love, what envious° streaks   *spiteful*
Do lace the severing° clouds in yonder east.   *parting*
Night's candles are burnt out, and jocund day
10   Stands tiptoe on the misty mountain tops.
I must be gone and live, or stay and die.
JULIET   Yon light is not daylight; I know it, I.
It is some meteor that the sun exhaled[1]
To be to thee this night a torchbearer
15   And light thee on thy way to Mantua.
Therefore stay yet. Thou need'st not to be gone.
ROMEO   Let me be ta'en, let me be put to death.
I am content, so° thou wilt have it so.   *as long as*
I'll say yon grey is not the morning's eye,
20   'Tis but the pale reflex° of Cynthia's° brow;   *reflection / the moon's*
Nor that is not the lark whose notes do beat
The vaulty heaven so high above our heads.
I have more care° to stay than will to go.   *desire*
Come, death, and welcome; Juliet wills it so.
25   How is't, my soul? Let's talk. It is not day.
JULIET   It is, it is. Hie hence, be gone, away.
It is the lark that sings so out of tune,
Straining° harsh discords and unpleasing sharps.[2]   *Distorting; tuning up*
Some say the lark makes sweet division;°   *variations on a melody*
30   This doth not so, for she divideth° us.   *separates*
Some say the lark and loathèd toad changed eyes.[3]
O, now I would they had changed voices, too,
Since arm from arm that voice doth us affray,°   *frighten*
Hunting thee hence with hunt's-up[4] to the day.
35   O, now be gone! More light and light it grows.
ROMEO   More light and light, more dark and dark our woes.

Enter NURSE *hastily*

NURSE   Madam.
JULIET   Nurse.
NURSE   Your lady mother is coming to your chamber.
40   The day is broke; be wary, look about.   [*Exit*]

3.5 Location: The upper acting area represents Juliet's
window or balcony. The main stage represents Capulet's
orchard until line 59, then the interior of Capulet's house
from line 64.
1. Breathed. Meteors were thought to be impure vapors
that the sun had drawn up from the earth and ignited,
and were usually considered bad omens.

2. Harsh sounds, too-high tones.
3. A folk explanation for the supposed ugliness of the
lark's eyes and the beauty of the toad's. *changed:*
exchanged.
4. Morning song used to wake the bride after the wedding night.

JULIET   Then, window, let day in, and let life out.

ROMEO   Farewell, farewell! One kiss, and I'll descend.

He [lets down the ladder of cords and] goes down

JULIET   Art thou gone so, love, lord, my husband, friend?°   lover

    I must hear from thee every day in the hour,

45   For in a minute there are many days.

    O, by this count I shall be much in years

    Ere I again behold my Romeo.

ROMEO   Farewell.

    I will omit no opportunity

50   That may convey my greetings, love, to thee.

JULIET   O, think'st thou we shall ever meet again?

ROMEO   I doubt it not, and all these woes shall serve

    For sweet discourses° in our times to come.   conversations

JULIET   O God, I have an ill-divining° soul!   a misfortune-predicting

55   Methinks I see thee, now thou art so low,

    As one dead in the bottom of a tomb.

    Either my eyesight fails, or thou look'st pale.

ROMEO   And trust me, love, in my eye so do you.

    Dry sorrow drinks our blood.[5] Adieu, adieu.   *Exit*

JULIET [*pulling up the ladder and weeping*]   O fortune, fortune,

60   all men call thee fickle.

    If thou art fickle, what dost thou with him

    That is renowned for faith?° Be fickle, fortune,   fidelity

    For then I hope thou wilt not keep him long,

    But send him back.

Enter [CAPULET'S WIFE below]

CAPULET'S WIFE   Ho, daughter, are you up?

65 JULIET   Who is't that calls? It is my lady mother.

    Is she not down° so late, or up so early?   in bed

    What unaccustomed cause procures° her hither?   brings

She goes down [and enters below]

CAPULET'S WIFE   Why, how now, Juliet?

JULIET   Madam, I am not well.

CAPULET'S WIFE   Evermore weeping for your cousin's death?

70   What, wilt thou wash him from his grave with tears?

    An if thou couldst, thou couldst not make him live,

    Therefore have done. Some grief shows much of love,

    But much of grief shows still° some want° of wit.   always / lack

JULIET   Yet let me weep for such a feeling° loss.   profound

75 CAPULET'S WIFE   So shall you feel° the loss, but not the friend°   experience; touch / kin

    Which you so weep for.

JULIET   Feeling so the loss,

    I cannot choose but ever weep the friend.°   lover

CAPULET'S WIFE   Well, girl, thou weep'st not so much for his death

    As that the villain lives which slaughtered him.

JULIET   What villain, madam?

80 CAPULET'S WIFE   That same villain Romeo.

JULIET [*aside*]   Villain and he be many miles asunder.

    [*To her mother*] God pardon him—I do, with all my heart,

    And yet no man like° he doth grieve my heart.   so much as; resembling

CAPULET'S WIFE   That is because the traitor murderer lives.

---

5. *Dry . . . blood:* Each sigh supposedly cost the heart a drop of blood and caused the blood's sorrowful heat to simmer away its fluids. Thus, the lovers are pale. *Dry:* Thirsty.

85 JULIET   Ay, madam, from the reach of these my hands.
         Would none but I might venge my cousin's death.
    CAPULET'S WIFE   We will have vengeance for it, fear thou not.
         Then weep no more. I'll send to one in Mantua,
         Where that same banished runagate doth live,
90   Shall give him such an unaccustomed dram
         That he shall soon keep Tybalt company;
         And then I hope thou wilt be satisfied.°   *sufficiently avenged*
    JULIET   Indeed, I never shall be satisfied
         With Romeo till I behold him, dead,
95   Is my poor heart⁶ so for a kinsman vexed.
         Madam, if you could find out but a man
         To bear a poison, I would temper° it   *mix; dilute*
         That Romeo should, upon receipt thereof,
         Soon sleep in quiet. O, how my heart abhors
100   To hear him named and cannot come to him
         To wreak the love I bore my cousin
         Upon his body that hath slaughtered him!
    CAPULET'S WIFE   Find thou the means, and I'll find such a man.
         But now I'll tell thee joyful tidings, girl.
105 JULIET   And joy comes well in such a needy time.
         What are they, I beseech your ladyship?
    CAPULET'S WIFE   Well, well, thou hast a careful° father, child;   *solicitous*
         One who, to put thee from thy heaviness,
         Hath sorted out a sudden° day of joy   *chosen an immediate*
110   That thou expect'st not, nor I looked not for.
    JULIET   Madam, in happy° time. What day is that?   *at a fortunate*
    CAPULET'S WIFE   Marry, my child, early next Thursday morn
         The gallant, young, and noble gentleman
         The County Paris at Saint Peter's Church
115   Shall happily make thee there a joyful bride.
    JULIET   Now, by Saint Peter's Church, and Peter too,
         He shall not make me there a joyful bride.
         I wonder° at this haste, that I must wed   *am astonished*
         Ere he that should be husband comes to woo.
120   I pray you, tell my lord and father, madam,
         I will not marry yet; and when I do, I swear
         It shall be Romeo—whom you know I hate—
         Rather than Paris. These are news indeed.
              Enter old CAPULET *and* NURSE
    CAPULET'S WIFE   Here comes your father. Tell him so yourself,
125   And see how he will take it at your hands.
    CAPULET   When the sun sets, the earth doth drizzle° dew,   *weep out*
         But for the sunset of my brother's son
         It rains downright.
         How now, a conduit,° girl? What, still in tears?   *fountain*
130   Evermore show'ring? In one little body
         Thou counterfeit'st a barque,° a sea, a wind,   *represent a ship*
         For still thy eyes—which I may call the sea—
         Do ebb and flow with tears. The barque thy body is,
         Sailing in this salt flood; the winds thy sighs,
135   Who,° raging with thy tears and they with them,   *Which*

---

6. *till . . . heart:* Juliet allows her mother to understand that she will not be satisfied "till I behold him dead," while privately meaning that until she beholds him, "dead is my poor heart."

Without a sudden calm will overset
Thy tempest-tossèd body.—How now, wife?
Have you delivered to her our decree?
CAPULET'S WIFE   Ay, sir, but she will none,° she gives you thanks.[7]   *not agree*
140   I would the fool° were married to her grave.   *peevish child*
CAPULET   Soft, take me with you,[8] take me with you, wife.
How, will she none? Doth she not give us thanks?
Is she not proud?° Doth she not count her blest,   *gratified*
Unworthy as she is, that we have wrought°   *contrived for*
145   So worthy a gentleman to be her bride?°   *bridegroom*
JULIET   Not proud you have, but thankful that you have.
Proud can I never be of what I hate,
But thankful even for hate° that is meant love.°   *a hateful thing / as love*
CAPULET   How, how, how, how—chopped logic?° What is this?   *mere sophistry*
150   'Proud', and 'I thank you', and 'I thank you not',
And yet 'not proud'? Mistress minion,° you,   *spoiled child*
Thank me no thankings, nor proud me no prouds,
But fettle° your fine joints 'gainst° Thursday next   *prepare / for*
To go with Paris to Saint Peter's Church,
155   Or I will drag thee on a hurdle[9] thither.
Out,[1] you green-sickness carrion! Out, you baggage,
You tallow-face!
CAPULET'S WIFE   Fie, fie, what, are you mad?
JULIET (*kneels down*)   Good father, I beseech you on my knees,
Hear me with patience but to speak a word.
160   CAPULET   Hang thee, young baggage, disobedient wretch!
I tell thee what: get thee to church o' Thursday,
Or never after look me in the face.
Speak not, reply not, do not answer me.
[JULIET *rises*]
My fingers itch. Wife, we scarce thought us blest
165   That God had lent us but this only child,
But now I see this one is one too much,
And that we have a curse in having her.
Out on her, hilding!°   *hussy*
NURSE   God in heaven bless her!
You are to blame, my lord, to rate° her so.   *berate*
170   CAPULET   And why, my lady Wisdom? Hold your tongue,
Good Prudence. Smatter° with your gossips,° go!   *Chatter / cronies*
NURSE   I speak no treason.
CAPULET   O, God-i'-good-e'en!°   *for God's sake*
NURSE   May not one speak?
CAPULET   Peace, you mumbling fool,
Utter your gravity° o'er a gossip's bowl,°   *wisdom / drinking bowl*
For here we need it not.
175   CAPULET'S WIFE   You are too hot.°   *irascible, rash*
CAPULET   God's bread,° it makes me mad. Day, night; work,   *By the communion bread*
     play;
Alone, in company, still my care° hath been   *business*
To have her matched; and having now provided
A gentleman of noble parentage,

---

7. A polite refusal.   execution.
8. Not so fast, let me understand you.   1. An expression of disgust and impatience.
9. A sledge used to draw traitors through the streets to

180   Of fair demesnes,° youthful, and nobly lined,°   *estates / descended*
      Stuffed, as they say, with honourable parts,°   *qualities*
      Proportioned as one's thought would wish a man²—
      And then to have a wretched puling fool,
      A whining maumet,° in her fortune's tender,³   *puppet*
185   To answer 'I'll not wed, I cannot love;
      I am too young, I pray you pardon me'!
      But an you will not wed, I'll pardon you!°   *excuse you (to leave)*
      Graze where you will, you shall not house with me.
      Look to't, think on't. I do not use° to jest.   *make it customary*
190   Thursday is near. Lay hand on heart.⁴ Advise.°   *Consider*
      An you be mine, I'll give you to my friend.
      An you be not, hang, beg, starve, die in the streets,
      For, by my soul, I'll ne'er acknowledge thee,
      Nor what is mine shall never do thee good.
195   Trust to't. Bethink you. I'll not be forsworn.   *Exit*
      JULIET   Is there no pity sitting in the clouds
      That sees into the bottom of my grief?
      O sweet my° mother, cast me not away!   *my sweet*
      Delay this marriage for a month, a week;
200   Or if you do not, make the bridal bed
      In that dim monument° where Tybalt lies.   *sepulchre*
      CAPULET'S WIFE   Talk not to me, for I'll not speak a word.
      Do as thou wilt, for I have done with thee.   *Exit*
      JULIET   O, God—O Nurse, how shall this be prevented?
205   My husband is on earth, my faith° in heaven.   *marriage vows*
      How shall that faith return again to earth
      Unless that husband send it me from heaven
      By leaving earth?⁵ Comfort me, counsel me.
      Alack, alack, that heaven should practise stratagems
210   Upon so soft a subject as myself!
      What sayst thou? Hast thou not a word of joy?
      Some comfort, Nurse.
      NURSE   Faith, here it is: Romeo
      Is banishèd, and all the world to nothing⁶
      That he dares ne'er come back to challenge you,
215   Or if he do, it needs must be by stealth.
      Then, since the case so stands as now it doth,
      I think it best you married with the County.
      O, he's a lovely gentleman!
      Romeo's a dishclout° to him. An eagle, madam,   *dishcloth*
220   Hath not so green, so quick, so fair an eye
      As Paris hath. Beshrew° my very heart,   *Curse*
      I think you are happy° in this second match,   *lucky*
      For it excels your first; or if it did not,
      Your first is dead, or 'twere as good he were
225   As living hence and you no use of him.
      JULIET   Speak'st thou from thy heart?
      NURSE   And from my soul, too, else beshrew them both.
      JULIET   Amen.
      NURSE   What?

2. Shaped as handsomely as you can imagine.   unless Romeo dies first, thus releasing me from my vows
3. When good fortune is offered her.   to him?
4. Ascertain your feelings.   6. And it's a sure bet.
5. *How . . . earth:* How can I swear marriage vows again

230 JULIET   Well, thou hast comforted me marvellous much.
      Go in; and tell my lady I am gone,
      Having displeased my father, to Laurence' cell
      To make confession and to be absolved.
NURSE   Marry, I will; and this is wisely done.   *[Exit]*
235 JULIET (*looks after* NURSE)   Ancient damnation![7] O most wicked fiend!
      Is it more sin to wish me thus forsworn,
      Or to dispraise my lord with that same tongue
      Which she hath praised him with above compare
      So many thousand times? Go, counsellor!
240   Thou and my bosom° henceforth shall be twain.°   *heart's contents / divided*
      I'll to the friar, to know his remedy.
      If all else fail, myself have power to die.   *Exit*

4.1

Enter FRIAR [LAURENCE] *and County* PARIS
FRIAR LAURENCE   On Thursday, sir? The time is very short.
PARIS   My father Capulet will have it so,
      And I am nothing slow[1] to slack his haste.
FRIAR LAURENCE   You say you do not know the lady's mind?
5   Uneven is the course.[2] I like it not.
PARIS   Immoderately she weeps for Tybalt's death,
      And therefore have I little talked of love,
      For Venus smiles not in a house of tears.
      Now, sir, her father counts it dangerous
10   That she do give her sorrow so much sway,
      And in his wisdom hastes our marriage
      To stop the inundation of her tears,
      Which, too much minded° by herself alone,   *brooded over*
      May be put from her by society.°   *company*
15   Now do you know the reason of this haste.
FRIAR LAURENCE [*aside*]   I would I knew not why it should be slowed.—
      Enter JULIET
      Look, sir, here comes the lady toward my cell.
PARIS   Happily met, my lady and my wife.
JULIET   That may be, sir, when I may be a wife.
20 PARIS   That 'may be' must be, love, on Thursday next.
JULIET   What must be shall be.
FRIAR LAURENCE   That's a certain text.
PARIS   Come you to make confession to this father?
JULIET   To answer that, I should confess to you.
PARIS   Do not deny to him that you love me.
25 JULIET   I will confess to you that I love him.
PARIS   So will ye, I am sure, that you love me.
JULIET   If I do so, it will be of more price,°   *value*
      Being spoke behind your back, than to your face.
PARIS   Poor soul, thy face is much abused with tears.
30 JULIET   The tears have got small victory by that,
      For it was bad enough before their spite.°   *injury*
PARIS   Thou wrong'st it more than tears with that report.
JULIET   That is no slander, sir, which is a truth,
      And what I spake, I spake it to my face.

---

7. Damnable old woman (with a hint of "original sin").
4.1 Location: Friar Laurence's cell.

1. Not reluctant; not trying to drag behind him.
2. The plan is irregular; this is a tricky road to follow.

35   PARIS   Thy face is mine, and thou hast slandered it.
    JULIET   It may be so, for it is not mine own.[3] —
        Are you at leisure, holy father, now,
        Or shall I come to you at evening mass?
    FRIAR LAURENCE   My leisure serves me, pensive° daughter, now.   *sorrowful*
40   My lord, we must entreat the time alone.
    PARIS   God shield° I should disturb devotion! —   *forbid*
        Juliet, on Thursday early will I rouse ye.
        [*Kissing her*] Till then, adieu, and keep this holy kiss.   *Exit*
    JULIET   O, shut the door, and when thou hast done so,
45   Come weep with me, past hope, past cure, past help!
    FRIAR LAURENCE   O Juliet, I already know thy grief.°   *grievous situation*
        It strains me past the compass° of my wits.   *limit*
        I hear thou must, and nothing may prorogue° it,   *postpone*
        On Thursday next be married to this County.
50   JULIET   Tell me not, friar, that thou hear'st of this,
        Unless thou tell me how I may prevent it.
        If in thy wisdom thou canst give no help,
        Do thou but call my resolution wise,
           [*She draws a knife*]
        And with this knife I'll help it presently.°   *immediately*
55   God joined my heart and Romeo's, thou our hands,
        And ere this hand, by thee to Romeo's sealed,
        Shall be the label[4] to another deed,
        Or my true heart with treacherous revolt
        Turn to another, this shall slay them both.
60   Therefore, out of thy long-experienced time,
        Give me some present counsel; or, behold,
        'Twixt my extremes° and me this bloody knife   *extreme difficulties*
        Shall play the umpire, arbitrating that
        Which the commission° of thy years and art°   *authority / learning*
65   Could to no issue of true honour bring.
        Be not so long to speak. I long to die
        If what thou speak'st speak not of remedy.
    FRIAR LAURENCE   Hold, daughter, I do spy a kind of hope
        Which craves as desperate° an execution[5]   *reckless*
70   As that is desperate° which we would prevent.   *hopeless*
        If, rather than to marry County Paris,
        Thou hast the strength of will to slay thyself,
        Then is it likely thou wilt undertake
        A thing like death to chide away this shame,
75   That cop'st° with death himself to scape from it;°   *Who wrestles / (shame)*
        And, if thou dar'st, I'll give thee remedy.
    JULIET   O, bid me leap, rather than marry Paris,
        From off the battlements of any tower,
        Or walk in thievish° ways, or bid me lurk   *thief-infested*
80   Where serpents are. Chain me with roaring bears,
        Or hide me nightly in a charnel house,
        O'ercovered quite with dead men's rattling bones,
        With reeky° shanks and yellow chapless[6] skulls;   *foully damp*

---

3. Because it belongs to Romeo; also because Juliet, in her ambiguous replies, is not showing Paris her true face.
4. Ribbon attaching a seal to a legal document (deed),
and so a pledge confirming another marriage.
5. A performance; a killing.
6. Without a lower jaw.

Or bid me go into a new-made grave
85 And hide me with a dead man in his tomb—
Things that, to hear them told, have made me tremble—
And I will do it without fear or doubt,° *dread*
To live an unstained wife to my sweet love.
FRIAR LAURENCE Hold, then; go home, be merry, give consent
90 To marry Paris. Wednesday is tomorrow.
Tomorrow night look° that thou lie alone. *be sure*
Let not the Nurse lie with thee in thy chamber.
Take thou this vial, being then in bed,
And this distilling° liquor drink thou off, *permeating*
95 When presently through all thy veins shall run
A cold and drowsy humour;° for no pulse *bodily fluid*
Shall keep his° native progress, but surcease.° *its / cease*
No warmth, no breath shall testify thou livest.
The roses in thy lips and cheeks shall fade
100 To wanny° ashes, thy eyes' windows° fall *pale / lids*
Like death when he shuts up the day of life.
Each part, deprived of supple government,° *control of movement*
Shall, stiff and stark and cold, appear like death;
And in this borrowed likeness of shrunk death
105 Thou shalt continue two-and-forty hours,
And then awake as from a pleasant sleep.
Now, when the bridegroom in the morning comes
To rouse thee from thy bed, there art thou dead.
Then, as the manner of our country is,
110 In thy best robes, uncovered on the bier
Thou shalt be borne to that same ancient vault
Where all the kindred of the Capulets lie.
In the meantime, against° thou shalt awake, *in preparation for when*
Shall Romeo by my letters know our drift,° *scheme*
115 And hither shall he come, and he and I
Will watch° thy waking, and that very night *keep vigil for*
Shall Romeo bear thee hence to Mantua.
And this shall free thee from this present shame,
If no inconstant toy° nor womanish fear *fickle whim*
120 Abate thy valour in the acting it.
JULIET Give me, give me! O, tell not me of fear!
FRIAR LAURENCE [*giving her the vial*] Hold, get you gone. Be
        strong and prosperous
In this resolve. I'll send a friar with speed
To Mantua with my letters° to thy lord. *letter*
125 JULIET Love give me strength, and strength shall help afford.
Farewell, dear father.   *Exeunt* [*severally*]

4.2

Enter old CAPULET, *his* WIFE, NURSE, *and two or three*
        SERVINGMEN
CAPULET [*giving a* SERVINGMAN *a paper*] So many guests invite
        as here are writ.   [*Exit* SERVINGMAN]
    [*To the other* SERVINGMAN] Sirrah, go hire me twenty
        cunning° cooks. *skillful*

4.2 Location: Capulet's house.

SERVINGMAN .You shall have none ill, sir, for I'll try° if they can   *test*
lick their fingers.
5   CAPULET   How canst thou try them so?
SERVINGMAN   Marry, sir, 'tis an ill cook that cannot lick his own
fingers, therefore he that cannot lick his fingers goes not with
me.
CAPULET   Go, be gone.   [*Exit* SERVINGMAN]
10   We shall be much unfurnished° for this time.   *unprepared*
[*To* NURSE] What, is my daughter gone to Friar Laurence?
NURSE   Ay, forsooth.
CAPULET   Well, he may chance to do some good on her.
A peevish,° self-willed harlotry° it° is.   *An obstinate / brat / she*
        Enter JULIET
15   NURSE   See where she comes from shrift° with merry look.   *absolution*
CAPULET [*to* JULIET]   How now, my headstrong, where have you
        been gadding?
JULIET   Where I have learned me to repent the sin
Of disobedient opposition
To you and your behests, and am enjoined
20   By holy Laurence to fall prostrate here
To beg your pardon. (*She kneels down*) Pardon, I beseech you.
Henceforward I am ever ruled by you.
CAPULET [*to* NURSE]   Send for the County; go tell him of this.
I'll have this knot knit up tomorrow morning.
25   JULIET   I met the youthful lord at Laurence' cell,
And gave him what becoming° love I might,   *suitable*
Not stepping o'er the bounds of modesty.
CAPULET   Why, I am glad on't.° This is well. Stand up.   *of it*
        [JULIET *rises*]
This is as't should be. Let me see the County.
30   [*To* NURSE] Ay, marry, go, I say, and fetch him hither.
Now, afore God, this reverend holy friar,
All our whole city is much bound to him.
JULIET   Nurse, will you go with me into my closet°   *chamber*
To help me sort such needful ornaments
35   As you think fit to furnish me tomorrow?
CAPULET'S WIFE   No, not till Thursday. There is time enough.
CAPULET   Go, Nurse, go with her. We'll to church tomorrow.
                    Exeunt JULIET *and* NURSE
CAPULET'S WIFE   We shall be short in our provision.
'Tis now near night.
CAPULET   Tush, I will stir about,
40   And all things shall be well, I warrant thee, wife.
Go thou to Juliet, help to deck up her.
I'll not to bed tonight. Let me alone.
I'll play the housewife for this once. What, ho!
They are all forth. Well, I will walk myself
45   To County Paris to prepare up him
Against tomorrow. My heart is wondrous light,
Since this same wayward girl is so reclaimed.[1]
                    Exeunt [*severally*]

1. Reformed; claimed in marriage.

4.3

Enter JULIET *and* NURSE [*with garments*]¹

JULIET Ay, those attires are best. But, gentle Nurse,
  I pray thee leave me to myself tonight,
  For I have need of many orisons
  To move the heavens to smile upon my state,
5 Which—well thou knowest—is cross° and full of sin.   *adverse*
    Enter [CAPULET'S WIFE]
CAPULET'S WIFE What, are you busy, ho? Need you my help?
JULIET No, madam, we have culled such necessaries
  As are behoveful° for our state° tomorrow.   *needful / ceremony*
  So please° you, let me now be left alone,   *If it pleases*
10 And let the Nurse this night sit up with you,
  For I am sure you have your hands full all
  In this so sudden business.
CAPULET'S WIFE   Good night.
  Get thee to bed, and rest, for thou hast need.
        Exeunt [CAPULET'S WIFE *and* NURSE]
JULIET Farewell. God knows when we shall meet again.
15 I have a faint cold fear thrills° through my veins   *pierces*
  That almost freezes up the heat of life.
  I'll call them back again to comfort me.
  Nurse!—What should she do here?
    [*She opens curtains, behind which is seen her bed*]
  My dismal° scene I needs must act alone.   *calamitous*
20 Come, vial. What if this mixture do not work at all?
  Shall I be married then tomorrow morning?
  No, no, this shall forbid it. Lie thou there.
    [*She lays down a knife*]
  What if it be a poison which the friar
  Subtly hath ministered to have me dead,
25 Lest in this marriage he should be dishonoured
  Because he married me before to Romeo?
  I fear it is—and yet methinks it should not,°   *not be*
  For he hath still° been tried° a holy man.   *always / proved*
  How if, when I am laid into the tomb,
30 I wake before the time that Romeo
  Come to redeem me? There's a fearful point.
  Shall I not then be stifled in the vault,
  To whose foul mouth no healthsome air breathes in,
  And there die strangled° ere my Romeo comes?   *suffocated*
35 Or, if I live, is it not very like°   *likely*
  The horrible conceit of death and night,
  Together with the terror of the place—
  As° in a vault, an ancient receptacle   *As it is*
  Where for this many hundred years the bones
40 Of all my buried ancestors are packed;
  Where bloody Tybalt, yet but green° in earth,   *newly*
  Lies fest'ring in his shroud; where, as they say,
  At some hours in the night spirits resort—
  Alack, alack, is it not like that I,
45 So early waking—what with loathsome smells,

4.3 Location: Capulet's house.
1. Juliet's chamber may be represented by a bed onstage for this scene and the next.

And shrieks like mandrakes² torn out of the earth,
That living mortals, hearing them, run mad—
O, if I wake, shall I not be distraught,
Environèd with all these hideous fears,
50 And madly play with my forefathers' joints,
And pluck the mangled Tybalt from his shroud,
And, in this rage,° with some great kinsman's bone   *insanity*
As with a club dash out my desp'rate brains?
O, look! Methinks I see my cousin's ghost
55 Seeking out Romeo that did spit his body
Upon a rapier's point. Stay, Tybalt, stay!
Romeo, Romeo, Romeo! Here's drink. I drink to thee.
            [*She drinks from the vial and*] *falls upon her bed within
            the curtains*

4.4

            Enter [CAPULET'S WIFE,] *and* NURSE *with herbs*
CAPULET'S WIFE   Hold, take these keys, and fetch more spices, Nurse.
NURSE   They call for dates and quinces in the pastry.°   *pastry kitchen*
            Enter old CAPULET
CAPULET   Come, stir, stir, stir! The second cock hath crowed.
      The curfew bell¹ hath rung. 'Tis three o'clock.
5   Look to the baked meats, good Angelica.²
      Spare not for cost.
NURSE   Go, you cot-quean,° go.   *old housewife*
      Get you to bed. Faith, you'll be sick tomorrow
      For this night's watching.°   *wakefulness*
CAPULET   No, not a whit. What, I have watched ere now
10   All night for lesser cause, and ne'er been sick.
CAPULET'S WIFE   Ay, you have been a mouse-hunt° in your time,   *skirt chaser*
      But I will watch° you from such watching now.   *guard*
                        Exeunt [CAPULET'S WIFE] *and* NURSE
CAPULET   A jealous-hood,³ a jealous-hood!
            Enter three or four SERVINGMEN, *with spits and logs and
            baskets*
                              Now, fellow, what is there?
FIRST SERVINGMAN   Things for the cook, sir, but I know not what.
CAPULET   Make haste, make haste.
                  [*Exit* FIRST SERVINGMAN *and one or two others*]
15   Sirrah, fetch drier logs.
      Call Peter. He will show thee where they are.
SECOND SERVINGMAN   I have a head, sir, that will find out logs⁴
      And never trouble Peter for the matter.
CAPULET   Mass,° and well said! A merry whoreson,° ha!   *By the mass / rogue*
      Thou shalt be loggerhead.°   *Exit* [SECOND SERVINGMAN]   *wooden-headed*
20   Good faith, 'tis day.
      The County will be here with music straight,
      For so he said he would.
            Play music [*within*]

2. Plants with forked roots thought to resemble a man.
Popular belief held that they uttered a death- or madness-
producing shriek upon being pulled up.
4.4 Location: Scene continues.
1. Also rung at daybreak.
2. Unclear whether Capulet refers to his wife or the
nurse.
3. Jealousy; jealous woman.
4. I have a good head for finding things, so I can certainly
find the logs; my head knows all about logs (I am a blockhead).

I hear him near.
Nurse! Wife! What ho, what, Nurse, I say!
         Enter NURSE
Go waken Juliet. Go and trim her up.
25 I'll go and chat with Paris. Hie, make haste,
Make haste, the bridegroom he is come already.
Make haste, I say.   [*Exit*]
NURSE Mistress, what, mistress! Juliet! Fast,° I warrant her, she.   *Asleep*
Why, lamb, why, lady! Fie, you slug-abed!
30 Why, love, I say, madam, sweetheart, why, bride!
What, not a word? You take your pennyworths° now.   *bits*
Sleep for a week, for the next night, I warrant,
The County Paris hath set up his rest⁵
That you shall rest but little. God forgive me!
35 Marry, and amen. How sound is she asleep!
I needs must wake her. Madam, madam, madam!
Ay, let the County take° you in your bed.   *catch; sexually possess*
He'll fright you up, i'faith. Will it not be?
         [*She draws back the curtains*]
What, dressed and in your clothes, and down again?
40 I must needs wake you. Lady, lady, lady!
Alas, alas! Help, help! My lady's dead.
O welladay,° that ever I was born!   *alas*
Some aqua-vitae, ho! My lord, my lady!
         Enter [CAPULET'S WIFE]
CAPULET'S WIFE What noise is here?
NURSE   O lamentable day!
CAPULET'S WIFE What is the matter?
45 NURSE   Look, look. O heavy day!
CAPULET'S WIFE O me, O me, my child, my only life!
Revive, look up, or I will die with thee.
Help, help, call help!
         Enter [CAPULET]
CAPULET For shame, bring Juliet forth. Her lord is come.
50 NURSE She's dead, deceased. She's dead, alack the day!
CAPULET'S WIFE Alack the day, she's dead, she's dead, she's dead!
CAPULET Ha, let me see her! Out,° alas, she's cold.   *Woe*
Her blood is settled,° and her joints are stiff.   *motionless*
Life and these lips have long been separated.
55 Death lies on her like an untimely frost
Upon the sweetest flower of all the field.
NURSE O lamentable day!
CAPULET'S WIFE   O woeful time!
CAPULET Death, that hath ta'en her hence to make me wail,
Ties up my tongue, and will not let me speak.
         Enter FRIAR [LAURENCE] *and* PARIS [*with Musicians*]
60 FRIAR LAURENCE Come, is the bride ready to go to church?
CAPULET Ready to go, but never to return.
[*To* PARIS] O son, the night before thy wedding day
Hath death lain with thy wife. See, there she lies,
Flower as she was, deflowerèd by him.
65 Death is my son-in-law, death is my heir.
My daughter he hath wedded. I will die,

---

5. Has resolved (from staking everything in the card game primero), with bawdy pun.

And leave him all. Life, living,° all is death's.   *property*
    All at once wring their hands and cry out
PARIS   Have I thought° long to see this morning's face,   *expected*
   And doth it give me such a sight as this?
70   Beguiled,° divorcèd, wrongèd, spited,° slain!   *Cheated / injured*
   Most detestable death, by thee beguiled,
   By cruel, cruel thee quite overthrown.
   O love, O life: not life, but love in death.
CAPULET'S WIFE   Accursed, unhappy, wretched, hateful day!
75   Most miserable hour that e'er time saw
   In lasting° labour of his pilgrimage!   *eternal*
   But one, poor one, one poor and loving child,
   But one thing to rejoice and solace in,
   And cruel death hath catched° it from my sight!   *seized*
80 NURSE   O woe! O woeful, woeful, woeful day!
   Most lamentable day! Most woeful day
   That ever, ever, I did yet behold!
   O day, O day, O day, O hateful day,
   Never was seen so black a day as this!
85   O woeful day, O woeful day!
CAPULET   Despised, distressèd, hated, martyred, killed!
   Uncomfortable° time, why cam'st thou now   *Comfortless*
   To murder, murder our solemnity?°   *festivity*
   O child, O child, my soul and not my child!⁶
90   Dead art thou, alack, my child is dead,
   And with my child my joys are burièd.
FRIAR LAURENCE   Peace, ho, for shame! Confusion's° cure lives   *Destruction's*
      not
   In these confusions.° Heaven and yourself   *commotions*
   Had part in this fair maid. Now heaven hath all,
95   And all the better is it for the maid.
   Your part in her you could not keep from death,
   But heaven keeps his part in eternal life.
   The most you sought was her promotion,°   *social advancement*
   For 'twas your heaven° she should be advanced,   *highest ambition*
100   And weep ye now, seeing she is advanced
   Above the clouds as high as heaven itself?
   O, in this love you love your child so ill
   That you run mad, seeing that she is well.
   She's not well married that lives married long,
105   But she's best married that dies married young.
   Dry up your tears, and stick your rosemary
   On this fair corpse, and, as the custom is,
   All in her best array bear her to church;
   For though fond° nature° bids us all lament,   *foolish; doting / affection*
110   Yet nature's tears are reason's merriment.°   *laughable idiocy*
CAPULET   All things that we ordainèd festival
   Turn from their office° to black funeral.   *due function*
   Our instruments to melancholy bells,
   Our wedding cheer° to a sad burial feast,   *fare*
115   Our solemn° hymns to sullen° dirges change;   *ceremonial / mournful*
   Our bridal flowers serve for a buried corpse,
   And all things change them to the contrary.
FRIAR LAURENCE   Sir, go you in; and madam, go with him,

6. *not my child*: because dead and only a corpse.

And go, Sir Paris. Everyone prepare
120 To follow this fair corpse unto her grave.
The heavens do lour° upon you for some ill.°   *hang threatening / offense*
Move° them no more by crossing their high will.   *Anger*

All but NURSE *go forth, casting rosemary on* JULIET *and*
shutting the curtains. Manent° NURSE *and* MUSICIANS   *Remain*

FIRST MUSICIAN   Faith, we may put° up our pipes and be gone.   *pack*
NURSE   Honest good fellows, ah, put up, put up,
125 For well you know this is a pitiful case.
FIRST MUSICIAN   Ay, by my troth, the case may be amended.[7]

                                  Exit [NURSE]

Enter PETER

PETER   Musicians, O, musicians! 'Heart's ease',° 'Heart's ease';   *(popular song)*
O, an you will have me live, play 'Heart's ease'.
FIRST MUSICIAN   Why 'Heart's ease'?
130 PETER   O, musicians, because my heart itself plays 'My heart is
full of woe'. O, play me some merry dump° to comfort me.   *sad tune*
FIRST MUSICIAN   Not a dump, we. 'Tis no time to play now.
PETER   You will not then?
FIRST MUSICIAN   No.
135 PETER   I will then give it you soundly.°   *thoroughly; in sound*
FIRST MUSICIAN   What will you give us?
PETER   No money, on my faith, but the gleek.[8] I will give you
the minstrel.[9]
FIRST MUSICIAN   Then will I give you the serving-creature.
140 PETER [*drawing his dagger*]   Then will I lay the serving-creature's
dagger on your pate. I will carry° no crochets.[1] I'll re you, I'll fa   *bear; sing*
you. Do you note° me?   *heed*
FIRST MUSICIAN   An you re us and fa us, you note° us.   *give notes to*
SECOND MUSICIAN   Pray you, put up your dagger and put out°   *show; quench*
145 your wit.
PETER   Then have at you with my wit. I will dry-beat° you with   *thrash*
an iron° wit, and put up my iron dagger. Answer[2] me like men.   *a merciless*
[*Sings*]   When griping grief the heart doth wound,
      And doleful dumps° the mind oppress,   *melancholy*
150   Then music with her silver sound[3] —
Why 'silver sound', why 'music with her silver sound'? What
say you, Matthew Minikin?°   *small lute string*
FIRST MUSICIAN   Marry, sir, because silver hath a sweet sound.
PETER   Prates!° What say you, Hugh Rebec?[4]   *Chatter*
155 SECOND MUSICIAN   I say 'silver sound' because musicians sound
for silver.
PETER   Prates too! What say you, Simon Soundpost?[5]
THIRD MUSICIAN   Faith, I know not what to say.
PETER   O, I cry you mercy,° you are the singer. I will say for you.   *beg your pardon*
160 It is 'music with her silver sound' because musicians have no
gold for sounding.[6]
[*Sings*]   Then music with her silver sound
        With speedy help doth lend redress.   *Exit*
FIRST MUSICIAN   What a pestilent knave is this same!

7. Things could be better; the instrument case can be repaired.
8. To "give the gleek" was to make a fool of or play a trick on.
9. I will insultingly call you a minstrel.
1. Whimsy; quarter notes.
2. Defy; respond to.

3. Lines from the song "In Commendation of Music."
4. Three-stringed instrument.
5. Supporting peg fixed between the sounding board and back of a stringed instrument.
6. We are given no gold for playing; we are poor and have no gold to jingle.

165 SECOND MUSICIAN Hang him, jack! Come, we'll in here, tarry
    for the mourners, and stay° dinner.   *Exeunt*   *await*

5.1

Enter ROMEO

ROMEO If I may trust the flattering° truth of sleep,   *encouraging*
    My dreams presage some joyful news at hand.
    My bosom's lord sits lightly in his throne,[1]
    And all this day an unaccustomed spirit
5   Lifts me above the ground with cheerful thoughts.
    I dreamt my lady came and found me dead—
    Strange dream, that gives a dead man leave to think!—
    And breathed such life with kisses in° my lips   *into*
    That I revived and was an emperor.
10   Ah me, how sweet is love itself possessed°   *enjoyed in reality*
    When but love's shadows° are so rich in joy!   *dreams; images*

Enter BALTHASAR, *his man, booted*

    News from Verona! How now, Balthasar?
    Dost thou not bring me letters from the friar?
    How doth my lady? Is my father well?
15   How fares my Juliet? That I ask again,
    For nothing can be ill if she be well.
BALTHASAR Then she is well, and nothing can be ill.
    Her body sleeps in Capel's monument,
    And her immortal part with angels lives.
20   I saw her laid low in her kindred's vault,
    And presently° took post[2] to tell it you.   *immediately*
    O, pardon me for bringing these ill news,
    Since you did leave it for my office,° sir.   *duty*
ROMEO Is it e'en so? Then I defy you, stars.
25   Thou knowest my lodging. Get me ink and paper,
    And hire posthorses. I will hence tonight.
BALTHASAR I do beseech you, sir, have patience.
    Your looks are pale and wild, and do import°   *signify*
    Some misadventure.
ROMEO   Tush, thou art deceived.
30   Leave me, and do the thing I bid thee do.
    Hast thou no letters to me from the friar?
BALTHASAR No, my good lord.
ROMEO   No matter. Get thee gone,
    And hire those horses. I'll be with thee straight.

Exit BALTHASAR

    Well, Juliet, I will lie with thee tonight.
35   Let's see for means. O mischief, thou art swift
    To enter in the thoughts of desperate men!
    I do remember an apothecary,
    And hereabouts a dwells, which late I noted,
    In tattered weeds,° with overwhelming° brows,   *clothes / overhanging*
40   Culling of simples.° Meagre were his looks.   *herbs*
    Sharp misery had worn him to the bones,
    And in his needy° shop a tortoise hung,   *poor*
    An alligator stuffed, and other skins

5.1 Location: A street in Mantua.   2. Set out on post horses.
1. Love rules in the heart; the heart is at ease in the chest.

Of ill-shaped fishes; and about his shelves
45 A beggarly account° of empty boxes,   *A sparse collection*
Green earthen pots, bladders, and musty seeds,
Remnants of packthread,° and old cakes of roses[3]   *twine*
Were thinly scattered to make up a show.
Noting this penury, to myself I said
50 'An if a man did need a poison now,
Whose sale is present death[4] in Mantua,
Here lives a caitiff° wretch would sell it him.'   *pitiful*
O, this same thought did but forerun my need,
And this same needy man must sell it me.
55 As I remember, this should be the house.
Being holiday, the beggar's shop is shut.
What ho, apothecary!
    Enter APOTHECARY
APOTHECARY   Who calls so loud?
ROMEO   Come hither, man. I see that thou art poor.
    [*He offers money*]
Hold, there is forty ducats.[5] Let me have
60 A dram of poison—such soon-speeding gear[6]
As will disperse itself through all the veins,
That the life-weary taker may fall dead,
And that the trunk° may be discharged of breath   *body*
As violently as hasty powder fired
65 Doth hurry from the fatal cannon's womb.
APOTHECARY   Such mortal drugs I have, but Mantua's law
Is death to any he° that utters° them.   *man / offers to sell*
ROMEO   Art thou so bare° and full of wretchedness,   *destitute*
And fear'st to die? Famine is in thy cheeks,
70 Need and oppression starveth in thy eyes,
Contempt and beggary hangs upon thy back.
The world is not thy friend, nor the world's law.
The world affords° no law to make thee rich.   *provides*
Then be not poor, but break it, and take this.
75 APOTHECARY   My poverty but not my will consents.
ROMEO   I pay thy poverty and not thy will.
APOTHECARY [*handing* ROMEO *poison*]   Put this in any liquid
    thing you will
And drink it off, and if you had the strength
Of twenty men it would dispatch you straight.°   *immediately*
ROMEO [*giving money*]   There is thy gold—worse poison to
80   men's souls,
Doing more murder in this loathsome world,
Than these poor compounds that thou mayst not sell.
I sell thee poison; thou hast sold me none.
Farewell, buy food, and get thyself in flesh.°   *grow fatter*
    [*Exit* APOTHECARY]
85 Come, cordial° and not poison, go with me   *restorative; heart's ease*
To Juliet's grave, for there must I use thee.   *Exit*

---

3. Rose petals pressed into cake form and used as a sachet.
4. Punishable by immediate death.
5. Various gold coins used at times in much of Europe, and Shakespeare's usual currency for plays not set in England.
6. Quick-working stuff; quick-killing stuff.

5.2

Enter FRIAR JOHN [*at one door*]

FRIAR JOHN   Holy Franciscan friar, brother, ho!

Enter FRIAR LAURENCE [*at another door*]

FRIAR LAURENCE   This same should be the voice of Friar John.
Welcome from Mantua! What says Romeo?
Or if his mind° be writ, give me his letter.   thoughts

5   FRIAR JOHN   Going to find a barefoot brother out—
One of our order—to associate me[1]
Here in this city visiting the sick,
And finding him, the searchers[2] of the town,
Suspecting that we both were in a house

10   Where the infectious pestilence did reign,
Sealed up the doors, and would not let us forth,
So that my speed to Mantua there was stayed.°   stopped

FRIAR LAURENCE   Who bare my letter then to Romeo?

FRIAR JOHN   I could not send it—here it is again—

15   Nor get a messenger to bring it thee,
So fearful were they of infection.°   contagion

FRIAR LAURENCE   Unhappy fortune! By my brotherhood,
The letter was not nice,° but full of charge,°   trivial / importance
Of dear import,° and the neglecting it   serious consequence

20   May do much danger. Friar John, go hence.
Get me an iron crow,° and bring it straight   crowbar
Unto my cell.

FRIAR JOHN   Brother, I'll go and bring it thee.   *Exit*

FRIAR LAURENCE   Now must I to the monument alone.
Within this three hours will fair Juliet wake.

25   She will beshrew° me much that Romeo   curse
Hath had no notice of these accidents.°   events
But I will write again to Mantua,
And keep her at my cell till Romeo come.
Poor living corpse, closed in a dead man's tomb!   *Exit*

5.3

Enter County PARIS *and his* PAGE, *with flowers, sweet*°   perfumed
water [*and a torch*]

PARIS   Give me thy torch, boy. Hence, and stand aloof.°   stay apart
Yet put it out, for I would not be seen.
    [*His* PAGE *puts out the torch*]
Under yon yew trees lay thee all along,°   stretched out
Holding thy ear close to the hollow ground.

5   So shall no foot upon the churchyard tread,
Being° loose, unfirm, with digging up of graves,   The ground being
But thou shalt hear it. Whistle then to me
As signal that thou hear'st something approach.
Give me those flowers. Do as I bid thee. Go.

10   PAGE [*aside*]   I am almost afraid to stand alone
Here in the churchyard, yet I will adventure.°   risk it
    [*He hides himself at a distance from* PARIS]

5.2 Location: Friar Laurence's cell.
1. Franciscan friars (barefoot because the order is sworn
to poverty) traveled only in pairs. *associate:* accompany.

2. Health officers appointed to examine corpses and
identify houses infected with the plague.
5.3 Location: The Capulet mausoleum.

PARIS (*strews the tomb with flowers*)   Sweet flower, with flowers
    thy bridal bed I strew.
       [*He sprinkles water*]
    O woe! Thy canopy° is dust and stones,   *covering; bed hangings*
    Which with sweet water nightly I will dew,
15   Or, wanting that, with tears distilled by moans.
    The obsequies that I for thee will keep°   *perform*
    Nightly shall be to strew thy grave and weep.
       [PAGE *whistles*]
    The boy gives warning. Something doth approach.
    What cursèd foot wanders this way tonight
20   To cross° my obsequies and true love's rite?   *thwart*
       Enter ROMEO *and* BALTHASAR, *with a torch, a mattock,*
       and a crow of iron
    What, with a torch? Muffle me, night, a while.
       [*He stands aside*]
ROMEO   Give me that mattock and the wrenching iron.
    Hold, take this letter. Early in the morning
    See thou deliver it to my lord and father.
25   Give me the light. Upon thy life I charge thee,
    Whate'er thou hear'st or seest, stand all aloof,
    And do not interrupt me in my course.
    Why I descend into this bed of death
    Is partly to behold my lady's face,
30   But chiefly to take thence from her dead finger
    A precious ring, a ring that I must use
    In dear° employment. Therefore hence, be gone.   *important; tender*
    But if thou, jealous,° dost return to pry   *suspicious*
    In what I farther shall intend to do,
35   By heaven, I will tear thee joint by joint,
    And strew this hungry churchyard with thy limbs.
    The time and my intents are savage-wild,
    More fierce and more inexorable far
    Than empty tigers or the roaring sea.
40 BALTHASAR   I will be gone, sir, and not trouble ye.
ROMEO   So shalt thou show me friendship. Take thou that.
       [*He gives money*]
    Live and be prosperous, and farewell, good fellow.
BALTHASAR [*aside*]   For all this same, I'll hide me hereabout.
    His looks I fear, and his intents I doubt.°   *suspect*
       [*He hides himself at a distance from* ROMEO.]
       ROMEO *begins to open the tomb*
45 ROMEO   Thou detestable maw, thou womb¹ of death,
    Gorged with the dearest morsel of the earth,
    Thus I enforce thy rotten jaws to open,
    And in despite° I'll cram thee with more food.   *defiant ill will*
PARIS [*aside*]   This is that banished haughty Montague
50   That murdered my love's cousin, with which grief
    It is supposèd the fair creature died;
    And here is come to do some villainous shame
    To the dead bodies. I will apprehend him.
    [*Drawing*] Stop thy unhallowed° toil, vile Montague!   *unholy*

---

1. Belly; also playing on the birthplace of Romeo's death.

55 Can vengeance be pursued further than death?
Condemnèd villain, I do apprehend thee.
Obey and go with me, for thou must die.
ROMEO   I must indeed, and therefore came I hither.
Good gentle youth, tempt not a desp'rate° man.   *despairing; violent*
60 Fly hence, and leave me. Think upon these gone.
Let them affright thee. I beseech thee, youth,
Put not another sin upon my head
By urging me to fury. O, be gone.
By heaven, I love thee better than myself,
65 For I come hither armed against myself.
Stay not, be gone. Live, and hereafter say
A madman's mercy bid thee run away.
PARIS   I do defy thy conjuration,°   *entreaty*
And apprehend thee for a felon here.
70 ROMEO [*drawing*]   Wilt thou provoke me? Then have at thee, boy.
          They fight
PAGE   O Lord, they fight! I will go call the watch.   [*Exit*]
PARIS   O, I am slain! If thou be merciful,
Open the tomb, lay me with Juliet.
ROMEO   In faith, I will.   [PARIS *dies*]
          Let me peruse this face.
75 Mercutio's kinsman, noble County Paris!
What said my man when my betossèd° soul   *storm-tossed*
Did not attend° him as we rode? I think   *listen to*
He told me Paris should have married Juliet.
Said he not so? Or did I dream it so?
80 Or am I mad, hearing him talk of Juliet,
To think it was so? O, give me thy hand,
One writ with me in sour misfortune's book.
I'll bury thee in a triumphant° grave.   *magnificent*
          [*He opens the tomb, revealing* JULIET]
A grave—O no, a lantern,° slaughtered youth,   *lighthouse*
85 For here lies Juliet, and her beauty makes
This vault a feasting presence² full of light.
          [*He bears the body of Paris to the tomb*]
Death, lie thou there, by a dead man interred.
How oft, when men are at the point of death,
Have they been merry, which their keepers call
90 A lightning before death! O, how may I
Call this a lightning? O my love, my wife!
Death, that hath sucked the honey of thy breath,
Hath had no power yet upon thy beauty.
Thou art not conquered.° Beauty's ensign° yet   *overpowered; seduced / flag*
95 Is crimson in thy lips and in thy cheeks,
And death's pale flag is not advancèd there.
Tybalt, liest thou there in thy bloody sheet?
O, what more favour can I do to thee
Than with that hand that cut thy youth in twain
100 To sunder his° that was thine enemy?   *the youth of him*
Forgive me, cousin. Ah, dear Juliet,
Why art thou yet so fair? Shall I believe
That unsubstantial° death is amorous,   *immaterial*

2. Festive royal chamber for receiving guests.

And that the lean abhorrèd monster keeps
105 Thee here in dark to be his paramour?
For fear of that I still will stay with thee,
And never from this pallet of dim night
Depart again. Here, here will I remain
With worms that are thy chambermaids. O, here
110 Will I set up my everlasting rest,³
And shake the yoke of inauspicious stars
From this world-wearied flesh. Eyes, look your last.
Arms, take your last embrace, and lips, O you
The doors of breath, seal with a righteous kiss
115 A dateless° bargain to engrossing⁴ death.   *An eternal*
        [*He kisses* JULIET, *then pours poison into the cup*]
Come, bitter conduct, come, unsavoury guide,
Thou desperate pilot, now at once run on
The dashing rocks thy seasick weary° barque!   *travel-weary*
Here's to my love.
        [*He drinks the poison*]
                    O true apothecary,
120 Thy drugs are quick!° Thus with a kiss I die.   *fast; vigorous*
        [*He kisses* JULIET,] *falls* [*and dies.*]
        Enter FRIAR [LAURENCE] *with lantern, crow,*
        and spade
FRIAR LAURENCE   Saint Francis be my speed!° How oft tonight   *help*
        Have my old feet stumbled at graves? Who's there?
BALTHASAR   Here's one, a friend, and one that knows you well.
FRIAR LAURENCE   Bliss be upon you. Tell me, good my friend,
125 What torch is yon that vainly lends his light
        To grubs and eyeless skulls? As I discern,
        It burneth in the Capels' monument.
BALTHASAR   It doth so, holy sir, and there's my master,
        One that you love.
FRIAR LAURENCE   Who is it?
BALTHASAR   Romeo.
FRIAR LAURENCE   How long hath he been there?
130 BALTHASAR   Full half an hour.
FRIAR LAURENCE   Go with me to the vault.
BALTHASAR   I dare not, sir.
        My master knows not but I am gone hence,
        And fearfully° did menace me with death   *fearsomely*
        If I did stay to look on his intents.
135 FRIAR LAURENCE   Stay then, I'll go alone. Fear comes upon me.
        O, much I fear some ill unthrifty° thing.   *unfortunate*
BALTHASAR   As I did sleep under this yew tree here
        I dreamt my master and another fought,
        And that my master slew him.
FRIAR LAURENCE   Romeo!
        [*He*] *stoops and looks on the blood and weapons*
140 Alack, alack, what blood is this which stains
        The stony entrance of this sepulchre?
        What mean these masterless and gory swords
        To lie discoloured by this place of peace?

3. Make my final determination.
4. Buying up in large quantities to monopolize; writing a legal document.

Romeo! O, pale! Who else? What, Paris, too,
145 And steeped in blood? Ah, what an unkind° hour   *unnatural; a cruel*
     Is guilty of this lamentable chance!°   *event*
                    JULIET [*awakes and*] *rises*
     The lady stirs.
     JULIET   O comfortable° friar, where is my lord?   *solace-giving*
     I do remember well where I should be,
150 And there I am. Where is my Romeo?
     FRIAR LAURENCE   I hear some noise. Lady, come from that nest
     Of death, contagion, and unnatural sleep.
     A greater power than we can contradict
     Hath thwarted our intents. Come, come away.
155 Thy husband in thy bosom there lies dead,
     And Paris, too. Come, I'll dispose of thee
     Among a sisterhood of holy nuns.
     Stay not to question, for the watch is coming.
     Come, go, good Juliet. I dare no longer stay.   *Exit*
160 JULIET   Go, get thee hence, for I will not away.
     What's here? A cup closed in my true love's hand?
     Poison, I see, hath been his timeless° end.   *untimely; lasting*
     O churl!—drunk all, and left no friendly drop
     To help me after? I will kiss thy lips.
165 Haply° some poison yet doth hang on them,   *Perhaps*
     To make me die with a restorative.[5]
                    [*She kisses Romeo's lips*]
     Thy lips are warm.
     CHIEF WATCHMAN [*within*]   Lead, boy. Which way?
     JULIET   Yea, noise? Then I'll be brief.
                    [*She takes Romeo's dagger*]
                                   O happy° dagger,   *fortunate*
     This is thy sheath! There rust, and let me die.
                    She stabs herself, falls [*and dies*]
                    Enter [PAGE] *and* WATCH
170 PAGE   This is the place, there where the torch doth burn.
     CHIEF WATCHMAN   The ground is bloody. Search about the churchyard.
     Go, some of you. Whoe'er you find, attach.°   *arrest*
                    [*Exeunt some* WATCHMEN]
     Pitiful sight! Here lies the County slain,
     And Juliet bleeding, warm, and newly dead,
175 Who here hath lain this two days burièd.
     Go tell the Prince. Run to the Capulets,
     Raise up the Montagues. Some others search.
                    [*Exeunt other* WATCHMEN *severally*]
     We see the ground° whereon these woes do lie,   *earth*
     But the true ground° of all these piteous woes   *cause*
180 We cannot without circumstance° descry.   *a fuller account*
                    Enter [WATCHMEN] *with Romeo's man* [BALTHASAR]
     SECOND WATCHMAN   Here's Romeo's man. We found him in
                    the churchyard.
     CHIEF WATCHMAN   Hold him in safety° till the Prince come   *securely*
                    hither.
                    Enter another WATCHMAN *with* FRIAR [LAURENCE]
     THIRD WATCHMAN   Here is a friar that trembles, sighs, and weeps.

---

5. Both the kiss, which is healing, and the poison, which restores them to each other.

We took this mattock and this spade from him

185 As he was coming from this churchyard's side.[6]

CHIEF WATCHMAN   A great suspicion. Stay° the friar, too.   *Hold*

      Enter PRINCE *with others*

PRINCE   What misadventure is so early up,

That calls our person from our morning rest?

      Enter old CAPULET *and his* WIFE

CAPULET   What should it be that is so shrieked abroad?

190 CAPULET'S WIFE   O, the people in the street cry 'Romeo',

Some 'Juliet', and some 'Paris', and all run

With open° outcry toward our monument.   *public; open-mouthed*

PRINCE   What fear is this which startles° in our ears?   *bursts out*

CHIEF WATCHMAN   Sovereign, here lies the County Paris slain,

195 And Romeo dead, and Juliet, dead before,

Warm, and new killed.

PRINCE   Search, seek, and know how this foul murder comes.

CHIEF WATCHMAN   Here is a friar, and slaughtered Romeo's man,

With instruments upon them fit to open

200 These dead men's tombs.

CAPULET   O heavens! O wife, look how our daughter bleeds!

This dagger hath mista'en, for lo, his house°   *scabbard*

Is empty on the back of Montague,

And it mis-sheathèd in my daughter's bosom.

205 CAPULET'S WIFE   O me, this sight of death is as a bell

That warns° my old age to a sepulchre.   *summons*

      Enter old MONTAGUE

PRINCE   Come, Montague, for thou art early up

To see thy son and heir more early down.

MONTAGUE   Alas, my liege, my wife is dead tonight.

210 Grief of my son's exile hath stopped her breath.

What further woe conspires against mine age?

PRINCE   Look, and thou shalt see.

MONTAGUE [*seeing Romeo's body*]   O thou untaught! What

      manners is in this,

To press before° thy father to a grave?   *To shove ahead of*

215 PRINCE   Seal up the mouth of outrage[7] for a while,

Till we can clear these ambiguities

And know their spring, their head, their true descent;

And then will I be general of your woes,

And lead you even to death. Meantime, forbear,

220 And let mischance be slave to° patience.   *overruled by*

Bring forth the parties of suspicion.

FRIAR LAURENCE   I am the greatest,° able to do least,   *most suspect*

Yet most suspected, as the time and place

Doth make against me, of this direful murder;

225 And here I stand, both to impeach and purge

Myself condemnèd and myself excused.[8]

PRINCE   Then say at once what thou dost know in this.

FRIAR LAURENCE   I will be brief, for my short date° of breath   *duration*

Is not so long as is a tedious tale.

230 Romeo, there dead, was husband to that Juliet,

And she, there dead, that Romeo's faithful wife.

---

6. This side of the churchyard.
7. Of impassioned exclamation.

8. *to . . . excused:* to accuse myself of what I am guilty of
and clear myself of what I am not.

I married them, and their stol'n marriage day
Was Tybalt's doomsday, whose untimely death
Banished the new-made bridegroom from this city,
235 For whom, and not for Tybalt, Juliet pined.
You, to remove that siege of grief from her,
Betrothed and would have married her perforce°   *forcibly*
To County Paris. Then comes she to me,
And with wild looks bid me devise some mean°   *method*
240 To rid her from this second marriage,
Or in my cell there would she kill herself.
Then gave I her—so tutored by my art⁹—
A sleeping potion, which so took effect
As I intended, for it wrought on her
245 The form° of death. Meantime I writ to Romeo   *appearance*
That he should hither come as this° dire night   *as this = this*
To help to take her from her borrowed grave,
Being the time the potion's force should cease.
But he which bore my letter, Friar John,
250 Was stayed by accident, and yesternight
Returned my letter back. Then all alone,
At the prefixèd° hour of her waking,   *prearranged*
Came I to take her from her kindred's vault,
Meaning to keep her closely° at my cell   *secretly*
255 Till I conveniently° could send to Romeo.   *befittingly*
But when I came, some minute ere the time
Of her awakening, here untimely lay
The noble Paris and true Romeo dead.
She wakes, and I entreated her come forth
260 And bear this work of heaven with patience.
But then a noise did scare me from the tomb,
And she, too desperate,° would not go with me,   *violent*
But, as it seems, did violence on herself.
All this I know, and to the marriage
265 Her nurse is privy; and if aught in this
Miscarried by my fault, let my old life
Be sacrificed, some hour before his° time,   *its*
Unto the rigour of severest law.
PRINCE   We still° have known thee for a holy man.   *always*
270   Where's Romeo's man? What can he say to this?
BALTHASAR   I brought my master news of Juliet's death,
And then in post° he came from Mantua   *haste*
To this same place, to this same monument.
This letter he early bid me give his father,
275 And threatened me with death, going in the vault,
If I departed not and left him there.
PRINCE   Give me the letter. I will look on it.
        [*He takes the letter*]
Where is the County's page that raised the watch?
Sirrah, what made° your master in this place?   *did*
280 PAGE   He came with flowers to strew his lady's grave,
And bid me stand aloof, and so I did.
Anon° comes one with light to ope the tomb,   *Soon*

9. As I knew through my medical study to do.

And by and by my master drew on him,
And then I ran away to call the watch.
285 PRINCE   This letter doth make good the friar's words,
Their course of love, the tidings of her death;
And here he writes that he did buy a poison
Of a poor 'pothecary, and therewithal
Came to this vault to die, and lie with Juliet.
290 Where be these enemies? Capulet, Montague,
See what a scourge is laid upon your hate,
That heaven finds means to kill your joys° with love.   *happiness; children*
And I, for winking at° your discords, too   *closing my eyes to*
Have lost a brace of kinsmen. All are punishèd.
295 CAPULET   O brother Montague, give me thy hand.
This is my daughter's jointure,° for no more   *marriage portion*
Can I demand.
MONTAGUE   But I can give thee more,
For I will raise her statue in pure gold,
That whiles Verona by that name is known
300 There shall no figure at such rate be set[1]
As that of true and faithful Juliet.
CAPULET   As rich shall Romeo's by his lady's lie,
Poor sacrifices of our enmity.
PRINCE   A glooming° peace this morning with it brings.   *frowning; dark*
305 The sun for sorrow will not show his head.
Go hence, to have more talk of these sad things.
Some shall be pardoned, and some punishèd;
For never was a story of more woe
Than this of Juliet and her Romeo.
                                      [*The tomb is closed.*] *Exeunt*

TEXTUAL VARIANTS

Control text: Q2 (Q1 for 1.2.51–1.3.36)

F: The Folio of 1623
Q1: The Quarto of 1597
Q2: The Quarto of 1599
Q3: The Quarto of 1609
Q4: The Quarto of 1623

Title: The . . . Iuliet [Q2 (title-page and head title above 1.1.)] *The most lamentable Tragedie of Romeo and Iuliet.* [Q2 (running title)]

s.p. CITIZENS OF THE WATCH [Q2's use of *Officer(s)* has been standardized throughout.]
s.p. CAPULET'S WIFE [Q2's use of *Capulet's Wife, Old Lady, Wife, Lady,* and *Mother* has been standardized throughout.]
s.p. MONTAGUE'S WIFE [Q2's use of *Wife* and *Wife. 2.* has been standardized throughout.]
s.p. CAPULET [Q2's use of *Capulet, I. Capulet,* and *Father* has been standardized throughout.]

---

1. No figure shall be valued; no figure shall be erected at such a price.

s.p. PETER [Q2's use of *Peter* and *Servingman* has been standardized throughout.]
s.p. CAPULET'S COUSIN [Q2's use of *2. Capulet* has been standardized throughout.]
s.p. FRIAR LAURENCE [Q2's use of *Friar* and *Lawrence* has been standardized throughout.]
s.p. FIRST SERVINGMAN [Q2's use of *1.*, *3.*, and *Fellow* has been standardized throughout.]
s.p. SECOND SERVINGMAN [Q2's use of *2.* has been standardized throughout.]
s.p. FIRST MUSICIAN [Q2's use of *Musician, Fiddler,* and *Minstrel* has been standardized throughout.]
s.p. SECOND MUSICIAN [Q2's use of *2. Musician, Fiddler,* and *2. Minstrel* has been standardized throughout.]
s.p. THIRD MUSICIAN [Q2's use of *3. Musician, 3. Fiddler,* and *3. Minstrel* has been standardized throughout.]
s.p. BALTHASAR [Q2's use of *Man* and *Balthasar* has been standardized throughout.]

1.1.24 in [Q1; not in Q2] **34 side** [Q1] sides **140 his** [Q3] is **146 sun** same **170 create** [Q1] created **172 well-seeming** [Q4] welseeing **185 lovers'** louing **195 Bid a . . . make** [Q1] A . . . makes **204 unharmed** [Q1] vncharmed **211 makes** [Q4] make
1.2.13 made [Q1; Q2 continues: "Earth hath swallowed all my hopes but she, / Shees the hopefull Lady of my earth"] **27 female** [Q1] femme **65 Vitruvio** Vtruuio **89 fires** fire
1.3.4 where is Wher's **68 honour** [Q1] houre **69 honour** [Q1] *houre* **101 it** [Q1; not in Q2]
1.4.6–8 crowkeeper . . . entrance. [Q1] Crowkeeper. **23 s.p. MERCUTIO** [Q4] *Horatio.* **31 deformity** [Q1] deformities **39 done** [Q3] dum **42 save your reverence** [F] saue you reuerence **45 like lights** lights lights **47 five** fine **54 s.p. BENVOLIO Queen . . . she?** [Q1; not in Q2] **55–91 She . . . bodes.** [Q2 omits 1.4.68–70 and prints "She . . . bodes" as prose.] **55 s.p. MERCUTIO** [not in Q2] **59 Athwart** [Q1] Ouer **62–64 Her . . . bone** her traces of the smallest spider web / her collors of the moonshines watry beams, her whip of Crickets bone **64 film** Philome **67 maid** [Q1] man **73 O'er** [Q1] On **straight;** [Q2 continues: "ore Lawyerrs fingers who strait dreame on fees"] **76 breaths** [Q1] breath **77 lawyer's** [Q1] Courtiers **lip** nose **81 dreams he** [Q1] he dreams **90 elf-locks** [Q1] Elklocks **92 face** [Q1] side **113 sail** [Q1] sute
1.5.6 marzipan March-pane **13 longest** longer **15 a bout** about **16 Aha** [Q1] Ah **91 gentler** gentle **92 ready** [Q1] did readie
2.0.4 matched [Q3] match
2.1.10 Pronounce [Q1] prouaunt **dove** [Q1] day **12 heir** [Q1] her **13 Adam** Abraham **trim** [Q1] true **38 open-arse** an open, or **58 do** [Q1] to **73 passing** [Q1] puffing **83–84 nor any . . . name** o be some other name / Belonging to a man. **87 were** [Q1] wene **107 kinsmen** [Q1] kismen **125 washed** [Q1] washeth **141 'haviour** [Q1] behauior **143 more cunning** [Q1] coying **152 circled** [Q1] circle **190 lord** L. **191 s.p. NURSE** [not in Q2] **193–95 thee . . . come.—** thee (by and by I come) Madam. **207 mine** [Q1; not in Q2] **108 Romeo's name. Romeo!** [Q1] *Romeo.* **212 My nyas** My Neece **225 silk** [Q1] silken **229–32 Parting . . . s.p. ROMEO Sleep . . . Would** Parting . . . *Iu⟨liet⟩.* Sleep . . . *Ro⟨meo⟩.* Would **232 rest.** [Q1; Q2 continues: "The grey eyde morne smiles on the frowning night, / checkring the Easterne Clouds with streaks of light / And darknesse fleckted like a drunkard reeles, / From forth daies pathway, made by *Tytans* wheeles."] **233 sire's close** Friers close
2.2.4 path and Titan's fiery [Q1] path, and *Titans* burning [Q2 (Version B)] pathway, made by Tytans [Q2 (Version A)] **22 sometime's** [Q1] sometime **26 slays** [Q1] staies **74 yet ring** [Q4] yet ringing
2.3.6 kinsman [Q1] kisman **16 s.p. BENVOLIO** [Q1] *Ro⟨meo⟩.* **23 hai** Hay **25–26 phantasims** phantacies **29 pardon-me's** [Q1] pardons mees **60 Switch . . . switch** Swits . . . swits **84 s.p. BENVOLIO** [not in Q2] **102 for** [Q1; not in Q2] **181–91 Well . . . letter** [prose in Q2] **179 I warrant** Warrant **192 Ah A dog's** [Q3] dog
2.4.11 three [Q3] there **15–19 And . . . away M. And** [Q2's M. is indented as a speech prefix]
2.5.27 music's [Q4] musicke **34 sum up** some sum up sum

3.1.2 Capels are [Q1] *Capels* **63 injured** [F] iniuried **69** *stoccado* stucatho **70 come
. . . walk** will you walke **85 s.p. PETRUCCIO Away, Tybalt!** Away Tybalt. [as stage direc-
tion] **87 both your** both **177 He gad** He gan **119 fire-eyed** [Q1] end **140 kinsman**
[Q1] kisman **145 fray** [Q1, F] bloudie fray **160 agent** aged **170 kinsman** [Q3] kisman **178 s.p. MONTAGUE** [Q4] *Capu⟨let⟩.* **182 hate's** [Q1] hearts **186 I** [Q1] It

3.2.1 s.p. JULIET [Q1, F; not in Q2] **9 By** [Q4] And by **15 grown** grow **19 on** vpon **73
s.p. JULIET O . . . face** [Q1; assigned to *Nur⟨se⟩.* in Q2] **76 Dove-feathered** Rauenous
douefeatherd **79 damned** [Q4] dimme **87 dissemblers all** all dissemblers **128 corpse**
course

3.3.15 Hence [Q1] Here **19 banished** [Q1] blanisht **40–43 But . . . death?** This may
flyes do, when I from this must flie, / And sayest thou yet, that exile is not death? / But
Romeo may not, he is banished. / Flies may do this, but I from this must flie: / They are
freemen, but I am banished.

3.3.52 Thou [Q1] Then **62 men** [Q1] man **82 Where is** [Q1] Wheres **109 denote** [Q1]
deuote **116 lives** lies **143 pout'st upon** [Q4] puts vp **167 disguised** [Q3] disguise

3.4.13 be [Q1] me **23 We'll** [Q1] Well

3.5.13 sun exhaled Sun exhale **19 the** [Q1] the the **31 changed** change **43 my** [Q1]
ay **82 him** [Q4; not in Q2] **106 I** [Q4; not in Q2] **139 gives** [Q3] giue **176 work,
play;** houre, tide, time, worke, play **180 lined** liand **225 hence** here

4.1.45 cure [Q1] care **72 slay** [Q1] stay **83 chapless** [Q1] chapels **85 tomb** [not in
Q2] **98 breath** [Q1] breast **100 wanny** many **110 In** [Q3] Is **bier** [Q2 continues: "Be
borne to buriall in thy kindreds graue"] **111 shalt** [Q3] shall **116 waking** [Q3] walking

4.2.14 self-willed harlotry [Q1] selfewield harlottry **26 becoming** becomd

4.3.48 wake [Q4] walke

4.4.20 faith [Q4] father **63 See** [not in Q2] **68 long** [Q1] loue **70–73 Beguiled . . .
death** [follows Nurse's speech 4.4.80–85] **82 behold** [Q3] bedold **92 cure** care **108
All in** And in **109 fond** some **126 by my** [Q1] my my **131 full of woe** [Q4] full **132
s.p. FIRST MUSICIAN** [Q1] *Minstrels.* **146 s.p. PETER Then . . . I** [Q4] Then . . . *Peter.
I.* **148 grief** [Q1] griefes **149 And . . . oppress** [Q1; not in Q2] **152 Matthew Minikin**
Simon Catling **157 Simon** [Q1] *Iames*

5.1.3 lord L. **15 fares my Juliet** [Q1] doth my Lady *Iuliet* **24 defy** [Q1] denie **77 pay**
[Q1] pray

5.3.3. yew trees [Q1] young tree **20 rite** right **40, 43 s.p. BALTHASAR** [Q1] *Pet⟨er⟩.* **68
conjuration** commiration **71 s.p. PAGE** [Q1; line not assigned to anyone in Q2] **102–
3 Shall I believe / That I will beleeue,** / Shall I beleeue that **108 Depart again.** [Q4]
Depart again, come lye thou in my arme. / Here's to thy health, where ere thou tumblest
in. / O true Appothecarie! / Thy drugs are quicke. Thus with a kisse I die. / Depart
againe **137 yew** yong **186 too** [F] too too **189 is so shrieked** is so shrike **193 our**
your **198 slaughtered** [Q4, F] slaughter **208 more early** [Q1] now earling **231 that**
[Q4] thats **298 raise** [Q4, F] raie

Julius Caesar

In any account of Roman history, Julius Caesar's life and death form a crucial chapter. Caesar's assassination, and the tumult that followed his death, produced institutional changes that affected Rome and its enormous territorial possessions for centuries to come. Such a story, simultaneously personal and political, might be expected to fascinate Shakespeare, perennially interested as he was in this small city once capable of ruling what seemed, from a European point of view, to be virtually the entire world. Some theater historians believe that *Julius Caesar* was the first play performed in the Globe theater, a large playhouse erected by Shakespeare's increasingly successful company in 1599. What better choice to inaugurate the new Globe than a story in which world dominion seems to be at stake?

Shakespeare's play opens in 44 B.C., when an astonishing sequence of conquests had made Rome the center of an empire that stretched from north Africa to Britain, from Persia to Spain. Despite its triumphs, however, the city itself was collapsing from within. Rome had long been governed by a senate, but as the city's military endeavors grew increasingly ambitious, its generals became far more powerful than the individually weak, factionalized senators to whom they supposedly owed allegiance. In addition, the Roman polity suffered from sharp class divisions. After a long struggle, the plebeians, or the working class, had won the right to elect their own "tribunes," or representatives, but all women and most plebeian men were still largely excluded from political power. Thus, although the republic was democratic in some respects, the majority of Rome's population did not have a strong interest in maintaining it.

As republican institutions came under increasing pressure, one man after another emerged with absolutist aspirations. Of these, Julius Caesar looked by far the most likely to succeed. He was a remarkable general who had subdued much of northwest Europe even while consolidating his popularity among the poorer classes at home. His combination of ability, charisma, ambition, and good luck made him both extremely valuable to the state and, at the same time, exceptionally dangerous. Those who supported the city's traditional form of government feared that the Rome that prided itself upon its victories abroad was likely to find itself enslaved by one of its own citizens. When legal and military attempts to curb Caesar's growing power failed, a group of conspirators led by Caius Cassius and Marcus Brutus summarily assassinated him. Civil war soon erupted in consequence. The armies loyal to the conspirators were defeated by an army led by Caesar's friend Mark Antony and his heir, Octavius. Eventually, after a power struggle among the victors (recounted in Shakespeare's *Antony and Cleopatra*), Octavius was installed as the emperor Augustus, and the senate was reduced to a merely ceremonial role.

Romans were never shy about acknowledging the importance of their own affairs, and Caesar's contemporaries immediately grasped the significance of his career and his demise. Virtually from the moment the conspirators pulled their swords from Caesar's bleeding corpse, the events Shakespeare treats in *Julius Caesar* were amply documented and their rationale debated. Different commentators from antiquity to the Renaissance, depending on their own political convictions, viewed the assassination as an act of heroism, expediency, or villainy and celebrated, excused, or denounced its perpetrators accordingly. While Michelangelo and Milton idealize Brutus as a selfless defender of human liberty, Dante plunges him, with Cassius, into the deepest pit of hell. It is not surprising that Shakespeare, ever alive to the dramatic possibilities inherent in multiple, conflicting perspectives, should choose to stage an incident that had been provoking debate for more than sixteen hundred years.

In Shakespeare's dramatization, the controversy over Caesar's rise and assassination arises from stubborn incompatibilities among various ideals or objectives, each admirable in itself. The play suggests questions like these: What limits can a community appropriately set on the activities of its most remarkable members? Are citizens allowed, or even obliged, to defend the rule of law against such an individual by resorting to extralegal violence? When the demands of civic responsibility apparently conflict with those of personal loyalty, as they do for Brutus, which ought to prevail? Ultimately these are questions not merely about individual choices and behaviors, but about the future of a society: do Rome's military conquests, which eventually demand stronger supervision than the senate can provide, eventually doom the republican political configuration that made those conquests possible in the first place?

For Shakespeare's contemporaries, such questions were not merely of antiquarian interest. Throughout early modern Europe, strong monarchs were attempting, with varying degrees of success, to consolidate their power. In England, these efforts threatened the traditional prerogatives of the aristocracy and of elected representatives in the House of Commons. For thinkers and writers saturated by their classical education in the antique past, it was easy to see the shift toward strong monarchy as replaying the shift from republican to imperial Rome. In England in 1599, moreover, concerns over the general nationalizing trend were exacerbated by more specific anxieties. Queen Elizabeth I had proven a remarkably durable queen—she had already survived several attempts on her life—but at sixty-six, she was a very old woman by Renaissance standards, and her reign was clearly soon to come to an end. Since, however, she had never begotten children or named an heir, it was unclear who would succeed her or how the new monarch would be selected. Conceivably England would revert, upon her death, to the kind of civil chaos through which it had suffered in the fifteenth century. In a state in which censorship made direct commentary on contemporary political affairs virtually impossible, the story of Caesar's death and its calamitous aftermath provided an opportunity to reflect, at a suitably prudent distance, upon what might happen when accepted methods of allocating and transferring sovereign power disintegrated.

Shakespeare's treatment of Caesar's career is deeply influenced by his main sources, the lives of Caesar and Brutus in Thomas North's English translation of Plutarch's *Lives of the Noble Greeks and Romans*. Writing in the first century A.D., Plutarch had construed the biographer's task as inextricable from the historian's, since in his view history recorded the achievements of great men. In the Roman Republic, he claimed, there was always more than one powerful person, but rarely more than a few. Shakespeare followed Plutarch in stressing the decisive roles played by the acknowledged leaders of Roman society, rather than dwelling on the frictions among larger social groups. Not that he was entirely unaware of the latter: the testiness of *Julius Caesar*'s opening scene makes the internal divisions in Roman society abundantly clear. But throughout the play, commoners are largely imagined from an upper-class perspective—as a politically unsophisticated mob that hardly seems to merit the scrupulous civic responsibility of its betters. The capacity for conscious and reflective political decision making rests in the hands of a small elite.

Plutarch's "great man" view of history conduces to compelling dramas involving a manageable number of characters. And Shakespeare's drastic condensation of narrative time frame in *Julius Caesar* has the effect of exaggerating Plutarch's emphases. In Plutarch, Caesar's triumph over Pompey's sons occurs in October, but Shakespeare makes it coincide with the Lupercalia in February, so that the assassination on the ides of March seems a direct response to a specific display of arrogance. Likewise, in Plutarch, Brutus and Cassius withdraw from Rome more than a year after Caesar's funeral, but in Shakespeare, their flight fol-

Julius Caesar. From Plutarch, *The Lives of the Noble Grecians and Romanes* (1595).

lows immediately upon Antony's brilliant incitement of the Roman mob. The effect is not only to escalate dramatic momentum but also to make the personal strengths and weaknesses of Rome's leaders seem matters of titanic consequence.

Not surprisingly, then, issues of characterization have traditionally dominated the critical reception of *Julius Caesar*. It is a play that, like the Roman Republic itself, no single hero can appropriate wholly to himself. Instead, *Julius Caesar* divides its attention among several characters, setting them off against one another, while the titular hero makes less claim upon the audience's attention than might be expected. Plutarch's biography emphasizes Caesar's military genius, his ruthless executive skill, and his astonishing capacity to rescue himself repeatedly from crushing adversity. Shakespeare's Caesar seems less outsized: we are informed of his ambition, but his accomplishments are not shown us or much alluded to, and much of what we do hear is filtered through the hostile reports of resentful observers. Onstage, Caesar seems sociable, ambitious, and egotistical—sometimes ridiculously so. But the plausibility of the conspirators' fears is never entirely clear.

Brutus, Caesar's friend and killer, is far more fully elaborated, especially in the soliloquies in which he carefully examines his motives and the possible consequences of his actions. Moreover, unlike the other characters, he appears to us in several guises: as a public figure, a husband, a master of servants, a military leader. Thus he experiences painfully in his own person the value conflicts that are elsewhere dispersed among various antagonists. How is Brutus, and how are we, to reconcile his tender regard for his family circle with his willingness to commit political murder? Does Brutus's intimacy with Caesar make his decision to assassinate him more truly noble, since it cannot be said to stem from self-interest? Or does it suggest a troubling insensitivity to the claims of friendship and to Caesar's genuinely exceptional character?

Most important, how is Brutus's idealism and his commitment to principle to be evaluated? Surely his habit of appealing to abstract moral and political tenets is an admirable trait, especially in a city in which selfishness seems the dominant passion. But repeatedly this practice leads him to commit disastrous tactical errors. Concerned to minimize bloodshed, he refuses to countenance Cassius's suggestion that Antony be killed along with Caesar. Then—once again ignoring Cassius's advice—he permits Antony to speak an unsupervised eulogy at Caesar's funeral, thus losing the "spin" on Caesar's death and unleashing the rage of the crowd against himself and his allies. Later, his indignation at what he believes to be Cassius's corrupt practices seriously endangers their alliance.

In all these cases, Brutus is concerned to diminish the extent to which any of his actions might conceivably serve his own self-interest, even though by doing so he risks and eventually dooms the cause he is attempting to serve. In comparison, the impulsive, unscrupulous Cassius is far more alert to the way the world really works, willingly stooping to expediency to get what he wants and what his cause needs. The contrast with Antony likewise clarifies the way in which Brutus's principles incapacitate him. Antony emerges as a formidable opponent not despite but because of traits that Brutus can see only as weaknesses: love of sensual indulgence, lack of principle, a tendency to live in the present without sufficient care for past or future. Antony's uninhibited, improvisatory nature suits him beautifully for swaying the plebeians. A marvelous actor, he exploits gestures, cunning rhetoric, props, and any other means that most fully serve the particular moment in which he finds himself. In fact, Antony's political astuteness seems to arise directly from his personal familiarity with passion, since much of politics is, as Brutus never quite realizes, a matter of assessing and responding to group desire.

Marc Antony. From Plutarch, *The Lives of the Noble Grecians and Romanes* (1595).

Unlike Antony on the one hand or Cassius on the other, both Caesar and Brutus attempt to live up to superhuman ideals, although the kind of transcendence they have in mind is rather different. Caesar wants absolute supremacy—less, apparently, because he has any particular vision for the Roman polity than because he yearns for the unqualified homage of others, both in the present and for eternity. Although epileptic and physically frail, he imagines himself as embodying a god-like permanence, "unshaked of motion" (3.1.70):

> I am constant as the Northern Star,
> Of whose true fixed and resting quality
> There is no fellow in the firmament.
> (3.1.60–62)

Brutus, though not entirely innocent of Caesar's love of dominion, generally frames his desire for constancy less in terms of power over others than in terms of personal self-control. By behaving according to immovable principles, he tries to give his life a stern but reassuring fixity.

Of course, both Caesar and Brutus end up paying for these aspirations with their lives; and even before they do so, their yearning for fixity appears misplaced in a play in which character seems complex and highly mutable. Often in *Julius Caesar*, the same scene provides a character with a variety of motives, permitting alternative descriptions of a single action. Thus when Brutus decides to participate in the conspiracy to kill Caesar, he believes he has carefully sequestered his self-interest from his convictions about the common good. But Cassius has meanwhile been tossing flattering messages through his window, so the theater audience must consider the possibility that Brutus is swayed by a personal ambition of which he may not be entirely aware. Elsewhere, Shakespeare complicates his portraits by what might be called a technique of gradual release. By slowly making details available to the audience, he forces it to revise its previous impressions to take account of new information. For instance, Antony's bravura eulogy reaches a climax when he reads Caesar's will, thus harnessing the plebeians' greed to the end of revenging Caesar's death. A mere two scenes later, he is shown in conference with Lepidus and Octavius, giving brisk orders to minimize the cost of Caesar's generosity. The incongruity between the first scene and the second makes Antony's original celebration of his friend's magnanimity seem, in retrospect, less sincere or spontaneous. Nonetheless, the two scenes do not force the audience to a single obvious conclusion. Does Antony's later parsimony indicate that he was simply hypocritical when he used Caesar's will to provoke a riot? Perhaps, but not necessarily; he could simply have been caught up in a wave of loyalty to Caesar and in the pathos of the situation, or he could have had vaguely ambitious but not yet fully articulated plans. In such cases, Shakespeare's cunning dramatic presentation enhances the complexity of his characterizations. The realistic illusion depends as much on what he withholds from the audience as on what he provides it.

Even while Shakespeare vividly differentiates his characters, he shows clearly how they derive from the particular social and intellectual culture they inhabit. Shakespeare was no antiquarian: he imagines the characters of *Julius Caesar* wearing Elizabethan doublet and hose, and he notoriously equips ancient Rome with a medieval invention, the mechanical clock. Nonetheless, his Romans share a set of distinctive values, ideals, and assumptions. When Antony, at the end of the play, calls Brutus "the noblest of the Romans," he is not simply praising Brutus as an individual. Instead, he is locating Brutus in a tradition of specifically "Roman" virtue, a virtue associated with the particular strengths of the republican form of government Brutus died attempting to defend.

What does this virtue entail? Brutus's willingness to identify his abstract principles with the common good, as well as his intense suspicion of anyone who appears self-aggrandizing, is wholly characteristic of an ethos that distinguishes sharply between duty and pleasure, between public and private. The heroes of the Roman Republic had always been celebrated for their incorruptibility and for their preference for public service, however thankless, over private goods like marriage, friendship, sensual pleasure, and personal enrichment. At the same time, Rome was in fact a hotbed of nepotism and unscrupulousness, and its venality grew along with its power. Thus pillars of the Roman Republic like Lucius Junius Brutus, Marcus Cato, Scipio Africanus, and Marcus Brutus himself were admired not merely because their propensity for self-sacrifice was socially valuable, but because such exemplars were rarer and more surprising than Romans liked to admit.

The sharp distinction Roman culture made between public and private concerns has important consequences in *Julius Caesar*. The public world is an all-male affair: bonds and rivalries provide both the glue that holds the Roman Republic together and a competitive petulancy that ordinarily precludes a single individual's gaining too much power. We are given a vivid picture of this complex interpersonal dynamic in Cassius's account of his swimming contest with Caesar, an incident of pure bravado in which friends test their toughness against one another, and in which one ends up saving the other's life. The same rivalrous intensity characterizes the almost erotically charged quarrel and reconciliation between Brutus and Cassius in 4.2.

Beside the fraught intensity of such relationships, the heterosexual connections in the play are rather pallid. Although Brutus loves Portia dearly, it does not occur to him to take her into his confidence until she struggles mightily for the privilege on the eve of the assassination; even then, all she requests is information, not permission to offer advice. Similarly, Decius easily shames Caesar into ignoring Calpurnia's foreboding dream:

> it were a mock
> Apt to be rendered for someone to say
> 'Break up the Senate till another time,
> When Caesar's wife shall meet with better dreams.'
> (2.2.96–99)

Even the most powerful man in the state, apparently, cannot risk being seen to be influenced by a mere wife. Most tellingly, in what is perhaps a sign of textual corruption but more probably a supreme instance of Shakespearean skill in delineating character, we are given two successive accounts of the way Brutus learns of Portia's suicide. In the first, Brutus divulges the loss himself to Cassius, expressing his grief in solitary conference with an old friend. Shortly thereafter, however, he tells his military subordinates that he has not received any news of Portia at all. Once informed that she has died "in strange manner," he affects a studied indifference, insisting that the tidings merely interfere with more important matters at hand. His ability to sequester domestic concerns from public and military ones elicits the admiration of those around him: for true "Romans" are willing to incur huge emotional costs for what they imagine is the greater good.

The sharp division between male and female, public and private, means that the arenas in which "virtue" can be exercised are almost entirely reserved for men. Even within the confines of the household, the women of *Julius Caesar* are unable to cultivate an alternative form of social value. Maternity, for instance, is not a source of power here: Calpurnia is declared to be barren, and Portia too is apparently childless. The "feminine intuition" both women possess in abundance has no practical effect. Nobility for these radically marginalized characters requires them to internalize values that for them have little use. Portia proves what she calls her "masculine" courage to her husband by the bizarre means of stabbing herself deliberately in the thigh, a gesture that suggests a self-castration, as if a woman were at best a slashed man. For the virtue she claims to possess is not truly her own possession; rather, it is a quality reflected from her male relatives that makes her superior to ordinary women. "Think you I am no stronger than my sex, / Being so fathered and so husbanded?" (2.1.295–96). Portia kills herself, typically, in an exceptionally painful way, by swallowing hot coals. While the fabled hardihood of Portia's father, Cato, or her husband, Brutus, has at least some military rationale, Portia's imitation of their fortitude seems pointlessly masochistic, serving neither their ends nor her own.

The pressure of Roman values on the characters of *Julius Caesar* suggests that its protagonists are not entirely free to invent themselves; they are limited to the cultural materials at hand. On other grounds too, a reading focusing purely on character seems finally inadequate. In oft-cited lines, Cassius pronounces: "The fault, dear Brutus, is not in our stars, / But in ourselves, that we are underlings" (1.2.141–42). It is not at all clear, however, that he is right. Plutarch emphasizes how the fates of his biographical subjects fail to reflect

Brutus falling on his sword. From Geffrey Whitney, *A Choice of Emblemes* (1586).

their virtues. Caesar, who had miraculously survived so many strange adventures in hostile foreign lands, can be dispatched in a few minutes by his erstwhile friends just moments after leaving his own house. Cicero, whose oratory had held sway in Rome for so many years, is obliterated by Antony and Octavius practically as an afterthought. The gifted and honorable Brutus meets death after a military defeat that seems almost accidental. Cassius's suicide is even more haphazard. The inscrutable workings of fate play at least as great a role as personality does in determining the outcome of the action.

For this reason, virtually all the characters find it impossible to achieve a reliable perspective on events in which they are immersed. In the play's most literal case of limited vision, the "thick-sighted" Cassius misinterprets victory as defeat and kills himself moments before his triumphant soldiers arrive hoping to congratulate him. Here and elsewhere, Shakespeare drums home the difference between the perspective of the theater audience, for whom the killing of Julius Caesar is an act centuries old now replayed for its entertainment value, and the perspective of the characters within the play, for whom it is unfolding in the present moment, its consequences both dire and unknown. Caesar pronounces upon his godlike permanence a moment before we know he is about to be ignominiously slaughtered. Once he is dead, Cassius exclaims:

> How many ages hence
> Shall this our lofty scene be acted over,
> In states unborn and accents yet unknown!
>
> (3.1.112–14)

In this striking moment, Cassius not only celebrates what he accurately imagines will be the eternal fame of Caesar's assassination but also obscurely anticipates his own impersonated presence on Shakespeare's stage. The durability of that "lofty scene" does not, however, as he imagines, bespeak the assassins' success. The conspiracy not only fails to accomplish its purpose but in fact opens the way for centuries of imperial rule more despotic than anything Julius ever imagined. Likewise, from the audience's point of view, when Antony plots with Octavius to eliminate Lepidus, he becomes the victim of an irony he cannot possibly comprehend. For the audience knows as Antony cannot that the cold, noncommittal Octavius will ultimately annihilate both his triumviral associates.

To be alive to such ironies, the characters would need to be able to look into the future. Struggling to understand their own place in history, they continually resort to augury, attempting—usually incorrectly—to comprehend the omens that shadow forth their fates.

In *Julius Caesar*, omens are always telling, but they are rarely intelligible except in retro-spect. No one knows what to make of the lions loose in the streets; the soothsayer arrives too late; Caesar's dream is misinterpreted; Cassius notices carrion birds on his standards but decides to disregard them. By emphasizing the analogies among personal, political, and natural forms of disruption, omens on the one hand intensify the significance of the play's characters: their decisions, quirks, and flaws affect the structure of the universe itself. On the other hand, the reliability of omens challenges the notion that history is the product of personal effort, since augury implies restrictions on free will, suggesting that individuals are caught in the toils of a historical process they cannot control or understand. Under-girding the other questions of authority, responsibility, and agency in *Julius Caesar* are unanswerable questions about who creates history, and what that history can possibly mean.

KATHARINE EISAMAN MAUS

TEXTUAL NOTE

The 1623 First Folio (F) provides the only authoritative text for *Julius Caesar*. The fullness of the stage directions, which specify sound effects as well as actors' exits and entrances, and the absence of Shakespearean spellings suggest that the Folio text was derived from the theater company's official promptbook rather than from Shakespeare's manuscript.

Despite the general reliability of the Folio *Julius Caesar*, there are a few editorial puzzles. In Act 4, there is some confusion about the parts played by the minor characters Titinius, Lucillius, and Lucius, leading some scholars to believe that Shakespeare revised these scenes. Two conundrums have more significant consequences for the play's charac-terizations. In 1614 and again in 1625, Shakespeare's contemporary Ben Jonson ridiculed a line in 3.1 in which Caesar supposedly proclaims: "Know Caesar doth not wrong but with just cause." F omits the last four words, but the currency of Jonson's joke even after the publication of the Folio suggests that they were retained in performance. Indeed the apparent illogic of Caesar's utterance (how can a wrong have a just cause?) seems to testify powerfully to the speaker's megalomaniac sense that he transcends the rules ordinary mortals must obey. The Oxford text restores the line as reported by Jonson rather than emending it to some more "reasonable" possibility. Some textual scholars see a similar lapse of logic in 4.2, in which Brutus's account of Portia's death to Cassius seems to contradict his claim, moments later, that he is ignorant of that death. Possibly Shakespeare revised the scene and forgot to cancel the rejected lines. However, as in 3.1, the seeming inconsistency might be justified as revealing an interesting aspect of Brutus's character or of Roman attitudes toward the difference between domestic and public domains.

SELECTED BIBLIOGRAPHY

Bloom, Harold, ed. *William Shakespeare's "Julius Caesar."* New York: Chelsea House, 1988.

Burckhardt, Sigurd. "How Not to Murder Caesar." *Shakespearean Meanings.* Princeton: Princeton University Press, 1968. 3–21.

Knights, L. C. "Shakespeare and Political Wisdom: A Note on the Personalism of *Julius Caesar* and *Coriolanus.*" *Sewanee Review* 61 (1953): 43–55.

Miles, Gary B. "How Roman Are Shakespeare's 'Romans'?" *Shakespeare Quarterly* 40 (1989): 257–83.

Miola, Robert S. "*Julius Caesar* and the Tyrannicide Debate." *Renaissance Quarterly* 38 (1985): 271–89.

Paster, Gail. " 'In the Spirit of Men There Is No Blood': Blood as a Trope of Gender in *Julius Caesar*." *Shakespeare Quarterly* 40 (1989): 284–98.

Rebhorn, Wayne. "The Crisis of the Aristocracy in *Julius Caesar*." *Renaissance Quarterly* 43 (1990): 75–111.

Taylor, Gary. "Bardicide." *Shakespeare and Cultural Traditions*. Ed. Tetsuo Kishi, Roger Pringle, and Stanley Wells. Newark: University of Delaware Press, 1991. 333–49.

Traversi, Derek. *"Julius Caesar." Shakespeare: The Roman Plays*. Stanford: Stanford University Press, 1963. 21–75.

The Tragedy of Julius Caesar

THE PERSONS OF THE PLAY

Julius CAESAR
CALPURNIA, his wife
Marcus BRUTUS, a noble Roman, opposed to Caesar
PORTIA, his wife
LUCIUS, his servant
Caius CASSIUS ⎫
CASCA
TREBONIUS
DECIUS Brutus ⎬ opposed to Caesar
METELLUS Cimber
CINNA
Caius LIGARIUS ⎭
Mark ANTONY ⎫
OCTAVIUS Caesar ⎬ rulers of Rome after Caesar's death
LEPIDUS ⎭
FLAVIUS ⎫ tribunes of the people
MURELLUS ⎭
CICERO ⎫
PUBLIUS ⎬ senators
POPILLIUS Laena ⎭
A SOOTHSAYER
ARTEMIDORUS
CINNA the Poet
PINDARUS, Cassius' bondman
TITINIUS, an officer in Cassius' army
LUCILLIUS ⎫
MESSALA
VARRUS
CLAUDIO
YOUNG CATO ⎬ officers and soldiers in Brutus' army
STRATO
VOLUMNIUS
FLAVIUS
DARDANIUS
CLITUS ⎭
A POET
A GHOST of Caesar
A COBBLER
A CARPENTER
Other PLEBEIANS
A MESSENGER
SERVANTS
Senators, soldiers, and attendants

1.1

Enter FLAVIUS, MURELLUS, *and certain commoners over
the stage*

FLAVIUS　Hence, home, you idle creatures, get you home!
　Is this a holiday? What, know you not,
　Being mechanical,° you ought not walk　　　　　　　*of the artisan class*
　Upon a labouring day without the sign°　　　　　　*tools and garments*
5　Of your profession? — Speak, what trade art thou?
CARPENTER　Why, sir, a carpenter.
MURELLUS　Where is thy leather apron and thy rule?
　What dost thou with thy best apparel on? —
　You, sir, what trade are you?
10　COBBLER　Truly, sir, in respect of° a fine workman I am but, as　　*in comparison with*
　you would say, a cobbler.[1]
MURELLUS　But what trade art thou? Answer me directly.
COBBLER　A trade, sir, that I hope I may use with a safe con-
　science, which is indeed, sir, a mender of bad soles.°　　　*(punning on "souls")*
15　FLAVIUS　What trade, thou knave? Thou naughty° knave, what trade?　　*wicked*
COBBLER　Nay, I beseech you, sir, be not out[2] with me. Yet if
　you be out, sir, I can mend you.
MURELLUS　What mean'st thou by that? Mend me, thou saucy fellow?
COBBLER　Why, sir, cobble you.
20　FLAVIUS　Thou art a cobbler, art thou?
COBBLER　Truly, sir, all that I live by is with the awl. I meddle
　with no tradesman's matters, nor women's matters,° but withal[3]　　*(a bawdy joke)*
　I am indeed, sir, a surgeon to old shoes: when they are in great
　danger I recover° them. As proper° men as ever trod upon　　*resole; cure / fine*
25　neat's leather° have gone° upon my handiwork.　　　　*cowhide / walked*
FLAVIUS　But wherefore art not in thy shop today?
　Why dost thou lead these men about the streets?
COBBLER　Truly, sir, to wear out their shoes to get myself into
　more work. But indeed, sir, we make holiday to see Caesar, and
30　to rejoice in his triumph.[4]
MURELLUS　Wherefore rejoice? What conquest brings he home?
　What tributaries° follow him to Rome　　　　　　*ransom payers*
　To grace in captive bonds his chariot wheels?[5]
　You blocks, you stones, you worse than senseless° things!　　*inanimate*
35　O, you hard hearts, you cruel men of Rome,
　Knew you not Pompey?[6] Many a time and oft
　Have you climbed up to walls and battlements,
　To towers and windows, yea to chimney-tops,
　Your infants in your arms, and there have sat
40　The livelong day with patient expectation
　To see great Pompey pass the streets of Rome.
　And when you saw his chariot but appear,
　Have you not made an universal shout,
　That Tiber[7] trembled underneath her banks
45　To hear the replication° of your sounds　　　　　　*echo*
　Made in her concave shores?

1.1　Location: A street in Rome.
1. Mender of shoes; bungler (the sense Murellus understands).
2. Angry; worn out, like shoes.
3. Nevertheless; punning on "awl."
4. Triumphal procession in honor of victory (by Roman
custom, over foreign enemies, but here over Caesar's

political adversaries, Pompey's sons).
5. Captives were tied to their conquerors' chariots.
6. Pompey the Great, who had shared rule of Rome with
Caesar and Crassus; he was defeated by Caesar after their
alliance disintegrated, and later assassinated.
7. River that flows through Rome.

And do you now put on your best attire?
And do you now cull out° a holiday?   *choose*
And do you now strew flowers in his way
50 That comes in triumph over Pompey's blood?°   *offspring*
Be gone!
Run to your houses, fall upon your knees,
Pray to the gods to intermit[8] the plague
That needs must light on this ingratitude.
55 FLAVIUS Go, go, good countrymen, and for this fault
Assemble all the poor men of your sort;°   *rank*
Draw them to Tiber banks, and weep your tears
Into the channel, till the lowest stream
Do kiss the most exalted shores of all.°   *tops of the riverbanks*
Exeunt all the commoners
60 See whe'er° their basest mettle be not moved.   *whether*
They vanish tongue-tied in their guiltiness.
Go you down that way towards the Capitol;[9]
This way will I. Disrobe the images
If you do find them decked with ceremonies.[1]
65 MURELLUS May we do so?
You know it is the Feast of Lupercal.[2]
FLAVIUS It is no matter. Let no images
Be hung with Caesar's trophies.° I'll about,   *ornaments*
And drive away the vulgar° from the streets;   *commoners*
70 So do you too where you perceive them thick.
These growing feathers plucked from Caesar's wing
Will make him fly an ordinary pitch,[3]
Who else° would soar above the view of men   *otherwise*
And keep us all in servile fearfulness.   *Exeunt*

1.2

[Loud music.] Enter CAESAR, ANTONY *[stripped] for the
course,*[1] CALPURNIA, PORTIA, DECIUS, CICERO, BRUTUS,
CASSIUS, CASCA, *a* SOOTHSAYER[*, a throng of citizens*];
after them, MURELLUS *and* FLAVIUS
CAESAR Calpurnia.
CASCA Peace, ho! Caesar speaks.
[Music ceases]
CAESAR Calpurnia.
CALPURNIA Here, my lord.
5 CAESAR Stand you directly in Antonio's way
When he doth run his course.—Antonio.
ANTONY Caesar, my lord.
CAESAR Forget not in your speed, Antonio,
To touch Calpurnia, for our elders say
10 The barren, touchèd in this holy chase,
Shake off their sterile curse.
ANTONY   I shall remember:
When Caesar says 'Do this', it is performed.

8. Withhold (plague was considered a divine punishment).
9. Hill on whose top was the Temple of Jupiter, where
victorious generals in a triumph offered sacrifice.
1. Caesar's followers had put imperial crowns ("ceremonies") on his statues.
2. Lupercalia, a festival celebrated February 15. Historically, Caesar's triumph took place in October.
3. At a medium height (an image from falconry).
1.2 Location: A public place in Rome.
1. During the Lupercalia, two celebrants ran naked
through Rome, striking those they met with goatskin
thongs.

CAESAR Set on,° and leave no ceremony out.   *Proceed*
      [*Music*]
SOOTHSAYER Caesar!
15 CAESAR Ha! Who calls?
CASCA Bid every noise be still. Peace yet again.
      [*Music ceases*]
CAESAR Who is it in the press° that calls on me?   *crowd*
  I hear a tongue shriller than all the music
  Cry 'Caesar!' Speak. Caesar is turned to hear.
SOOTHSAYER Beware the ides² of March.
20 CAESAR   What man is that?
BRUTUS A soothsayer bids you beware the ides of March.
CAESAR Set him before me; let me see his face.
CASSIUS Fellow, come from the throng; look upon Caesar.
      [*The* SOOTHSAYER *comes forward*]
CAESAR What sayst thou to me now? Speak once again.
25 SOOTHSAYER Beware the ides of March.
CAESAR He is a dreamer. Let us leave him. Pass!°   *Onward*
                  Sennet.° Exeunt. Manent° BRUTUS *and* CASSIUS   *Trumpet flourish / Remain*
CASSIUS Will you go see the order of the course?°   *running of the race*
BRUTUS Not I.
CASSIUS I pray you, do.
30 BRUTUS I am not gamesome;° I do lack some part   *fond of sport*
  Of that quick° spirit that is in Antony.   *lively*
  Let me not hinder, Cassius, your desires.
  I'll leave you.
CASSIUS Brutus, I do observe you now of late.
35 I have not from your eyes that gentleness
  And show of love as I was wont° to have.   *accustomed*
  You bear too stubborn and too strange° a hand³   *unfriendly*
  Over your friend that loves you.
BRUTUS   Cassius,
  Be not deceived. If I have veiled my look,°   *seemed less outgoing*
40 I turn the trouble of my countenance°   *my troubled looks*
  Merely° upon myself. Vexèd I am   *Wholly*
  Of late with passions of some difference,°   *conflicting kinds*
  Conceptions only proper° to myself,   *suitable*
  Which give some soil,° perhaps, to my behaviours.   *blemish*
45 But let not therefore my good friends be grieved—
  Among which number, Cassius, be you one—
  Nor construe any further° my neglect   *make any more of*
  Than that poor Brutus, with himself at war,
  Forgets the shows of love to other men.
50 CASSIUS Then, Brutus, I have much mistook your passion,°   *feelings*
  By means whereof⁴ this breast of mine hath buried°   *concealed*
  Thoughts of great value, worthy cogitations.
  Tell me, good Brutus, can you see your face?
BRUTUS No, Cassius, for the eye sees not itself
55 But by reflection, by some other things.
CASSIUS 'Tis just;°   *true*
  And it is very much lamented, Brutus,

---

2. The ides marked roughly the midpoint of every Roman month (usually the thirteenth); in March, the fifteenth.

3. Management of horse's reins (figurative).
4. In consequence of which mistake.

That you have no such mirrors as will turn
Your hidden worthiness into your eye,
60 That you might see your shadow.° I have heard   *reflection*
Where many of the best respect° in Rome—   *repute*
Except immortal Caesar—speaking of Brutus,
And groaning underneath this age's yoke,
Have wished that noble Brutus had his eyes.⁵
65 BRUTUS Into what dangers would you lead me, Cassius,
That you would have me seek into myself
For that which is not in me?
CASSIUS Therefor,° good Brutus, be prepared to hear.   *As to that*
And since you know you cannot see yourself
70 So well as by reflection, I, your glass,°   *mirror*
Will modestly discover° to yourself   *reveal*
That of yourself which you yet know not of.
And be not jealous on° me, gentle Brutus.   *suspicious of*
Were I a common laughter,° or did use   *object of ridicule*
75 To stale° with ordinary° oaths my love   *debase / cheap*
To every new protester;° if you know   *declarer of friendship*
That I do fawn on men and hug them hard,
And after scandal° them; or if you know   *defame*
That I profess myself° in banqueting   *declare friendship*
80 To all the rout:° then hold me dangerous.   *mob*
          Flourish, and shout [within]
BRUTUS What means this shouting? I do fear the people
Choose Caesar for their king.
CASSIUS   Ay, do you fear it?
Then must I think you would not have it so.
BRUTUS I would not, Cassius; yet I love him well.
85 But wherefore do you hold me here so long?
What is it that you would impart to me?
If it be aught toward the general good,
Set honour in one eye and death i'th' other,
And I will look on both indifferently;°   *impartially*
90 For let the gods so speed me as⁶ I love
The name of honour more than I fear death.
CASSIUS I know that virtue to be in you, Brutus,
As well as I do know your outward favour.°   *appearance*
Well, honour is the subject of my story.
95 I cannot tell what you and other men
Think of this life; but for my single self,
I had as lief not be,° as live to be   *I had rather be dead*
In awe of such a thing as I myself.
I was born free as Caesar, so were you.
100 We both have fed as well, and we can both
Endure the winter's cold as well as he.
For once upon a raw and gusty day,
The troubled Tiber chafing with° her shores,   *raging against*
Said Caesar to me 'Dar'st thou, Cassius, now
105 Leap in with me into this angry flood,
And swim to yonder point?'° Upon the word,   *promontory*
Accoutred° as I was I plungèd in,   *Dressed in armor*
And bade him follow. So indeed he did.

5. That is, could see properly.   6. Make me fortunate insofar as.

The torrent roared, and we did buffet it
110 With lusty sinews, throwing it aside,
And stemming° it with hearts of controversy.°   *confronting / rivalry*
But ere we could arrive° the point proposed,   *reach*
Caesar cried 'Help me, Cassius, or I sink!'
Ay, as Aeneas⁷ our great ancestor
115 Did from the flames of Troy upon his shoulder
The old Anchises bear, so from the waves of Tiber
Did I the tirèd Caesar. And this man
Is now become a god, and Cassius is
A wretched creature, and must bend his body°   *(must bow)*
120 If Caesar carelessly but nod on him.
He had a fever when he was in Spain,
And when the fit was on him, I did mark
How he did shake. 'Tis true, this god did shake.
His coward lips did from their colour fly;⁸
125 And that same eye whose bend° doth awe the world   *glance*
Did lose his° lustre. I did hear him groan,   *its*
Ay, and that tongue of his that bade the Romans
Mark him and write his speeches in their books,
'Alas!' it cried, 'Give me some drink, Titinius',
130 As a sick girl. Ye gods, it doth amaze me
A man of such a feeble temper° should   *constitution*
So get the start of° the majestic world,   *advantage over*
And bear the palm° alone!   *be victor*
              Shout [within]. Flourish
BRUTUS   Another general shout!
I do believe that these applauses are
135 For some new honours that are heaped on Caesar.
CASSIUS   Why, man, he doth bestride the narrow world
Like a Colossus,⁹ and we petty men
Walk under his huge legs, and peep about
To find ourselves dishonourable graves.
140 Men at sometime° were masters of their fates.   *formerly*
The fault, dear Brutus, is not in our stars,
But in ourselves, that we are underlings.
Brutus and Caesar: what should be in that 'Caesar'?
Why should that name be sounded more than yours?
145 Write them together: yours is as fair a name.
Sound them: it doth become the mouth as well.
Weigh them: it is as heavy. Conjure with 'em:
'Brutus' will start¹ a spirit as soon as 'Caesar'.
Now in the names of all the gods at once,
150 Upon what meat° doth this our Caesar feed   *food*
That he is grown so great? Age, thou art shamed.
Rome, thou hast lost the breed of noble bloods.
When went there by an age since the great flood,²
But it was famed with° more than with one man?   *renowned for*
155 When could they say till now, that talked of Rome,

---

7. Legendary Trojan warrior and founder of Rome; when the Greeks burned Troy, he carried his father, Anchises, out on his back.
8. Did turn pale; did desert their flag (Caesar suffered epileptic seizures).
9. Giant statue of Apollo, which straddled the harbor of Rhodes.
1. Raise (only the names of the gods were thought to be able to raise the dead).
2. A great flood was recorded in classical as well as biblical accounts.

That her wide walls encompassed but one man?
Now is it Rome indeed, and room° enough   *(pronounced like "Rome")*
When there is in it but one only man.
O, you and I have heard our fathers say
160   There was a Brutus once[3] that would have brooked°   *endured*
Th'eternal devil to keep his state° in Rome   *hold court*
As easily as a king.
BRUTUS   That you do love me I am nothing jealous.°   *not at all uncertain*
What you would work° me to I have some aim.°   *persuade / idea*
165   How I have thought of this and of these times
I shall recount hereafter. For this present,°   *present time*
I would not, so with love° I might entreat you,   *if in friendship*
Be any further moved.° What you have said   *persuaded*
I will consider. What you have to say
170   I will with patience hear, and find a time
Both meet° to hear and answer such high things.   *Fitting both*
Till then, my noble friend, chew upon this:
Brutus had rather be a villager
Than to repute himself a son of Rome
175   Under these hard conditions as this time
Is like to lay upon us.
CASSIUS   I am glad
That my weak words have struck but thus much show
Of fire from Brutus.
       [Music.] Enter CAESAR *and his train*°   *retinue*
BRUTUS   The games are done, and Caesar is returning.
180   CASSIUS   As they pass by, pluck Casca by the sleeve,[4]
And he will, after his sour fashion, tell you
What hath proceeded worthy° note today.   *worthy of*
BRUTUS   I will do so. But look you, Cassius,
The angry spot doth glow on Caesar's brow,
185   And all the rest look like a chidden° train.   *scolded*
Calpurnia's cheek is pale, and Cicero
Looks with such ferret[5] and such fiery eyes
As we have seen him in the Capitol
Being crossed in conference° by some senators.   *opposed in debate*
190   CASSIUS   Casca will tell us what the matter is.
CAESAR   Antonio.
ANTONY   Caesar.
CAESAR   Let me have men about me that are fat,
Sleek-headed men, and such as sleep a-nights.
195   Yon Cassius has a lean and hungry look.
He thinks too much. Such men are dangerous.
ANTONY   Fear him not, Caesar, he's not dangerous.
He is a noble Roman, and well given.°   *well disposed*
CAESAR   Would he were fatter! But I fear him not.
200   Yet if my name[6] were liable to fear,
I do not know the man I should avoid
So soon as that spare Cassius. He reads much,
He is a great observer, and he looks

---

3. Lucius Junius Brutus, an ancestor of Marcus Brutus and a founder of the Roman Republic, famed for his role in expelling the Tarquins, who had ruled Rome as kings.
4. Like "cloak" (line 216), "doublet" (line 262) and "unbraced" (1.3.48), this suggests a performance in Elizabethan dress.
5. Ferretlike (red and darting).
6. One of my name (that is, myself).

Quite through⁷ the deeds of men. He loves no plays,
205   As thou dost, Antony; he hears no music.⁸
       Seldom he smiles, and smiles in such a sort°   *manner*
       As if he mocked himself, and scorned his spirit
       That could be moved to smile at anything.
       Such men as he be never at heart's ease
210   Whiles they behold a greater than themselves,
       And therefore are they very dangerous.
       I rather tell thee what is to be feared
       Than what I fear, for always I am Caesar.
       Come on my right hand, for this ear is deaf,
215   And tell me truly what thou think'st of him.
              Sennet. Exeunt CAESAR *and his train.* [BRUTUS,
                          CASSIUS, *and* CASCA *remain*]
CASCA [*to* BRUTUS]   You pulled me by the cloak.° Would you   *pulled me aside*
       speak with me?
BRUTUS   Ay, Casca. Tell us what hath chanced today,
       That Caesar looks so sad.°   *serious*
220 CASCA   Why, you were with him, were you not?
BRUTUS   I should not then ask Casca what had chanced.
CASCA   Why, there was a crown offered him; and being offered
       him, he put it by with the back of his hand, thus; and then the
       people fell a-shouting.
225 BRUTUS   What was the second noise for?
CASCA   Why, for that too.
CASSIUS   They shouted thrice. What was the last cry for?
CASCA   Why, for that too.
BRUTUS   Was the crown offered him thrice?
230 CASCA   Ay, marry,° was't; and he put it by thrice, every time   *indeed*
       gentler than other; and at every putting by, mine honest°   *(sarcastic)*
       neighbours shouted.
CASSIUS   Who offered him the crown?
CASCA   Why, Antony.
BRUTUS   Tell us the manner of it, gentle° Casca.   *noble*
235 CASCA   I can as well be hanged as tell the manner of it. It was
       mere foolery,° I did not mark it. I saw Mark Antony offer him   *utter absurdity*
       a crown—yet 'twas not a crown neither, 'twas one of these coro-
       nets—and as I told you he put it by once; but for all that, to my
       thinking he would fain° have had it. Then he offered it to him   *gladly*
240   again; then he put it by again—but to my thinking he was very
       loath to lay his fingers off it. And then he offered it the third
       time; he put it the third time by. And still° as he refused it,   *continually*
       the rabblement hooted, and clapped their chapped hands, and
       threw up their sweaty nightcaps,⁹ and uttered such a deal of
245   stinking breath because Caesar refused the crown that it had
       almost choked Caesar; for he swooned and fell down at it. And
       for mine own part, I durst not laugh for fear of opening my lips
       and receiving the bad air.
CASSIUS   But soft, I pray you. What, did Caesar swoon?
250 CASCA   He fell down in the market-place, and foamed at mouth,
       and was speechless.

---

7. Completely into the motives of.   *Merchant of Venice.*
8. This was regarded as a sign of wickedness; see *The*   9. Artisans wore felt hats on holidays.

BRUTUS 'Tis very like: he hath the falling sickness.[1]

CASSIUS No, Caesar hath it not; but you and I
And honest Casca, we have the falling sickness.

255 CASCA I know not what you mean by that, but I am sure Caesar
fell down. If the tag-rag people° did not clap him and hiss him,   *riffraff*
according as he pleased and displeased them, as they use° to   *are accustomed*
do the players in the theatre, I am no true man.

BRUTUS What said he when he came unto himself?

260 CASCA Marry, before he fell down, when he perceived the common herd was glad he refused the crown, he plucked me ope[2]
his doublet° and offered them his throat to cut. An° I had been   *jacket / If*
a man of any occupation, if I would not have taken him at a°   *his*
word, I would I might go to hell among the rogues. And so he

265 fell. When he came to himself again, he said, if he had done
or said anything amiss, he desired their worships to think it was
his infirmity. Three or four wenches where I stood cried 'Alas,
good soul!' and forgave him with all their hearts. But there's no
heed to be taken of them: if Caesar had stabbed[3] their mothers

270 they would have done no less.

BRUTUS And after that he came thus sad away?

CASCA Ay.

CASSIUS Did Cicero say anything?

CASCA Ay, he spoke Greek.

275 CASSIUS To what effect?

CASCA Nay, an I tell you that, I'll ne'er look you i'th' face again.
But those that understood him smiled at one another, and
shook their heads. But for mine own part, it was Greek to me.
I could tell you more news, too. Murellus and Flavius, for pull-

280 ing scarves[4] off Caesar's images, are put to silence.° Fare you   *deprived of office*
well. There was more foolery yet, if I could remember it.

CASSIUS Will you sup with me tonight, Casca?

CASCA No, I am promised forth.°   *elsewhere*

CASSIUS Will you dine with me tomorrow?

285 CASCA Ay, if I be alive, and your mind hold,° and your dinner   *does not change*
worth the eating.

CASSIUS Good; I will expect you.

CASCA Do so. Farewell both.   *Exit*

BRUTUS What a blunt fellow is this grown to be!

290 He was quick mettle° when he went to school.   *of energetic spirit*

CASSIUS So is he now, in execution
Of any bold or noble enterprise,
However he puts on this tardy form.[5]
This rudeness° is a sauce to his good wit,°   *harshness / intelligence*

295 Which gives men stomach° to digest his words   *relish*
With better appetite.

BRUTUS And so it is. For this time I will leave you.
Tomorrow, if you please to speak with me,
I will come home to you; or if you will,

300 Come home to me and I will wait for you.

CASSIUS I will do so. Till then, think of the world.° *Exit* BRUTUS   *state of affairs*
Well, Brutus, thou art noble; yet I see

---

1. Epilepsy (Cassius puns on "collapse from power").
2. Pulled open ("me" is colloquial).
3. Playing on "sexually penetrated."

4. Decorations (see 1.1.63–64).
5. Although he feigns this indolent manner.

Thy honourable mettle may be wrought
From that it is disposed.[6] Therefore it is meet°   *fitting*
305 That noble minds keep ever with their likes;
For who so firm that cannot be seduced?
Caesar doth bear me hard,° but he loves Brutus.   *ill will*
If I were Brutus now, and he were Cassius,
He should not humour° me. I will this night   *influence*
310 In several hands° in at his windows throw—   *various handwritings*
As if they came from several citizens—
Writings, all tending to° the great opinion   *intimating*
That Rome holds of his name, wherein obscurely°   *cryptically*
Caesar's ambition shall be glancèd° at.   *hinted*
315 And after this, let Caesar seat him sure,[7]
For we will shake him, or worse days endure.   *Exit*

1.3

Thunder and lightning. Enter CASCA, [*at one door, with
his sword drawn,*] *and* CICERO [*at another*]

CICERO   Good even, Casca. Brought° you Caesar home?   *Escorted*
    Why are you breathless, and why stare you so?
CASCA   Are not you moved, when all the sway° of earth   *realm*
    Shakes like a thing unfirm? O Cicero,
5   I have seen tempests when the scolding winds
    Have rived° the knotty oaks, and I have seen   *split*
    Th'ambitious ocean swell and rage and foam
    To be exalted with° the threat'ning clouds;   *raised as high as*
    But never till tonight, never till now,
10   Did I go through a tempest dropping fire.
    Either there is a civil strife in heaven,
    Or else the world, too saucy° with the gods,   *insolent*
    Incenses them to send destruction.
CICERO   Why, saw you anything more° wonderful?   *else*
15 CASCA   A common slave—you know him well by sight—
    Held up his left hand, which did flame and burn
    Like twenty torches joined; and yet his hand,
    Not sensible of° fire, remained unscorched.   *Not feeling*
    Besides—I ha' not since put up° my sword—   *sheathed*
20   Against° the Capitol I met a lion   *Next to*
    Who glazed° upon me, and went surly by   *stared*
    Without annoying° me. And there were drawn   *harming*
    Upon a heap[1] a hundred ghastly° women,   *pallid*
    Transformèd with their fear, who swore they saw
25   Men all in fire walk up and down the streets.
    And yesterday the bird of night° did sit   *screech owl*
    Even at noonday upon the market-place,
    Hooting and shrieking. When these prodigies°   *abnormalities*
    Do so conjointly meet,° let not men say   *happen together*
30   'These are their reasons', 'they are natural',
    For I believe they are portentous things
    Unto the climate° that they point upon.   *region*
CICERO   Indeed it is a strange-disposèd time;

---

6. *wrought . . . disposed:* changed from its natural prop-   1.3 Location: A street in Rome.
erty (alluding to the alchemical transmutation of metals).   1. Huddled in a crowd.
7. Establish himself securely.

But men may construe things after their fashion,°   *in their own way*
35   Clean° from the purpose of the things themselves.   *Completely different*
Comes Caesar to the Capitol tomorrow?
CASCA   He doth, for he did bid Antonio
Send word to you he would be there tomorrow.
CICERO   Good night then, Casca. This disturbèd sky
Is not to walk in.
40   CASCA   Farewell, Cicero.   *Exit* CICERO
             Enter CASSIUS [*unbraced*]°   *with open doublet*
CASSIUS   Who's there?
CASCA   A Roman.
CASSIUS   Casca, by your voice.
CASCA   Your ear is good. Cassius, what night is this?
CASSIUS   A very pleasing night to honest men.
CASCA   Who ever knew the heavens menace so?
45   CASSIUS   Those that have known the earth so full of faults.
For my part, I have walked about the streets,
Submitting me unto the perilous night;
And thus unbracèd, Casca, as you see,
Have bared my bosom to the thunder-stone;°   *thunderbolt*
50   And when the cross° blue lightning seemed to open   *forked; hostile*
The breast of heaven, I did present myself
Even° in the aim and very flash of it.   *Exactly*
CASCA   But wherefore did you so much tempt the heavens?
It is the part of men to fear and tremble
55   When the most mighty gods by tokens° send   *signs*
Such dreadful heralds to astonish° us.   *dismay*
CASSIUS   You are dull, Casca, and those sparks of life
That should be in a Roman you do want,°   *lack*
Or else you use not. You look pale, and gaze,
60   And put on fear, and cast yourself in wonder,
To see the strange impatience of the heavens;
But if you would consider the true cause
Why all these fires, why all these gliding ghosts,
Why birds and beasts from quality and kind²—
65   Why old men, fools, and children calculate°—   *prophesy*
Why all these things change from their ordinance,°—   *usual order*
Their natures, and preformèd faculties,
To monstrous° quality—why, you shall find   *unnatural*
That heaven hath infused them with these spirits
70   To make them instruments of fear and warning
Unto some monstrous state.³ Now could I, Casca,
Name to thee a man most like this dreadful night,
That thunders, lightens, opens graves, and roars
As doth the lion in the Capitol;
75   A man no mightier than thyself or me
In personal action, yet prodigious° grown,   *ominous*
And fearful,° as these strange eruptions° are.   *terrifying / upheavals*
CASCA   'Tis Caesar that you mean, is it not, Cassius?
CASSIUS   Let it be who it is; for Romans now
80   Have thews° and limbs like to their ancestors.   *sinews*
But woe the while!° Our fathers' minds are dead,   *alas for these times*

---

2. *from quality and kind:* behaving contrary to their   3. Abnormal situation; atrocious government.
nature.

And we are governed with our mothers' spirits.
Our yoke and sufferance° show us womanish.   *servitude and patience*
CASCA   Indeed they say the senators tomorrow
85   Mean to establish Caesar as a king,
And he shall wear his crown by sea and land
In every place save here in Italy.
CASSIUS [*drawing his dagger*]   I know where I will wear this dagger then:
Cassius from bondage will deliver Cassius.
90   Therein, ye gods, you make the weak most strong;
Therein, ye gods, you tyrants do defeat.
Nor stony tower, nor walls of beaten brass,
Nor airless dungeon, nor strong links of iron,
Can be retentive to° the strength of spirit;   *Can imprison*
95   But life, being weary of these worldly bars,°   *hindrances*
Never lacks power to dismiss itself.
If I know this, know all the world besides,
That part of tyranny that I do bear
I can shake off at pleasure.
         Thunder still
CASCA   So can I.
100   So every bondman in his own hand bears
The power to cancel his captivity.
CASSIUS   And why should Caesar be a tyrant then?
Poor man, I know he would not be a wolf
But that he sees the Romans are but sheep.
105   He were no lion, were not Romans hinds.°   *female deer; servants*
Those that with haste will make a mighty fire
Begin it with weak straws. What trash is Rome,
What rubbish, and what offal,° when it serves   *wood chips; refuse*
For the base° matter to illuminate   *underlying; despicable*
110   So vile a thing as Caesar! But, O grief,
Where hast thou led me? I perhaps speak this
Before a willing bondman; then I know
My answer must be made.[4] But I am armed,°   *(physically and morally)*
And dangers are to me indifferent.°   *insignificant*
115 CASCA   You speak to Casca, and to such a man
That is no fleering° tell-tale. Hold.° My hand.   *sneering / Enough*
Be factious° for redress of all these griefs,   *Form a group*
And I will set this foot of mine as far
As who° goes farthest.   *whoever*
         [*They join hands*]
CASSIUS   There's a bargain made.
120   Now know you, Casca, I have moved° already   *persuaded*
Some certain of the noblest-minded Romans
To undergo° with me an enterprise   *undertake*
Of honourable-dangerous consequence.
And I do know by this° they stay° for me   *this time / wait*
125   In Pompey's Porch;[5] for now, this fearful night,
There is no stir or walking in the streets,
And the complexion of the element°   *disposition of the sky*
In favour's° like the work we have in hand,   *In appearance is*
Most bloody, fiery, and most terrible.
         Enter CINNA

---

4. I must pay the penalty.   5. Portico of a theater commissioned by Pompey.

130 CASCA   Stand close° a while, for here comes one in haste.   *concealed*
CASSIUS   'Tis Cinna; I do know him by his gait.
He is a friend.—Cinna, where haste you so?
CINNA   To find out you. Who's that? Metellus Cimber?
CASSIUS   No, it is Casca, one incorporate°   *a party*
135 To our attempts. Am I not stayed for,° Cinna?   *awaited*
CINNA   I am glad on't.[6] What a fearful night is this!
There's two or three of us have seen strange sights.
CASSIUS   Am I not stayed for? Tell me.
CINNA   Yes, you are.
140 O Cassius, if you could
But win the noble Brutus to our party—
CASSIUS   Be you content. Good Cinna, take this paper,
  [*He gives* CINNA *letters*]
And look you lay it in the Praetor's[7] Chair,
Where Brutus may but° find it; and throw this   *must surely*
145 In at his window. Set this up with wax
Upon old Brutus'° statue. All this done,   *Lucius Junius Brutus's*
Repair° to Pompey's Porch where you shall find us.   *Proceed*
Is Decius Brutus and Trebonius there?
CINNA   All but Metellus Cimber, and he's gone
150 To seek you at your house. Well, I will hie,°   *hasten*
And so bestow these papers as you bade me.
CASSIUS   That done, repair to Pompey's Theatre.   *Exit* CINNA
Come, Casca, you and I will yet ere day
See Brutus at his house. Three parts° of him   *quarters*
155 Is ours already, and the man entire
Upon the next encounter yields him ours.
CASCA   O, he sits high in all the people's hearts,
And that which would appear offence in us
His countenance, like richest alchemy,[8]
160 Will change to virtue and to worthiness.
CASSIUS   Him and his worth, and our great need of him,
You have right well conceited.° Let us go,   *understood*
For it is after midnight, and ere day
We will awake him and be sure of him.   *Exeunt*

2.1

Enter BRUTUS *in his orchard*
BRUTUS   What, Lucius, ho!—
I cannot by the progress of the stars
Give guess how near to day.—Lucius, I say!—
I would it were my fault to sleep so soundly.—
5 When, Lucius, when?° Awake, I say! What, Lucius!   *(expressing impatience)*
  Enter LUCIUS
LUCIUS   Called you, my lord?
BRUTUS   Get me a taper° in my study, Lucius.   *candle*
When it is lighted, come and call me here.
LUCIUS   I will, my lord.   *Exit*
10 BRUTUS   It must be by his° death. And for my part   *(Caesar's)*
I know no personal cause to spurn° at him,   *kick*

6. Cinna is responding to Cassius's information about   8. Alchemy attempted to change base metals into gold.
Casca.   *countenance:* approval; noble appearance.
7. Brutus was one of sixteen praetors, or chief magistrates,   **2.1** Location: Outside Brutus's house.
subordinate only to the two consuls.

But for the general.° He would be crowned. *common good*
How that might change his nature, there's the question.
It is the bright day that brings forth the adder,
15 And that craves° wary walking. Crown him: that! *calls for*
And then I grant we put a sting in him
That at his will he may do danger with.
Th'abuse of greatness is when it disjoins
Remorse° from power. And to speak truth of Caesar, *Conscience*
20 I have not known when his affections swayed° *passions ruled*
More than his reason. But 'tis a common proof° *experience*
That lowliness° is young ambition's ladder, *humility*
Whereto the climber-upward turns his face;
But when he once attains the upmost round,° *rung*
25 He then unto the ladder turns his back,
Looks in the clouds, scorning the base degrees[1]
By which he did ascend. So Caesar may.
Then lest he may, prevent. And since the quarrel
Will bear no colour for the thing he is,[2]
30 Fashion° it thus: that what he is, augmented, *Describe*
Would run to these and these extremities;
And therefore think him as a serpent's egg,
Which, hatched, would as his kind° grow mischievous,° *by its nature / harmful*
And kill him in the shell.
   Enter LUCIUS [*with a letter*]
35 LUCIUS The taper burneth in your closet,° sir. *private room*
Searching the window for a flint, I found
This paper, thus sealed up, and I am sure
It did not lie there when I went to bed.
   [*He*] *gives him the letter*
BRUTUS Get you to bed again; it is not day.
40 Is not tomorrow, boy, the ides of March?
LUCIUS I know not, sir.
BRUTUS Look in the calendar and bring me word.
LUCIUS I will, sir.   *Exit*
BRUTUS The exhalations° whizzing in the air *meteors*
45 Give so much light that I may read by them.
   [*He*] *opens the letter and reads*
'Brutus, thou sleep'st. Awake, and see thyself.
Shall Rome, et cetera? Speak, strike, redress.'—
'Brutus, thou sleep'st. Awake.'
Such instigations have been often dropped
50 Where I have took them up.
'Shall Rome, et cetera?' Thus must I piece it out:
Shall Rome stand under one man's awe? What, Rome?
My ancestors did from the streets of Rome
The Tarquin drive when he was called a king.[3]
55 'Speak, strike, redress.' Am I entreated
To speak and strike? O Rome, I make thee promise,
If the redress will follow,[4] thou receivest
Thy full petition at the hand of Brutus.
   Enter LUCIUS
LUCIUS Sir, March is wasted fifteen days.

1. Low rungs; contemptible means; lowly social ranks.
2. Will find no plausible pretext in his conduct so far.
3. See note to 1.2.160.
4. That is, if killing Caesar will restore the republic.

Knock within

60 BRUTUS 'Tis good. Go to the gate; somebody knocks. [*Exit* LUCIUS]
Since Cassius first did whet° me against Caesar   *incite*
I have not slept.
Between the acting of a dreadful thing
And the first motion,° all the interim is   *impulse*
65 Like a phantasma° or a hideous dream.   *nightmare*
The genius° and the mortal instruments[5]   *immortal spirit*
Are then in counsel, and the state of man,
Like to a little kingdom, suffers then
The nature of an insurrection.[6]

Enter LUCIUS

70 LUCIUS Sir, 'tis your brother Cassius[7] at the door,
Who doth desire to see you.
BRUTUS   Is he alone?
LUCIUS No, sir, there are more with him.
BRUTUS   Do you know them?
LUCIUS No, sir; their hats are plucked about their ears,
And half their faces buried in their cloaks,
75 That by no means I may discover° them   *identify*
By any mark of favour.°   *distinctive feature*
BRUTUS   Let 'em enter.   [*Exit* LUCIUS]
They are the faction. O conspiracy,
Sham'st thou to show thy dang'rous brow by night,
When evils are most free?° O then by day   *uninhibited*
80 Where wilt thou find a cavern dark enough
To mask thy monstrous visage? Seek none, conspiracy.
Hide it in smiles and affability;
For if thou put thy native semblance on,[8]
Not Erebus° itself were dim enough   *dark underworld region*
85 To hide thee from prevention.[9]

Enter the conspirators [*muffled*]: CASSIUS, CASCA,
DECIUS, CINNA, METELLUS, *and* TREBONIUS

CASSIUS I think we are too bold[1] upon your rest.
Good morrow, Brutus. Do we trouble you?
BRUTUS I have been up this hour, awake all night.
Know I these men that come along with you?
90 CASSIUS Yes, every man of them; and no man here
But honours you; and every one doth wish
You had but that opinion of yourself
Which every noble Roman bears of you.
This is Trebonius.
BRUTUS   He is welcome hither.
CASSIUS This, Decius Brutus.
95 BRUTUS   He is welcome too.
CASSIUS This, Casca; Cinna, this; and this, Metellus Cimber.
BRUTUS They are all welcome.
What watchful° cares do interpose themselves   *sleep-preventing*
Betwixt your eyes and night?
CASSIUS   Shall I entreat a word?
[CASSIUS *and* BRUTUS *stand aside and*] *whisper*

---

5. Bodily powers.
6. *the state . . . insurrection:* referring to a commonplace
analogy between disorder in man, in the body politic, and
in nature.
7. Cassius was married to Brutus's sister.
8. Display your natural appearance.
9. From being recognized and thwarted.
1. We intrude too presumptuously.

100 DECIUS Here lies the east. Doth not the day break here?
CASCA No.
CINNA O pardon, sir, it doth; and yon grey lines
    That fret° the clouds are messengers of day.   *interlace*
CASCA You shall confess that you are both deceived.
    [*He points his sword*]
105   Here, as I point my sword, the sun arises,
    Which is a great way growing° on the south,   *encroaching*
    Weighing° the youthful season of the year.   *On account of*
    Some two months hence up higher toward the north
    He first presents his fire, and the high° east   *due*
110   Stands, as the Capitol, directly here.
    [*He points his sword*]
    [BRUTUS *and* CASSIUS *join the other conspirators*]
BRUTUS Give me your hands all over, one by one.
    [*He shakes their hands*]
CASSIUS And let us swear our resolution.
BRUTUS No, not an oath. If not the face° of men,   *(grave) expressions*
    The sufferance° of our souls, the time's abuse² —   *suffering*
115   If these be motives weak, break off betimes,°   *at once*
    And every man hence to his idle° bed.   *unused; lazy*
    So let high-sighted° tyranny range on   *arrogant*
    Till each man drop by lottery.³ But if these,°   *these reasons*
    As I am sure they do, bear fire enough
120   To kindle cowards and to steel with valour
    The melting spirits of women, then, countrymen,
    What need we any spur but our own cause
    To prick us to redress? What other bond
    Than secret Romans,⁴ that have spoke the word
125   And will not palter?° And what other oath   *equivocate*
    Than honesty° to honesty engaged   *integrity*
    That this shall be or we will fall for it?
    Swear° priests and cowards and men cautelous,°   *Let swear / crafty; wary*
    Old feeble carrions,° and such suffering souls   *corpselike men*
130   That welcome wrongs;⁵ unto bad causes swear
    Such creatures as men doubt;° but do not stain   *suspect*
    The even° virtue of our enterprise,   *just; straightforward*
    Nor th'insuppressive° mettle of our spirits,   *the indomitable*
    To think that or° our cause or our performance   *either*
135   Did need an oath, when every drop of blood
    That every Roman bears, and nobly bears,
    Is guilty of a several bastardy⁶
    If he do break the smallest particle
    Of any promise that hath passed from him.
140 CASSIUS But what of Cicero? Shall we sound him?°   *find out his thoughts*
    I think he will stand very strong with us.
CASCA Let us not leave him out.
CINNA   No, by no means.
METELLUS O, let us have him, for his silver hairs
    Will purchase us a good opinion,°   *reputation*

---

2. The corruption of the present time.
3. Chance (the tyrant's caprice).
4. Than that we are Romans capable of secrecy.

5. That gladly submit to oppression.
6. Will show itself individually to be adulterated by non-Roman blood.

145   And buy men's voices to commend our deeds.
      It shall be said his judgement ruled our hands.
      Our youths and wildness shall no whit appear,
      But all be buried in his gravity.
      BRUTUS   O, name him not! Let us not break with° him,   *disclose our plans to*
150   For he will never follow anything
        That other men begin.
      CASSIUS   Then leave him out.
      CASCA   Indeed he is not fit.
      DECIUS   Shall no man else be touched, but only Caesar?
155   CASSIUS   Decius, well urged.° I think it is not meet°   *suggested / proper*
        Mark Antony, so well beloved of Caesar,
        Should outlive Caesar. We shall find of him
        A shrewd° contriver. And you know his means,   *malicious*
        If he improve° them, may well stretch so far   *make the most of*
160   As to annoy° us all; which to prevent,   *harm*
        Let Antony and Caesar fall together.
      BRUTUS   Our course⁷ will seem too bloody, Caius Cassius,
        To cut the head off and then hack the limbs,
        Like wrath in death and envy° afterwards—   *malice*
165   For Antony is but a limb of Caesar.
        Let's be sacrificers, but not butchers, Caius.
        We all stand up against the spirit of Caesar,
        And in the spirit of men there is no blood.
        O, that we then could come by° Caesar's spirit,   *obtain*
170   And not dismember Caesar! But, alas,
        Caesar must bleed for it. And, gentle friends,
        Let's kill him boldly, but not wrathfully.
        Let's carve him as a dish fit for the gods,
        Not hew him as a carcass fit for hounds.
175   And let our hearts, as subtle° masters do,   *cunning*
        Stir up their servants° to an act of rage,   *(that is, our hands)*
        And after seem to chide 'em. This shall make
        Our purpose necessary, and not envious;°   *malicious*
        Which so appearing to the common eyes,
180   We shall be called purgers,° not murderers.   *purifiers*
        And for Mark Antony, think not of him,
        For he can do no more than Caesar's arm
        When Caesar's head is off.
      CASSIUS   Yet I fear him;
        For in the engrafted° love he bears to Caesar—   *deep-rooted*
185   BRUTUS   Alas, good Cassius, do not think of him.
        If he love Caesar, all that he can do
        Is to himself: take thought,° and die for Caesar.   *succumb to melancholy*
        And that were much he should,⁸ for he is given
        To sports, to wildness, and much company.
190   TREBONIUS   There is no fear° in him. Let him not die;   *nothing to fear*
        For he will live, and laugh at this hereafter.
              Clock strikes
      BRUTUS   Peace, count the clock.⁹
      CASSIUS   The clock hath stricken three.

---

7. Punning on "corse," meaning "corpse."   9. The clock is an anachronism, like sleeves and dou-
8. And that is more than he is likely to do.   blets.

TREBONIUS   'Tis time to part.
CASSIUS   But it is doubtful yet
      Whether Caesar will come forth today or no;
195   For he is superstitious grown of late,
      Quite from the main° opinion he held once   *Contrary to the strong*
      Of fantasy, of dreams and ceremonies.
      It may be these apparent° prodigies,   *manifest*
      The unaccustomed terror of this night,
200   And the persuasion of his augurers,[1]
      May hold him from the Capitol today.
DECIUS   Never fear that. If he be so resolved
      I can o'ersway° him; for he loves to hear   *prevail upon*
      That unicorns may be betrayed with trees,[2]
205   And bears with glasses,[3] elephants with holes,°   *pits*
      Lions with toils,° and men with flatterers;   *nets*
      But when I tell him he hates flatterers;
      He says he does, being then most flattered. Let me work,
      For I can give his humour the true bent,[4]
210   And I will bring him to the Capitol.
CASSIUS   Nay, we will all of us be there to fetch him.
BRUTUS   By the eighth hour. Is that the uttermost?°   *latest*
CINNA   Be that the uttermost, and fail not then.
METELLUS   Caius Ligarius doth bear Caesar hard,°   *ill will*
215   Who rated° him for speaking well of Pompey.   *rebuked*
      I wonder none of you have thought of him.
BRUTUS   Now good Metellus, go along by him.°   *to his house*
      He loves me well, and I have given him reasons.
      Send him but hither, and I'll fashion° him.   *work upon*
220   CASSIUS   The morning comes upon's. We'll leave you, Brutus.
      And, friends, disperse yourselves; but all remember
      What you have said, and show yourselves true Romans.
BRUTUS   Good gentlemen, look fresh and merrily.
      Let not our looks put on° our purposes;   *display*
225   But bear it as our Roman actors do,
      With untired spirits and formal constancy.°   *decorous self-possession*
      And so good morrow to you every one.
                              Exeunt. Manet° BRUTUS   *Remains*
      Boy, Lucius!—Fast asleep? It is no matter.
      Enjoy the honey-heavy dew of slumber.
230   Thou hast no figures° nor no fantasies   *imaginings*
      Which busy care draws in the brains of men;
      Therefore thou sleep'st so sound.
                        Enter PORTIA
PORTIA   Brutus, my lord.
BRUTUS   Portia, what mean you? Wherefore rise you now?
      It is not for° your health thus to commit   *good for*
235   Your weak condition to the raw cold morning.
PORTIA   Nor for yours neither. You've ungently,° Brutus,   *unkindly*
      Stole from my bed; and yesternight at supper
      You suddenly arose, and walked about

1. Priests who interpreted "auguries," or omens.
2. The unicorn could supposedly be caught by tricking it
into impaling its horn on a tree.

3. Mirrors (imagined to bewilder bears).
4. Give his disposition the right direction.

Musing and sighing, with your arms across;[5]
240 And when I asked you what the matter was,
You stared upon me with ungentle looks.
I urged you further; then you scratched your head,
And too impatiently stamped with your foot.
Yet I insisted; yet you answered not,
245 But with an angry wafture° of your hand   *gesture*
Gave sign for me to leave you. So I did,
Fearing to strengthen that impatience
Which seemed too much enkindled, and withal°   *besides*
Hoping it was but an effect of humour,°   *moodiness*
250 Which sometime hath his° hour with every man.   *its*
It will not let you eat, nor talk, nor sleep;
And could it work so much upon your shape
As it hath much prevailed on your condition,°   *disposition*
I should not know you° Brutus. Dear my lord,   *recognize you as*
255 Make me acquainted with your cause of grief.
BRUTUS   I am not well in health, and that is all.
PORTIA   Brutus is wise, and were he not in health
He would embrace the means to come by it.
BRUTUS   Why, so I do. Good Portia, go to bed.
260 PORTIA   Is Brutus sick? And is it physical°   *curative*
To walk unbracèd° and suck up the humours[6]   *with open doublet*
Of the dank morning? What, is Brutus sick?
And will he steal out of his wholesome bed
To dare the vile contagion of the night,
265 And tempt the rheumy and unpurgèd° air   *moist and impure*
To add unto his sickness? No, my Brutus,
You have some sick offence° within your mind,   *disturbance*
Which by the right and virtue° of my place°   *perogative / (as a wife)*
I ought to know of. [*Kneeling*] And upon my knees,
270 I charm° you by my once-commended beauty,   *conjure*
By all your vows of love, and that great vow
Which did incorporate and make us one,
That you unfold to me, your self, your half,
Why you are heavy,° and what men tonight   *dejected*
275 Have had resort to you—for here have been
Some six or seven, who did hide their faces
Even from darkness.
BRUTUS   Kneel not, gentle Portia.
PORTIA [*rising*]   I should not need if you were gentle Brutus.
Within the bond of marriage, tell me, Brutus,
280 Is it excepted[7] I should know no secrets
That appertain to you? Am I your self
But as it were in sort or limitation?[8]
To keep with you at meals, comfort your bed,
And talk to you sometimes? Dwell I but in the suburbs[9]
285 Of your good pleasure? If it be no more,
Portia is Brutus' harlot, not his wife.
BRUTUS   You are my true and honourable wife,

---

5. Crossed (a sign of melancholy).
6. Inhale the mists.
7. Is it stipulated as a qualification that.
8. *in sort or limitation:* after a fashion or with restrictions

(like "excepted," "limited" is a legal term).
9. Outlying areas (where brothels were located in Shakespeare's time).

As dear to me as are the ruddy drops
That visit° my sad heart.   *afflict; come to*
290 PORTIA   If this were true, then should I know this secret.
I grant I am a woman, but withal°   *still*
A woman that Lord Brutus took to wife.
I grant I am a woman, but withal
A woman well reputed, Cato's daughter.[1]
295 Think you I am no stronger than my sex,
Being so fathered and so husbanded?
Tell me your counsels;° I will not disclose 'em.   *secrets*
I have made strong proof of my constancy,
Giving myself a voluntary wound
300 Here in the thigh. Can I bear that with patience,
And not my husband's secrets?
BRUTUS   O ye gods,
Render me worthy of this noble wife!
            Knock[ing within]
Hark, hark, one knocks. Portia, go in a while,
And by and by thy bosom shall partake
305 The secrets of my heart.
All my engagements° I will construe° to thee,   *commitments / explain*
All the charactery[2] of my sad brows.
Leave me with haste.   *Exit* PORTIA
                 Lucius, who's that knocks?
            Enter LUCIUS, *and* LIGARIUS [*with a kerchief round his
            head*][3]
LUCIUS   Here is a sick man that would speak with you.
310 BRUTUS   Caius Ligarius, that Metellus spake of. —
Boy, stand aside.   [*Exit* LUCIUS]
                 Caius Ligarius, how?°   *how are you*
LIGARIUS   Vouchsafe° good morrow from a feeble tongue.   *Deign to accept*
BRUTUS   O, what a time have you chose out, brave Caius,
To wear a kerchief! Would you were not sick!
315 LIGARIUS   I am not sick if Brutus have in hand
Any exploit worthy the name of honour.
BRUTUS   Such an exploit have I in hand, Ligarius,
Had you a healthful ear to hear of it.
LIGARIUS   By all the gods that Romans bow before,
I here discard my sickness.
            [*He pulls off his kerchief*]
320   Soul of Rome,
Brave son derived from honourable loins,
Thou like an exorcist° hast conjured up   *a magician*
My mortifièd° spirit. Now bid me run,   *deadened*
And I will strive with things impossible,
325 Yea, get the better of them. What's to do?
BRUTUS   A piece of work that will make sick men whole.°   *healthy*
LIGARIUS   But are not some whole that we must make sick?
BRUTUS   That must we also. What it is, my Caius,
I shall unfold to thee as we are going
To whom it must be done.

---

1. Marcus Porcius Cato was renowned for his strict moral
integrity; after Caesar's victory over Pompey, he killed
himself rather than submit to Caesar's rule.
2. Handwriting (the lines of care "inscribed" on his forehead).
3. Kerchiefs were commonly worn by the sick in Elizabethan England.

330 LIGARIUS   Set on° your foot,   *Advance*
And with a heart new-fired I follow you
To do I know not what; but it sufficeth
That Brutus leads me on.
BRUTUS   Follow me then.   *Exeunt*

2.2

Thunder and lightning.
Enter Julius CAESAR *in his nightgown°*   *dressing gown*
CAESAR   Nor heaven nor earth have been at peace tonight.
Thrice hath Calpurnia in her sleep cried out
'Help, ho! They murder Caesar!'—Who's within?
    Enter a SERVANT
SERVANT   My lord.
5 CAESAR   Go bid the priests do present° sacrifice,   *immediate*
And bring me their opinions of success.[1]
SERVANT   I will, my lord.   *Exit*
    Enter CALPURNIA
CALPURNIA   What mean you, Caesar? Think you to walk forth?
You shall not stir out of your house today.
10 CAESAR   Caesar shall forth. The things that threatened me
Ne'er looked but on my back; when they shall see
The face of Caesar, they are vanishèd.
CALPURNIA   Caesar, I never stood on ceremonies,°   *heeded omens*
Yet now they fright me. There is one within,
15 Besides the things that we have heard and seen,
Recounts most horrid sights seen by the watch.[2]
A lioness hath whelpèd in the streets,
And graves have yawned and yielded up their dead.
Fierce fiery warriors fight upon the clouds,
20 In ranks and squadrons and right form of war,°   *regular battle formation*
Which drizzled blood upon the Capitol.
The noise of battle hurtled in the air.
Horses do neigh, and dying men did groan,
And ghosts did shriek and squeal about the streets.
25 O Caesar, these things are beyond all use,°   *all normal experience*
And I do fear them.
CAESAR   What can be avoided
Whose end is purposed by the mighty gods?
Yet Caesar shall go forth, for these predictions
Are to° the world in general as to Caesar.   *Are as applicable to*
30 CALPURNIA   When beggars die there are no comets seen;
The heavens themselves blaze forth° the death of princes.   *flame out; proclaim*
CAESAR   Cowards die many times before their deaths;
The valiant never taste of death but once.
Of all the wonders that I yet have heard,
35 It seems to me most strange that men should fear,
Seeing that death, a necessary end,
Will come when it will come.
    Enter SERVANT
                    What say the augurers?
SERVANT   They would not have you to stir forth today.

2.2 Location: Caesar's house.
1. Of the outcome (good or bad), as determined by reading the entrails of the sacrificial animals.
2. Night watchmen (another anachronism).

Plucking the entrails of an offering forth,
40 They could not find a heart within the beast.
CAESAR   The gods do this in shame of cowardice.°   *to put cowardice to shame*
Caesar should be a beast without a heart
If he should stay at home today for fear.
No, Caesar shall not. Danger knows full well
45 That Caesar is more dangerous than he.
We are two lions littered in one day,
And I the elder and more terrible.
And Caesar shall go forth.
CALPURNIA   Alas, my lord,
Your wisdom is consumed in confidence.°   *overconfidence*
50 Do not go forth today. Call it my fear
That keeps you in the house, and not your own.
We'll send Mark Antony to the Senate House,
And he shall say you are not well today.
Let me upon my knee prevail in this.
      [*She kneels*]
55 CAESAR   Mark Antony shall say I am not well,
And for thy humour° I will stay at home.   *whim*
      Enter DECIUS
Here's Decius Brutus; he shall tell them so.
      [CALPURNIA *rises*]
DECIUS   Caesar, all hail! Good morrow, worthy Caesar.
I come to fetch you to the Senate House.
60 CAESAR   And you are come in very happy° time   *opportune*
To bear my greeting to the senators
And tell them that I will not come today.
Cannot is false, and that I dare not, falser.
I will not come today; tell them so, Decius.
CALPURNIA   Say he is sick.
65 CAESAR   Shall Caesar send a lie?
Have I in conquest stretched mine arm so far,
To be afeard to tell greybeards the truth?
Decius, go tell them Caesar will not come.
DECIUS   Most mighty Caesar, let me know some cause,
70 Lest I be laughed at when I tell them so.
CAESAR   The cause is in my will; I will not come.
That is enough to satisfy the Senate.
But for your private satisfaction,
Because I love you, I will let you know.
75 Calpurnia here, my wife, stays° me at home.   *keeps*
She dreamt tonight° she saw my statue,   *last night*
Which like a fountain with an hundred spouts
Did run pure blood; and many lusty° Romans   *joyful*
Came smiling and did bathe their hands in it.
80 And these does she apply° for warnings and portents   *interpret*
Of evils imminent, and on her knee
Hath begged that I will stay at home today.
DECIUS   This dream is all amiss interpreted.
It was a vision fair and fortunate.
85 Your statue spouting blood in many pipes,
In which so many smiling Romans bathed,
Signifies that from you great Rome shall suck
Reviving blood, and that great men shall press

For tinctures, stains, relics, and cognizance.[3]
90 This by Calpurnia's dream is signified.
CAESAR And this way have you well expounded it.
DECIUS I have, when you have heard what I can say.
And know it now: the Senate have concluded
To give this day a crown to mighty Caesar.
95 If you shall send them word you will not come,
Their minds may change. Besides, it were a mock
Apt to be rendered[4] for someone to say
'Break up the Senate till another time,
When Caesar's wife shall meet with better dreams.'
100 If Caesar hide himself, shall they not whisper
'Lo, Caesar is afraid'?
Pardon me, Caesar; for my dear dear love
To your proceeding° bids me tell you this,   advancement
And reason to my love is liable.[5]
105 CAESAR How foolish do your fears seem now, Calpurnia!
I am ashamèd I did yield to them.
Give me my robe, for I will go.
        Enter [CASSIUS,] BRUTUS, LIGARIUS, METELLUS, CASCA,
        TREBONIUS, *and* CINNA
And look where Cassius is come to fetch me.
CASSIUS Good morrow, Caesar.
CAESAR   Welcome, Cassius.—
110 What, Brutus, are you stirred so early too?—
Good morrow, Casca.—Caius Ligarius,
Caesar was ne'er so much your enemy
As that same ague° which hath made you lean.   fever
What is't o'clock?
BRUTUS   Caesar, 'tis strucken eight.
115 CAESAR I thank you for your pains and courtesy.
        Enter ANTONY
See, Antony that revels long a-nights
Is notwithstanding up. Good morrow, Antony.
ANTONY So to most noble Caesar.
CAESAR [*to* CALPURNIA]   Bid them prepare within.
I am to blame to be thus waited for.   [*Exit* CALPURNIA]
120 Now, Cinna.—Now, Metellus.—What, Trebonius!
I have an hour's talk in store for you.
Remember that you call on me today.
Be near me, that I may remember you.
TREBONIUS Caesar, I will, [*aside*] and so near will I be
125 That your best friends shall wish I had been further.
CAESAR Good friends, go in and taste some wine with me,
And we, like[6] friends, will straightway go together.
BRUTUS [*aside*] That every like is not the same, O Caesar,
The heart of Brutus ernes° to think upon.   *Exeunt*   grieves

2.3

        Enter ARTEMIDORUS, *reading a letter*
ARTEMIDORUS 'Caesar, beware of Brutus. Take heed of Cassius.

---

3. Heraldic colors and emblems ("tinctures," "stains,"
and "cognizance"); venerated properties of saints ("tinctures," "stains," and "relics").
4. *a mock . . . rendered:* a sarcastic reply likely to be made.

5. And prudence is subordinate to my affection.
6. As becomes (but Brutus plays on the senses "resem-
bling" and "equal to").
2.3 Location: A street near the Capitol.

Come not near Casca. Have an eye to Cinna. Trust not Trebonius. Mark well Metellus Cimber. Decius Brutus loves thee
not. Thou hast wronged Caius Ligarius. There is but one mind
5   in all these men, and it is bent against Caesar. If thou beest not
immortal, look about you. Security gives way to° conspiracy.   *Overconfidence permits*
The mighty gods defend thee!

                                   Thy lover,°   *friend*
                                 Artemidorus.'

10   Here will I stand till Caesar pass along,
      And as a suitor° will I give him this.   *petitioner*
      My heart laments that virtue cannot live
      Out of the teeth of emulation.[1]
      If thou read this, O Caesar, thou mayst live.
15   If not, the fates with traitors do contrive.°   *Exit*   *conspire*

2.4

Enter PORTIA *and* LUCIUS
PORTIA   I prithee, boy, run to the Senate House.
      Stay not to answer me, but get thee gone. —
      Why dost thou stay?
LUCIUS   To know my errand, madam.
PORTIA   I would have had thee there and here again
5   Ere I can tell thee what thou shouldst do there.
      [*Aside*] O constancy, be strong upon my side;
      Set a huge mountain 'tween my heart and tongue.
      I have a man's mind, but a woman's might.
      How hard it is for women to keep counsel!°   *a secret*
      [*To* LUCIUS] Art thou here yet?
10 LUCIUS   Madam, what should I do?
      Run to the Capitol, and nothing else?
      And so return to you, and nothing else?
PORTIA   Yes, bring me word, boy, if thy lord look well,
      For he went sickly forth; and take good note
15   What Caesar doth, what suitors press to him.
      Hark, boy, what noise is that?
LUCIUS   I hear none, madam.
PORTIA   Prithee, listen well.
      I heard a bustling rumour,° like a fray,   *disturbed clamor*
20   And the wind brings it from the Capitol.
LUCIUS   Sooth,° madam, I hear nothing.   *In truth*
      Enter the SOOTHSAYER
PORTIA   Come hither, fellow. Which way hast thou been?
SOOTHSAYER   At mine own house, good lady.
PORTIA   What is't o'clock?
25 SOOTHSAYER   About the ninth hour, lady.
PORTIA   Is Caesar yet gone to the Capitol?
SOOTHSAYER   Madam, not yet. I go to take my stand
      To see him pass on to the Capitol.
PORTIA   Thou hast some suit to Caesar, hast thou not?
30 SOOTHSAYER   That I have, lady. If it will please Caesar
      To be so good to Caesar as to hear me,
      I shall beseech him to befriend himself.
PORTIA   Why, know'st thou any harms intended towards him?

---

1. Beyond the danger of ambitious envy.   **2.4** Location: Brutus's house.

SOOTHSAYER   None that I know will be; much that I fear may chance.
Good morrow to you.
        [*He moves away*]
35   Here the street is narrow.
The throng that follows Caesar at the heels,
Of senators, of praetors, common suitors,
Will crowd a feeble man almost to death.
I'll get me to a place more void,° and there   *empty*
40   Speak to great Caesar as he comes along.   *Exit*
PORTIA [*aside*]   I must go in. Ay me! How weak a thing
The heart of woman is! O Brutus,
The heavens speed thee in thine enterprise!—
Sure the boy heard me. [*To* LUCIUS] Brutus hath a suit
45   That Caesar will not grant. [*Aside*] O, I grow faint!
[*To* LUCIUS] Run, Lucius, and commend me to my lord.
Say I am merry.° Come to me again,   *in good spirits*
And bring me word what he doth say to thee.
                              Exeunt [*severally*]°   *separately*

3.1

Enter [*at one door*] ARTEMIDORUS, *the* SOOTHSAYER [*and
citizens*]. *Flourish. Enter* [*at another door*] CAESAR, BRUTUS,
CASSIUS, CASCA, DECIUS, METELLUS, TREBONIUS, CINNA,
[LIGARIUS,] ANTONY, LEPIDUS, PUBLIUS[, POPILLIUS,
and other senators]

CAESAR [*to the* SOOTHSAYER]   The ides of March are come.
SOOTHSAYER   Ay, Caesar, but not gone.
ARTEMIDORUS   Hail, Caesar! Read this schedule.°   *document*
DECIUS [*to* CAESAR]   Trebonius doth desire you to o'er-read
5   At your best leisure this his humble suit.
ARTEMIDORUS   O Caesar, read mine first, for mine's a suit
That touches° Caesar nearer. Read it, great Caesar.   *concerns*
CAESAR   What touches us ourself shall be last served.°   *attended to*
ARTEMIDORUS   Delay not, Caesar, read it instantly.
CAESAR   What, is the fellow mad?
10   PUBLIUS [*to* ARTEMIDORUS]   Sirrah, give place.
CASSIUS [*to* ARTEMIDORUS]   What, urge you your petitions in the street?
Come to the Capitol.
        [*They walk about the stage*]¹
POPILLIUS [*aside to* CASSIUS]   I wish your enterprise today may thrive.
CASSIUS   What enterprise, Popillius?
POPILLIUS   Fare you well.
        [*He leaves* CASSIUS, *and makes to*° CAESAR]   *goes toward*
15   BRUTUS   What said Popillius Laena?
CASSIUS   He wished today our enterprise might thrive.
I fear our purpose is discoverèd.
BRUTUS   Look how he makes to Caesar. Mark him.
CASSIUS   Casca, be sudden,° for we fear prevention.°—   *swift / being thwarted*
20   Brutus, what shall be done? If this be known,
Cassius or Caesar never shall turn back,°   *return alive*
For I will slay myself.
BRUTUS   Cassius, be constant.°   *resolute*

3.1 Location: At the Capitol.
1. Indicating a movement from the street outside to the interior of the Capitol.

Popillius Laena speaks not of our purposes,
For look, he smiles, and Caesar doth not change.
25 CASSIUS   Trebonius knows his time, for look you, Brutus,
He draws Mark Antony out of the way. [*Exeunt* TREBONIUS *and* ANTONY]
DECIUS   Where is Metellus Cimber? Let him go
And presently prefer° his suit to Caesar.   *at once present*
[CAESAR *sits*]
BRUTUS   He is addressed.° Press near, and second him.   *ready*
30 CINNA   Casca, you are the first that rears your hand.
[*The conspirators and the other senators
take their places*]
CAESAR   Are we all ready? What is now amiss
That Caesar and his Senate must redress?
METELLUS [*coming forward and kneeling*]   Most high, most
mighty, and most puissant Caesar,
Metellus Cimber throws before thy seat
An humble heart.
35 CAESAR   I must prevent° thee, Cimber.   *thwart*
These couchings° and these lowly courtesies°   *stoopings / bows*
Might fire the blood° of ordinary men,   *passions*
And turn preordinance and first decree²
Into the law of children.° Be not fond³   *childish whims*
40 To think that Caesar bears such rebel° blood   *lawless*
That will be thawed from the true quality°   *proper constancy*
With that which melteth fools: I mean sweet words,
Low-crookèd° curtsies, and base spaniel fawning.   *Obsequious; dishonest*
Thy brother by decree is banishèd.
45 If thou dost bend and pray and fawn for him,
I spurn thee like a cur out of my way.
Know Caesar doth not wrong but with just cause,⁴
Nor without cause will he be satisfied.
METELLUS   Is there no voice more worthy than my own
50 To sound more sweetly in great Caesar's ear
For the repealing of my banished brother?
BRUTUS [*coming forward and kneeling*]   I kiss thy hand, but not
in flattery, Caesar,
Desiring thee that Publius Cimber may
Have an immediate freedom of repeal.°   *release from banishment*
CAESAR   What, Brutus?
CASSIUS [*coming forward and kneeling*]
55   Pardon, Caesar; Caesar, pardon.
As low as to thy foot doth Cassius fall
To beg enfranchisement° for Publius Cimber.   *liberation*
CAESAR   I could be well moved if I were as you.
If I could pray to move,° prayers would move me.   *make pleas*
60 But I am constant as the Northern Star,°   *polestar*
Of whose true fixed and resting° quality   *stationary*
There is no fellow° in the firmament.   *equal*
The skies are painted with unnumbered sparks;
They are all fire, and every one doth shine;
65 But there's but one in all doth hold his place.
So in the world: 'tis furnished well with men,

2. Established precedent and original rulings.   4. F reads merely, "Know Caesar doth not wrong." See
3. Do not be so foolish as.   Textual Note.

And men are flesh and blood, and apprehensive;°   *capable of understanding*
Yet in the number I do know but one
That unassailable holds on his rank,°   *maintains his place*
70   Unshaked of motion;[5] and that I am he
Let me a little show it even in this—
That I was constant° Cimber should be banished,   *resolute*
And constant do remain to keep him so.
CINNA [*coming forward and kneeling*]
    O Caesar!
CAESAR   Hence! Wilt thou lift up Olympus?[6]
DECIUS [*coming forward with* LIGARIUS *and kneeling*]
    Great Caesar!
75   CAESAR   Doth not Brutus bootless° kneel?   *in vain*
CASCA [*coming forward and kneeling*]
    Speak hands for me.[7]
        They stab CAESAR [CASCA *first,* BRUTUS *last*]
CAESAR   *Et tu, Bruté?*[8]—Then fall Caesar.
                             [*He*] *dies*
CINNA   Liberty! Freedom! Tyranny is dead!
  Run hence, proclaim, cry it about the streets.
CASSIUS   Some to the common pulpits,° and cry out   *public platforms (rostra)*
80   'Liberty, freedom, and enfranchisement!'
BRUTUS   People and senators, be not affrighted.
    [*Exeunt in a tumult* LEPIDUS, POPILLIUS, *other senators,*
                ARTEMIDORUS, SOOTHSAYER, *and citizens*]
  Fly not! Stand still! Ambition's debt is paid.
CASCA   Go to the pulpit, Brutus.
DECIUS   And Cassius too.
85   BRUTUS   Where's Publius?°   *(an elderly senator)*
CINNA   Here, quite confounded° with this mutiny.°   *confused / tumult*
METELLUS   Stand fast together, lest some friend of Caesar's
  Should chance—
BRUTUS   Talk not of standing.—Publius, good cheer!
90   There is no harm intended to your person,
  Nor to no Roman else—so tell them, Publius.
CASSIUS   And leave us, Publius, lest that the people,
  Rushing on us, should do your age some mischief.°   *injury*
BRUTUS   Do so; and let no man abide° this deed   *pay the penalty for*
95   But we the doers.   [*Exit* PUBLIUS]
    Enter TREBONIUS
CASSIUS   Where is Antony?
TREBONIUS   Fled to his house, amazed.
  Men, wives, and children stare, cry out, and run,
  As° it were doomsday.   *As if*
BRUTUS   Fates, we will know your pleasures.
100   That we shall die, we know; 'tis but the time
  And drawing days out that men stand upon.[9]
CASCA   Why, he that cuts off twenty years of life
  Cuts off so many years of fearing death.

---

5. Completely steady; unmoved by persuasion.
6. High mountain in Greece where the gods were supposed to dwell.
7. Let my hands beseech in prayer; let violent action take over where speech has failed.
8. Latin: And you, Brutus? According to Plutarch, Caesar

spoke these words in Greek and stopped defending himself when he saw Brutus among the conspirators.
9. *'tis . . . upon:* it is but the specific time of death and the possibility of extending their lives with which men concern themselves.

BRUTUS Grant that, and then is death a benefit.
105 So are we Caesar's friends, that have abridged
His time of fearing death. Stoop, Romans, stoop,
And let us bathe our hands in Caesar's blood
Up to the elbows, and besmear our swords;
Then walk we forth even to the market-place,°   *the Roman Forum*
110 And, waving our red weapons o'er our heads,
Let's all cry 'peace, freedom, and liberty!'
CASSIUS Stoop, then, and wash.
        [*They smear their hands with Caesar's blood*]
                                How many ages hence
Shall this our lofty scene be acted over,
In states unborn and accents° yet unknown!   *languages*
115 BRUTUS How many times shall Caesar bleed in sport,°   *for entertainment*
That now on Pompey's basis lies along,[1]
No worthier than the dust!
CASSIUS   So oft as that shall be,
So often shall the knot° of us be called   *group*
The men that gave their country liberty.
DECIUS What, shall we forth?
120 CASSIUS   Ay, every man away.
Brutus shall lead, and we will grace° his heels   *honor*
With the most boldest and best hearts of Rome.
        Enter [Antony's] SERVANT
BRUTUS Soft;° who comes here? A friend of Antony's.   *Wait*
SERVANT [*kneeling and falling prostrate*] Thus, Brutus, did my master bid
        me kneel.
125 Thus did Mark Antony bid me fall down,
And, being prostrate, thus he bade me say.
'Brutus is noble, wise, valiant, and honest.°   *honorable*
Caesar was mighty, bold, royal, and loving.
Say I love Brutus, and I honour him.
130 Say I feared Caesar, honoured him, and loved him.
If Brutus will vouchsafe that Antony
May safely come to him and be resolved°   *learn for certain*
How Caesar hath deserved to lie in death,
Mark Antony shall not love Caesar dead
135 So well as Brutus living, but will follow
The fortunes and affairs of noble Brutus
Thorough° the hazards of this untrod state[2]   *Through*
With all true faith.' So says my master Antony.
BRUTUS Thy master is a wise and valiant Roman.
140 I never thought him worse.
Tell him, so° please him come unto this place,   *if it should*
He shall be satisfied, and, by my honour,
Depart untouched.
SERVANT [*rising*]   I'll fetch him presently.°   *Exit*   *at once*
BRUTUS I know that we shall have him well to friend.°   *as a friend*
145 CASSIUS I wish we may. But yet have I a mind
That fears him much; and my misgiving still
Falls shrewdly to the purpose.[3]
        Enter ANTONY

---

1. Lies stretched out on the pedestal ("basis") of Pompey's statue.
2. These unprecedented circumstances.

3. *my ... purpose*: my suspicions always turn out to be unfortunately pertinent.

BRUTUS   But here comes Antony.—Welcome, Mark Antony.
ANTONY   O mighty Caesar! Dost thou lie so low?
150   Are all thy conquests, glories, triumphs, spoils,
Shrunk to this little measure? Fare thee well.—
I know not, gentlemen, what you intend—
Who else must be let blood, who else is rank.[4]
If I myself, there is no hour so fit
155   As Caesar's death's hour, nor no instrument
Of half that worth as those your swords, made rich
With the most noble blood of all this world.
I do beseech ye, if you bear me hard,°   *bear me ill will*
Now, whilst your purpled° hands do reek° and smoke,   *bloody / steam*
160   Fulfil your pleasure. Live° a thousand years,   *If I live*
I shall not find myself so apt° to die.   *ready*
No place will please me so, no mean° of death,   *manner*
As here by Caesar, and by you cut off,
The choice° and master spirits of this age.   *most select*
165   BRUTUS   O Antony, beg not your death of us!
Though now we must appear bloody and cruel,
As by our hands and this our present act
You see we do, yet see you but our hands,
And this the bleeding business they have done.
170   Our hearts you see not; they are pitiful;°   *full of pity*
And pity to the general wrong of Rome—
As fire drives out fire, so pity pity[5]—
Hath done this deed on Caesar. For your part,°   *As for you*
To you our swords have leaden° points, Mark Antony.   *blunt*
175   Our arms, unstrung of malice,[6] and our hearts
Of brothers' temper,° do receive you in   *disposition*
With all kind love, good thoughts, and reverence.
CASSIUS   Your voice° shall be as strong as any man's   *opinion*
In the disposing of new dignities.[7]
180   BRUTUS   Only be patient till we have appeased°   *calmed*
The multitude, beside themselves with fear,
And then we will deliver you the cause
Why I, that did love Caesar when I struck him,
Have thus proceeded.
ANTONY   I doubt not of your wisdom.
185   Let each man render me his bloody hand.
He shakes hands with the conspirators
First, Marcus Brutus, will I shake with you.—
Next, Caius Cassius, do I take your hand.—
Now, Decius Brutus, yours;—now yours, Metellus;—
Yours, Cinna;—and my valiant Casca, yours;—
190   Though last, not least in love, yours, good Trebonius.
Gentlemen all—alas, what shall I say?
My credit° now stands on such slippery ground   *credibility*
That one of two bad ways you must conceit° me: *judge*
Either a coward or a flatterer.
195   That I did love thee, Caesar, O, 'tis true.
If then thy spirit look upon us now,

4. Festering with disease; overgrown. *let blood:* have   6. Having given up their power to harm. (The image is
blood drawn off medically (that is, killed).   of a bow with its string loosened or removed.)
5. That is, pity for the state has driven out pity for Caesar.   7. Conferring new offices of state.

Shall it not grieve thee dearer° than thy death   *more keenly*
To see thy Antony making his peace,
Shaking the bloody fingers of thy foes—
200   Most noble!—in the presence of thy corpse?
Had I as many eyes as thou hast wounds,
Weeping as fast as they stream forth thy blood,
It would become me better than to close°   *agree*
In terms of friendship with thine enemies.
205   Pardon me, Julius. Here wast thou bayed,° brave hart;[8]   *brought to bay*
Here didst thou fall, and here thy hunters stand
Signed° in thy spoil° and crimsoned in thy lethe.[9]   *Marked / slaughter*
O world, thou wast the forest to this hart;
And this indeed, O world, the heart of thee.
210   How like a deer strucken by many princes
Dost thou here lie!

CASSIUS   Mark Antony.

ANTONY   Pardon me, Caius Cassius.
The enemies of Caesar shall say this;
215   Then in a friend it is cold modesty.°   *moderation*

CASSIUS   I blame you not for praising Caesar so;
But what compact° mean you to have with us?   *agreement*
Will you be pricked in number of° our friends,   *be counted among*
Or shall we on,° and not depend on you?   *proceed*

220 ANTONY   Therefore I took your hands, but was indeed
Swayed from the point by looking down on Caesar.
Friends am I with you all, and love you all
Upon this hope: that you shall give me reasons
Why and wherein Caesar was dangerous.

225 BRUTUS   Or else were this a savage spectacle.
Our reasons are so full of good regard,°   *sound considerations*
That were you, Antony, the son of Caesar,
You should be satisfied.

ANTONY   That's all I seek;
And am, moreover, suitor° that I may   *petitioner*
230   Produce° his body to the market-place,   *Bring out*
And in the pulpit,° as becomes a friend,   *rostrum*
Speak in the order° of his funeral.   *ceremony*

BRUTUS   You shall, Mark Antony.

CASSIUS   Brutus, a word with you.
[*Aside to* BRUTUS] You know not what you do. Do not consent
235   That Antony speak in his funeral.
Know you how much the people may be moved
By that which he will utter?

BRUTUS [*aside to* CASSIUS]   By your pardon,°   *With your permission*
I will myself into the pulpit first,
And show the reason of our Caesar's death.
240   What Antony shall speak I will protest°   *proclaim*
He speaks by leave and by permission;
And that we are contented Caesar shall
Have all true° rites and lawful ceremonies,   *proper*
It shall advantage° more than do us wrong.   *benefit*
245 CASSIUS [*aside to* BRUTUS]   I know not what may fall.° I like it not.   *happen*

---

8. Stag (punning on "heart").
9. Lost lifeblood (Lethe was the river of forgetfulness in the classical underworld).

BRUTUS   Mark Antony, here, take you Caesar's body.
You shall not in your funeral speech blame us;
But speak all good you can devise of Caesar,
And say you do't by our permission;

250   Else shall you not have any hand at all
About° his funeral. And you shall speak   *In*
In the same pulpit whereto I am going,
After my speech is ended.

ANTONY   Be it so;
255   I do desire no more.

BRUTUS   Prepare the body then, and follow us.

                              Exeunt. Manet ANTONY

ANTONY   O pardon me, thou bleeding piece of earth,
That I am meek and gentle with these butchers.
Thou art the ruins of the noblest man
260   That ever livèd in the tide of times.°   *flow of history*
Woe to the hand that shed this costly° blood!   *precious*
Over thy wounds now do I prophesy—
Which like dumb mouths do ope their ruby lips
To beg the voice and utterance of my tongue—
265   A curse shall light upon the limbs of men;
Domestic fury and fierce civil strife
Shall cumber° all the parts of Italy;   *oppress*
Blood and destruction shall be so in use,°   *so customary*
And dreadful objects so familiar,
270   That mothers shall but smile when they behold
Their infants quartered° with the hands of war,   *cut in pieces*
All pity choked with custom of fell° deeds;   *familiarity with cruel*
And Caesar's spirit, ranging° for revenge,   *roving like a wild beast*
With Ate° by his side come hot from hell,   *goddess of discord*
275   Shall in these confines° with a monarch's voice   *regions*
Cry 'havoc!'[1] and let slip° the dogs of war,   *unleash*
That this foul deed shall smell above the earth
With carrion men, groaning for burial.

                  Enter Octavius' SERVANT

You serve Octavius Caesar, do you not?
280   SERVANT   I do, Mark Antony.

ANTONY   Caesar did write for him to come to Rome.

SERVANT   He did receive his letters, and is coming,
And bid me say to you by word of mouth—
[*Seeing the body*] O Caesar!

285   ANTONY   Thy heart is big.° Get thee apart and weep.   *swollen with grief*
Passion,° I see, is catching, for mine eyes,   *Sorrow*
Seeing those beads of sorrow stand in thine,
Began to water. Is thy master coming?

SERVANT   He lies° tonight within seven leagues° of Rome.   *stays / 20 miles*
290   ANTONY   Post° back with speed and tell him what hath chanced.   *Ride quickly*
Here is a mourning Rome, a dangerous Rome,
No Rome of safety for Octavius yet.
Hie° hence and tell him so.—Yet stay awhile.   *Hasten*
Thou shalt not back till I have borne this corpse
295   Into the market-place. There shall I try°   *test*
In my oration how the people take

---

1. Military order for slaughter and pillage.

The cruel issue° of these bloody men;   *deed*
According to the which thou shalt discourse
To young Octavius of the state of things.
300 Lend me your hand.   *Exeunt [with Caesar's body]*

3.2

Enter BRUTUS *and* CASSIUS, *with the* PLEBEIANS
ALL THE PLEBEIANS   We will be satisfied!° Let us be satisfied!   *given an explanation*
BRUTUS   Then follow me, and give me audience, friends.
    [*Aside to* CASSIUS] Cassius, go you into the other street,
    And part the numbers.°   *divide the multitude*
5   [*To the* PLEBEIANS] Those that will hear me speak, let 'em stay here;
    Those that will follow Cassius, go with him;
    And public reasons shall be renderèd
    Of Caesar's death.
              BRUTUS [*ascends to*] *the pulpit*
FIRST PLEBEIAN   I will hear Brutus speak.
SECOND PLEBEIAN   I will hear Cassius, and compare their reasons
10 When severally° we hear them renderèd.   *separately*
                   [*Exit* CASSIUS, *with some* PLEBEIANS]
           [*Enter* BRUTUS *above in the pulpit*]
THIRD PLEBEIAN   The noble Brutus is ascended. Silence.
BRUTUS   Be patient till the last.°   *end of my address*
    Romans, countrymen, and lovers,° hear me for my cause, and   *dear friends*
    be silent that you may hear. Believe me for° mine honour, and   *on account of*
15 have respect to° mine honour, that you may believe. Censure°   *regard for / Judge*
    me in your wisdom, and awake your senses,° that you may the   *understanding*
    better judge. If there be any in this assembly, any dear friend
    of Caesar's, to him I say that Brutus' love to Caesar was no less
    than his. If then that friend demand why Brutus rose against
20 Caesar, this is my answer: not that I loved Caesar less, but that
    I loved Rome more. Had you rather Caesar were living, and
    die all slaves, than that Caesar were dead, to live all free men?
    As Caesar loved me, I weep for him. As he was fortunate, I
    rejoice at it. As he was valiant, I honour him. But as he was
25 ambitious, I slew him. There is tears for his love, joy for his
    fortune, honour for his valour, and death for his ambition. Who
    is here so base that would be a bondman? If any, speak, for him
    have I offended.° Who is here so rude° that would not be a   *wronged / barbarous*
    Roman? If any, speak, for him have I offended. Who is here so
30 vile that will not love his country? If any, speak, for him have I
    offended. I pause for a reply.
ALL THE PLEBEIANS   None, Brutus, none.
BRUTUS   Then none have I offended. I have done no more to
    Caesar than you shall do[1] to Brutus. The question of° his   *reasons for*
35 death is enrolled° in the Capitol, his glory not extenuated°   *recorded / diminished*
    wherein he was worthy, nor his offences enforced° for which   *unduly stressed*
    he suffered death.
            Enter Mark ANTONY, *with* [*others bearing*] *Caesar's*
            body [*in a coffin*]
    Here comes his body, mourned by Mark Antony, who, though
    he had no hand in his death, shall receive the benefit of his
40 dying: a place in the commonwealth—as which of you shall

3.2 Location: The Forum.   1. Should do (in such circumstances).

not? With this I depart: that as I slew my best lover° for the   *friend*
    good of Rome, I have the same dagger for myself when it shall
    please my country to need my death.
ALL THE PLEBEIANS   Live, Brutus, live, live!
45   FIRST PLEBEIAN   Bring him with triumph home unto his house.
FOURTH PLEBEIAN   Give him a statue with his ancestors.
THIRD PLEBEIAN   Let him be Caesar.
FIFTH PLEBEIAN   Caesar's better parts°   *faculties*
    Shall be crowned in Brutus.
FIRST PLEBEIAN   We'll bring him to his house with shouts and clamours.
BRUTUS   My countrymen.
50   FOURTH PLEBEIAN   Peace, silence. Brutus speaks.
FIRST PLEBEIAN   Peace, ho!
BRUTUS   Good countrymen, let me depart alone,
    And, for my sake, stay here with Antony.
    Do grace° to Caesar's corpse, and grace² his speech   *Pay respect*
55   Tending° to Caesar's glories, which Mark Antony,   *Relating*
    By our permission, is allowed to make.
    I do entreat you, not a man depart
    Save I alone till Antony have spoke.   *Exit*
FIRST PLEBEIAN   Stay, ho, and let us hear Mark Antony.
60   THIRD PLEBEIAN   Let him go up into the public chair.
    We'll hear him. Noble Antony, go up.
ANTONY   For Brutus' sake I am beholden to you.
        [ANTONY *ascends to the pulpit*]
FIFTH PLEBEIAN   What does he say of Brutus?
THIRD PLEBEIAN   He says, for Brutus' sake
    He finds himself beholden to us all.
65   FIFTH PLEBEIAN   'Twere best he speak no harm of Brutus here!
FIRST PLEBEIAN   This Caesar was a tyrant.
THIRD PLEBEIAN   Nay, that's certain.
    We are blessed that Rome is rid of him.
        [*Enter* ANTONY *in the pulpit*]
FOURTH PLEBEIAN   Peace, let us hear what Antony can say.
ANTONY   You gentle Romans.
ALL THE PLEBEIANS   Peace, ho! Let us hear him.
70   ANTONY   Friends, Romans, countrymen, lend me your ears.
    I come to bury Caesar, not to praise him.
    The evil that men do lives after them;
    The good is oft interrèd with their bones.
    So let it be with Caesar. The noble Brutus
75   Hath told you Caesar was ambitious.
    If it were so, it was a grievous fault,
    And grievously hath Caesar answered° it.   *paid the penalty for*
    Here, under leave° of Brutus and the rest—   *by permission*
    For Brutus is an honourable man,
80   So are they all, all honourable men—
    Come I to speak in Caesar's funeral.
    He was my friend, faithful and just to me.
    But Brutus says he was ambitious,
    And Brutus is an honourable man.
85   He hath brought many captives home to Rome,

2. Courteously hear.

Whose ransoms did the general coffers° fill.   *public treasury*
Did this in Caesar seem ambitious?
When that the poor have cried, Caesar hath wept.
Ambition should be made of sterner stuff.
90   Yet Brutus says he was ambitious,
And Brutus is an honourable man.
You all did see that on the Lupercal
I thrice presented him a kingly crown,
Which he did thrice refuse. Was this ambition?
95   Yet Brutus says he was ambitious,
And sure he is an honourable man.
I speak not to disprove what Brutus spoke,
But here I am to speak what I do know.
You all did love him once, not without cause.
100   What cause withholds you then to mourn for him?
O judgement, thou art fled to brutish beasts,
And men have lost their reason!
          [*He weeps*]
                                        Bear with me.
My heart is in the coffin there with Caesar,
And I must pause till it come back to me.
105   FIRST PLEBEIAN   Methinks there is much reason in his sayings.
FOURTH PLEBEIAN   If thou consider rightly of the matter,
     Caesar has had great wrong.
THIRD PLEBEIAN   Has he not, masters?
     I fear there will a worse come in his place.
FIFTH PLEBEIAN   Marked ye his words? He would not take the crown,
110   Therefore 'tis certain he was not ambitious.
FIRST PLEBEIAN   If it be found so, some will dear abide° it.   *pay dearly for*
FOURTH PLEBEIAN   Poor soul, his eyes are red as fire with weeping.
THIRD PLEBEIAN   There's not a nobler man in Rome than Antony.
FIFTH PLEBEIAN   Now mark him; he begins again to speak.
115   ANTONY   But° yesterday the word of Caesar might   *Only*
     Have stood against the world. Now lies he there,
     And none so poor to do him reverence.[3]
     O masters, if I were disposed to stir
     Your hearts and minds to mutiny° and rage,   *rebellion*
120   I should do Brutus wrong, and Cassius wrong,
     Who, you all know, are honourable men.
     I will not do them wrong. I rather choose
     To wrong the dead, to wrong myself and you,
     Than I will wrong such honourable men.
125   But here's a parchment with the seal of Caesar.
     I found it in his closet.° 'Tis his will.   *study*
     Let but the commons° hear this testament—   *commoners*
     Which, pardon me, I do not mean to read—
     And they would go and kiss dead Caesar's wounds,
130   And dip their napkins[4] in his sacred blood,
     Yea, beg a hair of him for memory,
     And, dying, mention it within their wills,
     Bequeathing it as a rich legacy
     Unto their issue.°   *children*

---

3. And no one is so lowly as to owe obeisance to him.
4. Handkerchiefs (implying that Caesar is a martyr whose bloody relics should be regarded as holy).

FIFTH PLEBEIAN We'll hear the will. Read it, Mark Antony.

ALL THE PLEBEIANS The will, the will! We will hear Caesar's will.

ANTONY Have patience, gentle friends, I must not read it.

    It is not meet° you know how Caesar loved you.   *fitting*

    You are not wood, you are not stones, but men;

140   And, being men, hearing the will of Caesar,

    It will inflame you, it will make you mad.

    'Tis good you know not that you are his heirs,

    For if you should, O what would come of it?

FIFTH PLEBEIAN Read the will. We'll hear it, Antony.

145   You shall read us the will, Caesar's will.

ANTONY Will you be patient? Will you stay a while?

    I have o'ershot myself[5] to tell you of it.

    I fear I wrong the honourable men

    Whose daggers have stabbed Caesar; I do fear it.

150 FIFTH PLEBEIAN They were traitors. Honourable men?

ALL THE PLEBEIANS The will, the testament!

FOURTH PLEBEIAN They were villains, murderers. The will, read

    the will!

ANTONY You will compel me then to read the will?

155   Then make a ring about the corpse of Caesar,

    And let me show you him that made the will.

    Shall I descend? And will you give me leave?

ALL THE PLEBEIANS

    Come down.

FOURTH PLEBEIAN Descend.

THIRD PLEBEIAN   You shall have leave.

    [ANTONY *descends from the pulpit*]

FIFTH PLEBEIAN   A ring.

    Stand round.

FIRST PLEBEIAN Stand from the hearse.° Stand from the body.   *bier*

160 FOURTH PLEBEIAN Room for Antony, most noble Antony!

    [*Enter* ANTONY *below*]

ANTONY Nay, press not so upon me. Stand farre° off.   *farther*

ALL THE PLEBEIANS Stand back! Room! Bear back!

ANTONY If you have tears, prepare to shed them now.

    You all do know this mantle. I remember

165   The first time ever Caesar put it on.

    'Twas on a summer's evening in his tent,

    That day he overcame the Nervii.[6]

    Look, in this place ran Cassius' dagger through.

    See what a rent the envious° Casca made.   *spiteful*

170   Through this the well-belovèd Brutus stabbed;

    And as he plucked his cursèd steel away,

    Mark how the blood of Caesar followed it,

    As° rushing out of doors to be resolved[7]   *As if*

    If Brutus so unkindly° knocked or no—   *cruelly; unnaturally*

175   For Brutus, as you know, was Caesar's angel.[8]

    Judge, O you gods, how dearly Caesar loved him!

    This was the most unkindest cut of all.

    For when the noble Caesar saw him stab,

---

5. I have gone too far (an image from archery).
6. Gallic tribe conquered by Caesar in 57 B.C.; it was an important victory, extravagantly celebrated in Rome.

7. To find out for sure.
8. Attendant spirit (that is, dearest friend).

Ingratitude, more strong than traitors' arms,
180 Quite vanquished him. Then burst his mighty heart,
And in his mantle muffling up his face,
Even at the base of Pompey's statue,
Which all the while ran blood, great Caesar fell.
O, what a fall was there, my countrymen!
185 Then I, and you, and all of us fell down,
Whilst bloody treason flourished[9] over us.
O now you weep, and I perceive you feel
The dint° of pity. These are gracious drops.   impression
Kind souls, what, weep you when you but behold
190 Our Caesar's vesture° wounded? Look you here.   garment
Here is himself, marred, as you see, with traitors.
        [*He uncovers Caesar's body*]
FIRST PLEBEIAN   O piteous spectacle!
FOURTH PLEBEIAN   O noble Caesar!
THIRD PLEBEIAN   O woeful day!
FIFTH PLEBEIAN   O traitors, villains!
FIRST PLEBEIAN   O most bloody sight!
195 FOURTH PLEBEIAN   We will be revenged.
ALL THE PLEBEIANS   Revenge! About!° Seek! Burn! Fire! Kill! Slay!   *To work*
   Let not a traitor live!
ANTONY   Stay, countrymen.
FIRST PLEBEIAN   Peace there, hear the noble Antony.
FOURTH PLEBEIAN   We'll hear him, we'll follow him, we'll die
200   with him!
ANTONY   Good friends, sweet friends, let me not stir you up
   To such a sudden flood of mutiny.
   They that have done this deed are honourable.
   What private griefs° they have, alas, I know not,   *personal grievances*
205   That made them do it. They are wise and honourable,
   And will no doubt with reasons answer you.
   I come not, friends, to steal away your hearts.
   I am no orator as Brutus is,
   But, as you know me all, a plain blunt man
210   That love my friend; and that they know full well
   That gave me public leave to speak[1] of him.
   For I have neither wit,° nor words, nor worth,°   *intelligence / stature*
   Action,° nor utterance, nor the power of speech,   *Gesture*
   To stir men's blood. I only speak right on.°   *straightforwardly*
215   I tell you that which you yourselves do know,
   Show you sweet Caesar's wounds, poor poor dumb mouths,
   And bid them speak for me. But were I Brutus,
   And Brutus Antony, there were an Antony
   Would ruffle° up your spirits, and put a tongue   *stir*
220   In every wound of Caesar that should move
   The stones of Rome to rise and mutiny.°   *riot*
ALL THE PLEBEIANS   We'll mutiny.
FIRST PLEBEIAN   We'll burn the house of Brutus.
THIRD PLEBEIAN   Away then! Come, seek the conspirators.
ANTONY   Yet hear me, countrymen, yet hear me speak.
225 ALL THE PLEBEIANS   Peace, ho! Hear Antony, most noble Antony.
ANTONY   Why, friends, you go to do you know not what.

9. Shook its sword; triumphed.   1. Permission to speak in public.

Wherein hath Caesar thus deserved your loves?
Alas, you know not. I must tell you then.
You have forgot the will I told you of.

230 ALL THE PLEBEIANS   Most true. The will. Let's stay and hear the will.

ANTONY   Here is the will, and under Caesar's seal.
To every Roman citizen he gives—
To every several° man—seventy-five drachmas.[2]   *individual*

FOURTH PLEBEIAN   Most noble Caesar! We'll revenge his death.

THIRD PLEBEIAN   O royal Caesar!

ANTONY   Hear me with patience.

235 ALL THE PLEBEIANS   Peace,° ho!   *Silence*

ANTONY   Moreover he hath left you all his walks,
His private arbours, and new-planted orchards,°   *gardens*
On this side Tiber. He hath left them you,
And to your heirs for ever—common pleasures°   *public parks*
240 To walk abroad and recreate yourselves.
Here was a Caesar. When comes such another?

FIRST PLEBEIAN   Never, never! Come, away, away!
We'll burn his body in the holy place,
And with the brands fire the traitors' houses.
245 Take up the body.

FOURTH PLEBEIAN   Go, fetch fire!

THIRD PLEBEIAN   Pluck down benches!

FIFTH PLEBEIAN   Pluck down forms,° windows,° anything!   *benches / shutters*

                    Exeunt PLEBEIANS [*with Caesar's body*]

ANTONY   Now let it work. Mischief, thou art afoot.
Take thou what course thou wilt.

                    Enter [*Octavius'*] SERVANT

250   How now, fellow?

SERVANT   Sir, Octavius is already come to Rome.

ANTONY   Where is he?

SERVANT   He and Lepidus are at Caesar's house.

ANTONY   And thither will I straight° to visit him.   *at once*
255 He comes upon a wish.° Fortune is merry,   *just as I wished*
And in this mood will give us anything.

SERVANT   I heard him say Brutus and Cassius
Are rid° like madmen through the gates of Rome.   *Have ridden*

ANTONY   Belike° they had some notice° of the people,   *Probably / warning*
260 How I had moved them. Bring me to Octavius.   *Exeunt*

3.3

                    Enter CINNA *the poet*

CINNA   I dreamt tonight° that I did feast with Caesar,   *last night*
And things unlucky charge my fantasy.[1]
I have no will to wander forth of doors,
Yet something leads me forth.

                    [*Enter*] *the* PLEBEIANS

5 FIRST PLEBEIAN   What is your name?

SECOND PLEBEIAN   Whither are you going?

THIRD PLEBEIAN   Where do you dwell?

FOURTH PLEBEIAN   Are you a married man or a bachelor?

SECOND PLEBEIAN   Answer every man directly.[2]

---

2. Greek silver coins.
3.3 Location: A street in Rome.

1. And bad omens oppress my imagination.
2. At once; speaking straightforwardly.

10 FIRST PLEBEIAN   Ay, and briefly.
FOURTH PLEBEIAN   Ay, and wisely.
THIRD PLEBEIAN   Ay, and truly, you were best.°   *you'd better*
CINNA   What is my name? Whither am I going? Where do I
    dwell? Am I a married man or a bachelor? Then to answer
15   every man directly and briefly, wisely and truly: wisely, I say, I
    am a bachelor.
SECOND PLEBEIAN   That's as much as to say they are fools that
    marry. You'll bear me a bang° for that, I fear. Proceed directly.   *get a blow from me*
CINNA   Directly I am going to Caesar's funeral.
20 FIRST PLEBEIAN   As a friend or an enemy?
CINNA   As a friend.
SECOND PLEBEIAN   That matter is answered directly.
FOURTH PLEBEIAN   For your dwelling—briefly.
CINNA   Briefly, I dwell by the Capitol.
25 THIRD PLEBEIAN   Your name, sir, truly.
CINNA   Truly, my name is Cinna.
FIRST PLEBEIAN   Tear him to pieces! He's a conspirator.
CINNA   I am Cinna the poet, I am Cinna the poet.
FOURTH PLEBEIAN   Tear him for his bad verses, tear him for his
30   bad verses.
CINNA   I am not Cinna the conspirator.
FOURTH PLEBEIAN   It is no matter, his name's Cinna. Pluck but
    his name out of his heart, and turn him going.°   *send him packing*
THIRD PLEBEIAN   Tear him, tear him!
    [*They set upon* CINNA]
35   Come, brands, ho! Firebrands! To Brutus', to Cassius'! Burn
    all! Some to Decius' house, and some to Casca's; some to Liga-
    rius'. Away, go!
                    Exeunt all the PLEBEIANS [*with* CINNA]

4.1

            Enter ANTONY [*with papers*], OCTAVIUS, *and* LEPIDUS
ANTONY   These many, then, shall die; their names are pricked.°   *marked down*
OCTAVIUS [*to* LEPIDUS]   Your brother too must die. Consent you, Lepidus?
LEPIDUS   I do consent.
OCTAVIUS   Prick him down, Antony.
LEPIDUS   Upon condition° Publius shall not live,   *Provided that*
5   Who is your sister's son, Mark Antony.
ANTONY   He shall not live. Look, with a spot I damn him.[1]
    But Lepidus, go you to Caesar's house;
    Fetch the will hither, and we shall determine
    How to cut off some charge in legacies.[2]
10 LEPIDUS   What, shall I find you here?
OCTAVIUS   Or° here or at the Capitol.   *Exit* LEPIDUS   *Either*
ANTONY   This is a slight, unmeritable° man,   *undeserving*
    Meet° to be sent on errands. Is it fit,   *Fit*
    The three-fold world divided,[3] he should stand
    One of the three to share it?
15 OCTAVIUS   So you thought him,
    And took his voice° who should be pricked to die   *accepted his opinion*

4.1 Location: Antony's house in Rome.
1. With a mark I condemn him to death.
2. Reduce the amount paid out to beneficiaries of Caesar's will.

3. Antony, Octavius, and Lepidus, in the second triumvirate, or joint rule of three, parceled out rule of Rome's
empire among themselves.

145 BRUTUS   A flatterer's would not, though they do appear
    As huge as high Olympus.
  CASSIUS   Come, Antony and young Octavius, come,
    Revenge yourselves alone on Cassius;
    For Cassius is aweary of the world,
150   Hated by one he loves, braved° by his brother,   *defied*
    Checked° like a bondman; all his faults observed,   *Rebuked*
    Set in a notebook, learned and conned by rote,°   *memorized*
    To cast into my teeth. O, I could weep
    My spirit from mine eyes! There is my dagger,
155   And here my naked breast; within, a heart
    Dearer° than Pluto's[4] mine, richer than gold.   *More valuable*
    If that thou beest a Roman, take it forth.
    I that denied thee gold will give my heart.
    Strike as thou didst at Caesar; for I know
160   When thou didst hate him worst, thou loved'st him better
    Than ever thou loved'st Cassius.
  BRUTUS   Sheathe your dagger.
    Be angry when you will; it shall have scope.°   *room for exercise*
    Do what you will; dishonour shall be humour.[5]
    O Cassius, you are yokèd° with a lamb   *allied*
165   That carries anger as the flint bears fire,
    Who, much enforcèd,° shows a hasty spark   *struck*
    And straight° is cold again.   *immediately*
  CASSIUS   Hath Cassius lived
    To be but mirth and laughter to his Brutus
    When grief and blood ill-tempered[6] vexeth him?
170 BRUTUS   When I spoke that, I was ill-tempered too.
  CASSIUS   Do you confess so much? Give me your hand.
  BRUTUS   And my heart too.
       [*They embrace*]
  CASSIUS   O Brutus!
  BRUTUS   What's the matter?
  CASSIUS   Have not you love enough to bear with me
    When that rash humour° which my mother gave me   *temperament*
    Makes me forgetful?
175 BRUTUS   Yes, Cassius, and from henceforth,
    When you are over-earnest with your Brutus,
    He'll think your mother chides, and leave you so.°   *let you alone*
       Enter [LUCILLIUS *and*] *a* POET
  POET   Let me go in to see the generals.
    There is some grudge between 'em; 'tis not meet
    They be alone.
180 LUCILLIUS   You shall not come to them.
  POET   Nothing but death shall stay me.
  CASSIUS   How now! What's the matter?
  POET   For shame, you generals, what do you mean?
    Love and be friends, as two such men should be,
    For I have seen more years, I'm sure, than ye.
185 CASSIUS   Ha, ha! How vilely doth this cynic[7] rhyme!

---

4. Roman god of riches (Plutus; often conflated with Pluto, god of the underworld).
5. Dishonorable actions shall be ascribed to moodiness.
6. Literally, badly mixed blood (thought to produce anger and melancholy).
7. Member of a philosophical school that refused to respect differences in social class.

BRUTUS [*to the* POET]   Get you hence, sirrah;° saucy fellow,   (*contemptuous address*)
    hence!
CASSIUS   Bear with him, Brutus, 'tis his fashion.
BRUTUS   I'll know his humour when he knows his time.[8]
    What should the wars do with these jigging° fools?   (*incompetently versifying*)
    [*To the* POET] Companion,° hence!   (*contemptuous*)
190 CASSIUS [*to the* POET]   Away, away, be gone!
                                                        Exit POET
BRUTUS   Lucillius and Titinius, bid the commanders
    Prepare to lodge their companies tonight.
CASSIUS   And come yourselves, and bring Messala with you
    Immediately to us.   [*Exeunt* LUCILLIUS *and* TITINIUS]
BRUTUS   Lucius, a bowl of wine.   [*Exit* LUCIUS]
195 CASSIUS   I did not think you could have been so angry.
BRUTUS   O Cassius, I am sick of° many griefs.   *suffering from*
CASSIUS   Of your philosophy you make no use,
    If you give place to accidental evils.[9]
BRUTUS   No man bears sorrow better. Portia is dead.
200 CASSIUS   Ha! Portia?
BRUTUS   She is dead.
CASSIUS   How scaped I killing° when I crossed you so?   *being killed*
    O insupportable and touching loss!
    Upon what sickness?
BRUTUS   Impatience of° my absence,   *Inability to tolerate*
205 And grief that young Octavius with Mark Antony
    Have made themselves so strong—for with° her death   *with the news of*
    That tidings came. With this, she fell distraught,
    And, her attendants absent, swallowed fire.[1]
CASSIUS   And died so?
BRUTUS   Even so.
CASSIUS   O ye immortal gods!
        Enter [LUCIUS] *with wine and tapers*°   *candles*
210 BRUTUS   Speak no more of her. [*To* LUCIUS] Give me a bowl of wine.
    [*To* CASSIUS] In this I bury all unkindness, Cassius.
        [*He*] *drinks*
CASSIUS   My heart is thirsty for that noble pledge.
    Fill, Lucius, till the wine o'erswell° the cup.   *overflow*
    I cannot drink too much of Brutus' love.
        [*He drinks*]   [*Exit* LUCIUS]
        Enter TITINIUS *and* MESSALA[2]
215 BRUTUS   Come in, Titinius; welcome, good Messala.
    Now sit we close about this taper here,
    And call in question° our necessities.   *discuss*
CASSIUS [*aside*]   Portia, art thou gone?
BRUTUS   No more, I pray you.
        [*They sit*]
    Messala, I have here receivèd letters
220 That young Octavius and Mark Antony
    Come down upon us with a mighty power,
    Bending their expedition° toward Philippi.[3]   *Pressing hastily*

---

8. I'll tolerate his eccentricity when he finds an appropriate time for it.
9. Brutus admired the Stoics, who taught that the wise
man should remain unaffected by circumstances outside
himself. *evils*: misfortunes.

1. Portia committed suicide by swallowing live embers.
2. Lucillius, who ought logically to return at this point
(see lines 193–94), is not mentioned, an inconsistency
that suggests Shakespearean revision of this scene.
3. City in northeastern Greece.

MESSALA Myself have letters of the selfsame tenor.
BRUTUS With what addition?
225 MESSALA That by proscription[4] and bills of outlawry
    Octavius, Antony, and Lepidus
    Have put to death an hundred senators.
BRUTUS Therein our letters do not well agree.
    Mine speak of seventy senators that died
230 By their proscriptions, Cicero being one.
CASSIUS Cicero one?
MESSALA   Ay, Cicero is dead,
    And by that order of proscription.
    [To BRUTUS] Had you your letters from your wife, my lord?
BRUTUS No, Messala.
235 MESSALA Nor nothing in your letters writ of her?
BRUTUS Nothing, Messala.
MESSALA   That methinks is strange.
BRUTUS Why ask you? Hear you aught of her in yours?
MESSALA No, my lord.
BRUTUS Now as you are a Roman, tell me true.
240 MESSALA Then like a Roman bear the truth I tell;
    For certain she is dead, and by strange manner.
BRUTUS Why, farewell, Portia.[5] We must die, Messala.
    With meditating that she must die once,°   *at some time*
    I have the patience to endure it now.
245 MESSALA Even so great men great losses should endure.
CASSIUS I have as much of this in art[6] as you,
    But yet my nature could not bear it so.
BRUTUS Well, to our work alive.[7] What do you think
    Of marching to Philippi presently?°   *at once*
CASSIUS I do not think it good.
BRUTUS   Your reason?
250 CASSIUS   This it is:
    'Tis better that the enemy seek us;
    So shall he waste his means, weary his soldiers,
    Doing himself offence; whilst we, lying still,
    Are full of rest, defence, and nimbleness.
255 BRUTUS Good reasons must of force° give place to better.   *of necessity*
    The people 'twixt Philippi and this ground
    Do stand but in a forced affection,
    For they have grudged us contribution.[8]
    The enemy marching along by them
260 By them shall make a fuller number up,
    Come on refreshed, new added,° and encouraged;   *reinforced*
    From which advantage shall we cut him off,
    If at Philippi we do face him there,
    These people at our back.
CASSIUS   Hear me, good brother.
265 BRUTUS Under your pardon.° You must note beside   *Allow me to continue*
    That we have tried the utmost of our friends;
    Our legions are brim-full, our cause is ripe.
    The enemy increaseth every day;

---

4. See note to 4.1.17.
5. On the apparent conflict between this passage and lines 199–210, see the Introduction and the Textual Note.
6. I have learned as much of this philosophy.
7. *alive:* of concern to those now living.
8. Money to support the army.

We at the height are ready to decline.
270 There is a tide in the affairs of men
Which, taken at the flood, leads on to fortune;
Omitted,° all the voyage of their life   *Once missed*
Is bound in° shallows and in miseries.   *confined to*
On such a full sea are we now afloat,
275 And we must take the current when it serves,
Or lose our ventures.[9]
CASSIUS   Then, with your will,° go on.   *as you wish*
We'll along ourselves, and meet them at Philippi.
BRUTUS   The deep of night is crept upon our talk,
And nature must obey necessity,
280 Which we will niggard° with a little rest.   *stint*
There is no more to say.
CASSIUS   No more. Good night.
Early tomorrow will we rise and hence.°   *depart*
BRUTUS   Lucius.
          Enter LUCIUS
                     My gown.°   [*Exit* LUCIUS]   *dressing gown*
                     Farewell, good Messala.
Good night, Titinius. Noble, noble, Cassius,
Good night and good repose.
285 CASSIUS   O my dear brother,
This was an ill beginning of the night!
Never come such division 'tween our souls.
Let it not, Brutus.
          Enter LUCIUS *with the gown*
BRUTUS   Everything is well.
CASSIUS   Good night, my lord.
BRUTUS   Good night, good brother.
TITINIUS *and* MESSALA   Good night, Lord Brutus.
290 BRUTUS   Farewell, every one.
                              Exeunt [CASSIUS, TITINIUS, *and* MESSALA]
Give me the gown.
          [*He puts on the gown*]
                     Where is thy instrument?°   *(probably a lute)*
LUCIUS   Here in the tent.
BRUTUS   What, thou speak'st drowsily.
Poor knave,° I blame thee not; thou art o'erwatched.[1]   *lad*
Call Claudio and some other of my men.
295 I'll have them sleep on cushions in my tent.
LUCIUS   Varrus and Claudio!
          Enter VARRUS *and* CLAUDIO
VARRUS   Calls my lord?
BRUTUS   I pray you, sirs, lie in my tent and sleep.
It may be I shall raise you° by and by   *get you up*
On business to my brother Cassius.
300 VARRUS   So please you, we will stand and watch your pleasure.[2]
BRUTUS   I will not have it so. Lie down, good sirs.
It may be I shall otherwise bethink me.°   *change my mind*
          [VARRUS *and* CLAUDIO *lie down to sleep*]
Look, Lucius, here's the book I sought for so.

9. Investments (in trading voyages).   2. And stay awake to attend to your wishes.
1. You have stayed up too long.

I put it in the pocket of my gown.

305 LUCIUS I was sure your lordship did not give it me.

BRUTUS Bear with me, good boy, I am much forgetful.
Canst thou hold up thy heavy eyes a while,
And touch thy instrument a strain or two?

LUCIUS Ay, my lord, an't° please you.   *if it*

BRUTUS   It does, my boy.

310 I trouble thee too much, but thou art willing.

LUCIUS It is my duty, sir.

BRUTUS I should not urge thy duty past thy might.
I know young bloods° look for a time of rest.   *youthful spirits*

LUCIUS I have slept, my lord, already.

315 BRUTUS It was well done, and thou shalt sleep again.
I will not hold thee long. If I do live,
I will be good to thee.

     [LUCIUS *plays*] *music and* [*sings*] *a song* [*and so falls*
     asleep]

This is a sleepy tune. O murd'rous slumber,
Lay'st thou thy leaden mace° upon my boy   *heavy staff of office*

320 That plays thee music?—Gentle knave, good night.
I will not do thee so much wrong to wake thee.
If thou dost nod thou break'st thy instrument;
I'll take it from thee, and, good boy, good night.

     [*He takes away Lucius' instrument, then opens the book*]

Let me see, let me see, is not the leaf turned down

325 Where I left reading? Here it is, I think.

     Enter the GHOST of Caesar

How ill this taper burns!³ Ha! Who comes here?
I think it is the weakness of mine eyes
That shapes this monstrous apparition.
It comes upon° me. Art thou any thing?   *toward*

330 Art thou some god, some angel, or some devil,
That mak'st my blood cold and my hair to stare?°   *stand on end*
Speak to me what thou art.

GHOST Thy evil spirit, Brutus.

BRUTUS Why com'st thou?

335 GHOST To tell thee thou shalt see me at Philippi.

BRUTUS Well; then I shall see thee again?

GHOST   Ay, at Philippi.

BRUTUS Why, I will see thee at Philippi then.   *Exit* GHOST
Now I have taken heart, thou vanishest.
Ill spirit, I would hold more talk with thee.—

340 Boy, Lucius, Varrus, Claudio, sirs, awake!
Claudio!

LUCIUS   The strings, my lord, are false.°   *out of tune*

BRUTUS He thinks he still is at his instrument.—
Lucius, awake!

LUCIUS My lord.

345 BRUTUS Didst thou dream, Lucius, that thou so cried'st out?

LUCIUS My lord, I do not know that I did cry.

BRUTUS Yes, that thou didst. Didst thou see anything?

LUCIUS Nothing, my lord.

BRUTUS Sleep again, Lucius.—Sirrah Claudio!

---

3. The dimming of a flame was held to indicate a ghost's presence.

[*To* VARRUS]   Fellow,
350 Thou, awake!
VARRUS My lord.
CLAUDIO My lord.
BRUTUS Why did you so cry out, sirs, in your sleep?
BOTH Did we, my lord?
BRUTUS   Ay. Saw you anything?
VARRUS No, my lord, I saw nothing.
355 CLAUDIO   Nor I, my lord.
BRUTUS Go and commend me° to my brother Cassius.   *send my regards*
    Bid him set on his powers betimes before,[4]
    And we will follow.
BOTH   It shall be done, my lord.
              Exeunt [VARRUS *and* CLAUDIO *at one door,* BRUTUS
                        and LUCIUS *at another door*]

5.1

              Enter OCTAVIUS, ANTONY, *and their army*
OCTAVIUS Now, Antony, our hopes are answerèd.
    You said the enemy would not come down,
    But keep the hills and upper regions.
    It proves not so; their battles° are at hand.   *forces*
5   They mean to warn° us at Philippi here,   *challenge*
    Answering before we do demand of them.
ANTONY Tut, I am in their bosoms,[1] and I know
    Wherefore they do it. They could be content
    To visit other places;° and come down   *To go elsewhere*
10 With fearful bravery,[2] thinking by this face°   *pretense; defiance*
    To fasten in our thoughts that they have courage;
    But 'tis not so.
              Enter a MESSENGER
MESSENGER   Prepare you, generals.
    The enemy comes on in gallant show.
    Their bloody sign° of battle is hung out,   *red flag*
15 And something to° be done immediately.   *is to*
ANTONY Octavius, lead your battle softly° on   *your army warily*
    Upon the left hand of the even field.
OCTAVIUS Upon the right hand, I; keep thou the left.
ANTONY Why do you cross° me in this exigent?°   *thwart / critical moment*
20 OCTAVIUS I do not cross you,[3] but I will do so.
              [*Drum.* ANTONY *and* OCTAVIUS] *march* [*with their army*].
              Drum [*within*]. *Enter* [*marching*] BRUTUS, CASSIUS, *and
              their army* [*amongst them* TITINIUS, LUCILLIUS, *and* MES-
              SALA]
              [*Octavius' and Antony's army makes a stand*]
BRUTUS They stand, and would have parley.
CASSIUS Stand fast, Titinius. We must out° and talk.   *go forward*
              [*Brutus' and Cassius' army makes a stand*]
OCTAVIUS Mark Antony, shall we give sign of battle?
ANTONY No, Caesar, we will answer on their charge.[4]

4. March off with his army before me.   fying display.
5.1 Location: The remainder of the play takes place on   3. March on the right side; dispute with you in the
the battlefield near Philippi.   future.
1. I know their secret thoughts.   4. We will meet them when they attack.
2. With a show of courage that conceals fear; with a terri-

25 Make forth,° the generals would have some words.   *Go forward*
    OCTAVIUS [*to his army*]   Stir not until the signal.
              [ANTONY *and* OCTAVIUS *meet* BRUTUS *and* CASSIUS]
    BRUTUS   Words before blows: is it so, countrymen?
    OCTAVIUS   Not that we love words better, as you do.
    BRUTUS   Good words are better than bad strokes, Octavius.
30 ANTONY   In your° bad strokes, Brutus, you give good words.   *As you deliver*
        Witness the hole you made in Caesar's heart,
        Crying 'Long live, hail Caesar'.
    CASSIUS   Antony,
        The posture° of your blows are yet unknown;   *quality*
        But for your words, they rob the Hybla⁵ bees,
35   And leave them honeyless.
    ANTONY   Not stingless too.
    BRUTUS   O yes, and soundless too,
        For you have stolen their buzzing, Antony,
        And very wisely threat before you sting.
40 ANTONY   Villains, you did not so when your vile daggers
        Hacked one another in the sides of Caesar.
        You showed your teeth like apes,° and fawned like hounds,   *You imitated smiles*
        And bowed like bondmen, kissing Caesar's feet,
        Whilst damnèd Casca, like a cur, behind,
45   Struck Caesar on the neck. O you flatterers!
    CASSIUS   Flatterers? Now, Brutus, thank yourself.
        This tongue had not offended so today
        If Cassius might have ruled.°   *had his way*
    OCTAVIUS   Come, come, the cause.° If arguing make us sweat,   *matter in hand*
50   The proof° of it will turn to redder drops.   *testing*
              [*He draws*]
        Look, I draw a sword against conspirators.
        When think you that the sword goes up again?
        Never till Caesar's three and thirty wounds
        Be well avenged, or till another Caesar⁶
55   Have added slaughter to⁷ the swords of traitors.
    BRUTUS   Caesar, thou canst not die by traitors' hands,
        Unless thou bring'st them with thee.°   *(Unless by your hand)*
    OCTAVIUS   So I hope.
        I was not born to die on Brutus' sword.
    BRUTUS   O, if thou wert the noblest of thy strain,°   *family*
60   Young man, thou couldst not die more honourable.
    CASSIUS   A peevish° schoolboy, worthless of such honour,   *silly*
        Joined with a masquer and a reveller!⁸
    ANTONY   Old Cassius still.
    OCTAVIUS   Come, Antony, away.
        Defiance, traitors, hurl we in your teeth.
65   If you dare fight today, come to the field.
        If not, when you have stomachs.°   *inclination; courage*
              Exeunt OCTAVIUS, ANTONY, *and* [*their*] *army*
    CASSIUS   Why, now blow wind, swell billow, and swim bark.°   *ship*
        The storm is up, and all is on the hazard.°   *at risk*
    BRUTUS   Ho, Lucillius! Hark, a word with you.

---

5. Sicilian town famous for honey.
6. That is, Octavius Caesar himself.
7. Has increased the slaughter committed by.

8. That is, Antony, who was noted for his love of extravagant entertainments and banquets.

LUCILLIUS   My lord.
    [He] stand[s] forth° [and speaks with BRUTUS]   *comes forward*
CASSIUS   Messala.
MESSALA *[standing forth]*   What says my general?
70   CASSIUS   Messala,
    This is my birthday; as° this very day   *on*
    Was Cassius born. Give me thy hand, Messala.
    Be thou my witness that, against my will,
    As Pompey was, am I compelled to set
75   Upon one battle all our liberties.
    You know that I held Epicurus strong,
    And his opinion.[9] Now I change my mind,
    And partly credit things that do presage.
    Coming from Sardis, on our former ensigns°   *foremost banners*
80   Two mighty eagles fell,° and there they perched,   *alighted*
    Gorging and feeding from our soldiers' hands,
    Who to Philippi here consorted° us.   *accompanied*
    This morning are they fled away and gone,
    And in their steads do ravens, crows, and kites[1]
85   Fly o'er our heads and downward look on us,
    As° we were sickly prey. Their shadows seem   *As if*
    A canopy most fatal,° under which   *ominous*
    Our army lies ready to give° the ghost.   *give up*
MESSALA   Believe not so.
CASSIUS   I but believe it partly,
90   For I am fresh of spirit, and resolved
    To meet all perils very constantly.°   *resolutely*
BRUTUS   Even so, Lucillius.
CASSIUS *[joining* BRUTUS]   Now, most noble Brutus,
    The gods° today stand friendly, that we may,   *May the gods*
    Lovers° in peace, lead on our days to age.   *Close friends*
95   But since the affairs of men rest still° incertain,   *always remain*
    Let's reason with° the worst that may befall.   *consider*
    If we do lose this battle, then is this
    The very last time we shall speak together.
    What are you then determinèd to do?
100   BRUTUS   Even by the rule of that philosophy[2]
    By which I did blame Cato[3] for the death
    Which he did give himself—I know not how,
    But I do find it cowardly and vile
    For fear of what might fall° so to prevent°   *happen / anticipate*
105   The time° of life—arming myself with patience   *natural limit*
    To stay° the providence of some high powers   *await*
    That govern us below.
CASSIUS   Then if we lose this battle,
    You are contented to be led in triumph[4]
    Thorough° the streets of Rome?   *Through*
110   BRUTUS   No, Cassius, no.
    Think not, thou noble Roman,

---

9. Epicurus, a Greek philosopher, thought the gods indifferent to human affairs and therefore disbelieved omens.
1. These are all scavenger birds, considered bad omens.
2. Brutus admired Plato, who rejected suicide.

3. See note to 2.1.294.
4. As a captive in a triumphal procession; see note to
1.1.30.

That ever Brutus will go bound to Rome.
He bears too great a mind. But this same day
Must end that work the ides of March begun;
115 And whether we shall meet again I know not.
Therefore our everlasting farewell take.
For ever and for ever farewell, Cassius.
If we do meet again, why, we shall smile.
If not, why then, this parting was well made.
120 CASSIUS For ever and for ever farewell, Brutus.
If we do meet again, we'll smile indeed.
If not, 'tis true this parting was well made.
BRUTUS Why then, lead on. O that a man might know
The end of this day's business ere it come!
125 But it sufficeth that the day will end,
And then the end is known.—Come, ho, away!   *Exeunt*

5.2

Alarum.° Enter BRUTUS *and* MESSALA   Offstage call to battle
BRUTUS Ride, ride, Messala, ride, and give these bills°   written orders
Unto the legions on the other side.°   (Cassius's wing)
Loud alarum
Let them set on° at once, for I perceive   advance
But cold demeanour° in Octavio's wing,   lack of fighting spirit
5 And sudden push gives them the overthrow.
Ride, ride, Messala; let them all come down.
                              Exeunt [severally]

5.3

Alarums. Enter CASSIUS [*with an ensign,*°] *and* TITINIUS   a banner
CASSIUS O look, Titinius, look: the villains° fly.   (Cassius's own men)
Myself have to mine own turned enemy:
This ensign° here of mine was turning back;   standard-bearer
I slew the coward, and did take it° from him.   (the standard)
5 TITINIUS O Cassius, Brutus gave the word too early,
Who, having some advantage on Octavius,
Took it too eagerly. His soldiers fell to spoil,°   looting
Whilst we by Antony are all enclosed.
Enter PINDARUS
PINDARUS Fly further off, my lord, fly further off!
10 Mark Antony is in your tents, my lord;
Fly therefore, noble Cassius, fly farre° off.   farther
CASSIUS This hill is far enough. Look, look, Titinius,
Are those my tents where I perceive the fire?
TITINIUS They are, my lord.
CASSIUS   Titinius, if thou lovest me,
15 Mount thou my horse, and hide thy spurs in him
Till he have brought thee up to yonder troops
And here again, that I may rest assured
Whether yon troops are friend or enemy.
TITINIUS I will be here again even with° a thought.   *Exit*   as fast as
20 CASSIUS Go, Pindarus, get higher on that hill.
My sight was ever thick.° Regard, Titinius,   dim
And tell me what thou not'st about the field. [*Exit* PINDARUS]
This day I breathèd first. Time is come round,

And where I did begin, there shall I end.
My life is run his compass.°   *its circuit*
     [*Enter* PINDARUS *above*]°   *(on the stage balcony)*
25   Sirrah, what news?
PINDARUS   O my lord!
CASSIUS   What news?
PINDARUS   Titinius is enclosèd round about
     With horsemen, that make to him on the spur.[1]
30   Yet he spurs on. Now they are almost on him.
     Now Titinius. Now some light.° O, he lights too.   *alight*
     He's ta'en.°   *taken*
          Shout [*within*]
     And hark, they shout for joy.
CASSIUS   Come down; behold no more.
                              [*Exit* PINDARUS]
     O coward that I am, to live so long
35   To see my best friend ta'en before my face!
          Enter PINDARUS [*below*]
     Come hither, sirrah. In Parthia° did I take thee prisoner,   *(modern Iran)*
     And then I swore thee, saving of[2] thy life,
     That whatsoever I did bid thee do
     Thou shouldst attempt it. Come now, keep thine oath.
40   Now be a freeman, and, with this good sword
     That ran through Caesar's bowels, search° this bosom.   *penetrate*
     Stand° not to answer. Here, take thou the hilts,°   *Delay / sword handle*
          [PINDARUS *takes the sword*]
     And when my face is covered, as 'tis now,
     Guide thou the sword.
          [PINDARUS *stabs him*]
                         Caesar, thou art revenged,
45   Even with the sword that killed thee.   [*He dies*]
PINDARUS   So, I am free, yet would not so have been
     Durst° I have done my will. O Cassius!   *Dared*
     Far from this country Pindarus shall run,
     Where never Roman shall take note of him.   *Exit*
          Enter TITINIUS [*wearing a wreath of victory*°] *and* MES-   *(made of laurel leaves)*
          SALA
50   MESSALA   It is but change,° Titinius, for Octavius   *an even exchange*
     Is overthrown by noble Brutus' power,
     As Cassius' legions are by Antony.
TITINIUS   These tidings will well comfort Cassius.
MESSALA   Where did you leave him?
TITINIUS   All disconsolate,
55   With Pindarus his bondman, on this hill.
MESSALA   Is not that he that lies upon the ground?
TITINIUS   He lies not like the living. —O my heart!
MESSALA   Is not that he?
TITINIUS   No, this was he, Messala;
     But Cassius is no more. O setting sun,
60   As in thy red rays thou dost sink tonight,
     So in his red blood Cassius' day is set.
     The sun of Rome is set. Our day is gone.

5.3
1. Who approach him at a gallop.   2. I made you swear, when I spared.

Clouds, dews, and dangers come. Our deeds are done.
Mistrust of my success³ hath done this deed.
65 MESSALA   Mistrust of good success hath done this deed.
O hateful Error, Melancholy's child,⁴
Why dost thou show to the apt° thoughts of men   *impressionable*
The things that are not? O Error, soon conceived,
Thou never com'st unto a happy birth,
70 But kill'st the mother° that engendered thee.   *(the melancholy person)*
TITINIUS   What, Pindarus! Where art thou, Pindarus?
MESSALA   Seek him, Titinius, whilst I go to meet
The noble Brutus, thrusting this report
Into his ears. I may say 'thrusting' it,
75 For piercing steel and darts° envenomèd   *spears*
Shall be as welcome to the ears of Brutus
As tidings of this sight.
TITINIUS   Hie you, Messala,
And I will seek for Pindarus the while.   [*Exit* MESSALA]
Why didst thou send me forth, brave Cassius?
80 Did I not meet thy friends, and did not they
Put on my brows this wreath of victory,
And bid me give it thee? Didst thou not hear their shouts?
Alas, thou hast misconstrued everything.
But hold thee, take this garland on thy brow.
85 Thy Brutus bid me give it thee, and I
Will do his bidding. Brutus, come apace,°   *quickly*
And see how I regarded° Caius Cassius.   *esteemed*
By your leave, gods, this is a Roman's part:
Come Cassius' sword, and find Titinius' heart.
                          [*He stabs himself, and*] *dies*
          Alarum. Enter BRUTUS, MESSALA, YOUNG CATO,⁵ STRATO,
              VOLUMNIUS, LUCILLIUS[, LABIO, *and* FLAVIO]
90 BRUTUS   Where, where, Messala, doth his body lie?
MESSALA   Lo yonder, and Titinius mourning it.
BRUTUS   Titinius' face is upward.
CATO   He is slain.
BRUTUS   O Julius Caesar, thou art mighty yet.
Thy spirit walks abroad, and turns our swords
In our own proper° entrails.   *our very own*
          Low° Alarums   *Soft*
95 CATO   Brave Titinius,
Look whe'er° he have not crowned dead Cassius.   *whether*
BRUTUS   Are yet two Romans living such as these?
The last of all the Romans, fare thee well.
It is impossible that ever Rome
100 Should breed thy fellow. Friends, I owe more tears
To this dead man than you shall see me pay.—
I shall find time, Cassius, I shall find time.—
Come, therefore, and to Thasos° send his body.   *an island near Phillippi*
His funerals shall not be in our camp,
105 Lest it discomfort° us. Lucillius, come;   *dishearten*
And come, young Cato. Let us to the field.
Labio and Flavio, set our battles° on.   *forces*

---

3. Doubt about the outcome of my mission.   5. The son of Brutus Portius Cato.
4. That is, bred from melancholy thoughts.

'Tis three o'clock, and, Romans, yet ere night
We shall try fortune in a second fight.

Exeunt [with the bodies]

5.4

Alarum. Enter BRUTUS, MESSALA, YOUNG CATO, LUCIL-
LIUS, *and* FLAVIUS

BRUTUS   Yet, countrymen, O yet hold up your heads.

[Exit with MESSALA *and* FLAVIUS]

CATO   What bastard° doth not? Who will go with me?   *untrue Roman*
I will proclaim my name about the field.
I am the son of Marcus Cato, ho!
5   A foe to tyrants, and my country's friend.
I am the son of Marcus Cato, ho!

Enter SOLDIERS, *and fight*

LUCILLIUS   And I am Brutus, Marcus Brutus, I,
Brutus, my country's friend. Know me for Brutus.

*[*SOLDIERS *kill* CATO]

O young and noble Cato, art thou down?
10   Why, now thou diest as bravely as Titinius,
And mayst be honoured, being Cato's son.

FIRST SOLDIER   Yield, or thou diest.

LUCILLIUS   Only I yield to die.¹
There is so much,² that thou wilt kill me straight:°   *immediately*
Kill Brutus, and be honoured in his death.

15   FIRST SOLDIER   We must not.—A noble prisoner.

SECOND SOLDIER   Room, ho! Tell Antony Brutus is ta'en.

Enter ANTONY

FIRST SOLDIER   I'll tell the news. Here comes the general.—
[To ANTONY] Brutus is ta'en, Brutus is ta'en, my lord.

ANTONY   Where is he?

20   LUCILLIUS   Safe, Antony, Brutus is safe enough.
I dare assure thee that no enemy
Shall ever take alive the noble Brutus.
The gods defend him from so great a shame.
When you do find him, or° alive or dead,   *either*
25   He will be found like Brutus, like himself.°   *true to his noble nature*

ANTONY *[to* FIRST SOLDIER]   This is not Brutus, friend, but, I assure you,
A prize no less in worth. Keep this man safe.
Give him all kindness. I had rather have
Such men my friends than enemies.
[To another SOLDIER]   Go on,
30   And see whe'er Brutus be alive or dead,
And bring us word unto Octavius' tent
How everything is chanced.°   *has happened*

Exeunt [the SOLDIER *at one door,* ANTONY,
LUCILLIUS *and other* SOLDIERS, *some bearing
Cato's body, at another door]*

5.4
1. I yield only so that I may die.   2. There is enough inducement.

5.5

Enter BRUTUS, DARDANIUS, CLITUS, STRATO, *and*
VOLUMNIUS

BRUTUS   Come, poor remains of friends, rest on this rock.
[*He sits.* STRATO *rests and falls asleep*]

CLITUS   Statillius[1] showed the torchlight, but, my lord,
He came not back. He is or ta'en° or slain.   *either captured*

BRUTUS   Sit thee down, Clitus. Slaying is the word:
5   It is a deed in fashion. Hark thee, Clitus.
[*He whispers*]

CLITUS   What I, my lord? No, not for all the world.

BRUTUS   Peace, then, no words.

CLITUS   I'll rather kill myself.
[*He stands apart*]

BRUTUS   Hark thee, Dardanius.
[*He whispers*]

DARDANIUS   Shall I do such a deed?
[*He joins* CLITUS]

CLITUS   O Dardanius!

10   DARDANIUS   O Clitus!

CLITUS   What ill request did Brutus make to thee?

DARDANIUS   To kill him, Clitus. Look, he meditates.

CLITUS   Now is that noble vessel full of grief,
That it runs over even at his eyes.

15   BRUTUS   Come hither, good Volumnius. List° a word.   *Listen to*

VOLUMNIUS   What says my lord?

BRUTUS   Why this, Volumnius.
The ghost of Caesar hath appeared to me
Two several° times by night—at Sardis once,   *different*
And this last night, here in Philippi fields.
I know my hour is come.

20   VOLUMNIUS   Not so, my lord.

BRUTUS   Nay, I am sure it is, Volumnius.
Thou seest the world, Volumnius, how it goes.
Our enemies have beat° us to the pit,[2]   *driven*
Low alarums
It is more worthy to leap in ourselves
25   Than tarry till they push us. Good Volumnius,
Thou know'st that we two went to school together.
Even for that, our love of old, I prithee,
Hold thou my sword hilts whilst I run on it.

VOLUMNIUS   That's not an office for a friend, my lord.
Alarum still

30   CLITUS   Fly, fly, my lord! There is no tarrying here.

BRUTUS   Farewell to you, and you, and you, Volumnius.—
Strato, thou hast been all this while asleep.
[STRATO *wakes*]
Farewell to thee too, Strato. Countrymen,
My heart doth joy that yet in all my life
35   I found no man but he was true to me.

5.5
1. A soldier sent ahead with instructions to signal by torchlight if all is well.
2. Animal trap; grave.

I shall have glory by this losing day,
More than Octavius and Mark Antony
By this vile conquest shall attain unto.
So fare you well at once, for Brutus' tongue
40   Hath almost ended his life's history.
Night hangs upon mine eyes. My bones would rest,
That have but laboured³ to attain this hour.
          Alarum. Cry within: 'Fly, fly, fly!'
CLITUS   Fly, my lord, fly!
BRUTUS   Hence; I will follow.
          [*Exeunt* CLITUS, DARDANIUS, *and* VOLUMNIUS]
I prithee, Strato, stay thou by thy lord.
45   Thou art a fellow of a good respect.°   *reputation*
Thy life hath had some smatch° of honour in it.   *relish*
Hold then my sword, and turn away thy face
While I do run upon it. Wilt thou, Strato?
STRATO   Give me your hand first. Fare you well, my lord.
BRUTUS   Farewell, good Strato.
          [STRATO *holds the sword, while* BRUTUS *runs on it*]
50   Caesar, now be still.
I killed not thee with half so good a will.   [*He*] *dies*
          *Alarum. Retreat.*⁴ *Enter* ANTONY, OCTAVIUS, MESSALA,
          LUCILLIUS, *and the army*
OCTAVIUS   What man is that?
MESSALA   My master's man. Strato, where is thy master?
STRATO   Free from the bondage you are in, Messala.
55   The conquerors can but make a fire of him,°   *burn his body*
For Brutus only overcame himself,⁵
And no man else hath honour by his death.
LUCILLIUS   So Brutus should be found. I thank thee, Brutus,
That thou hast proved Lucillius' saying true.
60   OCTAVIUS   All that served Brutus, I will entertain them.°   *take them into service*
[*To* STRATO] Fellow, wilt thou bestow° thy time with me?   *spend*
STRATO   Ay, if Messala will prefer° me to you.   *recommend*
OCTAVIUS   Do so, good Messala.
MESSALA   How died my master, Strato?
STRATO   I held the sword, and he did run on it.
65   MESSALA   Octavius, then take him to follow° thee,   *serve*
That did the latest° service to my master.   *last*
ANTONY   This was the noblest Roman of them all.
All the conspirators save only he
Did that° they did in envy of great Caesar.   *what*
70   He only in a general honest thought⁶
And common good to all⁷ made one of them.
His life was gentle,° and the elements⁸   *noble*
So mixed in him that nature might stand up
And say to all the world 'This was a man'.
75   OCTAVIUS   According° to his virtue let us use him,   *In accordance with*
With all respect and rites of burial.
Within my tent his bones tonight shall lie,
Most like a soldier, ordered° honourably.   *treated*

---

3. Labored for no other purpose than.
4. Trumpet signal to cease pursuit.
5. For only Brutus conquered Brutus.
6. With a virtuous, principled conviction.

7. And desire for the common good.
8. The four bodily humors, different combinations of which supposedly affected temperament; in the ideal individual, no single humor predominated.

So call the field to rest, and let's away
80   To part° the glories of this happy day.   *share*

Exeunt [with Brutus' body]

TEXTUAL VARIANTS

Control text: F

F: The Folio of 1623

1.2.104 Said Caesar *Caesar* saide **140 were** are **156 walls** Walkes
1.3.128 In favour's Is Fauors
2.1.40 ides first **67 of** of a **83 put** path **96 Cinna, this;** this, *Cinna;* **266 his** hit **312, 315, 319 s.p. LIGARIUS** *Cai⟨us⟩.*
2.2.46 are heare **81 Of** And **108 Cassius** *Publius* **109 s.p. CASSIUS** *Pub⟨lius⟩.* **Cassius** *Publius*
3.1.39 law lane **47 but with just cause** [not in F; line is quoted by Ben Jonson in *Timber, or Discoveries.*] **116 lies** lye **175 unstrung** in strength **286 for** from
3.2.50 s.p. FOURTH PLEBEIAN 2. **63 s.p. FIFTH PLEBEIAN** 4. **101 art** are **107 he not** hee **196–97 revenged. / ALL THE PLEBEIANS Revenge!** reueng'd: Reuenge **213 wit** writ
4.1.44 meinies meanes
4.2.2 s.p. SOLDIER *Lucil⟨lius⟩.* **34–36 s.p.'s FIRST SOLDIER, SECOND SOLDIER, THIRD SOLDIER** [not in F] **80 bay** baite **170 ill-tempered too.** ill remper'd too.s **204 Impatience** Impatient **269 to** ro **301 will** will it
5.1.42 teeth teethes **55 swords** Sword **79 ensigns** Ensigne **88 give** giue up **95 rest** rests
5.3.103 Thasos *Tharsus*
5.4.7 s.p. LUCILLIUS [not in F] **17 the** thee
5.5.76 With all Withall

Hamlet

"Who's there?" Shakespeare's most famous play begins. The question, turned back on the tragedy itself, has haunted audiences and readers for centuries. *Hamlet* is an enigma. Mountains of feverish speculation have only deepened the interlocking mysteries: Why does Hamlet delay avenging the murder of his father by Claudius, his father's brother? How much guilt does Hamlet's mother, Gertrude, who has since married Claudius, bear in this crime? How trustworthy is the ghost of Hamlet's father, who has returned from the grave to demand that Hamlet avenge his murder? Is vengeance morally justifiable in this play, or is it to be condemned? What exactly *is* the ghost, and where has it come from? Why is the ghost, visible to everyone in the first act, visible only to Hamlet in Act 3? Is Hamlet's madness feigned or true, a strategy masquerading as a reality or a reality masquerading as a strategy? Does Hamlet, who once loved Ophelia, continue to love her in spite of his apparent cruelty? Does Ophelia, crushed by that cruelty and driven mad by Hamlet's murder of her father, Polonius, actually intend to drown herself, or does she die accidentally? What enables Hamlet to pass from thoughts of suicide to faith in God's providence, from "To be, or not to be" to "Let be"? What was Hamlet trying to say before death stopped his speech at the close? *Hamlet*, as one critic has wittily remarked, is "the tragedy of an audience that cannot make up its mind."

Shakespeare probably wrote *Hamlet* in 1600 (shortly after *Julius Caesar*, to which Polonius seems to allude at 3.2.93), but the precise date of composition is uncertain, and this uncertainty is compounded by the exceptionally complex state of the text. *The Tragedie of Hamlet, Prince of Denmarke* is included in the First Folio of 1623, but most editions of the play since the eighteenth century have incorporated passages that appear only in an earlier text, the Second Quarto, dated 1604 and entitled *The Tragicall Historie of Hamlet, Prince of Denmarke*. In the present edition of the play, based on the Folio text, lines that appear only in the Second Quarto are indented and numbered separately, so that readers will be able to assess the difference between the two versions. The Second Quarto has come to be known as the good quarto—in contrast to the so-called bad quarto, the first known printed version of Shakespeare's play, published in 1603. This First Quarto, regarded by most scholars as a highly suspect text, is little more than half the length of the play we now read and even in what it includes contains many striking differences. (The Prince's most famous soliloquy, for example, begins "To be, or not to be, ay there's the point.") *Hamlet* is a monument of world literature, but it is a monument built on shifting sands.

With a text so fraught with uncertainty, it is tempting to think that our unresolved questions are largely the result of the perplexities that must inevitably come with the passage of time and the vagaries of editors. Yet the play in all its versions seems designed to provoke such perplexities. "What art thou?" Horatio asks the Ghost, and the question, unanswered, is echoed again and again until it seems to touch on everything: "Is it not like the King?" (1.1.57); "Why seems it so particular with thee?" (1.2.75); "What does this mean, my lord?" (1.4.8); "Whither wilt thou lead me?" (1.5.1); "What's Hecuba to him, or he to Hecuba, / That he should weep for her?" (2.2.536–37); "Why wouldst thou be a breeder of sinners?" (3.1.122–23); "What should such fellows as I do crawling between heaven and earth?" (3.1.127–28); "Do you see nothing there?" (3.4.122); "What is it ye would see?" (5.2.306). The dream of getting answers to such questions tantalizes many of the play's characters and drives them to scrutinize one another. But the task is maddeningly difficult. When Hamlet repeatedly asks Guildenstern, one of the school friends whom his uncle has set to spy on him, to play the recorder, Guildenstern protests that he does not

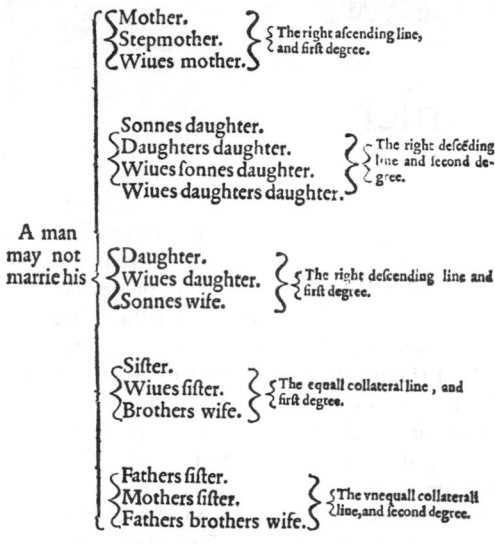

A man may not marrie his

Mother. Stepmother. Wiues mother.	The right afcending line, and firft degree.
Sonnes daughter. Daughters daughter. Wiues fonnes daughter. Wiues daughters daughter.	The right defcéding line and fecond degree.
Daughter. Wiues daughter. Sonnes wife.	The right defcending line and firft degree.
Sifter. Wiues fifter. Brothers wife.	The equall collateral line, and firft degree.
Fathers fifter. Mothers fifter. Fathers brothers wife.	The vnequall collateralll line, and fecond degree.

30 Therfore fhall ye keepe mine ordinances, that ye doe not any of the abhominable cuftomes, which haue been done before you.

Table of prohibited marriages. From William Clerke, *The Triall of Bastardie* (London, 1594).

know how. "You would play upon me," Hamlet returns, "you would seem to know my stops, you would pluck out the heart of my mystery. . . . do you think I am easier to be played on than a pipe?" (3.2.335–40).

Hamlet at once invites and resists interrogation. He is, more than any theatrical character before and perhaps since, a figure constructed around an unseen or secret core. Such a figure in the theater is something of a paradox, since all that exists of any character onstage is what is seen and heard there. But from his place onstage at the center of a courtly world in which he is "the observed of all observers" and hence a person allowed virtually no privacy, Hamlet insists that he has "that within which passeth show" (1.2.85). What is it that he has "within"? In the nineteenth century, following a suggestion by the German poet Johann Wolfgang von Goethe, critics frequently argued that Hamlet has within him the soul of a poet, too sensitive, delicate, and complex to endure the cruel pressures of a coarse world. In the twentieth century, following a suggestion by the founder of psychoanalysis, Sigmund Freud, many critics have speculated that Hamlet has within him an unresolved Oedipus complex, a sexual desire for his mother that prevents him from taking decisive action against the man who has done in reality the thing that Hamlet unconsciously desires to do: kill his father and marry his mother. On occasion, this psychological speculation has been challenged by a political one: Hamlet hides within himself a spirit of political resistance, a subversive challenge to a corrupt, illegitimate regime shored up by lies, spies, and treachery.

These recurrent attempts to pluck out the heart of Hamlet's mystery are a modern continuation of an interpretive activity that goes on throughout the play itself. Attempting to solve the riddle of Hamlet's strange behavior, Polonius speculates that the Prince is desperately lovesick for his daughter, but Claudius concludes, after spying on Hamlet's conversation with Ophelia, that "his affections do not that way tend" (3.1.161). Rosencrantz and Guildenstern propose that Hamlet is suffering from ambition—after all, though Denmark is an elective monarchy, the Prince could have hoped to succeed his father on the throne—but Hamlet vehemently refutes the charge: "O God, I could be bounded in a nutshell and count myself a king of infinite space, were it not that I have bad dreams" (2.2.248–50). Claudius doubts that Hamlet is mad and, though he never directly articulates this suspicion, seems to fear that the Prince somehow knows of his secret crime, but Hamlet's painful interiority, his melancholy insistence that he has something "within," is already clear from his first appearance, before the Ghost's revelation. Gertrude therefore seems wiser to argue that her son's distemper at least originates in "his father's death and our o'er-hasty marriage" (2.2.57).

As we first encounter him, Hamlet is a young man in deep mourning, which his mother and uncle both urge him to cease. The death of fathers is natural and inevitable, they point out, and while it is customary to grieve, it is unreasonable to persist obstinately in sorrow. Hamlet responds that his grief is not a theatrical performance, a mere costume to be put on and then discarded. When he is alone onstage a few moments later, he discloses, in the first of his famous soliloquies, a near-suicidal despair and a corrosive bitterness centered on the haste with which his mother has remarried. This bitterness is intensified by Hamlet's idealized image of his father and by painful memories of what had seemed to him his parents' perfect mutual love. As he broods on the brief time between his father's death and his mother's remarriage, Hamlet's tormented mind convulsively shortens the interval: "two months," "nay, not so much, not two," "within a month."

Hamlet's soliloquies are carefully crafted rhetorical performances. Thus, for example, the celebrated lines that begin "To be, or not to be; that is the question" (3.1.58ff.) have the structure of a formal academic debate on the subject of suicide: prudently considering both sides of the question and rehearsing venerable commonplaces, Hamlet does not once use the words "I" or "me." Yet here and elsewhere his words manage with astonishing vividness to convey the spontaneous rhythms of a mind in motion. Shakespeare had anticipated this achievement in such plays as *Richard II*, *1 Henry IV*, and *Julius Caesar*: King Richard, Prince Hal, and Brutus all have intimate moments in which they seem to disclose the troubled faces that are normally hidden behind expressionless social masks. But in its moral complexity, psychological depth, and philosophical power, *Hamlet* seems to mark an epochal shift not only in Shakespeare's own career but in Western drama; it is as if the play were giving birth to a whole new kind of literary subjectivity. This subjectivity—the sense of being inside a character's psyche and following its twists and turns—is to a large degree an effect of language, the product of dramatic poetry and prose of unprecedented intensity. In order to convey a traumatized mind straining to articulate perceptions of a shattered world, Shakespeare developed a complex syntax and a remarkably expanded diction. By one scholar's count, he introduced over six hundred words in *Hamlet* that he had not used before; many of these words do not appear, at least with the form or meaning they have here, in any previous English text. The innovative inwardness is not restricted to scenes in which Hamlet is alone onstage, nor is it restricted to the Prince himself; indeed, many of the deepest psychic revelations in the play are conveyed not in moments of isolation but in disturbing exchanges, intimate encounters in which love and poison are intertwined.

These innovations are not called for by the story itself. In *Hamlet*, as in so many of his plays, Shakespeare was recycling narratives long in circulation. The legendary tale of Hamlet (Amleth) was already recounted at length in the late-twelfth-century *Danish History* compiled in Latin by Saxo the Grammarian. In Saxo's version, which was adapted in French in François de Belleforest's *Histoires Tragiques* (1570), the unscrupulous Feng ambushes and kills his brother Horwendil and marries Horwendil's wife, Gerutha. Horwendil and Gerutha had a son, Amleth, who, though young and surrounded by Feng's henchmen, undertakes to avenge his father. The problem is survival: Amleth's every move is carefully watched. In order to avert suspicion and buy time, the cunning Amleth pretends to be feebleminded. His strategy works: with the active assistance of his mother, whom he has shamed into collaborating with him, Amleth eventually succeeds in killing his uncle, along with the uncle's followers, and is enthusiastically proclaimed King of Denmark. No ghost and no sickening uncertainty: the murder of Amleth's father is public knowledge, flimsily justified by Feng's claim that Horwendil was mistreating Gerutha. (In Belleforest's adaptation, Fengon and Geruth were having an adulterous affair.) Not only is there no problem of doubt for Amleth, there is also no problem of conscience, for in pre-Christian Denmark revenge was not a violation of the moral or religious law but a filial obligation.

This is the rough outline of the story Shakespeare inherited, along, it seems, with at least one other version about which we know tantalizingly little: by 1589, English audiences had evidently seen a play, now lost, on the theme of Hamlet. Apparently, this play—which scholars call the Ur (original)-*Hamlet*—featured a ghost who cried, "Hamlet, revenge!" On the basis of the barest shreds of contemporary evidence, scholars have constructed elaborate theories about this supposed source play, but there is little agreement among them. Further details have been pieced together speculatively by studying a German version of *Hamlet*, called *Der bestrafte Brudermord* (Fratricide Punished). The text of this crude version dates from 1710, long after Shakespeare, but some scholars conjecture that it was based on the Ur-*Hamlet*, perhaps as performed in Germany by an itinerant company of English actors. The text (which other scholars argue was based on Q1, the bad quarto) includes such features as the use of the play-within-the-play to test the truth of the ghost's tale, the sparing of the usurper king at prayer, Ophelia's madness, and the climactic slaughter resulting from poisoned sword and poisoned drink. Still other scholars, though a distinct minority, dispute the whole existence of a non-Shakespearean Ur-*Hamlet* and speculate instead that the bad quarto reflects a very early version of the play that Shakespeare himself authored and that gave rise to the smattering of early allusions to the Hamlet story.

Assuming that there was an Ur-*Hamlet*, an Elizabethan staging of the story that preceded Shakespeare's, its author remains unknown. Many scholars have assigned it to Thomas Kyd, who wrote *The Spanish Tragedy* (c. 1587), one of the most successful and enduring Elizabethan plays. *The Spanish Tragedy* itself has features that strikingly anticipate Shakespeare's tragedy, including a ghost impatient for revenge, a secret crime, a hero tormented by uncertainty and self-reproach, the strategic feigning of a madness that seems disturbingly close to the real thing, a woman who goes mad from grief and commits suicide, a play-within-the-play, and a final slaughter that wipes out much of the royal family and court, along with the avenger himself. Kyd's play is entirely structured around the problem of revenge—"wild justice," in Francis Bacon's haunting phrase—and gave rise to a whole genre of revenge plays in which *Hamlet* participates.

These plays generally share certain conventional assumptions. First, revenge is an individual response to an intolerable wrong or a public insult. It is an unauthorized, violent action in a world whose institutions seem unable or unwilling to satisfy a craving for justice. Second, since institutional channels are closed and since the criminal is usually either hidden or well protected, revenge almost always follows a devious path toward its violent end. Third, the revenger is in the grip of an inner compulsion: his course of action may be motivated by institutional failure—for example, the mechanisms of justice are in the hands of the criminals themselves—but even if these mechanisms were operating perfectly, they would not allow the psychic satisfactions of revenge. Fourth, revengers generally need their victims to know what is happening and why: satisfaction depends on a moment of declaration and vindication. And fifth, revenge is a universal imperative more powerful than the pious injunctions of any particular belief system, including Christianity itself.

Shakespeare had already produced a sensationally violent, crude version of these conventions in *Titus Andronicus*. In *Hamlet*, he at once reproduces them and calls them into question. The audience knows for certain—from Claudius's tortured attempt to pray in Act 3—that there has been a "foul murder," a fratricide successfully covered over by the story that a serpent stung the sleeping King. But Hamlet does not overhear Claudius's confession and has only the questionable testimony of the Ghost. That testimony is open to question because the nature of the Ghost is open to question. The Ghost speaks as if he were condemned to a term of suffering in the realm Catholics called purgatory:

> Doomed for a certain term to walk the night,
> And for the day confined to fast in fires
> Till the foul crimes done in my days of nature
> Are burnt and purged away
>
> (1.5.10–13).

But Protestant theologians vehemently denied that purgatory existed and argued that spirits thought to be ghosts were in fact devils sent to lure humans into sinful actions. Hamlet responds at first as if he believes the Ghost to be the authentic spirit of his father returned from the dead, but he subsequently expresses serious doubts, and in the play's most famous soliloquy he speaks of death as "the undiscovered country from whose bourn / No traveller returns" (3.1.81–82).

The test Hamlet devises to authenticate the Ghost's accusation—carefully watching the reaction of his uncle to *The Mousetrap*—appears to resolve any doubts: "I'll take the Ghost's word," Hamlet exults, after the King has stormed out in a rage, "for a thousand

The man in prayer. By Mair von Landshut (1499).

pound" (3.2.263–64). Yet even here Shakespeare introduces an occasion for uncertainty: after all, the murderer in the play-within-the play is "one Lucianus, nephew to the King" (3.2.223). Claudius's anger could have arisen from the spectacle of the player-nephew killing his player-uncle and not from the spectacle of his own hidden crime. The effect on the audience is not so much to cast doubt on the Ghost's word as to uncouple Hamlet's inner life once again from the external world, even at the moment that he himself thinks they are at last securely linked.

This uncoupling, this sense of inward thoughts and feelings painfully cut off from the world around him, haunts virtually all of Hamlet's relationships. When he speaks with his old school friends Rosencrantz and Guildenstern, with the courtier Osric or with Polonius, he is deliberately evasive, but his exchanges with Ophelia are equally oblique and baffling. Even with his intimate friend Horatio, there is some gap across which Hamlet struggles to speak: "There are more things in heaven and earth, Horatio," Hamlet says after his first encounter with the Ghost, "than are dreamt of in our philosophy" (1.5.168–69). (The quarto variant—"in your philosophy"—marks the gap between them still more sharply.) When Hamlet directly confronts his mother with the charge of murder, she reacts with astonishment. The painful words that follow, Hamlet's weird, tormented admonition to his mother to shun her husband's bed, do indeed seem to strike home: "These words like daggers," Gertrude exclaims, "enter in mine ears" (3.4.85). But the Ghost's sudden reappearance, visible this time only to Hamlet (and, of course, to the audience), convinces his mother that her son is mad. "Do you see nothing there?" asks Hamlet, to which his mother, certain that her son is hallucinating, replies steadfastly, "Nothing at all, yet all that is I see" (3.4.122–23).

Ironically, the distance between what Hamlet sees and what those around him see is smallest in the case of Claudius, since both share a knowledge of the secret crime that has poisoned the kingdom, and each maneuvers against the other throughout the play. But their fatal opposition never rises to view until the final violent seconds, nor does Hamlet ever establish unequivocal, unambiguous public confirmation of his uncle's guilt. It would have been easy for Shakespeare to provide such confirmation, for example in a last speech by the mortally wounded usurper, but he chooses instead to leave what Horatio calls "th' yet unknowing world" (5.2.323) in the dark. Until the explosion of treason and murder, the horrified bystanders know only a court in which the loving Claudius appeals to Hamlet as his "son" and wagers on his skill in fencing. Hamlet begins an explanation—"O I could tell you"—but he is cut short by death. The effect is to extend Hamlet's tragic isolation, his gnawing inward pain, all the way to his final silence.

What would it take to get rid of this pain? The possibility of cleansing, definitive action at once continually tantalizes and eludes the Prince. Such action is embodied in the soldier Fortinbras, but if Hamlet finds some way of easing his mental anguish, it is not through any comparable martial exploit, nor is it through the secret plotting undertaken by Laertes. The spiritual calm to which he gives voice near the play's close—"There's a special providence in the fall of a sparrow. If it be now, 'tis not to come. If it be not to come, it will be now. If it be not now, yet it will come. The readiness is all" (5.2.157–60)—descends upon him *before*, not as a result of, his revenge. The act of revenge itself happens in a flash of rage, without planning, without any self-vindicating declaration by Hamlet to Claudius, and without any public confession of guilt by the usurper. Revenge leaves the Prince not with inner satisfaction but with intense anxiety over his "wounded name."

Standing on a stage littered with corpses, Horatio promises to fulfill Hamlet's dying request to tell his story, but his account of "carnal, bloody, and unnatural acts," though it may be accurate, must be inadequate to the play we have just witnessed. For *Hamlet* situates the need for revenge in a context that goes beyond any crime, however heinous,

Swordsmen. From *Vincentio Saviolo his Practice* (London, 1595).

and that seems resistant to violent solutions. Before the Ghost disclosed his uncle's villainy, Hamlet was suffering from the traumas of mortality: the searing pain of his father's death, a troubled recognition of his mother's sexuality, a sickening awareness of the vulnerability and corruptibility of the flesh. There was a time, the play implies, when Hamlet embodied all the hopes and aspirations of his age and his own vision of human possibility was unbounded—"What a piece of work is a man!"—but that vision has given way to bitter disillusionment: "And yet to me what is this quintessence of dust?" (2.2.293–94, 297–98).

In Hamlet's melancholy consciousness, human existence has been reduced to dust at its dustiest. Though Claudius's secret crime is a political act that has poisoned the public sphere, the roots of Hamlet's despair seem to lie in a more intractably inward place, a place perhaps less consonant with revenge than with suicide. If there were only the evil usurper to depose, Hamlet might compass a straightforward course of action, but his soul-sickness has receding layers: beyond political corruption, there is the time-serving shallowness of his friends Rosencrantz and Guildenstern, and beyond this there is Ophelia's dismayingly compliant obedience to her father, and beyond this there is his mother's disturbing carnality, and beyond this there is the ongoing, endlessly transformative, morally indifferent cycle of life itself. For Hamlet, the quintessence of dust is not only the cold, inert matter produced by the nauseating triumph of death—the flesh of Alexander the Great metamorphosed into a plug of dirt stopping up a beer barrel—but also living matter pullulating with tenacious, ·meaningless vitality, produced by the equally nauseating triumph of life. "We fat all creatures else to fat us," Hamlet tells Claudius, "and we fat ourselves for maggots" (4.3.22–23).

In a world pervaded by decay, the process of natural renewal has come to seem grotesque and disgusting:

> 'Tis an unweeded garden
> That grows to seed; things rank and gross in nature
> Possess it merely.
>
> (1.2.135–37)

These lines immediately give way to bitter reflections on his mother's sexual appetite: in Hamlet's diseased consciousness, the spectacle of nature run riot, of uncontrolled breeding and feeding, centers on the body of woman. His bitterness at his mother's remarriage spreads like a stain to include all women, including the woman he had once ardently courted. "Get thee to a nunnery," Hamlet urges Ophelia, as if the only virtuous course of action were renunciation of the flesh. "Why wouldst thou be a breeder of sinners?" (3.1.122–23) Even this desperate advice seems to be undermined by Hamlet's obsessive sense of rampant female sexuality and of his own corruption, since in Elizabethan slang "nunnery" could also be a term for "brothel."

The fragile Ophelia begins to crack under the strain of Hamlet's misogynistic revulsion. Gertrude, who takes the full force of this revulsion, is evidently made of stronger stuff, but when confronted alone by her son, she fears for her life. Both women sense the violence and despair seething in Hamlet beneath what he calls his "antic disposition" (1.5.173). That disposition, manifested in his disordered dress and in the "wild and whirling words" (1.5.137) that he begins to speak after encountering the Ghost, casts Hamlet in the strange role of jester in the court in which he is the mourning son and the heir apparent. Of all Shakespeare's tragic heroes, he is at once the saddest and the funniest. His blend of sarcasm, riddling, and sly wordplay initially strikes those around him as folly, but this first impression continually gives way to an uneasy awareness of hidden meanings: Claudius, alert to danger, notes that "there's something in his soul / O'er which his melancholy sits on brood" (3.1.163–64). The "something" Claudius senses is in part the murderous design of the revenger, but it is also the philosophical meditation on life and death that haunts Hamlet throughout the play. This meditation reaches a climax in the graveyard, where Hamlet, trading zany quibbles with the gravediggers, directly confronts the corruption and decay that had obsessed him ever since his father's death. If there is any release for Hamlet from this obsession—and it is not clear that there is—it comes from an unflinching gaze at a skull, the skull of the jester Yorick, but also, by extension, his father's skull and his own.

STEPHEN GREENBLATT

TEXTUAL NOTE

Hamlet exists in three distinct early texts. The relations between these texts, along with a mountain of speculation about an earlier theatrical version of the story, now lost, have occupied scholars for decades. These are some of the bare facts. A printer named James Roberts placed an entry in the Stationers' Register on July 26, 1602, for "A booke called the Revenge of Hamlett Prince Denmarke as yt was latelie Acted by the Lord Chamberleyne his servantes." The first known edition (Q1) is a quarto dated 1603, printed not by Roberts but by Nicholas Ling and John Trundell. This edition, "*The Tragicall Historie of HAMLET Prince of Denmarke By William Shake-speare*," is a text markedly inferior, except for a few details, to the others and, at 2,200 type lines long, markedly shorter. Accordingly, it is often referred to as the "bad quarto." Only two copies of this quarto, first identified in 1823, are known to exist; one is in the British Library in London, the other in the Huntington Library in San Marino, California.

A second edition (Q2), dated 1604, was printed by James Roberts. The title page advertises itself as "Newly imprinted and enlarged to almost as much againe as it was, according to the true and perfect Coppie." At 3,800 type lines, Q2 makes good on its claim to substantial enlargement, and scholars tend to agree that the printer's shop set the text from the playwright's own handwritten draft, or "foul papers," occasionally supplemented by consultation with Q1. Q2 was reprinted once, without significant alteration, during Shakespeare's lifetime.

If Shakespeare's manuscript is behind Q2, what is the source of the substantially different Q1? The most widely accepted theory, first proposed in 1941 by G. I. Duthie (*The 'Bad' Quarto of Hamlet*), is that Q1 is the product of memorial reconstruction. That is, one or more actors in the play reported what they remembered to a scribe, who prepared copy for the printer. Scholars have conjectured that the principal reporter was the actor who played Marcellus and probably doubled as Valtemand and Lucianus, since the accuracy of the text, as measured by the subsequent editions, greatly improves whenever those characters are onstage. Along with virtually every other aspect of the textual history of *Hamlet*, this appeal to memorial reconstruction is a subject of continuing scholarly debate.

The third major version of the play appeared in 1623 in the First Folio (F), where it is entitled *The Tragedie of Hamlet, Prince of Denmarke*. This edition differs in important ways from Q2: there are a great many small changes, along with some substantial cuts and additions. Most recent editors believe that F was set not from the author's own draft but from a scribal transcript, possibly from a promptbook prepared while Shakespeare was still active in the company. Such a promptbook would normally have been made by annotating a fair copy of the author's foul papers. In other words, the text of *Hamlet* in F is probably closer than Q2 to the play as it was performed in the theater when Shakespeare was alive.

Traditionally, many editors regarded any changes introduced in the passage from the author's own draft to the transcript prepared for the prompter (and thus in the case of *Hamlet* from Q2 to F) as corruptions of the text. Their goal, then, was to remove the corruptions and restore the play to its original state, the text as the author had conceived it. But most if not all of the passages that appear in F and not in Q2 seem unmistakably by Shakespeare himself, while the passages that appear in Q2 and not in F seem equally authentic. Consequently, editors were forced to conjecture that the compositors of Q2 had in 1604 unaccountably omitted the passages that appear in F, while the compositors of the

Folio had similarly omitted those passages that only appear in Q2. As early as the eighteenth century, *Hamlet*'s editors routinely conflated Q2 and F, incorporating in a single text as much as possible of both versions of the play.

The Oxford editors broke with this tradition. They observed that Shakespeare was an active member of his company and therefore that the passage from foul papers to promptbook was not necessarily a corruption of his text. Rather, it could as easily have been the occasion for deliberate authorial revision, drawing upon his own second thoughts as well as the suggestions of his trusted professional colleagues. Close study of the differences between Q2 and F suggests the strong possibility of such revision, reflecting a coherent strategy. The Oxford editors hypothesized that Shakespeare himself prepared a fair copy of the foul papers from which Q2 was set, that in making that fair copy he revised the text in a number of ways, and that F derives, at one or possibly more removes, from that fair copy. Therefore, since the Oxford editors concluded that Shakespeare's own revisions are reflected in F, they adopted F as the control text.

In keeping with this decision, the *Oxford Shakespeare* relegated passages from Q2 that do not appear in F to an appendix. This format enables readers to imagine more readily the version of *Hamlet* thought to have been revised for performance during Shakespeare's own lifetime, but it has certain disadvantages, the principal of which is that only a reader extremely familiar with the play can easily imagine exactly how the Q2 passages functioned in what everyone agrees was a version of the play also written by Shakespeare. Moreover, since several of these passages have long been regarded as integral parts of the play, their relegation to an appendix makes it difficult for readers to participate fully in the great cultural conversation about *Hamlet* that has occupied artists, critics, and scholars for generations. Accordingly, the *Norton Shakespeare*, while following the Oxford text, has moved the Q2 passages from the appendix to the body of the play. But in order not to once again produce a conflated text, the Q2 passages are indented, printed in a different typeface, and numbered in such a way as to make clear their provenance. Also, at the points where the Folio and the Q2 passages directly overlap (3.4.70, 3.4.151, and 5.2.154), the overlapping lines are repeated. Those who wish to read the Folio version of *Hamlet* can thus simply skip over the offset Q2 passages, while at the same time it is possible for readers to see clearly the place that the Q2 passages occupy.

SELECTED BIBLIOGRAPHY

Booth, Stephen. "On the Value of *Hamlet*." *Reinterpretations of Elizabethan Drama: Selected Papers from the English Institute*. Ed. Norman Rabkin. New York: Columbia University Press, 1969. 137–77.

Bradley, A. C. *Shakespearean Tragedy: Lectures on "Hamlet," "Othello," "King Lear," "Macbeth."* 1904. 3rd ed. Basingstoke, Eng.: Macmillan, 1992.

Eliot, T. S. "Hamlet and His Problems." *The Sacred Wood*. London: Methuen, 1920.

Empson, William. "*Hamlet* When New." *Sewanee Review* 61 (1953): 15–42, 185–205.

Garber, Marjorie. "*Hamlet*: Giving Up the Ghost." *Shakespeare's Ghost Writers*. New York: Methuen, 1987. 124–76.

Granville-Barker, Harley. *Preface to "Hamlet."* 1936. Princeton: Princeton University Press, 1965.

Levin, Harry. *The Question of "Hamlet."* New York: Oxford University Press, 1959.

Mack, Maynard. "The World of *Hamlet*." *The Yale Review* 41 (1952): 502–23.

McGee, Arthur. *The Elizabethan Hamlet*. New Haven, Conn.: Yale University Press, 1987.

Wilson, J. Dover. *What Happens in "Hamlet."* Cambridge: Cambridge University Press, 1935 (rev. ed. 1951).

See also the creative uses of *Hamlet* in Johann Wolfgang von Goethe's *Wilhelm Meister's Apprenticeship* (1796); James Joyce's *Ulysses* (1922); and Tom Stoppard's *Rosencrantz and Guildenstern Are Dead* (1967).

The Tragedy of Hamlet, Prince of Denmark

THE PERSONS OF THE PLAY

GHOST of Hamlet, the late King of Denmark
KING CLAUDIUS, his brother
QUEEN GERTRUDE of Denmark, widow of King Hamlet, now
    wife of Claudius
Prince HAMLET, son of King Hamlet and Queen Gertrude
POLONIUS, a lord
LAERTES, son of Polonius
OPHELIA, daughter of Polonius
REYNALDO, servant of Polonius
HORATIO ⎫
ROSENCRANTZ ⎬ friends of Prince Hamlet
GUILDENSTERN ⎭
FRANCISCO ⎫
BARNARDO ⎬ soldiers
MARCELLUS ⎭
VALTEMAND ⎫
CORNELIUS ⎪
OSRIC ⎬ courtiers
GENTLEMEN ⎭
A SAILOR
TWO CLOWNS, a gravedigger and his companion
A PRIEST
FORTINBRAS, Prince of Norway
A CAPTAIN in his army
AMBASSADORS from England
PLAYERS, who play the parts of the PROLOGUE, PLAYER KING,
    PLAYER QUEEN, and LUCIANUS, in *The Mousetrap*
Lords, messengers, attendants, guards, soldiers, followers of
    Laertes, sailors

1.1

Enter BARNARDO *and* FRANCISCO, *two sentinels* [*at several° doors*]   separate

BARNARDO Who's there?
FRANCISCO Nay, answer me.[1] Stand and unfold° yourself.   identify
BARNARDO Long live the King!
FRANCISCO   Barnardo?
BARNARDO   He.
FRANCISCO You come most carefully° upon your hour.   dutifully; cautiously
5 BARNARDO 'Tis now struck twelve. Get thee to bed, Francisco.
FRANCISCO For this relief much thanks. 'Tis bitter cold,
And I am sick at heart.

1.1 Location: A guard platform at Elsinore Castle, Denmark.

1. Francisco, as sentry on duty, is responsible for challenging anyone who appears.

BARNARDO	Have you had quiet guard?	
FRANCISCO	Not a mouse stirring.	
BARNARDO	Well, good night.	

If you do meet Horatio and Marcellus,
10   The rivals° of my watch, bid them make haste.   *partners*
       Enter HORATIO *and* MARCELLUS
FRANCISCO   I think I hear them.—Stand! Who's there?
HORATIO   Friends to this ground.°   *country*
MARCELLUS   And liegemen° to the Dane.[2]   *sworn servants*
FRANCISCO   Give° you good night.   *God give*
MARCELLUS   O farewell, honest soldier. Who hath relieved you?
FRANCISCO   Barnardo has my place. Give you good night.   *Exit*
15 MARCELLUS   Holla, Barnardo!
BARNARDO   Say—what, is Horatio there?
HORATIO   A piece of him.
BARNARDO   Welcome, Horatio. Welcome, good Marcellus.
MARCELLUS[3]   What, has this thing appeared again tonight?
20 BARNARDO   I have seen nothing.
MARCELLUS   Horatio says 'tis but our fantasy,
    And will not let belief take hold of him
    Touching this dreaded sight twice seen of us.
    Therefore I have entreated him along
25   With us to watch the minutes of this night,
    That if again this apparition come
    He may approve° our eyes and speak to it.[4]   *verify the evidence of*
HORATIO   Tush, tush, 'twill not appear.
BARNARDO   Sit down a while,
    And let us once again assail your ears,
30   That are so fortified against our story,
    What we two nights have seen.
HORATIO   Well, sit we down,
    And let us hear Barnardo speak of this.
BARNARDO   Last night of all,°   *Just last night*
    When yon same star that's westward from the pole°   *polestar*
35   Had made his° course t'illume that part of heaven   *its*
    Where now it burns, Marcellus and myself,
    The bell then beating one—
       Enter the GHOST [*in complete armour, holding a trun-
       cheon, with his beaver up*][5]
MARCELLUS   Peace, break thee off. Look where it comes again.
BARNARDO   In the same figure like the King that's dead.
40 MARCELLUS [*to* HORATIO]   Thou art a scholar—speak to it, Horatio.
BARNARDO   Looks it not like the King?—Mark it, Horatio.
HORATIO   Most like. It harrows me with fear and wonder.
BARNARDO   It would° be spoke to.   *wishes to*
MARCELLUS   Question it, Horatio.
HORATIO [*to the* GHOST]   What art thou that usurp'st[6] this time of night,
45   Together with that fair and warlike form
    In which the majesty of buried Denmark°   *the buried King*

2. King of Denmark.
3. Q2 gives this line to Horatio.
4. A ghost was believed to speak only when spoken to. As a precaution, the experiment will be conducted by an educated man (Horatio) who knows Latin (the language effective for exorcising demonic spirits).
5. Holding a baton (military commander's sign of office), with his visor ("beaver") raised.
6. Wrongfully seize (both the night and the shape of the King). The familiar "thou" would be an inappropriate form of address for a real king.

Did sometimes° march? By heaven, I charge thee speak.   *formerly*
MARCELLUS   It is offended.
BARNARDO   See, it stalks away.
HORATIO [*to the* GHOST]   Stay, speak, speak, I charge thee speak.
                                                            Exit GHOST
50   MARCELLUS   'Tis gone, and will not answer.
BARNARDO   How now, Horatio? You tremble and look pale.
       Is not this something more than fantasy?
       What think you on't?°   *of it*
HORATIO   Before my God, I might not this believe
55   Without the sensible° and true avouch°   *sensory / testimony*
       Of mine own eyes.
MARCELLUS   Is it not like the King?
HORATIO   As thou art to thyself.
       Such was the very armour he had on
60   When he th'ambitious Norway° combated.   *King of Norway*
       So frowned he once when in an angry parley°   *debate*
       He smote the sledded Polacks[7] on the ice.
       'Tis strange.
MARCELLUS   Thus twice before, and just at this dead hour,
65   With martial stalk hath he gone by our watch.
HORATIO   In what particular thought to work[8] I know not,
       But in the gross and scope of my opinion[9]
       This bodes some strange eruption° to our state.   *calamity*
MARCELLUS   Good now,° sit down, and tell me, he that knows,   *(an entreaty)*
70   Why this same strict and most observant watch
       So nightly toils the subject of the land,[1]
       And why such daily cast° of brazen cannon,   *production*
       And foreign mart° for implements of war,   *trade*
       Why such impress° of shipwrights, whose sore task   *drafting*
75   Does not divide the Sunday from the week:
       What might be toward° that this sweaty haste   *impending*
       Doth make the night joint-labourer with the day,
       Who is't that can inform me?
HORATIO   That can I—
       At least the whisper goes so: our last king,
80   Whose image even but now appeared to us,
       Was as you know by Fortinbras of Norway,
       Thereto pricked° on by a most emulate° pride,   *spurred / rivalrous*
       Dared to the combat; in which our valiant Hamlet—
       For so this side of our known world esteemed him—
85   Did slay this Fortinbras, who by a sealed compact[2]
       Well ratified by law and heraldry[3]
       Did forfeit with his life all those his lands
       Which he stood seized on° to the conqueror;   *held possession of*
       Against the which a moiety competent°   *an equal portion*
90   Was gagèd° by our King, which had returned[4]   *staked*
       To the inheritance° of Fortinbras   *ownership*
       Had he been vanquisher, as by the same cov'nant
       And carriage of the article designed[5]

7. Poles who traveled by sled.
8. *In . . . work:* What precise theory to follow.
9. But in my considered opinion.
1. *So . . . land:* Requires the country's subjects to toil
every night.

2. A mutually agreed-upon contract ("compact") to
which each set his seal.
3. Properly ratified in accordance with heraldic law.
4. Which would have gone.
5. And execution of the contract's provision.

	His fell to Hamlet. Now sir, young Fortinbras,	
95	Of unimproved° mettle hot and full,	*untested; untrained*
	Hath in the skirts° of Norway here and there	*outlying parts*
	Sharked up a list[6] of landless[7] resolutes	
	For food and diet to some enterprise	
	That hath a stomach in't,[8] which is no other—	
100	And it doth well° appear unto our state—	*obviously*
	But to recover of us by strong hand[9]	
	And terms compulsative° those foresaid lands	*forcible*
	So by his father lost. And this, I take it,	
	Is the main motive of our preparations,	
105	The source of this our watch, and the chief head°	*source*
	Of this post-haste and rummage[1] in the land.[2]	
106.1	BARNARDO *I think it be no other but e'en so.*	
	Well may it sort° that this portentous figure	*be fitting*
	Comes armèd through our watch so like the king	
	That was and is the question° of these wars.	*cause*
106.5	HORATIO *A mote° it is to trouble the mind's eye.*	*speck of dust*
	In the most high and palmy° state of Rome,	*flourishing*
	A little ere the mightiest Julius fell,	
	The graves stood tenantless, and the sheeted° dead	*shrouded*
	Did squeak and gibber in the Roman streets	
106.10	*At stars with trains of fire,[3] and dews of blood,*	
	Disasters[4] in the sun; and the moist star,[5]	
	Upon whose influence Neptune's empire stands,°	*depends*
	Was sick almost to doomsday with eclipse.[6]	
	And even the like precurse° of feared events,	*forerunner*
106.15	*As harbingers° preceding still° the fates,*	*heralds / always*
	And prologue to the omen° coming on,	*disastrous event*
	Have heaven and earth together demonstrated	
	Unto our climature° and countrymen.	*region*
	Enter the GHOST [*as before*]	
	But soft,° behold—lo where it comes again!	*hush*
	I'll cross[7] it though it blast° me.—Stay, illusion.	*wither*
	[*The* GHOST] *spreads his arms*	
	If thou hast any sound or use of voice,	
110	Speak to me.	
	If there be any good thing to be done	
	That may to thee do ease and grace to me,	
	Speak to me.	
	If thou art privy to thy country's fate	
115	Which happily° foreknowing may avoid,	*perhaps; fortunately*
	O speak!	
	Or if thou hast uphoarded in thy life	
	Extorted treasure in the womb of earth—	

6. Gathered together indiscriminately (as a shark takes prey) a band ("list").
7. Q1, Q2 print "lawless," which accurately conveys Horatio's view of these men; F's "landless," however, provides a more specific motive for their enlistment. *stomach:* courageous action; challenge to the pride (of both the Prince and his men).
8. *For . . . in't:* The men will "feed" his enterprise, they are fed in return for their service. *stomach:* courageous action; challenge to the pride (of both the Prince and his men).
9. By main force (punning on the name "Fortinbras," literally "strong arm").
1. Of this feverish activity and commotion.

2. After this line, Q2 contains the following passage, 106.1–106.18, omitted in F.
3. At comets. "At" is emended from Q2's "As," which would require another verb.
4. Malevolent influences (astrological term).
5. The moon, thought to control tides by drawing water out of the sea ("Neptune's empire," line 106.12).
6. Eclipses of sun and moon would accompany Christ's return to earth on Judgment Day (see Revelation 6:12).
7. Confront, cross its path; also, make the sign of the cross (to counter its evil influence).

For which, they say, you spirits oft walk in death—
                    The cock crows
120   Speak of it, stay and speak.—Stop it, Marcellus.
MARCELLUS   Shall I strike at it with my partisan?°   spear-handled blade
HORATIO   Do, if it will not stand.
BARNARDO   'Tis here.
HORATIO   'Tis here.
                                                    Exit GHOST

MARCELLUS   'Tis gone.
        We do it wrong, being so majestical,
125   To offer it the show of violence,
        For it is as the air invulnerable,
        And our vain blows malicious mockery.
BARNARDO   It was about to speak when the cock crew.
HORATIO   And then it started like a guilty thing
130   Upon a fearful summons. I have heard
        The cock, that is the trumpet to the morn,
        Doth with his lofty and shrill-sounding throat
        Awake the god of day,⁸ and at his warning,
        Whether in sea or fire, in earth or air,
135   Th'extravagant and erring⁹ spirit hies°   hurries
        To his confine;° and of the truth herein   enclosure
        This present object° made probation.°   example / proof
MARCELLUS   It faded on the crowing of the cock.
        Some say that ever 'gainst° that season comes   always when
140   Wherein our saviour's birth is celebrated
        The bird of dawning singeth all night long;
        And then, they say, no spirit can walk abroad,
        The nights are wholesome; then no planets strike,¹
        No fairy takes,° nor witch hath power to charm,   bewitches
145   So hallowed and so gracious° is the time.   full of God's grace
HORATIO   So have I heard, and do in part believe it.
        But look, the morn in russet mantle clad
        Walks o'er the dew of yon high eastern hill.
        Break we our watch up, and by my advice
150   Let us impart what we have seen tonight
        Unto young Hamlet; for upon my life,
        This spirit, dumb to us, will speak to him.
        Do you consent we shall acquaint him with it,
        As needful in our loves,² fitting our duty?
155   MARCELLUS   Let's do't, I pray; and I this morning know
        Where we shall find him most conveniently.   *Exeunt*

1.2

Flourish. Enter CLAUDIUS, *King of Denmark,* GERTRUDE
the Queen, [*members of the*] *Council,* [*such*] *as* POLON-
IUS, *his son* LAERTES *and* [*daughter*] OPHELIA, [*Prince*]
HAMLET [*dressed in black*], *cum aliis*°   with others
KING CLAUDIUS   Though yet of Hamlet our¹ dear brother's death
        The memory be green, and that it us befitted

---

8. The sun god, Phoebus Apollo.
9. Wandering out of its boundaries.
1. When they were in certain unfavorable astrological positions, heavenly bodies were thought to exercise a negative influence on earthly events.

2. As necessary because of the love we have for him.
1.2 Location: The castle.
1. My. (Kings often referred to themselves in the plural, the royal "we," although in the lines that follow, Claudius may also be talking about Danes in general.)

To bear our hearts in grief and our whole kingdom
To be contracted in one brow of woe,[2]
5   Yet so far hath discretion fought with nature°   *natural love*
That we with wisest sorrow think on him
Together with remembrance of ourselves.[3]
Therefore our sometime° sister, now our queen,[4]   *former*
Th'imperial jointress° of this warlike state,   *joint possessor*
10   Have we as 'twere with a defeated joy,
With one auspicious and one dropping eye,[5]
With mirth in funeral and with dirge in marriage,
In equal scale weighing delight and dole,°   *sorrow*
Taken to wife. Nor have we herein barred°   *excluded; contradicted*
15   Your better wisdoms, which have freely gone
With this affair along. For all, our thanks.
Now follows that you know° young Fortinbras,   *should be informed that*
Holding a weak supposal° of our worth,   *a poor opinion*
Or thinking by our late dear brother's death
20   Our state to be disjoint° and out of frame,°   *fractured / order*
Co-leaguèd with the dream of his advantage,[6]
He hath not failed to pester us with message
Importing° the surrender of those lands   *Concerning*
Lost by his father, with all bonds° of law,   *legal procedures*
25   To our most valiant brother. So much for him.
         Enter VALTEMAND *and* CORNELIUS
Now for ourself, and for this time of meeting,
Thus much the business is: we have here writ
To Norway, uncle of young Fortinbras —
Who, impotent and bed-rid, scarcely hears
30   Of this his nephew's purpose — to suppress
His further gait° herein, in that the levies,   *progress*
The lists, and full proportions are all made
Out of his subject;[7] and we here dispatch
You, good Cornelius, and you, Valtemand,
35   For bearers of this greeting to old Norway,
Giving to you no further personal power
To business with the King more than the scope
Of these dilated articles allow.
Farewell, and let your haste commend your duty.[8]
40   VALTEMAND   In that and all things will we show our duty.
KING CLAUDIUS   We doubt it nothing,° heartily farewell.   *not at all*
         Exeunt VALTEMAND *and* CORNELIUS
And now, Laertes, what's the news with you?
You told us of some suit. What is't, Laertes?
You cannot speak of reason to the Dane°   *the Danish King*
45   And lose your voice. What wouldst thou beg, Laertes,

---

2. To be drawn together into a collective expression of mourning (playing on "the frowning brow of a mourner").
3. *we . . . ourselves:* "He is not wise that is not wise for himself" was proverbial.
4. English canon law forbade marriage between former brother- and sister-in-law (Leviticus 18:16; Book of Common Prayer); it was on this ground that Henry VIII annulled his marriage to his brother's widow and married Anne Boleyn, Queen Elizabeth's mother. The relationship between Claudius and Gertrude could thus be regarded as incestuous. In some early Germanic societies, however, a new king customarily married the late king's widow.
5. One eye looking hopefully, the other downcast, or "dropping" tears.
6. Reinforced by the illusion of his own advantageous position.
7. *in that . . . subject:* since the moneys, enlistments, and forces are made up of his (the King of Norway's) subjects.
8. Let your swift departure (rather than elaborate speeches) show your loyalty.

That shall not be my offer, not thy asking?[9]
The head is not more native[1] to the heart,
The hand more instrumental to the mouth,
Than is the throne of Denmark to thy father.
What wouldst thou have, Laertes?

50 LAERTES   Dread my° lord,   *My revered*
Your leave° and favour° to return to France,   *permission / approval*
From whence though willingly I came to Denmark
To show my duty in your coronation,
Yet now I must confess, that duty done,
55 My thoughts and wishes bend again towards France
And bow them to your gracious leave and pardon.[2]
KING CLAUDIUS   Have you your father's leave? What says Polonius?
POLONIUS   He hath, my lord, wrung from me my slow leave
By laboursome petition, and at last
60 Upon his will° I sealed my hard° consent.   *desire / reluctant*
I do beseech you give him leave to go.
KING CLAUDIUS   Take thy fair hour,[3] Laertes. Time be thine,
And thy best graces spend it at thy will.[4]
But now, my cousin[5] Hamlet, and my son—
65 HAMLET   A little more than kin and less than kind.[6]
KING CLAUDIUS   How is it that the clouds still hang on you?
HAMLET   Not so, my lord, I am too much i'th' sun.[7]
QUEEN GERTRUDE   Good Hamlet, cast thy nightly colour[8] off,
And let thine eye look like a friend on Denmark.[9]
70 Do not for ever with thy vailèd lids°   *downcast eyes*
Seek for thy noble father in the dust.
Thou know'st 'tis common—all that lives must die,
Passing through nature to eternity.
HAMLET   Ay, madam, it is common.[1]
QUEEN GERTRUDE   If it be,
75 Why seems it so particular° with thee?   *personal*
HAMLET   Seems, madam? Nay, it *is*. I know not 'seems'.
'Tis not alone my inky cloak, good-mother,[2]
Nor customary suits of solemn black,
Nor windy suspiration° of forced breath,   *sighs*
80 No, nor the fruitful° river in the eye,   *copious*
Nor the dejected haviour° of the visage,   *expression*
Together with all forms, moods, shows of grief
That can denote me truly. These indeed 'seem',
For they are actions that a man might play;
85 But I have that within which passeth show—
These but the trappings and the suits of woe.

---

9. *What wouldst . . . asking*: What could you ask of me that I would not offer before you asked?
1. Naturally connected; an allusion to the "body politic," headed by the king and having as its heart the king's council.
2. And humbly ask you to grant permission to depart.
3. Opportunity (while you are young).
4. *Time . . . will*: Your time is your own; use it in accordance with your best qualities.
5. Kinsman (outside one's immediate family).
6. "The nearer in kin the less in kindness" was proverbial. Hamlet's riddling comment indicates first that there is lit-

tle warmth in their new, only nominally closer relationship. Playing on "kind" in the sense of natural type or offspring, however, he also refers to the incestuousness of the marriage that has produced their unnatural kinship.
7. In the sunshine of Claudius's favor; also, feeling the burden of being his father's son (not Claudius's).
8. Black mourning garments and melancholic behavior.
9. Both the King of Denmark and the country.
1. Commonplace (?); crude (?).
2. Stepmother. The hyphen, an editorial addition to F's "good Mother," calls attention to the ironic implication of Hamlet's words.

KING CLAUDIUS   'Tis sweet and commendable in your nature, Hamlet,
To give these mourning duties to your father;
But you must know your father lost a father;
90   That father lost, lost his; and the survivor bound
In filial obligation for some term
To do obsequious sorrow.[3] But to persever
In obstinate condolement° is a course   *lamenting*
Of impious stubbornness, 'tis unmanly grief,
95   It shows a will most incorrect° to heaven,   *unsubmissive*
A heart unfortified, a mind impatient,[4]
An understanding simple° and unschooled;   *childish*
For what we know must be, and is as common
As any the most vulgar thing to sense,[5]
100   Why should we in our peevish opposition
Take it to heart? Fie, 'tis a fault to heaven,
A fault against the dead, a fault to nature,
To reason most absurd, whose common theme
Is death of fathers, and who still° hath cried   *always*
105   From the first corpse[6] till he that died today,
'This must be so'. We pray you throw to earth
This unprevailing° woe, and think of us   *unavailing*
As of a father; for let the world take note
You are the most immediate° to our throne,   *next in succession*
110   And with no less nobility° of love   *purity; generosity*
Than that which dearest father bears his son
Do I impart towards you. For your intent
In going back to school in Wittenberg,[7]
It is most retrograde° to our desire,   *contrary*
115   And we beseech you bend you° to remain   *yield, agree*
Here in the cheer and comfort of our eye,
Our chiefest courtier, cousin, and our son.
QUEEN GERTRUDE   Let not thy mother lose her prayers, Hamlet.
I pray thee stay with us, go not to Wittenberg.
120   HAMLET   I shall in all my best obey you, madam.
KING CLAUDIUS   Why, 'tis a loving and a fair reply.
Be as ourself in Denmark. [*To* GERTRUDE] Madam, come.
This gentle and unforced accord of Hamlet
Sits smiling to° my heart; in grace° whereof,   *Pleases / honor*
125   No jocund health that Denmark° drinks today   *the King*
But the great cannon to the clouds shall tell,°   *sound*
And the King's rouse[8] the heavens shall bruit again,°   *loudly echo*
Re-speaking earthly thunder. Come, away.
                    Flourish. Exeunt all but HAMLET
HAMLET   O that this too too solid[9] flesh would melt,
130   Thaw, and resolve° itself into a dew,   *dissolve*
Or that the Everlasting had not fixed
His canon° 'gainst self-slaughter! O God, O God,   *law*
How weary, stale, flat, and unprofitable

3. To mourn as befits obsequies, or funeral ceremonies.
4. A heart not strengthened (against emotion or misfortune), a mind unprepared to suffer.
5. As the most obvious and ordinary thing we perceive using our senses.
6. Of Abel, the first human to die. A particularly infelicitous example, since Abel was murdered by his brother, Cain.

7. The birthplace of Protestantism, the university of Luther and Faustus; many Danes studied there.
8. Bout of drinking.
9. F's reading; Q2 has "sallied," a possible spelling of "sullied." Editors have seen wordplay on "sallied," or salty, tear-soaked (salting was a method of preserving meat), and "sullied," or contaminated, ill-used. "Solid" accords best with "melt."

Seem to me all the uses° of this world!   *customs; business*
135 Fie on't, ah fie, fie! 'Tis an unweeded garden
That grows to seed; things rank and gross in nature
Possess it merely.° That it should come to this—   *entirely*
But two months dead—nay, not so much, not two—
So excellent a king, that was to this
140 Hyperion to a satyr,[1] so loving to my mother
That he might not beteem° the winds of heaven   *permit*
Visit her face too roughly! Heaven and earth,
Must I remember? Why, she would hang on him
As if increase of appetite had grown
145 By what it fed on, and yet within a month—
Let me not think on't; frailty, thy name is woman—
A little month, or ere° those shoes were old   *before*
With which she followed my poor father's body,
Like Niobe, all tears,[2] why she, even she—
150 O God, a beast that wants discourse of reason[3]
Would have mourned longer!—married with mine uncle,
My father's brother, but no more like my father
Than I to Hercules; within a month,
Ere yet the salt of most unrighteous tears
155 Had left the flushing of her gallèd° eyes,   *inflamed*
She married. O most wicked speed, to post°   *hurry*
With such dexterity to incestuous sheets!
It is not, nor it cannot come to good.
But break, my heart, for I must hold my tongue.
            Enter HORATIO, MARCELLUS, *and* BARNARDO
HORATIO   Hail to your lordship.
160 HAMLET   I am glad to see you well.
Horatio—or I do forget myself.
HORATIO   The same, my lord, and your poor servant ever.
HAMLET   Sir, my good friend; I'll change° that name with you.   *exchange*
And what make you from[4] Wittenberg, Horatio?—
Marcellus.
165 MARCELLUS   My good lord.
HAMLET   I am very glad to see you. [*To* BARNARDO]   Good even, sir.—
But what in faith make you from Wittenberg?
HORATIO   A truant disposition, good my lord.
HAMLET   I would not have your enemy say so,
170 Nor shall you do mine ear that violence
To make it truster of your own report
Against yourself. I know you are no truant.
But what is your affair in Elsinore?
We'll teach you to drink deep ere you depart.
175 HORATIO   My lord, I came to see your father's funeral.
HAMLET   I prithee do not mock me, fellow-student;
I think it was to see my mother's wedding.
HORATIO   Indeed, my lord, it followed hard upon.
HAMLET   Thrift, thrift, Horatio. The funeral baked meats°   *meat pies and pastries*
180 Did coldly° furnish forth the marriage tables.   *when cold*
Would I had met my dearest° foe in heaven   *most hated*

---

1. So . . . satyr: That King was to this as the sun god (Hyperion, a Titan) is to a lustful half goat (mythological companion of the wine god, Bacchus).
2. Niobe's fourteen children were killed by Apollo and Artemis to punish her for boasting about them. She continued to weep bitterly even after she was turned to stone.
3. That lacks the faculty of rational thought.
4. What are you doing away from.

Ere I had ever seen that day, Horatio.
My father—methinks I see my father.
HORATIO   O where, my lord?
HAMLET   In my mind's eye, Horatio.
185 HORATIO   I saw him once. A° was a goodly king.   *He*
HAMLET   A was a man. Take him for all in all,
   I shall not look upon his like again.
HORATIO   My lord, I think I saw him yesternight.
HAMLET   Saw? Who?
190 HORATIO   My lord, the King your father.
HAMLET   The King my father?
HORATIO   Season° your admiration° for a while   *Moderate / amazement*
   With an attent° ear till I may deliver,   *attentive*
   Upon the witness of these gentlemen,
   This marvel to you.
195 HAMLET   For God's love let me hear!
HORATIO   Two nights together had these gentlemen,
   Marcellus and Barnardo, on their watch,
   In the dead waste° and middle of the night,   *stillness*
   Been thus encountered. A figure like your father,
200 Armed at all points° exactly, cap-à-pie,°   *details / head to foot*
   Appears before them, and with solemn march
   Goes slow and stately by them. Thrice he walked
   By their oppressed and fear-surprisèd eyes
   Within his truncheon's[5] length, whilst they distilled°   *dissolved*
205 Almost to jelly with the act° of fear   *effect*
   Stand dumb and speak not to him. This to me
   In dreadful secrecy impart they did,
   And I with them the third night kept the watch,
   Where, as they had delivered, both in time,
210 Form of the thing, each word made true and good,
   The apparition comes. I knew your father;
   These hands are not more like.[6]
HAMLET   But where was this?
MARCELLUS   My lord, upon the platform where we watched.
HAMLET   Did you not speak to it?
HORATIO   My lord, I did,
215 But answer made it none; yet once methought
   It lifted up it° head and did address   *its*
   Itself to motion like as it would speak,[7]
   But even° then the morning cock crew loud,   *just*
   And at the sound it shrunk in haste away
   And vanished from our sight.
220 HAMLET   'Tis very strange.
HORATIO   As I do live, my honoured lord, 'tis true,
   And we did think it writ down° in our duty   *prescribed*
   To let you know of it.
HAMLET   Indeed, indeed, sirs; but this troubles me.—
   Hold you the watch tonight?
225 BARNARDO *and* MARCELLUS   We do, my lord.
HAMLET   Armed, say you?

5. Officer's baton (see stage direction at 1.1.37).
6. These hands are not more like each other than the
apparition was like King Hamlet.

7. *address . . . speak:* start to move as though it wished to
speak.

BARNARDO *and* MARCELLUS   Armed, my lord.
HAMLET   From top to toe?
BARNARDO *and* MARCELLUS   My lord, from head to foot.
HAMLET   Then saw you not his
    face.
HORATIO   O yes, my lord, he wore his beaver up.
HAMLET   What° looked he? Frowningly?   *How*
HORATIO   A countenance more
    In sorrow than in anger.
230   HAMLET   Pale or red?
HORATIO   Nay, very pale.
HAMLET   And fixed his eyes upon you?
HORATIO   Most constantly.
HAMLET   I would I had been there.
HORATIO   It would have much amazed you.
235   HAMLET   Very like, very like. Stayed it long?
HORATIO   While one with moderate haste might tell° a hundred.   *count*
BARNARDO *and* MARCELLUS   Longer, longer.
HORATIO   Not when I saw't.
HAMLET   His beard was grizzly,° no?   *gray*
240   HORATIO   It was as I have seen it in his life,
    A sable silvered.⁸
HAMLET   I'll watch tonight. Perchance
    'Twill walk again.
HORATIO   I warrant° you it will.   *guarantee*
HAMLET   If it assume my noble father's person
    I'll speak to it though hell itself should gape
245   And bid me hold my peace. I pray you all,
    If you have hitherto concealed this sight,
    Let it be treble⁹ in your silence still,
    And whatsoever else shall hap° tonight,   *occur*
    Give it an understanding but no tongue.
250   I will requite your loves. So fare ye well.
    Upon the platform 'twixt eleven and twelve
    I'll visit you.
ALL THREE   Our duty to your honour.
HAMLET   Your love, as mine to you. Farewell.
                              Exeunt [all but HAMLET]
    My father's spirit in arms! All is not well.
255   I doubt° some foul play. Would the night were come.   *suspect*
    Till then, sit still, my soul. Foul deeds will rise,
    Though all the earth o'erwhelm them, to men's eyes.   *Exit*

1.3

    Enter LAERTES *and* OPHELIA, *his sister*
LAERTES   My necessaries are inbarqued.° Farewell.   *aboard ship*
    And, sister, as the winds give benefit
    And convoy is assistant,¹ do not sleep
    But let me hear from you.
OPHELIA   Do you doubt that?
5   LAERTES   For Hamlet and the trifling of his favour,

---

8. Black sprinkled with white.
9. Triply (F's reading); most editors follow Q2's "tenable" (that is, able to be held).

1.3 Location: Polonius's apartments in the castle.
1. And means of transport is available.

Hold it a fashion and a toy in blood,
A violet in the youth of primy nature,
Forward[2] not permanent, sweet not lasting,
The perfume and suppliance° of a minute,   *diversion*
No more.

OPHELIA   No more but so?

10 LAERTES   Think it no more.
For nature crescent° does not grow alone   *growing*
In thews° and bulk, but as his temple° waxes   *muscles / body*
The inward service° of the mind and soul   *responsibility*
Grows wide withal.° Perhaps he loves you now,   *along with it*
15 And now no soil° nor cautel° doth besmirch   *stain / deception*
The virtue of his will;° but you must fear,   *intentions; desires*
His greatness weighed,[3] his will is not his own,
For he himself is subject to his birth.
He may not, as unvalued° persons do,   *common*
20 Carve for himself,[4] for on his choice depends
The sanity[5] and health of the whole state;
And therefore must his choice be circumscribed
Unto the voice° and yielding° of that body[6]   *vote / consent*
Whereof he is the head. Then if he says he loves you,
25 It fits° your wisdom so far to believe it   *befits*
As he in his peculiar sect and force[7]
May give his saying deed,[8] which is no further
Than the main° voice of Denmark goes withal.   *collective*
Then weigh what loss your honour may sustain
30 If with too credent° ear you list° his songs,   *trusting / listen to*
Or lose your heart, or your chaste treasure open
To his unmastered° importunity.   *uncontrolled*
Fear it, Ophelia, fear it, my dear sister,
And keep within the rear of your affection,[9]
35 Out of the shot and danger of desire.
The chariest° maid is prodigal enough   *most careful, modest*
If she unmask her beauty to the moon.[1]
Virtue itself scapes not calumnious strokes.
The canker galls the infants[2] of the spring
40 Too oft before their buttons be disclosed,°   *buds are open*
And in the morn and liquid dew of youth
Contagious blastments° are most imminent.   *blights*
Be wary then; best safety lies in fear;
Youth to itself rebels, though none else near.[3]
45 OPHELIA   I shall th'effect of this good lesson keep
As watchman to my heart; but, good my brother,
Do not, as some ungracious° pastors do,   *ungodly*
Show me the steep and thorny way to heaven
Whilst like a puffed° and reckless libertine   *proud*

---

2. *a toy . . . / Forward:* a passing sexual fancy, a flower of
his natural impulses in their prime, early blooming ("forward").
3. When his high rank is considered.
4. Help himself to his own choice of the roast (proverbially, to choose for himself).
5. Well-being, emended from F's "sanctity"; Q2 prints
"safety."
6. Body politic; nation.
7. His special rank and power (F). Q2 (and most editors)
give "particular act and place," which has been interpre-

ted as "power of action and social position."
8. May act on his promise.
9. And be restrained, despite the forward march of your
feelings.
1. *prodigal . . . moon:* risk-taking enough if she exposes
herself to the chaste moon. (Upper-class women wore
masks to screen their complexions from the sun.) Q2
introduces lines 36, 38, and 39 with quotation marks,
identifying these sentences as proverbial or noteworthy.
2. The cankerworm injures the shoots.
3. Young people are naturally rebellious.

50 Himself the primrose path of dalliance treads
    And recks° not his own rede.°   *heeds / advice*
    LAERTES   O fear me not.°   *fear not for me*
        Enter POLONIUS
    I stay too long—but here my father comes.
    A double blessing is a double grace;
    Occasion smiles upon a second leave.[4]
55 POLONIUS   Yet here, Laertes? Aboard, aboard, for shame!
    The wind sits in the shoulder° of your sail,   *at the back*
    And you are stayed° for. There—my blessing with thee,   *waited*
    And these few precepts in thy memory
    See thou character.° Give thy thoughts no tongue,   *inscribe*
60 Nor any unproportioned° thought his act.   *unruly*
    Be thou familiar° but by no means vulgar.[5]   *friendly*
    The friends thou hast, and their adoption tried,°   *their friendship tested*
    Grapple them to thy soul with hoops of steel,
    But do not dull° thy palm with entertainment[6]   *callous*
65 Of each new-hatched unfledged comrade. Beware
    Of entrance to a quarrel, but being in,
    Bear't° that th'opposèd may beware of thee.   *Manage it so*
    Give every man thine ear but few thy voice.
    Take each man's censure,° but reserve thy judgement.   *opinion*
70 Costly thy habit° as thy purse can buy,   *dress*
    But not expressed in fancy;° rich not gaudy;   *bizarre excess*
    For the apparel oft proclaims the man,
    And they in France of the best rank and station
    Are of all most select and generous chief in that.[7]
75 Neither a borrower nor a lender be,
    For loan oft loses both itself and friend,
    And borrowing dulls the edge of husbandry.°   *economy*
    This above all—to thine own self be true,
    And it must follow, as the night the day,
80 Thou canst not then be false to any man.
    Farewell—my blessing season° this in thee.   *mature*
    LAERTES   Most humbly do I take my leave, my lord.
    POLONIUS   The time invites you. Go; your servants tend.°   *wait*
    LAERTES   Farewell, Ophelia, and remember well
    What I have said to you.
85 OPHELIA   'Tis in my memory locked,
    And you yourself shall keep the key of it.
    LAERTES   Farewell.   *Exit*
    POLONIUS   What is't, Ophelia, he hath said to you?
    OPHELIA   So please you, something touching the Lord Hamlet.
90 POLONIUS   Marry,[8] well bethought.
    'Tis told me he hath very oft of late
    Given private time to you, and you yourself
    Have of your audience° been most free and bounteous.   *attention*
    If it be so—as so 'tis put on° me,   *suggested to*
95 And that in way of caution—I must tell you
    You do not understand yourself so clearly

---

4. Favorable circumstances provide us with a second
farewell.
5. Indiscriminately social.
6. Greeting (handshaking).

7. Are of all people the most adept at displaying rank in
fine appearance.
8. By the Virgin Mary, a mild oath.

As it behoves my daughter and your honour.
What is between you? Give me up the truth.
OPHELIA   He hath, my lord, of late made many tenders°   *offers*
100   Of his affection to me.
POLONIUS   Affection, pooh! You speak like a green girl
         Unsifted° in such perilous circumstance.   *Inexperienced*
         Do you believe his 'tenders' as you call them?
OPHELIA   I do not know, my lord, what I should think.
105   POLONIUS   Marry, I'll teach you: think yourself a baby
         That you have ta'en his tenders for true pay,
         Which are not sterling.⁹ Tender° yourself more dearly,   *Value; protect*
         Or—not to crack the wind of the poor phrase,
         Running it thus¹—you'll tender me a fool.²
110   OPHELIA   My lord, he hath importuned me with love
         In honourable fashion—
POLONIUS   Ay, fashion° you may call it. Go to,³ go to.   *conventional flattery*
OPHELIA   And hath given countenance° to his speech, my lord,   *authority*
         With all the vows of heaven.
115   POLONIUS   Ay, springes to catch woodcocks.⁴ I do know
         When the blood burns how prodigal° the soul   *lavishly*
         Lends the tongue vows. These blazes, daughter,
         Giving more light than heat, extinct° in both   *extinguished*
         Even in their promise as it is a-making,
120   You must not take for fire. From this time, daughter,
         Be somewhat scanter of your maiden presence.
         Set your entreatments at a higher rate
         Than a command to parley.⁵ For Lord Hamlet,
         Believe so much in° him, that he is young,   *concerning*
125   And with a larger tether may he walk
         Than may be given you. In few,° Ophelia,   *brief*
         Do not believe his vows, for they are brokers,°   *go-betweens*
         Not of the dye which their investments° show,   *clerical vestments*
         But mere imploratators° of unholy suits,   *solicitors*
130   Breathing° like sanctified and pious bawds   *Speaking*
         The better to beguile. This is for all—
         I would not, in plain terms, from this time forth
         Have you so slander° any moment leisure   *disgrace*
         As to give words or talk with the Lord Hamlet.
135   Look to't, I charge you. Come your ways.°   *Come along*
OPHELIA   I shall obey, my lord.   *Exeunt*

1.4

Enter [Prince] HAMLET, HORATIO, *and* MARCELLUS
HAMLET   The air bites shrewdly,° it is very cold.   *sharply*
HORATIO   It is a nipping and an eager° air.   *a bitter*
HAMLET   What hour now?
HORATIO   I think it lacks of twelve.
5   MARCELLUS   No, it is struck.
HORATIO   Indeed? I heard it not. Then it draws near the season°   *time*
         Wherein the spirit held his wont° to walk.   *was accustomed*

---

9. Genuine currency.
1. *crack . . . thus:* ruin the phrase with overworking (like
a "broken-winded" horse).
2. A multiple pun: make me look foolish; seem yourself
a fool; show me a baby (idiomatically, a "fool").

3. That's enough; come, come.
4. (Obvious) traps for proverbially gullible birds.
5. *Set . . . parley:* Do not negotiate a surrender (of your
chastity) just because he asks to speak with you.
1.4 Location: The castle's battlements.

A flourish of trumpets, and two pieces [of ordnance]°   cannons
goes off
What does this mean, my lord?
HAMLET   The King doth wake tonight and takes his rouse,
10   Keeps wassail, and the swagg'ring upspring reels,[1]
And as he drains his draughts of Rhenish° down   Rhine wine
The kettle-drum and trumpet thus bray out
The triumph of his pledge.[2]
HORATIO   Is it a custom?
15 HAMLET   Ay, marry is't,
And to my mind, though I am native here
And to the manner° born, it is a custom   custom
More honoured in the breach than the observance.[3]
18.1   *This heavy-headed revel east and west*
Makes us traduced and taxed of other nations.
They clepe° us drunkards, and with swinish phrase   call
Soil our addition;° and indeed it takes   reputation
18.5   *From our achievements, though performed at height,°*   excellently
The pith° and marrow of our attribute.°   heart / attributed glory
So, oft it chances in particular men
That, for some vicious mole of nature[4] in them—
As in their birth,° wherein they are not guilty,   parentage
18.10   *Since nature cannot choose his° origin,*   its
By the o'ergrowth of some complexion,[5]
Oft breaking down the pales° and forts of reason,   fences, boundaries
Or by some habit that too much o'erleavens
The form of plausive manners[6]—that these men,
18.15   *Carrying, I say, the stamp of one defect,*
Being nature's livery or fortune's star,[7]
His virtues else be they as pure as grace,
As infinite as man may undergo,°   sustain
Shall in the general censure° take corruption   the public opinion
18.20   *From that particular fault. The dram of evil[8]*
Doth all the noble substance over-daub[9]
To his own scandal.°   shame
Enter GHOST *[as before]*
HORATIO   Look, my lord, it comes.
20 HAMLET   Angels and ministers of grace defend us!
Be thou a spirit of health or goblin° damned,   demon
Bring with thee airs° from heaven or blasts[1] from hell,   gentle breezes
Be thy intents wicked or charitable,
Thou com'st in such a questionable shape
25 That I will speak to thee. I'll call thee Hamlet,
King, father, royal Dane. O answer me!

---

1. *The King . . . reels:* The King revels and carouses rather than sleeping, has a drinking party ("wassail"), and staggers ("reels") through a wild German dance.
2. His success in draining his cup upon making a toast.
3. Which is more honored in being broken than in being observed. After this line, Q2 has the following passage, 18.1–18.22, omitted in F (possibly in deference to the English queen, Anne of Denmark).
4. Natural blemish that tends to vice.
5. By the disproportionate amount of one humor (see note to 2.2.310–11), and thus an unbalanced personality.
6. *o'erleavens . . . manners:* changes the whole effect of otherwise pleasing ("plausive") manners for the worse (as

too much yeast ruins a batch of bread).
7. Being a congenital defect (the "livery," or clothing, given by nature) or a blemish caused by fortune (the influence of chance astrological events).
8. Tiny amount (eighth of an ounce) of bad qualities. This is a conjectural emendation of Q2's "eale," although there is no consensus on the correct reading.
9. *Doth . . . over-daub:* Obscures the virtuous essence with adhering dirt. Emended from Q2's "of a doubt," an incomplete thought; "often dout" (extinguish) is another plausible correction.
1. Pestilent gusts.

Let me not burst in ignorance, but tell
Why thy canonized° bones, hearsèd° in death,   consecrated / coffined
Have burst their cerements,° why the sepulchre   grave clothes
30 Wherein we saw thee quietly enurned°   entombed
Hath oped his ponderous and marble jaws
To cast thee up again. What may this mean,
That thou, dead corpse, again in complete steel,°   armor
Revisitst thus the glimpses of the moon,[2]
35 Making night hideous, and we fools of nature[3]
So horridly to shake our disposition°   mental foundations
With thoughts beyond the reaches of our souls?
Say, why is this? Wherefore? What should we do?
          GHOST *beckons* HAMLET
HORATIO   It beckons you to go away with it
40 As if it some impartment° did desire   communication
To you alone.
MARCELLUS [*to* HAMLET]   Look with what courteous action
It wafts° you to a more removèd ground.   beckons
But do not go with it.
HORATIO [*to* HAMLET]   No, by no means.
HAMLET   It will not speak. Then will I follow it.
HORATIO   Do not, my lord.
45 HAMLET   Why, what should be the fear?
I do not set my life at a pin's fee,°   value
And for my soul, what can it do to that,
Being a thing immortal as itself?
          [GHOST *beckons* HAMLET]
It waves me forth again. I'll follow it.
50 HORATIO   What if it tempt you toward the flood,° my lord,   sea
Or to the dreadful summit of the cliff
That beetles o'er° his base into the sea,   overhangs
And there assume some other horrible form
Which might deprive your sovereignty of reason
55 And draw you into madness? Think of it.[4]
55.1   *The very place puts toys of desperation,[5]*
          Without more motive,° into every brain   cause
          That looks so many fathoms to the sea
          And hears it roar beneath.
          [GHOST *beckons* HAMLET]
HAMLET   It wafts me still. [*To* GHOST] Go on, I'll follow thee.
MARCELLUS   You shall not go, my lord.
HAMLET   Hold off your hand.
HORATIO   Be ruled. You shall not go.
HAMLET   My fate cries out,
And makes each petty artere° in this body   artery
60 As hardy as the Nemean lion's[6] nerve.
          [GHOST *beckons* HAMLET]
Still am I called. Unhand me, gentlemen.
By heav'n, I'll make a ghost of him that lets° me.   hinders
I say, away! [*To* GHOST] Go on, I'll follow thee.
                    Exeunt GHOST *and* HAMLET

---

2. *glimpses of the moon:* (earth lit by) flickering moonlight.
3. Mere mortals (terrified by encounters with the supernatural).

4. After this line, Q2 has the following passage, 55.1–
55.4, omitted in F.
5. Imaginings of despair and suicide.
6. A ferocious beast killed by Hercules.

HORATIO   He waxes desperate with imagination.
65 MARCELLUS   Let's follow. 'Tis not fit thus to obey him.
HORATIO   Have after.° To what issue° will this come?   *Go on / end*
MARCELLUS   Something is rotten in the state of Denmark.
HORATIO   Heaven will direct it.°   *(the outcome)*
MARCELLUS   Nay, let's follow him.   *Exeunt*

1.5

Enter GHOST, *and* [*Prince*] HAMLET [*following*]

HAMLET   Whither wilt thou lead me? Speak. I'll go no further.
GHOST   Mark me.
HAMLET   I will.
GHOST   My hour is almost come
When I to sulph'rous and tormenting flames
Must render up myself.
HAMLET   Alas, poor ghost!
5 GHOST   Pity me not, but lend thy serious hearing
To what I shall unfold.
HAMLET   Speak, I am bound to hear.
GHOST   So art thou to revenge when thou shalt hear.
HAMLET   What?
GHOST   I am thy father's spirit,
10 Doomed for a certain term to walk the night,
And for the day confined to fast° in fires   *do penance*
Till the foul crimes done in my days of nature°   *my natural life*
Are burnt and purged away. But that I am forbid
To tell the secrets of my prison-house
15 I could a tale unfold whose lightest word
Would harrow up thy soul, freeze thy young blood,
Make thy two eyes like stars start from their spheres,
Thy knotty and combinèd locks to part,
And each particular hair to stand on end
20 Like quills upon the fretful porcupine.
But this eternal blazon¹ must not be
To ears of flesh and blood. List,° Hamlet, list, O list!   *Listen*
If thou didst ever thy dear father love—
HAMLET   O God!
25 GHOST   Revenge his foul and most unnatural murder.
HAMLET   Murder?
GHOST   Murder most foul, as in the best it is,
But this most foul, strange, and unnatural.
HAMLET   Haste, haste me to know it, that with wings as swift
30 As meditation or the thoughts of love
May sweep to my revenge.
GHOST   I find thee apt,
And duller shouldst thou be than the fat° weed   *gross*
That rots itself² in ease on Lethe wharf³
Wouldst thou not stir in this. Now, Hamlet, hear.
35 'Tis given out that, sleeping in mine orchard,
A serpent stung me. So the whole ear of Denmark
Is by a forgèd process° of my death   *a fabricated account*

1.5 Location: Scene continues.
1. Catalogue or display of the afterlife's mysteries.
2. Decays under its own excessive growth (F). Q1, Q2

print "roots itself," another possible reading.
3. In classical mythology, Lethe was the river of forgetfulness in Hades.

Rankly abused.° But know, thou noble youth,   *deceived*
The serpent that did sting thy father's life
40   Now wears his crown.
    HAMLET   O my prophetic soul! Mine uncle?
    GHOST   Ay, that incestuous, that adulterate° beast,   *adulterous*
    With witchcraft of his wit, with traitorous gifts°—   *abilities; presents*
    O wicked wit and gifts, that have the power
45   So to seduce!—won to his shameful lust
The will of my most seeming-virtuous queen.
O Hamlet, what a falling off was there!—
From me, whose love was of that dignity
That it went hand-in-hand even with the vow
50   I made to her in marriage, and to decline
Upon a wretch whose natural gifts were poor
To° those of mine.   *Compared to*
But virtue, as it never will be moved,
Though lewdness court it in a shape of heaven,
55   So lust, though to a radiant angel linked,
Will sate itself[4] in a celestial bed,
And prey on garbage.
But soft, methinks I scent the morning's air.
Brief let me be. Sleeping within mine orchard,
60   My custom always in the afternoon,
Upon my secure hour thy uncle stole
With juice of cursèd hebenon[5] in a vial,
And in the porches° of mine ears did pour   *entranceways*
The leperous distilment,[6] whose effect
65   Holds such an enmity with blood of man
That swift as quicksilver it courses through
The natural gates and alleys of the body,
And with a sudden vigour it doth posset°   *curdle*
And curd, like eager° droppings into milk,   *acid (like wine)*
70   The thin and wholesome blood. So did it mine;
And a most instant tetter° barked about,[7]   *scaly rash*
Most lazar-like,° with vile and loathsome crust,   *leperlike*
All my smooth body.
Thus was I, sleeping, by a brother's hand
75   Of life, of crown, of queen at once dispatched,°   *deprived*
Cut off even in the blossoms of my sin,[8]
Unhouseled, dis-appointed, unaneled,[9]
No reck'ning made, but sent to my account
With all my imperfections on my head.[1]
80   O horrible, O horrible, most horrible!
If thou hast nature° in thee, bear it not.   *natural feeling*
Let not the royal bed of Denmark be
A couch for luxury° and damnèd incest.   *lechery*
But howsoever thou pursuest this act,
85   Taint not thy mind,[2] nor let thy soul contrive
Against thy mother aught.° Leave her to heaven,   *any punishment*

---

4. Will become satiated (and unable to find further pleasure).
5. A poison, possibly henbane.
6. Distillation causing skin to become scaly (as in leprosy, a disease familiar in Elizabethan England).
7. Covered the body like bark.
8. Cut off when my sins were full-blown, flourishing.

9. Without the sacrament of the Eucharist, without death-bed confession and absolution, and without the ritual anointing of extreme unction.
1. No . . . head: Without having made restitution for my sins, but sent to the Last Judgment liable for all my faults.
2. Do not let yourself be corrupted.

And to those thorns that in her bosom lodge
To prick and sting her. Fare thee well at once.
The glow-worm shows the matin° to be near,   *morning*
90   And gins° to pale his uneffectual fire.   *begins*
Adieu, adieu, Hamlet. Remember me.   *Exit*
HAMLET   O all you host of heaven! O earth! What else?
And shall I couple° hell? O fie! Hold, hold, my heart,   *add*
And you, my sinews, grow not instant old,
95   But bear me stiffly up. Remember thee?
Ay, thou poor ghost, while memory holds a seat
In this distracted globe.³ Remember thee?
Yea, from the table° of my memory   *tablet, book*
I'll wipe away all trivial fond° records,   *foolish*
100   All saws of books, all forms, all pressures past,⁴
That youth and observation copied there,
And thy commandment all alone shall live
Within the book and volume of my brain
Unmixed with baser matter. Yes, yes, by heaven.
105   O most pernicious woman!
O villain, villain, smiling, damnèd villain!
My tables,⁵
My tables—meet it is I set it down
That one may smile and smile and be a villain.
110   At least I'm sure it may be so in Denmark.
        [*He writes*]
So, uncle, there you are. Now to my word:°   *watchword*
It is 'Adieu, adieu, remember me'.
I have sworn't.
HORATIO *and* MARCELLUS [*within*]   My lord, my lord.
        Enter HORATIO *and* MARCELLUS
115 MARCELLUS [*calling*]   Lord Hamlet!
HORATIO   Heaven secure him.
HAMLET   So be it.
HORATIO [*calling*]   Illo, ho, ho, my lord.
HAMLET   Hillo, ho, ho, boy; come, bird, come.
120 MARCELLUS   How is't, my noble lord?
HORATIO [*to* HAMLET]   What news, my lord?
HAMLET   O wonderful!
HORATIO   Good my lord, tell it.
HAMLET   No, you'll reveal it.
HORATIO   Not I, my lord, by heaven.
MARCELLUS   Nor I, my lord.
125 HAMLET   How say you then, would heart of man once think it?
    But you'll be secret?
HORATIO *and* MARCELLUS   Ay, by heav'n, my lord.
HAMLET   There's ne'er a villain dwelling in all Denmark
    But he's an arrant° knave.   *a downright*
HORATIO   There needs no ghost, my lord, come from the grave
    To tell us this.
130 HAMLET   Why, right, you are i'th' right,
    And so without more circumstance° at all   *elaborate speech*

---

3. Confused head; disordered world; often also taken as a reference to the Globe theater and the audience.
4. All adages from books, all images or customs, all past impressions.
5. Scholars and others might carry two writing tables hinged together, as a notebook.

I hold it fit that we shake hands and part,
You as your business and desires shall point you—
For every man has business and desire,
135 Such as it is—and for mine own poor part,
Look you, I'll go pray.
HORATIO   These are but wild and whirling words, my lord.
HAMLET   I'm sorry they offend you, heartily,
Yes, faith, heartily.
HORATIO   There's no offence, my lord.
140 HAMLET   Yes, by Saint Patrick,[6] but there is, Horatio,
And much offence,[7] too. Touching this vision here,
It is an honest° ghost, that let me tell you.   *a reliable; a genuine*
For your desire to know what is between us,
O'ermaster't as you may. And now, good friends,
145 As you are friends, scholars, and soldiers,
Give me one poor request.
HORATIO   What is't, my lord? We will.
HAMLET   Never make known what you have seen tonight.
HORATIO *and* MARCELLUS   My lord, we will not.
HAMLET   Nay, but swear't.
HORATIO   In faith, my lord, not I.[8]
MARCELLUS   Nor I, my lord, in faith.
HAMLET   Upon my sword.[9]
150 MARCELLUS   We have sworn, my lord, already.
HAMLET   Indeed, upon my sword, indeed.
              GHOST *cries under the stage*
GHOST   Swear.
HAMLET   Ah ha, boy, sayst thou so? Art thou there, truepenny?°—   *trusty fellow*
Come on. You hear this fellow in the cellarage.
Consent to swear.
HORATIO   Propose the oath, my lord.
155 HAMLET   Never to speak of this that you have seen,
Swear by my sword.
GHOST [*under the stage*]   Swear.
              [*They swear*][1]
HAMLET   *Hic et ubique?*[2] Then we'll shift our ground.—
Come hither, gentlemen,
160 And lay your hands again upon my sword.
Never to speak of this that you have heard,
Swear by my sword.
GHOST [*under the stage*]   Swear.
              [*They swear*]
HAMLET   Well said, old mole. Canst work i'th' earth so fast?
165 A worthy pioneer.[3]—Once more remove,° good friends.   *move*
HORATIO   O day and night, but this is wondrous strange!
HAMLET   And therefore as a stranger give it welcome.[4]
There are more things in heaven and earth, Horatio,
Than are dreamt of in our philosophy.[5] But come,

6. Perhaps because Patrick was thought to be keeper of purgatory.
7. Offense against the kingdom and morality.
8. I will indeed not reveal it.
9. Swearing on a sword was a fairly common practice because the hilt and blade form a cross.
1. Horatio and Marcellus may swear here on the crossed hilt of Hamlet's sword. (Alternatively, they may be reluc-

tant to swear until they are on safer ground.)
2. Here and everywhere (Latin).
3. Army trench digger.
4. As if it had a guest's right to courteous hospitality.
5. Human speculative knowledge. Q2 and most editors print "your philosophy"; F's "our" shows Hamlet himself still trying to reconcile his own understanding with the supernatural revelations.

170   Here as before, never, so help you mercy,
    How strange or odd soe'er I bear myself—
    As I perchance hereafter shall think meet
    To put an antic disposition on[6]—
    That you at such time seeing me never shall,
175   With arms encumbered° thus, or this headshake,   *folded*
    Or by pronouncing of some doubtful° phrase   *ambiguous*
    As 'Well, we know' or 'We could an if° we would',   *an if = if*
    Or 'If we list° to speak', or 'There be, an if they might',[7]   *liked*
    Or such ambiguous giving out, to note
180   That you know aught° of me—this not to do,   *anything*
    So grace and mercy at your most need help you, swear.
    GHOST [*under the stage*]   Swear.
              [*They swear*]
    HAMLET   Rest, rest, perturbèd spirit.—So, gentlemen,
    With all my love I do commend me to you,
185   And what so poor a man as Hamlet is
    May do t'express his love and friending° to you,   *friendship*
    God willing, shall not lack.° Let us go in together,   *be left undone*
    And still° your fingers on your lips, I pray.   *always*
    The time is out of joint.° O cursèd spite   *dislocated, disordered*
190   That ever I was born to set it right!
    Nay, come,[8] let's go together.   *Exeunt*

2.1

    Enter old POLONIUS *with his man* REYNALDO
    POLONIUS   Give him this money and these notes, Reynaldo.
    REYNALDO   I will, my lord.
    POLONIUS   You shall do marv'lous wisely, good Reynaldo,
    Before you visit him to make enquire
    Of his behaviour.
5   REYNALDO   My lord, I did intend it.
    POLONIUS   Marry, well said, very well said. Look you, sir,
    Enquire me° first what Danskers° are in Paris,   *for me / Danes*
    And how, and who, what means,° and where they keep,°   *wealth, income / lodge*
    What company, at what expense; and finding
10   By this encompassment and drift of question[1]
    That they do know my son, come you more nearer
    Than your particular demands will touch it.[2]
    Take you,° as 'twere, some distant knowledge of him,   *Pretend*
    As thus: 'I know his father and his friends,
15   And in part him'—do you mark this, Reynaldo?
    REYNALDO   Ay, very well, my lord.
    POLONIUS   'And in part him, but', you may say, 'not well,
    But if't be he I mean, he's very wild,
    Addicted so and so'; and there put on him°   *attribute to him*
20   What forgeries° you please—marry, none so rank[3]   *made-up tales*
    As may dishonour him, take heed of that—
    But, sir, such wanton,° wild, and usual slips   *unrestrained*

6. To assume the behavior of a madman.
7. There are those who would speak if they were allowed.
8. The others are politely waiting for Hamlet, the Prince, to lead the way; he insists on informality.
2.1 Location: Polonius's apartments in the castle.

1. By this roundabout and indirect way of inquiry.
2. *come . . . it:* you will come closer to the truth than by direct questions.
3. Excessive; foul.

As are companions noted and most known
To youth and liberty.
25 REYNALDO   As gaming, my lord?
POLONIUS   Ay, or drinking, fencing, swearing,
   Quarrelling, drabbing°—you may go so far.   *whoring*
REYNALDO   My lord, that would dishonour him.
POLONIUS   Faith, no, as you may season° it in the charge.   *mitigate*
30   You must not put another scandal on him,
   That he is open° to incontinency.°   *inclined / sexual excess*
   That's not my meaning—but breathe his faults so quaintly
   That they may seem the taints of liberty,[4]
   The flash and outbreak of a fiery mind,
35   A savageness in unreclaimèd° blood,   *unchecked*
   Of general assault.[5]
REYNALDO   But, my good lord—
POLONIUS   Wherefore should you do this?
REYNALDO   Ay, my lord.
   I would know that.
POLONIUS   Marry, sir, here's my drift,
   And I believe it is a fetch of warrant:[6]
40   You laying these slight sullies on my son,
   As 'twere a thing a little soiled i'th' working,[7]
   Mark you, your party° in converse, him you would sound,°   *partner / sound out*
   Having° ever seen in the prenominate crimes[8]   *If he has*
   The youth you breathe of guilty, be assured
45   He closes° with you in this consequence:[9]   *confides*
   'Good sir', or so, or 'friend', or 'gentleman',
   According to the phrase° and the addition[1]   *expression*
   Of man and country.
REYNALDO   Very good, my lord.
POLONIUS   And then, sir, does a° this—a does—   *he*
50   what was I about to say? By the mass, I was about to say some-
   thing. Where did I leave?
REYNALDO   At 'closes in the consequence', at 'friend,
   Or so', and 'gentleman'.
POLONIUS   At 'closes in the consequence'—ay, marry,
55   He closes with you thus: 'I know the gentleman,
   I saw him yesterday'—or t'other day,
   Or then, or then—'with such and such, and, as you say,
   There was a° gaming, there o'ertook in 's rouse,   *he*
   There falling out° at tennis', or perchance   *quarreling*
60   'I saw him enter such a house of sale',
   Videlicet,° a brothel, or so forth. See you now,   *That is to say*
   Your bait of falsehood takes this carp of truth;
   And thus do we of wisdom and of reach°   *wide understanding*
   With windlasses and with assays of bias[2]
65   By indirections find directions° out.   *real tendencies*
   So, by my former° lecture and advice,   *preceding*
   Shall you my son. You have me,° have you not?   *my meaning*

4. Faults resulting from freedom of action.
5. Which afflicts all young men.
6. *fetch of warrant*: justifiable trick (F). Q2 has "fetch of wit" (clever scheme).
7. Stained by education in the ways of the world, "shop soiled."
8. Aforesaid faults.
9. To the following effect.
1. Title of address.
2. And with indirect tests, like the curved line, or "bias," that a weighted bowling ball describes. *windlasses*: roundabout paths (a hunter's circuit to intercept game).

REYNALDO My lord, I have.
POLONIUS God b'wi' ye. Fare ye well.
70 REYNALDO Good my lord.
POLONIUS Observe his inclination in° yourself.   *for*
REYNALDO I shall, my lord.
POLONIUS And let him ply° his music.   *work at*
REYNALDO Well, my lord.

        Enter OPHELIA

POLONIUS Farewell.   *Exit* REYNALDO
75   How now, Ophelia, what's the matter?
OPHELIA Alas, my lord, I have been so affrighted.
POLONIUS With what, i'th' name of God?
OPHELIA My lord, as I was sewing in my chamber,
   Lord Hamlet, with his doublet all unbraced,°   *jacket all unfastened*
80   No hat upon his head, his stockings fouled,
   Ungartered, and down-gyvèd to his ankle,[3]
   Pale as his shirt, his knees knocking each other,
   And with a look so piteous in purport
   As if he had been loosèd out of hell
85   To speak of horrors, he comes before me.
POLONIUS Mad for thy love?
OPHELIA   My lord, I do not know,
   But truly I do fear it.
POLONIUS   What said he?
OPHELIA He took me by the wrist and held me hard,
   Then goes he to the length of all his arm,
90   And with his other hand thus o'er his brow
   He falls to such perusal of my face
   As a° would draw it. Long stayed he so.   *As if he*
   At last, a little shaking of mine arm,
   And thrice his head thus waving up and down,
95   He raised a sigh so piteous and profound
   That it did seem to shatter all his bulk
   And end his being. That done, he lets me go,
   And, with his head over his shoulder turned,
   He seemed to find his way without his eyes,
100   For out o' doors he went without their help,
   And to the last bended their light[4] on me.
POLONIUS Come, go with me. I will go seek the King.
   This is the very ecstasy° of love,   *insanity*
   Whose violent property fordoes° itself   *nature destroys*
105   And leads the will to desperate undertakings
   As oft as any passion under heaven
   That does afflict our natures. I am sorry—
   What, have you given him any hard words of late?
OPHELIA No, my good lord, but as you did command
110   I did repel his letters and denied
   His access to me.
POLONIUS   That hath made him mad.
   I am sorry that with better speed and judgement
   I had not quoted° him. I feared he did but trifle   *observed*

---

3. Fallen round his ankles, like a prisoner's fetters, or "gyves."

4. Sight was thought to result from both sending light out and taking it in through the eyes.

And meant to wreck thee.[5] But beshrew my jealousy!°   *curse my suspicion*
115   By heaven, it is as proper to our age
To cast beyond ourselves[6] in our opinions
As it is common for the younger sort
To lack discretion. Come, go we to the King.
This must be known, which, being kept close, might move
120   More grief to hide than hate to utter love.[7]   *Exeunt*

2.2

Flourish. Enter KING [CLAUDIUS] *and* QUEEN [GER-
TRUDE], ROSENCRANTZ *and* GUILDENSTERN,[1] *cum aliis*

KING CLAUDIUS   Welcome, dear Rosencrantz and Guildenstern.
Moreover° that we much did long to see you,   *Beyond the fact*
The need we have to use you did provoke
Our hasty sending.° Something have you heard   *summons*
5   Of Hamlet's transformation—so I call it,
Since not th'exterior nor the inward man
Resembles that° it was. What it should be,   *what*
More than his father's death, that thus hath put him
So much from th'understanding of himself,
10   I cannot deem of.[2] I entreat you both
That, being of so young days[3] brought up with him,
And since so neighboured° to his youth and humour,°   *familiar / temperament*
That you vouchsafe your rest[4] here in our court
Some little time, so by your companies
15   To draw him on to pleasures, and to gather,
So much as from occasions° you may glean,   *opportunities*
Whether aught to us unknown afflicts him thus
That, opened,° lies within our remedy.   *if disclosed*

QUEEN GERTRUDE   Good gentlemen, he hath much talked of you,
20   And sure I am two men there is not living
To whom he more adheres.[5] If it will please you
To show us so much gentry° and good will   *courtesy*
As to expend your time with us a while
For the supply and profit of our hope,[6]
25   Your visitation shall receive such thanks
As fits a king's remembrance.

ROSENCRANTZ   Both your majesties
Might, by the sovereign power you have of° us,   *over*
Put your dread° pleasures more into command   *reverend*
Than to entreaty.

GUILDENSTERN   But we both obey,
30   And here give up ourselves in the full bent[7]
To lay our service freely at your feet
To be commanded.

KING CLAUDIUS   Thanks, Rosencrantz and gentle Guildenstern.

---

5. To ruin you through seduction.
6. *as proper . . . ourselves:* as natural to us old men to go too far and (like hunting dogs) lose the scent, thus erring out of caution.
7. *which . . . love:* we may incur hatred by revealing (Hamlet's) love, but to conceal it may cause greater suffering. *close:* secret.
2.2 Location: A stateroom in the castle.
1. Historical figures with these names are mentioned in an ambassador's report to Queen Elizabeth sent from

Elsinore in 1588.
2. Judge (F). Q2 prints "dream."
3. From such an early age.
4. That you agree to stay.
5. To whom he is more attached.
6. *For . . . hope:* To provide support for and furtherance of our hope.
7. To the fullest extent (like an archer's bow, fully drawn).

QUEEN GERTRUDE   Thanks, Guildenstern and gentle Rosencrantz.
35   And I beseech you instantly to visit
        My too-much changèd son.—Go, some of ye,
        And bring the gentlemen where Hamlet is.
GUILDENSTERN   Heavens make our presence and our practices
        Pleasant and helpful to him.
QUEEN GERTRUDE   Ay, amen!
            Exeunt ROSENCRANTZ *and* GUILDENSTERN [*with others*]
            Enter POLONIUS
40 POLONIUS   Th'ambassadors from Norway, my good lord,
        Are joyfully returned.
KING CLAUDIUS   Thou still° hast been the father of good news.   *always*
POLONIUS   Have I, my lord? Assure you, my good liege,
        I hold my duty, as I hold my soul,
45   Both to my God and to my gracious King.
        And I do think—or else this brain of mine
        Hunts not the trail of policy° so sure   *cleverness*
        As it hath used to do—that I have found
        The very cause of Hamlet's lunacy.
50 KING CLAUDIUS   O speak of that, that I do long to hear!
POLONIUS   Give first admittance to th'ambassadors.
        My news shall be the fruit° to that great feast.   *dessert*
KING CLAUDIUS   Thyself do grace to them, and bring them in.
                                [*Exit* POLONIUS]
        He tells me, my sweet queen, that he hath found
55   The head° and source of all your son's distemper.   *origins; chief part*
QUEEN GERTRUDE   I doubt[8] it is no other but the main°—   *main matter*
        His father's death and our o'er-hasty marriage.
KING CLAUDIUS   Well, we shall sift him.°   *interrogate (Polonius)*
            Enter POLONIUS, VALTEMAND, *and* CORNELIUS
                            Welcome, my good friends.
        Say, Valtemand, what from our brother° Norway?   *fellow monarch*
60 VALTEMAND   Most fair return of greetings and desires.°   *good wishes*
        Upon our first[9] he sent out to suppress
        His nephew's levies, which to him appeared
        To be a preparation 'gainst the Polack;°   *King of Poland*
        But better looked into, he truly found
65   It was against your highness; whereat grieved
        That so his sickness, age, and impotence
        Was falsely borne in hand,[1] sends out arrests
        On Fortinbras,[2] which he, in brief, obeys,
        Receives rebuke from Norway, and, in fine,°   *conclusion*
70   Makes vow before his uncle never more
        To give th'essay of arms[3] against your majesty;
        Whereon old Norway, overcome with joy,
        Gives him three thousand crowns in annual fee°   *income*
        And his commission to employ those soldiers
75   So levied as before, against the Polack,
        With an entreaty herein further shown,
            [*He gives a letter to* CLAUDIUS]
        That it might please you to give quiet pass

8. Fear, suspect.
9. When we first raised the matter.
1. Disloyally taken advantage of, tricked.
2. *arrests / On Fortinbras*: orders commanding Fortinbras

to stop his preparations and (presumably) present himself
to explain them.
3. To mount a military challenge.

Through your dominions for his enterprise
On such regards of safety and allowance[4]
As therein are set down.

80 KING CLAUDIUS   It likes° us well,   *pleases*
    And at our more considered° time we'll read,   *suitable for thought*
    Answer, and think upon this business.
    Meantime we thank you for your well-took labour.
    Go to your rest; at night we'll feast together.
85   Most welcome home.

                   Exeunt [VALTEMAND *and* CORNELIUS]

POLONIUS   This business is very well ended.
    My liege, and madam, to expostulate°   *debate*
    What majesty should be, what duty is,
    Why day is day, night night, and time is time,
90   Were nothing but to waste night, day, and time.
    Therefore, since brevity is the soul of wit,
    And tediousness the limbs and outward flourishes,°   *rhetorical devices*
    I will be brief. Your noble son is mad—
    'Mad' call I it, for to define true madness,
95   What is't but to be nothing else but mad?
    But let that go.
QUEEN GERTRUDE   More matter with less art.
POLONIUS   Madam, I swear I use no art at all.
    That he is mad, 'tis true; 'tis true 'tis pity,
    And pity 'tis 'tis true—a foolish figure,°   *figure of speech*
100   But farewell it, for I will use no art.
    Mad let us grant him, then; and now remains
    That we find out the cause of this effect—
    Or rather say 'the cause of this *defect*',
    For this effect defective[5] comes by cause.
105   Thus it remains, and the remainder thus.
    Perpend.°   *Consider*
    I have a daughter—have whilst she is mine°—   *until she marries*
    Who in her duty and obedience, mark,
    Hath given me this. Now gather and surmise.

        [*He reads a*] *letter*
110   'To the celestial and my soul's idol, the most beautified Ophe-
    lia'— that's an ill phrase, a vile phrase, 'beautified' is a vile
    phrase. But you shall hear— 'these in° her excellent white   *these words unto*
    bosom, these'.
QUEEN GERTRUDE   Came this from Hamlet to her?
115 POLONIUS   Good madam, stay° a while. I will be faithful.[6]   *wait*
      'Doubt thou the stars are fire,
        Doubt that the sun doth move,
      Doubt° truth to be a liar,   *Suspect*
        But never doubt I love.
120   O dear Ophelia, I am ill at these numbers.[7] I have not art to
    reckon my groans.[8] But that I love thee best, O most best,
    believe it. Adieu.
      Thine evermore, most dear lady, whilst this
      machine is° to him,   *this body belongs*

---

4. *On . . . allowance:* Conditions regarding your realm's safety, subject to your approval.
5. This consequence showing a lack of something (Hamlet's reason).
6. I will accurately read out the letter's contents.
7. Hamlet is both bad at writing verse and lovesick while he is writing.
8. Count my groans; also, number my groans metrically.

Hamlet.'

125 This in obedience hath my daughter showed me,
And more above° hath his solicitings,   *in addition*
As they fell out° by time, by means, and place,   *occurred*
All given to mine ear.

KING CLAUDIUS   But how hath she
Received his love?

POLONIUS   What do you think of me?

130 KING CLAUDIUS   As of a man faithful and honourable.

POLONIUS   I would fain° prove so. But what might you think,   *be glad to*
When I had seen this hot love on the wing,
As I perceived it—I must tell you that—
Before my daughter told me, what might you,

135 Or my dear majesty your queen here, think,
If I had played the desk or table-book,⁹
Or given my heart a winking mute and dumb,¹
Or looked upon this love with idle sight—
What might you think? No, I went round° to work,   *directly*

140 And my young mistress thus I did bespeak:°   *address*
'Lord Hamlet is a prince out of thy star.°   *above your sphere*
This must not be'. And then I precepts gave her,
That she should lock herself from his resort,°   *visits*
Admit no messengers, receive no tokens;

145 Which done, she took the fruits of my advice,
And he, repulsèd—a short tale to make—
Fell into a sadness, then into a fast,
Thence to a watch,° thence into a weakness,   *an insomnia*
Thence to a lightness,° and, by this declension,°   *dizziness / decline*

150 Into the madness wherein now he raves,
And all we° wail for.   *of us*

KING CLAUDIUS [*to* GERTRUDE]   Do you think 'tis this?

QUEEN GERTRUDE   It may be; very likely.

POLONIUS   Hath there been such a time—I'd fain know that—

155 That I have positively said ' 'Tis so'
When it proved otherwise?

KING CLAUDIUS   Not that I know.

POLONIUS [*touching his head, then his shoulder*]
Take this from this if this be otherwise.
If circumstances lead me I will find
Where truth is hid, though it were hid indeed
Within the centre.°   *middle of the earth*

160 KING CLAUDIUS   How may we try° it further?   *test*

POLONIUS   You know sometimes he walks four hours together
Here in the lobby.

QUEEN GERTRUDE   So he does indeed.

POLONIUS   At such a time I'll loose my daughter to him.
[*To* CLAUDIUS] Be you and I behind an arras° then.   *a tapestry*

165 Mark the encounter. If he love her not,
And be not from his reason fall'n thereon,°   *on that account*

---

9. If I had recorded the perception (in my memory) but kept it hidden.   1. Or made my heart close its eyes and remain silent.

Let me be no assistant for a state,
But keep a farm and carters.°   *wagon drivers*
KING CLAUDIUS   We will try it.
    Enter [Prince] HAMLET, *[madly attired,] reading on a
    book*[2]
QUEEN GERTRUDE   But look where sadly° the poor wretch comes   *gravely*
    reading.
170 POLONIUS   Away, I do beseech you both, away.
    I'll board him presently.° O give me leave.[3]   *accost him immediately*
                              Exit KING *and* QUEEN
    How does my good Lord Hamlet?
HAMLET   Well, God-'a'-mercy.[4]
POLONIUS   Do you know me, my lord?
175 HAMLET   Excellent, excellent well. You're a fishmonger.
POLONIUS   Not I, my lord.
HAMLET   Then I would you were so honest a man.
POLONIUS   Honest, my lord?
HAMLET   Ay, sir. To be honest, as this world goes, is to be one
180 man picked out of ten thousand.
POLONIUS   That's very true, my lord.
HAMLET   For if the sun breed maggots in a dead dog, being a
    good kissing carrion[5]—have you a daughter?
POLONIUS   I have, my lord.
185 HAMLET   Let her not walk i'th' sun.[6] Conception[7] is a blessing,
    but not as your daughter may conceive. Friend, look to't.°   *take care*
POLONIUS   *[aside]*   How say you by that? Still harping on my
    daughter. Yet he knew me not at first—a° said I was a fish-   *he*
    monger. A is far gone, far gone, and truly, in my youth I suf-
190 fered much extremity for love, very near this. I'll speak to him
    again.—What do you read, my lord?
HAMLET   Words, words, words.
POLONIUS   What is the matter,[8] my lord?
HAMLET   Between who?
195 POLONIUS   I mean the matter you read, my lord.
HAMLET   Slanders, sir; for the satirical slave° says here that old   *scoundrel*
    men have grey beards, that their faces are wrinkled, their eyes
    purging° thick amber° or plum-tree gum, and that they have a   *discharging / resin*
    plentiful lack of wit,° together with most weak hams. All which,   *intellect*
200 sir, though I most powerfully and potently believe, yet I hold it
    not honesty° to have it thus set down; for you yourself, sir,   *honorable*
    should be old as I am—if, like a crab, you could go backward.
POLONIUS   *[aside]*   Though this be madness, yet there is method
    in't.—Will you walk out of the air,[9] my lord?
205 HAMLET   Into my grave.
POLONIUS   Indeed, that is out o'th' air. *[Aside]* How pregnant°   *meaningful*
    sometimes his replies are! A happiness° that often madness hits   *An appropriateness*

2. Hamlet possibly has two entrances here, the first at the inner stage ("lobby," line 162) and the second at the outer stage representing the audience chamber, where Claudius, Gertrude, and Polonius are talking. Hamlet would thus have overheard Polonius's plan before they notice him reading (line 169). (See 2.1.79–82 for Ophelia's description of Hamlet's attire.)
3. Excuse me (politely asking the King and Queen to leave).
4. Thank you (used with inferiors).
5. Piece of flesh good for kissing. Dead matter was thought to breed maggots, especially in sunlight.
6. Walk out in public or (as in 1.2.67) expose herself too much to a prince's (or son's) love.
7. The ability to form ideas; pregnancy.
8. Content, although Hamlet deliberately takes it as "subject of a quarrel."
9. Outdoor air was regarded as a hazard for the sick; Polonius may mean "out of the draughts," since the scene seems to be set indoors.

on, which reason and sanity could not so prosperously° be   *successfully*
delivered of. I will leave him, and suddenly° contrive the means   *immediately*
210 of meeting between him and my daughter.—My lord, I will
take my leave of you.
    HAMLET   You cannot, sir, take from me anything that I will more
willingly part withal°—except my life, my life, my life.   *with*
    POLONIUS [*going*]   Fare you well, my lord.
215 HAMLET   These tedious old fools!
              Enter GUILDENSTERN *and* ROSENCRANTZ[1]
    POLONIUS   You go to seek the Lord Hamlet. There he is.
    ROSENCRANTZ   God save you, sir.
    GUILDENSTERN [*to* POLONIUS]   Mine honoured lord.
                              [*Exit* POLONIUS]
    ROSENCRANTZ [*to* HAMLET]   My most dear lord.
220 HAMLET   My ex'llent good friends. How dost thou, Guildenstern? Ah, Rosencrantz—good lads, how do ye both?
    ROSENCRANTZ   As the indifferent° children of the earth.   *ordinary*
    GUILDENSTERN   Happy° in that we are not over-happy,   *Fortunate*
On Fortune's cap we are not the very button.°   *highest point*
225 HAMLET   Nor the soles of her shoe?
    ROSENCRANTZ   Neither, my lord.
    HAMLET   Then you live about her waist, or in the middle of her
favour?
    GUILDENSTERN   Faith, her privates[2] we.
230 HAMLET   In the secret parts of Fortune? O, most true, she is a
strumpet.° What's the news?   *whore*
    ROSENCRANTZ   None, my lord, but that the world's grown
honest.
    HAMLET   Then is doomsday near. But your news is not true. Let
235 me question more in particular. What have you, my good
friends, deserved at the hands of Fortune that she sends you to
prison hither?
    GUILDENSTERN   Prison, my lord?
    HAMLET   Denmark's a prison.
240 ROSENCRANTZ   Then is the world one.
    HAMLET   A goodly[3] one, in which there are many confines,°   *enclosures*
wards,° and dungeons, Denmark being one o'th' worst.   *cells*
    ROSENCRANTZ   We think not so, my lord.
    HAMLET   Why, then 'tis none to you, for there is nothing either
245 good or bad but thinking makes it so. To me it is a prison.
    ROSENCRANTZ   Why, then your ambition makes it one; 'tis too
narrow for your mind.
    HAMLET   O God, I could be bounded in a nutshell and count
myself a king of infinite space, were it not that I have bad
250 dreams.
    GUILDENSTERN   Which dreams indeed are ambition; for the very
substance of the ambitious is merely the shadow of a dream.
    HAMLET   A dream itself is but a shadow.
    ROSENCRANTZ   Truly, and I hold ambition of so airy and light a
255 quality that it is but a shadow's shadow.

---

1. In F, Rosencrantz and Guildenstern enter after line
215; in Q1, after line 211; in Q2, after line 213. Because
Polonius addresses them at line 216, this seems the best
place for their entry.

2. A triple pun: private persons holding no office; intimate friends; private parts, genitalia.
3. Spacious; fine.

HAMLET   Then are our beggars bodies, and our monarchs and
outstretched heroes the beggars' shadows.[4] Shall we to th'
court? For, by my fay,° I cannot reason.   *faith*

ROSENCRANTZ *and* GUILDENSTERN   We'll wait upon° you.   *accompany*

260   HAMLET   No such matter.° I will not sort° you with the rest of my   *Certainly not / class*
servants, for, to speak to you like an honest man, I am most
dreadfully attended.° But in the beaten way[5] of friendship, what   *waited upon*
make you° at Elsinore?   *are you doing*

ROSENCRANTZ   To visit you, my lord, no other occasion.

265   HAMLET   Beggar that I am, I am even poor in thanks, but I thank
you; and sure, dear friends, my thanks are too dear a halfpenny.[6] Were you not sent for? Is it your own inclining? Is it a
free° visitation? Come, deal justly with me. Come, come. Nay,   *voluntary*
speak.

270   GUILDENSTERN   What should we say, my lord?

HAMLET   Why, anything—but to th' purpose. You were sent for,
and there is a kind of confession in your looks which your mod-
esties[7] have not craft enough to colour.° I know the good King   *disguise*
and Queen have sent for you.

275   ROSENCRANTZ   To what end, my lord?

HAMLET   That you must teach me. But let me conjure° you by   *solemnly request*
the rights of our fellowship, by the consonancy° of our youth,   *harmonious friendship*
by the obligation of our ever-preserved love, and by what more
dear a better proposer could charge you withal, be even° and   *level*
280   direct with me whether you were sent for or no.

ROSENCRANTZ [*to* GUILDENSTERN]   What say you?

HAMLET   Nay then, I have an eye of° you—if you love me, hold   *on*
not off.

GUILDENSTERN   My lord, we were sent for.

285   HAMLET   I will tell you why. So shall my anticipation prevent°   *forestall*
your discovery, and your secrecy to the King and Queen moult
no feather.[8] I have of late—but wherefore I know not—lost all
my mirth, forgone all custom of exercise; and indeed it goes so
heavily with my disposition[9] that this goodly frame,° the earth,   *structure*
290   seems to me a sterile promontory. This most excellent canopy
the air, look you, this brave o'erhanging,[1] this majestical roof
fretted° with golden fire—why, it appears no other thing to me   *adorned*
than a foul and pestilent congregation° of vapours. What a   *mass*
piece of work is a man! How noble in reason, how infinite in
295   faculty,° in form and moving how express[2] and admirable, in   *natural powers*
action how like an angel, in apprehension how like a god—the
beauty of the world, the paragon of animals! And yet to me
what is this quintessence of dust?[3] Man delights not me—no,

4. *Then . . . shadows:* Then beggars, being without ambition, are not shadows but have substance; if monarchs and
heroes (who ambitiously "stretch" too far) are shadows
and only substantial bodies can cast shadows, they must
be the beggars' shadows.
5. Well-worn track (plain words).
6. Too expensive at a halfpenny (not worth a halfpenny);
perhaps also, too expensive by a halfpenny for me to give
in return for such worthless information.
7. Senses of decency.
8. Remain unimpaired. To pull the feathers off a reputation meant to detract from it.
9. *it goes . . . disposition:* I am so heavy with melancholy.

F, however, prints "heavenly" for Q2's "heavily," which if
accepted gives a startling image of Hamlet's impatient
world-weariness.
1. This splendid overhang (F). Most editions give Q2's
"o'erhanging firmament" (heavens). In either case, the
image may refer to the "heavens," the roof overhanging
the Elizabethan stage, which was decorated with stars.
2. Precise; expressive.
3. It was thought that the heavenly bodies were composed of a fifth element ("quintessence"), superior to the
other four (earth, air, fire, and water) and also the purest
distillation of earthly objects. Hamlet thinks of humanity
as dust at its dustiest.

300 nor woman neither, though by your smiling you seem to say
so.

ROSENCRANTZ   My lord, there was no such stuff in my thoughts.

HAMLET   Why did you laugh, then, when I said 'Man delights
not me'?

ROSENCRANTZ   To think, my lord, if you delight not in man what
305 lenten entertainment[4] the players shall receive from you. We
coted° them on the way, and hither are they coming to offer   *passed*
you service.

HAMLET   He that plays the King shall be welcome; his majesty
shall have tribute of me. The adventurous Knight shall use his
310 foil° and target,° the Lover shall not sigh gratis,° the Humorous   *sword / shield / for free*
Man shall end his part in peace,[5] the Clown shall make those
laugh whose lungs are tickled o'th' sear,[6] and the Lady shall say
her mind freely, or the blank verse shall halt for't.[7] What players are they?

315 ROSENCRANTZ   Even those you were wont to take delight in, the
tragedians° of the city.   *actors*

HAMLET   How chances it they travel? Their residence° both in   *(in the city)*
reputation and profit was better both ways.

ROSENCRANTZ   I think their inhibition comes by the means of
320 the late innovation.[8]

HAMLET   Do they hold the same estimation° they did when I was   *esteem*
in the city? Are they so followed?

ROSENCRANTZ   No, indeed, they are not.

HAMLET   How comes it? Do they grow rusty?

325 ROSENCRANTZ   Nay, their endeavour keeps° in the wonted° pace.   *continues / accustomed*
But there is, sir, an eyrie of children, little eyases,[9] that cry out
on the top of question[1] and are most tyrannically° clapped for't.   *outrageously*
These are now the fashion, and so berattle° the common   *noisily abuse*
stages[2]—so they call them—that many wearing rapiers are
330 afraid of goose-quills,[3] and dare scarce come thither.

HAMLET   What, are they children? Who maintains 'em? How are
they escoted?° Will they pursue the quality° no longer than   *provided for / profession*
they can sing?[4] Will they not say afterwards, if they should grow
themselves to common players—as it is like° most will, if their   *likely*
335 means° are not better—their writers do them wrong to make   *financial options*
them exclaim against their own succession?°   *later employment*

ROSENCRANTZ   Faith, there has been much to-do on both sides,
and the nation° holds it no sin to tarre° them to controversy.   *populace / goad*
There was for a while no money bid for argument unless the
340 poet and the player went to cuffs in the question.[5]

HAMLET   Is't possible?

---

4. Welcome. Lent was a period of penitence and fasting (when London theaters were closed).

5. *the Humorous . . . peace:* the eccentric (governed by excess of one humor, or mood-influencing bodily fluid) should be allowed to rant on without disturbance.

6. Whose lungs are primed to laugh. (The "sear" is the part of a gun holding back the hammer until the trigger releases it.)

7. *and the Lady . . . for't:* if the lady is not allowed to speak all her part, the poetry will "limp" (fail to scan).

8. Comes from recent fashion (probably the rage for boy-acting companies). An "inhibition" could be either a hin-drance or an official prohibition. (Elizabethan theaters

were commonly closed at signs of political instability.)

9. Young hawks. A company of boy actors flourished at the private Blackfriars theater, leased from the Burbages, from 1600 to 1608. *eyrie:* nest for a bird of prey.

1. That yell over their critics' voices.

2. Public theaters (such as the Globe).

3. That gentlemen are afraid of the poet's satirical pen.

4. Only until their voices break.

5. *no money . . . question:* nothing offered for the plot (or draft) of a play unless it added to the dispute between the children's dramatists and the public theater companies. *went to cuffs:* came to blows.

GUILDENSTERN   O, there has been much throwing about of
brains.[6]

HAMLET   Do the boys carry it° away?   *(the victory)*

345   ROSENCRANTZ   Ay, that they do, my lord, Hercules and his load
too.[7]

HAMLET   It is not strange; for mine uncle is King of Denmark,
and those that would make mows° at him while my father lived   *grimaces*
give twenty, forty, an hundred ducats apiece for his picture in

350   little.° 'Sblood,[8] there is something in this more than natural,   *miniature*
if philosophy could find it out.

A flourish[9] for the PLAYERS

GUILDENSTERN   There are the players.

HAMLET   Gentlemen, you are welcome to Elsinore. Your hands,
come. Th'appurtenance° of welcome is fashion and ceremony.   *fitting accompaniment*

355   Let me comply with you in the garb,[1] lest my extent° to the   *offering (of welcome)*
players— which, I tell you, must show fairly° outward—should   *courteously*
more appear like entertainment° than yours.   *(warm) welcome*

[*He shakes hands with them*]

You are welcome. But my uncle-father and aunt-mother are
deceived.

360   GUILDENSTERN   In what, my dear lord?

HAMLET   I am but mad north-north-west;[2] when the wind is
southerly, I know a hawk from a handsaw.[3]

Enter POLONIUS

POLONIUS   Well be with you, gentlemen.

HAMLET [*aside*]   Hark you, Guildenstern, and you too—at each

365   ear a hearer— that great baby you see there is not yet out of his
swathing-clouts.°   *swaddling clothes*

ROSENCRANTZ [*aside*]   Haply° he's the second time come to   *Perhaps*
them, for they say an old man is twice a child.

HAMLET [*aside*]   I will prophesy he comes to tell me of the play-

370   ers. Mark it.— You say right, sir, for o' Monday morning, 'twas
so indeed.

POLONIUS   My lord, I have news to tell you.

HAMLET   My lord, I have news to tell you. When Roscius[4] was
an actor in Rome—

375   POLONIUS   The actors are come hither, my lord.

HAMLET   Buzz, buzz.[5]

POLONIUS   Upon mine honour—

HAMLET   Then came each actor on his ass.

POLONIUS   The best actors in the world, either for tragedy, com-

380   edy, history, pastoral, pastorical-comical, historical-pastoral,
tragical-historical, tragical-comical-historical-pastoral, scene
individable[6] or poem unlimited.[7] Seneca cannot be too heavy,

---

6. A great battle of wits.
7. In the course of one of his labors, Hercules held up
the world on his shoulders while Atlas (its usual support)
ran an errand; Hercules bearing the world was the sign of
the Globe.
8. By God's blood.
9. Trumpet flourishes often heralded dramatic performances.
1. Let me follow accepted forms in the recognized manner (by shaking hands).
2. The smallest compass point away from true north, and
thus not far from sane; or possibly, only mad on occasions

when the wind blows from the north-northwest.
3. A small saw, and possibly a variant of "heronshaw"
(heron).
4. The most famous ancient Roman actor, a rather dated
news item.
5. A response to stale news.
6. Probably, play with no breaks in performance, or play
observing the unity of place (and presumably the other
classical unities). Shakespeare parodies the classifications
of contemporary dramatic theorists.
7. (Dramatic) poem unrestricted by classical rules.

nor Plautus too light.[8] For the law of writ and the liberty,[9] these
are the only men.

385   HAMLET   O Jephthah, judge of Israel, what a treasure hadst
thou![1]

POLONIUS   What a treasure had he, my lord?

HAMLET   Why,

    'One fair daughter and no more,

390   The which he lovèd passing° well'.   *surpassingly*

POLONIUS [*aside*]   Still on my daughter.

HAMLET   Am I not i'th' right, old Jephthah?

POLONIUS   If you call me Jephthah, my lord, I have a daughter
that I love passing well.

395   HAMLET   Nay, that follows not.[2]

POLONIUS   What follows then, my lord?

HAMLET   Why

            'As by lot°   *chance*

            God wot',°   *knows*

400   and then you know

            'It came to pass

            As most like° it was'—   *probable*

the first row° of the pious chanson° will show you more, for   *stanza / ballad*
look where my abridgements[3] come.

    Enter four or five PLAYERS

405   You're welcome, masters, welcome all.—I am glad to see thee
well.—Welcome, good friends.—O, my old friend! Thy face is
valanced° since I saw thee last. Com'st thou to beard° me in   *fringed (with beard) / defy*
Denmark?— What, my young lady and mistress.[4] By'r Lady,
your ladyship is nearer heaven than when I saw you last by the

410   altitude of a chopine.° Pray God your voice, like a piece of   *high platform shoe*
uncurrent gold, be not cracked within the ring.[5]—Masters, you
are all welcome. We'll e'en to't like French falc'ners,[6] fly at
anything we see. We'll have a speech straight.° Come, give us   *right away*
a taste of your quality.° Come, a passionate speech.   *professional skill*

415   FIRST PLAYER   What speech, my good lord?

HAMLET   I heard thee speak me a speech once, but it was never
acted, or, if it was, not above once; for the play, I remember,
pleased not the million. 'Twas caviare to the general.° But it   *populace*
was—as I received it, and others whose judgements in such

420   matters cried in the top of[7] mine—an excellent play, well
digested° in the scenes, set down with as much modesty° as   *organized / restraint*
cunning. I remember one said there was no sallets[8] in the lines
to make the matter savoury, nor no matter in the phrase that
might indict the author of affectation, but called it an honest

425   method, as wholesome as sweet, and by very much more handsome than fine.[9] One speech in it I chiefly loved, 'twas Aeneas'
tale to Dido, and thereabout of it especially where he speaks of

---

8. The best-known Roman playwrights, masters of tragedy and comedy, respectively.
9. For plays where classical rules are either observed or
abandoned.
1. Jephthah vowed that if he defeated the Ammonites, he
would sacrifice the first living thing he saw on his return.
He won, and his daughter became the sacrificial victim
(Judges 11).
2. Polonius's having a daughter is not a logical consequence of Hamlet's calling him Jephthah.
3. Those who cut me short; also, entertainments.

4. The boy who played female roles.
5. A coin was no longer legal tender if the circle or ring
enclosing the monarch's head was broken (by "clipping,"
or trimming off small amounts of gold).
6. We'll go to work at once. (French falconers seem to
have been regarded as experts, willing to try any potential
prey.)
7. *cried . . . of:* outweighed.
8. Literally, salads (seasoned dishes); highly flavored, or
"salty" (lecherous).
9. Beautifully crafted rather than showy.

Priam's slaughter.[1] If it live in your memory, begin at this
line—let me see, let me see:
430 'The rugged° Pyrrhus,[2] like th'Hyrcanian beast'°—   *savage / tiger*
'tis not so. It begins with Pyrrhus—
'The rugged Pyrrhus, he whose sable° arms,   *black*
Black as his purpose, did the night resemble
When he lay couchèd° in the ominous horse,[3]   *hidden*
435 Hath now this dread and black complexion° smeared   *appearance*
With heraldry° more dismal. Head to foot   *heraldic colors*
Now is he total gules,° horridly tricked°   *all red / inked over*
With blood of fathers, mothers, daughters, sons,
Baked and impasted with° the parching° streets,   *encrusted by / fiery*
440 That lend a tyrranous and damnèd light
To their vile murders. Roasted in wrath and fire,
And thus o'er-sizèd[4] with coagulate gore,
With eyes like carbuncles[5] the hellish Pyrrhus
Old grandsire Priam seeks.'
445 So, proceed you.
POLONIUS   Fore God, my lord, well spoken, with good accent
and good discretion.
FIRST PLAYER   'Anon° he finds him,   *Soon*
Striking too short at Greeks. His antique sword,
450 Rebellious to his arm, lies where it falls,
Repugnant° to command. Unequal match,   *Resistant*
Pyrrhus at Priam drives, in rage strikes wide;
But with the whiff and wind of his fell° sword   *fierce*
Th'unnervèd° father falls. Then senseless Ilium,[6]   *strengthless*
455 Seeming to feel his blow, with flaming top
Stoops to his° base, and with a hideous crash   *its*
Takes prisoner Pyrrhus' ear. For lo, his sword,
Which was declining° on the milky° head   *descending / white*
Of reverend Priam, seemed i'th' air to stick.
460 So, as a painted tyrant,[7] Pyrrhus stood,
And, like a neutral to his will and matter,[8]
Did nothing.
But as we often see against° some storm   *before*
A silence in the heavens, the rack° stand still,   *cloud banks*
465 The bold winds speechless, and the orb° below   *earth*
As hush as death, anon the dreadful thunder
Doth rend the region:° so, after Pyrrhus' pause,   *sky*
A rousèd vengeance sets him new a-work;
And never did the Cyclops'[9] hammers fall
470 On Mars his° armour, forged for proof eterne,[1]   *(Mars's)*
With less remorse° than Pyrrhus' bleeding sword   *pity; hesitation*
Now falls on Priam.
Out, out, thou strumpet Fortune! All you gods,
In general synod, take away her power,

---

1. The murder of the Trojan king Priam, at the end of
the Trojan War; adapted from Virgil's *Aeneid*, possibly via
Christopher Marlowe's *Dido, Queen of Carthage*.
2. Also known as Neoptolemus, he came to Troy to
avenge the death of his father, the Greek hero Achilles.
3. The Trojan horse, full of Greek warriors.
4. As though coated with sizing, the thick liquid used to
prepare a canvas for painting.
5. Gems supposed to glow with their own light.

6. The citadel of Troy.
7. Tyrant depicted in a painting and so incapable of
moving.
8. And as one indifferent toward his intention and the
action at hand.
9. The three one-eyed giants who served as armorers to
the classical gods and heroes.
1. To remain impenetrable forever.

475 Break all the spokes and fellies from her wheel,[2]
And bowl the round nave° down the hill of heaven,°   *wheel hub / Mt. Olympus*
As low as to the fiends!'
POLONIUS   This is too long.
HAMLET   It shall to the barber's, with your beard.° [*To* FIRST   *It shall be cut short*
480 PLAYER] Prithee, say on. He's for a jig[3] or a tale of bawdry, or
he sleeps. Say on, come to Hecuba.
FIRST PLAYER   'But who, O who had seen the mobbled°   *veiled, muffled*
    queen'—
HAMLET   'The mobbled queen'?
POLONIUS   That's good; 'mobbled queen' is good.
485 FIRST PLAYER   'Run barefoot up and down, threat'ning the flames
With bisson rheum;° a clout° upon that head   *blinding tears / cloth*
Where late the diadem stood, and for a robe,
About her lank and all o'er-teemèd[4] loins,
A blanket in th'alarm of fear caught up—
490 Who this had seen, with tongue in venom steeped,
'Gainst Fortune's state° would treason have pronounced.   *rule*
But if the gods themselves did see her then,
When she saw Pyrrhus make malicious sport
In mincing with his sword her husband's limbs,
495 The instant burst of clamour that she made—
Unless things mortal move them not at all—
Would have made milch° the burning eyes of heaven,   *milky, moist*
And passion° in the gods.'   *suffering; pity*
POLONIUS   Look whe'er° he has not turned his colour, and has   *whether*
500 tears in 's eyes. [*To* FIRST PLAYER] Prithee, no more.
HAMLET [*to* FIRST PLAYER]   'Tis well. I'll have thee speak out the
rest soon. [*To* POLONIUS] Good my lord, will you see the players
well bestowed?° Do ye hear?—let them be well used,° for they   *lodged / treated*
are the abstracts° and brief chronicles of the time. After your   *summaries*
505 death you were better have a bad epitaph than their ill
report while you live.
POLONIUS   My lord, I will use them according to their desert.
HAMLET   God's bodykins,° man, much better. Use every man   *By God's dear body*
after° his desert, and who should scape whipping? Use them   *according to*
510 after your own honour and dignity—the less they deserve, the
more merit is in your bounty. Take them in.
POLONIUS [*to* PLAYERS]   Come, sirs.   *Exit*
HAMLET [*to* PLAYERS]   Follow him, friends. We'll hear a play
tomorrow. Dost thou hear me, old friend? Can you play the
515 murder of Gonzago?
PLAYERS   Ay, my lord.
HAMLET   We'll ha't° tomorrow night. You could for a need° study   *have it / if necessary*
a speech of some dozen or sixteen lines which I would set down
and insert in't, could ye not?
520 PLAYERS   Ay, my lord.
HAMLET   Very well. Follow that lord, and look you mock him
not.

Exeunt PLAYERS[5]

2. The power of Fortune's ever-turning wheel, raising
and lowering men in succession, was proverbial. *fellies:*
curved sections of a wooden wheel rim.
3. A ridiculous piece of poetry, or the dance that followed
many plays (unrelated to the drama).
4. Completely worn out with childbearing. (Hecuba was

supposed to have borne seventeen or more children.)
5. In F and Q1, the players leave after line 524. In Q2,
they leave with Polonius after line 512. Their exit has
been relocated here to coincide with Hamlet's command
that they follow Polonius.

My good friends, I'll leave you till night. You are welcome to
Elsinore.
525 ROSENCRANTZ Good my lord.
HAMLET Ay, so. God b'wi' ye.   *Exeunt [all but]* HAMLET
                    Now I am alone.
O, what a rogue and peasant slave am I!
Is it not monstrous that this player here,
But° in a fiction, in a dream of passion,   *Merely*
530 Could force his soul so to his whole conceit[6]
That from her° working all his visage wanned,°   *(the soul's) / grew pale*
Tears in his eyes, distraction in 's aspect,
A broken voice, and his whole function suiting
With forms to his conceit?[7] And all for nothing.
535 For Hecuba!
What's Hecuba to him, or he to Hecuba,
That he should weep for her? What would he do
Had he the motive and the cue for passion
That I have? He would drown the stage with tears,
540 And cleave the general ear[8] with horrid speech,
Make mad the guilty and appal the free,°   *innocent*
Confound the ignorant, and amaze° indeed   *bewilder*
The very faculty of eyes and ears. Yet I,
A dull and muddy-mettled° rascal, peak°   *dull-spirited / mope*
545 Like John-a-dreams,° unpregnant of[9] my cause,   *a sleepy idler*
And can say nothing—no, not for a king
Upon whose property° and most dear life   *rightful sovereignty*
A damned defeat[1] was made. Am I a coward?
Who calls me villain, breaks my pate° across,   *head*
550 Plucks off my beard and blows it in my face,
Tweaks me by th' nose, gives me the lie i'th' throat
As deep as to the lungs?[2] Who does me this?
Ha? 'Swounds,° I should take it; for it cannot be   *By God's wounds*
But I am pigeon-livered and lack gall[3]
555 To make oppression bitter, or ere this
I should 'a' fatted all the region kites[4]
With this slave's offal. Bloody, bawdy villain!
Remorseless, treacherous, lecherous, kindless villain!
O, vengeance!—
560 Why, what an ass am I? Ay, sure, this is most brave,°   *fine*
That I, the son of the dear murderèd,°   *the dear murdered man*
Prompted to my revenge by heaven and hell,
Must, like a whore, unpack my heart with words
And fall a-cursing like a very drab,°   *whore*
565 A scullion![5] Fie upon't, foh!—About,° my brain.   *Go about it*
I have heard that guilty creatures sitting at a play
Have by the very cunning° of the scene   *artfulness*
Been struck so to the soul that presently°   *immediately*
They have proclaimed their malefactions;
570 For murder, though it have no tongue, will speak

---

6. Could make his innermost being conform so well with
his imagined situation.
7. *his whole . . . conceit:* the action of his whole body in
outward accord with his imagination.
8. The ears of people generally.
9. Not quickened into action by.

1. An act of overthrow worthy of damnation.
2. *gives . . . lungs:* calls me a thoroughgoing liar.
3. Pigeons were thought not to secrete gall, a bitter fluid
produced by the liver and the supposed source of anger.
4. All the kites (a bird of prey) in the sky ("region").
5. Kitchen servant.

With most miraculous organ. I'll have these players
Play something like the murder of my father
Before mine uncle. I'll observe his looks,
I'll tent° him to the quick. If a but blench,   probe (a wound)
575   I know my course. The spirit that I have seen
May be the devil, and the devil hath power
T'assume a pleasing shape; yea, and perhaps,
Out of my weakness and my melancholy—
As he is very potent with such spirits[6]—
580   Abuses° me to damn me. I'll have grounds   Deceives
More relative° than this. The play's the thing   relevant
Wherein I'll catch the conscience of the King.   *Exit*

3.1

Enter KING [CLAUDIUS], QUEEN [GERTRUDE], POLONIUS,
OPHELIA, ROSENCRANTZ, GUILDENSTERN, *and lords*
KING CLAUDIUS [*to* ROSENCRANTZ *and* GUILDENSTERN]
And can you by no drift of circumstance[1]
Get from him why he puts on this confusion,
Grating so harshly all his days of quiet
With turbulent and dangerous lunacy?
5   ROSENCRANTZ   He does confess he feels himself distracted,
But from what cause a will by no means speak.
GUILDENSTERN   Nor do we find him forward° to be sounded,°   eager / probed
But with a crafty madness keeps aloof
When we would bring him on to some confession
10   Of his true state.
QUEEN GERTRUDE   Did he receive you well?
ROSENCRANTZ   Most like a gentleman.
GUILDENSTERN   But with much forcing of his disposition.°   mood
ROSENCRANTZ   Niggard of question,[2] but of° our demands   to
Most free in his reply.
15   QUEEN GERTRUDE   Did you assay° him   try to persuade
To any pastime?
ROSENCRANTZ   Madam, it so fell out that certain players
We o'er-raught° on the way. Of these we told him,   passed
And there did seem in him a kind of joy
20   To hear of it. They are about the court,
And, as I think, they have already order
This night to play before him.
POLONIUS   'Tis most true,
And he beseeched me to entreat your majesties
To hear and see the matter.
25   KING CLAUDIUS   With all my heart; and it doth much content me
To hear him so inclined.—Good gentlemen,
Give him a further edge,° and drive his purpose on   stimulus; appetite
To these delights.
ROSENCRANTZ   We shall, my lord.
Exeunt ROSENCRANTZ *and* GUILDENSTERN
30   KING CLAUDIUS   Sweet Gertrude, leave us too,
For we have closely° sent for Hamlet hither,   privately

---

6. *Out of . . . spirits:* it was thought that those afflicted
with too much black bile, a humor (fluid), or "spirit" (distillation), became melancholy and subject to hallucina-
tions, which in turn made them easily tricked by the

devil. *potent with:* powerful over.
3.1 Location: The castle.
1. By no carefully directed conversation.
2. Reluctant to offer conversation.

That he, as 'twere by accident, may here
Affront° Ophelia.   *Confront*
Her father and myself, lawful espials,°   *spies*
35   Will so bestow ourselves that, seeing unseen,
We may of their encounter frankly judge,
And gather by him, as he is behaved,
If't be th'affliction of his love or no
That thus he suffers for.
QUEEN GERTRUDE   I shall obey you.
40   And for your part, Ophelia, I do wish
That your good beauties be the happy cause
Of Hamlet's wildness; so shall I hope your virtues
Will bring him to his wonted° way again,   *customary*
To both your honours.
OPHELIA   Madam, I wish it may.
                          [*Exit* GERTRUDE]
45   POLONIUS   Ophelia, walk you here. — Gracious,° so please you,   *Your Grace*
We will bestow ourselves. — Read on this book,
That show of such an exercise may colour
Your loneliness.[3] We are oft to blame in this:
'Tis too much proved° that with devotion's visage   *true in experience*
50   And pious action we do sugar o'er
The devil himself.
KING CLAUDIUS   O, 'tis too true.
[*Aside*] How smart° a lash that speech doth give my conscience.   *sharp*
The harlot's cheek, beautied with plast'ring° art,   *cosmetic; healing*
Is not more ugly to the thing that helps it[4]
55   Than is my deed to my most painted word.
O heavy burden!
POLONIUS   I hear him coming. Let's withdraw, my lord.
                 Exeunt [CLAUDIUS *and* POLONIUS]
      Enter [*Prince*] HAMLET
HAMLET   To be, or not to be; that is the question:
Whether 'tis nobler in the mind to suffer
60   The slings and arrows of outrageous fortune,
Or to take arms against a sea of troubles,
And, by opposing, end them. To die, to sleep—
No more, and by a sleep to say we end
The heartache and the thousand natural shocks
65   That flesh is heir to—'tis a consummation
Devoutly to be wished. To die, to sleep.
To sleep, perchance to dream. Ay, there's the rub,[5]
For in that sleep of death what dreams may come
When we have shuffled° off this mortal coil°   *cast / turmoil; flesh*
70   Must give us pause. There's the respect°   *consideration*
That makes calamity of so long life,[6]
For who would bear the whips and scorns of time,
Th'oppressor's wrong, the proud man's contumely,°   *scornful abuse*
The pangs of disprized° love, the law's delay,   *unvalued*
75   The insolence of office,° and the spurns[7]   *bureaucrats*

---

3. *may . . . loneliness:* may explain your solitude, and also give it a virtuous or pious look. The "book" is a prayer-book or devotional text.
4. *to . . . it:* compared to the artificially beautiful surface that covers it.

5. Obstacle in the game of bowls, an impediment to the ball's intended path.
6. Makes adversity so long-lived (as opposed to quickly ended in suicide).
7. Kicks, insults.

That patient merit of th'unworthy takes,[8]
When he himself might his quietus make[9]
With a bare bodkin?° Who would these fardels° bear,　　　　*mere dagger / burdens*
To grunt and sweat under a weary life,
80　　But that the dread of something after death,
The undiscovered country from whose bourn°　　　　　　　　*border*
No traveller returns, puzzles the will,
And makes us rather bear those ills we have
Than fly to others that we know not of?
85　　Thus conscience[1] does make cowards of us all,
And thus the native hue° of resolution　　　　　　　　　*ruddy complexion*
Is sicklied o'er with the pale cast° of thought,　　　　　　*tint*
And enterprises of great pith and moment[2]
With this regard° their currents turn awry,　　　　　　　*consideration*
90　　And lose the name of action. Soft you, now,[3]
The fair Ophelia!—Nymph, in thy orisons°　　　　　　　*prayers*
Be all my sins remembered.
OPHELIA　　　　　　　　　　　Good my lord,
How does your honour for this many a day?
HAMLET　I humbly thank you, well, well, well.
95　OPHELIA　My lord, I have remembrances of yours
That I have longèd long to redeliver.
I pray you now receive them.
HAMLET　No, no, I never gave you aught.
OPHELIA　My honoured lord, you know right well you did,
100　And with them words of so sweet breath composed
As made the things more rich. Their perfume lost,
Take these again; for to the noble mind
Rich gifts wax° poor when givers prove unkind.　　　　　*grow*
There, my lord.
105　HAMLET　Ha, ha? Are you honest?°　　　　　　　　*chaste; truthful*
OPHELIA　My lord.
HAMLET　Are you fair?
OPHELIA　What means your lordship?
HAMLET　That if you be honest and fair, your honesty should
110　admit no discourse to[4] your beauty.
OPHELIA　Could beauty, my lord, have better commerce° than　　*dealings*
with honesty?
HAMLET　Ay, truly, for the power of beauty will sooner transform
honesty from what it is to a bawd than the force of honesty can
115　translate beauty into his° likeness. This was sometime a para-　　*its (honesty's)*
dox, but now the time[5] gives it proof. I did love you once.
OPHELIA　Indeed, my lord, you made me believe so.
HAMLET　You should not have believed me, for virtue cannot so
inoculate our old stock but we shall relish of it.[6] I loved you
120　not.
OPHELIA　I was the more deceived.

---

8. That the deserving has to accept patiently from the unworthy.
9. A paid-off account was marked "Quietus est" ("laid to rest").
1. Both consciousness (introspective knowledge) and moral conscience.
2. Of profundity and importance (F). Q2 gives "pitch," meaning "height" (in the context of a falcon's flight).

3. Wait a moment (an expression of surprise).
4. No familiar conversation with.
5. This was formerly an uncredited opinion, but now the present age.
6. *You . . . it:* Virtue grafted onto fallen human nature cannot eradicate completely the taste ("relish") of original sin.

HAMLET   Get thee to a nunnery.[7] Why wouldst thou be a breeder
of sinners? I am myself indifferent honest,° but yet I could   *moderately virtuous*
accuse me of such things that it were better my mother had not
125   borne me. I am very proud, revengeful, ambitious, with more
offences at my beck° than I have thoughts to put them in, imag-   *command*
ination to give them shape, or time to act them in. What should
such fellows as I do crawling between heaven and earth? We
are arrant° knaves, all. Believe none of us. Go thy ways to a   *downright*
130   nunnery. Where's your father?
OPHELIA   At home, my lord.
HAMLET   Let the doors be shut upon him, that he may play the
fool nowhere but in 's own house. Farewell.
OPHELIA   O help him, you sweet heavens!
135   HAMLET   If thou dost marry, I'll give thee this plague for thy
dowry: be thou as chaste as ice, as pure as snow, thou shalt not
escape calumny. Get thee to a nunnery, go, farewell. Or if thou
wilt needs marry, marry a fool; for wise men know well enough
what monsters[8] you° make of them. To a nunnery, go, and   *you women*
140   quickly, too. Farewell.
OPHELIA   O heavenly powers, restore him!
HAMLET   I have heard of your paintings, too, well enough. God
hath given you one face, and you make yourselves another. You
jig, you amble, and you lisp,[9] and nickname God's creatures,[1]
145   and make your wantonness your ignorance.[2] Go to, I'll no
more on't.° It hath made me mad. I say we will have no more   *of it*
marriages. Those that are married already—all but one—shall
live. The rest shall keep as they are. To a nunnery, go.   *Exit*
OPHELIA   O what a noble mind is here o'erthrown!
150   The courtier's, soldier's, scholar's eye, tongue, sword,
Th'expectancy and rose of the fair state,
The glass° of fashion and the mould of form,[3]   *mirror image*
Th'observed of all observers, quite, quite, down!
And I, of ladies most deject and wretched,
155   That sucked the honey of his music vows,
Now see that noble and most sovereign reason
Like sweet bells jangled out of tune and harsh;
That unmatched form and feature of blown° youth   *fully blossoming*
Blasted° with ecstasy.° O woe is me,   *Withered / madness*
160   T'have seen what I have seen, see what I see!
      Enter KING [CLAUDIUS] *and* POLONIUS
KING CLAUDIUS   Love? His affections° do not that way tend,   *emotions*
Nor what he spake, though it lacked form a little,
Was not like madness. There's something in his soul
O'er which his melancholy sits on brood,
165   And I do doubt° the hatch and the disclose[4]   *fear*
Will be some danger; which to prevent
I have in quick determination
Thus set it down:° he shall with speed to England   *resolved it*
For the demand of our neglected tribute.

7. By entering a nunnery, Ophelia will take a vow of life-long chastity. But in Elizabethan slang, "nunnery" could also mean "brothel."
8. Alluding to the belief that cuckolds grew horns, but Hamlet may mean a more spiritual or psychological transformation as well.
9. *You jig . . . lisp:* You dance (or sing), walk with an

affectedly easy gait, and speak artificially.
1. Use new and fashionable names instead of the God-given ones.
2. *make . . . ignorance:* "play dumb" to excuse your (seductive) affectations.
3. Pattern of decorum.
4. Public disclosure.

170 Haply the seas and countries different,
     With variable objects,[5] shall expel
     This something-settled° matter in his heart,   *somewhat rooted*
     Whereon his brains still° beating puts him thus   *constantly*
     From fashion of himself.[6] What think you on't?
175 POLONIUS   It shall do well. But yet do I believe
     The origin and commencement of this grief
     Sprung from neglected° love. — How now, Ophelia?   *unrequited*
     You need not tell us what Lord Hamlet said;
     We heard it all. — My lord, do as you please,
180 But, if you hold it fit, after the play
     Let his queen mother all alone entreat him
     To show his griefs. Let her be round° with him,   *blunt*
     And I'll be placed, so please you, in the ear°   *within earshot*
     Of all their conference. If she find him not,[7]
185 To England send him, or confine him where
     Your wisdom best shall think.
     KING CLAUDIUS   It shall be so.
     Madness in great ones must not unwatched go.   *Exeunt*

3.2

Enter [Prince] HAMLET *and two or three of the* PLAYERS

HAMLET   Speak the speech, I pray you, as I pronounced it to
   you — trippingly on the tongue; but if you mouth it,[1] as many
   of your players do, I had as lief° the town-crier had spoke my   *willingly*
   lines. Nor do not saw the air too much with your hand, thus,
5 but use all gently; for in the very torrent, tempest, and as I may
   say the whirlwind of your passion, you must acquire and beget
   a temperance that may give it smoothness. O, it offends me to
   the soul to hear a robustious,° periwig-pated° fellow tear a pas- *bombastic / wig-wearing*
   sion to tatters, to very rags, to split the ears of the groundlings,[2]
10 who for the most part are capable of nothing but inexplicable
   dumb shows[3] and noise. I would have such a fellow whipped
   for o'erdoing Termagant. It out-Herods Herod.[4] Pray you avoid
   it.
   A PLAYER   I warrant your honour.[5]
15 HAMLET   Be not too tame, neither; but let your own discretion
   be your tutor. Suit the action to the word, the word to the
   action, with this special observance: that you o'erstep not the
   modesty° of nature. For anything so overdone is from° the pur-   *moderation / opposed to*
   pose of playing, whose end, both at the first and now, was and
20 is to hold as 'twere the mirror up to nature, to show virtue her
   own feature, scorn her own image, and the very age and body
   of the time his form and pressure.[6] Now this overdone, or come
   tardy° off, though it make the unskilful[7] laugh, cannot but   *faultily*
   make the judicious grieve; the censure of the which one[8] must

---

5. With different sights or interests.
6. *puts . . . himself:* makes him unlike his normal self.
7. If she fails to discover his secret.
3.2 Location: A stateroom of the castle.
1. If you speak exaggeratedly.
2. Spectators standing on the ground before the stage (the cheapest area).
3. Brief mimed scenes giving the plot of the scene to follow (see 3.2.122ff.). By Shakespeare's time, this once-
common device was out of fashion.
4. It surpasses the excesses of Herod, who, as a character

in medieval cycle plays, was famous for his ranting. Termagant, an imaginary deity supposedly worshipped by
Muslims, takes the form of a violent speaking idol in
medieval drama.
5. I assure your Honor (that we will avoid it).
6. *the very . . . pressure:* the true state of things at present,
in shape ("form") and likeness (as a stamp pressed in
wax).
7. Undiscriminating.
8. The judgment of one of whom (judicious persons).

25   in your allowance o'erweigh a whole theatre of others. O, there
    be players that I have seen play, and heard others praise, and
    that highly, not to speak it profanely,[9] that neither having the
    accent of Christians nor the gait of Christian, pagan, nor no
    man, have so strutted and bellowed that I have thought some
30   of nature's journeymen[1] had made men, and not made them
    well, they imitated humanity so abominably.

A PLAYER   I hope we have reformed that indifferently° with us,   *moderately well*
    sir.

HAMLET   O, reform it altogether. And let those that play your
35   clowns speak no more than is set down for them; for there be
    of° them that will themselves laugh to set° on some quantity of   *some of / urge*
    barren° spectators to laugh too, though in the mean time some   *unthinking*
    necessary question of the play be then to be considered. That's
    villainous, and shows a most pitiful ambition in the fool that
40   uses it. Go make you ready.   *Exeunt* PLAYERS
        Enter POLONIUS, GUILDENSTERN, *and* ROSENCRANTZ
    [*To* POLONIUS] How now, my lord? Will the King hear this
    piece of work?

POLONIUS   And the Queen too, and that presently.°   *immediately*

HAMLET   Bid the players make haste.   *Exit* POLONIUS
    Will you two help to hasten them?

45 ROSENCRANTZ *and* GUILDENSTERN   We will, my lord.   *Exeunt*

HAMLET   What ho, Horatio!
        Enter HORATIO

HORATIO   Here, sweet lord, at your service.

HAMLET   Horatio, thou art e'en as just° a man   *honest; balanced*
    As e'er my conversation coped withal.[2]

HORATIO   O my dear lord—

HAMLET   Nay, do not think I flatter;
50   For what advancement° may I hope from thee,   *political favors*
    That no revenue hast but thy good spirits
    To feed and clothe thee? Why should the poor be flattered?
    No, let the candied° tongue lick absurd pomp,   *flattering*
    And crook the pregnant° hinges of the knee   *ready (to bow)*
55   Where thrift may follow feigning.[3] Dost thou hear?—
    Since my dear soul was mistress of her choice
    And could of° men distinguish, her election   *between*
    Hath sealed thee for herself;[4] for thou hast been
    As one in suff'ring all that suffers nothing,
60   A man that Fortune's buffets and rewards
    Hath ta'en with equal thanks; and blest are those
    Whose blood° and judgement are so well commingled   *passion*
    That they are not a pipe for Fortune's finger
    To sound what stop she please. Give me that man
65   That is not passion's slave, and I will wear him
    In my heart's core, ay, in my heart of heart,
    As I do thee. Something too much of this.
    There is a play tonight before the King.
    One scene of it comes near the circumstance

9. Meaning no blasphemy (by implying as he goes on to
do that some humans were not created by God).
1. Hired assistants to the master craftsmen, still learning
their trade.
2. As I ever encountered in my dealings with men.

3. Where prosperity may result from (flattering) lies.
Most editions follow Q2's "fawning."
4. Has marked you as her own (on a document, a legal
sign of possession).

70   Which I have told thee of my father's death.
     I prithee, when thou seest that act afoot,
     Even with the very comment of thy soul⁵
     Observe mine uncle. If his occulted° guilt   *hidden*
     Do not itself unkennel in one speech,
75   It is a damnèd ghost that we have seen,
     And my imaginations are as foul
     As Vulcan's stithy.⁶ Give him heedful note,
     For I mine eyes will rivet to his face,
     And after, we will both our judgements join
     To censure of his seeming.⁷
80 HORATIO   Well, my lord.
     If a° steal aught the whilst this play is playing   *he*
     And scape detecting, I will pay the theft.
          Enter trumpets and kettle drums. Sound a flourish
   HAMLET   They are coming to the play. I must be idle.°   *mad; unoccupied*
     Get you a place.
          Danish march. Enter KING [CLAUDIUS], QUEEN [GER-
          TRUDE], POLONIUS, OPHELIA, ROSENCRANTZ, GUILDEN-
          STERN, *and other lords attendant, with* [*the King's*]
          guard carrying torches
   KING CLAUDIUS   How fares⁸ our cousin° Hamlet?   *kinsman*
85 HAMLET   Excellent, i'faith, of the chameleon's dish. I eat the air,
     promise-crammed.⁹ You cannot feed capons¹ so.
   KING CLAUDIUS   I have nothing with this answer, Hamlet. These
     words are not mine.
   HAMLET   No, nor mine now. [*To* POLONIUS] My lord, you played
90   once i'th' university, you say.
   POLONIUS   That I did, my lord, and was accounted a good actor.
   HAMLET   And what did you enact?
   POLONIUS   I did enact Julius Caesar. I was killed i'th' Capitol.²
     Brutus killed me.
95 HAMLET   It was a brute part of him to kill so capital a calf°   *such a prize fool*
     there. — Be the players ready?
   ROSENCRANTZ   Ay, my lord, they stay° upon your patience.   *wait*
   QUEEN GERTRUDE   Come hither, my good Hamlet. Sit by me.
   HAMLET   No, good-mother,° here's mettle³ more attractive.   *stepmother*
          [*He sits by* OPHELIA]
100 POLONIUS [*aside*]   O ho, do you mark that?
   HAMLET [*to* OPHELIA]   Lady, shall I lie in your lap?
   OPHELIA   No, my lord.
   HAMLET   I mean my head upon your lap?
   OPHELIA   Ay, my lord.
105 HAMLET   Do you think I meant country matters?⁴
   OPHELIA   I think nothing, my lord.
   HAMLET   That's a fair thought to lie between maids' legs.

5. With your utmost critical faculty.
6. Smithy, or forge, of Vulcan, the Roman blacksmith god.
7. To judge by his outward reaction.
8. How does; Hamlet's response puns on "fare" as food and drink.
9. The chameleon was supposed to live on air. Hamlet puns on "heir," referring to Claudius's insubstantial promise of the succession.
1. Castrated cocks, crammed or fattened for the table (and a term for a fool).
2. Perhaps an allusion to Shakespeare's own *Julius Caesar*; the actor who first played Polonius may also have played the part of Caesar.
3. A disposition (punning on magnetically attractive "metal").
4. Rustic doings (with an obscene pun on "cunt"). The punning continues in the following lines, where "nothing" suggests the female genitals (often linked to the shape of a zero), and "thing" the male genitals.

OPHELIA   What is, my lord?

HAMLET   No thing.

110   OPHELIA   You are merry, my lord.

HAMLET   Who, I?

OPHELIA   Ay, my lord.

HAMLET   O God, your only jig-maker![5] What should a man do
but be merry? For look you how cheerfully my mother looks,

115   and my father died within 's° two hours.   *these*

OPHELIA   Nay, 'tis twice two months, my lord.

HAMLET   So long? Nay then, let the devil wear black, for I'll have
a suit of sables.[6] O heavens, die two months ago and not forgotten yet! Then there's hope a great man's memory may outlive

120   his life half a year. But, by'r Lady, a must build churches then,
or else shall a suffer not thinking on,[7] with the hobby-horse,
whose epitaph is 'For O, for O, the hobby-horse is forgot.'[8]

Hautboys° play. *The dumb show enters. Enter a* KING   *Oboes*
and a QUEEN *very lovingly, the* QUEEN *embracing him.*
She kneels and makes show of protestation unto him. He
takes her up and declines° his head upon her neck. He   *leans*
lays him down upon a bank of flowers. She, seeing him
asleep, leaves him. Anon comes in a fellow, takes off his
crown, kisses it, and pours poison in the King's ears, and
exits. The QUEEN *returns, finds the* KING *dead, and*
makes passionate action. The poisoner, with some two or
three mutes,° comes in again, seeming to lament with   *nonspeaking actors*
her. The dead body is carried away. The poisoner woos
the QUEEN *with gifts. She seems loath and unwilling a*
while, but in the end accepts his love. Exeunt [the
PLAYERS]

OPHELIA   What means this, my lord?

HAMLET   Marry, this is miching *malhecho.°* That means mis-   *sneaking wrongdoing*

125   chief.

OPHELIA   Belike this show imports the argument° of the play.   *plot*

Enter PROLOGUE

HAMLET   We shall know by this fellow. The players cannot keep
counsel,° they'll tell all.   *a secret*

OPHELIA   Will a tell us what this show meant?

130   HAMLET   Ay, or any show that you'll show him. Be not you
ashamed to show, he'll not shame to tell you what it means.

OPHELIA   You are naught,° you are naught. I'll mark the play.   *indecent*

PROLOGUE   For us and for our tragedy
Here stooping to your clemency,

135   We beg your hearing patiently.   [*Exit*]

HAMLET   Is this a prologue, or the posy of a ring?[9]

OPHELIA   'Tis brief, my lord.

HAMLET   As woman's love.

*Enter the [*PLAYER*]* KING *and his* QUEEN

PLAYER KING   Full thirty times hath Phoebus' cart[1] gone round

---

5. The leading comic actor often devised and performed
the farcical song and dance concluding a play. *only:* unri-
valed.
6. Sable is both an expensive fur for cloaks and trim and
the heraldic term for "black"; Hamlet simultaneously for-
swears his ascetic mourning and vows to continue it.
7. He shall have to endure being forgotten.

8. The hobbyhorse, a man with a mock horse's body
strapped round his waist, was a figure in May Day morris
dances (under attack in Shakespeare's time by religious
reformers). "The hobby horse is forgot" seems to have
been a ballad refrain.
9. The motto engraved in a ring.
1. Apollo's chariot (the sun).

140   Neptune's salt wash and Tellus' orbèd ground,[2]
    And thirty dozen moons with borrowed sheen°   *reflected light*
    About the world have times twelve thirties been
    Since love our hearts and Hymen° did our hands   *goddess of marriage*
    Unite commutual in most sacred bands.
145 PLAYER QUEEN   So many journeys may the sun and moon
    Make us again count o'er ere love be done.
    But woe is me, you are so sick of late,
    So far from cheer and from your former state,
    That I distrust° you. Yet, though I distrust,   *am worried about*
150   Discomfort° you my lord it nothing must.   *Sadden*
    For women's fear and love holds quantity,[3]
    In neither aught, or in extremity.[4]
    Now what my love is, proof° hath made you know,   *experience*
    And as my love is sized,° my fear is so.[5]   *in quantity*
154.1   *Where love is great, the littlest doubts are fear:*
     Where little fears grow great, great love grows there.
155 PLAYER KING   Faith, I must leave thee, love, and shortly too.
    My operant° powers their functions leave° to do,   *vital / cease*
    And thou shalt live in this fair world behind,
    Honoured, beloved; and haply° one as kind   *perhaps*
    For husband shalt thou—
PLAYER QUEEN   O, confound the rest!
160   Such love must needs be treason in my breast.
    In second husband let me be accurst;
    None wed the second but who killed the first.
HAMLET   Wormwood,[6] wormwood.
PLAYER QUEEN   The instances° that second marriage move° *motives / prompt*
165   Are base respects of thrift,° but none of love. *considerations of profit*
    A second time I kill my husband dead
    When second husband kisses me in bed.
PLAYER KING   I do believe you think what now you speak;
    But what we do determine oft we break.
170   Purpose is but the slave to[7] memory,
    Of violent birth but poor validity,°   *enduring strength*
    Which now like fruit unripe sticks on the tree,
    But fall unshaken when they mellow be.
    Most necessary 'tis that we forget
175   To pay ourselves what to ourselves is debt.[8]
    What to ourselves in passion we propose,
    The passion ending, doth the purpose lose.
    The violence of either grief or joy
    Their own enactures with themselves destroy.[9]
180   Where joy most revels, grief doth most lament;
    Grief joys, joy grieves, on slender accident.[1]
    This world is not for aye,° nor 'tis not strange   *eternity*
    That even our loves should with our fortunes change;

2. *Neptune's . . . ground:* The salty flood of the sea god and the round foundation of Tellus (the earth).
3. Are in equal proportions. Q2 includes one other line before this one: "For women fear too much, even as they love / And women's fear . . ."
4. *In . . . extremity:* Either love and fear are both absent, or both are extremely strong.
5. After this line, Q2 has a couplet, 154.1–154.2, omitted in F.
6. A bitter herb taken medicinally (hence, "a bitter pill to swallow").
7. Our intentions serve and depend on.
8. *Most . . . debt:* It is inevitable (or necessary for our well-being) that we neglect to fulfill those promises made to ourselves.
9. *The violence . . . destroy:* Extreme grief and joy destroy themselves, and the motive for action vanishes with them.
1. On account of a small, unforeseen event.

For 'tis a question left us yet to prove
185 Whether love lead fortune or else fortune love.
The great man down, you mark his favourite flies;
The poor advanced° makes friends of enemies.   *promoted*
And hitherto° doth love on fortune tend,°   *to this extent / attend*
For who not needs shall never lack a friend,
190 And who in want a hollow friend doth try°   *test*
Directly seasons him² his enemy.
But orderly to end where I begun,
Our wills and fates do so contrary run³
That our devices still° are overthrown;   *our plans always*
195 Our thoughts are ours, their ends° none of our own.   *results*
So think thou wilt no second husband wed;
But die thy thoughts when thy first lord is dead.
PLAYER QUEEN   Nor earth to me give food, nor heaven light,
Sport and repose lock from me day and night,⁴
199.1   *To desperation turn my trust and hope;*
    An anchor's cheer⁵ in prison be my scope.°   *extent (of good)*
200 Each opposite⁶ that blanks° the face of joy   *makes pale*
Meet what I would have well and it destroy,
Both here and hence pursue me lasting strife
If, once a widow, ever I be wife.
HAMLET   If she should break it now!
PLAYER KING *[to* PLAYER QUEEN*]*
205   'Tis deeply sworn. Sweet, leave me here a while.
My spirits grow dull, and fain° I would beguile   *gladly*
The tedious day with sleep.
PLAYER QUEEN   Sleep rock thy brain,
And never come mischance between us twain.
                    *[*PLAYER KING*] sleeps. Exit [*PLAYER QUEEN*]*
HAMLET *[to* GERTRUDE*]*   Madam, how like you this play?
210 QUEEN GERTRUDE   The lady protests too much, methinks.
HAMLET   O, but she'll keep her word.
KING CLAUDIUS   Have you heard the argument?° Is there no   *plot*
offence in't?
HAMLET   No, no, they do but jest, poison in jest. No offence i'th'
215 world.
KING CLAUDIUS   What do you call the play?
HAMLET   *The Mousetrap.* Marry, how? Tropically.⁷ This play is
the image of a murder done in Vienna. Gonzago is the Duke's
name, his wife Baptista.⁸ You shall see anon. 'Tis a knavish
220 piece of work; but what o' that? Your majesty, and we that have
free° souls, it touches⁹ us not. Let the galled jade wince, our   *guiltless*
withers are unwrung.¹
     *Enter [*PLAYER*]* LUCIANUS
This is one Lucianus, nephew to the King.

---

2. Immediately hardens him, as timber is seasoned for use.
3. What we desire and what is destined to happen are so opposed.
4. After this line, Q2 has a couplet omitted in F, 199.1–199.2.
5. Food for an anchorite (ascetic religious hermit).
6. Each adverse force.
7. As a trope, or rhetorical figure (perhaps punning on "trap").
8. That is, the Player King and Queen (called "Duke" and "Duchess" throughout Q1). Shakespeare seems to base *The Moustrap* on an extremely muddled version of the Duke of Urbino's alleged 1538 murder by Luigi Gonzaga.
9. Wounds; concerns.
1. Let the chafed horse wince, our shoulders are not rubbed sore.

OPHELIA You are as good as a chorus,[2] my lord.

225 HAMLET I could interpret between you and your love if I could see the puppets dallying.[3]

OPHELIA You are keen,° my lord, you are keen. *sharply satirical*

HAMLET It would cost you a groaning to take off mine edge.[4]

OPHELIA Still better, and worse.[5]

230 HAMLET So you mis-take your husbands.[6] [*To* LUCIANUS] Begin, murderer. Pox, leave thy damnable° faces and begin. Come: *grimacing* 'the croaking raven doth bellow for revenge'.[7]

PLAYER LUCIANUS Thoughts black, hands apt, drugs fit, and time agreeing,
    Confederate° season, else no creature seeing; *Complicit*
235 Thou mixture rank° of midnight weeds collected, *foul*
    With Hecate's ban[8] thrice blasted, thrice infected,
    Thy natural magic and dire property° *quality*
    On wholesome life usurp immediately.

[*He*] *pours the poison in* [*the Player King's*] *ears*

HAMLET A poisons him i'th' garden for 's estate.° His name's *position; state*
240 Gonzago. The story is extant, and writ in choice Italian. You shall see anon how the murderer gets the love of Gonzago's wife.

OPHELIA The King rises.

HAMLET What, frighted with false fire?[9]

245 QUEEN GERTRUDE [*to* CLAUDIUS] How fares my lord?

POLONIUS Give o'er the play.

KING CLAUDIUS Give me some light. Away.

COURTIERS Lights, lights, lights![1]

Exeunt all but HAMLET *and* HORATIO

HAMLET Why, let the stricken deer go weep,[2]
250   The hart ungallèd° play, *unafflicted*
    For some must watch,° while some must sleep, *stay awake*
        So runs the world away.[3]
    Would not this,° sir, and a forest of feathers,[4] if the rest of my *(The Mousetrap)*
    fortunes turn Turk° with me, with two Provençal roses on my *renegade*
255 razed[5] shoes, get me a fellowship in a cry of players,[6] sir?

HORATIO Half a share.

HAMLET A whole one, I.
    For thou dost know, O Damon[7] dear,
    This realm dismantled° was *deprived*
260 Of Jove himself, and now reigns here
    A very, very—pajock.[8]

---

2. The Chorus explained the forthcoming action. In puppet shows, a choric narrator, or "interpreter," announced the characters' names and spoke the dialogue.
3. Flirting. Hamlet uses "interpret" here in the sense of acting as the go-between, or pander, for two lovers.
4. To satisfy my sexual appetite (leading to groaning in either sexual intercourse or childbirth).
5. Wittier, and more obscene.
6. With these false promises ("for better and for worse"), you take your husbands in marriage and cheat on them.
7. Misquoted from *The True Tragedy of Richard III* (c. 1591; not to be confused with Shakespeare's own *Richard III*).
8. Curse by the goddess of witchcraft.
9. Fireworks or blank cartridges.
1. This line is spoken by Polonius in Q2 and by "All"

in F.
2. A deer was thought to weep when mortally wounded. These four lines are probably from a lost ballad.
3. That's the way of the world.
4. Plumes, worn often onstage.
5. Decorated with slashes. *Provençal roses:* large rosettes concealing shoelaces.
6. *a fellowship . . . players:* a profit-sharing partnership in a pack ("cry") of actors (such as Shakespeare had in the Lord Chamberlain's Men).
7. Damon and Pythias were legendary ideals of friendship.
8. "Patchock" (rare, meaning something like "oaf"), or "peacock," emblem of the sin of pride. (The expected rhyme word would be "ass.")

HORATIO   You might have rhymed.

HAMLET   O good Horatio, I'll take the Ghost's word for a thousand pound. Didst perceive?

265 HORATIO   Very well, my lord.

HAMLET   Upon the talk of the pois'ning?

HORATIO   I did very well note him.

Enter ROSENCRANTZ *and* GUILDENSTERN

HAMLET   Ah ha! Come, some music, come, the recorders,
For if the King like not the comedy,

270 Why then, belike he likes it not, pardie.°   *indeed* (pardieu)
Come, some music.

GUILDENSTERN   Good my lord, vouchsafe me a word with you.

HAMLET   Sir, a whole history.

GUILDENSTERN   The King, sir—

275 HAMLET   Ay, sir, what of him?

GUILDENSTERN   Is in his retirement° marvellous distempered.   *withdrawal*

HAMLET   With drink, sir?

GUILDENSTERN   No, my lord, rather with choler.[9]

HAMLET   Your wisdom should show itself more richer° to signify   *resourceful*
280 this to his doctor, for for me to put him to his purgation[1] would
perhaps plunge him into far more choler.

GUILDENSTERN   Good my lord, put your discourse into some
frame,° and start° not so wildly from my affair.   *order / jump away*

HAMLET   I am tame, sir. Pronounce.

285 GUILDENSTERN   The Queen your mother, in most great affliction of spirit, hath sent me to you.

HAMLET   You are welcome.

GUILDENSTERN   Nay, good my lord, this courtesy is not of the
right breed.° If it shall please you to make me a wholesome°   *kind; nobility / sane*
290 answer, I will do your mother's commandment; if not, your
pardon° and my return shall be the end of my business.   *permission to go*

HAMLET   Sir, I cannot.

GUILDENSTERN   What, my lord?

HAMLET   Make you a wholesome answer. My wit's diseased. But,
295 sir, such answers as I can make, you shall command; or rather,
as you say, my mother. Therefore no more, but to the matter.
My mother, you say?

ROSENCRANTZ   Then thus she says: your behaviour hath struck
her into amazement and admiration.°   *bewilderment*

300 HAMLET   O wonderful son, that can so astonish a mother! But is
there no sequel at the heels of this mother's admiration?

ROSENCRANTZ   She desires to speak with you in her closet° ere   *private chamber*
you go to bed.

HAMLET   We shall obey, were she ten times our mother. Have
305 you any further trade with us?

ROSENCRANTZ   My lord, you once did love me.

HAMLET   So I do still, by these pickers and stealers.[2]

ROSENCRANTZ   Good my lord, what is your cause of distemper?

---

9. Both anger (Guildenstern's meaning) and indigestion
(Hamlet's). In Renaissance medical psychology, each was
a symptom of too much yellow bile—an imbalance ("distemper") of the bodily fluids (humors).
1. A complicated pun: bloodletting; spiritual purging
(confession and absolution); legal purging (clearing one-

self of a crime).
2. Hands. (The catechism in the Book of Common
Prayer includes a promise to "keep my hands from picking and stealing, and my tongue from evil speaking, lying,
and slandering.")

You do freely° bar the door of your own liberty if you deny your   *voluntarily*
310 griefs to your friend.
HAMLET   Sir, I lack advancement.
ROSENCRANTZ   How can that be when you have the voice of the
King himself for your succession in Denmark?
HAMLET   Ay, but 'while the grass grows . . .'³—the proverb is
315 something° musty.   *somewhat*
         Enter one with a recorder⁴
O, the recorder. Let me see. [To ROSENCRANTZ *and* GUILDEN-
STERN, *taking them aside*] To withdraw° with you, why do you   *speak privately*
go about to recover the wind of me as if you would drive me
into a toil?⁵
320 GUILDENSTERN   O my lord, if my duty be too bold, my love is
too unmannerly.⁶
HAMLET   I do not well understand that. Will you play upon this
pipe?
GUILDENSTERN   My lord, I cannot.
325 HAMLET   I pray you.
GUILDENSTERN   Believe me, I cannot.
HAMLET   I do beseech you.
GUILDENSTERN   I know no touch of it, my lord.
HAMLET   'Tis as easy as lying. Govern these ventages° with your   *finger holes*
330 fingers and thumb, give it breath with your mouth, and it will
discourse most excellent music. Look you, these are the stops.°   *finger holes; notes*
GUILDENSTERN   But these cannot I command to any utterance
of harmony. I have not the skill.
HAMLET   Why, look you now, how unworthy a thing you make
335 of me! You would play upon me, you would seem to know my
stops, you would pluck out the heart of my mystery, you would
sound° me from my lowest note to the top of my compass;° and   *fathom; play on / range*
there is much music, excellent voice in this little organ,° yet   *musical instrument*
cannot you make it speak. 'Sblood, do you think I am easier to
340 be played on than a pipe? Call me what instrument you will,
though you can fret⁷ me, you cannot play upon me.
         Enter POLONIUS
God bless you, sir.
POLONIUS   My lord, the Queen would speak with you, and presently.
345 HAMLET   Do you see yonder cloud that's almost in shape of a
camel?
POLONIUS   By th' mass, and 'tis: like a camel, indeed.
HAMLET   Methinks it is like a weasel.
POLONIUS   It is backed like a weasel.
350 HAMLET   Or like a whale.
POLONIUS   Very like a whale.
HAMLET   Then will I come to my mother by and by. [*Aside*]
They fool me to the top of my bent.⁸ [*To* POLONIUS] I will come
by and by.
355 POLONIUS   I will say so.
HAMLET   'By and by' is easily said.   *Exit* [POLONIUS]

---

3. "While the grass grows, the horse starves."
4. Q2 has "Enter the Players with Recorders."
5. *go . . . toil:* both conspire and take a roundabout
course in order to get to the windward (like a hunter
using his own smell to drive quarry to a waiting snare, or
"toil").

6. If I have been discourteous in pursuing what is my
duty, my love for you is to blame.
7. Irritate, punning on "frets of stringed instruments,"
which regulate fingering and pitch.
8. They go along with my foolishness to its limit, or to
the limit of my endurance.

Leave me, friends. [*Exeunt* ROSENCRANTZ *and* GUILDENSTERN]
'Tis now the very witching time of night,
When churchyards yawn, and hell itself breathes out
360 Contagion to this world. Now could I drink hot blood,
And do such bitter business as the day
Would quake to look on. Soft, now to my mother.
O heart, lose not thy nature!° Let not ever   *natural affection*
The soul of Nero[9] enter this firm° bosom.   *resolved*
365 Let me be cruel, not unnatural.
I will speak daggers to her, but use none.
My tongue and soul in this be hypocrites[1] —
How in my words somever[2] she be shent,°   *rebuked*
To give them seals[3] never my soul consent.   *Exit*

3.3

Enter KING [CLAUDIUS], ROSENCRANTZ, *and* GUILDEN-
STERN

KING CLAUDIUS   I like him not, nor stands it safe with us
To let his madness range. Therefore prepare you.
I your commission will forthwith dispatch,
And he to England shall along with you.
5 The terms of our estate[1] may not endure
Hazard so dangerous as doth hourly grow
Out of his lunacies.[2]
GUILDENSTERN   We will ourselves provide.
Most holy and religious fear° it is   *care*
To keep those many many bodies safe
10 That live and feed upon your majesty.
ROSENCRANTZ   The single° and peculiar° life is bound   *individual / private*
With all the strength and armour of the mind
To keep itself from noyance;° but much more   *harm*
That spirit upon whose weal° depends and rests   *well-being*
15 The lives of many. The cease° of majesty   *decease*
Dies not alone, but like a gulf° doth draw   *whirlpool*
What's near it with it. It is a massy° wheel   *massive*
Fixed on the summit of the highest mount,
To whose huge spokes ten thousand lesser things
20 Are mortised° and adjoined, which° when it falls   *affixed / so that*
Each small annexment, petty consequence,
Attends° the boist'rous ruin. Never alone   *Accompanies*
Did the King sigh, but with a general groan.
KING CLAUDIUS   Arm° you, I pray you, to this speedy voyage,   *Prepare*
25 For we will fetters put upon this fear
Which now goes too free-footed.
ROSENCRANTZ *and* GUILDENSTERN   We will haste us.
                               Exeunt [both]
    Enter POLONIUS
POLONIUS   My lord, he's going to his mother's closet.
Behind the arras° I'll convey myself   *wall tapestry*
To hear the process.° I'll warrant she'll tax him home.[3]   *proceedings*

---

9. The Roman emperor Nero reputedly murdered his mother, in one account, by cutting open her womb.
1. Let me appear and speak as if I intended violence (though I do not).
2. However much by my words.
3. To confirm them with visible deeds.

3.3 Location: The castle.
1. The responsibilities of our position.
2. Mad actions, apparently a revision in F of Q2's "browes" (an ambiguous term suggesting "brain," "expressions," or "effrontery").
3. I'm sure she will rebuke him thoroughly.

30   And, as you said—and wisely was it said—
        'Tis meet° that some more audience than a mother,   *fitting*
        Since nature makes them partial, should o'erhear
        The speech of vantage.° Fare you well, my liege.   *in addition*
        I'll call upon you ere you go to bed,
        And tell you what I know.
35   KING CLAUDIUS   Thanks, dear my lord.

                                                        Exit [POLONIUS]

        O, my offence is rank! It smells to heaven.
        It hath the primal eldest curse[4] upon't,
        A brother's murder. Pray can I not.
        Though inclination be as sharp as will,[5]
40   My stronger guilt defeats my strong intent,
        And like a man to double business bound[6]
        I stand in pause where I shall first begin,
        And both neglect. What if this cursèd hand
        Were thicker than itself with brother's blood,[7]
45   Is there not rain enough in the sweet heavens
        To wash it white as snow?[8] Whereto serves mercy
        But to confront the visage of offence?[9]
        And what's in prayer but this twofold force,
        To be forestallèd° ere we come to fall,   *prevented*
50   Or pardoned being down? Then I'll look up.
        My fault is past—but O, what form of prayer
        Can serve my turn? 'Forgive me my foul murder'?
        That cannot be, since I am still possessed
        Of those effects for which I did the murder—
55   My crown, mine own ambition, and my queen.
        May one be pardoned and retain th'offence?[1]
        In the corrupted currents of this world
        Offence's gilded° hand may shove by justice,   *bribing*
        And oft 'tis seen the wicked prize[2] itself
60   Buys out the law. But 'tis not so above.
        There is no shuffling,° there the action lies   *evasion*
        In his true nature,[3] and we ourselves compelled
        Even to the teeth and forehead of[4] our faults
        To give in evidence.[5] What then? What rests?°   *remains to be done*
65   Try what repentance can. What can it not?
        Yet what can it when one cannot repent?
        O wretched state, O bosom black as death,
        O limèd[6] soul that, struggling to be free,
        Art more engaged!° Help, angels! Make assay.°   *entangled / some attempt*
70   Bow, stubborn knees; and heart with strings of steel,

---

4. The first, oldest curse (God's curse on Cain for murdering his brother, Abel; see Genesis 4:10–12).
5. Though my desire (to pray) is as strong as my determination to do so.
6. Committed to two different goals.
7. Were covered with a layer of brother's blood deeper than the hand's thickness.
8. Compare Isaiah 1:15–18: "And though ye make many prayers, I will not hear: for your hands are full of blood. Wash you, make you clean; take away the evil of your works from before mine eyes. . . . though your sins were as crimson, they shall be made white as snow."
9. *Whereto . . . offence:* What purpose has mercy if not to oppose sin face to face?
1. And keep what was gained from the crime.
2. The profits from wickedness.
3. *the action . . . nature:* the deed appears in its true form; legal proceedings are properly conducted.
4. *Even . . . of:* Even face to face with. (English law provided for the confrontation of the accused and the witnesses.)
5. To testify. In English law, one cannot be forced to give evidence against oneself; heavenly justice is different.
6. Caught as if in birdlime, a sticky substance smeared on twigs to catch birds.

Be soft as sinews of the new-born babe.
All may be well.
    [*He kneels.*]
    Enter [*Prince*] HAMLET [*behind him*]
HAMLET Now might I do it pat,° now a° is praying,   *neatly / he*
And now I'll do't,
    [*He draws his sword*]
        and so a goes to heaven,
75 And so am I revenged. That would be scanned.[7]
A villain kills my father, and for that
I, his sole son, do this same villain send
To heaven.
O, this is hire and salary, not revenge!
80 A took my father grossly, full of bread,[8]
With all his crimes broad blown,[9] as flush° as May;   *vigorously thriving*
And how his audit° stands, who knows save heaven?   *spiritual account*
But in our circumstance and course of thought[1]
'Tis heavy with him. And am I then revenged
85 To take him in the purging of his soul,
When he is fit and seasoned° for his passage?   *made ready*
No.
    [*He sheathes his sword*]
Up, sword, and know thou a more horrid hint.°   *occasion*
When he is drunk asleep, or in his rage,
90 Or in th'incestuous pleasure of his bed,
At gaming, swearing, or about some act
That has no relish° of salvation in't,   *trace*
Then trip him that his heels may kick at heaven,
And that his soul may be as damned and black
95 As hell whereto it goes. My mother stays.°   *waits*
This physic[2] but prolongs thy sickly days.   *Exit*
KING CLAUDIUS My words fly up, my thoughts remain below.
Words without thoughts never to heaven go.   *Exit*

3.4

    Enter QUEEN GERTRUDE *and* POLONIUS
POLONIUS A will come straight.° Look you lay home to him.[1]   *immediately*
Tell him his pranks have been too broad° to bear with,   *outrageous*
And that your grace hath screened and stood between
Much heat and him. I'll silence me e'en here.
5 Pray you be round° with him.   *blunt*
HAMLET (*within*) Mother, mother, mother!
QUEEN GERTRUDE I'll warr'nt you. Fear° me not. Withdraw; I   *Doubt*
 hear him coming.
    [POLONIUS *hides behind the arras.*]
    Enter [*Prince*] HAMLET
HAMLET Now, mother, what's the matter?
QUEEN GERTRUDE Hamlet, thou hast thy father much offended.
10 HAMLET Mother, you have my father much offended.

---

7. That needs careful evaluation.
8. Not spiritually prepared. Compare Ezekiel 16:49: "Behold, this was the iniquity of thy sister Sodom, pride, fullness of bread, and abundance of idleness."
9. With all his sins in full bloom.
1. But in our indirect and limited way of knowing on earth.
2. Medicine (both Claudius's prayer and Hamlet's postponement of the revenge).
3.4 Location: The Queen's private chamber.
1. Be sure to rebuke him thoroughly.

QUEEN GERTRUDE   Come, come, you answer with an idle tongue.

HAMLET   Go, go, you question with a wicked tongue.

QUEEN GERTRUDE   Why, how now,° Hamlet?   *what's this*

HAMLET   What's the matter now?

QUEEN GERTRUDE   Have you forgot me?[2]

HAMLET   No, by the rood,° not so.   *Cross of Christ*

15   You are the Queen, your husband's brother's wife.
      But—would you were not so—you are my mother.

QUEEN GERTRUDE   Nay, then, I'll set those to you that can speak.[3]

HAMLET   Come, come, and sit you down. You shall not budge.
      You go not till I set you up a glass°   *mirror*

20   Where you may see the inmost part of you.

QUEEN GERTRUDE   What wilt thou do? Thou wilt not murder me?
      Help, help, ho!

POLONIUS [*behind the arras*]   What ho! Help, help, help!

HAMLET   How now, a rat? Dead for a ducat, dead.[4]

          [*He thrusts his sword through the arras.*] Kills POLONIUS

POLONIUS   O, I am slain!

QUEEN GERTRUDE [*to* HAMLET]   O me, what hast thou done?

25   HAMLET   Nay, I know not. Is it the King?

QUEEN GERTRUDE   O, what a rash and bloody deed is this!

HAMLET   A bloody deed—almost as bad, good-mother,°   *stepmother*
      As kill a king and marry with his brother.

QUEEN GERTRUDE   As kill a king?

HAMLET   Ay, lady, 'twas my word.

30   [*To* POLONIUS] Thou wretched, rash, intruding fool, farewell.
      I took thee for thy better. Take thy fortune.
      Thou find'st to be too busy° is some danger.—   *nosy*
      Leave wringing of your hands. Peace, sit you down,
      And let me wring your heart; for so I shall

35   If it be made of penetrable stuff,
      If damnèd custom° have not brassed it so   *sinful habit*
      That it is proof and bulwark against sense.[5]

QUEEN GERTRUDE   What have I done, that thou dar'st wag thy tongue
      In noise so rude against me?

HAMLET   Such an act

40   That blurs the grace and blush of modesty,
      Calls virtue hypocrite, takes off the rose
      From the fair forehead of an innocent love
      And sets a blister there,[6] makes marriage vows
      As false as dicers' oaths—O, such a deed

45   As from the body of contraction plucks
      The very soul, and sweet religion makes
      A rhapsody[7] of words. Heaven's face doth glow,°   *blush*
      Yea, this solidity and compound mass[8]
      With tristful° visage, as against the doom,[9]   *sad*
      Is thought-sick at the act.

50   QUEEN GERTRUDE   Ay me, what act,

---

2. Forgotten the respect you owe to me as your mother.
3. *that can speak*: who can deal with someone as impossibly rude as you.
4. I bet a ducat I have killed it.
5. *brassed . . . sense*: made it so brasslike (or brazen) that it is impenetrably fortified against natural feeling ("sense").

6. Prostitutes, among other criminals, were branded on the forehead during the sixteenth and seventeenth centuries.
7. Meaningless jumble.
8. Solid earth (a compound of the four elements).
9. As if preparing for the Last Judgment.

That roars so loud and thunders in the index?[1]

HAMLET   Look here upon this picture, and on this,
The counterfeit presentment° of two brothers.   *painted portrayal*
See what a grace was seated on this brow—
55   Hyperion's° curls, the front° of Jove himself,   *The sun god's / forehead*
An eye like Mars,° to threaten or command,   *the god of war*
A station like the herald Mercury[2]
New lighted° on a heaven-kissing hill;   *alighted*
A combination and a form indeed
60   Where every god did seem to set his seal
To give the world assurance of a man.
This *was* your husband. Look you now what follows.
Here *is* your husband, like a mildewed ear°   *ear of grain*
Blasting° his wholesome brother. Have you eyes?   *Infesting*
65   Could you on this fair mountain leave° to feed,   *cease*
And batten on this moor?[3] Ha, have you eyes?
You cannot call it love, for at your age
The heyday in the blood[4] is tame, it's humble,
And waits° upon the judgement; and what judgement   *follows*
70   Would step from this to this?[5]
70.1   *Sense[6] sure you have,*
          Else could you not have motion; but sure that sense
          Is apoplexed,° for madness would not err,   *paralyzed*
          Nor sense to ecstasy was ne'er so thralled
70.5   *But it reserved some quantity of choice*
          To serve in such a difference.[7] What devil was't
          That thus hath cozened you at hoodman-blind?[8]
          Eyes without feeling, feeling without sight,
          Ears without hands or eyes, smelling sans all,[9]
70.10   *Or but a sickly part of one true sense*
          Could not so mope.[1]
                              What devil was't
That thus hath cozened you at hood-man blind?[2]
O shame, where is thy blush? Rebellious hell,
If thou canst mutine° in a matron's bones,   *mutiny*
To flaming youth let virtue be as wax
75   And melt in her° own fire. Proclaim no shame   *(youth's)*
When the compulsive ardour gives the charge,°   *order to attack*
Since frost itself as actively doth burn,
And reason panders will.[3]

QUEEN GERTRUDE   O Hamlet, speak no more!
Thou turn'st mine eyes into my very soul,
80   And there I see such black and grainèd° spots   *engrained*
As will not leave their tinct.°   *lose their color*

HAMLET   Nay, but to live
In the rank sweat of an enseamèd° bed,   *a greasy*

1. Table of contents; preface.
2. A stance like the winged herald of the gods.
3. And glut yourself on this poor pastureland (possibly
punning on "blackamoor").
4. The excitement of sexual passion.
5. After "this?" Q2 has a longer version, 70.1–70.11, of
Hamlet's subsequent one and a half lines.
6. Sensation; the five senses (sight, smell, hearing, taste,
and touch).
7. *ne'er . . . difference*: never so enslaved by madness that

it did not retain some ability to choose between such different men ("sense" connoting "reason").
8. See note to line 71.
9. *sans all*: without any other sense.
1. Could not be so obtuse.
2. That in this way has cheated you in blindman's buff
(as if her second husband had been put in her way while
she was groping blindfolded).
3. And mature reason abets lust (rather than restraining
it).

Stewed in corruption, honeying and making love
Over the nasty sty—
QUEEN GERTRUDE   O, speak to me no more!
85   These words like daggers enter in mine ears.
No more, sweet Hamlet.
HAMLET   A murderer and a villain,
A slave that is not twenti'th part the tithe°   one-tenth
Of your precedent° lord, a vice[4] of kings,   previous
A cutpurse° of the empire and the rule,   pickpocket
90   That from a shelf the precious diadem stole
And put it in his pocket—
QUEEN GERTRUDE   No more.
HAMLET   A king of shreds and patches[5]—
        Enter GHOST in his nightgown[6]
Save me and hover o'er me with your wings,
95   You heavenly guards! [To GHOST] What would you, gracious figure?
QUEEN GERTRUDE   Alas, he's mad.
HAMLET [to GHOST]   Do you not come your tardy son to chide,
That, lapsed in time and passion,[7] lets go by
Th'important° acting of your dread command?   urgent
O, say!
100   GHOST   Do not forget. This visitation
Is but to whet thy almost blunted purpose.
But look, amazement on thy mother sits.
O, step between her and her fighting soul.
Conceit° in weakest bodies strongest works.   Imagination
105   Speak to her, Hamlet.
HAMLET   How is it with you, lady?
QUEEN GERTRUDE   Alas, how is't with you,
That you do bend your eye on vacancy,
And with th'incorporal° air do hold discourse?   bodiless
110   Forth at your eyes your spirits wildly peep,
And, as the sleeping soldiers in th'alarm,°   call to arms
Your bedded hair, like life in excrements,[8]
Start up and stand on end. O gentle son,
Upon the heat and flame of thy distemper°   unbalanced mind
115   Sprinkle cool patience! Whereon do you look?
HAMLET   On him, on him. Look you how pale he glares.
His form and cause conjoined,[9] preaching to stones,
Would make them capable. [To GHOST] Do not look
        upon me,
Lest with this piteous action you convert°   change (to mercy)
120   My stern effects.° Then what I have to do   intended acts
Will want true colour[1]—tears perchance° for blood.   perhaps
QUEEN GERTRUDE   To whom do you speak this?
HAMLET   Do you see nothing there?
QUEEN GERTRUDE   Nothing at all, yet all that is I see.
HAMLET   Nor did you nothing hear?
QUEEN GERTRUDE   No, nothing but ourselves.

4. In morality plays, the buffoon who personified evil.
5. *shreds and patches:* motley, the costume of a jester.
6. The nightgown is specified only in Q1; Q2 and F
leave open the possibility that the Ghost is appearing
again in his armor.
7. *lapsed . . . passion:* having allowed time to pass and

passionate dedication (to revenge) to fade.
8. In insensate outgrowths (used of nails and hair). *bedded:* (formerly) flat and inert.
9. His appearance joined with his reason for appearing.
1. Will not be as it should (since he cries colorless tears
instead of shedding red blood).

125 HAMLET   Why, look you there. Look how it steals away.
My father, in his habit² as° he lived.   *when; as if*
Look where he goes even now out at the portal.
                                                                    Exit GHOST
QUEEN GERTRUDE   This is the very coinage of your brain.
This bodiless creation ecstasy
Is very cunning in.³
130 HAMLET   Ecstasy?
My pulse as yours doth temperately keep time,
And makes as healthful music. It is not madness
That I have uttered. Bring me to the test,
And I the matter will reword,° which madness   *repeat exactly*
135 Would gambol° from. Mother, for love of grace   *skitter away*
Lay not a flattering unction⁴ to your soul
That not your trespass but my madness speaks.
It will but skin° and film the ulcerous place   *cover*
Whilst rank corruption, mining° all within,   *undermining*
140 Infects unseen. Confess yourself to heaven;
Repent what's past, avoid what is to come,
And do not spread the compost o'er the weeds
To make them ranker. Forgive me this my virtue,°   *virtuous exhortation*
For in the fatness° of these pursy° times   *grossness / flatulent*
145 Virtue itself of vice must pardon beg,
Yea, curb° and woo for leave° to do him good.   *bow / permission*
QUEEN GERTRUDE   O Hamlet, thou hast cleft my heart in twain!
HAMLET   O, throw away the worser part of it,
And live the purer with the other half!
150 Good night—but go not to mine uncle's bed.
Assume° a virtue if you have it not.⁵   *Put on (actions of)*
151.1   *That monster custom, who all sense doth eat,*
          Of habits devilish,⁶ is angel yet in this:
          That to the use° of actions fair and good   *habitual practice*
          He likewise gives a frock or livery
151.5   *That aptly° is put on. Refrain tonight,*   *quickly*
          And that shall lend a kind of easiness
          To the next abstinence, the next more easy—
          For use almost can change the stamp of nature—
          And either in° the devil, or throw him out   *let in*
151.10   *With wondrous potency.*
Refrain tonight,
And that shall lend a kind of easiness
To the next abstinence. Once more, good night;
155 And when you are desirous to be blest,
I'll blessing beg of you. For this same lord,
I do repent. But heaven hath pleased it so
To punish me with this, and this with me,
That I must be their scourge and minister.⁷
160 I will bestow° him, and will answer well⁸   *dispose of*
The death I gave him. So, again, good night.

2. Dress and bearing.
3. *This bodiless . . . in:* This type of hallucination is a particular skill ("cunning") of madness.
4. Do not apply an ointment that relieves pain but does not heal (contrasted to a sacramental unction that blesses the soul).

5. Q2 has the following longer version (151.1–151.10) of lines 152–54 *(Refrain . . . abstinence)*.
6. Emended from Q2's "devil," apparently in compressed opposition to "angel."
7. Heaven's agent of punishment.
8. Will take responsibility for.

I must be cruel only to be kind.
Thus bad begins, and worse remains behind.[9]
QUEEN GERTRUDE   What shall I do?
165 HAMLET   Not this, by no means, that I bid you do:
.   Let the bloat King tempt you again to bed,
Pinch wanton on your cheek, call you his mouse,
And let him for a pair of reechy° kisses,   *filthy*
Or paddling° in your neck with his damned fingers,   *fondly fingering*
170 Make you to ravel° all this matter out,   *disclose*
That I essentially am not in madness,
But mad in craft.° 'Twere good you let him know,   *cunning*
For who that's but° a queen, fair, sober, wise,   *only*
Would from a paddock,° from a bat, a gib,°   *toad / tomcat*
175 Such dear concernings° hide? Who would do so?   *Such vital affairs*
No, in despite of sense and secrecy,
Unpeg the basket on the house's top,
Let the birds fly, and, like the famous ape,
To try conclusions in the basket creep,
180 And break your own neck down.[1]
QUEEN GERTRUDE   Be thou assured, if words be made of breath,
And breath of life, I have no life to breathe
What thou hast said to me.
HAMLET   I must to England.
You know that?
QUEEN GERTRUDE   Alack, I had forgot.
185 'Tis so concluded on.[2]
185.1   HAMLET   *There's letters sealed, and my two schoolfellows—*
Whom I will trust as I will adders fanged—
They bear the mandate, they must sweep my way
And marshal me to knavery.[3] Let it work,°   *proceed*
185.5   *For 'tis the sport to have the engineer[4]*
Hoised with his own petard;[5] and't shall go hard
But I will delve one yard below their mines°   *military tunnels*
And blow them at the moon. O, 'tis most sweet
When in one line two crafts directly meet.[6]
HAMLET   This man shall set me packing.
I'll lug the guts into the neighbour room.
Mother, good night indeed. This counsellor
Is now most still, most secret, and most grave,
Who was in life a foolish prating knave.—
190 Come, sir, to draw toward an end with you.[7]—
Good night, mother.   *Exit, tugging in* POLONIUS

---

9. To follow. Q2 here adds, "One word more good Lady."
1. *like . . . down:* a tale presumably involving an ape who opened a wicker cage full of birds and released them from the rooftop; after climbing into the basket, he tried to imitate their flight to freedom but died in the fall. *try conclusions:* test the results.
2. Q2 contains the following additional passage.
3. *sweep . . . knavery:* prepare my path and escort me into

a trap (also, and provoke me to crime).
4. Designer and builder of "engines" (military devices).
5. Blown skyward by his own bomb (for breaching enemy fortifications).
6. That is, when two devious plots ("crafts") meet along the same path of tunneling (a standard technique in siege warfare).
7. To conclude my dealings with you (punning on "draw" as "drag").

4.1

Enter KING CLAUDIUS *to* QUEEN GERTRUDE[1]

KING CLAUDIUS   There's matter in these sighs, these profound heaves;
You must translate. 'Tis fit we understand them.
Where is your son?[2]

3.1   QUEEN GERTRUDE   *Bestow this place on us a little while.*
Exeunt [ROSENCRANTZ *and* GUILDENSTERN]
Ah, my good lord, what have I seen tonight!

5   KING CLAUDIUS   What, Gertrude? How does Hamlet?

QUEEN GERTRUDE   Mad as the sea and wind when both contend
Which is the mightier. In his lawless fit,
Behind the arras hearing something stir,
He whips his rapier out and cries 'A rat, a rat!',

10   And in his brainish apprehension° kills   *brain-sick notion*
The unseen good old man.

KING CLAUDIUS   O heavy deed!
It had been so with us° had we been there.   *me (royal "we")*
His liberty is full of threats to all—
To you yourself, to us, to everyone.

15   Alas, how shall this bloody deed be answered?°   *accounted for*
It will be laid to° us, whose providence°   *blamed on / foresight*
Should have kept short,° restrained, and out of haunt[3]   *closely tethered*
This mad young man. But so much was our love,
We would not understand what was most fit,

20   But, like the owner° of a foul disease,   *victim*
To keep it from divulging,° let it feed   *being seen*
Even on the pith of life. Where is he gone?

QUEEN GERTRUDE   To draw apart the body he hath killed,
O'er whom—his very madness, like some ore°   *vein of gold*
25   Among a mineral° of metals base,   *mine*
Shows itself pure—a° weeps for what is done.   *he*

KING CLAUDIUS   O Gertrude, come away!
The sun no sooner shall the mountains touch
But we will ship him hence; and this vile deed
30   We must with all our majesty and skill
Both countenance° and excuse.—Ho, Guildenstern!   *condone*
Enter ROSENCRANTZ *and* GUILDENSTERN
Friends both, go join you with some further aid.
Hamlet in madness hath Polonius slain,
And from his mother's closet hath he dragged him.
35   Go seek him out, speak fair, and bring the body
Into the chapel. I pray you haste in this.
Exeunt [ROSENCRANTZ *and* GUILDENSTERN]
Come, Gertrude, we'll call up our wisest friends
To let them know both what we mean to do
And what's untimely done.[4]

39.1   *So envious slander,*[5]
Whose whisper o'er the world's diameter,°   *whole extent*

4.1 Location: The castle.
1. The action continues, Gertrude remaining onstage. (Act divisions in the play are not authorial.) In Q2, Rosencrantz and Guildenstern enter with Claudius.
2. In Q2, Rosencrantz and Guildenstern, having entered with Claudius and Gertrude, can exit here (see line 3.1).
3. Public gatherings.
4. After "done," Q2 has the following passage, 39.1–39.5, omitted in F.
5. The phrase is conjectural. Q2 is missing a half line that contains the subject of the sentence.

As level as the cannon to his blank,[6]
Transports his poisoned shot, may miss our name
39.5   And hit the woundless° air.   *invulnerable*
                         O, come away!
40   My soul is full of discord and dismay.   *Exeunt*

4.2

Enter [Prince] HAMLET
HAMLET   Safely stowed.
ROSENCRANTZ and GUILDENSTERN (within) Hamlet, Lord Hamlet!
HAMLET   What noise? Who calls on Hamlet?
          Enter ROSENCRANTZ and GUILDENSTERN
                         O, here they come.
ROSENCRANTZ   What have you done, my lord, with the dead body?
5   HAMLET   Compounded° it with dust, whereto 'tis kin.   *Mixed*
ROSENCRANTZ   Tell us where 'tis, that we may take it thence
     And bear it to the chapel.
HAMLET   Do not believe it.
ROSENCRANTZ   Believe what?
10   HAMLET   That I can keep your counsel and not mine own.[1]
     Besides, to be demanded of° a sponge—what replication°   *questioned by / reply*
     should be made by the son of a king?
ROSENCRANTZ   Take you me for a sponge, my lord?
HAMLET   Ay, sir, that soaks up the King's countenance,° his   *favor*
15   rewards, his authorities. But such officers do the King best ser-
     vice in the end. He keeps them, like an ape an apple in the
     corner of his jaw, first mouthed to be last swallowed. When he
     needs what you have gleaned, it is but squeezing you, and,
     sponge, you shall be dry again.
20   ROSENCRANTZ   I understand you not, my lord.
HAMLET   I am glad of it. A knavish speech sleeps in a foolish
     ear.[2]
ROSENCRANTZ   My lord, you must tell us where the body is, and
     go with us to the King.
25   HAMLET   The body is with the King, but the King is not with the
     body.[3] The King is a thing—
GUILDENSTERN   A thing, my lord?
HAMLET   Of nothing. Bring me to him. Hide fox, and all after.[4]
               [Exit running, pursued by the others]

4.3

Enter KING [CLAUDIUS][1]
KING CLAUDIUS   I have sent to seek him, and to find the body.
     How dangerous is it that this man goes loose!
     Yet must not we put the strong law on him.
     He's loved of° the distracted° multitude,   *by / unreasonable*

6. As straight as the cannon at a target at point-blank
range. (The cannon would be tilted to aim at a distant
target.)
4.2 Location: Scene continues.
1. Hamlet plays on two senses of "counsel": That I can
follow your advice and not keep my secret.
2. An insulting remark is not perceived by a fool.
3. A riddle. Hamlet may mean that Polonius is gone to
the afterlife with King Hamlet but Claudius is still alive;
or he may refer to the legal theory of the "king's two bod-

ies" (one the king's natural body, the other the immortal
abstract body of the state).
4. From the children's game fox-and-hounds, similar to
hide-and-seek.
4.3 Location: Scene continues.
1. Q2 reads, "Enter King and two or three," thus allowing
the ensuing lines to be spoken to other characters rather
than treating them as a soliloquy or directed to the audience.

5   Who like not in their judgement but their eyes,[2]
And where 'tis so, th'offender's scourge° is weighed,   *punishment*
But never the offence. To bear° all smooth and even,   *manage*
This sudden sending him away must seem
Deliberate pause.° Diseases desperate grown   *Careful planning*
10 By desperate appliance° are relieved,   *remedy*
Or not at all.
            Enter ROSENCRANTZ
            How now, what hath befall'n?
ROSENCRANTZ   Where the dead body is bestowed, my lord,
We cannot get from him.
KING CLAUDIUS   But where is he?
ROSENCRANTZ   Without, my lord, guarded to know your pleasure.
15 KING CLAUDIUS   Bring him before us.
ROSENCRANTZ   Ho, Guildenstern! Bring in my lord.
            Enter [Prince] HAMLET *and* GUILDENSTERN
KING CLAUDIUS   Now, Hamlet, where's Polonius?
HAMLET   At supper.
KING CLAUDIUS   At supper? Where?
20 HAMLET   Not where he eats, but where a is eaten.[3] A certain
convocation of politic° worms are e'en° at him. Your worm is   *cunning / now*
your only emperor for diet.[4] We fat all creatures else° to fat us,   *besides ourselves*
and we fat ourselves for maggots. Your fat king and your lean
beggar is but variable service°—two dishes, but to one table.   *different courses*
25 That's the end.
KING CLAUDIUS   Alas, alas!
HAMLET   A man may fish with the worm that hath eat of a king,
and eat of the fish that hath fed of that worm.
KING CLAUDIUS   What dost thou mean by this?
30 HAMLET   Nothing but to show you how a king may go a progress°   *royal journey*
through the guts of a beggar.
KING CLAUDIUS   Where is Polonius?
HAMLET   In heaven. Send thither to see. If your messenger find
him not there, seek him i'th' other place yourself. But indeed,
35 if you find him not this month, you shall nose him as you go
up the stairs into the lobby.
KING CLAUDIUS [*to* ROSENCRANTZ]   Go seek him there.
HAMLET [*to* ROSENCRANTZ]   A will stay till ye come.
            [*Exit* ROSENCRANTZ]
KING CLAUDIUS   Hamlet, this deed of thine, for thine especial safety—
40 Which we do tender° as we dearly grieve   *value*
For that which thou hast done—must send thee hence
With fiery quickness. Therefore prepare thyself.
The barque is ready, and the wind at help,
Th'associates tend,° and everything is bent°   *companions wait / poised*
45 For England.
HAMLET   For England?
KING CLAUDIUS   Ay, Hamlet.

2. Who choose not by reason but by external appearance.
3. Possibly an allusion to the Eucharist (Lord's Supper), in which the body of Christ is consumed in the form of bread.
4. *Your worm . . . diet*: The average worm is the only creature with a diet superior to a king's. The Diet (Council) of Emperor Charles V at Worms in 1521 called on Luther to defend his new doctrine. A scholar at Hamlet's university at Wittenberg, Luther maintained that faith alone, rather than sacramental ritual, was the basis of salvation.

HAMLET Good.

KING CLAUDIUS So is it if thou knew'st our purposes.

50 HAMLET I see a cherub[5] that sees them. But come, for England.
　　Farewell, dear mother.

KING CLAUDIUS Thy loving father, Hamlet.

HAMLET My mother. Father and mother is man and wife, man
　　and wife is one flesh,[6] and so my mother. Come, for England.
　　　　　　　　　　　　　　　　　　　　　　　　　Exit

55 KING CLAUDIUS [*to* GUILDENSTERN] Follow him at foot.° Tempt　　　　*his heel*
　　him with speed aboard.
　　Delay it not. I'll have him hence tonight.
　　Away, for everything is sealed and done
　　That else leans° on th'affair. Pray you, make haste.　　　　　　　　*bears*
　　　　　　　　　　　　　　　　[*Exit* GUILDENSTERN]
　　And, England,[7] if my love thou hold'st at aught°—　　　　　　　*any value*
60　As my great power thereof may give thee sense,[8]
　　Since yet thy cicatrice° looks raw and red　　　　　　　　　　　*scar*
　　After the Danish sword, and thy free awe[9]
　　Pays homage to us—thou mayst not coldly set°　　　　　*indifferently view*
　　Our sovereign process, which imports at full,[1]
65　By letters conjuring to that effect,
　　The present° death of Hamlet. Do it, England,　　　　　　　　*immediate*
　　For like the hectic° in my blood he rages,　　　　　　　　　　*fever*
　　And thou must cure me. Till I know 'tis done,
　　Howe'er my haps,° my joys were ne'er begun.　　　*Exit*　　　*fortunes*

4.4

Enter FORTINBRAS *with a drum and his army over the*
stage

FORTINBRAS Go, captain, from me greet the Danish king.
　　Tell him that by his licence° Fortinbras　　　　　　　　　　*permission*
　　Claims the conveyance of° a promised march　　　　　　　　*escort for*
　　Over his kingdom. You know the rendezvous.
5　If that his majesty would aught with us,
　　We shall express our duty in his eye,°　　　　　　　　　　　*presence*
　　And let him know so.

CAPTAIN I will do't, my lord.　　　　　　　　　　　[*Exit*]

FORTINBRAS Go safely[1] on.　　　　　　　*Exeunt* [*marching*]
　　　Enter [*Prince*] HAMLET, ROSENCRANTZ, [GUILDENSTERN,] *etc.*

9.1　HAMLET [*to the* CAPTAIN] *Good sir, whose powers° are these?*　　*forces*

CAPTAIN *They are of Norway, sir.*

HAMLET　　　　　　　　　*How purposed, sir, I pray you?*

CAPTAIN *Against some part of Poland.*

HAMLET　　　　　　　　　*Who commands them, sir?*

CAPTAIN *The nephew to old Norway, Fortinbras.*

9.5　HAMLET *Goes it against the main° of Poland, sir,*　　　　　*heart*
　　Or for some frontier?

CAPTAIN *Truly to speak, and with no addition,°*　　　　　*exaggeration*

5. The keen-sighted second order of angels, cherubim
symbolized heavenly knowledge.
6. As stated in Genesis 2:23 and the marriage rite of the
Book of Common Prayer.
7. King of England.
8. May give you a reason to feel the value of that love.
9. Your respect unconstrained (by an army of occupa-

tion).
1. Our sovereign command, which signifies in detailed
instructions.
4.4 Location: The Danish coast.
1. In Q2, "softly" (that is, slowly, circumspectly). In Q2,
the captain remains onstage, and the scene continues
with the following passage, 9.1–9.56.

We go to gain a little patch of ground
That hath in it no profit but the name.
9.10   To pay five ducats, five, I would not farm° it,   *lease*
Nor will it yield to Norway or the Pole
A ranker rate, should it be sold in fee.[2]

HAMLET   Why then, the Polack never will defend it.
CAPTAIN   Yes, it is already garrisoned.
9.15   HAMLET   Two thousand souls and twenty thousand ducats
Will now[3] debate the question of this straw.°   *trifle*
This is th'imposthume° of much wealth and peace,   *abscess*
That inward breaks and shows no cause without[4]
Why the man dies. I humbly thank you, sir.
CAPTAIN   God buy° you, sir.   [Exit]   *be with*
9.20   ROSENCRANTZ   Will't please you go, my lord?
HAMLET   I'll be with you straight. Go a little before
                     [Exeunt all but HAMLET]
How all occasions do inform against° me   *accuse*
And spur my dull revenge! What is a man
If his chief good and market° of his time   *profit*
9.25   Be but to sleep and feed?—a beast, no more.
Sure, he that made us with such large discourse,°   *reasoning faculty*
Looking before and after,[5] gave us not
That capability° and god-like reason   *intelligence*
To fust° in us unused. Now whether it be   *grow moldy*
9.30   Bestial oblivion,[6] or some craven scruple
Of thinking too precisely on th'event—
A thought which, quartered, hath but one part wisdom
And ever three parts coward—I do not know
Why yet I live to say 'This thing's to do',
9.35   Sith° I have cause, and will, and strength, and means,   *Since*
To do't. Examples gross as earth exhort me,
Witness this army of such mass and charge,°   *cost*
Led by a delicate and tender° prince,   *young*
Whose spirit with divine ambition puffed°   *inspired*
9.40   Makes mouths at the invisible event,[7]
Exposing what is mortal and unsure
To all that fortune, death, and danger dare,
Even for an eggshell. Rightly to be great
Is not to stir without great argument,
9.45   But greatly to find quarrel in a straw
When honour's at the stake.[8] How stand I, then,
That have a father killed, a mother stained,
Excitements° of my reason and my blood,   *Urgings*
And let all sleep while, to my shame, I see
9.50   The imminent death of twenty thousand men
That, for a fantasy and trick° of fame,   *fragile trifle*
Go to their graves like beds, fight for a plot
Whereon the numbers cannot try the cause,[9]

---

2. Sold outright as a freehold. *ranker rate:* more generous return.
3. Oxford's emendation of Q2's "Will not."
4. That ruptures internally without external symptom.
5. Able to see past and future.
6. Animal-like inability to remember.

7. Shows a scornful face to unforeseeable outcomes.
8. *Rightly . . . stake:* these lines, syntactically ambiguous, seem to mean that true greatness lies not in rational restraint but in noble action. *the stake:* post to which a bull or bear was fastened for baiting.
9. Which is not big enough for the armies to fight on.

9.55   Which is not tomb enough and continent°   *container*
     To hide the slain. O, from this time forth
     My thoughts be bloody or be nothing worth!   *Exit*

4.5

Enter QUEEN GERTRUDE *and* HORATIO
QUEEN GERTRUDE   I will not speak with her.
HORATIO[1]   She is importunate,
   Indeed distraught. Her mood will needs be pitied.
QUEEN GERTRUDE   What would she have?
HORATIO   She speaks much of her father, says she hears
5   There's tricks i'th' world, and hems, and beats her heart,
     Spurns enviously at straws,[2] speaks things in doubt°   *obscurely*
     That carry but half sense. Her speech is nothing,
     Yet the unshapèd use° of it doth move   *incoherent manner*
     The hearers to collection.° They aim° at it,   *inference / guess*
10   And botch° the words up fit to° their own thoughts,   *patch / to match*
     Which,° as her winks and nods and gestures yield them,   *(words)*
     Indeed would make one think there might be thought,
     Though nothing sure, yet much unhappily.[3]
QUEEN GERTRUDE   'Twere good she were spoken with, for she may strew
15   Dangerous conjectures in ill-breeding minds.
     Let her come in.
            [HORATIO *withdraws to admit* OPHELIA]
QUEEN GERTRUDE   To my sick soul, as sin's true nature is,
     Each toy° seems prologue to some great amiss.°   *triviality / calamity*
     So full of artless jealousy° is guilt,   *uncontrolled suspicion*
20   It spills itself in fearing to be spilt.
        Enter OPHELIA *distracted, playing on a lute, and her*
        hair down, singing[4]
OPHELIA   Where is the beauteous majesty of Denmark?
QUEEN GERTRUDE   How now,° Ophelia?   *What's this*
OPHELIA *(sings)*   How should I your true love know
          From another one?—
25   By his cockle hat and staff,
          And his sandal shoon.[5]
QUEEN GERTRUDE   Alas, sweet lady, what imports° this song?   *means*
OPHELIA   Say you? Nay, pray you, mark.°   *listen*
   (Song)   He is dead and gone, lady,
30   He is dead and gone.
          At his head a grass-green turf,
          At his heels a stone.
QUEEN GERTRUDE   Nay, but Ophelia—
OPHELIA   Pray you, mark.
35   *(Song)*   White his shroud as the mountain snow—
        Enter KING [CLAUDIUS]
QUEEN GERTRUDE   Alas, look here, my lord.

4.5 Location: A public room of the castle.
1. As in F. In Q2, lines 1–2 and 4–13 are spoken by a "Gent.," while Horatio comments on them in 14–15 (assigned in F to Gertrude).
2. Kicks bitterly (takes offense) at the slightest thing.
3. Though they reveal nothing for certain, her words could lead to unfortunate impressions (because either unflatteringly wrong or too near the unflattering truth).
4. F simply notes that Ophelia enters distracted; the additional details are taken from Q1.
5. Shoes. *cockle hat:* a cockle-shell badge worn in the hat was a pilgrim's memento of St. James's shrine at Compostela in Spain.

OPHELIA *(Song)* Larded° with sweet flowers,   *Garnished*
    Which bewept to the grave did—not[6]—go
    With true-love showers.°   *tears*
40 KING CLAUDIUS How do ye, pretty lady?
OPHELIA Well, God'ield° you. They say the owl was a baker's   *God yield (reward)*
   daughter.[7] Lord, we know what we are, but know not what we
   may be. God be at your table!
KING CLAUDIUS [*to* GERTRUDE] Conceit° upon her father.   *Brooding imagination*
45 OPHELIA Pray you, let's have no words of this, but when they ask
   you what it means, say you this.
   (Song) Tomorrow is Saint Valentine's day,
      All in the morning betime,°   *early*
      And I a maid at your window
50   To be your Valentine.
      Then up he rose, and donned his clothes,
      And dupped° the chamber door;   *unlatched*
      Let in the maid, that out a maid
      Never departed more.
55 KING CLAUDIUS Pretty Ophelia—
OPHELIA Indeed, la? Without an oath, I'll make an end on't.°   *of it*
   (Song) By Gis,° and by Saint Charity,   *Jesus*
      Alack, and fie for shame!
      Young men will do't if they come to't,
60   By Cock,[8] they are to blame.
      Quoth she 'Before you tumbled me,
      You promised me to wed.'
      So would I 'a' done, by yonder sun,
      An° thou hadst not come to my bed.   *If*
65 KING CLAUDIUS [*to* GERTRUDE] How long hath she been thus?
OPHELIA I hope all will be well. We must be patient. But I cannot choose but weep to think they should lay him i'th' cold
   ground. My brother shall know of it. And so I thank you for
   your good counsel. Come, my coach! Good night, ladies, good
70   night, sweet ladies, good night, good night.   *Exit*
KING CLAUDIUS [*to* HORATIO] Follow her close. Give her good
   watch, I pray you.   [*Exit* HORATIO]
   O, this is the poison of deep grief! It springs
   All from her father's death. O Gertrude, Gertrude,
   When sorrows come they come not single spies,°   *scouts*
75   But in battalions. First, her father slain;
   Next, your son gone, and he most violent author
   Of his own just remove; the people muddied,°   *confused*
   Thick and unwholesome in their thoughts and whispers
   For good Polonius' death; and we have done but greenly°   *naively*
80   In hugger-mugger° to inter him; poor Ophelia   *secrecy*
   Divided from herself and her fair judgement,
   Without the which we are pictures or mere beasts;
   Last, and as much containing° as all these,   *and as important*
   Her brother is in secret come from France,

6. By adding "not," Ophelia changes the song's words and meter to fit the circumstances of Polonius's burial (see lines 79–80).
7. A folktale: Christ turned a baker's daughter into an owl because when he asked for food, she would give him only a small loaf.
8. A corruption of "God" in very mild swearing (playing on "penis").

85   Feeds on this wonder, keeps himself in clouds,°   *unverified suspicion*
        And wants° not buzzers° to infect his ear   *lacks / scandal mongers*
        With pestilent speeches of his father's death;
        Wherein necessity, of matter beggared,
        Will nothing stick our persons to arraign
90   In ear and ear.⁹ O my dear Gertrude, this,
        Like to a murd'ring-piece,¹ in many places
        Gives me superfluous° death.   *redundant*
                A noise within
QUEEN GERTRUDE   Alack, what noise is this?
KING CLAUDIUS   Where is my Switzers?² Let them guard the door.
                Enter a MESSENGER
        What is the matter?
MESSENGER   Save yourself, my lord.
95   The ocean, overpeering of his list,³
        Eats not the flats with more impetuous⁴ haste
        Than young Laertes, in a riotous head,°   *insurrection; tidal wave*
        O'erbears your officers. The rabble call him lord,
        And, as° the world were now but° to begin,   *as if / only now*
100   Antiquity forgot, custom not known,
        The ratifiers and props of every word,⁵
        They cry 'Choose we! Laertes shall be king.'
        Caps, hands, and tongues applaud it to the clouds,
        'Laertes shall be king, Laertes king.'
105 QUEEN GERTRUDE   How cheerfully on the false trail they cry!⁶
                A noise within
        O, this is counter,⁷ you false Danish dogs!
KING CLAUDIUS   The doors are broke.
                Enter LAERTES *with [his* FOLLOWERS *at the door]*
LAERTES   Where is the King?—Sirs, stand you all without.
ALL HIS FOLLOWERS   No, let's come in.
110 LAERTES   I pray you, give me leave.
ALL HIS FOLLOWERS   We will, we will.
LAERTES   I thank you. Keep the door.   [*Exeunt* FOLLOWERS]
                              O thou vile king,
        Give me my father.
QUEEN GERTRUDE   Calmly, good Laertes.
LAERTES   That drop of blood that's calm proclaims me bastard,
115   Cries cuckold to my father, brands the harlot
        Even here between the chaste unsmirchèd brow
        Of my true mother.
KING CLAUDIUS   What is the cause, Laertes,
        That thy rebellion looks so giant-like?—
        Let him go, Gertrude. Do not fear° our person.   *fear for*
120   There's such divinity doth hedge a king

9. *Wherein . . . ear:* In which affair, because they have no
real information and need to give some account, they will
not hesitate to whisper accusations against us.
1. Small cannon that fired shrapnel.
2. Company of Swiss mercenaries (employed as royal
bodyguards in many European countries).
3. Rising over its boundary at the shore.
4. Spelled "impittious" in F and "impitious" in Q2, probably meaning "merciless" as well as "rash." *flats:* low-lying

countryside.
5. *Antiquity . . . word:* Ignoring history and traditional
precedents, which give meaning, order, and stability to
society by fixing the agreed-upon meaning of political
contracts (and of any truth expressed in language).
6. How enthusiastically they run after the wrong scent
(like a pack of hounds hunting the murderer of Polonius).
7. This is following the quarry's trail, but in the wrong
direction.

That treason can but peep to what it would,[8]
Acts little of his will. —Tell me, Laertes,
Why thou art thus incensed. —Let him go, Gertrude. —
Speak, man.
LAERTES   Where is my father?
KING CLAUDIUS   Dead.
QUEEN GERTRUDE [*to* LAERTES]   But not by him.
125   KING CLAUDIUS   Let him demand his fill.
LAERTES   How came he dead? I'll not be juggled with.°   *deceived*
      To hell, allegiance! Vows to the blackest devil!
      Conscience and grace to the profoundest pit!
      I dare damnation. To this point° I stand,   *resolve*
130   That both the worlds I give to negligence,[9]
      Let come what comes. Only I'll be revenged
      Most throughly° for my father.   *thoroughly*
KING CLAUDIUS   Who shall stay° you?   *prevent*
LAERTES   My will, not all the world;
135   And for my means, I'll husband them so well
      They shall go far with little.
KING CLAUDIUS   Good Laertes,
      If you desire to know the certainty
      Of your dear father's death, is't writ in your revenge
      That, sweepstake,[1] you will draw° both friend and foe,   *take from*
140   Winner and loser?
LAERTES   None but his enemies.
KING CLAUDIUS   Will you know them then?
LAERTES   To his good friends thus wide I'll ope my arms,
      And, like the kind life-rend'ring pelican,
      Repast them with my blood.[2]
145   KING CLAUDIUS   Why, now you speak
      Like a good child and a true gentleman.
      That I am guiltless of your father's death,
      And am most sensibly° in grief for it,   *sympathetically*
      It shall as level° to your judgement pierce   *directly*
150   As day does to your eye.
            A noise within
VOICES [*within*]   Let her come in.[3]
LAERTES   How now, what noise is that?
            Enter OPHELIA [*as before*]
      O heat dry up my brains! Tears seven times salt
      Burn out the sense and virtue° of mine eye!   *natural power*
155   By heaven, thy madness shall be paid by weight
      Till our scale turns the beam.[4] O rose of May,
      Dear maid, kind sister, sweet Ophelia!
      O heavens, is't possible a young maid's wits
      Should be as mortal as an old man's life?
160   Nature is fine in love, and where 'tis fine

8. That treason can only glance furtively at what it would
like to do.
9. That both this world and the next do not matter to me.
1. Indiscriminately. (The winner of a sweepstake gained
the stakes of all other players.)
2. The female pelican was supposed to feed, and even
revive, its young with blood from a wound it pecked in its
own breast. *Repast:* Feed.
3. This line is assigned to no one in F but rather appears
in italic following the stage direction "A noise within."
Q2 gives the line to Laertes.
4. *shall . . . beam:* shall be atoned for until vengeance
outweighs the injury of madness (thus tilting the "scale"
of justice).

It sends some precious instance of itself
After the thing it loves.[5]

OPHELIA *(Song)*   They bore him barefaced on the bier,
            Hey non nony, nony, hey nony,
165   And on his grave rained many a tear—
Fare you well, my dove.

LAERTES Hadst thou thy wits and didst persuade° revenge,   *argue for*
It could not move thus.

OPHELIA You must sing 'Down, a-down', and you, 'Call him a
170 down-a'. O, how the wheel[6] becomes it! It is the false steward
that stole his master's daughter.[7]

LAERTES This nothing's more than matter.[8]

OPHELIA There's rosemary, that's for remembrance. Pray, love,
remember. And there is pansies; that's for thoughts.[9]

175 LAERTES A document in madness—thoughts and remembrance
fitted.

OPHELIA There's fennel for you, and columbines.[1] There's rue
for you, and here's some for me. We may call it herb-grace o'
Sundays. O, you must wear your rue with a difference.[2] There's
180 a daisy. I would give you some violets,[3] but they withered all
when my father died. They say a made a good end.
(Song)   For bonny sweet Robin is all my joy.

LAERTES Thought and affliction, passion, hell itself
She turns to favour° and to prettiness.   *beauty*

185 OPHELIA *(Song)*   And will a not come again,
            And will a not come again?
            No, no, he is dead,
            Go to thy death-bed,
            He never will come again.

190   His beard as white as snow,
            All flaxen° was his poll.°   *white / head*
            He is gone, he is gone,
            And we cast away moan.
            God 'a' mercy on his soul.

195 And of all Christian souls, I pray God. God b'wi' ye.
               Exeunt OPHELIA [*and* GERTRUDE]

LAERTES Do you see this, O God?

KING CLAUDIUS Laertes, I must commune with your grief,
Or you deny me right. Go but apart,
Make choice of whom° your wisest friends you will,   *whichever of*
200 And they shall hear and judge 'twixt you and me.
If by direct or by collateral° hand   *an agent's*
They find us touched,° we will our kingdom give,   *involved in guilt*

---

5. *Nature . . . loves:* Human nature is made ethereally pure by love and sends a precious token ("instance") of itself after the object of its love. Laertes struggles to say that because of Ophelia's great love for her father, her sanity departed with him.
6. Probably refrain, although possibly spinning wheel (at which women sang ballads) or Fortune's wheel. "Down, a-down" resembles the refrain of recorded ballads.
7. *false . . . daughter:* the tale is unknown; Laertes seems to recognize it.
8. This nonsense signifies more than coherent speech.
9. *There's . . . thoughts:* Ophelia, recalling the flowers' symbolic significance, distributes them to Laertes (rosemary and pansies?), Gertrude (fennel and columbines?), and Claudius (rue and daisies?).
1. Columbines were associated with ingratitude or marital infidelity, fennel with flattery.
2. In heraldry, minor branches of a family were distinguished by a "difference," a variation or addition to the coat of arms. Ophelia probably means "for a different reason." Rue is associated with repentance, and Ophelia identifies it with the "herb of grace" (wormwood), since penitence depended on and enabled God's blessing.
3. Representing faithfulness; daisies could symbolize dissembling seduction.

Our crown, our life, and all that we call ours,
To you in satisfaction.° But if not,   *recompense*
205 Be you content to lend your patience to us,
And we shall jointly labour with your soul
To give it due content.
LAERTES   Let this be so.
His means of death, his obscure burial—
No trophy, sword, nor hatchment[4] o'er his bones,
210 No noble rite nor formal ostentation°—   *rite of grief*
Cry to be heard, as 'twere from heaven to earth,
That I must call't in question.[5]
KING CLAUDIUS   So you shall;
And where th'offence is, let the great axe fall.
I pray you go with me.   *Exeunt*

4.6

Enter HORATIO *with* [*a* SERVANT]
HORATIO   What are they that would speak with me?
SERVANT   Sailors, sir. They say they have letters for you.
HORATIO   Let them come in.   [*Exit* SERVANT]
I do not know from what part of the world
5 I should be greeted if not from Lord Hamlet.
Enter SAILOR[S]
A SAILOR   God bless you, sir.
HORATIO   Let him bless thee too.
A SAILOR   A shall, sir, an't° please him. There's a letter for you,   *if it*
sir. It comes from th'ambassador that was bound for England—
10 if your name be Horatio, as I am let to know it is.
HORATIO *(reads)* 'Horatio, when thou shalt have overlooked°   *read*
this, give these fellows some means° to the King. They have   *access*
letters for him. Ere we were two days old at sea, a pirate of very
warlike appointment° gave us chase. Finding ourselves too slow   *equipment*
15 of sail, we put on a compelled valour, and in the grapple I
boarded them. On the instant they got clear of our ship, so I
alone became their prisoner. They have dealt with me like
thieves of mercy; but they knew what they did:[1] I am to do a
good turn for them. Let the King have the letters I have sent,
20 and repair thou° to me with as much haste as thou wouldst fly   *come*
death. I have words to speak in thine ear will make thee dumb,
yet are they much too light for the bore° of the matter. These   *caliber, size*
good fellows will bring thee where I am. Rosencrantz and Guildenstern hold their course for England. Of them I have much
25 to tell thee. Farewell.
He that thou knowest thine,
Hamlet.'
Come, I will give you way° for these your letters,   *means of delivery*
And do't the speedier that you may direct me
30 To him from whom you brought them.   *Exeunt*

---

4. Lozenge-shaped tablet bearing a coat of arms, carried
in funeral processions and deposited near the tomb. *trophy*: memorial (often consisting of real or symbolic weapons and armor).
5. I must demand an explanation of it.
4.6 Location: The castle.

1. *They have . . . did*: They have been merciful, but with
the expectation of a return. Hamlet recalls the thieves crucified next to Christ (one of whom he blessed) and
Christ's plea of forgiveness for those who "know not what
they do" (Luke 23:34–43).

4.7

Enter KING [CLAUDIUS] *and* LAERTES

KING CLAUDIUS   Now must your conscience my acquittance seal,[1]
And you must put me in your heart for friend,
Sith° you have heard, and with a knowing ear,   *Since*
That he which hath your noble father slain
5   Pursued my life.

LAERTES   It well appears. But tell me
Why you proceeded not against these feats,°   *acts*
So crimeful and so capital° in nature,   *punishable by death*
As by your safety, wisdom, all things else,
You mainly° were stirred up.   *greatly*

KING CLAUDIUS   O, for two special reasons,
10   Which may to you perhaps seem much unsinewed,°   *uncompelling*
And yet to me they're strong. The Queen his mother
Lives almost by his looks; and for myself—
My virtue or my plague, be it either which—
She's so conjunctive to my life and soul
15   That, as the star moves not but in his sphere,[2]
I could not but by her. The other motive
Why to a public count° I might not go   *accounting*
Is the great love the general gender° bear him,   *the common people*
Who, dipping all his faults in their affection,
20   Would, like the spring that turneth wood to stone,[3]
Convert his guilts to graces; so that my arrows,
Too slightly timbered for so loud a wind,
Would have reverted to my bow again,
And not where I had aimed them.

25   LAERTES   And so have I a noble father lost,
A sister driven into desp'rate terms,
Who has, if praises may go back again,[4]
Stood challenger, on mount, of all the age
For her perfections.[5] But my revenge will come.

30   KING CLAUDIUS   Break not your sleeps for that. You must not think
That we are made of stuff so flat and dull
That we can let our beard be shook with danger,[6]
And think it pastime. You shortly shall hear more.
I loved your father, and we love ourself.
35   And that, I hope, will teach you to imagine—

Enter a MESSENGER *with letters*

How now? What news?

MESSENGER   Letters, my lord, from Hamlet.
This to your majesty; this to the Queen.

KING CLAUDIUS   From Hamlet? Who brought them?

MESSENGER   Sailors, my lord, they say. I saw them not.
40   They were given me by Claudio. He received them.

KING CLAUDIUS   Laertes, you shall hear them.—Leave us.

Exit MESSENGER

4.7 Location: Claudius's private apartments.
1. *my acquaintance seal*: affirm my innocence (of Polonius's death).
2. According to Ptolemeic astronomy, heavenly bodies moved in hollow spheres. *conjunctive* (line 14): closely united (as two planets were said astronomically to be "in conjunction" when they appeared close).
3. In limestone-rich areas (such as south Warwickshire), concentrations in spring water may be great enough to petrify absorbent objects.
4. May refer to what was (but is no longer).
5. *Stood . . . perfections*: Conspicuously challenged the world to match her perfections.
6. That I can allow anyone to endanger me with contemptuous behavior.

[*Reads*] 'High and mighty, you shall know I am set naked° on   *destitute*
your kingdom. Tomorrow shall I beg leave to see your kingly
eyes, when I shall, first asking your pardon,° thereunto recount   *permission*
45 th'occasions of my sudden and more strange return.
                          Hamlet.'
What should this mean? Are all the rest come back?
Or is it some abuse,° and no such thing?   *deception*
LAERTES   Know you the hand?
KING CLAUDIUS   'Tis Hamlet's character.°   *handwriting*
50 'Naked'—and in a postscript here he says
'Alone'. Can you advise me?
LAERTES   I'm lost in it, my lord. But let him come.
It warms the very sickness in my heart
That I shall live and tell him to his teeth,
'Thus diddest thou'.[7]
55 KING CLAUDIUS   If it be so, Laertes—
As how should it be so, how otherwise?[8]—
Will you be ruled by me?
LAERTES   If so° you'll not o'errule me to a peace.   *Provided that*
KING CLAUDIUS   To thine own peace. If he be now returned,
60 As checking at[9] his voyage, and that he means
No more to undertake it, I will work him
To an exploit, now ripe in my device,°   *planning*
Under the which he shall not choose but fall;
And for his death no wind of blame shall breathe;
65 But even his mother shall uncharge° the practice°   *not accuse / connivance*
And call it accident.[1]
66.1   LAERTES   *My lord, I will be ruled,*
        The rather if you could devise it so
        That I might be the organ.°   *agent*
      KING CLAUDIUS   *It falls right.*
        You have been talked of, since your travel, much,
66.5   *And that in Hamlet's hearing, for a quality*
        Wherein they say you shine. Your sum of parts°   *abilities*
        Did not together pluck such envy from him
        As did that one, and that, in my regard,
        Of the unworthiest siege.°   *lowest rank*
      LAERTES   *What part is that, my lord?*
66.10   KING CLAUDIUS   *A very ribbon in the cap of youth,*
        Yet needful too, for youth no less becomes°   *is suited by*
        The light and careless livery that it wears
        Than settled age his sables and his weeds
        Importing health and graveness.[2]
                          Some two months since
Here was a gentleman of Normandy.
I've seen myself, and served against, the French,
And they can well° on horseback; but this gallant   *are skilled*
70 Had witchcraft in't. He grew into his seat,
And to such wondrous doing brought his horse

---

7. This which I do now to you, you did to my father.
8. *As . . . otherwise*: How could Hamlet be returning, and
yet how else could he have sent this letter?
9. As one who has been diverted from ("checking at" is a
term from falconry).

1. After "accident," Q2 has the following passage, 66.1–
66.14, omitted in F.
2. *his . . . graveness*: its rich gowns trimmed with sable,
garments ("weeds") signifying concern for prosperity and
dignity.

As had he been incorpsed and demi-natured[3]
With the brave beast. So far he passed my thought
That I in forgery of shapes and tricks[4]
Come short of what he did.

75 LAERTES   A Norman was't?

KING CLAUDIUS   A Norman.

LAERTES   Upon my life, Lamord.

KING CLAUDIUS   The very same.

LAERTES   I know him well. He is the brooch° indeed,   ornament
And gem, of all the nation.

KING CLAUDIUS   He made confession° of you,   testimonial
80   And gave you such a masterly report
For art and exercise in your defence,
And for your rapier most especially,
That he cried out 'twould be a sight indeed
If one could match you.[5]

84.1   *Th'escrimers° of their nation*   fencers
He swore had neither motion, guard, nor eye
If you opposed them.
                         Sir, this report of his
85   Did Hamlet so envenom with his envy
That he could nothing do but wish and beg
Your sudden° coming o'er to play with him.   immediate
Now, out of this—

LAERTES   What out of this, my lord?

KING CLAUDIUS   Laertes, was your father dear to you?
90   Or are you like the painting of a sorrow,
A face without a heart?

LAERTES   Why ask you this?

KING CLAUDIUS   Not that I think you did not love your father,
But that I know love is begun by time,°   circumstance
And that I see, in passages of proof,[6]
95   Time qualifies° the spark and fire of it.[7]   moderates
95.1   *There lives within the very flame of love*
A kind of wick or snuff[8] that will abate it,
And nothing is at a like° goodness still,°   an equal / always
For goodness, growing to a plurisy,[9]
95.5   *Dies in his own too much.° That we would do*   overabundance
We should do when we would, for this 'would' changes,
And hath abatements and delays as many
As there are tongues, are hands, are accidents;
And then this 'should' is like a spendthrift's sigh,
95.10   *That hurts by easing.[1] But to the quick° of th'ulcer—*   center
Hamlet comes back. What would you undertake
To show yourself your father's son in deed
More than in words?

LAERTES   To cut his throat i'th' church.

3. As if he had been in the same body and had half the nature of (the image of a centaur).
4. That I in my very imagination ("forgery") of figures and skillful feats of horsemanship.
5. After "you," Q2 has the following passage, 84.1–84.3, omitted in F.
6. From experiences that have tested this.
7. After this line, Q2 has the following passage, 95.1–

95.10, omitted in F.
8. Burned part of the wick (which causes smoke and reduces light if not removed).
9. A chest inflammation, metaphorically like a fire in the heart; thought to take its name from the Latin for "more" (*plus*) and to be caused by an excess of humors (and so playing on "excess").
1. A sigh was thought to use up a drop of blood.

KING CLAUDIUS   No place indeed should murder sanctuarize.[2]
100   Revenge should have no bounds. But, good Laertes,
      Will you do this?—keep close within your chamber.
      Hamlet returned shall know you are come home.
      We'll put on those shall[3] praise your excellence,
      And set a double varnish on the fame
105   The Frenchman gave you; bring you, in fine,° together,   *conclusion*
      And wager on your heads. He, being remiss,°   *unwary*
      Most generous,° and free from all contriving,   *noble*
      Will not peruse the foils; so that with ease,
      Or with a little shuffling, you may choose
110   A sword unbated, and, in a pass of practice,[4]
      Requite him for your father.
      LAERTES   I will do't,
      And for that purpose I'll anoint my sword.
      I bought an unction° of a mountebank°   *ointment / quack*
      So mortal that, but dip a knife in it,
115   Where it draws blood no cataplasm° so rare,   *poultice*
      Collected from all simples° that have virtue°   *herbs / potency*
      Under the moon, can save the thing from death
      That is but scratched withal.° I'll touch my point   *with it*
      With this contagion, that if I gall° him slightly,   *prick*
      It may be death.
120   KING CLAUDIUS   Let's further think of this;
      Weigh what convenience both of time and means
      May fit us to our shape.[5] If this should fail,
      And that our drift look° through our bad performance,   *our intention be seen*
      'Twere better not essayed. Therefore this project
125   Should have a back or second[6] that might hold
      If this should blast in proof.[7] Soft, let me see.
      We'll make a solemn wager on your cunnings . . .°   *skills*
      I ha't! When in your motion° you are hot and dry—   *exercise*
      As make your bouts more violent to that end—
130   And that he calls for drink, I'll have prepared him
      A chalice for the nonce,° whereon but sipping,   *occasion*
      If he by chance escape your venomed stuck,°   *thrust* (stoccado)
      Our purpose may hold there.—
            Enter QUEEN [GERTRUDE]
                              How now, sweet Queen?
      QUEEN GERTRUDE   One woe doth tread upon another's heel,
135   So fast they follow. Your sister's drowned, Laertes.
      LAERTES   Drowned? O, where?
      QUEEN GERTRUDE   There is a willow grows aslant a brook
      That shows his hoar leaves[8] in the glassy stream.
      Therewith fantastic garlands did she make
140   Of crow-flowers, nettles, daisies, and long purples,[9]

2. Give sanctuary to a murderer. In English tradition, a
criminal remained invulnerable to secular authority for
most crimes (save sacrilege and treason) so long as he
took refuge in a church.
3. *We'll . . . shall:* I shall incite some people to.
4. In a treacherous thrust. *unbated:* unblunted (as recreational or practice foils were).
5. May make us ready to put into effect our plot and to
assume the roles we are to play.
6. Should have reserve soldiers (another military meta-

phor for the plotting).
7. Should blow up in our faces when put to the test (like
a cannon).
8. The willow leaf is gray-white ("hoar") on the under-
sides (reflected from below by the water). The willow was
an emblem of mourning and of forsaken love.
9. Early purple orchises. *crow-flowers:* common name for
several wildflowers, including Ragged Robin and blue-
bells (often appearing beside long purples in woodland
and sharing their association with fertility).

That liberal shepherds give a grosser[1] name,
But our cold° maids do dead men's fingers call them. *chaste*
There on the pendent boughs her crownet° weeds *garlanded*
Clamb'ring to hang,[2] an envious sliver° broke, *a malicious twig*
145 When down the weedy trophies and herself
Fell in the weeping brook. Her clothes spread wide,
And mermaid-like a while they bore her up;
Which time she chanted snatches of old tunes,
As one incapable° of her own distress, *uncomprehending*
150 Or like a creature native and endued
Unto that element.[3] But long it could not be
Till that her garments, heavy with their drink,
Pulled the poor wretch from her melodious lay° *song*
To muddy death.
155 LAERTES   Alas, then is she drowned.
QUEEN GERTRUDE   Drowned, drowned.
LAERTES   Too much of water hast thou, poor Ophelia,
And therefore I forbid my tears. But yet
It is our trick;° nature her custom holds, *characteristic way*
Let shame say what it will.
        [*He weeps*]
160   When these are gone,
The woman will be out.[4] Adieu, my lord.
I have a speech of fire that fain° would blaze, *gladly*
But that this folly douts° it.   *Exit* *extinguishes*
KING CLAUDIUS   Let's follow, Gertrude.
How much I had to do to calm his rage!
165 Now fear I this will give it start again;
Therefore let's follow.   *Exeunt*

5.1

Enter two CLOWNS° *carrying a spade and a pickaxe* *rustics, peasants*
FIRST CLOWN   Is she to be buried in Christian burial that wilfully
    seeks her own salvation?[1]
SECOND CLOWN   I tell thee she is, and therefore make her grave
    straight.° The coroner hath sat on her,[2] and finds it Christian *right away*
5   burial.[3]
FIRST CLOWN   How can that be unless she drowned herself in
    her own defence?
SECOND CLOWN   Why, 'tis found so.
FIRST CLOWN   It must be *se offendendo*,[4] it cannot be else; for
10   here lies the point: if I drown myself wittingly, it argues an act;
    and an act hath three branches: it is to act, to do, and to per-
    form. Argal[5] she drowned herself wittingly.

1. More indecent. Among the recorded names for the
purple orchis are "priest's-pintle" (penis), "dog's cullions"
(testicles), "goat's cullions," and "fool's ballochs." *liberal:*
free-spoken.
2. Deserted lovers proverbially hung garlands on willows.
3. *native . . . element:* naturally fit to live in water.
4. *When . . . out:* When I have cried my tears, the feminine side of my nature will be gone with them.
5.1 Location: A churchyard.
1. Probably a mistake for "damnation"; suicide was a
mortal sin. Ordinarily, suicides would not receive a
"Christian burial" (in consecrated ground with the

church's blessing and ritual).
2. Conducted an inquest on the cause of her death.
3. And has given the verdict that she is eligible for a
Christian burial (in effect, a decision that Ophelia did not
drown herself).
4. A mangled version of *se defendendo*, the term for "killing in self-defense."
5. For "ergo," or "therefore." The argument parodies a
famous law case of 1554 concerning suicide by drowning,
in which the act was said to have three parts: imagination,
resolution, and perfection (accomplishment).

SECOND CLOWN   Nay, but hear you, Goodman Delver.[6]

FIRST CLOWN   Give me leave. Here lies the water—good. Here
15   stands the man—good. If the man go to this water and drown
himself, it is, will he nill he,° he goes. Mark you that. But if the   *willy-nilly*
water come to him and drown him, he drowns not himself;
argal he that is not guilty of his own death shortens not his own
life.

20   SECOND CLOWN   But is this law?

FIRST CLOWN   Ay, marry, is't: coroner's quest° law.   *inquest*

SECOND CLOWN   Will you ha' the truth on't? If this had not been
a gentlewoman, she should have been buried out o' Christian
burial.

25   FIRST CLOWN   Why, there thou sayst,° and the more pity that   *how right you are*
great folk should have count'nance° in this world to drown or   *privilege*
hang themselves more than their even° Christian. Come, my   *fellow*
spade. There is no ancient gentlemen but gardeners, ditchers,
and gravemakers; they hold up° Adam's profession.   *carry on*
[FIRST CLOWN *digs*]

30   SECOND CLOWN   Was he a gentleman?

FIRST CLOWN   A was the first that ever bore arms.[7]

SECOND CLOWN   Why, he had none.

FIRST CLOWN   What, art a heathen? How dost thou understand
the Scripture? The Scripture says Adam digged. Could he dig
35   without arms? I'll put another question to thee. If thou answer-
est me not to the purpose, confess thyself[8]—

SECOND CLOWN   Go to.[9]

FIRST CLOWN   What is he that builds stronger than either the
mason, the shipwright, or the carpenter?

40   SECOND CLOWN   The gallows-maker; for that frame° outlives a   *structure*
thousand tenants.

FIRST CLOWN   I like thy wit well, in good faith. The gallows does°   *serves*
well. But how does it well? It does well to those that do ill. Now
thou dost ill to say the gallows is built stronger than the church,
45   argal the gallows may do well to thee. To't again, come.

SECOND CLOWN   'Who builds stronger than a mason, a shipwright, or a carpenter?'

FIRST CLOWN   Ay, tell me that, and unyoke.[1]

SECOND CLOWN   Marry, now I can tell.

50   FIRST CLOWN   To't.

SECOND CLOWN   Mass,° I cannot tell.   *By the mass*
Enter [Prince] HAMLET *and* HORATIO *afar off*

FIRST CLOWN   Cudgel thy brains no more about it, for your dull
ass will not mend° his pace with beating; and when you are   *improve*
asked this question next, say 'a grave-maker'; the houses that he
55   makes lasts till doomsday. Go, get thee to Johan.[2] Fetch me a
stoup° of liquor.   [*Exit* SECOND CLOWN]   *flagon*
(*Sings*) In youth when I did love, did love,
Methought it was very sweet

6. Master Digger ("Goodman" was the ordinary title in
addressing a man by his occupation).
7. Those bearing a family coat of arms were officially recognized as gentlemen; playing on "limbs."
8. "Confess thyself and be hanged" was proverbial.

9. An expression of impatience.
1. Rest your wits from work (like draught animals).
2. *Johan:* unknown (presumably a neighborhood ale-
house keeper).

To contract°-O-the time for-a-my behove,°   *shorten / advantage*
60   O methought there-a-was nothing-a-meet.[3]

HAMLET   Has this fellow no feeling of his business that a sings at grave-making?

HORATIO   Custom hath made it in him a property of easiness.[4]

HAMLET   'Tis e'en so; the hand of little employment hath the
65   daintier sense.[5]

FIRST CLOWN (*sings*) But age with his stealing steps
       Hath caught me in his clutch,
       And hath shipped me intil the land,°   *into the earth*
       As if I had never been such.
       [*He throws up a skull*]

70 HAMLET   That skull had a tongue in it and could sing once. How
the knave jowls° it to th' ground as if 'twere Cain's jawbone,   *slams*
that did the first murder! This might be the pate of a politician
which this ass o'er-offices,[6] one that would circumvent God,
might it not?

75 HORATIO   It might, my lord.

HAMLET   Or of a courtier, which could say 'Good morrow, sweet
lord. How dost thou, good lord?' This might be my lord such a
one, that praised my lord such a one's horse when a meant to
beg it, might it not?

80 HORATIO   Ay, my lord.

HAMLET   Why, e'en so, and now my lady Worm's, chapless,° and   *lacking a lower jaw*
knocked about the mazard° with a sexton's spade. Here's fine   *head*
revolution,[7] an° we had the trick° to see't. Did these bones cost   *if / ability*
no more the breeding but to play at loggats with 'em?[8] Mine
85   ache to think on't.

FIRST CLOWN (*sings*) A pickaxe and a spade, a spade,
       For and° a shrouding-sheet;   *And also*
       O, a pit of clay for to be made
       For such a guest is meet.
       [*He throws up another skull*]

90 HAMLET   There's another. Why might not that be the skull of a
lawyer? Where be his quiddits[9] now, his quillets,° his cases, his   *quibbles*
tenures,° and his tricks? Why does he suffer this rude knave   *property titles*
now to knock him about the sconce° with a dirty shovel, and   *head*
will not tell him of his action of battery?[1] H'm! This fellow
95   might be in 's time a great buyer of land, with his statutes, his
recognizances, his fines, his double vouchers, his recoveries.[2]
Is this the fine° of his fines and the recovery° of his recoveries,   *end / profit*
to have his fine° pate full of fine° dirt? Will his vouchers vouch[3]   *subtle / fine-grained*
him no more of his purchases, and double ones too, than the

---

3. *meet*: suitable. The Clown sings garbled snatches of Thomas Lord Vaux's poem "The Aged Lover Renounceth Love," printed in *Tottel's Miscellany* (1557). The extrametrical "O"s and "A"s are probably grunts while digging.
4. *a property of easiness*: something he can do without distress.
5. Has more delicate feeling (because not hardened by callouses).
6. *o'er-offices*: lords it over because of his position, pulls rank on. A "politician" was a schemer for political advantage.
7. Reversal of fortune (literally, the turning of Fortune's

wheel).
8. Was it so inexpensive and easy to bring these bones to maturity that they can be treated as loggats (small wooden clubs thrown at a stake)?
9. Subtle distinctions.
1. Legal prosecution for assault.
2. Fines and recoveries were both kinds of lawsuits brought to make legal an agreement to transfer land ownership. The "double voucher" summoned two witnesses to attest to the land's ownership in these cases. *statutes*: mortgages on land, often linked with "recognizances" (bonds acknowledging a particular debt).
3. Guarantee.

100 length and breadth of a pair of indentures?[4] The very convey-
     ances° of his lands will hardly lie in this box;° and must th'in-   *deeds / deed box; coffin*
     heritor° himself have no more, ha?   *owner*

HORATIO   Not a jot more, my lord.

HAMLET   Is not parchment made of sheepskins?

105 HORATIO   Ay, my lord, and of calf-skins too.

HAMLET   They are sheep and calves° that seek out assurance[5] in   *simpletons and fools*
     that. I will speak to this fellow. [*To the* FIRST CLOWN] Whose
     grave's this, sirrah?[6]

FIRST CLOWN   Mine, sir.

110 (*Sings*)   O, a pit of clay for to be made
                      For such a guest is meet.

HAMLET   I think it be thine indeed, for thou liest in't.

FIRST CLOWN   You lie out on't, sir, and therefore it is not yours.
     For my part, I do not lie in't, and yet it is mine.

115 HAMLET   Thou dost lie in't, to be in't and say 'tis thine. 'Tis for
     the dead, not for the quick;° therefore thou liest.   *living*

FIRST CLOWN   'Tis a quick° lie, sir, 'twill away again from me to   *nimble*
     you.

HAMLET   What man dost thou dig it for?

120 FIRST CLOWN   For no man, sir.

HAMLET   What woman, then?

FIRST CLOWN   For none, neither.

HAMLET   Who is to be buried in't?

FIRST CLOWN   One that was a woman, sir; but, rest her soul, she's

125 dead.

HAMLET   How absolute° the knave is! We must speak by the   *precise*
     card,[7] or equivocation will undo us. By the Lord, Horatio, these
     three years I have taken note of it. The age is grown so picked°   *punctilious*
     that the toe of the peasant comes so near the heel of the court-

130 ier he galls his kibe.° [*To the* FIRST CLOWN] How long hast thou   *chafes his heel sore*
     been a grave-maker?

FIRST CLOWN   Of all the days i'th' year I came to't that day that
     our last King Hamlet o'ercame Fortinbras.

HAMLET   How long is that since?

135 FIRST CLOWN   Cannot you tell that? Every fool can tell that. It
     was the very day that young Hamlet was born—he that was
     mad and sent into England.

HAMLET   Ay, marry, why was he sent into England?

FIRST CLOWN   Why, because a was mad. A shall recover his wits

140 there; or if a do not, 'tis no great matter there.

HAMLET   Why?

FIRST CLOWN   'Twill not be seen in him there. There the men
     are as mad as he.

HAMLET   How came he mad?

145 FIRST CLOWN   Very strangely, they say.

HAMLET   How strangely?

FIRST CLOWN   Faith, e'en with losing his wits.

HAMLET   Upon what ground?[8]

---

4. The two copies of a document (written on one sheet
and separated by an irregular cut so that they could later
be proved to be part of one transaction). The dead man's
property (his grave) is hardly bigger than these elaborate
papers.
5. Security, playing on the legal conveyance of a property

title.
6. An address used with inferiors.
7. With precisely defined meanings (literally, by the
directions marked on a mariner's compass card).
8. From what cause? (The Clown takes him to mean "In
what country?")

FIRST CLOWN   Why, here in Denmark. I have been sexton here,
150   man and boy, thirty years.
HAMLET   How long will a man lie i'th' earth ere he rot?
FIRST CLOWN   I'faith, if a be not rotten before a die—as we have
      many pocky corpses nowadays, that will scarce hold the laying
      in[9]—a will last you some eight year or nine year. A tanner will
155   last you nine year.
HAMLET   Why he more than another?
FIRST CLOWN   Why, sir, his hide is so tanned with his trade that
      a will keep out water a great while, and your water is a sore
      decayer of your whoreson° dead body. Here's a skull, now. This   *vile*
160   skull has lain in the earth three-and-twenty years.
HAMLET   Whose was it?
FIRST CLOWN   A whoreson mad fellow's it was. Whose do you
      think it was?
HAMLET   Nay, I know not.
165   FIRST CLOWN   A pestilence on him for a mad rogue—a poured a
      flagon of Rhenish° on my head once! This same skull, sir, was   *Rhine wine*
      Yorick's skull, the King's jester.
HAMLET   This?
FIRST CLOWN   E'en that.
170   HAMLET   Let me see.
            [*He takes the skull*]
      Alas, poor Yorick. I knew him, Horatio—a fellow of infinite
      jest, of most excellent fancy. He hath borne me on his back a
      thousand times; and now, how abhorred my imagination is! My
      gorge rises at it. Here hung those lips that I have kissed I know
175   not how oft. Where be your gibes now, your gambols, your
      songs, your flashes of merriment that were wont to set the table
      on a roar? Not one now to mock your own grinning? Quite
      chop-fallen?[1] Now get you to my lady's chamber and tell her,
      let her paint an inch thick, to this favour° she must come. Make   *appearance*
180   her laugh at that. Prithee, Horatio, tell me one thing.
HORATIO   What's that, my lord?
HAMLET   Dost thou think Alexander looked o' this fashion i'th'
      earth?
HORATIO   E'en so.
185   HAMLET   And smelt so? Pah!
            [*He throws the skull down*]
HORATIO   E'en so, my lord.
HAMLET   To what base uses we may return, Horatio! Why may
      not imagination trace the noble dust of Alexander till a find it
      stopping a bung-hole?°   *opening of a cask*
190   HORATIO   'Twere to consider too curiously° to consider so.   *over-subtly*
HAMLET   No, faith, not a jot; but to follow him thither with mod-
      esty° enough, and likelihood to lead it, as thus: Alexander died,   *reasonable speculation*
      Alexander was buried, Alexander returneth into dust, the dust
      is earth, of earth we make loam,[2] and why of that loam whereto
195   he was converted might they not stop a beer-barrel?
      Imperial Caesar, dead and turned to clay,
      Might stop a hole to keep the wind away.
      O, that that earth which kept the world in awe

---

9. *pocky . . . in:* bodies riddled with venereal disease that   1. Dejected; also, with a dropped or lost lower jaw.
hardly keep from disintegrating during their burial rites.   2. A mix of clay and straw used as plaster.

Should patch a wall t'expel the winter's flaw!°   *violent wind*
But soft, but soft; aside.

> [HAMLET *and* HORATIO *stand aside.*] *Enter* KING [CLAU-
> DIUS], QUEEN [GERTRUDE], LAERTES, *and a coffin, with*
> [*a* PRIEST *and*] *lords attendant*

200   Here comes the King,
The Queen, the courtiers—who is that they follow,
And with such maimèd rites?[3] This doth betoken
The corpse they follow did with desp'rate hand
Fordo it° own life. 'Twas of some estate.°   *Bring down its / rank*
Couch we° a while, and mark.   *Let's lie low*

205 LAERTES   What ceremony else?
HAMLET [*aside to* HORATIO]   That is Laertes, a very noble youth. Mark.
LAERTES   What ceremony else?
PRIEST   Her obsequies have been as far enlarged
As we have warrantise.° Her death was doubtful,[4]   *proper sanction*
210 And but that great command o'ersways the order[5]
She should in ground unsanctified have lodged
Till the last trumpet. For° charitable prayers,   *Rather than*
Shards, flints, and pebbles should be thrown on her,
Yet here she is allowed her virgin rites,
215 Her maiden strewments,[6] and the bringing home
Of bell and burial.[7]
LAERTES   Must there no more be done?
PRIEST   No more be done.
We should profane the service of the dead
220 To sing sage° requiem and such rest to her   *solemn*
As to peace-parted° souls.   *peacefully deceased*
LAERTES   Lay her i'th' earth,
And from her fair and unpolluted flesh
May violets spring. I tell thee, churlish priest,
A minist'ring angel shall my sister be
225 When thou liest howling.°   *(in hell)*
HAMLET [*aside*]   What, the fair Ophelia!
QUEEN GERTRUDE [*scattering flowers*]   Sweets to the sweet. Farewell.
I hoped thou shouldst have been my Hamlet's wife.
I thought thy bride-bed to have decked, sweet maid,
And not t'have strewed thy grave.
230 LAERTES   O, treble woe
Fall ten times treble on that cursèd head
Whose wicked deed thy most ingenious sense[8]
Deprived thee of!—Hold off the earth a while,
Till I have caught her once more in mine arms.

> [LAERTES] *leaps into the grave*

235 Now our dust upon the quick and dead
Till of this flat a mountain you have made
To o'ertop old Pelion, or the skyish head
Of blue Olympus.[9]

---

3. Truncated ceremonies (ordinarily grand for a court funeral).
4. That is, possibly suicide.
5. And if royal authority had not prevailed over the usual ecclesiastical procedure.
6. Flowers strewed over the casket or grave. Throughout northern Europe, funerary flowers of an unmarried girl often included a special wreath that was sometimes after-ward hung in the church. (Q2's "crants" [garlands] for F's "rites" specifically evokes this practice.)
7. *the bringing . . . burial:* the taking her to her resting place with the ritual passing bells and funeral service.
8. Quick, perceptive intelligence.
9. In Greek mythology, giants piled Pelion (a mountain in Thessaly) on top of Mount Ossa in an attempt to climb Mount Olympus.

HAMLET [*coming forward*]   What is he whose grief
  Bears such an emphasis,[1] whose phrase° of sorrow   *rhetoric*
240 Conjures the wand'ring stars° and makes them stand   *planets*
  Like wonder-wounded° hearers? This is I,   *awestruck*
  Hamlet the Dane.[2]
          HAMLET *leaps in after* LAERTES
LAERTES   The devil take thy soul.
HAMLET   Thou pray'st not well.
245 I prithee take thy fingers from my throat,
  For though I am not splenative° and rash,   *quick-tempered*
  Yet have I something in me dangerous,
  Which let thy wiseness fear. Away thy hand.
KING CLAUDIUS [*to* LORDS]   Pluck them asunder.
QUEEN GERTRUDE   Hamlet, Hamlet!
ALL THE LORDS   Gentlemen!
250 HORATIO [*to* HAMLET]   Good my lord, be quiet.
HAMLET   Why, I will fight with him upon this theme
  Until my eyelids will no longer wag.°   *blink*
QUEEN GERTRUDE   O my son, what theme?
HAMLET   I loved Ophelia. Forty thousand brothers
255 Could not, with all their quantity of love,
  Make up my sum.—What wilt thou do for her?
KING CLAUDIUS   O, he is mad, Laertes.
QUEEN GERTRUDE [*to* LAERTES]   For love of God, forbear him.°   *let him alone*
HAMLET [*to* LAERTES]   'Swounds,° show me what thou'lt do.   *By Christ's wounds*
260 Woot° weep, woot fight, woot fast, woot tear thyself,   *Wilt thou*
  Woot drink up eisel,° eat a crocodile?   *vinegar*
  I'll do't. Dost thou come here to whine,
  To outface me with leaping in her grave?
  Be buried quick with her, and so will I.
265 And if thou prate of mountains, let them throw
  Millions of acres on us, till our ground,
  Singeing his pate° against the burning zone,°   *his head / sun's sphere*
  Make Ossa[3] like a wart. Nay, an° thou'lt mouth,°   *if / speak excessively*
  I'll rant as well as thou.
KING CLAUDIUS [*to* LAERTES]   This is mere madness,
270 And thus a while the fit will work on him.
  Anon,° as patient as the female dove   *Soon*
  When that her golden couplets are disclosed,°   *chicks are hatched*
  His silence will sit drooping.
HAMLET [*to* LAERTES]   Hear you, sir,
  What is the reason that you use me thus?
275 I loved you ever. But it is no matter.
  Let Hercules himself do what he may,
  The cat will mew, and dog will have his day.[4]   *Exit*
KING CLAUDIUS   I pray you, good Horatio, wait upon him.
                 [*Exit*] HORATIO
  [*To* LAERTES] Strengthen your patience in° our last night's   *with*
    speech.
280 We'll put the matter to the present push.°—   *the immediate trial*
  Good Gertrude, set some watch over your son.—

---

1. A violent expression.
2. Normally the title of the King of Denmark.
3. Greek mountain (see note to line 238).

4. *Let . . . day*: Despite Laertes' Herculean ranting, my
day will come.

This grave shall have a living monument.[5]
An hour of quiet shortly shall we see;
Till then, in patience our proceeding be.   *Exeunt*

5.2

Enter [Prince] HAMLET *and* HORATIO
HAMLET   So much for this, sir. Now, let me see, the other.°   *other matter*
    You do remember all the circumstance?°   *state of things then*
HORATIO   Remember it, my lord!
HAMLET   Sir, in my heart there was a kind of fighting
5   That would not let me sleep. Methought I lay
    Worse than the mutines in the bilboes.[1] Rashly°—   *Impulsively*
    And praised be rashness for it: let us know°   *acknowledge*
    Our indiscretion° sometime serves us well   *unreasoned action*
    When our dear plots do pall,° and that should teach us   *grow weak*
10   There's a divinity that shapes our ends,
    Rough-hew them° how we will—   *Form them roughly*
HORATIO   That is most certain.
HAMLET   Up from my cabin,
    My sea-gown scarfed about me in the dark,
15   Groped I to find out them, had my desire,
    Fingered° their packet, and in fine° withdrew   *Stole / finally*
    To mine own room again, making so bold,
    My fears forgetting manners, to unseal
    Their grand commission; where I found, Horatio—
20   O royal knavery!—an exact command,
    Larded° with many several° sorts of reasons   *Elaborated / different*
    Importing° Denmark's health, and England's, too,   *Concerning*
    With ho! such bugs and goblins in my life,[2]
    That on the supervise,° no leisure bated,°   *reading / allowed*
25   No, not to stay° the grinding of the axe,   *await*
    My head should be struck off.
HORATIO   Is't possible?
HAMLET [*giving it to him*]   Here's the commission. Read it at more leisure.
    But wilt thou hear me how I did proceed?
HORATIO   I beseech you.
30   HAMLET   Being thus benetted round with villainies—
    Ere I could make a prologue to my brains,
    They had begun the play[3]—I sat me down,
    Devised a new commission, wrote it fair.[4]
    I once did hold it, as our statists° do,   *statesmen*
35   A baseness to write fair, and laboured much
    How to forget that learning;[5] but, sir, now
    It did me yeoman's service.[6] Wilt thou know
    Th'effect of what I wrote?
HORATIO   Ay, good my lord.

5. A lasting memorial; hinting that Hamlet, now "living," will soon be sacrificed to Ophelia's memory.
5.2 Location: A stateroom of the castle.
1. Worse than the mutineers in the ankle fetters.
2. Such fanciful horrors that would result were I to remain alive. *bugs:* bugbears.
3. *Ere . . . play:* Hamlet's brains "acted" before he consciously thought out a plan.
4. In the professional handwriting of finished (published) documents.

5. *I once . . . learning:* in the sixteenth century, the upper echelons of government became increasingly professionalized; Hamlet implies that these newly elevated officials are prone to snobbish pretensions, covering up their education as common clerks, and he confesses that he once shared their snobbery.
6. It served me valiantly. English yeomen (free landholders) were famous for military strength, supposedly because they fought for their national interest rather than for base pay.

HAMLET   An earnest conjuration° from the King,   *appeal*
40   As England was his faithful tributary,
        As love between them like the palm should flourish,
        As peace should still her wheaten garland[7] wear
        And stand a comma[8] 'tween their amities,
        And many such like 'as'es of great charge,[9]
45   That on the view and know of these contents,
        Without debatement further more or less,
        He should the bearers put to sudden death,
        Not shriving-time[1] allowed.
HORATIO   How was this sealed?
HAMLET   Why, even in that was heaven ordinant.°   *guiding*
50   I had my father's signet in my purse,
        Which was the model of that Danish seal;
        Folded the writ up in the form of th'other,
        Subscribed° it, gave't th'impression,° placed it safely,   *Signed / seal (in wax)*
        The changeling[2] never known. Now the next day
55   Was our sea-fight; and what to this was sequent°   *subsequent*
        Thou know'st already.
HORATIO   So Guildenstern and Rosencrantz go to't.
HAMLET   Why, man, they did make love to this employment.
        They are not near my conscience. Their defeat°   *destruction*
60   Doth by their own insinuation grow.
        'Tis dangerous when the baser nature comes
        Between the pass and fell incensèd points[3]
        Of mighty opposites.°   *opponents*
HORATIO   Why, what a king is this!
HAMLET   Does it not, think'st thee, stand me now upon[4]—
65   He that hath killed my king and whored my mother,
        Popped in between th'election and my hopes,
        Thrown out his angle° for my proper° life,   *fish hook / own*
        And with such coz'nage°—is't not perfect conscience   *trickery*
        To quit° him with this arm? And is't not to be damned   *requite*
70   To let this canker° of our nature come   *cancerous sore*
        In° further evil?   *Into*
HORATIO   It must be shortly known to him from England
        What is the issue° of the business there.   *result*
HAMLET   It will be short. The interim's mine,
75   And a man's life's no more than to say 'one'.[5]
        But I am very sorry, good Horatio,
        That to Laertes I forgot myself;
        For by the image° of my cause I see   *mirror's reflection*
        The portraiture of his. I'll court his favours.
80   But sure, the bravery° of his grief did put me   *ostentation*
        Into a tow'ring passion.
HORATIO   Peace, who comes here?
        Enter young OSRIC, *a courtier [taking off his hat]*

7. Like the palm tree, an emblem of peace and prosperity.
8. And hold their interests separate but still connected
(unlike a period, which would cut off "amity").
9. Weighty clauses beginning with "as"; asses bearing
heavy loads.
1. Time for final confession and absolution, a part of the
state ritual of legal executions.

2. A malicious elf child substituted for an infant, as Hamlet swaps his counterfeit letter for their authentic one.
3. *the pass . . . points:* fencing language; the thrust
("pass") and fiercely angry ("fell") rapiers.
4. Rest incumbent upon me.
5. And life lasts no longer than it takes to pronounce
("say") the monosyllable "one."

OSRIC Your lordship is right welcome back to Denmark.

HAMLET I humbly thank you, sir. [*To* HORATIO] Dost know this
water-fly?

85 HORATIO No, my good lord.

HAMLET Thy state is the more gracious,° for 'tis a vice to know   *blessed*
him. He hath much land, and fertile. Let a beast be lord of
beasts, and his crib shall stand at the king's mess.[6] 'Tis a chuff,°   *rich boor; jackdaw*
but, as I say, spacious in the possession of dirt.

90 OSRIC Sweet lord, if your friendship were at leisure I should
impart a thing to you from his majesty.

HAMLET I will receive it, sir, with all diligence of spirit. Put your
bonnet° to his right use; 'tis for the head.   *hat*

OSRIC I thank your lordship, 'tis very hot.

95 HAMLET No, believe me, 'tis very cold. The wind is northerly.

OSRIC It is indifferent° cold, my lord, indeed.   *rather*

HAMLET Methinks it is very sultry and hot for my complexion.°   *constitution*

OSRIC Exceedingly, my lord. It is very sultry, as 'twere—I cannot
tell how. But, my lord, his majesty bade me signify to you that
100 a° has laid a great wager on your head. Sir, this is the matter.   *he*

HAMLET I beseech you, remember.[7]

OSRIC Nay, good my lord, for mine ease, in good faith.[8]

102.1 *Sir here is newly come to court Laertes, believe me, an*
absolute gentleman, full of most excellent differences,°   *superior qualities*
of very soft° society and great showing.° Indeed, to speak   *pleasing / appearance*
feelingly° of him, he is the card or calendar of gentry,[9]   *appreciatively*
102.5 *for you shall find in him the continent of what part[1]*
a gentleman would see.

HAMLET *Sir, his definement suffers no perdition in you,[2]*
though I know to divide him inventorially would dizzy
th'arithmetic of memory, and yet but yaw neither in
102.10 *respect of his quick sail.[3] But in the verity of extolment,°*   *in truthful praise*
I take him to be a soul of great article,[4] and his infusion°   *inborn essence*
of such dearth° and rareness as, to make true diction[5] of   *preciousness*
him, his semblable° is his mirror, and who else would   *likeness*
trace him his umbrage, nothing more.[6]

102.15 OSRIC *Your lordship speaks most infallibly of him.*

HAMLET *The concernancy,° sir? Why do we wrap the gen-*   *relevance (to us)*
tleman in our more rawer breath?[7]

OSRIC *Sir?*

HORATIO *Is't not possible to understand in another*
102.20 *tongue? You will to't, sir, rarely.[8]*

HAMLET *What imports the nomination° of this gentleman?*   *mention*

OSRIC *Of Laertes?*

6. *Let . . . mess:* If an animal owned enough herds, even
it might find a place at the King's table. *crib:* manger.
7. "Remember your courtesy," the conventional expression inviting a subordinate to put his hat back on.
8. A conventional expression declining Hamlet's invitation. Q2 adds the following passage, lines 102.1–102.34,
in place of lines 103–4, placing a comma instead of a
period after "faith."
9. The model of gentlemanly behavior. *card:* chart or
map. *calendar:* account book, directory.
1. Attribute or quality, playing on "region" (to which
Laertes is the "card"). *continent:* embodiment, continuing
the geographical pun.
2. Your picture of him ("definement") loses none of the
man's real excellence.

3. *to divide . . . sail:* to list his qualities individually would
confuse the memory's reckoning up (through recounting
vast numbers), and yet only steer erratically ("yaw")
around Laertes' skills; that is, the description would only
approximate his virtues.
4. Large scope (?); excellent qualities (?).
5. To speak truly.
6. And whoever imitates him is like his shadow
("umbrage"), not the real thing at all.
7. Our less refined words (since we are so much inferior
to Laertes).
8. *Is't . . . rarely:* Can't he understand his words in
another man's mouth? You will have your joke, sir, splendidly.

HORATIO [*aside to* HAMLET]   *His purse is empty already; all*
       's golden words are spent.

102.25   HAMLET [*to* OSRIC]   *Of him, sir.*

OSRIC   *I know you are not ignorant—*

HAMLET   *I would you did, sir; yet, in faith, if you did it*
       would not much approve° me. Well, sir?   commend

OSRIC   *You are not ignorant of what excellence Laertes is.*

102.30   HAMLET   *I dare not confess that, lest I should compare*
       with him in excellence.[9] *But to know a man well were*
       to know himself.[1]

OSRIC   *I mean, sir, for his weapon. But in the imputation*
       laid on him by them, in his meed° he's unfellowed.°   merit / unmatched

Sir, you are not ignorant of what excellence Laertes is at his
weapon.

105   HAMLET   What's his weapon?

OSRIC   Rapier and dagger.

HAMLET   That's two of his weapons. But well.

OSRIC   The King, sir, hath wagered with him six Barbary horses,
against the which he imponed,° as I take it, six French rapiers   staked

110   and poniards, with their assigns° as girdle,° hanger,[2] or so.   accessories / sword belt
Three of the carriages, in faith, are very dear to fancy, very
responsive to the hilts, most delicate carriages, and of very liberal conceit.[3]

HAMLET   What call you the carriages?[4]

114.1   HORATIO [*aside to* HAMLET]   *I know you must be edified*
       by the margin[5] *ere you had done.*

115   OSRIC   The carriages, sir, are the hangers.

HAMLET   The phrase would be more germane to the matter if we
could carry cannon by our sides. I would it might be hangers
till then. But on: six Barbary horses against six French swords,
their assigns, and three liberal-conceited carriages—that's the

120   French bet against the Danish. Why is this 'imponed', as you
call it?

OSRIC   The King, sir, hath laid,° sir, that in a dozen passes   placed his bet
between you and him he shall not exceed you three hits.[6] He
hath on't twelve for nine,[7] and it would come to immediate

125   trial if your lordship would vouchsafe the answer.[8]

HAMLET   How if I answer no?

OSRIC   I mean, my lord, the opposition of your person in trial.

HAMLET   Sir, I will walk here in the hall. If it please his majesty,
'tis the breathing° time of day with me. Let the foils be brought;   exercising

130   the gentleman willing, an° the King hold his purpose, I will   if
win for him an I can. If not, I'll gain nothing but my shame
and the odd hits.

OSRIC   Shall I re-deliver you e'en so?

HAMLET   To this effect, sir; after what flourish your nature will.

9. Claim to match him (since, proverbially, only excellence recognizes excellence).
1. For in order to know another man truly, one must
know oneself.
2. Attaching straps.
3. *are . . . conceit:* capture the imagination ("fancy") and
match or echo ("respond to") the ornamentation on the
rapiers' hilts; further, they are finely wrought ("delicate")
and of an elaborate ("liberal") design.
4. Osric's inflated term for "hangers," or straps. Here Q2
adds the following aside by Horatio, lines 114.1–114.2.

5. Must be informed by an explanatory note (from the
margin of a book).
6. Laertes must score three more "hits" than Hamlet out
of twelve bouts of swordplay to win the wager.
7. If "he" is Laertes, Osric may mean "He has bet twelve
passes for nine hits" (a greater challenge than the King's
terms, by which he would only need eight hits to win).
8. Would accept the challenge (Osric's meaning, and the
only honorable response). In the next line, Hamlet deliberately misunderstands "answer" as "(any) reply."

135 OSRIC I commend my duty° to your lordship.   *dedicate my service*

HAMLET Yours, yours.   [*Exit* OSRIC]

He does well to commend° it himself; there are no tongues   *recommend*
else for 's turn.°   *purpose*

HORATIO This lapwing runs away with the shell on his head.[9]

140 HAMLET A did comply with his dug[1] before a sucked it. Thus
has he—and many more of the same bevy that I know the
drossy° age dotes on— only got the tune of the time and out-   *worthless*
ward habit of encounter,[2] a kind of yeasty collection which
carries them through and through the most fanned and win-
145 nowed opinions;[3] and do but blow them to their trial, the bubbles are out.[4]

Enter a LORD

146.1 LORD [*to* HAMLET] *My lord, his majesty commended him
to you by young Osric, who brings back to him that you
attend him in the hall. He sends to know if your pleasure
hold to play with Laertes, or that you will take longer*
146.5 *time.*

HAMLET *I am constant to my purposes; they follow the
King's pleasure. If his fitness speaks, mine is ready, now
or whensoever, provided I be so able as now.*

LORD *The King and Queen and all are coming down.*

146.10 HAMLET *In happy time.*

LORD *The Queen desires you to use some gentle entertainment[5] to Laertes before you fall to play.*

HAMLET *She well instructs me.*   [*Exit* LORD]

HORATIO *You will lose, my lord.*

HORATIO You will lose this wager, my lord.

HAMLET I do not think so. Since he went into France, I have
been in continual practice. I shall win at the odds. But thou
150 wouldst not think how all here about my heart—but it is no
matter.

HORATIO Nay, good my lord—

HAMLET It is but foolery, but it is such a kind of gain-giving° as   *misgiving*
would perhaps trouble a woman.

155 HORATIO If your mind dislike anything, obey it. I will forestall
their repair° hither, and say you are not fit.   *coming*

HAMLET Not a whit. We defy augury. There's a special providence[6] in the fall of a sparrow. If it be now, 'tis not to come. If
it be not to come, it will be now. If it be not now, yet it will
160 come. The readiness is all. Since no man has aught of what he
leaves, what is't to leave betimes?[7]

---

9. The newly hatched chicks of the plover ("lapwing")
were supposed to scurry about still wearing their egg-
shells, a reference to the bonnet that Osric has finally put
back on as well as to the courtier's brainless chirping.
1. He bowed politely to his mother's breast.
2. *the tune . . . encounter*: the fashionable turns of speech
("tune of the time") and the formulas ('habit') of courteous conversation ("encounter").
3. *a kind of . . . opinions*: their empty clichés get them
through or pass for the most carefully considered wisdom
(which is "fanned and winnowed" like wheat separated
from chaff during threshing). *yeasty collection*: a frothy
and inflated repertoire of speech and behavior.
4. And if you test them by blowing on them—as Hamlet
does by speaking to Osric—they pop and dissolve. In Q2,
the following passage, lines 146.1–146.14, replaces Hora-

tio's line in F, "You will lose this wager, my lord."
5. To behave with conciliatory courtesy. Shakespeare
seems to have considered two alternative explanations for
Hamlet's final graciousness toward Laertes; here, in Q2,
the Queen's maternal guidance nudges him to it, while
F instead supplies Hamlet's own regret for his graveside
brawling in 5.2.76–81.
6. God's direction for a specific event (over and above
"general providence," the whole shape of God's design).
Compare Matthew 10:29.
7. Since man does not truly possess what he must leave
behind him (worldly things and earthly flesh), why does
it matter to leave them sooner ("betimes")? Q2 reads
"Since no man of ought he leaves, knows what is't to leave
betimes, let be."

Enter KING [CLAUDIUS], QUEEN [GERTRUDE], LAERTES,
and lords, with [OSRIC *and*] *other attendants with trum-*
pets, drums, cushions, foils, and gauntlets; a table, and
flagons of wine on it

KING CLAUDIUS Come, Hamlet, come, and take this hand from me.
HAMLET [*to* LAERTES] Give me your pardon, sir. I've done you wrong;
  But pardon't as you are a gentleman.
165 This presence° knows,   *royal company*
  And you must needs have heard, how I am punished
  With sore distraction. What I have done
  That might your nature, honour, and exception°   *disapproval*
  Roughly awake, I here proclaim was madness.
170 Was't Hamlet wronged Laertes? Never Hamlet.
  If Hamlet from himself be ta'en away,
  And when he's not himself does wrong Laertes,
  Then Hamlet does it not, Hamlet denies it.
  Who does it then? His madness. If't be so,
175 Hamlet is of the faction that is wronged.
  His madness is poor Hamlet's enemy.
  Sir, in this audience
  Let my disclaiming from a purposed evil[8]
  Free me so far in your most generous thoughts
180 That I have shot mine arrow o'er the house
  And hurt my brother.[9]
LAERTES   I am satisfied in nature,
  Whose motive in this case should stir me most
  To my revenge. But in my terms of honour[1]
  I stand aloof, and will no reconcilement
185 Till by some elder masters of known honour
  I have a voice and precedent of peace[2]
  To keep my name ungored;° but till that time   *my reputation intact*
  I do receive your offered love like love,
  And will not wrong it.
HAMLET   I do embrace it freely,
190 And will this brothers' wager frankly° play.—   *freely*
  [*To attendants*] Give us the foils. Come on.
LAERTES [*to attendants*]   Come, one for me.
HAMLET I'll be your foil,[3] Laertes. In mine ignorance
  Your skill shall, like a star i'th' darkest night,
  Stick° fiery off indeed.   *Sparkle; jab*
195 LAERTES You mock me, sir.
HAMLET No, by this hand.
KING CLAUDIUS Give them the foils, young Osric. Cousin Hamlet,
  You know the wager?
HAMLET   Very well, my lord.
  Your grace hath laid the odds o'th' weaker side.
200 KING CLAUDIUS I do not fear it; I have seen you both.
  But since he is bettered,° we have therefore odds.°   *favored / handicapping*
LAERTES [*taking a foil*] This is too heavy; let me see another.

---

8. Let my disavowal of evil intention.
9. F's reading is "mother."
1. But where my social standing as a man of honor is
concerned.
2. *Till . . . peace:* Until the consensus of men of authoritative standing, judging by the standards of tradition (precedent), holds that I can make an honorable peace.
3. Flattering contrast. Jewels were often set with a piece
of metal foil under them to increase their glitter.

HAMLET [*taking a foil*]   This likes° me well. These foils have all   *pleases*
       a° length?   *the same*

OSRIC   Ay, my good lord.
            [HAMLET *and* LAERTES] *prepare to play*

KING CLAUDIUS [*to attendants*]   Set me the stoups° of wine upon   *flagons*
205   that table.

If Hamlet give the first or second hit,
Or quit in answer of the third exchange,[4]
Let all the battlements their ordnance fire.
The King shall drink to Hamlet's better breath,°   *energy*
210 And in the cup an union[5] shall he throw
Richer than that which four successive kings
In Denmark's crown have worn. Give me the cups,
And let the kettle° to the trumpet speak,   *kettledrum*
The trumpet to the cannoneer without,
215 The cannons to the heavens, the heaven to earth,
'Now the King drinks to Hamlet'.
       Trumpets the while [*he drinks*]
                    Come, begin.

And you, the judges, bear a wary eye.

HAMLET [*to* LAERTES]   Come on, sir.

LAERTES   Come, my lord.
       They play
220 HAMLET   One.

LAERTES   No.

HAMLET [*to* OSRIC]   Judgement.

OSRIC   A hit, a very palpable hit.

LAERTES   Well, again.

225 KING CLAUDIUS   Stay.° Give me drink. Hamlet, this pearl is thine.   *Stop*
      Here's to thy health.—
       Drum [*and*] *trumpets sound, and shot goes off*
                  Give him the cup.

HAMLET   I'll play this bout first. Set it by a while.—
      Come.
       They play again
       Another hit. What say you?

LAERTES   A touch, a touch, I do confess.

KING CLAUDIUS   Our son shall win.

230 QUEEN GERTRUDE   He's fat° and scant of breath.—   *sweaty*
      Here, Hamlet, take my napkin.° Rub thy brows.   *handkerchief*
      The Queen carouses to thy fortune, Hamlet.

HAMLET   Good madam.

KING CLAUDIUS   Gertrude, do not drink.

QUEEN GERTRUDE   I will, my lord, I pray you pardon me.
       She drinks [*then offers the cup to* HAMLET]
235 KING CLAUDIUS [*aside*]   It is the poisoned cup; it is too late.

HAMLET   I dare not drink yet, madam; by and by.

QUEEN GERTRUDE [*to* HAMLET]   Come, let me wipe thy face.

LAERTES [*aside to* CLAUDIUS]   My lord, I'll hit him now.

KING CLAUDIUS [*aside to* LAERTES]   I do not think't.

240 LAERTES [*aside*]   And yet 'tis almost 'gainst my conscience.

---

4. Or repay Laertes' victories by winning the third bout.
5. A pearl, of exceptional quality. Claudius is perhaps   proposing to dissolve the gem, as Cleopatra did in a much-repeated legend.

HAMLET   Come for the third, Laertes, you but dally.
  I pray you pass° with your best violence.   *thrust*
  I am afeard you make a wanton° of me.   *spoiled child*
LAERTES   Say you so? Come on.
    [They] play
OSRIC   Nothing neither way.
LAERTES [*to* HAMLET]   Have at you now!
      [LAERTES *wounds* HAMLET.] *In scuffling, they change*
      rapiers[6] [*and* HAMLET *wounds* LAERTES]
245 KING CLAUDIUS [*to attendants*]   Part them, they are incensed.
HAMLET [*to* LAERTES]   Nay, come again.
      The QUEEN *falls down*[7]
OSRIC   Look to the Queen there, ho!
HORATIO   They bleed on both sides. [*To* HAMLET] How is't, my lord?
OSRIC   How is't, Laertes?
LAERTES   Why, as a woodcock to mine own springe,° Osric.   *snare*
250 I am justly killed with mine own treachery.
HAMLET   How does the Queen?
KING CLAUDIUS   She swoons to see them bleed.
QUEEN GERTRUDE   No, no, the drink, the drink! O my dear Hamlet,
  The drink, the drink—I am poisoned.   [*She dies*]
HAMLET   O villainy! Ho! Let the door be locked!   [*Exit* OSRIC]
255 Treachery, seek it out.
LAERTES   It is here, Hamlet. Hamlet, thou art slain.
  No med'cine in the world can do thee good.
  In thee there is not half an hour of life.
  The treacherous instrument is in thy hand,
260 Unbated° and envenomed. The foul practice   *Not blunted*
  Hath turned itself on me. Lo, here I lie,
  Never to rise again. Thy mother's poisoned.
  I can no more. The King, the King's to blame.
HAMLET   The point envenomed too? Then, venom, to thy work.
      [*He*] *hurts* KING [CLAUDIUS]
265 ALL THE COURTIERS   Treason, treason!
KING CLAUDIUS   O yet defend me, friends! I am but hurt.
HAMLET   Here, thou incestuous, murd'rous, damnèd Dane,
  Drink off this potion. Is thy union[8] here?
  Follow my mother.   KING [CLAUDIUS] *dies*
LAERTES   He is justly served.
270 It is a poison tempered° by himself.   *mixed*
  Exchange forgiveness with me, noble Hamlet.
  Mine and my father's death come not upon thee,[9]
  Nor thine on me.   LAERTES *dies*
HAMLET   Heaven make thee free of it! I follow thee.
275 I am dead, Horatio. Wretched Queen, adieu!
  You that look pale and tremble at this chance,
  That are but mutes° or audience to this act,   *nonspeaking actors*
  Had I but time—as this fell sergeant[1] Death
  Is strict in his arrest—O, I could tell you—

---

6. *In . . . rapiers*: from F. While Q2 lacks any stage direction here, Q1 has "They catch one another's Rapiers," suggesting that each combatant is trying to disarm the other with his free hand. Q1 also supplies daggers at line 161; these would presumably have been dropped so that each man would have a free hand.
7. This stage direction and the one at line 253 are taken

from Q1, where they occur together.
8. Referring to both the pearl and his incestuous marriage to Gertrude.
9. May your soul not be judged accountable for our murders.
1. As this fierce sheriff's officer.

280 But let it be. Horatio, I am dead,
Thou liv'st. Report me and my cause aright
To the unsatisfied.

HORATIO   Never believe it.
I am more an antique Roman than a Dane.[2]
Here's yet some liquor left.

HAMLET   As thou'rt a man,
285 Give me the cup. Let go. By heaven, I'll ha't.
O God, Horatio, what a wounded name,
Things standing thus unknown, shall live behind me!
If thou didst ever hold me in thy heart,
Absent thee from felicity a while,
290 And in this harsh world draw thy breath in pain
To tell my story.
      March afar off, and shout within
            What warlike noise is this?
      Enter OSRIC

OSRIC   Young Fortinbras, with conquest come from Poland,
To th'ambassadors of England gives
This warlike volley.°   *military salute*

HAMLET   O, I die, Horatio!
295 The potent poison quite o'ercrows[3] my spirit.
I cannot live to hear the news from England,
But I do prophesy th'election lights
On Fortinbras. He has my dying voice.[4]
So tell him, with th'occurrents,° more and less,   *events*
300 Which have solicited.[5] The rest is silence.
O, O, O, O!   HAMLET *dies*

HORATIO   Now cracks a noble heart. Good night, sweet prince,
And flights of angels sing thee to thy rest. —
Why does the drum come hither?
      Enter FORTINBRAS *with the English* AMBASSADORS, *with*
      drumme[r], colours, and attendants

305 FORTINBRAS   Where is this sight?

HORATIO   What is it ye would see?
If aught of woe or wonder, cease your search.

FORTINBRAS   This quarry cries on havoc.[6] O proud death,
What feast is toward° in thine eternal cell   *preparing*
310 That thou so many princes at a shot
So bloodily hast struck!

AMBASSADOR   The sight is dismal,
And our affairs from England come too late.
The ears are senseless that should give us hearing
To tell him° his commandment is fulfilled,   *(Claudius)*
315 That Rosencrantz and Guildenstern are dead.
Where should we have our thanks?

HORATIO   Not from his mouth,
Had it th'ability of life to thank you.

---

2. Ancient ("antique") Romans generally regarded suicide as preferable to dishonor; in particular, they believed that servants or retainers should not outlive their master's overthrow.
3. Announces triumph over, like the victorious rooster in a cockfight.
4. Vote. Because Denmark is an elective monarchy, Fortinbras can only become King by receiving the "voice,"
or vote, of electors like Hamlet.
5. Some editors assume that the sentence is grammatically incomplete, broken off by death. Hamlet seems to refer to the events that have moved ("solicited") him to have his story told and to give his support to Fortinbras.
6. All this slaughtered game ("quarry") proclaims a massacre.

He never gave commandment for their death.
But since so jump° upon this bloody question°   *immediately / matter*
320   You from the Polack wars, and you from England,
Are here arrived, give order that these bodies
High on a stage be placèd to the view;
And let me speak to th' yet unknowing world
How these things came about. So shall you hear
325   Of carnal, bloody, and unnatural acts,
Of accidental judgements,° casual° slaughters,   *retributions / chance*
Of deaths put on° by cunning and forced cause;   *instigated*
And, in this upshot, purposes mistook
Fall'n on th'inventors' heads. All this can I
Truly deliver.
330   FORTINBRAS   Let us haste to hear it,
And call the noblest to the audience.
For me, with sorrow I embrace my fortune.
I have some rights of memory[7] in this kingdom,
Which now to claim my vantage° doth invite me.   *favorable opportunity*
335   HORATIO   Of that I shall have also cause to speak,
And from his mouth whose voice will draw on more.[8]
But let this same be presently performed,
Even whiles men's minds are wild, lest more mischance
On° plots and errors happen.   *On top of*
FORTINBRAS   Let four captains
340   Bear Hamlet like a soldier to the stage,
For he was likely, had he been put on,°   *put to the test*
To have proved° most royally; and for his passage,   *shown himself; acted*
The soldiers' music and the rites of war
Speak loudly for him.
345   Take up the body. Such a sight as this
Becomes the field,[9] but here shows° much amiss.   *appears*
Go, bid the soldiers shoot.

> *Exeunt, marching [with the bodies]; after*
> *the which, a peal of ordnance are shot off*

TEXTUAL VARIANTS

Control text: F

F: The Folio of 1623
Fa, Fb: Successive states of F incorporating various print-shop corrections and changes
Q1: The Quarto of 1603 ("bad")
Q2: The Quarto of 1604 ("good")
Q2a, Q2b: Successive states of Q2 incorporating various print-shop corrections and changes
Q3: The Quarto of 1611

s.p. KING CLAUDIUS [F's use of *King* has been standardized throughout.]
s.p. QUEEN GERTRUDE [F's use of *Queen* has been standardized throughout.]
s.p. PLAYER KING [F's use of *King* has been standardized throughout.]

---

7. *of memory:* unforgotten; traditional.
8. Whose choice will induce more votes of support.
9. Is most appropriate to a battlefield.

s.p. PLAYER QUEEN [F's use of *Baptista* and *Queen* has been standardized throughout.]
s.p. FIRST CLOWN [F's use of *Clown* has been standardized throughout.]
s.p. SECOND CLOWN [F's use of *Other* has been changed throughout.]

Title: *The Tragedie of Hamlet Prince of Denmarke* [Q2 (head title, running titles), F (head title), Q1 (running titles)] THE Tragicall Historie of HAMLET, *Prince of Denmarke* [Q2 (title page)] *The Tragedie of Hamlet* [F (running titles, table of contents)] THE Tragicall Historie of HAMLET *Prince of Denmarke* [Q1 (title page, head title)]

1.1.60 **he** [Q1, Q2; not in F] 62 **Polacks** Pollax 93 **designed** designe 106.8 **tenantless** tennatlesse [Q2] 106.10 **At** As [Q2] 106.14 **feared** feare [Q2] 106.18 **climature** climatures [Q2] 131 **morn** [Q2] day 139 **say** [Q1, Q2] sayes 144 **takes** [Q1, Q2] talkes 155 **Let's** [Q1, Q2] Let

1.2.8 **sometime** [Q2] sometimes 21 **Co-leaguèd** Coleagued [Q2] Colleagued 34 **Valtemand** [Q2] *Voltemond* 35 **bearers** [Q1, Q2] bearing 58–60 **wrung . . . consent** [Q2; not in F] wrung from me a forced graunt [Q1; Oxford editor G. R. Hibbard argues that the "forced graunt" recollected by the Q1 reporter suggests that he was aware of Laertes' "laboursome petition" as it appears in Q2. The omission is therefore most likely an accident, not an authorial cut.] 77 **good-mother** good Mother 119 **pray thee** [Q2] prythee 132 **canon** cannon 134 **Seem** [Q2] Seemes 135 **ah** [Q2] Oh 141 **beteem** [Q2] beteene 150 **God** [Q1, Q2] Heauen 164 **Marcellus.** [Q2; F (text) indents, like a speech prefix; F (c.w.) is *"Mar-."*] 167 **Wittenberg** [Q2] *Wittemberge* 176 **prithee** [Q2] pray thee 186 **A** [Q2] He 195 **God's** [Q1, Q2] Heauens 204 **distilled** [Q1, Q2] bestil'd 209 **Where, as** [Q1] Whereas 237 **s.p. BARNARDO** *and* MARCELLUS *Both.* [Q2] *All.* [F] 242 **walk** [Q1, Q2] wake

1.3.1 **inbarqued** [Q1, Q2] imbark't 5 **favour** [Q2] fauours 8 **Forward** [Q2] Froward 9 **perfume and** [Q2; not in F] 16 **will** [Q2] feare 21 **sanity and** sanctity and **whole** [Q2] weole 40 **their** [Q2] the 46 **watchman** [Q2] watchmen 57 **thee** [Q1, Q2] you 65 **new-hatched** [Q2] vnhatch't 74 **all** a 109 **Running** Roaming 117 **Lends** [Q1, Q2] Giues 120 **From** [Q2] For 128 **dye** [Q2] eye 129 **imploratators** imploratators 130 **bawds** bonds

1.4.1 **it is** [Q2] is it 10 **wassail** [Q1, Q2] wassels 18.1 **revel** [Q3] reueale [Q2] 18.11 **the** their [Q2] 18.20 **evil** eale [Q2] 18.21 **over** of a [Q2] **daub** doubt [Q2] 23 **intents** [Q1, Q2] euents 26 **O** [Q1] Oh, oh 37 **the** [Q1, Q2] thee 51 **summit** [Q2] Sonnet 53 **assume** [Q1, Q2] assumes 59 **artere** Artire

1.5.1 **Whither** [Q1, Q2] Where 19 **on** [Q1] an 20 **porcupine** Porpentine 22 **List, Hamlet, list, O list!** list *Hamlet,* oh list 24 **God** [Q1, Q2] Heauen 35 **'Tis** [Q1, Q2] It's 43 **wit** wits **with traitorous gifts—** [Q2] hath Traitorous guifts. 45 **to his** [Q1, Q2] to to this 69 **eager** Aygre 71 **barked** bak'd 75 **of queen** [Q1, Q2] and Queene 93 **Hold, hold** [Q2] hold 117 **s.p. HAMLET** *Marcellus* 120 **is't** [Q1, Q2] ist't 137 **whirling** [Q1, Q2] hurling 140 **Horatio** [Q1, Q2] my Lord 158 **our** [Q1, Q2] for 164 **earth** [Q1, Q2] ground 175 **this headshake** [Q1, Q2] thus, head shake 178 **they** [Q1, Q2] there

2.1.1 **this** [Q1, Q2] his 3 **marv'lous** maruels 4 **to** [Q2] you **enquire** [Q2] inquiry 14 **As** [Q2] And 47 **and the addition** Addition 49 **does a this—a** does— [Q2] he this? / He does: 50 **By the mass** [Q2; not in F] 58 **a** [Q2] he 62 **carp** [Q2] Cape 69 **b'wi'** [Q2] buy 69 **Fare ye** [Q2] fare you 77 **i'th' name of God** [Q2] in the name of Heauen 92 **a** [Q2] he 98 **shoulder** [Q1, Q2] shoulders 102 **Come,** [Q2; not in F] 113 **feared** [Q2] feare 115 **By heaven** [Q1, Q2] It seemes

2.2.17 **Whether . . . thus** [Q2; not in F] 20 **is** [Q2] are 29 **But we** [Q2] We 31 **service** [Q2] Seruices 39 **Ay** [Q2; not in F] 45 **and** [Q1, Q2] one 48 **it hath** [Q2] I haue 52 **fruit** [Q2] Newes 58 **my** [Q2; not in F] 59 **Valtemand** [Q2] *Voltumand* 99 **'tis** 'tis [Q2] it is 126 **solicitings** [Q2] soliciting 150 **wherein** [Q2] whereon 162 **does** [Q2] ha's 168 **But** [Q2] And 180 **ten** [Q1, Q2] two 188 **a said** [Q2] he said 189 **A is** [Q2] he is 195 **read** [Q1, Q2] meane 199 **lack** [Q2] locke 200 **most** [Q2; not in F] 210–11 **My Lord, I will take** [Q1, Q2] My Honourable Lord, I will most humbly / Take 213 **except my life, my life, my life** except my life, my life 216 **the** [Q2] my 221 **Ah** [Q2]

Oh **272 of** [Q1, Q2; not in F] **286 discovery, and** [Q2] discovery of **289 heavily** [Q2] heauenly **302 then, when** [Q1, Q2] when **328 berattle** be-ratled **334 like most will** like most **350 'Sblood** [Q2; not in F] **367 Haply** [Q2] Happily **373 was** [Q1, Q2; not in F] **378 came** [Q2] can **382 individable** [Q2] indiuible **403 pious chanson** [Q2] *Pons Chanson* **407 valanced** [Q2] valiant **415 good** [Q1, Q2; not in F] **418 caviare** [Q1, Q2] *Cauiarie* **419 judgements** [Q1, Q2] iudgement **425–26 as wholesome as sweet, and . . . fine** [Q2; not in F] **426 One** [Q2] One cheefe **437 total** [Q1, Q2] to take **445 So, proceed you** [Q2; not in F] so goe on [Q1; probably an accidental omission. See variant at 1.2.58–60.] **449 antique** anticke [probably punning on "antic"] **470 armour** [Q2] Armours **479 to the** [Q1, Q2] to'th **482 mobbled** [Q1, Q2] inobled **484 mobbled** [Q1] Inobled **485 flames** [Q2] flame **499 whe'er** [Q2] whether **500 Prithee** [Q2] Pray you **506 live** [Q1, Q2] liued **508 much** [Q2; not in F] **516 s.p. PLAYERS** Play⟨ers⟩. **526 b'wi'** [F, Q2] buy **531 wanned** [Q2] warm'd **553 'Swounds** [Q2] Why **556 'a'** [Q1, Q2] haue **557 offal. Bloody, bawdy** [Q2] Offall, bloudy: a Bawdy **560 Why,** [Q2] Who? **561 the dear murderèd** Deere **574 a** [Q2] he

3.1.32 here [Q2] there **45 please you** [Q2] please ye **50 sugar** [Q2] surge **51 too true** [Q2] true **73 Th'** [Q2] The **proud** [Q2] poore **76 th'** [Q2] the **89 awry** [Q2] away **99 you know** [Q1, Q2] I know **101 Their perfume lost** then perfume left **112 with** [Q1, Q2] your **133 nowhere** [Q1, Q2] no way **142 paintings, too** [Q1] pratlings too **143 hath** [Q1, Q2] has **face** [Q1, Q2] pace **selves** [Q1, Q2] selfe **154 And** [Q2] Haue

3.2.4 with [Q1, Q2; not in F] **6 your** [Q2; not in F] **8 hear** [Q1, Q2] see **11 would** [Q1, Q2] could **17 o'erstep** [Q2] ore-stop **28–29 nor no man** or Norman **53 tongue lick** [Q2] tongue, like **55 feigning** faining **56 her** [Q2] my **72 thy** [Q2] my **77 stithy** [Q2] Stythe **heedful** [Q2] needfull **81 a** [Q2] he **89 mine now. My Lord, you** mine. Now my Lord, you **120 a must** [Q2] he must **121 a suffer** [Q2] he suffer **124 *mal-hecho*** *Malicho* **127 this fellow** [Q1, Q2] these Fellowes **129 a** [Q2] they **148 former** [Q2] forme **156 their** [Q2] my **178 either** [Q2] other **179 enactures** [Q2] enactors **186 favourite** [Q2] fauourites **198 me give** [Q2] giue me **199.2 An** And [Q2] **221 wince** [Q2] winch **222 unwrung** [Q2] vnrung **224 as good as a** [Q1, Q2] a good **228 mine** [Q2] my **230 mis-take** [Q2] mistake **your** [Q1, Q2; not in F] **239 A** [Q2] He **248 s.p. COURTIERS** *All.* **249 stricken** [F] strucken **268 Ah ha!** [Q2] Oh, ha? **296 as you** [Q2] you **298 struck** stroke **330 fingers** [Q2] finger **339 it speak.** [Q2] it **S'blood** [Q2] Why **I** [Q1, Q2] that I **345 yonder** [Q1, Q2] that **of** [Q1, Q2] like **347 mass** [Q2] Misse **and 'tis,** [Q2] and it's

3.3.14 weal [Q2] spirit **18 summit** Somnet **73 a** [Q2] he **74 a** [Q2] he **77 sole** [Q2] soule **80 A** [Q2] He **81 flush** [Q2] fresh **88 hint** hent

3.4.1 A [Q2] He **12 a wicked** [Q2] an idle **31 better** [Q2] Betters **36 brassed** braz'd **41 off** [Q2] of **43 sets** [Q2] makes **54 this** [Q2] his **64 brother** [Q2] breath **78 And** [Q2] As **108 you do** [Q2] you **109 th'incorporal** [Q2] their corporall **122 whom** [Q2] who **142 o'er** or **143 ranker** [Q2] ranke **144 these** this **151.1–2 eat, / Of habits devilish** eate / Of habits deuill [Q2] **151.5 Refrain tonight** [F] to refraine night [Q2] **151.9 either in** either [Q2] **166 bloat** [Q2] blunt **172 mad** [Q2] made **185.6 and't** an't [Q2]

4.1.1 matter [Q2] matters **6 sea** [Q1, Q2] Seas **11 O** [Q2] On **21 let** [Q2] let's **26 a** [Q2] He **34 mother's closet** [Q2] Mother Clossets **39.1 So envious slander** [not in Q2]

4.2.16 like an ape an apple like an Ape

4.3.7 never [Q2] neerer **20 a** [Q2] he **21 politic** [Q1, Q2; not in F] **23 ourselves** [Q2] our selfe **26–28 s.p. KING CLAUDIUS** Alas . . . that worm [Q2; not in F] **38 A will** [Q2] He will **44 is** [Q2] at **50 them** [Q2] him

4.4.9.16 now [not in Q2]

4.5.12 might [Q2] would **41 God'ield** God dil'd **65 thus** [Q2] this **74 sorrows come** [Q2] sorrowes comes **75 battalions** [Q2] Battaliaes **85 Feeds** [Q2] Keepes **this** [Q2]

his 88 **Wherein** [Q2] Where in 93 **is** [Q2] are 96 **impetuous** impittious 114 **that's calm** [Q2] that calmes 124 **Where is** [Q2] Where's 138 **is't** [Q2] if 139 **sweepstake** Soop-stake 144 **pelican** [Q2] Politician 148 **sensibly** [Q2] sensible 151 **s.p. VOICES** [not in F] 165 **rained** [Q2] *raines* 166 **Fare you well, my dove.** [F italicizes as part of the song.] 174 **pansies** [Q2] Paconcies 181 **a made** [Q2] he made 185–86 **a . . . a** [Q2] *he . . . he* 194 **God 'a' mercy** [Q1, Q2] *Gramercy* 196 **O God** [Q2] you Gods 197 **commune** common 212 **call't** [Q2] call

4.6.8 A [Q2] Hee 9 **ambassador** [Q2] Ambassadours 11 **Horatio** [Q2; not in F] 21 **thine** [Q2] *your*

4.7.11 they're [Q2] they are 21 **guilts** Gyues 24 **aimed** [Q2] arm'd 27 **Who has** Who was 48 **abuse, and** [Q2] abuse? Or 66 **since** [Q2] hence 69 **can** [Q2] ran 77 **Lamord** [Q2] *Lamound* 79 **the** [Q2] our **made** [Q2] mad 84.1 **Th'escrimers** the Scrimures [Q2] 84 **Sir, this** [Q2] Sir. This 88 **What** [Q2] Why 97 **in deed** indeed 114 **that, but dip** [Q2] I but dipt 127 **cunnings** [Q2] commings 129 **that** [Q2] the 133 **How now, sweet Queen?** how sweet Queene. 135 **they** [Q2] they'l 139 **Therewith** [Q2] There with **make** [Q2] come 143 **crownet** Coronet 152 **their** [Q1, Q2] her 153 **lay** [Q2] buy

5.1.4 coroner [Q2] Crowner 11 **to act** [Q2] an Act 23 **o'** [Q2] of 31 **A** [Q2] He 60 **there-a-was nothing-a** [Q2] *there was nothing* 61 **a** [Q2] he 71 **'twere** [Q2] it / were 72 **This** [Q2] It 73 **would** [Q2] could 78 **a** [Q2] he 83 **an** [Q2] if 90 **of** [Q1] of of 101–2 **th'inheritor** [Q2] the Inheritor 108 **sirrah** [Q2] Sir 129 **heel** [Q1, Q2] heeles 129–30 **the courtier** [Q1, Q2] our Courtier 139–40 **a . . . A . . . a . . .** [Q2] he . . . hee . . . he 140 **'tis** [Q2] it's 142 **him there. There** [Q2] him, there 149 **sexton** [Q2] sixteene 152 **a . . . a** [Q2] he . . . he 154 **a will** [Q2] he will 166 **This same skull, sir** [Q2] This same Scull Sir, this same Scull sir 173 **now, how** [Q1, Q2] how 177 **Not** [Q2] No **grinning** [Q2] leering 185 **Pah** puh 188 **a** [Q2] he 202 **rites** rights 204 **of** [Q2; not in F] 212 **prayers** [Q2] praier 230 **treble woe** [Q2] terrible woer 237 **To o'ertop** [Q2] To o'retop 238 **grief** [Q2] griefes 240 **Conjures** [Q2] Con-uire 246 **For** [Q1, Q2] Sir 250 **ALL THE LORDS** Gentlemen! [not in F] **s.p. HORATIO** [Q2] Gen. 259 **'Swounds** [Q2] Come 260 **woot fast** [Q2; not in F] 272 **couplets** [Q2] Cuplet 279 **your** [Q2] you

5.2.7 praised [Q2] praise 8 **sometime** [Q2] sometimes 9 **pall** paule 21 **reasons** [Q2] reason 30 **villainies** villaines 38 **Th'** [Q2] The **effect** [Q2] effects 41 **like** [Q2] as 49 **ordinant** [Q2] ordinate 52 **the form of th'** forme of the 55 **sequent** [Q2] sement 59 **defeat** [Q2] debate 79 **court** count 88 **chuff** Chowgh 89 **say** [Q2] saw 92 **sir** [Q2; not in F] 100 **a** [Q2] he 102 **Nay, good my Lord** [Q2] Nay, in good faith, 102.2 **gentleman** gentlemen [Q2] 102.4 **feelingly** [Q3] sellingly [Q2a] fellingly [Q2b] 102.8 **dizzy** [Q3] dazzie [Q2] 102.9 **yaw** [Q2a] raw [Q2b] 102.20 **to't** [Q2a] doo't [Q2b] **rarely** really [Q2] 102.34 **his** this [Q2] 108 **King, sir** [Q2] sir King **hath wagered** [Q2] ha's wag'd 110 **hanger** [Q2] Hangers 120 **bet** [Q2] but 122 **laid, sir** [Q2] laid 124 **on't one nine** [Q2] mine **it** [Q2] that 132 **and** [Q2] if 138 **turn** [Q2] tongue 140 **A** [Q2] He **a** [Q2] hee 141 **has** [Q2] had **many** [Q2] mine 144 **fanned** fond 145 **trial** [Q2] tryalls 150 **it** [Q2; not in F] 181 **brother** [Q1, Q2] Mother 187 **ungored** [Q2] vngorg'd 213 **trumpet speak** [Q2] Trumpets speake 219 **my lord** [Q2] on sir 227 **Set it** [Q1, Q2] set 231 **Here, Hamlet, take my** Heere's a 249 **mine own** [Q2] mine 254 **Ho!** [Q2] How? 265 **s.p. ALL THE COURTIERS** [Q2] *All.* 281 **cause aright** [Q2] causes right 285 **ha't** [Q2] haue't 286 **God** [Q2] good 299 **th'occurrents** [Q2] the occurents 302 **cracks** [Q2] cracke 308 **This** [Q2] His 310 **shot** [Q2] shoote 329 **th'inventors'** [Q2] the Inuentors 333 **rights** [Q1, Q2] Rites 334 **now** [Q1, Q2] are 335 **also** [Q2] alwayes

Othello

Little seems at stake in *Othello* (1603–4). The tragedies with which it is often compared — *Hamlet*, *King Lear*, and *Macbeth* — chronicle the fall of kings and princes, connecting familial and psychological concerns to the fate of nations. And *Othello* does feint in the same direction early on. The island of Cyprus is threatened by a Turkish fleet — a crucial event absent from Shakespeare's primary source, Giraldi Cinthio's *Gli Hecatommithi* (1565). (In general, *Othello* owes much of its plot to Cinthio but little of its language, characterization, or outlook.) By having the Venetian state send Othello to the island to protect Christian interests from the forces of Islam, Shakespeare projects his protagonist into one of the defining struggles of the age, particularly in the Mediterranean. But before Othello can arrive, a storm destroys the Turkish armada and temporarily eliminates the threat, and the remainder of the play concentrates on domestic concerns seemingly of small consequence for affairs of state.

Yet these concerns acquire an intensity rarely equaled in Shakespearean drama. The plot almost conforms to what Renaissance dramatic theorists considered the Aristotelian unities of time, place, and action; it deploys the smallest cast of characters in Shakespearean tragedy; and it concentrates on a single theme, jealousy. Further, that theme is explored in psychologically complex, disturbing racial and sexual terms that Shakespeare only accentuates in what is probably his revised, expanded version of the play preserved in the First Folio and followed here. (See the Textual Note.) The development of the plot seems both to undermine and to validate racist and misogynist stereotypes. Not surprisingly, the play, always one of Shakespeare's most popular on the stage, has produced powerful contradictory reactions.

In the opening scene, Iago, Othello's ensign, warns Brabanzio, a Venetian senator, that "an old black ram / Is tupping your white ewe" (1.1.88–89) — an allusion to the marriage of "black" Othello to Brabanzio's "white" daughter, Desdemona. Roderigo helpfully explains to Brabanzio that his "fair daughter" has been "transported . . . / To the gross clasps of a lascivious Moor" (1.1.123, 125–27). The strategy of playing upon the old man's fear of miscegenation proves effective. Brabanzio cannot believe, he tells Othello, that his daughter would ever have "run . . . to the sooty bosom / Of such a thing as thou" (1.2.71–72). The Folio revisions of Act 1 expand the roles of Roderigo and Brabanzio and emphasize the charge that Othello used magic to win Desdemona. The language of color here lacks the full racist import it has since acquired, but it certainly draws on a long-standing ethical association of blackness and evil, Elizabethan prejudice toward black Africans resident in England, and the early stages of the slave trade. Yet Shakespeare also followed less prominent, more sympathetic traditions that highlighted aristocratic Moors. The play quickly undermines Brabanzio's claim: Desdemona's love for Othello has led *her* to woo *him*, and the Venetian Senate duly ratifies their marriage. At this point, against the cultural norms of both Shakespeare's time and subsequent centuries, *Othello* celebrates its protagonist's grandeur, female assertiveness and autonomy, and their result: an interracial marriage between Venetian and Moor.

But, of course, Othello murders Desdemona, convinced by Iago that his wife has taken his lieutenant and second-in-command, Cassio, as a lover. The meaning of the play primarily depends on how one understands Othello's movement from nobly loving husband to insanely jealous killer. Critics and audiences alike have often agreed with Brabanzio, seeing in the conclusion the triumph of Othello's homicidal, inferior African essence over his civilized, Christian, European surface. When they have defended Desdemona's and Othello's nobility, they have denied that Othello was black. Basically, those who consid-

Two views of "the Moor," suggesting the range of images Shakespeare may have had in mind. On left: Moroccan ambassador to Queen Elizabeth I (1600); on right: "a Moor," from Cesare Vecellio, *Degli habiti* (1590).

ered Othello beastly thought he was black; those who found him noble were sure he was white. The compromise resolution—at odds with the preponderance of the evidence—suggests the underlying racist agreement between these seemingly antithetical conclusions about Othello's skin color: "Othello was an Oriental, not a Negro: a stately Arab of the best caste." These interpretations, though indicative of cultural mores and inadvertently faithful to Shakespeare's source, say little about *Othello* itself. Yet the play does link Othello's behavior to his ethnicity by making him simultaneously exotic and representative: his degeneration results from his partly external relationship to Europe, a position that encourages him to go "native"—not by reverting to African primitivism but, ironically, by internalizing the destructive norms of Christian society.

The agent of this internalization, Iago, speaks over two hundred lines more than Othello, freely offering motives for his behavior. In the opening scene, he explains his desire for revenge: Othello has chosen Cassio, an unproven gentleman, as his lieutenant rather than Iago, the battle-tested common soldier,

> of whom his eyes had seen the proof
> At Rhodes, at Cyprus, and on other grounds
> Christened and heathen.

(1.1.27–29)

His class-based resentment links him to other figures in Shakespearean tragedy who attack older men standing in the way of their social advancement—Edmund in *King Lear*, Octavius Caesar in *Antony and Cleopatra*, and Macbeth. Like them, he destroys his more archaic, chivalric foe by acting in a value-free fashion that turns others into mere instruments, mere means to his ends. But Iago, who in *Gli Hecatommithi* seeks revenge not on Othello but on Desdemona when she refuses to commit adultery with him, is also the resident misogynist of the play. He soon expresses the fear that Othello has made love to his own wife, Emilia:

> I do suspect the lusty Moor
> Hath leapt into my seat, the thought whereof
> Doth, like a poisonous mineral, gnaw my inwards.
> (2.1.282–84)

These assertions do not reveal the sole motivation, however. Iago also enjoys the sport of ruining Othello's life. In this respect, he descends from the Vice figure of the earlier morality plays—a semisecularized version of the devil who is colloquially intimate with the predominantly lower-class audience and who employs his comic verve to plot the downfall of his virtuous antagonists. (Richard III is Shakespeare's most extended earlier experiment in adapting this figure.) Iago's diabolism is emphasized throughout *Othello*. " 'Swounds [By Christ's wounds], sir, you are one of those that will not serve God if the devil bid you" (1.1.110–11), he tells Brabanzio with the linguistic duplicity and dramatic irony that mark his character: it almost *is* the devil who invokes God to urge Brabanzio not to "serve God" but to commit an ungodly act. Similarly, he explains,

> When devils will the blackest sins put on,
> They do suggest at first with heavenly shows,
> As I do now.
> (2.3.325–27)

Iago's use of the word "devil" gradually seems to infect the other characters. Cassio finds the devil in wine (2.3.263–86); Othello equates the devil with Desdemona (3.4.40; 4.1.41, 235, 239); both fail to detect Iago. Emilia, who has a more disabused view of human behavior, guesses what is happening though not until too late the identity of the perpetrator. As she tells Othello, "If any wretch ha' put this in your head, / Let heaven requite it with the serpent's curse" (4.2.16–17). She suspects that "some eternal villain," in order "to get some office," has slandered Desdemona, an act for which she urges that "hell gnaw his bones" (4.2.134–40). After Othello admits killing Desdemona but before Iago's role emerges, she accuses Othello of being a devil (5.2.140, 142). But it is Othello who ultimately draws the appropriate inference.

> OTHELLO   I look down towards his feet, but that's a fable.
> [*To* IAGO] If that thou beest a devil I cannot kill thee.
> [*He wounds* IAGO]
> . . . .
> IAGO   I bleed, sir, but not killed.
> (5.2.292–94)

The "fable" is that the devil's feet are cloven hooves. If Iago is the devil, he cannot die, a point he mockingly makes by insisting he is "not killed."

This imagery of diabolism enables the play to offer incompatible accounts of both Iago and Othello. The Romantic critic Samuel Taylor Coleridge accurately described the villain's behavior, without fully recognizing its duality, when he saw in Iago the "motive-hunting of a motiveless malignity." In one view, Iago is plausibly driven by resentment— "I know my price, I am worth no worse a place" (1.1.11)—and by an obsessive jealousy that "doth . . . gnaw my inwards" (2.1.284). He is thus part of the psychological drama, afflicting Othello with what he himself feels. But this realistic treatment inevitably turns Othello into the "gull," "dolt," "dull Moor," "murderous coxcomb," and "fool" Emilia accuses him of being (5.2.170, 232, 240). Similarly, all the virtuous characters are "credulous fools . . . caught" (4.1.42) in the trap of a merely clever young man. Alternatively, however, Iago has no fixed essence at all: "I am not what I am" (1.1.65). Operating inside and outside the narrative movement of the play, Iago, like the Vice before him, sometimes seems more a dramatic function than a psychologically realized character. As a devilish figure, not only does he interact with the audience and display improvisationally manipulative acting skills; he also raises the stakes and thus gives the play a religious cast in which the fate of Othello's soul is in the balance and Othello's failure, in repudiating his good "angel" (5.2.140) and succumbing to temptation, reenacts the Fall. Faced with a supernatural adversary, Othello's nobility is less tarnished. In short, the long-standing debate about the protagonist's character is partly inspired by the duality of Iago and hence cannot be resolved: Othello is both culpable dupe and noble victim.

His destruction is linked not only to Christian theology but also to Christian civilization's secular mores. Othello woos Desdemona by movingly narrating his adventures; Iago destroys Othello (and Desdemona) by persuading him to internalize different narratives of his life and her nature, composed out of the repugnant stereotypes of European society. Othello's degradation involves accepting the views of both Brabanzio and Iago. After failing to prevent Desdemona's marriage, Brabanzio warns Othello: "Look to her, Moor, if thou hast eyes to see. / She has deceived her father, and may thee" (1.3.291–92). Iago retrieves the thought:

> IAGO She did deceive her father, marrying you,
> And when she seemed to shake and fear your looks
> She loved them most.
> OTHELLO   And so she did.
>
> (3.3.210–12)

Similarly, Brabanzio accuses Othello of being a "foul thief" who has stolen his "jewel" (1.2.63, 1.3.194). This patriarchal view of women as objects possessed by men then informs Othello's lament:

> O curse of marriage,
> That we can call these delicate creatures ours
> And not their appetites!
>
> (3.3.272–74)

Again, Brabanzio's denial that Desdemona could possibly love Othello "against all rules of nature" (1.3.101) is effectively recycled by Iago, who accuses her of "thoughts unnatural" (3.3.238). Othello agrees literally—"Haply for I am black" (3.3.267)—and metaphorically, in a passage added in the Folio revision: "My name . . . is now begrimed and black / As mine own face" (3.3.391–93). And when Iago describes Cassio and Desdemona in the play's recurrent animal imagery—"as prime as goats, as hot as monkeys" (3.3.408)—Othello dutifully echoes, "Goats and monkeys!" (4.1.260).

But Othello's sexual loathing is also inspired by Desdemona's directness:

> That I did love the Moor to live with him,
> My downright violence and storm of fortunes
> May trumpet to the world.
>
> (1.3.247–49)

This erotic boldness, though it makes Desdemona more appealing, seems to unnerve Othello, who wants his wife with him not "to comply with heat . . . / But to be free and bounteous to her mind" (1.3.262–64). Christian doctrine sometimes considered excessive marital sexual pleasure to be a form of adultery. Othello registers both the allure and the threat of such excess when he is reunited with Desdemona on Cyprus:

> If it were now to die
> 'Twere now to be most happy. . . .
> . . . .
> I cannot speak enough of this content.
> It stops me here, it is too much of joy.
>
> (2.1.186–94)

Earlier, Iago plots "after some time to abuse Othello's ears / That he is too familiar with his wife" (1.3.377–78). "He" is presumably Cassio, to whom Iago has referred two lines earlier. But the more proximate mention of Othello and the confusion of pronouns—since "his" must refer to Othello—point toward the conclusion that Othello experiences his own sexual desire as adulterous, that immediately following what was presumably the initial sexual consummation of his marriage he projects this desire onto Cassio, and that he then punishes his feelings by punishing Desdemona.

The play offers various explanations for Othello's suggestibility. Most obviously, Iago expresses Othello's own unconscious racial and sexual anxieties. But Othello is also out of his element. A soldier since childhood, he knows little of peacetime urban existence. As a colonial possession of Venice and military outpost in what was for Christians the war between civilization and barbarism, Cyprus seems a place where Othello should feel at home. But when the Turkish threat fails to materialize, the island, though it remains the characteristic other world of Shakespearean drama in which fundamental change occurs, assumes several of the features of Venetian society. Othello thus has scant basis for challenging Iago's reductiveness: "In Venice they do let God see the pranks / They dare not show their husbands" (3.3.206–7). Such claims carry conviction partly because they are not entirely false.

> DESDEMONA   Dost thou in conscience think—tell me, Emilia—
>   That there be women do abuse their husbands
>   In such gross kind?
> EMILIA   There be some such, no question.
>   (4.3.59–61)

But Emilia, unlike Iago, considers female adultery not a sign of the depravity of women but tit for tat: "Then let them use us well, else let them know / The ills we do, their ills instruct us so" (4.3.100–01). Shakespeare's Folio revisions enlarge Emilia's part, stressing not only her denunciation of sexual inequality and the sexual double standard but also her concluding heroic defiance of Othello and Iago, a defiance that leads to Iago's undoing. These changes, like others in the Folio, reduce the cynical disillusionment of the play and increase the efficacy of virtue while underscoring the defects of the culture in which Othello and Desdemona operate.

Iago's racial insinuations influence Othello in part not because they are true but because they are the norm in Venetian society. Brabanzio's ravings are unwittingly echoed in the Duke's ostensible repudiation of them: "Your son-in-law is far more fair than black" (1.3.289)—where the praise depends on the negative connotations of blackness. Finally, Othello's willingness to trust circumstantial evidence is also standard: " 'Tis probable, and palpable to thinking," Brabanzio argues, that Othello has used magic on Desdemona (1.2.77). "I know not if't be true" that Othello is Emilia's lover, Iago concedes, "but I, for mere suspicion in that kind, / Will do as if for surety" (1.3.370–72). Thus Iago can get away without "ocular proof" (3.3.365):

>   But yet I say,
>   If imputation, and strong circumstances
>   Which lead directly to the door of truth,
>   Will give you satisfaction, you might ha't.
>   (3.3.410–13)

In short, with the passion of the recently converted, Othello is driven to murder not by reversion to African barbarism but by adherence to an extreme, perverse version of the logic of Christian society.

Why has Othello's failure been so deeply moving to audiences and readers since the seventeenth century? The answer is that *Othello*, unlike its source, emphasizes that Othello and Desdemona are special people who have done a special thing. Their unusual nobility of soul—supplemented in Shakespeare's reworking of his source by a comparable elevation in social status—leads most of the other characters to applaud a marriage that bridges gaps in age, nation, ethnicity, and culture. Especially when the central role is performed by actors of sub-Saharan descent, performances of *Othello*, despite the play's apparent indifference to politics, have seemed to strike a blow for freedom—on the European continent following the revolutions of 1848, in czarist Russia on the eve of the liberation of the serfs, in World War II America, and in the final years of South African apartheid. The 1943 American *Othello*, which featured the American theater's first kiss between a black actor and a white actress, was the longest-running production of any Shakespearean play in the United States.

The couple's nobility, however, is grist for Iago's mill. Desdemona's boldness and generosity of spirit are evidence of her affair with Cassio. Othello's "free and open nature, / That thinks men honest that but seem to be so," causes him to "be led by th' nose / As asses are" (1.3.381–84) by the ironically titled "honest Iago" (1.3.293 and elsewhere). Moreover, before Othello becomes jealous, he has touchingly but ominously staked everything on Desdemona:

> My life upon her faith.
>
> (1.3.293)

> Perdition catch my soul
> But I do love thee, and when I love thee not,
> Chaos is come again.
>
> (3.3.91–93)

Iago can also count on Othello's military resoluteness:

> I'll see before I doubt; when I doubt, prove;
> And on the proof, there is no more but this:
> Away at once with love or jealousy.
>
> (3.3.194–96)

But Othello's precipitousness leaves room for neither love nor jealousy. The play's famous dual time schemes preclude either development. On the one hand, Othello asserts that Desdemona "with Cassio hath the act of shame / A thousand times committed" (5.2.218–19). On the other, he apparently murders Desdemona the day after they arrive on Cyprus. These incompatible chronologies function like Iago's duality. Allusions to the passage of time make it physically possible for Desdemona to have committed adultery but turn Othello into a fool. By contrast, the compressed dramatized concatenation of events makes it psychologically plausible, as it is not in Shakespeare's source, for Othello to act before Iago's plot unravels.

The intensity of the short chronology is sustained by Othello's eloquent evocation of his predicament, a predicament that Shakespeare especially stresses in his revised version: "I think my wife be honest, and think she is not. / I think that thou art just, and think thou art not" (3.3.389–90). More generally, Othello renders his pathos in an imaginative, idealizing poetry that contrasts with Iago's prose and that earlier won Desdemona:

> O, now for ever
> Farewell the tranquil mind, farewell content,
> Farewell the plumèd troops and the big wars
> That makes ambition virtue!
>
> (3.3.352–55)

As he carries a torch into his bedroom to kill his sleeping wife, his simple language captures the symbolic significance of his intentions: "Put out the light, and then put out the light" (5.2.7). Correspondingly, as Othello's suspicions of Desdemona grow, the play emphasizes her innocence by dramatizing her obedience to Othello. This pattern climaxes just before her death:

DESDEMONA   O, falsely, falsely murdered!

. . . .

   A guiltless death I die.
EMILIA   O, who hath done this deed?
DESDEMONA   Nobody, I myself. Farewell.
   Commend me to my kind lord. O, farewell!
                        (5.2.126–34)

The meaning of her words is unclear, however. The Folio revisions increase Desdemona's part in Act 4 so as to emphasize her innocent victimization: a loyally subordinate Desdemona is more conventionally reassuring than the Desdemona who flouted convention to marry Othello. This diminution of female autonomy marks a retreat from the bolder position in the opening scenes of the play and arguably in the earlier version as a whole. On the other hand, Desdemona's final words may be seen as a masochistic submissiveness every bit as unsettling as her earlier, franker behavior.

A similar uncertainty characterizes the end of Othello's life. Othello believes that in killing Desdemona, he is administering secular justice or performing a religious ritual, but his rage forces him to "call what I intend to do / A murder, which I thought a sacrifice" (5.2.69–70). Faced with the truth about Desdemona, he again assumes the role of minister of justice, executing himself as he had earlier sought to execute his wife. The despairing bravery and moral scrupulousness of this act are antithetical to the morally furtive and anticlimactic behavior of the protagonist in *Gli Hecatommithi*. Yet if suicide conjures up disinterested justice or Roman heroism, it also suggests Christian despair and certainty of damnation. Similarly, one may or may not agree with Othello's concluding self-evaluation as "an honourable murderer" or as "one not easily jealous" (5.2.300, 354).

More striking still is the persistence of Othello's guilt about marital intercourse and the association of sex with death suggested by his earlier assertion "If it were now to die / 'Twere now to be most happy" (2.1.186–87). The fatal "napkin," or handkerchief, indicative of aristocratic privilege but important because of its very triviality, symbolically captures these inexpressible feelings. Presented, according to Othello, to his mother by "an Egyptian . . . charmer," the handkerchief combines the magic and ethnic exoticism that Othello earlier repudiates. It enabled his mother to "subdue my father / Entirely to her love" (3.4.54–58). Or perhaps it did not. At the end of the play, Othello offers a more prosaic, incompatible account: "It was a handkerchief, an antique token / My father gave my mother" (5.2.223–24). "Spotted with strawberries" (3.3.440) in *Othello* but not in Shakespeare's source, it evokes the blood Desdemona loses with her virginity on the marriage bed. Desdemona has Emilia "lay on my bed my wedding sheets" (4.2.108), a decision that inadvertently suggests Othello's underlying sexual loathing and self-loathing as

The manner of Turkish tyrannie over Christian flaves.

Compare Othello's last speech before killing himself (5.2.361–65). Woodcut, from F. Knight, *A Relation of Seaven Years Slaverie Under the Turkes of Argeire* (1640).

he comes to kill her: "Thy bed, lust-stained, shall with lust's blood be spotted" (5.1.37). This association between sexual pleasure and death is then grimly enacted. Overwhelmed by the attraction of his sleeping wife, Othello cannot resist kissing her: "Be thus when thou art dead, and I will kill thee / And love thee after" (5.2.18–19). He consciously echoes this necrophilic perversity at his own death: "I kissed thee ere I killed thee. No way but this: / Killing myself, to die upon a kiss" (5.2.368–69). In Renaissance English, to "die" could mean to "have an orgasm." Only in death can Othello guiltlessly experience the adulterous pleasure of marriage.

The alien connotations of the handkerchief are echoed by the ethnic rhetoric of Othello's last long speech, in which the conflict of civilizations reemerges in his identification with the exotic non-European, non-Christian world. He is "like the base Indian" who "threw a pearl away / Richer than all his tribe" (5.2.356–57). He "drops tears as fast as the Arabian trees / Their medicinable gum" (5.2.359–60). Most remarkably, he asks his listeners to remind the Venetian state

> that in Aleppo once,
> Where a malignant and a turbaned Turk
> Beat a Venetian and traduced the state,
> I took by th' throat the circumcisèd dog
> And smote him thus.
> *He stabs himself*
>
> (5.2.361–65)

In Act 1, Othello was asked to defend the Venetians from the Turks—that is, to defend Christianity against a Muslim people with whom Moors were traditionally linked on religious and military grounds. An orthodox Christian and loyal servant of the state, he readily agreed. Here, in Act 5, he recalls that he had also done so once before. But this recollection is the occasion for his suicide, a deed that splits him in two. Othello is both agent and object of justice, both servant and enemy of the Christian state. He is and is not the Turk. If Iago has always lacked a unitary inner essence, so too at the end does Othello. He half assumes an ethnic and religious otherness to indicate and exorcise his guilt. The gesture of self-scapegoating, which parallels the more general scapegoating of Iago, exonerates Christian society in a way that previous events do not justify. But his unwarranted projection of guilt beyond the confines of Europe is the precondition of that noble acceptance of responsibility with which Othello so memorably leaves the world, and the play.

WALTER COHEN

TEXTUAL NOTE

The Tragedy of Othello the Moore of Venice (1603–4) survives in two early authoritative versions—the First Quarto of 1622 (Q) and the First Folio of the following year (F). The quarto is probably based on a scribal copy of the author's original manuscript, the Folio on a scribal copy of what is here hypothesized to be Shakespeare's own revision. Accordingly, this edition is based on F. On the other hand, Q more accurately preserves Shakespeare's characteristic spelling and punctuation, its stage directions are fuller and more authorial (though some were probably added by the scribe), and it contains more than fifty oaths excluded from the Folio presumably in response to the Profanity Act of 1606. (It is also the only Shakespearean quarto with act divisions—possibly indicative of court or university performance.) In order to capture these features, the version printed here uses Q for these details. But it adds the roughly 160 lines from F not found in Q, and it usually prefers F to Q in the over one thousand places where their wording differs. In general, then, F is the primary source for the language, whereas Q provides the spelling, punctuation, oaths, and to some extent stage directions. Act divisions are the same in the two versions. Other modern editions of the play, though differing in their assumptions and in many details, produce broadly similar texts.

The Folio's additions fall into three main categories. In Act 1, Roderigo's and Brabanzio's accusations against Othello are lengthened. Second, beginning in Act 3, F provides Othello with somewhat greater opportunity to express his anguish. Finally and most important, the last two acts build up the parts of Desdemona (mainly by giving her the willow song in 4.3) and Emilia. The specific effects of these changes, which tend to move *Othello* away from cynicism and disillusionment, are discussed in the Introduction, and some of the more extensive additions or striking differences from Q are mentioned in the notes. By contrast, additions to Iago's role are minor and incidental. Interestingly, the hypothesized revisions of *Troilus and Cressida* and *King Lear*, plays initially composed within a couple of years of *Othello*, head in the same direction—away from satire and bitterness. It is tempting but speculative to conclude that the revisions, like the original versions, were clustered together in time. Though the excision of oaths places the scribal transcript for the Folio's version of *Othello* after 1606, no strong inference is possible about the date of Shakespeare's own revised manuscript. A weak one is, however. A few of the expurgations (most strikingly the replacement of Q's "Zouns" by F's "What dost thou meane?" at 3.3.159) go well beyond the Folio's standard procedure—the mere omission of the offending word or its simple replacement (for instance, "heaven" instead of the proscribed "God"). The simplest theory is that the Profanity Act necessitated certain limited revisions for a revival in 1606 or later and that at the same time Shakespeare took the opportunity to introduce more substantive changes—occasionally in the oaths, more often into the characters themselves.

SELECTED BIBLIOGRAPHY

Barthelemy, Anthony Gerard, ed. *Critical Essays on Shakespeare's "Othello."* New York: Hall, 1994.

Bloom, Harold, ed. *William Shakespeare's "Othello."* New York: Chelsea House, 1987.

Fiedler, Leslie A. *The Stranger in Shakespeare.* New York: Stein and Day, 1972. 139–96.

Greenblatt, Stephen. *Renaissance Self-Fashioning: From More to Shakespeare.* Chicago: University of Chicago Press, 1980. 222–54.

Hunter, G. K. "Othello and Colour Prejudice." *Proceedings of the British Academy* 53 (1967): 139–63.

Orkin, Martin, *Shakespeare Against Apartheid.* Craighall, South Africa: Ad. Donker, 1987. 59–129.

Parker, Patricia. "Fantasies of 'Race' and 'Gender': Africa, *Othello,* and Bringing to Light." *Women, "Race," and Writing in the Early Modern Period.* Ed. Margo Hendricks and Patricia Parker. London: Routledge, 1994. 84–100.

Snow, Edward A. "Sexual Anxiety and the Male Order of Things in *Othello*." *English Literary Renaissance* 10 (1980): 384–412.

Stallybrass, Peter. "Patriarchal Territories: The Body Enclosed." *Rewriting the Renaissance: The Discourses of Sexual Difference in Early Modern Europe.* Ed. Margaret W. Ferguson, Maureen Quilligan, and Nancy Vickers. Chicago: University of Chicago Press, 1986. 123–42.

Wain, John, ed. *Shakespeare: "Othello." A Casebook.* London: Macmillan, 1971.

The Tragedy of Othello, the Moor of Venice

THE PERSONS OF THE PLAY

OTHELLO, the Moor of Venice
DESDEMONA, his wife
Michael CASSIO, his lieutenant
BIANCA, a courtesan, in love with Cassio
IAGO, the Moor's ensign
EMILIA, Iago's wife
A CLOWN, a servant of Othello
The DUKE of Venice
BRABANZIO, Desdemona's father, a senator of Venice
GRAZIANO, Brabanzio's brother
LODOVICO, kinsman of Brabanzio
SENATORS of Venice
RODERIGO, a Venetian gentleman, in love with Desdemona
MONTANO, Governor of Cyprus
A HERALD
A MESSENGER
Attendants, officers, sailors, gentlemen of Cyprus, musicians

1.1

Enter IAGO[1] *and* RODERIGO

RODERIGO   Tush, never tell me!° I take it much unkindly   *You're kidding*
　　That thou, Iago, who hast had my purse
　　As if the strings were thine, shouldst know of this.[2]
IAGO   'Sblood,° but you'll not hear me!   *By Christ's blood*
5　　If ever I did dream of such a matter, abhor me.
RODERIGO   Thou told'st me thou didst hold him° in thy hate.   *(Othello)*
IAGO   Despise me
　　If I do not. Three great ones of the city,
　　In personal suit to make me his lieutenant,
10　　Off-capped° to him; and by the faith of man   *Took off their caps*
　　I know my price, I am worth no worse a place.
　　But he, as loving his own pride and purposes,
　　Evades them with a bombast circumstance[3]
　　Horribly stuffed with epithets of war,°   *military jargon*
15　　Nonsuits° my mediators; for 'Certes,'° says he,   *Denies / Certainly*
　　'I have already chose my officer.'
　　And what was he?
　　Forsooth, a great arithmetician,[4]
　　One Michael Cassio, a Florentine,

1.1 Location: A street in Venice.
1. Iago's name may be related to Santiago Matamoros,
St. James the Moorslayer, the patron saint of Spain.
2. Desdemona's marriage to Othello.
3. With an inflated circumlocution. *bombast*: cotton pad-

ding in clothes, a metaphor picked up by "stuffed" (line
14) and possibly "suit" (line 9) and "Nonsuits" (line 15).
4. Implying that Cassio's knowledge of war is purely theo-
retical.

20	A fellow almost damned in a fair wife,[5]	
	That° never set a squadron in the field	*Who*
	Nor the division° of a battle° knows	*ordering / battalion*
	More than a spinster°—unless the bookish theoric,°	*housewife / learning*
	Wherein the togaed consuls can propose[6]	
25	As masterly as he. Mere prattle without practice	
	Is all his soldiership; but he, sir, had th'election,	
	And I—of whom his° eyes had seen the proof	*(Othello's)*
	At Rhodes, at Cyprus, and on other grounds	
	Christened and heathen—must be beleed° and calmed°	*without wind / becalmed*
30	By debitor and creditor. This counter-caster,[7]	
	He in good time° must his lieutenant be,	*indeed (scornful)*
	And I—God bless the mark!°—his Moorship's ensign.[8]	*God help us*

RODERIGO   By heaven, I rather would have been his hangman.

IAGO   Why, there's no remedy. 'Tis the curse of service.

35	Preferment goes by letter and affection,[9]	
	And not by old gradation,° where each second	*traditional seniority*
	Stood heir to th' first. Now, sir, be judge yourself	
	Whether I in any just term am affined°	*bound in any just way*
	To love the Moor.[1]	

40	RODERIGO I would not follow him then.	
	IAGO O sir, content you.°	*be content*
	I follow him to serve my turn upon him.	
	We cannot all be masters, nor all masters	
	Cannot be truly followed. You shall mark	
45	Many a duteous and knee-crooking knave	
	That, doting on his own obsequious bondage,	
	Wears out his time much like his master's ass	
	For naught but provender,° and when he's old, cashiered.°	*animal feed / fired*
	Whip me° such honest knaves. Others there are	*The hell with*
50	Who, trimmed° in forms and visages of duty,	*outwardly decorated*
	Keep yet their hearts attending on themselves,	
	And, throwing but shows of service on their lords,	
	Do well thrive by 'em, and when they have lined their coats,	
	Do themselves homage. These fellows have some soul,	
55	And such a one do I profess myself—for, sir,	
	It is as sure as you are Roderigo,	
	Were I the Moor I would not be Iago.	
	In following him I follow but myself.[2]	
	Heaven is my judge, not I for° love and duty,	*I am not driven by*
60	But seeming so for my peculiar° end.	*personal*
	For when my outward action doth demonstrate	
	The native act and figure[3] of my heart	
	In compliment extern,° 'tis not long after	*outward appearance*

5. The meaning is obscure, since Cassio is unmarried and has not yet met Bianca, although the corresponding character in Shakespeare's source is married. Perhaps the point is that Cassio is a ladies' man.
6. In which the toga-wearing senators can debate.
7. *debitor and creditor, counter-caster*: pejorative terms for an accountant (Cassio).
8. As "ensign," Iago is something like a standard-bearer and Othello's third-in-command. He clearly ranks below "lieutenant" Cassio, the second-in-command.
9. Promotion comes through connections and favoritism.
1. A Moor was a Muslim of the mixed Berber and Arab people inhabiting northwest Africa. This term, like the

comparison of Othello to a "Barbary horse" (an Arab, line 113), formerly led to the denial of Othello's blackness. But the passages describing Othello's appearance—"thick-lips," "black ram," "sooty bosom," "black Othello," "I am black," "black / As mine own face" (1.1.66, 1.1.88, 1.2.71, 2.3.27–28, 3.3.267, 3.3.392–93)—seem to have greater weight. "Moor" often meant sub-Saharan African in the Renaissance.
2. I'd rather command than serve; I serve out of self-interest rather than duty. (See line 65 and note, 4.1.17, and the Introduction.)
3. The innate operation (or motivation) and shape (or nature).

But I will wear my heart upon my sleeve
65   For daws° to peck at. I am not what I am.[4]   *crowlike birds*
RODERIGO   What a full fortune does the thick-lips owe°   *(Othello) own*
    If he can carry't thus!°   *carry out the marriage*
IAGO   Call up her father,
    Rouse him, make after him, poison his delight,
    Proclaim him in the streets; incense her kinsmen,
70   And, though he in a fertile climate dwell,
    Plague him with flies.[5] Though that his joy be joy,
    Yet throw such chances of vexation on't
    As it may lose some colour.
RODERIGO   Here is her father's house. I'll call aloud.
75 IAGO   Do, with like timorous accent° and dire yell   *frightening tone*
    As when, by night and negligence, the fire
    Is spied in populous cities.
RODERIGO *[calling]*   What ho, Brabanzio, Signor Brabanzio, ho!
IAGO *[calling]*   Awake, what ho, Brabanzio, thieves, thieves, thieves!
80   Look to your house, your daughter, and your bags.
    Thieves, thieves!

        [Enter] BRABANZIO *[in his nightgown] at a window*
        above

BRABANZIO   What is the reason of this terrible summons?
    What is the matter there?
RODERIGO   Signor, is all your family within?
IAGO   Are your doors locked?
85 BRABANZIO   Why, wherefore ask you this?
IAGO   'Swounds,° sir, you're robbed. For shame, put on your   *By Christ's wounds*
    gown.
    Your heart is burst, you have lost half your soul.
    Even now, now, very now, an old black ram
    Is tupping° your white ewe. Arise, arise!   *copulating with*
90   Awake the snorting° citizens with the bell,   *snoring*
    Or else the devil will make a grandsire of you.
    Arise, I say.
BRABANZIO   What, have you lost your wits?
RODERIGO   Most reverend signor, do you know my voice?
BRABANZIO   Not I. What are you?
95 RODERIGO   My name is Roderigo.
BRABANZIO   The worser welcome.
    I have charged thee not to haunt about my doors.
    In honest plainness thou hast heard me say
    My daughter is not for thee, and now in madness,
100   Being full of supper and distempering° draughts,   *destabilizing*
    Upon malicious bravery° dost thou come   *defiance*
    To start° my quiet.   *upset*
RODERIGO   Sir, sir, sir.
BRABANZIO   But thou must needs be sure
105   My spirits and my place° have in their power   *senatorial rank*
    To make this bitter to thee.
RODERIGO   Patience, good sir.
BRABANZIO   What tell'st thou me of robbing? This is Venice.
    My house is not a grange.°   *country house*

---

4. I am not what I seem; I have no essential nature.
5. *though . . . flies:* though he (either Othello or Desde-   mona's father, Brabanzio) is fortunate, make his life
unpleasant.

RODERIGO   Most grave Brabanzio,
In simple and pure soul I come to you.

110 IAGO [to BRABANZIO]   'Swounds, sir, you are one of those that will
not serve God if the devil bid you.[6] Because we come to do you
service and you think we are ruffians, you'll have your daughter
covered with a Barbary horse,[7] you'll have your nephews° neigh   grandsons
to you, you'll have coursers for cousins and jennets for ger-

115 mans.[8]

BRABANZIO   What profane wretch art thou?

IAGO   I am one, sir, that comes to tell you your daughter and the
Moor are now making the beast with two backs.°   copulating

BRABANZIO   Thou art a villain.

IAGO   You are a senator.

120 BRABANZIO   This thou shalt answer.° I know thee, Roderigo.   account for

RODERIGO   Sir, I will answer anything. But I beseech you,
If't be your pleasure and most wise consent[9]—
As partly I find it is—that your fair daughter,
At this odd-even° and dull watch o'th' night,   late (around midnight)

125 Transported with no worse nor better guard
But with a knave of common° hire, a gondolier,   public
To the gross clasps of a lascivious Moor—
If this be known to you, and your allowance,°   allowed by you
We then have done you bold and saucy wrongs.

130 But if you know not this, my manners tell me
We have your wrong rebuke. Do not believe
That, from° the sense of all civility,   in opposition to
I thus would play and trifle with your reverence.
Your daughter, if you have not given her leave,

135 I say again hath made a gross revolt,
Tying her duty, beauty, wit, and fortunes
In an extravagant and wheeling stranger[1]
Of here and everywhere. Straight° satisfy yourself.   Immediately
If she be in her chamber or your house,

140 Let loose on me the justice of the state
For thus deluding you.

BRABANZIO [calling]   Strike on the tinder,° ho!   A light
Give me a taper,° call up all my people.   candle
This accident° is not unlike my dream;   event
Belief of it oppresses me already.
Light, I say, light!   Exit

145 IAGO   Farewell, for I must leave you.
It seems not meet° nor wholesome to my place   proper
To be producted°—as, if I stay, I shall—   presented as witness
Against the Moor, for I do know the state,
However this may gall him with some check,°   reprimand

150 Cannot with safety cast° him, for he's embarked   dismiss
With such loud reason to the Cyprus wars,[2]
Which even now stands in act,° that, for their souls,   are taking place
Another of his fathom° they have none   caliber

6. Iago is not encouraging Brabanzio to "serve God," but
ironically it is "the devil" who is urging him on. For the
religious and theatrical significance of the language of
diabolism, see the Introduction.
7. Horse from northwest coastal Africa; an Arab; suggesting barbarism; hence, Othello.
8. *coursers:* strong horses. *cousins:* kinsmen. *jennets:* small

Spanish horses. *germans:* close relatives.
9. Lines 122–138 do not appear in Q.
1. In a vagrant and vagabond foreigner (perhaps suggesting a planet wandering off course).
2. *he's . . . wars:* the choice of Othello to lead the fight in
Cyprus has received such vociferous ("loud") and entirely
appropriate support ("reason").

To lead their business, in which regard—
155 Though I do hate him as I do hell pains—
Yet for necessity of present life
I must show out a flag and sign of love,
Which is indeed but sign. That you shall surely find him,
Lead to the Sagittary³ the raisèd search,°   *awakened searchers*
160 And there will I be with him. So farewell.   *Exit*
    Enter [below] BRABANZIO *in his nightgown, and servants
    with torches*
BRABANZIO   It is too true an evil. Gone she is,
And what's to come of my despisèd time°   *lifetime*
Is naught but bitterness. Now, Roderigo,
Where didst thou see her?—O unhappy girl!—
165 With the Moor, sayst thou?—Who would be a father?—
How didst thou know 'twas she?—O, she deceives me
Past thought!—What said she to you? [*To servants*] Get more tapers,
Raise all my kindred.   [*Exit one or more*]
[*To* RODERIGO]   Are they married, think you?
RODERIGO   Truly, I think they are.
170 BRABANZIO   O heaven, how got she out? O, treason of the blood!
Fathers, from hence trust not your daughters' minds
By what you see them act. Is there not charms°   *magic*
By which the property° of youth and maidhood°   *attribute / virginity*
May be abused? Have you not read, Roderigo,
Of some such thing?
175 RODERIGO   Yes, sir, I have indeed.
BRABANZIO [*to servants*]   Call up my brother. [*To* RODERIGO] O,
    would you had had her.
[*To servants*] Some one way, some another. [*Exit one or more*]
[*To* RODERIGO]   Do you know
Where we may apprehend her and the Moor?
RODERIGO   I think I can discover him, if you please
180 To get good guard and go along with me.
BRABANZIO   Pray you lead on. At every house I'll call;
I may command° at most. [*Calling*] Get weapons, ho,   *demand help*
And raise some special officers of night.
On, good Roderigo. I will deserve° your pains.   *Exeunt*   *reward*

1.2

    Enter OTHELLO, IAGO, *and attendants with torches*
IAGO   Though in the trade of war I have slain men,
Yet do I hold it very stuff° o'th' conscience   *essence*
To do no contrived° murder. I lack iniquity,   *premeditated*
Sometime, to do me service. Nine or ten times
5 I had thought to've yerked him° here, under the ribs.   *stabbed (Roderigo)*
OTHELLO   'Tis better as it is.
IAGO   Nay, but he prated,
And spoke such scurvy and provoking terms
Against your honour
That, with the little godliness I have,

3. Perhaps indicating an inn named for the astrological sign Sagitarius, where Othello and Desdemona are staying. It may also suggest Othello himself, since Sagitarius is depicted as a centaur (a mythological being part man, part horse), and Iago has already likened Othello to a "Barbary horse."
1.2 Location: Another street in Venice, before Othello's lodgings.

10   I did full hard forbear him.[1] But I pray you, sir,
    Are you fast° married? Be assured of this: *legitimately*
    That the magnifico° is much beloved,   *(Brabanzio)*
    And hath in his effect a voice potential°   *powerful*
    As double as the Duke's. He will divorce you,
15   Or put upon you what restraint or grievance
    The law, with all his might to enforce it on,
    Will give him cable.°   *scope*
OTHELLO   Let him do his spite.
    My services which I have done the signory°   *Venetian government*
    Shall out-tongue his complaints. 'Tis yet to know°—   *not publicly known*
20   Which, when I know that boasting is an honour,
    I shall promulgate—I fetch my life and being
    From men of royal siege,° and my demerits°   *rank / deserts*
    May speak unbonneted[2] to as proud a fortune
    As this that I have reached. For know, Iago,
25   But that I love the gentle Desdemona
    I would not my unhousèd° free condition   *unconfined*
    Put into circumscription and confine
    For the seas' worth.
            Enter CASSIO *and officers, with torches*
            But look, what lights come yond?
IAGO   Those are the raisèd father and his friends.
    You were best go in.
30 OTHELLO   Not I. I must be found.
    My parts,° my title, and my perfect soul[3]   *qualities*
    Shall manifest me rightly. Is it they?
IAGO   By Janus,° I think no.   *two-faced Roman god*
OTHELLO   The servants of the Duke, and my lieutenant!
35   The goodness of the night upon you, friends.
    What is the news?
CASSIO   The Duke does greet you, general,
    And he requires your haste-post-haste appearance
    Even on the instant.
OTHELLO   What is the matter, think you?
CASSIO   Something from Cyprus, as I may divine;
40   It is a business of some heat.° The galleys   *urgency*
    Have sent a dozen sequent° messengers   *successive*
    This very night at one another's heels,
    And many of the consuls, raised and met,
    Are at the Duke's already. You have been hotly called for,
45   When, being not at your lodging to be found,
    The senate sent about three several quests
    To search you out.
OTHELLO   'Tis well I am found by you.
    I will but spend a word here in the house
    And go with you.   *[Exit]*
CASSIO   Ensign, what makes he here?
50 IAGO   Faith, he tonight hath boarded a land-carrack.
    If it prove lawful prize, he's made for ever.[4]
CASSIO   I do not understand.

---

1. I barely restrained myself from attacking him.
2. Without deference; modestly.
3. My clear conscience.
4. If the large Spanish merchant ship ("carrack," here

referring to Desdemona) Othello has "boarded" (as a pirate; sexually) turns out to be legitimately his, he's financially set for life.

IAGO He's married.

CASSIO To who?

Enter BRABANZIO, RODERIGO, *and* OFFICERS, *with lights and weapons*

IAGO Marry,° to— By Mary (mild oath)

[*Enter* OTHELLO]

[*To* OTHELLO] Come, captain, will you go?

OTHELLO Have with you.° Let's go

55 CASSIO Here comes another troop to seek for you.

IAGO It is Brabanzio. General, be advised.
He comes to bad intent.

OTHELLO Holla, stand, there!

RODERIGO [*to* BRABANZIO] Signor, it is the Moor.

BRABANZIO Down with him, thief!

IAGO [*drawing his sword*] You, Roderigo? Come, sir, I am for you.

60 OTHELLO Keep up° your bright swords, for the dew will rust 'em. Put away
[*To* BRABANZIO] Good signor, you shall more command with years
Than with your weapons.

BRABANZIO O thou foul thief, where hast thou stowed my daughter?
Damned as thou art, thou hast enchanted her,
65 For I'll refer me to all things of sense,⁵
If she in chains of magic were not bound,
Whether a maid so tender, fair, and happy,
So opposite to marriage that she shunned
The wealthy curlèd darlings of our nation,
70 Would ever have, t'incur a general mock,
Run from her guardage to the sooty bosom
Of such a thing as thou—to fear, not to delight.
Judge me the world if 'tis not gross in sense⁶
That thou hast practised on her with foul charms,
75 Abused her delicate youth with drugs or minerals
That weakens motion. I'll have't disputed on.° argued by experts
'Tis probable, and palpable to thinking.
I therefore apprehend and do attach° thee arrest
For an abuser° of the world, a practiser As a deceiver
80 Of arts inhibited and out of warrant.° prohibited and illegal
[*To* OFFICERS] Lay hold upon him. If he do resist,
Subdue him at his peril.

OTHELLO Hold your hands,
Both you of my inclining° and the rest. following
Were it my cue to fight, I should have known it
85 Without a prompter. Whither will you that I go
To answer this your charge?

BRABANZIO To prison, till fit time
Of law and course of direct session
Call thee to answer.

OTHELLO What if I do obey?
How may the Duke be therewith satisfied,
90 Whose messengers are here about my side
Upon some present business of the state
To bring me to him?

OFFICER [*to* BRABANZIO] 'Tis true, most worthy signor.

---

5. For I'll ask, relying on common sense.
6. If it is not patently obvious. Lines 73–78 do not appear in Q.

The Duke's in council, and your noble self,
I am sure, is sent for.
BRABANZIO   How, the Duke in council?
95 In this time of the night? Bring him away.°   *along*
Mine's not an idle° cause. The Duke himself,   *a trivial*
Or any of my brothers of the state,
Cannot but feel this wrong as 'twere their own;
For if such actions may have passage free,
100 Bondslaves and pagans shall our statesmen be.   *Exeunt*

1.3

Enter [the] DUKE *and* SENATORS *set at a table, with*
lights and OFFICERS
DUKE   There is no composition in these news
That gives them credit.[1]
FIRST SENATOR   Indeed, they are disproportioned.°   *inconsistent*
My letters say a hundred and seven galleys.
DUKE   And mine a hundred-forty.
SECOND SENATOR   And mine two hundred.
5   But though they jump not on a just account°—   *don't exactly agree*
As, in these cases, where the aim reports
'Tis oft with difference[2]—yet do they all confirm
A Turkish fleet, and bearing up to Cyprus.
DUKE   Nay, it is possible enough to judgement.
10 I do not so secure me in the error,
But the main article I do approve
In fearful sense.[3]
SAILOR *(within)*   What ho, what ho, what ho!
Enter [a] SAILOR
OFFICER   A messenger from the galleys.
DUKE   Now, what's the business?
SAILOR   The Turkish preparation° makes for Rhodes.   *battle-ready fleet*
15 So was I bid report here to the state
By Signor Angelo.[4]
DUKE *[to* SENATORS*]*   How say you by this change?
FIRST SENATOR   This cannot be,
By no assay° of reason—'tis a pageant   *test*
20 To keep us in false gaze. When we consider
The importancy of Cyprus to the Turk,
And let ourselves again but understand
That, as it more concerns the Turk than Rhodes,
So may he with more facile question bear it,[5]
25 For that it stands not in such warlike brace,
But altogether lacks th'abilities
That Rhodes is dressed in—if we make thought of this,
We must not think the Turk is so unskilful
To leave that latest° which concerns him first,   *last*
30 Neglecting an attempt of ease and gain
To wake and wage° a danger profitless.   *risk*

1.3 Location: A Venetian council room.
1. *There . . . credit*: The reports lack the consistency that would make them believable.
2. *where . . . difference*: where the reports are estimates, there are often discrepancies among them.
3. *I do not . . . sense*: I am not so reassured by the discrepancies as to dismiss the main concern—the approach of the Turkish fleet.
4. Not mentioned elsewhere in the play, Angelus Sorianus was a Venetian sea captain who received the Venetian ambassador bearing from Constantinople the Turkish ultimatum to surrender Cyprus shortly before its capture by the Turks in 1571.
5. So also can the Turkish fleet more easily win it.

DUKE   Nay, in all confidence, he's not for Rhodes.
OFFICER   Here is more news.

        Enter a MESSENGER

MESSENGER   The Ottomites,° reverend and gracious,   *Ottoman Turks*
35   Steering with due course toward the Isle of Rhodes,
Have there injointed them with an after° fleet.   *joined with another*
FIRST SENATOR   Ay, so I thought. How many, as you guess?
MESSENGER   Of thirty sail, and now they do restem°   *retrace*
Their backward course, bearing with frank appearance
40   Their purposes toward Cyprus. Signor Montano,
Your trusty and most valiant servitor,
With his free duty recommends you thus,[6]
And prays you to believe him.
DUKE   'Tis certain then for Cyprus.
Marcus Luccicos,[7] is not he in town?
45 FIRST SENATOR   He's now in Florence.
DUKE   Write from us to him post-post-haste. Dispatch.

        Enter BRABANZIO, OTHELLO, RODERIGO, IAGO, CASSIO,
        and officers

FIRST SENATOR   Here comes Brabanzio and the valiant Moor.
DUKE   Valiant Othello, we must straight° employ you   *immediately*
Against the general enemy° Ottoman.   *(to all Christendom)*
50   [*To* BRABANZIO] I did not see you. Welcome, gentle° signor.   *noble*
We lacked your counsel and your help tonight.
BRABANZIO   So did I yours. Good your grace, pardon me.
Neither my place,° nor aught I heard of business,   *official duty*
Hath raised me from my bed, nor doth the general care
55   Take hold on me; for my particular grief
Is of so floodgate and o'erbearing nature
That it engluts and swallows other sorrows,
And it is still itself.[8]
DUKE   Why, what's the matter?
BRABANZIO   My daughter, O, my daughter!
SENATORS   Dead?
BRABANZIO   Ay, to me.
60   She is abused,° stol'n from me, and corrupted   *deluded*
By spells and medicines bought of mountebanks.°   *quacks*
For nature so preposterously to err,
Being not deficient, blind, or lame of sense,
Sans° witchcraft could not.   *Without*
65 DUKE   Whoe'er he be that in this foul proceeding
Hath thus beguiled your daughter of herself
And you of her, the bloody book of law
You shall yourself read in the bitter letter
After your own sense, yea, though our proper son
Stood in your action.[9]
70 BRABANZIO   Humbly I thank your grace.
Here is the man, this Moor, whom now it seems
Your special mandate for the state affairs
Hath hither brought.
SENATORS   We are very sorry for't.

6. With his freely given loyalty reports to you thus.
7. Not mentioned elsewhere in the play.
8. *for my . . . itself:* other sorrows are so small compared with my torrential "grief" that mine can incorporate them without being affected.
9. *You shall . . . action:* You yourself shall interpret the law as you see fit even if my own son is the one you accuse.

DUKE [*to* OTHELLO]   What in your own part can you say to this?
75 BRABANZIO   Nothing but this is so.
OTHELLO   Most potent, grave, and reverend signors,
My very noble and approved good masters,
That I have ta'en away this old man's daughter,
It is most true, true I have married her.
80 The very head and front° of my offending   *height and breadth*
Hath this extent, no more. Rude° am I in my speech,   *Unpolished*
And little blessed with the soft phrase of peace,
For since these arms of mine had seven years' pith°   *strength*
Till now some nine moons wasted,° they have used   *Nine months ago*
85 Their dearest° action in the tented field,   *most valued*
And little of this great world can I speak
More than pertains to feats of broils° and battle.   *combats*
And therefore little shall I grace my cause
In speaking for myself. Yet, by your gracious patience,
90 I will a round° unvarnished tale deliver   *plain*
Of my whole course of love, what drugs, what charms,
What conjuration and what mighty magic —
For such proceeding I am charged withal° —   *with*
I won his daughter.
BRABANZIO   A maiden never bold,
95 Of spirit so still and quiet that her motion
Blushed at herself[1] — and she in spite of nature,
Of years, of country, credit,° everything,   *reputation*
To fall in love with what she feared to look on!
It is a judgement maimed and most imperfect
100 That will confess perfection so could err
Against all rules of nature, and must° be driven   *(we therefore) must*
To find out practices of cunning hell
Why this should be. I therefore vouch again
That with some mixtures powerful o'er the blood,°   *passions*
105 Or with some dram conjured° to this effect,   *enchanted dose*
He wrought upon her.
DUKE   To vouch this is no proof
Without more wider and more overt test
Than these thin habits and poor likelihoods
Of modern seeming do prefer against him.[2]
110 A SENATOR   But Othello, speak.
Did you by indirect and forcèd courses°   *means*
Subdue and poison this young maid's affections,
Or came it by request and such fair question°   *conversation*
As soul to soul affordeth?
OTHELLO   I do beseech you,
115 Send for the lady to the Sagittary,
And let her speak of me before her father.
If you do find me foul in her report,
The trust, the office I do hold of you
Not only take away, but let your sentence
Even fall upon my life.
120 DUKE [*to* OFFICERS]   Fetch Desdemona hither.

---

1. *her . . . herself:* she blushed at herself at the slightest provocation.
2. *Without . . . him:* Without fuller and more direct testi-mony than mere appearances and conjecture based on currently popular beliefs against him.

OTHELLO Ensign, conduct them. You best know the place.

Exit [IAGO *with*] *two or three* [*officers*]

And till she come, as truly as to heaven
I do confess the vices of my blood,°   *sins of passion*
So justly to your grave ears I'll present
125 How I did thrive in this fair lady's love,
And she in mine.

DUKE   Say it, Othello.

OTHELLO Her father loved me, oft invited me,
Still° questioned me the story of my life   *Constantly*
From year to year, the battles, sieges, fortunes
130 That I have passed.
I ran it through even from my boyish days
To th' very moment that he bade me tell it,
Wherein I spoke of most disastrous chances,°   *events*
Of moving accidents° by flood and field,   *events*
135 Of hair-breadth scapes i'th' imminent deadly breach,[3]
Of being taken by the insolent foe
And sold to slavery, of my redemption thence,
And portance° in my traveller's history,   *conduct*
Wherein of antres° vast and deserts idle,   *caves*
140 Rough quarries, rocks, and hills whose heads touch heaven,
It was my hint° to speak. Such was my process,°   *occasion / story*
And of the cannibals that each other eat,
The Anthropophagi,[4] and men whose heads
Do grow beneath their shoulders. These things to hear
145 Would Desdemona seriously incline,
But still the house affairs would draw her thence,
Which ever as° she could with haste dispatch   *Whenever*
She'd come again, and with a greedy ear
Devour up my discourse; which I observing,
150 Took once a pliant° hour, and found good means   *convenient*
To draw from her a prayer of earnest heart
That I would all my pilgrimage dilate,°   *relate*
Whereof by parcels she had something heard,
But not intentively.° I did consent,   *continuously*
155 And often did beguile her of her tears
When I did speak of some distressful stroke
That my youth suffered. My story being done,
She gave me for my pains a world of kisses.[5]
She swore in faith 'twas strange, 'twas passing° strange,   *exceptionally*
160 'Twas pitiful, 'twas wondrous pitiful.
She wished she had not heard it, yet she wished
That heaven had made her such a man.[6] She thankèd me,
And bade me, if I had a friend that loved her,
I should but teach him how to tell my story,
165 And that would woo her. Upon this hint I spake.
She loved me for the dangers I had passed,
And I loved her that she did pity them.
This only is the witchcraft I have used.

---

3. In the deadly gaps in a fortification.
4. Man-eaters. The term is from the Roman writer Pliny. Shakespeare was also indebted to the travel literature of the Middle Ages (*Mandeville's Travels*) and the Renaissance (Hakluyt's *Principal Navigations*, among others).

5. F reads "kisses," Q "sighs." It is hard to explain "kisses" as a textual error; its plausibility depends on how forward one imagines Desdemona to be.
6. Made her into such a man; made such a man for her.

Enter DESDEMONA, IAGO, *and attendants*
Here comes the lady. Let her witness it.
170 DUKE   I think this tale would win my daughter, too. —
Good Brabanzio,
Take up this mangled matter at the best.°   *Make the best of this*
Men do their broken weapons rather use
Than their bare hands.
BRABANZIO   I pray you hear her speak.
175 If she confess that she was half the wooer,
Destruction on my head if my bad blame
Light on the man! Come hither, gentle mistress.
Do you perceive in all this noble company
Where most you owe obedience?
DESDEMONA   My noble father,
180 I do perceive here a divided duty.
To you I am bound for life and education.
My life and education both do learn° me   *teach*
How to respect you. You are the lord of duty,
I am hitherto your daughter. But here's my husband,
185 And so much duty as my mother showed
To you, preferring you before her father,
So much I challenge° that I may profess   *assert*
Due to the Moor my lord.
BRABANZIO   God b'wi'you, I ha' done.
Please it your grace, on to the state affairs.
190 I had rather to adopt a child than get° it.   *beget*
Come hither, Moor.
I here do give thee that° with all my heart   *that which*
Which, but° thou hast already, with all my heart   *except that*
I would keep from thee. [*To* DESDEMONA] For your sake, jewel,
195 I am glad at soul I have no other child,
For thy escape would teach me tyranny,
To hang clogs⁷ on 'em. I have done, my lord.
DUKE   Let me speak like yourself, and lay a sentence°   *draw a moral*
Which, as a grece° or step, may help these lovers   *step*
200 Into your favour.
When remedies are past, the griefs are ended
By seeing the worst which late on hopes depended.⁸
To mourn a mischief that is past and gone
Is the next way to draw new mischief on.
205 What cannot be preserved when fortune takes,
Patience her injury a mockery makes.⁹
The robbed that smiles steals something from the thief;
He robs himself that spends a bootless° grief.   *pointless*
BRABANZIO   So let the Turk of Cyprus us beguile,
210 We lose it not so long as we can smile.
He bears the sentence° well that nothing bears   *saying; judgment*
But the free comfort which from thence he hears,
But he bears both the sentence and the sorrow
That, to pay grief, must of poor patience borrow.
215 These sentences, to sugar or to gall,°   *both sweet and bitter*

7. Blocks of wood tied to criminals' legs to keep them from escaping.
8. By seeing those things come to pass that caused grief in anticipation.
9. Patience laughs at what cannot be helped (and thus reduces the "injury").

Being strong on both sides, are equivocal.
But words are words. I never yet did hear
That the bruisèd heart was piercèd[1] through the ear. I humbly
beseech you proceed to th'affairs of state.

220 DUKE The Turk with a most mighty preparation makes for
Cyprus. Othello, the fortitude of the place is best known to
you, and though we have there a substitute of most allowed
sufficiency,° yet opinion, a more sovereign mistress of effects,   *known ability*
throws a more safer voice on you.[2] You must therefore be con-
225 tent to slubber° the gloss of your new fortunes with this more   *soil*
stubborn° and boisterous expedition.   *rougher*

OTHELLO The tyrant custom, most grave senators,
Hath made the flinty and steel couch of war
My thrice-driven° bed of down. I do agnize°   *sifted / acknowledge*
230 A natural and prompt alacrity
I find in hardness,° and do undertake   *hardship*
This present wars against the Ottomites.
Most humbly therefore bending to your state,°   *authority*
I crave fit disposition for my wife,
235 Due reference of place and exhibition,[3]
With such accommodation and besort°   *suitable attendance*
As levels with her breeding.

DUKE Why, at her father's!

BRABANZIO I will not have it so.

240 OTHELLO Nor I.

DESDEMONA Nor would I there reside,
To put my father in impatient thoughts
By being in his eye. Most gracious Duke,
To my unfolding° lend your prosperous° ear,   *proposal / receptive*
245 And let me find a charter° in your voice   *an authorization*
T'assist my simpleness.

DUKE   What would you, Desdemona?

DESDEMONA That I did love the Moor to live with him,
My downright violence and storm of fortunes[4]
May trumpet to the world. My heart's subdued
250 Even to the very quality of my lord.[5]
I saw Othello's visage in his mind,
And to his honours and his valiant parts°   *qualities*
Did I my soul and fortunes consecrate;
So that, dear lords, if I be left behind,
255 A moth of peace, and he go to the war,
The rites° for why I love him are bereft me,   *(of love); (of war?)*
And I a heavy interim shall support
By his dear absence. Let me go with him.

OTHELLO [*to the* DUKE] Let her have your voice.
260 Vouch with me heaven, I therefor beg it not
To please the palate of my appetite,
Nor to comply with heat°—the young affects[6]   *sexual passion*
In me defunct—and proper° satisfaction,   *personal; fitting*

1. Surgically lanced (and presumably cured).
2. *opinion . . . you:* public opinion, which determines what gets done, finds greater security with you.
3. Proper accommodation and maintenance.
4. My outright defiance of custom.
5. *My heart's . . . lord:* I love him for what he is (military,
adventurous). Q reads "utmost pleasure" for "very quality"—an openly sexual formulation that makes Desdemona's response one of subordination rather than of identification, sexual and otherwise.
6. The youthful desires.

But to be free° and bounteous to her mind;   *liberal*
265 And heaven defend your good souls that you think
  I will your serious and great business scant
  When she is with me. No, when light-winged toys°   *diversions*
  Of feathered Cupid seel° with wanton dullness   *blind*
  My speculative and officed instruments,[7]
270 That my disports° corrupt and taint my business,   *sexual pleasures*
  Let housewives make a skillet of my helm,
  And all indign° and base adversities   *undignified*
  Make head against my estimation.[8]
  DUKE Be it as you shall privately determine,
275 Either for her stay or going. Th'affair cries haste,
  And speed must answer it.
  A SENATOR [*to* OTHELLO] You must away tonight.
  DESDEMONA Tonight, my lord?
  DUKE   This night.
  OTHELLO   With all my heart.
  DUKE At nine i'th' morning here we'll meet again.
  Othello, leave some officer behind,
280 And he shall our commission bring to you,
  And such things else of quality and respect°   *weight and importance*
  As doth import° you.   *concern*
  OTHELLO   So please your grace, my ensign.
  A man he is of honesty[9] and trust.
  To his conveyance I assign my wife,
285 With what else needful your good grace shall think
  To be sent after me.
  DUKE   Let it be so.
  Good night to everyone. [*To* BRABANZIO] And, noble signor,
  If virtue no delighted° beauty lack,   *delightful*
  Your son-in-law is far more fair than black.
290 A SENATOR Adieu, brave Moor. Use Desdemona well.
  BRABANZIO Look to her,° Moor, if thou hast eyes to see. *Watch her carefully*
  She has deceived her father, and may thee.
      Exeunt [DUKE, BRABANZIO, CASSIO, SENATORS,
               and officers]
  OTHELLO My life upon her faith. Honest Iago,
  My Desdemona must I leave to thee.
295 I prithee let thy wife attend on her,
  And bring them after in the best advantage.[1]
  Come, Desdemona. I have but an hour
  Of love, of worldly matter and direction
  To spend with thee. We must obey the time.
      Exeunt [OTHELLO *the*] Moor *and* DESDEMONA
300 RODERIGO Iago.
  IAGO What sayst thou, noble heart?
  RODERIGO What will I do, think'st thou?
  IAGO Why, go to bed and sleep.
  RODERIGO I will incontinently° drown myself.   *immediately*
305 IAGO If thou dost, I shall never love thee after. Why, thou silly
  gentleman!

---

7. My duty-bound faculties of sense.
8. Raise an army against my good reputation.
9. The first of many references to Iago's "honesty," all of

them deeply ironic, some unwittingly so.
1. And bring them along at the most favorable moment.

RODERIGO It is silliness to live when to live is torment; and then
have we a prescription° to die when death is our physician.   *right; doctor's order*

310   IAGO O, villainous!° I ha' looked upon the world for four times   *absurd; immoral?*
seven years, and since I could distinguish betwixt a benefit and
an injury I never found man that knew how to love himself.
Ere I would say I would drown myself for the love of a guinea-
hen,° I would change my humanity with a baboon.   *woman*

RODERIGO What should I do? I confess it is my shame to be so
315   fond, but it is not in my virtue° to amend it.   *native ability*

IAGO Virtue? A fig!° 'Tis in ourselves that we are thus or thus.   *(an obscenity)*
Our bodies are our gardens, to the which our wills are garden-
ers; so that if we will plant nettles or sow lettuce, set hyssop° and   *mint herb*
weed up thyme, supply it with one gender of herbs or distract it
320   with many, either to have it sterile with idleness° or manured   *noncultivation*
with industry, why, the power and corrigible authority° of this   *ability to decide*
lies in our wills. If the beam° of our lives had not one scale of   *(as on a scale)*
reason to peise° another of sensuality, the blood and baseness   *counterweigh*
of our natures would conduct us to most preposterous conclu-
325   sions. But we have reason to cool our raging motions,° our car-   *appetites*
nal stings, our unbitted° lusts; whereof I take this that you call   *unrestrained*
love to be a sect or scion.°   *offshoot*

RODERIGO It cannot be.

IAGO It is merely a lust of the blood and a permission of the will.
330   Come, be a man. Drown thyself? Drown cats and blind pup-
pies. I have professed me thy friend, and I confess me knit to
thy deserving with cables of perdurable° toughness. I could   *durable*
never better stead° thee than now. Put money in thy purse.   *help*
Follow thou the wars, defeat thy favour with an usurped beard.²
335   I say, put money in thy purse. It cannot be long that Desdemona should continue her love to the Moor—put money in
thy purse—nor he his to her. It was a violent commencement°   *an abruptly begun affair*
in her, and thou shalt see an answerable sequestration³— put
but money in thy purse. These Moors are changeable in their
340   wills—fill thy purse with money. The food that to him now
is as luscious as locusts⁴ shall be to him shortly as bitter as
coloquintida.⁵ She must change for youth. When she is sated
with his body, she will find the error of her choice. Therefore
put money in thy purse. If thou wilt needs° damn thyself, do it   *If you must*
345   a more delicate way than drowning. Make all the money thou
canst. If sanctimony° and a frail vow betwixt an erring° barbar-   *holy rite / a wandering*
ian and a super-subtle° Venetian be not too hard for my wits   *highly sensitive*
and all the tribe of hell, thou shalt enjoy her; therefore make
money. A pox o' drowning thyself—it is clean out of the way.°   *of no use*
350   Seek thou rather to be hanged in compassing° thy joy than to   *encompassing*
be drowned and go without her.

RODERIGO Wilt thou be fast° to my hopes if I depend on the   *duty bound*
issue?°   *outcome*

IAGO Thou art sure of me. Go, make money. I have told thee
355   often, and I re-tell thee again and again, I hate the Moor. My
cause is hearted,° thine hath no less reason. Let us be conjunc-   *heartfelt*
tive° in our revenge against him. If thou canst cuckold him,   *joined*

2. Disguise your appearance with a fake beard.   5. Colocynth, a purgative—one of Iago's many refer-
3. A correspondingly abrupt separation.   ences to the digestive tract.
4. A sweet, exotic fruit, perhaps carob or honeysuckle.

thou dost thyself a pleasure, me a sport. There are many events
in the womb of time, which will be delivered. Traverse,° go,   *Go (to arms)*
360   provide thy money. We will have more of this tomorrow.
Adieu.
RODERIGO   Where shall we meet i'th' morning?
IAGO   At my lodging.
RODERIGO   I'll be with thee betimes.°   *early*
IAGO   Go to, farewell—
Do you hear, Roderigo?
RODERIGO   I'll sell all my land.   *Exit*
365   IAGO   Thus do I ever make my fool my purse—
For I mine own gained knowledge should profane
If I would time expend with such a snipe°   *fool*
But for my sport and profit. I hate the Moor,
And it is thought abroad° that 'twixt my sheets   *rumored*
370   He has done my office. I know not if't be true,
But I, for mere suspicion in that kind,
Will do° as if for surety. He holds° me well: *act / esteems*
The better shall my purpose work on him.
Cassio's a proper° man. Let me see now,   *handsome*
375   To get his place, and to plume up° my will   *gratify*
In double knavery—how, how? Let's see.
After some time to abuse Othello's ears
That he is too familiar with his wife;[6]
He hath a person and a smooth dispose°   *manner*
380   To be suspected, framed to make women false.
The Moor is of a free° and open nature,   *liberal*
That thinks men honest that but seem to be so,
And will as tenderly° be led by th' nose   *easily*
As asses are.
385   I ha't. It is ingendered. Hell and night
Must bring this monstrous birth to the world's light.   *Exit*

2.1

Enter [below] MONTANO, *Governor of Cyprus; two other*
GENTLEMEN *[above]*
MONTANO   What from the cape can you discern at sea?
FIRST GENTLEMAN   Nothing at all. It is a high-wrought flood.°   *very rough sea*
I cannot 'twixt the heaven and the main°   *sea*
Descry° a sail.   *Discern*
5   MONTANO   Methinks the wind hath spoke aloud at land.
A fuller blast ne'er shook our battlements.
If it ha' ruffianed° so upon the sea,   *raged*
What ribs of oak, when mountains melt on them,
Can hold the mortise?[1] What shall we hear of this?
10   SECOND GENTLEMAN   A segregation° of the Turkish fleet;   *separation*
For do but stand upon the foaming shore,
The chidden billow[2] seems to pelt the clouds,
The wind-shaked surge with high and monstrous mane

---

6. "He" is Cassio (as in line 379), but "his" refers to
Othello. This confusion of pronouns points to the guilt
Othello seems to feel over his sexual desire for Desdemona.
2.1 Location: A seaport in Cyprus; outdoors near the
harbor.

1. *What . . . mortise:* What ship (with "ribs of oak") can
hold its joints ("mortise") together when "mountains" of
water pour on it?
2. The surging ocean, rebuked ("chidden") by the wind
(or repulsed by the land).

Seems to cast water on the burning Bear

15 And quench the guards of th'ever-fixèd Pole.[3]

I never did like molestation view°   *see such a tumult*

On the enchafèd flood.

MONTANO   If that the Turkish fleet

Be not ensheltered and embayed, they are drowned.

It is impossible to bear it out.

Enter a THIRD GENTLEMAN

20 THIRD GENTLEMAN   News, lads! Our wars are done.

The desperate tempest hath so banged the Turks

That their designment° halts. A noble ship of Venice   *plan*

Hath seen a grievous wrack and sufferance

On most part of their fleet.

25 MONTANO   How, is this true?

THIRD GENTLEMAN   The ship is here put in,

A Veronessa.[4] Michael Cassio,

Lieutenant to the warlike Moor Othello,

Is come on shore; the Moor himself at sea,

30 And is in full commission here for Cyprus.

MONTANO   I am glad on't; 'tis a worthy governor.

THIRD GENTLEMAN   But this same Cassio, though he speak of comfort

Touching the Turkish loss, yet he looks sadly,°   *seriously*

And prays the Moor be safe, for they were parted

With foul and violent tempest.

35 MONTANO   Pray heavens he be,

For I have served him, and the man commands

Like a full soldier. Let's to the sea-side, ho!—

As well to see the vessel that's come in

As to throw out our eyes for brave Othello,

40 Even till we make the main and th'aerial blue

An indistinct regard.[5]

THIRD GENTLEMAN   Come, let's do so,

For every minute is expectancy

Of more arrivance.

Enter CASSIO

CASSIO   Thanks, you the valiant of this warlike isle

45 That so approve the Moor! O, let the heavens

Give him defence against the elements,

For I have lost him on a dangerous sea.

MONTANO   Is he well shipped?

CASSIO   His barque is stoutly timbered, and his pilot

50 Of very expert and approved allowance.°   *known ability*

Therefore my hopes, not surfeited to death,°   *not excessive*

Stand in bold cure.°   *likely to be rewarded*

VOICES *(within)*   A sail, a sail, a sail!

CASSIO   What noise?

A GENTLEMAN   The town is empty. On the brow° o'th' sea   *cliff at the edge*

55 Stand ranks of people, and they cry 'A sail!'

CASSIO   My hopes do shape him° for the governor.   *make it out to be*

A shot

---

3. *burning Bear:* the constellation Ursa Minor. *guards:*
probably two stars in the constellation that point in a line
to the polestar, also in Ursa Minor.
4. Meaning unclear: originally from Verona, though now

used by the Venetians; a cutter; possibly meant to modify
not "ship" but Cassio.
5. *Even . . . regard:* Until we can't distinguish sea from
sky.

A GENTLEMAN They do discharge their shot of courtesy—
  Our friends, at least.
CASSIO   I pray you, sir, go forth,
  And give us truth who 'tis that is arrived.
60 A GENTLEMAN I shall.   *Exit*
  MONTANO But, good lieutenant, is your general wived?
  CASSIO Most fortunately. He hath achieved a maid
    That paragons° description and wild fame,   stands above
    One that excels the quirks of blazoning° pens,   praise-giving
65 And in th'essential vesture of creation
    Does tire the engineer.⁶
        Enter GENTLEMAN
                  How now, who has put in?
  GENTLEMAN 'Tis one Iago, ensign to the general.
  CASSIO He's had most favourable and happy speed.
    Tempests themselves, high seas, and howling winds,
70 The guttered° rocks and congregated° sands,   jagged / accumulated
    Traitors ensteeped° to enclog the guiltless keel,   underwater
    As having sense of beauty do omit°   forgo
    Their mortal° natures, letting go safely by   deadly
    The divine Desdemona.
  MONTANO   What is she?
75 CASSIO She that I spake of, our great captain's captain,
    Left in the conduct of the bold Iago,
    Whose footing here anticipates our thoughts
    A sennight's speed.⁷ Great Jove, Othello guard,
    And swell his sail with thine own powerful breath,
80 That he may bless this bay with his tall ship,
    Make love's quick pants in Desdemona's arms,
    Give renewed fire to our extincted spirits,
    And bring all Cyprus comfort.
        Enter DESDEMONA, IAGO, EMILIA, *and* RODERIGO
                  O, behold,
    The riches of the ship is come on shore!
85 You men of Cyprus, let her have your knees.
        [MONTANO *and the* GENTLEMEN *make curtsy to*
        DESDEMONA]
    Hail to thee, lady, and the grace of heaven
    Before, behind thee, and on every hand
    Enwheel thee round!
  DESDEMONA   I thank you, valiant Cassio.
    What tidings can you tell me of my lord?
90 CASSIO He is not yet arrived, nor know I aught
    But that he's well and will be shortly here.
  DESDEMONA O, but I fear—how lost you company?
  CASSIO The great contention of the sea and skies
    Parted our fellowship.
95 VOICES (*within*) A sail, a sail!
  CASSIO But hark, a sail.
        [*A shot*]
  A GENTLEMAN They give their greeting to the citadel.
    This likewise is a friend.

6. *in . . . engineer:* whose natural beauty exhausts the   7. *Whose . . . speed:* Whose arrival predates our expecta-
poet's capacity to invent praise.   tions by a week.

CASSIO   See for the news. [*Exit* GENTLEMAN]
Good ensign, you are welcome. [*Kissing* EMILIA] Welcome, mistress.
100 Let it not gall your patience, good Iago,
That I extend my manners. 'Tis my breeding
That gives me this bold show of courtesy.
IAGO   Sir, would she give you so much of her lips
As of her tongue she oft bestows on me,
105 You would have enough.
DESDEMONA   Alas, she has no speech!⁸
IAGO   In faith, too much.
I find it still when I ha' leave to sleep.
Marry, before your ladyship, I grant,
110 She puts her tongue a little in her heart,⁹
And chides with thinking.
EMILIA   You ha' little cause to say so.
IAGO   Come on, come on. You are pictures out of door,
Bells in your parlours; wildcats in your kitchens,
Saints in your injuries; devils being offended,
115 Players in your housewifery, and hussies in your beds.¹
DESDEMONA   O, fie upon thee, slanderer!
IAGO   Nay, it is true, or else I am a Turk.
You rise to play and go to bed to work.
EMILIA   You shall not write my praise.
IAGO   No, let me not.
120 DESDEMONA   What wouldst write of me, if thou shouldst praise me?
IAGO   O, gentle lady, do not put me to't,
For I am nothing if not critical.
DESDEMONA   Come on, essay°—there's one gone to the harbour?   *try*
IAGO   Ay, madam.
125 DESDEMONA   I am not merry, but I do beguile°   *disguise*
The thing I am° by seeming otherwise.   *(worried for Othello)*
Come, how wouldst thou praise me?
IAGO   I am about it, but indeed my invention
Comes from my pate as birdlime² does from frieze°—   *coarse wool cloth*
130 It plucks out brains and all. But my muse labours,°   *(in childbirth)*
And thus she is delivered:
If she be fair and wise, fairness and wit,
The one's for use, the other useth it.³
DESDEMONA   Well praised! How if she be black and witty?
135 IAGO   If she be black and thereto have a wit,
She'll find a white that shall her blackness fit.⁴
DESDEMONA   Worse and worse.
EMILIA   How if fair and foolish?
IAGO   She never yet was foolish that was fair,
For even her folly° helped her to an heir.   *foolishness; lechery*
140 DESDEMONA   These are old fond° paradoxes, to make fools laugh   *foolish*
i'th' alehouse.

8. Perhaps: Alas, the accused scolding chatterbox is not even rising to her own defense (both a defense of Emilia and a prod for her to speak).
9. She keeps her (critical) thoughts to herself.
1. You are . . . beds: Iago shifts from Emilia to women generally in this speech. pictures: models of silent propriety. Bells: Noisy. kitchens: perhaps domestic affairs generally, rather than a specific room. Saints: Martyrs. Players

in your housewifery: Deceptive in managing household expenses. hussies: wanton (perhaps businesslike, or sparing of sexual favors).
2. Sticky substance used to trap small birds.
3. The one's . . . it: Intelligence makes use of beauty.
4. black: dark-haired or dark-complexioned; the latter meaning has special relevance in Othello. white: fair-skinned person ("wight" means "person"). fit: (sexual).

What miserable praise hast thou for her   ugly
That's foul° and foolish?   to boot
IAGO   There's none so foul and foolish thereunto,°   lascivious
145   But does foul° pranks which fair and wise ones do.
DESDEMONA   O heavy ignorance! Thou praisest the worst best.
    But what praise couldst thou bestow on a deserving woman
    indeed—one that, in the authority of her merit, did justly put
    on the vouch° of very malice itself?   compel the approval
150 IAGO   She that was ever fair and never proud,
    Had tongue at will and yet was never loud,
    Never lacked gold and yet went never gay,°   lavishly clothed
    Fled from her wish, and yet said 'Now I may';[5]
    She that, being angered, her revenge being nigh,
155   Bade her wrong stay° and her displeasure fly;   sense of injury end
    She that in wisdom never was so frail
    To change the cod's head for the salmon's tail;[6]
    She that could think and ne'er disclose her mind,
    See suitors following, and not look behind—
160   She was a wight, if ever such wights were—
DESDEMONA   To do what?
IAGO   To suckle fools, and chronicle small beer.[7]
DESDEMONA   O most lame and impotent conclusion! Do not
    learn of him, Emilia, though he be thy husband. How say you,
165   Cassio, is he not a most profane and liberal° counsellor?   outspoken
CASSIO   He speaks home, madam. You may relish him more in°   as
    the soldier than in the scholar.
       [CASSIO and DESDEMONA talk apart]
IAGO [aside]   He takes her by the palm. Ay, well said°—whisper.   well done
    With as little a web as this will I ensnare as great a fly as Cassio.
170   Ay, smile upon her, do. I will gyve° thee in thine own court-   shackle
    ship.° You say true, 'tis so indeed. If such tricks as these strip   courtliness
    you out of your lieutenantry, it had been better you had not
    kissed your three fingers[8] so oft, which now again you are most
    apt to play the sir° in. Very good, well kissed, an excellent   gentleman
175   curtsy, 'tis so indeed; yet again your fingers to your lips? Would
    they were clyster-pipes° for your sake.   enema tubes
       Trumpets within
    [Aloud] The Moor—I know his trumpet.
CASSIO   'Tis truly so.
DESDEMONA   Let's meet him and receive him.
CASSIO   Lo where he comes!
       Enter OTHELLO and attendants
OTHELLO [to DESDEMONA]   O my fair warrior!
DESDEMONA   My dear Othello.
180 OTHELLO   It gives me wonder great as my content
    To see you here before me. O my soul's joy,
    If after every tempest come such calms,
    May the winds blow till they have wakened death,
    And let the labouring barque° climb hills of seas   small ship

---

5. Voluntarily withstood temptation even when given the choice.
6. To make an unworthy exchange. Probably also suggesting sexual infidelity: "cod" means "penis," and "tail" equals "vulva."

7. To breast-feed babies and keep track of trivial domestic goods. That is, such perfect virtue suits only a dull, complacent, decidedly ungenteel housewife.
8. Kissing one's own hand was a common courtly gesture from a gentleman to a lady.

185   Olympus-high,⁹ and duck again as low
     As hell's from heaven. If it were now to die
     'Twere now to be most happy, for I fear
     My soul hath her content so absolute
     That not another comfort like to this
     Succeeds in unknown fate.°   *(after death)*
190 DESDEMONA   The heavens forbid
     But that our loves and comforts should increase
     Even as our days do grow.
    OTHELLO   Amen to that, sweet powers!
     I cannot speak enough of this content.
     It stops me here, it is too much of joy.
195   And this, *(they kiss)* and this, the greatest discords be
     That e'er our hearts shall make.
    IAGO [*aside*]   O, you are well tuned now,
     But I'll set down the pegs that make this music,¹
     As honest as I am.
    OTHELLO   Come, let us to the castle.
     News, friends: our wars are done, the Turks are drowned.
200   How does my old acquaintance of this isle?—
     Honey, you shall be well desired° in Cyprus,   *welcomed*
     I have found great love amongst them. O my sweet,
     I prattle out of fashion, and I dote
     In mine own comforts. I prithee, good Iago,
205   Go to the bay and disembark my coffers.
     Bring thou the master° to the citadel.   *captain*
     He is a good one, and his worthiness
     Does challenge° much respect. Come, Desdemona.—   *deserve*
     Once more, well met at Cyprus!
                   Exeunt OTHELLO *and* DESDEMONA
                   [*with all but* IAGO *and* RODERIGO]
210 IAGO [*to an attendant as he goes out*]   Do thou meet me pres-
     ently at the harbour. [*To* RODERIGO] Come hither. If thou beest
     valiant—as they say base° men being in love have then a nobil-   *lowly born*
     ity in their natures more than is native to them—list° me. The   *listen to*
     lieutenant tonight watches on the court of guard.² First, I
215   must tell thee this: Desdemona is directly in love with him.
    RODERIGO   With him? Why, 'tis not possible!
    IAGO   Lay thy finger thus,° and let thy soul be instructed. Mark   *Be silent*
     me with what violence she first loved the Moor, but for brag-
     ging and telling her fantastical lies. To love him still for prat-
220   ing?— let not thy discreet heart think it. Her eye must be fed,
     and what delight shall she have to look on the devil? When the
     blood is made dull with the act of sport, there should be again
     to inflame it, and to give satiety a fresh appetite, loveliness in
     favour,° sympathy in years, manners, and beauties, all which   *looks*
225   the Moor is defective in. Now, for want of these required con-
     veniences,° her delicate tenderness will find itself abused,°   *compatibilities / revolted*
     begin to heave the gorge,° disrelish and abhor the Moor. Very   *feel nausea*
     nature will instruct her in it and compel her to some second
     choice. Now, sir, this granted—as it is a most pregnant° and   *obvious; (sexual)*

---

9. Mount Olympus, home of the Greek gods and hence   strings of a musical instrument taut.
too high for mortals.   2. Cassio is in charge of the watch at the guardhouse.
1. I'll untune (by loosening) the "pegs" that hold the

230 unforced position—who stands so eminent in the degree of[3] *facile*
this fortune as Cassio does?—a knave very voluble,° no further *no more ethical*
conscionable° than in putting on the mere form of civil and *achievement / lewd*
humane seeming for the better compass° of his salt° and most *slippery*
hidden loose affection. Why, none; why, none—a slipper° and
235 subtle knave, a finder of occasion, that has an eye can stamp
and counterfeit advantages,[4] though true advantage never present itself, a devilish knave! Besides, the knave is handsome,
young, and hath all those requisites in him that folly° and green *wantonness*
minds look after. A pestilent° complete knave, and the woman *damnably*
240 hath found him already.

RODERIGO   I cannot believe that in her. She's full of most blessed
condition.

IAGO   Blessed fig's end!° The wine she drinks is made of grapes. *(obscene)*
If she had been blessed, she would never have loved the Moor.
245 Blessed pudding!° Didst thou not see her paddle with the palm *sausage*
of his hand? Didst not mark that?

RODERIGO   Yes, that I did, but that was but courtesy.

IAGO   Lechery, by this hand; an index and obscure prologue to
the history of lust and foul thoughts.[5] They met so near with
250 their lips that their breaths embraced together. Villainous
thoughts, Roderigo! When these mutualities so marshal the
way, hard at hand comes the master and main exercise,[6] th'in-
corporate° conclusion. Pish! But, sir, be you ruled by me. I have *in the flesh*
brought you from Venice. Watch you tonight. For the com-
255 mand, I'll lay't upon you.[7] Cassio knows you not; I'll not be far
from you. Do you find some occasion to anger Cassio, either
by speaking too loud, or tainting° his discipline, or from what *insulting*
other course you please, which the time shall more favourably
minister.° *provide*

260 RODERIGO   Well.

IAGO   Sir, he's rash and very sudden in choler, and haply° may *perhaps*
strike at you. Provoke him that he may, for even out of that will
I cause these of Cyprus to mutiny, whose qualification shall
come into no true taste again[8] but by the displanting of Cassio.
265 So shall you have a shorter journey to your desires by the means
I shall then have to prefer° them, and the impediment most *promote*
profitably removed, without the which there were no expectation of our prosperity.

RODERIGO   I will do this, if you can bring it to any opportunity.

270 IAGO   I warrant thee. Meet me by and by at the citadel. I must
fetch his necessaries° ashore. Farewell. *Othello's possessions*

RODERIGO   Adieu.   *Exit*

IAGO   That Cassio loves her, I do well believe it.
That she loves him, 'tis apt and of great credit.° *likely and believable*
275 The Moor—howbe't that I endure him not—
Is of a constant, loving, noble nature,
And I dare think he'll prove to Desdemona
A most dear° husband. Now I do love her too, *affectionate; costly*
Not out of absolute lust—though peradventure

---

3. *in the degree of*: as next in line for.
4. Who can (like a counterfeiter) create his own opportunities.
5. *an . . . thoughts*: the analogy is to a dirty book. *index*:
table of contents. *obscure*: encoded. *history*: story.

6. When these intimacies have cleared the way, the main
event follows close behind. Here, the analogy is to an
official procession.
7. Stand watch tonight. I'll see that you receive orders.
8. *whose . . . again*: who will not be adequately appeased.

280   I stand accountant° for as great a sin—   *accountable*
       But partly led to diet° my revenge   *feed*
       For that I do suspect the lusty Moor
       Hath leapt into my seat,° the thought whereof   *slept with my wife*
       Doth, like a poisonous mineral, gnaw my inwards;°   *innards*
285   And nothing can or shall content my soul
       Till I am evened with him, wife for wife—
       Or failing so, yet that I put the Moor
       At least into a jealousy so strong
       That judgement cannot cure, which thing to do,
290   If this poor trash of Venice whom I trace
       For his quick hunting stand the putting on,[9]
       I'll have our Michael Cassio on the hip,°   *at my mercy*
       Abuse° him to the Moor in the rank garb°—   *Slander / "hot" manner*
       For I fear Cassio with my nightcap,° too—   *(as sexual rival)*
295   Make the Moor thank me, love me, and reward me
       For making him egregiously an ass,
       And practising upon° his peace and quiet   *undermining*
       Even to madness. 'Tis here,° but yet confused.   *My plan is here*
       Knavery's plain face is never seen till used.   *Exit*

2.2

Enter Othello's HERALD *reading a proclamation*

HERALD   It is Othello's pleasure—our noble and valiant general—that, upon certain tidings now arrived importing the
mere perdition° of the Turkish fleet, every man put himself   *entire loss*
into triumph: some to dance, some to make bonfires, each man
5   to what sport and revels his addiction° leads him; for besides   *inclination*
these beneficial news, it is the celebration of his nuptial. So
much was his pleasure should be proclaimed. All offices° are   *storehouses*
open, and there is full liberty of feasting from this present hour
of five till the bell have told eleven. Heaven bless the isle of
10   Cyprus and our noble general, Othello!   *Exit*

2.3

Enter OTHELLO, DESDEMONA, CASSIO, *and attendants*

OTHELLO   Good Michael, look you to the guard tonight.
       Let's teach ourselves that honourable stop°   *self-restraint*
       Not to outsport° discretion.   *pass the limits of*
CASSIO   Iago hath direction what to do,
5   But notwithstanding, with my personal eye
       Will I look to't.
OTHELLO   Iago is most honest.
       Michael, good night. Tomorrow with your earliest
       Let me have speech with you. [*To* DESDEMONA] Come, my dear love,
       The purchase made, the fruits are to ensue.
10   That profit's yet to come 'tween me and you.[1]
       [*To* CASSIO] Good night.
                Exeunt OTHELLO, DESDEMONA [*and attendants*]
       Enter IAGO

---

9. *If . . . on:* If Roderigo, whom I follow (?), train (?), put
weights on to slow him down (?), is successfully set on the
hunt when incited.

2.2 Location: A street in Cyprus.
2.3 Location: The citadel at Cyprus.
1. We haven't yet consummated our marriage.

CASSIO Welcome, Iago. We must to the watch.

IAGO Not this hour, lieutenant; 'tis not yet ten o'th' clock. Our
general cast° us thus early for the love of his Desdemona, who   *dismissed*
15   let us not therefore blame. He hath not yet made wanton the
night with her, and she is sport for Jove.

CASSIO She's a most exquisite lady.

IAGO And I'll warrant her full of game.

CASSIO Indeed, she's a most fresh and delicate creature.

20 IAGO What an eye she has! Methinks it sounds a parley° to prov-   *(military) call*
ocation.

CASSIO An inviting eye, and yet, methinks, right modest.

IAGO And when she speaks, is it not an alarum° to love?   *a call (to arms)*

CASSIO She is indeed perfection.

25 IAGO Well, happiness to their sheets. Come, lieutenant. I have
a stoup° of wine, and here without are a brace° of Cyprus gal-   *two quarts / pair*
lants that would fain have a measure° to the health of black   *would like to drink*
Othello.

CASSIO Not tonight, good Iago. I have very poor and unhappy
30   brains for drinking. I could well wish courtesy would invent
some other custom of entertainment.

IAGO O, they are our friends! But one cup. I'll drink for you.

CASSIO I ha' drunk but one cup tonight, and that was craftily
qualified,° too, and behold what innovation° it makes here! I   *well diluted / disorder*
35   am infortunate in the infirmity, and dare not task my weakness
with any more.

IAGO What, man, 'tis a night of revels, the gallants desire it!

CASSIO Where are they?

IAGO Here at the door. I pray you call them in.

40 CASSIO I'll do't, but it dislikes me.°   *Exit*   *I don't like doing it*

IAGO If I can fasten but one cup upon him,
With that which he hath drunk tonight already
He'll be as full of quarrel and offence
As my young mistress' dog. Now my sick fool Roderigo,
45   Whom love hath turned almost the wrong side out,
To Desdemona hath tonight caroused
Potations pottle-deep, and he's to watch.[2]
Three else of Cyprus—noble swelling° spirits   *proud*
That hold their honours in a wary distance,[3]
50   The very elements° of this warlike isle—   *typical residents*
Have I tonight flustered with flowing cups,
And they watch too. Now 'mongst this flock of drunkards
Am I to put our Cassio in some action
That may offend the isle.

     Enter MONTANO, CASSIO, GENTLEMEN, *and [servants*
     with wine]

                     But here they come.
55   If consequence do but approve my dream,[4]
My boat sails freely both with wind and stream.°   *current*

CASSIO Fore God, they have given me a rouse° already.   *full draft*

MONTANO Good faith, a little one; not past a pint,
As I am a soldier.

IAGO   Some wine, ho!

---

2. *caroused . . . watch:* consumed drink to the bottom of the tankard, and he's assigned guard duty.

3. Who are touchy about their honor.

4. If events turn out as I hope.

60   [*Sings*]   And let me the cannikin° clink, clink,   *drinking vessel*
                     And let me the cannikin clink.
                       A soldier's a man,
                       O, man's life's but a span,
                       Why then, let a soldier drink.
65   Some wine, boys!
CASSIO   Fore God, an excellent song.
IAGO   I learned it in England, where indeed they are most potent
     in potting.[5] Your Dane, your German, and your swag°-bellied   *hanging*
     Hollander— drink, ho!—are nothing to your English.
70 CASSIO   Is your Englishman so exquisite in his drinking?
IAGO   Why, he drinks you with facility your Dane dead drunk.
     He sweats not to overthrow your Almain.° He gives your Hol-   *German*
     lander a vomit ere the next pottle° can be filled.   *tankard*
CASSIO   To the health of our general!
75 MONTANO   I am for it, lieutenant, and I'll do you justice.°   *match your drinking*
IAGO   O sweet England!
     [*Sings*]   King Stephen was and a worthy peer,
                     His breeches cost him but a crown;
                   He held them sixpence all too dear,
80   With that he called the tailor lown.°   *lout*
                   He was a wight of high renown,
                   And thou art but of low degree.
               'Tis pride° that pulls the country down,   *ostentatious clothing*
                   Then take thy auld cloak about thee.
85   Some wine, ho!
CASSIO   Fore God, this is a more exquisite song than the other.
IAGO   Will you hear't again?
CASSIO   No, for I hold him to be unworthy of his place that does
     those things. Well, God's above all, and there be souls must be
90   saved, and there be souls must not be saved.[6]
IAGO   It's true, good lieutenant.
CASSIO   For mine own part—no offence to the general, nor any
     man of quality°—I hope to be saved.   *rank*
IAGO   And so do I too, lieutenant.
95 CASSIO   Ay, but, by your leave, not before me. The lieutenant is
     to be saved before the ensign. Let's ha' no more of this. Let's to
     our affairs. God forgive us our sins. Gentlemen, let's look to
     our business. Do not think, gentlemen, I am drunk. This is my
     ensign, this is my right hand, and this is my left. I am not drunk
100   now. I can stand well enough, and I speak well enough.
GENTLEMEN   Excellent well.
CASSIO   Why, very well then. You must not think then that I am
     drunk.   *Exit*
MONTANO   To th' platform, masters. Come, let's set the watch.
                                   [*Exeunt* GENTLEMEN]
105 IAGO   You see this fellow that is gone before—
     He's a soldier fit to stand by Caesar
     And give direction; and do but see his vice.
     'Tis to his virtue a just equinox,°   *of equal size*
     The one as long as th'other. 'Tis pity of him.
110   I fear the trust Othello puts him in,

---

5. Most adept at drinking.
6. Referring to the idea of predestination, the belief held   by Calvinist Protestants that some souls are destined from
the outset to be saved and others damned.

On some odd time of his infirmity,
Will shake this island.
MONTANO   But is he often thus?
IAGO   'Tis evermore his prologue to his sleep.
     He'll watch the horologe a double set[7]
     If drink rock not his cradle.
115   MONTANO   It were well
     The general were put in mind of it.
     Perhaps he sees it not, or his good nature
     Prizes the virtue that appears in Cassio,
     And looks not on his evils. Is not this true?
         Enter RODERIGO
120   IAGO [*aside*]   How now, Roderigo!
     I pray you after the lieutenant, go.   *Exit* RODERIGO
     MONTANO   And 'tis great pity that the noble Moor
     Should hazard such a place as his own second
     With one of an engraffed° infirmity.   *ingrained*
125   It were an honest action to say so
     To the Moor.
IAGO   Not I, for this fair island!
     I do love Cassio well, and would do much
     To cure him of this evil.
VOICES (*within*)   Help, help!
IAGO   But hark, what noise?
         Enter CASSIO, *driving in* RODERIGO
130   CASSIO   'Swounds, you rogue, you rascal!
     MONTANO   What's the matter, lieutenant?
     CASSIO   A knave teach me my duty?—I'll beat the knave into a
       twiggen° bottle.   *wicker-cased*
     RODERIGO   Beat me?
135   CASSIO   Dost thou prate, rogue?
     MONTANO   Nay, good lieutenant, I pray you, sir, hold your hand.
     CASSIO   Let me go, sir, or I'll knock you o'er the mazard.°   *head*
     MONTANO   Come, come, you're drunk.
     CASSIO   Drunk?
         They fight
140   IAGO [*to* RODERIGO]   Away, I say. Go out and cry a mutiny.
                               [*Exit* RODERIGO]
     Nay, good lieutenant. God's will, gentlemen!
     Help, ho! Lieutenant! Sir! Montano! Sir!
     Help, masters. Here's a goodly watch indeed.
         A bell rung
     Who's that which rings the bell? Diablo,° ho!   *The devil*
145   The town will rise. God's will, lieutenant, hold.
     You'll be ashamed for ever.
         Enter OTHELLO *and attendants, with weapons*
OTHELLO   What is the matter here?
MONTANO   'Swounds, I bleed still. I am hurt to th' death.
         [*Attacking* CASSIO] He dies.
OTHELLO   Hold, for your lives!
IAGO   Hold, ho, lieutenant, sir, Montano, gentlemen!
150   Have you forgot all place of sense and duty?
     Hold, the general speaks to you. Hold, hold, for shame.

---

7. He'll stay up twice around the clock.

OTHELLO   Why, how now, ho? From whence ariseth this?
Are we turned Turks, and to ourselves do that
Which heaven hath forbid the Ottomites?°   *(by raising a storm)*
155   For Christian shame, put by this barbarous brawl.
He that stirs next to carve for his own rage°   *draw a sword in anger*
Holds his soul light. He dies upon his motion.
Silence that dreadful bell—it frights the isle
From her propriety.
            [*Bell stops*]
                      What is the matter, masters?
160   Honest Iago, that looks dead with grieving,
Speak. Who began this? On thy love I charge thee.
IAGO   I do not know. Friends all but now, even now,
In quarter° and in terms like bride and groom   *Under control*
Devesting them° for bed; and then but now—   *Getting undressed*
165   As if some planet° had unwitted men—   *astrological influence*
Swords out, and tilting one at others' breasts
In opposition bloody. I cannot speak
Any beginning to this peevish odds,°   *silly quarrel*
And would in action glorious I had lost
170   Those legs that brought me to a part of it.
OTHELLO   How comes it, Michael, you are thus forgot?
CASSIO   I pray you pardon me. I cannot speak.
OTHELLO   Worthy Montano, you were wont be° civil.   *you used to be*
The gravity and stillness of your youth
175   The world hath noted, and your name is great
In mouths of wisest censure.° What's the matter,   *judgment*
That you unlace your reputation thus,
And spend your rich opinion° for the name   *reputation*
Of a night-brawler? Give me answer to it.
180   MONTANO   Worthy Othello, I am hurt to danger.
Your officer Iago can inform you,
While I spare speech—which something now offends me°—   *somewhat now pains me*
Of all that I do know; nor know I aught
By me that's said or done amiss this night,
185   Unless self-charity° be sometimes a vice,   *care of oneself*
And to defend ourselves it be a sin
When violence assails us.
OTHELLO   Now, by heaven,
My blood begins my safer guides to rule,
And passion, having my best judgement collied,°   *darkened*
190   Essays to lead the way. 'Swounds, if I stir,
Or do but lift this arm, the best of you
Shall sink in my rebuke. Give me to know
How this foul rout began, who set it on,
And he that is approved in this offence,
195   Though he had twinned with me, both at a birth,
Shall lose me. What, in a town of war
Yet° wild, the people's hearts brimful of fear,   *Still*
To manage° private and domestic quarrel   *carry on*
In night, and on the court and guard of safety!⁸
200   'Tis monstrous. Iago, who began't?
MONTANO [*to* IAGO]   If partially affined° or leagued in office   *biased (for Cassio)*

---

8. And at the place where safety and security are at stake (on the night watch).

Thou dost deliver more or less than truth,
Thou art no soldier.
IAGO   Touch me not so near.
I had rather ha' this tongue cut from my mouth
205 Than it should do offence to Michael Cassio.
Yet I persuade myself to speak the truth
Shall nothing wrong him. This it is, general.
Montano and myself being in speech,
There comes a fellow crying out for help,
210 And Cassio following him with determined sword
To execute upon° him. Sir, this gentleman   *To attack*
Steps in to Cassio, and entreats his pause.
Myself the crying fellow did pursue,
Lest by his clamour, as it so fell out,
215 The town might fall in fright. He, swift of foot,
Outran my purpose, and I returned, the rather
For that I heard the clink and fall of swords
And Cassio high in oath, which till tonight
I ne'er might say before. When I came back—
220 For this was brief—I found them close together
At blow and thrust, even as again they were
When you yourself did part them.
More of this matter cannot I report,
But men are men. The best sometimes forget.
225 Though Cassio did some little wrong to him,
As men in rage strike those that wish them best,
Yet surely Cassio, I believe, received
From him that fled some strange indignity
Which patience could not pass.°   *let pass*
OTHELLO   I know, Iago,
230 Thy honesty and love doth mince° this matter,   *minimize*
Making it light to Cassio. Cassio, I love thee,
But never more be officer of mine.
              Enter DESDEMONA, *attended*
Look if my gentle love be not raised up.
I'll make thee an example.
235 DESDEMONA   What is the matter, dear?
OTHELLO   All's well now, sweeting.
Come away to bed. [*To* MONTANO] Sir, for your hurts
Myself will be your surgeon. [*To attendants*] Lead him off.
                    [*Exeunt attendants with* MONTANO]
Iago, look with care about the town,
240 And silence those whom this vile brawl distracted.
Come, Desdemona. 'Tis the soldier's life
To have their balmy slumbers waked with strife.
              Exeunt [OTHELLO *the*] *Moor,* DESDEMONA,
                              and attendants
IAGO   What, are you hurt, lieutenant?
CASSIO   Ay, past all surgery.
245 IAGO   Marry, God forbid.
CASSIO   Reputation, reputation, reputation—O, I ha' lost my rep-
    utation, I ha' lost the immortal part of myself, and what remains
    is bestial! My reputation, Iago, my reputation.
IAGO   As I am an honest man, I thought you had received some
250 bodily wound. There is more sense in that than in reputation.

Reputation is an idle and most false imposition,° oft got without *artificial notion*
merit and lost without deserving. You have lost no reputation
at all unless you repute yourself such a loser. What, man, there
are more ways to recover the general again. You are but now
255 cast in his mood—a punishment more in policy⁹ than in malice, even so as one would beat his offenceless dog to affright an
imperious lion. Sue to° him again, and he's yours.   *Petition*

CASSIO   I will rather sue to be despised than to deceive so good a
commander with so slight, so drunken, and so indiscreet an
260 officer. Drunk, and speak parrot,° and squabble? Swagger,   *rant on*
swear, and discourse fustian° with one's own shadow? O thou   *nonsense*
invisible spirit of wine, if thou hast no name to be known by,
let us call thee devil.

IAGO   What was he that you followed with your sword? What had
265 he done to you?

CASSIO   I know not.

IAGO   Is't possible?

CASSIO   I remember a mass of things, but nothing distinctly; a
quarrel, but nothing wherefore.° O God, that men should put   *but not why*
270 an enemy in their mouths° to steal away their brains! That we   *should drink*
should with joy, pleasance, revel, and applause transform our-
selves into beasts!

IAGO   Why, but you are now well enough. How came you thus
recovered?

275 CASSIO   It hath pleased the devil drunkenness to give place to
the devil wrath. One unperfectness shows me another, to make
me frankly despise myself.

IAGO   Come, you are too severe a moraller. As the time, the
place, and the condition of this country stands, I could heartily
280 wish this had not befallen; but since it is as it is, mend it for
your own good.

CASSIO   I will ask him for my place again. He shall tell me I am
a drunkard. Had I as many mouths as Hydra,¹ such an answer
would stop them all. To be now a sensible man, by and by a
285 fool, and presently a beast! O, strange! Every inordinate cup is
unblessed, and the ingredient is a devil.

IAGO   Come, come. Good wine is a good familiar creature, if it
be well used. Exclaim no more against it. And, good lieutenant,
I think you think I love you.

290 CASSIO   I have well approved° it, sir—I drunk?   *tested*

IAGO   You or any man living may be drunk at a time, man. I'll
tell you what you shall do. Our general's wife is now the general. I may say so in this respect, for that he hath devoted and
given up himself to the contemplation, mark, and denotement°   *observation*
295 of her parts° and graces. Confess yourself freely to her. Impor- *qualities*
tune her help to put you in your place again. She is of so free,°   *generous*
so kind, so apt, so blessed a disposition, she holds it a vice in
her goodness not to do more than she is requested. This broken
joint between you and her husband entreat her to splinter,°   *heal with a splint*
300 and, my fortunes against any lay° worth naming, this crack of   *wager*
your love shall grow stronger than it was before.

CASSIO   You advise me well.

---

9. *cast . . . policy:* dismissed in anger—a matter of policy   1. A mythical serpent with many heads who grew two
(of public example).   more when one was cut off.

IAGO   I protest,° in the sincerity of love and honest kindness.   *insist*

CASSIO   I think it freely, and betimes° in the morning I will   *early*
305   beseech the virtuous Desdemona to undertake for me. I am
desperate of my fortunes if they check° me here.   *stop*

IAGO   You are in the right. Good night, lieutenant. I must to the
watch.

CASSIO   Good night, honest Iago.   *Exit*

310   IAGO   And what's he then that says I play the villain,
When this advice is free I give, and honest,
Probal° to thinking, and indeed the course   *Wise*
To win the Moor again? For 'tis most easy
Th'inclining° Desdemona to subdue   *The well-disposed*
315   In any honest suit. She's framed as fruitful°   *generous*
As the free elements; and then for her
To win the Moor, were't to renounce his baptism,
All seals and symbols of redeemèd sin,
His soul is so enfettered to her love
320   That she may make, unmake, do what she list,
Even as her appetite° shall play the god   *wishes*
With his weak function.° How am I then a villain,   *faculties*
To counsel Cassio to this parallel° course   *suitable*
Directly to his good? Divinity° of hell: *Theology*
325   When devils will the blackest sins put on,
They do suggest at first with heavenly shows,
As I do now; for whiles this honest fool
Plies Desdemona to repair his fortune,
And she for him pleads strongly to the Moor,
330   I'll pour this pestilence into his ear:
That she repeals him° for her body's lust,   *appeals for him*
And by how much she strives to do him good
She shall undo her credit with the Moor.
So will I turn her virtue into pitch,²
335   And out of her own goodness make the net
That shall enmesh them all.
     Enter RODERIGO
              How now, Roderigo?

RODERIGO   I do follow here in the chase, not like a hound that
hunts, but one that fills up the cry.° My money is almost spent,   *a pack follower*
I ha' been tonight exceedingly well cudgelled, and I think the
340   issue will be I shall have so much° experience for my pains: *only so much*
and so, with no money at all and a little more wit, return again
to Venice.

IAGO   How poor are they that ha' not patience!
What wound did ever heal but by degrees?
345   Thou know'st we work by wit and not by witchcraft,
And wit depends on dilatory° time.   *drawn-out*
Does't not go well? Cassio hath beaten thee,
And thou by that small hurt hast cashiered° Cassio.   *dismissed*
Though other things grow fair against the sun,
350   Yet fruits that blossom first will first be ripe.³
Content thyself a while. By the mass,° 'tis morning.   *(a mild oath)*

---

2 Black, sticky substance used as a snare. The more the
thing caught in it tries to escape, the more stuck it
becomes.

3. *Though . . . ripe:* Although others may appear to be
prospering, your plan will be successful soonest because
started first.

Pleasure and action make the hours seem short.
Retire thee. Go where thou art billeted.
Away, I say. Thou shalt know more hereafter.
Nay, get thee gone.   *Exit* RODERIGO
355   Two things are to be done.
My wife must move for Cassio to her mistress.
I'll set her on.
Myself a while to draw the Moor apart,
And bring him jump° when he may Cassio find   exactly
360 Soliciting his wife. Ay, that's the way.
Dull not device by coldness and delay.[4]   *Exit*

3.1

Enter CASSIO *with* MUSICIANS

CASSIO   Masters, play here—I will content° your pains—   reward
Something that's brief, and bid 'Good morrow, general'.
          [*Music.*] *Enter* CLOWN

CLOWN   Why, masters, ha' your instruments been in Naples, that
they speak i'th' nose thus?[1]

5 MUSICIAN   How, sir, how?

CLOWN   Are these, I pray you, wind instruments?[2]

MUSICIAN   Ay, marry are they, sir.

CLOWN   O, thereby hangs a tail.

MUSICIAN   Whereby hangs a tale, sir?

10 CLOWN   Marry, sir, by many a wind instrument that I know. But
masters, here's money for you, and the general so likes your
music that he desires you, for love's sake, to make no more
noise with it.

MUSICIAN   Well, sir, we will not.

15 CLOWN   If you have any music that may not° be heard, to't again;   cannot
but, as they say, to hear music the general does not greatly care.

MUSICIAN   We ha' none such, sir.

CLOWN   Then put up your pipes in your bag, for I'll away. Go,
vanish into air, away.   *Exeunt* MUSICIANS

20 CASSIO   Dost thou hear, my honest friend?

CLOWN   No, I hear not your honest friend, I hear you.

CASSIO   Prithee, keep up thy quillets.° There's a poor piece of   pack up your puns
gold for thee. If the gentlewoman that attends the general's wife
be stirring, tell her there's one Cassio entreats her a little favour

25 of speech. Wilt thou do this?

CLOWN   She is stirring, sir. If she will stir hither, I shall seem° to   arrange
notify unto her.

CASSIO   Do, good my friend.   *Exit* CLOWN
          Enter IAGO
                          In happy time,° Iago.   Well met

IAGO   You ha' not been abed, then.

CASSIO   Why, no. The day had broke

30 Before we parted. I ha' made bold, Iago,
To send in to your wife. My suit to her

---

4. Don't let sluggishness and slowness to act weaken the plot.
3.1 Location: Outside Othello and Desdemona's room.
1. That they sound so nasal; perhaps a reference to vene-real disease, often associated with Naples, or a phallic or

anal joke.
2. The exchange that follows depends on the connec-tions between wind instruments, flatulence, and "tale/tail."

Is that she will to virtuous Desdemona
Procure me some access.
IAGO   I'll send her to you presently,
35   And I'll devise a mean to draw the Moor
Out of the way, that your converse and business
May be more free.
CASSIO   I humbly thank you for't.   *Exit* IAGO
I never knew a Florentine more kind and honest.
    Enter EMILIA
EMILIA   Good morrow, good lieutenant. I am sorry
40   For your displeasure, but all will sure be well.
The general and his wife are talking of it,
And she speaks for you stoutly. The Moor replies
That he you hurt is of great fame in Cyprus,
And great affinity,° and that in wholesome wisdom   *well connected*
45   He might not but refuse you. But he protests he loves you,
And needs no other suitor but his likings
To take the saf'st occasion by the front°   *forelock*
To bring you in again.
CASSIO   Yet I beseech you,
If you think fit, or that it may be done,
50   Give me advantage of some brief discourse
With Desdemon alone.
EMILIA   Pray you come in.
I will bestow you where you shall have time
To speak your bosom° freely.   *heart*
CASSIO   I am much bound to you.
                            Exeunt

3.2

    Enter OTHELLO, IAGO, *and* GENTLEMEN
OTHELLO   These letters give, Iago, to the pilot,
And by him do my duties° to the senate.   *send my respects*
That done, I will be walking on the works.°   *fortifications*
Repair there to me.
IAGO   Well, my good lord, I'll do't.   [*Exit*]
5 OTHELLO   This fortification, gentlemen—shall we see't?
A GENTLEMAN   We'll wait upon your lordship.   *Exeunt*

3.3

    Enter DESDEMONA, CASSIO, *and* EMILIA
DESDEMONA   Be thou assured, good Cassio, I will do
All my abilities in thy behalf.
EMILIA   Good madam, do. I warrant it grieves my husband
As if the cause were his.
5 DESDEMONA   O, that's an honest fellow. Do not doubt, Cassio,
But I will have my lord and you again
As friendly as you were.
CASSIO   Bounteous madam,
Whatever shall become of Michael Cassio
He's never anything but your true servant.
10 DESDEMONA   I know't. I thank you. You do love my lord.
You have known him long, and be you well assured

3.2 Location: The citadel.   3.3 Location: The citadel's garden.

He shall in strangeness stand no farther off
Than in a politic distance.[1]
CASSIO   Ay, but, lady,
  That policy may either last so long,
15 Or feed upon such nice and wat'rish diet,
  Or breed itself so out of circumstance,[2]
  That, I being absent and my place supplied,°   *filled*
  My general will forget my love and service.
DESDEMONA Do not doubt° that. Before Emilia here   *fear*
20 I give thee warrant° of thy place. Assure thee,   *assurance*
  If I do vow a friendship I'll perform it
  To the last article. My lord shall never rest.
  I'll watch him tame, and talk him out of patience.[3]
  His bed shall seem a school, his board a shrift.°   *confessional*
25 I'll intermingle everything he does
  With Cassio's suit. Therefore be merry, Cassio,
  For thy solicitor° shall rather die   *advocate*
  Than give thy cause away.°   *up (ironically prophetic)*
      Enter OTHELLO *and* IAGO
EMILIA   Madam, here comes my lord.
CASSIO Madam, I'll take my leave.
DESDEMONA   Why, stay, and hear me speak.
30 CASSIO Madam, not now. I am very ill at ease,
  Unfit for mine own purposes.
DESDEMONA Well, do your discretion.   *Exit* CASSIO
IAGO Ha! I like not that.
OTHELLO What dost thou say?
35 IAGO Nothing, my lord. Or if, I know not what.
OTHELLO Was not that Cassio parted from my wife?
IAGO Cassio, my lord? No, sure, I cannot think it,
  That he would steal away so guilty-like
  Seeing your coming.
40 OTHELLO I do believe 'twas he.
DESDEMONA How now, my lord?
  I have been talking with a suitor here,
  A man that languishes in your displeasure.
OTHELLO Who is't you mean?
45 DESDEMONA Why, your lieutenant, Cassio; good my lord,
  If I have any grace or power to move you,
  His present reconciliation take;°   *Accept him now*
  For if he be not one that truly loves you,
  That errs in ignorance and not in cunning,°   *not knowingly*
50 I have no judgement in an honest face.
  I prithee call him back.
OTHELLO Went he hence now?
DESDEMONA Yes, faith, so humbled
  That he hath left part of his grief with me
55 To suffer with him. Good love, call him back.
OTHELLO Not now, sweet Desdemon. Some other time.
DESDEMONA But shall't be shortly?
OTHELLO   The sooner, sweet, for you.

---

1. *He ... distance:* He will distance himself from you only as much as good diplomacy requires.
2. *Or feed ... circumstance:* Or persist based on such unimportant and poor justifications, or continue by chance.
3. I'll keep him awake until he obeys me, and talk to him beyond his endurance.

DESDEMONA   Shall't be tonight at supper?
OTHELLO   No, not tonight.
DESDEMONA   Tomorrow dinner,° then?   *midday meal*
OTHELLO   I shall not dine at home.
60   I meet the captains at the citadel.
DESDEMONA   Why then, tomorrow night, or Tuesday morn,
      On Tuesday noon, or night, on Wednesday morn—
      I prithee name the time, but let it not
      Exceed three days. In faith, he's penitent,
65   And yet his trespass, in our common reason°—   *normal judgment*
      Save that, they say, the wars must make example
      Out of her° best—is not almost a fault   *(war's)*
      T'incur a private check.⁴ When shall he come?
      Tell me, Othello. I wonder in my soul
70   What you would ask me that I should deny,
      Or stand so mamm'ring° on? What, Michael Cassio,   *hesitating*
      That came a-wooing with you, and so many a time
      When I have spoke of you dispraisingly
      Hath ta'en your part—to have so much to-do
75   To bring him in?° By'r Lady, I could do much.⁵   *into favor*
OTHELLO   Prithee, no more. Let him come when he will.
      I will deny thee nothing.
DESDEMONA   Why, this is not a boon.
      'Tis as I should entreat you wear your gloves,
      Or feed on nourishing dishes, or keep you warm,
80   Or sue to you to do a peculiar° profit   *particular*
      To your own person. Nay, when I have a suit
      Wherein I mean to touch your love indeed,
      It shall be full of poise° and difficult weight,   *balanced judgment*
      And fearful to be granted.
OTHELLO   I will deny thee nothing,
85   Whereon I do beseech thee grant me this:
      To leave me but a little to myself.
DESDEMONA   Shall I deny you? No. Farewell, my lord.
OTHELLO   Farewell, my Desdemona. I'll come to thee straight.°   *immediately*
DESDEMONA   Emilia, come. [*To* OTHELLO] Be as your fancies
            teach° you.   *as your whims lead*
90   Whate'er you be, I am obedient.
                              Exeunt DESDEMONA *and* EMILIA
OTHELLO   Excellent wretch!° Perdition catch my soul   *(affectionate)*
      But I do love thee, and when I love thee not,
      Chaos is come again.
IAGO   My noble lord.
95   OTHELLO   What dost thou say, Iago?
IAGO   Did Michael Cassio, when you wooed my lady,
      Know of your love?
OTHELLO   He did, from first to last. Why dost thou ask?
IAGO   But for a satisfaction of my thought,
      No further harm.
100   OTHELLO   Why of thy thought, Iago?
IAGO   I did not think he had been acquainted with her.
OTHELLO   O yes, and went between us very oft.
IAGO   Indeed?

---

4. *is . . . check:* is barely worth even private criticism.   5. Do much to make you regret your reluctance (?).

OTHELLO Indeed? Ay, indeed. Discern'st thou aught in that?
105　Is he not honest?
IAGO　Honest, my lord?
OTHELLO　Honest? Ay, honest.
IAGO　My lord, for aught I know.
OTHELLO　　　　　　　　　What dost thou think?
IAGO　Think, my lord?
110　OTHELLO　'Think, my lord?' By heaven, thou echo'st me
　　As if there were some monster in thy thought
　　Too hideous to be shown! Thou dost mean something.
　　I heard thee say even now thou liked'st not that,
　　When Cassio left my wife. What didst not like?
115　And when I told thee he was of my counsel°　　　　　　　　　*in my confidence*
　　In my whole course of wooing, thou cried'st 'Indeed?'
　　And didst contract and purse thy brow together
　　As if thou then hadst shut up in thy brain
　　Some horrible conceit.° If thou dost love me,　　　　　　　　　*thought*
120　Show me thy thought.
IAGO　My lord, you know I love you.
OTHELLO　I think thou dost,
　　And for° I know thou'rt full of love and honesty,　　　　　　　　*since*
　　And weigh'st thy words before thou giv'st them breath,
125　Therefore these stops° of thine fright me the more;　　　　　　　*reluctances*
　　For such things in a false disloyal knave
　　Are tricks of custom,° but in a man that's just,　　　　　　　　*habitual*
　　They're close dilations,[6] working from the heart
　　That passion cannot rule.°　　　　　　　　　　　　　　　　*control*
IAGO　　　　　　　　　　For Michael Cassio,
130　I dare be sworn I think that he is honest.
OTHELLO　I think so too.
IAGO　　　　　　　　Men should be what they seem,
　　Or those that be not, would they might seem none.[7]
OTHELLO　Certain, men should be what they seem.
IAGO　Why then, I think Cassio's an honest man.
135　OTHELLO　Nay, yet there's more in this.
　　I prithee speak to me as to thy thinkings,
　　As thou dost ruminate, and give thy worst of thoughts
　　The worst of words.
IAGO　　　　　　　　Good my lord, pardon me.
　　Though I am bound to every act of duty,
140　I am not bound to that all slaves are free to.[8]
　　Utter my thoughts? Why, say they are vile and false,
　　As where's that palace whereinto foul things
　　Sometimes intrude not? Who has that breast so pure
　　But some uncleanly apprehensions
145　Keep leets and law-days, and in sessions sit
　　With meditations lawful?[9]
OTHELLO　Thou dost conspire against thy friend,° Iago,　　　　　*(Othello)*
　　If thou but think'st him wronged and mak'st his ear
　　A stranger to thy thoughts.
IAGO　　　　　　　　　I do beseech you,

6. Involuntary revelations of interior, close-kept secrets.
7. *Or . . . none:* If only those who are not what they seem didn't seem to be what they are not.
8. I am not obligated to reveal my inner thoughts, some-

thing about which even slaves have a choice.
9. *uncleanly . . . lawful:* illegitimate thoughts meet in court ("leets") from time to time (on "law-days") and debate (in court "sessions") with legitimate ones.

150 Though I perchance am vicious° in my guess— *mistaken*
As I confess it is my nature's plague
To spy into abuses, and oft my jealousy
Shapes faults that are not—that your wisdom then,
From one that so imperfectly conceits,° *imagines*
155 Would take no notice, nor build yourself a trouble
Out of his scattering° and unsure observance. *incoherent*
It were not for your quiet nor your good,
Nor for my manhood, honesty, and wisdom,
To let you know my thoughts.
OTHELLO What dost thou mean?
160 IAGO Good name in man and woman, dear my lord,
Is the immediate jewel of their souls.
Who steals my purse steals trash; 'tis something, nothing;
'Twas mine, 'tis his, and has been slave to thousands.
But he that filches from me my good name
165 Robs me of that which not enriches him
And makes me poor indeed.
OTHELLO By heaven, I'll know thy thoughts.
IAGO You cannot, if my heart were in your hand;
Nor shall not whilst 'tis in my custody.
OTHELLO Ha!
IAGO O, beware, my lord, of jealousy.
170 It is the green-eyed monster which doth mock
The meat it feeds on.[1] That cuckold lives in bliss
Who, certain of his fate, loves not his wronger.[2]
But O, what damnèd minutes tells he o'er
Who dotes yet doubts, suspects yet fondly loves!
175 OTHELLO O misery!
IAGO Poor and content is rich, and rich enough,
But riches fineless° is as poor as winter *boundless*
To him that ever fears he shall be poor.
Good God the souls of all my tribe defend
From jealousy!
180 OTHELLO Why, why is this?
Think'st thou I'd make a life of jealousy,
To follow still the changes of the moon° *To renew endlessly*
With fresh suspicions? No, to be once in doubt
Is once to be resolved.° Exchange me for a goat *to be finally settled*
185 When I shall turn the business of my soul
To such exsufflicate and blowed° surmises *inflated and blown-up*
Matching thy inference. 'Tis not to make me jealous
To say my wife is fair, feeds well, loves company,
Is free of speech, sings, plays, and dances well.
190 Where virtue is, these are more virtuous,
Nor from mine own weak merits will I draw
The smallest fear or doubt of her revolt,° *or fear of her betrayal*
For she had eyes and chose me. No, Iago,
I'll see before I doubt; when I doubt, prove;
195 And on the proof, there is no more but this:
Away at once with love or jealousy.

1. *which . . . on:* that tortures, as it consumes, the heart of
the jealous person.
2. Who, knowing it is his fate to be cuckolded, doesn't
love his wife; who, certain that his wife is faithful even
when she is not, does not knowingly love the cuckolder.

IAGO I am glad of this, for now I shall have reason
   To show the love and duty that I bear you
   With franker spirit. Therefore, as I am bound,
200   Receive it from me. I speak not yet of proof.
   Look to your wife. Observe her well with Cassio.
   Wear your eyes thus: not jealous, nor secure.
   I would not have your free and noble nature
   Out of self-bounty be abused.³ Look to't.
205   I know our country disposition well.
   In Venice they do let God see the pranks
   They dare not show their husbands; their best conscience
   Is not to leave't undone, but keep't unknown.
OTHELLO Dost thou say so?
210   IAGO She did deceive her father, marrying you,
   And when she seemed to shake and fear your looks
   She loved them most.
OTHELLO   And so she did.
IAGO   Why, go to,° then.   *that's it*
   She that so young could give out such a seeming,
   To seel her father's eyes up close as oak,⁴
215   He thought 'twas witchcraft! But I am much to blame.
   I humbly do beseech you of your pardon
   For too much loving you.
OTHELLO   I am bound to thee for ever.
IAGO I see this hath a little dashed your spirits.
OTHELLO Not a jot, not a jot.
IAGO   I'faith, I fear it has.
220   I hope you will consider what is spoke
   Comes from my love. But I do see you're moved.
   I am to pray you not to strain my speech
   To grosser issues,° nor to larger reach   *greater conclusions*
   Than to suspicion.
225   OTHELLO I will not.
IAGO Should you do so, my lord,
   My speech should fall into such vile success
   Which my thoughts aimed not. Cassio's my worthy friend.
   My lord, I see you're moved.
OTHELLO   No, not much moved.
230   I do not think but Desdemona's honest.
IAGO Long live she so, and long live you to think so!
OTHELLO And yet how nature, erring from itself—
IAGO Ay, there's the point; as, to be bold with you,
   Not to affect° many proposèd matches   *desire*
235   Of her own clime, complexion, and degree,
   Whereto we see in all things nature tends.
   Foh, one may smell in such a will most rank,
   Foul disproportions, thoughts unnatural!
   But pardon me. I do not in position°   *argument*
240   Distinctly speak of her, though I may fear
   Her will,° recoiling° to her better judgement,   *desire / submitting*
   May fall to match you with her country forms⁵
   And happily° repent.   *perhaps*

3. Be deceived on account of your own goodness.   eyes as tightly as oak (a fine-grained wood).
4. Perhaps: To cover ("seel" means "to blind") her father's   5. May happen to compare you with Venetian standards.

OTHELLO   Farewell, farewell.
If more thou dost perceive, let me know more.
245   Set on thy wife to observe. Leave me, Iago.
IAGO [*going*] My lord, I take my leave.
OTHELLO Why did I marry? This honest creature doubtless
Sees and knows more, much more, than he unfolds.
IAGO [*returning*] My lord, I would I might entreat your honour
250   To scan this thing no farther. Leave it to time.
Although 'tis fit that Cassio have his place—
For sure he fills it up with great ability—
Yet, if you please to hold him off a while,
You shall by that perceive him and his means.[6]
255   Note if your lady strain his entertainment°   *urge his reception*
With any strong or vehement importunity.
Much will be seen in that. In the mean time,
Let me be thought too busy° in my fears—   *meddlesome*
As worthy cause I have to fear I am—
260   And hold her free,° I do beseech your honour.   *believe her innocent*
OTHELLO Fear not my government.°   *self-conduct*
IAGO   I once more take my leave.
                                          Exit
OTHELLO This fellow's of exceeding honesty,
And knows all qualities° with a learned spirit   *(human) types*
Of human dealings. If I do prove her haggard,°   *wild (falconry)*
265   Though that her jesses were my dear heart-strings
I'd whistle her off and let her down the wind
To prey at fortune.[7] Haply for° I am black,   *Perhaps because*
And have not those soft parts of conversation°   *easy manners*
That chamberers° have; or for I am declined   *gallants*
270   Into the vale of years—yet that's not much—
She's gone. I am abused,° and my relief   *deceived*
Must be to loathe her. O curse of marriage,
That we can call these delicate creatures ours
And not their appetites! I had rather be a toad
275   And live upon the vapour of a dungeon
Than keep a corner in the thing I love
For others' uses. Yet 'tis the plague of great ones;
Prerogatived° are they less than the base.°   *Privileged / lowborn*
'Tis destiny unshunnable, like death.
280   Even then this forkèd plague is fated to us
When we do quicken.[8]
          Enter DESDEMONA *and* EMILIA
                Look where she comes.
If she be false, O then heaven mocks itself!
I'll not believe't.
DESDEMONA   How now, my dear Othello?
Your dinner, and the generous° islanders   *noble*
285   By you invited, do attend° your presence.   *wait for*
OTHELLO I am to blame.
DESDEMONA Why do you speak so faintly? Are you not well?
OTHELLO I have a pain upon my forehead here.°   *(from cuckold's horns)*

---

6. Method (for restoring himself to favor).
7. *Though . . . fortune:* Even if what tied her ("jesses"
were leg straps put on a hawk) were my own heartstrings,
I'd set her loose downwind forever to hunt on her own.

8. *Even . . . quicken:* The "plague" of horns (imagined to
grow from the forehead of a cuckold) is our fate as soon
as we live.

DESDEMONA   Faith, that's with watching.[9] 'Twill away again.
290   Let me but bind it hard, within this hour
       It will be well.
OTHELLO   Your napkin° is too little.   *handkerchief*
       [*He puts the napkin from him. It drops*]
       Let it alone. Come, I'll go in with you.
DESDEMONA   I am very sorry that you are not well.
                        Exeunt OTHELLO *and* DESDEMONA
EMILIA [*taking up the napkin*]   I am glad I have found this napkin.
295   This was her first remembrance from the Moor.
       My wayward husband hath a hundred times
       Wooed me to steal it, but she so loves the token—
       For he conjured her[1] she should ever keep it—
       That she reserves it evermore about her
300   To kiss and talk to. I'll ha' the work ta'en out,°   *embroidery copied*
       And give't Iago. What he will do with it,
       Heaven knows, not I.
       I nothing,° but to please his fantasy.   *intend nothing*
           Enter IAGO
IAGO   How now, what do you here alone?
305   EMILIA   Do not you chide. I have a thing for you.
IAGO   You have a thing for me? It is a common thing.[2]
EMILIA   Ha?
IAGO   To have a foolish wife.
EMILIA   O, is that all? What will you give me now
310   For that same handkerchief?
IAGO   What handkerchief?
EMILIA   What handkerchief?
       Why, that the Moor first gave to Desdemona,
       That which so often you did bid me steal.
315   IAGO   Hast stol'n it from her?
EMILIA   No, faith, she let it drop by negligence,
       And to th'advantage° I, being here, took't up.   *taking the occasion*
       Look, here 'tis.
IAGO   A good wench! Give it me.
EMILIA   What will you do with it, that you have been so earnest
       To have me filch it?
320   IAGO   Why, what is that to you?
       [*He takes the napkin*]
EMILIA   If it be not for some purpose of import,
       Give't me again. Poor lady, she'll run mad
       When she shall lack it.
IAGO   Be not acknown on't.° I have use for it. Go, leave me.   *Don't let it be known*
                        Exit EMILIA
325   I will in Cassio's lodging lose this napkin,
       And let him find it. Trifles light as air
       Are to the jealous confirmations strong
       As proofs of holy writ. This may do something.
       The Moor already changes with my poison.
330   Dangerous conceits° are in their natures poisons,   *ideas*
       Which at the first are scarce found to distaste,

---

9. Staying awake; unbeknownst to Desdemona, "watching" may also refer to Othello's fantasy of seeing Desdemona have intercourse with Cassio.
1. Made her swear; perhaps also an unwitting backward glance at Brabanzio's charge in 1.3 that Othello employed witchcraft to win Desdemona.
2. It is a vagina ("thing") available to all.

But, with a little act° upon the blood,   *effect*
Burn like the mines of sulphur.[3]
    Enter OTHELLO
                        I did say so.
Look where he comes. Not poppy nor mandragora[4]

335 Nor all the drowsy syrups of the world
Shall ever medicine thee to that sweet sleep
Which thou owedst° yesterday.   *owned*
OTHELLO   Ha, ha, false to me?
IAGO   Why, how now, general? No more of that.

340 OTHELLO   Avaunt, be gone. Thou hast set me on the rack.
I swear 'tis better to be much abused°   *mistreated; deceived*
Than but to know't a little.
IAGO   How now, my lord?
OTHELLO   What sense had I of her stol'n hours of lust?
I saw't not, thought it not; it harmed not me.

345 I slept the next night well, fed well, was free and merry.
I found not Cassio's kisses on her lips.
He that is robbed, not wanting° what is stol'n,   *missing*
Let him not know't and he's not robbed at all.
IAGO   I am sorry to hear this.

350 OTHELLO   I had been happy if the general camp,
Pioneers° and all, had tasted her sweet body,   *Manual laborers*
So° I had nothing known. O, now for ever   *If*
Farewell the tranquil mind, farewell content,
Farewell the plumèd troops and the big wars

355 That makes ambition virtue! O, farewell,
Farewell the neighing steed and the shrill trump,
The spirit-stirring drum, th'ear-piercing fife,
The royal banner, and all quality,°   *aspects*
Pride,° pomp, and circumstance° of glorious war!   *Magnificence / ceremony*

360 And O, you mortal engines° whose rude throats   *deadly cannons*
Th'immortal Jove's dread clamours° counterfeit,   *thunderclaps*
Farewell! Othello's occupation's gone.
IAGO   Is't possible, my lord?
OTHELLO [*taking* IAGO *by the throat*]   Villain, be sure thou prove
    my love a whore.

365 Be sure of it. Give me the ocular proof,
Or, by the worth of mine eternal soul,
Thou hadst been better have been born a dog
Than answer my waked wrath.
IAGO   Is't come to this?
OTHELLO   Make me to see't, or at the least so prove it

370 That the probation° bear no hinge nor loop   *proof*
To hang a doubt on, or woe upon thy life.
IAGO   My noble lord.
OTHELLO   If thou dost slander her and torture me,
Never pray more; abandon all remorse,

375 On horror's head horrors accumulate,
Do deeds to make heaven weep, all earth amazed,
For nothing canst thou to damnation add
Greater than that.

---

3. Pliny describes two islands of sulfur between mainland Italy and Sicily that were rumored to be always on fire.

4. A sleep-inducing substance made from the mandrake root.

IAGO   O grace, O heaven forgive me!
Are you a man? Have you a soul or sense?
God buy you, take mine office.⁵ O wretched fool,°   *(to himself)*
That lov'st to make thine honesty a vice!°   *fault*
O monstrous world, take note, take note, O world,
To be direct and honest is not safe!
I thank you for this profit,° and from hence   *profitable lesson*
I'll love no friend, sith° love breeds such offence.   *since*

OTHELLO   Nay, stay. Thou shouldst be honest.
IAGO   I should be wise, for honesty's a fool,
And loses that° it works for.   *what*
OTHELLO   By the world,⁶
I think my wife be honest, and think she is not.
I think that thou art just, and think thou art not.
I'll have some proof. My name, that was as fresh
As Dian's⁷ visage, is now begrimed and black
As mine own face. If there be cords, or knives,
Poison, or fire, or suffocating streams,
I'll not endure it. Would I were satisfied!
IAGO   I see, sir, you are eaten up with passion.
I do repent me that I put it to you.
You would be satisfied?
OTHELLO   Would? Nay, and I will.
IAGO   And may. But how, how satisfied, my lord?
Would you, the supervisor,° grossly gape on,   *observer*
Behold her topped?
OTHELLO   Death and damnation! O!
IAGO   It were a tedious° difficulty, I think,   *painful*
To bring them to that prospect. Damn them then
If ever mortal eyes do see them bolster°   *share a pillow*
More° than their own!° What then, how then?   *Other / own eyes*
What shall I say? Where's satisfaction?
It is impossible you should see this,
Were they as prime° as goats, as hot as monkeys,   *lustful*
As salt as wolves in pride,⁸ and fools as gross
As ignorance made drunk. But yet I say,
If imputation, and strong circumstances⁹
Which lead directly to the door of truth,
Will give you satisfaction, you might ha't.
OTHELLO   Give me a living reason she's disloyal.
IAGO   I do not like the office,
But sith I am entered in this cause so far,
Pricked to't° by foolish honesty and love,   *Prodded on*
I will go on. I lay with Cassio lately,
And being troubled with a raging tooth,
I could not sleep. There are a kind of men
So loose of soul that in their sleeps
Will mutter their affairs. One of this kind is Cassio.
In sleep I heard him say 'Sweet Desdemona,
Let us be wary, let us hide our loves',
And then, sir, would he grip and wring my hand,

---

5. Goodbye, I resign my official position (ensign).
6. Othello's speech (lines 388–95) does not appear in Q.
7. Diana, goddess of chastity and of the (pale) moon. The
Second Quarto (1630) replaces "My" (line 391) with

"Her," a plausible but arguably less powerful reading that
lacks textual authority.
8. As lecherous as wolves in heat.
9. If inference and strong circumstantial evidence.

Cry 'O, sweet creature!', then kiss me hard,
As if he plucked up kisses by the roots,
That grew upon my lips, lay his leg o'er my thigh,
And sigh, and kiss, and then cry 'Cursèd fate,
430   That gave thee to the Moor!'
OTHELLO   O, monstrous, monstrous!
IAGO   Nay, this was but his dream.
OTHELLO   But this denoted a foregone conclusion.°   *an earlier event*
IAGO   'Tis a shrewd doubt,° though it be but a dream,   *reasonable fear*
435   And this may help to thicken other proofs
That do demonstrate thinly.
OTHELLO   I'll tear her all to pieces.
IAGO   Nay, yet be wise; yet we see nothing done.
She may be honest yet. Tell me but this:
Have you not sometimes seen a handkerchief
440   Spotted with strawberries in your wife's hand?
OTHELLO   I gave her such a one. 'Twas my first gift.
IAGO   I know not that, but such a handkerchief—
I am sure it was your wife's—did I today
See Cassio wipe his beard with.
OTHELLO   If it be that—
445   IAGO   If it be that, or any that was hers,
It speaks against her with the other proofs.
OTHELLO   O that the slave° had forty thousand lives!   *(Cassio)*
One is too poor, too weak for my revenge.
Now do I see 'tis true. Look here, Iago.
450   All my fond love thus do I blow to heaven—'tis gone.
Arise, black vengeance, from the hollow hell.
Yield up, O love, thy crown and hearted throne°   *rule of the heart*
To tyrannous hate! Swell, bosom, with thy freight,°   *burden*
For 'tis of aspics'° tongues.   *poison snakes'*
IAGO   Yet be content.
OTHELLO   O, blood, blood, blood!
455   IAGO   Patience, I say. Your mind may change.
OTHELLO   Never, Iago. Like to the Pontic Sea,°   *Black Sea*
Whose icy current and compulsive course
Ne'er knows retiring ebb, but keeps due on
To the Propontic and the Hellespont,[1]
460   Even so my bloody thoughts with violent pace
Shall ne'er look back, ne'er ebb to humble love,
Till that a capable° and wide revenge   *capacious*
Swallow them up.
      [*He kneels*]
              Now, by yon marble heaven,
In the due reverence of a sacred vow
I here engage my words.
465   IAGO   Do not rise yet.
      IAGO *kneels*[2]
Witness you ever-burning lights above,
You elements that clip° us round about,   *embrace (sexual?)*
Witness that here Iago doth give up

1. The Propontic was the body of water bounded by the straits of Bosphorus and the Dardanelles (Hellespont), the latter strait leading to the Aegean.
2. This parody of the marriage ceremony suggests a homoerotic or, more probably, a homosocial bond between Othello and Iago. But it also anticipates Desdemona's kneeling before Iago (4.2.155–65).

The execution° of his wit, hands, heart   *command*
470 To wronged Othello's service. Let him command,
And to obey shall be in me remorse,°   *pity (for Othello)*
What bloody business ever.°   *soever*
    [*They rise*]
OTHELLO   I greet thy love,
Not with vain thanks, but with acceptance bounteous,
And will upon the instant put thee to't.° *immediately test it*
475 Within these three days let me hear thee say
That Cassio's not alive.
IAGO   My friend is dead.
'Tis done at your request; but let her live.
OTHELLO Damn her, lewd minx!° O, damn her, damn her! *wanton*
Come, go with me apart. I will withdraw
480 To furnish me with some swift means of death
For the fair devil. Now art thou my lieutenant.
IAGO I am your own for ever.   *Exeunt*

3.4

   Enter DESDEMONA, EMILIA, *and the* CLOWN
DESDEMONA Do you know, sirrah,[1] where Lieutenant Cassio
 lies?
CLOWN I dare not say he lies anywhere.
DESDEMONA Why, man?
5 CLOWN He's a soldier, and for me to say a soldier lies, 'tis stabbing.
DESDEMONA Go to. Where lodges he?
CLOWN To tell you where he lodges is to tell you where I lie.
DESDEMONA Can anything be made of this?
10 CLOWN I know not where he lodges, and for me to devise a
 lodging and say he lies here, or he lies there, were to lie in
 mine own throat.°   *lie outrageously*
DESDEMONA Can you enquire him out, and be edified by
 report?
15 CLOWN I will catechize the world for him; that is, make questions, and by them answer.
DESDEMONA Seek him, bid him come hither, tell him I have
 moved° my lord on his behalf, and hope all will be well. *petitioned*
CLOWN To do this is within the compass° of man's wit, and *scope*
20 therefore I will attempt the doing it.   *Exit*
DESDEMONA Where should° I lose the handkerchief, Emilia? *did*
EMILIA I know not, madam.
DESDEMONA Believe me, I had rather have lost my purse
Full of crusadoes,° and but° my noble Moor *gold coins / but that*
25 Is true of mind, and made of no such baseness
As jealous creatures are, it were enough
To put him to ill thinking.
EMILIA   Is he not jealous?
DESDEMONA Who, he? I think the sun where he was born
Drew all such humours from him.
    Enter OTHELLO
EMILIA   Look where he comes.
30 DESDEMONA I will not leave him now till Cassio

3.4 Location: Before the citadel.   1. A form of address to an inferior.

Be called to him. How is't with you, my lord?
OTHELLO   Well, my good lady. [*Aside*] O hardness to dissemble!—
How do you, Desdemona?
DESDEMONA   Well, my good lord.
OTHELLO   Give me your hand. This hand is moist, my lady.
35 DESDEMONA   It hath felt no age, nor known no sorrow.
OTHELLO   This argues fruitfulness and liberal heart.[2]
Hot, hot and moist—this hand of yours requires
A sequester from liberty; fasting, and prayer,
Much castigation, exercise devout,
40 For here's a young and sweating devil here
That commonly rebels. 'Tis a good hand,
A frank° one.   (sexually) open
DESDEMONA   You may indeed say so,
For 'twas that hand that gave away my heart.
OTHELLO   A liberal hand. The hearts of old gave hands,
45 But our new heraldry is hands, not hearts.[3]
DESDEMONA   I cannot speak of this. Come now, your promise.
OTHELLO   What promise, chuck?°   woodchuck (affectionate)
DESDEMONA   I have sent to bid Cassio come speak with you.
OTHELLO   I have a salt and sorry rheum° offends me.   badly watering eyes
Lend me thy handkerchief.
50 DESDEMONA [*offering a handkerchief*]   Here, my lord.
OTHELLO   That which I gave you.
DESDEMONA   I have it not about me.
OTHELLO   Not?
DESDEMONA   No, faith, my lord.
OTHELLO   That's a fault. That handkerchief
Did an Egyptian to my mother give.
55 She was a charmer,° and could almost read   sorceress
The thoughts of people. She told her, while she kept it
'Twould make her amiable,° and subdue my father   desirable
Entirely to her love; but if she lost it,
Or made a gift of it, my father's eye
60 Should hold her loathèd, and his spirits should hunt
After new fancies. She, dying, gave it me,
And bid me, when my fate would have me wived,
To give it her.° I did so, and take heed on't.   to my wife
Make it a darling, like your precious eye.
65 To lose't or give't away were such perdition°   loss; damnation
As nothing else could match.
DESDEMONA   Is't possible?
OTHELLO   'Tis true. There's magic in the web of it.
A sibyl° that had numbered in the world   female prophet
The sun to course two hundred compasses[4]
70 In her prophetic fury sewed the work.
The worms were hallowed that did breed the silk,
And it was dyed in mummy,[5] which the skilful
Conserved of° maidens' hearts.   Preserved out of
DESDEMONA   I'faith, is't true?

2. This demonstrates fertility (perhaps, by implication, lust) and a generous (loose) heart. A moist hand was thought to be a sign of active desire.
3. These days the joining of hands doesn't signify the joining of hearts.
4. *that . . . compasses*: who was two hundred years old.
5. Fluid drained from mummified bodies, supposedly magical.

OTHELLO Most veritable. Therefore look to't well.

75 DESDEMONA Then would to God that I had never seen it!

OTHELLO Ha, wherefore?

DESDEMONA Why do you speak so startingly and rash?

OTHELLO Is't lost? Is't gone? Speak, is't out o'th' way?

DESDEMONA Heaven bless us!

80 OTHELLO Say you?

DESDEMONA It is not lost, but what an if° it were?   *an if = if*

OTHELLO How?

DESDEMONA I say it is not lost.

OTHELLO   Fetch't, let me see't.

DESDEMONA Why, so I can, sir, but I will not now.

85   This is a trick to put me from my suit.

        Pray you let Cassio be received again.

OTHELLO Fetch me the handkerchief. My mind misgives.

DESDEMONA Come, come, you'll never meet a more sufficient° man.   *complete*

OTHELLO The handkerchief.

DESDEMONA   I pray, talk me of Cassio.

OTHELLO The handkerchief.

90 DESDEMONA   A man that all his time

        Hath founded his good fortunes on your love,

        Shared dangers with you —

OTHELLO The handkerchief.

DESDEMONA I'faith, you are to blame.

95 OTHELLO 'Swounds!   *Exit*

EMILIA Is not this man jealous?

DESDEMONA   I ne'er saw this before.

        Sure there's some wonder in this handkerchief.

        I am most unhappy in the loss of it.

EMILIA 'Tis not a year or two shows us a man.[6]

100   They are all but° stomachs, and we all but food.   *nothing but*

        They eat us hungrily, and when they are full,

        They belch us.

                Enter IAGO *and* CASSIO

                Look you, Cassio and my husband.

IAGO [*to* CASSIO] There is no other way. 'Tis she must do't,

        And lo, the happiness![7] Go and importune her.

105 DESDEMONA How now, good Cassio? What's the news with you?

CASSIO Madam, my former suit. I do beseech you

        That by your virtuous means I may again

        Exist and be a member of his love

        Whom I, with all the office of my heart,

110   Entirely honour. I would not be delayed.

        If my offence be of such mortal° kind   *deadly*

        That nor° my service past, nor present sorrows,   *neither*

        Nor purposed merit in futurity

        Can ransom me into his love again,

115   But to know so° must be my benefit.   *Even to know this*

        So° shall I clothe me in a forced content,   *If so*

        And shut° myself up in some other course   *give*

        To fortune's alms.

DESDEMONA   Alas, thrice-gentle Cassio!

---

6. Probably: It doesn't take long to see what men are   you'll rarely find a true man.
made of. Possibly: It takes a long time to know a man;   7. What a happy coincidence (seeing Desdemona).

My advocation is not now in tune.[8]
120 My lord is not my lord, nor should I know him
Were he in favour° as in humour altered.   *appearance*
So help me every spirit sanctified
As I have spoken for you all my best,
And stood within the blank of° his displeasure   *in the aim of*
125 For my free speech! You must a while be patient.
What I can do I will, and more I will
Than for myself I dare. Let that suffice you.
IAGO   Is my lord angry?
EMILIA   He went hence but now,
And certainly in strange unquietness.
130 IAGO   Can he be angry? I have seen the cannon
When it hath blown his ranks into the air,
And, like the devil, from his very arm
Puffed his own brother;[9] and is he angry?
Something of moment then. I will go meet him.
135 There's matter in't indeed, if he be angry.
DESDEMONA   I prithee do so.   *Exit* IAGO
                 Something sure of state,[1]
Either from Venice or some unhatched practice°   *unfinished plot*
Made demonstrable here in Cyprus to him,
Hath puddled his clear spirit; and in such cases
140 Men's natures wrangle with inferior things,
Though great ones are their object. 'Tis even so;
For let our finger ache and it indues°   *induces*
Our other, healthful members even to a sense
Of pain. Nay, we must think men are not gods,
145 Nor of them look for such observancy°   *careful attention*
As fits the bridal.° Beshrew me° much, Emilia,   *wedding / (mild curse)*
I was—unhandsome° warrior as I am—   *unskilled*
Arraigning his unkindness with my soul;
But now I find I had suborned the witness,
And he's indicted falsely.[2]
150 EMILIA   Pray heaven it be
State matters, as you think, and no conception
Nor no jealous toy° concerning you.   *whim*
DESDEMONA   Alas the day, I never gave him cause.
EMILIA   But jealous souls will not be answered so.
155 They are not ever jealous for the cause,
But jealous for they're jealous. It is a monster
Begot upon itself, born on itself.
DESDEMONA   Heaven keep the monster from Othello's mind.
EMILIA   Lady, amen.
160 DESDEMONA   I will go seek him. Cassio, walk here about.
If I do find him fit I'll move your suit,
And seek to effect it to my uttermost.
CASSIO   I humbly thank your ladyship.
           Exeunt DESDEMONA *and* EMILIA

---

8. My advocacy isn't working properly.
9. Blew up his own brother (and Othello wasn't angry even then).

1. Surely some official business.
2. *suborned . . . falsely:* made the witness lie and so accused Othello falsely.

Enter BIANCA[3]

BIANCA Save you,° friend Cassio.   *God save you*

CASSIO   What make° you from home?   *brings*

165   How is't with you, my most fair Bianca?

I'faith, sweet love, I was coming to your house.

BIANCA   And I was going to your lodging, Cassio.

What, keep a week away? Seven days and nights,

Eightscore-eight hours, and lovers' absent hours

170   More tedious than the dial eightscore times![4]

O weary reckoning!°   *calculating*

CASSIO   Pardon me, Bianca,

I have this while with leaden thoughts been pressed,

But I shall in a more continuate° time   *opportune*

Strike off° this score of absence. Sweet Bianca,   *Make up*

Take me this work out.°   *Copy this embroidery*

[*He gives her Desdemona's napkin*]

175 BIANCA   O Cassio, whence came this?

This is some token from a newer friend.

To the felt absence now I feel a cause.

Is't come to this? Well, well.

CASSIO   Go to,° woman.   *Stop it*

Throw your vile guesses in the devil's teeth,

180   From whence you have them. You are jealous now

That this is from some mistress, some remembrance.

No, by my faith, Bianca.

BIANCA   Why, whose is it?

CASSIO   I know not, neither. I found it in my chamber.

I like the work well. Ere it be demanded°—   *sought out*

185   As like° enough it will—I would have it copied.   *likely*

Take it, and do't, and leave me for this time.

BIANCA   Leave you? Wherefore?

CASSIO   I do attend here on the general,

And think it no addition,° nor my wish,   *(to my cause)*

To have him see me womaned.

190 BIANCA   Why, I pray you?

CASSIO   Not that I love you not.

BIANCA   But that you do not love me.

I pray you bring me on the way a little,

And say if I shall see you soon at night.

CASSIO   'Tis but a little way that I can bring you,

195   For I attend here; but I'll see you soon.

BIANCA   'Tis very good. I must be circumstanced.[5]

Exeunt

4.1

Enter IAGO *and* OTHELLO

IAGO   Will you think so?

OTHELLO   Think so, Iago?

IAGO   What, to kiss in private?

OTHELLO   An unauthorized kiss.

---

3. "Bianca" means "white" in Italian—perhaps part of the play's ironic reversal of conventional color imagery, given that Bianca is a "customer" (courtesan, 4.1.117). But Bianca is shabbily treated by Cassio and Iago, and so Emilia's critique of the sexual double standard (4.3.82–

101) may be relevant.
4. *lovers' . . . times:* each hour lovers are parted is eight score (160) times more tedious than normal clock time.
5. Content with what circumstances offer.
4.1 Location: Before the citadel.

IAGO Or to be naked with her friend in bed
    An hour or more, not meaning any harm?
5 OTHELLO Naked in bed, Iago, and not mean harm?
    It is hypocrisy against the devil.[1]
    They that mean virtuously and yet do so,
    The devil their virtue tempts, and they tempt heaven.[2]
IAGO If they do nothing, 'tis a venial slip.°   *an excusable sin*
10   But if I give my wife a handkerchief—
OTHELLO What then?
IAGO Why then, 'tis hers, my lord, and being hers,
    She may, I think, bestow't on any man.
OTHELLO She is protectress of her honour, too.
15   May she give that?
IAGO Her honour is an essence that's not seen.
    They° have it very oft that have it not.   *They are reputed to*
    But for the handkerchief—
OTHELLO By heaven, I would most gladly have forgot it.
20   Thou said'st—O, it comes o'er my memory
    As doth the raven o'er the infectious house,[3]
    Boding to all!—he had my handkerchief.
IAGO Ay, what of that?
OTHELLO   That's not so good now.
IAGO What if I had said I had seen him do you wrong,
25   Or heard him say—as knaves be such abroad,[4]
    Who having by their own importunate suit
    Or voluntary dotage of some mistress
    Convincèd or supplied° them, cannot choose   *Seduced or satisfied*
    But they must blab—
OTHELLO   Hath he said anything?
30 IAGO He hath, my lord. But, be you well assured,
    No more than he'll unswear.
OTHELLO   What hath he said?
IAGO Faith, that he did—I know not what he did.
OTHELLO What, what?
IAGO   Lie—
OTHELLO   With her?
IAGO   With her, on her, what
    you will.
OTHELLO Lie with her? Lie on her? We say 'lie on her' when
35   they belie° her. Lie with her? 'Swounds, that's fulsome!° *slander / nauseating*
    Handkerchief—confessions—hankerchief. To[5] confess and be
    hanged for his labour. First to be hanged and then to confess!
    I tremble at it. Nature would not invest herself in such shadow-
    ing passion without some instruction.[6] It is not words that
40   shakes me thus. Pish! Noses, ears, and lips! Is't possible? Con-
    fess? Handkerchief? O devil!
        He falls down in a trance

---

1. *Naked . . . devil:* By showing every sign of committing adultery but then stopping just in time, they deliberately mislead the devil, who wrongly takes their apparent intention to sin at face value (just as an ordinary hypocrite deceives by professing virtue).
2. *They . . . heaven:* Those who mean well ("virtuously") but act in this lascivious fashion ("so") make it easy for the devil successfully to tempt them, and they push heaven to the point where it may not be able to forgive them (?).
3. The raven was thought to be an ill omen and a carrier of plague. *infectious:* plague-infested.
4. As such knaves do exist in the world.
5. Lines 36–41 do not appear in Q. Arguably, these lines provide more time for Othello to drive himself to distraction and hence make his collapse more plausible.
6. *Nature . . . instruction:* It isn't natural that I would feel such overwhelming ("shadowing") emotion (jealousy) unless there were some cause for it.

IAGO Work on; my medicine works. Thus credulous fools are caught,
And many worthy and chaste dames even thus,
All guiltless, meet reproach. What ho, my lord!
My lord, I say. Othello!
    Enter CASSIO

45   How now, Cassio?
CASSIO What's the matter?
IAGO My lord is fall'n into an epilepsy.
This is his second fit. He had one yesterday.
CASSIO Rub him about the temples.
IAGO   No, forbear.
50   The lethargy° must have his° quiet course.   *trance / its*
If not, he foams at mouth, and by and by
Breaks out to savage madness. Look, he stirs.
Do you withdraw yourself a little while,
He will recover straight.° When he is gone   *immediately*
55   I would on great occasion° speak with you.   [*Exit* CASSIO]   *important matters*
How is it, general? Have you not hurt your head?[7]
OTHELLO Dost thou mock me?
IAGO   I mock you not, by heaven.
Would you would bear your fortune like a man.
OTHELLO A hornèd man's a monster and a beast.
60   IAGO There's many a beast then in a populous city,
And many a civil° monster.   *city-dwelling*
OTHELLO Did he confess it?
IAGO Good sir, be a man.
Think every bearded fellow that's but yoked
65   May draw with you.[8] There's millions now alive
That nightly lie in those unproper beds
Which they dare swear peculiar.[9] Your case is better.
O, 'tis the spite of hell, the fiend's arch-mock,°   *devil's greatest mock*
To lip° a wanton in a secure° couch   *kiss / an unsuspected*
70   And to suppose her chaste! No, let me know,
And knowing what I am,° I know what she shall be.   *(a cuckold)*
OTHELLO O, thou art wise, 'tis certain.
IAGO   Stand you a while apart.
Confine yourself but in a patient list.°   *boundary*
Whilst you were here, o'erwhelmèd with your grief—
75   A passion most unsuiting such a man—
Cassio came hither. I shifted him away,
And laid good 'scuse upon your ecstasy,°   *for your fit*
Bade him anon return and here speak with me,
The which he promised. Do but encave° yourself,   *hide*
80   And mark the fleers,° the gibes and notable scorns   *sneers*
That dwell in every region of his face.
For I will make him tell the tale anew,
Where, how, how oft, how long ago, and when
He hath and is again to cope° your wife.   *copulate with*
85   I say, but mark his gesture. Marry, patience,
Or I shall say you're all-in-all in spleen,°   *completely impulsive*
And nothing of a man.

---

7. Othello takes this as suggesting that he has grown cuckold's horns.
8. *every . . . you:* every married man ("yoked," like an ox, to his wife and hence to cuckoldry) labors ("draws")

under the same fate.
9. *That . . . peculiar:* Who lie in beds that don't belong entirely to them but that they would swear are exclusively their own.

OTHELLO   Dost thou hear, Iago?
I will be found most cunning in my patience,
But—dost thou hear?—most bloody.
IAGO   That's not amiss,
90   But yet keep time° in all. Will you withdraw?   *maintain control*
        [OTHELLO *stands apart*]
Now will I question Cassio of Bianca,
A hussy that by selling her desires
Buys herself bread and cloth. It is a creature
That dotes on Cassio—as 'tis the strumpet's plague
95   To beguile many and be beguiled by one.
He, when he hears of her, cannot restrain
From the excess of laughter.
        Enter CASSIO
                          Here he comes.
As he shall smile, Othello shall go mad;
And his unbookish° jealousy must conster°   *ignorant / construe*
100   Poor Cassio's smiles, gestures, and light behaviours
Quite in the wrong. How do you now, lieutenant?
CASSIO   The worser that you give me the addition
Whose want even kills me.
IAGO   Ply Desdemona well and you are sure on't.
105   Now, if this suit lay in Bianca's power,
How quickly should you speed!
CASSIO [*laughing*]   Alas, poor caitiff!°   *wretch*
OTHELLO [*aside*]   Look how he laughs already.
IAGO   I never knew a woman love man so.
110   CASSIO   Alas, poor rogue! I think i'faith she loves me.
OTHELLO [*aside*]   Now he denies it faintly, and laughs it out.
IAGO   Do you hear, Cassio?
OTHELLO [*aside*]   Now he importunes him
To tell it o'er. Go to, well said, well said.
IAGO   She gives it out that you shall marry her.
Do you intend it?
115   CASSIO   Ha, ha, ha!
OTHELLO [*aside*]   Do ye triumph, Roman,¹ do you triumph?
CASSIO   I marry! What, a customer?° Prithee, bear some charity   *courtesan*
to my wit°— do not think it so unwholesome. Ha, ha, ha!   *sense*
OTHELLO [*aside*]   So, so, so, so. They laugh that wins.
120   IAGO   Faith, the cry goes that you marry her.
CASSIO   Prithee, say true.
IAGO   I am a very villain else.°   *if it's not true*
OTHELLO [*aside*]   Ha' you scored° me? Well.   *scored off*
CASSIO   This is the monkey's own giving out.°   She is persuaded   *Bianca's own story*
125   I will marry her out of her own love and flattery, not out of my
promise.
OTHELLO [*aside*]   Iago beckons me. Now he begins the story.
        [OTHELLO *draws closer*]
CASSIO   She was here even now. She haunts me in every place.
I was the other day talking on the sea-bank with certain Vene-
130   tians, and thither comes the bauble,° and falls me thus about   *toy*
my neck.

---

1. Perhaps Othello draws on associations either with Rome's imperial successes (and subsequent collapse) or with the Roman practice of holding celebratory processions.

OTHELLO [*aside*]   Crying 'O dear Cassio!' as it were. His gesture
imports° it.   indicates

CASSIO   So hangs and lolls and weeps upon me, so shakes and
135   pulls me—ha, ha, ha!

OTHELLO [*aside*]   Now he tells how she plucked him to my
chamber. O, I see that nose of yours, but not that dog I shall
throw it to!²

CASSIO   Well, I must leave her company.
      Enter BIANCA

140   IAGO   Before me, look where she comes.

CASSIO   'Tis such another fitchew!³ Marry, a perfumed one. [*To*
BIANCA] What do you mean by this haunting of me?

BIANCA   Let the devil and his dam° haunt you. What did you   mother
mean by that same handkerchief you gave me even now? I was
145   a fine fool to take it. I must take out° the whole work—a likely   copy
piece of work,° that you should find it in your chamber and   an implausible story
know not who left it there. This is some minx's token, and I
must take out the work. There, give it your hobby-horse.° [*Giv-*   loose woman
ing CASSIO *the napkin*] Wheresoever you had it, I'll take out
150   no work on't.

CASSIO   How now, my sweet Bianca, how now, how now?

OTHELLO [*aside*]   By heaven, that should° be my handkerchief.   must

BIANCA   An° you'll come to supper tonight, you may. An you will   If
not, come when you are next prepared for.⁴   *Exit*

155   IAGO   After her, after her.

CASSIO   Faith, I must, she'll rail in the streets else.

IAGO   Will you sup there?

CASSIO   Faith, I intend so.

IAGO   Well, I may chance to see you, for I would very fain speak
160   with you.

CASSIO   Prithee, come, will you?

IAGO   Go to, say no more.   *Exit* CASSIO

OTHELLO   How shall I murder him, Iago?

IAGO   Did you perceive how he laughed at his vice?

165   OTHELLO   O Iago!

IAGO   And did you see the handkerchief?

OTHELLO   Was that mine?

IAGO   Yours, by this hand. And to see how he prizes the foolish
woman your wife. She gave it him, and he hath given it his
170   whore.

OTHELLO   I would have him nine years a-killing.⁵ A fine woman,
a fair woman, a sweet woman.

IAGO   Nay, you must forget that.

OTHELLO   Ay, let her rot and perish, and be damned tonight, for
175   she shall not live. No, my heart is turned to stone; I strike it,
and it hurts my hand. O, the world hath not a sweeter creature!
She might lie by an emperor's side, and command him tasks.

IAGO   Nay, that's not your way.°   (the way to think)

OTHELLO   Hang her, I do but say what she is—so delicate with
180   her needle, an admirable musician. O, she will sing the savageness out of a bear! Of so high and plenteous wit and invention.°   imagination

---

2. *I see . . . to:* I'm envisioning my revenge, but the time
is not yet quite right. Cutting off the enemy's nose was
understood as a form of retribution.
3. Polecat, associated with prostitutes because of its bad

smell and presumed lecherousness.
4. Come next time I prepare for you (never).
5. I would spend nine years killing him.

IAGO   She's the worse for all this.

OTHELLO   O, a thousand, a thousand times! And then of so gen-
tle° a condition.   *highly born*

185   IAGO   Ay, too gentle.°   *generous (sexually)*

OTHELLO   Nay, that's certain. But yet the pity of it, Iago. O, Iago,
the pity of it, Iago!

IAGO   If you are so fond° over her iniquity, give her patent° to   *foolish / license*
offend; for if it touch not you, it comes near nobody.

190   OTHELLO   I will chop her into messes.° Cuckold me!   *pieces of food*

IAGO   O, 'tis foul in her.

OTHELLO   With mine officer.

IAGO   That's fouler.

OTHELLO   Get me some poison, Iago, this night. I'll not expostu-

195   late with her, lest her body and beauty unprovide my mind°   *weaken my resolve*
again. This night, Iago.

IAGO   Do it not with poison. Strangle her in her bed, even the
bed she hath contaminated.

OTHELLO   Good, good, the justice of it pleases, very good.

200   IAGO   And for Cassio, let me be his undertaker.° You shall hear   *murderer*
more by midnight.

OTHELLO   Excellent good.

        A trumpet

What trumpet is that same?

IAGO   I warrant, something from Venice.

        Enter LODOVICO, DESDEMONA, *and attendants*

205   'Tis Lodovico. This comes from the Duke. See, your wife's with
him.

LODOVICO   God save the worthy general.

OTHELLO   With all my heart,° sir.   *Thank you*

LODOVICO [*giving* OTHELLO *a letter*]   The Duke and the senators

210   of Venice greet you.

OTHELLO   I kiss the instrument° of their pleasures.°   *bearer / commands*

        [*He reads the letter*]

DESDEMONA   And what's the news, good cousin Lodovico?

IAGO [*to* LODOVICO]   I am very glad to see you, signor. Welcome
to Cyprus.

215   LODOVICO   I thank you. How does Lieutenant Cassio?

IAGO   Lives, sir.

DESDEMONA   Cousin, there's fall'n between him and my lord
An unkind° breach. But you shall make all well.   *unnatural*

OTHELLO   Are you sure of that?

220   DESDEMONA   My lord.

OTHELLO [*reads*]   'This fail you not to do as you will'—

LODOVICO   He did not call, he's busy in the paper.
Is there division 'twixt my lord and Cassio?

DESDEMONA   A most unhappy one. I would do much

225   T'atone° them, for the love I bear to Cassio.   *To reconcile*

OTHELLO   Fire and brimstone!

DESDEMONA   My lord?

OTHELLO   Are you wise?

DESDEMONA   What, is he angry?

LODOVICO   Maybe the letter moved him,
For, as I think, they do command him home,
Deputing Cassio in his government.°   *official position*

230   DESDEMONA   By my troth, I am glad on't.

OTHELLO   Indeed!
DESDEMONA   My lord?
OTHELLO [*to* DESDEMONA]   I am glad to see you mad.[6]
DESDEMONA   Why, sweet Othello!
235 OTHELLO   Devil!
           [*He strikes her*]
DESDEMONA   I have not deserved this.
LODOVICO   My lord, this would not be believed in Venice,
    Though I should swear I saw't. 'Tis very much.°   *going too far*
    Make her amends, she weeps.
OTHELLO   O, devil, devil!
240 If that the earth could teem with° woman's tears,   *become pregnant by*
    Each drop she falls would prove a crocodile.[7]
    Out of my sight!
DESDEMONA [*going*]   I will not stay to offend you.
LODOVICO   Truly, an obedient lady.
    I do beseech your lordship call her back.
245 OTHELLO   Mistress!
DESDEMONA [*returning*]   My lord?
OTHELLO [*to* LODOVICO]   What would you° with her, sir?   *do you wish*
LODOVICO   Who, I, my lord?
OTHELLO   Ay, you did wish that I would make her turn.°   *return*
250 Sir, she can turn and turn,° and yet go on   *(sexually)*
    And turn again, and she can weep, sir, weep,
    And she's obedient, as you say, obedient,
    Very obedient. [*To* DESDEMONA] Proceed you in your tears.
    [*To* LODOVICO] Concerning this, sir—[*To* DESDEMONA] O well
        painted passion!
    [*To* LODOVICO] I am commanded home. [*To* DESDEMONA] Get
255   you away.
    I'll send for you anon. [*To* LODOVICO] Sir, I obey the mandate,
    And will return to Venice. [*To* DESDEMONA] Hence, avaunt!°   *begone*
                                          [*Exit* DESDEMONA]
    [*To* LODOVICO] Cassio shall have my place, and, sir, tonight
    I do entreat that we may sup together.
260 You are welcome, sir, to Cyprus. Goats and monkeys![8]   *Exit*
LODOVICO   Is this the noble Moor whom our full senate
    Call all-in-all sufficient? Is this the nature
    Whom passion could not shake, whose solid virtue
    The shot of accident nor dart of chance
    Could neither graze nor pierce?
265 IAGO   He is much changed.
LODOVICO   Are his wits safe? Is he not light of brain?
IAGO   He's that he is. I may not breathe my censure
    What he might be. If what he might he is not,
    I would to heaven he were.[9]
LODOVICO   What, strike his wife!
270 IAGO   Faith, that was not so well. Yet would I knew

---

6. Perhaps Othello is pleased that she's rejoicing in Cas-sio's promotion and hence revealing their adulterous affair, which she would be "mad" to do in public and in front of him.
7. Each drop would cause the earth to conceive a croco-dile (crocodiles proverbially wept false tears for their vic-tims). The imagery of maternity ("teem with") and the idea of deception denote sexual betrayal. Maternity gener-ally carries negative connotations in the play.
8. Symbols of lust. Othello picks up the animal imagery Iago earlier used to express sexual loathing (3.3.408).
9. *I may . . . were*: I won't express my judgment on whether he is sane. If he is sane, I wish he were insane (because only that would excuse his bad behavior); if he is not sane, I wish he were.

That stroke would prove the worst.

LODOVICO   Is it his use,°   *custom*
  Or did the letters work upon his blood°   *passions*
  And new-create his fault?

IAGO   Alas, alas.
  It is not honesty in me to speak
275   What I have seen and known. You shall observe him,
  And his own courses° will denote him so   *actions*
  That I may save my speech. Do but go after,
  And mark how he continues.

LODOVICO   I am sorry that I am deceived in him.   *Exeunt*

4.2

Enter OTHELLO *and* EMILIA

OTHELLO   You have seen nothing then?

EMILIA   Nor ever heard, nor ever did suspect.

OTHELLO   Yes, you have seen Cassio and she together.

EMILIA   But then I saw no harm, and then I heard
5   Each syllable that breath made up between 'em.

OTHELLO   What, did they never whisper?

EMILIA   Never, my lord.

OTHELLO   Nor send you out o'th' way?

EMILIA   Never.

10 OTHELLO   To fetch her fan, her gloves, her mask, nor nothing?

EMILIA   Never, my lord.

OTHELLO   That's strange.

EMILIA   I durst, my lord, to wager she is honest,
  Lay down my soul at stake. If you think other,
15   Remove your thought; it doth abuse your bosom.
  If any wretch ha' put this in your head,
  Let heaven requite it with the serpent's curse,[1]
  For if she be not honest, chaste, and true,
  There's no man happy; the purest of their wives
  Is foul as slander.

20 OTHELLO   Bid her come hither. Go.   *Exit* EMILIA
  She says enough, yet she's a simple bawd
  That cannot say as much.[2] This is a subtle whore,
  A closet lock and key° of villainous secrets,   *A hider*
  And yet she'll kneel and pray—I ha' seen her do't.

Enter DESDEMONA *and* EMILIA

DESDEMONA   My lord, what is your will?

25 OTHELLO   Pray you, chuck, come hither.

DESDEMONA   What is your pleasure?

OTHELLO   Let me see your eyes.
  Look in my face.

DESDEMONA   What horrible fancy's this?

OTHELLO [*to* EMILIA]   Some of your function,[3] mistress.
30   Leave procreants° alone, and shut the door,   *copulators*
  Cough or cry 'Hem' if anybody come.
  Your mystery, your mystery°—nay, dispatch.   *Exit* EMILIA   *profession*

DESDEMONA   Upon my knees, what doth your speech import?

4.2 Location: The citadel.
1. The curse that God laid on the serpent in Genesis who deceived Eve.

2. *yet . . . much*: yet it would be a simpleminded go-between who can't say as much as she did.
3. Fulfill your bawd's function by guarding the door.

I understand a fury in your words,
But not the words.

35 OTHELLO   Why, what art thou?

DESDEMONA   Your wife, my lord, your true and loyal wife.

OTHELLO   Come, swear it, damn thyself,
Lest, being° like one of heaven, the devils themselves   *appearing*
Should fear to seize thee. Therefore be double-damned:
Swear thou art honest.

40 DESDEMONA   Heaven doth truly know it.

OTHELLO   Heaven truly knows that thou art false as hell.

DESDEMONA   To whom, my lord? With whom? How am I false?

OTHELLO [*weeping*]   Ah, Desdemon, away, away, away!

DESDEMONA   Alas, the heavy day! Why do you weep?
45 Am I the motive of these tears, my lord?
If haply° you my father do suspect   *perhaps*
An instrument of this your calling back,
Lay not your blame on me. If you have lost him,
I have lost him too.

OTHELLO   Had it pleased God
50 To try me with affliction; had He rained
All kind of sores and shames on my bare head,
Steeped me in poverty to the very lips,
Given to captivity me and my utmost hopes,
I should have found in some place of my soul
55 A drop of patience. But, alas, to make me
The fixèd figure for the time of scorn
To point his slow and moving finger at[4]—
Yet could I bear that too, well, very well.
But there where I have garnered° up my heart,   *stored*
60 Where either I must live or bear no life,
The fountain[5] from the which my current runs
Or else dries up—to be discarded thence,
Or keep it as a cistern for foul toads
To knot and gender° in! Turn thy complexion there,   *To couple and engender*
65 Patience,[6] thou young and rose-lipped cherubin,
Ay, here look grim as hell.

DESDEMONA   I hope my noble lord esteems me honest.

OTHELLO   O, ay—as summer flies are in the shambles,°   *slaughterhouse*
That quicken even with blowing.[7] O thou weed,
70 Who art so lovely fair, and smell'st so sweet,
That the sense aches at thee—would thou hadst ne'er been born!

DESDEMONA   Alas, what ignorant sin have I committed?

OTHELLO   Was this fair paper, this most goodly book,
Made to write 'whore' upon? What committed?
75 Committed?[8] O thou public commoner,°   *prostitute*
I should make very forges of my cheeks,
That would to cinders burn up modesty,
Did I but speak thy deeds. What committed?

---

4. *The fixed . . . at*: The designated object of scorn for this scornful time to point (as on a clock face) its slowly moving hand at.
5. Spring. The language here imagines Desdemona as the source of Othello's potential offspring.
6. *Turn . . . / Patience*: Change color at the thought of that, Patience. Or perhaps Patience and the "cherubin"

(end of line) are Desdemona, whom Othello directs to gaze at his own face or a mirror.
7. Who come to life (or bring their offspring to life and hence make the meat foul) as soon as the eggs are deposited. The point seems to be the speed of breeding, inferred from Desdemona's supposed infidelity.
8. Lines 75–78 do not appear in Q.

Heaven stops the nose at it, and the moon winks;°   *closes its eyes*
80   The bawdy° wind, that kisses all it meets,   *promiscuous*
   Is hushed within the hollow mine of earth°   *within a cave*
   And will not hear't. What committed?
DESDEMONA   By heaven, you do me wrong.
OTHELLO   Are not you a strumpet?
85   DESDEMONA   No, as I am a Christian.
   If to preserve this vessel for my lord
   From any other foul unlawful touch
   Be not to be a strumpet, I am none.
OTHELLO   What, not a whore?
DESDEMONA   No, as I shall be saved.
90   OTHELLO   Is't possible?
DESDEMONA   O heaven forgive us!
OTHELLO   I cry you mercy° then.   *I beg your pardon*
   I took you for that cunning whore of Venice
   That married with Othello. [*Calling*] You, mistress,
95   That have the office opposite to Saint Peter
   And keeps the gate of hell,
      Enter EMILIA
               you, you, ay, you.
   We ha' done our course.° [*Giving money*] There's money for your pains.   *business*
   I pray you, turn the key and keep our counsel.   *Exit*
EMILIA   Alas, what does this gentleman conceive?°   *believe*
100   How do you, madam? How do you, my good lady?
DESDEMONA   Faith, half asleep.
EMILIA   Good madam, what's the matter with my lord?
DESDEMONA   With who?
EMILIA   Why, with my lord, madam.
DESDEMONA   Who is thy lord?
EMILIA   He that is yours, sweet lady.
105   DESDEMONA   I ha' none. Do not talk to me, Emilia.
   I cannot weep, nor answers have I none
   But what should go by water.° Prithee tonight   *appear in tears*
   Lay on my bed my wedding sheets, remember.
   And call thy husband hither.
EMILIA   Here's a change indeed.   *Exit*
110   DESDEMONA   'Tis meet° I should be used so, very meet.   *fitting*
   How have I been behaved, that he might stick
   The small'st opinion on my least misuse?[9]
      Enter IAGO *and* EMILIA
IAGO   What is your pleasure, madam? How is't with you?
DESDEMONA   I cannot tell. Those that do teach young babes
115   Do it with gentle means and easy tasks.
   He might ha' chid me so, for, in good faith,
   I am a child to chiding.
IAGO   What is the matter, lady?
EMILIA   Alas, Iago, my lord hath so bewhored her,°   *called her whore*
   Thrown such despite° and heavy terms upon her,   *spite*
120   That true hearts cannot bear it.
DESDEMONA   Am I that name, Iago?
IAGO   What name, fair lady?
DESDEMONA   Such as she said my lord did say I was.

9. *that . . . misuse:* perhaps, which would cause him to suspect even slightly the least fault.

EMILIA   He called her whore. A beggar in his drink
125   Could not have laid such terms upon his callet.°   *whore*
IAGO   Why did he so?
DESDEMONA   I do not know. I am sure I am none such.
IAGO   Do not weep, do not weep. Alas the day!
EMILIA   Hath she forsook so many noble matches,
130   Her father and her country and her friends,
        To be called whore? Would it not make one weep?
DESDEMONA   It is my wretched fortune.
IAGO   Beshrew° him for't.   *Curse*
        How comes this trick° upon him?   *behavior*
DESDEMONA   Nay, heaven doth know.
EMILIA   I will be hanged if some eternal villain,
135   Some busy° and insinuating rogue,   *meddling*
        Some cogging,° cozening° slave, to get some office,   *deceiving / cheating*
        Have not devised this slander. I will be hanged else.
IAGO   Fie, there is no such man. It is impossible.
DESDEMONA   If any such there be, heaven pardon him.
140   EMILIA   A halter° pardon him, and hell gnaw his bones!   *hangman's noose*
        Why should he call her whore? Who keeps her company?
        What place, what time, what form, what likelihood?
        The Moor's abused by some most villainous knave,
        Some base, notorious knave, some scurvy fellow.
145   O heaven, that such companions thou'dst unfold,°   *reveal*
        And put in every honest hand a whip
        To lash the rascals naked through the world,
        Even from the east to th' west!
IAGO   Speak within door.°   *more softly*
EMILIA   O, fie upon them. Some such squire° he was   *fellow*
150   That turned your wit the seamy side without,°   *wrong side out*
        And made you to suspect me with the Moor.
IAGO   You are a fool. Go to.
DESDEMONA   O God, Iago,
        What shall I do to win my lord again?
        Good friend, go to him; for by this light of heaven,
        I know not how I lost him.
        [*She kneels*]
155   Here I kneel.¹
        If e'er my will did trespass 'gainst his love,
        Either in discourse of thought or actual deed,
        Or that mine eyes, mine ears, or any sense
        Delighted them in any other form,²
160   Or that I do not yet,° and ever did,   *still*
        And ever will—though he do shake me off
        To beggarly divorcement—love him dearly,
        Comfort forswear me.° Unkindness may do much,   *Deny me divine solace*
        And his unkindness may defeat my life,
        But never taint my love.
        [*She rises*]
165   I cannot say 'whore'.
        It does abhor me³ now I speak the word.

1. Lines 155–68 (beginning with "Here") do not appear   3. Fill me with abhorrence, perhaps with a pun on "ab-
in Q.   whore," make me whorelike (to speak the word).
2. Took pleasure in anyone but him.

To do the act that might the addition° earn,   *label*
Not the world's mass of vanity° could make me.   *all worldly splendor*
IAGO   I pray you, be content. 'Tis but his humour.°   *mood*
170   The business of the state does him offence,
And he does chide with you.
DESDEMONA   If 'twere no other!
IAGO   It is but so, I warrant.
            [*Flourish within*]
Hark how these instruments summon you to supper.
175   The messengers of Venice stays the meat.°   *are waiting to eat*
Go in, and weep not. All things shall be well.
                                              Exeunt DESDEMONA *and* EMILIA
      Enter RODERIGO
How now, Roderigo?
RODERIGO   I do not find that thou deal'st justly with me.
IAGO   What in the contrary?
180   RODERIGO   Every day thou daff'st me with some device,[4] Iago,
      and rather, as it seems to me now, keep'st from me all conve-
      niency° than suppliest me with the least advantage of hope. I   *opportunity*
      will indeed no longer endure it, nor am I yet persuaded to put
      up in peace what already I have foolishly suffered.
185   IAGO   Will you hear me, Roderigo?
RODERIGO   Faith, I have heard too much, for your words and
      performances are no kin together.
IAGO   You charge me most unjustly.
RODERIGO   With naught but truth. I have wasted myself out of
190   my means. The jewels you have had from me to deliver Desde-
      mona would half have corrupted a votarist.° You have told me   *nun*
      she hath received 'em, and returned me expectations and com-
      forts of sudden respect and acquaintance, but I find none.
IAGO   Well, go to,° very well.   *be patient*
195   RODERIGO   'Very well', 'go to'! I cannot go to,° man, nor 'tis not   *succeed in wooing*
      very well. Nay, I think it is scurvy, and begin to find myself
      fopped° in it.   *made a fool*
IAGO   Very well.
RODERIGO   I tell you 'tis not very well. I will make myself known
200   to Desdemona. If she will return me my jewels, I will give
      over my suit and repent my unlawful solicitation. If not, assure
      yourself I will seek satisfaction of you.
IAGO   You have said° now.   *finished*
RODERIGO   Ay, and said nothing but what I protest intendment
205   of doing.
IAGO   Why, now I see there's mettle in thee, and even from this
      instant do build on thee a better opinion than ever before. Give
      me thy hand, Roderigo. Thou hast taken against me a most just
      exception, but yet I protest I have dealt most directly in thy
210   affair.
RODERIGO   It hath not appeared.
IAGO   I grant, indeed, it hath not appeared, and your suspicion
      is not without wit and judgement. But, Roderigo, if thou hast
      that in thee indeed which I have greater reason to believe now
215   than ever—I mean purpose, courage, and valour—this night
      show it. If thou the next night following enjoy not Desdemona,

4. You put me off with some trick.

take me from this world with treachery, and devise engines for°
   my life.   *plots against*

RODERIGO   Well, what is it? Is it within reason and compass?°   *possibility*

220 IAGO   Sir, there is especial commission come from Venice to
   depute Cassio in Othello's place.

RODERIGO   Is that true? Why then, Othello and Desdemona
   return again to Venice.

IAGO   O no, he goes into Mauritania,[5] and takes away with him
225   the fair Desdemona, unless his abode be lingered here by some
   accident, wherein none can be so determinate° as the remov-   *effectual*
   ing of Cassio.

RODERIGO   How do you mean 'removing' of him?

IAGO   Why, by making him uncapable of Othello's place—
230   knocking out his brains.

RODERIGO   And that you would have me to do.

IAGO   Ay, if you dare do yourself a profit and a right. He sups
   tonight with a harlotry, and thither will I go to him. He knows
   not yet of his honourable fortune.° If you will watch his going   *his promotion*
235   thence, which I will fashion° to fall out between twelve and   *arrange*
   one, you may take him at your pleasure. I will be near, to sec-
   ond your attempt, and he shall fall between us. Come, stand
   not amazed at it, but go along with me. I will show you such a
   necessity in his death that you shall think yourself bound to put
240   it on him. It is now high supper-time, and the night grows to
   waste. About it.

RODERIGO   I will hear further reason for this.

IAGO   And you shall be satisfied.   *Exeunt*

4.3

Enter OTHELLO, DESDEMONA, LODOVICO, EMILIA, *and
   attendants*

LODOVICO   I do beseech you, sir, trouble yourself no further.

OTHELLO   O, pardon me, 'twill do me good to walk.

LODOVICO [*to* DESDEMONA]   Madam, good night. I humbly thank
   your ladyship.

DESDEMONA   Your honour is most welcome.

OTHELLO   Will you walk, sir?
5   O, Desdemona!

DESDEMONA   My lord?

OTHELLO   Get you to bed on th'instant. I will be returned forthwith. Dismiss your attendant there. Look't be done.

DESDEMONA   I will, my lord.
                  Exeunt [OTHELLO, LODOVICO, *and attendants*]
10 EMILIA   How goes it now? He looks gentler than he did.

DESDEMONA   He says he will return incontinent.°   *immediately*
   He hath commanded me to go to bed,
   And bid me to dismiss you.

EMILIA   Dismiss me?

DESDEMONA   It was his bidding. Therefore, good Emilia,
15   Give me my nightly wearing, and adieu.
   We must not now displease him.

EMILIA   I would you had never seen him.

DESDEMONA   So would not I. My love doth so approve him

---

5. Country in the western Sahara.   4.3 Location: Scene continues.

That even his stubbornness, his checks, his frowns—
20   Prithee unpin me—have grace and favour in them.
        [EMILIA *helps* DESDEMONA *to undress*]
EMILIA   I have laid those sheets you bade me on the bed.
DESDEMONA   All's one.° Good faith, how foolish are our minds!   *It doesn't matter*
    If I do die before thee, prithee shroud me
    In one of these same sheets.
EMILIA   Come, come, you talk.
25   DESDEMONA   My mother had a maid called Barbary.[1]
    She was in love, and he she loved proved mad
    And did forsake her. She had a song of willow.
    An old thing 'twas, but it expressed her fortune,
    And she died singing it. That song tonight
30   Will not go from my mind. I[2] have much to do
    But to[3] go hang my head all at one side
    And sing it, like poor Barbary. Prithee, dispatch.
EMILIA   Shall I go fetch your nightgown?
DESDEMONA   No. Unpin me here.
    This Lodovico is a proper man.
EMILIA   A very handsome man.
35   DESDEMONA   He speaks well.
EMILIA   I know a lady in Venice would have walked barefoot to
    Palestine for a touch of his nether lip.
DESDEMONA [*sings*]   'The poor soul sat sighing by a sycamore tree,
    Sing all a green willow.[4]
40   Her hand on her bosom, her head on her knee,
    Sing willow, willow, willow.
    The fresh streams ran by her and murmured her moans,
    Sing willow, willow, willow.
    Her salt tears fell from her and softened the stones,
45   Sing willow'—
    Lay by these.—
                  'willow, willow.'
    Prithee, hie thee.° He'll come anon.   *hurry*
    'Sing all a green willow must be my garland.
50   'Let nobody blame him, his scorn I approve'—
    Nay, that's not next. Hark, who is't that knocks?
EMILIA   It's the wind.
DESDEMONA [*sings*]   'I called my love false love, but what said he then?[5]
    Sing willow, willow, willow.
55   If I court more women, you'll couch with more men.'
    So, get thee gone. Good night. Mine eyes do itch.
    Doth that bode weeping?
EMILIA   'Tis neither here nor there.
DESDEMONA   I have heard it said so. O, these men, these men![6]
    Dost thou in conscience think—tell me, Emilia—
60   That there be women do abuse their husbands
    In such gross kind?°   *fashion*
EMILIA   There be some such, no question.
DESDEMONA   Wouldst thou do such a deed for all the world?
EMILIA   Why, would not you?

---

1. Iago compares Othello to a "Barbary horse" in 1.1.113.
The reference here lends an exotic, non-European aura
to Desdemona in her victimization.
2. Lines 30–51 ("I . . . next") do not appear in Q.

3. I can barely bring myself not to.
4. A conventional symbol of disappointed love.
5. Lines 53–55 do not appear in Q.
6. Lines 58–61 do not appear in Q.

DESDEMONA   No, by this heavenly light.

EMILIA   Nor I neither, by this heavenly light. I might do't as well
65   i'th' dark.

DESDEMONA   Wouldst thou do such a deed for all the world?

EMILIA   The world's a huge thing. It is a great price for a small
vice.

DESDEMONA   In truth, I think thou wouldst not.

70   EMILIA   In truth, I think I should, and undo't when I had done.
Marry, I would not do such a thing for a joint ring,[7] nor for
measures of lawn,° nor for gowns, petticoats, nor caps, nor any   *linen*
petty exhibition;° but for all the whole world? Ud's° pity, who   *gift / God's*
would not make her husband a cuckold to make him a mon-
75   arch? I should venture purgatory for't.

DESDEMONA   Beshrew me if I would do such a wrong
For the whole world.

EMILIA   Why, the wrong is but a wrong i'th' world, and having
the world for your labour, 'tis a wrong in your own world, and
80   you might quickly make it right.

DESDEMONA   I do not think there is any such woman.

EMILIA   Yes, a dozen, and as many
To th' vantage as would store the world they played for.[8]
But I do think it is their husbands' faults[9]
85   If wives do fall. Say that they slack their duties,°   *marital duties*
And pour our treasures into foreign laps,[1]
Or else break out in peevish jealousies,
Throwing restraint upon us; or say they strike us,
Or scant our former having in despite:[2]
90   Why, we have galls;° and though we have some grace,   *tempers*
Yet have we some revenge. Let husbands know
Their wives have sense like them. They see, and smell,
And have their palates both for sweet and sour,
As husbands have. What is it that they do
95   When they change us for others? Is it sport?
I think it is. And doth affection° breed it?   *lust*
I think it doth. Is't frailty that thus errs?
It is so, too. And have not we affections,
Desires for sport, and frailty, as men have?
100   Then let them use us well, else let them know
The ills we do, their ills instruct us so.

DESDEMONA   Good night, good night. God me such uses° send   *habits*
Not to pick bad from bad, but by bad mend![3]   *Exeunt*

5.1

Enter IAGO *and* RODERIGO

IAGO   Here, stand behind this bulk.° Straight° will he come.   *shop stall / Right away*
Wear thy good rapier bare, and put it home.°   *drive it into him*
Quick, quick, fear nothing. I'll be at thy elbow.
It makes us or it mars us. Think on that,
5   And fix most firm thy resolution.

RODERIGO   Be near at hand. I may miscarry in't.

---

7. A cheap ring in separable halves.
8. *and . . . for:* and as many more as it would take to pop-
ulate the world they gained by doing it.
9. Lines 84–101 do not appear in Q.
1. And give the semen that belongs to us to other women.

2. Or reduce our allowances out of spite.
3. Not to take bad behavior as an example, but to know
what to avoid.
5.1 Location: A street in Cyprus.

IAGO   Here at thy hand. Be bold, and take thy stand.
RODERIGO [*aside*]   I have no great devotion to the deed,
    And yet he hath given me satisfying reasons.
10   'Tis but a man gone. Forth my sword—he dies!
IAGO [*aside*]   I have rubbed this young quat° almost to the sense,°   *pimple / to the quick*
    And he grows angry. Now, whether he kill Cassio
    Or Cassio him, or each do kill the other,
    Every way makes my gain. Live Roderigo,°   *If Roderigo lives*
15   He calls me to a restitution large
    Of gold and jewels that I bobbed from him°   *defrauded him of*
    As gifts to Desdemona.
    It must not be. If Cassio do remain,
    He hath a daily beauty in his life
20   That makes me ugly; and besides, the Moor
    May unfold° me to him—there stand I in much peril.   *reveal*
    No, he must die. But so, I hear him coming.
        Enter CASSIO
RODERIGO   I know his gait, 'tis he. [*Attacking* CASSIO] Villain, thou diest.
CASSIO   That thrust had been mine enemy indeed,
25   But that my coat is better° than thou know'st.   *thicker; more armored*
    I will make proof of° thine.   *test*
        [*He stabs* RODERIGO, *who falls*]
RODERIGO   O, I am slain!
        [IAGO *wounds* CASSIO *in the leg from behind. Exit* IAGO]
CASSIO [*falling*]   I am maimed for ever. Help, ho, murder, murder!
        Enter OTHELLO [*above*]
OTHELLO   The voice of Cassio. Iago keeps his word.
RODERIGO   O, villain that I am!
30   OTHELLO   It is even so.
CASSIO   O, help, ho! Light, a surgeon!
OTHELLO   'Tis he. O brave Iago, honest and just,
    That hast such noble sense of thy friend's wrong—
    Thou teachest me. Minion,° your dear lies dead,   *Hussy*
35   And your unblessed fate hies.° Strumpet, I come.   *damnation hurries on*
    Forth of° my heart those charms, thine eyes, are blotted.   *Out of*
    Thy bed, lust-stained, shall with lust's blood be spotted.   *Exit*
        Enter LODOVICO *and* GRAZIANO
CASSIO   What ho, no watch, no passage?° Murder, murder!   *passersby*
GRAZIANO   'Tis some mischance. The voice is very direful.
40   CASSIO   O, help!
LODOVICO   Hark.
RODERIGO   O wretched villain!
LODOVICO   Two or three groan. 'Tis heavy° night.   *dark*
    These may be counterfeits. Let's think't unsafe
45   To come into° the cry without more help.   *go near*
RODERIGO   Nobody come? Then shall I bleed to death.
        Enter IAGO *with a light*
LODOVICO   Hark.
GRAZIANO   Here's one comes in his shirt, with light and weapons.
IAGO   Who's there? Whose noise is this that cries on murder?
LODOVICO   We do not know.
50   IAGO   Do not you hear a cry?
CASSIO   Here, here. For heaven's sake, help me.
IAGO   What's the matter?
GRAZIANO [*to* LODOVICO]   This is Othello's ensign, as I take it.

LODOVICO   The same indeed, a very valiant fellow.

IAGO [*to* CASSIO]   What are you here that cry so grievously?

55 CASSIO   Iago—O, I am spoiled, undone by villains.
   Give me some help.

IAGO   O me, lieutenant, what villains have done this?

CASSIO   I think that one of them is hereabout
   And cannot make away.

IAGO   O treacherous villains!
   [*To* LODOVICO *and* GRAZIANO] What are you there? Come in
60   and give some help.

RODERIGO   O, help me there!

CASSIO   That's one of 'em.

IAGO [*stabbing* RODERIGO]   O murderous slave! O villain!

RODERIGO   O damned Iago! O inhuman dog!

65 IAGO   Kill men i'th' dark? Where be these bloody thieves?
   How silent is this town! Ho, murder, murder!
   [*To* LODOVICO *and* GRAZIANO] What may you be? Are you of
     good or evil?

LODOVICO   As you shall prove us, praise us.

IAGO   Signor Lodovico.

LODOVICO   He, sir.

70 IAGO   I cry you mercy. Here's Cassio hurt by villains.

GRAZIANO   Cassio?

IAGO   How is't, brother?

CASSIO   My leg is cut in two.

IAGO   Marry, heaven forbid!

75   Light, gentlemen. I'll bind it with my shirt.
            Enter BIANCA

BIANCA   What is the matter, ho? Who is't that cried?

IAGO   Who is't that cried?

BIANCA   O my dear Cassio,
   My sweet Cassio, O, Cassio, Cassio!

IAGO   O notable strumpet! Cassio, may you suspect
80   Who they should be that have thus mangled you?

CASSIO   No.

GRAZIANO   I am sorry to find you thus. I have been to seek you.

IAGO   Lend me a garter. So. O for a chair,°   litter
   To bear him easily hence!

85 BIANCA   Alas, he faints. O, Cassio, Cassio, Cassio!

IAGO   Gentlemen all, I do suspect this trash
   To be a party in this injury.
   Patience a while, good Cassio. Come, come,
   Lend me a light. [*Going to* RODERIGO] Know we this face or no?
90   Alas, my friend, and my dear countryman.
   Roderigo? No—yes, sure—O heaven, Roderigo!

GRAZIANO   What, of Venice?

IAGO   Even he, sir. Did you know him?

GRAZIANO   Know him? Ay.

95 IAGO   Signor Graziano, I cry your gentle pardon.
   These bloody accidents must excuse my manners
   That so neglected you.

GRAZIANO   I am glad to see you.

IAGO   How do you, Cassio? O, a chair, a chair!

GRAZIANO   Roderigo.

IAGO   He, he, 'tis he.

[Enter attendants with a chair]

100   O, that's well said, the chair!
     Some good man bear him carefully from hence.
     I'll fetch the general's surgeon. *[To* BIANCA*]* For you, mistress,
     Save you your labour. He that lies slain here, Cassio,
     Was my dear friend. What malice was between you?

105 CASSIO   None in the world, nor do I know the man.
     IAGO *[to* BIANCA*]*   What, look you pale? *[To attendants]* O, bear
         him out o'th' air.[1]
     [To LODOVICO *and* GRAZIANO*]* Stay you, good gentlemen.

               [Exeunt attendants with CASSIO *in the chair*
                    and with Roderigo's body]

     [To BIANCA*]*   Look you pale, mistress?
     [To LODOVICO *and* GRAZIANO*]* Do you perceive the ghastness° of her eye?   *terror*
     [To BIANCA*]* Nay, an° you stare we shall hear more anon.   *if*

110   *[To* LODOVICO *and* GRAZIANO*]* Behold her well; I pray you look upon her.
     Do you see, gentlemen? Nay, guiltiness
     Will speak, though tongues were out of use.

         Enter EMILIA

     EMILIA   Alas, what is the matter? What is the matter, husband?
     IAGO   Cassio hath here been set on in the dark

115   By Roderigo and fellows that are scaped.
     He's almost slain, and Roderigo dead.
     EMILIA   Alas, good gentleman! Alas, good Cassio!
     IAGO   This is the fruits of whoring. Prithee, Emilia,
     Go know of Cassio where he supped tonight.

120   *[To* BIANCA*]* What, do you shake at that?
     BIANCA   He supped at my house, but I therefore shake not.
     IAGO   O, did he so? I charge you go with me.
     EMILIA *[to* BIANCA*]*   O, fie upon thee, strumpet!
     BIANCA   I am no strumpet, but of life as honest
     As you that thus abuse me.

125 EMILIA   As I? Fough, fie upon thee!
     IAGO   Kind gentlemen, let's go see poor Cassio dressed.
     [To BIANCA*]* Come, mistress, you must tell's another tale.
     Emilia, run you to the citadel
     And tell my lord and lady what hath happed.
     Will you go on afore?   *[Exit* EMILIA*]*

130   *[Aside]*   This is the night
     That either makes me or fordoes° me quite.   *Exeunt*   *undoes*

5.2

Enter OTHELLO *with a light. [He draws back a curtain,*
revealing] DESDEMONA *[asleep] in her bed*

     OTHELLO   It is the cause,[1] it is the cause, my soul.
     Let me not name it to you, you chaste stars.
     It is the cause. Yet I'll not shed her blood,
     Nor scar that whiter skin of hers than snow,

5   And smooth as monumental alabaster.°   *stone used in tombs*
     Yet she must die, else she'll betray more men.
     Put out the light, and then put out the light.[2]

---

1. Out of the open air (thought to be bad for wounds).
5.2 Location: Desdemona and Othello's bedroom.
1. What matters is Desdemona's infidelity; the "cause" of
justice, which Othello sees himself defending, as in the

subsequent lines.
2. This and the following lines compare the light of
Othello's lamp or torch to Desdemona's "light" of life.

If I quench thee, thou flaming minister,°   *light that serves me*
I can again thy former light restore
Should I repent me; but once put out thy light,
Thou cunning'st pattern of excelling nature,[3]
I know not where is that Promethean heat[4]
That can thy light relume.° When I have plucked thy rose   *relight*
I cannot give it vital growth again.
It needs must wither. I'll smell thee on the tree.
    [*He kisses her*]
O balmy breath, that dost almost persuade
Justice to break her sword! One more, one more.
Be thus when thou art dead, and I will kill thee
And love thee after. One more, and that's the last.
    He kisses her
So sweet was ne'er so fatal. I must weep,
But they are cruel tears. This sorrow's heavenly,
It strikes where it doth love.[5] She wakes.
DESDEMONA   Who's there? Othello?
OTHELLO   Ay, Desdemona.
DESDEMONA   Will you come to bed, my lord?
OTHELLO   Have you prayed tonight, Desdemon?
DESDEMONA   Ay, my lord.
OTHELLO   If you bethink yourself of any crime
Unreconciled as yet to heaven and grace,
Solicit° for it straight.   *Ask forgiveness*
DESDEMONA   Alack, my lord, what may you mean by that?
OTHELLO   Well, do it, and be brief. I will walk by.
I would not kill thy unpreparèd spirit.
No, heavens forfend! I would not kill thy soul.
DESDEMONA   Talk you of killing?
OTHELLO   Ay, I do.
DESDEMONA   Then heaven
Have mercy on me.
OTHELLO   Amen, with all my heart.
DESDEMONA   If you say so, I hope you will not kill me.
OTHELLO   Hum!
DESDEMONA   And yet I fear you, for you're fatal then
When your eyes roll so. Why I should fear I know not,
Since guiltiness I know not, but yet I feel I fear.
OTHELLO   Think on thy sins.
DESDEMONA   They are loves I bear to you.[6]
OTHELLO   Ay, and for that thou diest.
DESDEMONA   That death's unnatural that kills for loving.
Alas, why gnaw you so your nether lip?
Some bloody passion shakes your very frame.
These are portents, but yet I hope, I hope
They do not point on me.
OTHELLO   Peace, and be still.
DESDEMONA   I will so. What's the matter?
OTHELLO   That handkerchief
Which I so loved and gave thee, thou gav'st to Cassio.

3. You most cleverly wrought example of nature's work.
4. Life-giving fire. In Greek myth, Prometheus stole fire from heaven to give it to humankind; in a different tradition, he is credited with animating humankind from clay.
5. See Hebrews 12:6: "For whom the Lord loveth, he chasteneth."
6. Perhaps because Desdemona loves Othello more than God.

DESDEMONA   No, by my life and soul. Send for the man
  And ask him.
OTHELLO   Sweet soul, take heed, take heed of perjury.
55   Thou art on thy deathbed.
DESDEMONA   Ay, but not yet to die.
OTHELLO   Presently.°   *Immediately*
  Therefore confess thee freely of thy sin,
  For to deny each article with oath
60   Cannot remove nor choke the strong conception
  That I do groan withal.[7] Thou art to die.
DESDEMONA   Then Lord have mercy on me.
OTHELLO   I say amen.
DESDEMONA   And have you mercy, too. I never did
  Offend you in my life, never loved Cassio
65   But with such general warranty of heaven
  As I might love. I never gave him token.
OTHELLO   By heaven, I saw my handkerchief in's hand.
  O perjured woman! Thou dost stone° my heart,   *harden*
  And makes me call what I intend to do
70   A murder, which I thought a sacrifice.
  I saw the handkerchief.
DESDEMONA   He found it, then.
  I never gave it him. Send for him hither.
  Let him confess a truth.
OTHELLO   He hath confessed.
DESDEMONA   What, my lord?
OTHELLO   That he hath usèd thee.
75   DESDEMONA   How, unlawfully?
OTHELLO   Ay.
DESDEMONA   He will not say so.
OTHELLO   No, his mouth is stopped.
  Honest Iago hath ta'en order for't.
80   DESDEMONA   O, my fear interprets! What, is he dead?
OTHELLO   Had all his hairs been lives, my great revenge
  Had stomach for 'em all.
DESDEMONA [*weeping*]   Alas, he is betrayed, and I undone.
OTHELLO   Out, strumpet! Weep'st thou for him to my face?
85   DESDEMONA   O, banish me, my lord, but kill me not.
OTHELLO [*attacking her*]   Down, strumpet.
DESDEMONA   Kill me tomorrow; let me live tonight.
OTHELLO   Nay, an you strive—
DESDEMONA   But half an hour.
90   OTHELLO   Being done, there is no pause.[8]
DESDEMONA   But while I say one prayer.
OTHELLO   It is too late.
        He smothers her
DESDEMONA   O Lord, Lord, Lord!
        EMILIA *at the door*
EMILIA (*within*)   My lord, my lord, what ho, my lord, my lord!
95   OTHELLO   What noise is this? Not dead? Not yet quite dead?
  I that am cruel am yet merciful.

---

7. *Cannot . . . withal:* Cannot stop the strong conviction
I have in your guilt (or the firm plan to kill you), which

makes me groan so. The metaphor is from childbirth.
8. Now that I've started, there's no stopping.

I would not have thee linger in thy pain.
So, so.
EMILIA [*within*]   What ho, my lord, my lord!
OTHELLO   Who's there?
EMILIA [*within*]   O, good my lord, I would speak a word with you.
OTHELLO [*calling*]   Yes. — 'Tis Emilia. [*Calling*] By
100   and by! — She's dead.
'Tis like she comes to speak of Cassio's death.
The noise was high.° Ha! No more moving.   *commotion was loud*
Still as the grave. Shall she come in? Were't good?
I think she stirs again. No. What's best to do?
105   If she come in, she'll sure speak to my wife.
My wife, my wife! What wife? I ha' no wife.
O insupportable, O heavy hour!
Methinks it should be now a huge eclipse
Of sun and moon, and that th'affrighted globe
Should yawn at alteration.⁹
110   EMILIA [*within*]   I do beseech you
That I may speak with you. O, good my lord!
OTHELLO   I had forgot thee. — O, come in, Emilia. —
Soft,° by and by. Let me the curtains draw.   *Quiet*
      [*He closes the bed-curtains*]
Where art thou?
      [*He opens the door.*] *Enter* EMILIA
                  What's the matter with thee now?
115   EMILIA   O my good lord, yonder's foul murder's done.
OTHELLO   What, now?
EMILIA   But° now, my lord.   *Just*
OTHELLO   It is the very error° of the moon,   *deviation*
She comes more nearer earth than she was wont,
120   And makes men mad.
EMILIA   Cassio, my lord, hath killed a young Venetian
Called Roderigo.
OTHELLO   Roderigo killed
And Cassio killed?
EMILIA   No, Cassio is not killed.
OTHELLO   Not Cassio killed? Then murder's out of tune,
125   And sweet revenge grows harsh.
DESDEMONA   O, falsely, falsely murdered!
EMILIA   O Lord, what cry is that?
OTHELLO   That? What?
EMILIA   Out and alas, that was my lady's voice!
      [*She opens the bed-curtains*]
130   Help, help, ho, help! O lady, speak again!
Sweet Desdemona, O sweet mistress, speak!
DESDEMONA   A guiltless death I die.
EMILIA   O, who hath done this deed?
DESDEMONA   Nobody, I myself. Farewell.
Commend me to my kind lord. O, farewell!   *She dies*
OTHELLO   Why, how should she be murdered?
135   EMILIA   Alas, who knows?
OTHELLO   You heard her say herself it was not I.
EMILIA   She said so, I must needs report the truth.

---

9. Should gape at the change. Earthquakes were associated with eclipses.

OTHELLO   She's like a liar gone to burning hell.
'Twas I that killed her.
140 EMILIA   O, the more angel she, and you the blacker devil!
OTHELLO   She turned to folly,° and she was a whore.   *wantonness*
EMILIA   Thou dost belie her, and thou art a devil.
OTHELLO   She was false as water.
EMILIA   Thou art rash as fire
To say that she was false. O, she was heavenly true!
145 OTHELLO   Cassio did top her. Ask thy husband else.°   *if you doubt it*
O, I were damned beneath all depth in hell
But that I did proceed upon just grounds
To this extremity! Thy husband knew it all.
EMILIA   My husband?
OTHELLO   Thy husband.
EMILIA   That she was false to wedlock?
150 OTHELLO   Ay, with Cassio. Had she been true,
If heaven would make me such another world
Of one entire and perfect chrysolite°   *topaz*
I'd not have sold her for it.
EMILIA   My husband?
OTHELLO   Ay, 'twas he that told me on her first.
155 An honest man he is, and hates the slime
That sticks on filthy deeds.
EMILIA   My husband?
OTHELLO   What needs this iterance?° Woman, I say thy husband.   *repetition*
EMILIA   O mistress, villainy hath made mocks with° love.[1]   *at*
My husband say she was false?
OTHELLO   He, woman.
160 I say thy husband. Dost understand the word?
My friend, thy husband, honest, honest Iago.
EMILIA   If he say so, may his pernicious soul
Rot half a grain a day. He lies to th' heart.
She was too fond of her most filthy bargain.
165 OTHELLO   Ha?
EMILIA   Do thy worst.
This deed of thine is no more worthy heaven
Than thou wast worthy her.
OTHELLO   Peace, you were best.°   *it would be best for you*
EMILIA   Thou hast not half that power to do me harm
170 As I have to be hurt. O gull,° O dolt,   *fool*
As ignorant as dirt! Thou hast done a deed —
I care not for thy sword, I'll make thee known
Though I lost twenty lives. Help, help, ho! Help!
The Moor hath killed my mistress. Murder, murder!
Enter MONTANO, GRAZIANO, *and* IAGO
175 MONTANO   What is the matter? How now, general?
EMILIA   O, are you come, Iago? You have done well,
That men must lay their murders on your neck.
GRAZIANO   What is the matter?
EMILIA [*to* IAGO]   Disprove this villain if thou beest a man.
180 He says thou told'st him that his wife was false.
I know thou didst not. Thou'rt not such a villain.
Speak, for my heart is full.

---

1. Lines 158–61 do not appear in Q.

IAGO   I told him what I thought, and told no more
    Than what he found himself was apt and true.
185 EMILIA   But did you ever tell him she was false?
IAGO   I did.
EMILIA   You told a lie, an odious, damnèd lie,
    Upon my soul a lie, a wicked lie.
    She false with Cassio? Did you say with Cassio?
190 IAGO   With Cassio, mistress. Go to, charm° your tongue.   *silence*
EMILIA   I will not charm my tongue. I am bound to speak.
    My mistress here lies murdered in her bed.[2]
MONTANO *and* GRAZIANO   O heavens forfend!
EMILIA [*to* IAGO]   And your reports have set the murder on.
195 OTHELLO   Nay, stare not, masters. It is true indeed.
GRAZIANO   'Tis a strange truth.
MONTANO   O monstrous act!
EMILIA   Villainy, villainy, villainy!
    I think upon't, I think. I smell't. O villainy!
    I thought so then. I'll kill myself for grief.
200   O villainy, villainy!
IAGO   What, are you mad? I charge you get you home.
EMILIA   Good gentlemen, let me have leave to speak.
    'Tis proper I obey him, but not now.
    Perchance, Iago, I will ne'er go home.
OTHELLO   O, O, O!
           OTHELLO *falls on the bed*
205 EMILIA   Nay, lay thee down and roar,
    For thou hast killed the sweetest innocent
    That e'er did lift up eye.°   *(to heaven)*
OTHELLO [*rising*]   O, she was foul!
    [*To* GRAZIANO] I scarce did know you, uncle. There lies your niece,
    Whose breath indeed these hands have newly stopped.
210   I know this act shows° horrible and grim.   *appears*
GRAZIANO   Poor Desdemon, I am glad thy father's dead.
    Thy match was mortal to him, and pure grief
    Shore his old thread in twain.[3] Did he live now
    This sight would make him do a desperate turn,°   *act*
215   Yea, curse his better angel from his side,
    And fall to reprobance.[4]
OTHELLO   'Tis pitiful. But yet Iago knows
    That she with Cassio hath the act of shame
    A thousand times committed. Cassio confessed it,
220   And she did gratify his amorous works
    With that recognizance° and pledge of love   *token*
    Which I first gave her. I saw it in his hand.
    It was a handkerchief, an antique token
    My father gave my mother.
EMILIA   O God! O heavenly God!
IAGO   'Swounds, hold your peace!
225 EMILIA   'Twill out, 'twill out. I peace?
    No, I will speak as liberal as the north.[5]
    Let heaven, and men, and devils, let 'em all,
    All, all cry shame against me, yet I'll speak.

---

2. Lines 192–200 do not appear in Q.
3. Cut the thread of his life.
4. Suicide, the unforgivably sinful act of despair.
5. As freely as the north wind.

IAGO   Be wise and get you home.

230   EMILIA   I will not.

> [IAGO *draws his sword*]

GRAZIANO [*to* IAGO]   Fie, your sword upon a woman?

EMILIA   O thou dull Moor, that handkerchief thou speak'st of
  I found by fortune and did give my husband,
  For often, with a solemn earnestness—
235   More than indeed belonged to such a trifle—
  He begged of me to steal't.

IAGO   Villainous whore!

EMILIA   She give it Cassio? No, alas, I found it,
  And I did give't my husband.

IAGO   Filth, thou liest.

EMILIA   By heaven I do not, I do not, gentlemen.

240   O murderous coxcomb!° What should such a fool   *fool*
  Do with so good a wife?

OTHELLO   Are there no stones° in heaven   *thunderbolts*
  But what serves for the thunder? Precious° villain!   *Absolute*

> *The Moor runs at* IAGO. [MONTANO *disarms* OTHELLO.]
> IAGO [*wounds*] *his wife*

GRAZIANO   The woman falls. Sure he hath killed his wife.

EMILIA   Ay, ay. O, lay me by my mistress' side!   *Exit* IAGO

245   GRAZIANO   He's gone, but his wife's killed.

MONTANO   'Tis a notorious villain. Take you this weapon
  Which I have here recovered from the Moor.
  Come, guard the door without. Let him not pass,
  But kill him rather. I'll after that same villain,
  For 'tis a damnèd slave.   *Exeunt* MONTANO *and* GRAZIANO

250   OTHELLO   I am not valiant neither,
  But every puny whipster° gets my sword.   *insignificant person*
  But why should honour outlive honesty?[6]
  Let it go all.

EMILIA   What did thy song bode, lady?[7]
  Hark, canst thou hear me? I will play the swan,
255   And die in music. [*Sings*] 'Willow, willow, willow.'—
  Moor, she was chaste. She loved thee, cruel Moor.
  So come my soul to bliss as I speak true.
  So, speaking as I think, alas, I die.   *She dies*

OTHELLO   I have another weapon in this chamber.
260   It was a sword of Spain, the ice-brook's temper.°   *tempered in icy water*
  O, here it is. [*Calling*] Uncle, I must come forth.

GRAZIANO (*within*)   If thou attempt it, it will cost thee dear.
  Thou hast no weapon, and perforce must suffer.

OTHELLO   Look in upon me then, and speak with me,
265   Or, naked° as I am, I will assault thee.   *unarmed*

> [*Enter* GRAZIANO]

GRAZIANO   What is the matter?

OTHELLO   Behold, I have a weapon;
  A better never did itself sustain
  Upon a soldier's thigh. I have seen the day
  That, with this little arm and this good sword,
270   I have made my way through more impediments

---

6. Why should military reputation outlive integrity?
7. Lines 253–55 ("What . . . willow.'—") do not appear in Q.

Than twenty times your stop.° But O, vain boast!   *power to stop*
Who can control his fate? 'Tis not so now.
Be not afraid, though you do see me weaponed.
Here is my journey's end, here is my butt[8]
275   And very sea-mark° of my utmost sail.   *beacon*
Do you go back dismayed? 'Tis a lost° fear.   *an unnecessary*
Man but a rush° against Othello's breast   *Aim even a reed*
And he retires. Where should Othello go?
[*To* DESDEMONA] Now, how dost thou look now? O ill-starred wench,
280   Pale as thy smock! When we shall meet at count°   *Judgment Day*
This look of thine will hurl my soul from heaven,
And fiends will snatch at it.
          [*He touches her*]
                         Cold, cold, my girl,
Even like thy chastity. O cursèd, cursèd slave!
Whip me, ye devils,
285   From the possession of this heavenly sight.
Blow me about in winds, roast me in sulphur,
Wash me in steep-down gulfs of liquid fire!
O Desdemon! Dead Desdemon! Dead! O! O!
          Enter LODOVICO, MONTANO, IAGO [*guarded by*] *officers,*
          with CASSIO *in a chair*
LODOVICO   Where is this rash and most unfortunate man?
290   OTHELLO   That's he that was Othello. Here I am.
LODOVICO   Where is that viper? Bring the villain forth.
OTHELLO   I look down towards his feet,[9] but that's a fable.
          [*To* IAGO] If that thou beest a devil I cannot kill thee.
               [*He wounds* IAGO]
LODOVICO   Wrench his sword from him.
               [*Officers disarm* OTHELLO]
IAGO   I bleed, sir, but not killed.
295   OTHELLO   I am not sorry, neither. I'd have thee live,
For in my sense° 'tis happiness to die.   *state of feeling*
LODOVICO   O thou Othello, that was once so good,
Fall'n in the practice° of a cursèd slave,   *plot*
What shall be said to thee?
OTHELLO   Why, anything;
300   An honourable murderer, if you will,
For naught I did in hate, but all in honour.
LODOVICO   This wretch hath part confessed his villainy.
Did you and he consent in Cassio's death?
OTHELLO   Ay.
305   CASSIO   Dear general, I never gave you cause.
OTHELLO   I do believe it, and I ask your pardon.
Will you, I pray, demand that demi-devil
Why he hath thus ensnared my soul and body?
IAGO   Demand me nothing. What you know, you know.
310   From this time forth I never will speak word.
LODOVICO [*to* IAGO]   What, not to pray?
GRAZIANO [*to* IAGO]   Torments° will ope your lips.   *Tortures*
OTHELLO   Well, thou dost best.
LODOVICO   Sir, you shall understand what hath befall'n,
315   Which as, I think, you know not. Here is a letter,

8. Goal. Lines 273–79 do not appear in Q.   9. To look for the devil's cloven feet.

Found in the pocket of the slain Roderigo,
And here another. The one of them imports
The death of Cassio, to be undertook
By Roderigo.
320 OTHELLO   O villain!
CASSIO   Most heathenish and most gross.°   *monstrous*
LODOVICO   Now here's another discontented paper
Found in his pocket too, and this it seems
Roderigo meant to've sent this damnèd villain,
325 But that, belike,° Iago in the interim   *most likely*
Came in and satisfied him.
OTHELLO [to IAGO]   O thou pernicious caitiff!°   *wretch*
How came you, Cassio, by that handkerchief
That was my wife's?
CASSIO   I found it in my chamber,
330 And he himself confessed it, but even now,
That there he dropped it for a special purpose
Which wrought to his desire.
OTHELLO   O fool, fool, fool!
CASSIO   There is besides in Roderigo's letter
How he upbraids Iago, that he made him
335 Brave° me upon the watch, whereon it came   *Defy*
That I was cast;° and even but now he spake   *dismissed*
After long seeming dead, Iago hurt him,
Iago set him on.
LODOVICO [to OTHELLO]   You must forsake this room and go with us.
340 Your power and your command is taken off,
And Cassio rules in Cyprus. For this slave,
If there be any cunning cruelty
That can torment him much and hold him° long,   *(alive)*
It shall be his. You shall close° prisoner rest   *tightly confined*
345 Till that the nature of your fault be known
To the Venetian state. [To officers] Come, bring away.
OTHELLO   Soft you,° a word or two before you go.   *Wait*
I have done the state some service, and they know't.
No more of that. I pray you, in your letters,
350 When you shall these unlucky deeds relate,
Speak of me as I am. Nothing extenuate,
Nor set down aught in malice. Then must you speak
Of one that loved not wisely but too well,
Of one not easily jealous but, being wrought,
355 Perplexed in the extreme; of one whose hand,
Like the base Indian, threw a pearl away
Richer than all his tribe;¹ of one whose subdued° eyes,   *(by grief)*
Albeit unusèd to the melting mood,
Drops tears as fast as the Arabian trees
360 Their medicinable gum.° Set you down this,   *myrrh*
And say besides that in Aleppo once,
Where a malignant and a turbaned Turk
Beat a Venetian and traduced the state,
I took by th' throat the circumcisèd dog

---

1. Othello supposes an uncivilized "Indian" unaware of the value of a pearl. Compare this reading from Q with F's "Judean," which may suggest malice rather than ignorance by alluding to Judas (betrayer of Christ) or perhaps Herod (who killed his wife Mariamne out of jealousy). "Judean" also anticipates "circumcisèd" (line 364) and hence an identification of Othello with Jews.

365 And smote him thus.
       He stabs himself
LODOVICO   O bloody period!°   *conclusion; sentence*
GRAZIANO   All that is spoke is marred.
OTHELLO [*to* DESDEMONA]   I kissed thee ere I killed thee. No way but this:
    Killing myself, to die upon a kiss.[2]   *He* [*kisses* DESDEMONA *and*] *dies*
370 CASSIO   This did I fear, but thought he had no weapon,
    For he was great of heart.
LODOVICO [*to* IAGO]   O Spartan dog,°   *notoriously savage*
    More fell° than anguish, hunger, or the sea,   *cruel*
    Look on the tragic loading of this bed.
    This is thy work. The object poisons sight.
    Let it be hid.
        [*They close the bed-curtains*]
375   Graziano, keep the house,
    And seize upon the fortunes of the Moor,
    For they succeed on you. [*To* CASSIO] To you, Lord Governor,
    Remains the censure° of this hellish villain.   *sentence*
    The time, the place, the torture, O, enforce it!
380   Myself will straight aboard, and to the state
    This heavy act with heavy heart relate.   *Exeunt* [*with Emilia's body*]

TEXTUAL VARIANTS

Control text: F

F: The Folio of 1623
Q: The Quarto of 1622
Fa, Fb, Qc, Qd: Successive states of F or Q incorporating various print-shop corrections and changes

Title: *The Tragedy of* Othello *the Moore of Venice* [Q] *Tragoedy* [Q title page] THE TRAGEDIE OF Othello, the Moore of Venice [F, Stationers' Register entry]

1.1.1 Tush [Q; not in F] **4 'Sblood** [Q; not in F] **24 togaed** [Q] Tongued **28 other** [Q] others **32 God** [Q; not in F] **53 'em** [Q] them **66 full** [Q] fall **79 thieves, thieves thieves** [Q] Theeues, Theeues **86 'Swounds, sir** [Q] Sir **101 bravery** [Q] knauerie **110 'Swounds, sir** [Q] Sir **118 now** [Q; not in F] **183 night** [Q] might
1.2.34 Duke [Q] Dukes **46 sent** [Q] hath sent **55 comes another** [Q] come another [Fa] come sanother [Fb] **59 Roderigo? Come** [Q, Fa] *Rodorigoc?* Cme [Fb] **60 'em** [Q] them **69 darlings** [Q] Deareling **88 I** [Q; not in F]
1.3.1 There is [Q] There's **these** [Q] this **53 nor** [Q] hor **73 s.p. SENATORS** All. **90 tale** [Q] u Tale **106 upon** [Q] vp on **s.p. DUKE** [Q ⟨Du⟨ke⟩⟩; not in F] **107 overt** [Q] over **129 battles** [Q] Battaile **fortunes** [Q] Fortune **139 antres** [Q ⟨Antrees⟩] Antars **140 and hills whose heads** [Q] Hills, whose head **142 other** [Q] others **143 Anthropophagi** [Q] *Antropophague* **144 Do grow** [Q] Grew **146 thence** [Q] hence **154 intentively** [Q] instinctiuely **188 b'wi'you** [Q (bu'y)] be with you **197 'em** [Q] them **200 Into your favour** [Q; not in F] **218 ear** [Q] eares **228 couch** [Q] Coach **247 I did** [Q] I **263 me** my **269 instruments** [Q] Instrument **277 DESDE-**

---

2. At 5.2.244, the dying Emilia says, "O, lay me by my mistress' side." She then addresses Desdemona in a way that suggests that her wish has been granted. If it has, however, the presence of her body intrudes upon the concluding tableau of the dead Desdemona being kissed by the dying Othello, where "die" in line 369 has the secondary sense of "orgasm."

MONA . . . This night [Q; not in F] 299 the [Q] the the 309 ha' [Q] haue 322 beam braine 326 our unbitted [Q] or vnbitted 343 error [Q] errors 347 a super-subtle [Q] super-subtle 349 pox o' [Q] pox of 367 a [Q; not in F] 370 He has She ha's 385 ha't [Q] haue't

2.1.7 ha' [Q] hath 13 mane [Q (mayne)] Maine 27 Veronessa [Q] *Verennessa* 34 prays [Q] praye 41 s.p. THIRD GENTLEMAN [Q *(3 Gent.)*] *Gent.* 43 arrivance [Q] Arriuancie 44 this [Q] the 52 s.p. / s.d. VOICES *(within) Within* [s.p.] 83 And bring all Cyprus comfort [Q; not in F] 89 me [Q; not in F] 95 VOICES *(within)* A sail, a sail! *Within.*, A Saile, a Saile. [after line 96] 97 their [Q] this 108 ha' [Q] haue 111 ha' [Q] haue 115 hussies Huswiues 123 essay assay 174 an [Q] and 211 hither [Q] thither 222 again [Q] a game 235 has [Q] he's 251 mutualities [Q] mutabilities 293 rank [Q] right

2.2.5 addiction addition 9 Heaven bless [Q] Blesse

2.3.33 ha' [Q] haue 53 to put [Q] put to 57 God [Q] heauen 66 God [Q] Heauen 70 Englishman [Q] Englishmen 84 Then [Q] *And* 86 Fore God [Q] Why 89 God's [Q] heau'ns 96 ha' [Q] haue 97 God forgive [Q] Forgiue 124 engraffed ingraft 129 VOICES *(within)* Help, help! [Q *(Helpe, helpe, within.)*; not in F] 130 'Swounds, you [Q] You 141 God's will [Q] Alas 142 Sir! Montano! Sir! [Q] Sir *Montano:* 145 God's will [Q] Fie, fie hold [Q; not in F] 147 'Swounds [Q; not in F] 151 Hold, hold [Q] hold 173 be [Q] to be 190 'Swounds, if I [Q] If I once 201 leagued [Q] league 204 ha' [Q] haue 216 the [Q] then 236 now [Q; not in F] 245 God [Q] Heauen 246 ha' [Q] haue 247 ha' [Q] haue 249 thought [Q] had thought 269 O God [Q] Oh 291 I'll [Q] I 294 denotement deuotement 306 here [Q; not in F] 317 were't [Q] were 339 ha' [Q] haue 343 ha' [Q] haue 348 hast [Q] hath 351 By the mass [Q] Introth

3.1.3 ha' [Q] haue 8–9 tail . . . tale tale . . . tale 17 ha' [Q] haue 20 my [Q] me, mine 23 general's wife Cenerals wife [Q] Generall 28 CASSIO Do, good my friend [Q; not in F] 29 ha' [Q] haue 30 ha' [Q] haue 47 To take the saf'st occasion by the front [Q; not in F]

3.3.16 circumstance [Q] Circumstances 53 Yes, faith [Q] I sooth 61 or [Q] on 75 By'r Lady [Q] Trust me 96 you [Q] he 110 By heaven [Q] Alas 116 In [Q] Of 140 free to [Q] free 144 But some [Q] Wherein 152 oft [Q] of 153 that your wisdom then I intreate you then [Q] that your wisedome 166 By heaven [Q; not in F] 174 fondly soundly 179 God [Q] Heauen 184 once [Q; not in F] 189 well [Q; not in F] 206 God [Q] Heauen 208 keep't kept 219 I'faith [Q] Trust me 221 my [Q] your 253 hold [Q; not in F] 263 qualities [Q] Quantities 277 of [Q] to 282 O then heaven mocks [Q] Heauen mock'd 289 Faith [Q] Why 300 ha' [Q] haue 316 faith [Q] but 319 with it [Q] with't 343 of [Q] in 396 sir [Q; not in F] 400 supervisor [Q] super-vision 413 ha't [Q] haue't 428 lay laid 434 s.p. IAGO [Q *(Iag⟨o⟩.)*. Prefixed to line 435 *(Iago.)*: in other words, F gives line 434 to Othello.] 445 that was it was 458 knows keepes 463 s.d. *He kneels* [Q; not in F]

3.4.53 faith [Q] indeed 73 I'faith [Q] Indeed? 75 God [Q] Heauen seen it [Q] seene't 79 Heaven bless [Q] Blesse 84 sir [Q; not in F] 89–90 DESDEMONA I pray, talk me of Cassio. / OTHELLO The handkerchief. [Q; not in F] 94 I'faith [Q] Insooth 95 'Swounds [Q] Away 166 I'faith [Q] Indeed 182 by my faith [Q] in good troth

4.1.32 Faith [Q] Why 35 'Swounds, [Q; not in F] 49 No, forbear [Q; not in F] 75 unsuiting [Qd] vnfitting [Qc] resulting 77 'scuse [Q] scuses 92 hussy huswife 99 conster [Q] conserue 101 now [Q; not in F] 105 power [Q] dowre 109 a woman [Q] woman 110 i'faith [Q] indeed 120 Faith [Q] Why 123 Ha' [Q] Haue 127 beckons [Q] becomes 129 the sea- [Fb] the the Sea- [Fa] 145 whole [Q; not in F] 153 An . . . An [Q] If . . . if 156 Faith [Q; not in F] 158 Faith [Q] Yes 179 so [Fb] fo [Fa] 207 God save the [Q] Save you 227 the letter [Q] thle etter [Fa] thLetter [Fb] 230 By my troth [Q] Trust me 243 an [Q; not in F] 276 denote [Q] deonte [Fa] deuote [Fb]

4.2.5 'em [Q] them **16 ha'** [Q] haue **24 ha'** [Q] haue **32 nay** [Q] May **33 knees** [Q] knee **35 But not the words** [Q; not in F] **49 God** Heauen **50 He** [Q] they **71 ne'er** [Q] neuer **97 ha'** [Q] haue **105 ha'** [Q] haue **116 ha'** [Q] haue **120 hearts** [Fb] heart [Fa] **145 heaven** [Q] Heauens **152 O God** O Good [Q] Alas **159 them in** them: or **171 And he does chide with you** [Q; not in F] **186 Faith** [Q; not in F] **I have heard too much, for your words, and** [Q] And hell gnaw his bones, [Fa] I haue heard too much: and your words and [Fb] **192 'em** [Q] them **224 takes** [Q] taketh **228 of** [Q; not in F]

4.3.12 He [Q] And **20 in them** [Q; not in F] **22 faith** [Q] Father **23 thee** [Q; not in F] **37 nether** [Fb] neither [Fa] **38 soul sat** [Fb] *Sonle set* [Fa] **sighing** *sining* [Fa] singing [Fb] **73 Ud's pity** [Q] why **102 God** [Q] Heauen

5.1.1 bulk [Q] Barke **22 hear** [Q] heard **34 dear** [Q] deere **36 Forth** [Q] For **51 heaven's** heauen **62 'em** [Q] them **91 O heaven** [Q] yes, 'tis **106 out** [Q; not in F] **109 an** [Q] if **116 dead** [Q] quite dead **125 Fough** [Q; not in F]

5.2.37 so [Q; not in F] **62 Then Lord** [Q] O Heauen **82 'em** [Q] them **88 an** [Q] if **93 DESDEMONA O Lord, Lord, Lord!** [Q; not in F] **96 that am** [Fb] am that [Fa] **106 ha'** [Q] haue **110 Should** [Q] Did **127 O Lord,** [Q] Alas! **136 heard** [Q] heare **166 worst** [Q] wotst **224 God! O heavenly God!** [Q] Heauen! oh heauenly Powres! **225 'Swounds** [Q] come **227 'em** [Q] them **247 here** [Q; not in F] **260 ice-brook's** Isebrookes [Q] Ice brookes **356 Indian** [Q] Iudean

The Life of Timon of Athens

In a jewelry advertisement, a handsome man and a beautiful woman share a rapturous embrace. A large diamond sparkles on the woman's finger; apparently, the impressive ring symbolizes a love equally grand. Although the deliberate confusion of emotional and financial investments seems crass, the ad can only succeed if it captures something people know, or wish, to be true. What does love have to do with money? How closely entwined are friendship and material self-interest? Are persons esteemed for intrinsic personal characteristics, or for the glamor of their possessions? Are affluent communities or social classes especially likely to confuse sheer wealth with other forms of value?

Timon of Athens asks such questions with a relentlessness unusual for Shakespeare. To many readers and audiences, the play has seemed uncharacteristic in other respects as well: its schematic plot and vivid but rather static characters evoke the morality drama of Shakespeare's predecessors, or the satiric drama of his contemporaries, more closely than the other tragedies Shakespeare was writing at about the same time. Some argue that *Timon of Athens* was never finished; others suggest that the play is a collaborative work, about a third of which was written by Shakespeare's fellow dramatist Thomas Middleton. Nonetheless, some connections between *Timon* and Shakespeare's other plays are clear enough. The plot derives from that Shakespearean favorite Plutarch's *Lives*, which also provided the sources for *Julius Caesar, Antony and Cleopatra*, and *Coriolanus*. *Timon* has strong affinities to *The Merchant of Venice* in its concern with the connections between affectional and monetary bonds, and between material and intangible goods. The play's jaundiced view of ancient Greece recalls *Troilus and Cressida*, and so does its evasion of ordinary generic categories: although its protagonist dies at the end, its title does not promise a tragedy but merely a "life." The hero's sensational degradation from preeminence to utter penury, and his ferociously misanthropic reaction to that humiliation, has often prompted comparison with *King Lear*.

Timon opens on a panorama of glittering abundance. Purveyors of luxury goods—art, poems, jewels, textiles—flock to Timon's palace in hope of reward. Like advertisers today, they claim that their goods have a symbolic significance that goes beyond their obvious beauty or utility: these items give concrete expression to the ineffable virtues of their possessor. "Things of like value differing in the owners / Are prized by their masters," fawns the Jeweller. "You mend the jewel by the wearing it" (1.1.174–75, 176). The guests at Timon's sumptuous banquet are likewise loud in their admiration for their host. Their conversation turns almost obsessively upon Timon's apparently inexhaustible fortune.

And no wonder—for Timon seems not merely rich but unique. His generosity is characterized by what the Poet calls "magic of bounty," an outflow uncannily unbalanced by any apparent countereffort at acquisition. While ordinary owners have the power merely to transfer, not actually to generate, new goods, Timon seems freed from such basic material laws. He dispenses his "bounty" as if he were a god empowered to create wealth from nothing. But Timon's "magic" relies on a trick that he himself resolutely ignores. Using his lands as collateral, he borrows the money he needs to buy rich presents and keep a lavish table. The recipients of his hospitality are often the same men to whom he is indebted.

To Timon's surprise but hardly to the audience's, his elaborate charade collapses in the play's second act. Why has he behaved so self-destructively? We are given clues to his motives when, in the course of his banquet, he and his guests explicitly and implicitly offer several theories about the relationship of his "bounty" both to the social weal and to his own self-conception. Timon desires love and admiration, and in Athenian society as in many others, money proves a potent way of getting both. The adjectives "good," "worthy," "free," "kind," "gentle," and "noble" echo through the first act—their simultaneously economic and moral significance tending to break down any difference between the two domains. When Ventidius offers to return the large sum that Timon has spent releasing him from prison, Timon refuses:

> You mistake my love.
> I gave it freely ever, and there's none
> Can truly say he gives if he receives.
> (1.2.8–12)

Typically, love and money are here almost inextricable. Is the "it" that Timon freely gives the love to which he refers in the previous line or the money he has bestowed upon Ventidius? Moreover, Timon's generosity is entangled with pride and with a desire for mastery. By always giving, never receiving, Timon attempts to force his beneficiaries into an endlessly grateful and therefore subordinate role. His conduct recalls that of the chiefs of the native American tribes of the Pacific Northwest, who consolidated their status by "potlatches," great parties at which they would give away virtually all their possessions, thus compelling their guests to serve them in the future. In such a system, divesting oneself of wealth, not accumulating it, is the primary mode of acquiring status.

In the socioeconomic world of the potlatch, in which the recipient of a gift is profoundly obliged to the donor, Timon might well escape serious financial danger. His "courtiers" would attempt to repay him, in kind or in loyal service, relieving themselves of the burden of gratitude and thus restoring the social balance. Goods would circulate swiftly through such a community; and the reasons for desiring property would differ fundamentally from the motives that drive the inhabitants of more acquisitive cultures. Timon briefly imagines such a system when he rhapsodizes at his dinner party: "We are born to do benefits; and what better or properer can we call our own than the riches of our friends? O, what a precious comfort 'tis to have so many like brothers commanding one another's fortunes!" (1.2.95–98). Unfortunately, not only is this communitarian vision at odds with Timon's insistence on entirely unilateral gift-giving, but it is grossly out of kilter with the covetous society in which he actually lives. When Timon pays Ventidius's debt, Ventidius's messenger declares that "your lordship ever binds him" (1.1.106); likewise the First Lord claims to be "virtuously bound" by Timon's generosity (1.2.221). Yet by the middle of Act 2, they have already lost any sense of commitment to their erstwhile benefactor. Timon's "bonds," the legal instruments that enable his lenders to seize his lands when he forfeits cash repayment, turn out to be more "binding" than the unwritten ties of gratitude. In Athens, tangible goods are considered more real than intangible ones, legal commitments more real than obligations informally imposed.

Apemantus, the Cynic philosopher, hovering on the margins of Timon's dinner party, introduces an alternative economic language early in the play: the audience's perception of the entire banquet extravaganza is filtered through his commentary. For Timon, magnanimity apparently comes naturally, and gifts express sociability. For Apemantus, by contrast, people are naturally greedy and antisocial: protestations of friendship and gratitude hypocritically conceal an impulse to accumulate wealth at the expense of another, just as lavishness hypocritically conceals a desire for adulation. In such circumstances, the Cynic philosopher preserves his safety and integrity by repudiating his need both for property and for other people.

> Immortal gods, I crave no pelf.
> I pray for no man but myself.
> Grant I may never prove so fond
> To trust a man on his oath or bond,
> Or a harlot for her weeping,
> Or a dog that seems a-sleeping,

Or a keeper with my freedom,
Or my friends if I should need 'em.
(1.2.61–68)

To Timon's generous trustfulness, Apemantus counterpoises a self-protective suspicion. The difference in the way the two men conceive of human nature correlates with a difference in the way they imagine the material world. Timon believes that wealth is endlessly renewable and thus endlessly sharable without decrease. Apemantus believes that resources are strictly limited and that one person's gain must entail another person's loss. Thus what Timon sees as banquet pleasantries amount, in Apemantus's view, to a form of cannibalism. "O you gods, what a number of men eats Timon, and he sees 'em not! It grieves me to see so many dip their meat in one man's blood" (1.2.38–40). Both of these apparently opposite attitudes, however—Timon's romanticism and Apemantus's reductiveness—are actually rooted in a conviction that one's possessions, or the lack of them, centrally determine the way one thinks of oneself and interacts with other people. Arguably, Apemantus's cannibal imagery makes the shared materialism of the two men's attitudes especially obvious to a Christian audience; for that vision of Timon's banquet parodies, in grotesquely literal terms, the dispersal of Christ's spiritual body in the communion ceremony.

Most scholars believe that *Timon of Athens* was written between 1605 and 1608, several years after the accession of James I to the English throne. There are good reasons why Timon's particular economic dilemma would interest dramatists observing the contemporary scene in these years. If the play was, as many argue, left unfinished and unproduced, perhaps it was too incendiary to be safely performed in Jacobean England: although most of Shakespeare's plays reflect to some extent the time in which they were written, *Timon* is unusual in its brutally direct topical relevance. In the first decade of the seventeenth century, the traditional aristocratic virtues of openhanded generosity and carelessness of expense were coming into increasingly acute conflict with the limited means upon which the great nobles could actually draw. As England became an international trading power, luxuries once unheard-of became available to people with the money to buy them. As tastes grew more sophisticated, noblemen who wished to impress peers and subordinates with the splendor of their "bounty" were forced into ever greater expenditures. The result was an extraordinary expansion in the credit markets. The worst offender in this respect was King James, who—rather like Timon—showered his favorites with expensive gifts, a habit that created staggering

Penthesilea, Queen of the Amazons. From *The Masque of Queenes*, by Inigo Jones.

deficits in the Royal Exchequer. By 1608, royal indebtedness had reached crisis proportions, and other members of the upper aristocracy were likewise floating on a sea of debt and credit.

Shakespeare, or Shakespeare and Middleton, thus bear witness to a society in the process of a crucial economic transition—a transition that affects more than financial matters narrowly defined. In an earlier age, informal provisions among friends had often sufficed to meet relatively infrequent needs for ready money. In the first act, Timon assumes that he is living in such a world, as does Bassanio in the first scenes of The Merchant of Venice—their money transactions are accompanied by affection on the part of the giver and gratitude on the part of the recipient. In an informal credit system, the difference between love and money, and between loans and gifts, tends to become blurred. In Jacobean England, however, the inability of the upper classes to live within their means overstrained the limits of "friendly understanding": for few people then or now lend really substantial sums of money out of sheer amiability. Borrowing and lending thus increasingly became business matters transacted between relative strangers, divorced from rather than continuous with friendship and patronage relationships. Usury, a practice traditionally deplored and even illegal, was nonetheless widespread and increasingly accepted as a necessary fact of life.

The fiscally prudent son of a leatherworker, Shakespeare may well have been shocked on occasion at the profligacy of the patrons upon whose expansiveness he and his theater company partly depended. Certainly he recognized acutely that the motives of the Poet and the Painter do not differ from the motives of the other courtiers: "artists" in Athens are as venal as everybody else. What seems to have intrigued him most, however, is the way in which an apparently rather limited social phenomenon—aristocratic reliance on credit— necessarily affects social and even biological relations that seem far removed from money-lending. Uniquely among Shakespeare's plays, Timon is nearly bereft of women. The few who do briefly appear—the Amazons of Act 1, Alcibiades' whores in Act 4—are pointedly excluded from the "normal" marital relationships in which most socially useful reproductive activity traditionally takes place. In this nearly all-male world, the language of erotic intimacy is reserved for interactions among men, and new life seems the consequence of financial rather than sexual transactions.

> If I would sell my horse and buy twenty more
> Better than he, why, give my horse to Timon—
> Ask nothing, give it him—it foals me straight,
> And able horses.
>
> (2.1.7–10)

Exchanges of money and commodities take over some of the functions of procreative sexual intimacy, an appropriation that can easily be construed as perverse or depraved. Lending money at interest seems especially corrupt: Timon of Athens draws upon an ancient tradition of imagining usury to be a form of unnatural "breeding." After his disillusionment, Timon continually and deliberately conflates lust with greed, the venereal with the venal. Syphilis and its symptoms are not merely analogies for but are perhaps even the consequences of economic iniquity.

Despite the virtual absence of actual women, allegorical representations of female power play an important rhetorical role in Timon of Athens. The first half of the play is dominated by the allegorical figure of Dame Fortune. The Poet describes her as a "sovereign lady . . . upon a high and pleasant hill" (1.1.69, 64), huge, omnipotent, and whimsical, raising and crushing her struggling male subjects for no apparent reason. In the second half of the play, "Mother Earth" has some of the same threatening demeanor. The ruined Timon forsakes Athens for the wilderness outside it, rather as Shakespeare's lovers had done in that drastically different play A Midsummer Night's Dream. In Dream, the woods outside Athens are a lushly sexual place, but in Timon, roughly the same geographical locale is unusually harsh and minimalist. Like the whores to whom Timon compares her, Mother Earth is barren, refusing to surrender the roots for which Timon digs and instead yielding only the gold he had hoped to flee. Thus, for all the energy spent exposing the "unnaturalness" of Athenians' economic relations, a potentially restorative "natural" alternative is wholly lacking.

In many respects, Timon's disillusioned ferocity simply inverts, recoils from, the generous courtesy he had manifested throughout Act 1. Yet not everything changes: there is a clear continuity to Timon's personality in the first and second half of the play. Initially, as a wealthy patron and benefactor, Timon isolates himself from others by making himself a god of generosity. Later, as an indigent, he similarly sets himself apart, cursing mankind with all the immoderation with which he once blessed it. Shakespeare was fascinated throughout his career by self-absorbed, almost solipsistic characters: Adonis in *Venus and Adonis*, the young man of the sonnets, Malvolio in *Twelfth Night* "sick of self love." Timon exemplifies an extreme version of this egocentrism, his sense of his own separateness untouched even after his conception of human nature has been poisoned at its source. He not only dies alone, but mysteriously manages to bury himself and engrave his own epitaph: an epitaph that typically, and perversely, both demands that passersby remember him and orders them to "seek not my name" (5.5.73).

The necessarily social medium of the drama finds true hermits impossible to accommodate. For most of Acts 4 and 5, various acquaintances crowd to Timon's cave as they once crowded to his palace, enduring and in some cases responding to his predictable vituperation. The sense of separateness Timon has always possessed makes satiric alienation congenial to him; but like many satirists, he is an ambiguous figure. The satirist can tell truths about society because his disengagement gives him the standing to criticize practices he regards as corrupt. At the same time, his observational acuteness—his refusal to accept the complacencies of the majority—bespeaks a certain imbalance. The satirist's misanthropy coexists curiously with an inability to mind his own business. Insofar as Timon's ironies so often threaten to turn upon him, the tone of the play's latter acts becomes equivocal. Are we supposed to agree with Timon that virtually all human values and activities can be plausibly reduced to money and the greed for it? Certainly the action of the play gives us ample reason to share his disgust at his erstwhile friends. Or is his rage disproportionate to the adversities he endures? Just as the Timon of the early acts can be variously characterized as noble and foolish, the later Timon has seemed to some critics a sublimely disappointed idealist, to others a petulant whiner.

A few characters suggest that Timon's unmitigated misanthropy is too simple and incomplete. Flavius's loyalty to his former master defies the terms of Timon's blanket condemnation of all humankind, as Timon reluctantly acknowledges.

> Forgive my general and exceptless rashness,
> You perpetual sober gods! I do proclaim
> One honest man—mistake me not, but one,
> No more, I pray—and he's a steward.
> (4.3.487–90)

But even as he recognizes Flavius's virtue, Timon instantly blunts the force of that recognition by insisting that Flavius is exceptional. He apparently cannot bear considering that there might be more than a single selfless person; he also specifies that Flavius is a mere servant, which apparently makes the example count for less. Throughout *Timon*, low-ranking characters—having less to gain from greed—display an acute sense of gratitude and obligation sadly lacking in their "betters." All Timon's servants, not merely Flavius, seem dismayed by their master's ruin; and in 3.4, the usurers' servants, talking among themselves, quite freely condemn the commands they are forced to carry out. But Timon prefers to believe that rapacity is a universal human trait, not a more limited, class-linked phenomenon. Reduced to rags and roots though he is, Timon cannot help being a snob. And to some extent, his status consciousness seems justified: for if the servants are kindhearted, they are also ineffectual, disqualified by low rank from remedying the social problems they witness.

Alcibiades provides a more formidable alternative to the Athenian usurers, although

Dame Fortune, blind, standing on a ball with wings (to show how quickly her favors may fly away). From George Wither, *A Collection of Emblems, Ancient and Modern* (1635).

the connection between this subplot and the main action is sketchy. Certainly he does not escape, or seek to disentangle, the interconnections between love and money that eventually seem so poisonous to Timon: when he visits Timon in the cave, he comes with a prostitute on each arm. Nonetheless, in his brief appearances, Alcibiades testifies to the existence of a less restricted, more complex sociopolitical world than the one we witness for most of the play. Whereas, for instance, Timon's function in Athens seems mainly to give expensive dinner parties, Alcibiades insists that Timon has performed important military services for the state: that his "bounty" has had a political and executive, as well as sheerly economic, aspect. Unfortunately, the relationship between Timon and Alcibiades, as well as the relationship between the city's politics and its social organization, is left largely undeveloped in the text of the play as it has come down to us. The soldier, pursuing his vocation in the bleak world beyond the city walls, is imagined as partly outside the economic system in which other characters are enmeshed. Like the hermit-satirist, he has the special credibility that comes with distance. But whereas Timon's detachment is the product of a merely negative disgust, Alcibiades' involves allegiance to a rather different set of positive values. In 3.6, not only does he risk himself to defend a friend, but the terms of his defense hint at a code of behavior divorced from cash rewards and penalties.

At the end of the play, after Timon's death, the Athenian senators invite Alcibiades and his army back into the city. He will, they hope, "approach the fold and cull th'infected forth" (5.5.43), as a shepherd kills the sick animals of his flock in order to keep disease from spreading to the remainder. The senators argue that greed is merely the failing of a degenerate few, not the universal human trait Timon had believed it to be. But the play entertains this alternative view of Timon's plight too late and too hastily to carry much conviction, and the apparent optimism of the conclusion thus seems unearned. How Alcibiades' invasion will reform Athens is hard to imagine.

Katharine Eisaman Maus

TEXTUAL NOTE

The only source for *Timon* is the First Folio of 1623 (F), and the circumstances of its publication seem to have been unusual. Evidently the decision to include *Timon* in Shakespeare's collected works was made quite late; it was inserted into a space early in F that had been originally designated for the longer *Troilus and Cressida*, a play for which the printer initially had trouble obtaining copyright. This peculiarity, especially when viewed in light of the play's many rough edges and inconsistencies, has led scholars to speculate that *Timon* seemed, to the Folio compilers, to be marginal to Shakespeare's oeuvre. Some scholars believe, on the basis of analyzing vocabulary, stage directions, spelling, and style, that *Timon* is a collaborative text jointly authored by Shakespeare and Thomas Middleton. Others suggest that whatever its authorship, the play was abandoned before it reached the final stages of revision. There is no evidence that the play was ever performed, but such firm evidence is often lacking in the scanty surviving documents: the record is similarly silent on such plays as *As You Like It*, *Troilus and Cressida*, *All's Well That Ends Well*, and *Antony and Cleopatra*.

SELECTED BIBLIOGRAPHY

Chorost, Michael. "Biological Finance in Shakespeare's *Timon of Athens*." *English Literary Renaissance* 21 (1991): 349–70.

Empson, William. "Timon's Dog." *The Structure of Complex Words*. London: Chatto and Windus, 1951.

Kahn, Coppelia. " 'Magic of Bounty': *Timon of Athens*, Jacobean Patronage, and Maternal Power." *Shakespeare Quarterly* 38 (1987): 34–57.

Knights, L. C. "*Timon of Athens*." *The Morality of Art*. Ed. D. W. Jefferson. London: Routledge and Kegan Paul, 1969. 1–17.

Nuttall, A. D. *Timon of Athens*. Harvester New Critical Introductions to Shakespeare. New York: Harvester Wheatsheaf, 1989.

Paster, Gail. *The Idea of the City in the Age of Shakespeare*. Athens: University of Georgia Press, 1985. 91–108.

The Life of Timon of Athens

THE PERSONS OF THE PLAY

TIMON of Athens
A POET
A PAINTER
A JEWELLER
A MERCHANT
A mercer
LUCILIUS, one of Timon's servants
An OLD ATHENIAN
LORDS and SENATORS of Athens
VENTIDIUS, one of Timon's false friends
ALCIBIADES, an Athenian captain
APEMANTUS, a churlish philosopher
One dressed as CUPID in the masque
LADIES dressed as Amazons in the masque
FLAVIUS, Timon's steward
FLAMINIUS ⎱
SERVILIUS ⎰ Timon's servants
Other SERVANTS of Timon
A FOOL
A PAGE
CAPHIS
ISIDORE'S SERVANT ⎫ servants to Timon's creditors
Two of VARRO'S SERVANTS ⎭
LUCULLUS ⎫
LUCIUS ⎬ flattering lords
SEMPRONIUS ⎭
LUCULLUS' SERVANT
LUCIUS' SERVANT
Three STRANGERS, one called Hostillius
TITUS' SERVANT ⎫
HORTENSIUS' SERVANT ⎬ other servants to Timon's creditors
PHILOTUS' SERVANT ⎭
PHRYNIA ⎱
TIMANDRA ⎰ whores with Alcibiades
The banditti, THIEVES
SOLDIER of Alcibiades' army
Messengers, attendants, soldiers

1.1

Enter POET [*at one door*], PAINTER [*carrying a picture at
another door, followed by*] JEWELLER, MERCHANT, *and
Mercer, at several doors*
POET Good day, sir.
PAINTER   I am glad you're well.
POET I have not seen you long. How goes the world?

1.1 Location: Timon's house, Athens.

PAINTER It wears,° sir, as it grows.°		*wears out / ages*
POET Ay, that's well known.		
But what particular rarity, what strange,		
5 Which manifold record° not matches? — See,		*all recorded history*
Magic of bounty,° all these spirits thy power		*generosity*
Hath conjured to attend.		

       [MERCHANT *and* JEWELLER *meet. Mercer passes over the*
       stage, and exits]
                           I know the merchant.

PAINTER I know them both. Th'other's a jeweller.		
MERCHANT [*to* JEWELLER] O, 'tis a worthy lord!°		*(Timon)*
JEWELLER Nay, that's most fixed.°		*definite*
10 MERCHANT A most incomparable man, breathed,° as it were,		*trained; inspired*
To an untirable and continuate° goodness.		*habitual*
He passes.°		*excels*
JEWELLER [*showing a jewel*] I have a jewel here.		
MERCHANT O, pray, let's see't. For the Lord Timon, sir?		
JEWELLER If he will touch the estimate.° But for that—		*meet the price*
15 POET [*to himself*] 'When we for recompense have praised the vile,		
It stains the glory in that happy° verse		*appropriate*
Which aptly sings the good.'		
MERCHANT [*to* JEWELLER] 'Tis a good form.°		*shape*
JEWELLER And rich. Here is a water,° look ye.		*luster*
PAINTER [*to* POET] You are rapt, sir, in some work, some dedication		
To the great lord.[1]		
20 POET A thing slipped idly from me.		
Our poesy is as a gum° which oozes		*sap*
From whence 'tis nourished. The fire i'th' flint		
Shows not till it be struck; our gentle flame		
Provokes° itself, and like the current flies		*Generates*
25 Each bound it chafes.[2] What have you there?		
PAINTER A picture, sir. When comes your book forth?		
POET Upon the heels of my presentment,[3] sir.		
Let's see your piece.		
PAINTER [*showing the picture*] 'Tis a good piece.		
POET So 'tis. This comes off well and excellent.		
PAINTER Indifferent.°		*So-so*
30 POET Admirable. How this grace		
Speaks his own standing![4] What a mental power		
This eye shoots forth! How big imagination		
Moves in this lip! To th' dumbness° of the gesture		*muteness*
One might interpret.°		*supply words*
35 PAINTER It is a pretty mocking° of the life.		*imitation*
Here is a touch; is't good?		
POET I will say of it,		
It tutors nature. Artificial strife°		*The striving of art*
Lives in these touches livelier than life.		

       Enter certain Senators

PAINTER How this lord is followed!		
40 POET The senators of Athens. Happy man!		
PAINTER Look, more.		

---

1. Poets dedicated their volumes to wealthy patrons in
hopes of financial reward.
2. *like . . . chafes:* like the river overflows restricting

banks.
3. As soon as I have presented it formally (to Timon).
4. Imparts the dignity of his estate.

[*The Senators pass over the stage, and exeunt*]
POET   You see this confluence, this great flood of visitors.
I have in this rough work shaped out a man
Whom this beneath[5] world doth embrace and hug
45   With amplest entertainment.° My free drift°   hospitality / meaning
Halts not particularly,[6] but moves itself
In a wide sea of tax.[7] No levelled malice
Infects one comma in the course I hold,
But flies an eagle flight, bold and forth° on,   straight
50   Leaving no tract° behind.   trace
PAINTER   How shall I understand you?
POET   I will unbolt° to you.   disclose
You see how all conditions, how all minds,
As well of glib and slipp'ry creatures as
55   Of grave and austere quality, tender° down   give
Their service to Lord Timon. His large fortune,
Upon his good and gracious nature hanging,
Subdues and properties° to his love and tendance°   appropriates / attendance
All sorts of hearts; yea, from the glass-faced[8] flatterer
60   To Apemantus, that few things loves better
Than to abhor himself; even he drops down
The knee before him, and returns° in peace,   leaves
Most rich in Timon's nod.
PAINTER   I saw them speak together.
POET   Sir, I have upon a high and pleasant hill
65   Feigned° Fortune to be throned. The base o'th' mount   Imagined
Is ranked with all deserts,[9] all kind of natures
That labour on the bosom of this sphere
To propagate their states.° Amongst them all   improve their fortunes
Whose eyes are on this sovereign lady fixed
70   One do I personate of Lord Timon's frame,
Whom Fortune with her ivory hand wafts° to her,   beckons
Whose present grace° to present slaves and servants   graciousness
Translates his rivals.[1]
PAINTER   'Tis conceived to scope.°   correctly
This throne, this Fortune, and this hill, methinks,
75   With one man beckoned from the rest below,
Bowing his head against the steepy mount
To climb his happiness,° would be well expressed   good fortune
In our condition.[2]
POET   Nay, sir, but hear me on.
All those which were his fellows° but of late,   equals
80   Some better than his value, on the moment
Follow his strides, his lobbies fill with tendance,[3]
Rain sacrificial° whisperings in his ear,   respectful
Make sacred even his stirrup,[4] and through him
Drink the free air.

5. Sublunar (in Ptolomaic astronomy, the earth was the center of the universe and the moon its closest satellite; things beyond the moon were eternally fixed, but things in the sublunar "sphere" died or changed).
6. Does not criticize individuals.
7. In general satire (the Oxford editors substitute "tax" [criticism] for F's "wax"). *levelled*: aimed (at a particular person).
8. Reflecting his patron's moods.

9. Is lined with people of all degrees of virtue.
1. *to present . . . rivals*: instantly converts Timon's rivals to his slaves and servants.
2. *would . . . condition*: would be a good expression of the human condition; would make a good design for a painter.
3. *his . . . tendance*: crowd his rooms to visit him.
4. By holding it reverently as he mounts.

PAINTER	Ay, marry, what of these?	

85 POET   When Fortune in her shift and change of mood
    Spurns° down her late belovèd, all his dependants,   *Kicks*
    Which laboured after him to the mountain's top
    Even on their knees and hands, let him fall down,
    Not one accompanying his declining foot.
90 PAINTER   'Tis common.
    A thousand moral paintings I can show
    That shall demonstrate these quick blows of Fortune's
    More pregnantly° than words. Yet you do well   *forcibly*
    To show Lord Timon that mean° eyes have seen   *base people's*
95   The foot above the head.

        Trumpets sound. Enter TIMON [*wearing a rich jewel*],
        with a MESSENGER *from Ventidius;* LUCILIUS *and other*
        Servants attending. TIMON *address[es] himself courte-*
        ously to every suitor [*then speaks to the* MESSENGER]

TIMON   Imprisoned is he, say you?
MESSENGER   Ay, my good lord. Five talents[5] is his debt,
    His means most short, his creditors most strait.°   *severe*
    Your honourable letter he desires
100   To those° have shut him up, which failing,   *those who*
    Periods° his comfort.   *Ends*
TIMON   Noble Ventidius! Well,
    I am not of that feather° to shake off   *sort*
    My friend when he must need me. I do know him
    A gentleman that well deserves a help,
105   Which he shall have. I'll pay the debt and free him.
MESSENGER   Your lordship ever binds° him.   *obligates*
TIMON   Commend me to him. I will send his ransom;
    And, being enfranchised,° bid him come to me.   *set free*
    'Tis not enough to help the feeble up,
110   But to support him after. Fare you well.
MESSENGER   All happiness to your honour.   *Exit*

        Enter an OLD ATHENIAN

OLD ATHENIAN   Lord Timon, hear me speak.
TIMON   Freely, good father.
OLD ATHENIAN   Thou hast a servant named Lucilius.
TIMON   I have so. What of him?
115 OLD ATHENIAN   Most noble Timon, call the man before thee.
TIMON   Attends he here or no? Lucilius!
LUCILIUS [*coming forward*]   Here at your lordship's service.
OLD ATHENIAN   This fellow here, Lord Timon, this thy creature,
    By night frequents my house. I am a man
120   That from my first have been inclined to thrift,
    And my estate deserves an heir more raised°   *exalted*
    Than one which holds a trencher.[6]
TIMON   Well, what further?
OLD ATHENIAN   One only daughter have I, no kin else
    On whom I may confer what I have got.
125   The maid is fair, o'th' youngest for a bride,
    And I have bred her° at my dearest cost   *brought her up*

---

5. A large unit of money, usually taken as equivalent to several thousand dollars. Shakespeare seems undecided about how much a "talent" is worth in *Timon*, and his inconsistencies are often cited as evidence for incomplete revision of the text.
6. Platter (one who waits on table).

In qualities of the best. This man of thine
Attempts her love. I prithee, noble lord,
Join with me to forbid him her resort.°   *company*
130 Myself have spoke in vain.
TIMON The man is honest.
OLD ATHENIAN Therefore he will be,[7] Timon.
His honesty rewards him in itself;
It must not bear° my daughter.   *carry off*
135 TIMON Does she love him?
OLD ATHENIAN She is young and apt.°   *impressionable*
Our own precedent° passions do instruct us   *former*
What levity's in youth.
TIMON [*to* LUCILIUS] Love you the maid?
LUCILIUS Ay, my good lord, and she accepts of it.
140 OLD ATHENIAN If in her marriage my consent be missing,
I call the gods to witness, I will choose
Mine heir from forth the beggars of the world,
And dispossess her all.
TIMON   How shall she be endowed° *What dowry will she have*
If she be mated with an equal husband?
145 OLD ATHENIAN Three talents on the present; in future, all.
TIMON This gentleman of mine hath served me long.
To build his fortune I will strain a little,
For 'tis a bond° in men. Give him thy daughter. *duty of friendship*
What you bestow in him I'll counterpoise,
And make him weigh with her.
150 OLD ATHENIAN   Most noble lord,
Pawn me to this your honour,[8] she is his.
TIMON My hand to thee; mine honour on my promise.
LUCILIUS Humbly I thank your lordship. Never may
That state or fortune fall into my keeping
155 Which is not owed to you.

      Exeunt [LUCILIUS *and* OLD ATHENIAN]
POET [*presenting a poem to* TIMON] Vouchsafe° my labour, and *Accept*
long live your lordship!
TIMON I thank you. You shall hear from me anon.°   *soon*
Go not away. [*To* PAINTER] What have you there, my friend?
PAINTER A piece of painting, which I do beseech
Your lordship to accept.
160 TIMON   Painting is welcome.
The painting is almost the natural° man;   *actual*
For since dishonour traffics° with man's nature, *has dealings*
He is but outside;° these pencilled figures are *only superficial*
Even such as they give out.[9] I like your work,
165 And you shall find I like it. Wait attendance
Till you hear further from me.
PAINTER   The gods preserve ye!
TIMON Well fare you, gentleman. Give me your hand.
We must needs dine together. [*To* JEWELLER] Sir, your jewel
Hath suffered under[1] praise.
JEWELLER   What, my lord, dispraise?

7. He will behave honorably (and chastely).
8. If you pledge your honor to do this.
9. Just what they profess to be.

1. Has been inundated by (but the Jeweller misunderstands).

170 TIMON A mere° satiety of commendations.   *An utter*
 If I should pay you for't as 'tis extolled
 It would unclew° me quite.   *ruin*
JEWELLER   My lord, 'tis rated
 As those which sell would give;² but you well know
 Things of like value differing in the owners
175 Are prizèd by their masters.³ Believe't, dear lord,
 You mend° the jewel by the wearing it.   *improve*
TIMON Well mocked.°   *You're kidding*
MERCHANT No, my good lord, he speaks the common tongue°   *general opinion*
 Which all men speak with him.
    Enter APEMANTUS
TIMON   Look who comes here.
180 Will you be chid?
JEWELLER We will bear,° with your lordship.   *suffer*
MERCHANT He'll spare none.
TIMON Good morrow to thee, gentle Apemantus.
APEMANTUS Till I be gentle, stay thou for thy good morrow—
185 When thou art Timon's dog, and these knaves honest.⁴
TIMON Why dost thou call them knaves? Thou know'st them not.
APEMANTUS Are they not Athenians?
TIMON Yes.
APEMANTUS Then I repent not.
190 JEWELLER You know me, Apemantus?
APEMANTUS Thou know'st I do. I called thee by thy name.
TIMON Thou art proud, Apemantus!
APEMANTUS Of nothing so much as that I am not like Timon.
TIMON Whither art going?
195 APEMANTUS To knock out an honest Athenian's brains.
TIMON That's a deed thou'lt die for.
APEMANTUS Right, if doing nothing⁵ be death by th' law.
TIMON How likest thou this picture, Apemantus?
APEMANTUS The best for the innocence.⁶
200 TIMON Wrought he not well that painted it?
APEMANTUS He wrought better that made the painter, and yet
 he's but a filthy piece of work.
PAINTER You're a dog.⁷
APEMANTUS Thy mother's of my generation. What's she, if I be a dog?
205 TIMON Wilt dine with me, Apemantus?
APEMANTUS No, I eat not⁸ lords.
TIMON An° thou shouldst, thou'dst anger ladies.   *If*
APEMANTUS O, they eat lords. So they come by great bellies.
TIMON That's a lascivious apprehension.⁹
210 APEMANTUS So thou apprehend'st it; take it for thy labour.
TIMON How dost thou like this jewel, Apemantus?
APEMANTUS Not so well as plain dealing, which will not cost a
 man a doit.°   *tiny coin*
TIMON What dost thou think 'tis worth?

2. At what a merchant would pay (the wholesale price).
3. Are valued as their owners are valued.
4. *stay . . . honest*: wait for a polite greeting until you are
changed into your own dog or (an equally likely prospect)
these crooks become honest.
5. Since there are no honest Athenians.

6. For its inability to harm anyone.
7. "Dog" is not merely a term of contempt; Apemantus
was a Cynic philosopher, a school whose name derived
from the Greek *kynē*, "dog."
8. I do not devour the substance of.
9. Interpretation; grasping.

APEMANTUS   Not worth my thinking.
215   How now, poet?
POET   How now, philosopher?
APEMANTUS   Thou liest.
POET   Art not one?
APEMANTUS   Yes.
220   POET   Then I lie not.
APEMANTUS   Art not a poet?
POET   Yes.
APEMANTUS   Then thou liest. Look in thy last work, where thou
       hast feigned him° a worthy fellow.   (Timon)
225   POET   That's not feigned, he is so.
APEMANTUS   Yes, he is worthy of thee, and to pay thee for thy
       labour. He that loves to be flattered is worthy o'th' flatterer.
       Heavens, that I were a lord!
TIMON   What wouldst do then, Apemantus?
230   APEMANTUS   E'en as Apemantus does now: hate a lord with my heart.
TIMON   What, thyself?
APEMANTUS   Ay.
TIMON   Wherefore?
APEMANTUS   That I had no augury¹ but to be a lord.— Art not
235   thou a merchant?
MERCHANT   Ay, Apemantus.
APEMANTUS   Traffic confound° thee, if the gods will not!   May business ruin
MERCHANT   If traffic do it, the gods do it.
APEMANTUS   Traffic's thy god, and thy god confound thee!
              Trumpet sounds. Enter a MESSENGER
240   TIMON   What trumpet's that?
MESSENGER   'Tis Alcibiades, and some twenty horse°   horsemen
       All of companionship.°   in one group
TIMON [*to Servants*]   Pray entertain them. Give them guide to us.
                         [*Exit one or more Servants*]
       [*To* JEWELLER] You must needs dine with me.
       [*To* POET]   Go not you hence
245   Till I have thanked you. [*To* PAINTER] When dinner's done
       Show me this piece. [*To all*] I am joyful of your sights.°   to see you
              Enter ALCIBIADES *with* [*his horsemen*]
       Most welcome, sir!
APEMANTUS [*aside*]   So, so, there.
       Aches contract and starve° your supple joints!   ruin
250   That there should be small love 'mongst these sweet knaves,
       And all this courtesy! The strain of man's bred out°   degenerated
       Into baboon and monkey.
ALCIBIADES [*to* TIMON]   Sir, you have saved my longing,° and I   anticipated my desire
       feed
       Most hungrily on your sight.
TIMON   Right welcome, sir!
255   Ere we depart, we'll share a bounteous time
       In different pleasures. Pray you, let us in.
                         Exeunt [*all but* APEMANTUS]
              Enter two LORDS
FIRST LORD   What time o' day is't, Apemantus?
APEMANTUS   Time to be honest.

1. Foresight (so I could avoid it).

FIRST LORD	That time serves still.°	*always*
APEMANTUS	The most accursèd thou, that still omitt'st° it.	*do not take advantage of*
260 SECOND LORD	Thou art going to Lord Timon's feast?	
APEMANTUS	Ay, to see meat fill knaves, and wine heat fools.	
SECOND LORD	Fare thee well, fare thee well.	
APEMANTUS	Thou art a fool to bid me farewell twice.	
SECOND LORD	Why, Apemantus?	

APEMANTUS   Shouldst have kept one to thyself, for I mean to give
265   thee none.
FIRST LORD   Hang thyself!
APEMANTUS   No, I will do nothing at thy bidding. Make thy
    requests to thy friend.

270 SECOND LORD   Away, unpeaceable dog, or I'll spurn° thee hence.   *kick*
APEMANTUS   I will fly, like a dog, the heels o'th' ass.   *Exit*
FIRST LORD   He's opposite° to humanity. Come, shall we in,   *antagonistic*
  And taste Lord Timon's bounty? He outgoes°   *surpasses*
  The very heart° of kindness.   *essence*
275 SECOND LORD   He pours it out. Plutus the god of gold
  Is but his steward; no meed° but he repays   *gift*
  Sevenfold above itself; no gift to him
  But breeds the giver a return exceeding
  All use of quittance.°   *customary interest rates*
FIRST LORD   The noblest mind he carries
280   That ever governed man.
SECOND LORD   Long may he live in fortunes! Shall we in?
FIRST LORD   I'll keep you company.   *Exeunt*

1.2

Hautboys° playing loud music. A great banquet served in   *Oboes*
[FLAVIUS *and Servants attending*]; *and then enter*
TIMON, [ALCIBIADES,] *the* [SENATORS], *the Athenian*
LORDS, [*and*] VENTIDIUS *which* TIMON *redeemed from*
prison. Then comes, dropping° after all, APEMANTUS, *dis-*   *entering casually*
contentedly, like himself°   *in everyday clothes*

VENTIDIUS   Most honoured Timon, it hath pleased the gods to
    remember
  My father's age and call him to long peace.°   *eternal rest*
  He is gone happy, and has left me rich.
  Then, as in grateful virtue I am bound
5   To your free° heart, I do return those talents,   *generous*
  Doubled with thanks and service, from whose help
  I derived liberty.
TIMON   O, by no means,
  Honest Ventidius. You mistake my love.
  I gave it freely ever, and there's none
10   Can truly say he gives if he receives.
  If our betters play at that game,° we must not dare   *pretend generosity*
  To imitate them. Faults that are rich° are fair.   *of rich people*
VENTIDIUS   A noble spirit!
        [*The* LORDS *stand with ceremony*]
TIMON   Nay, my lords,
  Ceremony was but devised at first
15   To set a gloss on¹ faint deeds, hollow welcomes,

1.2 Location: Timon's banqueting room.   1. To give a fine appearance to.

Recanting goodness,[2] sorry ere 'tis shown;
But where there is true friendship, there needs none.°   *no ceremony*
Pray sit. More welcome are ye to my fortunes
Than my fortunes to me.
         [*They sit*]

20   FIRST LORD   My lord, we always have confessed it.
APEMANTUS   Ho, ho, confessed it? Hanged it, have you not?
TIMON   O, Apemantus! You are welcome.
APEMANTUS   No,
    You shall not make me welcome.
    I come to have thee° thrust me out of doors.   *provoke you to*
25   TIMON   Fie, thou'rt a churl.° Ye've got a humour there   *rude one*
    Does not become a man; 'tis much to blame.
    They say, my lords, *Ira furor brevis est,*[3]
    But yon man is ever angry.
    Go, let him have a table by himself,
30   For he does neither affect° company   *like*
    Nor is he fit for't, indeed.
APEMANTUS   Let me stay at thine apperil,° Timon.   *risk*
    I come to observe, I give thee warning on't.
TIMON   I take no heed of thee; thou'rt an Athenian,
35   Therefore welcome. I myself would have no power:[4]
    Prithee, let my meat make thee silent.
APEMANTUS   I scorn thy meat. 'Twould choke me, for I should
    ne'er flatter thee. O you gods, what a number of men eats
    Timon, and he sees 'em not! It grieves me to see so many dip
40   their meat in one man's blood; and all° the madness is, he   *the height of*
    cheers them up,° too.   *encourages them*
    I wonder men dare trust themselves with men.
    Methinks they should invite them without knives:[5]
    Good for their meat, and safer for their lives.
45   There's much example for't. The fellow that sits next him, now
    parts° bread with him, pledges the breath of him in a divided   *shares*
    draught,[6] is the readiest man to kill him. 'T'as been proved. If
    I were a huge° man, I should fear to drink at meals,   *great*
    Lest they should spy my windpipe's dangerous notes.[7]
50   Great men should drink with harness° on their throats.   *armor*
TIMON [*drinking to a* LORD]   My lord, in heart; and let the
    health° go round.   *shared cup*
SECOND LORD   Let it flow° this way, my good lord.   *circulate*
APEMANTUS   'Flow this way'? A brave° fellow; he keeps his tides[8]   *fine (ironic)*
55   well. Those healths will make thee and thy state look ill,
    Timon.
    Here's that which is too weak to be a sinner:
    Honest water, which ne'er left man i'th' mire.
    This and my food are equals; there's no odds.
60   Feasts are too proud to give thanks to the gods.
          Apemantus' grace
    Immortal gods, I crave no pelf.°   *property (contemptuous)*

---

2. Generosity that demands repayment, or that is immediately revoked.
3. Anger is brief insanity (Latin).
4. Wish no power to silence you.
5. Renaissance dinner guests brought their own silverware.

6. *pledges . . . draught:* toasts his health in a shared cup.
7. *my . . . notes:* the indications, when I drink, of where
my windpipe is (so they can cut my throat).
8. He observes his opportunity (joking, with wordplay on
"flow," that the Second Lord is ensuring that he gets
plenty to drink).

I pray for no man but myself.
Grant I may never prove so fond°   *foolish*
To trust man on his oath or bond,
65   Or a harlot for her weeping,
Or a dog that seems a-sleeping,
Or a keeper° with my freedom,   *jailer*
Or my friends if I should need 'em.
Amen. So fall to't.
70   Rich men sin, and I eat root.
        [*He eats*]
Much good dich° thy good heart, Apemantus.   *may it do*
TIMON   Captain Alcibiades, your heart's in the field° now.   *battlefield*
ALCIBIADES   My heart is ever at your service, my lord.
TIMON   You had rather be at a breakfast of enemies° than a din-   *(at a battle)*
75   ner of friends.
ALCIBIADES   So they were bleeding new, my lord; there's no
meat like 'em. I could wish my best friend at such a feast.
APEMANTUS   Would all those flatterers were thine enemies then,
That thou mightst kill 'em and bid me to 'em.
80   FIRST LORD [*to* TIMON]   Might we but have that happiness, my
lord, that you would once use our hearts,⁹ whereby we might
express some part of our zeals,° we should think ourselves for   *love*
ever perfect.°   *happy*
TIMON   O, no doubt, my good friends, but the gods themselves
85   have provided that I shall have much help from you. How had
you been my friends else? Why have you that charitable title°   *loving name*
from thousands, did not you chiefly belong to my heart? I have
told more of you to myself than you can with modesty speak in
your own behalf; and thus far I confirm you.¹ 'O you gods,'
90   think I, 'what need we have any friends if we should ne'er have
need of 'em? They were the most needless creatures living,
should we ne'er have use for 'em, and would most resemble
sweet instruments hung up in cases, that keeps their sounds to
themselves.' Why, I have often wished myself poorer, that I
95   might come nearer to you. We are born to do benefits; and
what better or properer° can we call our own than the riches of   *more suitably*
our friends? O, what a precious comfort 'tis to have so many
like brothers commanding° one another's fortunes! O, joy's   *having at their command*
e'en made away° ere't can be born: mine eyes cannot hold out   *destroyed (by tears)*
100   water, methinks. To forget their° faults, I drink to you.   *(my eyes')*
APEMANTUS   Thou weep'st to make them drink, Timon.
SECOND LORD [*to* TIMON]   Joy had the like° conception in our eyes,   *some kind of*
And at that instant like a babe sprung up.
APEMANTUS   Ho, ho, I laugh to think that babe a bastard.²
105 THIRD LORD [*to* TIMON]   I promise you, my lord, you moved me much.
APEMANTUS   Much!
        [*A*] tucket° sound[*s within*]   *trumpet flourish*
TIMON   What means that trump?
        Enter SERVANT
How now?
SERVANT   Please you, my lord, there are certain ladies most desir-
110   ous of admittance.

---

9. Would make trial of our affection.   2. That is, the guests' tears are illegitimate.
1. In your claim to be my friends.

TIMON   Ladies? What are their wills?

SERVANT   There comes with them a forerunner, my lord, which
bears that office° to signify their pleasures.°   *function / desires*

TIMON   I pray let them be admitted.

Enter [one as] CUPID

115   CUPID   Hail to thee, worthy Timon, and to all
That of his bounties taste! The five best senses
Acknowledge thee their patron, and come freely
To gratulate° thy plenteous bosom.° Th'ear,   *greet / generous heart*
Taste, touch, smell, all, pleased from thy table rise.

120   They° only now come but to feast thine eyes.   *(the masques)*

TIMON   They're welcome all. Let 'em have kind admittance.
Music make their welcome!   [*Exit* CUPID]

FIRST LORD   You see, my lord, how ample you're beloved.

[*Music.*] *Enter a masque of* LADIES [*as*] *Amazons, with
lutes in their hands, dancing and playing*

APEMANTUS   Hey-day, what a sweep of vanity comes this way!

125   They dance? They are madwomen.
Like madness is the glory° of this life   *vainglory*
As this pomp shows to a little oil and root.³
We make ourselves fools to disport° ourselves,   *amuse*
And spend our flatteries to drink° those men   *toast; drink up*

130   Upon whose age we void° it up again   *old age we spit*
With poisonous spite and envy.
Who lives that's not depravèd or depraves?
Who dies that bears not one spurn° to their graves   *insult*
Of their friends' gift?°   *giving*

135   I should fear those that dance before me now
Would one day stamp upon me. 'T'as been done.
Men shut their doors against a setting sun.

The LORDS *rise from table with much adoring of* TIMON;
*and to show their loves each singles out an Amazon, and
all dance, men with women, a lofty strain or two to the
hautboys, and cease*

TIMON   You have done our pleasures much grace, fair ladies,
Set a fair fashion on° our entertainment,   *Made elegant*

140   Which was not half so beautiful and kind.
You have added worth unto't and lustre,
And entertained me with mine own device.⁴
I am to thank you for't.

FIRST LADY   My lord, you take us even at the best.⁵

145   APEMANTUS   Faith; for the worst is filthy, and would not hold
taking,⁶ I doubt me.

TIMON   Ladies, there is an idle° banquet 'tends you.   *a trifling*
Please you to dispose° yourselves.   *seat*

ALL LADIES   Most thankfully, my lord.   *Exeunt* [LADIES]

150   TIMON   Flavius.

FLAVIUS   My lord.

TIMON   The little casket bring me hither.

FLAVIUS   Yes, my lord. [*Aside*] More jewels yet?
There is no crossing him in's humour,°   *whim*

---

3. As this feast compares to a meager meal.
4. Plan. Timon may be implying that he himself
arranged the entertainment, or merely that it was
designed for him by his admirers.

5. You consider our efforts in the best possible light.
6. Would not be worth noting; would not endure sexual
penetration (because of venereal disease).

155 Else I should tell him well, i'faith I should.
When all's spent, he'd be crossed⁷ then, an° he could.   *if*
'Tis pity bounty had not eyes behind,⁸
That man might ne'er be wretched for his mind.⁹   *Exit*
FIRST LORD   Where be our men?
160 SERVANT   Here, my lord, in readiness.
SECOND LORD   Our horses.   [*Exit* SERVANT]
          [*Enter* FLAVIUS *with the casket. He gives it to* TIMON *and
          exits*]
TIMON   O my friends, I have one word to say to you.
          Look you, my good lord,
          I must entreat you honour me so much
165   As to advance° this jewel. Accept and wear it,   *improve (by your worth)*
          Kind my lord.
FIRST LORD   I am so far already in your gifts.
ALL LORDS   So are we all.
          [TIMON *gives them jewels.*]
          Enter a SERVANT
FIRST SERVANT   My lord, there are certain nobles of the senate
170   newly alighted and come to visit you.
TIMON   They are fairly° welcome.   [*Exit* SERVANT]   *graciously*
          Enter FLAVIUS
FLAVIUS   I beseech your honour, vouchsafe me a word; it does
          concern you near.
TIMON   Near? Why then, another time I'll hear thee. I prithee,
175   let's be provided to show them entertainment.
FLAVIUS   I scarce know how.
          Enter a [SECOND SERVANT]
SECOND SERVANT   May it please your honour, Lord Lucius
          Out of his free love hath presented to you
          Four milk-white horses trapped° in silver.   *bedecked*
180 TIMON   I shall accept them fairly. Let the presents
          Be worthily entertained.°   [*Exit* SERVANT]   *accepted*
          Enter a [THIRD SERVANT]
          How now, what news?
THIRD SERVANT   Please you, my lord, that honourable gentleman
          Lord Lucullus entreats your company tomorrow to hunt with
          him, and has sent your honour two brace° of greyhounds.   *pairs*
185 TIMON   I'll hunt with him, and let them be received
          Not without fair reward.   [*Exit* SERVANT]
FLAVIUS [*aside*]   What will this come to?
          He commands us to provide and give great gifts,
          And all out of an empty coffer;
          Nor will he know his purse, or yield° me this: *allow*
190   To show him what a beggar his heart is,
          Being of no power to make his wishes good.
          His promises fly so beyond his state°   *estate*
          That what he speaks is all in debt, he owes
          For every word. He is so kind that he now
195   Pays interest for't. His land's put to their books.°   *mortgaged*
          Well, would I were gently put out of office
          Before I were forced out.

7. He'd want to have his debts canceled.   9. *for his mind:* because of his (generous) intentions.
8. 'Tis a pity generosity is not more careful.

Happier is he that has no friend to feed
Than such that do e'en enemies exceed.[1]
I bleed inwardly for my lord.   *Exit*

200 TIMON [*to the* LORDS]   You do yourselves
Much wrong, you bate° too much of your own merits.   *undervalue*
[*To* SECOND LORD] Here, my lord, a trifle of our love.
SECOND LORD   With more than common thanks I will receive it.
THIRD LORD   O, he's the very soul of bounty!

205 TIMON [*to* FIRST LORD]   And now I remember, my lord, you gave
good words the other day of a bay courser I rode on. 'Tis yours,
because you liked it.
FIRST LORD   O I beseech you pardon me, my lord, in that.[2]
TIMON   You may take my word, my lord, I know no man

210 Can justly praise but what he does affect.°   *desire*
I weigh my friends' affection with mine own.
I'll tell you true, I'll call to° you.   *on*
ALL LORDS   O, none so welcome.
TIMON   I take all and your several visitations

So kind to heart, 'tis not enough to give.
215 Methinks I could deal kingdoms to my friends,
And ne'er be weary. Alcibiades,
Thou art a soldier, therefore seldom rich.
[*Giving a present*] It comes in charity to thee, for all thy living
Is 'mongst the dead, and all the lands thou hast
Lie in a pitched field.

220 ALCIBIADES   Ay, defiled[3] land, my lord.
FIRST LORD   We are so virtuously bound—
TIMON   And so am I to you.
SECOND LORD   So infinitely endeared°—   *obliged*
TIMON   All to you. Lights, more lights!

225 FIRST LORD   The best of happiness, honour, and fortunes
Keep with you, Lord Timon.
TIMON   Ready for his friends.
                    Exeunt [*all but* TIMON *and* APEMANTUS]
APEMANTUS   What a coil's° here,   *commotion is*
Serving of becks° and jutting-out of bums!   *bowing*

230 I doubt whether their legs° be worth the sums   *curtsies*
That are given for 'em. Friendship's full of dregs.
Methinks false hearts should never have sound legs.
Thus honest fools lay out their wealth on curtseys.
TIMON   Now, Apemantus, if thou wert not sullen

235 I would be good to thee.
APEMANTUS   No, I'll nothing; for if I should be bribed too, there
would be none left to rail upon thee, and then thou wouldst
sin the faster. Thou giv'st so long, Timon, I fear me thou wilt
give away thyself in paper° shortly. What needs these feasts,   *promissory notes*

240 pomps, and vainglories?
TIMON   Nay, an you begin to rail on society once, I am sworn
not to give regard° to you.   *pay attention*
Farewell, and come with better music.   *Exit*

---

1. Who ruin themselves faster than enemies could.
2. That is, I wasn't hinting for the horse.
3. Lined with ranks of soldiers; punning on Ecclesias-   ticus 13:1, "He that toucheth pitch, shall be defiled with it."

APEMANTUS   So.
Thou wilt not hear me now, thou shalt not then.
245   I'll lock thy heaven° from thee. O, that men's ears should be   *(my redemptive guidance)*
To counsel deaf, but not to flattery!   *Exit*

2.1
Enter a SENATOR [*with bonds*]

SENATOR   And late five thousand. To Varro and to Isidore
He owes nine thousand, besides my former sum,
Which makes it five-and-twenty. Still in motion
Of raging waste!¹ It cannot hold,° it will not.   *last*
5   If I want gold, steal but a beggar's dog
And give it Timon, why, the dog coins gold.
If I would sell my horse and buy twenty more
Better than he, why, give my horse to Timon—
Ask nothing, give it him—it foals me straight,²
10   And able horses.³ No porter³ at his gate,
But rather one that smiles and still invites
All that pass by. It cannot hold. No reason
Can sound his state in safety.⁴ Caphis ho!
Caphis, I say!
      Enter CAPHIS

CAPHIS   Here, sir. What is your pleasure?
15   SENATOR   Get on your cloak and haste you to Lord Timon.
Importune him for my moneys. Be not ceased°   *put off*
With slight denial, nor then silenced when
'Commend me to your master', and the cap
Plays in the right hand,⁵ thus; but tell him
20   My uses cry to me, I must serve my turn
Out of mine own,⁶ his days and times are past,
And my reliances on his fracted° dates   *broken*
Have smit° my credit. I love and honour him,   *hurt*
But must not break my back to heal his finger.
25   Immediate are my needs, and my relief
Must not be tossed and turned⁷ to me in words,
But find supply immediate. Get you gone.
Put on a most importunate aspect,
A visage of demand, for I do fear
30   When every feather sticks in his own wing⁸
Lord Timon will be left a naked gull,°   *an unfledged bird; dupe*
Which flashes now a phoenix. Get you gone.
CAPHIS   I go, sir.
SENATOR [*giving him bonds*]   Take the bonds along with you,
And have the dates in count.°   *reckoned up*
CAPHIS   I will, sir.
SENATOR   Go.
                 Exeunt [*severally*]°   *separately*

2.1 Location: A Senator's house.
1. *Still . . . waste:* Still keeping up unending extravagance.
2. It immediately gives birth.
3. Gatekeeper (who restricts entrance). *able horses:* full-grown horses (not "foals," baby horses).
4. *No reason . . . safety:* No rational person can investi-
gate his financial situation and believe it safe.
5. *when . . . hand:* that is, with friendly speech and gestures.
6. *serve . . . own:* pay for my needs with my own money.
7. Returned (like a tennis ball).
8. When everything is returned to its proper owner.

2.2

Enter [FLAVIUS *the*] *Steward, with many bills in his hand*

FLAVIUS No care, no stop; so senseless of expense
That he will neither know how to maintain it
Nor cease his flow of riot,° takes no account   *his wastefulness*
How things go from him, nor resumes° no care   *takes*
5   Of what is to continue. Never mind
Was to be so unwise to be so kind.¹
What shall be done? He will not hear till feel.°   *he suffers*
[*A sound of horns within*]
I must be round° with him, now he comes from hunting.   *frank*
Fie, fie, fie, fie!
Enter CAPHIS [*at one door*] *and* [SERVANTS *of*] *Isidore and Varro* [*at another door*]
10   CAPHIS Good even, Varro. What, you come for money?
VARRO'S SERVANT Is't not your business too?
CAPHIS It is; and yours too, Isidore?
ISIDORE'S SERVANT   It is so.
CAPHIS Would we were all discharged.
VARRO'S SERVANT   I fear it.
CAPHIS   Here comes the lord.
Enter TIMON *and his train* [*amongst them* ALCIBIADES, *as from hunting*]
TIMON So soon as dinner's done we'll forth again,
My Alcibiades.
[CAPHIS *meets* TIMON]
15   With me? What is your will?
CAPHIS My lord, here is a note of certain dues.°   *debts*
TIMON Dues? Whence are you?
CAPHIS Of Athens here, my lord.
TIMON Go to my steward.
20   CAPHIS Please it your lordship, he hath put me off,
To the succession of new days, this month.°   *every day for a month*
My master is awaked° by great occasion°   *driven / need*
To call upon his own,° and humbly prays you   *own money*
That with your other noble parts you'll suit²
In giving him his right.
25   TIMON   Mine honest friend,
I prithee but repair° to me next morning.   *come back*
CAPHIS Nay, good my lord.
TIMON   Contain thyself, good friend.
VARRO'S SERVANT One Varro's servant, my good lord.
ISIDORE'S SERVANT [*to* TIMON] From Isidore. He humbly prays
your speedy payment.
30   CAPHIS [*to* TIMON] If you did know, my lord, my master's wants—
VARRO'S SERVANT [*to* TIMON] 'Twas due on forfeiture,³ my lord,
six weeks and past.
ISIDORE'S SERVANT [*to* TIMON] Your steward puts me off, my
lord, and I
Am sent expressly to your lordship.

2.2 Location: Before Timon's house.
1. *Never . . . kind:* Never was anyone so idiotically generous.

2. That you'll act in accordance with your noble qualities.
3. On penalty of forfeiting the security.

TIMON   Give me breath.—
    I do beseech you, good my lords, keep on.°   *go ahead*
    I'll wait upon you instantly.
                      [*Exeunt* ALCIBIADES *and Timon's train*]
35   [*To* FLAVIUS]   Come hither. Pray you,
    How goes the world, that I am thus encountered
    With clamorous demands of broken bonds
    And the detention of° long-since-due debts,   *failure to pay*
    Against my honour?
FLAVIUS [*to* SERVANTS]   Please you, gentlemen,
40   The time is unagreeable to this business;
    Your importunacy cease till after dinner,
    That I may make his lordship understand
    Wherefore you are not paid.
TIMON [*to* SERVANTS]   Do so, my friends.
    [*To* FLAVIUS] See them well entertained.   *Exit*
FLAVIUS   Pray draw near. *Exit*
       Enter APEMANTUS *and* FOOL
45   CAPHIS   Stay, stay, here comes the fool with Apemantus.
    Let's ha' some sport with 'em.
VARRO'S SERVANT   Hang him, he'll abuse us.
ISIDORE'S SERVANT   A plague upon him, dog!
VARRO'S SERVANT   How dost, fool?
50   APEMANTUS   Dost dialogue with thy shadow?[4]
VARRO'S SERVANT   I speak not to thee.
APEMANTUS   No, 'tis to thyself. [*To* FOOL] Come away.
ISIDORE'S SERVANT [*to* VARRO'S SERVANT]   There's the fool[5] hangs
    on your back already.
55   APEMANTUS   No, thou stand'st single:° thou'rt not on him yet.   *alone (in being a fool)*
CAPHIS [*to* ISIDORE'S SERVANT]   Where's the fool now?
APEMANTUS   He last asked the question. Poor rogues' and usu-
    rers' men, bawds between gold and want.[6]
ALL SERVANTS   What are we, Apemantus?
60   APEMANTUS   Asses.
ALL SERVANTS   Why?
APEMANTUS   That you ask me what you are, and do not know
    yourselves. Speak to 'em, fool.
FOOL   How do you, gentlemen?
65   ALL SERVANTS   Gramercies,° good fool. How does your mistress?   *Many thanks*
FOOL   She's e'en° setting on water to scald such chickens[7] as you   *just now*
    are. Would we could see you at Corinth.[8]
APEMANTUS   Good; gramercy.
       Enter PAGE [*with two letters*]
FOOL   Look you, here comes my mistress' page.
70   PAGE   Why, how now, captain? What do you in this wise com-
    pany? How dost thou, Apemantus?
APEMANTUS   Would I had a rod[9] in my mouth, that I might
    answer thee profitably.

---

4. With your reflection (implying that Varro's Servant is also a fool).

5. The name "fool." In Renaissance England, wrong-doers were punished by being made to wear signs declaring their offenses.

6. *bawds . . . want:* go-betweens making deals between moneylenders and those who need loans.

7. In order to remove the feathers (a "plucked bird" was a hoodwinked fool; compare 2.1.31); also, syphilitics were "sweated" in tubs of very hot water.

8. Greek city famous for prostitution.

9. From Proverbs 26:3–4: "Unto the horse belongeth a whip, to the ass a bridle, and a rod to the fool's back. Answer not a fool according to his foolishness, lest thou also be like him."

PAGE Prithee, Apemantus, read me the superscription° of these   *address*
75 letters. I know not which is which.
APEMANTUS Canst not read?
PAGE No.
APEMANTUS There will little learning die then that day thou art
hanged. This is to Lord Timon, this to Alcibiades. Go, thou
80 wast born a bastard, and thou'lt die a bawd.
PAGE Thou wast whelped a dog, and thou shalt famish° a dog's   *die*
death. Answer not; I am gone.   *Exit*
APEMANTUS E'en so thou outrunn'st grace.[1] Fool, I will go with
you to Lord Timon's.
85 FOOL Will you leave me there?
APEMANTUS If Timon stay at home.[2] [*To* SERVANTS] You three
serve three usurers?
ALL SERVANTS Ay. Would they served us.°   *treated us well*
APEMANTUS So would I: as good a trick as ever hangman served
90 thief.
FOOL Are you three usurers' men?
ALL SERVANTS Ay, fool.
FOOL I think no usurer but has a fool to his servant. My mistress
is one,[3] and I am her fool. When men come to borrow of your
95 masters they approach sadly and go away merry, but they enter
my mistress's house merrily and go away sadly.[4] The reason of
this?
VARRO'S SERVANT I could render one.
APEMANTUS Do it then, that we may account thee a whore-
100 master and a knave, which notwithstanding thou shalt be no
less esteemed.
VARRO'S SERVANT What is a whoremaster, fool?
FOOL A fool in good clothes, and something like thee. 'Tis a
spirit; sometime 't appears like a lord, sometime like a lawyer,
105 sometime like a philosopher with two stones[5] more than's° arti-   *than his*
ficial one. He is very often like a knight; and generally in all
shapes that man goes up and down in from fourscore to thirteen, this spirit walks in.
VARRO'S SERVANT Thou art not altogether a fool.
110 FOOL Nor thou altogether a wise man. As much foolery as I
have, so much wit thou lack'st.
APEMANTUS That answer might have become° Apemantus.   *suited*
          Enter TIMON *and* [FLAVIUS *the*] Steward
ALL SERVANTS Aside, aside, here comes Lord Timon.
APEMANTUS Come with me, fool, come.
115 FOOL I do not always follow lover, elder brother, and woman:[6]
sometime the philosopher.   [*Exeunt* APEMANTUS *and* FOOL]
FLAVIUS [*to* SERVANTS] Pray you, walk near. I'll speak with you
anon.   *Exeunt* [SERVANTS]
TIMON You make me marvel wherefore ere this time
120 Had you not fully laid my state before me,[7]
That I might so have rated° my expense   *regulated*
As I had leave of means.°   *As means permitted*

---

1. You run away from profitable instruction.
2. There will be a fool at Timon's house as long as he is at home.
3. She is a "usurer" in the sense that she lends her body for financial gain; the connection between usury and prostitution was traditional.
4. According to Aristotle, all creatures are sad after sexual intercourse.
5. Testicles. In alchemy, the "philosopher's stone" was thought to turn base metals into gold.
6. All figures associated with folly.
7. Described my financial status.

FLAVIUS   You would not hear me.
    At many leisures I proposed—
TIMON   Go to.°   *(impatient exclamation)*
    Perchance some single vantages° you took,   *isolated opportunities*
125 When my indisposition° put you back,   *disinclination*
    And that unaptness made your minister°   *allowed you*
    Thus to excuse yourself.
FLAVIUS   O my good lord,
    At many times I brought in my accounts,
    Laid them before you; you would throw them off
130 And say you summed them in mine honesty.[8]
    When for some trifling present you have bid me
    Return so much,° I have shook my head and wept,   *a large sum*
    Yea, 'gainst th'authority of manners° prayed you   *with rude bluntness*
    To hold your hand more close. I did endure
135 Not seldom nor no slight checks° when I have   *rebukes*
    Prompted you in° the ebb of your estate   *Urged you to note*
    And your great flow of debts. My lovèd lord—
    Though you hear now too late, yet now's a time°—   *better late than never*
    The greatest of your having[9] lacks a half
    To pay your present debts.
140 TIMON   Let all my land be sold.
FLAVIUS 'Tis all engaged,° some forfeited and gone,   *mortgaged*
    And what remains will hardly stop the mouth
    Of present dues.° The future comes apace.   *debts*
    What shall defend the interim, and at length°   *in the long term*
145 How goes our reck'ning?
TIMON   To Lacedaemon° did my land extend.   *Sparta*
FLAVIUS   O my good lord, the world is but a word.
    Were it all yours to give it in a breath,
    How quickly were it gone.
TIMON   You tell me true.
150 FLAVIUS   If you suspect my husbandry° or falsehood,   *household management*
    Call me before th'exactest auditors
    And set me on the proof. So the gods bless me,
    When all our offices° have been oppressed   *kitchens and workrooms*
    With riotous feeders, when our vaults have wept
155 With drunken spilth° of wine, when every room   *spilling*
    Hath blazed with lights and brayed with minstrelsy,
    I have retired me to a wasteful cock,[1]
    And set mine eyes at flow.
TIMON   Prithee, no more.
FLAVIUS   'Heavens,' have I said, 'the bounty of this lord!
160 How many prodigal bits° have slaves and peasants   *extravagant morsels*
    This night englutted! Who is not Timon's?°   *devoted to Timon*
    What heart, head, sword, force, means, but is Lord Timon's?
    Great Timon, noble, worthy, royal Timon!
    Ah, when the means are gone that buy this praise,
165 The breath is gone whereof this praise is made.
    Feast won, fast° lost; one cloud of winter show'rs,   *quickly; while fasting*
    These flies are couched.'°   *lying unseen*
TIMON   Come, sermon me no further.

---

8. You gauged their accuracy by my honesty.
9. The most generous estimate of your wealth.

1. I have sat down beside a wine spout, left wastefully flowing.

No villainous° bounty yet hath passed my heart.   *shameful*
Unwisely, not ignobly, have I given.
170 Why dost thou weep? Canst thou the conscience° lack   *conviction*
To think I shall lack friends? Secure thy heart.
If I would broach° the vessels of my love   *tap (like a wine barrel)*
And try the argument° of hearts by borrowing,   *test the contents*
Men and men's fortunes could I frankly° use   *as freely*
As I can bid thee speak.
175 FLAVIUS   Assurance bless your thoughts!²
TIMON   And in some sort° these wants of mine are crowned°   *respect / exalted*
That I account them blessings, for by these
Shall I try friends. You shall perceive how you
Mistake my fortunes. I am wealthy in my friends.—
180 Within there, Flaminius, Servilius!
        Enter [FLAMINIUS, SERVILIUS, *and a* THIRD] SERVANT
ALL SERVANTS   My lord, my lord.
TIMON   I will dispatch you severally,°   *separately*
        [*To* SERVILIUS] You to Lord Lucius,
        [*To* FLAMINIUS]   to Lord Lucullus you—
        I hunted with his honour today—
        [*To* THIRD SERVANT] You to Sempronius. Commend me to
            their loves,
185 And I am proud, say, that my occasions° have   *needs*
Found time° to use 'em toward a supply of money.   *occasion*
Let the request be fifty talents.°   *(a huge sum)*
FLAMINIUS   As you have said, my lord.   [*Exeunt* SERVANTS]
FLAVIUS   Lord Lucius and Lucullus? Hmh!
190 TIMON   Go you, sir, to the senators,
Of whom, even to the state's best health,³ I have
Deserved this hearing. Bid 'em send o'th' instant
A thousand talents to me.
FLAVIUS   I have been bold,
For that I knew it the most general° way,   *usual*
195 To them, to use your signet⁴ and your name;
But they do shake their heads, and I am here
No richer in return.
TIMON   Is't true? Can't be?
FLAVIUS   They answer in a joint and corporate voice
That now they are at fall,° want° treasure, cannot   *low ebb / lack*
200 Do what they would, are sorry, you are honourable,
But yet they could have wished—they know not—
Something hath been amiss—a noble nature
May catch a wrench°—would all were well—'tis pity;   *suffer a misfortune*
And so, intending° other serious matters,   *pretending; attending to*
205 After distasteful looks and these hard fractions,°   *phrases*
With certain half-caps° and cold moving nods   *reluctant salutations*
They froze me into silence.
TIMON   You gods reward them!
Prithee, man, look cheerly.° These old fellows   *cheerful*
Have their ingratitude in them hereditary.
210 Their blood is caked, 'tis cold, it seldom flows.
'Tis lack of kindly⁵ warmth they are not kind;

---

2. May your hopes be well-founded.   4. Signet ring (token of authorization).
3. Greatest welfare (see 4.3.92–95).   5. Natural (punning on "caring").

And nature as it grows again toward earth°   *the grave*
Is fashioned for the journey dull and heavy.
Go to Ventidius. Prithee, be not sad.
215 Thou art true and honest—ingenuously° I speak—   *candidly*
No blame belongs to thee. Ventidius lately
Buried his father, by whose death he's stepped
Into a great estate. When he was poor,
Imprisoned, and in scarcity of friends,
220 I cleared him with five talents. Greet him from me.
Bid him suppose some good° necessity   *urgent*
Touches his friend, which craves to be remembered
With° those five talents. That had, give't these fellows   *By return of*
To whom 'tis instant due. Ne'er speak or think
225 That Timon's fortunes 'mong his friends can sink.
FLAVIUS I would I could not think it. That thought is bounty's foe:
Being free° itself, it thinks all others so.   *Exeunt [severally]*   *generous*

3.1

[Enter] FLAMINIUS, *[with a box under his cloak,] waiting*
to speak with [LUCULLUS]. *From his master, enters a* SER-
VANT *to him*
LUCULLUS' SERVANT I have told my lord of you. He is coming
down to you.
FLAMINIUS I thank you, sir.
Enter LUCULLUS
LUCULLUS' SERVANT Here's my lord.
5 LUCULLUS *[aside]* One of Lord Timon's men? A gift, I warrant.
Why, this hits right; I dreamt of a silver basin and ewer°   *pitcher*
tonight.—Flaminius, honest Flaminius, you are very respec-
tively° welcome, sir. *[To his* SERVANT] Fill me some wine.   *respectfully*
[Exit SERVANT]
And how does that honourable, complete, free-hearted gentle-
10 man of Athens, thy very bountiful good lord and master?
FLAMINIUS His health is well, sir.
LUCULLUS I am right glad that his health is well, sir. And what
hast thou there under thy cloak, pretty Flaminius?
FLAMINIUS Faith, nothing but an empty box, sir, which in my
15 lord's behalf I come to entreat your honour to supply, who,
having great and instant° occasion to use fifty talents, hath sent   *urgent*
to your lordship to furnish him, nothing doubting your present°   *immediate*
assistance therein.
LUCULLUS La, la, la, la, 'nothing doubting' says he? Alas, good
20 lord! A noble gentleman 'tis, if he would not keep so good a
house.° Many a time and often I ha' dined with him and told   *such lavish hospitality*
him on't, and come again to supper to him of purpose to have
him[1] spend less; and yet he would embrace no counsel, take
no warning by my coming. Every man has his fault, and hon-
25 esty° is his. I ha' told him on't, but I could ne'er get him from't.   *generosity*
Enter SERVANT, *with wine*
SERVANT Please your lordship, here is the wine.
LUCULLUS Flaminius, I have noted thee always wise.
[Drinking] Here's to thee!
FLAMINIUS Your lordship speaks your pleasure.°   *It pleases you to say so*

3.1 Location: Lucullus's house.   1. *of . . . him:* in order to persuade him to.

30 LUCULLUS   I have observed thee always for a towardly° prompt   *promising*
spirit, give thee thy due, and one that knows what belongs to
reason;° and canst use the time well if the time use thee well.²   *is reasonable*
[*Drinking*] Good parts in thee!³
[*To his* SERVANT] Get you gone, sirrah.   [*Exit* SERVANT]
35 Draw nearer, honest Flaminius. Thy lord's a bountiful gentleman; but thou art wise, and thou know'st well enough,
although thou com'st to me, that this is no time to lend money,
especially upon bare° friendship without security. [*Giving*   *mere*
coins] Here's three solidares° for thee. Good boy, wink at me,⁴   *shillings*
40 and say thou saw'st me not. Fare thee well.
FLAMINIUS   Is't possible the world should so much differ,°   *alter*
And we alive that lived?
      [*He throws the coins at* LUCULLUS]
          Fly, damnèd baseness,
To him that worships thee.
LUCULLUS   Ha! Now I see thou art a fool, and fit for thy master.
                                Exit
45 FLAMINIUS   May these add to the number that may scald thee.°   *(in hell)*
Let molten coin be thy damnation,
Thou disease of a friend, and not himself.°   *not a true friend*
Has friendship such a faint and milky heart
It turns° in less than two nights? O you gods,   *curdles*
50 I feel my master's passion!° This slave   *suffering*
Unto this hour has my lord's meat in him.
Why should it thrive and turn to nutriment,
When he is turned to poison?
O, may diseases only work upon't;
55 And when he's sick to death, let not that part of nature
Which my lord paid for be of any power
To expel sickness, but prolong his hour.°   *Exit*   *(of suffering)*

3.2

Enter LUCIUS, *with three* STRANGERS
LUCIUS   Who, the Lord Timon? He is my very good friend, and
an honourable gentleman.
FIRST STRANGER   We know him for no less, though we are but
strangers to him. But I can tell you one thing, my lord, and
5 which I hear from common rumours: now Lord Timon's happy
hours are done and past, and his estate shrinks from him.
LUCIUS   Fie, no, do not believe it. He cannot want for money.
SECOND STRANGER   But believe you this, my lord, that not long
ago one of his men was with the Lord Lucullus to borrow so
10 many talents—nay, urged extremely for't, and showed what
necessity belonged to't, and yet was denied.
LUCIUS   How?
SECOND STRANGER   I tell you, denied, my lord.
LUCIUS   What a strange case was that! Now before the gods, I am
15 ashamed on't. Denied that honourable man? There was very
little honour showed in't. For my own part, I must needs confess I have received some small kindnesses from him, as money,
plate, jewels, and suchlike trifles—nothing comparing to his;

2. *canst . . . thee well:* know how to use an opportunity.
3. To your good qualities (a toast).
4. Close your eyes to me.
3.2 Location: A public place.

yet had he not mistook him[1] and sent to me, I should ne'er
20   have denied his occasion so many talents.
          Enter SERVILIUS
SERVILIUS [*aside*]   See, by good hap yonder's my lord. I have
          sweat° to see his honour. [*To* LUCIUS] My honoured lord!   *hurried*
LUCIUS   Servilius! You are kindly met, sir. Fare thee well. Com-
          mend me to thy honourable virtuous lord, my very exquisite°   *extraordinary*
25   friend.
SERVILIUS   May it please your honour, my lord hath sent—
LUCIUS   Ha! What has he sent? I am so much endeared° to that   *obliged*
          lord, he's ever sending. How shall I thank him, think'st thou?
          And what has he sent now?
30   SERVILIUS   He's only sent his present occasion now, my lord,
          requesting your lordship to supply his instant use with so many
          talents.
LUCIUS   I know his lordship is but merry with me.
          He cannot want fifty-five hundred[2] talents.
35   SERVILIUS   But in the mean time he wants less, my lord.
          If his occasion were not virtuous
          I should not urge it half so faithfully.
LUCIUS   Dost thou speak seriously, Servilius?
SERVILIUS   Upon my soul, 'tis true, sir.
40   LUCIUS   What a wicked beast was I to disfurnish myself against
          such a good time[3] when I might ha' shown myself honourable!
          How unluckily it happened that I should purchase the day
          before a little part,° and undo a great deal of honour! Servilius,   *small investment*
          now before the gods I am not able to do, the more beast I, I
45   say. I was sending to use° Lord Timon myself—these gentle-   *make use of*
          men can witness—but I would not for the wealth of Athens I
          had done't now. Commend me bountifully to his good lord-
          ship; and I hope his honour will conceive the fairest° of me   *think the best*
          because I have no power to be kind. And tell him this from me:
50   I count it one of my greatest afflictions, say, that I cannot plea-
          sure° such an honourable gentleman. Good Servilius, will you   *gratify*
          befriend me so far as to use mine own words to him?
SERVILIUS   Yes, sir, I shall.
LUCIUS   I'll look you out° a good turn, Servilius. *Exit* SERVILIUS   *seek to do you*
55   True as you said: Timon is shrunk indeed;
          And he that's once denied will hardly speed.°   *Exit*   *prosper*
FIRST STRANGER   Do you observe this, Hostilius?
SECOND STRANGER   Ay, too well.
FIRST STRANGER   Why, this is the world's soul,° and just of the   *essence*
          same piece°   *(of cloth)*
          Is every flatterer's spirit. Who can call him his friend
60   That dips in the same dish?[4] For, in my knowing,
          Timon has been this lord's father°   *patron*
          And kept his° credit with his purse,   *sustained (Lucius's)*
          Supported his estate; nay, Timon's money
          Has paid his men their wages. He ne'er drinks,
65   But Timon's silver treads upon his lip;
          And yet—O see the monstrousness of man

1. Not overestimated Lucullus's generosity.
2. This number possibly retains Shakespeare's revision
from "five hundred" to "fifty" or vice versa.
3. *disfurnish . . . time:* be unprepared for such a fine occasion.
4. Alluding to Judas's betrayal of Christ after the Last
Supper.

When he looks out° in an ungrateful shape!— | *shows himself*
He does deny him, in respect of his,[5]
What charitable men afford to beggars.

THIRD STRANGER   Religion groans at it.

70 FIRST STRANGER   For mine own part,
I never tasted° Timon in my life, | *had experience of*
Nor came any of his bounties over me
To mark me for his friend; yet I protest,
For his right noble mind, illustrious virtue,
75 And honourable carriage,° | *conduct*
Had his necessity made use of me
I would have put my wealth into donation° | *given my wealth*
And the best half should have returned to him,
So much I love his heart. But I perceive
80 Men must learn now with pity to dispense,
For policy° sits above conscience.   *Exeunt* | *calculation*

3.3

Enter [Timon's] THIRD SERVANT, with SEMPRONIUS,
another of Timon's friends

SEMPRONIUS   Must he needs trouble me in't? Hmh! 'Bove all others?
He might have tried Lord Lucius or Lucullus;
And now Ventidius is wealthy too,
Whom he redeemed from prison. All these
Owes their estates unto him.
5 SERVANT   My lord,
They have all been touched° and found base metal, | *tested for purity*
For they have all denied him.
SEMPRONIUS   How, have they denied him?
Has Ventidius and Lucullus denied him,
And does he send to me? Three? Hmh!
10 It shows but little love or judgement in him.
Must I be his last refuge? His friends, like physicians,
Thrive, give him over;[1] must I take th' cure upon me?
He's much disgraced me in't. I'm angry at him,
That might have known my place.[2] I see no sense for't
15 But his occasions might have wooed me first,
For, in my conscience,° I was the first man | *on my word*
That e'er receivèd gift from him.
And does he think so backwardly of me now
That I'll requite it last? No.
20 So it may prove an argument° of laughter | *a subject*
To th' rest, and I 'mongst lords be thought a fool.
I'd rather than the worth of thrice the sum
He'd sent to me first, but for my mind's sake.[3]
I'd such a courage to do him good. But now return,
25 And with their faint reply this answer join:
Who bates° mine honour shall not know my coin.   *Exit* | *undervalues*
SERVANT   Excellent. Your lordship's a goodly villain. The devil
knew not what he did when he made man politic°— he | *calculating*
crossed[4] himself by't, and I cannot think but in the end the

---

5. In proportion to what he owns.
3.3 Location: Sempronius's house.
1. Thrive, while abandoning him to death.
2. That is, his place in Timon's list of friends.

3. If only on account of my disposition to him.
4. Thwarted (by making men his equal); canceled from the list of debtors.

30 villainies of man will set him clear.[5] How fairly° this lord strives   *fully; speciously*
    to appear foul! Takes virtuous copies° to be wicked, like those[6]   *precepts*
    that under hot ardent zeal would set whole realms on fire; of
    such a nature is his politic love.
    This was my lord's best hope. Now all are fled
35 Save only the gods. Now his friends are dead.
    Doors that were ne'er acquainted with their wards°   *locks*
    Many a bounteous year must be employed
    Now to guard sure° their master;   *safely*
    And this is all a liberal° course allows: *generous*
40 Who cannot keep his wealth must keep his house.[7]   *Exit*

3.4

Enter Varro's [two SERVANTS*], meeting others, all [*SER-
VANTS *of]* Timon's *creditors, to wait for his coming out.
Then enter [*SERVANTS *of]* Lucius, *[*Titus,*] and Horten-
sius*

VARRO'S FIRST SERVANT Well met; good morrow, Titus and
    Hortensius.
TITUS' SERVANT The like to you, kind Varro.
HORTENSIUS' SERVANT Lucius, what, do we meet together?
LUCIUS' SERVANT Ay, and I think one business does command
    us all,
    For mine is money.
5 TITUS' SERVANT   So is theirs and ours.
    Enter [a SERVANT *of]* Philotus
LUCIUS' SERVANT And Sir Philotus too!
PHILOTUS' SERVANT   Good day at once.
LUCIUS' SERVANT Welcome, good brother. What do you think
    the hour?
PHILOTUS' SERVANT Labouring for° nine.   *Approaching*
LUCIUS' SERVANT So much?
10 PHILOTUS' SERVANT Is not my lord seen yet?
LUCIUS' SERVANT Not yet.
PHILOTUS' SERVANT I wonder on't; he was wont to shine° at   *used to rise*
    seven.
LUCIUS' SERVANT Ay, but the days are waxed shorter with him.
    You must consider that a prodigal course
15 Is like the sun's,[1]
    But not, like his,° recoverable. I fear   *(the sun's)*
    'Tis deepest winter in Lord Timon's purse; that is,
    One may reach deep enough, and yet find little.
PHILOTUS' SERVANT I am of° your fear for that.   *I share*
20 TITUS' SERVANT I'll show you how t'observe a strange event.
    Your lord sends now for money?
HORTENSIUS' SERVANT   Most true, he does.
TITUS' SERVANT And he wears jewels now of Timon's gift,
    For° which I wait for money.   *For the purchase of*
HORTENSIUS' SERVANT It is against my heart.°   *desire*
25 LUCIUS' SERVANT Mark how strange it shows.
    Timon in this should pay more than he owes,

---

5. Will make him look innocent; will free him from debt.   7. Must stay indoors (for fear of arrest).
6. Religious fanatics; perhaps alludes to the Catholic   3.4 Location: Timon's house.
Gunpowder Plot to blow up king and Parliament.   1. That is, waning after the summer solstice.

And e'en° as if your lord should wear rich jewels   *just*
And send for money for 'em.[2]
HORTENSIUS' SERVANT   I'm weary of this charge,° the gods can   *task*
   witness.
30   I know my lord hath spent of Timon's wealth,
   And now ingratitude makes it worse than stealth.°   *stealing*
VARRO'S FIRST SERVANT
   Yes; mine's three thousand crowns. What's yours?
LUCIUS' SERVANT   Five thousand, mine.
VARRO'S FIRST SERVANT   'Tis much° deep, and it should seem by th' sum   *very*
   Your master's confidence was above mine,°   *(my master's)*
   Else surely his° had equalled.   *(my master's loan)*
        Enter FLAMINIUS
35   TITUS' SERVANT   One of Lord Timon's men.
LUCIUS' SERVANT   Flaminius! Sir, a word. Pray, is my lord
   Ready to come forth?
FLAMINIUS   No, indeed he is not.
TITUS' SERVANT   We attend his lordship.
   Pray signify so much.
40   FLAMINIUS   I need not tell
   Him that; he knows you are too diligent.
       Enter [FLAVIUS *the*] *Steward, muffled in a cloak*
LUCIUS' SERVANT   Ha, is not that his steward muffled so?
   He goes away in a cloud.° Call him, call him.   *concealed; in trouble*
TITUS' SERVANT [*to* FLAVIUS]   Do you hear, sir?
45   VARRO'S SECOND SERVANT [*to* FLAVIUS]   By your leave, sir.
FLAVIUS   What do ye ask of me, my friend?
TITUS' SERVANT   We wait for certain money here, sir.
FLAVIUS   Ay,
   If money were as certain as your waiting,
   'Twere sure enough.
50   Why then preferred° you not your sums and bills   *brought forward*
   When your false masters ate of my lord's meat?
   Then they could smile and fawn upon his debts,
   And take down th'int'rest into their glutt'nous maws.
   You do yourselves but wrong to stir me up.
55   Let me pass quietly.
   Believe't, my lord and I have made an end.°   *finished with each other*
   I have no more to reckon, he to spend.
LUCIUS' SERVANT   Ay, but this answer will not serve.
FLAVIUS   If 'twill not serve[3] 'tis not so base as you,
60   For you serve knaves.   *Exit*
VARRO'S FIRST SERVANT   How? What does his cashiered° worship   *dismissed*
   mutter?
VARRO'S SECOND SERVANT   No matter what; he's poor, and that's
   revenge enough. Who can speak broader[4] than he that has no
65   house to put his head in? Such may rail against great buildings.
       Enter SERVILIUS
TITUS' SERVANT   O, here's Servilius. Now we shall know some
   answer.
SERVILIUS   If I might beseech you, gentlemen, to repair° some   *return*

---

2. And demand payment from Timon for supplying them.   4. More freely; more out-of-doors.
3. Suffice (but in line 60, "wait on").

other hour, I should derive° much from't; for, take't of my soul,   *gain*
70 my lord leans wondrously to discontent. His comfortable° tem-   *cheerful*
per has forsook him. He's much out of health, and keeps his
chamber.
LUCIUS' SERVANT   Many do keep their chambers are not sick,[5]
And if it be so far beyond his health
75 Methinks he should the sooner pay his debts
And make a clear way to the gods.
SERVILIUS   Good gods!
TITUS' SERVANT   We cannot take this for an answer, sir.
FLAMINIUS [*within*]   Servilius, help! My lord, my lord!
      Enter TIMON *in a rage*
TIMON   What, are my doors opposed against my passage?
80 Have I been ever free,° and must my house   *at liberty; generous*
Be my retentive° enemy, my jail?   *confining; niggardly*
The place which I have feasted, does it now,
Like all mankind, show me an iron heart?
LUCIUS' SERVANT   Put in° now, Titus.   *Make your claim*
TITUS' SERVANT   My lord, here is my bill.
LUCIUS' SERVANT   Here's mine.
85 HORTENSIUS' SERVANT   And mine, my lord.
VARRO'S FIRST *and* SECOND SERVANTS   And ours, my lord.
PHILOTUS' SERVANT   All our bills.
TIMON   Knock me down with 'em, cleave me to the girdle.[6]
LUCIUS' SERVANT   Alas, my lord.
90 TIMON   Cut my heart in° sums.   *into*
TITUS' SERVANT   Mine fifty talents.
TIMON   Tell° out my blood.   *Count*
LUCIUS' SERVANT   Five thousand crowns, my lord.
TIMON   Five thousand drops pays that. What yours? And yours?
VARRO'S FIRST SERVANT   My lord—
95 VARRO'S SECOND SERVANT   My lord—
TIMON   Tear me, take me, and the gods fall upon you.   *Exit*
HORTENSIUS' SERVANT   Faith, I perceive our masters may throw
their caps at° their money. These debts may well be called des-   *cease pursuing*
perate° ones, for a madman owes 'em.   *Exeunt*   *hopeless; insane*

3.5

    Enter TIMON [*and* FLAVIUS]
TIMON   They have e'en put[1] my breath from me, the slaves.
Creditors? Devils!
FLAVIUS   My dear lord—
TIMON   What if it should be so?[2]
5 FLAVIUS   My lord—
TIMON   I'll have it so. My steward!
FLAVIUS   Here, my lord.
TIMON   So fitly?° Go bid all my friends again: *conveniently*
Lucius, Lucullus, and Sempronius—all luxors,° all.   *lechers*
I'll once more feast the rascals.
FLAVIUS   O my lord,
10 You only speak from your distracted soul.

---

5. That is, they are avoiding arrest for debt.
6. Timon puns on "bills" (line 87) as weapons (halberds).
3.5 Location: Scene continues.

1. Have taken (referring to Timon's breathlessness and to
the proverb "Air is free").
2. Timon is referring to a plan he has just thought of.

There is not so much left to furnish out
A moderate table.
TIMON   Be it not in thy care.°   *your responsibility*
Go, I charge thee, invite them all. Let in the tide
Of knaves once more. My cook and I'll provide.

Exeunt [severally]

3.6

Enter three SENATORS *at one door*

FIRST SENATOR   My lords, you have my voice to't.° The fault's°   *vote for it / crime is*
bloody.
'Tis necessary he should die.
Nothing emboldens sin so much as mercy.
SECOND SENATOR   Most true; the law shall bruise 'im.

[Enter] ALCIBIADES *[at another door], with attendants*

5 ALCIBIADES   Honour, health, and compassion to the senate!
FIRST SENATOR   Now, captain.
ALCIBIADES   I am an humble suitor to your virtues;
For pity is the virtue° of the law,   *essence*
And none but tyrants use it cruelly.
10   It pleases time and fortune to lie heavy
Upon a friend of mine, who in hot blood
Hath stepped into° the law, which is past depth   *(as into quicksand)*
To those that without heed do plunge into't.
He is a man, setting his feat° aside,   *deed*
15   Of comely virtues;
Nor did he soil the fact with cowardice —
An honour in him which buys out his fault°—   *redeems his crime*
But with a noble fury and fair spirit,
Seeing his reputation touched to death,°   *fatally besmirched*
20   He did oppose his foe;
And with such sober and unnoted[1] passion
He did behave° his anger, ere 'twas spent,   *control*
As if he had but proved an argument.
FIRST SENATOR   You undergo° too strict a paradox,   *undertake*
25   Striving to make an ugly deed look fair.
Your words have took such pains as if they laboured
To bring manslaughter into form,[2] and set quarrelling
Upon the head° of valour—which indeed   *In the category of*
Is valour misbegot, and came into the world
30   When sects and factions were newly born.
He's truly valiant that can wisely suffer
The worst that man can breathe,° and make his wrongs his   *utter*
outsides°   *merely external things*
To wear them like his raiment carelessly,
And ne'er prefer° his injuries to his heart   *promote*
35   To bring it into danger.
If wrongs be evils and enforce us kill,
What folly 'tis to hazard life for ill!
ALCIBIADES   My lord—
FIRST SENATOR   You cannot make gross sins look clear.
To revenge is no valour, but to bear.°   *endure (is valor)*

3.6 Location: The Senate house.   2. To make manslaughter legal.
1. Unnoticed (because moderate).

40   ALCIBIADES   My lords, then, under favour,° pardon me   *by your leave*
      If I speak like a captain.
      Why do fond° men expose themselves to battle,   *foolish*
      And not endure all threats, sleep upon't,
      And let the foes quietly cut their throats
45   Without repugnancy?° If there be   *resistance*
      Such valour in the bearing,° what make we   *enduring*
      Abroad?³ Why then, women are more valiant
      That stay at home if bearing carry it,°   *wins the day*
      And the ass more captain than the lion, the felon
50   Loaden with irons° wiser than the judge,   *shackles*
      If wisdom be in suffering. O my lords,
      As you are great, be pitifully good.°   *good in showing pity*
      Who cannot condemn rashness in cold blood?
      To kill, I grant, is sin's extremest gust,°   *outburst*
55   But in defence, by mercy,⁴ 'tis most just.
      To be in anger is impiety,
      But who is man that is not angry?
      Weigh but the crime with this.
  SECOND SENATOR   You breathe in vain.
  ALCIBIADES   In vain?
      His service done at Lacedaemon and Byzantium
60   Were a sufficient briber for his life.
  FIRST SENATOR   What's that?
  ALCIBIADES   Why, I say, my lords, he's done fair° service,   *fine*
      And slain in fight many of your enemies.
      How full of valour did he bear himself
      In the last conflict, and made plenteous wounds!
65   SECOND SENATOR   He has made too much plenty with 'em.
      He's a sworn rioter;° he has a sin   *committed reveler*
      That often drowns him and takes his valour prisoner.⁵
      If there were no foes, that were enough
      To overcome him. In that beastly fury
70   He has been known to commit outrages
      And cherish factions.° 'Tis inferred° to us   *foster dissension / alleged*
      His days are foul and his drink dangerous.
  FIRST SENATOR   He dies.
  ALCIBIADES   Hard fate! He might have died in war.
      My lords, if not for any parts° in him—   *good qualities*
75   Though his right arm might purchase his own time⁶
      And be in debt to none—yet more to move you,
      Take° my deserts to his and join 'em both.   *Combine*
      And for I know
      Your reverend ages love security,⁷
80   I'll pawn my victories, all my honour to you
      Upon his good returns.°   *repayment (of your money)*
      If by this crime he owes the law his life,
      Why, let the war receive't in valiant gore,
      For law is strict, and war is nothing more.
85   FIRST SENATOR   We are for law; he dies. Urge it no more,
      On height of our° displeasure. Friend or brother,   *At risk of our highest*

---

3. *what make we / Abroad:* why do we (men) go outdoors?
4. But self-defense, considered mercifully.
5. *sin . . . prisoner:* that is, drunkenness.

6. Though performance in battle might redeem him for the duration of his life.
7. Collateral (as on a loan); safety.

He forfeits his own blood that spills another.
ALCIBIADES   Must it be so? It must not be.
  My lords, I do beseech you know me.
SECOND SENATOR   How?
ALCIBIADES   Call me to your remembrances.
90 THIRD SENATOR   What?
ALCIBIADES   I cannot think but your age has forgot me.
  It could not else° be I should prove so base   otherwise
  To sue and be denied such common grace.
  My wounds ache at you.
FIRST SENATOR   Do you dare our anger?
95 'Tis in few words, but spacious° in effect: great
  We banish thee for ever.
ALCIBIADES   Banish me?
  Banish your dotage, banish usury
  That makes the senate ugly.
FIRST SENATOR   If after two days' shine
  Athens contain thee, attend our weightier judgement;
100 And, not to swell your spirit,° he shall be   anger
  Executed presently.°   *Exeunt* [SENATORS *and attendants*]   immediately
ALCIBIADES   Now the gods keep you old enough that you may live
  Only in bone,° that none may look on you!   as skeletons
  I'm worse than mad. I have kept back their foes
105 While they have told° their money and let out   counted
  Their coin upon large interest—I myself,
  Rich only in large hurts. All those for this?
  Is this the balsam° that the usuring senate   ointment
  Pours into captains' wounds? Banishment!
110 It comes not ill; I hate not to be banished.
  It is a cause worthy my spleen and fury,
  That I may strike at Athens. I'll cheer up
  My discontented troops, and lay for hearts.°   win their support
  'Tis honour with most lands° to be at odds.   the richest
115 Soldiers should brook° as little wrongs as gods.   *Exit*   endure

3.7

Enter divers [of Timon's] friends, [amongst them LUCUL-
LUS, LUCIUS, SEMPRONIUS, *and other* LORDS *and Sena-*
tors,] at several doors
FIRST LORD   The good time of day to you, sir.
SECOND LORD   I also wish it to you. I think this honourable lord
  did but try° us this other day.   test
FIRST LORD   Upon that were my thoughts tiring[1] when we
5 encountered.° I hope it is not so low with him as he made it   met
  seem in the trial of his several friends.
SECOND LORD   It should not be, by the persuasion° of his new   evidence
  feasting.
FIRST LORD   I should think so. He hath sent me an earnest invit-
10 ing, which many my near occasions° did urge me to put off, but   my many urgent affairs
  he hath conjured me beyond them, and I must needs appear.
SECOND LORD   In like manner was I in debt° to my importunate   I needed to atttend
  business, but he would not hear my excuse. I am sorry when
  he sent to borrow of me that my provision was out.

3.7 Location: Timon's house.   1. Feeding (as a hawk tears flesh).

15   FIRST LORD   I am sick of that grief too, as I understand how all
things go.²
SECOND LORD   Every man hears so. What would he have bor-
rowed of you?
FIRST LORD   A thousand pieces.
20   SECOND LORD   A thousand pieces?
FIRST LORD   What of you?
SECOND LORD   He sent to me, sir—
[*Loud music.*] *Enter* TIMON *and attendants*
Here he comes.
TIMON   With all my heart, gentlemen both; and how fare you?
25   FIRST LORD   Ever at the best, hearing well of your lordship.
SECOND LORD   The swallow follows not summer more willing
than we your lordship.
TIMON [*aside*]   Nor more willingly leaves winter, such summer
birds are men.—Gentlemen, our dinner will not recompense
30   this long stay. Feast your ears with the music a while, if they   sustain themselves
will fare° so harshly o'th' trumpets' sound; we shall to't
presently.
FIRST LORD   I hope it remains not unkindly with your lordship
that I returned you an empty messenger.
35   TIMON   O sir, let it not trouble you.
SECOND LORD   My noble lord—
TIMON   Ah, my good friend, what cheer?
[*A table and stools are*] *brought in*
SECOND LORD   My most honourable lord, I am e'en° sick of   utterly
shame that when your lordship this other day sent to me I was
40   so unfortunate a beggar.
TIMON   Think not on't, sir.
SECOND LORD   If you had sent but two hours before—
TIMON   Let it not cumber° your better remembrance.— Come,   burden
bring in all together.
[*Enter Servants with covered dishes*]
45   SECOND LORD   All covered dishes.
FIRST LORD   Royal cheer,° I warrant you.   dining
THIRD LORD   Doubt not that, if money and the season can yield it.
FIRST LORD   How do you? What's the news?
THIRD LORD   Alcibiades is banished. Hear you of it?
50   FIRST and SECOND LORDS   Alcibiades banished?
THIRD LORD   'Tis so, be sure of it.
FIRST LORD   How, how?
SECOND LORD   I pray you, upon what?°   what grounds
TIMON   My worthy friends, will you draw near?
55   THIRD LORD   I'll tell you more anon. Here's a noble feast
toward.°   coming up
SECOND LORD   This is the old³ man still.
THIRD LORD   Will't hold, will't hold?°   last
SECOND LORD   It does; but time will°—and so—   "time will tell"
60   THIRD LORD   I do conceive.°   understand
TIMON   Each man to his stool with that spur° as he would to the   speed
lip of his mistress. Your diet shall be in all places alike. Make

---

2. *as . . . go*: now that I understand the real situation.   3. Familiar (in his generosity).

not a city feast[4] of it, to let the meat cool ere we can agree upon
the first place.° Sit, sit. The gods require our thanks.   *place of honor*
          They sit
65   You great benefactors, sprinkle our society with thankfulness.
For your own gifts make yourselves praised; but reserve still[5] to
give, lest your deities be despised. Lend to each man enough
that one need not lend to another; for were your godheads to
borrow of men, men would forsake the gods. Make the meat
70   be beloved more than the man that gives it. Let no assembly of
twenty be without a score of villains. If there sit twelve women
at the table, let a dozen of them be as they are. The rest of your
foes, O gods—the senators of Athens, together with the
common tag° of people—what is amiss in them, you gods,   *mob*
75   make suitable for destruction. For these my present friends, as
they are to me nothing, so in nothing bless them; and to nothing are they welcome.—Uncover, dogs, and lap.
          [*The dishes are uncovered, and seen to be full of
          steaming water and stones*]
SOME LORDS   What does his lordship mean?
OTHER LORDS   I know not.
80 TIMON   May you a better feast never behold,
          You knot of mouth-friends.[6] Smoke and lukewarm water
          Is your perfection. This is Timon's last,
          Who, stuck and spangled with your flattery,
          Washes it off, and sprinkles in your faces
          Your reeking° villainy.   *steaming; stinking*
          [*He throws water in their faces*]
85   Live loathed and long,
          Most smiling, smooth, detested parasites,
          Courteous destroyers, affable wolves, meek bears,
          You fools of fortune, trencher-friends,° time's flies,[7]   *mealtime friends*
          Cap-and-knee° slaves, vapours, and minute-jacks![8]   *Sycophantic*
90   Of man and beast the infinite malady[9]
          Crust you quite o'er.
          [*A* LORD *is going*]
                                  What, dost thou go?
          Soft,° take thy physic° first. Thou too, and thou.   *Wait / medicine*
          [*He beats them*]
          Stay, I will lend thee money, borrow none.
          [*Exeunt* LORDS, *leaving caps and gowns*]
          What, all in motion? Henceforth be no feast
95   Whereat a villain's not a welcome guest.
          Burn house! Sink Athens! Henceforth hated be
          Of Timon man and all humanity!   *Exit*
          Enter the Senators [and] other LORDS
FIRST LORD   How now, my lords?
SECOND LORD   Know you the quality° of Lord Timon's fury?   *nature*
THIRD LORD   Push!° Did you see my cap?   *(impatient expression)*
100 FOURTH LORD   I have lost my gown.
FIRST LORD   He's but a mad lord, and naught but humours°   *unstable moods*

---

4. Feast as given by London dignitaries, in which seating
arrangements were thought socially significant.
5. But always hold back something.
6. You group of insincere (or gluttonous) friends.

7. That is, vanishing in cold weather.
8. Mannekins that strike bells on medieval clocks; hence,
timeservers.
9. May every disease of man and beast.

sways him. He gave me a jewel th'other day, and now he has
beat it out of my hat.
Did you see my jewel?

THIRD LORD   Did you see my cap?

SECOND LORD   Here 'tis.

FOURTH LORD   Here lies my gown.

105   FIRST LORD   Let's make no stay.

SECOND LORD   Lord Timon's mad.

THIRD LORD   I feel't upon my bones.

FOURTH LORD   One day he gives us diamonds, next day stones.

Exeunt

4.1

Enter TIMON

TIMON   Let me look back upon thee. O thou wall
That girdles in those wolves, dive in the earth,
And fence not Athens! Matrons, turn incontinent!°   *unchaste*
Obedience fail in children! Slaves and fools,
5   Pluck the grave wrinkled senate from the bench
And minister in their steads! To general filths°   *common whores*
Convert o'th' instant, green¹ virginity!
Do't in your parents' eyes. Bankrupts, hold fast!°   *refuse to pay*
Rather than render back, out with your knives,
10   And cut your trusters'° throats. Bound° servants, steal!   *creditors' / Indentured*
Large-handed robbers your grave masters are,
And pill° by law. Maid, to thy master's bed!   *plunder*
Thy mistress is o'th' brothel. Son of sixteen,
Pluck the lined° crutch from thy old limping sire;   *padded*
15   With it beat out his brains! Piety and fear,
Religion to the gods, peace, justice, truth,
Domestic awe,² night rest, and neighbourhood,°   *neighborliness*
Instruction, manners, mysteries,° and trades,   *crafts*
Degrees,° observances,³ customs, and laws,   *Social ranks*
20   Decline to your confounding° contraries,   *destroying*
And let confusion live! Plagues incident to men,
Your potent and infectious fevers heap
On Athens, ripe for stroke!° Thou cold sciatica,°   *to be struck / nerve pain*
Cripple our senators, that their limbs may halt°   *limp*
25   As lamely as their manners! Lust and liberty,°   *licentiousness*
Creep in the minds and marrows⁴ of our youth,
That 'gainst the stream of virtue they may strive
And drown themselves in riot!° Itches, blains,°   *debauchery / sores*
Sow all th'Athenian bosoms, and their crop
30   Be general leprosy! Breath infect breath,
That their society,° as their friendship, may   *company*
Be merely° poison!   *wholly*

He tears off his clothing

              Nothing I'll bear from thee
But nakedness, thou detestable town;
Take thou that too, with multiplying bans.°   *curses*
35   Timon will to the woods, where he shall find

4.1 Location: Outside the walls of Athens.
1. Young, newly menstruating girls often suffered anemia, then called "greensickness" and thought to be cur-
able by sexual satisfaction.

2. Household government.
3. Respectful customs.
4. Thought to be the site of vigor; proverbially melted by
lust.

Th'unkindest beast more kinder⁵ than mankind.
The gods confound—hear me you good gods all—
Th'Athenians, both within and out that wall;
And grant, as Timon grows, his hate may grow
40 To the whole race of mankind, high and low.
Amen.   *Exit*

4.2

Enter [FLAVIUS *the*] *Steward, with two or three* SERVANTS
FIRST SERVANT   Hear you, master steward, where's our master?
Are we undone, cast off, nothing remaining?
FLAVIUS   Alack, my fellows, what should I say to you?
Let me be recorded: by the righteous gods,
I am as poor as you.
5 FIRST SERVANT   Such a house broke,
So noble a master fall'n? All gone, and not
One friend to take his° fortune by the arm   *(Timon's)*
And go along with him?
SECOND SERVANT   As we do turn our backs
From our companion thrown into his grave,
10 So his familiars to¹ his buried fortunes
Slink all away, leave their false vows with him
Like empty purses picked; and his poor self,
A dedicated° beggar to the air,   *Abandoned as a*
With his disease of all-shunned poverty,
Walks like contempt alone.
Enter other SERVANTS
15   More of our fellows.
FLAVIUS   All broken implements of a ruined house.
THIRD SERVANT   Yet do our hearts wear Timon's livery.°   *servants' uniforms*
That see I by our faces. We are fellows still,
Serving alike in sorrow. Leaked is our barque,°   *sailboat*
20 And we, poor mates, stand on the dying° deck   *sinking*
Hearing the surges'° threat. We must all part   *waves*
Into this sea of air.
FLAVIUS   Good fellows all,
The latest° of my wealth I'll share amongst you.   *last bit*
Wherever we shall meet, for Timon's sake
25 Let's yet be fellows. Let's shake our heads and say,
As 'twere a knell unto our master's fortunes,
'We have seen better days.'
[*He gives them money*]
                                    Let each take some.
Nay, put out all your hands. Not one word more.
Thus part we rich in sorrow, parting poor.
[*They*] *embrace, and* [*the* SERVANTS] *part several ways*
30 O, the fierce° wretchedness that glory brings us!   *excessive*
Who would not wish to be from wealth exempt,
Since riches point to misery and contempt?
Who would be so mocked with glory, or to live
But in a dream of friendship,

---

5. Gentler; more natural; more nearly akin.
4.2 Location: Timon's house.

1. So his intimate friends from (a "familiar" could also be
a flattering devil).

35 To have his pomp and all what state compounds[2]
But only painted like his varnished friends?
Poor honest lord, brought low by his own heart,
Undone by goodness! Strange, unusual blood°   *disposition*
When man's worst sin is he does too much good!
40 Who then dares to be half so kind again?
For bounty, that makes° gods, does still mar men.   *characterizes*
My dearest lord, blessed to be most accursed,
Rich only to be wretched, thy great fortunes
Are made thy chief afflictions. Alas, kind lord!
45 He's flung in rage from this ingrateful seat°   *residence*
Of monstrous friends;
Nor has he with him to supply° his life,   *resources to maintain*
Or that° which can command it.   *(money)*
I'll follow and enquire him out.
50 I'll ever serve his mind with my best will.
Whilst I have gold I'll be his steward still.   *Exit*

4.3

Enter TIMON *[from his cave] in the woods [half naked,*
and with a spade]

TIMON   O blessèd breeding sun,[1] draw from the earth
Rotten° humidity; below thy sister's[2] orb   *Putrid*
Infect the air. Twinned brothers of one womb,
Whose procreation, residence,° and birth   *time in the womb*
5 Scarce is dividant,° touch them with several° fortunes,   *separable / different*
The greater scorns the lesser. Not nature,
To whom all sores° lay siege, can bear great fortune   *afflictions*
But by contempt of nature.[3]
It is the pasture lards[4] the brother's sides,
10 The want that makes him lean.
Raise me[5] this beggar and demit that lord,
The senator shall bear contempt hereditary,°   *as if he had inherited it*
The beggar native° honour. Who dares, who dares   *inborn*
In purity of manhood stand upright
15 And say 'This man's a flatterer'? If one be,
So are they all, for every grece° of fortune   *step on the staircase*
Is smoothed by that below.[6] The learnèd pate°   *head*
Ducks° to the golden fool. All's obliquy;°   *Bows / deviousness*
There's nothing level° in our cursèd natures   *straight, consistent*
20 But direct villainy. Therefore be abhorred
All feasts, societies, and throngs of men.
His semblable,° yea, himself, Timon disdains.   *His own image*
Destruction fang° mankind. Earth, yield me roots.   *seize*
       [He digs]
Who seeks for better of thee, sauce his palate
With thy most operant° poison.   *potent*
       [He finds gold]
                              What is here?
25

2. And all that splendor is made of.
4.3 Location: Outside Athens.
1. The sun was supposed to be able to generate vermin spontaneously and to foment infection.
2. The moon's; see note to 1.1.44.
3. Without scorning those of like nature.

4. Fattens ("pasture" suggests both owning and eating from the land).
5. This "me" is an example of the so-called ethic dative (literally, "for me"), used to emphasize the verb. See also line 112.
6. By the people standing on the step below.

Gold? Yellow, glittering, precious gold?
No, gods, I am no idle° votarist: *frivolous*
Roots, you clear heavens. Thus much of this will make
Black white, foul fair, wrong right,
30 Base noble, old young, coward valiant.
Ha, you gods! Why this, what, this, you gods? Why, this
Will lug your priests and servants from your sides,
Pluck stout men's pillows from below their heads.°   *(to kill them)*
This yellow slave
35 Will knit and break religions, bless th'accursed,
Make the hoar° leprosy adored, place° thieves,   *gray / appoint to office*
And give them title, knee,° and approbation   *kneeling*
With senators on the bench. This is it
That makes the wappered° widow wed again.   *worn out*
40 She whom the spittle house° and ulcerous sores   *hospital*
Would cast the gorge° at, this embalms and spices   *vomit*
To th' April day⁷ again. Come, damnèd earth,°   *gold*
Thou common whore of mankind, that puts odds°   *quarrels?*
Among the rout° of nations; I will make thee   *rabble*
Do⁸ thy right nature.
    March afar off
45   Ha, a drum! Thou'rt quick;⁹
But yet I'll bury thee.
    [He buries gold]
            Thou'lt go, strong thief,
When gouty keepers of thee cannot stand.
    [He keeps some gold]
Nay, stay thou out for earnest.°   *as a pledge*
    Enter ALCIBIADES, *with [soldiers playing] drum and fife,*
    in warlike manner; and PHRYNIA *and* TIMANDRA
ALCIBIADES   What art thou there? Speak.
TIMON   A beast, as thou art. The canker¹ gnaw thy heart
50   For showing me again the eyes of man.
ALCIBIADES   What is thy name? Is man so hateful to thee
  That art thyself a man?
TIMON   I am Misanthropos,° and hate mankind.   *man-hater (Greek)*
  For thy part, I do wish thou wert a dog,
  That I might love thee something.°   *somewhat*
55 ALCIBIADES   I know thee well,
  But in thy fortunes am unlearned and strange.²
TIMON   I know thee too, and more than that I know thee
  I not desire° to know. Follow thy drum.   *do not desire*
  With man's blood paint the ground gules,° gules.   *red (heraldic term)*
60   Religious canons, civil laws, are cruel;
  Then what should war be? This fell° whore of thine   *dreadful*
  Hath in her more destruction than thy sword,
  For all her cherubin look.
PHRYNIA   Thy lips rot off!°   *(as in syphilis)*
TIMON   I will not kiss thee; then the rot returns
65   To thine own lips again.
ALCIBIADES   How came the noble Timon to this change?

---

7. To youthful freshness.
8. Act according to (by concealing gold and yielding roots).
9. Swift to bring strife; alive.
1. Spreading ulcer; cankerworm.
2. Am ignorant and unacquainted.

TIMON   As the moon does, by wanting° light to give.   *lacking*
　　But then renew I could not like the moon;
　　There were no suns to borrow of.
70 ALCIBIADES   Noble Timon, what friendship may I do thee?
TIMON   None but to maintain my opinion.
ALCIBIADES   What is it, Timon?
TIMON   Promise me friendship, but perform none. If thou wilt
　　promise, the gods plague thee, for thou art a man. If thou dost
75 　not perform, confound° thee, for thou art a man.   *damn*
ALCIBIADES   I have heard in some sort° of thy miseries.   *to some extent*
TIMON   Thou saw'st them when I had prosperity.
ALCIBIADES   I see them now; then was a blessèd time.
TIMON   As thine is now, held with a brace° of harlots.   *pair*
80 TIMANDRA   Is this th'Athenian minion,° whom the world   *favorite*
　　Voiced° so regardfully?   *Spoke of*
TIMON   Art thou Timandra?
TIMANDRA   Yes.
TIMON   Be a whore still. They love thee not that use thee.
　　Give them diseases, leaving with thee their lust.
85 　Make use of thy salt° hours: season° the slaves   *lecherous / prepare*
　　For tubs and baths,³ bring down rose-cheeked youth
　　To the tub-fast and the diet.
TIMANDRA   Hang thee, monster!
ALCIBIADES   Pardon him, sweet Timandra, for his wits
　　Are drowned and lost in his calamities.
90 　I have but little gold of late, brave Timon,
　　The want whereof doth daily make° revolt   *cause*
　　In my penurious band. I have heard and grieved
　　How cursèd Athens, mindless of thy worth,
　　Forgetting thy great deeds, when neighbour states
95 　But for thy sword and fortune trod upon them⁴—
TIMON   I prithee, beat thy drum and get thee gone.
ALCIBIADES   I am thy friend, and pity thee, dear Timon.
TIMON   How dost thou pity him whom thou dost trouble?
　　I had rather be alone.
ALCIBIADES   Why, fare thee well.
　　Here is some gold for thee.
100 TIMON   Keep it. I cannot eat it.
ALCIBIADES   When I have laid proud Athens on a heap—
TIMON   Warr'st thou 'gainst Athens?
ALCIBIADES   Ay, Timon, and have cause.
TIMON   The gods confound them all in thy conquest,
　　And thee after, when thou hast conquerèd.
ALCIBIADES   Why me, Timon?
105 TIMON   That by killing of villains
　　Thou wast born to conquer my country.
　　Put up thy gold.
　　　　[*He gives* ALCIBIADES *gold*]
　　　　　　Go on; here's gold; go on.
　　Be as a planetary plague⁵ when Jove
　　Will o'er some high-viced city hang his poison

3. Used, with "diet" (line 87), to treat venereal disease.
4. Alcibiades suggests that Timon's money and military expertise saved Athens in the past.
5. Plagues were thought to be caused by the influence of the other planets.

110   In the sick air. Let not thy sword skip one.
        Pity not honoured age for his white beard;
        He is an usurer. Strike me° the counterfeit matron;   *Strike for me*
        It is her habit° only that is honest,   *attire*
        Herself's a bawd. Let not the virgin's cheek
115   Make soft thy trenchant° sword; for those milk paps°   *cutting / breasts*
        That through the window-bars° bore at men's eyes   *openwork bodice*
        Are not within the leaf° of pity writ;   *page*
        But set them down horrible traitors. Spare not the babe
        Whose dimpled smiles from fools exhaust° their mercy.   *draw out*
120   Think it a bastard whom the oracle
        Hath doubtfully° pronounced thy throat shall cut,   *ambiguously*
        And mince it sans° remorse. Swear against objects.⁶   *without*
        Put armour on thine ears and on thine eyes
        Whose proof° nor yells of mothers, maids, nor babes,   *strength*
125   Nor sight of priests in holy vestments bleeding,
        Shall pierce a jot. There's gold to pay thy soldiers.
        Make large confusion, and, thy fury spent,
        Confounded be thyself. Speak not. Be gone.
      ALCIBIADES   Hast thou gold yet? I'll take the gold thou giv'st me,
130   Not all thy counsel.
      TIMON   Dost thou or dost thou not, heaven's curse upon thee!
      PHRYNIA *and* TIMANDRA   Give us some gold, good Timon. Hast
            thou more?
      TIMON   Enough to make a whore forswear her trade,
        And to make wholesomeness a bawd. Hold up, you sluts,
        Your aprons mountant.⁷
            [*He throws gold into their aprons*]
135   You are not oathable,⁸
        Although I know you'll swear, terribly swear,
        Into strong shudders and to heavenly agues°   *fevers*
        Th'immortal gods that hear you. Spare your oaths;
        I'll trust to your conditions.° Be whores still,   *occupations; characters*
140   And he whose pious breath seeks to convert you,
        Be strong in whore, allure him, burn him up.°   *inflame him; infect him*
        Let your close° fire predominate his smoke;⁹   *secret*
        And be no turncoats. Yet may your pain-sick months
        Be quite contrary,° and thatch your poor thin roofs   *Make you suffer intensely*
145   With burdens of the dead¹—some that were hanged,
        No matter. Wear them, betray with them; whore still;
        Paint° till a horse may mire° upon your face.   *Use cosmetics / get stuck*
        A pox of wrinkles!
      PHRYNIA *and* TIMANDRA   Well, more gold; what then?
        Believe't that we'll do anything for gold.
150   TIMON   Consumptions° sow   *Diseases*
        In hollow bones of man, strike their sharp shins,²
        And mar men's spurring.³ Crack the lawyer's voice,
        That he may never more false title plead
        Nor sound his quillets° shrilly. Hoar the flamen⁴   *quibbles (wordplay)*

6. Vow not to listen to protests.
7. Your skirts lifted ("mountant," a heraldic term, puns
on "sexual mounting").
8. Capable of being bound on oath.
9. Overcome his "pious breath" (line 140).
1. *thatch . . . dead:* wear wigs made of corpses' hair to
cover your syphilitic baldness.
2. Syphilis causes bone degeneration.
3. Horseback riding; sexual intercourse. *Crack:* Ruin (an
ulcerous larynx is an effect of syphilis).
4. Whiten the priest (with syphilis or leprosy).

155   That scolds against the quality° of flesh   *nature*

        And not believes himself. Down with the nose,

        Down with it flat;⁵ take the bridge quite away

        Of him that his particular° to foresee   *self-interest*

        Smells from the general weal.⁶ Make curled-pate ruffians bald,

160   And let the unscarred braggarts of the war

        Derive some pain from you. Plague all,

        That your activity may defeat and quell

        The source of all erection.⁷ There's more gold.

        Do you damn others, and let this damn you;

165   And ditches grave you all!⁸

PHRYNIA *and* TIMANDRA   More counsel with more money, boun-

        teous Timon.

TIMON   More whore, more mischief first; I have given you earnest.°   *a down payment*

ALCIBIADES   Strike up the drum towards Athens. Farewell,

        Timon.

        If I thrive well, I'll visit thee again.

170 TIMON   If I hope well, I'll never see thee more.

ALCIBIADES   I never did thee harm.

TIMON   Yes, thou spok'st well of me.

ALCIBIADES   Call'st thou that harm?

TIMON   Men daily find it.° Get thee away,   *discover it to be so*

        And take thy beagles° with thee.   *fawning curs (the whores)*

175 ALCIBIADES   We but offend him. Strike!

                Exeunt [to drum and fife, all but TIMON]

TIMON   That nature, being sick of° man's unkindness,   *through excess of*

        Should yet be hungry!

        [*He digs the earth*]

                  Common° mother—thou   *Universal*

        Whose womb unmeasurable and infinite breast

        Teems° and feeds all, whose selfsame mettle°   *Breeds / substance*

180   Whereof thy proud child, arrogant man, is puffed

        Engenders the black toad and adder blue,

        The gilded newt and eyeless venomed worm,

        With all th'abhorrèd births below crisp° heaven   *clear*

        Whereon Hyperion's quick'ning° fire doth shine—   *the sun's life-giving*

185   Yield him who all thy human sons do hate

        From forth thy plenteous bosom, one poor root.

        Ensear° thy fertile and conceptious womb;   *Dry up*

        Let it no more bring out ingrateful man.

        Go great° with tigers, dragons, wolves, and bears;   *pregnant*

190   Teem with new monsters whom thy upward° face   *upturned*

        Hath to the marbled mansion° all above   *heavens*

        Never presented.

        [*He finds a root*]

                  O, a root! Dear thanks.

        Dry up thy marrows,° vines, and plough-torn leas,°   *pulpy fruits / fields*

        Whereof ingrateful man with liquorish draughts⁹

195   And morsels unctuous° greases his pure mind,   *oily*

        That from it all consideration° slips!—   *rationality*

---

5. Syphilis sometimes caused the bridge of the nose to collapse.
6. The image suggests a dog leaving the pack to pursue its own quarry.

7. Sexual erection; social advancement.
8. May you all suffer squalid deaths.
9. Sweet, lust-inducing drinks.

Enter APEMANTUS
More man? Plague, plague!

APEMANTUS   I was directed hither. Men report
Thou dost affect° my manners, and dost use them.   *like; imitate*

200 TIMON   'Tis then because thou dost not keep a dog
Whom I would imitate. Consumption catch thee!

APEMANTUS   This is in thee a nature but infected,[1]
A poor unmanly melancholy, sprung
From change of fortune. Why this spade, this place,

205 This slave-like habit,° and these looks of care?   *costume*
Thy flatterers yet wear silk, drink wine, lie soft,
Hug their diseased perfumes,° and have forgot   *perfumed women*
That ever Timon was. Shame not these woods
By putting on the cunning of a carper.[2]

210 Be thou a flatterer now, and seek to thrive
By that which has undone thee. Hinge thy knee,
And let his very breath whom thou'lt observe°   *pay court to*
Blow off thy cap. Praise his most vicious strain,°   *trait*
And call it excellent. Thou wast told thus.

215 Thou gav'st thine ears like tapsters° that bade welcome   *bartenders*
To knaves and all approachers. 'Tis most just
That thou turn rascal.° Hadst thou wealth again,   *knave; solitary deer*
Rascals should have't. Do not assume my likeness.

TIMON   Were I like thee, I'd throw away myself.

220 APEMANTUS   Thou hast cast away thyself being like thyself—
A madman so long, now a fool. What, think'st
That the bleak air, thy boisterous chamberlain,°   *personal servant*
Will put thy shirt on warm? Will these mossed trees
That have outlived the eagle page° thy heels   *follow at*

225 And skip when thou point'st out?[3] Will the cold brook,
Candied° with ice, caudle thy morning taste[4]   *Encrusted*
To cure thy o'ernight's surfeit? Call the creatures
Whose naked natures live in° all the spite   *exposed to*
Of wreakful° heaven, whose bare unhousèd trunks°   *vengeful / bodies*

230 To the conflicting elements exposed
Answer° mere nature; bid them flatter thee.   *Obey*
O, thou shalt find—

TIMON   A fool of thee! Depart.

APEMANTUS   I love thee better now than e'er I did.

TIMON   I hate thee worse.

APEMANTUS   Why?

TIMON   Thou flatter'st misery.

235 APEMANTUS   I flatter not, but say thou art a caitiff.°   *wretch*

TIMON   Why dost thou seek me out?

APEMANTUS   To vex thee.

TIMON   Always a villain's office, or a fool's.
Dost please thyself in't?

APEMANTUS   Ay.

TIMON   What, a knave too?

APEMANTUS   If thou didst put this sour cold habit° on   *dress; disposition*
240 To castigate thy pride, 'twere well; but thou

---

1. That is, not innately so or converted by philosophical argument.
2. The knowledge of a faultfinder.

3. And jump to get whatever you indicate.
4. Give you a hot drink in the morning.

Dost it enforcèdly.° Thou'dst courtier be again   *by compulsion*
Wert thou not beggar. Willing misery
Outlives incertain° pomp, is crowned⁵ before.   *insecure*
The one° is filling still,° never complete;   *("incertain pomp") / always*
245   The other at high wish.⁶ Best state, contentless,⁷
Hath a distracted and most wretched being,
Worse than the worst, content.⁸
Thou shouldst desire to die, being miserable.
TIMON   Not by his breath that is more miserable.⁹
250   Thou art a slave whom fortune's tender arm
With favour never clasped, but bred a dog.
Hadst thou like us from our first swathe proceeded¹
The sweet degrees² that this brief world affords
To such as° may the passive drudges of it   *To those who*
255   Freely command, thou wouldst have plunged thyself
In general riot,° melted down thy youth   *debauchery*
In different beds of lust, and never learned
The icy precepts of respect,° but followed   *restraint; judgment*
The sugared game° before thee. But myself,   *sweet quarry*
260   Who had the world as my confectionary,
The mouths, the tongues, the eyes and hearts of men
At duty,° more than I could frame° employment,   *my service / provide*
That numberless upon me stuck, as leaves
Do on the oak, have with one winter's brush
265   Fell from their boughs, and left me open, bare
For every storm that blows—I to bear this,
That never knew but better,° is some burden.   *anything but good fortune*
Thy nature did commence in sufferance,° time   *suffering*
Hath made thee hard° in't. Why shouldst thou hate men?   *hardened*
270   They never flattered thee. What hast thou given?
If thou wilt curse, thy father, that poor rag,°   *wretch*
Must be thy subject, who in spite put stuff
To³ some she-beggar and compounded° thee   *constituted*
Poor rogue hereditary.° Hence, be gone.   *by birth*
275   If thou hadst not been born the worst of men
Thou hadst been a knave and flatterer.
APEMANTUS   Art thou proud yet?
TIMON   Ay, that I am not thee.
APEMANTUS   I that I was
No prodigal.
280   TIMON   I that I am one now.
Were all the wealth I have shut up° in thee   *contained*
I'd give thee leave to hang it. Get thee gone.
That° the whole life of Athens were in this!   *Would that*
Thus would I eat it.
[*He bites the root*]
APEMANTUS [*offering food*]   Here, I will mend° thy feast.   *improve*
285   TIMON   First mend my company: take away thyself.
APEMANTUS   So I shall mend mine own by th' lack of thine.

---

5. Finds fulfillment.
6. (Misery) at the height of its wish.
7. The greatest prosperity, if not contented.
8. The least prosperity, living contented.
9. Not at the command of someone even unhappier

than I.
1. From our swaddling clothes mounted.
2. Social ranks; steps on Fortune's ladder.
3. *put stuff / To*: ejaculated into.

TIMON 'Tis not well mended so, it is but botched;[4]
If not, I would it were.

APEMANTUS   What wouldst thou have to[5] Athens?

TIMON Thee thither in a whirlwind. If thou wilt,
290   Tell them there I have gold. Look, so I have.

APEMANTUS Here is no use for gold.

TIMON   The best and truest,
For here it sleeps and does no hirèd harm.

APEMANTUS Where liest a-nights, Timon?

TIMON Under that's above me.° Where feed'st thou a-days,   *(the sky)*
295   Apemantus?

APEMANTUS Where my stomach finds meat;° or rather, where I eat it.   *food*

TIMON Would poison were obedient, and knew my mind!

APEMANTUS Where wouldst thou send it?

TIMON To sauce thy dishes.

300 APEMANTUS The middle of humanity thou never knewest, but
the extremity of both ends. When thou wast in thy gilt and thy
perfume, they mocked thee for too much curiosity;° in thy rags   *delicacy*
thou know'st none, but art despised for the contrary. There's a
medlar[6] for thee; eat it.

305 TIMON On what I hate I feed not.

APEMANTUS Dost hate a medlar?

TIMON Ay, though it look like thee.

APEMANTUS An° thou'dst hated meddlers sooner, thou shouldst   *If*
have loved thyself better now. What man didst thou ever know
310   unthrift° that was beloved after[7] his means?   *prodigal*

TIMON Who, without those means thou talk'st of, didst thou ever
know beloved?

APEMANTUS Myself.

TIMON I understand thee: thou hadst some means to keep a dog.[8]

315 APEMANTUS What things in the world canst thou nearest compare to thy flatterers?

TIMON Women nearest; but men, men are the things them
selves. What wouldst thou do with the world, Apemantus, if it
lay in thy power?

320 APEMANTUS Give it the beasts, to be rid of the men.

TIMON Wouldst thou have thyself fall in the confusion° of men,   *overthrow*
and remain a beast with the beasts?

APEMANTUS Ay, Timon.

TIMON A beastly ambition, which the gods grant thee t'attain to.
325   If thou wert the lion, the fox would beguile thee. If thou wert
the lamb, the fox would eat thee. If thou wert the fox, the lion
would suspect thee when peradventure° thou wert accused by   *perchance*
the ass. If thou wert the ass, thy dullness would torment thee,
and still° thou lived'st but as a breakfast to the wolf. If thou wert   *always*
330   the wolf, thy greediness would afflict thee, and oft thou
shouldst hazard thy life for thy dinner. Wert thou the unicorn,
pride and wrath would confound thee, and make thine own
self the conquest of thy fury.[9] Wert thou a bear, thou wouldst

---

4. It is fixed badly (because Apemantus will still have to
endure himself).
5. Have conveyed to (but Timon changes the meaning).
6. A pear eaten when rotten; with puns in the following
lines on "lecher," "whore," and "interfering person."
7. In proportion to; after losing. *means:* money.

8. Which flattered its master for meager reward (or perhaps "dog" refers to Apemantus himself).
9. The legendary unicorn could be trapped by a hunter
who stood in front of a tree; when the unicorn charged,
the hunter stepped aside, and the unicorn's horn stuck
fast in the tree.

be killed by the horse.[1] Wert thou a horse, thou wouldst be
335   seized by the leopard. Wert thou a leopard, thou wert german°   *related*
to the lion, and the spots of thy kindred[2] were jurors on thy life;
all thy safety were remotion,° and thy defence absence. What   *remaining away*
beast couldst thou be that were not subject to a beast? And
what a beast art thou already, that seest not thy loss in transfor-
340   mation![3]

APEMANTUS   If thou couldst please me with speaking to me, thou
mightst have hit upon it here.[4] The commonwealth of Athens
is become a forest of beasts.

TIMON   How, has the ass broke the wall, that thou art out of the city?

345 APEMANTUS   Yonder comes a poet and a painter.[5] The plague of
company light upon thee! I will fear to catch it, and give way.°   *go away*
When I know not what else to do, I'll see thee again.

TIMON   When there is nothing living but thee, thou shalt be welcome. I had rather be a beggar's dog than Apemantus.

350 APEMANTUS   Thou art the cap[6] of all the fools alive.

TIMON   Would thou wert clean enough to spit upon.

APEMANTUS   A plague on thee! Thou art too bad to curse.

TIMON   All villains that do stand by thee are pure.°   *(by comparison)*

APEMANTUS   There is no leprosy but what thou speak'st.

355 TIMON   If I name thee.
I'd beat thee, but I should infect my hands.

APEMANTUS   I would my tongue could rot them off.

TIMON   Away, thou issue° of a mangy dog!   *offspring; discharge*
Choler does kill me that thou art alive.

360 I swoon to see thee.

APEMANTUS   Would thou wouldst burst!

TIMON   Away, thou tedious rogue!
    [*He throws a stone at* APEMANTUS]
I am sorry I shall lose a stone by thee.

APEMANTUS   Beast!

365 TIMON   Slave!

APEMANTUS   Toad!

TIMON   Rogue, rogue, rogue!
I am sick of this false world, and will love naught
But even° the mere necessities upon't.   *Except*

370 Then, Timon, presently° prepare thy grave.   *at once*
Lie where the light foam of the sea may beat
Thy gravestone daily. Make thine epitaph,
That death in° me at others' lives may laugh.   *through*
    [*He looks on the gold*]
O, thou sweet king-killer, and dear divorce

375 'Twixt natural son and sire; thou bright defiler
Of Hymen's° purest bed; thou valiant Mars;[7]   *god of marriage*
Thou ever young, fresh, loved, and delicate wooer,
Whose blush° doth thaw the consecrated snow[8]   *glow*
That lies on Dian's lap; thou visible god,

380 That sold'rest close impossibilities[9]

1. Bears were supposedly hated by horses.
2. Lion's crimes; leopard's spots.
3. Being transformed to a beast.
4. *thou . . . here*: what you've just said would please me.
5. They do not appear until 5.1 (perhaps a sign of revision).
6. Supreme instance (with wordplay on "fool's cap").
7. Adulterous lover of Venus and the god of war.
8. The snow of chastity, of which the goddess Diana was patroness.
9. That tightly solders together incompatible things.

And mak'st them kiss, that speak'st with every tongue
To every purpose; O thou touch° of hearts: *touchstone*
Think thy slave man rebels, and by thy virtue°   *power*
Set them into confounding odds,° that beasts   *men at ruinous strife*
May have the world in empire.
385 APEMANTUS   Would 'twere so,
But not till I am dead. I'll say thou'st gold.
Thou wilt be thronged to shortly.
TIMON   Thronged to?
APEMANTUS   Ay.
TIMON Thy back,[1] I prithee.
APEMANTUS   Live, and love thy misery.
TIMON Long live so, and so die. I am quit.°   *rid of you*
        Enter the Banditti [THIEVES]
390 APEMANTUS More things like men. Eat, Timon, and abhor
them.   *Exit*
FIRST THIEF Where should he have° this gold? It is some poor   *have obtained; have put*
fragment, some slender ort° of his remainder. The mere want   *scrap*
of gold and the falling-from of his friends drove him into this
395 melancholy.
SECOND THIEF It is noised° he hath a mass of treasure.   *rumored*
THIRD THIEF Let us make the assay° upon him. If he care not   *test; assault*
for't, he will supply us easily. If he covetously reserve it, how
shall 's get it?
400 SECOND THIEF True, for he bears it not about him; 'tis hid.
FIRST THIEF Is not this he?
OTHER THIEVES Where?
SECOND THIEF 'Tis his description.
THIRD THIEF He, I know him.
405 ALL THIEVES [*coming forward*] Save° thee, Timon.   *God save*
TIMON Now, thieves.
ALL THIEVES Soldiers, not thieves.
TIMON   Both, too, and women's sons.
ALL THIEVES We are not thieves, but men that much do want.°   *are very needy*
TIMON Your greatest want is, you want much of meat.°   *food*
410 Why should you want? Behold, the earth hath roots.
Within this mile break forth a hundred springs.
The oaks bear mast,° the briars scarlet hips.[2]   *acorns (fed to swine)*
The bounteous housewife nature on each bush
Lays her full mess° before you. Want? Why want?   *serving*
415 FIRST THIEF We cannot live on grass, on berries, water,
As beasts and birds and fishes.
TIMON Nor on the beasts themselves, the birds and fishes;
You must eat men. Yet thanks I must you con°   *render*
That you are thieves professed, that you work not
420 In holier shapes; for there is boundless theft
In limited° professions. [*Giving gold*] Rascal thieves,   *legitimate*
Here's gold. Go suck the subtle° blood o'th' grape   *delicate; deceptive*
Till the high fever seethe° your blood to froth,   *boil (by drunkenness)*
And so scape hanging.° Trust not the physician;   *(by dying of a fever)*
425 His antidotes are poison, and he slays
More than you rob. Take wealth and lives together.
Do villainy; do, since you protest° to do't,   *openly profess*

1. Show me your back (go away).   2. Rose hips (sour fruit).

Like workmen.° I'll example you with[3] thievery.   *skilled artisans*
The sun's a thief, and with his great attraction°   *power to draw up*
430 Robs the vast sea. The moon's an arrant[4] thief,
And her pale fire she snatches from the sun.
The sea's a thief, whose liquid surge resolves°   *melts*
The moon into salt tears.[5] The earth's a thief,
That feeds and breeds by a composture° stol'n   *manure*
435 From gen'ral° excrement. Each thing's a thief.   *universal*
The laws, your curb and whip,° in their rough power   *restraint and punishment*
Has unchecked theft.[6] Love not yourselves. Away,
Rob one another. There's more gold. Cut throats;
All that you meet are thieves. To Athens go,
440 Break open shops; nothing can you steal
But thieves do lose it. Steal no less for° this I give you,   *because of*
And gold confound you howsoe'er.° Amen.   *whatever you do*
THIRD THIEF He's almost charmed me from my profession by
persuading me to it.
445 FIRST THIEF 'Tis in the malice° of mankind that he thus advises   *out of hatred*
us, not to have us thrive in our mystery.°   *profession*
SECOND THIEF I'll believe him as[7] an enemy, and give over my
trade.
FIRST THIEF Let us first see peace in Athens.° There is no time   *(an unlikely prospect)*
450 so miserable but a man may be true.°   *Exeunt* THIEVES   *may repent*
    Enter [FLAVIUS *the*] *Steward to* TIMON
FLAVIUS O you gods!
Is yon despised and ruinous° man my lord,   *ruined*
Full of decay and failing? O monument
And wonder of good deeds evilly bestowed![8]
455 What an alteration of honour has desp'rate want made!
What viler thing upon the earth than friends,
Who can bring noblest minds to basest ends!
How rarely does it meet with this time's guise,
When man was wished to love his enemies![9]
460 Grant I may ever love and rather woo
Those that would mischief me than those that do![1]
    [TIMON *sees him*]
He's caught me in his eye. I will present
My honest grief unto him, and as my lord
Still serve him with my life.—My dearest master.
TIMON Away! What art thou?
465 FLAVIUS   Have you forgot me, sir?
TIMON Why dost ask that? I have forgot all men;
Then if thou grant'st thou'rt man, I have forgot thee.
FLAVIUS An honest poor servant of yours.
TIMON Then I know thee not. I never had
470 Honest man about me; ay, all I kept were knaves,
To serve in meat° to villains.   *serve food*
FLAVIUS   The gods are witness,
Ne'er did poor steward wear a truer grief

---

3. I'll give you precedents for.
4. Unmitigated; a wandering. The moon was considered auspicious to thieves.
5. Tides supposedly resulted from the sea drawing moisture from the moon.
6. Have unlimited power to steal.
7. As I would an enemy (that is, not at all).

8. Bestowed on ungrateful people.
9. *How . . . enemies:* How perfectly it accords with the customary exhortation to love one's enemies (since friends are one's undoing).
1. Those who would like to injure me, rather than those who really do so.

For his undone lord than mine eyes for you.

TIMON What, dost thou weep? Come nearer then; I love thee
475   Because thou art a woman,° and disclaim'st   *(in weeping)*
      Flinty mankind whose eyes do never give°   *succumb*
      But thorough° lust and laughter. Pity's sleeping.   *through*
      Strange times, that weep with laughing, not with weeping!

FLAVIUS I beg of you to know me, good my lord,
      T'accept my grief,
          [*He offers his money*]
480   and whilst this poor wealth lasts
      To entertain° me as your steward still.   *employ*

TIMON Had I a steward
      So true, so just, and now so comfortable?°   *comforting*
      It almost turns my dangerous° nature mild.   *savage*
485   Let me behold thy face. Surely this man
      Was born of woman.
      Forgive my general and exceptless° rashness,   *indiscriminate*
      You perpetual sober gods! I do proclaim
      One honest man—mistake me not, but one,
490   No more, I pray—and he's a steward.
      How fain° would I have hated all mankind,   *willingly*
      And thou redeem'st thyself! But all save thee
      I fell° with curses.   *cut down*
      Methinks thou art more honest now than wise,
495   For by oppressing and betraying me
      Thou mightst have sooner got another service;
      For many so arrive at second masters
      Upon° their first lord's neck. But tell me true—   *By stepping on*
      For I must ever doubt, though ne'er so sure—
500   Is not thy kindness subtle,° covetous,   *treacherous*
      A usuring kindness, and, as rich men deal gifts,
      Expecting in return twenty for one?

FLAVIUS No, my most worthy master, in whose breast
      Doubt and suspect,° alas, are placed too late.   *suspicion*
505   You should have feared false times when you did feast.
      Suspect still° comes where an estate is least.   *always*
      That which I show, heaven knows, is merely love,
      Duty and zeal to your unmatchèd mind,
      Care of your food and living; and, believe it,
510   My most honoured lord,
      For° any benefit that points to me,   *As for*
      Either in hope° or present, I'd exchange   *the future*
      For this one wish: that you had power and wealth
      To requite° me by making rich yourself.   *repay*
515 TIMON Look thee, 'tis so. Thou singly honest man,
          [*He gives* FLAVIUS *gold*]
      Here, take. The gods, out of my misery,
      Has sent thee treasure. Go, live rich and happy,
      But thus conditioned:[2] thou shalt build from° men,   *away from*
      Hate all, curse all, show charity to none,
520   But let the famished flesh slide from the bone
      Ere thou relieve the beggar. Give to dogs
      What thou deniest to men. Let prisons swallow 'em,

2. But on this condition.

Debts wither 'em to nothing; be men° like blasted woods,　　　　　　　*let men be*
And may diseases lick up their false bloods.
And so farewell, and thrive.

525　FLAVIUS　　　　　　　　　　O, let me stay
And comfort you, my master.
TIMON　　　　　　　　　　If thou hat'st curses,
Stay not. Fly whilst thou art blest and free.
Ne'er see thou man, and let me ne'er see thee.

Exeunt [TIMON *into his cave,* FLAVIUS *another way*]

5.1

Enter POET *and* PAINTER

PAINTER　As I took note of the place, it cannot be far where he
abides.
POET　What's to be thought of him? Does the rumour hold for
true that he's so full of gold?
5　PAINTER　Certain. Alcibiades reports it. Phrynia and Timandra
had gold of him. He likewise enriched poor straggling soldiers
with great quantity. 'Tis said he gave unto his steward a mighty
sum.
POET　Then this breaking° of his has been but a try° for his　　*bankruptcy / test*
10　friends?
PAINTER　Nothing else. You shall see him a palm[1] in Athens
again, and flourish with the highest. Therefore 'tis not amiss
we tender our loves to him in this supposed distress of his. It
will show honestly in us, and is very likely to load our purposes°　　*to reward our efforts*
15　with what they travail° for, if it be a just and true report that　　*labor; travel*
goes° of his having.°　　*circulates / property*
POET　What have you now to present unto him?
PAINTER　Nothing at this time, but my visitation; only I will
promise him an excellent piece.
20　POET　I must serve him so too, tell him of an intent that's coming
toward him.
PAINTER　Good as the best.°　　*That's excellent*

Enter TIMON *from his cave* [*unobserved*]

Promising is the very air° o'th' time; it opens the eyes of expec-　　*fashion*
tation. Performance is ever the duller for his° act, and but in　　*its*
25　the plainer and simpler kind of people the deed of saying° is　　*doing what one says*
quite out of use. To promise is most courtly and fashionable.
Performance is a kind of will or testament which argues a great
sickness in his judgement that makes it.[2]
TIMON [*aside*]　Excellent workman, thou canst not paint a man
30　so bad as is thyself.
POET [*to* PAINTER]　I am thinking what I shall say I have provided
for him. It must be a personating° of himself, a satire against　　*representation*
the softness of prosperity, with a discovery° of the infinite flat-　　*revelation*
teries that follow youth and opulency.
35　TIMON [*aside*]　Must thou needs stand° for a villain in thine own　　*model*
work? Wilt thou whip thine own faults in other men? Do so; I
have gold for thee.
POET [*to* PAINTER]　Nay, let's seek him.

5.1 Location: Outside Athens.　　　　　　2. That is, only those close to death worry about fulfilling
1. The highest tree: alluding to Psalm 92:12, "The righ-　their vows.
teous shall flourish like a palm tree."

Then do we sin against our own estate°   condition in life
40   When we may profit meet° and come too late.   make a profit
PAINTER   True.
When the day serves,° before black-cornered night,   allows
Find what thou want'st by free and offered light.
Come.
45   TIMON [aside]   I'll meet you at the turn.[3] What a god's gold,
That he is worshipped in a baser temple
Than where swine feed!
'Tis thou that rigg'st the barque° and plough'st the foam,   puts sails on the boat
Settlest admirèd reverence in a slave.[4]
50   To thee be worship, and thy saints for aye°   ever
Be crowned with plagues, that thee alone obey.
Fit° I meet them.   It is fit
         [He comes forward to them]
POET   Hail, worthy Timon!
PAINTER   Our late noble master!
TIMON   Have I once° lived to see two honest men?   really
55   POET   Sir, having often of your open bounty tasted,
Hearing you were retired,° your friends fall'n off,   had gone away
Whose thankless natures, O abhorrèd spirits,
Not all the whips of heaven are large enough —
What, to you,
60   Whose star-like nobleness gave life and influence[5]
To their whole being! I am rapt,° and cannot cover   overwhelmed
The monstrous bulk of this ingratitude
With any size[6] of words.
TIMON   Let it go naked; men may see't the better.
65   You that are honest, by being what you are
Make them° best seen and known.   (the "abhorrèd spirits")
PAINTER   He and myself
Have travelled° in the great show'r of your gifts,   walked
And sweetly felt it.
TIMON   Ay, you are honest men.
PAINTER   We are hither come to offer you our service.
70   TIMON   Most honest men. Why, how shall I requite you?
Can you eat roots and drink cold water? No.
POET and PAINTER   What we can do we'll do to do you service.
TIMON   You're honest men. You've heard that I have gold,
I am sure you have. Speak truth; you're honest men.
75   PAINTER   So it is said, my noble lord, but therefor
Came not my friend nor I.
TIMON   Good honest men. [To PAINTER] Thou draw'st a counterfeit°   picture; fake
Best in all Athens; thou'rt indeed the best;
Thou counterfeit'st most lively.
PAINTER   So so, my lord.
80   TIMON   E'en so, sir, as I say. [To POET] And for thy fiction,°   poetry; lying
Why, thy verse swells with stuff so fine and smooth
That thou art even natural° in thine art.   lifelike; idiotic
But for all this, my honest-natured friends,
I must needs say you have a little fault.

3. I'll meet you when you come around the corner; I'll   thought to stream forth from stars and affect events on
trick you in return.   earth.
4. Makes an unworthy person be revered.   6. Amount; sizing, a layer applied to walls prior to
5. Explained astrologically, "influence" was a substance   painting.

85   Marry, 'tis not monstrous in you, neither wish I
       You take much pains to mend.
POET *and* PAINTER   Beseech your honour
       To make it known to us.
TIMON   You'll take it ill.
POET *and* PAINTER   Most thankfully, my lord.
TIMON   Will you indeed?
90   POET *and* PAINTER   Doubt it not, worthy lord.
TIMON   There's never a one of you but trusts a knave
       That mightily deceives you.
POET *and* PAINTER   Do we, my lord?
TIMON   Ay, and you hear him cog,° see him dissemble,   *cheat*
       Know his gross patchery,° love him, feed him,   *roguery*
95   Keep° in your bosom; yet remain assured   *Keep him*
       That he's a made-up° villain.   *complete*
PAINTER   I know none such, my lord.
POET   Nor I.
TIMON   Look you, I love you well. I'll give you gold,
100   Rid me these villains from your companies.
       Hang them or stab them, drown them in a draught,°   *stream; cesspool*
       Confound° them by some course, and come to me,   *Destroy*
       I'll give you gold enough.
POET *and* PAINTER   Name them, my lord, let's know them.
TIMON   You that way and you this—but two in company—
105   Each man apart, all single and alone,
       Yet an arch-villain keeps him company.[7]
       [*To* PAINTER] If where thou art two villains shall not be,
       Come not near him. [*To* POET] If thou wouldst not reside
       But where one villain is, then him abandon.
110   Hence; pack!° [*Striking him*] There's gold. You came for gold,   *go away*
         ye slaves.
       [*Striking* PAINTER] You have work for me; there's payment.
         Hence!
       [*Striking* POET]   You are an alchemist;[8] make gold of that.
       Out, rascal dogs!   *Exeunt* [POET *and* PAINTER *one way,*
                                   TIMON *into his cave*]

5.2

Enter [FLAVIUS *the*] *Steward and two* SENATORS
FLAVIUS   It is in vain that you would speak with Timon,
       For he is set so only to himself°   *so self-isolated*
       That nothing but himself which looks like man
       Is friendly with° him.   *congenial to*
FIRST SENATOR   Bring us to his cave.
5   It is our part and promise to th' Athenians
       To speak with Timon.
SECOND SENATOR   At all times alike
       Men are not still° the same. 'Twas time and griefs   *always*
       That framed him thus. Time with his fairer hand
       Offering the fortunes of his former days,
10   The former man may make him. Bring us to him,
       And chance it as it may.

7. That is, both of you are archvillains.
8. That is, one who can translate base metal (the beating) into gold.

5.2 Location: Scene continues.

FLAVIUS   Here is his cave.
 [*Calling*] Peace and content be here! Lord Timon, Timon,
 Look out and speak to friends. Th'Athenians
 By two of their most reverend senate greet thee.
15 Speak to them, noble Timon.
     Enter TIMON *out of his cave*
TIMON Thou sun that comforts, burn! Speak and be hanged.
 For each true word a blister, and each false°   *let each false word*
 Be as a cantherizing° to the root o'th' tongue,   *cauterizing*
 Consuming it with speaking.
FIRST SENATOR   Worthy Timon—
20 TIMON Of none but such as you, and you of Timon.[1]
FIRST SENATOR The senators of Athens greet thee, Timon.
TIMON I thank them, and would send them back the plague
 Could I but catch it for them.
FIRST SENATOR   O, forget
 What we are sorry for, ourselves in thee.[2]
25 The senators with one consent of° love   *unanimous*
 Entreat thee back to Athens, who have thought
 On special dignities° which vacant lie   *titles; offices*
 For thy best use and wearing.
SECOND SENATOR   They confess
 Toward thee forgetfulness too general-gross,°   *obvious and extreme*
30 Which now the public body,° which doth seldom   *republic*
 Play the recanter,° feeling in itself   *Change its mind*
 A lack of Timon's aid, hath sense withal
 Of it own fail,° restraining° aid to Timon;   *failure / witholding*
 And send forth us to make their sorrowed render,°   *to apologize sadly*
35 Together with a recompense more fruitful
 Than their offence can weigh down by the dram;[3]
 Ay, even such heaps and sums of love and wealth
 As shall to thee blot out what wrongs were theirs,
 And write in thee the figures[4] of their love,
 Ever to read them thine.
40 TIMON   You witch° me in it,   *bewitch*
 Surprise me to the very brink of tears.
 Lend me a fool's heart and a woman's eyes,
 And I'll beweep these comforts, worthy senators.
FIRST SENATOR Therefore so please thee to return with us,
45 And of our Athens, thine and ours, to take
 The captainship, thou shalt be met with thanks,
 Allowed° with absolute power, and thy good name   *Vested*
 Live with authority. So soon we shall drive back
 Of Alcibiades th'approaches wild,
50 Who, like a boar too savage, doth root up
 His country's peace.
SECOND SENATOR   And shakes his threat'ning sword
 Against the walls of Athens.
FIRST SENATOR   Therefore, Timon—
TIMON Well, sir, I will; therefore I will, sir, thus.
 If Alcibiades kill my countrymen,
55 Let Alcibiades know this of Timon:

---

1. That is, we deserve each other.
2. In the injuries we did you.

3. Can outweigh even by painstaking calculation.
4. Distinctive marks; numbers in an account book.

That Timon cares not. But if he sack fair Athens,
And take our goodly agèd men by th' beards,
Giving our holy virgins to the stain°   *(by rape)*
Of contumelious,° beastly, mad-brained war,   *insolent*
60   Then let him know, and tell him Timon speaks it
In pity of our agèd and our youth,
I cannot choose but tell him that I care not;
And—let him take't at worst⁵—for their knives care not
While you have throats to answer.° For myself,   *suitable for cutting*
65   There's not a whittle° in th' unruly camp   *pocket knife*
But I do prize it at my love before
The reverend'st throat in Athens. So I leave you
To the protection of the prosperous gods,
As thieves to keepers.
FLAVIUS [*to* SENATORS]   Stay not; all's in vain.
70   TIMON   Why, I was writing of my epitaph.
It will be seen tomorrow. My long sickness
Of health and living now begins to mend,
And nothing° brings me all things. Go; live still.   *oblivion*
Be Alcibiades your plague, you his,
And last so long enough.
75   FIRST SENATOR   We speak in vain.
TIMON   But yet I love my country, and am not
One that rejoices in the common wrack°   *ruin*
As common bruit° doth put it.   *rumor*
FIRST SENATOR   That's well spoke.
TIMON   Commend me to my loving countrymen—
FIRST SENATOR   These words become your lips as they pass
80   through them.
SECOND SENATOR   And enter in our ears like great triumphers⁶
In their applauding gates.⁷
TIMON   Commend me to them,
And tell them that to ease them of their griefs,
Their fears of hostile strokes, their aches, losses,
85   Their pangs of love, with other incident throes°   *natural torments*
That nature's fragile vessel doth sustain
In life's uncertain voyage, I will some kindness do them.
I'll teach them to prevent° wild Alcibiades' wrath.   *forestall*
FIRST SENATOR [*aside*]   I like this well; he will return again.
90   TIMON   I have a tree which grows here in my close°   *enclosure*
That mine own use° invites me to cut down,   *purpose*
And shortly must I fell it. Tell my friends,
Tell Athens, in the sequence of degree°   *in order of rank*
From high to low throughout, that whoso please
95   To stop affliction, let him take his haste,
Come hither ere my tree hath felt the axe,
And hang himself. I pray you do my greeting.
FLAVIUS [*to* SENATORS]   Trouble him no further. Thus you still
            shall find him.
TIMON   Come not to me again, but say to Athens,
100   Timon hath made his everlasting mansion°   *(his grave)*
Upon the beachèd verge° of the salt flood,°   *edge / sea*

5. Interpret what I say in the worst possible way.   7. Gates full of applauding fellow citizens.
6. Like conquerors returning home.

Who once a day with his embossèd° froth — *foaming*
The turbulent surge shall cover. Thither come,
And let my gravestone be your oracle.° — *source of revelation*
105 Lips, let four° words go by, and language end. — *(that is, few)*
What is amiss, plague and infection mend.
Graves only be men's works, and death their gain.
Sun, hide thy beams. Timon hath done his reign.

Exit [into his cave]

FIRST SENATOR   His discontents are unremovably
110 Coupled to nature.° — *Intrinsic to his nature*
SECOND SENATOR   Our hope in him is dead. Let us return,
And strain what other means is left unto us
In our dear peril.
FIRST SENATOR   It requires swift foot.   *Exeunt*

5.3

Enter two other SENATORS, with a MESSENGER

THIRD SENATOR   Thou hast painfully discovered.[1] Are his files° — *troops*
As full as thy report?
MESSENGER   I have spoke the least.° — *estimated low*
Besides, his expedition° promises — *speed*
Present° approach. — *Immediate*
5 FOURTH SENATOR   We stand much hazard if they bring not Timon.
MESSENGER   I met a courier, one mine ancient friend,
Whom, though in general part° we were opposed, — *public matters*
Yet our old love made° a particular force — *exerted*
And made us speak like friends. This man was riding
10 From Alcibiades to Timon's cave
With letters of entreaty which imported° — *urged*
His fellowship i'th' cause against your city,
In part for his sake moved.

Enter the other SENATORS

THIRD SENATOR   Here come our brothers.
FIRST SENATOR   No talk of Timon; nothing of him expect.
15 The enemy's drum is heard, and fearful scouring° — *hostile action*
Doth choke the air with dust. In, and prepare.
Ours is the fall, I fear, our foe's the snare.   *Exeunt*

5.4

Enter a SOLDIER, in the woods, seeking TIMON

SOLDIER   By all description, this should be the place.
Who's here? Speak, ho! No answer?
[*He discovers a gravestone*]
                        What is this?
Dead, sure, and this his grave. What's on this tomb
I cannot read. The character I'll take with wax.[1]
5 Our captain hath in every figure° skill, — *kind of writing*
An aged° interpreter, though young in days. — *experienced*
Before proud Athens he's set down by this,° — *laid siege by this time*
Whose fall the mark° of his ambition is.   *Exit* — *goal*

5.3 Location: Outside the walls of Athens.   5.4 Location: Outside Athens.
1. Carefully reconnoitered; told us painful news.   1. By making an impression of the letters.

5.5

Trumpets sound. Enter ALCIBIADES *with his powers,°*　　　　army
before Athens

ALCIBIADES　Sound° to this coward and lascivious town　　　*Proclaim*
　　Our terrible approach.
　　　　　　A parley¹ sound[s]. The SENATORS *appear upon the*
　　　　　　walls²
　　Till now you have gone on and filled the time
　　With all licentious measure,³ making your wills
5　　The scope of justice.⁴ Till now myself and such
　　As slept° within the shadow of your power　　　　　*dwelled*
　　Have wandered with our traversed⁵ arms, and breathed
　　Our sufferance⁶ vainly. Now the time is flush
　　When crouching marrow,° in the bearer strong,　　　*latent vigor*
10　　Cries of itself 'No more'; now breathless° wrong　　　*exhausted*
　　Shall sit and pant in your great chairs of ease,
　　And pursy° insolence shall break his wind°　　　*short-winded / pant; fail*
　　With fear and horrid° flight.　　　　　　　　　　*terrified*
FIRST SENATOR　　　　　　　　Noble and young,
　　When thy first griefs were but a mere conceit,°　　　*only merely imagined*
15　　Ere thou hadst power or we had cause of fear,
　　We sent to thee to give thy rages balm,
　　To wipe out our ingratitude with loves
　　Above their quantity.⁷
SECOND SENATOR　　　　So did we woo
　　Transformèd Timon to our city's love
20　　By humble message and by promised means.°　　　*wealth*
　　We were not all unkind, nor all deserve
　　The common° stroke of war.　　　　　　　　　　*indiscriminate*
FIRST SENATOR　　　　　　　These walls of ours
　　Were not erected by their hands from whom
　　You have received your grief; nor are they such
25　　That these great tow'rs, trophies,° and schools⁸ should fall　　*monuments*
　　For private faults in them.°　　　　　　　　　　*(the offenders)*
SECOND SENATOR　　　　　　Nor are they living
　　Who were the motives that you first went out.⁹
　　Shame that they wanted° cunning, in excess,　　　*lacked*
　　Hath broke their hearts. March, noble lord,
30　　Into our city with thy banners spread.
　　By decimation and a tithèd death,¹
　　If thy revenges hunger for that food
　　Which nature loathes, take thou the destined tenth,
　　And by the hazard of the spotted die
　　Let die the spotted.²
35　FIRST SENATOR　　　　All have not offended.
　　For those that were,° it is not square° to take,　　　*(living) / fair*
　　On those that are, revenges. Crimes like lands
　　Are not inherited. Then, dear countryman,
　　Bring in thy ranks, but leave without° thy rage.　　　*outside*

5.5 Location: Outside the walls of Athens.　　　　6. *breathed / Our sufferance:* voiced our grievances.
1. Trumpet call to negotiate.　　　　　　　　　　7. *loves . . . quantity:* friendly gestures greater than your
2. Probably on the upper gallery at stage rear.　　grievances.
3. All kinds of licentious conduct.　　　　　　　8. Public buildings.
4. *making . . . justice:* making justice conform to your　9. Who were those who prompted your banishment.
whims.　　　　　　　　　　　　　　　　　1. Killing one of every ten person, chosen by lot.
5. Crossed (as part of military training).　　　　2. Corrupt (punning on the spots of dice).

40 Spare thy Athenian cradle° and those kin   *birthplace*
Which, in the bluster of thy wrath, must fall
With those that have offended. Like a shepherd
Approach the fold and cull th'infected forth,°   *pick out the corrupt*
But kill not all together.
SECOND SENATOR   What thou wilt,
45 Thou rather shalt enforce it with thy smile
Than hew to't with thy sword.
FIRST SENATOR   Set but thy foot
Against our rampired° gates and they shall ope,   *barricaded*
So° thou wilt send thy gentle heart before   *If*
To say thou'lt enter friendly.
SECOND SENATOR   Throw thy glove,
50 Or any token° of thine honour else,   *pledge*
That thou wilt use the wars as thy redress,
And not as our confusion.° All thy powers°   *ruin / army*
Shall make their harbour° in our town till we   *lodging*
Have sealed° thy full desire.   *satisfied*
ALCIBIADES [*throwing up a glove*]   Then there's my glove.
55 Descend, and open your unchargèd ports.°   *unattacked gates*
Those enemies of Timon's and mine own
Whom you yourselves shall set out for reproof°   *select for punishment*
Fall, and no more; and to atone° your fears   *appease*
With my more noble meaning, not a man°   *soldier*
60 Shall pass his quarter° or offend the stream   *leave his assigned place*
Of regular justice³ in your city's bounds
But shall be remedied to° your public laws   *punished according to*
At heaviest answer.°   *penalty*
BOTH SENATORS   'Tis most nobly spoken.
65 ALCIBIADES   Descend, and keep your words.
          [*Trumpets sound. Exeunt* SENATORS *from the walls.*]
          Enter [SOLDIER, *with a tablet of wax*]
SOLDIER   My noble general, Timon is dead,
Entombed upon the very hem° o'th' sea;   *edge*
And on his gravestone this insculpture,° which   *inscription*
With wax I brought away, whose soft impression
70 Interprets for my poor ignorance.
          ALCIBIADES *reads the Epitaph*
ALCIBIADES   'Here lies a wretched corpse,
          Of wretched soul bereft.
     Seek not my name. A plague consume
          You wicked caitiffs° left!   *wretches*
75 Here lie I, Timon, who alive
          All living men did hate.
     Pass by and curse thy fill, but pass
          And stay not here thy gait.'
These well express in thee thy latter spirits.°   *sentiments*
80 Though thou abhorred'st in us our human griefs,
Scorned'st our brains' flow⁴ and those our droplets which
From niggard⁵ nature fall, yet rich conceit°   *imagination*
Taught thee to make vast Neptune weep for aye°   *ever*
On thy low grave, on faults forgiven. Dead

---

3. *offend . . . justice:* violate the ordinary laws.
4. Tears were thought to exude from the brain.

5. "Niggard" because teardrops are tiny compared with
the sea, Neptune (line 83).

85   Is noble Timon, of whose memory
    Hereafter more.
              [*Enter* SENATORS *through the gates*]
              Bring me into your city,
    And I will use the olive° with my sword,   *(symbol of peace)*
    Make war breed peace, make peace stint° war, make each   *stop*
    Prescribe to other as each other's leech.[6]
90   Let our drums strike.   [*Drums.*] *Exeunt* [*through the gates*]

TEXTUAL VARIANTS

Control text: F

F: The Folio of 1623

s.p. ISIDORE'S SERVANT [F's use of *Isid.* has been changed throughout.]
s.p. VARRO'S SERVANT [F's use of *Var.* has been changed throughout.]
s.p. VARRO'S SECOND SERVANT [F's use of *2. Var.* has been changed throughout.]
s.p. LUCIUS' SERVANT [F's use of *Luci.* has been changed throughout.]
s.p. FIRST LORD, SECOND LORD [F's use of *1, 2* has been changed throughout.]
s.p. FIRST STRANGER, SECOND STRANGER, THIRD STRANGER [F's use of *1, 2, 3* has been changed throughout.]
s.p. FIRST THIEF [F's use of *1* has been changed throughout.]

1.1.21 gum which oozes Gowne, which vses 25 chafes chases 40 man men   47 tax wax 56 service services 88 hands hand fall sit 212 cost cast 235 augury but angry wit 250 'mongst amongst 272 Come Comes 273 taste raste 283 s.p. FIRST LORD [not in F]
1.2.28 ever verie 79 thou then thou 119 smell, all all 123 s.p. FIRST LORD *Luc.* 144 s.p. LADY *Lord.* 147 'tends attends 165 Accept Accept it
2.1.33 Take I go sir? / Take 34 in count in. Come
2.2.4 resumes resume 37 broken debt, broken 59, 61, 65, 88, 92 s.p. ALL SERVANTS *Al., All.* 69 mistress' Masters 123 proposed propose 130 summed sound 181 s.p. ALL SERVANTS *Ser.* 199 treasure Treature
3.1.51 this hour his Honor
3.2.19 not mistook mistooke 23 s.p. LUCIUS *Lucil⟨ius⟩.* 43 before a before for a 44 I, I I 59 spirit sport
3.3.21 I 'mongst lords 'mong'st Lords
3.4.59 If I['t 77 an answer answer 85 s.p. HORTENSIUS' SERVANT *1 Var⟨ro⟩.* 86 s.p. VARRO'S FIRST *and* SECOND SERVANTS *2. Var⟨ro⟩.*
3.5.8 Sempronius—all luxors, *Sempronius Ullorxa:* 11 There is There's
3.6.1 lords Lord 17 An And 22 behave his behoove his 49 felon fellow 61 Why, I Why 65 'em him 100 your our
3.7.73 foes *Fees* 74 tag *legge* 83 with your flattery you with Flatteries 99 the rhe 104 s.p. THIRD *2* 105 s.p. SECOND *3*
4.1.6 steads steeds 13 Son Some 21 let yet
4.2.41 does do
4.3.9–10, 11–13 It . . . lean. / Raise . . . honour. Raise . . . Honor. / It . . . leaue: 11 demit deny't 12 senator Senators 15 say fay 39 wappered wappen'd 41 at, this at. This 73–75 If thou wilt promise . . . If thou dost not perform If thou wilt not promise

---

6. Physician (because war purges peace of its decadence, and peace purges war of its violence).

. . . if thou do'st performe   87 **tub-fast** Fubfast   116 **bars** Barne   121 **thy** the   132, 148, 166 **s.p.** PHYRNIA *and* TIMANDRA *Both.*   134 **wholesomeness** Whores   143 **pain-sick** paines six   155 **scolds** scold'st   185 **thy** the   204 **fortune** future   223 **mossed** moyst   255 **command** command'st   285 **my** thy   375 **son and sire** Sunne and fire   391 **them** then   402 **s.p.** OTHER THIEVES *All.*   427 **villainy** villaine   441 **Steal no** Steal   446 **us,** vs   467 **grant'st thou'rt man,** grunt'st, th'art a man.   484 **mild** wilde   501 **A** If not a

5.1.5 Phrynia *Phrinica*   **Timandra** *Timandylo*   50 **worship** worshipt   68 **men** man   105 **apart** a part

5.2.1 is in is   11 **chance** chanc'd   32 **sense** since

5.3.1 s.p. THIRD SENATOR I   4 **s.p.** FOURTH SENATOR 2   14 **s.p.** FIRST SENATOR 3

5.4.2 this? this? / *Tymon* is dead, who hath out-stretcht his span, / Some beast read this; / There do's not liue a Man.

5.5.37 revenges Reuenge   55 **Descend** Defend   66 **s.p.** SOLDIER *Mes⟨senger⟩.*

King Lear

You have, King James told his eldest son a few years before Shakespeare wrote *King Lear*, a double obligation to love God: first because He made you a man, and second because He made you "a little God to sit on his Throne, and rule over other men." Whatever the realities of Renaissance kingship—realities that included the stern necessity of compromise, reciprocity, and restraint—the idea of sovereignty was closely linked to fantasies of divine omnipotence. From his exalted height, the sovereign looked down upon the tiny figures of the ordinary mortals below him. Their hopes, the material conditions of their miserable existence, their names, were of little interest, and yet the king knew that they too were looking back up at him. "For Kings being public persons," James uneasily acknowledged, are set "upon a public stage, in the sight of all the people; where all the beholders' eyes are attentively bent to look and pry in the least circumstance of their secretist drifts." Under such circumstances, the sovereign's dream was to command, like God, not only unquestioning obedience but unqualified love.

In *King Lear*, Shakespeare explores the dark consequences of this dream not only in the state but also in the family, where the Renaissance father increasingly styled himself "a little God." If, as the play opens, the aged Lear, exercising his imperious will and demanding professions of devotion, is "every inch a king," he is also by the same token every inch a father, the absolute ruler of a family that conspicuously lacks the alternative authority of a mother. Shakespeare's play invokes this royal and paternal sovereignty only to chronicle its destruction in scenes of astonishing cruelty and power. The very words "every inch a king" are spoken not by the confident figure of supreme authority whom we glimpse in the first moments but by the ruined old man who perceives in his feverish rage and madness that the fantasy of omnipotence is a fraud: "When the rain came to wet me once, and the wind to make me chatter; when the thunder would not peace at my bidding, there I found 'em, there I smelt 'em out. Go to, they are not men o' their words. They told me I was everything; 'tis a lie, I am not ague-proof" (4.5.98–102; all quotations, except where noted, are from *The Tragedy of King Lear*).

"They told me I was everything": Shakespeare's culture continually staged public rituals of deference to authority. These rituals—kneeling, bowing, uncovering the head, and so forth—enacted respect for wealth, caste, power, and, at virtually every level of society, age. Jacobean England had a strong official regard for the rights and privileges of age. It told itself that, by the will of God and the natural order of things, authority gravitated to old men, and it contrived to ensure that this proper, sanctified arrangement of society be everywhere respected.

"'Tis a lie": Shakespeare's culture continually told itself at the same time that without the control of property and the threat of punishment, any claim to authority was chillingly vulnerable to the ruthless ambitions of the young, the restless, and the discontented. The incessant, ritualized spectacles of sovereignty have a nervous air, as if no one quite believed all the grand claims to divine sanction for the rule of kings and fathers, as if those who ruled both states and families secretly feared that the elaborate hierarchical structure could vanish like a mirage exposing their shivering, defenseless bodies. *King Lear* relentlessly stages this horrifying descent toward what the ruined King, contemplating the filthy, naked body of a mad beggar, calls "the thing itself": "Unaccommodated man is no more but such a poor, bare, forked animal as thou art" (3.4.95–97). Lear and the Earl of Gloucester, another old man whose terrible fate closely parallels Lear's, repeatedly look up at the heavens and call upon the gods for help, but the gods are silent. The despairing Gloucester concludes that the universe is actively malevolent—"As flies to wanton boys are we to th'gods; / They kill us for their sport" (4.1.37–38)—but the awful silence of the gods may equally be a sign of their indifference or their nonexistence.

The story of King Lear and his three daughters had been often told when Shakespeare undertook to make it the subject of a tragedy. The play, performed at court in December 1605, was probably written and first performed somewhat earlier, though not before 1603, since it contains allusions to a book published in that year. The book is Samuel Harsnett's *Declaration of Egregious Popish Impostures*, a florid piece of anti-Catholic propaganda from which Shakespeare took the colorful names of the "foul fiends" by whom the mad beggar claims to be possessed. Thus scholars generally assign Shakespeare's composition of *King Lear* to 1604–5, shortly after *Othello* (c. 1603–4) and before *Macbeth* (c. 1606): an astounding succession of tragic masterpieces.

King Lear first appeared in print in a quarto published in 1608 entitled *M. William Shak-speare His Historie, of King Lear*; a substantially different text, entitled *The Tragedie of King Lear* and grouped with the other tragedies, was printed in the 1623 First Folio. From the eighteenth century, when the difference between the two texts was first noted, editors, assuming that they were imperfect versions of the identical play, customarily conflated them, blending together the approximately one hundred Folio lines not printed in the quarto with the approximately three hundred quarto lines not printed in the Folio and selecting as best they could among the hundreds of particular alternative readings. But there is a growing scholarly consensus that the 1608 text of *Lear* represents the play as Shakespeare first wrote it and that the 1623 text represents a substantial revision. (See the Textual Note for further discussion.) Since this revision includes significant structural changes as well as many local details, the two texts provide a precious opportunity to glimpse Shakespeare's creative process as an artist and the collaborative work of his theater company. Accordingly, the *Norton Shakespeare* prints *The History of King Lear* and *The Tragedy of King Lear* on facing pages; in addition, a modern conflated version of the play follows, so that readers will be able to judge for themselves the effects of the familiar editorial practice of stitching together the two texts.

When *King Lear* was first performed, it may have struck contemporaries as strangely timely in the wake of a lawsuit that had occurred in late 1603. The two elder daughters of a doddering gentleman named Sir Brian Annesley attempted to get their father legally certified as insane, thereby enabling themselves to take over his estate, while his youngest daughter vehemently protested on her father's behalf. The youngest daughter's name happened to be Cordell, a name uncannily close to that of Lear's youngest daughter, Cordelia, who tries to save her father from the malevolent designs of her older sisters.

Cordeilla Queene. From Raphael Holinshed, *The First Volume of the Chronicles of England, Scotlande, and Irelande* (1577).

The Annesley case is worth invoking not only because it may have caught Shakespeare's attention but also because it directs our own attention to the ordinary family tensions and fears around which *King Lear*, for all of its wildness, violence, and strangeness, is constructed. Though the Lear story has the mythic quality of a folktale (specifically, it resembles both the tale of Cinderella and the tale of a daughter who falls into disfavor for telling her father she loves him as much as salt), it was rehearsed in Shakespeare's time as a piece of authentic British history from the very ancient past (c. 800 B.C.) and as an admonition to contemporary fathers not to put too much trust in the flattery of their children:

"Remember what happened to old King Lear . . ." In some versions of the story, including Shakespeare's, the warning centers on a decision to retire.

Retirement has come to seem a routine event, but in the patriarchal, gerontocratic culture of Tudor and Stuart England, it was generally shunned. When through illness or extreme old age it became unavoidable, retirement put a severe strain on the politics and psychology of deference by driving a wedge between status—what Lear at society's pinnacle calls "the name and all th'addition to a king" (1.1.134)—and power. In both the state and the family, the strain could be somewhat eased by transferring power to the eldest legitimate male successor, but as the families of both the legendary Lear and the real Brian Annesley showed, such a successor did not always exist. In the absence of a male heir, the aged Lear, determined to "shake all cares and business" from himself and confer them on "younger strengths," attempts to divide his kingdom equally among his daughters so that, as he puts it, "future strife / May be prevented now" (1.1.37–38, 42–43). But this attempt is a disastrous failure. Critics have often argued that the roots of the failure lie in the division of the kingdom, that any parceling out of the land on a map would itself have provoked in the audience an ominous shudder, as it is clearly meant to do when the rebels spread out a map in anticipation of a comparable division in *1 Henry IV*. Early seventeenth-century audiences had reason to fear the dissolution of the realm into competing fragments. But the focus of Shakespeare's tragedy seems to lie elsewhere: Lear's folly is not that he retires or that he divides his kingdom—the play opens with the Earl of Gloucester and the Earl of Kent commenting without apparent disapproval on the scrupulous equality of the shares—but rather that he rashly disinherits the only child who truly loves him, his youngest daughter.

Shakespeare contrives moreover to show that the problem with which his characters are grappling does not simply result from the absence of a son and heir. In his most brilliant and complex use of a double plot, he intertwines the story of Lear and his three daughters with the story of Gloucester and his two sons, a tale he adapted from an episode in Philip Sidney's prose romance *Arcadia*. Gloucester has a legitimate heir, his elder son Edgar, as well as an illegitimate son, Edmond, and in this family the tragic conflict originates not in an unusual manner of transferring property from one generation to another but rather in the reverse: Edmond seethes with murderous resentment at the disadvantage entirely customary for someone in his position, both as a younger son and as what was called a "base" or "natural" child. "Thou, nature, art my goddess," he declares:

> Wherefore should I
> Stand in the plague of custom and permit
> The curiosity of nations to deprive me
> For that I am some twelve or fourteen moonshines
> Lag of a brother? Why 'bastard'? Wherefore 'base'?
> (1.2.1–6)

For Edmond, the social order and the language used to articulate it are merely arbitrary constraints, obstacles to the triumph of his will. He schemes to tear down the obstacles by playing on his father's fears, cleverly planting a forged letter in which his older brother appears to be plotting against his father's life. The letter's chilling sentences express Edmond's own impatience, his hatred of the confining power of custom, his disgusted observation of "the oppression of aged tyranny, who sways not as it hath power but as it is suffered" (1.2.48–49). Gloucester is predictably horrified and incensed; these are, as Edmond cunningly knows, the cold sentiments that the aged fear lie just beneath the surface of deference and flattery. The forged letter reflects back as well on the scene in which Gloucester himself has just participated: a scene in which everyone, with the exception of the Earl of Kent, has tamely suffered a tyrannical old man to banish his youngest daughter for her failure to flatter him.

Why does Lear, who has already drawn up the map dividing the kingdom, stage the love test? In Shakespeare's principal source, an anonymous play called *The True Chronicle*

Star-gazing. From John Cypriano, *A Most Strange and Wonderfulle Prophesie* (1595). "I should have been that I am had the maidenliest star in the firmament twinkled on my bastardizing" (1.2.119–21).

History of King Leir (published in 1605 but dating from 1594 or earlier), there is a gratifyingly clear answer. Leir's strong-willed daughter Cordella has vowed that she will only marry a man whom she herself loves; Leir wishes her to marry the man he chooses for his own dynastic purposes. He stages the love test, anticipating that in competing with her sisters Cordella will declare that she loves her father best, at which point Leir will demand that she prove her love by marrying the suitor of his choice. The stratagem backfires, but its purpose is clear.

By stripping his character of a comparable motive, Shakespeare makes Lear's act seem stranger, at once more arbitrary and more rooted in deep psychological needs. His Lear is a man who has determined to retire from power but who cannot endure dependence. Unwilling to lose his identity as an absolute authority both in the state and in the family, he arranges a public ritual—"Which of you shall we say doth love us most?" (1.1.49)—whose aim seems to be to allay his own anxiety by arousing it in his children. Since the shares have already been apportioned, Lear evidently wants his daughters to engage in a competition for his bounty without having to endure any of the actual consequences of such a competition; he wants, that is, to produce in them something like the effect of theater, where emotions run high and their practical effects are negligible. But in this absolutist theater Cordelia refuses to perform: "What shall Cordelia speak? Love and be silent" (1.1.60). When she says "Nothing," a word that echoes darkly throughout the play, Lear hears what he most dreads: emptiness, loss of respect, the extinction of identity. And when, under further interrogation, she declares that she loves her father "according to my bond" (1.1.91), Lear understands these words too to be the equivalent of "nothing."

As Cordelia's subsequent actions demonstrate, his youngest daughter's bond is in reality a sustaining, generous love, but it is a love that ultimately leads to her death. Here Shakespeare makes an even more startling departure not only from *The True Chronicle History of King Leir* but from all his known sources. The earliest of these, the account in Geoffrey of Monmouth's twelfth-century *Historia Regum Britanniae*, sets the pattern repeated in John Higgins's *Mirror for Magistrates* (1574 edition), William Warner's *Albion's England* (1586), Raphael Holinshed's *Chronicles of England, Scotland, and Ireland* (2nd ed., 1587), and Edmund Spenser's *Faerie Queene* (1590, 2.10.27–32): the aged Lear is overthrown by his wicked daughters and their husbands, but he is restored to the throne by the army of his good daughter's husband, the King of France. The story then is one of loss and restoration: Lear resumes his reign, and when, "made ripe for death" by old age, as Spenser puts it, he dies, he is succeeded by Cordelia. The conclusion is not unequivocally happy; in all of the known chronicles, Cordelia rules worthily for several years and then, after being deposed and imprisoned by her nephews, in despair commits suicide. But Shakespeare's ending is unprecedented in its tragic devastation. When in Act 5 Lear suddenly enters with the lifeless body of Cordelia in his arms, the original audience, secure in the expectation of a very different resolution, must have been doubly shocked, a shock cruelly reinforced when the signs that she might be reviving—"This feather stirs. She lives" (5.3.239)—all prove false. Lear apparently dies in the grip of the illusion that he detects some breath on his daughter's lips, but we know that Cordelia will, as he says a moment earlier, "come no more. / Never, never, never, never, never" (5.3.283–84).

Those five reiterated words, the bleakest pentameter line Shakespeare ever wrote, are the climax of an extraordinary poetics of despair that is set in motion when Lear disinherits Cordelia and when Gloucester credits Edmond's lies about Edgar. *King Lear* has seemed to many modern readers and audiences the greatest of Shakespeare's tragedies precisely because of its anguished look into the heart of darkness, but its vision of suffering and evil has not always commanded unequivocal admiration. In the eighteenth century, Samuel Johnson wrote, "I was many years ago so shocked by Cordelia's death that I know not whether I ever endured to read again the last scenes of the play till I undertook to revise them as an editor." Johnson's contemporaries preferred a revision of Shakespeare's tragedy undertaken in 1681 by Nahum Tate. Finding the play "a Heap of Jewels, unstrung, and unpolisht," Tate proceeded to restring them in order to save Cordelia's life and to produce the unambiguous and happy triumph of the forces of good.

Only in the nineteenth century was Shakespeare's deeply pessimistic ending—the old generation dead or dying, the survivors shaken to the core, the ruling families all broken with no impending marriage to promise renewal—generally restored to theatrical performance and the tragedy's immense power fully acknowledged. Even passionate admirers of *King Lear*, however, continued to express deep uneasiness, repeatedly noting not only its unbearably painful close but also what Johnson first called the "improbability of Lear's conduct" and Samuel Taylor Coleridge termed the plot's "glaring absurdity." Above all, critics questioned whether the tragedy was suitable for the stage. Coleridge compared the suffering Lear to one of Michelangelo's titanic figures, but the grandeur invoked by the comparison led his contemporary Charles Lamb to conclude flatly that "Lear is essentially impossible to be represented on stage." "To see Lear acted," Lamb wrote, "to see an old man tottering about the stage with a walking stick, turned out of doors by his daughters in a rainy night, has nothing in it but what is painful and disgusting." In such a view, *King Lear* could only be staged successfully in the imagination; there alone would Lear's passion be perceived not like ordinary human suffering but rather, in the marvelous characterization of another Romantic critic, William Hazlitt, "like a sea, swelling, chafing, raging, without bound, without hope, without beacon, or anchor." In the theater of the mind, Shakespeare's play could assume its true, stupendous proportions, enabling the reader to grasp its ultimate meaning. That meaning, the great early twentieth-century critic A. C. Bradley wrote, is that we must "renounce the world, hate it, and lose it gladly. The only real thing in it is the soul, with its courage, patience, devotion. And nothing outward can touch that." Splendid; but what about the body?

A succession of brilliant stage performances and, more recently, films has not only belied the view that *King Lear* is unactable but also underscored the crucial importance in the play of the body. If Shakespeare explores the extremes of the mind's anguish and the soul's devotion, he never forgets that his characters have bodies as well, bodies that have needs, cravings, and terrible vulnerabilities. When in this tragedy characters fall from high station, they plunge unprotected into a world of violent storms, murderous cruelty, and physical horror. The old King wanders raging on the heath, through a wild night of thunder and rain. Disguised as Poor Tom, a mad beggar possessed by demons, Gloucester's son Edgar enacts a life of utmost degradation: "Poor Tom, that eats the swimming frog, the toad, the tadpole, the wall-newt and the water; that in the fury of his heart, when the foul fiend rages, eats cowdung for salads, swallows the old rat and the ditch-dog, drinks the green mantle of the standing pool" (3.4.115–19). Gloucester's fate is even more terrible: betrayed by his son Edmond, he is seized in his own house by Lear's reptilian daughter Regan and her husband, Cornwall, tied to a chair, brutally interrogated, blinded, and then thrust bleeding out of doors.

Mental anguish in *King Lear*, then, is closely intertwined with physical anguish; the terrifying forces that are released by Lear's folly crash down upon both body and soul, just as the storm that rages on the heath seems at once an objective event and a symbolic representation of Lear's innermost being. The greatest expression of this intertwining in the play is Lear's madness, which brings together a devastating loss of identity, a relentless, radical assault on the hypocrisies of authority, and a demented, nauseated loathing of female sexuality. The loathing culminates in a fit of retching—"Fie, fie, fie; pah, pah!"—followed by Lear's delusional attempt to find a physical remedy for his psychic pain: "Give me an ounce of civet, good apothecary, sweeten my imagination" (4.5.123–24). In fact, relief from the chaotic rage of madness comes in the wake of a deep, restorative sleep and a change of garments.

The body in *King Lear* is a site not only of abject misery, nausea, and pain but of care and a nascent moral awareness. In the midst of his mad ravings, Lear turns to the shivering Fool and asks, "Art cold?" (3.2.67). The simple question anticipates his recognition a few moments later that there is more suffering in the world than his own:

> Poor naked wretches, wheresoe'er you are,
> That bide the pelting of this pitiless storm,
> How shall your houseless heads and unfed sides,
> Your looped and windowed raggedness, defend you
> From seasons such as these? O, I have ta'en
> Too little care of this.
>
> (3.4.28–33)

And if the world seems largely unjust and indifferent to human suffering, there are nonetheless throughout the play constant manifestations of generosity of body as well as soul.

Tom Durie (1614). By Marcus Gheeraerts the Younger. Durie was the jester of Anne of Denmark, who was married to James I.

"Help me, help me!" cries the frightened Fool, to which Kent (disguised in order to serve the King who has banished him) says simply, "Give me thy hand" (3.4.39–40). "What are you?" says the blind Gloucester to the son he has unjustly disinherited, to which the son, also in disguise, replies similarly, "Give me your hand" (4.5.213, 216). (In a moving moment from *The History of King Lear*, absent from the Folio version, two of Gloucester's servants not only react with horror to their master's blinding but also resolve to assist him: "Go thou. I'll fetch some flax and whites of eggs / To apply to his bleeding face. Now heaven help him!" [14.103–4].) Such signs of goodness and empathy do not outweigh the harshness of the physical world of the play, let alone cancel out the vicious cruelty of certain of its inhabitants, but they do qualify its moral bleakness.

It is possible to detect in *King Lear* one of the great structural rhythms of Christianity: a passage though suffering, humiliation, and pain to a transcendent wisdom and love. Lear's initial actions were blind and selfish, but he comes to acknowledge his folly and, in an immensely poignant scene, to kneel down before the daughter he has wronged. Gloucester too learns that he was blind, even when his eyes could see, and he passes, by means of Edgar's strange deception at the imaginary cliff, from suicidal despair to patient resignation. "Men must endure / Their going hence even as their coming hither," Edgar wisely counsels his father. "Ripeness is all" (5.2.9–11). For a time, evil seems to flourish in the world, but the wicked do not ultimately triumph. The sadistic Duke of Cornwall is fatally wounded by his own morally upright servant, Edmond is killed by the brother he had tried to destroy, the loathsome Oswald is clubbed to death trying to murder Gloucester, one wicked sister poisons the other and then kills herself. Against self-interest and in the face of intolerable pressure, goodness shines forth. The Earl of Kent, banished by the rash Lear, dons a disguise in order to serve his king and master, and there are comparable acts of devoted service and self-sacrificing love from Edgar, Cordelia, and that remarkable figure the Fool. In one of the comic masterpieces of the sixteenth century, *The Praise of Folly*, the great Dutch humanist Erasmus used the fool as an emblem of the deepest Christian wisdom, revealed only when the pride, cruelty, and ambition of the world are shattered by a cleansing laughter. The shattering in *King Lear* is tragically violent and deadly, but the presence of the truth-telling Fool seems to point toward a comparable revelation.

Yet *King Lear*, set in a pagan world, resists the redemptive optimism that underlies the Christian vision (an optimism that led Dante to call his poem of damnation and salvation *The Divine Comedy*). The Fool's unnervingly perceptive observations sound far more corrosive than loving—he is, in Lear's words, "a bitter fool" (1.4.122)—and he disappears altogether in the third act. His moments of insight and those of all the other characters in the play are radically unstable, like brilliant flashes of lightning in a vast, dark landscape. Hence, for example, Lear's recognition of his folly in banishing Cordelia for her "most small fault" (1.4.228) is immediately followed by his hideous cursing of Goneril. His moving acknowledgment of the suffering of the poor naked wretches is immediately followed by his inability to see the poor naked wretch before him in any terms but his own: "Didst thou give all to thy two daughters, / And art thou come to this?" (3.4.47–48). And his appeal to patient resignation—"When we are born, we cry that we are come / To this great stage of fools" (4.5.172–73)—is immediately followed by a mad fantasy of revenge: "Then kill, kill, kill, kill, kill, kill!" Every time we seem to have reached firm moral ground, the ground shifts, and we are kept, as Johnson observed, in "a perpetual tumult of indignation, pity, and hope." There are moments of apparent resolution: "Let's away to prison," says Lear to the weeping Cordelia, when they are captured by the enemy. "We two alone will sing like birds i'th'cage" (5.3.8–9). But a more terrible fate lies before them. "Some good I mean to do," says the dying Edmond, "despite of mine own nature" (5.3.217–18). But his attempt to send a reprieve and therefore in some measure to redeem himself comes too late. The play's nightmarish events continually lurch ahead of intentions, and even efforts to say "I have seen the worst" are frustrated.

The tragedy is not only that the intervals of moral resolution, mental lucidity, and spiritual calm are so brief, continually giving way to feverish grief and rage, but also that the modest human understandings, moving in their simplicity, cost such an enormous amount of pain. Edgar saves his father from despair but also in some sense breaks his father's heart. Cordelia's steadfast honesty, her refusal to flatter the father she loves, is admirable but has disastrous consequences, and her attempt to save Lear only leads to her own death. For a sublime moment, Lear actually *sees* his daughter, understands her separateness, acknowledges her existence —

> Do not laugh at me,
> For as I am a man, I think this lady
> To be my child, Cordelia —

but it has taken the destruction of virtually his whole world for him to reach this recognition (4.6.61–63).

An apocalyptic dream of last judgment and redemption hovers over the entire tragedy, but it is a dream forever deferred. At the sight of the howling Lear with the dead Cordelia in his arms, the bystanders can only ask a succession of stunned questions:

> KENT   Is this the promised end?
> EDGAR   Or image of that horror?
>
>   (5.3.237–38)

Lear's own question a moment later seems the most terrible and the most important: "Why should a dog, a horse, a rat have life, / And thou no breath at all?" (5.3.281–82). It is a sign of *King Lear*'s astonishing freedom from orthodoxy that it refuses to offer any of the conventional answers to this question, answers that largely serve to conceal or deflect the mourner's anguish. Shakespeare's tragedy asks us not to turn away from evil, folly, and unbearable human pain but, seeing them face-to-face, to strengthen our capacity to endure and to love.

STEPHEN GREENBLATT

TEXTUAL NOTE

The textual traces of *King Lear* have probably given scholars more cause for debate than any of Shakespeare's other works. The debate centers on the relative authority of the two early texts of the tragedy, the First Quarto (Q1) and the First Folio (F), and the relationship between them. Q1 contains approximately three hundred lines that do not appear in F; F prints approximately one hundred lines that are not in Q1. There are also hundreds of individual variants, some apparently negligible but others highly significant. To take a single instance, the closing lines of the play—by convention assigned to the person who will now govern the state—are in Q1 spoken by Albany, in F spoken by Edgar.

Q1 was first printed in December and January of 1607–8 in the shop of Nicholas Okes, a London printer, under the following title:

> M William Shak-speare: His True Chronicle Historie of the life and death of King Lear and his three Daughters. With the vnfortunate life of Edgar, sonne and heire to the Earle of Gloster, and his sullen and assumed humor of Tom of Bedlam: As it was played before the Kings Maiestie at Whitehall vpon S. Stephens night in Christmas Hollidayes. By his Maiesties seruants playing vsually at the Gloabe on the Bancke-side. London, Printed for Nathaniel Butter, and are to be sold at his shop in Pauls Church-yard at the signe of the Pide Bull neere St. Austins Gate. 1608.

Of the print run, only twelve copies have been found. Q1 was set, most scholars agree, from Shakespeare's own draft, his "foul papers." That Q1 was printed from such a draft and not from a scribe's copy or a promptbook promises strong authority. However, there are difficulties.

Peculiarities within the text and variations among the twelve copies suggest that Okes's printing shop was not quite up to the task set by this long, complex play. *King Lear* appears indeed to have been the first play Okes attempted. There was clearly a shortage of typeface, particularly of full stops and colons: this may help to explain anomalous aspects of lineation and punctuation. Evidently, two compositors worked together on the play, one perhaps reading aloud while the other set the type; this may have caused what often appear to be aural errors in the text. And these errors, which may have been compounded by difficulties in reading the copy, might have been avoided had the printer's copy come from an experienced scribe rather than from Shakespeare's own handwriting, which appears at some points to have been illegible. The result is a text of great importance but tantalizing uncertainty. While no critics doubt that Q1 represents a legitimate early version of *King Lear*, it is a version whose authority is compromised by a succession of readings that are often confusing and sometimes nonsensical.

At a time when it was generally accepted that Q1 and F were, for all their differences, derived from one original text, now lost, these textual difficulties were relatively easily handled: the editor, positing a single ideal form of the play "behind" or "before" the versions that were printed, would conflate the two texts, weaving together the lines that appear in only one or the other version and correcting Q1 with reference to F or (in a much smaller number of instances) F with reference to Q1. The Oxford editors, upon whose work this edition is based, broke decisively with this tradition of conflation. Instead, they edited and printed Q1 and F as separate and distinct texts. In so doing, they gave up the luxury of editorial cross-referencing. As the principal Oxford editor of *King Lear*, Gary Taylor, points out, "The entire purpose of editing Q and F separately is to preserve the integrity of each, and such a purpose is not well served by importing revised readings into an unrevised fabric." Oxford therefore sought, insofar as possible, to emend Q1, where necessary, as if F did not exist.

Such emendation is almost unnecessary in the altogether more straightforward text of the First Folio, which appeared in 1623 as *The Tragedie of King Lear*. In contrast to Q1, F differentiates carefully between prose and verse, shows consistency in spelling, and offers detailed stage directions. The Folio also characteristically divides the play into acts and scenes. These differences, along with the cuts and the additional passages, are all the more striking if F is basically derived, as Oxford contends, from the text known as Q2. For this second quarto, printed in 1619 (three years after Shakespeare's death) although falsely dated 1608, is only a slightly improved copy of Q1. While spelling and punctuation were somewhat corrected and some attempts were made to emend difficult words and phrases, no independent manuscript was used to prepare Q2. Therefore, when the compositors sat down to print F, their copy of Q2, Oxford maintains, must have been annotated using an independent manuscript. What was the source of this manuscript? The Oxford editors think it likely that the manuscript was a scribal copy, perhaps a promptbook, that derived ultimately from Q1.

Though F is thus linked, if indirectly, to Q1, the fact remains that two quite different texts of the play exist. Efforts over the years to conflate them in the search for a hypothetical master text have been partly responsible for the neglect that Q1 has generally suffered and for the failure to explore fully the extraordinary opportunity that the survival of these distinct versions of the play presents. Each version has its own integrity; each contains passages intrinsically its own. In addition, the quarto may give us a precious glimpse, as the Oxford editor notes, of the play "as Shakespeare first conceived it, probably before it was performed," while the Folio represents a revision made probably two or three years after the play had been first written and performed. The Folio, then, with its substantial cuts and its small additions, its streamlining and its subtle shifts in emphasis, is the more theatrical text.

The *Norton Shakespeare* presents Q1 and F on facing pages so that readers can compare them easily. In order to make it possible to read them independently of one another, both texts are glossed and footnoted. In addition, we offer a conflated version of *King Lear*, prepared by Barbara K. Lewalski, so that readers can encounter the tragedy in the form that it assumed in most editions from the eighteenth century until very recently.

SELECTED BIBLIOGRAPHY

Booth, Stephen. "On the Greatness of *King Lear.*" *"King Lear," "Macbeth," Indefinition and Tragedy.* New Haven, Conn.: Yale University Press, 1983. 1–57.

Cavell, Stanley, "The Avoidance of Love: A Reading of *King Lear.*" *Disowning Knowledge in Six Plays of Shakespeare.* Cambridge: Cambridge University Press, 1987. 39–124.

Colie, Rosalie, ed. *Some Facets of "King Lear."* Toronto: University of Toronto Press, 1969.

Dollimore, Jonathan. "*King Lear* (c. 1605–6) and Essentialist Humanism." *Shakespearean Tragedy.* Ed. John Drakakis. Harlow, Essex, 1992. 194–207.

Elton, William. *"King Lear" and the Gods.* San Marino, Ca.: Huntington Library, 1966.

Greenblatt, Stephen. "Shakespeare and the Exorcists." *Shakespearean Negotiations.* Berkeley: University of California Press, 1988. 94–128.

Kahn, Coppélia. "The Absent Mother in *King Lear.*" *Rewriting the Renaissance: The Discourses of Sexual Difference in Early Modern Europe.* Ed. Margaret Ferguson, Maureen Quilligan, and Nancy J. Vickers. Chicago: University of Chicago Press, 1986. 33–49.

Kott, Jan. "*King Lear,* or Endgame." *Shakespeare Our Contemporary.* Trans. Boleslaw Taborski. 2nd ed. London: Methuen, 1967. 100–33.

Mack, Maynard. *"King Lear" in Our Time.* Berkeley: University of California Press, 1966.

Rosenberg, Marvin. *The Masks of "King Lear."* Berkeley: University of California Press, 1972.

The History of King Lear

Scene 1

*Enter [the Earl of] KENT, [the Earl of] GLOUCESTER,[1]
and Bastard [EDMUND]*

KENT I thought the King had more affected° the Duke of
Albany° than Cornwall.   favored / Scotland

GLOUCESTER It did always seem so to us, but now in the division
of the kingdoms it appears not° which of the Dukes he values   is not clear
5   most; for equalities° are so weighed° that curiosity in neither   shares / equal
can make choice of either's moiety.[2]

KENT Is not this your son, my lord?

GLOUCESTER His breeding,° sir, hath been at my charge.[3] I have   upbringing
so often blushed to acknowledge him that now I am brazed° to   hardened
10   it.

KENT I cannot conceive° you.   comprehend

GLOUCESTER Sir, this young fellow's mother could,[4] whereupon
she grew round-wombed and had indeed, sir, a son for her cradle ere she had a husband for her bed. Do you smell a fault?[5]

Scene 1 Location: King Lear's court.
1. Pronounced "Gloster."
2. *that . . . moiety:* that careful scrutiny ("curiosity") of
both parts cannot determine which portion ("moiety") is
preferable.

3. My responsibility; at my cost.
4. Could conceive; punning on biological conception.
5. Sin, wrongdoing; female genitals.

The Tragedy of King Lear

THE PERSONS OF THE PLAY

LEAR, King of Britain
GONERIL, Lear's eldest daughter
Duke of ALBANY, her husband
REGAN, Lear's second daughter
Duke of CORNWALL, her husband
CORDELIA, Lear's youngest daughter
King of FRANCE }
Duke of BURGUNDY } suitors of Cordelia
Earl of KENT, later disguised as Caius
Earl of GLOUCESTER
EDGAR, elder son of Gloucester, later disguised as Tom o' Bedlam
EDMOND, bastard son of Gloucester
OLD MAN, Gloucester's tenant
CURAN, Gloucester's retainer
Lear's FOOL
OSWALD, Goneril's steward
A SERVANT of Cornwall
A KNIGHT
A HERALD
A CAPTAIN
Gentlemen, servants, soldiers, attendants, messengers

1.1

Enter [the Earl of] KENT, [the Earl of] GLOUCESTER,[1]
and EDMOND

KENT I thought the King had more affected° the Duke of   favored
Albany° than Cornwall.   Scotland
GLOUCESTER It did always seem so to us, but now in the division
of the kingdom it appears not° which of the Dukes he values   is not clear
5   most; for qualities are so weighed that curiosity in neither can
make choice of either's moiety.[2]
KENT Is not this your son, my lord?
GLOUCESTER His breeding,° sir, hath been at my charge.[3] I have upbringing
so often blushed to acknowledge him that now I am brazed°   hardened
10   to't.
KENT I cannot conceive° you.   comprehend
GLOUCESTER Sir, this young fellow's mother could,[4] whereupon
she grew round-wombed and had indeed, sir, a son for her cradle ere she had a husband for her bed. Do you smell a fault?[5]

1.1 Location: King Lear's court.
1. Pronounced "Gloster."
2. *for . . . moiety*: because their qualities are so evenly
weighted that careful scrutiny ("curiosity") of both parts

cannot determine which portion ("moiety") is preferable.
3. My responsibility; at my cost.
4. Could conceive; punning on "biological conception."
5. Sin, wrongdoing; female genitals.

15 KENT I cannot wish the fault undone, the issue° of it being so
    proper.°

      GLOUCESTER But I have, sir, a son by order of law,° some year
    elder than this, who yet is no dearer in my account.° Though
    this knave° came something saucily⁶ into the world before he
20 was sent for, yet was his mother fair, there was good sport at his
    making, and the whoreson° must be acknowledged. [*To*
    EDMUND] Do you know this noble gentleman, Edmund?

      EDMUND No, my lord.

      GLOUCESTER [*to* EDMUND] My lord of Kent. Remember him
25 hereafter as my honourable friend.

      EDMUND [*to* KENT] My services to your lordship.

      KENT I must love you, and sue° to know you better.

      EDMUND Sir, I shall study deserving.°

      GLOUCESTER [*to* KENT] He hath been out° nine years, and away
30 he shall again.

            Sound a sennet°
          The King is coming.
            Enter one bearing a coronet, then [King] LEAR, *then the*
            Dukes of ALBANY *and* CORNWALL; *next* GONORIL, REGAN,
            CORDELIA, *with followers*

      LEAR Attend° my lords of France and Burgundy, Gloucester.

      GLOUCESTER I shall, my liege.°   [*Exit*]

      LEAR Meantime we° will express our darker° purposes.
35 The map there. Know we have divided
    In three our kingdom, and 'tis our first intent
    To shake all cares and business off our state,°
    Confirming them on younger years.
    The two great princes, France and Burgundy—
40 Great rivals in our youngest daughter's love—
    Long in our court have made their amorous sojourn,
    And here are to be answered. Tell me, my daughters,
    Which of you shall we say doth love us most,
    That° we our largest bounty° may extend
45 Where merit doth most challenge it?°
    Gonoril, our eldest born, speak first.

      GONORIL Sir, I do love you more than words can wield° the matter;
    Dearer than eyesight, space,° or liberty;
    Beyond what can be valued, rich or rare;
50 No less than life; with grace, health, beauty, honour;
    As much as child e'er loved, or father, friend;°
    A love that makes breath° poor and speech unable.
    Beyond all manner of so much° I love you.

      CORDELIA [*aside*] What shall Cordelia do? Love and be silent.
55 LEAR [*to* GONORIL] Of all these bounds even from this line to this,
    With shady forests and wide skirted meads,°

offspring; result
handsome; right
legitimate
estimation
scamp; fellow

rogue; bastard

ask
shall learn to deserve
away; abroad

fanfare of trumpets

Attend upon; escort
feudal superior
(royal "we") / more secret

position (as King)

So that / generosity
best claims it

convey
freedom of movement

or friend
language
Beyond all comparison

broad meadows

6. Somewhat rudely; somewhat shamefully.

15 KENT   I cannot wish the fault undone, the issue° of it being so   *offspring; result*
  proper.°   *handsome; right*
  GLOUCESTER   But I have a son, sir, by order of law,° some year   *legitimate*
  older than this, who yet is no dearer in my account.° Though   *estimation*
  this knave° came something saucily⁶ to the world before he was   *scamp; fellow*
20 sent for, yet was his mother fair, there was good sport at his
  making, and the whoreson° must be acknowledged. [*To*   *rogue; bastard*
  EDMOND] Do you know this noble gentleman, Edmond?
  EDMOND   No, my lord.
  GLOUCESTER [*to* EDMOND]   My lord of Kent. Remember him
25 hereafter as my honourable friend.
  EDMOND [*to* KENT]   My services to your lordship.
  KENT   I must love you, and sue° to know you better.   *ask*
  EDMOND   Sir, I shall study deserving.°   *shall learn to deserve*
  GLOUCESTER [*to* KENT]   He hath been out° nine years, and away   *away; abroad*
30 he shall again.
    Sennet°   *Fanfare of trumpets*
  The King is coming.
    Enter King LEAR, [*the Dukes of*] CORNWALL [*and*]
    ALBANY, GONERIL, REGAN, CORDELIA, *and attendants*
  LEAR   Attend° the lords of France and Burgundy, Gloucester.   *Attend upon; escort*
  GLOUCESTER   I shall, my lord.   *Exit*
  LEAR   Meantime we° shall express our darker° purpose.   *(royal "we") / more secret*
35 Give me the map there. Know that we have divided
  In three our kingdom, and 'tis our fast° intent   *steadfast*
  To shake all cares and business from our age,
  Conferring them on younger strengths while we
  Unburdened crawl toward death. Our son° of Cornwall,   *son-in-law*
40 And you, our no less loving son of Albany,
  We have this hour a constant will to publish⁷
  Our daughters' several dowers,° that future strife   *individual dowries*
  May be prevented now. The princes France and Burgundy—
  Great rivals in our youngest daughter's love—
45 Long in our court have made their amorous sojourn,
  And here are to be answered. Tell me, my daughters—
  Since now we will divest us both of rule,
  Interest° of territory, cares of state—   *Legal title*
  Which of you shall we say doth love us most,
50 That° we our largest bounty° may extend   *So that / generosity*
  Where nature doth with merit challenge?⁸ Goneril,
  Our eldest born, speak first.
  GONERIL   Sir, I love you more than words can wield° the matter;   *convey*
  Dearer than eyesight, space,° and liberty;   *freedom of movement*
55 Beyond what can be valued, rich or rare,
  No less than life; with grace, health, beauty, honour;
  As much as child e'er loved or father found;
  A love that makes breath° poor and speech unable.   *language*
  Beyond all manner of so much° I love you.   *Beyond all comparison*
  CORDELIA [*aside*]   What shall Cordelia speak? Love and be
60   silent.
  LEAR [*to* GONERIL]   Of all these bounds even from this line to this,
  With shadowy forests and with champains riched,°   *enriched plains*
  With plenteous rivers and wide-skirted meads,°   *broad meadows*

---

6. Somewhat rudely; somewhat shamefully.
7. A fixed determination to announce publicly.

8. *Where . . . challenge:* To the one whose natural love
and good deeds mutually enhance one another.

We make thee lady. To thine and Albany's issue°   *children, heirs*
Be this perpetual.—What says our second daughter?
Our dearest Regan, wife to Cornwall, speak.

60   REGAN   Sir, I am made
Of the self-same mettle° that my sister is,   *spirit; substance*
And prize me at her worth.° In my true heart   *believe myself her equal*
I find she names my very deed of love—
Only she came short, that° I profess   *in that*

65   Myself an enemy to all other joys
Which the most precious square of sense possesses,[7]
And find I am alone felicitate°   *am only made happy*
In your dear highness' love.

CORDELIA [*aside*]   Then poor Cordelia—
And yet not so, since I am sure my love's

70   More richer than my tongue.

LEAR [*to* REGAN]   To thee and thine hereditary ever
Remain this ample third of our fair kingdom,
No less in space, validity,° and pleasure   *value*
Than that confirmed° on Gonoril. [*To* CORDELIA] But now our joy,   *fixed*

75   Although the last, not least in our dear love:
What can you say to win a third more opulent
Than your sisters?

CORDELIA   Nothing, my lord.

LEAR   How? Nothing can come of nothing.[8] Speak again.

80   CORDELIA   Unhappy that I am, I cannot heave
My heart into my mouth. I love your majesty
According to my bond,° nor more nor less.   *filial duty*

LEAR   Go to, go to, mend your speech a little
Lest it may mar your fortunes.

CORDELIA   Good my lord,

85   You have begot me, bred me, loved me.
I return those duties back as are right fit—
Obey you, love you, and most honour you.
Why have my sisters husbands if they say
They love you all? Haply° when I shall wed   *Perhaps; if lucky*

90   That lord whose hand must take my plight° shall carry   *marriage vow; condition*
Half my love with him, half my care and duty.
Sure, I shall never marry like my sisters,
To love my father all.°   *completely*

LEAR   But goes this with thy heart?

95   CORDELIA   Ay, good my lord.

LEAR   So young and so untender?

CORDELIA   So young, my lord, and true.°   *honest; faithful*

LEAR   Well, let it be so. Thy truth then be thy dower;
For by the sacred radiance of the sun,

100   The mysteries of Hecate[9] and the night,
By all the operation of the orbs
From whom we do exist and cease to be,[1]

---

7. *Which . . . possesses:* That the body can enjoy. *precious square of sense:* measure of sensibility; or, perhaps, balanced and sensitive perception. The square may represent the even mixture of the body's four fluids, or humors.
8. *Ex nihilo nihil fit* was an Aristotelian maxim. This was accepted by the Christian Middle Ages with the single exception of God having created the world out of nothing.

9. A classical goddess of the moon and the patron of witchcraft, she was associated with the underworld, Hades.
1. *By all . . . be:* referring to the belief that the movements of stars and planets ("orbs") corresponded to physical and spiritual motions in a person, and thus controlled his or her fate.

We make thee lady. To thine and Albany's issues°   *children, heirs*
65   Be this perpetual.—What says our second daughter?
Our dearest Regan, wife of Cornwall?
REGAN   I am made of that self° mettle° as my sister,   *same / spirit; substance*
And prize me at her worth.° In my true heart   *believe myself her equal*
I find she names my very deed of love—
70   Only she comes too short, that° I profess   *in that*
Myself an enemy to all other joys
Which the most precious square of sense possesses,[9]
And find I am alone felicitate°   *am only made happy*
In your dear highness' love.
CORDELIA [*aside*]   Then poor Cordelia—
75   And yet not so, since I am sure my love's
More ponderous° than my tongue.   *weighty*
LEAR [*to* REGAN]   To thee and thine hereditary ever
Remain this ample third of our fair kingdom,
No less in space, validity,° and pleasure   *value*
80   Than that conferred on Goneril. [*To* CORDELIA] Now our joy,
Although our last and least,° to whose young love   *youngest; smallest*
The vines of France and milk of Burgundy
Strive to be interested:° what can you say to draw   *given access to*
A third more opulent than your sisters? Speak.
85 CORDELIA   Nothing, my lord.
LEAR   Nothing?
CORDELIA   Nothing.
LEAR   Nothing will come of nothing.[1] Speak again.
CORDELIA   Unhappy that I am, I cannot heave
90   My heart into my mouth. I love your majesty
According to my bond,° no more nor less.   *filial duty*
LEAR   How, how, Cordelia? Mend your speech a little
Lest you may mar your fortunes.
CORDELIA   Good my lord,
You have begot me, bred me, loved me.
95   I return those duties back as are right fit—
Obey you, love you, and most honour you.
Why have my sisters husbands if they say
They love you all? Haply° when I shall wed   *Perhaps; if lucky*
That lord whose hand must take my plight° shall carry   *marriage vow; condition*
100   Half my love with him, half my care and duty.
Sure, I shall never marry like my sisters.
LEAR   But goes thy heart with this?
CORDELIA   Ay, my good lord.
LEAR   So young and so untender?
105 CORDELIA   So young, my lord, and true.°   *honest; faithful*
LEAR   Let it be so. Thy truth then be thy dower;
For by the sacred radiance of the sun,
The mysteries of Hecate[2] and the night,
By all the operation of the orbs
110   From whom we do exist and cease to be,[3]

---

9. Which . . . possesses: That the body can enjoy. *precious square of sense*: measure of sensibility; or, perhaps, balanced and sensitive perception. The square may represent the even mixture of the body's four fluids, or humors.
1. *Ex nihilo nihil fit* was an Aristotelian maxim. This was accepted by the Christian Middle Ages with the single exception of God having created the world out of nothing.

2. A classical goddess of the moon and the patron of witchcraft, she was associated with the underworld, Hades.
3. *By all . . . be:* referring to the belief that the movements of stars and planets ("orbs") corresponded to physical and spiritual motions in a person, and thus controlled his or her fate.

Here I disclaim all my paternal care,
Propinquity,° and property of blood,°   *Closeness / kinship*
105   And as a stranger to my heart and me
Hold thee from this° for ever. The barbarous Scythian,[2]   *this time*
Or he that makes his generation
Messes[3] to gorge his appetite,
Shall be as well neighboured, pitied, and relieved
As thou, my sometime° daughter.   *former*
110   KENT   Good my liege—
    LEAR   Peace, Kent. Come not between the dragon and his wrath.
I loved her most, and thought to set my rest[4]
On her kind nursery.° [*To* CORDELIA] Hence, and avoid my sight!—   *care*
So be my grave my peace[5] as here I give
115   Her father's heart from her. Call France. Who stirs?[6]
Call Burgundy.   [*Exit one or more*]
                 Cornwall and Albany,
With my two daughters' dowers digest° this third.   *incorporate*
Let pride, which she calls plainness,° marry her.   *directness*
I do invest you jointly in my power,
120   Pre-eminence, and all the large effects°   *outward shows; trappings*
That troop with° majesty. Ourself by monthly course,   *accompany*
With reservation° of an hundred knights   *legal right to retain*
By you to be sustained, shall our abode
Make with you by due turns. Only we still retain
125   The name and all the additions° to a king.   *prerogatives*
The sway,° revenue, execution of the rest,   *power*
Belovèd sons, be yours; which to confirm,
This crownet[7] part betwixt you.
    KENT   Royal Lear,
Whom I have ever honoured as my king,
130   Loved as my father, as my master followed,
As my great patron thought on in my prayers—
    LEAR   The bow is bent and drawn; make from° the shaft.   *get clear of*
    KENT   Let it fall° rather, though the fork° invade   *strike here / arrowhead*
The region of my heart. Be Kent unmannerly
135   When Lear is mad. What wilt thou do, old man?
Think'st thou that duty shall have dread to speak
When power to flattery bows? To plainness° honour's bound   *plain speaking*
When majesty stoops to folly. Reverse thy doom,°   *Revoke your sentence*
And in thy best consideration check°   *halt*
140   This hideous rashness. Answer my life my judgement,[8]
Thy youngest daughter does not love thee least,
Nor are those empty-hearted whose low sound
Reverbs no hollowness.°   *Echoes no insincerity*
    LEAR   Kent, on thy life, no more!
    KENT   My life I never held but as a pawn°   *chess piece; stake*
145   To wage° against thy enemies, nor fear to lose it,   *wager*
Thy safety being the motive.

---

2. Notoriously savage Crimean nomads of classical antiquity.
3. *he . . . / Messes*: he who makes meals of his parents or his children.
4. To secure my repose; to stake my all, as in the card game known as primero.

5. So may I rest in peace (probably an oath).
6. Does nobody stir? An order, with the force of "Get moving."
7. Cordelia's crown, symbol of the endowment she has forsworn.
8. *Answer . . . judgement*: I'll stake my life on my opinion.

Here I disclaim all my paternal care,
Propinquity,° and property of blood,°   *Closeness / kinship*
And as a stranger to my heart and me
Hold thee from this° for ever. The barbarous Scythian,[4]   *this time*
115 Or he that makes his generation messes[5]
To gorge his appetite, shall to my bosom
Be as well neighboured, pitied, and relieved
As thou, my sometime° daughter.   *former*
KENT   Good my liege—
LEAR   Peace, Kent.
120 Come not between the dragon and his wrath.
I loved her most, and thought to set my rest[6]
On her kind nursery.° [*To* CORDELIA] Hence, and avoid my sight!—   *care*
So be my grave my peace[7] as here I give
Her father's heart from her. Call France. Who stirs?[8]
Call Burgundy.   [*Exit one or more*]
125   Cornwall and Albany,
With my two daughters' dowers digest° the third.   *incorporate*
Let pride, which she calls plainness,° marry her.   *directness*
I do invest you jointly with my power,
Pre-eminence, and all the large effects°   *outward shows, trappings*
130 That troop with° majesty. Ourself by monthly course,   *accompany*
With reservation° of an hundred knights   *legal right to retain*
By you to be sustained, shall our abode
Make with you by due turn. Only we shall retain
The name and all th'addition° to a king. The sway,°   *prerogatives / power*
135 Revenue, execution of the rest,
Belovèd sons, be yours; which to confirm,
This crownet[9] part between you.
KENT   Royal Lear,
Whom I have ever honoured as my king,
Loved as my father, as my master followed,
140 As my great patron thought on in my prayers—
LEAR   The bow is bent and drawn; make from° the shaft.   *get clear of*
KENT   Let it fall° rather, though the fork° invade   *strike here / arrowhead*
The region of my heart. Be Kent unmannerly
When Lear is mad. What wouldst thou do, old man?
145 Think'st thou that duty shall have dread to speak
When power to flattery bows? To plainness° honour's bound   *plain speaking*
When majesty falls to folly. Reserve° thy state,°   *Retain / rule; position*
And in thy best consideration check°   *halt*
This hideous rashness. Answer my life my judgement,[1]
150 Thy youngest daughter does not love thee least,
Nor are those empty-hearted whose low sounds
Reverb no hollowness.°   *Echo no insincerity*
LEAR   Kent, on thy life, no more!
KENT   My life I never held but as a pawn°   *chess piece; stake*
To wage° against thine enemies, ne'er feared to lose it,   *wager*
Thy safety being motive.°   *(my) motivation*

---

4. Notoriously savage Crimean nomads of classical antiquity.
5. *he . . . messes*: he who makes meals of his parents or his children.
6. To secure my repose; to stake my all, as in the card game known as primero.
7. So may I rest in peace (probably an oath).
8. Does nobody stir? An order, with the force of "Get moving."
9. Cordelia's crown, symbol of the endowment she has forsworn.
1. *Answer . . . judgement*: I'll stake my life on my opinion.

LEAR   Out of my sight!

KENT   See better, Lear, and let me still° remain   *always*
  The true blank° of thine eye.   *precise bull's-eye*

LEAR   Now, by Apollo—

KENT   Now, by Apollo, King, thou swear'st thy gods in vain.[9]

LEAR [*making to strike him*]   Vassal, recreant!°   *villain; unbeliever*

150 KENT   Do, kill thy physician,
  And the fee bestow upon the foul disease.[1]
  Revoke thy doom, or whilst I can vent clamour
  From my throat I'll tell thee thou dost evil.

LEAR   Hear me; on thy allegiance hear me!
155 Since thou hast sought to make us break our vow,
  Which we durst never yet, and with strayed° pride   *wayward, erring*
  To come between our sentence and our power,
  Which nor our nature nor our place[2] can bear,
  Our potency made good° take thy reward: *demonstrated*
160 Four days we do allot thee for provision
  To shield thee from dis-eases° of the world,   *discomforts*
  And on the fifth to turn thy hated back
  Upon our kingdom. If on the next day following
  Thy banished trunk° be found in our dominions,   *body*
165 The moment is thy death. Away! By Jupiter,
  This shall not be revoked.

KENT   Why, fare thee well, King; since thus thou wilt appear,
  Friendship lives hence, and banishment is here.
  [*To* CORDELIA] The gods to their protection take thee, maid,
170 That rightly thinks, and hast most justly said.
  [*To* GONORIL *and* REGAN] And your large speeches may your deeds approve,[3]
  That good effects may spring from words of love.
  Thus Kent, O princes, bids you all adieu;
  He'll shape his old course in a country new.   [*Exit*]
          Enter [*the King of*] FRANCE *and* [*the Duke of*] BUR-
          GUNDY, *with* GLOUCESTER

175 GLOUCESTER   Here's France and Burgundy, my noble lord.

LEAR   My lord of Burgundy,
  We first address towards you, who with a king
  Hath rivalled for our daughter: what in the least
  Will you require in present dower with her
  Or cease your quest of love?

180 BURGUNDY   Royal majesty,
  I crave no more than what your highness offered;
  Nor will you tender° less.   *offer*

LEAR   Right noble Burgundy,
  When she was dear to us we did hold her so;
  But now her price is fallen. Sir, there she stands.
185 If aught within that little seeming substance,[4]
  Or all of it, with our displeasure pieced,°   *joined*
  And nothing else, may fitly like° your grace,   *please*
  She's there, and she is yours.

---

9. You invoke your gods falsely and without effect. Lear's blindness and misdirected imprecations are particularly inapt for Apollo, god of the sun and of archery.
1. *kill . . . disease:* you would not only kill the doctor but hand his fee over to the disease.

2. Which neither my temperament nor my royal position.
3. And let your actions live up to your fine words.
4. *little seeming substance:* one who appears more substantial than she is; one who will not pretend.

155   LEAR   Out of my sight!

KENT   See better, Lear, and let me still° remain   *always*

    The true blank° of thine eye.   *precise bull's-eye*

    LEAR   Now, by Apollo—

KENT   Now, by Apollo, King, thou swear'st thy gods in vain.[2]

LEAR [*making to strike him*]   O vassal! Miscreant!°   *Villain; unbeliever*

ALBANY *and* CORDELIA   Dear sir, forbear.

160   KENT [*to* LEAR]   Kill thy physician, and thy fee bestow

    Upon the foul disease.[3] Revoke thy gift,

    Or whilst I can vent clamour from my throat

    I'll tell thee thou dost evil.

    LEAR   Hear me, recreant;° on thine allegiance hear me!   *traitor*

165   That thou hast sought to make us break our vows,

    Which we durst never yet, and with strained° pride   *overblown*

    To come betwixt our sentence and our power,

    Which nor our nature nor our place[4] can bear,

    Our potency made good° take thy reward: *demonstrated*

170   Five days we do allot thee for provision

    To shield thee from disasters of the world,

    And on the sixth to turn thy hated back

    Upon our kingdom. If on the seventh day following

    Thy banished trunk° be found in our dominions,   *body*

175   The moment is thy death. Away! By Jupiter,

    This shall not be revoked.

    KENT   Fare thee well, King; sith° thus thou wilt appear,   *since*

    Freedom lives hence, and banishment is here.

    [*To* CORDELIA] The gods to their dear shelter take thee, maid,

180   That justly think'st, and hast most rightly said.

    [*To* GONERIL *and* REGAN] And your large speeches may your deeds approve,[5]

    That good effects may spring from words of love.

    Thus Kent, O princes, bids you all adieu;

    He'll shape his old course in a country new.   *Exit*

          Flourish.° Enter GLOUCESTER *with* [*the King of*]   *Fanfare of trumpets*

          FRANCE, [*the Duke of*] BURGUNDY, *attendants*

185   CORDELIA   Here's France and Burgundy, my noble lord.

    LEAR   My lord of Burgundy,

    We first address toward you, who with this King

    Hath rivalled for our daughter: what in the least

    Will you require in present dower with her

    Or cease your quest of love?

190   BURGUNDY   Most royal majesty,

    I crave no more than hath your highness offered;

    Nor will you tender° less.   *offer*

    LEAR   Right noble Burgundy,

    When she was dear to us we did hold her so;

    But now her price is fallen. Sir, there she stands.

195   If aught within that little seeming substance,[6]

    Or all of it, with our displeasure pieced,°   *joined*

    And nothing more, may fitly like° your grace,   *please*

    She's there, and she is yours.

---

2. You invoke your gods falsely and without effect. Lear's blindness and misdirected imprecations are particularly inapt for Apollo, god of the sun and of archery.
3. *Kill . . . disease:* You would not only kill the doctor but hand his fee over to the disease.

4. Which neither my temperament nor my royal position.
5. And let your actions live up to your fine words.
6. *little seeming substance:* one who appears more substantial than she is; one who will not pretend.

BURGUNDY   I know no answer.

LEAR   Sir, will you with those infirmities she owes,°   *owns*

190   Unfriended, new-adopted to our hate,

Covered with our curse and strangered° with our oath,   *estranged*

Take her or leave her?

BURGUNDY   Pardon me, royal sir.

Election makes not up on such conditions.[5]

LEAR   Then leave her, sir; for by the power that made me,

195   I tell you° all her wealth. [*To* FRANCE] For° you, great King,   *inform you of / As for*

I would not from your love make such a stray°   *stray so far*

To° match you where I hate, therefore beseech you   *As to*

To avert your liking° a more worthier way   *To turn your affections*

Than on a wretch whom nature is ashamed

200   Almost to acknowledge hers.

FRANCE   This is most strange, that she that even but now

Was your best object, the argument° of your praise,   *theme*

Balm of your age, most best, most dearest,

Should in this trice° of time commit a thing   *moment*

205   So monstrous to dismantle°   *as to strip off, disrobe*

So many folds of favour. Sure, her offence

Must be of such unnatural degree

That monsters it,° or your fore-vouched affections   *makes it monstrous*

Fall'n into taint;[6] which to believe of her

210   Must be a faith that reason without miracle

Could never plant in me.

CORDELIA [*to* LEAR]   I yet beseech your majesty,

If for I want° that glib and oily art   *because I lack*

To speak and purpose not°—since what I well intend,   *and not intend*

215   I'll do't before I speak—that you acknow°   *acknowledge*

It is no vicious blot, murder, or foulness,

No unclean action or dishonoured step

That hath deprived me of your grace and favour,

But even the want of that for which I am rich—

220   A still-soliciting° eye, and such a tongue   *An always-begging*

As I am glad I have not, though not to have it

Hath lost me in your liking.

LEAR   Go to, go to.

Better thou hadst not been born than not to have pleased me better.

FRANCE   Is it no more but this—a tardiness in nature,

225   That often leaves the history unspoke

That it intends to do?[7] —My lord of Burgundy,

What say you to the lady? Love is not love

When it is mingled with respects° that stands   *considerations*

Aloof from the entire point. Will you have her?

She is herself a dower.

230   BURGUNDY   Royal Lear,

Give but that portion which yourself proposed,

And here I take Cordelia by the hand,

Duchess of Burgundy—

LEAR   Nothing. I have sworn.

---

5. A choice cannot be made under those terms.
6. *or . . . taint:* or else the love you earlier swore for Cordelia must be regarded with suspicion. "Or" may also mean "before," in which case the phrase would mean "before the love you once proclaimed could have decayed."
7. *a tardiness . . . do:* a natural reserve that inhibits voicing one's intentions.

BURGUNDY   I know no answer.

LEAR   Will you with those infirmities she owes,°   *owns*

200   Unfriended, new adopted to our hate,

Dowered with our curse and strangered° with our oath,   *estranged*

Take her or leave her?

BURGUNDY   Pardon me, royal sir.

Election makes not up in such conditions.[7]

LEAR   Then leave her, sir; for by the power that made me,

205   I tell you° all her wealth. [*To* FRANCE] For° you, great King,   *inform you of / As for*

I would not from your love make such a stray°   *stray so far*

To° match you where I hate, therefore beseech you   *As to*

T'avert your liking° a more worthier way   *To turn your affections*

Than on a wretch whom nature is ashamed

Almost t'acknowledge hers.

210   FRANCE   This is most strange,

That she whom even but now was your best object,

The argument° of your praise, balm of your age,   *theme*

The best, the dear'st, should in this trice° of time   *moment*

Commit a thing so monstrous to dismantle°   *as to strip off, disrobe*

215   So many folds of favour. Sure, her offence

Must be of such unnatural degree

That monsters it,° or your fore-vouched affection   *makes it monstrous*

Fall into taint;[8] which to believe of her

Must be a faith that reason without miracle

220   Should never plant in me.

CORDELIA [*to* LEAR]   I yet beseech your majesty,

If for I want° that glib and oily art   *because I lack*

To speak and purpose not°—since what I well intend,   *and not intend*

I'll do't before I speak—that you make known

225   It is no vicious blot, murder, or foulness,

No unchaste action or dishonoured step

That hath deprived me of your grace and favour,

But even the want of that for which I am richer—

A still-soliciting° eye, and such a tongue   *An always-begging*

230   That I am glad I have not, though not to have it

Hath lost me in your liking.

LEAR   Better thou

Hadst not been born than not t'have pleased me better.

FRANCE   Is it but this—a tardiness in nature,

Which often leaves the history unspoke

235   That it intends to do?[9]—My lord of Burgundy,

What say you to the lady? Love's not love

When it is mingled with regards° that stands   *considerations*

Aloof from th'entire point. Will you have her?

She is herself a dowry.

BURGUNDY [*to* LEAR]   Royal King,

240   Give but that portion which yourself proposed,

And here I take Cordelia by the hand,

Duchess of Burgundy.

LEAR   Nothing. I have sworn. I am firm.

7. A choice cannot be made under those terms.
8. *or . . . taint:* or else the love you earlier swore for Cordelia must be regarded with suspicion. "Or" may also
mean "before," in which case the phrase would mean

"before the love you once proclaimed could have
decayed."
9. *a tardiness . . . do:* a natural reserve that inhibits voicing one's intentions.

BURGUNDY [*to* CORDELIA]   I am sorry, then, you have so lost a father
235   That you must lose a husband.
CORDELIA   Peace be with Burgundy; since that respects
   Of fortune are his love, I shall not be his wife.
FRANCE   Fairest Cordelia, that art most rich, being poor;
   Most choice, forsaken; and most loved, despised:
240   Thee and thy virtues here I seize upon.
   Be it lawful, I take up what's cast away.
   Gods, gods! 'Tis strange that from their cold'st neglect
   My love should kindle to inflamed respect.°—   *ardent regard*
   Thy dowerless daughter, King, thrown to my chance,
245   Is queen of us, of ours, and our fair France.
   Not all the dukes in wat'rish° Burgundy   *irrigated; watery, weak*
   Shall buy this unprized° precious maid of me.—   *unappreciated*
   Bid them farewell, Cordelia, though unkind.°   *though they are unkind*
   Thou losest here,° a better where° to find.   *this place / place*
250   LEAR   Thou hast her, France. Let her be thine, for we
   Have no such daughter, nor shall ever see
   That face of hers again. Therefore be gone,
   Without our grace, our love, our benison.°—   *blessing*
   Come, noble Burgundy.
                    [*Flourish.*] *Exeunt* LEAR *and* BURGUNDY [*then*
                    ALBANY, CORNWALL, GLOUCESTER, EDMUND,
                              and followers]
   FRANCE [*to* CORDELIA]   Bid farewell to your sisters.
255   CORDELIA   Ye jewels of our father, with washed eyes
   Cordelia leaves you. I know you what you are,
   And like a sister am most loath to call
   Your faults as they are named.° Use well our father.   *are properly called*
   To your professèd bosoms° I commit him.   *publicly proclaimed love*
260   But yet, alas, stood I within his grace
   I would prefer° him to a better place.   *promote; recommend*
   So farewell to you both.
   GONORIL   Prescribe not us our duties.
   REGAN   Let your study
265   Be to content your lord, who hath received you
   At fortune's alms.[8] You have obedience scanted,°   *stinted on*
   And well are worth the worst that you have wanted.[9]
   CORDELIA   Time shall unfold what pleated cunning hides.
   Who covers faults, at last shame them derides.[1]
   Well may you prosper.
270   FRANCE   Come, fair Cordelia.
                    Exeunt FRANCE *and* CORDELIA
   GONORIL   Sister, it is not a little I have to say of what most nearly
   appertains to us both. I think our father will hence tonight.
   REGAN   That's most certain, and with you. Next month with us.
   GONORIL   You see how full of changes° his age is. The observa-   *fickleness*
275   tion we have made of it hath not been little.[2] He always loved
   our sister most, and with what poor judgement he hath now
   cast her off appears too gross.°   *blatant*

---

8. As a charitable gift from Dame Fortune.
9. And you deserve to get no more love (from your husband) than you have given (to your father). "Want" plays
on its alternative meanings of "lack" and "desire."

1. *Who . . . derides*: Those who hide their faults will in
the end be put to shame.
2. We have observed it more than a little.

BURGUNDY [*to* CORDELIA]   I am sorry, then, you have so lost a father
    That you must lose a husband.
245 CORDELIA   Peace be with Burgundy;
    Since that respect and fortunes are his love,
    I shall not be his wife.
FRANCE   Fairest Cordelia, that art most rich, being poor;
    Most choice, forsaken; and most loved, despised:
250   Thee and thy virtues here I seize upon.
    Be it lawful, I take up what's cast away.
    Gods, gods! 'Tis strange that from their cold'st neglect
    My love should kindle to inflamed respect.°—   *ardent regard*
    Thy dowerless daughter, King, thrown to my chance,
255   Is queen of us, of ours, and our fair France.
    Not all the dukes of wat'rish° Burgundy   *irrigated; watery, weak*
    Can buy this unprized° precious maid of me.—   *unappreciated*
    Bid them farewell, Cordelia, though unkind.°   *though they are unkind*
    Thou losest here,° a better where° to find.   *this place / place*
260 LEAR   Thou hast her, France. Let her be thine, for we
    Have no such daughter, nor shall ever see
    That face of hers again. Therefore be gone,
    Without our grace, our love, our benison.°—   *blessing*
    Come, noble Burgundy.
                   Flourish. Exeunt [all but FRANCE
                            and the sisters]
FRANCE   Bid farewell to your sisters.
265 CORDELIA   Ye jewels of our father, with washed eyes
    Cordelia leaves you. I know you what you are,
    And like a sister am most loath to call
    Your faults as they are named.° Love well our father.   *are properly called*
    To your professèd bosoms° I commit him.   *publicly proclaimed love*
270   But yet, alas, stood I within his grace
    I would prefer° him to a better place.   *promote; recommend*
    So farewell to you both.
REGAN   Prescribe not us our duty.
GONERIL   Let your study
275   Be to content your lord, who hath received you
    At fortune's alms.[1] You have obedience scanted,°   *stinted on*
    And well are worth the want that you have wanted.[2]
CORDELIA   Time shall unfold what pleated cunning hides,
    Who covert faults at last with shame derides.[3]
    Well may you prosper.
280 FRANCE   Come, my fair Cordelia.
                    Exeunt FRANCE *and* CORDELIA
GONERIL   Sister, it is not little I have to say of what most nearly
    appertains to us both. I think our father will hence tonight.
REGAN   That's most certain, and with you. Next month with us.
GONERIL   You see how full of changes° his age is. The observa-   *fickleness*
285   tion we have made of it hath been little.° He always loved our   *meticulous*
    sister most, and with what poor judgement he hath now cast
    her off appears too grossly.°   *blatantly*

1. As a charitable gift from Dame Fortune.
2. And you deserve to get no more love (from your husband) than you have given (to your father). "Want" plays
on its alternative meanings of "lack" and "desire."
3. *Time . . . derides*: Time eventually exposes and shames
all hidden faults.

REGAN 'Tis the infirmity of his age; yet he hath ever but slen-
derly known himself.

280 GONORIL The best and soundest of his time hath been but rash;[3]
then° must we look to receive from his age not alone the imper-   *therefore*
fection of long-engrafted condition,° but therewithal unruly   *deep-rooted habit*
waywardness that infirm and choleric years bring with them.

REGAN Such unconstant starts[4] are we like° to have from him as   *likely*
285 this of Kent's banishment.

GONORIL There is further compliment° of leave-taking between   *ceremony*
France and him. Pray, let's hit° together. If our father carry   *join; strike*
authority with such dispositions[5] as he bears, this last surrender°   *abdication*
of his will but offend° us.   *harm*

290 REGAN We shall further think on't.

GONORIL We must do something, and i'th' heat.°   *Exeunt*   *while the iron is hot*

Scene 2

Enter Bastard [EDMUND]

EDMUND Thou, nature, art my goddess. To thy law
My services are bound.[1] Wherefore° should I   *Why*
Stand in the plague of custom[2] and permit
The curiosity° of nations to deprive me   *legal niceties*
5 For that° I am some twelve or fourteen moonshines°   *Because / months*
Lag of° a brother? Why 'bastard'? Wherefore 'base',   *Younger than*
When my dimensions are as well compact,°   *composed*
My mind as generous,° and my shape as true   *noble*
As honest° madam's issue?   *married; chaste*
10 Why brand they us with 'base, base bastardy',
Who in the lusty stealth of nature take
More composition and fierce quality[3]
Than doth within a stale, dull-eyed bed go
To the creating a whole tribe of fops°   *fools*
15 Got° 'tween a sleep and wake? Well then,   *Begotten*
Legitimate Edgar, I must have your land.
Our father's love is to° the bastard Edmund   *as much to*
As to the legitimate. Well, my legitimate, if
This letter speed° and my invention° thrive,   *succeed / plot*
20 Edmund the base shall to° th' legitimate.   *match up to; usurp*
I grow, I prosper. Now gods, stand up for bastards!

Enter GLOUCESTER. [EDMUND *reads a letter*]

GLOUCESTER Kent banished thus, and France in choler parted,°   *in anger departed*
And the King gone tonight,° subscribed° his power,   *last night / limited*
Confined to exhibition[4]—all this done
25 Upon the gad?°—Edmund, how now? What news?   *spur of the moment*

EDMUND So please your lordship, none.

---

3. *The . . . rash:* Even in the prime of his life he was
impetuous.
4. Such impulsive outbursts.
5. Frame of mine.
Scene 2 Location: The Earl of Gloucester's house.
1. Edmund declares the raw force of unsocialized and
uregulated existence, as opposed to human law, to be his
ruler; ironically, "nature" also means "natural filial
affection." A "natural" was another word for "bastard"
(illegitimate child).
2. Submit to the imposition of inheritance law.

3. *Who . . . quality:* Whose begetting, by reason of its furtiveness and heightened excitement, requires better execution and more vigor. Alternatively (with "take" having
the meaning "give"), whose begetting produces (a person
of) more mixture and vigor. "Composition," or mixture,
may refer to the belief that the perfect offspring was conceived from an equal quantity of male and female essence
and that physical and mental abnormalities were caused
by a predominance of one or the other.
4. Pension; mere show without force.

REGAN   'Tis the infirmity of his age; yet he hath ever but slen-
derly known himself.

290 GONERIL   The best and soundest of his time hath been but rash;[4]
then° must we look from his age to receive not alone the imper-   *therefore*
fections of long-engrafted condition,° but therewithal the   *deep-rooted habit*
unruly waywardness that infirm and choleric years bring with
them.

295 REGAN   Such unconstant starts[5] are we like° to have from him as   *likely*
this of Kent's banishment.

GONERIL   There is further compliment° of leave-taking between   *ceremony*
France and him. Pray you, let us sit together. If our father carry
authority with such disposition[6] as he bears, this last surrender°   *abdication*
300 of his will but offend° us.   *harm*

REGAN   We shall further think of it.

GONERIL   We must do something, and i'th' heat.°   *Exeunt*   *while the iron is hot*

1.2

Enter Bastard [EDMOND]

EDMOND   Thou, nature, art my goddess. To thy law
My services are bound.[1] Wherefore° should I   *Why*
Stand in the plague of custom[2] and permit
The curiosity° of nations to deprive me   *legal niceties*
5 For that° I am some twelve or fourteen moonshines°   *Because / months*
Lag of° a brother? Why 'bastard'? Wherefore 'base',   *Younger than*
When my dimensions are as well compact,°   *composed*
My mind as generous,° and my shape as true   *noble*
As honest° madam's issue? Why brand they us   *married; chaste*
10 With 'base', with 'baseness, bastardy—base, base'—
Who in the lusty stealth of nature take
More composition and fierce quality[3]
Than doth within a dull, stale, tirèd bed
Go to th' creating a whole tribe of fops°   *fools*
15 Got° 'tween a sleep and wake? Well then,   *Begotten*
Legitimate Edgar, I must have your land.
Our father's love is to° the bastard Edmond   *as much to*
As to th' legitimate. Fine word, 'legitimate'.
Well, my legitimate, if this letter speed°   *succeed*
20 And my invention° thrive, Edmond the base   *plot*
Shall to° th' legitimate. I grow, I prosper.   *match up to; usurp*
Now gods, stand up for bastards!

Enter GLOUCESTER. [EDMOND *reads a letter*]

GLOUCESTER   Kent banished thus, and France in choler parted,°   *in anger departed*
And the King gone tonight,° prescribed° his power,   *last night / limited*
25 Confined to exhibition[4]—all this done
Upon the gad?°—Edmond, how now? What news?   *spur of the moment*

EDMOND   So please your lordship, none.

---

4. *The . . . rash:* Even in the prime of his life he was impetuous.
5. Such impulsive outbursts.
6. Frame of mind.
1.2 Location: The Earl of Gloucester's house.
1. Edmond declares the raw force of unsocialized and unregulated existence, as opposed to human law, to be his ruler; ironically, "nature" also means "natural filial affection." A "natural" was another word for "bastard" (illegitimate child).
2. Submit to the imposition of inheritance law.

3. *Who . . . quality:* Whose begetting, by reason of its furtiveness and heightened excitement, requires better execution and more vigor. Alternatively (with "take" having the meaning "give"), whose begetting produces (a person of) more mixture and vigor. "Composition," or mixture, may refer to the belief that the perfect offspring was conceived from an equal quantity of male and female essence and that physical and mental abnormalities were caused by a predominance of one or the other.
4. Pension; mere show without force.

GLOUCESTER   Why so earnestly seek you to put up that letter?
EDMUND   I know no news, my lord.
GLOUCESTER   What paper were you reading?
30 EDMUND   Nothing, my lord.
GLOUCESTER   No? What needs then that terrible dispatch° of it   *frightened haste*
   into your pocket? The quality of nothing hath not such need
   to hide itself. Let's see. Come, if it be nothing I shall not need
   spectacles.
35 EDMUND   I beseech you, sir, pardon me. It is a letter from my
   brother that I have not all o'er-read; for so much as I have
   perused, I find it not fit for your liking.°   *pleasure*
GLOUCESTER   Give me the letter, sir.
EDMUND   I shall offend either to detain or give it. The contents,
40 as in part I understand them, are to blame.
GLOUCESTER   Let's see, let's see.
EDMUND   I hope for my brother's justification he wrote this but
   as an assay or taste[5] of my virtue.
      [*He gives* GLOUCESTER] *a letter*
GLOUCESTER (*reads*)   'This policy of age makes the world bitter
45   to the best of our times,[6] keeps our fortunes from us till our
   oldness cannot relish them. I begin to find an idle and fond°   *a useless and foolish*
   bondage in the oppression of aged tyranny, who sways not as it
   hath power but as it is suffered.[7] Come to me, that of this I may
   speak more. If our father would sleep till I waked him, you
50   should enjoy half his revenue for ever and live the beloved of
   your brother,
                                                   Edgar.'
   Hum, conspiracy! 'Slept till I waked him, you should enjoy half
   his revenue'—my son Edgar! Had he a hand to write this, a
55   heart and brain to breed it in? When came this to you? Who
   brought it?
EDMUND   It was not brought me, my lord, there's the cunning of
   it. I found it thrown in at the casement° of my closet.°   *window / private room*
GLOUCESTER   You know the character° to be your brother's?   *handwriting*
60 EDMUND   If the matter° were good, my lord, I durst swear it were   *content*
   his; but in respect of that, I would fain° think it were not.   *gladly*
GLOUCESTER   It is his.
EDMUND   It is his hand, my lord, but I hope his heart is not in
   the contents.
65 GLOUCESTER   Hath he never heretofore sounded you° in this   *sounded you out*
   business?
EDMUND   Never, my lord; but I have often heard him maintain
   it to be fit that, sons at perfect age° and fathers declining, his   *at maturity*
   father should be as ward[8] to the son, and the son manage the
70   revenue.
GLOUCESTER   O villain, villain—his very opinion in the letter!
   Abhorred villain, unnatural, detested, brutish villain—worse
   than brutish! Go, sir, seek him, ay, apprehend him. Abominable villain! Where is he?

---

5. *but . . . taste:* simply as a proof or test. Both terms
derive from metallurgy.
6. The established primacy of the elderly embitters us at
the prime of our lives. *policy:* statecraft; craftiness; established order.

7. *who . . . suffered:* which rules not because it is powerful
but because it is permitted to ("suffered").
8. A child under eighteen years who was legally dependent, often orphaned.

GLOUCESTER   Why so earnestly seek you to put up that letter?

EDMOND   I know no news, my lord.

30   GLOUCESTER   What paper were you reading?

EDMOND   Nothing, my lord.

GLOUCESTER   No? What needed then that terrible dispatch° of it   *frightened haste*
into your pocket? The quality of nothing hath not such need
to hide itself. Let's see. Come, if it be nothing I shall not need
35   spectacles.

EDMOND   I beseech you, sir, pardon me. It is a letter from my
brother that I have not all o'er-read; and for so much as I have
perused, I find it not fit for your o'erlooking.

GLOUCESTER   Give me the letter, sir.

40   EDMOND   I shall offend either to detain or give it. The contents,
as in part I understand them, are to blame.

GLOUCESTER   Let's see, let's see.

EDMOND   I hope for my brother's justification he wrote this but
as an assay or taste⁵ of my virtue.

[*He gives* GLOUCESTER *a letter*]

45   GLOUCESTER   (*reads*)   'This policy and reverence of age makes
the world bitter to the best of our times,⁶ keeps our fortunes
from us till our oldness cannot relish them. I begin to find an
idle and fond° bondage in the oppression of aged tyranny, who   *a useless and foolish*
sways not as it hath power but as it is suffered.⁷ Come to me,
50   that of this I may speak more. If our father would sleep till I
waked him, you should enjoy half his revenue for ever and live
the beloved of your brother,
                                                    Edgar.'
Hum, conspiracy! 'Sleep till I wake him, you should enjoy half
55   his revenue'—my son Edgar! Had he a hand to write this, a
heart and brain to breed it in? When came you to this? Who
brought it?

EDMOND   It was not brought me, my lord, there's the cunning of
it. I found it thrown in at the casement° of my closet.°   *window / private room*

60   GLOUCESTER   You know the character° to be your brother's?   *handwriting*

EDMOND   If the matter° were good, my lord, I durst swear it were   *content*
his; but in respect of that, I would fain° think it were not.   *gladly*

GLOUCESTER   It is his.

EDMOND   It is his hand, my lord, but I hope his heart is not in
65   the contents.

GLOUCESTER   Has he never before sounded° you in this   *sounded you out*
business?

EDMOND   Never, my lord; but I have heard him oft maintain it
to be fit that, sons at perfect age° and fathers declined, the   *at maturity*
70   father should be as ward⁸ to the son, and the son manage his
revenue.

GLOUCESTER   O villain, villain—his very opinion in the letter!
Abhorred villain, unnatural, detested, brutish villain—worse
than brutish! Go, sirrah,⁹ seek him. I'll apprehend him. Abomi-
75   nable villain! Where is he?

---

5. *but . . . taste:* simply as a proof or test. Both terms
derive from metallurgy.
6. The established primacy of the elderly embitters us at
the prime of our lives. *policy:* statecraft; craftiness; established order.
7. *who . . . suffered:* which rules not because it is powerful
but because it is permitted to ("suffered").
8. A child under eighteen years who was legally dependent, often orphaned.
9. A form of address used with children or social inferiors.

75   EDMUND   I do not well know, my lord. If it shall please you to
      suspend your indignation against my brother till you can derive
      from him better testimony of this intent, you should run a cer-
      tain° course; where° if you violently proceed against him, mis-   *safe, reliable / whereas*
      taking his purpose, it would make a great gap in your own
80   honour and shake in pieces the heart of his obedience. I dare
      pawn down° my life for him he hath wrote this to feel° my   *I dare stake / feel out*
      affection to your honour, and to no further pretence of danger.⁹
      GLOUCESTER   Think you so?
      EDMUND   If your honour judge it meet,° I will place you where   *appropriate*
85   you shall hear us confer of this, and by an auricular assurance
      have your satisfaction, and that without any further delay than
      this very evening.
      GLOUCESTER   He cannot be such a monster.
      EDMUND   Nor is not, sure.
90   GLOUCESTER   To his father, that so tenderly and entirely loves
      him— heaven and earth! Edmund seek him out, wind me into
      him.¹ I pray you, frame° your business after your own wisdom.   *arrange*
      I would unstate myself to be in a due resolution.²
      EDMUND   I shall seek him, sir, presently,° convey° the business   *immediately / carry out*
95   as I shall see means, and acquaint you withal.°   *therewith*
      GLOUCESTER   These late° eclipses in the sun and moon portend   *recent*
      no good to us.³ Though the wisdom of nature can reason thus
      and thus, yet nature finds itself scourged by the sequent
      effects.⁴ Love cools, friendship falls off, brothers divide; in cities
100   mutinies, in countries discords, palaces treason, the bond
      cracked between son and father. Find out this villain, Edmund;
      it shall lose thee nothing. Do it carefully. And the noble and
      true-hearted Kent banished, his offence honesty! Strange,
      strange!   [*Exit*]
105   EDMUND   This is the excellent foppery° of the world: that when   *foolishness*
      we are sick in fortune—often the surfeit° of our own behav-   *excesses*
      iour— we make guilty of° our disasters the sun, the moon, and   *we hold responsible for*
      the stars, as if we were villains by necessity, fools by heavenly
      compulsion, knaves, thieves, and treacherers by spherical pre-
110   dominance,⁵ drunkards, liars, and adulterers by an enforced
      obedience of planetary influence, and all that we are evil in by
      a divine thrusting on.° An admirable° evasion of whoremaster   *imposition / amazing*
      man, to lay his goatish disposition to the charge of stars!⁶ My
      father compounded° with my mother under the Dragon's tail   *coupled*
115   and my nativity was under Ursa Major,⁷ so that it follows I am
      rough and lecherous. Fut!° I should have been that° I am had   *By Christ's foot / what*
      the maidenliest star of the firmament twinkled on my bastardy.
      Edgar . . .

9. No further intention to do harm.
1. Worm your way into his confidence (with "me" as an
intensifier); worm your way into his confidence for me
("me" as a dative of respect).
2. I would give up everything to have my doubts resolved.
3. Lunar and solar eclipses that were seen in London
about a year before the play's first recorded performance
would have added spice to this superstitious belief in the
role of heavenly bodies as augurs of misfortune.
4. *Though . . . effects:* Though natural science may explain the eclipses this way or that, nature (and family
bonds) suffers in the effects that follow.
5. By the ascendancy of a particular planet. In the universe as conceived by Ptolemy, the planets revolved about
the earth on crystalline spheres.
6. *to lay . . . stars:* to hold the stars responsible for his
lustful desires. In Greek mythology, the satyr, a creature
with goatlike characteristics, was notoriously lecherous.
7. Constellations: *Dragon's tail* = Draco, and *Ursa
Major* = Great Bear.

EDMOND   I do not well know, my lord. If it shall please you to
suspend your indignation against my brother till you can derive
from him better testimony of his intent, you should run a cer-
tain° course; where° if you violently proceed against him, mis-   *safe, reliable / whereas*
80   taking his purpose, it would make a great gap in your own
honour and shake in pieces the heart of his obedience. I dare
pawn down° my life for him that he hath writ this to feel° my   *I dare stake / feel out*
affection to your honour, and to no other pretence of danger.[1]
GLOUCESTER   Think you so?
85   EDMOND   If your honour judge it meet,° I will place you where   *appropriate*
you shall hear us confer of this, and by an auricular assurance
have your satisfaction, and that without any further delay than
this very evening.
GLOUCESTER   He cannot be such a monster. Edmond, seek him
90   out, wind me into him,[2] I pray you. Frame° the business after   *Arrange*
your own wisdom. I would unstate myself to be in a due
resolution.[3]
EDMOND   I will seek him, sir, presently,° convey° the business as   *immediately / carry out*
I shall find means, and acquaint you withal.°   *therewith*
95   GLOUCESTER   These late° eclipses in the sun and moon portend   *recent*
no good to us.[4] Though the wisdom of nature can reason it
thus and thus, yet nature finds itself scourged by the sequent
effects.[5] Love cools, friendship falls off, brothers divide; in
cities, mutinies; in countries, discord; in palaces, treason; and
100   the bond cracked 'twixt son and father. This villain of mine
comes under the prediction: there's son against father. The
King falls from bias of nature:[6] there's father against child. We
have seen the best of our time. Machinations, hollowness,°   *insincerity*
treachery, and all ruinous disorders follow us disquietly to our
105   graves. Find out this villain, Edmond; it shall lose thee nothing.
Do it carefully. And the noble and true-hearted Kent banished,
his offence honesty! 'Tis strange.   *Exit*
EDMOND   This is the excellent foppery° of the world: that when   *foolishness*
we are sick in fortune—often the surfeits° of our own behav-   *excesses*
110   iour—we make guilty of° our disasters the sun, the moon, and   *we hold responsible for*
stars, as if we were villains on necessity, fools by heavenly
compulsion, knaves, thieves, and treachers by spherical predominance,[7] drunkards, liars, and adulterers by an enforced
obedience of planetary influence, and all that we are evil in by
115   a divine thrusting on.° An admirable° evasion of whoremaster   *imposition / amazing*
man, to lay his goatish disposition on the charge of a star![8] My
father compounded° with my mother under the Dragon's tail   *coupled*
and my nativity was under Ursa Major,[9] so that it follows I
am rough and lecherous. Fut!° I should have been that° I am   *By Christ's foot / what*
120   had the maidenliest star in the firmament twinkled on my
bastardizing.

1. No other intention to do harm.
2. Worm your way into his confidence (with "me" as an intensifier); worm your way into his confidence for me ("me" as a dative of respect).
3. I would give up everything to have my doubts resolved.
4. Lunar and solar eclipses that were seen in London about a year before the play's first recorded performance would have added spice to this superstitious belief in the role of heavenly bodies as augurs of misfortune.
5. *Though . . . effects:* Though natural science may explain the eclipses this way or that, nature (and family bonds) suffers in the effects that follow.

6. The King deviates from his natural inclination. In the game of bowls, the "bias" ("course") is the eccentric path taken by the weighted ball when thrown.
7. By the ascendancy of a particular planet. In the universe as conceived by Ptolemy, the planets revolved about the earth on crystalline spheres.
8. *to lay . . . star:* to hold a star responsible for his lustful desires. In Greek mythology, the satyr, a creature with goatlike characteristics, was notoriously lecherous.
9. Constellations: *Dragon's tail* = Draco, and *Ursa Major* = Great Bear.

Enter EDGAR

and on's cue out he comes, like the catastrophe° of the old   *resolution*
120   comedy; mine° is villainous melancholy, with a sigh like them   *my cue; my role*
of Bedlam.[8]—O, these eclipses do portend these divisions.

EDGAR   How now, brother Edmund, what serious contemplation
are you in?

EDMUND   I am thinking, brother, of a prediction I read this other
125   day, what should follow these eclipses.

EDGAR   Do you busy yourself about that?

EDMUND   I promise you, the effects he writ of succeed° unhap-   *follow*
pily, as of unnaturalness between the child and the parent,
death, dearth, dissolutions of ancient amities, divisions in state,
130   menaces and maledictions against king and nobles, needless
diffidences,° banishment of friends, dissipation of cohorts,[9]   *baseless suspicions*
nuptial breaches, and I know not what.

EDGAR   How long have you been a sectary astronomical?°   *a devotee of astrology*

EDMUND   Come, come, when saw you my father last?

135   EDGAR   Why, the night gone by.

EDMUND   Spake you with him?

EDGAR   Two hours together.

EDMUND   Parted you in good terms? Found you no displeasure
in him by word or countenance?°   *appearance; demeanor*

140   EDGAR   None at all.

EDMUND   Bethink yourself wherein you may have offended him,
and at my entreaty forbear° his presence till some little time   *avoid*
hath qualified° the heat of his displeasure, which at this instant   *mollified*
so rageth in him that with the mischief of your person it would
145   scarce allay.[1]

EDGAR   Some villain hath done me wrong.

EDMUND   That's my fear, brother. I advise you to the best. Go
armed. I am no honest man if there be any good meaning
towards you. I have told you what I have seen and heard but
150   faintly, nothing like the image and horror of it. Pray you, away.

EDGAR   Shall I hear from you anon?

EDMUND   I do serve you in this business.   *Exit* EDGAR
A credulous father, and a brother noble,
Whose nature is so far from doing harms
155   That he suspects none; on whose foolish honesty
My practices° ride easy. I see the business.[2]   *plots*
Let me, if not by birth, have lands by wit.°   *intelligence*
All with me's meet that I can fashion fit.[3]   *Exit*

---

8. Like the inmates of Bedlam. "Bethlehem," shortened to "Bedlam," was the name of the oldest and best-known London madhouse.
9. Scattering of forces.
1. *with . . . allay:* even harming you bodily would hardly relieve his anger; alternatively, with the irritant of your presence, it (Gloucester's anger) would not be abated.
2. It is now clear to me what needs to be done.
3. Anything is fine by me as long as I can make it serve my purpose. *meet:* justifiable; appropriate.

Enter EDGAR

Pat° he comes, like the catastrophe° of the old comedy. My cue   *On cue / resolution*
is villainous melancholy, with a sigh like Tom o' Bedlam.[1]
    [*He reads a book*]
—O, these eclipses do portend these divisions. Fa, so, la, mi.[2]

125   EDGAR   How now, brother Edmond, what serious contemplation
      are you in?

EDMOND   I am thinking, brother, of a prediction I read this other
      day, what should follow these eclipses.

EDGAR   Do you busy yourself with that?

130   EDMOND   I promise you, the effects he writes of succeed° unhap-   *follow*
      pily. When saw you my father last?

EDGAR   The night gone by.

EDMOND   Spake you with him?

EDGAR   Ay, two hours together.

135   EDMOND   Parted you in good terms? Found you no displeasure
      in him by word nor countenance?°   *appearance; demeanor*

EDGAR   None at all.

EDMOND   Bethink yourself wherein you may have offended him,
      and at my entreaty forbear° his presence until some little time   *avoid*
140   hath qualified° the heat of his displeasure, which at this instant   *modified*
      so rageth in him that with the mischief of your person it would
      scarcely allay.[3]

EDGAR   Some villain hath done me wrong.

EDMOND   That's my fear. I pray you have a continent forbear-
145   ance° till the speed of his rage goes slower; and, as I say, retire   *restrained absence*
      with me to my lodging, from whence I will fitly° bring you to   *when suitable*
      hear my lord speak. Pray ye, go. There's my key. If you do stir
      abroad, go armed.

EDGAR   Armed, brother?

150   EDMOND   Brother, I advise you to the best. I am no honest man
      if there be any good meaning toward you. I have told you what
      I have seen and heard but faintly, nothing like the image and
      horror of it. Pray you, away.

EDGAR   Shall I hear from you anon?

155   EDMOND   I do serve you in this business.   *Exit* [EDGAR]
      A credulous father, and a brother noble,
      Whose nature is so far from doing harms
      That he suspects none; on whose foolish honesty
      My practices° ride easy. I see the business.[4]   *plots*
160   Let me, if not by birth, have lands by wit.°   *intelligence*
      All with me's meet that I can fashion fit.[5]   *Exit*

---

1. The usual name for lunatic beggars; "Bethlehem," shortened to "Bedlam," was the name of the oldest and best-known London madhouse.
2. The portion of the scale Edmund sings is an augmented fourth, an interval considered at this time very discordant; it was sometimes referred to as "the devil in music." *divisions:* social fractures; melodic embellishments.

3. *with . . . allay:* even harming you bodily ("mischief") would hardly relieve his anger; alternatively, with the irritant of your presence, it (Gloucester's anger) would not be abated.
4. It is now clear to me what needs to be done.
5. Anything is fine by me as long as I can make it serve my purpose. *meet:* justifiable; appropriate.

Scene 3

Enter GONORIL *and Gentleman* [OSWALD]

GONORIL   Did my father strike my gentleman
For chiding of his fool?

OSWALD   Yes, madam.

GONORIL   By day and night he wrongs me. Every hour
He flashes into one gross crime° or other   *offense*
5   That sets us all at odds. I'll not endure it.
His knights grow riotous, and himself upbraids us
On every trifle. When he returns from hunting
I will not speak with him. Say I am sick.
If you come slack of former services[1]
10   You shall do well; the fault of it I'll answer.°   *answer for*
          [*Hunting horns within*]

OSWALD   He's coming, madam. I hear him.

GONORIL   Put on what weary negligence you please,
You and your fellow servants. I'd have it come in° question.   *into*
If he dislike it, let him to our sister,
15   Whose mind and mine I know in that are one,
Not to be overruled. Idle° old man,   *Foolish*
That still would manage those authorities
That he hath given away! Now, by my life,
Old fools are babes again, and must be used
20   With checks as flatteries, when they are seen abused.[2]
Remember what I tell you.

OSWALD   Very well, madam.

GONORIL   And let his knights have colder looks among you.
What grows of it, no matter. Advise your fellows so.
I would breed from hence occasions, and I shall,
25   That I may speak.[3] I'll write straight° to my sister   *straightaway*
To hold my very° course. Go prepare for dinner.   *exact*
                              Exeunt [*severally*]°   *separately*

Scene 4

Enter KENT [*disguised*]

KENT   If but as well[1] I other accents borrow
That can my speech diffuse,° my good intent   *disguise*
May carry through itself to that full issue°   *result*
For which I razed my likeness.[2] Now, banished Kent,
5   If thou canst serve where thou dost stand condemned,
Thy master, whom thou lov'st, shall find thee full of labour.°   *ready for work*
          Enter LEAR [*and servants from hunting*]

LEAR   Let me not stay° a jot for dinner. Go get it ready.   *wait*
                              [*Exit one*]
[*To* KENT] How now, what° art thou?   *who*

KENT   A man, sir.

10   LEAR   What dost thou profess?[3] What wouldst thou with us?

KENT   I do profess to be no less than I seem, to serve him truly

---

Scene 3 Location: The Duke of Albany's castle.
1. If you offer him less service (and respect) than before.
2. *Old . . . abused*: When foolish old men act like children, rebukes are the kindest treatment when kind treatment is abused.
3. *I would . . . speak*: I wish to foster situations, and I
shall, in which to speak my mind.

Scene 4 Location: As before.
1. As well as disguising my appearance.
2. Disguised my appearance; shaved off my beard (with a
pun on "razor").
3. What is your job (profession)? Kent, in reply, uses
"profess" punningly to mean "claim."

1.3

Enter GONERIL *and Steward* [OSWALD]

GONERIL   Did my father strike my gentleman
For chiding of his fool?

OSWALD   Ay, madam.

GONERIL   By day and night he wrongs me. Every hour
He flashes into one gross crime° or other   *offense*
5   That sets us all at odds. I'll not endure it.
His knights grow riotous, and himself upbraids us
On every trifle. When he returns from hunting
I will not speak with him. Say I am sick.
If you come slack of former services¹
10   You shall do well; the fault of it I'll answer.°   *answer for*
        [*Horns within*]

OSWALD   He's coming, madam. I hear him.

GONERIL   Put on what weary negligence you please,
You and your fellows.° I'd have it come to question.   *servants*
If he distaste° it, let him to my sister,   *dislike*
15   Whose mind and mine I know in that are one.
Remember what I have said.

OSWALD   Well, madam.

GONERIL   And let his knights have colder looks among you.
What grows of it, no matter. Advise your fellows so.
I'll write straight° to my sister to hold my course.   *straightaway*
20   Prepare for dinner.   *Exeunt* [*severally*]°   *separately*

1.4

Enter KENT [*disguised*]

KENT   If but as well¹ I other accents borrow
That can my speech diffuse,° my good intent   *disguise*
May carry through itself to that full issue°   *result*
For which I razed my likeness.² Now, banished Kent,
5   If thou canst serve where thou dost stand condemned,
So may it come° thy master, whom thou lov'st,   *come to pass*
Shall find thee full of labours.°   *helpful; keen*
        Horns within.° Enter LEAR *and attendants* [*from*   Hunting horns offstage
        hunting]³

LEAR   Let me not stay° a jot for dinner. Go get it ready.   *wait*
        [*Exit one*]
    [*To* KENT] How now, what° art thou?   *who*
10   KENT   A man, sir.

LEAR   What dost thou profess?⁴ What wouldst thou with us?

KENT   I do profess to be no less than I seem, to serve him truly

---

1.3 Location: The Duke of Albany's castle.
1. If you offer him less service (and respect) than before.
1.4 Location: As before.
1. As well as disguising my appearance.
2. Disguised my appearance; shaved off my beard (with a pun on "razor").

3. The attendants include at least one knight. Critics of James I complained that he devalued honors by granting too many knighthoods and that he squandered too much time in hunting.
4. What is your job (profession)? Kent, in reply, uses "profess" punningly to mean "claim."

that will put me in trust, to love him that is honest, to converse°   *associate*
with him that is wise and says little, to fear judgement, to fight
when I cannot choose,° and to eat no fish.[4]   *when I must*

15 LEAR   What art thou?

KENT   A very honest-hearted fellow, and as poor as the King.

LEAR   If thou be as poor for a subject as he is for a king, thou'rt
poor enough. What wouldst thou?

KENT   Service.

20 LEAR   Who wouldst thou serve?

KENT   You.

LEAR   Dost thou know me, fellow?

KENT   No, sir, but you have that in your countenance which I
would fain° call master.   *gladly*

25 LEAR   What's that?

KENT   Authority.

LEAR   What services canst do?

KENT   I can keep honest counsel,° ride, run, mar a curious tale   *keep secrets*
in telling it, and deliver a plain message bluntly. That which
30 ordinary men are fit for I am qualified in; and the best of me is
diligence.

LEAR   How old art thou?

KENT   Not so young to love a woman for singing, nor so old to
dote on her for anything. I have years on my back forty-eight.

35 LEAR   Follow me. Thou shalt serve me, if I like thee no worse
after dinner. I will not part from thee yet. — Dinner, ho, dinner!
Where's my knave, my fool? Go you and call my fool hither.
                                                             [*Exit one*]

        Enter steward [OSWALD]
You, sirrah, where's my daughter?

OSWALD   So please you —   [*Exit*]

40 LEAR   What says the fellow there? Call the clotpoll° back.   *blockhead*
                                        [*Exeunt* SERVANT *and* KENT]
Where's my fool? Ho, I think the world's asleep.
        [*Enter* KENT *and a* SERVANT]
How now, where's that mongrel?

KENT   He says, my lord, your daughter is not well.

LEAR   Why came not the slave back to me when I called him?

45 SERVANT   Sir, he answered me in the roundest° manner he   *bluntest; rudest*
would not.

LEAR   A° would not?   *He*

SERVANT   My lord, I know not what the matter is, but to my
judgement your highness is not entertained with that ceremo-
50 nious affection as you were wont.° There's a great abatement   *accustomed to*
appears as well in the general dependants° as in the Duke him-   *servants*
self also, and your daughter.

LEAR   Ha, sayst thou so?

SERVANT   I beseech you pardon me, my lord, if I be mistaken, for
55 my duty cannot be silent when I think your highness wronged.

---

4. And not to be a Catholic or penitent (Catholics were obliged to eat fish on specified occasions and as penance);
alternatively, to be a manly man, meat eater.

that will put me in trust, to love him that is honest, to converse°   *associate*
with him that is wise and says little, to fear judgement, to fight
15   when I cannot choose,° and to eat no fish.[5]   *when I must*

LEAR   What art thou?

KENT   A very honest-hearted fellow, and as poor as the King.

LEAR   If thou be'st as poor for a subject as he's for a king, thou'rt
poor enough. What wouldst thou?

20   KENT   Service.

LEAR   Who wouldst thou serve?

KENT   You.

LEAR   Dost thou know me, fellow?

KENT   No, sir, but you have that in your countenance which I
25   would fain° call master.   *gladly*

LEAR   What's that?

KENT   Authority.

LEAR   What services canst do?

KENT   I can keep honest counsel,° ride, run, mar a curious tale   *keep secrets*
30   in telling it, and deliver a plain message bluntly. That which
ordinary men are fit for I am qualified in; and the best of me is
diligence.

LEAR   How old art thou?

KENT   Not so young, sir, to love a woman for singing, nor so old
35   to dote on her for anything. I have years on my back forty-eight.

LEAR   Follow me. Thou shalt serve me, if I like thee no worse
after dinner. I will not part from thee yet. Dinner, ho, dinner!
Where's my knave, my fool? Go you and call my fool hither.
                                                        [Exit one]

       Enter Steward [OSWALD]

You, you, sirrah, where's my daughter?

40   OSWALD   So please you—   *Exit*

LEAR   What says the fellow there? Call the clotpoll° back.   *blockhead*
                                                  [Exit a knight]

Where's my fool? Ho, I think the world's asleep.
       [Enter a KNIGHT]

How now? Where's that mongrel?

KNIGHT   He says, my lord, your daughter is not well.

45   LEAR   Why came not the slave back to me when I called him?

KNIGHT   Sir, he answered me in the roundest° manner he would   *bluntest; rudest*
not.

LEAR   A° would not?   *He*

KNIGHT   My lord, I know not what the matter is, but to my judge-
50   ment your highness is not entertained with that ceremonious
affection as you were wont.° There's a great abatement of kind-   *accustomed to*
ness appears as well in the general dependants° as in the Duke   *servants*
himself also, and your daughter.

LEAR   Ha, sayst thou so?

55   KNIGHT   I beseech you pardon me, my lord, if I be mistaken, for
my duty cannot be silent when I think your highness wronged.

---

5. And not to be a Catholic or penitent (Catholics were obliged to eat fish on specified occasions and as penance); alternatively, to be a manly man, a meat eater.

LEAR   Thou but rememberest° me of mine own conception.° I   *remind / perception*
have perceived a most faint neglect of late, which I have rather
blamed as mine own jealous curiosity[5] than as a very pretence°   *a true intention*
and purport of unkindness. I will look further into't. But
60   where's this fool? I have not seen him these two days.
SERVANT   Since my young lady's going into France, sir, the fool
hath much pined away.
LEAR   No more of that, I have noted it. Go you and tell my
daughter I would speak with her.   [*Exit one*]
65   Go you, call hither my fool.   [*Exit one*]
                [*Enter* OSWALD *crossing the stage*]
O you, sir, you, sir, come you hither. Who am I, sir?
OSWALD   My lady's father.
LEAR   My lady's father? My lord's knave, you whoreson dog, you
slave, you cur!
70   OSWALD   I am none of this, my lord, I beseech you pardon me.
LEAR   Do you bandy looks with me, you rascal?
                [LEAR *strikes him*]
OSWALD   I'll not be struck, my lord —
KENT [*tripping him*]   Nor tripped neither, you base football
player.[6]
75   LEAR [*to* KENT]   I thank thee, fellow. Thou serv'st me, and I'll
love thee.
KENT [*to* OSWALD]   Come, sir, I'll teach you differences.° Away,   *(of rank)*
away. If you will measure your lubber's length again,[7] tarry; but
away if you have wisdom.   [*Exit* OSWALD]
80   LEAR   Now, friendly knave, I thank thee.
                Enter [*Lear's*] FOOL
There's earnest of° thy service.   *downpayment for*
                [*He gives* KENT *money*]
FOOL   Let me hire him, too. [*To* KENT] Here's my coxcomb.°   *fool's cap*
LEAR   How now, my pretty knave, how dost thou?
FOOL [*to* KENT]   Sirrah, you were best take my coxcomb.
85   KENT   Why, fool?
FOOL   Why, for taking one's part that's out of favour. Nay, an
thou canst not smile as the wind sits, thou'lt catch cold shortly.[8]
There, take my coxcomb. Why, this fellow hath banished two
on's daughters[9] and done the third a blessing against his will. If
90   thou follow him, thou must needs wear my coxcomb. [*To*
LEAR] How now, nuncle?° Would I had two coxcombs and two   *(mine) uncle*
daughters.
LEAR   Why, my boy?
FOOL   If I gave them my living° I'd keep my coxcombs myself.[1]   *goods*
95   There's mine; beg another off thy daughters.
LEAR   Take heed, sirrah — the whip.

5. *jealous curiosity*: paranoid concern with niceties.
6. Football was a rough street game played by the poor.
7. If you will be stretched out by me again. *lubber*:
clumsy oaf.
8. *an . . . shortly*: if you can't keep in with those in power,

you will soon find yourself left out in the cold.
9. By abdicating, Lear has in effect prevented his daughters from any longer being his subjects, just as if he had
"banished" them.
1. I'd be twice as much a fool.

LEAR   Thou but rememberest° me of mine own conception.° I   *remind / perception*
have perceived a most faint neglect of late, which I have rather
blamed as mine own jealous curiosity[6] than as a very pretence°   *a true intention*
60   and purpose of unkindness. I will look further into't. But
where's my fool? I have not seen him these two days.

KNIGHT   Since my young lady's going into France, sir, the fool
hath much pined away.

LEAR   No more of that, I have noted it well. Go you and tell my
65   daughter I would speak with her.   [*Exit one*]
Go you, call hither my fool.   [*Exit one*]
        Enter Steward [OSWALD *crossing the stage*]
O you, sir, you, come you hither, sir, who am I, sir?

OSWALD   My lady's father.

LEAR   My lady's father? My lord's knave, you whoreson dog, you
70   slave, you cur!

OSWALD   I am none of these, my lord, I beseech your pardon.

LEAR   Do you bandy looks with me, you rascal?
        [LEAR *strikes him*]

OSWALD   I'll not be strucken, my lord.

KENT [*tripping him*]   Nor tripped neither, you base football
75   player.[7]

LEAR [*to* KENT]   I thank thee, fellow. Thou serv'st me, and I'll
love thee.

KENT [*to* OSWALD]   Come, sir, arise, away. I'll teach you differences.° Away, away. If you will measure your lubber's length   *(of rank)*
80   again,[8] tarry; but away, go to. Have you wisdom? So.
                                            [*Exit* OSWALD]

LEAR   Now, my friendly knave, I thank thee.
        Enter [*Lear's*] FOOL
There's earnest of° thy service.   *downpayment for*
        [*He gives* KENT *money*]

FOOL   Let me hire him, too. [*To* KENT] Here's my coxcomb.°   *fool's cap*

LEAR   How now, my pretty knave, how dost thou?

85   FOOL [*to* KENT]   Sirrah, you were best take my coxcomb.

LEAR   Why, my boy?

FOOL   Why? For taking one's part that's out of favour. [*To* KENT]
Nay, an thou canst not smile as the wind sits, thou'lt catch cold
shortly.[9] There, take my coxcomb. Why, this fellow has
90   banished two on's daughters[1] and did the third a blessing
against his will. If thou follow him, thou must needs wear my
coxcomb. [*To* LEAR] How now, nuncle?° Would I had two cox-   *(mine) uncle*
combs and two daughters.

LEAR   Why, my boy?

95   FOOL   If I gave them all my living° I'd keep my coxcombs   *goods*
myself.[2] There's mine; beg another off thy daughters.

LEAR   Take heed, sirrah—the whip.

---

6. *jealous curiosity:* paranoid concern with niceties.
7. Football was a rough street game played by the poor.
8. If you will be stretched out by me again. *lubber:* clumsy oaf.
9. *an . . . shortly:* if you can't keep in with those in power,
you will soon find yourself left out in the cold.
1. By abdicating, Lear has in effect prevented his daughters from any longer being his subjects, just as if he had "banished" them.
2. I'd be twice as much a fool.

FOOL   Truth is a dog that must to° kennel. He must be whipped   *go to*
out when Lady the brach² may stand by the fire and stink.

LEAR   A pestilent gall° to me!   *annoyance; bitterness*

100 FOOL [*to* KENT]   Sirrah, I'll teach thee a speech.

LEAR   Do.

FOOL   Mark it, uncle.

    Have more than thou showest,
    Speak less than thou knowest,

105   Lend less than thou owest,°   *own*
    Ride more than thou goest,°   *walk*
    Learn° more than thou trowest,°   *Hear / believe*
    Set less than thou throwest,³
    Leave thy drink and thy whore,

110   And keep in-a-door,
    And thou shalt have more
    Than two tens to a score.⁴

LEAR   This is nothing, fool.

FOOL   Then, like the breath° of an unfee'd° lawyer, you gave me   *speech / unpaid*

115 nothing for't. Can you make no use of nothing, uncle?

LEAR   Why no, boy. Nothing can be made out of nothing.

FOOL [*to* KENT]   Prithee, tell him so much the rent of his land
comes to.⁵ He will not believe a fool.

LEAR   A bitter fool.

120 FOOL   Dost know the difference, my boy, between a bitter fool
and a sweet fool?

LEAR   No, lad. Teach me.

FOOL [*sings*]   That lord that counselled thee
    To give away thy land,

125   Come, place him here by me;
    Do thou for him stand.°   *represent him*
    The sweet and bitter fool
    Will presently appear,
    The one in motley⁶ here,

130   The other found out there.

LEAR   Dost thou call me fool, boy?

FOOL   All thy other titles thou hast given away. That thou wast
born with.

KENT [*to* LEAR]   This is not altogether fool,° my lord.   *foolish, folly*

135 FOOL   No, faith; lords and great men will not let me. If I had a
monopoly out, they would have part on't, and ladies too, they
will not let me have all the fool to myself—they'll be snatching.
Give me an egg, nuncle, and I'll give thee two crowns.

LEAR   What two crowns shall they be?

140 FOOL   Why, after I have cut the egg in the middle and eat up
the meat,° the two crowns of the egg. When thou clovest° thy   *edible part / cleaved*
crown i'th' middle and gavest away both parts, thou borest° thy   *you carried*
ass o'th'° back o'er the dirt. Thou hadst little wit° in thy bald   *on your / sense*
crown when thou gavest thy golden one away. If I speak like

145 myself° in this, let him be whipped that first finds it so.⁷   *(like a fool)*

---

2. *Lady the bitch.* Pet dogs were often called "Lady" such-and-such. The allusion is to Regan and Gonoril, who are now being preferred to truthful Cordelia.
3. Don't gamble everything on a single cast of the dice.
4. *And thou . . . score:* And there will be more than two tens in your twenty; that is, you will become richer.

5. Remind him that no land means no rent; with a pun on "rent" meaning "torn, divided."
6. Multicolored dress of a court jester.
7. *that . . . so:* who first discovers for himself that this is true; colloquially, who deserves to be whipped as a fool.

FOOL   Truth's a dog must to° kennel. He must be whipped out   *go to*
    when the Lady Brach³ may stand by th' fire and stink.
100 LEAR   A pestilent gall° to me!   *annoyance; bitterness*
FOOL *[to* KENT*]*   Sirrah, I'll teach thee a speech.
LEAR   Do.
FOOL   Mark it, nuncle:
            Have more than thou showest,
105   Speak less than thou knowest,
            Lend less than thou owest,°   *own*
            Ride more than thou goest,°   *walk*
            Learn° more than thou trowest,°   *Hear / believe*
            Set less than thou throwest,⁴
110   Leave thy drink and thy whore,
            And keep in-a-door,
            And thou shalt have more
            Than two tens to a score.⁵
KENT   This is nothing, fool.
115 FOOL   Then 'tis like the breath° of an unfee'd° lawyer: you gave   *speech / unpaid*
    me nothing for't. *[To* LEAR*]* Can you make no use of nothing,
    nuncle?
LEAR   Why no, boy. Nothing can be made out of nothing.
FOOL *[to* KENT*]*   Prithee, tell him so much the rent of his land
120   comes to.⁶ He will not believe a fool.
LEAR   A bitter fool.
FOOL   Dost know the difference, my boy, between a bitter fool
    and a sweet one?
LEAR   No, lad. Teach me.

125 FOOL   Nuncle, give me an egg, and I'll give thee two crowns.
LEAR   What two crowns shall they be?
FOOL   Why, after I have cut the egg i'th' middle and eat up the
    meat,° the two crowns of the egg. When thou clovest° thy   *edible part / cleaved*
    crown i'th' middle and gavest away both parts, thou borest°   *you carried*
130   thine ass o'th'° back o'er the dirt. Thou hadst little wit° in thy   *on your / sense*
    bald crown when thou gavest thy golden one away. If I speak
    like myself° in this, let him be whipped that first finds it so.⁷   *(like a fool)*

---

3. Lady Bitch. Pet dogs were often called "Lady" such-and-such. The allusion is to Regan and Goneril, who are now being preferred to truthful Cordelia.
4. Don't gamble everything on a single cast of the dice.
5. *And thou . . . score:* And there will be more than two

tens in your twenty; that is, you will become richer.
6. Remind him that no land means no rent; with a pun on "rent" meaning "torn, divided."
7. *that . . . so:* who first discovers for himself that this is true; colloquially, who deserves to be whipped as a fool.

[*Sings*]   Fools had ne'er less wit in a year,
      For wise men are grown foppish.[8]
      They know not how their wits do wear,
      Their manners are so apish.°   *stupid; imitative*

150   LEAR   When were you wont° to be so full of songs, sirrah?   *accustomed*
    FOOL   I have used° it, nuncle, ever since thou madest thy daugh-   *practiced*
    ters thy mother; for when thou gavest them the rod and puttest
    down thine own breeches,
    [*Sings*]   Then they for sudden joy did weep,
155   And I for sorrow sung,
              That such a king should play bo-peep°   *a child's game*
              And go the fools among.
    Prithee, nuncle, keep a schoolmaster that can teach thy fool to
    lie. I would fain learn to lie.
160   LEAR   An° you lie, we'll have you whipped.   .   *If*
    FOOL   I marvel what kin° thou and thy daughters are. They'll   *how alike*
    have me whipped for speaking true, thou wilt have me whipped
    for lying, and sometime I am whipped for holding my peace. I
    had rather be any kind of thing than a fool; and yet I would not
165   be thee, nuncle. Thou hast pared thy wit o' both sides and left
    nothing in the middle.
             Enter GONORIL
    Here comes one of the parings.
    LEAR   How now, daughter, what makes that frontlet[9] on?
    Methinks you are too much o' late i'th' frown.
170   FOOL   Thou wast a pretty fellow when thou hadst no need to
    care for her frown. Now thou art an O without a figure.[1] I am
    better than thou art, now. I am a fool; thou art nothing. [*To*
    GONORIL] Yes, forsooth, I will hold my tongue; so your face
    bids me, though you say nothing.
175   [*Sings*]   Mum, mum.
            He that keeps neither crust nor crumb,
              Weary of all, shall want° some.   *lack, be in need of*
    That's a shelled peascod.°   *empty pea pod; nothing*
    GONORIL [*to* LEAR]   Not only, sir, this your all-licensed° fool,   *unrestrained*
180   But other of your insolent retinue
    Do hourly carp and quarrel, breaking forth
    In rank° and not-to-be-endurèd riots.   *foul; spreading*
    Sir, I had thought by making this well known unto you
    To have found a safe° redress, but now grow fearful,   *sure*
185   By what yourself too late° have spoke and done,   *recently*
    That you protect this course, and put it on°   *encourage it*
    By your allowance; which if you should, the fault
    Would not scape censure, nor the redress sleep
    Which in the tender of a wholesome weal
190   Might in their working do you that offence,
    That else were shame, that then necessity
    Must call discreet proceedings.[2]

---

8. *Fools . . . foppish*: Professional fools have gone out of favor ("grace") since wise men have lately outdone them in idiocy.
9. Band worn on the forehead; here, a metaphor for "frown."
1. A zero without a preceding digit; nothing.
2. *which if you . . . proceedings*: if you do approve (of your

attendants' behavior), you will not escape criticism, nor will it be without retribution, which for the common good will cause you pain. While this would otherwise be improper, it will be seen as a prudent ("discreet") action under the circumstances. *tender of*: concern for. *weal*: state, commonwealth. *then necessity*: the demands of the time.

[*Sings*] Fools had ne'er less grace in a year,		
For wise men are grown foppish,[8]		
135	And know not how their wits to wear,	
Their manners are so apish.°	*stupid; imitative*

LEAR   When were you wont° to be so full of songs, sirrah?   *accustomed*

FOOL   I have used° it, nuncle, e'er since thou madest thy daugh-   *practiced*
ters thy mothers; for when thou gavest them the rod and puttest
140   down thine own breeches,

[*Sings*]   Then they for sudden joy did weep,
And I for sorrow sung,
That such a king should play bo-peep°   *a child's game*
And go the fools among.

145   Prithee, nuncle, keep a schoolmaster that can teach thy fool to
lie. I would fain learn to lie.

LEAR   An° you lie, sirrah, we'll have you whipped.   *If*

FOOL   I marvel what kin° thou and thy daughters are. They'll   *how alike*
have me whipped for speaking true, thou'lt have me whipped
150   for lying, and sometimes I am whipped for holding my peace.
I had rather be any kind o' thing than a fool; and yet I would
not be thee, nuncle. Thou hast pared thy wit o' both sides and
left nothing i'th' middle.

Enter GONERIL

Here comes one o' the parings.

155   LEAR   How now, daughter? What makes that frontlet[9] on?
You are too much of late i'th' frown.

FOOL   Thou wast a pretty fellow when thou hadst no need to
care for her frowning. Now thou art an O without a figure.[1] I
am better than thou art, now. I am a fool; thou art nothing. [*To*
160   GONERIL] Yes, forsooth, I will hold my tongue; so your face bids
me, though you say nothing.

[*Sings*]   Mum, mum.
He that keeps nor crust nor crumb,
Weary of all, shall want° some.   *lack, be in need of*

165   That's a shelled peascod.°   *empty pea pod; nothing*

GONERIL [*to* LEAR]   Not only, sir, this your all-licensed° fool,   *unrestrained*
But other of your insolent retinue
Do hourly carp and quarrel, breaking forth
In rank° and not-to-be-endurèd riots. Sir,   *foul; spreading*
170   I had thought by making this well known unto you
To have found a safe° redress, but now grow fearful,   *sure*
By what yourself too late° have spoke and done,   *recently*
That you protect this course, and put it on°   *encourage it*
By your allowance; which if you should, the fault
175   Would not scape censure, nor the redresses sleep
Which in the tender of a wholesome weal
Might in their working do you that offence,
Which else were shame, that then necessity
Will call discreet proceeding.[2]

---

8. *Fools . . . foppish:* Professional fools have gone out of
favor ("grace") since wise men have lately outdone them
in idiocy.
9. Band worn on the forehead; here, a metaphor for
"frown."
1. A zero without a preceding digit; nothing.
2. *which if you . . . proceeding:* if you do approve (of your

attendants' behavior), you will not escape criticism, nor
will it be without retribution, which for the common
good will cause you pain. While this would otherwise be
improper, it will be seen as a prudent ("discreet") action
under the circumstances. *tender of:* concern for. *weal:*
state, commonwealth. *then necessity:* the demands of the
time.

FOOL [*to* LEAR]   For, you trow, nuncle,
   [*Sings*] The hedge-sparrow fed the cuckoo³ so long
195   That it had it° head bit off by it young;°   *its / (the young cuckoo)*
   so out went the candle, and we were left darkling.°   *in the dark*
LEAR [*to* GONORIL]   Are you our daughter?
GONORIL   Come, sir, I would you would make use of that good wisdom
   Whereof I know you are fraught,° and put away   *full*
200   These dispositions° that of late transform you   *moods, attitudes*
   From what you rightly are.
FOOL   May not an ass know when the cart draws the horse?
   [*Sings*] 'Whoop, jug,⁴ I love thee!'
LEAR   Doth any here know me? Why, this is not Lear.
205   Doth Lear walk thus, speak thus? Where are his eyes?
   Either his notion° weakens, or his discernings   *intellect*
   Are lethargied. Sleeping or waking, ha?
   Sure, 'tis not so.
   Who is it that can tell me who I am?
210   Lear's shadow? I would° learn that, for by the marks°   *wish to / evidence*
   Of sovereignty, knowledge, and reason
   I should be false persuaded I had daughters.
FOOL   Which° they will make an obedient father.   *Whom*
LEAR [*to* GONORIL]   Your name, fair gentlewoman?
GONORIL   Come, sir,
215   This admiration° is much of the savour   *excessive amazement*
   Of other your new pranks. I do beseech you
   Understand my purposes aright,
   As you are old and reverend, should° be wise.   *you should*
   Here do you keep a hundred knights and squires,
220   Men so disordered,° so debauched and bold   *disorderly*
   That this our court, infected with their manners,
   Shows° like a riotous inn, epicurism°   *Appears / gluttony*
   And lust make more like to a tavern, or brothel,
   Than a great palace. The shame itself doth speak
225   For instant remedy. Be thou desired,
   By her that else will take the thing she begs,
   A little to disquantity your train,°   *to reduce your retinue*
   And the remainder that shall still depend°   *be retained*
   To be such men as may besort° your age,   *befit*
   That know themselves° and you.   *Who know their place*
230 LEAR   Darkness and devils!
   Saddle my horses, call my train together!— [*Exit one or more*]
   Degenerate bastard, I'll not trouble thee.
   Yet° have I left a daughter.   *Still*
GONORIL   You strike my people, and your disordered rabble
235   Make servants of their betters.
      Enter Duke [*of* ALBANY]

---

3. The cuckoo lays its eggs in other birds' nests.   4. Nickname for "Joan"; sobriquet for a whore.

180 FOOL [*to* LEAR]   For, you know, nuncle,
    [*Sings*] The hedge-sparrow fed the cuckoo³ so long
        That it's had° head bit off by it young;°   *its / (the young cuckoo)*
    so out went the candle, and we were left darkling.°   *in the dark*
    LEAR [*to* GONERIL]   Are you our daughter?
185 GONERIL   I would you would make use of your good wisdom,
      Whereof I know you are fraught,° and put away   *full*
      These dispositions° which of late transport you   *moods, attitudes*
      From what you rightly are.
    FOOL   May not an ass know when the cart draws the horse?
190   [*Sings*] 'Whoop, jug,⁴ I love thee!'
    LEAR   Does any here know me? This is not Lear.
    Does Lear walk thus, speak thus? Where are his eyes?
    Either his notion° weakens, his discernings   *intellect*
    Are lethargied—ha, waking?° 'Tis not so.   *am I awake*
195 Who is it that can tell me who I am?
    FOOL   Lear's shadow.

    LEAR [*to* GONERIL]   Your name, fair gentlewoman?
    GONERIL   This admiration,° sir, is much o'th' savour   *excessive amazement*
      Of other your new pranks. I do beseech you
200   To understand my purposes aright,
      As you are old and reverend, should° be wise.   *you should*
      Here do you keep a hundred knights and squires,
      Men so disordered,° so debauched and bold   *disorderly*
      That this our court, infected with their manners,
205   Shows° like a riotous inn. Epicurism° and lust   *Appears / Gluttony*
      Makes it more like a tavern or a brothel
      Than a graced° palace. The shame itself doth speak   *an honored*
      For instant remedy. Be then desired,
      By her that else will take the thing she begs,
210   A little to disquantity your train,°   *to reduce your retinue*
      And the remainders that shall still depend°   *be retained*
      To be such men as may besort° your age,   *befit*
      Which know themselves° and you.   *Who know their place*
    LEAR   Darkness and devils!
    Saddle my horses, call my train together!— [*Exit one or more*]
215 Degenerate bastard, I'll not trouble thee.
    Yet° have I left a daughter.   *Still*
    GONERIL   You strike my people, and your disordered rabble
      Make servants of their betters.
      Enter ALBANY

---

3. The cuckoo lays its eggs in other birds' nests.   4. Nickname for "Joan"; sobriquet for a whore.

LEAR We that too late repent's—O sir, are you come?
    Is it your will that we—prepare my horses. [*Exit one or more*]
    Ingratitude, thou marble-hearted fiend,
    More hideous when thou show'st thee in a child
240   Than the sea-monster—[*to* GONORIL] detested kite,° thou liest.   carrion-eating hawk
    My train are men of choice and rarest parts,°   qualities
    That all particulars of duty know,
    And in the most exact regard support
    The worships of° their name. O most small fault,   honor accorded
245   How ugly didst thou in Cordelia show,
    That, like an engine, wrenched my frame of nature
    From the fixed place,⁵ drew from my heart all love,
    And added to the gall! O Lear, Lear!
    Beat at this gate° that let thy folly in   (his head)
250   And thy dear° judgement out.—Go, go, my people!   precious
ALBANY My lord, I am guiltless as I am ignorant.
LEAR It may be so, my lord. Hark, nature, hear:
    Dear goddess, suspend thy purpose if
    Thou didst intend to make this creature fruitful.
255   Into her womb convey sterility.
    Dry up in her the organs of increase,
    And from her derogate° body never spring   debased
    A babe to honour her. If she must teem,°   breed
    Create her child of spleen,° that it may live   malice
260   And be a thwart disnatured° torment to her.   a perverse unnatural
    Let it stamp wrinkles in her brow of youth,
    With cadent° tears fret° channels in her cheeks,   flowing / carve
    Turn all her mother's pains and benefits°   cares and kind actions
    To laughter and contempt, that she may feel—
265   That she may feel
    How sharper than a serpent's tooth it is
    To have a thankless child.—Go, go, my people!
        [*Exeunt* LEAR, KENT, FOOL, *and servants*]
ALBANY Now, gods that we adore, whereof comes this?
GONORIL Never afflict yourself to know the cause,
270   But let his disposition have that scope
    That dotage gives it.
        [*Enter* LEAR *and* FOOL]
LEAR What, fifty of my followers at a clap?
    Within a fortnight?
ALBANY   What is the matter, sir?
LEAR I'll tell thee. [*To* GONORIL] Life and death! I am ashamed
275   That thou hast power to shake my manhood thus,
    That these hot tears, that break from me perforce°   against my will
    And should make thee—worst blasts and fogs upon thee!
    Untented woundings° of a father's curse   Undressed wounds
    Pierce every sense about thee! Old fond° eyes,   foolish

---

5. *like . . . place*: as a machine (or lever) dislocated my natural affections from their proper foundations.

LEAR   Woe that° too late repents!   *Woe to him who*
  Is it your will? Speak, sir.—Prepare my horses.
                                    [*Exit one or more*]
220   Ingratitude, thou marble-hearted fiend,
      More hideous when thou show'st thee in a child
      Than the sea-monster—
ALBANY   Pray sir, be patient.
LEAR [*to* GONERIL]   Detested kite,° thou liest.   *carrion-eating hawk*
225   My train are men of choice and rarest parts,°   *qualities*
      That all particulars of duty know,
      And in the most exact regard support
      The worships of° their name. O most small fault,   *honors accorded*
      How ugly didst thou in Cordelia show,
230   Which, like an engine, wrenched my frame of nature
      From the fixed place,⁵ drew from my heart all love,
      And added to the gall! O Lear, Lear, Lear!
      Beat at this gate° that let thy folly in   *(his head)*
      And thy dear° judgement out.—Go, go, my people!   *precious*
235 ALBANY   My lord, I am guiltless, as I am ignorant
      Of what hath moved you.
LEAR   It may be so, my lord.
      Hear, nature; hear, dear goddess, hear:
      Suspend thy purpose if thou didst intend
      To make this creature fruitful.
240   Into her womb convey sterility.
      Dry up in her the organs of increase,
      And from her derogate° body never spring   *debased*
      A babe to honour her. If she must teem,°   *breed*
      Create her child of spleen,° that it may live   *malice*
245   And be a thwart disnatured° torment to her.   *a perverse unnatural*
      Let it stamp wrinkles in her brow of youth,
      With cadent° tears fret° channels in her cheeks,   *flowing / carve*
      Turn all her mother's pains and benefits°   *cares and kind actions*
      To laughter and contempt, that she may feel—
250   That she may feel
      How sharper than a serpent's tooth it is
      To have a thankless child. Away, away!
                          Exeunt [LEAR, KENT, *and attendants*]
ALBANY   Now, gods that we adore, whereof comes this?
GONERIL   Never afflict yourself to know more of it,
255   But let his disposition have that scope
      As° dotage gives it.   *Which*
            Enter LEAR
LEAR   What, fifty of my followers at a clap?
      Within a fortnight?
ALBANY   What's the matter, sir?
LEAR   I'll tell thee. [*To* GONERIL] Life and death! I am ashamed
260   That thou hast power to shake my manhood thus,
      That these hot tears, which break from me perforce,°   *against my will*
      Should make thee worth them. Blasts and fogs upon thee!
      Th'untented woundings° of a father's curse   *The undressed wounds*
      Pierce every sense about thee! Old fond° eyes,   *foolish*

5. *like . . . place*: as a machine (or lever) dislocated my natural affections from their proper foundations.

280 Beweep° this cause again I'll pluck you out   *If you weep over*
And cast you, with the waters that you make,
To temper° clay. Yea,   *soften*
Is't come to this? Yet have I left a daughter
Whom, I am sure, is kind and comfortable.°   *comforting*
285 When she shall hear this of thee, with her nails
She'll flay thy wolvish visage. Thou shalt find
That I'll resume the shape which thou dost think
I have cast off for ever; thou shalt, I warrant thee.   *[Exit]*
GONORIL   Do you mark that, my lord?
290 ALBANY   I cannot be so partial,° Gonoril,   *biased*
    To° the great love I bear you—   *Because of*
GONORIL   Come, sir, no more.—
    You, more knave than fool, after your master!
FOOL   Nuncle Lear, nuncle Lear, tarry, and take the fool with
    thee.
295   A fox when one has caught her,
               And such a daughter,
               Should sure° to the slaughter,   *surely be sent*
               If my cap would buy a halter.°   *collar; noose*
               So, the fool follows after.   *[Exit]*

300 GONORIL   What, Oswald, ho!
             [Enter OSWALD*]*
OSWALD   Here, madam.
GONORIL   What, have you writ this letter to my sister?
OSWALD   Yes, madam.
GONORIL   Take you some company, and away to horse.
305 Inform her full of my particular fears,
And thereto add such reasons of your own
As may compact° it more. Get you gone,   *compound*
And after, your retinue.   *[Exit* OSWALD*]*
               Now, my lord,
This milky gentleness and course of yours,
310 Though I dislike not, yet under pardon°   *begging your pardon*
You're much more ataxed° for want of wisdom   *taken to task; censured*
Than praised for harmful mildness.
ALBANY   How far your eyes may pierce° I cannot tell.   *foresee*
    Striving to better aught,° we mar what's well.   *anything*
315 GONORIL   Nay, then—
ALBANY   Well, well, the event.°   *Exeunt*   *time will tell*

265	Beweep° this cause again I'll pluck ye out	*If you weep over*
	And cast you, with the waters that you loose,°	*let loose*
	To temper° clay. Ha! Let it be so.	*soften*
	I have another daughter	
	Who, I am sure, is kind and comfortable.°	*comforting*
270	When she shall hear this of thee, with her nails	
	She'll flay thy wolvish visage. Thou shalt find	
	That I'll resume the shape which thou dost think	
	I have cast off for ever.	*Exit*

GONERIL   Do you mark that?

ALBANY   I cannot be so partial,° Goneril,   *biased*

275   To° the great love I bear you—   *Because of*

GONERIL   Pray you, content.° What, Oswald, ho!—   *be quiet*
        You, sir, more knave than fool, after your master.

FOOL   Nuncle Lear, nuncle Lear,
            Tarry, take the fool with thee.

280   A fox when one has caught her,
            And such a daughter,
            Should sure° to the slaughter,   *surely be sent*
            If my cap would buy a halter.°   *collar; noose*
            So, the fool follows after.   *Exit*

285   GONERIL   This man hath had good counsel—a hundred knights?
        'Tis politic° and safe to let him keep   *prudent*
        At point° a hundred knights, yes, that on every dream,   *Armed*
        Each buzz,° each fancy, each complaint, dislike,   *rumor*
        He may enguard° his dotage with their powers   *protect*

290   And hold our lives in mercy.—Oswald, I say!

ALBANY   Well, you may fear too far.

GONERIL   Safer than trust too far.
        Let me still° take away the harms I fear,   *always*
        Not° fear still to be taken. I know his heart.   *Rather than*
        What he hath uttered I have writ my sister.

295   If she sustain him and his hundred knights
        When I have showed th'unfitness°—   *unwillingness*
                Enter Steward [OSWALD]
                                How now, Oswald?
        What, have you writ that letter to my sister?

OSWALD   Ay, madam.

GONERIL   Take you some company, and away to horse.

300   Inform her full of my particular fear,
        And thereto add such reasons of your own
        As may compact° it more. Get you gone,   *compound*
        And hasten your return.   [*Exit* OSWALD]
                No, no, my lord,
        This milky gentleness and course of yours,

305   Though I condemn not, yet under pardon°   *begging your pardon*
        You are much more attasked° for want of wisdom   *taken to task; censured*
        Than praised for harmful mildness.

ALBANY   How far your eyes may pierce° I cannot tell.   *foresee*
        Striving to better, oft we mar what's well.

310   GONERIL   Nay, then—

ALBANY   Well, well, th'event.°   *Exeunt*   *time will tell*

Scene 5

Enter LEAR, KENT [*disguised, and* FOOL]

LEAR [*to* KENT] Go you before° to Gloucester[1] with these letters.   *on ahead*
Acquaint my daughter no further with anything you know than
comes from her demand out of the letter.[2] If your diligence be
not speedy, I shall be there before you.

5 KENT I will not sleep, my lord, till I have delivered your letter.

                                           Exit

FOOL If a man's brains were in his heels, were't not in danger of
kibes?°   *chilblains*

LEAR Ay, boy.

FOOL Then, I prithee, be merry: thy wit shall ne'er go slipshod.[3]

10 LEAR Ha, ha, ha!

FOOL Shalt° see thy other daughter will use thee kindly, for   *Thou shalt*
though she's as like this as a crab° is like an apple, yet I   *crab apple, sour apple*
con° what I can tell.   *know*

LEAR Why, what canst thou tell, my boy?

15 FOOL She'll taste as like this as a crab doth to a crab. Thou canst
not tell why one's nose stands in the middle of his face?

LEAR No.

FOOL Why, to keep his eyes on either side 's nose, that what a
man cannot smell out, a° may spy into.   *he*

20 LEAR I did her° wrong.   *(Cordelia)*

FOOL Canst tell how an oyster makes his shell?

LEAR No.

FOOL Nor I neither; but I can tell why a snail has a house.

LEAR Why?

25 FOOL Why, to put his head in, not to give it away to his daughter
and leave his horns without a case.[4]

LEAR I will forget my nature.° So kind a father!   *lose my fatherly feelings*
Be my horses ready?

FOOL Thy asses° are gone about them. The reason why the   *(servants)*
30 seven stars° are no more than seven is a pretty reason.   *the Pleiades*

LEAR Because they are not eight.

FOOL Yes. Thou wouldst make a good fool.

LEAR To take't again perforce[5]—monster ingratitude!

FOOL If thou wert my fool, nuncle, I'd have thee beaten for
35 being old before thy time.

LEAR How's that?

FOOL Thou shouldst not have been old before thou hadst been
wise.

LEAR O, let me not be mad, sweet heaven!
40 I would not be mad.
Keep me in temper.° I would not be mad.   *sane*

Scene 5 Location: Before Albany's castle.
1. To the city of Gloucester.
2. *than . . . letter:* other than such questions as are
prompted by the letter.
3. Literally, your brains will not wear slippers (to warm
feet that are afflicted with chilblains); feet of any intelligence would not walk toward Regan.

4. Protective covering for his head, or concealment for
his horns (horns were the conventional sign of a cuckold).
The Fool reflects the cynical view, common in the
period, that all married men are inevitably cuckolded.
5. To take it back by force. Lear may refer to Gonoril's
treachery, or he may be contemplating resuming his
authority.

1.5

Enter LEAR, KENT [*disguised, the First*] GENTLEMAN, *and*
FOOL

LEAR [*to the* GENTLEMAN,[1] *giving him a letter*]   Go you before° to   *on ahead*
Gloucester[2] with these letters.   [*Exit* GENTLEMAN]
[*To* KENT, *giving him a letter*] Acquaint my daughter no further
with anything you know than comes from her demand out
5   of the letter.[3] If your diligence be not speedy, I shall be there
afore you.

KENT   I will not sleep, my lord, till I have delivered your letter.
                                                      Exit

FOOL   If a man's brains were in's heels, were't not in danger of
kibes?°   *chilblains*

10   LEAR   Ay, boy.

FOOL   Then, I prithee, be merry: thy wit shall not go slipshod.[4]

LEAR   Ha, ha, ha!

FOOL   Shalt° see thy other daughter will use thee kindly, for   *Thou shalt*
though she's as like this as a crab's° like an apple, yet I can tell   *crab apple, sour apple*
15   what I can tell.

LEAR   What canst tell, boy?

FOOL   She will taste as like this as a crab does to a crab. Thou
canst tell why one's nose stands i'th' middle on 's° face?   *of one's*

LEAR   No.

20   FOOL   Why, to keep one's eyes of either side 's nose, that what a
man cannot smell out, a° may spy into.   *he*

LEAR   I did her° wrong.   *(Cordelia)*

FOOL   Canst tell how an oyster makes his shell?

LEAR   No.

25   FOOL   Nor I neither; but I can tell why a snail has a house.

LEAR   Why?

FOOL   Why, to put 's head in, not to give it away to his daughters
and leave his horns without a case.[5]

LEAR   I will forget my nature.° So kind a father!   *lose my fatherly feelings*

30   Be my horses ready?

FOOL   Thy asses° are gone about 'em. The reason why the seven   *(servants)*
stars° are no more than seven is a pretty reason.   *the Pleiades*

LEAR   Because they are not eight.

FOOL   Yes, indeed, thou wouldst make a good fool.

35   LEAR   To take't again perforce[6]—monster ingratitude!

FOOL   If thou wert my fool, nuncle, I'd have thee beaten for
being old before thy time.

LEAR   How's that?

FOOL   Thou shouldst not have been old till thou hadst been
40   wise.

LEAR   O, let me not be mad, not mad, sweet heaven!
Keep me in temper.° I would not be mad.   *sane*

1.5 Location: Before Albany's castle.
1. Most editors address this entire speech to Kent, since
in Q the first gentleman does not appear here.
2. To the city of Gloucester.
3. *than . . . letter:* other than such questions as are
prompted by the letter.
4. Literally, your brains will not wear slippers (to warm
feet that are afflicted with chilblains); feet of any intelli-

gence would not walk toward Regan.
5. Protective covering for his head, or concealment for
his horns (horns were the conventional sign of a cuckold).
The Fool reflects the cynical view, common in the
period, that all married men are inevitably cuckolded.
6. To take it back by force. Lear may refer to Goneril's
treachery, or he may be contemplating resuming his
authority.

[*Enter a* SERVANT]
Are the horses ready?
SERVANT   Ready, my lord.
LEAR [*to* FOOL]   Come, boy.   *Exeunt* [LEAR *and* SERVANT]
FOOL   She that is maid now, and laughs at my departure,
45   Shall not be a maid long, except things be cut shorter.⁶   *Exit*

Scene 6

Enter Bastard [EDMUND] *and* CURAN, *meeting*
EDMUND   Save° thee, Curan.   *God save*
CURAN   And you, sir. I have been with your father, and given
    him notice that the Duke of Cornwall and his duchess will be
    here with him tonight.
5   EDMUND   How comes that?
CURAN   Nay, I know not. You have heard of the news abroad?—
    I mean the whispered ones, for there are yet but ear-bussing
    arguments.¹
EDMUND   Not. I pray you, what are they?
10   CURAN   Have you heard of no likely wars towards° twixt the two   *impending*
    Dukes of Cornwall and Albany?
EDMUND   Not a word.
CURAN   You may then in time. Fare you well, sir.   [*Exit*]
EDMUND   The Duke be here tonight! The better, best.
15   This weaves itself perforce into my business.
        Enter EDGAR [*at a window above*]
    My father hath set guard to take my brother,
    And I have one thing of a queasy question²
    Which must ask briefness. Wit and fortune help!—
    Brother, a word. Descend, brother, I say.
        [EDGAR *climbs down*]
20   My father watches. O, fly this place.
    Intelligence is given where you are hid.
    You have now the good advantage of the night.
    Have you not spoken 'gainst the Duke of Cornwall aught?°   *anything*
    He's coming hither now, in the night, i'th' haste,
25   And Regan with him. Have you nothing said
    Upon his party° against the Duke of Albany?   *On his (Cornwall's) side*
    Advise you°—   *Consider carefully*
EDGAR   I am sure on't,° not a word.   *of it*
EDMUND   I hear my father coming. Pardon me.
    In cunning I must draw my sword upon you.
30   Seem to defend yourself. Now, quit you° well.   *acquit yourself*
    [*Calling*] Yield, come before my father. Light here, here!
    [*To* EDGAR] Fly, brother, fly! [*Calling*] Torches, torches! [*To*
      EDGAR] So, farewell.   [*Exit* EDGAR]
    Some blood drawn on me would beget opinion°   *produce the impression*
    Of my more fierce endeavour.
        He wounds his arm

---

6. *She . . . shorter*: A girl who would laugh at my leaving would be so foolish that she could not remain a virgin for long; "things" refers both to the unfolding event and to penises.

Scene 6 Location: Gloucester's castle.
1. Barely whispered affairs. *bussing*: buzzing.
2. And I have a hazardous and delicate problem.

[*Enter the* FIRST GENTLEMAN]

How now, are the horses ready?

FIRST GENTLEMAN   Ready, my lord.

LEAR [*to* FOOL]   Come, boy.

45 FOOL   She that's a maid now, and laughs at my departure,
Shall not be a maid long, unless things be cut shorter.[7]

Exeunt

2.1

Enter Bastard [EDMOND] *and* CURAN, *severally*

EDMOND   Save° thee, Curan.   *God save*

CURAN   And you, sir. I have been with your father, and given
him notice that the Duke of Cornwall and Regan his duchess
will be here with him this night.

5 EDMOND   How comes that?

CURAN   Nay, I know not. You have heard of the news abroad? —
I mean the whispered ones, for they are yet but ear-kissing
arguments.[1]

EDMOND   Not I. Pray you, what are they?

10 CURAN   Have you heard of no likely wars toward° twixt the Dukes   *impending*
of Cornwall and Albany?

EDMOND   Not a word.

CURAN   You may do then in time. Fare you well, sir.   *Exit*

EDMOND   The Duke be here tonight! The better, best.

15 This weaves itself perforce into my business.

Enter EDGAR [*at a window above*]

My father hath set guard to take my brother,
And I have one thing of a queasy question[2]
Which I must act. Briefness and fortune work!° —   *be with me*
Brother, a word, descend. Brother, I say.

[EDGAR *climbs down*]

20 My father watches. O sir, fly this place.
Intelligence is given where you are hid.
You have now the good advantage of the night.
Have you not spoken 'gainst the Duke of Cornwall?
He's coming hither, now, i'th' night, i'th' haste,

25 And Regan with him. Have you nothing said
Upon his party° 'gainst the Duke of Albany?   *On his (Cornwall's) side*
Advise yourself.°   *Consider carefully*

EDGAR   I am sure on't,° not a word.   *of it*

EDMOND   I hear my father coming. Pardon me.
In cunning I must draw my sword upon you.

30 Draw. Seem to defend yourself. Now, quit you° well.   *acquit yourself*
[*Calling*] Yield, come before my father. Light ho, here!
[*To* EDGAR] Fly, brother! [*Calling*] Torches, torches!
[*To* EDGAR]   So, farewell.

Exit EDGAR

Some blood drawn on me would beget opinion°   *produce the impression*
Of my more fierce endeavour.

[*He wounds his arm*]

---

7. *She . . . shorter:* A girl who would laugh at my leaving
would be so foolish that she could not remain a virgin for
long; "things" refers both to the unfolding event and to
penises.

2.1 Location: Gloucester's castle.
1. Barely whispered affairs.
2. And I have a hazardous and delicate problem.

I have seen

35 Drunkards do more than this in sport. [*Calling*] Father, father!
Stop, stop! Ho, help!

Enter GLOUCESTER [*and others*]

GLOUCESTER   Now, Edmund, where is the villain?
EDMUND   Here stood he in the dark, his sharp sword out,
Warbling of wicked charms, conjuring the moon
To stand 's° auspicious mistress.   *To act as his*
GLOUCESTER   But where is he?
EDMUND   Look, sir, I bleed.
40 GLOUCESTER   Where is the villain, Edmund?
EDMUND   Fled this way, sir, when by no means he could—
GLOUCESTER   Pursue him, go after.   [*Exeunt others*]

By no means what?

EDMUND   Persuade me to the murder of your lordship,
But that° I told him the revengive gods   *In response to that*
45 'Gainst parricides did all their thunders bend,
Spoke with how manifold and strong a bond
The child was bound to the father. Sir, in fine,°   *finally*
Seeing how loathly opposite° I stood   *opposed*
To his unnatural purpose, with fell° motion,   *deadly*
50 With his preparèd sword he charges home°   *strikes to the heart of*
My unprovided° body, lanced° mine arm;   *unprotected / struck*
But when he saw my best alarumed spirits
Bold in the quarrel's rights,³ roused to the encounter,
Or° whether ghasted° by the noise I made   *Either / frightened*
55 Or [   ] I know not,⁴
But suddenly he fled.
GLOUCESTER   Let him fly far,
Not in this land shall he remain uncaught,
And found, dispatch.° The noble Duke my master,   *And once found, killed*
My worthy arch° and patron, comes tonight.   *lord*
60 By his authority I will proclaim it
That he which finds him shall deserve our thanks,
Bringing the murderous caitiff° to the stake;⁵   *wretch*
He that conceals him, death.
EDMUND   When I dissuaded him from his intent
65 And found him pitched° to do it, with curst° speech   *resolved / bitter*
I threatened to discover° him. He replied,   *expose*
'Thou unpossessing bastard, dost thou think
If I would stand against thee, could the reposure°   *placing*
Of any trust, virtue, or worth in thee
70 Make thy words faithed?° No, what I should deny—   *credible*
As this I would, ay, though thou didst produce
My very character⁶—I'd turn it all
To⁷ thy suggestion, plot, and damnèd pretence,°   *intent*
And thou must make a dullard of the world
75 If they not thought the profits of my death

---

3. *my best . . . rights:* that I was fully roused to action, made brave by righteousness.
4. From the jumbled syntax, it appears likely that Q has accidentally omitted a verse line that, in the Oxford editors' conjecture, would have begun with "Or" and ended with "I know not."

5. Treachery and rebellion were crimes for which one could be burned.
6. Handwriting; but also, a true summary of my character.
7. *I'd . . . / To:* I'd blame it all on.

                    I have seen drunkards
35 Do more than this in sport. [*Calling*] Father, father!
   Stop, stop! Ho, help!
              Enter GLOUCESTER, *and servants with torches*
   GLOUCESTER   Now, Edmond, where's the villain?
   EDMOND   Here stood he in the dark, his sharp sword out,
     Mumbling of wicked charms, conjuring the moon
     To stand 's° auspicious mistress.   *To act as his*
   GLOUCESTER   But where is he?
   EDMOND   Look, sir, I bleed.
40 GLOUCESTER   Where is the villain, Edmond?
   EDMOND   Fled this way, sir, when by no means he could—
   GLOUCESTER   Pursue him, ho! Go after.   [*Exeunt servants*]
                         By no means what?
   EDMOND   Persuade me to the murder of your lordship,
     But that° I told him the revenging gods   *In response to that*
45 'Gainst parricides did all the thunder bend,
     Spoke with how manifold and strong a bond
     The child was bound to th' father. Sir, in fine,°   *finally*
     Seeing how loathly opposite° I stood   *opposed*
     To his unnatural purpose, in fell° motion   *deadly*
50 With his preparèd sword he charges home°   *strikes to the heart of*
     My unprovided° body, latched° mine arm;   *unprotected / struck*
     And when he saw my best alarumed spirits
     Bold in the quarrel's right,[3] roused to th'encounter,
     Or whether ghasted° by the noise I made,   *frightened*
     Full suddenly he fled.
55 GLOUCESTER   Let him fly far,
     Not in this land shall he remain uncaught,
     And found, dispatch.° The noble Duke my master,   *And once found, killed*
     My worthy arch° and patron, comes tonight.   *lord*
     By his authority I will proclaim it
60 That he which finds him shall deserve our thanks,
     Bringing the murderous coward to the stake;[4]
     He that conceals him, death.
   EDMOND   When I dissuaded him from his intent
     And found him pitched° to do it, with curst° speech   *resolved / bitter*
65 I threatened to discover° him. He replied,   *expose*
     'Thou unpossessing bastard, dost thou think
     If I would stand against thee, would the reposal°   *placing*
     Of any trust, virtue, or worth in thee
     Make thy words faithed?° No, what I should deny—   *credible*
70 As this I would, ay, though thou didst produce
     My very character[5]—I'd turn it all
     To[6] thy suggestion, plot, and damnèd practice,°   *scheming*
     And thou must make a dullard of the world
     If they not thought the profits of my death

3. *my best . . . right*: that I was fully roused to action,   5. Handwriting; but also, a true summary of my char-
made brave by righteousness.   acter.
4. Treachery and rebellion were crimes for which one   6. *I'd . . . / To*: I'd blame it all on.
could be burned.

Were very pregnant and potential spurs
To make thee seek it.'[8]
GLOUCESTER   Strong° and fastened° villain!   *Flagrant / incorrigible*
Would he deny his letter? I never got° him.   *begot*
     [*Trumpets within*]
Hark, the Duke's trumpets. I know not why he comes.
80   All ports° I'll bar. The villain shall not scape.   *seaports; exits*
The Duke must grant me that; besides, his picture
I will send far and near, that all the kingdom
May have note of him[9]—and of my land,
Loyal and natural° boy, I'll work the means   *loving; illegitimate*
85   To make thee capable.°   *legally able to inherit*
     Enter the Duke of CORNWALL [*and* REGAN]
CORNWALL   How now, my noble friend? Since I came hither,
     Which I can call but now, I have heard strange news.
REGAN   If it be true, all vengeance comes too short
     Which can pursue the offender. How dost, my lord?
90   GLOUCESTER   Madam, my old heart is cracked, is cracked.
REGAN   What, did my father's godson seek your life?
     He whom my father named, your Edgar?
GLOUCESTER   Ay, lady, lady; shame would have it hid.
REGAN   Was he not companion with the riotous knights
95   That tend° upon my father?   *attend*
GLOUCESTER   I know not, madam. 'Tis too bad, too bad.
EDMUND   Yes, madam, he was.
REGAN   No marvel, then, though° he were ill affected.°   *that / ill disposed*
     'Tis they have put him on° the old man's death,   *have urged him to seek*
100 To have the spoil and waste of his revenues.
     I have this present evening from my sister
     Been well informed of them, and with such cautions
     That if they come to sojourn at my house
     I'll not be there.
CORNWALL   Nor I, assure thee, Regan.
105 Edmund, I heard that you have shown your father
     A childlike office.°   *filial service*
EDMUND   'Twas my duty, sir.
GLOUCESTER [*to* CORNWALL]   He did betray his practice,°   *uncover his (Edgar's) plot*
          and received
     This hurt you see striving to apprehend him.
CORNWALL   Is he pursued?
GLOUCESTER   Ay, my good lord.
110 CORNWALL   If he be taken, he shall never more
     Be feared of doing harm. Make your own purpose
     How in my strength you please.[1] For you, Edmund,
     Whose virtue and obedience doth this instant
     So much commend itself, you shall be ours.
115 Natures of such deep trust we shall much need.
     You we first seize on.
EDMUND   I shall serve you truly,
     However else.°   *If nothing else*
GLOUCESTER [*to* CORNWALL]   For him I thank your grace.

---

8. *And thou . . . it:* And do you think the world so stupid
that it could not see the benefit you would get from my
death (and thus a motive for plotting to kill me)? *pregnant:* full. *potential spurs:* powerful temptations.
9. Likenesses of outlaws were drawn up, printed, and
publicly displayed, sometimes with an offer of reward
in "Wanted" posters.
1. *Make . . . please:* Devise your plots making use of
forces and authority as you see fit.

75   Were very pregnant and potential spirits
       To make thee seek it.'[7]
       GLOUCESTER   O strange° and fastened° villain!   *unnatural / incorrigible*
       Would he deny his letter, said he?
                Tucket° within   *Flourish of trumpets*
       Hark, the Duke's trumpets. I know not why he comes.
       All ports° I'll bar. The villain shall not scape.   *seaports; exits*
80   The Duke must grant me that; besides, his picture
       I will send far and near, that all the kingdom
       May have due note of him[8]—and of my land,
       Loyal and natural° boy, I'll work the means   *loving; illegitimate*
       To make thee capable.°   *legally able to inherit*
                Enter CORNWALL, REGAN, *and attendants*
85   CORNWALL   How now, my noble friend? Since I came hither,
       Which I can call but now, I have heard strange news.
       REGAN   If it be true, all vengeance comes too short
       Which can pursue th'offender. How dost, my lord?
       GLOUCESTER   O madam, my old heart is cracked, it's cracked.
90   REGAN   What, did my father's godson seek your life?
       He whom my father named, your Edgar?
       GLOUCESTER   O lady, lady, shame would have it hid!
       REGAN   Was he not companion with the riotous knights
       That tend° upon my father?   *attend*
95   GLOUCESTER   I know not, madam. 'Tis too bad, too bad.
       EDMOND   Yes, madam, he was of that consort.°   *company*
       REGAN   No marvel, then, though° he were ill affected.°   *that / ill disposed*
       'Tis they have put him on° the old man's death,   *have urged him to seek*
       To have th'expense° and spoil of his revenues.   *use*
100   I have this present evening from my sister
       Been well informed of them, and with such cautions
       That if they come to sojourn at my house
       I'll not be there.
       CORNWALL   Nor I, assure thee, Regan.
       Edmond, I hear that you have shown your father
       A childlike office.°   *filial service*
105   EDMOND   It was my duty, sir.
       GLOUCESTER [*to* CORNWALL]   He did bewray his practice,°   *uncover his (Edgar's) plot*
            and received
       This hurt you see striving to apprehend him.
       CORNWALL   Is he pursued?
       GLOUCESTER   Ay, my good lord.
       CORNWALL   If he be taken, he shall never more
110   Be feared of doing harm. Make your own purpose
       How in my strength you please.[9] For you, Edmond,
       Whose virtue and obedience doth this instant
       So much commend itself, you shall be ours.
       Natures of such deep trust we shall much need.
       You we first seize on.
115   EDMOND   I shall serve you, sir,
       Truly, however else.°   *if nothing else*
       GLOUCESTER [*to* CORNWALL] For him I thank your grace.

---

7. *And thou . . . it:* And do you think the world so stupid
that it could not see the benefit you would get from my
death (and thus a motive for plotting to kill me)? *pregnant:* full. *potential spirits:* powerful temptations.
8. Likenesses of outlaws were drawn up, printed, and

publicly displayed, sometimes with an offer of reward as
in "Wanted" posters.
9. *Make . . . please:* Devise your plots making use of my
forces and authority as you see fit.

CORNWALL   You know not why we came to visit you—
REGAN   This out-of-season threat'ning dark-eyed night—
      Occasions, noble Gloucester, of some poise,°   *weight*
120   Wherein we must have use of your advice.
      Our father he hath writ, so hath our sister,
      Of differences° which I least thought it fit   *quarrels*
      To answer from our home. The several° messengers   *various*
      From hence attend° dispatch. Our good old friend,   *await*
125   Lay comforts to your bosom, and bestow
      Your needful° counsel to our business,   *badly needed*
      Which craves the instant use.[2]
GLOUCESTER   I serve you, madam.
      Your graces are right welcome.   *Exeunt*

Scene 7

Enter KENT, *[disguised, at one door,] and Steward*
*[*OSWALD *at another door]*

OSWALD   Good even° to thee, friend. Art° of the house?   *evening / Are you a servant*
KENT   Ay.
OSWALD   Where may we set our horses?
KENT   I'th' mire.
5 OSWALD   Prithee, if thou love me,° tell me.   *if you will be so kind*
KENT   I love thee not.
OSWALD   Why then, I care not for thee.
KENT   If I had thee in Lipsbury pinfold[1] I would make thee care
    for me.
10 OSWALD   Why dost thou use° me thus? I know thee not.   *treat*
KENT   Fellow, I know thee.
OSWALD   What dost thou know me for?
KENT   A knave, a rascal, an eater of broken meats,° a base, proud,   *scraps*
    shallow, beggarly, three-suited, hundred-pound, filthy worsted-
15   stocking knave;[2] a lily-livered, action-taking knave; a whoreson,
    glass-gazing, superfinical rogue; one-trunk-inheriting slave;[3]
    one that wouldst be a bawd in way of good service,[4] and art
    nothing but the composition° of a knave, beggar, coward, pan-   *combination*
    der, and the son and heir of a mongrel bitch, whom I will beat
20   into clamorous whining if thou deny the least syllable of the
    addition.[5]
OSWALD   What a monstrous fellow art thou, thus to rail on one
    that's neither known of° thee nor knows thee!   *by*
KENT   What a brazen-faced varlet° art thou, to deny thou   *rascal*
25   knowest me! Is it two days ago since I beat thee and tripped up
    thy heels before the King? Draw, you rogue; for though it be
    night, the moon shines.
          [He draws his sword]

---

2. Which requires immediate attention.
Scene 7 Location: Before Gloucester's house.
1. If I had you in the enclosure of my mouth (gripped in my teeth). Lipsbury is probably an invented place-name. *pinfold*: pen, animal enclosure.
2. *three-suited . . . knave*: Oswald is being called a poor imitation of a gentleman. Servants were permitted three suits a year; one hundred pounds was the minimum qualification for the purchase of one of King James's knighthoods; a gentleman would wear silk, not "worsted" (of

thick woolen material), stockings.
3. *lily-livered*: cowardly. *action-taking*: litigious, one who would rather use the law than his fists. *glass-gazing*: mirror-gazing. *superfinical*: overly finicky, fastidious. *one-trunk inheriting*: owning only what would fill one trunk.
4. *one that . . . service*: one who would even be a pimp if called upon.
5. Of the descriptions Kent has just applied to him. *addition*: title (used ironically).

CORNWALL   You know not why we came to visit you—
REGAN   Thus out of season, threading dark-eyed night—
120   Occasions, noble Gloucester, of some poise,°   *weight*
Wherein we must have use of your advice.
Our father he hath writ, so hath our sister,
Of differences° which I least thought it fit   *quarrels*
To answer from our home. The several° messengers   *various*
125   From hence attend° dispatch. Our good old friend,   *await*
Lay comforts to your bosom, and bestow
Your needful° counsel to our businesses,   *badly needed*
Which craves the instant use.¹
GLOUCESTER   I serve you, madam.
130   Your graces are right welcome.   *Flourish. Exeunt*

2.2

Enter KENT, [*disguised,*] *and steward* [OSWALD], *severally*
OSWALD   Good dawning to thee, friend. Art° of this house?   *Are you a servant*
KENT   Ay.
OSWALD   Where may we set our horses?
KENT   I'th' mire.
5   OSWALD   Prithee, if thou lov'st me,° tell me.   *if you will be so kind*
KENT   I love thee not.
OSWALD   Why then, I care not for thee.
KENT   If I had thee in Lipsbury pinfold¹ I would make thee care
for me.
10   OSWALD   Why dost thou use° me thus? I know thee not.   *treat*
KENT   Fellow, I know thee.
OSWALD   What dost thou know me for?
KENT   A knave, a rascal, an eater of broken meats,° a base, proud,   *scraps*
shallow, beggarly, three-suited, hundred-pound, filthy worsted-
15   stocking knave;² a lily-livered, action-taking, whoreson, glass-
gazing, super-serviceable, finical rogue; one-trunk-inheriting
slave;³ one that wouldst be a bawd in way of good service,⁴ and
art nothing but the composition° of a knave, beggar, coward,   *combination*
pander, and the son and heir of a mongrel bitch, one whom I
20   will beat into clamorous whining if thou deniest the least syllable of thy addition.⁵
OSWALD   Why, what a monstrous fellow art thou, thus to rail on
one that is neither known of° thee nor knows thee!   *by*
KENT   What a brazen-faced varlet° art thou, to deny thou   *rascal*
25   knowest me! Is it two days since I tripped up thy heels and beat
thee before the King? Draw, you rogue; for though it be night,
yet the moon shines.
[*He draws his sword*]

---

1. Which require immediate attention.
2.2 Location: Before Gloucester's house.
1. If I had you in the enclosure of my mouth (gripped in my teeth). Lipsbury is probably an invented place-name. *pinfold*: pen, animal enclosure.
2. *three-suited . . . knave*: Oswald is being called a poor imitation of a gentleman. Servants were permitted three suits a year; one hundred pounds was the minimum qualification for the purchase of one of King James's knighthoods; a gentleman would wear silk, not "worsted" (of

thick woolen material), stockings.
3. *lily-livered*: cowardly. *action-taking*: litigious, one who would rather use the law than his fists. *glass-gazing*: mirror-gazing. *super-serviceable*: overly officious, or too ready to serve. *finical*: finicky, fastidious. *one-trunk inheriting*: owning only what would fill one trunk.
4. *one that . . . service*: one who would even be a pimp if called upon.
5. Of the descriptions Kent has just applied to him. *addition*: title (used ironically).

I'll make a sop of the moonshine[6] o' you. Draw, you whoreson,
cullionly barber-monger,[7] draw!

30　OSWALD　Away. I have nothing to do with thee.

KENT　Draw, you rascal. You bring letters against the King, and
take Vanity the puppet's part against the royalty of her father.[8]
Draw, you rogue, or I'll so carbonado[9] your shanks—draw, you
rascal, come your ways!°　　　　　　　　　　　　　　　　　　　　*come forward*

35　OSWALD　Help, ho, murder, help!

KENT　Strike, you slave! Stand, rogue! Stand, you neat° slave,　　*elegant; foppish*
strike!

OSWALD　Help, ho, murder, help!

Enter EDMUND *with his rapier drawn,* [*then*] GLOUCES-
TER, [*then*] *the Duke* [CORNWALL] *and Duchess*
[REGAN]

EDMUND　[*parting them*]　How now, what's the matter?

40　KENT　With you, goodman boy. An° you please come, I'll flesh　　*If*
you.[1] Come on, young master.

GLOUCESTER　Weapons? Arms? What's the matter here?

CORNWALL　Keep peace, upon your lives. He dies that strikes
again. What's the matter?

45　REGAN　The messengers from our sister and the King.

CORNWALL　[*to* KENT *and* OSWALD]　What's your difference?
Speak.

OSWALD　I am scarce in breath, my lord.

KENT　No marvel, you have so bestirred your valour, you cow-

50　ardly rascal. Nature disclaims° in thee; a tailor[2] made thee.　　*disowns her part*

CORNWALL　Thou art a strange fellow—a tailor make a man?

KENT　Ay, a tailor, sir. A stone-cutter or a painter could not have
made him so ill° though he had been but two hours at the　　*so badly*
trade.

55　GLOUCESTER　Speak yet; how grew your quarrel?

OSWALD　This ancient ruffian, sir, whose life I have spared at suit
of° his grey beard—　　　　　　　　　　　　　　　　　　　　　　*on account of*

KENT　Thou whoreson Z,[3] thou unnecessary letter—[*to* CORN-
WALL] my lord, if you'll give me leave I will tread this unboulted°　　*unsifted, coarse*

60　villain into mortar and daub the walls of a jakes° with him. [*To*　　*privy, toilet*
OSWALD] Spare my grey beard, you wagtail?[4]

CORNWALL　Peace, sir. You beastly knave, have you no
reverence?°　　　　　　　　　　　　　　　　　　　　　　　　　　　　*respect*

KENT　Yes, sir, but anger has a privilege.

65　CORNWALL　Why art thou angry?

KENT　That such a slave as this should wear a sword,
That° wears no honesty. Such smiling rogues　　　　　　　　　　　*Who*
As these, like rats, oft bite those cords[5] in twain
Which are too entrenched° to unloose, smooth° every passion　　*intricate / flatter*

70　That in the natures of their lords rebel,

---

6. Kent proposes so to skewer and pierce Oswald that his
body might soak up moonlight. *sop:* piece of bread to be
steeped or dunked in soup.
7. *cullionly barber-monger:* despicable frequenter of hair-
dressers. *cullion:* testicle.
8. *and take . . . father:* and support Gonoril, here depicted as a dressed-up doll whose pride is contrasted with
Lear's kingliness.
9. Slash or score as one would the surface of meat in
preparation for broiling.

1. I'll blood you (as a hunting dog); I'll initiate you into
fighting.
2. Tailors, considered effeminate, were stock objects of
mockery.
3. The letter Z (zed) was considered superfluous and
omitted from many dictionaries.
4. A common English bird that takes its name from the
up-and-down flicking of its tail; this, and its characteristic
hopping from foot to foot, causes it to appear nervous.
5. Bonds of kinship, affection, marriage, or rank.

I'll make a sop o'th' moonshine of you,[6] you whoreson, cullionly barber-monger,[7] draw!
30 OSWALD   Away. I have nothing to do with thee.
KENT   Draw, you rascal. You come with letters against the King,
and take Vanity the puppet's part against the royalty of her
father.[8] Draw, you rogue, or I'll so carbonado[9] your shanks—
draw, you rascal, come your ways!°   come forward
35 OSWALD   Help, ho, murder, help!
KENT   Strike, you slave! Stand, rogue! Stand, you neat° slave,   elegant; foppish
strike!
OSWALD   Help, ho, murder, murder!
        Enter Bastard [EDMOND], [then] CORNWALL, REGAN,
            GLOUCESTER, [and] servants
EDMOND   How now, what's the matter? Part.
40 KENT   With you, goodman boy. If you please, come, I'll flesh
ye.[1] Come on, young master.
GLOUCESTER   Weapons? Arms? What's the matter here?
CORNWALL   Keep peace, upon your lives. He dies that strikes again.
What is the matter?
45 REGAN   The messengers from our sister and the King.
CORNWALL [to KENT and OSWALD]   What is your difference?
Speak.
OSWALD   I am scarce in breath, my lord.
KENT   No marvel, you have so bestirred your valour, you cow-
50 ardly rascal. Nature disclaims° in thee; a tailor[2] made thee.   disowns her part
CORNWALL   Thou art a strange fellow—a tailor make a man?
KENT   A tailor, sir. A stone-cutter or a painter could not have
made him so ill° though they had been but two years o'th'°   so badly / at the
trade.
55 CORNWALL   Speak yet; how grew your quarrel?
OSWALD   This ancient ruffian, sir, whose life I have spared at suit
of° his grey beard—   on account of
KENT   Thou whoreson Z,[3] thou unnecessary letter—[to CORN-
WALL] my lord, if you'll give me leave I will tread this unbolted°   unsifted, coarse
60 villain into mortar and daub the wall of a jakes° with him. [To   privy, toilet
OSWALD] Spare my grey beard, you wagtail?[4]
CORNWALL   Peace, sirrah.
You beastly knave, know you no reverence?°   respect
KENT   Yes, sir, but anger hath a privilege.
65 CORNWALL   Why art thou angry?
KENT   That such a slave as this should wear a sword,
Who wears no honesty. Such smiling rogues as these,
Like rats, oft bite the holy cords[5] a-twain
Which are too intrince° t'unloose, smooth° every passion   intricate / flatter
70 That in the natures of their lords rebel;

6. Kent proposes so to skewer and pierce Oswald that his body might soak up moonlight. *sop*: piece of bread to be steeped or dunked in soup.
7. *cullionly barber-monger*: despicable frequenter of hair-dressers. *cullion*: testicle.
8. *and take ... father*: and support Goneril, here depicted as a dressed-up doll whose pride is contrasted with Lear's kingliness.
9. Slash or score as one would the surface of meat in preparation for broiling.

1. I'll blood you (as a hunting dog); I'll initiate you into fighting.
2. Tailors, considered effeminate, were stock objects of mockery.
3. The letter Z (zed) was considered superfluous and omitted from many dictionaries.
4. A common English bird that takes its name from the up-and-down flicking of its tail; this, and its characteristic hopping from foot to foot, causes it to appear nervous.
5. Bonds of kinship, affection, marriage, or rank.

Bring oil to fire, snow to their colder moods,
Renege,° affirm, and turn their halcyon beaks[6]   *Deny*
With every gale and vary° of their masters,   *mood*
Knowing naught, like dogs, but following.
75   [*To* OSWALD] A plague upon your epileptic° visage!   *distorted, grimacing*
Smile you° my speeches as° I were a fool?   *Do you smile at / as if*
Goose, an I had you upon Sarum Plain
I'd send you cackling home to Camelot.[7]
CORNWALL   What, art thou mad, old fellow?
GLOUCESTER [*to* KENT]   How fell you out?
80   Say that.
KENT   No contraries° hold more antipathy   *opposites*
Than I and such a knave.
CORNWALL   Why dost thou call him knave?
What's his offence?
KENT   His countenance likes° me not.   *pleases*
CORNWALL   No more perchance does mine, or his, or hers.
85   KENT   Sir, 'tis my occupation to be plain:
I have seen better faces in my time
Than stands on any shoulder that I see
Before me at this instant.
CORNWALL   This is a fellow
Who, having been praised for bluntness, doth affect
90   A saucy roughness, and constrains the garb
Quite from his nature.[8] He cannot flatter, he.
He must be plain, he must speak truth.
An they will take't, so; if not, he's plain.[9]
These kind of knaves I know, which in this plainness
95   Harbour more craft and more corrupter ends
Than twenty silly-ducking observants
That stretch their duties nicely.[1]
KENT   Sir, in good sooth, or in sincere verity,
Under the allowance of your grand aspect,[2]
100   Whose influence, like the wreath of radiant fire
In flickering Phoebus' front°—   *the sun god's forehead*
CORNWALL   What mean'st thou by this?
KENT   To go out of my dialect,° which you discommend so   *normal mode of speech*
much. I know, sir, I am no flatterer. He that beguiled you in a
plain accent was a plain knave, which for my part I will not be,
105   though I should win your displeasure to entreat me to't.[3]
CORNWALL [*to* OSWALD]   What's the offence you gave him?

---

6. It was believed that the kingfisher (in Greek, *halcyon*) could be used as a weather vane when dead: suspended by a fine thread, its beak would turn whatever way the wind blew.
7. *Goose . . . Camelot:* comparing him to a cackling goose, Kent tells Oswald that if he had him on Salisbury Plain, he would drive him all the way to Camelot, legendary home of King Arthur.
8. *and constrains . . . nature:* and assumes the appearance though it is untrue to his real self. Alternatively (with "his" meaning "its"), and distorts the true shape of plainness from what it naturally is (by turning it into disrespect).
9. If they will accept (Kent's attitude), well and good; if

not, he is a plainspoken man (and does not care).
1. *Than . . . nicely:* Than twenty obsequious attendants who constantly bow idiotically, and who perform their functions with excessive diligence ("nicely").
2. With the permission of your great countenance. "Aspect" also refers to the astrological position of a planet; Kent's bombastic language here raises Cornwall to the mock-heroic proportions of a heavenly body.
3. *He that . . . to't:* The person who tried to hoodwink you with plain speaking was, indeed, a pure knave—something I won't be, even if you were to beg me to be one (a plain knave, or flatterer).

Being oil to fire, snow to the colder moods,
Renege,° affirm, and turn their halcyon beaks[6]   *Deny*
With every gall and vary° of their masters,   *irritation and mood*
Knowing naught, like dogs, but following.
75   [*To* OSWALD] A plague upon your epileptic° visage!   *distorted, grimacing*
Smile you° my speeches as° I were a fool?   *Do you smile at / as if*
Goose, an I had you upon Sarum Plain
I'd drive ye cackling home to Camelot.[7]
CORNWALL   What, art thou mad, old fellow?
GLOUCESTER [*to* KENT]   How fell you out?
80   Say that.
KENT   No contraries° hold more antipathy   *opposites*
Than I and such a knave.
CORNWALL   Why dost thou call him knave?
What is his fault?°   *offense*
KENT   His countenance likes° me not.   *pleases*
CORNWALL   No more perchance does mine, nor his, nor hers.
85   KENT   Sir, 'tis my occupation to be plain:
I have seen better faces in my time
Than stands on any shoulder that I see
Before me at this instant.
CORNWALL   This is some fellow
Who, having been praised for bluntness, doth affect
90   A saucy roughness, and constrains the garb
Quite from his nature.[8] He cannot flatter, he;
An honest mind and plain, he must speak truth.
An they will take't, so; if not, he's plain.[9]
These kind of knaves I know, which in this plainness
95   Harbour more craft and more corrupter ends
Than twenty silly-ducking observants
That stretch their duties nicely.[1]
KENT   Sir, in good faith, in sincere verity,
Under th'allowance of your great aspect,[2]
100   Whose influence, like the wreath of radiant fire
On flick'ring Phoebus' front°—   *the sun god's forehead*
CORNWALL   What mean'st by this?
KENT   To go out of my dialect,° which you discommend so   *normal mode of speech*
much. I know, sir, I am no flatterer. He that beguiled you in a
plain accent was a plain knave, which for my part I will not be,
105   though I should win your displeasure to entreat me to't.[3]
CORNWALL [*to* OSWALD]   What was th'offence you gave him?

---

6. It was believed that the kingfisher (in Greek, *halcyon*) could be used as a weather vane when dead: suspended by a fine thread, its beak would turn whatever way the wind blew.
7. *Goose . . . Camelot*: comparing him to a cackling goose, Kent tells Oswald that if he had him on Salisbury Plain, he would drive him all the way to Camelot, legendary home of King Arthur.
8. *and constrains . . . nature*: and assumes the appearance though it is untrue to his real self. Alternatively (with "his" meaning "its"), and distorts the true shape of plainness from what it naturally is (by turning it into disrespect).
9. If they will accept (Kent's attitude), well and good; if

not, he is a plainspoken man (and does not care).
1. *Than . . . nicely*: Than twenty obsequious attendants who constantly bow idiotically, and who perform their functions with excessive diligence ("nicely").
2. With the permission of your great countenance. "Aspect" also refers to the astrological position of a planet; Kent's bombastic language here raises Cornwall to the mock-heroic proportions of a heavenly body.
3. *He that . . . to't*: The person who tried to hoodwink you with plain speaking was, indeed, a pure knave—something I won't be, even if you were to beg me to be one (a plain knave, or flatterer).

OSWALD   I never gave him any.
It pleased the King his master very late°   *lately*
To strike at me upon his misconstruction,°   *misunderstanding (me)*
When he, conjunct,° and flattering his displeasure,   *in league with*
110 Tripped me behind; being down, insulted,° railed,   *I being down, he insulted*
And put upon him such a deal of man
That worthied him,[4] got praises of the King
For him attempting who was self-subdued,[5]
And in the fleshment° of this dread exploit   *excitement; flush*
Drew on me here again.
115 KENT   None of these rogues and cowards
But Ajax is their fool.[6]
CORNWALL [*calling*]   Bring forth the stocks, ho! —
You stubborn, ancient knave, you reverend° braggart,   *old; revered*
We'll teach you.
KENT   I am too old to learn.
Call not your stocks for me. I serve the King,
120 On whose employments I was sent to you.
You should do small respect, show too bold malice
Against the grace° and person° of my master,   *majesty / personal honor*
Stocking° his messenger.   *By stocking*
CORNWALL [*calling*]   Fetch forth the stocks! —
As I have life and honour, there shall he sit till noon.
125 REGAN Till noon? — till night, my lord, and all night too.
KENT Why, madam, if I were your father's dog
You could not use me so.
REGAN   Sir, being° his knave, I will.   *since you are*
        [*Stocks brought out*]
CORNWALL This is a fellow of the selfsame nature
Our sister° speaks of. — Come, bring away the stocks.   *sister-in-law*
130 GLOUCESTER Let me beseech your grace not to do so.
His fault is much, and the good King his master
Will check° him for't. Your purposed° low correction   *reprimand / intended*
Is such as basest and contemnèd wretches
For pilf'rings and most common trespasses
135 Are punished with. The King must take it ill
That he's so slightly valued in his messenger,
Should have him thus restrained.
CORNWALL   I'll answer° that.   *be responsible for*
REGAN My sister may receive it much more worse
To have her gentlemen abused, assaulted,
140 For following° her affairs. Put in his legs.   *carrying out*
        [*They put* KENT *in the stocks*]
Come, my good lord, away!
        [*Exeunt all but* GLOUCESTER *and* KENT]
GLOUCESTER I am sorry for thee, friend. 'Tis the Duke's pleasure,
Whose disposition, all the world well knows,
Will not be rubbed° nor stopped. I'll entreat for thee.   *obstructed*

---

4. *And put . . . him:* And put on such a show of manliness
that he was thought a worthy fellow.
5. For attacking a man who had already surrendered
(Kent attacking Oswald).

6. *None . . . fool:* Such rogues and cowards as these talk
as if they were greater warriors (and blusterers) than Ajax;
such rogues always make even mighty Ajax out to be a
fool.

OSWALD   I never gave him any.
　　It pleased the King his master very late°   *lately*
　　To strike at me upon his misconstruction,°   *misunderstanding (me)*
　　When he, compact,° and flattering his displeasure,   *in league with*
110　　Tripped me behind; being down, insulted,° railed,   *I being down, he insulted*
　　And put upon him such a deal of man
　　That worthied him,[4] got praises of the King
　　For him attempting who was self-subdued,[5]
　　And in the fleshment° of this dread exploit   *excitement; flush*
　　Drew on me here again.
115　KENT   None of these rogues and cowards
　　But Ajax is their fool.[6]
CORNWALL   Fetch forth the stocks!
　　　　　　　　　　　　　　　　　　[*Exeunt some servants*]
　　You stubborn, ancient knave, you reverend° braggart,   *old; revered*
　　We'll teach you.
KENT   Sir, I am too old to learn.
　　Call not your stocks for me. I serve the King,
120　　On whose employment I was sent to you.
　　You shall do small respect, show too bold malice
　　Against the grace° and person° of my master,   *majesty / personal honor*
　　Stocking° his messenger.   *By stocking*
CORNWALL [*calling*]   Fetch forth the stocks!—
　　As I have life and honour, there shall he sit till noon.
125　REGAN   Till noon?—till night, my lord, and all night too.
KENT   Why, madam, if I were your father's dog
　　You should not use me so.
REGAN   Sir, being° his knave, I will.   *since you are*
　　　　　　　[*Stocks brought out*]
CORNWALL   This is a fellow of the selfsame colour°   *character*
　　Our sister° speaks of.—Come, bring away the stocks.   *sister-in-law*
130　GLOUCESTER   Let me beseech your grace not to do so.
　　The King his master needs must take it ill
　　That he, so slightly valued in his messenger,
　　Should have him thus restrained.
CORNWALL   I'll answer° that.   *be responsible for*
　　　　　　　[*They put* KENT *in the stocks*]
REGAN   My sister may receive it much more worse
135　　To have her gentlemen abused, assaulted.
CORNWALL   Come, my good lord, away!
　　　　　　　　　　　　Exeunt [*all but* GLOUCESTER *and* KENT]
GLOUCESTER   I am sorry for thee, friend. 'Tis the Duke's pleasure,
　　Whose disposition, all the world well knows,
　　Will not be rubbed° nor stopped. I'll entreat for thee.   *obstructed*

---

4. *And put . . . him:* And put on such a show of manliness
that he was thought a worthy fellow.
5. For attacking a man who had already surrendered
(Kent attacking Oswald).

6. *None . . . fool:* Such rogues and cowards as these talk
as if they were greater warriors (and blusterers) than Ajax;
such rogues always make even mighty Ajax out to be a
fool.

145 KENT   Pray you, do not, sir. I have watched° and travelled hard.   *gone without sleep*
      Some time I shall sleep out; the rest I'll whistle.
      A good man's fortune may grow out at heels.[7]
      Give° you good morrow.   *God give*
    GLOUCESTER   The Duke's to blame in this; 'twill be ill took.
                                               [*Exit*]

150 KENT   Good King, that must approve° the common say:°   *prove / saying*
      Thou out of heaven's benediction com'st
      To the warm sun.[8]
        [*He takes out a letter*]
      Approach, thou beacon[9] to this under globe,
      That by thy comfortable beams I may
155   Peruse this letter. Nothing almost sees miracles
      But misery.[1] I know 'tis from Cordelia,
      Who hath now fortunately been informed
      Of my obscurèd° course, and shall find time   *hidden, disguised*
      From this enormous state,° seeking to give   *awful state of affairs*
160   Losses their remedies. All weary and overwatched,°   *too long awake*
      Take vantage,° heavy eyes, not to behold   *the opportunity*
      This shameful lodging. Fortune, good night;
      Smile; once more turn thy wheel.   *Sleeps*
        Enter EDGAR

    EDGAR   I heard myself proclaimed,°   *declared an outlaw*
      And by the happy° hollow of a tree   *opportune*
165   Escaped the hunt. No port° is free, no place   *seaport; exit*
      That guard and most unusual vigilance
      Does not attend my taking.° While° I may scape   *await my capture / if*
      I will preserve myself, and am bethought°   *resolved*
      To take the basest and most poorest shape
170   That ever penury in contempt of° man
      Brought near to beast. My face I'll grime with filth,
      Blanket my loins, elf all my hair with knots,
      And with presented° nakedness outface
      The wind and persecution of the sky.
175   The country gives me proof and precedent
      Of Bedlam beggars who with roaring voices
      Strike° in their numbed and mortified° bare arms
      Pins, wooden pricks, nails, sprigs of rosemary,
      And with this horrible object from low farms,
180   Poor pelting villages, sheep-cotes and mills
      Sometime with lunatic bans, sometime with prayer
      Enforce their charity. 'Poor Turlygod! Poor Tom!'
      That's something yet. Edgar I nothing am.[5]   *Exit*
        Enter LEAR [*and*] FOOL, and a KNIGHT

    LEAR   'Tis strange that they should so depart from home,
      And not send back my messenger.

---

7. The fortunes of even good men sometimes wear thin.
8. Thou . . . sun: You come from the blessing of heaven into the heat of the sun (go from good to bad).
9. It is arguable whether Kent here refers to the sun or the moon.
1. Nothing . . . misery: Only those suffering misery are granted miracles; any comfort seems miraculous to those who are miserable.

2. The goddess Fortune, whose wheel, to signify her mutability, was believed to take people to the top of her wheel . . .
3. Tangle the hair into knots, in imitation of madness . . .
4. A word of unknown . . .
5. Edgar I am . . .

140 KENT   Pray do not, sir. I have watched° and travelled hard.   *gone without sleep*
       Some time I shall sleep out; the rest I'll whistle.
       A good man's fortune may grow out at heels.[7]
       Give° you good morrow.   *God give*
   GLOUCESTER   The Duke's to blame in this; 'twill be ill taken.
                                                                          Exit
145 KENT   Good King, that must approve° the common say:°   *prove / saying*
       Thou out of heaven's benediction com'st
       To the warm sun.[8]
           [*He takes out a letter*]
       Approach, thou beacon[9] to this under globe,
       That by thy comfortable beams I may
150   Peruse this letter. Nothing almost sees miracles
       But misery.[1] I know 'tis from Cordelia,
       Who hath now fortunately been informed
       Of my obscurèd° course, and shall find time   *hidden, disguised*
       For this enormous state,° seeking to give   *awful state of affairs*
155   Losses their remedies. All weary and o'erwatched,°   *too long awake*
       Take vantage,° heavy eyes, not to behold   *the opportunity*
       This shameful lodging. Fortune, good night;
       Smile once more; turn thy wheel.[2]   [*He sleeps*]
           Enter EDGAR
   EDGAR   I heard myself proclaimed,°   *declared an outlaw*
       And by the happy° hollow of a tree   *opportune*
160   Escaped the hunt. No port° is free, no place   *seaport; exit*
       That guard and most unusual vigilance
       Does not attend my taking.° Whiles° I may scape   *await my capture / Until*
       I will preserve myself, and am bethought°   *resolved*
       To take the basest and most poorest shape
165   That ever penury in contempt of° man   *for*
       Brought near to beast. My face I'll grime with filth,
       Blanket my loins, elf all my hairs in knots,[3]
       And with presented° nakedness outface   *exposed*
       The winds and persecutions of the sky.
170   The country gives me proof and precedent
       Of Bedlam beggars who with roaring voices
       Strike° in their numbed and mortifièd° arms   *Stick / deadened*
       Pins, wooden pricks, nails, sprigs of rosemary,
       And with this horrible object° from low farms,   *spectacle*
175   Poor pelting° villages, sheep-cotes and mills   *paltry; contemptible*
       Sometime with lunatic bans,° sometime with prayers   *curses*
       Enforce their charity. 'Poor Tuelygod,[4] Poor Tom.'
       That's something yet. Edgar I nothing am.[5]   *Exit*
           Enter LEAR, FOOL, *and* [*the* FIRST] GENTLEMAN[6]
   LEAR   'Tis strange that they should so depart from home
       And not send back my messenger.

---

7. The fortunes of even good men sometimes wear thin.
8. *Thou . . . sun:* you come from the blessing of heaven into the heat of the sun (go from good to bad).
9. It is arguable whether Kent here refers to the sun or the moon.
1. *Nothing . . . misery:* Only those suffering misery are granted miracles; any comfort seems miraculous to those who are miserable.
2. The goddess Fortune was traditionally depicted with a wheel to signify her mutability and caprice. She was believed to take pleasure in arbitrarily lowering those at the top of her wheel and raising those at the bottom.
3. Tangle the hair into "elf locks," supposed to be a favorite trick of malicious elves.
4. A word of unknown origin.
5. Edgar, I am nothing; I am no longer Edgar.
6. F seems to reserve "a Gentleman" (referred to as "First Gentleman" in this edition) for this particular character, who returns in 5.3.

185 KNIGHT   As I learned,
    The night before there was no purpose°   intention
    Of his remove.°   change of residence
    KENT [waking]   Hail to thee, noble master.
    LEAR   How! Mak'st thou this shame thy pastime?
    FOOL   Ha, ha, look, he wears cruel garters![6] Horses are tied by
190 the heads, dogs and bears by th' neck, monkeys by th' loins,
    and men by th' legs. When a man's over-lusty at legs,[7] then he
    wears wooden nether-stocks.°   knee socks
    LEAR [to KENT]   What's° he that hath so much thy place° mistook   Who's / position
    To set thee here?
    KENT   It is both he and she:
    Your son° and daughter.   son-in-law
    LEAR   No.
    KENT   Yes.
195 LEAR   No, I say.
    KENT   I say yea.
    LEAR   No, no, they would not.
    KENT   Yes, they have.
    LEAR   By Jupiter, I swear no. They durst not do't,
    They would not, could not do't. 'Tis worse than murder,
    To do upon respect[8] such violent outrage.
200 Resolve° me with all modest° haste which way   Inform / reasonable
    Thou mayst deserve or they propose this usage,
    Coming from us.
    KENT   My lord, when at their home
    I did commend° your highness' letters to them,   deliver
    Ere I was risen from the place that showed
205 My duty kneeling, came there a reeking° post   steaming
    Stewed in his haste, half breathless, panting forth
    From Gonoril, his mistress, salutations,
    Delivered letters spite of intermission,[9]
    Which presently° they read, on whose contents   immediately
210 They summoned up their meiny,° straight° took horse,   retinue / straightaway
    Commanded me to follow and attend
    The leisure of their answer, gave me cold looks;
    And meeting here the other messenger,
    Whose welcome I perceived had poisoned mine—
215 Being the very° fellow that of late   same
    Displayed so saucily° against your highness—   Acted so insolently
    Having more man° than wit° about me, drew.   courage / sense
    He raised the house with loud and coward cries.
    Your son and daughter found this trespass worth°   deserving of
220 This shame which here it suffers.

---

6. Worsted garters, punning on "crewel," a thin yarn.   8. To do to one who deserves respect.
The Fool is actually referring to the stocks in which   9. Regardless of interrupting me; despite the interrup-
Kent's feet are held.   tions in his account (as he gasped for breath).
7. When a man's liable to run away.

180 FIRST GENTLEMAN   As I learned,
      The night before there was no purpose in them°   *they had no intention*
      Of this remove.°   *change of residence*
      KENT [*waking*]   Hail to thee, noble master.
      LEAR   Ha! Mak'st thou this shame thy pastime?
      KENT   No, my lord.
      FOOL   Ha, ha, he wears cruel garters![7] Horses are tied by the
185   heads, dogs and bears by th' neck, monkeys by th' loins, and
      men by th' legs. When a man's overlusty at legs,[8] then he wears
      wooden nether-stocks.°   *knee socks*
      LEAR [*to* KENT]   What's° he that hath so much thy place° mistook   *Who's / position*
      To set thee here?
      KENT   It is both he and she:
      Your son° and daughter.   *son-in-law*
      LEAR   No.
      KENT   Yes.
190 LEAR   ·   No, I say.
      KENT   I say yea.
      LEAR   By Jupiter, I swear no.
      KENT   By Juno,[9] I swear ay.
      LEAR   They durst not do't,
      They could not, would not do't. 'Tis worse than murder,
      To do upon respect[1] such violent outrage.
195   Resolve° me with all modest° haste which way   *Inform / reasonable*
      Thou mightst deserve or they impose this usage,
      Coming from us.
      KENT   My lord, when at their home
      I did commend° your highness' letters to them,   *deliver*
      Ere I was risen from the place that showed
200   My duty kneeling, came there a reeking° post   *steaming*
      Stewed in his haste, half breathless, painting° forth   *panting*
      From Goneril, his mistress, salutations,
      Delivered letters spite of intermission,[2]
      Which presently° they read, on whose contents   *immediately*
205   They summoned up their meiny,° straight° took horse,   *retinue / straightaway*
      Commanded me to follow and attend
      The leisure of their answer, gave me cold looks;
      And meeting here the other messenger,
      Whose welcome I perceived had poisoned mine—
210   Being the very° fellow which of late   *same*
      Displayed so saucily° against your highness—   *Acted so insolently*
      Having more man° than wit° about me, drew.   *courage / sense*
      He raised the house with loud and coward cries.
      Your son and daughter found this trespass worth°   *deserving of*
215   The shame which here it suffers.

7. Worsted garters, punning on "crewel," a thin yarn. The Fool is actually referring to the stocks in which Kent's feet are held.
8. When a man's liable to run away.
9. Queen of the Roman gods and wife of Jupiter, with whom she constantly quarreled.
1. To do to one who deserves respect.
2. Regardless of interrupting me; despite the interruptions in his account (as he gasped for breath).

LEAR   O, how this mother° swells up toward my heart!   *hysteria*
      Histerica passio, down, thou climbing sorrow;[1]
      Thy element's° below.—Where is this daughter?   *natural place is*
KENT   With the Earl, sir, within.
LEAR   Follow me not; stay there.
                            [Exit]
KNIGHT *[to* KENT*]*   Made you no more offence than what you
225   speak of?
KENT   No. How chance the King comes with so small a train?
FOOL   An° thou hadst been set in the stocks for that question,   *If*
      thou hadst well deserved it.
KENT   Why, fool?
230 FOOL   We'll set thee to school to an ant, to teach thee there's no
      labouring in the winter.[2] All that follow their noses are led by
      their eyes but blind men, and there's not a nose among a hun-
      dred but can smell him that's stinking.° Let go thy hold when   *(as his fortunes decay)*
      a great wheel runs down a hill, lest it break thy neck with fol-
235   lowing it; but the great one that goes up the hill,[3] let him draw
      thee after. When a wise man gives thee better counsel, give me
      mine again. I would have none but knaves follow it, since a
      fool gives it.
      [Sings]   That sir that serves for gain
240   And follows but for form,
             Will pack° when it begin to rain,   *pack up and go*
             And leave thee in the storm.

             But I will tarry, the fool will stay,
             And let the wise man fly.
245   The knave turns fool that runs away,[4]
             The fool no knave, pardie.°   *by God (pardieu)*
KENT   Where learnt you this, fool?
FOOL   Not in the stocks.
      Enter LEAR *and* GLOUCESTER
LEAR   Deny to speak with me? They're sick, they're weary?
250 They travelled hard tonight?—mere insolence,
      Ay, the images of revolt and flying off.[5]
      Fetch me a better answer.

---

1. *Histerica . . . sorrow: Hysterica passio* (a Latin expression originating in the Greek *steiros*, "suffering in the womb") was an inflammation of the senses. In Renaissance medicine, vapors from the abdomen were thought to rise up through the body, and in women, the uterus itself to wander around.
2. Ants, proverbially prudent, do not work in winter.

Implicitly, a wise person should know better than to look for sustenance to an old man who has fallen on wintry times.
3. A great wheel is a figure for Lear and of Fortune's wheel itself, which has swung downward.
4. The scoundrel who runs away is the real fool.
5. *images of:* signs of. *flying off:* desertion; insurrection.

FOOL   Winter's not gone yet if the wild geese fly that way.[3]
   [*Sings*]   Fathers that wear rags
            Do make their children blind,[4]
         But fathers that bear bags
220   Shall see their children kind.
         Fortune, that arrant whore,
            Ne'er turns the key° to th' poor.   *opens the door*
   But for all this thou shalt have as many dolours[5] for thy daugh-
   ters as thou canst tell° in a year.   *count*
225 LEAR   O, how this mother° swells up toward my heart!   *hysteria*
   Histerica passio down, thou climbing sorrow;[6]
   Thy element's° below.—Where is this daughter?   *natural place is*
KENT   With the Earl, sir, here within.
LEAR   Follow me not; stay here.
                               Exit
FIRST GENTLEMAN [*to* KENT]   Made you no more offence but
       what you speak of?
230 KENT   None.
   How chance the King comes with so small a number?
FOOL   An° thou hadst been set i'th' stocks for that question,   *If*
   thou'dst well deserved it.
KENT   Why, Fool?
235 FOOL   We'll set thee to school to an ant, to teach thee there's no
   labouring i'th' winter.[7] All that follow their noses are led by
   their eyes but blind men, and there's not a nose among twenty
   but can smell him that's stinking.° Let go thy hold when a great   *(as his fortunes decay)*
   wheel runs down a hill,[8] lest it break thy neck with following;
240   but the great one that goes upward, let him draw thee after.
   When a wise man gives thee better counsel, give me mine
   again. I would have none but knaves follow it, since a fool gives
   it.
   [*Sings*]   That sir which serves and seeks for gain
245   And follows but for form,
         Will pack° when it begin to rain,   *pack up and go*
            And leave thee in the storm.

         But I will tarry, the fool will stay,
            And let the wise man fly.
250   The knave turns fool that runs away,[9]
            The fool no knave, pardie.°   *by God* (pardieu)
KENT   Where learned you this, Fool?
FOOL   Not i'th' stocks, fool.
       Enter LEAR *and* GLOUCESTER
LEAR   Deny to speak with me? They are sick, they are weary,
255   They have travelled all the night?—mere fetches,°   *ruses, pretexts*
   The images of revolt and flying off.[1]
   Fetch me a better answer.

---

3. That is, things will get worse before they get better.
4. Blind to their father's needs.
5. Pain, sorrow; punning on "dollar," the English term for the German "thaler," a large silver coin.
6. Histerica . . . *sorrow*: *Hysterica passio* (a Latin expression originating in the Greek *steiros*, "suffering in the womb") was an inflammation of the senses. In Renaissance medicine, vapors from the abdomen were thought to rise up through the body, and in women, the uterus itself to wander around.
7. Ants, proverbially prudent, do not work in winter. Implicitly, a wise person should know better than to look for sustenance to an old man who has fallen on wintry times.
8. A great wheel is a figure for Lear and of Fortune's wheel itself, which has swung downward.
9. The scoundrel who runs away is the real fool.
1. *images of*: signs of. *flying off*: desertion; insurrection.

GLOUCESTER   My dear lord,
  You know the fiery quality° of the Duke,   *disposition*
  How unremovable and fixed he is
  In his own course.
255   LEAR   Vengeance, death, plague, confusion!°   *destruction*
  What 'fiery quality'? Why, Gloucester, Gloucester, I'd
  Speak with the Duke of Cornwall and his wife.
GLOUCESTER   Ay, my good lord.
LEAR   The King would speak with Cornwall; the dear father
260   Would with his daughter speak, commands, tends° service.   *awaits*
  'Fiery'? The Duke?—tell the hot Duke that Lear—
  No, but not yet. Maybe he is not well.
  Infirmity doth still° neglect all office°   *always / obligation*
  Whereto our health is bound. We are not ourselves
265   When nature, being oppressed, commands the mind
  To suffer with the body. I'll forbear,
  And am fallen out with my more headier will,[6]
  To take° the indisposed and sickly fit   *mistake*
  For the sound man.—Death on my state,[7]
270   Wherefore° should he sit here? This act persuades me   *Why*
  That this remotion° of the Duke and her   *remoteness, aloofness*
  Is practice° only. Give me my servant forth.   *trickery*
  Tell the Duke and 's wife I'll speak with them,
  Now, presently.° Bid them come forth and hear me,   *at once*
275   Or at their chamber door I'll beat the drum
  Till it cry sleep to death.[8]
GLOUCESTER   I would have all well
  Betwixt you.   [*Exit*]
LEAR   O, my heart, my heart!
FOOL   Cry to it, nuncle, as the cockney° did to the eels when she   *Londoner (city woman)*
  put 'em i'th' paste° alive. She rapped 'em o'th' coxcombs° with   *pie; pastry / heads*
280   a stick, and cried 'Down, wantons,° down!' 'Twas her brother   *rogues*
  that, in pure kindness to his horse, buttered his hay.[9]
          Enter Duke [of CORNWALL] *and* REGAN [GLOUCESTER,*
          and others]
LEAR   Good morrow to you both.
CORNWALL   Hail to your grace.
         [KENT *here set at liberty*]
REGAN   I am glad to see your highness.
285   LEAR   Regan, I think you are. I know what reason
  I have to think so. If thou shouldst not be glad
  I would divorce me from thy mother's shrine,
  Sepulchring° an adultress. [*To* KENT] Yea, are you free?   *Because it entombed*
  Some other time for that.—Belovèd Regan,
290   Thy sister is naught.° O, Regan, she hath tied   *wicked; nothing*
  Sharp-toothed unkindness like a vulture here.[1]
  I can scarce speak to thee. Thou'lt not believe
  Of how deplored a quality—O, Regan!

6. And disagree with my (earlier) more rash intention.
7. May my royal authority end (an oath). Ironically, this has already happened.
8. Till the noise kills sleep.
9. Like that of his sister (who wanted to make eel pie without killing the eels), his kindness was misplaced: horses will not eat buttered hay. Lear's earlier kindness to his daughters was equally foolish.
1. Lear probably gestures to his heart.

GLOUCESTER   My dear lord,
    You know the fiery quality° of the Duke,   *disposition*
    How unremovable and fixed he is
    In his own course.
260 LEAR   Vengeance, plague, death, confusion!°   *destruction*
    'Fiery'? What 'quality'? Why, Gloucester, Gloucester,
    I'd speak with the Duke of Cornwall and his wife.
  GLOUCESTER   Well, my good lord, I have informed them so.
  LEAR   'Informed them'? Dost thou understand me, man?
265 GLOUCESTER   Ay, my good lord.
  LEAR   The King would speak with Cornwall; the dear father
    Would with his daughter speak, commands, tends° service.   *awaits*
    Are they 'informed' of this? My breath and blood—
    'Fiery'? The 'fiery' Duke—tell the hot Duke that—
270   No, but not yet. Maybe he is not well.
    Infirmity doth still° neglect all office°   *always / obligation*
    Whereto our health is bound. We are not ourselves
    When nature, being oppressed, commands the mind
    To suffer with the body. I'll forbear,
275   And am fallen out with my more headier will,[2]
    To take° the indisposed and sickly fit   *mistake*
    For the sound man.—Death on my state,[3] wherefore°   *why*
    Should he sit here? This act persuades me
    That this remotion° of the Duke and her   *remoteness, aloofness*
280   Is practice° only. Give me my servant forth.   *trickery*
    Go tell the Duke and 's wife I'd speak with them,
    Now, presently.° Bid them come forth and hear me,   *at once*
    Or at their chamber door I'll beat the drum
    Till it cry sleep to death.[4]
  GLOUCESTER   I would have all well betwixt you.

                                        Exit

285 LEAR   O me, my heart! My rising heart! But down.
  FOOL   Cry to it, nuncle, as the cockney° did to the eels when she   *Londoner (city woman)*
    put 'em i'th' paste° alive. She knapped 'em o'th' coxcombs°   *pie; pastry / heads*
    with a stick, and cried 'Down, wantons,° down!' 'Twas her   *rogues*
    brother that, in pure kindness to his horse, buttered his hay.[5]

         Enter CORNWALL, REGAN, GLOUCESTER, [*and*] *servants*

290 LEAR   Good morrow to you both.
  CORNWALL   Hail to your grace.

        KENT *here set at liberty*

  REGAN   I am glad to see your highness.
  LEAR   Regan, I think you are. I know what reason
    I have to think so. If thou shouldst not be glad
295   I would divorce me from thy mother's shrine,
    Sepulchring° an adultress. [*To* KENT] O, are you free?   *Because it entombed*
    Some other time for that.   [*Exit* KENT]
                    Belovèd Regan,
    Thy sister's naught.° O, Regan, she hath tied   *wicked; nothing*
    Sharp-toothed unkindness like a vulture here.[6]
300   I can scarce speak to thee. Thou'lt not believe
    With how depraved a quality—O, Regan!

---

2. And disagree with my (earlier) more rash intention.
3. May my royal authority end (an oath). Ironically, this has already happened.
4. Till the noise kills sleep.
5. Like that of his sister (who wanted to make eel pie without killing the eels), his kindness was misplaced: horses will not eat buttered hay. Lear's earlier kindness to his daughters was equally foolish.
6. Lear probably gestures to his heart.

REGAN   I pray you, sir, take patience. I have hope
295　　　You less know how to value her desert
　　　　Than she to slack her duty.[2]

LEAR   My curses on her.
REGAN   O sir, you are old.
　　　　Nature° in you stands on the very verge　　　　　　　　　　　*Life*
300　　　Of her confine.° You should be ruled and led　　　　　　　*Of its limit*
　　　　By some discretion° that discerns your state　　　　　　　*discreet person*
　　　　Better than you yourself. Therefore I pray
　　　　That to our sister you do make return;
　　　　Say you have wronged her, sir.
LEAR　　　　　　　　　　　　　　Ask her forgiveness?
305　　　Do you mark how this becomes the house?[3]
　　　　[*Kneeling*] 'Dear daughter, I confess that I am old.
　　　　Age° is unnecessary. On my knees I beg　　　　　　　　　*An old man*
　　　　That you'll vouchsafe me raiment,° bed, and food.'　　　*promise me clothing*
REGAN   Good sir, no more. These are unsightly tricks.
　　　　Return you to my sister.
310　LEAR [*rising*]　　　　　　　　No, Regan.
　　　　She hath abated° me of half my train,　　　　　　　　　*deprived*
　　　　Looked black upon me, struck me with her tongue
　　　　Most serpent-like upon the very heart.
　　　　All° the stored vengeances of heaven fall　　　　　　　*Let all*
315　　　On her ungrateful top!° Strike her young bones,　　　　*head*
　　　　You taking° airs, with lameness!　　　　　　　　　　　*infectious; malignant*
CORNWALL　　　　　　　　　　　Fie, fie, sir.
LEAR   You nimble lightnings, dart your blinding flames
　　　　Into her scornful eyes. Infect her beauty,
　　　　You fen-sucked fogs drawn by the pow'rful sun[4]
　　　　To fall and blast her pride.
320　REGAN　　　　　　　　　　　O, the blest gods!
　　　　So will you wish on me when the rash mood—
LEAR   No, Regan. Thou shalt never have my curse.
　　　　Thy tender-hested° nature shall not give　　　　　　　*pledged to tenderness*
　　　　Thee o'er to harshness. Her eyes are fierce, but thine
325　　　Do comfort and not burn. 'Tis not in thee
　　　　To grudge my pleasures, to cut off my train,
　　　　To bandy hasty words, to scant my sizes,°　　　　　　　*reduce my allowances*
　　　　And, in conclusion, to oppose the bolt°　　　　　　　　*to lock the door*
　　　　Against my coming in. Thou better know'st
330　　　The offices° of nature, bond of childhood,　　　　　　　*duties*
　　　　Effects° of courtesy, dues of gratitude.　　　　　　　　*Actions*
　　　　Thy half of the kingdom hast thou not forgot,
　　　　Wherein I thee endowed.

2. *I have . . . duty:* I expect that you are worse at valuing
her deservings than she is at neglecting her duty. The
double negative here ("less," "scant") is acceptable Jacobean usage.

3. Do you see how appropriate this is among members of
a family (spoken ironically)?
4. The sun was thought to suck poisonous vapors from
marshy ground.

REGAN   I pray you, sir, take patience. I have hope
    You less know how to value her desert
    Than she to scant her duty.[7]
LEAR   Say, how is that?
305   REGAN   I cannot think my sister in the least
    Would fail her obligation. If, sir, perchance
    She have restrained the riots of your followers,
    'Tis on such ground and to such wholesome end
    As clears her from all blame.
310   LEAR   My curses on her.
    REGAN   O sir, you are old.
    Nature° in you stands on the very verge   *Life*
    Of his confine.° You should be ruled and led   *Of its limit*
    By some discretion° that discerns your state   *discreet person*
315   Better than you yourself. Therefore I pray you
    That to our sister you do make return;
    Say you have wronged her.
    LEAR   Ask her forgiveness?
    Do you but mark how this becomes the house?[8]
    [*Kneeling*] 'Dear daughter, I confess that I am old.
320   Age° is unnecessary. On my knees I beg   *An old man*
    That you'll vouchsafe me raiment,° bed, and food.' *promise me clothing*
    REGAN   Good sir, no more. These are unsightly tricks.
    Return you to my sister.
    LEAR [*rising*]   Never, Regan.
    She hath abated° me of half my train,   *deprived*
325   Looked black upon me, struck me with her tongue
    Most serpent-like upon the very heart.
    All° the stored vengeances of heaven fall   *Let all*
    On her ingrateful top!° Strike her young bones,   *head*
    You taking° airs, with lameness!   *infectious; malignant*
    CORNWALL   Fie, sir, fie.
330   LEAR   You nimble lightnings, dart your blinding flames
    Into her scornful eyes. Infect her beauty,
    You fen-sucked fogs drawn by the pow'rful sun[9]
    To fall and blister.
    REGAN   O, the blest gods!
    So will you wish on me when the rash mood is on.
335   LEAR   No, Regan. Thou shalt never have my curse.
    Thy tender-hafted[1] nature shall not give
    Thee o'er to harshness. Her eyes are fierce, but thine
    Do comfort and not burn. 'Tis not in thee
    To grudge my pleasures, to cut off my train,
340   To bandy hasty words, to scant my sizes,°   *reduce my allowances*
    And, in conclusion, to oppose the bolt°   *to lock the door*
    Against my coming in. Thou better know'st
    The offices° of nature, bond of childhood,   *duties*
    Effects° of courtesy, dues of gratitude.   *Actions*
345   Thy half o'th' kingdom hast thou not forgot,
    Wherein I thee endowed.

---

7. *I have . . . duty:* I expect that you are worse at valuing
her deservings than she is at neglecting her duty. The
double negative here ("less," "scant") is acceptable Jacobean usage.
8. Do you see how appropriate this is among members of

a family (spoken ironically)?
9. The sun was thought to suck poisonous vapors from
marshy ground.
1. Tender-handled; firmly set in a tender disposition (as
a knife blade into its haft).

REGAN   Good sir, to th' purpose.°   *get to the point*
LEAR   Who put my man i'th' stocks?
       [*Trumpets within*]
CORNWALL   What trumpet's that?
       Enter Steward [OSWALD]
335   REGAN   I know't, my sister's. This approves° her letters   *confirms*
       That she would soon be here. [*To* OSWALD] Is your lady come?
       LEAR   This is a slave whose easy-borrowed pride⁵
       Dwells in the fickle grace of her a° follows.   *he*
       [*He strikes* OSWALD]
       Out, varlet,° from my sight!   *wretch*
CORNWALL   What means your grace?
       Enter GONORIL
340   GONORIL   Who struck my servant? Regan, I have good hope
       Thou didst not know on't.°   *of it*
       LEAR   Who comes here? O heavens,
       If you do love old men, if your sweet sway
       Allow obedience, if yourselves are old,
       Make it your cause! Send down and take my part.
345   [*To* GONORIL] Art not ashamed to look upon this beard?
       O Regan, wilt thou take her by the hand?
       GONORIL   Why not by the hand, sir? How have I offended?
       All's not offence that indiscretion finds
       And dotage terms so.
       LEAR   O sides,⁶ you are too tough!
350   Will you yet hold? — How came my man i'th' stocks?
       CORNWALL   I set him there, sir; but his own disorders°   *disorderly behavior*
       Deserved much less advancement.⁷
       LEAR   You? Did you?
       REGAN   I pray you, father, being weak, seem so.°   *behave so*
       If till the expiration of your month
355   You will return and sojourn with my sister,
       Dismissing half your train, come then to me.
       I am now from home, and out of that provision
       Which shall be needful for your entertainment.
       LEAR   Return to her, and fifty men dismissed?
360   No, rather I abjure all roofs, and choose
       To be a comrade with the wolf and owl,
       To wage against the enmity of the air
       Necessity's sharp pinch.⁸ Return with her?
       Why, the hot-blood in France that dowerless took
365   Our youngest born — I could as well be brought
       To knee° his throne and, squire-like, pension beg   *kneel to*
       To keep base life afoot. Return with her?
       Persuade me rather to be slave and sumpter°   *pack horse*
       To this detested groom.°   *(Oswald)*
       GONORIL   At your choice, sir.
370   LEAR   Now I prithee, daughter, do not make me mad.
       I will not trouble thee, my child. Farewell.
       We'll no more meet, no more see one another.
       But yet thou art my flesh, my blood, my daughter—

---

5. Unmerited and unpaid-for arrogance; "pride" may also refer to Oswald's fine clothing received for his services to Gonoril.
6. Chest, where Lear's heart is swelling with emotion.
7. Deserved far worse treatment.

8. *To wage . . . pinch:* To counter the harshness of the elements with the hardness brought on by necessity. *pinch:* stress, pressure. Oxford has transposed lines 361 and 362.

REGAN   Good sir, to th' purpose.°   *get to the point*

LEAR   Who put my man i'th' stocks?

       Tucket within

CORNWALL   What trumpet's that?

       Enter Steward [OSWALD]

REGAN   I know't, my sister's. This approves° her letter   *confirms*

     That she would soon be here. [*To* OSWALD] Is your lady come?

350   LEAR   This is a slave whose easy-borrowed pride[2]

     Dwells in the sickly grace of her a° follows.   *he*

     [*To* OSWALD] Out, varlet,° from my sight!   *wretch*

CORNWALL   What means your grace?

       Enter GONERIL

LEAR   Who stocked my servant? Regan, I have good hope

     Thou didst not know on't.° Who comes here? O heavens,   *of it*

355   If you do love old men, if your sweet sway

     Allow obedience, if you yourselves are old,

     Make it your cause! Send down and take my part.

     [*To* GONERIL] Art not ashamed to look upon this beard?

     O Regan, will you take her by the hand?

360   GONERIL   Why not by th' hand, sir? How have I offended?

     All's not offence that indiscretion finds

     And dotage terms so.

LEAR   O sides,[3] you are too tough!

     Will you yet hold? — How came my man i'th' stocks?

CORNWALL   I set him there, sir; but his own disorders°   *disorderly behavior*

     Deserved much less advancement.[4]

365   LEAR   You? Did you?

REGAN   I pray you, father, being weak, seem so.°   *behave so*

     If till the expiration of your month

     You will return and sojourn with my sister,

     Dismissing half your train, come then to me.

370   I am now from home, and out of that provision

     Which shall be needful for your entertainment.

LEAR   Return to her, and fifty men dismissed?

     No, rather I abjure all roofs, and choose

     To be a comrade with the wolf and owl,

375   To wage against the enmity o'th' air

     Necessity's sharp pinch.[5] Return with her?

     Why, the hot-blooded France, that dowerless took

     Our youngest born — I could as well be brought

     To knee° his throne and, squire-like, pension beg   *kneel to*

380   To keep base life afoot. Return with her?

     Persuade me rather to be slave and sumpter°   *pack horse*

     To this detested groom.°   *(Oswald)*

GONERIL   At your choice, sir.

LEAR   I prithee, daughter, do not make me mad.

     I will not trouble thee, my child. Farewell.

385   We'll no more meet, no more see one another.

     But yet thou art my flesh, my blood, my daughter —

---

2. Unmerited and unpaid-for arrogance; "pride" may also refer to Oswald's fine clothing received for his services to Goneril.
3. Chest, where Lear's heart is swelled with emotion.
4. Deserved far worse treatment.

5. *To wage . . . pinch:* To counter the harshness of the elements with the hardness brought on by necessity. *pinch:* stress, pressure. Oxford has transposed lines 375 and 376.

Or rather a disease that lies within my flesh,
375 Which I must needs call mine. Thou art a boil,
A plague-sore, an embossèd° carbuncle   *a swollen*
In my corrupted blood. But I'll not chide thee.
Let shame come when it will, I do not call° it.   *call upon*
I do not bid the thunder-bearer° shoot,   *(Jove)*
380 Nor tell tales of thee to high-judging Jove.
Mend° when thou canst; be better at thy leisure.   *Make amends*
I can be patient, I can stay with Regan,
I and my hundred knights.

REGAN   Not altogether so, sir.
I look not for° you yet, nor am provided   *I did not expect*
385 For your fit welcome. Give ear, sir, to my sister;
For those that mingle reason with your passion[9]
Must be content to think you are old, and so—
But she knows what she does.

LEAR   Is this well° spoken now?   *earnestly*

REGAN   I dare avouch° it, sir. What, fifty followers?   *vouch for*
390 Is it not well? What should you need of more,
Yea, or so many, sith° that both charge° and danger   *since / expense*
Speaks 'gainst so great a number? How in a house
Should many people under two commands
Hold amity? 'Tis hard, almost impossible.

395 GONORIL   Why might not you, my lord, receive attendance
From those that she calls servants, or from mine?

REGAN   Why not, my lord? If then they chanced to slack° you,   *neglect*
We could control them. If you will come to me—
For now I spy a danger—I entreat you
400 To bring but five-and-twenty; to no more
Will I give place or notice.°   *acknowledgment*

LEAR   I gave you all.

REGAN   And in good time° you gave it.   *it was about time*

LEAR   Made you my guardians, my depositaries,°   *trustees*
405 But kept a reservation° to be followed   *reserved a right*
With such a number. What, must I come to you
With five-and-twenty, Regan? Said you so?

REGAN   And speak't again, my lord. No more with me.

LEAR   Those wicked creatures yet do seem well favoured°   *attractive*
410 When others are more wicked. Not being the worst
Stands in some rank of praise.[1] [*To* GONORIL] I'll go with thee.
Thy fifty yet doth double five-and-twenty,
And thou art twice her love.

GONORIL   Hear me, my lord.
What need you five-and-twenty, ten, or five,
415 To follow in a house where twice so many
Have a command to tend you?

REGAN   What needs one?

LEAR   O, reason not the need! Our basest beggars
Are in the poorest thing superfluous.[2]
Allow not° nature more than nature needs,   *If you don't allow*
420 Man's life is cheap as beast's. Thou art a lady.

9. For those who temper your passionate argument with
their own calm reasoning.
1. Deserves some degree ("rank") of praise.

2. *Our . . . superfluous:* Even the lowliest beggars have
something more than the barest minimum.

Or rather a disease that's in my flesh,
Which I must needs call mine. Thou art a boil,
A plague-sore or embossèd° carbuncle   *swollen*
390 In my corrupted blood. But I'll not chide thee.
Let shame come when it will, I do not call° it.   *call upon*
I do not bid the thunder-bearer° shoot,   *(Jove)*
Nor tell tales of thee to high-judging Jove.
Mend° when thou canst; be better at thy leisure.   *Make amends*
395 I can be patient, I can stay with Regan,
I and my hundred knights.
REGAN   Not altogether so.
I looked not for° you yet, nor am provided   *I did not expect*
For your fit welcome. Give ear, sir, to my sister;
For those that mingle reason with your passion[6]
400 Must be content to think you old, and so—
But she knows what she does.
LEAR   Is this well° spoken?   *earnestly*
REGAN   I dare avouch° it, sir. What, fifty followers?   *vouch for*
Is it not well? What should you need of more,
Yea, or so many, sith° that both charge° and danger   *since / expense*
405 Speak 'gainst so great a number? How in one house
Should many people under two commands
Hold amity? 'Tis hard, almost impossible.
GONERIL   Why might not you, my lord, receive attendance
From those that she calls servants, or from mine?
410 REGAN   Why not, my lord? If then they chanced to slack° ye,   *neglect*
We could control them. If you will come to me—
For now I spy a danger—I entreat you
To bring but five and twenty; to no more
Will I give place or notice.°   *acknowledgment*
415 LEAR   I gave you all.
REGAN   And in good time° you gave it.   *it was about time*
LEAR   Made you my guardians, my depositaries,°   *trustees*
But kept a reservation° to be followed   *reserved a right*
With such a number. What, must I come to you
420 With five and twenty? Regan, said you so?
REGAN   And speak't again, my lord. No more with me.
LEAR   Those wicked creatures yet do look well favoured°   *attractive*
When others are more wicked. Not being the worst
Stands in some rank of praise.[7] [*To* GONERIL] I'll go with thee.
425 Thy fifty yet doth double five and twenty,
And thou art twice her love.
GONERIL   Hear me, my lord.
What need you five and twenty, ten, or five,
To follow in a house where twice so many
Have a command to tend you?
REGAN   What need one?
430 LEAR   O, reason not the need! Our basest beggars
Are in the poorest thing superfluous.[8]
Allow not° nature more than nature needs,   *If you don't allow*
Man's life is cheap as beast's. Thou art a lady.

6. For those who temper your passionate argument with   8. *Our . . . superfluous:* Even the lowliest beggars have
their own calm reasoning.   something more than the barest minimum.
7. Deserves some degree ("rank") of praise.

If only to go warm were gorgeous,
Why, nature needs not what thou, gorgeous, wearest,
Which scarcely keeps thee warm.³ But for true need—
You heavens, give me that patience,° patience I need.   *endurance*
425 You see me here, you gods, a poor old fellow,
As full of grief as age, wretchèd in both.
If it be you that stirs these daughters' hearts
Against their father, fool me not so much
To bear it tamely.⁴ Touch me with noble anger.
430 O, let not women's weapons, water-drops,
Stain my man's cheeks! No, you unnatural hags,
I will have such revenges on you both
That all the world shall—I will do such things—
What they are, yet I know not; but they shall be
435 The terrors of the earth. You think I'll weep.
No, I'll not weep.
                    [*Storm within*]
I have full cause of weeping, but this heart
Shall break into a hundred thousand flaws°   *fragments*
Or ere° I'll weep.—O fool, I shall go mad!   *Before*
        Exeunt LEAR, [GLOUCESTER,] KENT, [KNIGHT,] *and* FOOL
440 CORNWALL   Let us withdraw. 'Twill be a storm.
REGAN   This house is little. The old man and his people
    Cannot be well bestowed.°   *lodged*
GONORIL   'Tis his own blame;
    Hath put himself from° rest, and must needs taste his folly.   *deprived himself of*
REGAN   For his particular° I'll receive him gladly,   *single self*
445 But not one follower.
CORNWALL   So am I purposed. Where is my lord of Gloucester?
REGAN   Followed the old man forth.
        Enter GLOUCESTER
                        He is returned.
GLOUCESTER   The King is in high rage, and will I know not whither.
REGAN   'Tis good to give him way. He leads himself.
450 GONORIL [*to* GLOUCESTER]   My lord, entreat him by no means to stay.
GLOUCESTER   Alack, the night comes on, and the bleak winds
    Do sorely rustle. For many miles about
    There's not a bush.
REGAN   O sir, to wilful men
    The injuries that they themselves procure
455 Must be their schoolmasters. Shut up your doors.
    He is attended with a desperate° train,   *violent*
    And what they may incense° him to, being apt   *incite*
    To have his ear abused,° wisdom bids fear.   *deceived*
CORNWALL   Shut up your doors, my lord. 'Tis a wild night.
460 My Regan counsels well. Come out o'th' storm.   *Exeunt*

---

3. *If . . . thee warm:* If gorgeousness in clothes is mea-   4. *fool . . . tamely:* do not make me so foolish as to accept
sured by the warmth they provide, your elaborate clothes   it meekly.
are superfluous, for they barely cover your body.

If only to go warm were gorgeous,
435 Why, nature needs not what thou, gorgeous, wear'st,
Which scarcely keeps thee warm.⁹ But for true need—
You heavens, give me that patience,° patience I need.   *endurance*
You see me here, you gods, a poor old man,
As full of grief as age, wretchèd in both.
440 If it be you that stirs these daughters' hearts
Against their father, fool me not so much
To bear it tamely.¹ Touch me with noble anger,
And let not women's weapons, water-drops,
Stain my man's cheeks. No, you unnatural hags,
445 I will have such revenges on you both
That all the world shall—I will do such things—
What they are, yet I know not; but they shall be
The terrors of the earth. You think I'll weep.
No, I'll not weep. I have full cause of weeping,
          Storm and tempest
450 But this heart shall break into a hundred thousand flaws°   *fragments*
Or ere° I'll weep.—O Fool, I shall go mad!   *Before*
          Exeunt [LEAR, FOOL, GENTLEMAN, *and* GLOUCESTER]
CORNWALL   Let us withdraw. 'Twill be a storm.
REGAN   This house is little. The old man and 's people
Cannot be well bestowed.°   *lodged*
GONERIL   'Tis his own blame;
455 Hath put himself from° rest, and must needs taste his folly.   *deprived himself of*
REGAN   For his particular° I'll receive him gladly,   *single self*
But not one follower.
GONERIL   So am I purposed.
Where is my lord of Gloucester?
CORNWALL   Followed the old man forth.
          Enter GLOUCESTER
                    He is returned.
GLOUCESTER   The King is in high rage.
460 CORNWALL   Whither is he going?
GLOUCESTER   He calls to horse, but will I know not whither.
CORNWALL   'Tis best to give him way. He leads himself.
GONERIL [*to* GLOUCESTER]   My lord, entreat him by no means to stay.
GLOUCESTER   Alack, the night comes on, and the high winds
465 Do sorely ruffle.° For many miles about   *bluster*
There's scarce a bush.
REGAN   O sir, to wilful men
The injuries that they themselves procure
Must be their schoolmasters. Shut up your doors.
He is attended with a desperate° train,   *violent*
470 And what they may incense° him to, being apt   *incite*
To have his ear abused,° wisdom bids fear.   *deceived*
CORNWALL   Shut up your doors, my lord. 'Tis a wild night.
My Regan counsels well. Come out o'th' storm.   *Exeunt*

9. *If . . . thee warm:* If gorgeousness in clothes is mea-   1. *fool . . . tamely:* do not make me so foolish as to accept
sured by the warmth they provide, your elaborate clothes   it meekly.
are superfluous, for they barely cover your body.

Scene 8

[*Storm.*] *Enter* KENT [*disguised,*] *and* [FIRST] GENTLE-
MAN, *at several doors*

KENT   What's here, beside foul weather?

FIRST GENTLEMAN   One minded like the weather,
    Most unquietly.

KENT   I know you. Where's the King?

FIRST GENTLEMAN   Contending with the fretful element;
    Bids the wind blow the earth into the sea

5   Or swell the curlèd waters 'bove the main,°   *mainland*
    That things might change or cease; tears his white hair,
    Which the impetuous blasts, with eyeless rage,
    Catch in their fury and make nothing of;
    Strives in his little world of man to outstorm

10   The to-and-fro-conflicting wind and rain.
    This night, wherein the cub-drawn bear would couch,[1]
    The lion and the belly-pinchèd wolf
    Keep their fur dry, unbonneted° he runs,   *hatless; uncrowned*
    And bids what will take all.

KENT   But who is with him?

15 FIRST GENTLEMAN   None but the fool, who labours to outjest
    His heart-struck injuries.[2]

KENT   Sir, I do know you,
    And dare upon the warrant of my art[3]
    Commend a dear° thing to you. There is division,   *Entrust a crucial*
    Although as yet the face of it be covered

20   With mutual cunning, 'twixt Albany and Cornwall;
    But true it is. From France there comes a power
    Into this scattered kingdom, who already,
    Wise in° our negligence, have secret feet   *Aware of*
    In some of our best ports, and are at point°   *ready*

25   To show their open banner. Now to you:
    If on my credit you dare build° so far   *If you trust me*
    To make your speed to Dover, you shall find
    Some that will thank you, making just° report   *accurate*
    Of how unnatural and bemadding° sorrow   *maddening*

30   The King hath cause to plain.°   *complain*
    I am a gentleman of blood and breeding,
    And from some knowledge and assurance offer
    This office° to you.   *role; duty*

FIRST GENTLEMAN   I will talk farther with you.

35 KENT   No, do not.
    For confirmation that I am much more
    Than my out-wall,° open this purse, and take   *outward appearance*
    What it contains. If you shall see Cordelia—
    As fear not but you shall—show her this ring

40   And she will tell you who your fellow° is,   *(Kent himself)*

Scene 8 Location: Bare, open country.
1. In which even the bear, though starving, having been
sucked dry ("drawn") by its cub, would not go out to
forage.

2. *to outjest:* to relieve with laughter; to exorcise through
ridicule. *heart-struck injuries:* injuries (from the betrayal
of his paternal love) that penetrated to the heart.
3. On the basis of my skill (at judging people).

3.1

Storm still. Enter KENT *[disguised] and [the* FIRST*]* GEN-
TLEMAN, *severally*

KENT   Who's there, besides foul weather?
FIRST GENTLEMAN   One minded like the weather,
    Most unquietly.
KENT   I know you. Where's the King?
FIRST GENTLEMAN   Contending with the fretful elements;
    Bids the wind blow the earth into the sea
5   Or swell the curlèd waters 'bove the main,°   *mainland*
    That things might change or cease.

KENT   But who is with him?
FIRST GENTLEMAN   None but the Fool, who labours to outjest
    His heart-struck injuries.[1]
KENT   Sir, I do know you,
    And dare upon the warrant of my note[2]
10   Commend a dear° thing to you. There is division,   *Entrust a crucial*
    Although as yet the face of it is covered
    With mutual cunning, 'twixt Albany and Cornwall,
    Who have—as who have not that their great stars
    Throned and set high[3]—servants, who seem no less,°   *who appear as such*
15   Which are to France the spies and speculations°   *observers*
    Intelligent of[4] our state. What hath been seen,
    Either in snuffs and packings° of the Dukes,   *quarrels and plots*
    Or the hard rein° which both of them hath borne   *treatment*
    Against the old kind King; or something deeper,
20   Whereof perchance these are but furnishings°—   *pretexts*

FIRST GENTLEMAN   I will talk further with you.
KENT   No, do not.
    For confirmation that I am much more
    Than my out-wall,° open this purse, and take   *outward appearance*
    What it contains. If you shall see Cordelia—
25   As fear not but you shall—show her this ring
    And she will tell you who that fellow° is   *(Kent himself)*

3.1 Location: Bare, open country.
1. *to outjest:* to relieve with laughter; to exorcise through ridicule. *heart-struck injuries:* injuries (from the betrayal of his paternal love) that penetrated to the heart.

2. On the basis of my skill (at judging people).
3. *as . . . high:* as has everybody who has been favored by destiny.
4. Supplying intelligence about; too well informed of.

That yet you do not know. Fie on this storm!
I will go seek the King.
FIRST GENTLEMAN   Give me your hand.
Have you no more to say?
KENT   Few words, but to effect°   *but in importance*
More than all yet: that when we have found the King—
45   In which endeavour I'll° this way, you that—   *I'll go*
He that first lights on him holla the other.   *Exeunt severally*

Scene 9

[*Storm.*] *Enter* LEAR *and* FOOL
LEAR   Blow, wind, and crack your cheeks! Rage, blow,
     You cataracts and hurricanoes,[1] spout
     Till you have drenched the steeples, drowned the cocks!°   *weather vanes*
     You sulphurous and thought-executing fires,[2]
5   Vaunt-couriers° to oak-cleaving thunderbolts,   *Forerunners*
     Singe my white head; and thou all-shaking thunder,
     Smite flat the thick rotundity of the world,
     Crack nature's mould, all germens° spill at once   *seeds*
     That make ingrateful man.
10   FOOL   O nuncle, court holy water[3] in a dry house is better than
     this rain-water out o' door. Good nuncle, in, and ask thy daugh-
     ters blessing. Here's a night pities neither wise man nor fool.
     LEAR   Rumble thy bellyful; spit, fire; spout, rain.
     Nor rain, wind, thunder, fire are my daughters.
15   I tax° not you, you elements, with unkindness.   *blame*
     I never gave you kingdom, called you children.
     You owe me no subscription.° Why then, let fall   *obedience, allegiance*
     Your horrible pleasure. Here I stand your slave,
     A poor, infirm, weak and despised old man,
20   But yet I call you servile ministers,°   *agents*
     That have with two pernicious daughters joined
     Your high engendered battle° 'gainst a head   *heaven-bred forces*
     So old and white as this. O, 'tis foul!
     FOOL   He that has a house to put his head in has a good
25   headpiece.°   *hat; brain*
     [*Sings*]   The codpiece that will house
                              Before the head has any,
                         The head and he shall louse,
                              So beggars marry many.[4]
30   The man that makes his toe
                              What he his heart should make
                         Shall have a corn cry woe,
                              And turn his sleep to wake[5]—
     for there was never yet fair woman but she made mouths in a
35   glass.[6]

Scene 9 Location: As before.
1. *cataracts*: floodgates of the heavens. *hurricanoes*: water-spouts (water from both sky and sea).
2. *thought-executing fires*: lightning that strikes as swiftly as thought.
3. Sprinkled blessings of a courtier, flattery.
4. *The codpiece . . . many*: Whoever finds his penis a lodging before providing shelter for his head will end up in lice-infested poverty and live in married beggary. *cod-piece*: a pouchlike covering for the male genitals, often

conspicuous, particularly in the costume of a fool.
5. *The man . . . wake*: The man who values an inferior part of his body over the part that is truly valuable (as Lear privileged Gonoril and Regan over Cordelia) will suffer from and lose sleep over that inferior part.
6. She practiced making pretty faces in a mirror. The Fool probably refers to Regan's and Gonoril's vanity, or the line may be thrown in to soften the harshness of his satire.

That yet you do not know. Fie on this storm!
I will go seek the King.

FIRST GENTLEMAN   Give me your hand. Have you no more to say?

30 KENT   Few words, but to effect° more than all yet: *but in importance*
That when we have found the King—in which your pain
That way, I'll this⁵—he that first lights on him
Holla the other.   *Exeunt [severally]*

3.2

Storm still. Enter LEAR *and* FOOL

LEAR   Blow, winds, and crack your cheeks! Rage, blow,
You cataracts and hurricanoes,¹ spout
Till you have drenched our steeples, drowned the cocks!°   *weather vanes*
You sulph'rous and thought-executing fires,²
5   Vaunt-couriers° of oak-cleaving thunderbolts,   *Forerunners*
Singe my white head; and thou all-shaking thunder,
Strike flat the thick rotundity o'th' world,
Crack nature's moulds, all germens° spill at once   *seeds*
That makes ingrateful man.

10 FOOL   O nuncle, court holy water³ in a dry house is better than
this rain-water out o' door. Good nuncle, in, ask thy daughters
blessing. Here's a night pities neither wise men nor fools.

LEAR   Rumble thy bellyful; spit, fire; spout, rain.
Nor rain, wind, thunder, fire are my daughters.
15 I tax° not you, you elements, with unkindness.   *blame*
I never gave you kingdom, called you children.
You owe me no subscription.° Then let fall   *obedience, allegiance*
Your horrible pleasure. Here I stand your slave,
A poor, infirm, weak and despised old man,
20 But yet I call you servile ministers,°   *agents*
That will with two pernicious daughters join
Your high-engendered battles° 'gainst a head   *heaven-bred forces*
So old and white as this. O, ho, 'tis foul!

FOOL   He that has a house to put 's head in has a good
25 headpiece.°   *hat; brain*
[*Sings*]   The codpiece that will house
Before the head has any,
The head and he shall louse,
So beggars marry many.⁴
30   The man that makes his toe
What he his heart should make
Shall of a corn cry woe,
And turn his sleep to wake⁵—
for there was never yet fair woman but she made mouths in a
35 glass.⁶

---

5. *in which ... this*: in which effort you will go that way
and I this way.
3.2 Location: As before.
1. *cataracts*: floodgates of the heavens. *hurricanoes*: water-
spouts (water from both sky and sea).
2. *thought-executing fires*: lightning that strikes as swiftly
as thought.
3. Sprinkled blessings of a courtier; flattery.
4. *The codpiece ... many*: Whoever finds his penis a
lodging before providing shelter for his head will end up
in lice-infested poverty and live in married beggary. *cod-*

piece: a pouchlike covering for the male genitals, often
conspicuous, particularly in the costume of a fool.
5. *The man ... wake*: The man who values an inferior
part of his body over the part that is truly valuable (as Lear
privileged Goneril and Regan over Cordelia) will suffer
from and lose sleep over that inferior part.
6. She practiced making pretty faces in a mirror. The
Fool probably refers to Regan's and Goneril's vanity, or
the line may be thrown in to soften the harshness of his
satire.

LEAR   No, I will be the pattern of all patience.
        [He sits.] Enter KENT *[disguised]*
  I will say nothing.
KENT   Who's there?
FOOL   Marry, here's grace and a codpiece—that's a wise man
40   and a fool.⁷
KENT *[to* LEAR*]*   Alas, sir, sit you here? Things that love night
  Love not such nights as these. The wrathful skies
  Gallow° the very wanderers of the dark   *Frighten*
  And makes them keep° their caves. Since I was man   *keep inside*
45 Such sheets of fire, such bursts of horrid thunder,
  Such groans of roaring wind and rain I ne'er
  Remember to have heard. Man's nature cannot carry°   *bear*
  The affliction nor the force.
LEAR   Let the great gods,
  That keep this dreadful pother° o'er our heads,   *commotion*
50 Find out their enemies now. Tremble, thou wretch
  That hast within thee undivulgèd crimes
  Unwhipped of° justice; hide thee, thou bloody hand,   *Unpunished by*
  Thou perjured and thou simular° man of virtue   *simulating; pretending*
  That art incestuous; caitiff,° in pieces shake,   *wretch*
55 That under covert and convenient seeming°   *fitting hypocrisy*
  Hast practised on° man's life;   *against*
  Close° pent-up guilts, rive° your concealèd centres   *Secret / split open*
  And cry these dreadful summoners grace.⁸
  I am a man more sinned against than sinning.
60 KENT   Alack, bare-headed?
  Gracious my lord, hard by here is a hovel.
  Some friendship will it lend you 'gainst the tempest.
  Repose you there whilst I to this hard house—
  More hard than is the stone whereof 'tis raised,
65 Which° even but now, demanding° after you,   *Who / I demanding*
  Denied me to come in—return and force
  Their scanted° courtesy.   *niggardly*
LEAR   My wit begins to turn.
  [To FOOL*]* Come on, my boy. How dost, my boy? Art cold?
  I am cold myself.—Where is this straw, my fellow?
70 The art° of our necessities is strange,   *skill; alchemy*
  That can make vile things precious. Come, your hovel.—
  Poor fool and knave, I have one part of my heart
  That sorrows yet for thee.
FOOL *[sings]*⁹ He that has a little tiny wit,°   *sense*
75   With heigh-ho, the wind and the rain,
           Must make content with his fortunes fit,
           For the rain it raineth every day.
LEAR   True, my good boy. *[To* KENT*]* Come, bring us to this hovel.
                        [Exeunt]

---

7. The supposedly wise King is symbolized by royal grace, the Fool by his codpiece (here, slang for "penis"). The Fool speaks ironically: the King, as he has pointed out, is now the foolish one. *Marry:* By the Virgin Mary (a mild oath).

8. And pray for mercy from these elements that bring you to justice.
9. The following song is an adaptation of one sung by Feste at the end of *Twelfth Night*.

Enter KENT [*disguised*]

LEAR No, I will be the pattern of all patience.
I will say nothing.

KENT Who's there?

FOOL Marry, here's grace and a codpiece—that's a wise man
40 and a fool.[7]

KENT [*to* LEAR] Alas, sir, are you here? Things that love night
Love not such nights as these. The wrathful skies
Gallow° the very wanderers of the dark   *Frighten*
And make them keep° their caves. Since I was man   *keep inside*
45 Such sheets of fire, such bursts of horrid thunder,
Such groans of roaring wind and rain I never
Remember to have heard. Man's nature cannot carry°   *bear*
Th'affliction nor the fear.

LEAR   Let the great gods,
That keep this dreadful pother° o'er our heads,   *commotion*
50 Find out their enemies now. Tremble, thou wretch
That hast within thee undivulgèd crimes
Unwhipped of° justice; hide thee, thou bloody hand,   *Unpunished by*
Thou perjured and thou simular° of virtue   *simulator; pretender*
That art incestuous; caitiff,° to pieces shake,   *wretch*
55 That under covert and convenient seeming°   *fitting hypocrisy*
Has practised on° man's life; close° pent-up guilts,   *against / secret*
Rive° your concealing continents° and cry   *Split open / coverings*
These dreadful summoners grace.[8] I am a man
More sinned against than sinning.

KENT   Alack, bare-headed?
60 Gracious my lord, hard by here is a hovel.
Some friendship will it lend you 'gainst the tempest.
Repose you there while I to this hard house—
More harder than the stones whereof 'tis raised,
Which° even but now, demanding° after you,   *Who / I demanding*
65 Denied me to come in—return and force
Their scanted° courtesy.   *niggardly*

LEAR   My wits begin to turn.
[*To* FOOL] Come on, my boy. How dost, my boy? Art cold?
I am cold myself.—Where is this straw, my fellow?
The art° of our necessities is strange,   *skill; alchemy*
70 And can make vile things precious. Come, your hovel.—
Poor fool and knave, I have one part in my heart
That's sorry yet for thee.

FOOL [*Sings*][9] He that has and° a little tiny wit,°   *even / sense*
With heigh-ho, the wind and the rain,
75 Must make content with his fortunes fit,
Though the rain it raineth every day.

LEAR True, boy. [*To* KENT] Come, bring us to this hovel.

Exeunt [LEAR *and* KENT]

---

7. The supposedly wise King is symbolized by royal grace, the Fool by his codpiece (here, slang for "penis"). The Fool speaks ironically: the King, as he has pointed out, is now the foolish one. *Marry:* By the Virgin Mary (a mild oath).

8. *and cry . . . grace:* and pray for mercy from these elements that bring you to justice.
9. The following song is an adaptation of one sung by Feste at the end of *Twelfth Night.*

Scene 10

Enter GLOUCESTER *and the Bastard* [EDMUND], *with
lights*

GLOUCESTER   Alack, alack, Edmund, I like not this
Unnatural dealing. When I desired their leave
That I might pity° him, they took from me   *relieve*
The use of mine own house, charged me on pain
5   Of their displeasure neither to speak of him,
Entreat for him, nor any way sustain him.
EDMUND   Most savage and unnatural!
GLOUCESTER   Go to,° say you nothing. There's a division betwixt   *(an expletive)*
the Dukes, and a worse matter than that. I have received a
10   letter this night—'tis dangerous to be spoken— I have locked
the letter in my closet.° These injuries the King now bears will   *private chamber*
be revenged home.° There's part of a power° already landed.   *to the hilt / an army*
We must incline to¹ the King. I will seek him and privily°   *secretly, privately*
relieve him. Go you and maintain talk with the Duke, that my
15   charity be not of him perceived. If he ask for me, I am ill and
gone to bed. Though I die for't—as no less is threatened me—
the King my old master must be relieved. There is some strange
thing toward.° Edmund, pray you be careful.   *Exit*   *coming*
EDMUND   This courtesy,° forbid° thee, shall the Duke   *act of kindness / forbidden*
20   Instantly know, and of that letter too.
This seems a fair deserving,² and must draw me
That which my father loses: no less than all.
The younger rises when the old do fall.   *Exit*

Scene 10 Location: At Gloucester's castle.   2. This seems an action that deserves to be rewarded.
1. We must take the side of.

FOOL   This is a brave night to cool a courtesan.[1] I'll speak a
    prophecy ere I go:[2]

80
      When priests are more in word than matter;°   *real virtue*
      When brewers mar their malt with water;
      When nobles are their tailors' tutors,[3]
      No heretics burned, but wenches' suitors,[4]
      Then shall the realm of Albion°   *Britain*
85
      Come to great confusion.°   *decay*

      When every case in law is right;°   *just*
      No squire in debt nor no poor knight;
      When slanders do not live in tongues,
      Nor cutpurses° come not to throngs;   *pickpockets*
90
      When usurers tell their gold i'th' field,[5]
      And bawds and whores do churches build,
      Then comes the time, who lives to see't,
      That going° shall be used° with feet.   *walking / practiced*
    This prophecy Merlin shall make; for I live before his time.[6]
                                                       Exit

3.3

Enter GLOUCESTER *and* EDMOND

GLOUCESTER   Alack, alack, Edmond, I like not this unnatural
    dealing. When I desired their leave that I might pity° him, they   *relieve*
    took from me the use of mine own house, charged me on pain
    of perpetual displeasure neither to speak of him, entreat for
5   him, or any way sustain him.
EDMOND   Most savage and unnatural!
GLOUCESTER   Go to,° say you nothing. There is division between   *(an expletive)*
    the Dukes, and a worse matter than that. I have received a
    letter this night—'tis dangerous to be spoken— I have locked
10   the letter in my closet.° These injuries the King now bears will   *private chamber*
    be revenged home.° There is part of a power already footed.[1]   *to the hilt*
    We must incline to[2] the King. I will look° him and privily°   *seek / secretly, privately*
    relieve him. Go you and maintain talk with the Duke, that my
    charity be not of him perceived. If he ask for me, I am ill and
15   gone to bed. If I die for't—as no less is threatened me—the
    King my old master must be relieved. There is strange things
    toward,° Edmond; pray you be careful.   *Exit*   *coming*
EDMOND   This courtesy,° forbid° thee, shall the Duke   *act of kindness / forbidden*
    Instantly know, and of that letter too.
20   This seems a fair deserving,[3] and must draw me
    That which my father loses: no less than all.
    The younger rises when the old doth fall.   *Exit*

---

1. To cool even the hot lusts of a prostitute.
2. What follows is a parody of the pseudo-Chaucerian "Merlin's Prophecy" from *Arte of English Poesie*. In F, lines 84–85 follow line 91.
3. When noblemen follow fashion more closely than their tailors do.
4. When the only heretics burned are faithless lovers, who burn from venereal disease.
5. When usurers can count their profits openly (because

they have no shady dealings to hide).
6. Merlin was the great wizard at the legendary court of King Arthur. Lear's Britain is set in an even more distant past.
3.3 Location: At Gloucester's castle.
1. Part of an army already landed.
2. We must take the side of.
3. This seems an action that deserves to be rewarded.

Scene 11

[Storm.] Enter LEAR, KENT *[disguised], and* FOOL

KENT   Here is the place, my lord. Good my lord, enter.
The tyranny of the open night's too rough
For nature° to endure.   *human weakness*

LEAR   Let me alone.

KENT   Good my lord, enter here.

LEAR   Wilt break my heart?

5   KENT   I had rather break mine own. Good my lord, enter.

LEAR   Thou think'st 'tis much that this contentious storm
Invades us to the skin. So 'tis to thee;
But where the greater malady is fixed,°   *rooted*
The lesser is scarce felt. Thou'dst shun a bear,
10   But if thy flight lay toward the roaring sea
Thou'dst meet the bear i'th' mouth. When the mind's free,°   *unburdened*
The body's delicate.° This tempest in my mind   *sensitive*
Doth from my senses take all feeling else
Save° what beats there: filial ingratitude.   *Except*
15   Is it not as° this mouth should tear this hand   *as if*
For lifting food to't? But I will punish sure.
No, I will weep no more.—
In such a night as this! O Regan, Gonoril,
Your old kind father, whose frank heart gave you all—
20   O, that way madness lies. Let me shun that.
No more of that.

KENT   Good my lord, enter.

LEAR   Prithee, go in thyself. Seek thy own ease.
This tempest will not give me leave to° ponder   *allow me to*
On things would hurt me more; but I'll go in.   *[Exit* FOOL*]*
25   Poor naked wretches, wheresoe'er you are,
That bide° the pelting of this pitiless night,   *endure; dwell in*
How shall your houseless heads and unfed sides,°   *starved ribs*
Your looped and windowed[1] raggedness, defend you
From seasons such as these? O, I have ta'en
30   Too little care of this. Take physic, pomp,[2]
Expose thyself to feel what wretches feel,
That thou mayst shake the superflux[3] to them
And show the heavens more just.
      [Enter FOOL*]*

FOOL   Come not in here, nuncle; here's a spirit. Help me, help
35   me!

KENT   Give me thy hand. Who's there?

FOOL   A spirit. He says his name's Poor Tom.

KENT   What art thou that dost grumble there in the straw?
Come forth.

Scene 11 Location: Open country, before a cattle shed.
1. *looped and windowed*: full of holes and vents; "windowed" could also refer to cloth worn through to semi-
transparency, like the oilcloth window "panes" of the
poor.

2. Cure yourself, pompous person.
3. Superfluity; bodily discharge, suggested by "physic"
(which also has the meaning of "purgative") in line 30.
Excess here is also excess of wealth.

3.4

Enter LEAR, KENT [*disguised*], *and* FOOL

KENT   Here is the place, my lord. Good my lord, enter.
The tyranny of the open night's too rough
For nature° to endure.   *human weakness*
       Storm still

LEAR   Let me alone.

KENT   Good my lord, enter here.

LEAR   Wilt break my heart?

5   KENT   I had rather break mine own. Good my lord, enter.

LEAR   Thou think'st 'tis much that this contentious storm
Invades us to the skin. So 'tis to thee;
But where the greater malady is fixed,°   *rooted*
The lesser is scarce felt. Thou'dst shun a bear,
10   But if thy flight lay toward the roaring sea
Thou'dst meet the bear i'th' mouth. When the mind's free,°   *unburdened*
The body's delicate.° This tempest in my mind   *sensitive*
Doth from my senses take all feeling else
Save° what beats there: filial ingratitude.   *Except*
15   Is it not as° this mouth should tear this hand   *as if*
For lifting food to't? But I will punish home.°   *thoroughly*
No, I will weep no more.—In such a night
To shut me out? Pour on, I will endure.
In such a night as this! O Regan, Goneril,
20   Your old kind father, whose frank heart gave all—
O, that way madness lies. Let me shun that.
No more of that.

KENT   Good my lord, enter here.

LEAR   Prithee, go in thyself. Seek thine own ease.
This tempest will not give me leave to° ponder   *allow me to*
25   On things would hurt me more; but I'll go in.
[*To* FOOL] In, boy; go first. [*Kneeling*] You houseless poverty°—   *poor*
Nay, get thee in. I'll pray, and then I'll sleep.   *Exit* [FOOL]
Poor naked wretches, wheresoe'er you are,
That bide° the pelting of this pitiless storm,   *endure; dwell in*
30   How shall your houseless heads and unfed sides,°   *starved ribs*
Your looped and windowed[1] raggedness, defend you
From seasons such as these? O, I have ta'en
Too little care of this. Take physic, pomp,[2]
Expose thyself to feel what wretches feel,
35   That thou mayst shake the superflux[3] to them
And show the heavens more just.
       Enter FOOL, *and* EDGAR [*as a Bedlam beggar in the*
       hovel]

EDGAR   Fathom and half![4] Fathom and half! Poor Tom!

FOOL   Come not in here, nuncle. Here's a spirit. Help me, help
me!

40   KENT   Give my thy hand. Who's there?

FOOL   A spirit, a spirit. He says his name's Poor Tom.

KENT   What art thou that dost grumble there i'th' straw?
Come forth.

3.4 Location: Open country, before a cattle shed.
1. *looped and windowed*: full of holes and vents; "windowed" could also refer to cloth worn through to semi-transparency, like the oilcloth window "panes" of the poor.
2. Cure yourself, pompous person.

3. Superfluity; bodily discharge, suggested by "physic" (which also has the meaning of "purgative") in line 33. Excess here is also excess of wealth.
4. "Nine feet," a sailor's cry when taking soundings to gauge the depth of water.

[*Enter* EDGAR *as a Bedlam beggar*]

40 EDGAR Away, the foul fiend follows me. Through the sharp hawthorn blows the cold wind.[4] Go to thy cold bed and warm
thee.[5]

LEAR Hast thou given all to thy two daughters,
And art thou come to this?

45 EDGAR Who gives anything to Poor Tom, whom the foul fiend
hath led through fire and through ford and whirlypool, o'er bog
and quagmire; that has laid knives under his pillow and halters
in his pew, set ratsbane by his potage,[6] made him proud of
heart to ride on a bay trotting-horse over four-inched bridges,[7]
50 to course° his own shadow for° a traitor. Bless thy five wits,[8]   hunt / as
Tom's a-cold! Bless thee from whirlwinds, star-blasting, and taking.[9] Do Poor Tom some charity, whom the foul fiend vexes.
There could I have him, now, and there, and there again.[1]

LEAR What, has his daughters brought him to this pass?
55 [*To* EDGAR] Couldst thou save nothing? Didst thou give them all?

FOOL Nay, he reserved a blanket, else we had been all shamed.

LEAR [*to* EDGAR] Now all the plagues that in the pendulous° air   overhanging; portentous
Hang fated o'er men's faults fall on thy daughters!

KENT He hath no daughters, sir.

60 LEAR Death, traitor! Nothing could have subdued nature
To such a lowness but his unkind daughters.
[*To* EDGAR] Is it the fashion that discarded fathers
Should have thus little mercy on their flesh?
Judicious punishment: 'twas this flesh begot
65 Those pelican[2] daughters.

EDGAR Pillicock sat on pillicock's hill; a lo, lo, lo.[3]

FOOL This cold night will turn us all to fools and madmen.

EDGAR Take heed o'th' foul fiend; obey thy parents; keep thy
word justly; swear not; commit not with man's sworn spouse:
70 set not thy sweet heart on proud array.[4] Tom's a-cold.

LEAR What hast thou been?

EDGAR A servingman, proud in heart and mind, that curled my
hair, wore gloves in my cap,[5] served the lust of my mistress'
heart, and did the act of darkness with her; swore as many oaths
75 as I spake words, and broke them in the sweet face of heaven;
one that slept in the contriving of lust, and waked to do it. Wine
loved I deeply, dice dearly, and in woman out-paramoured the
Turk.[6] False of heart, light of ear,° bloody of hand; hog in sloth,   rumor-hungry
fox in stealth, wolf in greediness, dog in madness, lion in prey.
80 Let not the creaking of shoes[7] nor the rustlings of silks betray

---

4. *Through . . . wind*: perhaps a fragment from a ballad.
5. *Go . . . thee*: this expression is also used by the drunken
beggar Christopher Sly in *The Taming of the Shrew*,
Induction 1.
6. *laid knives . . . potage*: these are all means by which
the foul fiend tempts Tom to commit suicide. *halters*:
nooses. *ratsbane*: rat poison. *potage*: soup.
7. Impossibly narrow, and probably suicidal to attempt
without diabolical help.
8. The five wits were common wit, imagination, fantasy,
estimation, and memory (from medieval and Renaissance
cognitive theory).
9. *whirlwinds, star-blasting*: malign astrological influences capable of causing sickness or death. *taking*: infection; bewitchment.

1. As Edgar speaks this sentence, he might kill vermin on
his body as if they were devils.
2. Greedy. Young pelicans were reputed to feed on blood
from the wounds they made in their mother's breast; in
some versions, they first killed their father.
3. A fragment of an old rhyme, followed by hunting cries
or a ballad refrain; "Pillicock" was both a term of endearment and a euphemism for "penis."
4. *obey . . . array*: these are fragments from the Ten Com-
mandments.
5. Favors from his mistress. In Petrarchan poetry, wooers
are "servants" to their ladies.
6. And had more women than the sultan had in his royal
harem.
7. Creaking shoes were a fashionable affectation.

[EDGAR *comes forth*]

EDGAR Away, the foul fiend follows me. Thorough the sharp
45 hawthorn blow the winds.⁵ Hm! Go to thy cold bed and warm
thee.⁶

LEAR Didst thou give all to thy two daughters,
And art thou come to this?

EDGAR Who gives anything to Poor Tom, whom the foul fiend
50 hath led through fire and through flame, through ford and
whirlpool, o'er bog and quagmire; that hath laid knives under
his pillow and halters in his pew, set ratsbane by his porridge,⁷
made him proud of heart to ride on a bay trotting-horse over
four-inched⁸ bridges, to course° his own shadow for° a traitor.   *hunt / as*
55 Bless thy five wits,⁹ Tom's a-cold! O, do, de, do, de, do de. Bless
thee from whirlwinds, star-blasting, and taking.¹ Do Poor Tom
some charity, whom the foul fiend vexes. There could I have
him now, and there, and there again, and there.²

Storm still

LEAR Has his daughters brought him to this pass?
60 [*To* EDGAR] Couldst thou save nothing? Wouldst thou give 'em all?

FOOL Nay, he reserved a blanket, else we had been all shamed.

LEAR [*to* EDGAR] Now all the plagues that in the pendulous° air   *overhanging; portentous*
Hang fated o'er men's faults light on thy daughters!

KENT He hath no daughters, sir.

65 LEAR Death, traitor! Nothing could have subdued nature
To such a lowness but his unkind daughters.
[*To* EDGAR] Is it the fashion that discarded fathers
Should have thus little mercy on their flesh?
Judicious punishment: 'twas this flesh begot
70 Those pelican³ daughters.

EDGAR Pillicock sat on Pillicock Hill; alow, alow, loo, loo.⁴

FOOL This cold night will turn us all to fools and madmen.

EDGAR Take heed o'th' foul fiend; obey thy parents; keep thy
words' justice; swear not; commit not with man's sworn spouse;
75 set not thy sweet heart on proud array.⁵ Tom's a-cold.

LEAR What hast thou been?

EDGAR A servingman, proud in heart and mind, that curled my
hair, wore gloves⁶ in my cap, served the lust of my mistress'
heart, and did the act of darkness with her; swore as many oaths
80 as I spake words, and broke them in the sweet face of heaven;
one that slept in the contriving of lust, and waked to do it. Wine
loved I deeply, dice dearly, and in woman out-paramoured the
Turk.⁷ False of heart, light of ear,° bloody of hand; hog in sloth,   *rumor-hungry*
fox in stealth, wolf in greediness, dog in madness, lion in prey.
85 Let not the creaking of shoes⁸ nor the rustling of silks betray

---

5. *Thorough . . . winds:* perhaps a fragment from a ballad.
6. *Go . . . thee:* this expression is also used by the drunken
beggar Christopher Sly in *The Taming of the Shrew,*
Induction 1.
7. *laid knives . . . porridge:* these are all means by which
the foul fiend tempts Tom to commit suicide. *halters:*
nooses. *ratsbane:* rat poison.
8. Impossibly narrow, and probably suicidal to attempt
without diabolical help.
9. The five wits were common wit, imagination, fantasy,
estimation, and memory (from medieval and Renaissance
cognitive theory).
1. *whirlwinds, star-blasting:* malign astrological influences capable of causing sickness or death. *taking:* infection; bewitchment.

2. As Edgar speaks this sentence, he might kill vermin on
his body as if they were devils.
3. Greedy. Young pelicans were reputed to feed on blood
from the wounds they made in their mother's breast; in
some versions, they first killed their father.
4. A fragment of an old rhyme, followed by hunting cries
or a ballad refrain; "Pillicock" was both a term of endearment and a euphemism for "penis."
5. *obey . . . array:* these are fragments from the Ten Com-
mandments.
6. Favors from his mistress. In Petrarchan poetry, wooers
are "servants" to their ladies.
7. And had more women than the sultan had in his royal
harem.
8. Creaking shoes were a fashionable affectation.

thy poor heart to women. Keep thy foot[8] out of brothel, thy
hand out of placket,[9] thy pen from lender's book, and defy the
foul fiend. Still through the hawthorn blows the cold wind.
Heigh no nonny. Dolphin, my boy, my boy! Cease, let him trot
85   by.[1]

LEAR   Why, thou wert better in thy grave than to answer° with   *encounter*
thy uncovered body this extremity of the skies.° Is man no more   *violent weather*
but this? Consider him well. Thou owest the worm no silk, the
beast no hide, the sheep no wool, the cat[2] no perfume. Here's
90   three on 's° are sophisticated; thou art the thing itself. Unac-   *of us*
commodated[3] man is no more but such a poor, bare, forked°   *two-legged*
animal as thou art. Off, off, you lendings!° Come on, be true.   *borrowed clothes*

FOOL   Prithee, nuncle, be content. This is a naughty° night to   *foul*
swim in. Now a little fire in a wild° field were like an old lech-   *barren; lustful*
95   er's heart—a small spark, all the rest on 's° body cold. Look,   *of his*
here comes a walking fire.

Enter GLOUCESTER [*with a torch*]

EDGAR   This is the foul fiend Flibbertigibbet.[4] He begins at cur-
few° and walks till the first cock.° He gives the web and the   *9:00 P.M. / midnight*
pin,[5] squinies° the eye, and makes the harelip; mildews the   *causes squints in*
100   white° wheat, and hurts the poor creature of earth.   *near-ripe*
[*Sings*]   Swithin footed thrice the wold,[6]
A met the night mare and her nine foal;[7]
Bid her alight
And her troth plight,°   *And gave her word*
105   And aroint thee,° witch, aroint thee!   *begone*

KENT [*to* LEAR]   How fares your grace?

LEAR   What's° he?   *Who's*

KENT [*to* GLOUCESTER]   Who's there? What is't you seek?

GLOUCESTER   What are you there? Your names?

EDGAR   Poor Tom, that eats the swimming frog, the toad, the
110   tadpole, the wall-newt and the water;° that in the fury of his   *water newt*
heart, when the foul fiend rages, eats cowdung for salads,° swal-   *savories*
lows the old rat and the ditch-dog,[8] drinks the green mantle° of   *scum*
the standing pool; who is whipped from tithing° to tithing, and   *parish*
stock-punished,° and imprisoned; who hath had three suits to   *put in stocks*
115   his back, six shirts to his body,
Horse to ride, and weapon to wear.
But mice and rats and such small deer[9]
Hath been Tom's food for seven long year—
Beware my follower. Peace, Smolking;° peace, thou fiend!   *a Harsnett devil*
120   GLOUCESTER [*to* LEAR]   What, hath your grace no better company?

EDGAR   The Prince of Darkness is a gentleman;
Modo he's called, and Mahu[1]—

8. Punning on the French *foutre* ("fuck").
9. Slits in skirts or petticoats.
1. These phrases are probably snatches from songs and
proverbs. "Dolphin" is an imagined animal or devil or the
heir to the French throne ("dauphin," which Shakespeare
usually Anglicizes), or all three.
2. Civet cat, in Shakespeare's time the major source of
musk for perfume.
3. Naked; without the trappings of civilization.
4. A devil drawn from folk beliefs, but famous for his
prominent place in Samuel Harsnett's *Declaration of
Egregious Popish Impostures* (1603); the frequent borrowings from Harsnett in *King Lear* set the earliest possi-

ble composition date for the play.
5. *web and the pin:* cataract.
6. Swithin, an early English saint famous for healing, traversed the hilly countryside three times.
7. *night mare:* a demon that is not necessarily in the
shape of a horse; "foal" can also signify the folds, or coils,
of a snake. A: He.
8. A dog found dead in a ditch.
9. *deer:* animals. These verses are adapted from a
romance popular in Shakespeare's time, *Bevis of
Hampton.*
1. Modo and Mahu, more Harsnett devils, were commanding generals of the hellish troops.

thy poor heart to woman. Keep thy foot[9] out of brothels, thy
hand out of plackets,[1] thy pen from lenders' books, and defy
the foul fiend. Still through the hawthorn blows the cold wind,
says suum, mun, nonny. Dauphin, my boy! Boy, *cessez;*° let   *stop*
90   him trot by.[2]
       Storm still
LEAR   Thou wert better in a grave than to answer° with thy uncov-   *encounter*
       ered body this extremity of the skies.° Is man no more than this?   *violent weather*
       Consider him well. Thou owest the worm no silk, the beast
       no hide, the sheep no wool, the cat[3] no perfume. Ha, here's
95   three on 's° are sophisticated; thou art the thing itself. Unac-   *of us*
       commodated[4] man is no more but such a poor, bare, forked°   *two-legged*
       animal as thou art. Off, off, you lendings!° Come, unbutton   *borrowed clothes*
       here.
       Enter GLOUCESTER *with a torch*
FOOL   Prithee, nuncle, be contented. 'Tis a naughty° night to   *foul*
100   swim in. Now a little fire in a wild° field were like an old lech-   *barren; lustful*
       er's heart—a small spark, all the rest on 's° body cold. Look,   *of his*
       here comes a walking fire.
EDGAR This is the foul fiend Flibbertigibbet.[5] He begins at cur-
       few° and walks till the first cock.° He gives the web and the   *9:00 P.M.* / *midnight*
105   pin,[6] squints the eye, and makes the harelip; mildews the
       white° wheat, and hurts the poor creature of earth.   *near-ripe*
       [*Sings*]   Swithin footed thrice the wold,[7]
                A met the night mare and her nine foal,[8]
                Bid her alight
110   And her troth plight,°   *And gave her word*
                And aroint thee,° witch, aroint thee!   *begone*
KENT [*to* LEAR]   How fares your grace?
LEAR   What's° he?   *Who's*
KENT [*to* GLOUCESTER]   Who's there? What is't you seek?
GLOUCESTER   What are you there? Your names?
115 EDGAR   Poor Tom, that eats the swimming frog, the toad, the
       tadpole, the wall-newt and the water;° that in the fury of his   *water newt*
       heart, when the foul fiend rages, eats cowdung for salads,° swal-   *savories*
       lows the old rat and the ditch-dog,[9] drinks the green mantle° of   *scum*
       the standing pool; who is whipped from tithing° to tithing, and   *parish*
120   stocked,° punished, and imprisoned; who hath had three suits   *put in stocks*
       to his back, six shirts to his body,
                Horse to ride, and weapon to wear;
                But mice and rats and such small deer[1]
                Have been Tom's food for seven long year.
125   Beware my follower. Peace, Smulkin;° peace, thou fiend!   *a Harsnett devil*
GLOUCESTER [*to* LEAR]   What, hath your grace no better company?
EDGAR   The Prince of Darkness is a gentleman.
       Modo he's called, and Mahu.[2]

---

9. Punning on the French *foutre* ("fuck").
1. Slits in skirts or petticoats.
2. These phrases are probably snatches from songs and proverbs. *Dauphin:* the heir to the French throne, sometimes identified with the devil by the English.
3. Civet cat, in Shakespeare's time the major source of musk for perfume.
4. Naked; without the trappings of civilization.
5. A devil drawn from folk beliefs, but famous for his prominent place in Samuel Harsnett's *Declaration of Egregious Popish Impostures* (1603); the frequent borrowings from Harsnett in *King Lear* set the earliest possible composition date for the play.

6. *web and the pin:* cataract.
7. Swithin, an early English saint famous for healing, traversed the hilly countryside three times.
8. *night mare:* a demon that is not necessarily in the shape of a horse; "foal" can also signify the folds, or coils, of a snake. A: He.
9. A dog found dead in a ditch.
1. *deer:* animals. These verses are adapted from a romance popular in Shakespeare's time, *Bevis of Hampton.*
2. Modo and Mahu, more Harsnett devils, were commanding generals of the hellish troops.

GLOUCESTER [*to* LEAR]   Our flesh and blood is grown so vile, my lord,
    That it doth hate what gets° it.   *begets*
EDGAR   Poor Tom's a-cold.
125 GLOUCESTER [*to* LEAR]   Go in with me. My duty cannot suffer°   *permit me*
    To obey in all your daughters' hard commands.
    Though their injunction be to bar my doors
    And let this tyrannous night take hold upon you,
    Yet have I ventured to come seek you out
130   And bring you where both food and fire is ready.
LEAR   First let me talk with this philosopher.
    [*To* EDGAR] What is the cause of thunder?
KENT   My good lord,
    Take his offer; go into the house.
LEAR   I'll talk a word with this most learnèd Theban.°   *Greek sage*
135 [*To* EDGAR] What is your study?°   *field of expertise*
EDGAR   How to prevent the fiend, and to kill vermin.
LEAR   Let me ask you one word in private.
      [*They converse apart*]
KENT [*to* GLOUCESTER]   Importune him to go, my lord.
    His wits begin to unsettle.
GLOUCESTER   Canst thou blame him?
140   His daughters seek his death. O, that good Kent,
    He said it would be thus, poor banished man!
    Thou sayst the King grows mad; I'll tell thee, friend,
    I am almost mad myself. I had a son,
    Now outlawed° from my blood; a° sought my life   *disowned / he*
145   But lately, very late.° I loved him, friend;   *recently*
    No father his son dearer. True to tell thee,
    The grief hath crazed my wits. What a night's this!
    [*To* LEAR] I do beseech your grace—
LEAR   O, cry you mercy.°   *beg your pardon*
    [*To* EDGAR] Noble philosopher, your company.
EDGAR   Tom's a-cold.
150 GLOUCESTER   In, fellow, there in t'hovel; keep thee warm.
LEAR   Come, let's in all.
KENT   This way, my lord.
LEAR   With him!
    I will keep still with my philosopher.
KENT [*to* GLOUCESTER]   Good my lord, soothe° him; let him take   *humor*
    the fellow.
155 GLOUCESTER   Take him you on.°   *on ahead*
KENT [*to* EDGAR]   Sirrah, come on. Go along with us.
LEAR [*to* EDGAR]   Come, good Athenian.°   *Greek philosopher*
GLOUCESTER   No words, no words. Hush.
EDGAR   Child Roland² to the dark tower come,
    His word° was still° 'Fie, fo, and fum;   *motto / always*
160   I smell the blood of a British³ man.'
              [*Exeunt*]

---

2. *Child:* an aspirant to knighthood. Roland is the famous
hero of the Charlemagne legends.
3. "An Englishman" usually appears in this rhyme from
the cycle of tales of which "Jack and the Beanstalk" is the
best-known. The alteration befits Lear's ancient Britain.

GLOUCESTER [*to* LEAR]   Our flesh and blood, my lord, is grown so vile

That it doth hate what gets° it.   *begets*

130 EDGAR   Poor Tom's a-cold.

GLOUCESTER [*to* LEAR]   Go in with me. My duty cannot suffer°   *permit me*

T'obey in all your daughters' hard commands.

Though their injunction be to bar my doors

And let this tyrannous night take hold upon you,

135 Yet have I ventured to come seek you out

And bring you where both fire and food is ready.

LEAR   First let me talk with this philosopher.

[*To* EDGAR] What is the cause of thunder?

KENT   Good my lord, take his offer; go into th' house.

140 LEAR   I'll talk a word with this same learnèd Theban.°   *Greek sage*

[*To* EDGAR] What is your study?°   *field of expertise*

EDGAR   How to prevent the fiend, and to kill vermin.

LEAR   Let me ask you one word in private.

           [*They converse apart*]

KENT [*to* GLOUCESTER]   Importune him once more to go, my lord.

His wits begin t'unsettle.

145 GLOUCESTER   Canst thou blame him?

           Storm still

His daughters seek his death. Ah, that good Kent,

He said it would be thus, poor banished man!

Thou sayst the King grows mad; I'll tell thee, friend,

I am almost mad myself. I had a son,

150 Now outlawed° from my blood; a° sought my life   *disowned / he*

But lately, very late.° I loved him, friend;   *recently*

No father his son dearer. True to tell thee,

The grief hath crazed my wits. What a night's this!

[*To* LEAR] I do beseech your grace—

LEAR   O, cry you mercy,° sir!   *beg your pardon*

[*To* EDGAR] Noble philosopher, your company.

155 EDGAR   Tom's a-cold.

GLOUCESTER   In, fellow, there in t'hovel; keep thee warm.

LEAR   Come, let's in all.

KENT   This way, my lord.

LEAR   With him!

I will keep still with my philosopher.

KENT [*to* GLOUCESTER]   Good my lord, soothe° him; let him take   *humor*

           the fellow.

160 GLOUCESTER   Take him you on.°   *on ahead*

KENT [*to* EDGAR]   Sirrah, come on. Go along with us.

LEAR [*to* EDGAR]   Come, good Athenian.°   *Greek philosopher*

GLOUCESTER   No words, no words. Hush.

EDGAR   Child Roland[3] to the dark tower came,

His word° was still° 'Fie, fo, and fum;   *motto / always*

165 I smell the blood of a British[4] man.'   *Exeunt*

---

3. *Child*: an aspirant to knighthood. Roland is the famous hero of the Charlemagne legends.
4. "An Englishman" usually appears in this rhyme from the cycle of tales of which "Jack and the Beanstalk" is the best-known. The alteration befits Lear's ancient Britain.

Scene 12

Enter CORNWALL *and Bastard* [EDMUND]

CORNWALL   I will have my revenge ere I depart the house.

EDMUND   How, my lord, I may be censured,° that nature° thus   *judged / kinship*
gives way to loyalty, something fears me° to think of.   *I am somewhat afraid*

CORNWALL   I now perceive it was not altogether your brother's
5   evil disposition made him seek his° death, but a provoking   *(Gloucester's)*
merit set a-work by a reprovable badness in himself.[1]

EDMUND   How malicious is my fortune, that I must repent to
be just! This is the letter he spoke of, which approves him an
intelligent party to the advantages of France.[2] O heavens, that
10   his treason were not, or not I the detector!

CORNWALL   Go with me to the Duchess.

EDMUND   If the matter of this paper be certain, you have mighty
business in hand.

CORNWALL   True or false, it hath made thee Earl of Gloucester.
15   Seek out where thy father is, that he may be ready for our
apprehension.°   *arrest*

EDMUND [*aside*]   If I find him comforting the King, it will stuff
his° suspicion more fully. [*To* CORNWALL] I will persever in my   *(Cornwall's)*
course of loyalty, though the conflict be sore between that and
20   my blood.°   *filial duty*

CORNWALL   I will lay trust upon thee, and thou shalt find a
dearer father in my love.   *Exeunt*

Scene 13

Enter GLOUCESTER *and* LEAR, KENT [*disguised*], FOOL,
and EDGAR [*as a Bedlam beggar*]

GLOUCESTER   Here is better than the open air; take it thankfully.
I will piece° out the comfort with what addition I can. I will   *pad*
not be long from you.

KENT   All the power of his wits have given way to impatience;[1]
5   the gods° discern your kindness!   [*Exit* GLOUCESTER]   *may the gods*

EDGAR   Frateretto° calls me, and tells me Nero is an angler in   *a Harsnett devil*
the lake of darkness.[2] Pray, innocent; beware the foul fiend.

FOOL [*to* LEAR]   Prithee, nuncle, tell me whether a madman be
a gentleman or a yeoman.[3]

10   LEAR   A king, a king! To have a thousand
With red burning spits come hissing in upon them!

EDGAR   The foul fiend bites my back.

FOOL [*to* LEAR]   He's mad that trusts in the tameness of a wolf, a
horse's health, a boy's love, or a whore's oath.

15   LEAR   It shall be done. I will arraign° them straight.°   *prosecute / immediately*
[*To* EDGAR] Come, sit thou here, most learnèd justicer.
[*To* FOOL] Thou sapient sir, sit here.—No, you she-foxes—

EDGAR   Look where he stands and glares. Want'st thou eyes at
troll-madam?[4]

Scene 12 Location: At Gloucester's castle.
1. *a provoking . . . himself*: Gloucester's own wickedness
deservedly triggered the blameworthy evil in Edgar.
2. *which . . . France*: which proves him a spy and
informer in the aid of France; "party," or faction, was usually a term of opprobrium in the Renaissance.
Scene 13 Location: Within an outbuilding of Gloucester's.
1. Rage; inability to bear more suffering.

2. In Chaucer's *Monk's Tale*, the infamously cruel
Roman emperor Nero is found fishing in hell (lines 485–
86).
3. A free landowner but not a member of the gentry, lacking official family arms and the distinctions they confer.
Shakespeare seems to have procured a coat of arms for his
father in 1596.
4. *troll*: a board game using small balls. *eyes*: eyeballs (?)
to troll: to fish; to sing.

3.5

Enter CORNWALL *and* EDMOND

CORNWALL   I will have my revenge ere I depart his house.

EDMOND   How, my lord, I may be censured,° that nature° thus
    gives way to loyalty, something fears me° to think of.

judged / kinship
I am somewhat afraid

CORNWALL   I now perceive it was not altogether your brother's

5   evil disposition made him seek his° death, but a provoking
    merit set a-work by a reprovable badness in himself.[1]

(Gloucester's)

EDMOND   How malicious is my fortune, that I must repent to be
    just! This is the letter which he spoke of, which approves him
    an intelligent party to the advantages of France.[2] O heavens,

10   that this treason were not, or not I the detector!

CORNWALL   Go with me to the Duchess.

EDMOND   If the matter of this paper be certain, you have mighty
    business in hand.

CORNWALL   True or false, it hath made thee Earl of Gloucester.

15   Seek out where thy father is, that he may be ready for our
    apprehension.°

arrest

EDMOND [*aside*]   If I find him comforting the King, it will stuff
    his° suspicion more fully. [*To* CORNWALL] I will persever in my
    course of loyalty, though the conflict be sore between that and

(Cornwall's)

20   my blood.°

filial duty

CORNWALL   I will lay trust upon thee, and thou shalt find a
    dearer father in my love.   *Exeunt*

3.6

Enter KENT [*disguised*], *and* GLOUCESTER

GLOUCESTER   Here is better than the open air; take it thankfully.
    I will piece° out the comfort with what addition I can. I will
    not be long from you.

pad

KENT   All the power of his wits have given way to his impa-

5   tience;[1] the gods° reward your kindness!   *Exit* GLOUCESTER

may the gods

Enter LEAR, EDGAR [*as a Bedlam beggar*], *and* FOOL

EDGAR   Fraterretto° calls me, and tells me Nero is an angler in the
    lake of darkness.[2] Pray, innocent, and beware the foul fiend.

a Harsnett devil

FOOL   Prithee, nuncle, tell me whether a madman be a gentle-
    man or a yeoman.[3]

10 LEAR   A king, a king!

FOOL   No, he's a yeoman that has a gentleman to his son; for
    he's a mad yeoman that sees his son a gentleman before him.

LEAR   To have a thousand with red burning spits
    Come hissing in upon 'em!

3.5 Location: At Gloucester's castle.

1. *a provoking . . . himself:* Gloucester's own wickedness
deservedly triggered the blameworthy evil in Edgar.

2. *which . . . France:* which proves him a spy and
informer in the aid of France; "party," or faction, was usually a term of opprobrium in the Renaissance.

3.6 Location: Within an outbuilding of Gloucester's.

1. Rage; inability to bear more suffering.

2. In Chaucer's *Monk's Tale,* the infamously cruel
Roman emperor Nero is found fishing in hell (lines 485–
86).

3. A free landowner but not a member of the gentry, lacking official family arms and the distinctions they confer.
Shakespeare seems to have procured a coat of arms for his
father in 1596.

20   [*Sings*]   Come o'er the burn, Bessy, to me.[5]
      FOOL [*sings*]   Her boat hath a leak,[6]
                        And she must not speak
                        Why she dares not come over to thee.
      EDGAR   The foul fiend haunts Poor Tom in the voice of a night-   *a demon / fresh*
25   ingale. Hoppedance° cries in Tom's belly for two white° her-
      ring. Croak° not, black angel: I have no food for thee.   *Growl*
      KENT [*to* LEAR]   How do you, sir? Stand you not so amazed.
      Will you lie down and rest upon the cushions?
      LEAR   I'll see their trial first. Bring in the evidence.
30   [*To* EDGAR] Thou robèd man of justice, take thy place;
      [*to* FOOL] And thou, his yokefellow of equity,°   *partner of law*
      Bench° by his side. [*To* KENT] You are o'th' commission,°   *Sit / judiciary*
      Sit you, too.
      EDGAR   Let us deal justly.
35   [*Sings*]   Sleepest or wakest thou, jolly shepherd?
                   Thy sheep be in the corn,°   *grain*
                   And for one blast of thy minikin° mouth   *dainty*
                   Thy sheep shall take no harm.
      Purr, the cat[7] is grey.
40   LEAR   Arraign her first. 'Tis Gonoril. I here take my oath before
      this honourable assembly she kicked the poor King her father.
      FOOL   Come hither, mistress. Is your name Gonoril?
      LEAR   She cannot deny it.
      FOOL   Cry you mercy, I took you for a join-stool.[8]
45   LEAR   And here's another, whose warped looks proclaim
      What store° her heart is made on.° Stop her there.   *material / of*
      Arms, arms, sword, fire, corruption in the place!
      False justicer, why hast thou let her scape?
      EDGAR   Bless thy five wits.
50   KENT [*to* LEAR]   O pity! Sir, where is the patience now
      That you so oft have boasted to retain?
      EDGAR [*aside*]   My tears begin to take his part so much
      They'll mar my counterfeiting.
      LEAR   The little dogs and all,°   *Even the little dogs*
      Tray, Blanch, and Sweetheart—see, they bark at me.
55   EDGAR   Tom will throw his head at° them.—Avaunt,° you curs!   *will threaten? / Begone*
      Be thy mouth or° black or white,   *either*
      Tooth that poisons° if it bite,   *gives rabies*
      Mastiff, greyhound, mongrel grim,
      Hound or spaniel, brach° or him,   *bitch*
60   Bobtail tyke or trundle-tail,[9]
      Tom will make them weep and wail;
      For with throwing thus my head,
      Dogs leap the hatch,[1] and all are fled.
      Loudla, doodla! Come, march to wakes° and fairs   *parish festivals*
65   And market towns. Poor Tom, thy horn is dry.[2]

---

5. From an old song. *burn*: a small stream.
6. She has venereal disease; punning on "boat" as body
and "burn" as genital discomfort.
7. Purr the cat is another devil; such devils in the shape
of cats were the familiars of witches.
8. I beg your pardon, I mistook you for a stool. An idiom
of the day expressing annoyance at being slighted. Here

the part of Gonoril is actually being played by a stool.
9. Short-tailed mongrel or long-tailed.
1. Dogs leap over the lower half of a divided door.
2. A begging formula that refers to the horn vessel that
vagabonds carried for drink; the covert sense is that Edgar
has run out of Bedlamite inspiration.

EDGAR   Bless thy five wits.

15   KENT [*to* LEAR]   O, pity! Sir, where is the patience now
      That you so oft have boasted to retain?
     EDGAR [*aside*]   My tears begin to take his part so much
      They mar my counterfeiting.

     LEAR   The little dogs and all,°   *Even the little dogs*
      Tray, Blanch, and Sweetheart—see, they bark at me.

20   EDGAR   Tom will throw his head at° them.—Avaunt,° you curs!   *will threaten? / Begone*
      Be thy mouth or° black or white,   *either*
      Tooth that poisons° if it bite,   *gives rabies*
      Mastiff, greyhound, mongrel grim,
      Hound or spaniel, brach° or him,   *bitch*

25   Bobtail tyke or trundle-tail,[4]
      Tom will make him weep and wail;
      For with throwing thus my head,
      Dogs leapt the hatch,[5] and all are fled.
      Do, de, de, de. Sese![6] Come, march to wakes° and fairs   *parish festivals*

30   And market towns. Poor Tom, thy horn is dry.[7]

---

4. Short-tailed mongrel or long-tailed.
5. Dogs leaped over the lower half of a divided door.
6. Apparently nonsense, although "Sese" may be a version of the French *cessez* ("stop" or "hush").

7. A begging formula that refers to the horn vessel that vagabonds carried for drink; the covert sense is that Edgar has run out of Bedlamite inspiration.

LEAR   Then let them anatomize° Regan; see what breeds about   *dissect*
her heart. Is there any cause in nature that makes this hardness?
[*To* EDGAR] You, sir, I entertain° you for one of my hundred,   *retain*
only I do not like the fashion of your garments. You'll say they
70   are Persian° attire; but let them be changed.   *oriental; splendid*
KENT   Now, good my lord, lie here a while.
LEAR   Make no noise, make no noise. Draw the curtains.° So, so,   *bed curtains*
so. We'll go to supper i'th' morning. So, so, so.
           [*He sleeps.*] *Enter* GLOUCESTER
GLOUCESTER [*to* KENT]   Come hither, friend. Where is the King
75   my master?
KENT   Here, sir, but trouble him not; his wits are gone.
GLOUCESTER   Good friend, I prithee take him in thy arms.
I have o'erheard a plot of death upon° him.   *against*
There is a litter ready. Lay him in't
80   And drive towards Dover, friend, where thou shalt meet
Both welcome and protection. Take up thy master.
If thou shouldst dally half an hour, his life,
With thine and all that offer to defend him,
Stand in assurèd loss.° Take up, take up,   *Are certainly doomed*
85   And follow me, that will to some provision
Give thee quick conduct.³
KENT [*to* LEAR]   Oppressèd nature sleeps.
This rest might yet have balmed° thy broken sinews°   *soothed / nerves*
Which, if convenience° will not allow,   *circumstances*
Stand in hard cure.° [*To* FOOL] Come, help to bear thy   *Will be hard to cure*
master.
Thou must not stay behind.
90   GLOUCESTER   Come, come away.
                     Exeunt [*all but* EDGAR]
EDGAR   When we our betters see bearing our° woes,   *our same*
We scarcely think our miseries our foes.
Who alone suffers, suffers most i'th' mind,
Leaving free° things and happy shows° behind.   *carefree / scenes*
95   But then the mind much sufferance doth o'erskip
When grief hath mates, and bearing° fellowship.   *pain, suffering*
How light and portable my pain seems now,
When that which makes me bend, makes the King bow.
He° childed as I fathered. Tom, away.   *He is*
100   Mark the high noises,° and thyself bewray°   *important rumors / reveal*
When false opinion, whose wrong thoughts defile thee,
In thy just proof repeals and reconciles thee.⁴
What° will hap° more tonight, safe scape the King!   *Whatever / chance*
Lurk, lurk.   [*Exit*]

3. *that . . . conduct:* who will quickly guide you to some   4. *In . . . thee:* When true evidence pardons you and rec-
supplies.   onciles you (with your father).

LEAR Then let them anatomize° Regan; see what breeds about   *dissect*
her heart. Is there any cause in nature that makes these hard-
hearts? [*To* EDGAR] You, sir, I entertain° for one of my hundred,   *retain*
only I do not like the fashion of your garments. You will say
35 they are Persian;° but let them be changed.   *oriental; splendid*
KENT Now, good my lord, lie here and rest a while.
LEAR Make no noise, make no noise. Draw the curtains.° So, so.   *bed curtains*
We'll go to supper i'th' morning.
       [*He sleeps*]
FOOL And I'll go to bed at noon.
       Enter GLOUCESTER
GLOUCESTER [*to* KENT] Come hither, friend. Where is the King
40   my master?
KENT Here, sir, but trouble him not; his wits are gone.
GLOUCESTER Good friend, I prithee take him in thy arms.
I have o'erheard a plot of death upon° him.   *against*
There is a litter ready. Lay him in't
45 And drive toward Dover, friend, where thou shalt meet
Both welcome and protection. Take up thy master.
If thou shouldst dally half an hour, his life,
With thine and all that offer to defend him,
Stand in assurèd loss.° Take up, take up,   *Are certainly doomed*
50 And follow me, that will to some provision
Give thee quick conduct.[8] Come, come away.
       Exeunt [KENT *carrying* LEAR *in his arms*]

---

8. *that . . . conduct:* who will quickly guide you to some supplies.

Scene 14

Enter CORNWALL *and* REGAN, *and* GONORIL *and Bastard*
[EDMUND, *and* SERVANTS]

CORNWALL [*to* GONORIL]   Post° speedily to my lord your husband.   Ride
Show him this letter. The army of France is landed.
[*To* SERVANTS] Seek out the villain Gloucester. [*Exeunt some*]
REGAN   Hang him instantly.
GONORIL   Pluck out his eyes.
CORNWALL   Leave him to my displeasure.—
5   Edmund, keep you our sister° company. The revenges we are   *sister-in-law*
        bound¹ to take upon your traitorous father are not fit for your
        beholding. Advise the Duke where you are going, to a most
        festinate preparation;² we are bound° to the like. Our posts°   *committed / messengers*
        shall be swift, and intelligence° betwixt us.—   *convey information*
10   Farewell, dear sister. Farewell, my lord of Gloucester.
                Enter Steward [OSWALD]
        How now, where's the King?
OSWALD   My lord of Gloucester hath conveyed him hence.
        Some five- or six-and-thirty of his° knights,   *(Lear's)*
        Hot questants° after him, met him at gate,   *searchers*
15   Who, with some other of the lord's° dependants,   *(Gloucester's)*
        Are gone with him towards Dover, where they boast
        To have well-armèd friends.
CORNWALL   Get horses for your mistress.   [*Exit* OSWALD]
GONORIL   Farewell, sweet lord, and sister.
CORNWALL   Edmund, farewell.
                Exeunt GONORIL *and Bastard* [EDMUND]
20   [*To* SERVANTS]   Go seek the traitor Gloucester.
        Pinion him° like a thief; bring him before us.   *Tie his arms*
                            [*Exeunt other* SERVANTS]
        Though we may not pass° upon his life   *pass sentence*
        Without the form° of justice, yet our power   *official proceedings*
        Shall do a curtsy³ to our wrath, which men
25   May blame but not control. Who's there—the traitor?
                Enter GLOUCESTER *brought in by two or three*
REGAN   Ingrateful fox, 'tis he.
CORNWALL [*to* SERVANTS]   Bind fast his corky° arms.   *withered*
GLOUCESTER   What means your graces? Good my friends, consider
        You are my guests. Do me no foul play, friends.
CORNWALL [*to* SERVANTS]   Bind him, I say—
REGAN   Hard, hard! O filthy traitor!
30   GLOUCESTER   Unmerciful lady as you are, I am true.
CORNWALL [*to* SERVANTS]   To this chair bind him. [*To* GLOUCES-
        TER] Villain, thou shalt find—
                [REGAN *plucks Gloucester's beard*]°   *(an extreme insult)*
GLOUCESTER   By the kind gods, 'tis most ignobly done,
        To pluck me by the beard.
REGAN   So white,° and such a traitor!   *white-haired; venerable*

Scene 14 Location: At Gloucester's castle.   the Duke to prepare quickly.
1. Bound by duty; expected by destiny.   3. Shall allow a courtesy, or indulgence; shall bow to.
2. *Advise . . . preparation:* When you reach Albany, tell

3.7

Enter CORNWALL, REGAN, GONERIL, *Bastard* [EDMOND],
and SERVANTS

CORNWALL [*to* GONERIL]   Post° speedily to my lord your husband.   *Ride*
  show him this letter. the army of France is landed.
  [*To* SERVANTS] Seek out the traitor Gloucester. [*Exeunt some*]
REGAN   Hang him instantly.
GONERIL   Pluck out his eyes.
CORNWALL   Leave him to my displeasure.
5   Edmond, keep you our sister° company.   *sister-in-law*
  The revenges we are bound[1] to take upon your traitorous father
  are not fit for your beholding. Advise the Duke where you are
  going, to a most festinate preparation;[2] we are bound° to the   *committed*
  like. Our posts° shall be swift and intelligent° betwixt us. [*To*   *messengers / well-informed*
10   GONERIL]   Farewell, dear sister. [*To* EDMOND] Farewell, my
  lord of Gloucester.
      Enter Steward [OSWALD]
  How now, where's the King?
OSWALD   My lord of Gloucester hath conveyed him hence.
  Some five or six and thirty of his° knights,   *(Lear's)*
15   Hot questrists° after him, met him at gate,   *searchers*
  Who, with some other of the lord's° dependants,   *(Gloucester's)*
  Are gone with him toward Dover, where they boast
  To have well-armèd friends.
CORNWALL   Get horses for your mistress.   *Exit* [OSWALD]
20 GONERIL   Farewell, sweet lord, and sister.
CORNWALL   Edmond, farewell. [*Exeunt* GONERIL *and* EDMOND]
  [*To* SERVANTS]   Go seek the traitor Gloucester.
  Pinion him° like a thief; bring him before us.   *Tie his arms*
                    [*Exeunt other* SERVANTS]
  Though well we may not pass° upon his life   *pass sentence*
  Without the form° of justice, yet our power   *official proceedings*
25   Shall do a curtsy[3] to our wrath, which men
  May blame but not control.
      Enter GLOUCESTER *and* SERVANTS
              Who's there—the traitor?
REGAN   Ingrateful fox, 'tis he.
CORNWALL [*to* SERVANTS]   Bind fast his corky° arms.   *withered*
GLOUCESTER   What means your graces? Good my friends, consider
  You are my guests. Do me no foul play, friends.
CORNWALL [*to* SERVANTS]   Bind him, I say.
30   REGAN   Hard, hard! O filthy traitor!
GLOUCESTER   Unmerciful lady as you are, I'm none.
CORNWALL [*to* SERVANTS]   To this chair bind him. [*To* GLOUCES-
    TER] Villain, thou shalt find—
      [REGAN *plucks Gloucester's beard*]°   *(an extreme insult)*
GLOUCESTER   By the kind gods, 'tis most ignobly done,
  To pluck me by the beard.
35 REGAN   So white,° and such a traitor?   *white-haired; venerable*

3.7 Location: At Gloucester's castle.
1. Bound by duty; expected by destiny.
2. *Advise . . . preparation*: When you reach Albany, tell

the Duke to prepare quickly.
3. Shall allow a courtesy, or indulgence; shall bow to.

35	GLOUCESTER Naughty° lady,	*Wicked*
	These hairs which thou dost ravish from my chin	
	Will quicken° and accuse thee. I am your host.	*come alive*
	With robbers' hands my hospitable favours°	*features*
	You should not ruffle° thus. What will you do?	*snatch at*
40	CORNWALL Come, sir, what letters had you late° from France?	*lately*
	REGAN Be simple,° answerer, for we know the truth.	*direct*
	CORNWALL And what confederacy have you with the traitors	
	Late footed° in the kingdom?	*landed*
	REGAN To whose hands	
	You have sent the lunatic King. Speak.	
45	GLOUCESTER I have a letter guessingly set down,[4]	
	Which came from one that's of a neutral heart,	
	And not from one opposed.	
	CORNWALL Cunning.	
	REGAN And false.	
	CORNWALL Where hast thou sent the King?	
	GLOUCESTER To Dover.	
	REGAN Wherefore° to Dover? Wast thou not charged° at peril—	*Why / commanded*
50	CORNWALL Wherefore to Dover? Let him first answer that.	
	GLOUCESTER I am tied to th' stake, and I must stand the course.[5]	
	REGAN Wherefore to Dover, sir?	
	GLOUCESTER Because I would not see thy cruel nails	
	Pluck out his poor old eyes, nor thy fierce sister	
55	In his anointed[6] flesh rash° boarish fangs.	*slash, cut*
	The sea, with such a storm as his bowed head	
	In hell-black night endured, would have buoyed° up	*risen*
	And quenched the stellèd° fires. Yet, poor old heart,	*stars'*
	He holped° the heavens to rage.	*helped*
60	If wolves had at thy gate howled that dern° time,	*dreary; dreadful*
	Thou shouldst have said 'Good porter, turn the key;°	*(to open the door)*
	All cruels I'll subscribe.'[7] But I shall see	
	The wingèd vengeance[8] overtake such children.	
	CORNWALL See't shalt thou never.—Fellows,° hold the chair.—	*Servants*
65	Upon those eyes of thine I'll set my foot.	
	GLOUCESTER He that will think° to live till he be old	*Whoever hopes*
	Give me some help!—O cruel! O ye gods!	
	[CORNWALL *pulls out one of Gloucester's eyes and*	
	stamps on it]	
	REGAN [*to* CORNWALL] One side will mock another; t'other, too.	
	CORNWALL [*to* GLOUCESTER] If you see vengeance—	
	SERVANT Hold your hand, my lord.	
70	I have served you ever since I was a child,	
	But better service have I never done you	
	Than now to bid you hold.	
	REGAN How now, you dog!	

---

4. Written without confirmation; speculative.
5. An image from bearbaiting, in which a bear on a short tether had to fight off the assault of dogs.
6. Consecrated with holy oils (as part of a king's coronation).
7. The cruelty of all creatures (but not yours) I can

accept ("subscribe"). Oxford emends F ("else subscribe") and Q ("else subscrib'd"); the line is usually paraphrased "All other cruel beasts would have pity, but not you."
8. Swift or heaven-sent revenge; either an angel of God or the Furies, who were flying executors of divine vengeance in classical myth.

GLOUCESTER Naughty° lady,   *Wicked*
These hairs which thou dost ravish from my chin
Will quicken° and accuse thee. I am your host.   *come alive*
With robbers' hands my hospitable favours°   *features*
40 You should not ruffle° thus. What will you do?   *snatch at*
CORNWALL Come, sir, what letters had you late° from France?   *lately*
REGAN Be simple-answered,° for we know the truth.   *straightforward*
CORNWALL And what confederacy have you with the traitors
Late footed° in the kingdom?   *landed*
REGAN   To whose hands
45 You have sent the lunatic King. Speak.
GLOUCESTER I have a letter guessingly set down,[4]
Which came from one that's of a neutral heart,
And not from one opposed.
CORNWALL   Cunning.
REGAN   And false.
CORNWALL Where hast thou sent the King?
GLOUCESTER   To Dover.
50 REGAN Wherefore° to Dover? Wast thou not charged° at peril—   *Why / commanded*
CORNWALL Wherefore to Dover?—Let him answer that.
GLOUCESTER I am tied to th' stake, and I must stand the course.[5]
REGAN Wherefore to Dover?
GLOUCESTER Because I would not see thy cruel nails
55 Pluck out his poor old eyes, nor thy fierce sister
In his anointed[6] flesh stick boarish fangs.
The sea, with such a storm as his bare head
In hell-black night endured, would have buoyed° up   *risen*
And quenched the stellèd° fires.   *stars'*
60 Yet, poor old heart, he holp° the heavens to rain.   *helped*
If wolves had at thy gate howled that stern time,
Thou shouldst have said 'Good porter, turn the key;°   *(to open the door)*
All cruels I'll subscribe.'[7] But I shall see
The wingèd vengeance[8] overtake such children.
65 CORNWALL See't shalt thou never.—Fellows,° hold the chair.—   *Servants*
Upon these eyes of thine I'll set my foot.
GLOUCESTER He that will think° to live till he be old   *Whoever hopes*
Give me some help!—O cruel! O you gods!
        [CORNWALL *pulls out one of Gloucester's eyes and*
        stamps on it]
REGAN [*to* CORNWALL] One side will mock another; th'other, too.
CORNWALL [*to* GLOUCESTER] If you see vengeance—
70 SERVANT   Hold your hand, my lord.
I have served you ever since I was a child,
But better service have I never done you
Than now to bid you hold.
REGAN   How now, you dog!

---

4. Written without confirmation; speculative.
5. An image from bearbaiting, in which a bear on a short
tether had to fight off the assault of dogs.
6. Consecrated with holy oils (as part of a king's coronation).
7. The cruelty of all creatures (but not yours) I can

accept ("subscribe"). Oxford emends F ("else subscribe")
and Q ("else subscrib'd"); the line is usually paraphrased
as "All other cruel beasts would have pity, but not you."
8. Swift or heaven-sent revenge; either an angel of God
or the Furies, who were flying executors of divine vengeance in classical myth.

SERVANT   If you did wear a beard upon your chin
    I'd shake it on this quarrel.[9] [*To* CORNWALL] What do you mean?°   *intend*
75 CORNWALL   My villein!°   *servant; villain*
SERVANT   Why then, come on, and take the chance of anger.[1]
    [*They*] *draw and fight*
REGAN [*to another* SERVANT]   Give me thy sword. A peasant stand up thus!
    She takes a sword and runs at him behind
SERVANT [*to* GLOUCESTER]   O, I am slain, my lord! Yet have you one eye left
    To see some mischief° on him.   *injury*
    [REGAN *stabs him again*]
             O!   [*He dies*]
80 CORNWALL   Lest it see more, prevent it. Out, vile jelly!
    [*He pulls out Gloucester's other eye*]
    Where is thy lustre now?
GLOUCESTER   All dark and comfortless. Where's my son Edmund?
    Edmund, enkindle all the sparks of nature[2]
    To quite° this horrid act.   *requite; avenge*
REGAN   Out, villain!
85 Thou call'st on him that hates thee. It was he
    That made the overture° of thy treasons to us,   *revelation*
    Who is too good to pity thee.
GLOUCESTER   O, my follies! Then Edgar was abused.°   *slandered*
    Kind gods, forgive me that, and prosper him!
90 REGAN [*to* SERVANTS]   Go thrust him out at gates, and let him smell
    His way to Dover. [*To* CORNWALL] How is't, my lord? How
        look you?°   *How do you feel*
CORNWALL   I have received a hurt. Follow me, lady.
    [*To* SERVANTS] Turn out that eyeless villain. Throw this slave
    Upon the dunghill.
        [*Exit one or more with* GLOUCESTER *and the body*]
        Regan, I bleed apace.
95 Untimely comes this hurt. Give me your arm.
             Exeunt [CORNWALL *and* REGAN]
SECOND SERVANT   I'll never care what wickedness I do
    If this man come to good.[3]
THIRD SERVANT   If she live long
    And in the end meet the old° course of death,   *usual*
    Women will all turn monsters.
100 SECOND SERVANT   Let's follow the old Earl and get the bedlam
    To lead him where he would. His roguish madness
    Allows itself to anything.
THIRD SERVANT   Go thou. I'll fetch some flax and whites of eggs
    To apply to his bleeding face. Now heaven help him!
             Exeunt [*severally*]

---

9. I'd pluck it over this point; I'd issue a challenge.
1. Take the risk of fighting when angry; take the fortune
of one who is governed by his anger.
2. All the warmth of filial love; all the anger that your

father has received such treatment.
3. *I'll . . . good:* Because this may be a sign that evil goes
unpunished. *this man:* Cornwall.

SERVANT   If you did wear a beard upon your chin
I'd shake it on this quarrel.[9] [*To* CORNWALL] What do you mean?°   *intend*
CORNWALL   My villein!°   *servant; villain*
SERVANT   Nay then, come on, and take the chance of anger.[1]
            [*They draw and fight*]
REGAN [*to another* SERVANT]   Give me thy sword. A peasant stand up thus!
            [*She*] *kills him*
SERVANT [*to* GLOUCESTER]   O, I am slain. My lord, you have one eye left
To see some mischief° on him.   *injury*
            [REGAN *stabs him again*]
                                    O!   [*He dies*]
CORNWALL   Lest it see more, prevent it. Out, vile jelly!
            [*He pulls out Gloucester's other eye*]
Where is thy lustre now?
GLOUCESTER   All dark and comfortless. Where's my son Edmond?
Edmond, enkindle all the sparks of nature[2]
To quite° this horrid act.   *requite, avenge*
REGAN   Out, treacherous villain!
Thou call'st on him that hates thee. It was he
That made the overture° of thy treasons to us,   *revelation*
Who is too good to pity thee.
GLOUCESTER   O, my follies! Then Edgar was abused.°   *slandered*
Kind gods, forgive me that, and prosper him!
REGAN [*to* SERVANTS]   Go thrust him out at gates, and let him smell
His way to Dover.   *Exit* [*one or more*] *with* GLOUCESTER
                        How is't, my lord? How look you?°   *How do you feel*
CORNWALL   I have received a hurt. Follow me, lady.
            [*To* SERVANTS] Turn out that eyeless villain. Throw this slave
Upon the dunghill. Regan, I bleed apace.
Untimely comes this hurt. Give me your arm.
                                    Exeunt [*with the body*]

9. I'd pluck it over this point; I'd issue a challenge.
1. Take the risk of fighting when angry; take the fortune
of one who is governed by his anger.

2. All the warmth of filial love; all the anger that your
father has received such treatment.

Scene 15

Enter EDGAR [*as a Bedlam beggar*]

EDGAR   Yet better thus and known to be contemned°   despised
　　　Than still° contemned and flattered. To be worst,   always
　　　The low'st and most dejected thing of fortune,
　　　Stands still in esperance, lives not in fear.[1]
5　　　The lamentable change is from the best;
　　　The worst returns to laughter.[2]
　　　　　　Enter GLOUCESTER *led by an* OLD MAN
　　　Who's here? My father, parti-eyed?[3] World, world, O world!
　　　But that thy strange mutations make us hate thee,
　　　Life would not yield to age.[4]
　　　　　　[EDGAR *stands aside*]
OLD MAN [*to* GLOUCESTER]　　　O my good lord,
10　　　I have been your tenant and your father's tenant
　　　This fourscore —
GLOUCESTER   Away, get thee away, good friend, be gone.
　　　Thy comforts° can do me no good at all;   assistance
　　　Thee they may hurt.
15 OLD MAN   Alack, sir, you cannot see your way.
GLOUCESTER   I have no way, and therefore want no eyes.
　　　I stumbled when I saw. Full oft 'tis seen
　　　Our means secure us, and our mere defects
　　　Prove our commodities.[5] Ah dear son Edgar,
20　　　The food° of thy abusèd° father's wrath —   fuel; prey / despised
　　　Might I but live to see thee in° my touch   through
　　　I'd say I had eyes again.
OLD MAN　　　　　　How now? Who's there?
EDGAR [*aside*]   O gods! Who is't can say 'I am at the worst'?
　　　I am worse than e'er I was.
OLD MAN　　　　　　'Tis poor mad Tom.
25 EDGAR [*aside*]   And worse I may be yet. The worst is not
　　　As long as we can say 'This is the worst.'
OLD MAN [*to* EDGAR]   Fellow, where goest?
GLOUCESTER   Is it a beggarman?
OLD MAN   Madman and beggar too.
30 GLOUCESTER   A° has some reason, else he could not beg.   He
　　　In the last night's storm I such a fellow saw,
　　　Which made me think a man a worm. My son
　　　Came then into my mind, and yet my mind
　　　Was then scarce friends with him. I have heard more since.
35　　　As flies to wanton° boys are we to th' gods;   playful; careless
　　　They kill us for their sport.

Scene 15 Location: Open country.
1. *Stands . . . fear:* Remains in hope ("esperance") because there is no fear of falling further.
2. *The lamentable . . . laughter:* The change to be lamented is one that alters the best of circumstances; the worst luck can only improve.
3. Multicolored like a fool's costume (red with blood under white dressings).
4. *But . . . age:* If there were no strange reversals of fortune to make the world hateful, we would not consent to aging and death.
5. *Our means . . . commodities:* Our wealth makes us overconfident, and our utter deprivation proves to be beneficial.

4.1

Enter EDGAR [*as a Bedlam beggar*]

EDGAR Yet better thus and known to be contemned°   *despised*
    Than still° contemned and flattered. To be worst,   *always*
    The low'st and most dejected thing of fortune,
    Stands still in esperance, lives not in fear.[1]
5   The lamentable change is from the best;
    The worst returns to laughter.[2] Welcome, then,
    Thou unsubstantial air that I embrace.
    The wretch that thou hast blown unto the worst
    Owes nothing° to thy blasts.   *(because he can't pay)*

Enter GLOUCESTER [*led by*] *an* OLD MAN

                         But who comes here?
10   My father, parti-eyed?[3] World, world, O world!
    But that thy strange mutations make us hate thee,
    Life would not yield to age.[4]

    [EDGAR *stands aside*]

OLD MAN [*to* GLOUCESTER]   O my good lord,
    I have been your tenant and your father's tenant
    These fourscore years.
15 GLOUCESTER Away, get thee away, good friend, be gone.
    Thy comforts° can do me no good at all;   *assistance*
    Thee they may hurt.
OLD MAN   You cannot see your way.
GLOUCESTER I have no way, and therefore want no eyes.
    I stumbled when I saw. Full oft 'tis seen
20   Our means secure us, and our mere defects
    Prove our commodities.[5] O dear son Edgar,
    The food° of thy abusèd° father's wrath—   *fuel; prey / deceived*
    Might I but live to see thee in° my touch   *through*
    I'd say I had eyes again.
OLD MAN   How now? Who's there?
25 EDGAR [*aside*] O gods! Who is't can say 'I am at the worst'?
    I am worse than e'er I was.
OLD MAN [*to* GLOUCESTER]   'Tis poor mad Tom.
EDGAR [*aside*] And worse I may be yet. The worst is not
    So long as we can say 'This is the worst.'
OLD MAN [*to* EDGAR]   Fellow, where goest?
30 GLOUCESTER Is it a beggarman?
OLD MAN Madman and beggar too.
GLOUCESTER A° has some reason, else he could not beg.   *He*
    I'th' last night's storm I such a fellow saw,
    Which made me think a man a worm. My son
35   Came then into my mind, and yet my mind
    Was then scarce friends with him. I have heard more since.
    As flies to wanton° boys are we to th' gods;   *playful; careless*
    They kill us for their sport.

4.1 Location: Open country.

1. *Stands . . . fear:* Remains in hope ("esperance") because there is no fear of falling further.

2. *The lamentable . . . laughter:* The change to be lamented is one that alters the best of circumstances; the worst luck can only improve.

3. Multicolored like a fool's costume (red with blood under white dressings).

4. *But . . . age:* If there were no strange reversals of fortune to make the world hateful, we would not consent to aging and death.

5. *Our means . . . commodities:* Our wealth makes us overconfident, and our utter deprivation proves to be beneficial.

EDGAR [*aside*]   How should this be?
  Bad is the trade that must play fool to sorrow,[6]
  Ang'ring itself and others.
       [*He comes forward*]
                   Bless thee, master.
GLOUCESTER   Is that the naked fellow?
OLD MAN   Ay, my lord.
40 GLOUCESTER   Then prithee, get thee gone. If for my sake
  Thou wilt o'ertake us hence a mile or twain
  I'th' way toward Dover, do it for ancient love,[7]
  And bring some covering for this naked soul,
  Who I'll entreat to lead me.
OLD MAN   Alack, sir, he is mad.
45 GLOUCESTER   'Tis the time's plague when[8] madmen lead the blind.
  Do as I bid thee; or rather do thy pleasure.
  Above the rest, be gone.

OLD MAN I'll bring him the best 'parel° that I have,		*apparel, clothing*
Come on't what will. [*Exit*]		

GLOUCESTER   Sirrah, naked fellow!
50 EDGAR   Poor Tom's a-cold. I cannot dance it farther.[9]
GLOUCESTER   Come hither, fellow.
EDGAR   Bless thy sweet eyes, they bleed.
GLOUCESTER   Know'st thou the way to Dover?

EDGAR Both stile and gate, horseway and footpath. Poor Tom		
hath been scared out of his good wits. Bless thee, goodman,°		*commoner*
from the foul fiend. Five fiends have been in Poor Tom at		
once, as Obidicut of lust, Hobbididence prince of dumbness,		
Mahu of stealing, Modo of murder, Flibbertigibbet of mocking		
and mowing,° who since possesses chambermaids and waiting-		*making faces*
women. So bless thee, master.		

55, 60

GLOUCESTER Here, take this purse, thou whom the heavens' plagues		
Have humbled to all strokes.° That I am wretched		*to accept all blows*
Makes thee the happier. Heavens deal so still.°		*always*
Let the superfluous and lust-dieted man[1]		
That stands° your ordinance,° that will not see		*resists / authority*
Because he does not feel, feel your power quickly.		
So distribution should undo excess,		
And each man have enough. Dost thou know Dover?		

65

EDGAR   Ay, master.

70 GLOUCESTER There is a cliff whose high and bending° head		*overhanging*
Looks saucily in the confinèd deep.[2]		
Bring me but to the very brim of it		
And I'll repair the misery thou dost bear		
With something rich about me. From that place		
I shall no leading need.		

75

EDGAR   Give me thy arm.
  Poor Tom shall lead thee.   [*Exit* EDGAR *guiding* GLOUCESTER]

---

6. It is a bad business to have to play the fool in the face of sorrow.
7. For the sake of our long and loyal relationship (as master and servant).
8. The time is truly sick when.
9. I cannot continue the charade.
1. Let the overprosperous man who indulges his appetite.
2. Looks fearsomely into the straits below.

EDGAR [*aside*] How should this be?
Bad is the trade that must play fool to sorrow,[6]
Ang'ring itself and others.
  [*He comes forward*]
40 Bless thee, master.
GLOUCESTER Is that the naked fellow?
OLD MAN Ay, my lord.
GLOUCESTER Get thee away. If for my sake
  Thou wilt o'ertake us hence a mile or twain
  I'th' way toward Dover, do it for ancient love,[7]
45 And bring some covering for this naked soul,
  Which I'll entreat to lead me.
OLD MAN Alack, sir, he is mad.
GLOUCESTER 'Tis the time's plague when[8] madmen lead the blind.
  Do as I bid thee; or rather do thy pleasure.
  Above the rest, be gone.
50 OLD MAN I'll bring him the best 'parel° that I have,   apparel, clothing
  Come on't what will.   Exit
GLOUCESTER Sirrah, naked fellow!
EDGAR Poor Tom's a-cold. [*Aside*] I cannot daub it further.[9]
GLOUCESTER Come hither, fellow.
EDGAR [*aside*] And yet I must.
  [*To* GLOUCESTER] Bless thy sweet eyes, they bleed.
GLOUCESTER Know'st thou the way to Dover?
55 EDGAR Both stile and gate, horseway and footpath. Poor Tom
  hath been scared out of his good wits. Bless thee, goodman's°   commoner's
  son, from the foul fiend.
GLOUCESTER Here, take this purse, thou whom the heavens' plagues
  Have humbled to all strokes.° That I am wretched   to accept all blows
60 Makes thee the happier. Heavens deal so still.°   always
  Let the superfluous and lust-dieted man[1]
  That slaves° your ordinance,° that will not see   defers to/ authority
  Because he does not feel, feel your power quickly.
  So distribution should undo excess,
65 And each man have enough. Dost thou know Dover?
EDGAR Ay, master.
GLOUCESTER There is a cliff whose high and bending° head   overhanging
  Looks fearfully in the confinèd deep.[2]
  Bring me but to the very brim of it
70 And I'll repair the misery thou dost bear
  With something rich about me. From that place
  I shall no leading need.
EDGAR Give me thy arm.
  Poor Tom shall lead thee.   *Exit* [EDGAR *guiding* GLOUCESTER]

6. It is a bad business to have to play the fool in the face
of sorrow.
7. For the sake of our long and loyal relationship (as master and servant).
8. The time is truly sick when.
9. I cannot continue the charade. *daub*: mask, plaster.
1. Let the overprosperous man who indulges his appetite.
2. Looks fearsomely into the straits below.

Scene 16

Enter [at one door] GONORIL *and Bastard* [EDMUND]

GONORIL Welcome, my lord. I marvel our mild husband
Not° met us on the way.   *Has not*

Enter [at another door] Steward [OSWALD]

                 Now, where's your master?

OSWALD Madam, within; but never man so changed.
I told him of the army that was landed;
5 He smiled at it. I told him you were coming;
His answer was 'The worse.' Of Gloucester's treachery
And of the loyal service of his son
When I informed him, then he called me sot,°   *fool*
And told me I had turned the wrong side out.[1]
10 What he should most defy seems pleasant to him;
What like, offensive.

GONORIL [*to* EDMUND] Then shall you go no further.
It is the cowish° terror of his spirit   *cowardly*
That dares not undertake. He'll not feel wrongs
Which tie him to an answer.[2] Our wishes on the way
15 May prove effects.[3] Back, Edmund, to my brother.°   *brother-in-law*
Hasten his musters° and conduct his powers.°   *call-up of troops / armies*
I must change arms at home, and give the distaff[4]
Into my husband's hands. This trusty servant
Shall pass between us. Ere long you are like° to hear,   *likely*
20 If you dare venture in your own behalf,
A mistress's° command. Wear this. Spare speech.   *(playing on "lover's")*
Decline your head. This kiss, if it durst speak,
Would stretch thy spirits up into the air.
       [*She kisses him*]
Conceive,° and fare you well.   *Understand (my meaning)*
25 EDMUND Yours in° the ranks of death.   *even in*
GONORIL My most dear Gloucester.   [*Exit* EDMUND]
   To thee a woman's services are due;
My foot usurps my body.[5]
OSWALD   Madam, here comes my lord.   *Exit*
       [*Enter* ALBANY]
GONORIL I have been worth the whistling.[6]
ALBANY   O Gonoril,
30 You are not worth the dust which the rude wind
Blows in your face. I fear your disposition.
That nature which contemns it° origin   *despises its*
Cannot be bordered certain° in itself.   *be defended securely*
She that herself will sliver and disbranch°   *split*
35 From her material sap perforce must wither,
And come to deadly use.[7]

Scene 16 Location: Before Albany's castle.
1. I had reversed things (by mistaking loyalty for treachery).
2. *He'll . . . answer:* He'll ignore insults that would provoke him to retaliate.
3. May be put into action.
4. A device used in spinning and so emblematic of the female role. To "change arms," therefore, is to swap the insignia of male and female identity.
5. Continuing the inversion of roles, Albany, who should

be the head of the family, is seen by Gonoril as a subservient member with no right to control her.
6. At one time, you would have come to welcome me home; referring to the proverb "It is a poor dog that is not worth the whistling."
7. *She . . . use:* The allusion is probably biblical: "But that which beareth thorns and briers is reproved, and is near unto cursing; whose end is to be burned" (Hebrews 6:8). *come to deadly use:* be destroyed; be used for burning.

4.2

Enter GONERIL *[and] Bastard* [EDMOND *at one door]*
and Steward [OSWALD *at another]*

GONERIL   Welcome, my lord. I marvel our mild husband
  Not° met us on the way. [*To* OSWALD] Now, where's your master?   *Has not*
OSWALD   Madam, within; but never man so changed.
  I told him of the army that was landed;
5 He smiled at it. I told him you were coming;
  His answer was 'The worse'. Of Gloucester's treachery
  And of the loyal service of his son
  When I informed him, then he called me sot,°   *fool*
  And told me I had turned the wrong side out.[1]
10 What most he should dislike seems pleasant to him;
  What like, offensive.
GONERIL [*to* EDMOND]   Then shall you go no further.
  It is the cowish° terror of his spirit   *cowardly*
  That dares not undertake. He'll not feel wrongs
  Which tie him to an answer.[2] Our wishes on the way
15 May prove effects.[3] Back, Edmond, to my brother.°   *brother-in-law*
  Hasten his musters° and conduct his powers.°   *call-up of troops / armies*
  I must change names° at home, and give the distaff[4]   *exchange roles*
  Into my husband's hands. This trusty servant
  Shall pass between us. Ere long you are like° to hear,   *likely*
20 If you dare venture in your own behalf,
  A mistress's° command. Wear this. Spare speech.   *(playing on "lover's")*
  Decline your head. This kiss, if it durst speak,
  Would stretch thy spirits up into the air.
      [*She kisses him*]
  Conceive,° and fare thee well.   *Understand (my meaning)*
25 EDMOND   Yours in° the ranks of death.   *even in*
GONERIL   My most dear Gloucester.   *Exit* [EDMOND]
  O, the difference of man and man!
  To thee a woman's services are due;
  My fool usurps my body.[5]
OSWALD   Madam, here comes my lord.
      Enter ALBANY
GONERIL   I have been worth the whistling.[6]
30 ALBANY   O Goneril,
  You are not worth the dust which the rude wind
  Blows in your face.

4.2 Location: Before Albany's castle.
1. I had reversed things (by mistaking loyalty for treachery).
2. *He'll . . . answer:* He'll ignore insults that would provoke him to retaliate.
3. May be put into action.

4. Spinning staff, the female insignia that she wishes to exchange for Albany's manly sword.
5. My idiot husband presumes to possess me.
6. At one time, you would have come to welcome me home; referring to the proverb "It is a poor dog that is not worth the whistling."

GONORIL   No more. The text is foolish.
ALBANY   Wisdom and goodness to the vile seem vile;
        Filths savour but themselves. What have you done?
        Tigers, not daughters, what have you performed?
40   A father, and a gracious, agèd man,
        Whose reverence even the head-lugged° bear would lick,   *dragged by the head*
        Most barbarous, most degenerate, have you madded.
        Could my good-brother° suffer you to do it—   *brother-in-law*
        A man, a prince by him so benefacted?
45   If that the heavens do not their visible spirits
        Send quickly down to tame these vile offences,
        It will come,
        Humanity must perforce° prey on itself,   *inevitably*
        Like monsters of the deep.
GONORIL   Milk-livered° man,   *Cowardly*
50   That bear'st a cheek for blows, a head for wrongs;[8]
        Who hast not in thy brows an eye discerning
        Thine honour from thy suffering;[9] that not know'st
        Fools do those villains pity who are punished
        Ere they have done their mischief: where's thy drum?°   *(to muster troops)*
55   France spreads his banners in our noiseless° land,   *peaceful*
        With plumèd helm thy flaxen biggin° threats,   *nightcap; child's cap*
        Whiles thou, a moral° fool, sits still and cries   *moralizing*
        'Alack, why does he so?'
ALBANY   See thyself, devil.
        Proper deformity shows not in the fiend
        So horrid as in woman.[1]
60 GONORIL   O vain° fool!   *useless*
ALBANY   Thou changèd and self-covered[2] thing, for shame
        Bemonster not thy feature. Were't my fitness°   *If it were appropriate*
        To let these hands obey my blood,
        They are apt enough to dislocate and tear
65   Thy flesh and bones. Howe'er° thou art a fiend,   *Although*
        A woman's shape doth shield thee.
GONORIL   Marry your manhood, mew[3]—
                Enter [SECOND] GENTLEMAN
ALBANY   What news?
SECOND GENTLEMAN   O my good lord, the Duke of Cornwall's dead,
        Slain by his servant going to put out
        The other eye of Gloucester.
70 ALBANY   Gloucester's eyes?
SECOND GENTLEMAN   A servant that he bred, thralled with
                remorse,°   *shaken with pity*
        Opposed against the act, bending° his sword   *directing*
        To° his great master, who thereat enraged   *Against*

---

8. *for wrongs:* fit for abuse; ready for cuckold's horns.
9. *discerning . . . suffering:* that can distinguish between an insult to your honor and something you should patiently endure.
1. *Proper . . . woman:* Deformity (of morals) is appropriate in the devil and so less horrid than in woman, from whom virtue is expected. Albany may hold a mirror in front of Gonoril, since Jacobean women sometimes wore small mirrors attached to their dresses.
2. Altered and with your true (womanly) self concealed.
3. Get control of your manhood—restrain ("mew") it. Alternatively, assert your feeble masculinity (with a derisive catcall, "mew").

GONERIL   Milk-livered° man,   *Cowardly*
That bear'st a cheek for blows, a head for wrongs;[7]
Who hast not in thy brows an eye discerning
Thine honour from thy suffering[8]—

35   ALBANY   See thyself, devil.
Proper deformity shows not in the fiend
So horrid as in woman.[9]
GONERIL   O vain° fool!   *useless*

        Enter a MESSENGER
MESSENGER   O my good lord, the Duke of Cornwall's dead,
Slain by his servant going to put out
The other eye of Gloucester.
40   ALBANY   Gloucester's eyes?
MESSENGER   A servant that he bred, thrilled with remorse,°   *shaken with pity*
Opposed against the act, bending° his sword   *directing*
To° his great master, who thereat enraged   *Against*

7. *for wrongs:* fit for abuse; ready for cuckold's horns.
8. *discerning . . . suffering:* that can distinguish between
an insult to your honor and something you should
patiently endure.
9. *Proper . . . woman:* Deformity (of morals) is appropriate in the devil and so less horrid than in woman, from
whom virtue is expected. Albany may hold a mirror in
front of Goneril, since Jacobean women sometimes wore
small mirrors attached to their dresses.

Flew on him, and amongst them felled him dead,
75 But not without that harmful stroke which since
Hath plucked him after.[4]
ALBANY   This shows you are above,
You justicers,° that these our nether crimes[5]   judges
So speedily can venge. But O, poor Gloucester!
Lost he his other eye?
SECOND GENTLEMAN   Both, both, my lord.
80 [*To* GONORIL] This letter, madam, craves a speedy answer.
'Tis from your sister.
GONORIL [*aside*]   One way I like this well;[6]
But being° widow, and my Gloucester with her,   her being
May all the building on my fancy pluck
Upon my hateful life.[7] Another way
85 The news is not so took.[8] — I'll read and answer.   *Exit*
ALBANY   Where was his son when they did take his eyes?
SECOND GENTLEMAN   Come with my lady hither.
ALBANY   He is not here.
SECOND GENTLEMAN   No, my good lord; I met him back° again.   *returning*
ALBANY   Knows he the wickedness?
90 SECOND GENTLEMAN   Ay, my good lord; 'twas he informed against him,
And quit the house on purpose that their punishment
Might have the freer course.
ALBANY   Gloucester, I live
To thank thee for the love thou showed'st the King,
And to revenge thy eyes. — Come hither, friend.
95 Tell me what more thou knowest.   *Exeunt*

Scene 17
Enter KENT [*disguised,*] *and* [FIRST] GENTLEMAN
KENT   Why the King of France is so suddenly gone back know
you no reason?
FIRST GENTLEMAN   Something he left imperfect° in the state   *unsettled*
Which, since his coming forth, is thought of;° which   *remembered*
5 Imports° to the kingdom so much fear and danger   *Portends*
That his personal return was most required
And necessary.
KENT   Who hath he left behind him general?
FIRST GENTLEMAN   The Maréchal° of France, Monsieur la Far.   *Marshall*
10 KENT   Did your letters pierce the Queen to any demonstration
of grief?
FIRST GENTLEMAN   Ay, sir. She took them, read them in my presence,
And now and then an ample tear trilled down
Her delicate cheek. It seemed she was a queen
15 Over her passion who,° most rebel-like,   *which*
Sought to be king o'er her.

---

4. Has sent him to follow his servant into death.
5. Lower crimes, and so committed on earth, but also suggesting that the deeds smack of the netherworld of hell.
6. Because a political rival has been eliminated.

7. *May . . . life:* May pull down all of my built-up fantasies and thus make my life hateful.
8. The news may be taken otherwise.
Scene 17 Location: Near the French camp at Dover.

Flew on him, and amongst them felled him dead,
45 But not without that harmful stroke which since
Hath plucked him after.[1]
ALBANY   This shows you are above,
You justicers,° that these our nether crimes[2]   *judges*
So speedily can venge. But O, poor Gloucester!
Lost he his other eye?
MESSENGER   Both, both, my lord.—
50 This letter, madam, craves a speedy answer.
'Tis from your sister.
GONERIL [*aside*]   One way I like this well;[3]
But being° widow, and my Gloucester with her,   *her being*
May all the building in my fancy pluck
Upon my hateful life.[4] Another way
55 The news is not so tart.°—I'll read and answer.   *bitter*
                                        [*Exit with* OSWALD]
ALBANY   Where was his son when they did take his eyes?
MESSENGER   Come with my lady hither.
ALBANY   He is not here.
MESSENGER   No, my good lord; I met him back° again.   *returning*
ALBANY   Knows he the wickedness?
60 MESSENGER   Ay, my good lord; 'twas he informed against him,
And quit the house on purpose that their punishment
Might have the freer course.
ALBANY   Gloucester, I live
To thank thee for the love thou showed'st the King,
And to revenge thine eyes.—Come hither, friend.
65 Tell me what more thou know'st.   *Exeunt*

1. Has sent him to follow his servant into death.
2. Lower crimes, and so committed on earth, but also suggesting that the deeds smack of the netherworld of hell.
3. Because a political rival has been eliminated.
4. *May . . . life*: May pull down all of my built-up fantasies and thus make my life hateful.

KENT   O, then it moved her.
FIRST GENTLEMAN   Not to a rage. Patience and sorrow strove
    Who should express her goodliest.[1] You have seen
    Sunshine and rain at once; her smiles and tears
20   Were like, a better way. Those happy smilets
    That played on her ripe lip seemed not to know
    What guests were in her eyes, which parted thence
    As pearls from diamonds dropped. In brief,
    Sorrow would be a rarity° most beloved   *gem*
    If all could so become it.[2]
25 KENT   Made she no verbal question?
FIRST GENTLEMAN   Faith, once or twice she heaved the name of 'father'
    Pantingly forth as if it pressed her heart,
    Cried 'Sisters, sisters, shame of ladies, sisters,
    Kent, father, sisters, what, i'th' storm, i'th' night,
30   Let piety not be believed!'[3] There she shook
    The holy water from her heavenly eyes
    And clamour° mastered, then away she started°   *crying / sprang*
    To deal with grief alone.
KENT   It is the stars,
    The stars above us govern our conditions,
35   Else one self mate and make[4] could not beget
    Such different issues.° You spoke not with her since?   *offspring*
FIRST GENTLEMAN   No.
KENT   Was this before the King returned?
FIRST GENTLEMAN   No, since.
KENT   Well, sir, the poor distressèd Lear's i'th' town,
40   Who sometime in his better tune° remembers   *state of mind*
    What we are come about, and by no means
    Will yield° to see his daughter.   *consent*
FIRST GENTLEMAN   Why, good sir?
KENT   A sovereign shame so elbows° him: his own unkindness, *prods, nudges*
    That stripped her from his benediction, turned her
45   To foreign casualties,° gave her dear rights   *risks*
    To his dog-hearted daughters—these things sting
    His mind so venomously that burning shame
    Detains him from Cordelia.
FIRST GENTLEMAN   Alack, poor gentleman!
KENT   Of Albany's and Cornwall's powers you heard not?
50 FIRST GENTLEMAN   'Tis so; they are afoot.
KENT   Well, sir, I'll bring you to our master Lear,
    And leave you to attend him. Some dear cause°   *Some important reason*
    Will in concealment wrap me up a while.
    When I am known aright you shall not grieve°   *repent*
55   Lending me this acquaintance.° I pray you go   *news*
    Along with me.   *Exeunt*

---

1. Which should best express her feelings.
2. If everyone wore it so beautifully.
3. Never believe in piety (pity, or filial respect); piety cannot exist.
4. Or else the same pair of spouses; "mate" and "make"
may describe either partner.

Scene 18

Enter [Queen] CORDELIA, DOCTOR, *and others*

CORDELIA   Alack, 'tis he! Why, he was met even now,
     As mad as the racked sea, singing aloud,
     Crowned with rank fumitor and furrow-weeds,[1]
     With burdocks, hemlock, nettles, cuckoo-flowers,
5   Darnel, and all the idle° weeds that grow   *useless*
     In our sustaining corn. The centuries° send forth.   *battalions*
     Search every acre in the high-grown field,
     And bring him to our eye.   [*Exit one or more*]
                              What can man's wisdom
     In the restoring° his bereavèd sense,   *Do to restore*
10   He that can help him
     Take all my outward° worth.   *material*
DOCTOR   There is means, madam.
     Our foster-nurse of nature[2] is repose,
     The which he lacks. That to provoke in him
15   Are many simples operative,[3] whose power
     Will close the eye of anguish.
CORDELIA   All blest secrets,
     All you unpublished virtues° of the earth,   *obscure healing plants*
     Spring with my tears, be aidant and remediate°   *healing and remedial*
     In the good man's distress!—Seek, seek for him,
20   Lest his ungoverned rage dissolve the life
     That wants° the means to lead it.   *lacks*
                    Enter MESSENGER
MESSENGER   News, madam.
     The British powers° are marching hitherward.   *armies*
CORDELIA   'Tis known before; our preparation stands
     In expectation of them.—O dear father,
25   It is thy business that I go about;[4]
     Therefore great France
     My mourning and important° tears hath pitied.   *urgent; solicitous*
     No blown° ambition doth our arms incite,   *inflated*
     But love, dear love, and our aged father's right.[5]
30   Soon may I hear and see him!   *Exeunt*

Scene 18 Location: The French camp at Dover.
1. Fumitor was used against brain sickness. Furrow-weeds, like the other weeds in the following lines, grow in the furrows of plowed fields.
2. *Our . . . nature*: That which comforts and nourishes human nature.
3. *That . . . operative*: To induce that ("repose") in him,

there are many effective medicinal herbs.
4. The line echoes Christ's explanation of his mission in Luke 2:49, "I must go about my father's business."
5. *No . . . right*: 1 Corinthians 13:4–5 in the Bishops' Bible says that love "swelleth not, dealeth not dishonestly, seeketh not her own."

4.3

Enter with drum and colours, [Queen] CORDELIA, GEN-
TLEMEN, *and soldiers*

CORDELIA   Alack, 'tis he! Why, he was met even now,
As mad as the vexed sea, singing aloud,
Crowned with rank fumitor and furrow-weeds,[1]
With burdocks, hemlock, nettles, cuckoo-flowers,
5   Darnel, and all the idle° weeds that grow   *useless*
In our sustaining corn. A century° send forth.   *battalion (100 men)*
Search every acre in the high-grown field,
And bring him to our eye.   [*Exit one or more*]
                                    What can man's wisdom
In the restoring° his bereavèd sense,   *Do to restore*
10   He that helps him take all my outward° worth.   *material*
FIRST GENTLEMAN   There is means, madam.
Our foster-nurse of nature[2] is repose,
The which he lacks. That to provoke in him
Are many simples operative,[3] whose power
Will close the eye of anguish.
15   CORDELIA   All blest secrets,
All you unpublished virtues° of the earth,   *obscure healing plants*
Spring with my tears, be aidant and remediate°   *healing and remedial*
In the good man's distress! — Seek, seek for him,
Lest his ungoverned rage dissolve the life
That wants° the means to lead it.   *lacks*
                    Enter [a] MESSENGER
20   MESSENGER   News, madam.
The British powers° are marching hitherward.   *armies*
CORDELIA   'Tis known before; our preparation stands
In expectation of them. — O dear father,
It is thy business that I go about;[4]
25   Therefore great France
My mourning and importuned° tears hath pitied.   *importunate; solicitous*
No blown° ambition doth our arms incite,   *inflated*
But love, dear love, and our aged father's right.[5]
Soon may I hear and see him!   *Exeunt*

4.3 Location: The French camp at Dover.
1. Fumitor was used against brain sickness. Furrow-weeds, like the other weeds in the following lines, grow in the furrows of plowed fields.
2. *Our ... nature:* That which comforts and nourishes human nature.
3. *That ... operative:* To induce that ("repose") in him,

there are many effective medicinal herbs.
4. The line echoes Christ's explanation of his mission in Luke 2:49, "I must go about my father's business."
5. *No ... right:* 1 Corinthians 13:4–5 in the Bishops' Bible says that love "swelleth not, dealeth not dishonestly, seeketh not her own."

Scene 19

Enter REGAN *and Steward* [OSWALD]

REGAN	But are my brother's powers° set forth?	*(Albany's forces)*
OSWALD	Ay, madam.	
REGAN	Himself in person?	
OSWALD	Madam, with much ado.°	*trouble*
	Your sister is the better soldier.	
REGAN	Lord Edmund spake not with your lord at home?	

5   OSWALD   No, madam.

REGAN   What might import° my sister's letters to him?   *mean*

OSWALD   I know not, lady.

REGAN   Faith, he is posted° hence on serious matter.   *hurried*

It was great ignorance, Gloucester's eyes being out,

10   To let him live. Where he arrives he moves

All hearts against us. Edmund, I think, is gone,

In pity of his misery,° to dispatch   *(ironic)*

His 'nighted° life, moreover to descry°   *darkened / investigate*

The strength o'th' army.

15   OSWALD   I must needs after° with my letters, madam.   *go after*

REGAN   Our troop sets forth tomorrow. Stay with us.

The ways are dangerous.

OSWALD   I may not, madam.

My lady charged° my duty in this business.   *commanded*

REGAN   Why should she write to Edmund? Might not you

20   Transport her purposes by word? Belike°—   *Perhaps*

Something, I know not what. I'll love° thee much: *reward*

Let me unseal the letter.

OSWALD   Madam, I'd rather—

REGAN   I know your lady does not love her husband.

I am sure of that, and at her late° being here   *recently*

25   She gave strange oeillades° and most speaking looks   *amorous glances*

To noble Edmund. I know you are of her bosom.°   *in her confidence*

OSWALD   I, madam?

REGAN   I speak in understanding,° for I know't.   *with certainty*

Therefore I do advise you take this note.°   *take note of this*

30   My lord is dead. Edmund and I have talked,

And more convenient° is he for my hand   *appropriate*

Than for your lady's. You may gather° more.   *infer*

If you do find him, pray you give him this,[1]

And when your mistress hears thus much from you,

35   I pray desire her call her wisdom to her.[2]

So, farewell.

If you do chance to hear of that blind traitor,

Preferment falls on him that cuts him off.°   *cuts his life short*

OSWALD   Would I could meet him, madam. I would show

What lady I do follow.

40   REGAN   Fare thee well.   *Exeunt* [*severally*]

Scene 19 Location: At Gloucester's castle.   2. *desire . . . to her*: tell her to come to her senses.
1. This information, but possibly another letter or token.

4.4

Enter REGAN *and Steward* [OSWALD]

REGAN But are my brother's powers° set forth?   (*Albany's forces*)

OSWALD   Ay, madam.

REGAN Himself in person there?

OSWALD   Madam, with much ado.°   *trouble*
    Your sister is the better soldier.

REGAN Lord Edmond spake not with your lord at home?

5 OSWALD No, madam.

REGAN What might import° my sister's letters to him?   *mean*

OSWALD I know not, lady.

REGAN Faith, he is posted° hence on serious matter.   *hurried*
    It was great ignorance, Gloucester's eyes being out,

10   To let him live. Where he arrives he moves
    All hearts against us. Edmond, I think, is gone,
    In pity of his misery,° to dispatch   (*ironic*)
    His 'nighted° life, moreover to descry°   *darkened / investigate*
    The strength o'th' enemy.

15 OSWALD I must needs after,° madam, with my letter.   *go after*

REGAN Our troops set forth tomorrow. Stay with us.
    The ways are dangerous.

OSWALD   I may not, madam.
    My lady charged° my duty in this business.   *commanded*

REGAN Why should she write to Edmond? Might not you

20   Transport her purposes by word? Belike°—   *Perhaps*
    Some things—I know not what. I'll love° thee much: *reward*
    Let me unseal the letter.

OSWALD   Madam, I had rather—

REGAN I know your lady does not love her husband.
    I am sure of that, and at her late° being here   *recently*

25   She gave strange oeillades° and most speaking looks   *amorous glances*
    To noble Edmond. I know you are of her bosom.°   *in her confidence*

OSWALD I, madam?

REGAN I speak in understanding.° Y'are, I know't.   *with certainty*
    Therefore I do advise you take this note.°   *take note of this*

30   My lord is dead. Edmond and I have talked,
    And more convenient° is he for my hand   *appropriate*
    Than for your lady's. You may gather° more.   *infer*
    If you do find him, pray you give him this,[1]
    And when your mistress hears thus much from you,

35   I pray desire her call her wisdom to her.[2]
    So, fare you well.
    If you do chance to hear of that blind traitor,
    Preferment falls on him that cuts him off.°   *cuts his life short*

OSWALD Would I could meet him, madam. I should show
    What party I do follow.

40 REGAN   Fare thee well.   *Exeunt* [*severally*]

4.4 Location: At Gloucester's castle.   2. *desire . . . to her*: tell her to come to her senses.
1. This information, but possibly another letter or token.

Scene 20

Enter EDGAR [*disguised as a peasant, with a staff, guid-*
ing the blind] GLOUCESTER

GLOUCESTER   When shall we come to th' top of that same° hill?   *agreed-upon*
EDGAR   You do climb up it now. Look how we labour.
GLOUCESTER   Methinks the ground is even.
EDGAR   Horrible steep.
       Hark, do you hear the sea?
GLOUCESTER   No, truly.
5   EDGAR   Why, then your other senses grow imperfect
       By your eyes' anguish.
GLOUCESTER   So may it be indeed.
       Methinks thy voice is altered, and thou speak'st
       With better phrase and matter° than thou didst.   *sense*
EDGAR   You're much deceived. In nothing am I changed
       But in my garments.
10   GLOUCESTER   Methinks you're better spoken.
EDGAR   Come on, sir, here's the place. Stand still. How fearful
       And dizzy 'tis to cast one's eyes so low!
       The crows and choughs° that wing the midway air[1]   *jackdaws*
       Show° scarce so gross° as beetles. Halfway down   *Appear / big*
15   Hangs one that gathers samphire,° dreadful trade!   *seaweed*
       Methinks he seems no bigger than his head.
       The fishermen that walk upon the beach
       Appear like mice, and yon tall anchoring barque°   *ship*
       Diminished to her cock,° her cock a buoy   *dinghy*
20   Almost too small for sight. The murmuring surge
       That on the unnumbered° idle pebble chafes   *innumerable*
       Cannot be heard, it's so high. I'll look no more,
       Lest my brain turn and the° deficient sight   *my*
       Topple° down headlong.   *Topple me*
GLOUCESTER   Set me where you stand.
25   EDGAR   Give me your hand. You are now within a foot
       Of th'extreme verge. For all beneath the moon
       Would I not leap upright.[2]
GLOUCESTER   Let go my hand.
       Here, friend, 's another purse; in it a jewel
       Well worth a poor man's taking. Fairies and gods
30   Prosper it[3] with thee! Go thou farther off.
       Bid me farewell, and let me hear thee going.
EDGAR   Now fare you well, good sir.
       [*He stands aside*]
GLOUCESTER   With all my heart.
EDGAR [*aside*]   Why I do trifle thus with his despair
       Is done to cure it.
GLOUCESTER   O you mighty gods,
       He kneels
35   This world I do renounce, and in your sights
       Shake patiently my great affliction off!

Scene 20 Location: Near Dover.   balance).
1. The air between cliff and sea.   3. Make it increase. Fairies were sometimes held to
2. I would not jump up and down (for fear of losing my hoard and multiply treasure.

4.5

Enter EDGAR [*disguised as a peasant, with a staff, guiding the blind*] GLOUCESTER

GLOUCESTER   When shall I come to th' top of that same° hill?   *agreed-upon*
EDGAR   You do climb up it now. Look how we labour.
GLOUCESTER   Methinks the ground is even.
EDGAR   Horrible steep.
   Hark, do you hear the sea?
GLOUCESTER   No, truly.
5   EDGAR   Why, then your other senses grow imperfect
   By your eyes' anguish.
GLOUCESTER   So may it be indeed.
   Methinks thy voice is altered, and thou speak'st
   In better phrase and matter° than thou didst.   *sense*
EDGAR   You're much deceived. In nothing am I changed
   But in my garments.
10   GLOUCESTER   Methinks you're better spoken.
EDGAR   Come on, sir, here's the place. Stand still. How fearful
   And dizzy 'tis to cast one's eyes so low!
   The crows and choughs° that wing the midway air[1]   *jackdaws*
   Show° scarce so gross° as beetles. Halfway down   *Appear / big*
15   Hangs one that gathers samphire,° dreadful trade!   *seaweed*
   Methinks he seems no bigger than his head.
   The fishermen that walk upon the beach
   Appear like mice, and yon tall anchoring barque°   *ship*
   Diminished to her cock,° her cock a buoy   *dinghy*
20   Almost too small for sight. The murmuring surge
   That on th'unnumbered° idle pebble chafes   *innumerable*
   Cannot be heard so high. I'll look no more,
   Lest my brain turn and the° deficient sight   *my*
   Topple° down headlong.   *Topple me*
GLOUCESTER   Set me where you stand.
25   EDGAR   Give me your hand. You are now within a foot
   Of th'extreme verge. For all beneath the moon
   Would I not leap upright.[2]
GLOUCESTER   Let go my hand.
   Here, friend, 's another purse; in it a jewel
   Well worth a poor man's taking. Fairies and gods
30   Prosper it[3] with thee! Go thou further off.
   Bid me farewell, and let me hear thee going.
EDGAR   Now fare ye well, good sir.
     [*He stands aside*]
GLOUCESTER   With all my heart.
EDGAR [*aside*]   Why I do trifle thus with his despair
   Is done to cure it.
GLOUCESTER [*kneeling*] O you mighty gods,
35   This world I do renounce, and in your sights
   Shake patiently my great affliction off!

4.5 Location: Near Dover.
1. The air between cliff and sea.
2. I would not jump up and down (for fear of losing my
balance).
3. Make it increase. Fairies were sometimes held to
hoard and multiply treasure.

If I could bear it longer, and not fall
To quarrel° with your great opposeless wills,   *Into conflict*
My snuff and loathèd part of nature[4] should
40 Burn itself out. If Edgar live, O bless him!—
Now, fellow, fare thee well.
EDGAR   Gone, sir. Farewell.
        [GLOUCESTER] *falls [forward]*
[*Aside*] And yet I know not how conceit may rob
The treasury of life, when life itself
Yields to the theft.[5] Had he been where he thought,
45 By this° had thought been past.—Alive or dead?   *now*
[*To* GLOUCESTER] Ho you, sir; hear you, sir? Speak.
[*Aside*] Thus might he pass° indeed. Yet he revives.   *pass away*
[*To* GLOUCESTER] What are you, sir?
GLOUCESTER   Away, and let me die.
EDGAR Hadst thou been aught° but goss'mer, feathers, air,   *anything*
50 So many fathom down precipitating°   *plunging*
Thou hadst shivered° like an egg. But thou dost breathe,   *shattered*
Hast heavy substance, bleed'st not, speak'st, art sound.
Ten masts a-length° make not the altitude   *end to end*
Which thou hast perpendicularly fell.
55 Thy life's a miracle. Speak yet again.
GLOUCESTER But have I fallen, or no?
EDGAR From the dread summit of this chalky bourn.[6]
Look up a-height. The shrill-gorged° lark so far   *shrill-throated*
Cannot be seen or heard. Do but look up.
60 GLOUCESTER Alack, I have no eyes.
Is wretchedness deprived° that benefit   *deprived of*
To end itself by death? 'Twas yet some comfort
When misery could beguile° the tyrant's rage   *cheat*
And frustrate his proud will.
EDGAR   Give me your arm.
65 Up. So, how now? Feel you your legs? You stand.
GLOUCESTER Too well, too well.
EDGAR   This is above all strangeness.
Upon the crown of the cliff what thing was that
Which parted from you?
GLOUCESTER   A poor unfortunate beggar.
EDGAR As I stood here below, methoughts his eyes
70 Were two full moons. A had a thousand noses,
Horns whelked° and wavèd like the enridgèd sea.   *twisted*
It was some fiend. Therefore, thou happy father,°   *lucky old man*
Think that the clearest° gods, who made their honours   *purest; most illustrious*
Of men's impossibilities,[7] have preserved thee.
75 GLOUCESTER I do remember now. Henceforth I'll bear
Affliction till it do cry out itself
'Enough, enough,' and die. That thing you speak of,
I took it for a man. Often would it say

---

4. The scorched and hateful remnant of my lifetime.
snuff: end of a candle wick.
5. *And yet . . . theft:* Edgar worries that the imagined scenario ("conceit") he has invented may be enough to kill
his father, particularly as Gloucester wishes for ("yields

to") his own death.
6. The white chalk cliffs of Dover, which make a boundary ("bourn") between land and sea.
7. *who . . . impossibilities:* who attained honor for themselves by performing deeds impossible to men.

If I could bear it longer, and not fall
To quarrel° with your great opposeless wills,   *Into conflict*
My snuff and loathèd part of nature⁴ should
40 Burn itself out. If Edgar live, O bless him!—
Now, fellow, fare thee well.
EDGAR   Gone, sir. Farewell.
    [GLOUCESTER *falls forward*]
    [*Aside*] And yet I know not how conceit may rob
The treasury of life, when life itself
Yields to the theft.⁵ Had he been where he thought,
45 By this° had thought been past.—Alive or dead?   *now*
    [*To* GLOUCESTER] Ho, you, sir, friend; hear you, sir? Speak.
    [*Aside*] Thus might he pass° indeed. Yet he revives.   *pass away*
    [*To* GLOUCESTER] What are you, sir?
GLOUCESTER   Away, and let me die.
EDGAR   Hadst thou been aught° but gossamer, feathers, air,   *anything*
50 So many fathom down precipitating°   *plunging*
Thou'dst shivered° like an egg. But thou dost breathe,   *shattered*
Hast heavy substance, bleed'st not, speak'st, art sound.
Ten masts a-length° make not the altitude   *end to end*
Which thou hast perpendicularly fell.
55 Thy life's a miracle. Speak yet again.
GLOUCESTER   But have I fall'n, or no?
EDGAR   From the dread summit of this chalky bourn.⁶
Look up a-height. The shrill-gorged° lark so far   *shrill-throated*
Cannot be seen or heard. Do but look up.
60 GLOUCESTER   Alack, I have no eyes.
Is wretchedness deprived° that benefit   *deprived of*
To end itself by death? 'Twas yet some comfort
When misery could beguile° the tyrant's rage   *cheat*
And frustrate his proud will.
EDGAR   Give me your arm.
65 Up, so. How is't? Feel you your legs? You stand.
GLOUCESTER   Too well, too well.
EDGAR   This is above all strangeness.
Upon the crown o'th' cliff what thing was that
Which parted from you?
GLOUCESTER   A poor unfortunate beggar.
EDGAR   As I stood here below, methoughts his eyes
70 Were two full moons. He had a thousand noses,
Horns whelked° and wavèd like the enragèd sea.   *twisted*
It was some fiend. Therefore, thou happy father,°   *lucky old man*
Think that the clearest° gods, who make them honours   *purest; most illustrious*
Of men's impossibilities,⁷ have preserved thee.
75 GLOUCESTER   I do remember now. Henceforth I'll bear
Affliction till it do cry out itself
'Enough, enough,' and die. That thing you speak of,
I took it for a man. Often 'twould say

---

4. The scorched and hateful remnant of my lifetime.
snuff: end of a candle wick.
5. *And yet . . . theft*: Edgar worries that the imagined scenario ("conceit") he has invented may be enough to kill
his father, particularly as Gloucester wishes for ("yields
to") his own death.
6. The white chalk cliffs of Dover, which make a boundary ("bourn") between land and sea.
7. *who . . . impossibilities*: who attain honor for themselves by performing deeds impossible to men.

'The fiend, the fiend!' He led me to that place.

EDGAR   Bear free and patient thoughts.

Enter LEAR *mad [crowned with weeds and flowers]*

80   But who comes here?
The safer sense will ne'er accommodate
His master thus.[8]

LEAR   No, they cannot touch me for coining.[9] I am the King
himself.

85   EDGAR   O thou side-piercing sight!

LEAR   Nature is above art in that respect.[1] There's your press-
money.[2] That fellow handles his bow like a crow-keeper.[3] Draw
me a clothier's yard.[4] Look, look, a mouse! Peace, peace, this
toasted cheese will do it.° There's my gauntlet. I'll prove it on   *(lure the mouse)*
90   a giant.[5] Bring up the brown bills.[6] O, well flown, bird,° in the   *arrow*
air. Ha! Give the word.°   *password*

EDGAR   Sweet marjoram.[7]

LEAR   Pass.

GLOUCESTER   I know that voice.

95   LEAR   Ha, Gonoril! Ha, Regan! They flattered me like a dog,°   *fawningly*
and told me I had white hairs in my beard ere the black ones
were there.[8] To say 'ay' and 'no' to everything I said 'ay' and
'no' to was no good divinity.[9] When the rain came to wet me
once, and the wind to make me chatter, when the thunder
100   would not peace at my bidding, there I found° them, there I   *understood*
smelt them out. Go to, they are not men of their words. They
told me I was everything; 'tis a lie, I am not ague-proof.°   *immune to illness*

GLOUCESTER   The trick° of that voice I do well remember.   *peculiarity*
Is't not the King?

LEAR   Ay, every inch a king.

                        [GLOUCESTER *kneels*]

105   When I do stare, see how the subject quakes!
I pardon that man's life. What was thy cause?°   *crime*
Adultery? Thou shalt not die for adultery.
No, the wren goes to't, and the small gilded fly
Does lecher in my sight.

110   Let copulation thrive, for Gloucester's bastard son
Was kinder to his father than my daughters
Got 'tween the lawful sheets. To't, luxury,° pell-mell,   *lechery*
For I lack soldiers. Behold yon simp'ring dame,
Whose face between her forks presageth snow,[1]

115   That minces° virtue, and does shake the head   *affects*
To hear of° pleasure's name: *even of*
The fitchew nor the soilèd horse[2] goes to't
With a more riotous appetite. Down from the waist

---

8. *The . . . thus:* A sane mind would never allow its possessor to dress up this way.
9. Because minting money was the prerogative of the
king, nobody could overtake or equal ("touch") him.
1. My true feelings will always outvalue others' hypocrisy;
my natural supremacy surpasses any attempt to create a
false new reign. This image may also be based on coining
(see note 9 above).
2. Fee paid to a soldier impressed, or forced, into the
army.
3. A person hired as a scarecrow, and thus unfit for anything else.
4. Draw the bowstring the full length of the arrow (a standard English arrow was a cloth yard [thirty-seven inches]

long).
5. I'll defend my stand even against a giant. To throw
down an armored glove ("gauntlet") was to issue a challenge.
6. Brown painted pikes; the soldiers carrying them.
7. Used medicinally against madness.
8. Told me I had wisdom before age.
9. *no good divinity:* poor theology (because insincere);
from James 5:12, "Let your yea be yea; nay, nay."
1. Whose expression implies cold chastity. "Face" refers
to the area between her legs ("forks"), as well as to her
literal facial expression as framed by the aristocratic lady's
starched headpiece, also called a "fork."
2. Neither the polecat nor a horse full of fresh grass.

'The fiend, the fiend!' He led me to that place.
EDGAR Bear free and patient thoughts.
          Enter LEAR [*mad, crowned with weeds and flowers*]
80   But who comes here?
The safer sense will ne'er accommodate
His master thus.[8]
LEAR No, they cannot touch me° for crying. I am the King   lay hands on me
     himself.
85 EDGAR O thou side-piercing sight!
LEAR Nature's above art in that respect.[9] There's your press-
     money.[1] That fellow handles his bow like a crow-keeper.[2] Draw
     me a clothier's yard.[3] Look, look, a mouse! Peace, peace, this
     piece of toasted cheese will do't.° There's my gauntlet. I'll   (lure the mouse)
90   prove it on a giant.[4] Bring up the brown bills.[5] O, well flown,
     bird,° i'th' clout,° i'th' clout! Whew! Give the word.°   arrow / bull's-eye / password
EDGAR Sweet marjoram.[6]
LEAR Pass.
GLOUCESTER I know that voice.
95 LEAR Ha! Goneril with a white beard? They flattered me like a
     dog,° and told me I had the white hairs in my beard ere the   fawningly
     black ones were there.[7] To say 'ay' and 'no' to everything that I
     said 'ay' and 'no' to was no good divinity.[8] When the rain came
     to wet me once, and the wind to make me chatter; when the
100 thunder would not peace at my bidding, there I found° 'em,   understood
     there I smelt 'em out. Go to, they are not men o' their words.
     They told me I was everything; 'tis a lie, I am not ague-proof.°   immune to illness
GLOUCESTER The trick° of that voice I do well remember.   peculiarity
     Is't not the King?
LEAR   Ay, every inch a king.
          [GLOUCESTER *kneels*]
105 When I do stare, see how the subject quakes!
I pardon that man's life. What was thy cause?°   crime
Adultery? Thou shalt not die. Die for adultery!
No, the wren goes to't, and the small gilded fly
Does lecher in my sight. Let copulation thrive,
110 For Gloucester's bastard son
Was kinder to his father than my daughters
Got 'tween the lawful sheets. To't, luxury,° pell-mell,   lechery
For I lack soldiers. Behold yon simp'ring dame,
Whose face between her forks presages snow,[9]
115 That minces° virtue, and does shake the head   affects
To hear of° pleasure's name.   even of
The fitchew nor the soilèd horse[1] goes to't
With a more riotous appetite. Down from the waist

8. *The . . . thus:* A sane mind would never allow its possessor to dress up this way.
9. My true feelings will always outvalue others' hypocrisy;
my natural supremacy surpasses any attempt to create a
false new reign. This image may also be based on coining.
1. Fee paid to a soldier impressed, or forced, into the
army.
2. A person hired as a scarecrow, and thus unfit for anything else.
3. Draw the bowstring the full length of the arrow (a standard English arrow was a cloth yard [thirty-seven inches]
long).
4. I'll defend my stand even against a giant. To throw

down an armored glove ("gauntlet") was to issue a challenge.
5. Brown painted pikes; the soldiers carrying them.
6. Used medicinally against madness.
7. Told me I had wisdom before age.
8. *no good divinity:* poor theology (because insincere);
from James 5:12, "Let your yea be yea; nay, nay."
9. Whose expression implies cold chastity. "Face" refers
to the area between her legs ("forks") as well as to her
literal facial expression as framed by the aristocratic lady's
starched headpiece, also called a "fork."
1. Neither the polecat nor a horse full of fresh grass.

	They're centaurs,[3] though women all above.	
120	But° to the girdle° do the gods inherit;°	*Only / waist / own*
	Beneath is all the fiend's. There's hell,[4] there's darkness,	
	There's the sulphury pit, burning, scalding,	
	Stench, consummation. Fie, fie, fie; pah, pah!	
	Give me an ounce of civet,[5] good apothecary,	
125	To sweeten my imagination.	
	There's money for thee.	

GLOUCESTER   O, let me kiss that hand!

LEAR   Here, wipe it first; it smells of mortality.

GLOUCESTER   O ruined piece° of nature! This great world   *masterpiece*
Shall so wear out to naught.[6] Do you know me?

130   LEAR   I remember thy eyes well enough. Dost thou squiny°   *squint*
on me?
No, do thy worst, blind Cupid, I'll not love.
Read thou that challenge. Mark the penning of 't.

GLOUCESTER   Were all the letters suns, I could not see one.

135   EDGAR [*aside*]   I would not take° this from report; it is,   *believe*
And my heart breaks at it.

LEAR [*to* GLOUCESTER]   Read.

GLOUCESTER   What—with the case° of eyes?   *sockets*

LEAR   O ho, are you there with me?[7] No eyes in your head, nor
140   no money in your purse? Your eyes are in a heavy case,[8] your
purse in a light; yet you see how this world goes.

GLOUCESTER   I see it feelingly.°   *by touch; painfully*

LEAR   What, art mad? A man may see how the world goes with
no eyes; look with thy ears. See how yon justice rails upon yon
145   simple° thief. Hark in thy ear: handy-dandy,[9] which is the thief,   *lowly; innocent*
which is the justice? Thou hast seen a farmer's dog bark at a
beggar?

GLOUCESTER   Ay, sir.

LEAR   An the creature° run from the cur, there thou mightst   *If the wretch*
150   behold the great image of authority. A dog's obeyed in office.
Thou rascal beadle,[1] hold° thy bloody hand.   *restrain*
Why dost thou lash that whore? Strip thine own back.
Thy blood as hotly lusts to use her in that kind°   *way*
For which thou whip'st her. The usurer hangs the cozener.[2]
155   Through tattered rags small vices do appear;
Robes and furred gowns hides all. Get thee glass eyes,
And, like a scurvy politician,[3] seem
To see the things thou dost not. No tears, now.
Pull off my boots. Harder, harder! So.

160   EDGAR [*aside*]   O, matter and impertinency° mixed—   *sense and nonsense*
Reason in madness!

---

3. Lecherous mythological creatures that have a human
body to the waist and the legs and torso of a horse below.
4. Shakespeare's frequent term for female genitals.
5. Exotic perfume derived from the sex glands of the
civet cat.
6. Shall decay to nothing in the same way. In Renaissance philosophy, humans were perfectly analogous to
the cosmos, standing for the whole in miniature and as its
masterpiece.

7. Is that what you are telling me?
8. In a sad condition; playing on "case" as "sockets."
9. Pick a hand, as in a child's game.
1. The parish officer responsible for whippings.
2. The ruinous moneylender, prosperous enough to be
made a judge, convicts the ordinary cheat.
3. A vile schemer. In early modern England, "politician"
meant an ambitious, even Machiavellian, upstart.

They're centaurs,[2] though women all above.

120 But° to the girdle° do the gods inherit;°   *Only / waist / own*
Beneath is all the fiend's. There's hell,[3] there's darkness, there
is the sulphurous pit, burning, scalding, stench, consumption.
Fie, fie, fie; pah, pah! Give me an ounce of civet,[4] good apothe-
cary, sweeten my imagination.
There's money for thee.

125 GLOUCESTER   O, let me kiss that hand!

LEAR   Let me wipe it first; it smells of mortality.

GLOUCESTER   O ruined piece° of nature! This great world   *masterpiece*
Shall so wear out to naught.[5] Dost thou know me?

LEAR   I remember thine eyes well enough. Dost thou squiny°   *squint*
130 at me?
No, do thy worst, blind Cupid, I'll not love.
Read thou this challenge. Mark but the penning of it.

GLOUCESTER   Were all thy letters suns, I could not see.

EDGAR [*aside*]   I would not take° this from report; it is,   *believe*
135 And my heart breaks at it.

LEAR [*to* GLOUCESTER]   Read.

GLOUCESTER   What—with the case° of eyes?   *socket*

LEAR   O ho, are you there with me?[6] No eyes in your head, nor
no money in your purse? Your eyes are in a heavy case,[7] your
140 purse in a light; yet you see how this world goes.

GLOUCESTER   I see it feelingly.°   *by touch; painfully*

LEAR   What, art mad? A man may see how this world goes with
no eyes; look with thine ears. See how yon justice rails upon
yon simple° thief. Hark in thine ear: change places, and handy-   *lowly; innocent*
145 dandy,[8] which is the justice, which is the thief? Thou hast seen
a farmer's dog bark at a beggar?

GLOUCESTER   Ay, sir.

LEAR   An the creature° run from the cur, there thou mightst   *If the wretch*
behold the great image of authority. A dog's obeyed in office.
150 Thou rascal beadle,[9] hold° thy bloody hand.   *restrain*
Why dost thou lash that whore? Strip thy own back.
Thou hotly lusts to use her in that kind°   *way*
For which thou whip'st her. The usurer hangs the cozener.[1]
Through tattered clothes great vices do appear;
155 Robes and furred gowns hide all. Plate° sin with gold,   *Armor; gild*
And the strong lance of justice hurtless° breaks;   *harmlessly*
Arm it in rags, a pygmy's straw does pierce it.
None does offend, none, I say none. I'll able° 'em.   *authorize*
Take that of me, my friend, who have the power
160 To seal th'accuser's lips. Get thee glass eyes,
And, like a scurvy politician,[2] seem
To see the things thou dost not. Now, now, now, now!
Pull off my boots. Harder, harder! So.

EDGAR [*aside*]   O, matter and impertinency° mixed—   *sense and nonsense*
165 Reason in madness!

---

2. Lecherous mythological creatures that have a human
body to the waist and the legs and torso of a horse below.
3. Shakespeare's frequent term for female genitals.
4. Exotic perfume derived from the sex glands of the
civet cat.
5. Shall decay to nothing in the same way. In Renaissance philosophy, humans were perfectly analogous to
the cosmos, standing for the whole in miniature and as its
masterpiece.

6. Is that what you are telling me?
7. In a sad condition; playing on "case" as "sockets."
8. Pick a hand, as in a child's game.
9. The parish officer responsible for whippings.
1. The ruinous moneylender, prosperous enough to be
made a judge, convicts the ordinary cheat.
2. A vile schemer. In early modern England, "politician"
meant an ambitious, even Machiavellian, upstart.

LEAR   If thou wilt weep my fortune, take my eyes.
    I know thee well enough: thy name is Gloucester.
    Thou must be patient. We came crying hither.
165   Thou know'st the first time that we smell the air
    We wail and cry. I will preach to thee. Mark me.
GLOUCESTER   Alack, alack, the day!
LEAR [*removing his crown of weeds*][4]   When we are born, we cry
        that we are come
    To this great stage of fools. This'° a good block.[5]   *This is*
170   It were a delicate° stratagem to shoe   *subtle*
    A troop of horse with felt;[6] and when I have stole upon
    These son-in-laws, then kill, kill, kill, kill, kill, kill!

            Enter three GENTLEMEN

FIRST GENTLEMAN   O, here he is. Lay hands upon him, sirs.
    [*To* LEAR] Your most dear—
175   LEAR   No rescue? What, a prisoner? I am e'en
    The natural fool[7] of fortune. Use° me well.   *Treat*
    You shall have ransom. Let me have a surgeon;
    I am cut to the brains.
FIRST GENTLEMAN   You shall have anything.
180   LEAR   No seconds?° All myself?   *supporters*
    Why, this would make a man a man of salt,[8]
    To use his eyes for garden water-pots,
    Ay, and laying° autumn's dust.   *settling*
FIRST GENTLEMAN   Good sir—
LEAR   I will die bravely,[9] like a bridegroom.
185   What, I will be jovial. Come, come,
    I am a king, my masters, know you that?
FIRST GENTLEMAN   You are a royal one, and we obey you.
LEAR   Then there's life° in't. Nay, an° you get it, you shall get it   *hope / if*
    with running.   *Exit running* [*pursued by two* GENTLEMEN]
190   FIRST GENTLEMAN   A sight most pitiful in the meanest wretch,
    Past speaking in a king. Thou hast one daughter
    Who redeems nature from the general curse
    Which twain hath brought her to.[1]
EDGAR   Hail, gentle° sir.   *noble*
195   FIRST GENTLEMAN   Sir, speed you.° What's your will?   *God speed you*
EDGAR   Do you hear aught of a battle toward?°   *coming*
FIRST GENTLEMAN   Most sure and vulgar,° everyone hears that   *commonly known*
    That can distinguish sense.°   *Who can understand*
EDGAR   But, by your favour,
200   How near's the other army?
FIRST GENTLEMAN   Near and on speedy foot, the main;°   *main army*
        descriers°   *scouts*
    Stands on the hourly thoughts.°   *Are expected forthwith*
EDGAR   I thank you, sir. That's all.

---

4. Like a preacher, removing his hat in the pulpit.
5. Stage (often called "scaffold" and hence linked to executioner's block); block used to shape a felt hat (such as
the hat removed by a preacher before a sermon); mounting block (such as the stump or stock Lear may have sat
on to remove his boots).
6. Hat material, to muffle the sound of the approaching
cavalry.
7. Born plaything; playing on "natural" as "mentally
deficient."

8. A man reduced to nothing but the salt his tears
deposit.
9. With courage; showily. "Die" plays on the Renaissance sense of "have an orgasm."
1. Who . . . *to*: Who restores proper meaning and order
to a universe plagued by the crimes of the other two
daughters; alluding to the fall of humankind and the natural world caused by the sin of Adam and Eve and to the
universal redemption brought about by Christ's sacrifice.

LEAR   If thou wilt weep my fortunes, take my eyes.
I know thee well enough: thy name is Gloucester.
Thou must be patient. We came crying hither.
Thou know'st the first time that we smell the air
170   We waul and cry. I will preach to thee. Mark.
GLOUCESTER   Alack, alack the day!
LEAR [*removing his crown of weeds*][3]   When we are born, we cry
    that we are come
To this great stage of fools. This°° a good block.[4]   This is
It were a delicate° stratagem to shoe   subtle
175   A troop of horse with felt.[5] I'll put't in proof,°   to the test
And when I have stol'n upon these son-in-laws,
Then kill, kill, kill, kill, kill, kill!
            Enter a GENTLEMAN
FIRST GENTLEMAN   O, here he is. Lay hand upon him. [*To* LEAR] Sir,
Your most dear daughter—
180   LEAR   No rescue? What, a prisoner? I am even
The natural fool[6] of fortune. Use° me well.   Treat
You shall have ransom. Let me have surgeons;
I am cut to th' brains.
FIRST GENTLEMAN   You shall have anything.
185   LEAR   No seconds?° All myself?   supporters
Why, this would make a man a man of salt,[7]
To use his eyes for garden water-pots.
I will die bravely,[8] like a smug° bridegroom. What,   an elegant
I will be jovial. Come, come, I am a king.
190   Masters, know you that?
FIRST GENTLEMAN   You are a royal one, and we obey you.
LEAR   Then there's life° in't. Come, an° you get it, you shall get   hope / if
    it by running. Sa, sa, sa, sa![9]
                                    Exit [*running*]
FIRST GENTLEMAN   A sight most pitiful in the meanest wretch,
195   Past speaking in a king. Thou hast a daughter
Who redeems nature from the general curse
Which twain have brought her to.[1]
EDGAR   Hail, gentle° sir.   noble
FIRST GENTLEMAN   Sir, speed you.° What's your will?   God speed you
200   EDGAR   Do you hear aught, sir, of a battle toward?°   coming
FIRST GENTLEMAN   Most sure and vulgar,° everyone hears that   commonly known
That can distinguish sound.
EDGAR   But, by your favour,
How near's the other army?
205   FIRST GENTLEMAN   Near and on speedy foot. The main descry°   appearance
Stands in the hourly thought.°   Is expected forthwith
EDGAR   I thank you, sir. That's all.

---

3. Like a preacher removing his hat in the pulpit.
4. Stage (often called "scaffold" and hence linked to executioner's block); block used to shape a felt hat (such as the hat removed by a preacher before a sermon); mounting block (such as the stump or stock Lear may have sat on to remove his boots).
5. Hat material, to muffle the sound of the approaching cavalry.
6. Born plaything; playing on "natural" as "mentally deficient."

7. A man reduced to nothing but the salt his tears deposit.
8. With courage; showily. "Die" plays on the Renaissance sense of "have an orgasm."
9. A cry to encourage dogs in the hunt.
1. *Who . . . to:* Who restores proper meaning and order to a universe plagued by the crimes of the other two daughters; alluding to the fall of humankind and the natural world caused by the sin of Adam and Eve and to the universal redemption brought about by Christ's sacrifice.

FIRST GENTLEMAN   Though that the Queen on° special cause°
        is here,
    Her army is moved on.   *for / reason*
EDGAR   I thank you, sir.   *Exit* GENTLEMAN
205 GLOUCESTER   You ever gentle gods, take my breath from me.
    Let not my worser spirit[2] tempt me again
    To die before you please.
EDGAR   Well pray you, father.[3]
GLOUCESTER   Now, good sir, what are you?
210 EDGAR   A most poor man, made lame by fortune's blows,
    Who by the art of known and feeling° sorrows   *profound*
    Am pregnant to° good pity. Give me your hand,   *disposed to feel*
    I'll lead you to some biding.°   *resting place*
GLOUCESTER [*rising*]   Hearty thanks.
    The bounty and the benison of heaven
    To send thee boot to boot.[4]
        Enter Steward [OSWALD]
215 OSWALD   A proclaimed prize![5] Most happy!°   *lucky*
    That eyeless head of thine was first framed° flesh   *made of*
    To raise my fortunes. Thou most unhappy traitor,
    Briefly thyself remember.[6] The sword is out
    That must destroy thee.
GLOUCESTER   Now let thy friendly hand
    Put strength enough to't.
220 OSWALD [*to* EDGAR]   Wherefore, bold peasant,
    Durst thou support a published° traitor? Hence,   *proclaimed*
    Lest the infection° of his fortune take   *(deathly) sickness*
    Like° hold on thee. Let go his arm.   *The same*
EDGAR   'Chill[7] not let go, sir, without 'cagion.°   *occasion*
225 OSWALD   Let go, slave, or thou diest.
EDGAR   Good gentleman, go your gate.° Let poor volk pass. An   *be on your way*
    'chud° have been swaggered out of my life, it would not have   *If I could*
    been so long by a vortnight. Nay, come not near the old man.
    Keep out, 'che vor' ye, or I'll try whether your costard or my
230 baton be the harder;[8] I'll be plain with you.
OSWALD   Out, dunghill!
        They fight
EDGAR   'Chill pick your teeth, sir. Come, no matter for your
    foins.°   *sword thrusts*
        [EDGAR *knocks him down*]
OSWALD   Slave, thou hast slain me. Villain, take my purse.
235 If ever thou wilt thrive, bury my body,
    And give the letters which thou find'st about me
    To Edmund, Earl of Gloucester. Seek him out
    Upon° the British party. O untimely death! Death!   *He dies*   *Within*

---

2. Wicked inclination; bad angel.
3. A term of respect for an elderly man.
4. To send you reward in addition (to my thanks).
5. A wanted man, with a bounty on his life.
6. Recollect and pray forgiveness for your sins.

7. I will; dialect from Somerset was a stage convention
for peasant dialogue.
8. *'che vor' ye ... harder*: I warrant you, or I'll test
whether your head or my cudgel is harder. *costard*: a kind
of apple.

FIRST GENTLEMAN   Though that the Queen on° special cause° is   *for / reason*
    here,
    Her army is moved on.
EDGAR   I thank you, sir.   *Exit* [GENTLEMAN]
GLOUCESTER   You ever gentle gods, take my breath from me.
210   Let not my worser spirit² tempt me again
    To die before you please.
EDGAR   Well pray you, father.³
GLOUCESTER   Now, good sir, what are you?
EDGAR   A most poor man, made tame to fortune's blows,
215   Who by the art of known and feeling° sorrows   *profound*
    Am pregnant to° good pity. Give me your hand,   *disposed to feel*
    I'll lead you to some biding.°   *resting place*
GLOUCESTER [*rising*]   Hearty thanks.
    The bounty and the benison of heaven
    To boot and boot.⁴
            Enter Steward [OSWALD]
OSWALD   A proclaimed prize!⁵ Most happy!°   *lucky*
220   That eyeless head of thine was first framed° flesh   *made of*
    To raise my fortunes. Thou old unhappy traitor,
    Briefly thyself remember.⁶ The sword is out
    That must destroy thee.
GLOUCESTER   Now let thy friendly hand
    Put strength enough to't.
OSWALD [*to* EDGAR]   Wherefore, bold peasant,
225   Durst thou support a published° traitor? Hence,   *proclaimed*
    Lest that th'infection° of his fortune take   *(deathly) sickness*
    Like° hold on thee. Let go his arm.   *The same*
EDGAR   'Chill⁷ not let go, sir, without vurther 'cagion.°   *further occasion*
OSWALD   Let go, slave, or thou diest.
230   EDGAR   Good gentleman, go your gate,° and let poor volk pass.   *be on your way*
    An 'chud ha'° been swaggered out of my life, 'twould not ha'   *If I could have*
    been so long as 'tis by a vortnight. Nay, come not near th'old
    man. Keep out, 'che vor' ye, or I's' try whether your costard or
    my baton be the harder;⁸ I'll be plain with you.
235   OSWALD   Out, dunghill!
EDGAR   'Chill pick your teeth, sir. Come, no matter vor your
    foins.°   *sword thrusts*
            [EDGAR *knocks him down*]
OSWALD   Slave, thou hast slain me. Villain, take my purse.
    If ever thou wilt thrive, bury my body,
240   And give the letters which thou find'st about me
    To Edmond, Earl of Gloucester. Seek him out
    Upon° the English party. O untimely death! Death!   [*He dies*]   *Within*

2. Wicked inclination; bad angel.
3. A term of respect for an elderly man.
4. In addition to my thanks, and may it bring you some
worldly reward.
5. A wanted man, with a bounty on his life.
6. Recollect and pray forgiveness for your sins.

7. I will; dialect from Somerset was a stage convention
for peasant dialogue.
8. *'che vor' ye . . . harder:* I warrant you, or I shall test
whether your head or my cudgel is harder. *costard:* a kind
of apple.

EDGAR I know thee well—a serviceable° villain,   *an officious*
240   As duteous to the vices of thy mistress
         As badness would desire.
GLOUCESTER What, is he dead?
EDGAR Sit you down, father. Rest you.
         [GLOUCESTER *sits*]
         Let's see his pockets. These letters that he speaks of
245   May be my friends. He's dead; I am only sorrow°   *sorry*
         He had no other deathsman.° Let us see.   *executioner*
         Leave,° gentle wax;⁹ and manners, blame us not.   *By your leave*
         To know our enemies' minds we'd rip their hearts;
         Their° papers is more lawful.   *To rip their*
         [*He reads*] *a letter*
250   'Let your reciprocal vows be remembered. You have many
         opportunities to cut him off. If your will want° not, time and   *lacks*
         place will be fruitfully offered. There is nothing done° if he   *accomplished*
         return the conqueror; then am I the prisoner, and his bed my
         jail, from the loathed warmth whereof, deliver me, and supply°   *fill*
255   the place for your labour.¹
              Your—wife, so I would say—your affectionate
                 servant, and for you her own for venture,²
                                                                    Gonoril.'
         O indistinguished space of woman's wit³—
260   A plot upon her virtuous husband's life,
         And the exchange° my brother!—Here in the sands   *substitute*
         Thee I'll rake up,° the post unsanctified°   *cover up / unholy messenger*
         Of murderous lechers, and in the mature time°   *when the time is ripe*
         With this ungracious° paper strike the sight   *ungodly*
265   Of the death-practisèd Duke.⁴ For him 'tis well
         That of thy death and business I can tell. [*Exit with the body*]
GLOUCESTER The King is mad. How stiff is my vile sense,⁵
         That I stand up and have ingenious feeling⁶
         Of my huge sorrows! Better I were distraught;°   *mad*
270   So should my thoughts be fencèd from my griefs,
         And woes by wrong° imaginations lose   *false*
         The knowledge of themselves.
              A drum afar off. [*Enter* EDGAR]
EDGAR   Give me your hand.
         Far off methinks I hear the beaten drum.
         Come, father, I'll bestow° you with a friend.   *lodge*
                        Exit [EDGAR *guiding* GLOUCESTER]

---

9. The wax seal on the letter.
1. *for your labour:* as a reward for your endeavors, and for
further sexual exertion.
2. *for you . . . venture:* one willing to risk all for you; all
yours, if you dare be so bold.

3. Limitless extent of woman's cunning.
4. Of the Duke whose death is plotted.
5. How obstinate is my unwanted power of reason.
6. That I remain upright and firm in my sanity and have
rational perceptions.

EDGAR   I know thee well—a serviceable° villain,   *an officious*
   As duteous to the vices of thy mistress
245   As badness would desire.
GLOUCESTER   What, is he dead?
EDGAR   Sit you down, father. Rest you.
      [GLOUCESTER *sits*]
   Let's see these pockets. The letters that he speaks of
   May be my friends. He's dead; I am only sorrow°   *sorry*
250   He had no other deathsman.° Let us see.   *executioner*
   Leave,° gentle wax,⁹ and manners; blame us not.   *By your leave*
   To know our enemies' minds we rip their hearts;
   Their° papers is more lawful.   *To rip their*
         Reads the letter
   'Let our reciprocal vows be remembered. You have many
255   opportunities to cut him off. If your will want° not, time and   *lacks*
   place will be fruitfully offered. There is nothing done° if he   *accomplished*
   return the conqueror; then am I the prisoner, and his bed my
   jail, from the loathed warmth whereof, deliver me, and supply°   *fill*
   the place for your labour.¹
260   Your—wife, so I would say,—affectionate
               servant, and for you her own for venture,²
                           Goneril.'
   O indistinguished space of woman's will³—
   A plot upon her virtuous husband's life,
265   And the exchange° my brother!—Here in the sands   *substitute*
   Thee I'll rake up,° the post unsanctified°   *cover up / unholy messenger*
   Of murderous lechers, and in the mature time°   *when the time is ripe*
   With this ungracious° paper strike the sight   *ungodly*
   Of the death-practised Duke.⁴ For him 'tis well
270   That of thy death and business I can tell.   [*Exit with the body*]
GLOUCESTER   The King is mad. How stiff is my vile sense,⁵
   That I stand up and have ingenious feeling⁶
   Of my huge sorrows! Better I were distraught,°   *mad*
   So should my thoughts be severed from my griefs,
         Drum afar off
275   And woes by wrong° imaginations lose   *false*
   The knowledge of themselves.
         [*Enter* EDGAR]
EDGAR   Give me your hand.
   Far off methinks I hear the beaten drum.
   Come, father, I'll bestow° you with a friend.   *lodge*
                  Exit [EDGAR *guiding* GLOUCESTER]

---

9. The wax seal on the letter.
1. *for your labour*: as a reward for your endeavors, and for further sexual exertion.
2. *for you . . . venture*: one willing to risk all for you; all yours, if you dare be so bold.
3. Limitless extent of woman's wilfullness. As with "hell"
in line 121, "will" might also refer to a woman's genitals.
4. Of the Duke whose death is plotted.
5. How obstinate is my unwanted power of reason.
6. That I remain upright and firm in my sanity and have rational perceptions.

Scene 21

[*Soft music.*] *Enter* CORDELIA, *and* KENT [*disguised*]

CORDELIA O thou good Kent,
How shall I live and work to match thy goodness?
My life will be too short, and every measure° fail me.   *attempt*
KENT To be acknowledged, madam, is o'erpaid.°   *is more than enough*
5   All my reports go[1] with the modest truth,
Nor more, nor clipped, but so.[2]
CORDELIA   Be better suited.°   *attired*
These weeds° are memories of those worser hours.   *clothes*
I prithee put them off.
KENT   Pardon me, dear madam.
Yet to be known shortens my made intent.[3]
10 My boon I make it[4] that you know° me not   *acknowledge*
Till time and I think meet.°   *suitable*
CORDELIA   Then be't so, my good lord.
[*Enter* DOCTOR *and* FIRST GENTLEMAN]
How does the King?
DOCTOR   Madam, sleeps still.
CORDELIA   O you kind gods,
Cure this great breach in his abusèd nature;
The untuned and hurrying senses O wind up[5]
Of this child-changèd[6] father!
15 DOCTOR   So please your majesty
That we may wake the King? He hath slept long.
CORDELIA Be governed by your knowledge, and proceed
I'th' sway° of your own will. Is he arrayed?°   *By the authority / clothed*
FIRST GENTLEMAN Ay, madam. In the heaviness of his sleep
20 We put fresh garments on him.
DOCTOR Good madam, be by when we do awake him.
I doubt not of his temperance.°   *calmness*
CORDELIA   Very well.
DOCTOR Please you draw near. Louder the music there!
[LEAR *is discovered*° *asleep*]   *revealed*
CORDELIA O my dear father, restoration hang
25 Thy medicine on my lips, and let this kiss
Repair those violent harms that my two sisters
Have in thy reverence° made!   *aged dignity*
KENT   Kind and dear princess!
CORDELIA Had you not[7] been their father, these white flakes°   *locks of hair*
Had challenged° pity of them. Was this a face   *Would have provoked*
30 To be exposed against the warring winds,
To stand against the deep dread-bolted thunder
In the most terrible and nimble stroke
Of quick cross-lightning, to watch°—poor *perdu*[8]—   *to stand guard*

Scene 21 Location: The French camp at Dover.
1. May all accounts of me agree.
2. Not greater or less, but exactly the modest amount I deserve.
3. Revealing myself now would abort my designs.
4. The reward I beg is.
5. *The . . . up:* Reorder his confused and delirious mind.

The image is of tightening the strings of a lute.
6. Changed by his children; changed into a child; playing on a musical key change.
7. Even if you had not.
8. Lost one; in military terms, a dangerously exposed sentry.

4.6

Enter CORDELIA, KENT [*disguised*], *and* [*the* FIRST] GEN-
TLEMAN

CORDELIA   O thou good Kent, how shall I live and work
To match thy goodness? My life will be too short,
And every measure° fail me.   *attempt*

KENT   To be acknowledged, madam, is o'erpaid.°   *is more than enough*

5   All my reports go¹ with the modest truth,
Nor more, nor clipped, but so.²

CORDELIA   Be better suited.°   *attired*
These weeds° are memories of those worser hours.   *clothes*
I prithee put them off.

KENT   Pardon, dear madam.
Yet to be known shortens my made intent.³

10   My boon I make it⁴ that you know° me not   *acknowledge*
Till time and I think meet.°   *suitable*

CORDELIA   Then be't so, my good lord. —
How does the King?

FIRST GENTLEMAN   Madam, sleeps still.

CORDELIA   O you kind gods,
Cure this great breach in his abusèd nature;
Th'untuned and jarring senses O wind up⁵
Of this child-changèd⁶ father!

15   FIRST GENTLEMAN   So please your majesty
That we may wake the King? He hath slept long.

CORDELIA   Be governed by your knowledge, and proceed
I'th' sway° of your own will. Is he arrayed?°   *By the authority / clothed*

FIRST GENTLEMAN   Ay, madam. In the heaviness of sleep

20   We put fresh garments on him.
Enter LEAR [*asleep,*] *in a chair carried by servants*
Be by, good madam, when we do awake him.
I doubt not of his temperance.°   *calmness*

CORDELIA   O my dear father, restoration hang
Thy medicine on my lips, and let this kiss

25   Repair those violent harms that my two sisters
Have in thy reverence° made!   *aged dignity*

KENT   Kind and dear princess!

CORDELIA   Had you not⁷ been their father, these white flakes°   *locks of hair*
Did challenge° pity of them. Was this a face   *Would have provoked*
To be opposed against the warring winds?

4.6 Location: The French camp at Dover.
1. May all accounts of me agree.
2. Not greater or less, but exactly the modest amount I deserve.
3. Revealing myself now would abort my designs.
4. The reward I beg is.

5. Th'untuned . . . up: Reorder his confused and delirious mind. The image is of tightening the strings of a lute.
6. Changed by his children; changed into a child; playing on a musical key change.
7. Even if you had not.

With this thin helm?° Mine injurer's mean'st dog,   helmet (of hair)
35   Though he had bit me, should have stood that night
     Against my fire. And wast thou fain,° poor father,   glad
     To hovel thee with swine and rogues forlorn
     In short° and musty straw? Alack, alack,   scant; broken
     'Tis wonder that thy life and wits at once
40   Had not concluded all!° [To DOCTOR] He wakes. Speak to him.   altogether
DOCTOR   Madam, do you; 'tis fittest.
CORDELIA [to LEAR]   How does my royal lord? How fares your majesty?
LEAR   You do me wrong to take me out o'th' grave.
     Thou art a soul in bliss, but I am bound
45   Upon a wheel of fire, that mine own tears
     Do scald like molten lead.[9]
CORDELIA   Sir, know me.
LEAR   You're a spirit, I know. Where did you die?
CORDELIA [to the DOCTOR]   Still, still far wide!°   unbalanced
DOCTOR   He's scarce awake. Let him alone a while.
50   LEAR   Where have I been? Where am I? Fair daylight?
     I am mightily abused.° I should e'en die with pity   wronged; deceived
     To see another thus. I know not what to say.
     I will not swear these are my hands. Let's see:
     I feel this pin prick. Would I were assured
     Of my condition.
55   CORDELIA [kneeling]   O look upon me, sir,
     And hold your hands in benediction o'er me.
     No, sir, you must not kneel.
     LEAR   Pray do not mock.
     I am a very foolish, fond° old man,   silly
     Fourscore and upward, and to deal plainly,
60   I fear I am not in my perfect mind.
     Methinks I should know you, and know this man;
     Yet I am doubtful, for I am mainly° ignorant   entirely
     What place this is; and all the skill I have
     Remembers not these garments; nor I know not
65   Where I did lodge last night. Do not laugh at me,
     For as I am a man, I think this lady
     To be my child, Cordelia.
CORDELIA   And so I am.
LEAR   Be your tears wet?[1] Yes, faith. I pray, weep not.
     If you have poison for me, I will drink it.
70   I know you do not love me; for your sisters
     Have, as I do remember, done me wrong.
     You have some cause; they have not.
CORDELIA   No cause, no cause.

---

9. *but I . . . lead:* Lear puts himself in either hell or purgatory, both places of such punishment in medieval

accounts.
1. Are your tears real?; is this really happening?

30   Mine enemy's dog, though he had bit me, should have stood
    That night against my fire. And wast thou fain,° poor father,   *glad*
    To hovel thee with swine and rogues forlorn
    In short° and musty straw? Alack, alack,   *scant; broken*
    'Tis wonder that thy life and wits at once
35   Had not concluded all!° [*To the* GENTLEMAN] He wakes. Speak   *altogether*
      to him.
FIRST GENTLEMAN   Madam, do you; 'tis fittest.
CORDELIA [*to* LEAR]   How does my royal lord? How fares your majesty?
LEAR   You do me wrong to take me out o'th' grave.
    Thou art a soul in bliss, but I am bound
40   Upon a wheel of fire, that mine own tears
    Do scald like molten lead.[8]
CORDELIA   Sir, do you know me?
LEAR   You are a spirit, I know. Where did you die?
CORDELIA [*to the* GENTLEMAN]   Still, still far wide!°   *unbalanced*
FIRST GENTLEMAN   He's scarce awake. Let him alone a while.
45 LEAR   Where have I been? Where am I? Fair daylight?
    I am mightily abused.° I should ev'n die with pity   *wronged; deceived*
    To see another thus. I know not what to say.
    I will not swear these are my hands. Let's see:
    I feel this pin prick. Would I were assured
    Of my condition.
50 CORDELIA [*kneeling*]   O look upon me, sir,
    And hold your hands in benediction o'er me.
    You must not kneel.
LEAR   Pray do not mock.
    I am a very foolish, fond° old man,   *silly*
    Fourscore and upward,
55   Not an hour more nor less; and to deal plainly,
    I fear I am not in my perfect mind.
    Methinks I should know you, and know this man;
    Yet I am doubtful, for I am mainly° ignorant   *entirely*
    What place this is; and all the skill I have
60   Remembers not these garments; nor I know not
    Where I did lodge last night. Do not laugh at me,
    For as I am a man, I think this lady
    To be my child, Cordelia.
CORDELIA   And so I am, I am.
LEAR   Be your tears wet?[9] Yes, faith. I pray, weep not.
65   If you have poison for me, I will drink it.
    I know you do not love me; for your sisters
    Have, as I do remember, done me wrong.
    You have some cause; they have not.
CORDELIA   No cause, no cause.

---

8. *but I . . . lead:* Lear puts himself in either hell or purgatory, both places of such punishment in medieval accounts.
9. Are your tears real?; is this really happening?

LEAR   Am I in France?
KENT   In your own kingdom, sir.
75   LEAR   Do not abuse° me.   *deceive; mock*
DOCTOR   Be comforted, good madam. The great rage
   You see is cured in him, and yet it is danger
   To make him even o'er° the time he has lost.   *go over*
   Desire him to go in; trouble him no more
80   Till further settling.°   *Until his mind eases*
CORDELIA [*to* LEAR]   Will't please your highness walk?
LEAR   You must bear with me.
   Pray now, forget and forgive. I am old
   And foolish.   *Exeunt. Manent*° KENT *and* [FIRST] GENTLEMAN   *Remain*
FIRST GENTLEMAN   Holds it true, sir, that the Duke
   Of Cornwall was so slain?
85   KENT   Most certain, sir.
FIRST GENTLEMAN   Who is conductor° of his people?   *commander*
KENT   As 'tis said,
   The bastard son of Gloucester.
FIRST GENTLEMAN   They say Edgar,
   His banished son, is with the Earl of Kent
   In Germany.
KENT   Report° is changeable.   *Rumor*
90   'Tis time to look about.° The powers of the kingdom   *prepare defenses*
   Approach apace.
FIRST GENTLEMAN   The arbitrement° is   *encounter*
   Like to be bloody. Fare you well, sir.   [*Exit*]
KENT   My point and period[2] will be throughly wrought,
   Or° well or ill, as this day's battle's fought.   *Exit*   *For*

Scene 22
Enter EDMUND, REGAN, *and their powers*
EDMUND   Know° of the Duke if his last purpose hold,[1]   *Inquire*
   Or whether since he is advised by aught[2]
   To change the course. He's full of abdication[3]
   And self-reproving. Bring his constant pleasure.°   *his settled intent*
                                    [*Exit one or more*]
5   REGAN   Our sister's man is certainly miscarried.[4]
EDMUND   'Tis to be doubted,° madam.   *feared*
REGAN   Now, sweet lord,
   You know the goodness I intend upon you.
   Tell me but truly—but then speak the truth—
   Do you not love my sister?
EDMUND   Ay: honoured° love.   *honorable*
10   REGAN   But have you never found my brother's way
   To the forfended[5] place?

---

2. The purpose and end of my life; literally, the full stop.
Scene 22 Location: The British camp near Dover.
1. If his previous intention (to wage war) remains firm.
2. Since then anything has persuaded him.

3. A tendency to give up his intentions or put aside his responsibilities.
4. Has surely come to grief by some accident.
5. Forbidden (to Edmund, because it is adulterous).

LEAR Am I in France?
70 KENT In your own kingdom, sir.
LEAR Do not abuse° me.   *deceive; mock*
FIRST GENTLEMAN Be comforted, good madam. The great rage
   You see is killed in him. Desire him to go in.
   Trouble him no more till further settling.°   *until his mind eases*
75 CORDELIA [*to* LEAR] Will't please your highness walk?
LEAR You must bear with me. Pray you now, forget
   And forgive. I am old and foolish.   *Exeunt*

5.1

Enter with drum and colours EDMOND, REGAN, GENTLE-
MEN, *and soldiers*
EDMOND Know° of the Duke if his last purpose hold,[1]   *Inquire*
   Or whether since he is advised by aught[2]
   To change the course. He's full of abdication[3]
   And self-reproving. Bring his constant pleasure.°   *his settled intent*
                                   [*Exit one or more*]
5 REGAN Our sister's man is certainly miscarried.[4]
EDMOND 'Tis to be doubted,° madam.   *feared*
REGAN   Now, sweet lord,
   You know the goodness I intend upon you.
   Tell me but truly—but then speak the truth—
   Do you not love my sister?
EDMOND   In honoured° love.   *honorable*
10 REGAN But have you never found my brother's way
   To the forfended[5] place?

5.1 Location: The British camp near Dover.   responsibilities.
1. If his previous intention (to wage war) remains firm.   4. Has surely come to grief by some accident.
2. Since then anything has persuaded him.   5. Forbidden (to Edmond, because it is adulterous).
3. A tendency to give up his intentions or put aside his

EDMUND   That thought abuses° you.   *deceives*
REGAN   I am doubtful
   That you have been conjunct° and bosomed with° her,   *complicit / enamored of*
   As far as we call hers.⁶
15   EDMUND   No, by mine honour, madam.
REGAN   I never shall endure her. Dear my lord,
   Be not familiar° with her.   *intimate*
EDMUND   Fear° me not.   *Doubt*
   She and the Duke her husband—
          Enter ALBANY and GONORIL with troops
20   GONORIL [*aside*]   I had rather lose the battle than that sister
   Should loosen° him and me.   *disunite*
ALBANY [*to* REGAN]   Our very loving sister, well bemet,°   *met*
   For this I hear: the King is come to his daughter,
   With others whom the rigour° of our state°   *harshness / government*
25   Forced to cry out. Where I could not be honest°   *honorable*
   I never yet was valiant. For this business,
   It touches° us as France invades our land;   *concerns*
   Yet bold's the King, with others whom I fear.⁷
   Most just and heavy causes make oppose.⁸
EDMUND   Sir, you speak nobly.
30   REGAN   Why is this reasoned?⁹
GONORIL   Combine together 'gainst the enemy;
   For these domestic poor particulars°   *minor details*
   Are not to° question here.   *the*
ALBANY   Let us then determine with the ensign° of war   *experienced officer(s)*
   On our proceedings.
35   EDMUND   I shall attend you
   Presently° at your tent.   *[Exit with his powers]*   *In a moment*
REGAN   Sister, you'll go with us?
GONORIL   No.
REGAN   'Tis most convenient.° Pray you go with us.¹   *suitable*
GONORIL [*aside*]   O ho, I know the riddle!° [*To* REGAN] I will go. *disguised meaning*
          Enter EDGAR [disguised as a peasant]
40   EDGAR [*to* ALBANY]   If e'er your grace had speech with man so poor,
   Hear me one word.
ALBANY [*to the others*]   I'll overtake you.
                    Exeunt [all but ALBANY and EDGAR]
                    Speak.
EDGAR   Before you fight the battle, ope this letter.
   If you have victory, let the trumpet sound
   For him that brought it. Wretched though I seem,
45   I can produce a champion that will prove°   *defend*
   What is avouchèd° there. If you miscarry,°   *maintained / perish*
   Your business of the world hath so an end.
   Fortune love you—
ALBANY   Stay till I have read the letter.

---

6. In total intimacy; all the way.
7. Albany expresses his ambivalence. The invasion concerns us insofar as we are facing a French army in our lands. On the other hand, King Lear, along with other powerful forces, is boldly claiming his own land.

8. Fair and serious causes are driven into opposition.
9. What is the point of this kind of speech?
1. Regan wants Gonoril to go with Albany and her, rather than with Edmund.

EDMOND   No, by mine honour, madam.
REGAN   I never shall endure her. Dear my lord,
    Be not familiar° with her.   *intimate*
EDMOND   Fear° me not.   *Doubt*
15 She and the Duke her husband—
            Enter with drum and colours ALBANY, GONERIL, [*and*]
            soldiers
ALBANY [*to* REGAN]   Our very loving sister, well bemet.°   *met*
    [*To* EDMOND] Sir, this I heard: the King is come to his daughter,
    With others whom the rigour° of our state°   *harshness / government*
    Forced to cry out.

REGAN   Why is this reasoned?°⁶
20 GONERIL   Combine together 'gainst the enemy;
    For these domestic and particular broils°   *minor details*
    Are not the question here.
ALBANY   Let's then determine with th'ensign° of war   *experienced officer(s)*
    On our proceeding.
REGAN   Sister, you'll go with us?⁷
25 GONERIL   No.
REGAN   'Tis most convenient.° Pray go with us.   *suitable*
GONERIL [*aside*]   O ho, I know the riddle!° [*To* REGAN] I will go.   *disguised meaning*
            Enter EDGAR [*disguised as a peasant*]
EDGAR [*to* ALBANY]   If e'er your grace had speech with man so poor,
    Hear me one word.
ALBANY [*to the others*]   I'll overtake you. *Exeunt both the armies*
                                              Speak.
30 EDGAR   Before you fight the battle, ope this letter.
    If you have victory, let the trumpet sound
    For him that brought it. Wretched though I seem,
    I can produce a champion that will prove°   *defend*
    What is avouchèd° there. If you miscarry,°   *maintained / perish*
35 Your business of the world hath so an end,
    And machination° ceases. Fortune love you.   *plotting*
ALBANY   Stay till I have read the letter.

6. What is the point of this kind of speech?
7. Regan wants Goneril to go with Albany and her, rather than with Edmond.

50 EDGAR I was forbid it.
    When time shall serve, let but the herald cry,
    And I'll appear again.
    ALBANY Why, fare thee well.
    I will o'erlook the paper.   *Exit* [EDGAR]
    Enter EDMUND
55 EDMUND The enemy's in view; draw up your powers.°   *troops*
    [*He offers* ALBANY *a paper*]
    Here is the guess° of their great strength and forces   *estimate*
    By diligent discovery;° but your haste   *spying*
    Is now urged on you.
    ALBANY   We will greet the time.[2]   *Exit*
    EDMUND To both these sisters have I sworn my love,
60   Each jealous° of the other as the stung   *suspicious*
    Are of the adder. Which of them shall I take?—
    Both?—one?—or neither? Neither can be enjoyed
    If both remain alive. To take the widow
    Exasperates, makes mad, her sister Gonoril,
65   And hardly° shall I carry out my side,°   *with difficulty / plan*
    Her husband being alive. Now then, we'll use
    His countenance[3] for the battle, which being done,
    Let her that would be rid of him devise
    His speedy taking off. As for his mercy
70   Which he intends to Lear and to Cordelia,
    The battle done, and they within our power,
    Shall° never see his pardon; for my state°   *They shall / condition*
    Stands on° me to defend, not to debate.   *Exit*   *Obliges*

Scene 23

Alarum.[1] *Enter the powers of France over the stage* [*led*
by] CORDELIA *with her father in her hand.* [*Then*] *enter*
EDGAR [*disguised as a peasant, guiding*] GLOUCESTER
EDGAR Here, father,[2] take the shadow of this bush
    For your good host;° pray that the right may thrive.   *shelter*
    If ever I return to you again
    I'll bring you comfort.   *Exit*
    GLOUCESTER   Grace go with you, sir.
    Alarum and retreat.° [*Enter* EDGAR]   *trumpet signal*
5 EDGAR Away, old man. Give me thy hand. Away.
    King Lear hath lost, he and his daughter ta'en.
    Give me thy hand. Come on.
    GLOUCESTER No farther, sir. A man may rot even° here.   *right*
    EDGAR What, in ill thoughts again? Men must endure
10   Their going hence even as their coming hither.
    Ripeness is all.[3] Come on. [*Exit* EDGAR *guiding* GLOUCESTER]

---

2. We will be ready to meet the occasion.
3. Authority or backing; also suggesting "face," to be used
like a mask for Edmund's ambition.
Scene 23 Location: The rest of the play takes place near
the battlefield.
1. Trumpet call to battle.

2. See note to 20.208.
3. To await the destined time is the most important
thing, as fruit falls only when ripe (playing on Gloucester's "rot," line 8); readiness for death is our only duty
(compare *Hamlet* 5.2.160, "The readiness is all").

EDGAR   I was forbid it.
  When time shall serve, let but the herald cry,
  And I'll appear again.
40 ALBANY   Why, fare thee well.
  I will o'erlook thy paper.   *Exit* [EDGAR]
     Enter EDMOND
EDMOND   The enemy's in view; draw up your powers.°   *troops*
  [*He offers* ALBANY *a paper*]
  Here is the guess° of their true strength and forces   *estimate*
  By diligent discovery;° but your haste   *spying*
  Is now urged on you.
45 ALBANY   We will greet the time.[8]   *Exit*
EDMOND   To both these sisters have I sworn my love,
  Each jealous° of the other as the stung   *suspicious*
  Are of the adder. Which of them shall I take?—
  Both?—one?—or neither? Neither can be enjoyed
50 If both remain alive. To take the widow
  Exasperates, makes mad, her sister Goneril,
  And hardly° shall I carry out my side,°   *with difficulty / plan*
  Her husband being alive. Now then, we'll use
  His countenance[9] for the battle, which being done,
55 Let her who would be rid of him devise
  His speedy taking off. As for the mercy
  Which he intends to Lear and to Cordelia,
  The battle done, and they within our power,
  Shall° never see his pardon; for my state°   *They shall / condition*
60 Stands on° me to defend, not to debate.   *Exit*   *Obliges*

5.2

    Alarum within.[1] *Enter with drum and colours* LEAR, COR-
    DELIA, *and soldiers over the stage; and exeunt. Enter*
    EDGAR [*disguised as a peasant, guiding*] GLOUCESTER
EDGAR   Here, father,[2] take the shadow of this tree
  For your good host;° pray that the right may thrive.   *shelter*
  If ever I return to you again
  I'll bring you comfort.
GLOUCESTER   Grace go with you, sir.   *Exit* [EDGAR]
    Alarum and retreat° within. Enter EDGAR   *trumpet signal*
5 EDGAR   Away, old man. Give me thy hand. Away.
  King Lear hath lost, he and his daughter ta'en.
  Give me thy hand. Come on.
GLOUCESTER   No further, sir. A man may rot even° here.   *right*
EDGAR   What, in ill thoughts again? Men must endure
10 Their going hence even as their coming hither.
  Ripeness is all.[3] Come on.
GLOUCESTER   And that's true, too.
    [*Exit* EDGAR *guiding* GLOUCESTER]

---

8. We will be ready to meet the occasion.
9. Authority or backing; also suggesting "face," to be used
like a mask for Edmond's ambition.
5.2 Location: The rest of the play takes place near the
battlefield.
1. Trumpet call to battle (backstage).

2. See note to 4.5.212.
3 To await the destined time is the most important thing,
as fruit falls only when ripe (playing on Gloucester's "rot,"
line 8); readiness for death is our only duty (compare
Hamlet 5.2.160, "The readiness is all").

Scene 24

Enter EDMUND *with* LEAR *and* CORDELIA *prisoners[, a*
CAPTAIN, *and soldiers*]

EDMUND   Some officers take them away. Good guard
    Until their greater pleasures[1] best be known
    That are to censure° them.   *judge*
CORDELIA [*to* LEAR]   We are not the first
    Who with best meaning° have incurred the worst.   *intention*
5   For thee, oppressèd King, am I cast down,°   *(into unhappiness)*
    Myself could else outfrown false fortune's frown.[2]
    Shall we not see these daughters and these sisters?
LEAR   No, no. Come, let's away to prison.
    We two alone will sing like birds i'th' cage.
10   When thou dost ask me blessing, I'll kneel down
    And ask of thee forgiveness; so we'll live,
    And pray, and sing, and tell old tales, and laugh
    At gilded butterflies,[3] and hear poor rogues
    Talk of court news, and we'll talk with them too—
15   Who loses and who wins, who's in, who's out,
    And take upon 's the mystery of things
    As if we were God's spies; and we'll wear out°   *outlast*
    In a walled prison packs and sects of great ones
    That ebb and flow by th' moon.[4]
EDMUND [*to soldiers*]   Take them away.
20 LEAR [*to* CORDELIA]   Upon such sacrifices,[5] my Cordelia,
    The gods themselves throw incense. Have I caught thee?
    He that parts us shall bring a brand from heaven
    And fire us hence like foxes.[6] Wipe thine eyes.
    The goodyear shall devour 'em, flesh and fell,[7]
25   Ere they shall make us weep. We'll see 'em starve first. Come.
                [*Exeunt all but* EDMUND *and* CAPTAIN]
EDMUND   Come hither, captain. Hark.
    Take thou this note. Go follow them to prison.
    One step I have advanced° thee; if thou dost   *promoted*
    As this instructs thee, thou dost make thy way
30   To noble fortunes. Know thou this: that men
    Are as the time is. To be tender-minded
    Does not become a sword.° Thy great employment   *befit a swordsman*
    Will not bear question.° Either say thou'lt do't,   *discussion*
    Or thrive by other means.
CAPTAIN   I'll do't, my lord.
35 EDMUND   About it, and write 'happy' when thou hast done.[8]
    Mark, I say, instantly, and carry it° so   *carry it out*
    As I have set it down.
CAPTAIN   I cannot draw a cart,
    Nor eat dried oats.° If it be man's work, I'll do't.   [*Exit*]   *(like a horse)*

Scene 24
1. *Good . . . pleasures:* Guard them well until the desires
of those greater persons.
2. Otherwise, I could be defiant in the face of bad fortune.
3. Gaudy and ephemeral courtiers; trivial matters.
4. *packs . . . moon:* followers and factions of important
people whose position at court varies as the tide.
5. Upon such sacrifices as we are, or as you have made.

6. *shall . . . foxes:* must have divine aid to do so. The
image is of using a torch to smoke foxes out of their holes,
or, in the case of Lear and Cordelia, prison cells.
7. *flesh and fell:* meat and skin; entirely. The precise
meaning of "goodyear" has not been explained; it may
signify simply the passage of time or may suggest some
ominous, destructive power.
8. Go to it, and call yourself happy when you are done.

5.3

Enter in conquest with drum and colours EDMOND; LEAR
and CORDELIA *as prisoners; soldiers; a* CAPTAIN

EDMOND   Some officers take them away. Good guard
    Until their greater pleasures[1] first be known
    That are to censure° them.   *judge*
CORDELIA [*to* LEAR]   We are not the first
    Who with best meaning° have incurred the worst.   *intention*
5   For thee, oppressèd King, I am cast down,°   *(into unhappiness)*
    Myself could else outfrown false fortune's frown.[2]
    Shall we not see these daughters and these sisters?
LEAR   No, no, no, no. Come, let's away to prison.
    We two alone will sing like birds i'th' cage.
10   When thou dost ask me blessing, I'll kneel down
    And ask of thee forgiveness; so we'll live,
    And pray, and sing, and tell old tales, and laugh
    At gilded butterflies,[3] and hear poor rogues
    Talk of court news, and we'll talk with them too —
15   Who loses and who wins, who's in, who's out,
    And take upon 's the mystery of things
    As if we were God's spies; and we'll wear out°   *outlast*
    In a walled prison packs and sects of great ones
    That ebb and flow by th' moon.[4]
EDMOND [*to soldiers*]   Take them away.
20 LEAR   Upon such sacrifices,[5] my Cordelia,
    The gods themselves throw incense. Have I caught thee?
    He that parts us shall bring a brand from heaven
    And fire us hence like foxes.[6] Wipe thine eyes.
    The goodyear shall devour them, flesh and fell,[7]
25   Ere they shall make us weep. We'll see 'em starved first. Come.
                      Exeunt [all but EDMOND *and* CAPTAIN]
EDMOND   Come hither, captain. Hark.
    Take thou this note. Go follow them to prison.
    One step I have advanced° thee; if thou dost   *promoted*
    As this instructs thee, thou dost make thy way
30   To noble fortunes. Know thou this: that men
    Are as the time is. To be tender-minded
    Does not become a sword.° Thy great employment   *befit a swordsman*
    Will not bear question.° Either say thou'lt do't,   *discussion*
    Or thrive by other means.
CAPTAIN   I'll do't, my lord.
35 EDMOND   About it, and write 'happy' when thou'st done.[8]
    Mark, I say, instantly, and carry it° so   *carry it out*
    As I have set it down.   *Exit* CAPTAIN

5.3
1. *Good . . . pleasures:* Guard them well until the desires
of those greater persons.
2. Otherwise, I could be defiant in the face of bad fortune.
3. Gaudy and ephemeral courtiers; trivial matters.
4. *packs . . . moon:* followers and factions of important
people whose position at court varies as the tide.
5. Upon such sacrifices as we are, or as you have made.

6. *shall . . . foxes:* must have divine aid to do so. The
image is of using a torch to smoke foxes out of their holes,
or, in the case of Lear and Cordelia, prison cells.
7. *flesh and fell:* meat and skin; entirely. The precise
meaning of "goodyear" has not been explained; it may
signify simply the passage of time or may suggest some
ominous, destructive power.
8. Go to it, and call yourself happy when you are done.

Enter Duke [of ALBANY], *the two ladies [*GONORIL *and*
REGAN, *another* CAPTAIN], *and others*

ALBANY [*to* EDMUND]   Sir, you have showed today your valiant
    strain,°   *qualities; birth*
40   And fortune led you well. You have the captives
    That were the opposites° of this day's strife.   *opponents*
    We do require then of you, so to use° them   *treat*
    As we shall find their merits and our safety
    May equally determine.

EDMUND   Sir, I thought it fit
45   To send the old and miserable King
    To some retention° and appointed guard,   *confinement*
    Whose° age has charms in it, whose title more,   *(Lear's)*
    To pluck the common bosom[9] on his side
    And turn our impressed lances° in our eyes   *conscripted lancers*
50   Which[1] do command them. With him I sent the Queen,
    My reason all the same, and they are ready
    Tomorrow, or at further space,° to appear   *at a future point*
    Where you shall hold your session.° At this time   *court of judgment*
    We sweat and bleed. The friend hath lost his friend,
55   And the best quarrels in the heat are cursed
    By those that feel their sharpness.[2]
    The question of Cordelia and her father
    Requires a fitter place.

ALBANY   Sir, by your patience,
    I hold you but a subject of° this war,   *in waging*
    Not as a brother.

60   REGAN   That's as we list° to grace him.   *like*
    Methinks our pleasure should have been demanded[3]
    Ere you had spoke so far. He led our powers,°   *armies*
    Bore the commission of my place and person,
    The which immediate° may well stand up   *close connection*
    And call itself your brother.

65   GONORIL   Not so hot.°   *Not so fast*
    In his own grace° he doth exalt himself   *merit*
    More than in your advancement.[4]

REGAN   In my right
    By me invested, he compeers° the best.   *equals*
GONORIL   That were the most[5] if he should husband you.
REGAN   Jesters do oft prove prophets.
70   GONORIL   Holla, holla—
    That eye that told you so looked but asquint.[6]
REGAN   Lady, I am not well, else I should answer
    From a full-flowing stomach.° [*To* EDMUND] General,   *anger*
    Take thou my soldiers, prisoners, patrimony.
75   Witness the world that I create thee here
    My lord and master.

---

9. To garner the affection of the populace.
1. *in our eyes / Which:* in the eyes of us who.
2. *And . . . sharpness:* And in the heat of battle, even the most just wars are cursed by those who must suffer the fighting.

3. I think you should have inquired into my wishes.
4. In the honors you confer upon him.
5. That investiture would be complete.
6. Squinting was a proverbial effect of jealousy, because of the tendency to look suspiciously at potential rivals.

Flourish. Enter ALBANY, GONERIL, REGAN, [*drummer,*
trumpeter and] *soldiers*

ALBANY   Sir, you have showed today your valiant strain,°   qualities; birth
And fortune led you well. You have the captives
40   Who were the opposites° of this day's strife.   opponents
I do require them of you, so to use° them   treat
As we shall find their merits and our safety
May equally determine.
EDMOND   Sir, I thought it fit
To send the old and miserable King
45   To some retention° and appointed guard,   confinement
Whose° age had charms in it, whose title more,   (Lear's)
To pluck the common bosom[9] on his side
And turn our impressed lances° in our eyes   conscripted lancers
Which[1] do command them. With him I sent the Queen,
50   My reason all the same, and they are ready
Tomorrow, or at further space,° t'appear   at a future point
Where you shall hold your session.°   court of judgment

ALBANY   Sir, by your patience,
I hold you but a subject of° this war,   in waging
Not as a brother.
REGAN   That's as we list° to grace him.   like
55   Methinks our pleasure might have been demanded[2]
Ere you had spoke so far. He led our powers,°   armies
Bore the commission of my place and person,
The which immediacy° may well stand up   close connection
And call itself your brother.
GONERIL   Not so hot.°   Not so fast
60   In his own grace° he doth exalt himself   merit
More than in your addition.[3]
REGAN   In my rights
By me invested, he compeers° the best.   equals
ALBANY   That were the most[4] if he should husband you.
REGAN   Jesters do oft prove prophets.
GONERIL   Holla, holla—
65   That eye that told you so looked but asquint.[5]
REGAN   Lady, I am not well, else I should answer
From a full-flowing stomach.° [*To* EDMOND] General,   anger
Take thou my soldiers, prisoners, patrimony.
Dispose of them, of me. The walls° is thine.   fortress of my heart
70   Witness the world that I create thee here
My lord and master.

9. To garner the affection of the populace.
1. *in our eyes / Which*: in the eyes of us who.
2. I think you should have inquired into my wishes.
3. In the honors you confer upon him.

4. That investiture would be complete.
5. Squinting was a proverbial effect of jealousy, because
of the tendency to look suspiciously at potential rivals.

GONORIL   Mean you to enjoy him, then?
ALBANY   The let-alone° lies not in your good will.   *veto*
EDMUND   Nor in thine, lord.
ALBANY   Half-blooded° fellow, yes.   *Bastard*
EDMUND   Let the drum strike[7] and prove my title good.
80   ALBANY   Stay yet, hear reason. Edmund, I arrest thee
       On capital treason, and in thine attaint[8]
       This gilded serpent. [*To* REGAN] For your claim, fair sister,°   *sister-in-law*
       I bar it in the interest of my wife.
       'Tis she is subcontracted to this lord,
85   And I, her husband, contradict the banns.°   *announcement of marriage*
       If you will marry, make your love to me.
       My lady is bespoke.—Thou art armed, Gloucester.
       If none appear to prove upon thy head
       Thy heinous, manifest, and many treasons,
            [*He throws down a glove*]
90   There is my pledge. I'll prove it on thy heart,
       Ere I taste bread, thou art in nothing less°   *in no way less guilty*
       Than I have here proclaimed thee.
REGAN   Sick, O sick!
GONORIL [*aside*]   If not, I'll ne'er trust poison.
EDMUND [*to* ALBANY, *throwing down a glove*]
95   There's my exchange. What° in the world he is   *Whoever*
       That names me traitor, villain-like he lies.
       Call by thy trumpet. He that dares, approach;
       On him, on you—who not?—I will maintain
       My truth and honour firmly.
100   ALBANY   A herald, ho!
EDMUND   A herald, ho, a herald!
ALBANY   Trust to thy single virtue,° for thy soldiers,   *your unassisted power*
       All levied in my name, have in my name
       Took their discharge.
REGAN   This sickness grows upon me.
105   ALBANY   She is not well. Convey her to my tent.
                  [*Exit one or more with* REGAN]
       [*Enter a* HERALD *and a trumpeter*]
       Come hither, herald. Let the trumpet sound,
       And read out this.

---

7. Perhaps to announce the betrothal, or a challenge.
8. And in order to accuse you; and as one who shares your corruption or crime.

GONERIL   Mean you to enjoy him?
ALBANY   The let-alone° lies not in your good will.   veto
EDMOND   Nor in thine, lord.
ALBANY   Half-blooded° fellow, yes.   Bastard
REGAN [to EDMOND]   Let the drum strike[6] and prove my title thine.
75 ALBANY   Stay yet, hear reason. Edmond, I arrest thee
      On capital treason, and in thy attaint[7]
      This gilded serpent. [To REGAN] For your claim, fair sister,°   sister-in-law
      I bar it in the interest of my wife.
      'Tis she is subcontracted to this lord,
80   And I, her husband, contradict your banns.°   announcement of marriage
      If you will marry, make your loves to me.
      My lady is bespoke.
GONERIL   An interlude!°   A farce
ALBANY   Thou art armed, Gloucester. Let the trumpet sound.
      If none appear to prove upon thy person
85   Thy heinous, manifest, and many treasons,
      There is my pledge.
            [He throws down a glove]
                              I'll make° it on thy heart,   prove
      Ere I taste bread, thou art in nothing less°   in no way less guilty
      Than I have here proclaimed thee.
REGAN   Sick, O sick!
90 GONERIL [aside]   If not, I'll ne'er trust medicine.°   poison (euphemistic)
EDMOND [to ALBANY, throwing down a glove]   There's my
            exchange. What° in the world he is   Whoever
      That names me traitor, villain-like he lies.
      Call by the trumpet. He that dares, approach;
      On him, on you,—who not?—I will maintain
      My truth and honour firmly.
95 ALBANY   A herald, ho!
            Enter a HERALD
      [To EDMOND] Trust to thy single virtue,° for thy soldiers,   your unassisted power
      All levied in my name, have in my name
      Took their discharge.
REGAN   My sickness grows upon me.
ALBANY   She is not well. Convey her to my tent.
                        [Exit one or more with REGAN]
100   Come hither, herald. Let the trumpet sound,
      And read out this.

---

6. Perhaps to announce the betrothal, or a challenge.
7. And in order to accuse you; and as one who shares your corruption or crime.

SECOND CAPTAIN   Sound, trumpet!
     [*Trumpeter sounds*]
HERALD [*reads*] 'If any man of quality or degree in the host of
110   the army will maintain upon Edmund, supposed Earl of
Gloucester, that he's a manifold traitor, let him appear at the
third sound of the trumpet. He is bold in his defence.'
EDMUND   Sound! [*Trumpeter sounds*] Again!
     Enter EDGAR, [*armed*,] *at the third sound, a trumpet*
     before him
ALBANY [*to the* HERALD]   Ask him his purposes, why he appears
    Upon this call o'th' trumpet.

115 HERALD [*to* EDGAR] What° are you?	*Who*
Your name and quality,° and why you answer	*degree, rank*
This present summons?	
EDGAR O, know my name is lost,	
By treason's tooth bare-gnawn and canker-bit.°	*worm-eaten*
Yet ere I move't,° where is the adversary	*make my declaration*
I come to cope withal?°	*to encounter with*
120 ALBANY Which is that adversary?	

EDGAR   What's he that speaks for Edmund, Earl of Gloucester?
EDMUND   Himself. What sayst thou to him?

EDGAR Draw thy sword,	
That° if my speech offend a noble heart	*So that*
Thy arm may do thee justice. Here is mine.	
[*He draws his sword*]	
125 Behold, it is the privilege of my tongue,	
My oath, and my profession. I protest,	
Maugre° thy strength, youth, place, and eminence,	*Despite*
Despite thy victor-sword and fire-new° fortune,	*newly minted*
Thy valour and thy heart,° thou art a traitor,	*courage*
130 False to thy gods, thy brother, and thy father,	
Conspirant 'gainst this high illustrious prince,	
And from th'extremest upward° of thy head	*top*
To the descent° and dust beneath thy feet	*lowest part; sole*
A most toad-spotted[9] traitor. Say thou no,	
135 This sword, this arm, and my best spirits are bent°	*ready*
To prove upon thy heart, whereto I speak,	
Thou liest.	
EDMUND In wisdom I should ask thy name,	
But since thy outside looks so fair and warlike,	
And that° thy tongue some say[1] of breeding breathes,	*since*
140 My right of knighthood° I disdain and spurn.	*(to ask your name)*
Here do I toss those treasons to thy head,	
With the hell-hated° lie o'erturn thy heart,	*hated as much as hell*

---

9. Venomous, like a toad; spotted with disgrace.   1. Taste (from "assay"); utterance.

A trumpet sounds

HERALD [*reads*]   'If any man of quality or degree within the lists
of the army will maintain upon Edmond, supposed Earl of
Gloucester, that he is a manifold traitor, let him appear by the
105   third sound of the trumpet. He is bold in his defence.'

First trumpet

Again.

Second trumpet

Again.

Third trumpet

Trumpet answers within. Enter EDGAR, *armed*

ALBANY [*to the* HERALD]   Ask him his purposes, why he appears
Upon this call o'th' trumpet.

HERALD [*to* EDGAR]   What° are you?   *Who*
110   Your name, your quality,° and why you answer   *degree, rank*
This present summons?

EDGAR   Know, my name is lost,
By treason's tooth bare-gnawn and canker-bit.°   *worm-eaten*
Yet am I noble as the adversary
I come to cope.°   *to encounter*

ALBANY   Which is that adversary?

115   EDGAR   What's he that speaks for Edmond, Earl of Gloucester?

EDMOND   Himself. What sayst thou to him?

EDGAR   Draw thy sword,
That° if my speech offend a noble heart   *So that*
Thy arm may do thee justice. Here is mine.
[*He draws his sword*]
Behold, it is the privilege of mine honour,
120   My oath, and my profession. I protest,
Maugre° thy strength, place, youth, and eminence,   *Despite*
Despite thy victor-sword and fire-new° fortune,   *newly minted*
Thy valour and thy heart,° thou art a traitor,   *courage*
False to thy gods, thy brother, and thy father,
125   Conspirant 'gainst this high illustrious prince,
And from th'extremest upward° of thy head   *top*
To the descent° and dust below thy foot   *lowest part; sole*
A most toad-spotted⁸ traitor. Say thou no,
This sword, this arm, and my best spirits are bent°   *ready*
130   To prove upon thy heart, whereto I speak,
Thou liest.

EDMOND   In wisdom I should ask thy name,
But since thy outside looks so fair and warlike,
And that° thy tongue some say⁹ of breeding breathes,   *since*
What safe and nicely I might well demand
135   By rule of knighthood I disdain and spurn.¹
Back do I toss those treasons to thy head,
With the hell-hated° lie o'erwhelm thy heart,   *hated as much as hell*

8. Venomous, like a toad; spotted with disgrace.
9. Taste (from "assay"); utterance.
1. *What . . . spurn*: What I have a right to know and what
would be prudent and technically correct to ask, I disdain
to inquire about.

Which, for° they yet glance by and scarcely bruise,   *since*
This sword of mine shall give them instant way°   *access*
145 Where they shall rest for ever. Trumpets, speak!
    [*Flourish. They fight.* EDMUND *is vanquished*]
ALL[2] Save° him, save him!   *Spare*
GONORIL   This is mere practice,° Gloucester. *trickery*
 By the law of arms thou art not bound to answer
 An unknown opposite.° Thou art not vanquished, *opponent*
 But cozened and beguiled.°   *cheated and deceived*
ALBANY   Stop your mouth, dame,
150 Or with this paper shall I stopple° it.   *plug*
 Thou worse than anything, read thine own evil.
 Nay, no tearing, lady. I perceive you know't.
GONORIL Say if I do, the laws are mine, not thine.
 Who shall arraign° me for't?   *prosecute*
ALBANY   Most monstrous!
 Know'st thou this paper?
155 GONORIL   Ask me not what I know. *Exit*
ALBANY Go after her. She's desperate. Govern° her. *Restrain*
        [*Exit one or more*]
EDMUND What you have charged me with, that have I done,
 And more, much more. The time will bring it out.
 'Tis past, and so am I. [*To* EDGAR] But what art thou,
160 That hast this fortune on me?[3] If thou beest noble,
 I do forgive thee.
EDGAR   Let's exchange charity.° *forgiveness*
 I am no less in blood than thou art, Edmund.
 If more, the more ignobly thou hast wronged me.
    [*He takes off his helmet*]
 My name is Edgar, and thy father's son.
165 The gods are just, and of our pleasant vices
 Make instruments to scourge us.
 The dark and vicious place where thee he got[4]
 Cost him his eyes.
EDMUND   Thou hast spoken truth.
 The wheel° is come full circled. I am here.[5] *Fortune's wheel*
170 ALBANY [*to* EDGAR] Methought thy very gait did prophesy
 A royal nobleness. I must embrace thee.
 Let sorrow split my heart if I did ever hate
 Thee or thy father.
EDGAR Worthy prince, I know't.
175 ALBANY Where have you hid yourself?
 How have you known the miseries of your father?
EDGAR By nursing them, my lord. List° a brief tale, *Listen to*
 And when 'tis told, O that my heart would burst!
 The bloody proclamation to escape[6]
180 That followed me so near—O, our lives' sweetness,

---

2. Both Q and F give this speech to "Alb." (for "Albany"), which may be a compositor's mistake for "All."
3. Who have this good fortune at my expense.
4. The adulterous bed in which you were born; or, possi-

bly, the vagina. *got*: begot.
5. Back at the lowest point.
6. In order to escape the sentence of death.

Which, for° they yet glance by and scarcely bruise,   *since*
This sword of mine shall give them instant way°   *access*
140   Where they shall rest for ever. Trumpets, speak!
　　　　Alarums. [They] fight. [EDMOND is vanquished]
ALL² Save° him, save him!   *Spare*
GONERIL   This is practice,° Gloucester.   *trickery*
By th' law of arms thou wast not bound to answer
An unknown opposite.° Thou art not vanquished,   *opponent*
But cozened and beguiled.°   *cheated and deceived*
ALBANY   Shut your mouth, dame,
145   Or with this paper shall I stopple° it.   *plug*
　　　[*To* EDMOND] Hold,° sir, thou worse than any name: read   *Behold*
　　　　　thine own evil.
　　　[*To* GONERIL] No tearing, lady. I perceive you know it.
GONERIL   Say if I do, the laws are mine, not thine.
Who can arraign° me for't?   *Exit*   *prosecute*
ALBANY   Most monstrous!—
O, know'st thou this paper?
150   EDMOND   Ask me not what I know.
ALBANY   Go after her. She's desperate. Govern° her.   *Restrain*
　　　　　　　　　　　　　　　　　　　[*Exit one or more*]
EDMOND   What you have charged me with, that have I done,
And more, much more. The time will bring it out.
'Tis past, and so am I. [*To* EDGAR] But what art thou,
155   That hast this fortune on me?³ If thou'rt noble,
I do forgive thee.
EDGAR   Let's exchange charity.°   *forgiveness*
I am no less in blood than thou art, Edmond.
If more, the more thou'st wronged me.
　　　　[*He takes off his helmet*]
My name is Edgar, and thy father's son.
160   The gods are just, and of our pleasant vices
Make instruments to plague us.
The dark and vicious place where thee he got⁴
Cost him his eyes.
EDMOND   Thou'st spoken right. 'Tis true.
The wheel° is come full circle. I am here.⁵   *Fortune's wheel*
165   ALBANY [*to* EDGAR]   Methought thy very gait did prophesy
A royal nobleness. I must embrace thee.
Let sorrow split my heart if ever I
Did hate thee or thy father.
EDGAR   Worthy prince, I know't.
170   ALBANY   Where have you hid yourself?
How have you known the miseries of your father?
EDGAR   By nursing them, my lord. List° a brief tale,   *Listen to*
And when 'tis told, O that my heart would burst!
The bloody proclamation to escape⁶
175   That followed me so near—O, our lives' sweetness,

---

2. Both Q and F give this speech to "Alb." (for "Albany"),
which may be a compositor's mistake for "All."
3. Who have this good fortune at my expense.
4. The adulterous bed in which you were born; or, possibly, the vagina. got: begot.
5. Back at the lowest point.
6. In order to escape the sentence of death.

That with the pain of death would hourly die
Rather than die at once!⁷—taught me to shift
Into a madman's rags, to assume a semblance
That very° dogs disdained; and in this habit   *even*
185   Met I my father with his bleeding rings,°   *sockets*
The precious stones° new-lost; became his guide,   *eyes*
Led him, begged for him, saved him from despair;
Never—O father!—revealed myself unto him
Until some half hour past, when I was armed.
190   Not sure, though hoping, of this good success,°   *conclusion*
I asked his blessing, and from first to last
Told him my pilgrimage; but his flawed° heart—   *cracked*
Alack, too weak the conflict to support—
'Twixt two extremes of passion, joy and grief,
Burst smilingly.
195   EDMUND   This speech of yours hath moved me,
And shall perchance do good. But speak you on—
You look as you had something more to say.
ALBANY   If there be more, more woeful, hold it in,
For I am almost ready to dissolve,°   *melt into tears*
Hearing of this.
200   EDGAR   This would have seemed a period°   *conclusion*
To such as love not sorrow; but another
To amplify,° too much would make much more,   *enlarge, extend*
And top extremity.
Whilst I was big in clamour° came there in a man   *lamenting loudly*
205   Who, having seen me in my worst estate,
Shunned my abhorred society; but then, finding
Who 'twas that so endured, with his strong arms
He fastened on my neck and bellowed out
As he'd burst heaven; threw him on my father,
210   Told the most piteous tale of Lear and him°   *himself*
That ever ear received, which in recounting
His grief grew puissant° and the strings of life   *powerful*
Began to crack. Twice then the trumpets sounded,
And there I left him tranced.
ALBANY   But who was this?
215   EDGAR   Kent, sir, the banished Kent, who in disguise
Followed his enemy king,⁸ and did him service
Improper° for a slave.   *Unfit even*
           Enter [SECOND GENTLEMAN] *with a bloody knife*
SECOND GENTLEMAN   Help, help!
ALBANY   What kind of help?
What means that bloody knife?
SECOND GENTLEMAN   It's hot, it smokes.
It came even from the heart of—
ALBANY   Who, man? Speak.
220   SECOND GENTLEMAN   Your lady, sir, your lady; and her sister
By her is poisonèd—she hath confessed it.

---

7. *our . . . once*: how sweet must life be that we prefer the   8. Because Lear had previously banished him. *enemy:*
constant pain of dying to death itself.   hostile.

That we the pain of death would hourly die
Rather than die at once!⁷—taught me to shift
Into a madman's rags, t'assume a semblance
That very° dogs disdained; and in this habit   *even*
180   Met I my father with his bleeding rings,°   *sockets*
Their precious stones° new-lost; became his guide,   *eyes*
Led him, begged for him, saved him from despair;
Never—O fault!—revealed myself unto him
Until some half hour past, when I was armed.
185   Not sure, though hoping, of this good success,°   *conclusion*
I asked his blessing, and from first to last
Told him our pilgrimage; but his flawed° heart—   *cracked*
Alack, too weak the conflict to support—
'Twixt two extremes of passion, joy and grief,
Burst smilingly.
190 EDMOND   This speech of yours hath moved me,
And shall perchance do good. But speak you on—
You look as you had something more to say.
ALBANY   If there be more, more woeful, hold it in,
For I am almost ready to dissolve,°   *melt into tears*
195   Hearing of this.

Enter a GENTLEMAN [*with a bloody knife*]
GENTLEMAN   Help, help, O help!
EDGAR   What kind of help?
ALBANY   Speak, man.
EDGAR   What means this bloody knife?
GENTLEMAN   'Tis hot, it smokes.
It came even from the heart of—O, she's dead!
ALBANY   Who dead? Speak, man.
200 GENTLEMAN   Your lady, sir, your lady; and her sister
By her is poisoned. She confesses it.

---

7. *our . . . once:* how sweet must life be that we prefer the constant pain of dying to death itself.

EDMUND I was contracted to them both; all three
Now marry° in an instant.   *unite (in death)*
ALBANY Produce their bodies, be they alive or dead.
225   This justice of the heavens, that makes us tremble,
Touches us not with pity.
                              Enter KENT [*as himself*]
EDGAR   Here comes Kent, sir.
ALBANY O, 'tis he; the time will not allow
The compliment that very manners urges.⁹
KENT I am come
230   To bid my king and master aye° good night.   *forever*
Is he not here?
ALBANY   Great thing of° us forgot! —   *by*
Speak, Edmund; where's the King, and where's Cordelia?
          The bodies of GONORIL *and* REGAN *are brought in*
Seest thou this object,° Kent?   *spectacle*
KENT Alack, why thus?
235 EDMUND Yet° Edmund was beloved.   *Despite all*
The one the other poisoned for my sake,
And after slew herself.
ALBANY   Even so. — Cover their faces.
EDMUND I pant for life. Some good I mean to do,
Despite of my own nature. Quickly send,
240   Be brief° in't, to th' castle; for my writ¹   *speedy*
Is on the life of Lear and on Cordelia.
Nay, send in time.
ALBANY   Run, run, O run!
EDGAR To who, my lord? Who hath the office?° Send   *commission*
Thy token of reprieve.
245 EDMUND Well thought on! Take my sword. The captain,
Give it the° captain.   *to the*
ALBANY   Haste thee for thy life.
                                        [*Exit* SECOND CAPTAIN]
EDMUND He hath commission from thy wife and me
To hang Cordelia in the prison, and
To lay the blame upon her own despair,
250   That she fordid herself.²
ALBANY The gods defend her! — Bear him hence a while.
                                        [*Exeunt some with* EDMUND]
          Enter LEAR *with* CORDELIA *in his arms* [*followed by the*
          SECOND CAPTAIN]
LEAR Howl, howl, howl, howl! O, you are men of stones.
Had I your tongues and eyes, I would use them so
That heaven's vault should crack. She's gone for ever.
255   I know when one is dead and when one lives.
She's dead as earth.

9. The ceremony that barest custom demands.   texts for the play, Cordelia does in fact kill herself after
1. Order of execution.   reigning for some years.
2. Destroyed herself. In most of Shakespeare's source

EDMOND   I was contracted to them both; all three
  Now marry° in an instant.   *unite (in death)*
EDGAR   Here comes Kent.
       Enter KENT [*as himself*]
ALBANY   Produce the bodies, be they alive or dead.
       Goneril's and Regan's bodies brought out
205   This judgement of the heavens, that makes us tremble,
  Touches us not with pity.—O, is this he?
  [*To* KENT] The time will not allow the compliment
  Which very manners urges.⁸
KENT   I am come
  To bid my king and master aye° good night.   *forever*
  Is he not here?
210   ALBANY   Great thing of° us forgot!—   *by*
  Speak, Edmond; where's the King, and where's Cordelia?—
  Seest thou this object,° Kent?   *spectacle*
KENT   Alack, why thus?
EDMOND   Yet° Edmond was beloved.   *Despite all*
215   The one the other poisoned for my sake,
  And after slew herself.
ALBANY   Even so.—Cover their faces.
EDMOND   I pant for life. Some good I mean to do,
  Despite of mine own nature. Quickly send,
  Be brief° in it, to th' castle; for my writ⁹   *speedy*
220   Is on the life of Lear and on Cordelia.
  Nay, send in time.
ALBANY   Run, run, O run!
EDGAR   To who, my lord?—Who has the office?° Send   *commission*
  Thy token of reprieve.
EDMOND   Well thought on! Take my sword. The captain,
  Give it the° captain.   *to the*
225   EDGAR   Haste thee for thy life.
                            [*Exit the* GENTLEMAN]
EDMOND [*to* ALBANY]   He hath commission from thy wife and me
  To hang Cordelia in the prison, and
  To lay the blame upon her own despair,
  That she fordid herself.¹
230   ALBANY   The gods defend her!—Bear him hence a while.
                            [*Exeunt some with* EDMOND]
       Enter LEAR *with* CORDELIA *in his arms* [*followed by the*
       GENTLEMAN]
LEAR   Howl, howl, howl, howl! O, you are men of stones.
  Had I your tongues and eyes, I'd use them so
  That heaven's vault should crack. She's gone for ever.
  I know when one is dead and when one lives.
  She's dead as earth.

8. *the compliment . . . urges:* the ceremony that barest custom demands.
9. Order of execution.

1. Destroyed herself. In most of Shakespeare's source texts for the play, Cordelia does in fact kill herself after reigning for some years.

[*He lays her down*]
                    Lend me a looking-glass.
If that her breath will mist or stain the stone,[3]
Why, then she lives.
KENT   Is this the promised end?[4]
EDGAR   Or image of that horror?
ALBANY   Fall and cease.[5]

260   LEAR   This feather stirs. She lives. If it be so,
It is a chance which does redeem all sorrows
That ever I have felt.
KENT [*kneeling*][6]   Ah, my good master!
LEAR   Prithee, away.
EDGAR   'Tis noble Kent, your friend.
LEAR   A plague upon you, murderous traitors all.
265   I might have saved her; now she's gone for ever. —
Cordelia, Cordelia: stay a little. Ha?
What is't thou sayst? — Her voice was ever soft,
Gentle, and low, an excellent thing in women. —
I killed the slave that was a-hanging thee.
SECOND CAPTAIN   'Tis true, my lords, he did.
270   LEAR   Did I not, fellow?
I have seen the day with my good biting falchion°   *light sword*
I would have made them skip. I am old now,
And these same crosses spoil me.[7] [*To* KENT] Who are you?
Mine eyes are not o' the best, I'll tell you straight.°   *recognize you soon*
275   KENT   If fortune bragged of two she loved or hated,[8]
One of them we behold.
LEAR   Are not you Kent?
KENT   The same, your servant Kent. Where is your servant
Caius?°   *(Kent's pseudonym)*
LEAR   He's a good fellow, I can tell you that.
He'll strike, and quickly too. He's dead and rotten.
280   KENT   No, my good lord, I am the very man —
LEAR   I'll see that straight.[9]
KENT   That from your first of difference and decay[1]
Have followed your sad steps.
LEAR   You're welcome hither.
KENT   Nor no man else.[2] All's cheerless, dark, and deadly.°   *deathly*
285   Your eldest daughters have fordone° themselves,   *destroyed*
And desperately° are dead.   *in despair*
LEAR   So think I, too.

---

3. Mica, or stone polished to a mirror finish.
4. Doomsday; expected end of the play. In no version of the story previous to Shakespeare's does Cordelia die at this point.
5. Let the world collapse and end.
6. Lear probably kneels over Cordelia's body during most of the scene, and Kent kneels here partly in submission, partly to catch Lear's attention.
7. And these recent adversities have weakened me; and these parries I could once match would now destroy me.

8. If Fortune bragged of two she treated only with good or terrible extremes; "or" may be a variant of "ere," giving the meaning "loved before she hated."
9. I'll attend to that shortly; I'll comprehend that in a moment.
1. Who from the beginning of your alteration and deterioration.
2. No, neither I nor anyone else is welcome; that is, this is not a welcoming sight.

[*He lays her down*]

235   Lend me a looking-glass.
    If that her breath will mist or stain the stone,[2]
    Why, then she lives.
KENT   Is this the promised end?[3]
EDGAR   Or image of that horror?
ALBANY   Fall and cease.[4]
LEAR   This feather stirs. She lives. If it be so,
240   It is a chance which does redeem all sorrows
    That ever I have felt.
KENT [*kneeling*][5]   O, my good master!
LEAR   Prithee, away.
EDGAR   'Tis noble Kent, your friend.
LEAR   A plague upon you, murderers, traitors all.
    I might have saved her; now she's gone for ever.—
245   Cordelia, Cordelia: stay a little. Ha?
    What is't thou sayst?—Her voice was ever soft,
    Gentle, and low, an excellent thing in woman.—
    I killed the slave that was a-hanging thee.
GENTLEMAN   'Tis true, my lords, he did.
LEAR   Did I not, fellow?
250   I have seen the day with my good biting falchion°   *light sword*
    I would have made them skip. I am old now,
    And these same crosses spoil me.[6] [*To* KENT] Who are you?
    Mine eyes are not o'th' best, I'll tell you straight.°   *recognize you soon*
KENT   If fortune brag of two she loved and hated,
    One of them we behold.[7]
255 LEAR   This' a dull sight.[8]
    Are you not Kent?
KENT   The same, your servant Kent.
    Where is your servant Caius?°   *(Kent's pseudonym)*
LEAR   He's a good fellow, I can tell you that.
260   He'll strike, and quickly too. He's dead and rotten.
KENT   No, my good lord, I am the very man—
LEAR   I'll see that straight.[9]
KENT   That from your first of difference and decay[1]
    Have followed your sad steps.
LEAR   You're welcome hither.
265 KENT   Nor no man else.[2] All's cheerless, dark, and deadly.°   *deathly*
    Your eldest daughters have fordone° themselves,   *destroyed*
    And desperately° are dead.   *in despair*
LEAR   Ay, so think I.

2. Mica, or stone polished to a mirror finish.
3. Doomsday; expected end of the play. In no version of the story previous to Shakespeare's does Cordelia die at this point.
4. Let the world collapse and end.
5. Lear probably kneels over Cordelia's body during most of the scene, and Kent kneels here partly in submission, partly to catch his attention.
6. And these recent adversities have weakened me; and these parries I could once match would now destroy me.
7. *If . . . behold*: If there were only two supreme examples

in the world of Fortune's ability to raise up and cast down, Lear would be one; alternatively, we are each of us one (Lear and Kent are here looking at each other).
8. This is a sad sight; my vision is failing.
9. I'll attend to that shortly; I'll comprehend that in a moment.
1. Who from the beginning of your alteration and deterioration.
2. No, neither I nor anyone else is welcome; that is, this is not a welcoming sight.

ALBANY   He knows not what he sees; and vain° it is   *in vain*
      That we present us to him.
EDGAR   Very bootless.°   *futile*
            Enter [another] CAPTAIN
THIRD CAPTAIN *[to* ALBANY*]*   Edmund is dead, my lord.
ALBANY   That's but a trifle here.—
290   You lords and noble friends, know our intent.
      What comfort to this great decay° may come   *ruin, destruction*
      Shall be applied; for us, we will resign
      During the life of this old majesty
      To him our absolute power; *[to* EDGAR *and* KENT*]* you to your rights,
295   With boot° and such addition° as your honours   *reward / distinction*
      Have more than merited. All friends shall taste
      The wages of their virtue, and all foes
      The cup of their deservings.—O see, see!
LEAR   And my poor fool[3] is hanged. No, no life.
300   Why should a dog, a horse, a rat have life,
      And thou no breath at all? O, thou wilt come no more.
      Never, never, never.—Pray you, undo
      This button. Thank you, sir. O, O, O, O!
EDGAR   He faints. *[To* LEAR*]* My lord, my lord!
305 LEAR   Break, heart, I prithee break.
EDGAR   Look up, my lord.
KENT   Vex not his ghost.[4] O, let him pass. He hates him
      That would upon the rack[5] of this tough world
      Stretch him out longer.
            *[*LEAR *dies]*
EDGAR   O, he is gone indeed.
310 KENT   The wonder is he hath endured so long.
      He but usurped his life.[6]
ALBANY *[to attendants]*   Bear them from hence. Our present business
      Is to general woe. *[To* KENT *and* EDGAR*]* Friends of my soul, you twain
      Rule in this kingdom, and the gored° state sustain.   *wounded, bloody*
315 KENT   I have a journey, sir, shortly to go:
      My master calls, and I must not say no.
ALBANY   The weight of this sad time we must obey,
      Speak what we feel, not what we ought to say.
      The oldest have borne most. We that are young
320   Shall never see so much, nor live so long.
                  [Exeunt carrying the bodies]

---

3. A term of endearment, here used for Cordelia.   5. Instrument of torture, used to stretch its victims.
4. Do not disturb his departing soul.   6. From death, which already had a claim on it.

ALBANY   He knows not what he says; and vain° is it   *in vain*
    That we present us to him.
             Enter a MESSENGER
EDGAR   Very bootless.°   *futile*
MESSENGER [*to* ALBANY]   Edmond is dead, my lord.
270   ALBANY   That's but a trifle here.—
    You lords and noble friends, know our intent.
    What comfort to this great decay° may come   *ruin, destruction*
    Shall be applied; for us, we will resign
    During the life of this old majesty
    To him our absolute power;
275   [*To* EDGAR *and* KENT]   you to your rights,
    With boot° and such addition° as your honours   *reward / distinction*
    Have more than merited. All friends shall taste
    The wages of their virtue, and all foes
    The cup of their deservings.—O see, see!
280   LEAR   And my poor fool[3] is hanged. No, no, no life?
    Why should a dog, a horse, a rat have life,
    And thou no breath at all? Thou'lt come no more.
    Never, never, never, never, never.
    [*To* KENT] Pray you, undo this button. Thank you, sir.
285   Do you see this? Look on her. Look, her lips.
    Look there, look there.   *He dies*
EDGAR   He faints. [*To* LEAR] My lord, my lord!
KENT [*to* LEAR]   Break, heart, I prithee break.
EDGAR [*to* LEAR]   Look up, my lord.
KENT   Vex not his ghost.[4] O, let him pass. He hates him
    That would upon the rack[5] of this tough world
    Stretch him out longer.
290   EDGAR   He is gone indeed.
KENT   The wonder is he hath endured so long.
    He but usurped his life.[6]
ALBANY   Bear them from hence. Our present business
    Is general woe. [*To* EDGAR *and* KENT] Friends of my soul, you twain
295   Rule in this realm, and the gored° state sustain.   *wounded, bloody*
KENT   I have a journey, sir, shortly to go:
    My master calls me; I must not say no.
EDGAR   The weight of this sad time we must obey,
    Speak what we feel, not what we ought to say.
300   The oldest hath borne most. We that are young
    Shall never see so much, nor live so long.
              Exeunt with a dead march [*carrying the bodies*]

---

3. A term of endearment, here used for Cordelia.
4. Do not disturb his departing soul.

5. Instrument of torture, used to stretch its victims.
6. From death, which already had a claim on it.

TEXTUAL VARIANTS: HISTORY

Control text: Q1

F: The Folio of 1623
F2: The Folio of 1632
Q1: The Quarto of 1608
Q2: The Quarto of 1619
Qa, Qb: Successive printings of Q1 incorporating various print-shop corrections and
    changes

Title: The Historie of King Lear [Q running title] M. William Shak-speare / HIS /
Historie, of King Lear. [Q head title, Stationers' Register] M. William Shak-speare: / HIS /
True Chronicle Historie of the life and / death of King LEAR and his three / Daughters. /
With the vnfortunate life of Edgar, *sonne* / and heire to the Earle of Gloster, and his /
sullen and assumed humor of / TOM of Bedlam: [Q title page]

s.p. EDMUND [Q's use of *Bastard* has been standardized throughout.]
s.p. OSWALD [Q's use of *Oswald, Gentleman,* and *Steward* has been standardized
    throughout.]
s.p. ALBANY [Q's use of *Duke* and *Albany* has been standardized throughout.]
s.p. CORNWALL [Q's use of *Duke* and *Cornwall* has been standardized throughout.]
s.p. FIRST GENTLEMAN, SECOND GENTLEMAN [Q only uses *Gentleman.*]
s.p. SECOND CAPTAIN, THIRD CAPTAIN [Q only uses *Captain.*]

1.37 **off** of 51 **as** [F] a 100 **mysteries** [F2] mistresse **night** [F] might 117 **dowers** [F]
  dower 128 **crownet** Coronet 135 **mad** [Q2, F] man 163 **next** tenth 208 **your** [F]
  you 215 **acknow** may know 219 **the** for 230 **a** [F] and 244 **my** [F] thy 255 **Ye**
  The 267 **the worst** the worth

2.13 **dull-eyed** dull lyed 14 **creating** [F] creating of 15 **then** [F] the 35 s.p. **EDMUND**
  Ba⟨*stard*⟩. [Qb; not in Qa] 73 **ay** I 103 **honesty** [F] honest 109 **spherical** [F] spiritu-
  all 119 **on's cue** out out 120 **sigh** sithe

4.2 **diffuse** defuse 60 **these** this 79 **if you have** you haue 94 **my** any 95 **off** of 98 **Lady
  the brach** Ladie oth'e brach 99 **gall** [F] gull 136 **ladies** [Qb] lodes [Qa] 159 **learn to**
  [Qb] learne [Qa] 171 **Now** [Qb] thou [Qa] 186 **it** [F; not in Q] 207 **lethargied** [F]
  lethergie 223 **more like to** more like 237 **my** any 241 **are** [F] and 260 **thwart**
  thourt **disnatured** [F] disuetur'd 262 **cadent** [F] accent 277 **And** [not in Q] 278
  Untented [Qb] vntender [Qa] 279 **Pierce** [Qb] peruse [Qa] **thee!** the 281 **cast you**
  [F] you cast 294 **thee** [F; not in Q] 308 **And after** [Qa] & hasten [Qb] **retinue**
  returne 309 **milky** [Qb] mildie [Qa] 311 **ataxed** alapt [Qa] attaskt [Qb] **for want**
  [Qb] want [Qa] 312 **praised** [F] praise

5.6 **were** [Q2] where 16 **stands** [Q2] stande

6.18 **Wit** [not in Q] 27 **you** your 29 **cunning** [F] crauing 36 **Ho** no 47 **fine** [F] a
  fine 51 **lanced** lancht 54 **ghasted** gasted 55 **Or . . . I know not** [not in Q] 65
  pitched pight 95 **tend** tends 100 **the spoil and waste** these—and wast [Qa, Q2] **his**
  [Qb] this his [Qa] 118 **This** Thus 119 **poise** [Qb] prise [Qa] 122 **differences** [Qb]
  defences [Qa] **least** [Qb] best [Qa] 123 **home** [Qb, F] hand [Qa]

7.58 **Z** Zedd 62 **have you** you haue 69 **entrenched** intrench **unloose,** [F] inloose
  71 **fire** [F] stir 74 **dogs** [F] dayes 76 **Smile** Smoile 78 **Camelot** [F] Camulet
  87 **Than** [Q2, F] That 90 **roughness** [F] ruffines 101 **flickering** flitkering 102
  dialect [F] dialogue 114 **fleshment** [F] flechuent 117 **ancient** [F] ausrent [Qa] miscreant [Qb] 123 **Stocking** [F] Stobing [Qa] Stopping [Qb] 129 **speaks** [Q2, F]
  speake 133 **contemnèd** temnest [Qb] 146 **out** [Q2, F] ont 150 **say** [Qa] saw
  [Qb] 155 **miracles** [F] my rackles [Qa] my wracke [Qb] 157 **now** not [Qa] most
  [Qb] 159 **For** From 160 **their** [Qb] and [Qa] **overwatched** [Q2, F] ouer-
  watch 161 **Take** [Qb] Late [Qa] 163 **heard** [F] heare 167 **Does** [F] Dost 172 **elf**

[F] else **177 and** [Qb; not in Qa] **178 Pins** [Qb] Pies [Qa] **179 farms** [F] ser-
uice **182 Tuelygod** [Qa] *Turlygod* [Qb] **184 home** [F] hence **189 cruel** [F] crewell
190 heads [F] heeles **201 propose** purpose **210 meiny** [F] men **222 *Histerica***
Historica **246 pardie** perdy **250 insolence** Iustice **259 father** [Qb] fate [Qa] **260 his**
[Qb] the [Qa] **commands** [Qb] come and [Qa] **tends** [Qa] her [Qb] **261 'Fiery'?**
The The fierie [Qa] Fierie [Qb] **265 commands** [Q2] Cōmand **287 divorce** [Qb]
deuose [Qa] **shrine, tombe 293 deplored** deptoued [Qa] depriued [Qb] **294 you**
[F; not in Q] **299 in** [F] on **317 s.p. LEAR** [Q2; not in Q1, which does indent the
line as though it were the beginning of a speech] **323 Thy** [F] The **342 your** [F]
you **361–62 To be . . . air** [In Q, the lines appear in the opposite order: "To be . . .
owle" after "To wage . . . Ayre."] **366 beg** [Q2, F] bag **375 boil** bile **417 need**
[F] deed **420 life is** [F] life as **428 so** [F] to **429 tamely** [F] lamely **438 into** [F]
in **flaws** [F] flowes
8.9 outstorm outscorne **36 am** [F; not in Q] **45 In which endeavor** [not in Q]
9.2 cataracts [F] caterickes **hurricanoes** [F] Hicanios **8 germens** Germains **15 tax** [F]
taske **34 but** [Qb] hut [Qa] **43 wanderers** [F] wanderer **59 than** [F] their **65 you** [F]
me **71 your** [F] you **74 tiny** tine
10.3 took [Q2, F] tooke me **23 The** [F] then
11.2 The [Qb] the/the [Qa] **4 here** [F; not in Q] **6 contentious** [F] crulentious [Qa]
tempestious [Qb] **10 roaring** [Qb, F] raging [Qa] **12 This** [Qb] the [Qa] **14 beats**
[Qb, F] beares [Qa] **22 own** one **51 star-blasting** [F] starre-blusting **53 there, and**
[Q2] there, and / and **54 has his** [F2] his **69 word** words **84 no nonny** [F] no on
ny **92 lendings** [Qb] leadings [Qa] **on, be true** [Qa] on [Qb] **95 on 's** [F] in **97
Flibbertigibbet** [F] fliberdegibek **98 gives** [Qb] gins [Qa] **and the** [Qb] the [Qa] **99
pin, squinies** pin- / queues [Qa] pin, / squemes [Qb] **hare** [Qb] harte [Qa] **101
Swithin** Swithald **wold** old **102 A** [Qa] he [Qb] **met the** [Qb] nellthu [Qa] **mare**
[Qb] more [Qa] **foal** fold **103 her alight** [F] her, O light **105 witch** [Qb] with
[Qa] **110 tadpole** tod pole **wall-newt** [Qb] wall-wort [Qa] **119 Smolking** snul-
bug **122 Mahu** [F] ma hu **158 tower** [F] towne
12.10 were not [F] were
13.5 discern deserue **6 Frateretto** [F] *Fretereto* **16 justicer** Iustice **19 troll** tral **20
burn** broome **28 cushions** cushings **29 the** their **30 robèd** robbed **41 she** [Q2; not
in Q1] **44 join-stool** ioyne stoole **46 on** an **58 mongrel** mungril **58–59 grim, /
Hound** [F] grim-hound **84 Take up, take up** [F] Take vp to keepe [Qa] take vp the
King [Qb]
14.5 revenges [F] reuenge **8 festinate** [F2] festuent **posts** [F] post **14 questants**
questrits **55 anointed** [Qb] aurynted [Qa] **56 as** [F] of [Qa] on [Qb] **bowed** lou'd
[Qa] lowd [Qb] **57 bouyed** [F] layd [Qa] bod [Qb] **58 stellèd** [Qb, F] steeled [Qa] **60
howled** [F] heard **62 I'll subscribe** else subscrib'd **70 you** [Q2, F; not in Q1] **83
enkindle** [F] vnbridle **84 quite** quit **96 s.p. SECOND** [not in Q] **97 s.p. THIRD
2 100 s.p. SECOND I 101 roguish** [Qa; not in Qb]
15.4 esperance [F] experience **7 parti-eyed** [Qb] poorlie, leed [Qa] **35 to** [F] are
toth' **36 kill** [F] bitt **37 play fool** [F] play the / foole **41 hence** [F] here **55 thee**
the **57 as . . . lust,** Of lust, as *Obidicut,* **58 Flibbertiggibet** *Stiberdigebit* mocking
Mobing, **59 mowing** *Mohing* **67 undo** [F] vnder **71 saucily** firmly
16.10 defy desire **12 terror** [Qb, F] curre [Qa, Q2] **15 Edmund** [Q2, F] *Edgar* **21
command** [Qb, F] coward [Qa, Q2] **27 a** [Qb; not in Qa] **28 My foot usurps my
body** [Qa] A Foole vsurps my bed [Qb] **29 whistling** [Qb] whistle [Qa] **44 benefacted**
beniflicted [Qa] benifited [Qb] **46 these** [Qb] the [Qa] **48 Humanity** [Qb] Humanly
[Qa] **51 discerning** [F] deseruing **55 noiseless** [Qb] noystles [Qa] **56 flaxen big-
gin threats** thy flayer begin threats [Qa] thy state begins thereat [Qb] **59 shows** [Qb]
seemes [Qa] **64 dislocate** dislecate [Qa] **67 mew** [Qb] now [Qa] **77 You** [Qb] your
[Qa] **justicers** [Qb] Iustices [Qa]
17.9 Maréchal Marshall **12 sir** say **17 strove** streme **21 seemed** seeme **30 Let piety
not be believed** Let pitie not be beleeft **32 mastered** moystened her

18.2 racked vent **3 fumitor** femiter **4 burdocks** hor-docks **6 The centuries** a centurie is **send** [F] sent **28 incite** [Q2] in sight

19.4 Lord [F] Lady **11 Edmund** [F] and now **15 after** after him **letters, madam.** letters **27 I, madam?** [F] I Madam.

20.2 up it now [F] it vpnow **39 snuff** [Q2] snurff **40 bless him** [F] blesse **42 may** [Q2, F] my **53 a-length** at each **57 summit** [F] sommons **65 how now** how **68 beggar** [Q2, F] bagger **81 ne'er** neare **91 Ha!** hagh **102 ague-proof** [F] argue-proofe **104 every** [Q2, F] euer **109 Does** [F] doe **115 does** [F] do **116 To** [F; not in Q] **117 The** [F] to **129 Shall** [F] should **133 of't** oft **149 An** And **150 dog's obeyed** [F] dogge, so bade **153 Thy blood as** thy bloud **155 tattered** tottered **158 No tears, now** no now **170 shoe** [F] shoot **171 felt** [F] fell **181 a man a man** [F] a man **183 s.p. FIRST GENTLEMAN** Good Sir— [not in Q1] **191 speaking** speaking of **201 speedy foot** [F] speed fort **descriers** descryes **202 Stands** [F] Standst **214 bounty** [Qb, Q2, F] bornet [Qa] **the benison** [Qb, Q2, F] beniz [Qa] **215 send thee** saue thee [Qa; not in Qb] **boot to boot** [Qb, Q2; not in Qa] **216 first** [Qb, Q2, F; not in Qa] **228 vortnight** [Qb, Q2, F] fortnight [Qa] **229 costard** [Qb, Q2, F] coster [Qa] **230 baton** bat- / tero [Qa] bat [Qb] **257 venture** *Venter*

21.19–21 s.p. FIRST GENTLEMAN . . . DOCTOR *Doct⟨or⟩. . . .Gent⟨leman⟩.* **33 perdu** Per du **34 injurer's** iniurious **mean'st** [not in Q]

22.3 abdication [Qa] alteration [Qb] **28 Yet** Not **bold's** bolds **32 poor** dore **56 Here** [F] Hard **59 sisters** [Q2, F] sister **60 stung** [F] sting

24.24 goodyear good **45 send** [Qb, Q2, F] saue [Qa] **46 and appointed guard,** [Qb, Q2; not in Q1] **48 common** coren? **bosom** [Qa] bossome [Qb] **on** [F] of **54 We** [Qb] mee **56 sharpness** [Qb] sharpes **83 bar** bare **85 banns** banes **119 ere** are **128 fortune** [F] fortun'd **131 Conspirant** [F] Conspicuate **135 are** [F] As **139 tongue** [F] being **140 My** by **142 hated** lie [F] hatedly **o'erturn** oreturnd **146 s.p. ALL** *Alb⟨any⟩.* **163 ignobly** [not in Q] **165 vices** [F] vertues, **209 him** me **264 you** [Q2, F] your **278 you** [F; not in Q] **282 from your first** [F] from your life **285 fordone** [F] foredoome **291 great** [F; not in Q] **295 honours** [Q2, F] honor **300 have** [Q2, F] of

---

TEXTUAL VARIANTS: TRAGEDY

Control text: F

F1: The Folio of 1623
F2: The Folio of 1632
Q1: The Quarto of 1608
Q2: The Quarto of 1619
Qa, Qb, Fa, Fb: Successive printings of Q1 and F incorporating various print-shop corrections and changes

s.p. EDMOND [F's use of *Edmond* and *Bastard* are standardized throughout.]
s.p. OSWALD [F only uses *Steward.*]
s.p. FIRST GENTLEMAN [F uses only *Gentleman.*]
s.p. LEAR [F uses *Kear* once.]
s.p. KENT [F uses *Lent* once.]

1.1.53 words [Q] word **72 possesses** [Q] professes **98 Haply** Happily **108 mysteries** [F2] miseries **137 crownet** Coronet **153 a** [Q, F2; not in F1] **154 ne'er feared** nere feare **159 s.p. ALBANY and CORDELIA** *Alb⟨any⟩. Cor⟨delia⟩.* **167 sentence** [Q] sentences **173 seventh** tenth **213 best** [Q; not in F] **dear'st** deerest **223 well** [Q] will **228 the** for **265 Ye** The **278 pleated** plighted **279 covert** couers
1.2.119 Fut! [Q; not in F]

1.4.1 well [Q] will **2 diffuse** defuse **18 thou'rt** [Q1] thou art **28 canst** [Q1] canst thou **44 Daughter** [Q] daughters **48 A** [Q1] he **61 these** this **96 off** of **122 know** [Q1] thou know **129 crown** [Q] crownes **130 o'th'** [Q1] on thy **144 fools** [Q] foole **145 Prithee** [Q] Pry'thy **163 nor crumb,** [Q] not crum **249–50 that she may feel—** / **That she may feel** That she may feele, **306 You** [F1] your [F2] **attasked** [Qb] at task
1.5.21 a may [Q1] he may
2.1.2 you [Q] your **36 Ho** no **39 stand** 's [Q1] stand **54 ghasted** gasted **69 I should** [Q] should I **70 ay,** [Q; not in F] **78 why** [Q] wher **86 strange news** [Q] strangenesse **94 tend** tended **99 spoil** [Qb] wast **120 poise** [Qb] prize **123 least** [Qb] best thought [Q] though
2.2.20 clamorous [Q] clamours **59 you'll** [Q1] you will **68 holy** [Fb] holly [Fa] **72 Renege** [Q] Reuenge **77 an** [Q1] if **93 take't** [Q1] take it **101 flick'ring** flicking **114 dread** [Q] dead **121 respect** [Q] respects **136 good** [Q1; not in F] **137 Duke's** [Q] Duke **144 to** [Q1] too **145 say** [Qa] saw **152 now** most **154 For** From **161 unusual** [Q1] vnusall **175 sheep-cotes** [Q] sheeps-coates **176 Sometime** [Q] sometimes **177 Tuelygod** [Qa] *Turlygod* **180 messenger** [Q] Messengers **186 man's** [Q] man **204 whose** [Q] those **216 wild** wil'd **226 Histerica** *Historica* **231 the** [Q] the the **242 gives** [Q, Fb] giue [Fa] **have** [Q] hause **246 begin** [Q1] begins **293 you** [Q] your **295 mother's** [Q] Mother **shrine** tombe **336 tender-hafted** tender-hefted **351 sickly** fickly **a** [Q1] he **374–75 To be a comrade with the wolf and owl,** / **To wage against the enmity o'th' air** To wage against the enmity oth'ayre, / To be a Comrade with the Wolfe, and Owle, **377 hot-blooded** [Fa] hot-bloodied [Fb] **451 mad** [Q, Fb] mads [Fa] **471 to** [Q1] too **472 wild** [Q] wil'd
3.1.2 s.p. FIRST GENTLEMAN Gen⟨tleman⟩. [The stage direction calls for "a Gentleman," and F uses this combination to mean this specific character who reappears in 5.3.196–249.]
3.2.3 drowned [Q] drown **49 pother** pudder **84–85 Then . . . confusion.** [in F, after 3.2.91]
3.3.15 for't [Q1] for it
3.4.10 thy [Q] they **12 This** [Qb] the **31 looped** lop'd **44 Thorough** [Q1] through **45 cold** [Q; not in F] **47 two** [Q; not in F] **50 led through** [Q] led though **ford** [Q] Sword **55 Bless** Blisse **82 deeply** [Q2] deerely **89 Dauphin** Dolphin *cessez* Sesey **103 fiend** [Q; not in F] **104 till the** [Q] at **107 Swithin** *Swithold* **wold** old **108 A** [Qa] he **nine foal,** nine-fold **120 had** [Q; not in F] **150 a** [Q1] he **156 in t'** [Q1] into th'
3.5.22 dearer [Q] deere
3.6.25 Bobtail [Q] Or Bobtaile **tyke** [Q] tight **trundle** [Q2] Troudle **32 makes** [Q] make
3.7.8 festinate festiuate **63 cruels I'll subscribe** Cruels else subscribe
4.1.10 parti-eyed [Qb] poorly led **32 A** [Q1] He
4.2.30 whistling [Qb] whistle **36 shows** [Qb] seemes **43 threat enraged** [Q, F2] threat-enrag'd **47 justicers** [Qb] Iustices
4.3.3 fumitor [Q] Fenitar **4 burdocks** Hardokes **18 distress** [Q] desires **good man's** [Q] Goodmans
4.4.6 letters [Q1] Letter **15 after, madam** after him, Madam **39 him** [Q, F2; not in F1]
4.5.7 speak'st [Q2] speakest **17 walk** [Q] walk'd **53 a-length** at each **69 methoughts** [Q1] me thought **119 They're** [Q1] they are **154 Through** [Q] Tho- / rough [F's unmetrical substitution straddles a page break in a passage set as justified prose; "Through" could not be split, and the compositor almost certainly added the "o" for reasons of page makeup.] **155 Plate sin** Place sinnes **178 s.p. FIRST GENTLEMAN** Gent. ⟨leman⟩. **195 speaking** speaking of **201–2 hears that** / **That** [Q] heares that, which **206 in** on **225 Durst** [Q1] Dar'st **228 'cagion** [Q] 'casion **231 swaggered** [Q1] zwaggerd **232 so** [Q1] zo **234 baton** Ballow **I'll** [Q1] chill **236 sir** [Q1] zir **249 sorrow** [Q1] sorry **261 and for you her own** for venture, [Q1; not in F]

4.6 Scaena Septima 22 **not of** [Q] of 29 **warring** [Q] iarring 51 **your hands** [Q] yours hand [Fa] your hand [Fb] 52 **mock** [Q1] mocke me

5.1.3 abdication [Qa] alteration 14 **me** [Q; not in F] 36 **love** [Q] loues

5.3.24 goodyear good yeares 45 **and appointed guard,** [Qb, Q2; not in F] 76 **attaint** [Q] arrest 77 **sister** [Q] Sisters 91 **he is** [Q] hes 119 **Behold, it is the privilege** [Q] Behold it is my priuiledge, / The priuiledge **honour** Honours 122 **Despite** [Q] Despise 134 **well demand** well delay 136 **those** [Q1] these 141 **s.p.** ALL Alb⟨any⟩. 142 **arms** [Q] Warre 145 **stopple** [Q1] stop 224 **The captain,** [Q1; not in F] 231 **Howl, howl, howl, howl** [Q] Howle, howle, howle **you** [Q] your 251 **them** [Q] him 255 **This'** this is 264 **You're** [Q1] Your are 267 **think I** [Q1] I thinke

King Lear

A CONFLATED TEXT

THE PERSONS OF THE PLAY

LEAR, King of Britain
GONERIL, Lear's eldest daughter
Duke of ALBANY, her husband
REGAN, Lear's second daughter
Duke of CORNWALL, her husband
CORDELIA, Lear's youngest daughter
King of FRANCE } suitors of Cordelia
Duke of BURGUNDY
Earl of KENT, later disguised as Caius
Earl of GLOUCESTER
EDGAR, elder son of Gloucester, later disguised as Tom o' Bedlam
EDMUND, bastard son of Gloucester
OLD MAN, Gloucester's tenant
CURAN, Gloucester's retainer
Lear's FOOL
OSWALD, Goneril's steward
A DOCTOR
A CAPTAIN
A GENTLEMAN
A HERALD
SERVANTS to Cornwall
Knights, officers, messengers, soldiers, attendants

1.1

Enter KENT, GLOUCESTER,[1] *and* EDMUND

KENT I thought the king had more affected° the Duke of Albany° than Cornwall. | favored / Scotland

GLOUCESTER It did always seem so to us; but now, in the division of the kingdom, it appears not° which of the dukes he 5 values most; for equalities° are so weighed,° that curiosity in neither can make choice of either's moiety.[2] | is not clear / shares / equal

KENT Is not this your son, my lord?

GLOUCESTER His breeding,° sir, hath been at my charge.[3] I have so often blushed to acknowledge him, that now I am brazed° 10 to it. | upbringing / hardened

KENT I cannot conceive° you. | comprehend

GLOUCESTER Sir, this young fellow's mother could;[4] whereupon she grew round-wombed, and had, indeed, sir, a son for her cradle ere she had a husband for her bed. Do you smell a 15 fault?[5]

1.1 Location: King Lear's court.
1. Pronounced "Gloster."
2. *that . . . moiety:* that careful scrutiny ("curiosity") of both parts cannot determine which portion ("moiety") is preferable.
3. My responsibility; at my cost.
4. Could conceive; punning on "biological conception."
5. Sin, wrongdoing; female genitals.

KENT   I cannot wish the fault undone, the issue° of it being so
proper.°

GLOUCESTER   But I have, sir, a son by order of law,° some year
elder than this, who yet is no dearer in my account.° Though
20   this knave° came something saucily⁶ into the world before he
was sent for, yet was his mother fair; there was good sport at his
making, and the whoreson° must be acknowledged. Do you
know this noble gentleman, Edmund?

EDMUND   No, my lord.

25   GLOUCESTER   My lord of Kent. Remember him hereafter as my
honorable friend.

EDMUND   My services to your lordship.

KENT   I must love you, and sue° to know you better.

EDMUND   Sir, I shall study deserving.°

30   GLOUCESTER   He hath been out° nine years, and away he shall
again. (*Sound a sennet*)° The king is coming.

  Enter one bearing a coronet, then King LEAR, CORN-
  WALL, ALBANY, GONERIL, REGAN, CORDELIA, *and attendants*

LEAR   Attend the lords of France and Burgundy, Gloucester.

GLOUCESTER   I shall, my liege.°

  Exeunt GLOUCESTER *and* EDMUND

LEAR   Meantime we° shall express our darker° purpose.
35   Give me the map there. Know that we have divided
In three our kingdom; and 'tis our fast° intent
To shake all cares and business from our age,
Conferring them on younger strengths, while we
Unburthened crawl toward death. Our son° of Cornwall,
40   And you, our no less loving son of Albany,
We have this hour a constant will to publish⁷
Our daughters' several dowers,° that future strife
May be prevented now. The princes, France and Burgundy,
Great rivals in our youngest daughter's love,
45   Long in our court have made their amorous sojourn,
And here are to be answered. Tell me, my daughters—
Since now we will divest us, both of rule,
Interest° of territory, cares of state—
Which of you shall we say doth love us most?
50   That° we our largest bounty° may extend
Where nature doth with merit challenge.⁸ Goneril,
Our eldest-born, speak first.

GONERIL   Sir, I love you more than words can wield° the matter;
Dearer than eye-sight, space,° and liberty;
55   Beyond what can be valued, rich or rare;
No less than life, with grace, health, beauty, honor;
As much as child e'er loved, or father found;
A love that makes breath° poor, and speech unable;
Beyond all manner of so much° I love you.

60   CORDELIA (*aside*)   What shall Cordelia speak? Love, and be silent.

LEAR   Of all these bounds, even from this line to this,
With shadowy forests and with champains riched,°
With plenteous rivers and wide-skirted meads,°

Glosses (right margin):
- offspring; result
- handsome; right
- legitimate
- estimation
- scamp; fellow
- rogue; bastard
- ask
- shall learn to deserve
- away; abroad
- fanfare of trumpets
- feudal superior
- (royal "we") / more secret
- steadfast
- son-in-law
- individual dowries
- Legal title
- So that / generosity
- convey
- freedom of movement
- language
- Beyond all comparison
- enriched plains
- broad meadows

---

6. Somewhat rudely; somewhat shamefully.
7. A fixed determination to announce publicly.

8. *Where . . . challenge:* To the one whose natural love
and good deeds mutually enhance one another.

We make thee lady: to thine and Albany's issue° — children, heirs
65 Be this perpetual. What says our second daughter,
Our dearest Regan, wife to Cornwall? Speak.
REGAN   Sir, I am made
Of the self-same metal° that my sister is, — spirit; substance
And prize me at her worth.° In my true heart — believe myself her equal
70 I find she names my very deed of love;
Only she comes too short, that° I profess — in that
Myself an enemy to all other joys,
Which the most precious square of sense possesses,[9]
And find I am alone felicitate° — am only made happy
In your dear highness' love.
75 CORDELIA (aside)   Then poor Cordelia!
And yet not so; since, I am sure, my love's
More ponderous° than my tongue. — weighty
LEAR   To thee and thine hereditary ever
Remain this ample third of our fair kingdom;
80 No less in space, validity,° and pleasure, — value
Than that conferred on Goneril. Now, our joy,
Although our last and least;° to whose young love — youngest; smallest
The vines of France and milk of Burgundy
Strive to be interested,° what can you say to draw — given access to
85 A third more opulent than your sisters? Speak.
CORDELIA   Nothing, my lord.
LEAR   Nothing?
CORDELIA   Nothing.
LEAR   Nothing will come of nothing,[1] speak again.
90 CORDELIA   Unhappy that I am, I cannot heave
My heart into my mouth. I love your majesty
According to my bond;° nor more nor less. — filial duty
LEAR   How, how, Cordelia! mend your speech a little,
Lest it may mar your fortunes.
CORDELIA   Good my lord,
95 You have begot me, bred me, loved me; I
Return those duties back as are right fit,
Obey you, love you, and most honor you.
Why have my sisters husbands, if they say
They love you all? Haply,° when I shall wed, — Perhaps; if lucky
100 That lord whose hand must take my plight° shall carry — marriage vow; condition
Half my love with him, half my care and duty.
Sure, I shall never marry like my sisters,
To love my father all.° — completely
LEAR   But goes thy heart with this?
105 CORDELIA   Ay, good my lord.
LEAR   So young, and so untender?
CORDELIA   So young, my lord, and true.° — honest; faithful
LEAR   Let it be so! Thy truth, then, be thy dower!
For, by the sacred radiance of the sun,
110 The mysteries of Hecate,[2] and the night;

9. Which . . . possesses: That the body can enjoy. precious square of sense: measure of sensibility; or, perhaps, balanced and sensitive perception. The square may represent the even mixture of the body's four fluids, or humors. 1. Ex nihilo nihil fit was an Aristotelian maxim. This was accepted by the Christian Middle Ages with the single exception of God having created the world out of nothing. 2. A classical goddess of the moon and the patron of witchcraft, she was associated with the underworld, Hades.

By all the operation of the orbs
From whom we do exist and cease to be;[3]
Here I disclaim all my paternal care,
Propinquity° and property of blood,°   *Closeness / kinship*
115   And as a stranger to my heart and me
Hold thee, from this,° for ever. The barbarous Scythian,[4]   *this time*
Or he that makes his generation messes[5]
To gorge his appetite, shall to my bosom
Be as well neighbored, pitied, and relieved,
As thou my sometime° daughter.   *former*
120   KENT   Good my liege—
     LEAR   Peace, Kent!
Come not between the dragon and his wrath.
I loved her most, and thought to set my rest[6]
On her kind nursery.° Hence, and avoid my sight!   *care*
125   So be my grave my peace,[7] as here I give
Her father's heart from her! Call France; who stirs?[8]
Call Burgundy. Cornwall and Albany,
With my two daughters' dowers digest° this third: *incorporate*
Let pride, which she calls plainness,° marry her.   *directness*
130   I do invest you jointly with my power,
Pre-eminence, and all the large effects°   *outward shows, trappings*
That troop with° majesty. Ourself, by monthly course,   *accompany*
With reservation° of an hundred knights,   *legal right to retain*
By you to be sustained, shall our abode
135   Make with you by due turns. Only we still retain
The name, and all the additions° to a king;   *prerogatives*
The sway,° revenue, execution of the rest,   *power*
Beloved sons, be yours; which to confirm,
This coronet[9] part betwixt you.
     KENT   Royal Lear,
140   Whom I have ever honored as my king,
Loved as my father, as my master followed,
As my great patron thought on in my prayers—
     LEAR   The bow is bent and drawn, make from° the shaft.   *get clear of*
     KENT   Let it fall° rather, though the fork° invade   *strike home / arrowhead*
145   The region of my heart: be Kent unmannerly,
When Lear is mad. What wilt thou do, old man?
Think'st thou that duty shall have dread to speak,
When power to flattery bows? To plainness° honor's bound,   *plain speaking*
When majesty stoops to folly. Reverse thy doom,°   *Revoke your sentence*
150   And, in thy best consideration, check°   *halt*
This hideous rashness. Answer my life my judgment,[1]
Thy youngest daughter does not love thee least;
Nor are those empty-hearted whose low sounds
Reverb no hollowness.°   *Echo no insincerity*
     LEAR   Kent, on thy life, no more.
155   KENT   My life I never held but as a pawn°   *chess piece; stake*

---

3. *By all . . . be:* Referring to the belief that the movements of stars and planets ("orbs") corresponded to physical and spiritual motions in a person, and thus controlled his or her fate.
4. Notoriously savage Crimean nomads of classical antiquity.
5. *he . . . messes:* he who makes meals of his parents or his children.

6. To secure my repose; to stake my all, as in the card game known as primero.
7. So may I rest in peace (probably an oath).
8. Does nobody stir? An order, with the force of "Get moving."
9. Cordelia's crown, symbol of the endowment she has forsworn.
1. *Answer . . . judgment:* I'll stake my life on my opinion.

To wage° against thy enemies; nor fear to lose it,   *wager*
Thy safety being the motive.
LEAR   Out of my sight!
KENT   See better, Lear; and let me still° remain   *always*
The true blank° of thine eye.   *precise bull's-eye*
LEAR   Now, by Apollo—
160   KENT   Now, by Apollo, king,
Thou swear'st thy gods in vain²
LEAR   O, vassal! miscreant!°   *villain; unbeliever*

Laying his hand on his sword

ALBANY   }
CORNWALL } Dear sir, forbear.
KENT   Do;
Kill thy physician, and the fee bestow
165   Upon thy foul disease.³ Revoke thy doom;
Or, whilst I can vent clamor from my throat,
I'll tell thee thou dost evil.
LEAR   Hear me, recreant!°   *traitor*
On thine allegiance, hear me!
Since thou hast sought to make us break our vow,
170   Which we durst never yet, and with strained° pride   *overblown*
To come between our sentence and our power,
Which nor our nature nor our place⁴ can bear,
Our potency made good,° take thy reward.   *demonstrated*
Five days we do allot thee, for provision
175   To shield thee from diseases of the world;
And on the sixth to turn thy hated back
Upon our kingdom: if, on the tenth day following,
Thy banished trunk° be found in our dominions,   *body*
The moment is thy death. Away! by Jupiter,
180   This shall not be revoked.
KENT   Fare thee well, king. Sith° thus thou wilt appear,   *Since*
Freedom lives hence, and banishment is here.
(*To* CORDELIA) The gods to their dear shelter take thee, maid,
That justly think'st, and hast most rightly said!
185   (*To* REGAN *and* GONERIL) And your large speeches may your deeds approve.⁵
That good effects may spring from words of love.
Thus Kent, O princes, bids you all adieu;
He'll shape his old course in a country new.   *Exit*
       Flourish.° Re-enter GLOUCESTER, *with* FRANCE, BUR-   *Fanfare of trumpets*
       GUNDY, *and attendants*
GLOUCESTER   Here's France and Burgundy, my noble lord.
190   LEAR   My lord of Burgundy,
We first address towards you, who with this king
Hath rivaled for our daughter. What, in the least,
Will you require in present dower with her,
Or cease your quest of love?
BURGUNDY   Most royal majesty,
195   I crave no more than what your highness offered,
Nor will you tender° less.   *offer*
LEAR   Right noble Burgundy,

---

2. You invoke your gods falsely and without effect. Lear's
blindness and misdirected imprecations are particularly
inapt for Apollo, god of the sun and of archery.
3. *Kill . . . disease:* You would not only kill the doctor but

hand his fee over to the disease.
4. Which neither my temperament nor my royal position.
5. And let your actions live up to your fine words.

When she was dear to us, we did hold her so;
But now her price is fallen. Sir, there she stands;
If aught within that little seeming substance,[6]
200 Or all of it, with our displeasure pieced,°   *joined*
And nothing more, may fitly like° your grace,   *please*
She's there, and she is yours.
BURGUNDY   I know no answer.
LEAR   Will you, with those infirmities she owes,°   *owns*
Unfriended, new-adopted to our hate,
205 Dowered with our curse, and strangered° with our oath,   *estranged*
Take her, or leave her?
BURGUNDY   Pardon me, royal sir;
Election makes not up on such conditions.[7]
LEAR   Then leave her, sir; for, by the power that made me,
I tell you° all her wealth. (*To* FRANCE) For° you, great king,   *inform you of / As for*
210 I would not from your love make such a stray°   *stray so far*
To° match you where I hate; therefore beseech you   *As to*
To avert your liking° a more worthier way   *To turn your affections*
Than on a wretch whom nature is ashamed
Almost to acknowledge hers.
FRANCE   This is most strange,
215 That she, whom even but now was your best object,
The argument° of your praise, balm of your age,   *theme*
Most best, most dearest, should in this trice° of time   *moment*
Commit a thing so monstrous, to dismantle°   *as to strip off, disrobe*
So many folds of favor. Sure, her offense
220 Must be of such unnatural degree,
That monsters it,° or your fore-vouched affection   *makes it monstrous*
Fall'n into taint;[8] which to believe of her,
Must be a faith that reason without miracle
Could never plant in me.
CORDELIA   I yet beseech your majesty—
225 If for I want° that glib and oily art,   *because I lack*
To speak and purpose not°—since what I well intend,   *and not intend*
I'll do't before I speak—that you make known
It is no vicious blot, murder, or foulness,
No unchaste action, or dishonored step,
230 That hath deprived me of your grace and favor;
But even for want of that for which I am richer,
A still-soliciting° eye, and such a tongue   *An always-begging*
As I am glad I have not, though not to have it
Hath lost me in your liking.
LEAR   Better thou
235 Hadst not been born than not to have pleased me better.
FRANCE   Is it but this—a tardiness in nature
Which often leaves the history unspoke
That it intends to do?[9] My lord of Burgundy,
What say you to the lady? Love's not love
240 When it is mingled with regards° that stands   *considerations*

---

6. *little seeming substance*: one who appears more substantial than she is; one who will not pretend.
7. A choice cannot be made under those terms.
8. *or . . . taint*: or else the love you earlier swore for Cordelia must be regarded with suspicion. "Or" may also mean "before," in which case the phrase would mean "before the love you once proclaimed could have decayed."
9. *a tardiness . . . do*: a natural reserve that inhibits voicing one's intentions.

Aloof from th' entire point. Will you have her?
She is herself a dowry.
BURGUNDY   Royal Lear,
Give but that portion which yourself proposed,
And here I take Cordelia by the hand,
245   Duchess of Burgundy.
LEAR   Nothing! I have sworn; I am firm.
BURGUNDY   I am sorry, then, you have so lost a father
That you must lose a husband.
CORDELIA   Peace be with Burgundy!
Since that respects of fortune are his love,
250   I shall not be his wife.
FRANCE   Fairest Cordelia, that art most rich, being poor;
Most choice, forsaken; and most loved, despised!
Thee and thy virtues here I seize upon:
Be it lawful I take up what's cast away.
255   Gods, gods! 't is strange that from their cold'st neglect
My love should kindle to inflamed respect.°   *ardent regard*
Thy dowerless daughter, king, thrown to my chance,
Is queen of us, of ours, and our fair France.
Not all the dukes of waterish° Burgundy   *irrigated; watery, weak*
260   Can buy this unprized° precious maid of me.   *unappreciated*
Bid them farewell, Cordelia, though unkind;°   *though they are unkind*
Thou losest here,° a better where° to find.   *this place / place*
LEAR   Thou hast her, France; let her be thine; for we
Have no such daughter, nor shall ever see
265   That face of hers again. Therefore be gone
Without our grace, our love, our benison.°   *blessing*
Come, noble Burgundy.
> *Flourish. Exeunt all but* FRANCE, GONERIL, REGAN, *and*
> CORDELIA
FRANCE   Bid farewell to your sisters.
CORDELIA   The jewels of our father, with washed eyes
270   Cordelia leaves you. I know you what you are,
And like a sister am most loath to call
Your faults as they are named.° Love well our father.   *are properly called*
To your professed bosoms° I commit him;   *publicly proclaimed love*
But yet, alas, stood I within his grace,
275   I would prefer° him to a better place.   *promote; recommend*
So, farewell to you both.
REGAN   Prescribe not us our duties.
GONERIL   Let your study
Be to content your lord, who hath received you
At fortune's alms.[1] You have obedience scanted,°   *stinted on*
280   And well are worth the want that you have wanted.[2]
CORDELIA   Time shall unfold what pleated cunning hides:
Who cover faults, at last shame them derides.[3]
Well may you prosper!
FRANCE   Come, my fair Cordelia.
> *Exeunt* FRANCE *and* CORDELIA

---

1. As a charitable gift from Dame Fortune.
2. And you deserve to get no more love (from your husband) than you have given (to your father). "Want" plays
on its alternative meanings of "lack" and "desire."
3. Those who hide their faults will in the end be put to shame.

GONERIL   Sister, it is not a little I have to save of what most nearly
285   appertains to us both. I think our father will hence to-night.
REGAN   That's most certain, and with you; next month with us.
GONERIL   You see how full of changes° his age is; the observation   *fickleness*
    we have made of it hath not been little:[4] he always loved our
    sister most; and with what poor judgment he hath now cast her
290   off appears too grossly.°   *blatantly*
REGAN   'Tis the infirmity of his age; yet he hath ever but slen-
    derly known himself.
GONERIL   The best and soundest of his time hath been but rash;[5]
    then° must we look to receive from his age, not alone the   *therefore*
295   imperfections of long-engraffed condition,° but therewithal the   *deep-rooted habit*
    unruly waywardness that infirm and choleric years bring with
    them.
REGAN   Such unconstant starts[6] are we like° to have from him as   *likely*
    this of Kent's banishment.
300   GONERIL   There is further compliment° of leave-taking between   *ceremony*
    France and him. Pray you, let's hit° together: if our father carry   *join; strike*
    authority with such dispositions[7] as he bears, this last surrender°   *abdication*
    of his will but offend° us.   *harm*
REGAN   We shall further think on 't.
305   GONERIL   We must do something, and i' the heat.°   *Exeunt*   *while the iron is hot*

1.2

Enter EDMUND, *with a letter*

EDMUND   Thou, nature, art my goddess; to thy law
    My services are bound.[1] Wherefore° should I   *Why*
    Stand in the plague of custom,[2] and permit
    The curiosity° of nations to deprive me,   *legal niceties*
5   For that° I am some twelve or fourteen moonshines°   *Because / months*
    Lag of° a brother? Why bastard? wherefore base?   *Younger than*
    When my dimensions are as well compact,°   *composed*
    My mind as generous° and my shape as true,   *noble*
    As honest° madam's issue? Why brand they us   *married; chaste*
10   With base? with baseness? bastardy? base, base?
    Who, in the lusty stealth of nature, take
    More composition and fierce quality[3]
    Than doth, within a dull, stale, tired bed,
    Go to creating a whole tribe of fops,°   *fools*
15   Got° 'tween asleep and wake? Well, then,   *Begotten*
    Legitimate Edgar, I must have your land.
    Our father's love is to° the bastard Edmund   *as much to*
    As to the legitimate. Fine word—'legitimate'!
    Well, my legitimate, if this letter speed,°   *succeed*
20   And my invention° thrive, Edmund the base   *plot*

4. We have observed it more than a little.
5. *The . . . rash:* Even in the prime of his life he was impetuous.
6. Such impulsive outbursts.
7. Frame of mind.
1.2 Location: The Earl of Gloucester's house.
1. Edmund declares the raw force of unsocialized and unregulated existence, as opposed to human law, to be his ruler; ironically, "nature" also means "natural filial affection." A "natural" was another word for "bastard" (illegitimate child).
2. Submit to the imposition of inheritance law.
3. *Who . . . quality:* Whose begetting, by reason of its furtiveness and heightened excitement, requires better execution and more vigor. Alternatively (with "take" having the meaning "give"), whose begetting produces (a person of) more mixture and vigor. "Composition," or mixture, may refer to the belief that the perfect offspring was conceived from an equal quantity of male and female essence and that physical and mental abnormalities were caused by a predominance of one or the other.

Shall top° the legitimate. I grow; I prosper. *overcome; usurp*
Now, gods, stand up for bastards!
      Enter GLOUCESTER
GLOUCESTER   Kent banished thus? and France in choler
      parted?° *in anger departed*
And the king gone tonight?° subscribed° his power? *last night / limited*
25 Confirmed to exhibition?[4] All this done
      Upon the gad?° Edmund, how now! what news? *spur of the moment*
EDMUND   So please your lordship, none.   *Putting up the letter*
GLOUCESTER   Why so earnestly seek you to put up that letter?
EDMUND   I know no news, my lord.
30 GLOUCESTER   What paper were you reading?
EDMUND   Nothing, my lord.
GLOUCESTER   No? What needed, then, that terrible dispatch° of *frightened haste*
      it into your pocket? The quality of nothing hath not such need
      to hide itself. Let's see. Come, if it be nothing, I shall not need
35   spectacles.
EDMUND   I beseech you, sir, pardon me. It is a letter from my
      brother, that I have not all o'er-read; and for so much as I have
      perused, I find it not fit for your o'er-looking.
GLOUCESTER   Give me the letter, sir.
40 EDMUND   I shall offend, either to detain or give it. The contents,
      as in part I understand them, are to blame.
GLOUCESTER   Let's see, let's see.
EDMUND   I hope, for my brother's justification, he wrote this but
      as an essay or taste[5] of my virtue.
45 GLOUCESTER *(reads)* "This policy and reverence of age makes
      the world bitter to the best of our times;[6] keeps our fortunes
      from us till our oldness cannot relish them. I begin to find an
      idle and fond° bondage in the oppression of aged tyranny; who *a useless and foolish*
      sways, not as it hath power, but as it is suffered.[7] Come to me,
50   that of this I may speak more. If our father would sleep till I
      waked him, you should enjoy half his revenue for ever, and live
      the beloved of your brother, Edgar."
      Hum—conspiracy!—"Sleep till I waked him—you should
      enjoy half his revenue"—My son Edgar! Had he a hand to
55   write this? a heart and brain to breed it in?—When came this
      to you? who brought it?
EDMUND   It was not brought me, my lord; there's the cunning of
      it; I found it thrown in at the casement° of my closet.° *window / private room*
GLOUCESTER   You know the character° to be your brother's? *handwriting*
60 EDMUND   If the matter° were good, my lord, I durst swear it were *content*
      his; but, in respect of that, I would fain° think it were not. *gladly*
GLOUCESTER   It is his.
EDMUND   It is his hand, my lord; but I hope his heart is not in
      the contents.
65 GLOUCESTER   Hath he never heretofore sounded you° in this *sounded you out*
      business?
EDMUND   Never, my lord. But I have heard him oft maintain it
      to be fit, that, sons at perfect age,° and fathers declining, the *at maturity*

---

4. Established as mere show; relegated to pension.
5. *but . . . taste:* simply as a proof or test. Both terms derive from metallurgy.
6. The established primacy of the elderly embitters us at

the prime of our lives. *policy:* statecraft; craftiness; established order.
7. *who . . . suffered:* which rules not because it is powerful but because it is permitted to ("suffered").

father should be as ward[8] to the son, and the son manage his
70   revenue.

GLOUCESTER   O villain, villain! His very opinion in the letter!
Abhorred villain! Unnatural, detested, brutish villain! worse
than brutish! Go, sirrah,[9] seek him. I'll apprehend him. Abominable villain! Where is he?

75   EDMUND   I do not well know, my lord. If it shall please you to
suspend your indignation against my brother till you can derive
from him better testimony of his intent, you shall run a certain°   *safe, reliable*
course; where,° if you violently proceed against him, mistaking   *whereas*
his purpose, it would make a great gap in your own honor and
80   shake in pieces the heart of his obedience. I dare pawn down°   *I dare stake*
my life for him that he hath wrote this to feel° my affection to   *feel out*
your honor, and to no further pretense of danger.[1]

GLOUCESTER   Think you so?

EDMUND   If your honor judge it meet,° I will place you where   *appropriate*
85   you shall hear us confer of this, and by an auricular assurance
have your satisfaction; and that without any further delay than
this very evening.

GLOUCESTER   He cannot be such a monster—

EDMUND   Nor is not, sure.

90   GLOUCESTER   To his father, that so tenderly and entirely loves
him. Heaven and earth! Edmund, seek him out; wind me into
him,[2] I pray you; frame° the business after your own wisdom. I   *arrange*
would unstate myself, to be in a due resolution.[3]

EDMUND   I will seek him, sir, presently;° convey° the business as   *immediately / carry out*
95   I shall find means, and acquaint you withal.°   *therewith*

GLOUCESTER   These late° eclipses in the sun and moon portend   *recent*
no good to us.[4] Though the wisdom of nature can reason it
thus and thus, yet nature finds itself scourged by the sequent
effects.[5] Love cools, friendship falls off, brothers divide; in
100   cities, mutinies; in countries, discord; in palaces, treason; and
the bond cracked 'twixt son and father. This villain of mine
comes under the prediction; there's son against father. The
king falls from bias of nature;[6] there's father against child. We
have seen the best of our time. Machinations, hollowness,°   *insincerity*
105   treachery, and all ruinous disorders, follow us disquietly to our
graves. Find out this villain, Edmund; it shall lose thee nothing; do it carefully. And the noble and true-hearted Kent banished! his offence, honesty! 'Tis strange.   *Exit*

EDMUND   This is the excellent foppery° of the world, that, when   *foolishness*
110   we are sick in fortune, often the surfeit° of our own behavior,   *excesses*
we make guilty of° our disasters the sun, the moon, and the   *we hold responsible for*
stars; as if we were villains by necessity; fools by heavenly compulsion; knaves, thieves, and treachers, by spherical predomi-

---

8. A child under eighteen years who was legally dependent, often orphaned.
9. A form of address used with children or social inferiors.
1. No further intention to do harm.
2. Worm your way into his confidence (with "me" as an
intensifier); worm your way into his confidence for me
("me" as a term of respect).
3. I would give up everything to have my doubts resolved.
4. Lunar and solar eclipses that were seen in London

about a year before the play's first recorded performance
would have added spice to this superstitious belief in the
role of heavenly bodies as augurs of misfortune.
5. *Though . . . effects:* Though natural science may
explain the eclipses this way or that, nature (and family
bonds) suffers in the effects that follow.
6. The King deviates from his natural inclination. In the
game of bowls, the "bias" ("course") is the eccentric path
taken by the weighted ball when thrown.

nance;[7] drunkards, liars, and adulterers, by an enforced
115 obedience of planetary influence; and all that we are evil in, by
a divine thrusting on.° An admirable° evasion of whore-master   *imposition / amazing*
man, to lay his goatish disposition to the charge of a star![8] My
father compounded° with my mother under the dragon's tail,   *coupled*
and my nativity was under Ursa Major,[9] so that it follows, I am
120 rough and lecherous. Fut!° I should have been that° I am, had   *By Christ's foot / what*
the maidenliest star in the firmament twinkled on my bastardiz-
ing. Edgar—
    Enter EDGAR
and pat° he comes like the catastrophe° of the old comedy. My   *on cue / resolution*
cue is villainous melancholy, with a sigh like Tom o' Bedlam.[1]
125 O, these eclipses do portend these divisions! Fa, sol, la, mi.[2]
EDGAR   How now, brother Edmund? What serious contempla-
    tion are you in?
EDMUND   I am thinking, brother, of a prediction I read this other
    day, what should follow these eclipses.
130 EDGAR   Do you busy yourself about that?
EDMUND   I promise you, the effects he writes of succeed° unhap-   *follow*
    pily; as of unnaturalness between the child and the parent;
    death, dearth, dissolutions of ancient amities; divisions in state,
    menaces and maledictions against king and nobles; needless
135   diffidences,° banishment of friends, dissipation of cohorts,[3]   *baseless suspicions*
    nuptial breaches, and I know not what.
EDGAR   How long have you been a sectary astronomical?°   *a devotee of astrology*
EDMUND   Come, come! When saw you my father last?
EDGAR   Why, the night gone by.
140 EDMUND   Spake you with him?
EDGAR   Ay, two hours together.
EDMUND   Parted you in good terms? Found you no displeasure
    in him by word or countenance?°   *appearance; demeanor*
EDGAR   None at all.
145 EDMUND   Bethink yourself wherein you may have offended him;
    and at my entreaty forbear° his presence till some little time   *avoid*
    hath qualified° the heat of his displeasure; which at this instant   *mollified*
    so rageth in him, that with the mischief of your person it would
    scarcely allay.[4]
150 EDGAR   Some villain hath done me wrong.
EDMUND   That's my fear. I pray you, have a continent forbear-
    ance° till the speed of his rage goes slower; and, as I say, retire   *restrained absence*
    with me to my lodging, from whence I will fitly° bring you to   *when suitable*
    hear my lord speak. Pray ye, go! There's my key. If you do stir
155   abroad, go armed.
EDGAR   Armed, brother?
EDMUND   Brother, I advise you to the best. Go armed. I am no
    honest man if there be any good meaning towards you. I have

7. By the ascendancy of a particular planet. In the universe as conceived by Ptolemy, the planets revolved about
the earth on crystalline spheres.
8. *to lay . . . star:* to hold a star responsible for his lustful
desires. In Greek mythology, the satyr, a creature with
goatlike characteristics, was notoriously lecherous.
9. Constellations: *Dragon's tail* = Draco, and *Ursa
Major* = Great Bear.
1. The usual name for lunatic beggars; "Bethlehem,"
shortened to "Bedlam," was the name of the oldest and

best-known London madhouse.
2. The portion of the scale Edmund sings is an augmented fourth, an interval considered at this time very
discordant; it was sometimes referred to as "the devil in
music." *divisions:* social fractures; melodic embellishments.
3. Scattering of forces.
4. *with . . . allay:* even harming you bodily would hardly
relieve his anger; alternatively, with the irritant of your
presence, it (Gloucester's anger) would not be abated.

told you what I have seen and heard; but faintly, nothing like
160   the image and horror of it. Pray you, away!
EDGAR   Shall I hear from you anon?
EDMUND   I do serve you in this business.   *Exit* EDGAR
   A credulous father, and a brother noble,
   Whose nature is so far from doing harms,
165   That he suspects none; on whose foolish honesty
   My practices° ride easy! I see the business.[5]   *plots*
   Let me, if not by birth, have lands by wit:°   *intelligence*
   All with me's meet that I can fashion fit.[6]   *Exit*

1.3

Enter GONERIL, *and* OSWALD, *her steward*

GONERIL   Did my father strike my gentleman for chiding of his fool?
OSWALD   Yes, madam.
GONERIL   By day and night he wrongs me; every hour
   He flashes into one gross crime° or other,   *offense*
5   That sets us all at odds. I'll not endure it.
   His knights grow riotous, and himself upbraids us
   On every trifle. When he returns from hunting,
   I will not speak with him. Say I am sick.
   If you come slack of former services,[1]
10   You shall do well; the fault of it I'll answer.°   *answer for*
OSWALD   He's coming, madam; I hear him.
          Horns within°   *Hunting horns offstage*
GONERIL   Put on what weary negligence you please,
   You and your fellows.° I'd have it come to question.   *servants*
   If he dislike it, let him to our sister,
15   Whose mind and mine, I know, in that are one,
   Not to be overruled. Idle° old man,   *Foolish*
   That still would manage those authorities
   That he hath given away! Now, by my life,
   Old fools are babes again, and must be used
20   With checks as flatteries, when they are seen abused.[2]
   Remember what I tell you.
OSWALD   Well, madam.
GONERIL   And let his knights have colder looks among you.
   What grows of it, no matter; advise your fellows so.
   I would breed from hence occasions, and I shall,
25   That I may speak.[3] I'll write straight° to my sister,   *straightaway*
   To hold my very° course. Prepare for dinner.   *Exeunt*   *exact*

1.4

Enter KENT, *disguised*

KENT   If but as well[1] I other accents borrow,
   That can my speech defuse,° my good intent   *disguise*
   May carry through itself to that full issue°   *result*
   For which I razed my likeness.[2] Now, banished Kent,

---

5. It is now clear to me what needs to be done.
6. Anything is fine by me as long as I can make it serve
my purpose. *meet:* justifiable; appropriate.
1.3 Location: The Duke of Albany's castle.
1. If you offer him less service (and respect) than before.
2. *Old . . . abused:* When foolish old men act like children, rebukes are the kindest treatment when kind treat-

ment is abused.
3. *I would . . . speak:* I wish to foster situations, and I
shall, in which to speak my mind.
1.4 Location: As before.
1. As well as disguising my appearance.
2. Disguised my appearance; shaved off my beard (with a
pun on "razor").

5   If thou canst serve where thou dost stand condemned,
     So may it come,° thy master, whom thou lovest,   come to pass
     Shall find thee full of labors.°   helpful; keen
                    Horns within. Enter LEAR, *knights, and attendants*[3]
     LEAR Let me not stay° a jot for dinner; go get it ready.   wait
                                                 Exit an attendant
     How now! What° art thou?   Who
10   KENT A man, sir.
     LEAR What dost thou profess?[4] What wouldst thou with us?
     KENT I do profess to be no less than I seem; to serve him truly
        that will put me in trust; to love him that is honest; to converse°   associate
        with him that is wise and says little; to fear judgment; to fight
15   when I cannot choose;° and to eat no fish.[5]   when I must
     LEAR What art thou?
     KENT A very honest-hearted fellow, and as poor as the king.
     LEAR If thou be as poor for a subject as he is for a king, thou art
        poor enough. What wouldst thou?
20   KENT Service.
     LEAR Who wouldst thou serve?
     KENT You.
     LEAR Dost thou know me, fellow?
     KENT No, sir; but you have that in your countenance which I
25   would fain° call master.   gladly
     LEAR What's that?
     KENT Authority.
     LEAR What services canst thou do?
     KENT I can keep honest counsel,° ride, run, mar a curious tale   keep secrets
30   in telling it, and deliver a plain message bluntly. That which
        ordinary men are fit for, I am qualified in; and the best of me
        is diligence.
     LEAR How old art thou?
     KENT Not so young, sir, to love a woman for singing, nor so old
35   to dote on her for anything. I have years on my back forty-eight.
     LEAR Follow me; thou shalt serve me. If I like thee no worse
        after dinner, I will not part from thee yet. Dinner, ho dinner!
        Where's my knave? my fool? Go you, and call my fool hither.
                                                 Exit an attendant
                    Enter OSWALD
     You, you, sirrah, where's my daughter?
40   OSWALD So please you—   *Exit*
     LEAR What says the fellow there? Call the clotpoll° back. (*Exit*   blockhead
        a KNIGHT) Where's my fool, ho? I think the world's asleep.
                    Re-enter KNIGHT
     How now! where's that mongrel?
     KNIGHT He says, my lord, your daughter is not well.
45   LEAR Why came not the slave back to me when I called him?
     KNIGHT Sir, he answered me in the roundest° manner, he would   bluntest; rudest
        not.
     LEAR He would not!
     KNIGHT My lord, I know not what the matter is; but, to my judg-

---

3. The attendants include at least one knight. Critics of
James I complained that he devalued honors by granting
too many knighthoods and that he squandered too much
time in hunting.
4. What is your job (profession)? Kent, in reply, uses

"profess" punningly to mean "claim."
5. And not to be a Catholic or penitent (Catholics were
obliged to eat fish on specified occasions and as penance);
alternatively, to be a manly man, a meat eater.

50 ment, your highness is not entertained with that ceremonious
affection as you were wont,° there's a great abatement of kind-   *accustomed to*
ness appears as well in the general dependants° as in the duke   *servants*
himself also and your daughter.
LEAR Ha! sayest thou so?
55 KNIGHT I beseech you pardon me, my lord, if I be mistaken; for
my duty cannot be silent when I think your highness wronged.
LEAR Thou but rememberest° me of mine own conception.° I   *remind / perception*
have perceived a most faint neglect of late; which I have
rather blamed as mine own jealous curiosity[6] than as a very
60 pretense° and purpose of unkindness. I will look further into 't.   *a true intention*
But where's my fool? I have not seen him this two days.
KNIGHT Since my young lady's going into France, sir, the fool
hath much pined away.
LEAR No more of that; I have noted it well. Go you and tell my
65 daughter I would speak with her.   *Exit* KNIGHT
Go you, call hither my fool.   *Exit an attendant*
            Re-enter OSWALD
O, you sir, you! Come you hither, sir. Who am I, sir?
OSWALD My lady's father.
LEAR "My lady's father"! My lord's knave! You whoreson dog!
70 you slave! you cur!
OSWALD I am none of these, my lord; I beseech your pardon.
LEAR Do you bandy looks with me, you rascal? (*Striking him*)
OSWALD I'll not be struck, my lord.
KENT Nor tripped neither, you base foot-ball player.[7]
            Tripping up his heels
75 LEAR I thank thee, fellow; thou servest me, and I'll love thee.
KENT Come, sir, arise, away! I'll teach you differences.° Away,   *(of rank)*
away! If you will measure your lubber's length again,[8] tarry; but
away! Go to! Have you wisdom? so.   *Pushes* OSWALD *out*
LEAR Now, my friendly knave, I thank thee: there's earnest of°   *downpayment for*
80 thy service. (*Giving* KENT *money*)
            Enter FOOL
FOOL Let me hire him too. Here's my coxcomb.°   *fool's cap*
            Offering KENT *his cap*
LEAR How now, my pretty knave! How dost thou?
FOOL Sirrah, you were best take my coxcomb.
KENT Why, fool?
85 FOOL Why, for taking one's part that's out of favor. Nay, an thou
canst not smile as the wind sits, thou'lt catch cold shortly.[9]
There, take my coxcomb! Why, this fellow has banished two
on's daughters,[1] and did the third a blessing against his will. If
thou follow him, thou must needs wear my coxcomb. How
90 now, nuncle!° Would I had two coxcombs and two daughters!   *(mine) uncle*
LEAR Why, my boy?
FOOL If I gave them all my living,° I'd keep my coxcombs   *goods*
myself.[2] There's mine; beg another of thy daughters.
LEAR Take heed, sirrah; the whip.
95 FOOL Truth's a dog must to° kennel; he must be whipped out,   *go to*

---

6. *jealous curiosity:* paranoid concern with niceties.
7. Football was a rough street game played by the poor.
8. If you will be stretched out by me again. *lubber:* clumsy oaf.
9. *an . . . shortly:* if you can't keep in with those in power,
you will soon find yourself left out in the cold.
1. By abdicating, Lear has in effect prevented his daughters from any longer being his subjects, just as if he had "banished" them.
2. I'd be twice as much a fool.

when Lady the brach³ may stand by the fire and stink.

LEAR A pestilent gall° to me!   *annoyance; bitterness*

FOOL Sirrah, I'll teach thee a speech.

LEAR Do.

100 FOOL Mark it, nuncle:

> Have more than thou showest,
> Speak less than thou knowest,
> Lend less than thou owest,°   *own*
> Ride more than thou goest,°   *walk*
> 105 Learn° more than thou trowest,°   *Hear / believe*
> Set less than thou throwest,⁴
> Leave thy drink and thy whore,
> And keep in-a-door,
> And thou shalt have more
> 110 Than two tens to a score.⁵

KENT This is nothing, fool.

FOOL Then 'tis like the breath° of an unfeed° lawyer; you gave   *speech / unpaid*
me nothing for 't. Can you make no use of nothing, nuncle?

LEAR Why, no, boy; nothing can be made out of nothing.

115 FOOL (*to* KENT) Prithee, tell him, so much the rent of his land
comes to.⁶ He will not believe a fool.

LEAR A bitter fool!

FOOL Dost thou know the difference, my boy, between a bitter
fool and a sweet fool?

120 LEAR No, lad; teach me.

FOOL
> That lord that counseled thee
>   To give away thy land,
> Come place him here by me,
>   Do thou for him stand:°   *represent him*
> 125 The sweet and bitter fool
>   Will presently appear;
> The one in motley⁷ here,
>   The other found out there.

LEAR Dost thou call me fool, boy?

130 FOOL All thy other titles thou hast given away; that thou wast
born with.

KENT This is not altogether fool,° my lord.   *foolish, folly*

FOOL No, faith, lords and great men will not let me; if I had a
monopoly out, they would have part on 't: and ladies too, they
135 will not let me have all fool to myself; they'll be snatching.
Give me an egg, nuncle, and I'll give thee two crowns.

LEAR What two crowns shall they be?

FOOL Why, after I have cut the egg i' the middle, and eat up the
meat,° the two crowns of the egg. When thou clovest° thy   *edible part / cleaved*
140 crown i' the middle, and gavest away both parts, thou borest°   *you carried*
thy ass on thy back o'er the dirt. Thou hadst little wit° in thy   *sense*
bald crown, when thou gavest thy golden one away. If I speak
like myself° in this, let him be whipped that first finds it so.⁸   *(like a fool)*

---

3. Lady the bitch. Pet dogs were often called "Lady" such-and-such. The allusion is to Regan and Goneril, who are now being preferred to truthful Cordelia.
4. Don't gamble everything on a single cast of the dice.
5. *And thou . . . score:* And there will be more than two tens in your twenty; that is, you will become richer.
6. Remind him that no land means no rent; with a pun on "rent" meaning "torn, divided."
7. Multicolored dress of a court jester.
8. *that . . . so:* who first discovers for himself that this is true; colloquially, who deserves to be whipped as a fool.

Singing
    Fools had ne'er less wit in a year;
145   For wise men are grown foppish,⁹
    They know not how their wits to wear,
        Their manners are so apish.°   *stupid; imitative*

LEAR When were you wont° to be so full of songs, sirrah?   *accustomed*

FOOL I have used° it, nuncle, ever since thou madest thy daugh-   *practiced*
150 ters thy mother; for when thou gavest them the rod, and put'st
    down thine own breeches,

Singing
    Then they for sudden joy did weep,
        And I for sorrow sung,
    That such a king should play bo-peep,°   *a child's game*
155   And go the fools among.
    Prithee, nuncle, keep a schoolmaster that can teach thy fool to
    lie. I would fain learn to lie.

LEAR An° you lie, sirrah, we'll have you whipped.   *If*

FOOL I marvel what kin° thou and thy daughters are. They'll   *how alike*
160 have me whipped for speaking true, thou'lt have me whipped
    for lying; and sometimes I am whipped for holding my peace.
    I had rather be any kind o' thing than a fool; and yet I would
    not be thee, nuncle; thou hast pared thy wit o' both sides, and
    left nothing i' the middle. Here comes one o' the parings.

Enter GONERIL
165 LEAR How now, daughter! What makes that frontlet¹ on?
    Methinks you are too much of late i' the frown.

FOOL Thou wast a pretty fellow when thou hadst no need to
    care for her frowning; now thou art an O without a figure.² I
    am better than thou art now; I am a fool, thou art nothing. [*To*
170 GONERIL] Yes, forsooth, I will hold my tongue; so your face bids
    me, though you say nothing. Mum, mum,
        He that keeps nor crust nor crum,
        Weary of all, shall want° some.   *lack, be in need of*
    (*Pointing to* LEAR) That's a shealed peascod.°   *empty pea pod; nothing*

175 GONERIL Not only, sir, this your all-licensed° fool,   *unrestrained*
    But other of your insolent retinue
    Do hourly carp and quarrel, breaking forth
    In rank° and not-to-be-endured riots. Sir,   *foul; spreading*
    I had thought, by making this well known unto you,
180 To have found a safe° redress; but now grow fearful,   *sure*
    By what yourself too late° have spoke and done,   *recently*
    That you protect this course, and put it on°   *encourage it*
    By your allowance; which if you should, the fault
    Would not 'scape censure, nor the redresses sleep,
185 Which, in the tender of a wholesome weal,
    Might in their working do you that offense,
    Which else were shame, that then necessity
    Will call discreet proceeding.³

---

9. *Fools . . . foppish:* Professional fools have gone out of
favor ("grace") since wise men have lately outdone them
in idiocy.
1. Band worn on the forehead; here, a metaphor for
"frown."
2. A zero without a preceding digit; nothing.
3. *which if you . . . proceeding:* if you do approve (of your

attendants' behavior), you will not escape criticism, nor
will it be without retribution, which for the common
good will cause you pain. While this would otherwise be
improper, it will be seen as a prudent ("discreet") action
under the circumstances. *tender of:* concern for. *weal:*
state, commonwealth. *then necessity:* the demands of the
time.

FOOL   For, you know, nuncle,
190   The hedge-sparrow fed the cuckoo[4] so long,
                       That it had it° head bit off by it young.°   *its / (the young cuckoo)*
            So, out went the candle, and we were left darkling.°   *in the dark*
LEAR   Are you our daughter?
GONERIL   Come, sir.
195   I would you would make use of that good wisdom,
            Whereof I know you are fraught,° and put away   *full*
            These dispositions,° that of late transform you   *moods, attitudes*
            From what you rightly are.
FOOL   May not an ass know when the cart draws the horse?
200   Whoop, Jug![5] I love thee.
LEAR   Doth any here know me? This is not Lear.
            Doth Lear walk thus? speak thus? Where are his eyes?
            Either his notion° weakens, his discernings   *intellect*
            Are lethargied—Ha! waking?° 'Tis not so.   *am I awake*
205   Who is it that can tell me who I am?
FOOL   Lear's shadow.
LEAR   I would° learn that; for, by the marks° of sovereignty,   *wish to / evidence*
            knowledge, and reason, I should be false persuaded I had
            daughters.
210   FOOL   Which° they will make an obedient father.   *Whom*
LEAR   Your name, fair gentlewoman?
GONERIL   This admiration,° sir, is much o' the savor   *excessive amazement*
            Of other your new pranks. I do beseech you
            To understand my purposes aright.
215   As you are old and reverend, you should be wise.
            Here do you keep a hundred knights and squires;
            Men so disordered,° so deboshed° and bold,   *disorderly / debauched*
            That this our court, infected with their manners,
            Shows° like a riotous inn. Epicurism° and lust   *Appears / Gluttony*
220   Make it more like a tavern or a brothel
            Than a graced° palace. The shame itself doth speak   *an honored*
            For instant remedy; be then desired
            By her, that else will take the thing she begs,
            A little to disquantity your train;°   *to reduce your retinue*
225   And the remainder that shall still depend,°   *be retained*
            To be such men as may besort° your age,   *befit*
            And know themselves° and you.   *know their place*
LEAR   Darkness and devils!
            Saddle my horses! call my train together!
            Degenerate bastard! I'll not trouble thee.
230   Yet° have I left a daughter.   *Still*
GONERIL   You strike my people, and your disordered rabble
            Make servants of their betters.
                    Enter ALBANY
LEAR   Woe that° too late repents!—(*To* ALBANY)   *Woe to him who*
            O, sir, are you come?
235   Is it your will? Speak, sir. Prepare my horses!
            Ingratitude, thou marble-hearted fiend,
            More hideous when thou show'st thee in a child
            Than the sea-monster!

4. The cuckoo lays its eggs in other birds' nests.   5. Nickname for "Joan"; sobriquet for a whore.

ALBANY   Pray, sir, be patient.
LEAR (*to* GONERIL)   Detested kite!° thou liest: *carrion-eating hawk*
240   My train are men of choice and rarest parts,°   *qualities*
        That all particulars of duty know,
        And in the most exact regard support
        The worships of° their name. O most small fault,   *honors accorded*
        How ugly didst thou in Cordelia show!
245   That, like an engine, wrench'd my frame of nature
        From the fixed place;⁶ drew from my heart all love,
        And added to the gall. O Lear, Lear, Lear!
        Beat at this gate, that let thy folly in, (*striking his head*)
        And thy dear° judgment out! Go, go, my people.   *precious*
250 ALBANY   My lord, I am guiltless, as I am ignorant
        Of what hath moved you.
LEAR   It may be so, my lord.
        Hear, Nature, hear! dear goddess, hear!
        Suspend thy purpose, if thou didst intend
        To make this creature fruitful!
255   Into her womb convey sterility!
        Dry up in her the organs of increase;
        And from her derogate° body never spring   *debased*
        A babe to honor her! If she must teem,°   *breed*
        Create her child of spleen,° that it may live   *malice*
260   And be a thwart, disnatured° torment to her!   *a perverse unnatural*
        Let it stamp wrinkles in her brow of youth;
        With cadent° tears fret° channels in her cheeks;   *flowing / carve*
        Turn all her mother's pains and benefits°   *cares and kind actions*
        To laughter and contempt, that she may feel
265   How sharper than a serpent's tooth it is
        To have a thankless child! Away, away!   *Exit*
ALBANY   Now, gods that we adore, whereof comes this?
GONERIL   Never afflict yourself to know the cause;
        But let his disposition have that scope
270   That dotage gives it.
              Re-enter LEAR
LEAR   What, fifty of my followers at a clap?
        Within a fortnight?
ALBANY   What's the matter, sir?
LEAR   I'll tell thee. (*To* GONERIL) Life and death! I am ashamed
        That thou hast power to shake my manhood thus;
275   That these hot tears, which break from me perforce,°   *against my will*
        Should make thee worth them. Blasts and fogs upon thee!
        The untented woundings° of a father's curse   *The undressed wounds*
        Pierce every sense about thee! Old fond° eyes,   *foolish*
        Beweep° this cause again, I'll pluck ye out,   *If you weep over*
280   And cast you, with the waters that you lose,
        To temper° clay. Yea, is it come to this?   *soften*
        Let it be so. Yet have I left a daughter,
        Who, I am sure, is kind and comfortable.°   *comforting*
        When she shall hear this of thee, with her nails
285   She'll flay thy wolvish visage. Thou shalt find
        That I'll resume the shape which thou dost think
        I have cast off for ever; thou shalt, I warrant thee.

6. *like . . . place:* as a machine (or lever) dislocated my natural affections from their proper foundations.

Exeunt LEAR, KENT, *and attendants*

GONERIL. Do you mark that, my lord?

ALBANY   I cannot be so partial,° Goneril,   *biased*
290   To° the great love I bear you—   *Because of*

GONERIL   Pray you, content.° What, Oswald, ho! (*To the* FOOL)   *be quiet*
You sir, more knave than fool, after your master!

FOOL   Nuncle Lear, nuncle Lear, tarry and take the fool with
thee.

295   A fox, when one has caught her,
And such a daughter,
Should sure° to the slaughter,   *surely be sent*
If my cap would buy a halter:°   *collar; noose*
So the fool follows after.   *Exit*

GONERIL   This man hath had good counsel!—a hundred
300   knights?
'Tis politic° and safe to let him keep   *prudent*
At point° a hundred knights? Yes, that on every dream,   *Armed*
Each buzz,° each fancy, each complaint, dislike,   *rumor*
He may enguard° his dotage with their powers,   *protect*
305   And hold our lives in mercy. Oswald, I say!

ALBANY   Well, you may fear too far.

GONERIL   Safer than trust too far:
Let me still° take away the harms I fear,   *always*
Not° fear still to be taken. I know his heart.   *Rather than*
What he hath uttered I have writ my sister.
310   If she sustain him and his hundred knights,
When I have showed the unfitness°—   *unwillingness*
          Re-enter OSWALD
                                    How now, Oswald!
What, have you writ that letter to my sister?

OSWALD   Yes, madam.

GONERIL   Take you some company, and away to horse!
315   Inform her full of my particular fear,
And thereto add such reasons of your own
As may compact° it more. Get you gone,   *compound*
And hasten your return.   *Exit* OSWALD
No, no, my lord,
320   This milky gentleness and course of yours
Though I condemn not, yet, under pardon,°   *begging your pardon*
You are much more attaxed° for want of wisdom   *taken to task; censured*
Than praised for harmful mildness.

ALBANY   How far your eyes may pierce° I cannot tell: *foresee*
325   Striving to better, oft we mar what's well.

GONERIL   Nay, then—

ALBANY   Well, well; the event.°   *Exeunt*   *time will tell*

1.5

Enter LEAR, KENT, *and* FOOL

LEAR   Go you before° to Gloucester¹ with these letters. Acquaint   *on ahead*
    my daughter no further with any thing you know than comes
    from her demand out of the letter.² If your diligence be not
    speedy, I shall be there afore you.

5 KENT   I will not sleep, my lord, till I have delivered your letter.

                                                    Exit

FOOL   If a man's brains were in 's heels, were't not in danger of
    kibes?°   *chilblains*

LEAR   Ay, boy.

FOOL   Then, I prithee, be merry; thy wit shall ne'er go slip-shod.³

10 LEAR   Ha, ha, ha!

FOOL   Shalt° see thy other daughter will use thee kindly; for   *Thou shalt*
    though she's as like this as a crab's° like an apple, yet I can tell   *crab apple, sour apple*
    what I can tell.

LEAR   Why, what canst thou tell, my boy?

15 FOOL   She will taste as like this as a crab does to a crab. Thou
    canst tell why one's nose stands i' the middle on's° face?   *of one's*

LEAR   No.

FOOL   Why, to keep one's eyes of either side's nose, that what a
    man cannot smell out, 'a° may spy into.   *he*

20 LEAR   I did her° wrong—   *(Cordelia)*

FOOL   Canst tell how an oyster makes his shell?

LEAR   No.

FOOL   Nor I neither; but I can tell why a snail has a house.

LEAR   Why?

25 FOOL   Why, to put his head in; not to give it away to his daugh-
    ters, and leave his horns without a case.⁴

LEAR   I will forget my nature.° So kind a father! Be my horses   *lose my fatherly feelings*
    ready?

FOOL   Thy asses° are gone about 'em. The reason why the seven   *(servants)*
30   stars° are no more than seven is a pretty reason.   *the Pleiades*

LEAR   Because they are not eight?

FOOL   Yes, indeed. Thou wouldst make a good fool.

LEAR   To take 't again perforce!⁵ Monster ingratitude!

FOOL   If thou wert my fool, nuncle, I'd have thee beaten for
35   being old before thy time.

LEAR   How's that?

FOOL   Thou shouldst not have been old till thou hadst been wise.

LEAR   O, let me not be mad, not mad, sweet heaven!
    Keep me in temper;° I would not be mad!   *sane*

            Enter GENTLEMEN

40 How now! Are the horses ready?

GENTLEMEN   Ready, my lord.

LEAR   Come, boy.

FOOL   She that's a maid now, and laughs at my departure,
    Shall not be a maid long, unless things be cut shorter.⁶

                                           Exeunt

1.5 Location: Before Albany's castle.
1. To the city of Gloucester.
2. *than . . . letter*: other than such questions as are prompted by the letter.
3. Literally, your brains will not wear slippers (to warm feet that are afflicted with chilblains); feet of any intelligence would not walk toward Regan.
4. Protective covering for his head or concealment for his horns (horns were the conventional sign of a cuckold).

The Fool reflects the cynical view, common in the period, that all married men are inevitably cuckolded.
5. To take it back by force. Lear may refer to Goneril's treachery, or he may be contemplating resuming his authority.
6. *She . . . shorter*: A girl who would laugh at my leaving would be so foolish that she could not remain a virgin for long; "things" refers both to the unfolding event and to penises.

2.1

Enter EDMUND *and* CURAN *meeting*

EDMUND   Save° thee, Curan.   *God save*

CURAN   And you, sir. I have been with your father, and given
   him notice that the Duke of Cornwall and Regan his duchess
   will be here with him this night.

5   EDMUND   How comes that?

CURAN   Nay, I know not. You have heard of the news abroad—
   I mean the whispered ones, for they are yet but ear-bussing
   arguments?[1]

EDMUND   Not I. Pray you, what are they?

10   CURAN   Have you heard of no likely wars toward,° 'twixt the   *impending*
   Dukes of Cornwall and Albany?

EDMUND   Not a word.

CURAN   You may do, then, in time. Fare you well, sir.   *Exit*

EDMUND   The duke be here tonight? The better! best!

15   This weaves itself perforce into my business.
   My father hath set guard to take my brother;
   And I have one thing, of a queasy question,[2]
   Which I must act. Briefness and fortune, work!°   *be with me*
   Brother, a word! Descend! Brother, I say!

      Enter EDGAR

20   My father watches. O sir, fly this place!
   Intelligence is given where you are hid.
   You have now the good advantage of the night.
   Have you not spoken 'gainst the Duke of Cornwall?
   He's coming hither; now, i' the night, i' the haste,

25   And Regan with him: have you nothing said
   Upon his party° 'gainst the Duke of Albany?   *On his (Cornwall's) side*
   Advise yourself.°   *Consider carefully*

EDGAR   I am sure on't,° not a word.   *of it*

EDMUND   I hear my father coming. Pardon me!
   In cunning I must draw my sword upon you:

30   Draw; seem to defend yourself; now quit you° well.   *acquit yourself*
   Yield! Come before my father. Light, ho, here!
   Fly, brother. Torches, torches! So farewell.   *Exit* EDGAR
   Some blood drawn on me would beget opinion°   *produce the impression*
      (*wounds his arm*)
   Of my more fierce endeavor. I have seen drunkards

35   Do more than this in sport. Father, father!
   Stop, stop! No help?

      Enter GLOUCESTER, *and servants with torches*

GLOUCESTER   Now, Edmund, where's the villain?

EDMUND   Here stood he in the dark, his sharp sword out,
   Mumbling of wicked charms, conjuring the moon
   To stand° auspicious mistress,—   *To act as his*

40   GLOUCESTER   But where is he?

EDMUND   Look, sir, I bleed.

GLOUCESTER   Where is the villain, Edmund?

EDMUND   Fled this way, sir. When by no means he could—

GLOUCESTER   Pursue him, ho! Go after.   *Exeunt some servants*
   By no means what?

2.1 Location: Gloucester's castle.   2. And I have a hazardous and delicate problem.
1. Barely whispered affairs. *bussing*: buzzing.

45	EDMUND Persuade me to the murder of your lordship;
	But that° I told him, the revenging gods
	'Gainst parricides did all their thunders bend;
	Spoke, with how manifold and strong a bond
	The child was bound to the father; sir, in fine,°
50	Seeing how loathly opposite° I stood
	To his unnatural purpose, in fell° motion,
	With his prepared sword, he charges home°
	My unprovided° body, lanched° mine arm:
	But when he saw my best alarumed spirits,
55	Bold in the quarrel's right,³ roused to the encounter,
	Or whether gasted° by the noise I made,
	Full suddenly he fled.
	GLOUCESTER Let him fly far.
	Not in this land shall he remain uncaught;
	And found—dispatch.° The noble duke my master,
60	My worthy arch° and patron, comes to-night:
	By his authority I will proclaim it,
	That he which finds him shall deserve our thanks,
	Bringing the murderous caitiff° to the stake;⁴
	He that conceals him, death.
65	EDMUND When I dissuaded him from his intent,
	And found him pight° to do it, with curst° speech
	I threatened to discover° him. He replied,
	"Thou unpossessing bastard! dost thou think
	If I would stand against thee, would the reposal°
70	Of any trust, virtue, or worth in thee
	Make thy words faithed?° No. What I should deny—
	As this I would; ay, though thou didst produce
	My very character⁵—I'd turn it all
	To⁶ thy suggestion, plot, and damned practice:°
75	And thou must make a dullard of the world,
	If they not thought the profits of my death
	Were very pregnant and potential spurs
	To make thee seek it."⁷
	GLOUCESTER Strong° and fast'ned° villain!
	Would he deny his letter? I never got° him.
	Tucket° within
80	Hark, the Duke's trumpets! I know not why he comes.
	All ports° I'll bar; the villain shall not 'scape;
	The duke must grant me that. Besides, his picture⁸
	I will send far and near, that all the kingdom
	May have due note of him; and of my land,
85	Loyal and natural° boy, I'll work the means
	To make thee capable.°
	Enter CORNWALL, REGAN, _and attendants_
	CORNWALL How now, my noble friend! Since I came hither,
	(Which I can call but now) I have heard strange news.

Right-margin glosses:

In response to that

finally

opposed
deadly
strikes to the heart of
unprotected / struck

frightened

And once found—killed
lord

wretch

resolved / bitter
expose

placing

credible

scheming

Flagrant / incorrigible
begot
Flourish of trumpets

seaports; exits

loving; illegitimate
legally able to inherit

3. *my best . . . right:* that I was fully roused to action, made brave by righteousness.
4. Treachery and rebellion were crimes for which one could be burned.
5. Handwriting; but also, a true summary of my character.
6. *I'd . . . / To:* I'd blame it all on.

7. *And thou . . . it:* And do you think the world so stupid that it could not see the benefit you would get from my death (and thus a motive for plotting to kill me)? *pregnant:* full. *potential spurs:* powerful temptations.
8. Likenesses of outlaws were drawn up, printed, and publicly displayed, sometimes with an offer of reward as in "Wanted" posters.

REGAN   If it be true, all vengeance comes too short
90   Which can pursue the offender. How dost, my lord?
GLOUCESTER   O, madam, my old heart is cracked, is cracked!
REGAN   What, did my father's godson seek your life?
       He whom my father named? Your Edgar?
GLOUCESTER   O, lady, lady, shame would have it hid!
95 REGAN   Was he not companion with the riotous knights
       That tend° upon my father?   *attend*
GLOUCESTER   I know not, madam. 'Tis too bad, too bad!
EDMUND   Yes, madam, he was of that consórt.°   *company*
REGAN   No marvel, then, though° he were ill affected.°   *that / ill disposed*
100   'Tis they have put him on° the old man's death,   *have urged him to seek*
       To have th' expense° and waste of his revénues.   *use*
       I have this present evening from my sister
       Been well informed of them; and with such cautions
       That if they come to sojourn at my house,
       I'll not be there.
105 CORNWALL   Nor I, assure thee, Regan.
       Edmund, I hear that you have shown your father
       A child-like office.°   *filial service*
EDMUND   'Twas my duty, sir.
GLOUCESTER   He did bewray his practice,° and received   *uncover his (Edgar's) plot*
       This hurt you see, striving to apprehend him.
CORNWALL   Is he pursued?
110 GLOUCESTER   Ay, my good lord.
CORNWALL   If he be taken, he shall never more
       Be feared of doing harm. Make your own purpose,
       How in my strength you please.⁹ For you, Edmund,
       Whose virtue and obedience doth this instant
115   So much commend itself, you shall be ours.
       Natures of such deep trust we shall much need;
       You we first seize on.
EDMUND   I shall serve you, sir,
       Truly, however else.°   *if nothing else*
GLOUCESTER   For him I thank your grace.
CORNWALL   You know not why we came to visit you—
120 REGAN   Thus out of season, threading dark-eyed night.
       Occasions, noble Gloucester, of some poise,°   *weight*
       Wherein we must have use of your advice:
       Our father he hath writ, so hath our sister,
       Of differences,° which I least thought of fit   *quarrels*
125   To answer from our home. The several° messengers   *various*
       From hence attend° dispatch. Our good old friend,   *await*
       Lay comforts to your bosom, and bestow
       Your needful° counsel to our business,   *badly needed*
       Which craves the instant use.¹
GLOUCESTER   I serve you, madam.
130   Your graces are right welcome.   *Exeunt*

9. *Make . . . please*: Devise your plots making use of my   1. Which requires immediate attention.
forces and authority as you see fit.

2.2

Enter KENT *and* OSWALD, *severally°*   *separately*

OSWALD   Good dawning to thee, friend. Art° of this house?   *Are you a servant*

KENT   Ay.

OSWALD   Where may we set our horses?

KENT   I' the mire.

5   OSWALD   Prithee, if thou lovest me,° tell me.   *if you will be so kind*

KENT   I love thee not.

OSWALD   Why, then, I care not for thee.

KENT   If I had thee in Lipsbury pinfold,[1] I would make thee care
for me.

10   OSWALD   Why dost thou use° me thus? I know thee not.   *treat*

KENT   Fellow, I know thee.

OSWALD   What dost thou know me for?

KENT   A knave; a rascal; an eater of broken meats;° a base, proud,   *scraps*
shallow, beggarly, three-suited, hundred-pound, filthy, worsted-

15   stocking knave;[2] a lily-livered, action-taking knave; a whoreson,
glass-gazing, superserviceable, finical rogue; one-trunk-inheriting slave;[3] one that wouldst be a bawd in way of good service,[4]
and art nothing but the composition° of a knave, beggar, cow-   *combination*
ard, pandar, and the son and heir of a mongrel bitch; one

20   whom I will beat into clamorous whining, if thou deniest the
least syllable of thy addition.[5]

OSWALD   Why, what a monstrous fellow art thou, thus to rail on
one that is neither known of° thee nor knows thee!   *by*

KENT   What a brazen-faced varlet° art thou, to deny thou   *rascal*

25   knowest me! Is it two days ago since I tripped up thy heels, and
beat thee before the king? Draw, you rogue! For, though it be
night, yet the moon shines. I'll make a sop of the moonshine[6]
of you. Draw, you whoreson cullionly barber-monger,[7] draw!
Drawing his sword

OSWALD   Away! I have nothing to do with thee.

30   KENT   Draw, you rascal! You come with letters against the king,
and take Vanity the puppet's part against the royalty of her
father.[8] Draw, you rogue, or I'll so carbonado[9] your shanks!
Draw, you rascal! Come your ways!°   *Come forward*

OSWALD   Help, ho! murther! help!

35   KENT   Strike, you slave! Stand, rogue! Stand, you neat° slave!   *elegant; foppish*
Strike! [*Beating him*]

OSWALD   Help, ho! muther! murther!

Enter EDMUND *with his rapier drawn,* CORNWALL,
REGAN, GLOUCESTER, *and servants*

2.2 Location: Before Gloucester's house.

1. If I had you in the enclosure of my mouth (gripped in my teeth). Lipsbury is probably an invented place-name. *pinfold:* pen, animal enclosure.

2. *three-suited . . . knave:* Oswald is being called a poor imitation of a gentleman. Servants were permitted three suits a year; one hundred pounds was the minimum qual-ification for the purchase of one of King James's knight-hoods; a gentleman would wear silk, not "worsted" (of thick woolen material), stockings.

3. *lily-livered:* cowardly. *action-taking:* litigious, one who would rather use the law than his fists. *glass-gazing:* mir-ror-gazing. *superserviceable:* overly officious, or too ready to serve. *finical:* finicky, fastidious. *one-trunk inheriting:* owning only what would fill one trunk.

4. *one that . . . service:* one who would even be a pimp if called upon.

5. Of the descriptions Kent has just applied to him. *addi-tion:* title (used ironically).

6. Kent proposes so to skewer and pierce Oswald that his body might soak up moonlight. *sop:* piece of bread to be steeped or dunked in soup.

7. *cullionly barber-monger:* despicable frequenter of hair-dressers. *cullion:* testicle.

8. *and take . . . father:* and support Goneril, here depicted as a dressed-up doll whose pride is contrasted with Lear's kingliness.

9. Slash or score as one would the surface of meat in preparation for broiling.

EDMUND   How now! What's the matter?
      Parts them

KENT   With you, goodman boy, an° you please! Come, I'll flesh   *if*
40   ye!¹ Come, on, young master!

GLOUCESTER   Weapons! arms! What's the matter here?

CORNWALL   Keep peace, upon your lives!
    He dies that strikes again. What is the matter?

REGAN   The messengers from our sister and the king.

45 CORNWALL   What is your difference? Speak.

OSWALD   I am scarce in breath, my lord.

KENT   No marvel, you have so bestirred your valor. You cowardly
    rascal, nature disclaims° in thee; a tailor made thee.   *disowns her part*

CORNWALL   Thou art a strange fellow. A tailor² make a man?

50 KENT   Ay, a tailor, sir. A stone-cutter or a painter could not have
    made him so ill,° though he had been but two hours at the   *so badly*
    trade.

CORNWALL   Speak yet, how grew your quarrel?

OSWALD   This ancient ruffian, sir, whose life I have spared at suit
55   of° his gray beard—   *on account of*

KENT   Thou whoreson zed!³ thou unnecessary letter! My lord, if
    you will give me leave, I will tread this unbolted° villain into   *unsifted, coarse*
    mortar, and daub the walls of a jakes° with him. Spare my gray   *privy, toilet*
    beard, you wagtail?⁴

60 CORNWALL   Peace, sirrah!
    You beastly knave, know you no reverence?°   *respect*

KENT   Yes, sir, but anger hath a privilege.

CORNWALL   Why art thou angry?

KENT   That such a slave as this should wear a sword,
65   Who wears no honesty. Such smiling rogues as these,
    Like rats, oft bite the holy cords⁵ a-twain
    Which are too intrinse° t' unloose; smooth° every passion   *intricate / flatter*
    That in natures of their lords rebel;
    Bring oil to fire, snow to their colder moods;
70   Renege,° affirm, and turn their halcyon beaks⁶   *Deny*
    With every gale and vary° of their masters,   *mood*
    Knowing nought, like dogs, but following.
    A plague upon your epileptic° visage!   *distorted, grimacing*
    Smile you° my speeches, as° I were a fool?   *Do you smile at / as if*
75   Goose, if I had you upon Sarum plain
    I'd drive ye cackling home to Camelot.⁷

CORNWALL   What, art thou mad, old fellow?

GLOUCESTER   How fell you out? say that.

KENT   No contraries° hold more antipathy   *opposites*
80   Than I and such a knave.

CORNWALL   Why dost thou call him knave? What's his offense?

KENT   His countenance likes° me not.   *pleases*

CORNWALL   No more, perchance, does mine, nor his, nor hers.

---

1. I'll blood you (as a hunting dog); I'll initiate you into
fighting.
2. Tailors, considered effeminate, were stock objects of
mockery.
3. The letter Z (zed) was considered superfluous and
omitted from many dictionaries.
4. A common English bird that takes its name from the
up-and-down flicking of its tail; this, and its characteristic
hopping from foot to foot, causes it to appear nervous.

5. Bonds of kinship, affection, marriage, or rank.
6. It was believed that the kingfisher (in Greek, *halcyon*)
could be used as a weather vane when dead: suspended
by a fine thread, its beak would turn whatever way the
wind blew.
7. *Goose . . . Camelot*: comparing him to a cackling
goose, Kent tells Oswald that if he had him on Salisbury
Plain, he would drive him all the way to Camelot, legendary home of King Arthur.

KENT   Sir, 'tis my occupation to be plain.
85   I have seen better faces in my time
       Than stands on any shoulder that I see
       Before me at this instant.
CORNWALL   This is some fellow,
       Who, having been praised for bluntness, doth affect
       A saucy roughness, and constrains the garb
90   Quite from his nature.[8] He cannot flatter, he,
       An honest mind and plain, he must speak truth!
       An they will take it, so; if not, he's plain.[9]
       These kind of knaves I know, which in this plainness
       Harbor more craft and more corrupter ends
95   Than twenty silly ducking observants
       That stretch their duties nicely.[1]
KENT   Sir, in good sooth, in sincere verity,
       Under the allowance of your great aspect,[2]
       Whose influence, like the wreath of radiant fire
       On flickering Phoebus' front,°   the sun god's forehead
100 CORNWALL   What mean'st by this?
KENT   To go out of my dialect,° which you discommend so   normal mode of speech
       much. I know, sir, I am no flatterer. He that beguiled you in a
       plain accent was a plain knave; which for my part I will not be,
       though I should win your displeasure to entreat me to 't.[3]
105 CORNWALL   What was the offense you gave him?
OSWALD   I never gave him any:
       It pleased the king his master very late°   lately
       To strike at me, upon his misconstruction,°   misunderstanding (me)
       When he, conjunct,° and flattering his displeasure,   in league with
110   Tripped me behind; being down, insulted,° railed,   I being down, he insulted
       And put upon him such a deal of man,
       That worthied him,[4] got praises of the king
       For him attempting who was self-subdued;[5]
       And, in the fleshment° of this dread exploit,   excitement; flush
       Drew on me here again.
115 KENT   None of these rogues and cowards
       But Ajax is their fool.[6]
CORNWALL   Fetch forth the stocks!
       You stubborn miscreant knave, you reverent° braggart,   old; revered
       We'll teach you—
KENT   Sir, I am too old to learn.
120   Call not your stocks for me. I serve the king;
       On whose employment I was sent to you:
       You shall do small respect, show too bold malice
       Against the grace° and person° of my master,   majesty / personal honor

8. *and constrains . . . nature*: and assumes the appearance
though it is untrue to his real self. Alternatively (with "his"
meaning "its"), and distorts the true shape of plainness
from what it naturally is (by turning it into disrespect).
9. If they will accept (Kent's attitude), well and good; if
not, he is a plainspoken man (and does not care).
1. *Than . . . nicely*: Than twenty obsequious attendants
who constantly bow idiotically, and who perform their
functions with excessive diligence ("nicely").
2. With the permission of your great countenance.
"Aspect" also refers to the astrological position of a planet;
Kent's bombastic language here raises Cornwall to the
mock-heroic proportions of a heavenly body.

3. *He that . . . to 't*: The person who tried to hoodwink
you with plain speaking was, indeed, a pure knave—
something I won't be, even if you were to beg me to be
one (a plain knave, or flatterer).
4. *And put . . . him*: And put on such a show of manliness
that he was thought a worthy fellow.
5. For attacking a man who had already surrendered
(Kent attacking Oswald).
6. *None . . . fool*: Such rogues and cowards as these talk
as if they were greater warriors (and blusterers) than Ajax;
such rogues always make even mighty Ajax out to be a
fool.

Stocking° his messenger.   *By stocking*

125 CORNWALL   Fetch forth the stocks! As I have life and honor.

There shall he sit till noon.

REGAN   Till noon? Till night, my lord, and all night too!

KENT   Why, madam, if I were your father's dog,

You should not use me so.

REGAN   Sir, being° his knave, I will.   *since you are*

130 CORNWALL   This is a fellow of the self-same color°   *character*

Our sister° speaks of. Come, bring away the stocks!   *sister-in-law*

       Stocks brought out

GLOUCESTER   Let me beseech your grace not to do so.

His fault is much, and the good king his master

Will check° him for't. Your purposed° low correction   *reprimand / intended*

135 Is such as basest and contemned'st wretches

For pilferings and most common trespasses

Are punished with: the king must take it ill,

That he, so slightly valued in his messenger,

Should have him thus restrained.

CORNWALL   I'll answer° that.   *be responsible for*

140 REGAN   My sister may receive it much more worse,

To have her gentleman abused, assaulted,

For following° her affairs. Put in his legs.   *carrying out*

       KENT *is put in the stocks*

Come, my good lord, away.

       Exeunt all but GLOUCESTER *and* KENT

GLOUCESTER   I am sorry for thee, friend: 'tis the duke's pleasure,

145 Whose disposition, all the world well knows,

Will not be rubbed° nor stopped: I'll entreat for thee.   *obstructed*

KENT   Pray, do not sir. I have watched° and traveled hard;   *gone without sleep*

Some time I shall sleep out, the rest I'll whistle.

A good man's fortune may grow out at heels:[7]

150 Give° you good morrow!   *God give*

GLOUCESTER   The duke's to blame in this; 't will be ill-taken.

       Exit

KENT   Good king, that must approve° the common saw,°   *prove / saying*

Thou out of heaven's benediction comest

To the warm sun![8]

155 Approach, thou beacon[9] to this under globe,

That by thy comfortable beams I may

Peruse this letter! Nothing almost sees miracles

But misery.[1] I know 'tis from Cordelia,

Who hath most fortunately been informed

160 Of my obscuréd° course; (*reads*) "and shall find time   *hidden, disguised*

From this enormous state,° seeking to give   *awful state of affairs*

Losses their remedies." All weary and o'er-watched,°   *too long awake*

Take vantage,° heavy eyes, not to behold   *the opportunity*

This shameful lodging.

165 Fortune, good night; smile once more; turn thy wheel![2]

       Sleeps

---

7. The fortunes of even good men sometimes wear thin.
8. *Thou . . . sun:* You come from the blessing of heaven into the heat of the sun (go from good to bad).
9. It is arguable whether Kent here refers to the sun or the moon.
1. *Nothing . . . misery:* Only those suffering misery are

granted miracles; any comfort seems miraculous to those who are miserable.
2. The goddess Fortune was traditionally depicted with a wheel to signify her mutability and caprice. She was believed to take pleasure in arbitrarily lowering those at the top of her wheel and raising those at the bottom.

2.3

Enter EDGAR

EDGAR   I heard myself proclaimed;°   *declared an outlaw*
      And by the happy° hollow of a tree   *opportune*
      Escaped the hunt. No port° is free; no place,   *seaport; exit*
      That guard, and most unusual vigilance,
5   Does not attend my taking.° Whiles° I may 'scape,   *await my capture / Until*
      I will preserve myself; and am bethought°   *resolved*
      To take the basest and most poorest shape
      That ever penury, in contempt of° man,   *for*
      Brought near to beast. My face I'll grime with filth,
10   Blanket my loins, elf[1] all my hair in knots,
      And with presented° nakedness out-face   *exposed*
      The winds and persecutions of the sky.
      The country gives me proof and precedent
      Of Bedlam beggars, who, with roaring voices,
15   Strike° in their numbed and mortified° bare arms   *Stick / deadened*
      Pins, wooden pricks, nails, sprigs of rosemary;
      And with this horrible object,° from low farms,   *spectacle*
      Poor pelting° villages, sheep-cotes, and mills,   *paltry; contemptible*
      Sometime with lunatic bans,° sometime with prayers,   *curses*
20   Enforce their charity. Poor Turlygod![2] poor Tom!
      That's something yet! Edgar I nothing am.[3]   *Exit*

2.4

Enter LEAR, FOOL, *and* GENTLEMAN[1]

LEAR   'Tis strange that they should so depart from home,
      And not send back my messenger.

GENTLEMAN   As I learned,
      The night before there was no purpose in them°   *they had no intention*
      Of this remove.°   *change of residence*

KENT   Hail to thee, noble master!

5 LEAR   Ha!
      Makest thou this shame thy pastime?

KENT   No, my lord.

FOOL   Ha, ha! he wears cruel garters.[2] Horses are tied by the
      heads, dogs and bears by the neck, monkeys by the loins, and
      men by the legs. When a man's over-lusty at legs,[3] then he
10   wears wooden nether-stocks.°   *knee socks*

LEAR   What's° he that hath so much thy place° mistook   *Who's / position*
      To set thee here?

KENT   It is both he and she;
      Your son° and daughter.   *son-in-law*

LEAR   No.

15 KENT   Yes.

LEAR   No, I say.

KENT   I say, yea.

LEAR   No, no, they would not!

KENT   Yes, yes, they have!

2.3 Location: As before.
1. Tangle the hair into "elf locks," supposed to be a favorite trick of malicious elves.
2. A word of unknown origin.
3. Edgar, I am nothing; I am no longer Edgar.
2.4 Location: As before.

1. F seems to reserve "a Gentleman" for this particular character, who returns in 5.3.
2. Worsted garters, punning on "crewel," a thin yarn. The Fool is actually referring to the stocks in which Kent's feet are held.
3. When a man's liable to run away.

20 LEAR   By Jupiter, I swear, no!
   KENT   By Juno,[4] I swear, aye!
   LEAR   They durst not do 't;
      They would not, could not do 't. 'Tis worse than murder,
      To do upon respect[5] such violent outrage.
      Resolve° me, with all modest° haste, which way   *Inform / reasonable*
25   Thou mightst deserve, or they impose, this usage,
      Coming from us.
   KENT   My lord, when at their home
      I did commend° your highness' letters to them,   *deliver*
      Ere I was risen from the place that showed
      My duty kneeling, came there a reeking° post,   *steaming*
30   Stewed in his haste, half breathless, panting forth
      From Goneril his mistress, salutations;
      Delivered letters, spite of intermission,[6]
      Which presently° they read; on whose conténts,   *immediately*
      They summoned up their meiny,° straight° took horse;   *retinue / straightaway*
35   Commanded me to follow, and attend
      The leisure of their answer, gave me cold looks,
      And meeting here the other messenger,
      Whose welcome, I perceived, had poisoned mine—
      Being the very° fellow that of late   *same*
40   Displayed so saucily° against your highness—   *Acted so insolently*
      Having more man° than wit° about me, drew.   *courage / sense*
      He raised the house with loud and coward cries.
      Your son and daughter found this trespass worth°   *deserving of*
      The shame which here it suffers.
45 FOOL   Winter's not gone yet, if the wild-geese fly that way.[7]
                        Fathers that wear rags
                           Do make their children blind;[8]
                        But fathers that bear bags
                           Shall see their children kind.
50   Fortune, that arrant whore,
                           Ne'er turns the key° to the poor.   *opens the door*
      But, for all this, thou shalt have as many dolors[9] for thy daugh-
      ters as thou canst tell° in a year.   *count*
   LEAR   O, how this mother° swells up toward my heart!   *hysteria*
55   *Hysterica passio*, down, thou climbing sorrow,[1]
      Thy element's° below! Where is this daughter?   *natural place is*
   KENT   With the earl, sir, here within.
   LEAR   Follow me not; stay here.
                                                          Exit
   GENTLEMAN   Made you no more offenses but what you speak of?
   KENT   None. How chance the king comes with so small a train?
60 FOOL   An° thou hadst been set i' the stocks for that question,   *If*
      thou hadst well deserved it.
   KENT   Why, fool?
   FOOL   We'll set thee to school to an ant, to teach thee there's no

4. Queen of the Roman gods and wife of Jupiter, with whom she constantly quarreled.
5. To do to one who deserves respect.
6. Regardless of interrupting me; despite the interruptions in his account (as he gasped for breath).
7. That is, things will get worse before they get better.
8. Blind to their father's needs.
9. Pains, sorrows; punning on "dollar," the English term

for the German "thaler," a large silver coin.
1. Hysterica . . . *sorrow*: *Hysterica passio* (a Latin expression originating in the Greek *steiros*, "suffering in the womb") was an inflammation of the senses. In Renaissance medicine, vapors from the abdomen were thought to rise up through the body, and in women, the uterus itself to wander around.

laboring i' the winter.[2] All that follow their noses are led by
their eyes but blind men, and there's not a nose among twenty
but can smell him that's stinking.° Let go thy hold when a great   *(as his fortunes decay)*
wheel runs down a hill,[3] lest it break thy neck with following
it; but the great one that goes up the hill, let him draw thee
after. When a wise man gives thee better counsel, give me
mine again. I would have none but knaves follow it, since a
fool gives it.

    That sir which serves and seeks for gain,
     And follows but for form,
    Will pack° when it begins to rain,   *pack up and go*
     And leave thee in the storm.
    But I will tarry; the fool will stay,
     And let the wise man fly.
    The knave turns fool that runs away;[4]
     The fool no knave, perdy.°   *by God (pardieu)*

KENT Where learned you this, fool?
FOOL Not i' the stocks, fool.
    Re-enter LEAR, *with* GLOUCESTER
LEAR Deny to speak with me? They are sick? they are weary?
They have traveled all the night? Mere fetches;°   *ruses, pretexts*
The images of revolt and flying off.[5]
Fetch me a better answer.
GLOUCESTER   My dear lord,
You know the fiery quality° of the duke;   *disposition*
How unremoveable and fixed he is
In his own course.
LEAR Vengeance! plague! death! confusion!°   *destruction*
Fiery? what quality? Why, Gloucester, Gloucester,
I'd speak with the Duke of Cornwall and his wife.
GLOUCESTER Well, my good lord, I have informed them so.
LEAR Informed them! Dost thou understand me, man?
GLOUCESTER Ay, my good lord.
LEAR The king would speak with Cornwall; the dear father
Would with his daughter speak, commands her service.
Are they informed of this? My breath and blood!
Fiery? the fiery duke? Tell the hot duke that—
No, but not yet. May be he is not well.
Infirmity doth still° neglect all office°   *always / obligation*
Whereto our health is bound; we are not ourselves
When nature, being oppressed, commands the mind
To suffer with the body. I'll forbear;
And am fallen out with my more headier will,[6]
To take° the indisposed and sickly fit   *mistake*
For the sound man. Death on my state![7] Wherefore°   *Why*
    looking on KENT
Should he sit here? This act persuades me
That this remotion° of the duke and her   *remoteness, aloofness*
Is practice° only. Give me my servant forth.   *trickery*

---

2. Ants, proverbially prudent, do not work in winter.
Implicitly, a wise person should know better than to look
for sustenance to an old man who has fallen on wintry
times.
3. A great wheel is a figure for Lear and of Fortune's
wheel itself, which has swung downward.

4. The scoundrel who runs away is the real fool.
5. *images of*: signs of. *flying off*: desertion; insurrection.
6. And disagree with my (earlier) more rash intention.
7. May my royal authority end (an oath). Ironically, this
has already happened.

110 Go tell the duke and 's wife I'd speak with them,
Now, presently!° Bid them come forth and hear me,   *at once*
Or at their chamber-door I'll beat the drum
Till it cry sleep to death.[8]

GLOUCESTER   I would have all well betwixt you.   *Exit*

115 LEAR   O me, my heart, my rising heart! but, down!

FOOL   Cry to it, nuncle, as the cockney° did to the eels when she   *Londoner (city woman)*
put 'em i' the paste° alive; she knapped 'em o' the coxcombs°   *pie; pastry / heads*
with a stick, and cried "Down, wantons,° down!" 'Twas her   *rogues*
brother that, in pure kindness to his horse, buttered his hay.[9]

     Enter CORNWALL, REGAN, GLOUCESTER, *and servants*

LEAR   Good morrow to you both.

120 CORNWALL   Hail to your grace!

      KENT *is set at liberty*

REGAN   I am glad to see your highness.

LEAR   Regan, I think you are; I know what reason
I have to think so. If thou shouldst not be glad,
I would divorce me from thy mother's tomb,

125 Sepulchring° an adultress. (*To* KENT) O, are you free?   *Because it entombed*
Some other time for that. Belovéd Regan,
Thy sister's naught.° O Regan, she hath tied   *wicked; nothing*
Sharp-toothed unkindness, like a vulture, here!

      Points to his heart

I can scarce speak to thee; thou'lt not believe

130 With how depraved a quality—O Regan!

REGAN   I pray you, sir, take patience. I have hope
You less know how to value her desert
Than she to scant her duty.[1]

LEAR   Say, how is that?

REGAN   I cannot think my sister in the least

135 Would fail her obligation. If, sir, perchance
She have restrained the riots of your followers,
'Tis on such ground, and to such wholesome end,
As clears her from all blame.

LEAR   My curses on her!

REGAN   O, sir, you are old;

140 Nature° in you stands on the very verge   *Life*
Of her confine.° You should be ruled and led   *Of its limit*
By some discretion,° that discerns your state   *discreet person*
Better than you yourself. Therefore, I pray you,
That to our sister you do make return;
Say you have wronged her, sir.

145 LEAR   Ask her forgiveness?
Do you but mark how this becomes the house:[2]
"Dear daughter, I confess that I am old; (*kneeling*)
Age° is unnecessary. On my knees I beg   *An old man*
That you'll vouchsafe me raiment,° bed, and food."   *promise me clothing*

150 REGAN   Good sir, no more! These are unsightly tricks.
Return you to my sister.

---

8. Till the noise kills sleep.
9. Like that of his sister (who wanted to make eel pie without killing the eels), his kindness was misplaced: horses will not eat buttered hay. Lear's earlier kindness to his daughters was equally foolish.
1. *I have . . . duty:* I expect that you are worse at valuing

her deservings than she is at neglecting her duty. The double negative here ("less," "scant") is acceptable Jacobean usage.
2. Do you see how appropriate this is among members of a family (spoken ironically)?

LEAR (*rising*)   Never, Regan!
     She hath abated° me of half my train;   *deprived*
     Looked black upon me; struck me with her tongue
     Most serpent-like, upon the very heart.
155   All° the stored vengeances of heaven fall   *Let all*
     On her ingrateful top!° Strike her young bones,   *head*
     You taking° airs, with lameness!   *infectious; malignant*
   CORNWALL   Fie, sir, fie!
LEAR   You nimble lightnings, dart your blinding flames
     Into her scornful eyes! Infect her beauty,
160   You fen-sucked fogs, drawn by the powerful sun,[3]
     To fall and blast her pride!
   REGAN   O the blest gods! so will you wish on me,
     When the rash mood is on.
   LEAR   No, Regan, thou shalt never have my curse.
165   Thy tender-hefted[4] nature shall not give
     Thee o'er to harshness. Her eyes are fierce; but thine
     Do comfort and not burn. 'Tis not in thee
     To grudge my pleasures, to cut off my train,
     To bandy hasty words, to scant my sizes,°   *reduce my allowances*
170   And in conclusion to oppose the bolt°   *to lock the door*
     Against my coming in. Thou better know'st
     The offices° of nature, bond of childhood,   *duties*
     Effects° of courtesy, dues of gratitude;   *Actions*
     Thy half o' the kingdom hast thou not forgot,
     Wherein I thee endowed.
175   REGAN   Good sir, to the purpose.°   *get to the point*
   LEAR   Who put my man i' the stocks?
        Tucket within
   CORNWALL   What trumpet's that?
   REGAN   I know't, my sister's. This approves° her letter,   *confirms*
     That she would soon be here.
        Enter OSWALD
                Is your lady come?
   LEAR   This is a slave, whose easy-borrowed pride[5]
180   Dwells in the fickle grace of her he follows.
     Out varlet,° from my sight!   *wretch*
   CORNWALL   What means your grace?
   LEAR   Who stocked my servant? Regan, I have good hope
     Thou didst not know on 't.°   *of it*
        Enter GONERIL
     Who comes here? O heavens,
185   If you do love old men, if your sweet sway
     Allow obedience, if yourselves are old,
     Make it your cause! Send down, and take my part!
     (*To* GONERIL) Art not ashamed to look upon this beard?
     O Regan, wilt thou take her by the hand?
190 GONERIL   Why not by the hand, sir? How have I offended?
     All's not offense that indiscretion finds
     And dotage terms so.
   LEAR   O sides,[6] you are too tough!

---

3. The sun was thought to suck poisonous vapors from marshy ground.
4. Tenderly placed; firmly set in a tender disposition (as a knife blade into its haft).
5. Unmerited and unpaid-for arrogance; "pride" may also refer to Oswald's fine clothing received for his services to Goneril.
6. Chest, where Lear's heart is swelling with emotion.

Will you yet hold? How came my man i' the stocks?

CORNWALL   I set him there, sir; but his own disorders°   *disorderly behavior*
Deserved much less advancement.[7]

195 LEAR   You! did you?

REGAN   I pray you, father, being weak, seem so.°   *behave so*
If, till the expiration of your month,
You will return and sojourn with my sister,
Dismissing half your train, come then to me.

200 I am now from home, and out of that provision
Which shall be needful for your entertainment.

LEAR   Return to her, and fifty men dismissed?
No, rather I abjure all roofs, and choose
To wage against the enmity o' the air;

205 To be a comrade with the wolf and owl—
Necessity's sharp pinch![8] Return with her?
Why, the hot-blooded France, that dowerless took
Our youngest born, I could as well be brought
To knee° his throne, and, squire-like, pension beg   *kneel to*

210 To keep base life afoot. Return with her?
Persuade me rather to be slave and sumpter°   *pack horse*
To this detested groom. (*Pointing at* OSWALD)

GONERIL   At your choice, sir.

LEAR   I prithee, daughter, do not make me mad.
I will not trouble thee, my child; farewell.

215 We'll no more meet, no more see one another.
But yet thou art my flesh, my blood, my daughter;
Or rather a disease that's in my flesh,
Which I must needs call mine. Thou art a boil,
A plague-sore, an embossed° carbuncle,   *a swollen*

220 In my corrupted blood. But I'll not chide thee;
Let shame come when it will, I do not call° it.   *call upon*
I do not bid the Thunder-bearer° shoot,   *(Jove)*
Nor tell tales of thee to high-judging Jove.
Mend° when thou canst; be better at thy leisure.   *Make amends*

225 I can be patient, I can stay with Regan,
I and my hundred knights.

REGAN   Not altogether so.
I looked not for° you yet, nor am provided   *I did not expect*
For your fit welcome. Give ear, sir, to my sister;
For those that mingle reason with your passion[9]

230 Must be content to think you old, and so—
But she knows what she does.

LEAR   Is this well° spoken?   *earnestly*

REGAN   I dare avouch° it, sir. What, fifty followers?   *vouch for*
Is it not well? What should you need of more?
Yea, or so many, sith° that both charge° and danger   *since / expense*

235 Speak 'gainst so great a number? How, in one house,
Should many people, under two commands,
Hold amity? 'T is hard; almost impossible.

GONERIL   Why might not you, my lord, receive attendance
From those that she calls servants, or from mine?

---

7. Deserved far worse treatment.
8. *To wage . . . pinch:* To counter, like predators, the harshness of the elements with the hardness brought on by necessity. *pinch:* stress, pressure.
9. For those who temper your passionate argument with their own calm reasoning.

240 REGAN   Why not, my lord? If then they chanced to slack° you,   *neglect*
       We could control them. If you will come to me—
       For now I spy a danger—I entreat you
       To bring but five-and-twenty. To no more
       Will I give place or notice.°   *acknowledgment*
     LEAR   I gave you all—
245 REGAN   And in good time° you gave it.   *it was about time*
     LEAR   Made you my guardians, my depositaries;°   *trustees*
       But kept a reservation° to be followed   *reserved a right*
       With such a number. What, must I come to you
       With five-and-twenty, Regan? Said you so?
250 REGAN   And speak't again, my lord; no more with me.
     LEAR   Those wicked creatures yet do look well-favored,°   *attractive*
       When others are more wicked; not being the worst
       Stands in some rank of praise.[1] (*To* GONERIL) I'll go with thee:
       Thy fifty yet doth double five-and-twenty,
       And thou art twice her love.
255 GONERIL   Hear me, my lord.
       What need you five-and-twenty, ten, or five,
       To follow in a house where twice so many
       Have a command to tend you?
     REGAN   What need one?
     LEAR   O, reason not the need! Our basest beggars
260   Are in the poorest thing superfluous.[2]
       Allow not° nature more than nature needs,   *If you don't allow*
       Man's life's as cheap as beast's. Thou art a lady;
       If only to go warm were gorgeous,
       Why, nature needs not what thou gorgeous wear'st,
265   Which scarcely keeps thee warm.[3] But, for true need—
       You heavens, give me that patience,° patience I need!   *endurance*
       You see me here, you gods, a poor old man,
       As full of grief as age; wretched in both!
       If it be you that stirs these daughters' hearts
270   Against their father, fool me not so much
       To bear it tamely;[4] touch me with noble anger,
       And let not women's weapons, water-drops,
       Stain my man's cheeks! No, you unnatural hags,
       I will have such revenges on you both,
275   That all the world shall—I will do such things—
       What they are, yet I know not; but they shall be
       The terrors of the earth! You think I'll weep;
       No, I'll not weep.
       I have full cause of weeping, but this heart
280   Shall break into a hundred thousand flaws°   *fragments*
       Or ere° I'll weep. O fool, I shall go mad!   *Before*
                    Exeunt LEAR, GLOUCESTER, KENT, *and* FOOL.
                              Storm and tempest
     CORNWALL   Let us withdraw; 't will be a storm.
     REGAN   This house is little; the old man and his people
       Cannot be well bestowed.°   *lodged*

---

1. Deserves some degree ("rank") of praise.
2. *Our . . . superfluous:* Even the lowliest beggars have
something more than the barest minimum.
3. *If . . . thee warm:* If gorgeousness in clothes is mea-

sured by the warmth they provide, your elaborate clothes
are superfluous, for they barely cover your body.
4. *fool . . . tamely:* do not make me so foolish as to accept
it meekly.

285 GONERIL   'Tis his own blame; hath put himself from° rest,   *deprived himself of*
 And must needs taste his folly.
 REGAN   For his particular,° I'll receive him gladly,   *single self*
 But not one follower.
 GONERIL   So am I purposed.
 Where is my lord of Gloucester?
290 CORNWALL   Followed the old man forth. He is returned.
          Re-enter GLOUCESTER
 GLOUCESTER   The king is in high rage.
 CORNWALL   Whither is he going?
 GLOUCESTER   He calls to horse, but will I know not whither.
 CORNWALL   'Tis best to give him way; he leads himself.
 GONERIL   My lord, entreat him by no means to stay.
295 GLOUCESTER   Alack, the night comes on, and the bleak winds
 Do sorely ruffle.° For many miles about   *bluster*
 There's scarce a bush.
 REGAN   O, sir, to willful men,
 The injuries that they themselves procure
 Must be their schoolmasters. Shut up your doors.
300 He is attended with a desperate° train;   *violent*
 And what they may incense° him to, being apt   *incite*
 To have his ear abused,° wisdom bids fear.   *deceived*
 CORNWALL   Shut up your doors, my lord; 'tis a wild night.
 My Regan counsels well. Come out o' the storm.   *Exeunt*

3.1

 Storm still. Enter KENT *and a* GENTLEMAN, *at several*
 doors
 KENT   Who's there, besides foul weather?
 GENTLEMAN   One minded like the weather, most unquietly.
 KENT   I know you. Where's the king?
 GENTLEMAN   Contending with the fretful elements;
5 Bids the wind blow the earth into the sea,
 Or swell the curléd waters 'bove the main,°   *mainland*
 That things might change or cease; tears his white hair,
 Which the impetuous blasts, with eyeless rage,
 Catch in their fury, and make nothing of;
10 Strives in his little world of man to out-scorn
 The to-and-fro-conflicting wind and rain.
 This night, wherein the cub-drawn bear would couch,[1]
 The lion and the belly-pinchéd wolf
 Keep their fur dry, unbonneted° he runs,   *hatless; uncrowned*
 And bids what will take all.
15 KENT   But who is with him?
 GENTLEMAN   None but the fool, who labors to out-jest
 His heart-struck injuries.[2]
 KENT   Sir, I do know you;
 And dare, upon the warrant of my note,[3]
 Commend a dear° thing to you. There is division,   *Entrust a crucial*
20 Although as yet the face of it be covered

3.1 Location: Bare, open country.
1. In which even the bear, though starving, having been
sucked dry ("drawn") by its cub, would not go out to
forage.

2. *to out-jest:* to relieve with laughter; to exorcise through
ridicule. *heart-struck injuries:* injuries (from the betrayal
of his paternal love) that penetrated to the heart.
3. On the basis of my skill (at judging people).

With mutual cunning, 'twixt Albany and Cornwall;
Who have—as who have not, that their great stars
Throned and set high?[4]—servants, who seem no less,°   who appear as such
Which are to France the spies and speculations°   observers
25   Intelligent of[5] our state. What hath been seen,
Either in snuffs and packings° of the dukes,   quarrels and plots
Or the hard rein° which both of them have borne   treatment
Against the old kind king; or something deeper,
Whereof perchance these are but furnishings;°   pretexts
30   But, true it is, from France there comes a power
Into this scattered kingdom; who already,
Wise in° our negligence, have secret feet   Aware of
In some of our best ports, and are at point°   ready
To show their open banner. Now to you:
35   If on my credit you dare build° so far   If you trust me
To make your speed to Dover, you shall find
Some that will thank you, making just° report   accurate
Of how unnatural and bemadding° sorrow   maddening
The king hath cause to plain.°   complain
40   I am a gentleman of blood and breeding;
And, from some knowledge and assurance, offer
This office° to you.   role; duty
GENTLEMAN   I will talk further with you.
KENT   No, do not.
For confirmation that I am much more
45   Than my out-wall,° open this purse, and take   outward appearance
What it contains. If you shall see Cordelia—
As fear not but you shall—show her this ring,
And she will tell you who your fellow° is   (Kent himself)
That yet you do not know. Fie on this storm!
50   I will go seek the king.
GENTLEMAN   Give me your hand. Have you no more to say?
KENT   Few words, but, to effect,° more than all yet;   in importance
That, when we have found the king—in which your pain
That way, I'll this[6]—he that first lights on him
55   Holla the other.   *Exeunt severally*

3.2

Enter LEAR *and* FOOL. *Storm still*
LEAR   Blow, winds, and crack your cheeks! rage! blow!
You cataracts and hurricanoes,[1] spout
Till you have drenched our steeples, drowned the cocks!°   weather vanes
You sulphurous and thought-executing fires,[2]
5   Vaunt-couriers° to oak-cleaving thunderbolts,   Forerunners
Singe my white head! And thou, all-shaking thunder,
Smite flat the thick rotundity o' the world!
Crack Nature's molds, all germens° spill at once,   seeds
That make ingrateful man!

---

4. *as . . . high:* as has everybody who has been favored by
destiny.
5. Supplying intelligence about; too well informed of.
6. *in which . . . this:* in which effort you will go that way
and I this way.

3.2 Location: As before.
1. *cataracts:* floodgates of the heavens. *hurricanoes:* water-
spouts (water from both sky and sea).
2. *thought-executing fires:* lightning that strikes as swiftly
as thought.

10   FOOL   O nuncle, court holy-water³ in a dry house is better than
         this rain-water out o' door. Good nuncle, in, and ask thy daugh-
         ters' blessing! Here's a night pities neither wise man nor fool.
    LEAR   Rumble thy bellyful! Spit, fire! spout, rain!
         Nor rain, wind, thunder, fire, are my daughters:

15   I tax° not you, you elements, with unkindness;   *blame*
         I never gave you kingdom, called you children,
         You owe me no subscription.° Then let fall   *obedience, allegiance*
         Your horrible pleasure. Here I stand, your slave,
         A poor, infirm, weak, and despised old man.

20   But yet I call you servile ministers,°   *agents*
         That have with two pernicious daughters joined
         Your high engendered battles° 'gainst a head   *heaven-bred forces*
         So old and white as this. O! O! 't is foul!
    FOOL   He that has a house to put 's head in has a good head-

25   piece.°   *hat; brain*

                     The cod-piece that will house
                     Before the head has any,
                     The head and he shall louse;
                     So beggars marry many.⁴

30   The man that makes his toe
                     What he his heart should make
                     Shall of a corn cry woe,
                     And turn his sleep to wake.⁵
         For there was never yet fair woman but she made mouths in a

35   glass.⁶
    LEAR   No, I will be the pattern of all patience; I will say nothing.
           Enter KENT
    KENT   Who's there?
    FOOL   Marry, here's grace and a cod-piece; that's a wise man and
         a fool.⁷

40   KENT   Alas, sir, are you here? things that love night
         Love not such nights as these; the wrathful skies
         Gallow° the very wanderers of the dark,   *Frighten*
         And make them keep° their caves. Since I was man,   *keep inside*
         Such sheets of fire, such bursts of horrid thunder,

45   Such groans of roaring wind and rain, I never
         Remember to have heard. Man's nature cannot carry°   *bear*
         The affliction nor the fear.
    LEAR   Let the great gods,
         That keep this dreadful pother° o'er our heads,   *commotion*
         Find out their enemies now. Tremble, thou wretch,

50   That hast within thee undivulgéd crimes,
         Unwhipped of° justice. Hide thee, thou bloody hand;   *Unpunished by*
         Thou perjured, and thou simular° of virtue   *simulator; pretender*

---

3. Sprinkled blessings of a courtier; flattery.
4. *The cod-piece . . . many:* Whoever finds his penis a
lodging before providing shelter for his head will end up
in lice-infested poverty and live in married beggary. *cod-piece:* a pouchlike covering for the male genitals, often
conspicuous, particularly in the costume of a fool.
5. *The man . . . wake:* The man who values an inferior
part of his body over the part that is truly valuable (as Lear
privileged Goneril and Regan over Cordelia) will suffer
from and lose sleep over that inferior part.

6. She practiced making pretty faces in a mirror. The
Fool probably refers to Regan's and Goneril's vanity, or
the line may be thrown in to soften the harshness of his
satire.
7. The supposedly wise King is symbolized by royal
grace, the Fool by his codpiece (here, slang for "penis").
The Fool speaks ironically: the King, as he has pointed
out, is now the foolish one. *Marry:* By the Virgin Mary (a
mild oath).

That are incestuous. Caitiff,° to pieces shake,   *Wretch*
That under covert and convenient seeming°   *fitting hypocrisy*
55   Hast practiced on° man's life. Close° pent-up guilts   *against / Secret*
Rive° your concealing continents,° and cry   *Split open / coverings*
These dreadful summoners grace.⁸ I am a man
More sinned against than sinning.
KENT   Alack, bare-headed?
Gracious my lord, hard by here is a hovel;
60   Some friendship will it lend you 'gainst the tempest.
Repose you there, while I to this hard house—
More harder than the stones whereof 'tis raised,
Which° even but now, demanding° after you,   *Who / I demanding*
Denied me to come in—return, and force
Their scanted° courtesy.   *niggardly*
65   LEAR   My wits begin to turn.
Come on, my boy. How dost, my boy? Art cold?
I am cold myself. Where is this straw, my fellow?
The art° of our necessities is strange,   *skill; alchemy*
That can make vile things precious. Come, your hovel.
70   Poor fool and knave, I have one part in my heart
That's sorry yet for thee.
FOOL (*singing*)⁹
He that has and° a little tiny wit°—   *even / sense*
With hey, ho, the wind and the rain—
Must make content with his fortunes fit,
75   Though the rain it raineth every day.
LEAR   True, boy. Come, bring us to this hovel.
                                        Exeunt LEAR and KENT
FOOL   This is a brave night to cool a courtesan.¹
I'll speak a prophecy ere I go:²
When priests are more in word than matter;°   *real virtue*
80   When brewers mar their malt with water;
When nobles are their tailors' tutors;³
No heretics burned, but wenches' suitors;⁴
When every case in law is right;°   *just*
No squire in debt, nor no poor knight;
85   When slanders do not live in tongues,
Nor cutpurses° come not to throngs;   *pickpockets*
When usurers tell their gold i' the field,⁵
And bawds and whores do churches build;
Then shall the realm of Albion°   *Britain*
90   Come to great confusion.°   *decay*
Then comes the time, who lives to see 't,
That going° shall be used° with feet.   *walking / practiced*
This prophecy Merlin shall make; for I live before his time.⁶
                                        Exit

8. *and cry . . . grace:* and pray for mercy from these elements that bring you to justice.
9. The following song is an adaptation of one sung by
Feste at the end of *Twelfth Night.*
1. To cool even the hot lusts of a prostitute.
2. What follows is a parody of the pseudo-Chaucerian
"Merlin's Prophecy" from *Arte of English Poesie.*
3. When noblemen follow fashion more closely than

their tailors do.
4. When the only heretics burned are faithless lovers,
who burn from venereal disease.
5. When usurers can count their profits openly (because
they have no shady dealings to hide).
6. Merlin was the great wizard at the legendary court of
King Arthur. Lear's Britain is set in an even more distant
past.

3.3

Enter GLOUCESTER *and* EDMUND

GLOUCESTER Alack, alack, Edmund, I like not this unnatural
dealing. When I desired their leave that I might pity° him, they   *relieve*
took from me the use of mine own house; charged me, on pain
of their perpetual displeasure, neither to speak of him, entreat
5 for him, nor any way sustain him.

EDMUND Most savage and unnatural!

GLOUCESTER Go to;° say you nothing. There's a division betwixt   *(an expletive)*
the dukes, and a worse matter than that. I have received a letter
this night; 'tis dangerous to be spoken; I have locked the letter
10 in my closet.° These injuries the king now bears will be   *private chamber*
revenged home;° there's part of a power already footed;[1] we   *to the hilt*
must incline to[2] the king. I will seek him, and privily° relieve   *secretly, privately*
him. Go you and maintain talk with the duke, that my charity
be not of him perceived if he ask for me, I am ill, and gone to
15 bed. Though I die for it, as no less is threatened me, the king
my old master must be relieved. There is some strange thing
toward,° Edmund; pray you, be careful.   *Exit*   *coming*

EDMUND This courtesy,° forbid° thee, shall the duke   *act of kindness / forbidden*
Instantly know, and of that letter too.
20 This seems a fair deserving,[3] and must draw me
That which my father loses—no less than all.
The younger rises when the old doth fall.   *Exit*

3.4

Enter LEAR, KENT, *and* FOOL

KENT Here is the place, my lord; good my lord, enter:
The tyranny of the open night's too rough
For nature° to endure.   *human weakness*

        Storm still

LEAR Let me alone.

KENT Good my lord, enter here.

5 LEAR   Wilt break my heart?

KENT I had rather break mine own. Good my lord, enter.

LEAR Thou think'st 'tis much that this contentious storm
Invades us to the skin. So 'tis to thee;
But where the greater malady is fixed,°   *rooted*
10 The lesser is scarce felt. Thou'dst shun a bear;
But if thy flight lay toward the raging sea,
Thou'dst meet the bear i' the mouth. When the mind's free,°   *unburdened*
The body's delicate.° The tempest in my mind   *sensitive*
Doth from my senses take all feeling else
15 Save° what beats there. Filial ingratitude!   *Except*
Is it not as° this mouth should tear this hand   *as if*
For lifting food to 't? But I will punish home.°   *thoroughly*
No, I will weep no more. In such a night
To shut me out! Pour on; I will endure.
20 In such a night as this! O Regan, Goneril!
Your old kind father, whose frank heart gave all—
O, that way madness lies; let me shun that;
No more of that.

3.3 Location: At Gloucester's castle.   3. This seems an action that deserves to be rewarded.
1. Part of an army already landed.   3.4 Location: Open country, before a cattle shed.
2. We must take the side of.

KENT   Good my lord, enter here.

LEAR   Prithee, go in thyself; seek thine own ease:

25 This tempest will not give me leave to° ponder   *allow me to*
On things would hurt me more. But I'll go in.
(*To the* FOOL) In, boy; go first. You houseless poverty°—   *poor*
Nay, get thee in. I'll pray, and then I'll sleep.

         FOOL *goes in*

Poor naked wretches, whereso'er you are,

30 That bide° the pelting of this pitiless storm,   *endure; dwell in*
How shall your houseless heads and unfed sides,°   *starved ribs*
Your looped and windowed[1] raggedness, defend you
From seasons such as these? O, I have ta'en
Too little care of this! Take physic, pomp;[2]

35 Expose thyself to feel what wretches feel,
That thou mayst shake the superflux[3] to them,
And show the heavens more just.

EDGAR (*within*)   Fathom and half,[4] fathom and half!
Poor Tom!

        The FOOL *runs out from the hovel*

40 FOOL   Come not in here, nuncle, here's a spirit.
Help me, help me!

KENT   Give me thy hand. Who's there?

FOOL   A spirit, a spirit! He says his name's poor Tom.

KENT   What art thou that dost grumble there i' the straw? Come
45 forth.

        Enter EDGAR *disguised as a madman*

EDGAR   Away! the foul fiend follows me!
Through the sharp hawthorn blows the cold wind.[5]
Humh! go to thy cold bed, and warm thee.[6]

LEAR   Hast thou given all to thy two daughters? And art thou
50 come to this?

EDGAR   Who gives any thing to poor Tom? whom the foul fiend
hath led through fire and through flame, through ford and
whirlpool, o'er bog and quagmire; that hath laid knives under
his pillow and halters in his pew; set ratsbane by his porridge;[7]
55 made him proud of heart, to ride on a bay trotting-horse over
four-inched bridges,[8] to course° his own shadow for° a traitor.   *hunt / as*
Bless thy five wits![9] Tom's a-cold—O, do, de, do de, do de.
Bless thee from whirlwinds, star-blasting, and taking![1] Do poor
Tom some charity, whom the foul fiend vexes: there could I
60 have him now—and there—and there again, and there.[2]

        Storm still

LEAR   What, has his daughters brought him to this pass?
Couldst thou save nothing? Didst thou give them all?

---

1. *looped and windowed*: full of holes and vents; "windowed" could also refer to cloth worn through to semi-transparency, like the oilcloth window "panes" of the poor.
2. Cure yourself, pompous person.
3. Superfluity; bodily discharge, suggested by "physic" (which also has the meaning of "purgative") in line 34. Excess here is also excess of wealth.
4. "Nine feet," a sailor's cry when taking soundings to gauge the depth of water.
5. *Through . . . wind*: perhaps a fragment from a ballad.
6. *go . . . thee*: this expression is also used by the drunken beggar Christopher Sly in *The Taming of the Shrew*, Induction 1.

7. *laid knives . . . porridge*: these are all means by which the foul fiend tempts Tom to commit suicide. *halters*: nooses. *ratsbane*: rat poison.
8. Impossibly narrow, and probably suicidal to attempt without diabolical help.
9. The five wits were common wit, imagination, fantasy, estimation, and memory (from medieval and Renaissance cognitive theory).
1. *whirlwinds, star-blasting*: malign astrological influences capable of causing sickness or death. *taking*: infection; bewitchment.
2. As Edgar speaks this sentence, he might kill vermin on his body as if they were devils.

FOOL   Nay, he reserved a blanket, else we had been all shamed.

LEAR   Now, all the plagues that in the pendulous° air   *overhanging; portentous*
65   Hang fated o'er men's faults light on thy daughters!

KENT   He hath no daughters, sir.

LEAR   Death, traitor! nothing could have subdued nature
        To such a lowness but his unkind daughters.
        Is it the fashion that discarded fathers
70   Should have thus little mercy on their flesh?
        Judicious punishment! 't was this flesh begot
        Those pelican[3] daughters.

EDGAR   Pillicock sat on Pillicock-hill.
         Halloo, halloo, loo, loo![4]

75 FOOL   This cold night will turn us all to fools and madmen.

EDGAR   Take heed o' the foul fiend; obey thy parents; keep thy
         word justly; swear not; commit not with man's sworn spouse;
         set not thy sweet heart on proud array.[5] Tom's a-cold.

LEAR   What hast thou been?

80 EDGAR   A serving-man, proud in heart and mind; that curled my
         hair; wore gloves in my cap;[6] served the lust of my mistress'
         heart, and did the act of darkness with her; swore as many oaths
         as I spake words, and broke them in the sweet face of heaven:
         one that slept in the contriving of lust, and waked to do it. Wine
85   loved I deeply, dice dearly; and in woman out-paramoured the
         Turk.[7] False of heart, light of ear,° bloody of hand; hog in sloth,   *rumor-hungry*
         fox in stealth, wolf in greediness, dog in mad- ness, lion in prey.
         Let not the creaking of shoes[8] nor the rustling of silks betray
         thy poor heart to woman. Keep thy foot[9] out of brothels, thy
90   hand out of plackets,[1] thy pen from lenders' books, and defy
         the foul fiend. Still through the hawthorn blows the cold wind:
         Says suum, mun, ha, no, nonny. Dolphin my boy, my boy,
         sessa! let him trot by.[2]
             Storm still

LEAR   Why, thou wert better in thy grave than to answer° with thy   *encounter*
95   uncovered body this extremity of the skies.° Is man no more   *violent weather*
        than this? Consider him well. Thou owest the worm no silk, the
        beast no hide, the sheep no wool, that cat[3] no perfume. Ha! here's
        three on's° are sophisticated! Thou art the thing itself; unac-   *of us*
        commodated[4] man is no more but such a poor, bare, forked°   *two-legged*
100   animal as thou art. Off, off, you lendings!° come unbutton   *borrowed clothes*
        here.
            Tearing off his clothes

FOOL   Prithee, nuncle, be contented; 'tis a naughty° night to   *foul*
        swim in. Now a little fire in a wild° field were like an old lech-   *barren; lustful*
        er's heart; a small spark, all the rest on's° body cold. Look, here   *of his*
105   comes a walking fire.
            Enter GLOUCESTER, *with a torch*

3. Greedy. Young pelicans were reputed to feed on blood
from the wounds they made in their mother's breast; in
some versions, they first killed their father.
4. A fragment of an old rhyme, followed by hunting cries
or a ballad refrain; "Pillicock" was both a term of endearment and a euphemism for "penis."
5. *obey . . . array*: these are fragments from the Ten Com-
mandments.
6. Favors from his mistress. In Petrarchan poetry, wooers
are "servants" to their ladies.
7. And had more women than the sultan had in his royal

harem.
8. Creaking shoes were a fashionable affectation.
9. Punning on the French *foutre* ("fuck").
1. Slits in skirts or petticoats.
2. These phrases are probably snatches from songs and
proverbs. "Dolphin" is an imagined animal or devil or the
heir to the French throne ("dauphin," which Shakespeare
usually Anglicized), or all three.
3. Civet cat, in Shakespeare's time the major source of
musk for perfume.
4. Naked; without the trappings of civilization.

EDGAR   This is the foul fiend Flibbertigibbet.[5] He begins at cur-
few,° and walks till the first cock.° He gives the web and the   *9:00 P.M. / midnight*
pin,[6] squinies[7] the eye, and makes the hare-lip; mildews the
white° wheat, and hurts the poor creature of earth.   *near-ripe*

110   St. Withold footed thrice the old;[8]
                 He met the night-mare and her nine-fold;[9]
                 Bid her alight,
                 And her troth plight,°   *And gave her word*
                 And, aroint thee,° witch, aroint thee!   *begone*
115 KENT   How fares your grace?
    LEAR   What's° he?   *Who's*
    KENT   Who's there? What is't you seek?
    GLOUCESTER   What are you there? Your names?
    EDGAR   Poor Tom, that eats the swimming frog, the toad, the
120 tadpole, the wall-newt and the water;° that in the fury of his   *water newt*
heart, when the foul fiend rages, eats cow-dung for sallets;°   *savories*
swallows the old rat and the ditch-dog;[1] drinks the green man-
tle° of the standing-pool; who is whipped from tithing to tith-   *scum*
ing,° and stock-punished,° and imprisoned; who hath had three   *parish / put in stocks*
125 suits to his back, six shirts to his body, horse to ride, and weapon
to wear;
                 But mice and rats, and such small deer,[2]
                 Have been Tom's food for seven long year.
           Beware my follower. Peace, Smulkin;° peace, thou fiend!   *a Harsnett devil*
130 GLOUCESTER   What, hath your grace no better company
    EDGAR   The prince of darkness is a gentleman. Modo he's call'd,
and Mahu.[3]
    GLOUCESTER   Our flesh and blood is grown so vile, my lord,
           That it doth hate what gets° it.   *begets*
135 EDGAR   Poor Tom's a-cold.
    GLOUCESTER   Go in with me. My duty cannot suffer°   *permit me*
           To obey in all your daughters' hard commands:
           Though their injunction be to bar my doors,
           And let this tyrannous night take hold upon you
140   Yet have I ventured to come seek you out.
           And bring you where both fire and food is ready.
    LEAR   First let me talk with this philosopher.
           What is the cause of thunder?
    KENT   Good my lord, take his offer; go into the house.
145 LEAR   I'll take a word with this same learned Theban.°   *Greek sage*
           What is your study?°   *field of expertise*
    EDGAR   How to prevent the fiend, and to kill vermin.
    LEAR   Let me ask you one word in private.
    KENT   Importune him once more to go, my lord;
           His wits begin to unsettle.
150 GLOUCESTER   Canst thou blame him?
        Storm still

---

5. A devil drawn from folk beliefs, but famous for his prominent place in Samuel Harsnett's *Declaration of Egregious Popish Impostures* (1603); the frequent borrowings from Harsnett in *King Lear* set the earliest possible composition date for the play.
6. *web and the pin*: cataract.
7. Causes squints in.
8. St. Withold traversed the hilly countryside three times. *old*: wold, uplands.
9. *night-mare*: a demon that is not necessarily in the shape of a horse. *fold*: familiar, demon.
1. A dog found dead in a ditch.
2. *deer*: animals. These verses are adapted from a romance popular in Shakespeare's time, *Bevis of Hampton*.
3. Modo and Mahu, more Harsnett devils, were commanding generals of the hellish troops.

His daughters seek his death; ah, that good Kent!
He said it would be thus, poor banished man!
Thou say'st the king grows mad; I'll tell thee, friend,
I am almost mad myself. I had a son,
155 Now outlawed° from my blood. He sought my life. *disowned*
But lately, very late.° I loved him, friend; *recently*
No father his son dearer. True to tell thee,
The grief hath crazed my wits. What a night's this!
I do beseech your grace—
LEAR   O, cry you mercy,° sir. *beg your pardon*
160 Noble philosopher, your company.
EDGAR   Tom's a-cold.
GLOUCESTER   In, fellow, there, into the hovel; keep thee warm.
LEAR   Come, let's in all.
                    This way, my lord.
KENT   With him!
LEAR   I will keep still with my philosopher.
165 KENT   Good my lord, soothe° him; let him take the fellow. *humor*
GLOUCESTER   Take him you on.° *on ahead*
KENT   Sirrah, come on; go along with us.
LEAR   Come, good Athenian.° *Greek philosopher*
GLOUCESTER   No words, no words: hush.
170 EDGAR   Child Rowland⁴ to the dark tower came,
His word° was still°—Fie, foh, and fum, *motto / always*
I smell the blood of a British⁵ man.   *Exeunt*

3.5

Enter CORNWALL *and* EDMUND
CORNWALL   I will have my revenge ere I depart his house.
EDMUND   How, my lord, I may be censured,° that nature° thus *judged / kinship*
gives way to loyalty, something fears me° to think of. *I am somewhat afraid*
CORNWALL   I now perceive, it was not altogether your brother's
5 evil disposition made him seek his° death; but a provoking *(Gloucester's)*
merit, set a-work by a reproveable badness in himself.¹
EDMUND   How malicious is my fortune, that I must repent to
be just! This is the letter he spoke of, which approves him an
intelligent party to the advantages of France.² O heavens! that
10 this treason were not, or not I the detector!
CORNWALL   Go with me to the duchess.
EDMUND   If the matter of this paper be certain, you have mighty
business in hand.
CORNWALL   True or false, it hath made thee Earl of Gloucester.
15 Seek out where thy father is, that he may be ready for our
apprehension.° *arrest*
EDMUND (*aside*)   If I find him comforting the king, it will stuff
his° suspicion more fully.—I will perséver in my course of loy- *(Cornwall's)*
alty, though the conflict be sore between that and my blood.° *filial duty*
20 CORNWALL   I will lay trust upon thee, and thou shalt find a
dearer father in my love.   *Exeunt*

---

4. *Child*: an aspirant to knighthood. Roland is the famous
hero of the Charlemagne legends.
5. "An Englishman" usually appears in this rhyme from
the cycle of tales of which "Jack and the Beanstalk" is the
best-known. The alteration befits Lear's ancient Britain.
3.5 Location: At Gloucester's castle.

1. *a provoking . . . himself*: Gloucester's own wickedness
deservedly triggered the blameworthy evil in Edgar.
2. *which . . . France*: which proves him a spy and
informer in the aid of France; "party," or faction, was usually a term of opprobrium in the Renaissance.

3.6

Enter GLOUCESTER, LEAR, KENT, FOOL, *and* EDGAR

GLOUCESTER   Here is better than the open air; take it thankfully.
I will piece° out the comfort with what addition I can; I will   *pad*
not be long from you.

KENT   All the power of his wits have given sway to his impa-
5   tience:[1] the gods° reward your kindness!   *Exit* GLOUCESTER   *may the gods*

EDGAR   Fraterretto° calls me; and tells me Nero is an angler in the   *a Harsnett devil*
lake of darkness.[2] Pray, innocent, and beware the foul fiend.

FOOL   Prithee, nuncle, tell me whether a madman be a gentleman or a yeoman?[3]

10   LEAR   A king, a king!

FOOL   No, he's a yeoman that has a gentleman to his son; for
he's a mad yeoman that sees his son a gentleman before him.

LEAR   To have a thousand with red burning spits
Come hissing in upon 'em—

15   EDGAR   The foul fiend bites my back.

FOOL   He's mad that trusts in the tameness of a wolf, a horse's
health, a boy's love, or a whore's oath.

LEAR   It shall be done; I will arraign° them straight.°   *prosecute / immediately*
(*To* EDGAR) Come, sit thou here, most learned justicer;
20   (*to the* FOOL) Thou, sapient sir, sit here. Now, you she foxes!

EDGAR   Look, where he stands and glares! Wantest thou eyes° at   *observers*
trial, madam?

FOOL   Come o'er the bourn, Bessy, to me[4]—
Her boat hath a leak,[5]
25   And she must not speak
Why she dares not come over to thee.

EDGAR   The foul fiend haunts poor Tom in the voice of a night-
ingale. Hopdance° cries in Tom's belly for two white° herring.   *a demon / fresh*
Croak° not, black angel; I have no food for thee.   *Growl*

30   KENT   How do you, sir? Stand you not so amazed:
Will you lie down and rest upon the cushions?

LEAR   I'll see their trial first. Bring in the evidence.
(*To* EDGAR) Thou robed man of justice, take thy place;
(*to the* FOOL) And thou, his yoke-fellow of equity,°   *partner of law*
35   Bench° by his side. (*To* KENT) You are o' the commission,°   *Sit / judiciary*
Sit you too.

EDGAR   Let us deal justly.
Sleepest or wakest thou, jolly shepherd?
Thy sheep be in the corn;°   *grain*
40   And for one blast of thy minikin° mouth,   *dainty*
Thy sheep shall take no harm.
Pur! the cat[6] is gray.

LEAR   Arraign her first; 'tis Goneril. I here take my oath before
this honorable assembly, she kicked the poor king her father.

45   FOOL   Come hither, mistress. Is your name Goneril?

LEAR   She cannot deny it.

3.6 Location: Within an outbuilding of Gloucester's.
1. Rage; inability to bear more suffering.
2. In Chaucer's *Monk's Tale*, the infamously cruel Roman emperor Nero is found fishing in hell (lines 485–86).
3. A free landowner but not a member of the gentry, lacking official family arms and the distinctions they confer.

Shakespeare seems to have procured a coat of arms for his father in 1596.
4. From an old song. *bourn*: a small stream.
5. She has venereal disease; punning on "boat" as body and "burn" as genital discomfort.
6. Pur the cat is another devil; such devils in the shape of cats were the familiars of witches.

FOOL   Cry you mercy, I took you for a joint-stool.[7]
LEAR   And here's another, whose warped looks proclaim
        What store° her heart is made on.° Stop her there!   *material / of*
50   Arms, arms, sword, fire! Corruption in the place!
        False justicer, why hast thou let her 'scape?
EDGAR   Bless thy five wits!
KENT   O pity! Sir, where is the patience now,
        That you so oft have boasted to retain?
55 EDGAR (*aside*)   My tears begin to take his part so much,
        They'll mar my counterfeiting.
LEAR   The little dogs and all,°   *Even the little dogs*
        Tray, Blanch, and Sweet-heart, see, they bark at me.
EDGAR   Tom will throw his head at° them. Avaunt,° you curs!   *will threaten? / Begone*
60   Be thy mouth or° black or white,   *either*
            Tooth that poisons° if it bite;   *gives rabies*
            Mastiff, greyhound, mongrel grim,
            Hound or spaniel, brach° or lym,   *bitch*
            Or bobtail tike or trundle-tail.[8]
65   Tom will make them weep and wail:
            For, with throwing thus my head,
            Dogs leap the hatch,[9] and all are fled.
        Do de, de, de. Sessa![1] Come, march to wakes° and fairs and   *parish festivals*
        market-towns. Poor Tom, thy horn is dry.[2]
70 LEAR   Then let them anatomize° Regan; see what breeds about   *dissect*
        her heart. Is there any cause in nature that makes these hard
        hearts? (*To* EDGAR) You, sir, I entertain° for one of my hundred;   *retain*
        I do not like the fashion of your garments. You will say they are
        Persian;° but let them be changed.   *oriental; splendid*
75 KENT   Now, good my lord, lie there and rest awhile.
LEAR   Make no noise, make no noise; draw the curtains.° So, so,   *bed curtains*
        so. We'll go to supper i' the morning.
FOOL   And I'll go to bed at noon.
            [*Re-enter* GLOUCESTER]
GLOUCESTER   Come hither, friend. Where is the king my master?
80 KENT   Here, sir; but trouble him not; his wits are gone.
GLOUCESTER   Good friend, I prithee, take him in thy arms;
        I have o'erheard a plot of death upon° him: *against*
        There is a litter ready; lay him in 't
        And drive towards Dover, friend, where thou shalt meet
85   Both welcome and protection. Take up thy master.
        If thou shouldst dally half an hour, his life,
        With thine, and all that offer to defend him,
        Stand in assured loss.° Take up, take up!   *Are certainly doomed*
        And follow me, that will to some provision
        Give thee quick conduct.[3]
90 KENT   Oppressèd nature sleeps:
        This rest might yet have balmed° thy broken sinews,°   *soothed / nerves*
        Which, if convenience will not allow,

---

7. I beg your pardon, I mistook you for a stool. An idiom of the day expressing annoyance at being slighted. Here the part of Goneril is actually being played by a stool.
8. Short-tailed mongrel or long-tailed.
9. Dogs leap over the lower half of a divided door.
1. Apparently nonsense, although "Sessa" may be a version of the French *cessez* ("stop" or "hush").
2. A begging formula that refers to the horn vessel that vagabonds carried for drink; the covert sense is that Edgar has run out of Bedlamite inspiration.
3. *that . . . conduct:* who will quickly guide you to some supplies.

Stand in hard cure.° (*To the* FOOL) Come, help to bear thy   *Will be hard to cure*
    master:
Thou must not stay behind.
GLOUCESTER   Come come, away.
                      Exeunt all but EDGAR
95 EDGAR   When we our betters see bearing our° woes,   *our same*
    We scarcely think our miseries our foes.
    Who alone suffers suffers most i' the mind,
    Leaving free° things and happy shows° behind: *carefree / scenes*
    But then the mind much sufferance doth o'erskip
100   When grief hath mates, and bearing° fellowship.   *pain, suffering*
    How light and portable my pain seems now,
    When that which makes me bend makes the king bow;
    He° childed as I fathered! Tom, away!   *He is*
    Mark the high noises,° and thyself bewray°   *important rumors / reveal*
105   When false opinion, whose wrong thought defiles thee,
    In thy just proof repeals and reconciles thee.[4]
    What° will hap° more tonight, safe 'scape the king!   *Whatever / chance*
    Lurk, lurk.   *Exit*

3.7

Enter CORNWALL, REGAN, GONERIL, EDMUND, *and ser-*
    vants
CORNWALL (*to* GONERIL) Post° speedily to my lord your hus-   *Ride*
    band; show him this letter. The army of France is landed. Seek
    out the villain Gloucester.   *Exeunt some of the servants*
REGAN   Hang him instantly.
5 GONERIL   Pluck out his eyes.
CORNWALL   Leave him to my displeasure. Edmund, keep you
    our sister° company. The revenges we are bound[1] to take   *sister-in-law*
    upon your traitorous father are not fit for your beholding.
    Advise the duke, where you are going, to a most festinate prep-
10 aration.[2] We are bound° to the like. Our posts° shall be swift and   *committed / messengers*
    intelligent° betwixt us. Farewell, dear sister: farewell, my lord of   *well-informed*
    Gloucester.
        Enter OSWALD
    How now! Where's the king?
OSWALD   My lord of Gloucester hath conveyed him hence.
15 Some five or six and thirty of his° knights,   *(Lear's)*
    Hot questrists° after him, met him at gate;   *searchers*
    Who, with some other of the lords° dependants,   *(Gloucester's)*
    Are gone with him towards Dover; where they boast
    To have well-armed friends.
CORNWALL   Get horses for your mistress.
20 GONERIL   Farewell, sweet lord, and sister.
CORNWALL   Edmund, farewell.
        Exeunt GONERIL, EDMUND, *and* OSWALD
    Go seek the traitor Gloucester,
    Pinion him° like a thief, bring him before us.   *Tie his arms*
                Exeunt other servants
    Though well we may not pass° upon his life   *pass sentence*

---

4. *In . . . thee:* When true evidence pardons you and reconciles you (with your father).
3.7 Location: At Gloucester's castle.

1. Bound by duty; expected by destiny.
2. *Advise . . . preparation:* When you reach Albany, tell
the Duke to prepare quickly.

25	Without the form° of justice, yet our power	*official proceedings*
	Shall do a courtesy³ to our wrath, which men	
	May blame, but not control. Who's there? the traitor?	

       Enter GLOUCESTER, *brought in by two or three*

REGAN   Ingrateful fox! 'tis he.

	CORNWALL Bind fast his corky° arms.	*withered*
30	GLOUCESTER What mean your graces? Good my friends, consider	
	You are my guests. Do me no foul play, friends.	

CORNWALL   Bind him, I say.

       Servants bind him

REGAN   Hard, hard. O filthy traitor!

GLOUCESTER   Unmerciful lady as you are, I'm none.

CORNWALL   To this chair bind him. Villain, thou shalt find—

REGAN *plucks his beard°*	*(an extreme insult)*

35 GLOUCESTER By the kind gods, 'tis most ignobly done	
To pluck me by the beard.	

	REGAN So white,° and such a traitor!	*white-haired; venerable*
	GLOUCESTER Naughty° lady,	*Wicked*
	These hairs, which thou dost ravish from my chin,	
	Will quicken,° and accuse thee. I am your host.	*come alive*
40	With robbers' hands my hospitable favors°	*features*
	You should not ruffle° thus. What will you do?	*snatch at*
	CORNWALL Come, sir, what letters had you late° from France?	*lately*
	REGAN Be simple° answered, for we know the truth.	*straightforwardly*
	CORNWALL And what confederacy have you with the traitors	
45	Late footed° in the kingdom?	*landed*

REGAN   To whose hands have you sent the lunatic king? Speak.

GLOUCESTER   I have a letter guessingly set down,⁴

    Which came from one that's of a neutral heart,

    And not from one opposed.

CORNWALL   Cunning.

REGAN   And false.

50	CORNWALL Where hast thou sent the king?	
	GLOUCESTER To Dover.	
	REGAN Wherefore° to Dover? Wast thou not charged° at peril—	*Why / commanded*

CORNWALL   Wherefore to Dover? Let him first answer that.

GLOUCESTER I am tied to the stake, and I must stand the	
55 course.⁵	

REGAN   Wherefore to Dover?

	GLOUCESTER Because I would not see thy cruel nails	
	Pluck out his poor old eyes; nor thy fierce sister	
	In his anointed⁶ flesh stick boarish fangs.	
60	The sea, with such a storm as his bare head	
	In hell-black night endured, would have buoyed° up,	*risen*
	And quenched the stellèd° fires.	*stars'*
	Yet, poor old heart, he holp° the heavens to rage.	*helped*
	If wolves had at thy gate howled that dern° time,	*dreary; dreadful*
65	Thou shouldst have said "Good porter, turn the key."°	*(to open the door)*
	All cruels else subscribed.⁷ But I shall see	
	The wingèd vengeance⁸ overtake such children.	

---

3. Shall allow a courtesy, or indulgence; shall bow to.
4. Written without confirmation; speculative.
5. An image from bearbaiting, in which a bear on a short tether had to fight off the assault of dogs.
6. Consecrated with holy oils (as part of a king's corona-

tion).
7. All other cruel creatures yielded to compassion.
8. Swift or heaven-sent revenge; either an angel of God or the Furies, who were flying executors of divine vengeance in classical myth.

CORNWALL   See 't shalt thou never. Fellows,° hold the chair. *Servants*
    Upon these eyes of thine I'll set my foot.
70 GLOUCESTER   He that will think° to live till he be old, *Whoever hopes*
    Give me some help! O cruel! O ye gods!
REGAN   One side will mock another. The other too!
CORNWALL   If you see vengeance—
FIRST SERVANT   Hold your hand, my lord:
    I have served you ever since I was a child;
75   But better service have I never done you
    Than now to bid you hold.
REGAN   How now, you dog!
FIRST SERVANT   If you did wear a beard upon your chin,
    I'd shake it on this quarrel.[9]
80 REGAN   What do you mean?° *intend*
CORNWALL   My villain!° *servant; villain*
FIRST SERVANT   Why, then, come on, and take the chance of anger.[1]
REGAN   Give me thy sword. A peasant stand up thus!
            CORNWALL *is wounded.*
            Takes a sword, and runs at him behind
FIRST SERVANT   O, I am slain! My lord, you have one eye left
85   To see some mischief° on him. O!   *Dies* *injury*
CORNWALL   Lest it see more, prevent it. Out, vile jelly!
    Where is thy luster now?
GLOUCESTER   All dark and comfortless. Where's my son Edmund?
    Edmund, enkindle all the sparks of nature,[2]
    To quit° this horrid act. *requite, avenge*
90 REGAN   Out, treacherous villain!
    Thou call'st on him that hates thee. It was he
    That made the overture° of thy treasons to us; *revelation*
    Who is too good to pity thee.
GLOUCESTER   O my follies! Then Edgar was abused.° *slandered*
95   Kind gods, forgive me that, and prosper him!
REGAN   Go thrust him out at gates, and let him smell
    His way to Dover.   *Exit one with* GLOUCESTER
    How is't, my lord? how look you?° *how do you feel*
CORNWALL   I have received a hurt. Follow me, lady;
100   Turn out that eyeless villain. Throw this slave
    Upon the dunghill. Regan, I bleed apace.
    Untimely comes this hurt. Give me your arm.
            Exit CORNWALL *led by* REGAN
SECOND SERVANT   I'll never care what wickedness I do,
    If this man come to good.[3]
THIRD SERVANT   If she live long,
105   And in the end meet the old° course of death, *usual*
    Woman will all turn monsters.
SECOND SERVANT   Let's follow the old earl, and get the Bedlam
    To lead him where he would. His roguish madness
    Allows itself to any thing.
110 THIRD SERVANT   Go thou; I'll fetch some flax and whites of eggs
    To apply to his bleeding face. Now, heaven help him!
            Exeunt severally

9. I'd pluck it over this point; I'd issue a challenge.
1. Take the risk of fighting when angry; take the fortune of one who is governed by his anger.
2. All the warmth of filial love; all the anger that your father has received such treatment.
3. *I'll . . . good*: because this may be a sign that evil goes unpunished. *this man*: Cornwall.

4.1

Enter EDGAR

EDGAR Yet better thus, and known to be contemned°   *despised*
Than still° contemned and flattered. To be worst,   *always*
The lowest and most dejected thing of fortune,
Stands still in esperance, lives not in fear.[1]
5 The lamentable change is from the best;
The worst returns to laughter.[2] Welcome, then,
Thou unsubstantial air that I embrace!
The wretch that thou hast blown unto the worst
Owes nothing° to thy blasts. But who comes here?   *(because he can't pay)*

Enter GLOUCESTER, *led by an* OLD MAN

10 My father, parti-eyed?[3] World, world, O world!
But that thy strange mutations make us hate thee,
Life would not yield to age.[4]

OLD MAN O, my good lord, I have been your tenant, and your
father's tenant, these fourscore years.

15 GLOUCESTER Away, get thee away! Good friend, be gone.
Thy comforts° can do me no good at all;   *assistance*
Thee they may hurt.

OLD MAN Alack, sir, you cannot see your way.

GLOUCESTER I have no way, and therefore want no eyes;
20 I stumbled when I saw. Full oft 'tis seen,
Our means secure us, and our mere defects
Prove our commodities.[5] O dear son Edgar,
The food° of thy abusèd° father's wrath!   *fuel; prey / despised*
Might I but live to see thee in° my touch,   *through*
I'd say I had eyes again!

25 OLD MAN   How now! Who's there?

EDGAR *(aside)* O gods! Who is't can say "I am at the worst"?
I am worse than e'er I was.

OLD MAN   'Tis poor mad Tom.

EDGAR *(aside)* And worse I may be yet: the worst is not
So long as we can say "This is the worst."

OLD MAN Fellow, where goest?

30 GLOUCESTER   Is it a beggar-man?

OLD MAN Madman and beggar too.

GLOUCESTER He has some reason, else he could not beg.
I' the last night's storm I such a fellow saw;
Which made me think a man a worm. My son
35 Came then into my mind, and yet my mind
Was then scarce friends with him. I have heard more since.
As flies to wanton° boys are we to the gods;   *playful; careless*
They kill us for their sport.

EDGAR *(aside)*   How should this be?
Bad is the trade that must play fool to sorrow,[6]
40 Angering itself and others.—Bless thee, master!

GLOUCESTER Is that the naked fellow?

4.1 Location: Open country.
1. *Stands ... fear:* Remains in hope ("esperance") because there is no fear of falling further.
2. *The lamentable ... laughter:* The change to be lamented is one that alters the best of circumstances; the worst luck can only improve.
3. Multicolored like a fool's costume (red with blood under white dressings).

4. *But ... age:* If there were no strange reversals of fortune to make the world hateful, we would not consent to aging and death.
5. *Our means ... commodities:* Our wealth makes us overconfident, and our utter deprivation proves to be beneficial.
6. It is a bad business to have to play the fool in the face of sorrow.

OLD MAN   Ay, my lord.
GLOUCESTER   Then, prithee, get thee gone. If, for my sake,
    Thou wilt o'ertake us, hence a mile or twain,
    I' the way toward Dover, do it for ancient love;[7]
45   And bring some covering for this naked soul,
    Who I'll entreat to lead me.
OLD MAN   Alack, sir, he is mad.
GLOUCESTER   'Tis the times' plague, when[8] madmen lead the blind.
    Do as I bid thee, or rather do thy pleasure;
    Above the rest, be gone.
50 OLD MAN   I'll bring him the best 'parel° that I have,   *apparel, clothing*
    Come on 't what will.   *Exit*
GLOUCESTER   Sirrah, naked fellow—
EDGAR   Poor Tom's a-cold. *(Aside)* I cannot daub it further.[9]
GLOUCESTER   Come hither, fellow.
55 EDGAR *(aside)*   And yet I must.—Bless thy sweet eyes, they bleed.
GLOUCESTER   Know'st thou the way to Dover?
EDGAR   Both stile and gate, horse-way and foot-path. Poor Tom
    hath been scared out of his good wits. Bless thee, good man's
    son, from the foul fiend! Five fiends have been in Poor Tom at
60   once; of lust, as Obidicut; Hobbididance, prince of dumbness;
    Mahu, of stealing; Modo, of murder; Flibbertigibbet, of mop-
    ping and mowing,° who since possesses chambermaids and   *making faces*
    waiting-women. So, bless thee, master!
GLOUCESTER   Here, take this purse, thou whom the heavens' plagues
65   Have humbled to all strokes.° That I am wretched   *to accept all blows*
    Makes thee the happier. Heavens, deal so still!°   *always*
    Let the superfluous and lust-dieted man,[1]
    That slaves° your ordinance,° that will not see   *defers to / authority*
    Because he doth not feel, feel your power quickly;
70   So distribution should undo excess,
    And each man have enough. Dost thou know Dover?
EDGAR   Ay, master.
GLOUCESTER   There is a cliff, whose high and bending° head   *overhanging*
    Looks fearfully in the confinéd deep.[2]
75   Bring me but to the very brim of it,
    And I'll repair the misery thou dost bear
    With something rich about me. From that place
    I shall no leading need.
EDGAR   Give me thy arm.
    Poor Tom shall lead thee.   *Exeunt*

4.2

Enter GONERIL *and* EDMUND
GONERIL   Welcome, my lord. I marvel our mild husband
    Not° met us on the way.   *Has not*
    Enter OSWALD
                    Now where's your master?
OSWALD   Madam, within, but never man so changed.
    I told him of the army that was landed;
5   He smiled at it. I told him you were coming;

---

7. For the sake of our long and loyal relationship (as master and servant).
8. The time is truly sick when.
9. I cannot continue the charade. *daub:* mask, plaster.

1. Let the overprosperous man who indulges his appetite.
2. Looks fearsomely into the straits below.
4.2 Location: Before Albany's castle.

His answer was "The worse." Of Gloucester's treachery,
And of the loyal service of his son,
When I informed him, then he called me sot,°   *fool*
And told me I had turned the wrong side out.[1]
10   What most he should dislike seems pleasant to him;
What like, offensive.
GONERIL (*to* EDMUND)   Then shall you go no further.
It is the cowish° terror of his spirit,   *cowardly*
That dares not undertake. He'll not feel wrongs
Which tie him to an answer.[2] Our wishes on the way
15   May prove effects.[3] Back, Edmund, to my brother;°   *brother-in-law*
Hasten his musters° and conduct his powers.°   *call-up of troops / armies*
I must change arms at home, and give the distaff[4]
Into my husband's hands. This trusty servant
Shall pass between us. Ere long you are like° to hear,   *likely*
20   If you dare venture in your own behalf,
A mistress's° command. Wear this; spare speech;   *(playing on "lover's")*
     (*giving a favor*)
Decline your head. This kiss, if it durst speak,
Would stretch thy spirits up into the air.
Conceive,° and fare thee well.   *Understand my meaning*
EDMUND   Yours in° the ranks of death.   *even in*
25   GONERIL   My most dear Gloucester!
                             Exit EDMUND

O, the difference of man and man!
To thee a woman's services are due:
My fool usurps my body.[5]
OSWALD   Madam, here comes my lord.   *Exit*
     Enter ALBANY
GONERIL   I have been worth the whistling.[6]
30   ALBANY   O Goneril!
You are not worth the dust which the rude wind
Blows in your face. I fear your disposition.
That nature, which contemns it° origin,   *despises its*
Cannot be bordered certain° in itself.   *be defended securely*
35   She that herself will sliver and disbranch°   *split*
From her material sap, perforce must wither
And come to deadly use.[7]
GONERIL   No more; the text is foolish.
ALBANY   Wisdom and goodness to the vile seem vile;
40   Filths savor but themselves. What have you done?
Tigers, not daughters, what have you performed?
A father, and a gracious aged man,
Whose reverence even the head-lugged° bear would lick,   *dragged by the head*
Most barbarous, most degenerate, have you madded.
45   Could my good brother° suffer you to do it?   *brother-in-law*
A man, a prince, by him so benefited!

---

1. I had reversed things (by mistaking loyalty for treachery).
2. *He'll . . . answer:* He'll ignore insults that would provoke him to retaliate.
3. May be put into action.
4. A device used in spinning and so emblematic of the female role. To "change arms," therefore, is to swap the insignia of male and female identity.
5. My idiot husband presumes to possess me.

6. At one time, you would have come to welcome me home; referring to the proverb "It is a poor dog that is not worth the whistling."
7. *She . . . use:* The allusion is probably biblical: "But that which beareth thorns and briers is reproved, and is near unto cursing; whose end is to be burned" (Hebrews 6:8). *come to deadly use:* be destroyed; be used for burning.

If that the heavens do not their visible spirits
Send quickly down to tame these vild° offenses,   *wild; vile*
It will come,
50 Humanity must perforce° prey on itself,   *inevitably*
Like monsters of the deep.
GONERIL   Milk-livered° man!   *Cowardly*
That bear'st a cheek for blows, a head for wrongs:[8]
Who hast not in thy brows an eye discerning
Thine honor from thy suffering;[9] that not know'st
55 Fools do those villains pity who are punished
Ere they have done their mischief. Where's thy drum?°   *(to muster troops)*
France spreads his banners in our noiseless° land,   *peaceful*
With pluméd helm thy state begins to threat;
Whiles thou, a moral° fool, sit'st still, and criest   *moralizing*
"Alack, why does he so?"
60 ALBANY   See thyself, devil!
Proper deformity shows not in the fiend
So horrid as in woman.[1]
GONERIL   O vain° fool!   *useless*
ALBANY   Thou changéd and self-covered[2] thing, for shame,
Be-monster not thy feature. Were't my fitness°   *If it were appropriate*
65 To let these hands obey my blood,
They are apt enough to dislocate and tear
Thy flesh and bones. Howe'er° thou art a fiend,   *Although*
A woman's shape doth shield thee.
GONERIL   Marry, your manhood! mew![3]
            Enter a MESSENGER
70 ALBANY   What news?
MESSENGER   O, my good lord, the Duke of Cornwall's dead;
Slain by his servant, going to put out
The other eye of Gloucester.
ALBANY   Gloucester's eyes?
MESSENGER   A servant that he bred, thrilled with remorse,°   *shaken with pity*
75 Opposed against the act, bending° his sword   *directing*
To° his great master; who, thereat enraged,   *Against*
Flew on him, and amongst them felled him dead;
But not without that harmful stroke, which since
Hath plucked him after.[4]
ALBANY   This shows you are above,
80 You justicers,° that these our nether crimes[5]   *judges*
So speedily can venge! But, O poor Gloucester!
Lost he his other eye?
MESSENGER   Both, both, my lord.
This letter, madam, craves a speedy answer;
'T is from your sister.
85 GONERIL (*aside*)   One way I like this well;[6]
But being° a widow, and my Gloucester with her,   *her being*

---

8. *for wrongs:* fit for abuse; ready for cuckold's horns.
9. *discerning . . . suffering:* that can distinguish between
an insult to your honor and something you should
patiently endure.
1. *Proper . . . woman:* Deformity (of morals) is appropriate in the devil and so less horrid than in woman, from
whom virtue is expected. Albany may hold a mirror in
front of Goneril, since Jacobean women sometimes wore
small mirrors attached to their dresses.

2. Altered and with your true (womanly) self concealed.
3. Some manhood! (spoken derisively). *Marry:* By the
Virgin Mary. *mew:* a derisive catcall.
4. Has sent him to follow his servant into death.
5. Lower crimes, and so committed on earth, but also
suggesting that the deeds smack of the netherworld of
hell.
6. Because a political rival has been eliminated.

May all the building in my fancy pluck
Upon my hateful life.[7] Another way,
The news is not so tart.°—I'll read, and answer.   *Exit*   *bitter*
90 ALBANY Where was his son when they did take his eyes?
MESSENGER Come with my lady hither.
ALBANY   He is not here.
MESSENGER No, my good lord; I met him back° again.   *returning*
ALBANY Knows he the wickedness?
MESSENGER Ay, my good lord; 'twas he informed against him;
95 And quit the house on purpose, that their punishment
Might have the freer course.
ALBANY   Gloucester, I live
To thank thee for the love thou show'dst the king,
And to revenge thine eyes. Come hither, friend.
Tell me what more thou know'st.   *Exeunt*

4.3

Enter KENT *and a* GENTLEMAN
KENT Why the King of France is so suddenly gone back know
you the reason?
GENTLEMAN Something he left imperfect° in the state, which   *unsettled*
since his coming forth is thought of;° which imports° to the   *remembered / portends*
5 kingdom so much fear and danger, that his personal return was
most required and necessary.
KENT Who hath he left behind him general?
GENTLEMAN The Marshall of France, Monsieur LaFar.
KENT Did your letters pierce the queen to any demonstration of grief?
10 GENTLEMAN Ay, sir. She took them, in my presence;
And now and then an ample tear trilled down
Her delicate cheek. It seemed she was a queen
Over her passion, who,° most rebel-like,   *which*
Sought to be king o'er her.
KENT   O, then it moved her.
15 GENTLEMAN Not to a rage. Patience and sorrow strove
Who should express her goodliest.[1] You have seen
Sunshine and rain at once: her smiles and tears
Were like a° better way. Those happy smilets,   *Were similar in a*
That played on her ripe lip, seemed not to know
20 What guests were in her eyes, which parted thence,
As pearls from diamonds dropped. In brief,
Sorrow would be a rarity° most beloved,   *gem*
If all could so become it.[2]
KENT   Made she no verbal question?
GENTLEMAN 'Faith, once or twice she heaved the name of "father"
25 Pantingly forth, as if it pressed her heart;
Cried "Sisters! sisters! Shame of ladies! sisters!
Kent! father! sisters! What, i' the storm? i' the night?
Let pity not be believed!"[3] There she shook
The holy water from her heavenly eyes,
30 And clamor moistened.[4] Then away she started°   *sprang*
To deal with grief alone.

7. *May . . . life:* May pull down all of my built-up fantasies and thus make my life hateful.
4.3 Location: Near the French camp at Dover.
1. Which should best express her feelings.

2. If everyone wore it so beautifully.
3. Never believe in pity; compassion cannot exist.
4. And moistened her anguish (with tears).

KENT   It is the stars,
   The stars above us, govern our conditions;
   Else one self mate and make⁵ could not beget
   Such different issues.° You spoke not with her since?   *offspring*
35   GENTLEMAN   No.
   KENT   Was this before the king returned?
   GENTLEMAN   No, since.
   KENT   Well, sir, the poor distressed Lear's i' the town;
   Who sometime, in his better tune,° remembers   *state of mind*
   What we are come about, and by no means
   Will yield° to see his daughter.   *consent*
40   GENTLEMAN   Why, good sir?
   KENT   A sovereign shame so elbows° him; his own unkindness,   *prods, nudges*
   That stripped her from his benediction, turned her
   To foreign casualties,° gave her dear rights   *risks*
   To his dog-hearted daughters, these things sting
45   His mind so venomously, that burning shame
   Detains him from Cordelia.
   GENTLEMAN   Alack, poor gentleman!
   KENT   Of Albany's and Cornwall's powers you heard not?
   GENTLEMAN   'Tis so, they are afoot.
   KENT   Well, sir, I'll bring you to our master Lear,
50   And leave you to attend him. Some dear cause°   *Some important reason*
   Will in concealment wrap me up awhile;
   When I am known aright, you shall not grieve°   *repent*
   Lending me this acquaintance.° I pray you, go   *news*
   Along with me.   *Exeunt*

4.4

*Enter, with drum and colors, CORDELIA, DOCTOR, and
soldiers*

CORDELIA   Alack, 'tis he! Why, he was met even now
   As mad as the vexed sea; singing aloud;
   Crowned with rank fumiter and furrow-weeds,¹
   With hor-docks, hemlock, nettles, cuckoo-flowers,
5   Darnel, and all the idle° weeds that grow   *useless*
   In our sustaining corn. A century° send forth;   *battalion (100 men)*
   Search every acre in the high-grown field,
   And bring him to our eye.   *Exit an officer*
   What can man's wisdom
10   In the restoring° his bereaved sense?   *Do to restore*
   He that helps him take all my outward° worth.   *material*
   DOCTOR   There is means, madam.
   Our foster-nurse of nature² is repose,
   The which he lacks. That to provoke in him,
15   Are many simples operative,³ whose power
   Will close the eye of anguish.
   CORDELIA   All blest secrets,
   All you unpublished virtues° of the earth,   *obscure healing plants*
   Spring with my tears! be aidant and remediate°   *healing and remedial*

---

5. Or else the same pair of spouses; "mate" and "make"
may describe either partner.
4.4 Location: The French camp at Dover.
1. Fumiter was used against brain sickness. Furrow-
weeds, like the other weeds in the following lines, grow

in the furrows of plowed fields.
2. *Our . . . nature*: That which comforts and nourishes
human nature.
3. *That . . . operative*: To induce that ("repose") in him,
there are many effective medicinal herbs.

In the good man's distress! Seek, seek for him;
20 Lest his ungoverned rage dissolve the life
That wants° the means to lead it.   *lacks*
       Enter a MESSENGER
MESSENGER   News, madam;
The British powers° are marching hitherward.   *armies*
CORDELIA   'Tis known before; our preparation stands
In expectation of them. O dear father,
25 It is thy business that I go about;[4]
Therefore great France
My mourning and importuned° tears hath pitied.   *importunate; solicitous*
No blown° ambition doth our arms incite,   *inflated*
But love, dear love, and our aged father's right.[5]
30 Soon may I hear and see him!   *Exeunt*

4.5

       Enter REGAN *and* OSWALD
REGAN   But are my brother's powers° set forth?   *(Albany's forces)*
OSWALD   Ay, madam.
REGAN   Himself in person there?
OSWALD   Madam, with much ado.°   *trouble*
Your sister is the better soldier.
5 REGAN   Lord Edmund spake not with your lord at home?
OSWALD   No, madam.
REGAN   What might import° my sister's letter to him?   *mean*
OSWALD   I know not, lady.
REGAN   Faith, he is posted° hence on serious matter.   *hurried*
10 It was great ignorance, Gloucester's eyes being out,
To let him live. Where he arrives he moves
All hearts against us. Edmund, I think, is gone,
In pity of his misery,° to dispatch   *(ironic)*
His nighted° life; moreover, to descry°   *darkened / investigate*
15 The strength o' the enemy.
OSWALD   I must needs after° him, madam, with my letter.   *go after*
REGAN   Our troops set forth tomorrow. Stay with us;
The ways are dangerous.
OSWALD   I may not, madam:
My lady charged° my duty in this business.   *commanded*
20 REGAN   Why should she write to Edmund? Might not you
Transport her purposes by word? Belike,°   *Perhaps*
Something—I know not what. I'll love° thee much,   *reward*
Let me unseal the letter.
OSWALD   Madam, I had rather—
REGAN   I know your lady does not love her husband;
25 I am sure of that; and at her late° being here   *recently*
She gave strange oeillades° and most speaking looks   *amorous glances*
To noble Edmund. I know you are of her bosom.°   *in her confidence*
OSWALD   I, madam?
REGAN   I speak in understanding;° y'are, I know't.   *with certainty*
30 Therefore I do advise you, take this note:°   *take note of this*
My lord is dead; Edmund and I have talked;

---

4. The line echoes Christ's explanation of his mission in
Luke 2:49: "I must go about my father's business."
5. *No ... right:* 1 Corinthians 13:4–5 in the Bishops'

Bible says that love "swelleth not, dealeth not dishonestly,
seeketh not her own."
4.5 Location: At Gloucester's castle.

And more convenient° is he for my hand   *appropriate*
Than for your lady's. You may gather° more.   *infer*
If you do find him, pray you, give him this;[1]
35   And when your mistress hears thus much from you,
I pray, desire her call her wisdom to her.[2]
So, fare you well.
If you do chance to hear of that blind traitor,
Preferment falls on him that cuts him off.°   *cuts his life short*
40   OSWALD   Would I could meet him, madam! I should show
What party I do follow.
REGAN   Fare thee well.   *Exeunt*

4.6

Enter GLOUCESTER, *and* EDGAR *dressed like a peasant*
GLOUCESTER   When shall we come to the top of that same° hill?   *agreed-upon*
EDGAR   You do climb up it now. Look how we labor.
GLOUCESTER   Methinks the ground is even.
EDGAR   Horrible steep.
Hark, do you hear the sea?
GLOUCESTER   No, truly.
5   EDGAR   Why, then, your other senses grow imperfect
By your eyes' anguish.
GLOUCESTER   So may it be, indeed.
Methinks thy voice is altered, and thou speakest
In better phrase and matter° than thou didst.   *sense*
EDGAR   Y'are much deceived. In nothing am I changed
But in my garments.
10   GLOUCESTER   Methinks y'are better spoken.
EDGAR   Come on, sir; here's the place. Stand still. How fearful
And dizzy 'tis, to cast one's eyes so low!
The crows and choughs° that wing the midway air[1]   *jackdaws*
Show° scarce so gross° as beetles. Halfway down   *Appear / big*
15   Hangs one that gathers sampire,° dreadful trade!   *seaweed*
Methinks he seems no bigger than his head.
The fishermen, that walk upon the beach,
Appear like mice; and yond tall anchoring bark,°   *ship*
Diminished to her cock;° her cock, a buoy   *dinghy*
20   Almost too small for sight. The murmuring surge,
That on the unnumbered° idle pebble chafes,   *innumerable*
Cannot be heard so high. I'll look no more,
Lest my brain turn, and the° deficient sight   *my*
Topple° down headlong.   *Topple me*
GLOUCESTER   Set me where you stand.
25   EDGAR   Give me your hand. You are now within a foot
Of th' extreme verge. For all beneath the moon
Would I not leap upright.[2]
GLOUCESTER   Let go my hand.
Here, friend, 's another purse; in it a jewel
Well worth a poor man's taking. Fairies and gods
30   Prosper it[3] with thee! Go thou farther off;
Bid me farewell, and let me hear thee going.

---

1. This information, but possibly another letter or token.
2. *desire . . . to her*: tell her to come to her senses.
4.6 Location: Near Dover.
1. The air between cliff and sea.

2. I would not jump up and down (for fear of losing my balance).
3. Make it increase. Fairies were sometimes held to hoard and multiply treasure.

EDGAR   Now fare you well, good sir.

GLOUCESTER   With all my heart.

EDGAR (*aside*)   Why I do trifle thus with his despair
    Is done to cure it.

GLOUCESTER (*kneeling*)   O you mighty gods!

35   This world I do renounce, and, in your sights,
    Shake patiently my great affliction off.
    If I could bear it longer, and not fall
    To quarrel° with your great opposeless wills,   *Into conflict*
    My snuff and loathéd part of nature[4] should

40   Burn itself out. If Edgar live, O, bless him!
    Now, fellow, fare thee well.

           He falls forward and swoons

EDGAR   Gone, sir; farewell.—
    And yet I know not how conceit may rob
    The treasury of life, when life itself
    Yields to the theft.[5] Had he been where he thought,

45   By this° had thought been past. Alive or dead?   *now*
    Ho, you sir! friend! Hear you, sir? speak!
    Thus might he pass° indeed. Yet he revives.   *pass away*
    What are you, sir?

GLOUCESTER   Away, and let me die.

EDGAR   Hadst thou been aught° but gossamer, feathers, air,   *anything*

50   So many fathom down precipitating,°   *plunging*
    Thou'dst shivered° like an egg; but thou dost breathe;   *shattered*
    Hast heavy substance; bleed'st not; speak'st; art sound.
    Ten masts at each° make not the altitude   *end to end*
    Which thou hast perpendicularly fell.

55   Thy life's a miracle. Speak yet again.

GLOUCESTER   But have I fallen, or no?

EDGAR   From the dread summit of this chalky bourn.[6]
    Look up a-height; the shrill-gorged° lark so far   *shrill-throated*
    Cannot be seen or heard. Do but look up.

60 GLOUCESTER   Alack, I have no eyes.
    Is wretchedness deprived° that benefit,   *deprived of*
    To end itself by death? 'Twas yet some comfort,
    When misery could beguile° the tyrant's rage,   *cheat*
    And frustrate his proud will.

EDGAR   Give me your arm.

65   Up—so. How is 't? Feel you your legs? You stand.

GLOUCESTER   Too well, too well.

EDGAR   This is above all strangeness.
    Upon the crown o' the cliff, what thing was that
    Which parted from you?

GLOUCESTER   A poor unfortunate beggar.

EDGAR   As I stood here below, methought his eyes

70   Were two full moons; he had a thousand noses,
    Horns whelked° and waved like the enridgéd sea: *twisted*
    It was some fiend. Therefore, thou happy father,°   *lucky old man*
    Think that the clearest° gods, who make them honors   *purest; most illustrious*
    Of men's impossibilities,[7] have preserved thee.

4. The scorched and hateful remnant of my lifetime. *snuff*: end of a candle wick.
5. *And yet . . . theft*: Edgar worries that the imagined scenario ("conceit") he has invented may be enough to kill his father, particularly as Gloucester wishes for ("yields to") his own death.
6. The white chalk cliffs of Dover, which make a boundary ("bourn") between land and sea.
7. *who . . . impossibilities*: who attain honor for themselves by performing deeds impossible to men.

75 GLOUCESTER I do remember now. Henceforth I'll bear
 Affliction till it do cry out itself
 "Enough, enough," and die. That thing you speak of,
 I took it for a man; often 't would say
 "The fiend, the fiend"—he led me to that place.

80 EDGAR Bear free and patient thoughts. But who comes here?
   Enter LEAR, *fantastically dressed with wild flowers*
 The safer sense will ne'er accommodate
 His master thus.[8]

LEAR No, they cannot touch me for coining;[9] I am the king
 himself.

85 EDGAR O thou side-piercing sight!

LEAR Nature's above art in that respect.[1] There's your press-
 money.[2] That fellow handles his bow like a crow-keeper.[3] Draw
 me a clothier's yard.[4] Look, look, a mouse! Peace, peace; this
 piece of toasted cheese will do 't.° There's my gauntlet; I'll   *(lure the mouse)*
90 prove it on a giant.[5] Bring up the brown bills.[6] O, well flown,
 bird!° i' the clout,° i' the clout. Hewgh! Give the word.°   *arrow / bull's-eye / password*

EDGAR Sweet marjoram.[7]

LEAR Pass.

GLOUCESTER I know that voice.

95 LEAR Ha! Goneril, with a white beard! They flattered me like a
 dog;° and told me I had white hairs in my beard ere the black   *fawningly*
 ones were there.[8] To say "aye" and "no" to everything that I
 said!—"Aye" and "no" too was no good divinity.[9] When the
 rain came to wet me once, and the wind to make me chatter;
100 when the thunder would not peace at my bidding; there I
 found° 'em, there I smelt 'em out. Go to, they are not men o'   *understood*
 their words! They told me I was everything. 'Tis a lie, I am not
 ague-proof.°   *immune to illness*

GLOUCESTER The trick° of that voice I do well remember.   *peculiarity*
 Is 't not the king?

105 LEAR   Aye, every inch a king!
 When I do stare, see how the subject quakes.
 I pardon that man's life. What was thy cause?°   *crime*
 Adultery?
 Thou shalt not die. Die for adultery? No.
110 The wren goes to 't, and the small gilded fly
 Does lecher in my sight.
 Let copulation thrive; for Gloucester's bastard son
 Was kinder to his father than my daughters
 Got 'tween the lawful sheets. To 't luxury,° pell-mell!   *lechery*
115 For I lack soldiers. Behold yond simpering dame,
 Whose face between her forks presages snow;[1]

---

8. *The . . . thus:* A sane mind would never allow its possessor to dress up this way.
9. Because minting money was the prerogative of the king, nobody could overtake or equal ("touch") him.
1. My true feelings will always outvalue others' hypocrisy; my natural supremacy surpasses any attempt to create a false new reign. This image may also be based on coining (see note 9 above).
2. Fee paid to a soldier impressed, or forced, into the army.
3. A person hired as a scarecrow, and thus unfit for anything else.
4. Draw the bowstring the full length of the arrow (a standard English arrow was a cloth yard [thirty-seven inches]

long).
5. I'll defend my stand even against a giant. To throw down an armored glove ("gauntlet") was to issue a challenge.
6. Brown painted pikes; or, the soldiers carrying them.
7. Used medicinally against madness.
8. Told me I had wisdom before age.
9. *no good divinity:* poor theology (because insincere); from James 5:12, "Let your yea be yea; nay, nay."
1. Whose expression implies cold chastity. "Face" refers to the area between her legs ("forks"), as well as to her literal facial expression as framed by the aristocratic lady's starched headpiece, also called a "fork."

That minces° virtue, and does shake the head   *affects*
To hear of° pleasure's name;   *even of*
The fitchew, nor the soiléd horse,[2] goes to 't
120 With a more riotous appetite.
Down from the waist they are Centaurs,[3]
Though women all above.
But° to the girdle° do the gods inherit.°   *Only / waist / own*
Beneath is all the fiends'; there's hell,[4] there's darkness,
125 There's the sulphurous pit, burning, scalding,
Stench, consumption! Fie, fie, fie! pah! pah!
Give me an ounce of civet,[5] good apothecary,
To sweeten my imagination.
There's money for thee.
130 GLOUCESTER   O, let me kiss that hand!
LEAR   Let me wipe it first; it smells of mortality.
GLOUCESTER   O ruined piece° of nature! This great world   *masterpiece*
Shall so wear out to nought.[6] Dost thou know me?
LEAR   I remember thine eyes well enough. Dost thou squiny° at   *squint*
135 me? No, do thy worst, blind Cupid; I'll not love. Read thou this
challenge; mark but the penning of it.
GLOUCESTER   Were all the letters suns, I could not see one.
EDGAR (*aside*)   I would not take° this from report. It is,   *believe*
And my heart breaks at it.
140 LEAR   Read.
GLOUCESTER   What, with the case° of eyes?   *socket*
LEAR   O, ho, are you there with me?[7] No eyes in your head, nor
no money in your purse? Your eyes are in a heavy case,[8] your
purse in a light. Yet you see how this world goes.
145 GLOUCESTER   I see it feelingly.°   *by touch; painfully*
LEAR   What, art mad? A man may see how this world goes with
no eyes. Look with thine ears. See how yond justice rails upon
yond simple° thief. Hark, in thine ear. Change places and,   *lowly; innocent*
handy-dandy,[9] which is the justice, which is the thief? Thou
150 hast seen a farmer's dog bark at a beggar?
GLOUCESTER   Aye, sir.
LEAR   And the creature° run from the cur? There thou mightst   *wretch*
behold the great image of authority: a dog's obeyed in office.
Thou rascal beadle,[1] hold° thy bloody hand!   *restrain*
155 Why dost thou lash that whore? Strip thine own back;
Thou hotly lusts to use her in that kind°   *way*
For which thou whipp'st her. The usurer hangs the cozener.[2]
Through tattered clothes small vices do appear;
Robes and furred gowns hide all. Plate° sin with gold,   *Armor; gild*
160 And the strong lance of justice hurtless° breaks;   *harmlessly*
Arm it in rags, a pigmy's straw does pierce it.
None does offend, none, I say, none; I'll able° 'em;   *authorize*
Take that of me, my friend, who have the power
To seal the accuser's lips. Get thee glass eyes;

2. Neither the polecat nor a horse full of fresh grass.
3. Lecherous mythological creatures that have a human body to the waist and the legs and torso of a horse below.
4. Shakespeare's frequent term for female genitals.
5. Exotic perfume derived from the sex glands of the civet cat.
6. Shall decay to nothing in the same way. In Renaissance philosophy, humans were perfectly analogous to the cosmos, standing for the whole in miniature and as its masterpiece.
7. Is that what you are telling me?
8. In a sad condition; playing on "case" as "sockets."
9. Pick a hand, as in a child's game.
1. The parish officer responsible for whippings.
2. The ruinous moneylender, prosperous enough to be made a judge, convicts the ordinary cheat.

165   And, like a scurvy politician,[3] seem
        To see the things thou dost not. Now, now, now, now!
        Pull off my boots. Harder, harder! So.
      EDGAR   O, matter and impertinency° mixed!   *sense and nonsense*
        Reason in madness!
170   LEAR   If thou wilt weep my fortunes, take my eyes.
        I know thee well enough; thy name is Gloucester:
        Thou must be patient. We came crying hither;
        Thou know'st, the first time that we smell the air,
        We wail and cry. I will preach to thee. Mark.
             LEAR *takes off his crown of weeds and flowers*[4]
175   GLOUCESTER   Alack, alack the day!
      LEAR   When we are born, we cry that we are come
        To this great stage of fools. This'° a good block;[5]   *This is*
        It were a delicate° stratagem, to shoe   *subtle*
        A troop of horse with felt.[6] I'll put 't in proof;°   *to the test*
180   And when I have stol'n upon these sons-in-law,
        Then, kill, kill, kill, kill, kill, kill!
            Enter a GENTLEMAN, *with attendants*
    GENTLEMAN   O, here he is; lay hand upon him. Sir,
        Your most dear daughter—
      LEAR   No rescue? What, a prisoner? I am even
185   The natural fool[7] of fortune. Use° me well;   *Treat*
        You shall have ransom. Let me have surgeons;
        I am cut to the brains.
    GENTLEMAN   You shall have any thing.
      LEAR   No seconds?° all myself?   *supporters*
        Why, this would make a man a man of salt,[8]
190   To use his eyes for garden water-pots,
        Aye, and laying° autumn's dust.   *settling*
    GENTLEMAN   Good sir—
      LEAR   I will die bravely,[9] like a smug° bridegroom. What!   *an elegant*
        I will be jovial. Come, come; I am a king,
        My masters, know you that?
195   GENTLEMAN   You are a royal one, and we obey you.
      LEAR   Then there's life° in't. Nay, if you get it, you shall get it   *hope*
        with running. Sa, sa, sa, sa.[1]   (*Exit running; attendants follow*)
    GENTLEMAN   A sight most pitiful in the meanest wretch,
        Past speaking of in a king! Thou hast one daughter,
200   Who redeems nature from the general curse
        Which twain have brought her to.[2]
      EDGAR   Hail, gentle° sir.   *noble*
    GENTLEMAN   Sir, speed you.° What's your will?   *God speed you*
      EDGAR   Do you hear aught, sir, of a battle toward?°   *coming*
    GENTLEMAN   Most sure and vulgar.° Everyone hears that,   *commonly known*
        Which° can distinguish sound.   *Who*

---

3. A vile schemer. In early modern England, "politician" meant an ambitious, even Machiavellian, upstart.
4. Like a preacher, removing his hat in the pulpit.
5. Stage (often called "scaffold" and hence linked to executioner's block); block used to shape a felt hat (such as the hat removed by a preacher before a sermon); mounting block (such as the stump or stock Lear may have sat on to remove his boots).
6. Hat material, to muffle the sound of the approaching cavalry.
7. Born plaything; playing on "natural" as "mentally

deficient."
8. A man reduced to nothing but the salt his tears deposit.
9. With courage; showily. "Die" plays on the Renaissance sense of "have an orgasm."
1. A cry to encourage dogs in the hunt.
2. *Who . . . to:* Who restores proper meaning and order to a universe plagued by the crimes of the other two daughters; alluding to the fall of humankind and the natural world caused by the sin of Adam and Eve and to the universal redemption brought about by Christ's sacrifice.

205 EDGAR   But, by your favor,
How near's the other army?
GENTLEMAN   Near and on speedy foot. The main descry°   *appearance*
Stands on the hourly thought.°   *Is expected forthwith*
EDGAR   I thank you, sir. That's all.
210 GENTLEMAN   Though that the queen on° special cause° is here,   *for / reason*
Her army is moved on.
EDGAR   I thank you, sir.   *Exit* GENTLEMAN
GLOUCESTER   You ever-gentle gods, take my breath from me;
Let not my worser spirit[3] tempt me again
To die before you please!
EDGAR   Well pray you, father.[4]
215 GLOUCESTER   Now, good sir, what are you?
EDGAR   A most poor man, made tame to fortune's blows;
Who, by the art of known and feeling° sorrows,   *profound*
Am pregnant to° good pity. Give me your hand,   *disposed to feel*
I'll lead you to some biding.°   *resting place*
GLOUCESTER   Hearty thanks.
220 The bounty and the benison of heaven
To boot, and boot!°   *As well, what's more*
       Enter OSWALD
OSWALD   A proclaimed prize![5] Most happy!°   *lucky*
That eyeless head of thine was first framed° flesh   *made of*
To raise my fortunes. Thou old unhappy traitor,
225 Briefly thyself remember.[6] The sword is out
That must destroy thee.
GLOUCESTER   Now let thy friendly hand
Put strength enough to 't.
      EDGAR *interposes*
OSWALD   Wherefore, bold peasant.
Darest thou support a published° traitor? Hence,   *proclaimed*
Lest that the infection° of his fortune take   *(deathly) sickness*
230 Like° hold on thee. Let go his arm.   *The same*
EDGAR   Chill[7] not let go, zir, without vurther 'casion.°   *further occasion*
OSWALD   Let go, slave, or thou diest!
EDGAR   Good gentleman, go your gait,° and let poor volk pass.   *walk on*
An chud ha'° bin zwaggered out of my life, 't would not ha' bin   *If I could have*
235 zo long as 'tis by a vortnight. Nay, come not near th' old man;
keep out, che vor ye, or ise try whether your costard or my
ballow be the harder.[8] Chill be plain with you.
OSWALD   Out, dunghill!
EDGAR   Chill pick your teeth, zir. Come! No matter vor your
240 foins.°   *sword thrusts*
     They fight, and EDGAR *knocks him down*
OSWALD   Slave, thou hast slain me. Villain, take my purse.
If ever thou wilt thrive, bury my body;
And give the letters which thou find'st about me
To Edmund earl of Gloucester. Seek him out
245 Upon° the British party. O, untimely death!   *Within*
Death!   *He dies*

---

3. Wicked inclination; bad angel.
4. A term of respect for an elderly man.
5. A wanted man, with a bounty on his life.
6. Recollect and pray forgiveness for your sins.
7. I will; dialect from Somerset was a stage convention
for peasant dialogue.
8. *che vor ye . . . harder:* I warrant you, or I shall test whether your head or my cudgel is harder. *costard:* a kind of apple.

EDGAR   I know thee well: a serviceable° villain;   *an officious*
As duteous to the vices of thy mistress
As badness would desire.

GLOUCESTER   What, is he dead?

250 EDGAR   Sit you down, father; rest you.
Let's see his pockets; the letters that he speaks of
May be my friends. He's dead; I am only sorry
He had no other death'sman.° Let us see.   *executioner*
Leave,° gentle wax;⁹ and, manners blame us not.   *By your leave*
255 To know our enemies' minds, we'd rip their hearts;
Their° papers, is more lawful.   *To rip their*
(*Reads*) "Let our reciprocal vows be remembered. You have
many opportunities to cut him off. If your will want° not, time   *lacks*
and place will be fruitfully offered. There is nothing done,° if   *accomplished*
260 he return the conqueror. Then am I the prisoner, and his bed
my jail; from the loathed warmth whereof deliver me, and sup-
ply° the place for your labor.¹   *fill*

Your—wife, so I would say—
Affectionate servant,
265   Goneril."

O undistinguished space of woman's will!²
A plot upon her virtuous husband's life;
And the exchange° my brother! Here, in the sands,   *substitute*
Thee I'll rake up,° the post unsanctified°   *cover up / unholy messenger*
270 Of murderous lechers; and in the mature time°   *when the time is ripe*
With this ungracious° paper strike the sight   *ungodly*
Of the death-practiced duke.³ For him 'tis well
That of thy death and business I can tell.

GLOUCESTER   The king is mad. How stiff is my vile sense,⁴
275 That I stand up, and have ingenious feeling⁵
Of my huge sorrows! Better I were distract;°   *mad*
So should my thoughts be severed from my griefs,
And woes by wrong° imaginations lose   *false*
The knowledge of themselves.
                Drum afar off

EDGAR   Give me your hand.
280 Far off, methinks, I hear the beaten drum.
Come, father, I'll bestow° you with a friend.   *Exeunt*   *lodge*

4.7

Enter CORDELIA, KENT, DOCTOR, *and a* GENTLEMAN

CORDELIA   O thou good Kent, how shall I live and work,
To match thy goodness? My life will be too short,
And every measure° fail me.   *attempt*

KENT   To be acknowledged, madam, is o'erpaid.°   *is more than enough*
5 All my reports go¹ with the modest truth;
Nor more nor clipped, but so.²

CORDELIA   Be better suited.°   *attired*
These weeds° are memories of those worser hours.   *clothes*
I prithee, put them off.

---

9. The wax seal on the letter.
1. *for your labor:* as a reward for your endeavors, and for
further sexual exertion.
2. Limitless extent of woman's wilfullness. As with "hell"
in line 124, "will" might also refer to a woman's genitals.
3. Of the Duke whose death is plotted.
4. How obstinate is my unwanted power of reason.

5. That I remain upright and firm in my sanity and have
rational perceptions.
4.7 Location: The French camp at Dover.
1. May all accounts of me agree.
2. Not greater or less, but exactly the modest amount I
deserve.

KENT   Pardon me, dear madam;
    Yet to be known shortens my made intent.[3]
10 My boon I make it,[4] that you know° me not   *acknowledge*
    Till time and I think meet.°   *suitable*
CORDELIA   Then be 't so, my good lord. (*To the* DOCTOR) How
    does the king?
DOCTOR   Madam, sleeps still.
CORDELIA   O you kind gods,
15 Cure this great breach in his abuséd nature!
    The untuned and jarring senses, O, wind up[5]
    Of this child-changéd[6] father!
DOCTOR   So please your majesty
    That we may wake the king? He hath slept long.
CORDELIA   Be governed by your knowledge, and proceed
20 I' the sway° of your own will. Is he arrayed?°   *By the authority / clothed*
    Enter LEAR *in a chair carried by servants*
GENTLEMAN   Aye, madam. In the heaviness of his sleep
    We put fresh garments on him.
DOCTOR   Be by, good madam, when we do awake him;
    I doubt not of his temperance.°   *calmness*
CORDELIA   Very well.
    Music
25 DOCTOR   Please you, draw near. Louder the music there!
CORDELIA   O my dear father! Restoration hang
    Thy medicine on my lips; and let this kiss
    Repair those violent harms that my two sisters
    Have in thy reverence° made!   *aged dignity*
KENT   Kind and dear princess!
30 CORDELIA   Had you not[7] been their father, these white flakes°   *locks of hair*
    Had challenged° pity of them. Was this a face   *Would have provoked*
    To be opposed against the warring winds?
    To stand against the deep dread-bolted thunder?
    In the most terrible and nimble stroke
35 Of quick, cross lightning? to watch°—poor perdu![8]—   *to stand guard*
    With this thin helm?° Mine enemy's dog,   *helmet (of hair)*
    Though he had bit me, should have stood that night
    Against my fire; and wast thou fain,° poor father,   *glad*
    To hovel thee with swine, and rogues forlorn,
40 In short° and musty straw? Alack, alack!   *scant; broken*
    'Tis wonder that thy life and wits at once
    Had not concluded all.° He wakes; speak to him.   *altogether*
DOCTOR   Madam, do you; 'tis fittest.
CORDELIA   How does my royal lord? How fares your majesty?
45 LEAR   You do me wrong to take me out o' the grave.
    Thou art a soul in bliss; but I am bound
    Upon a wheel of fire, that mine own tears
    Do scald like molten lead.[9]
CORDELIA   Sir, do you know me?
LEAR   You are a spirit, I know. When did you die?
50 CORDELIA   Still, still, far wide!°   *unbalanced*

3. Revealing myself now would abort my designs.
4. The reward I beg is.
5. *The . . . up*: Reorder his confused and delirious mind.
The image is of tightening the strings of a lute.
6. Changed by his children; changed into a child; playing on a musical key change.

7. Even if you had not.
8. Lost one; in military terms, a dangerously exposed
sentry.
9. *but I . . . lead*: Lear puts himself in either hell or purgatory, both places of such punishment in medieval
accounts.

DOCTOR   He's scarce awake. Let him alone awhile.
LEAR   Where have I been? Where am I? Fair daylight?
　I am mightily abused.° I should e'en die with pity,   *wronged; deceived*
　To see another thus. I know not what to say.
55　I will not swear these are my hands. Let's see.
　I feel this pin prick. Would I were assured
　Of my condition!
CORDELIA　　　　　O, look upon me, sir,
　And hold your hands in benediction o'er me:
　No, sir, you must not kneel.
60　LEAR   Pray, do not mock me.
　I am a very foolish fond° old man,   *silly*
　Fourscore and upward, not an hour more nor less;
　And, to deal plainly,
　I fear I am not in my perfect mind.
65　Methinks I should know you, and know this man;
　Yet I am doubtful; for I am mainly° ignorant   *entirely*
　What place this is; and all the skill I have
　Remembers not these garments; nor I know not
　Where I did lodge last night. Do not laugh at me;
70　For, as I am a man, I think this lady
　To be my child Cordelia.
CORDELIA　　　　　　And so I am, I am.
LEAR   Be your tears wet?[1] Yes, faith. I pray, weep not.
　If you have poison for me, I will drink it.
　I know you do not love me; for your sisters
75　Have, as I do remember, done me wrong.
　You have some cause, they have not.
CORDELIA　　　　　　　　No cause, no, cause.
LEAR   Am I in France?
KENT　　　　　In your own kingdom, sir.
LEAR   Do not abuse° me.   *deceive; mock*
DOCTOR   Be comforted, good madam. The great rage,
80　You see, is killed in him; and yet it is danger
　To make him even o'er° the time he has lost.   *go over*
　Desire him to go in. Trouble him no more
　Till further settling.°   *Until his mind eases*
CORDELIA   Will't please your highness walk?
LEAR　　　　　　　You must bear with me:
85　Pray you now, forget and forgive. I am old and foolish.
　　　　　　　Exeunt all but KENT *and* GENTLEMAN
GENTLEMAN   Holds it true, sir, that the Duke of Cornwall was so
　slain?
KENT   Most certain, sir.
GENTLEMAN   Who is conductor° of his people?   *commander*
90　KENT   As 'tis said, the bastard son of Gloucester.
GENTLEMAN   They say Edgar, his banished son, is with the Earl
　of Kent in Germany.
KENT   Report° is changeable. 'Tis time to look about.° The pow-   *Rumor / prepare defenses*
　ers of the kingdom approach apace.
95　GENTLEMAN   The arbitrement° is like to be bloody. Fare you   *encounter*
　well, sir.　　　　　　　　　　　　　　　　　*Exit*
KENT   My point and period[2] will be throughly wrought,
　Or° well or ill, as this day's battle's fought.　　*Exit*   *For*

---

1. Are your tears real?; is this really happening?　　2. The purpose and end of my life; literally, the full stop.

5.1

Enter, with drum and colors, EDMUND, REGAN, GENTLE-
MAN, *and soldiers*

EDMUND Know° of the duke if his last purpose hold,[1]   *Inquire*
Or whether since he is advised by aught[2]
To change the course. He's full of alteration°   *indecision*
And self-reproving. Bring his constant pleasure.°   *his settled intent*
          To a GENTLEMAN, *who goes out*

5 REGAN Our sister's man is certainly miscarried.[3]
EDMUND 'Tis to be doubted,° madam.   *feared*
REGAN   Now, sweet lord,
You know the goodness I intend upon you.
Tell me—but truly—but then speak the truth,
Do you not love my sister?
EDMUND   In honored° love.   *honorable*
10 REGAN But have you never found my brother's way
To the forfended[4] place?
EDMUND   That thought abuses° you.   *deceives*
REGAN I am doubtful that you have been conjunct°   *complicit*
And bosomed with° her, as far as we call hers.[5]   *enamored of*
EDMUND No, by mine honor, madam.
15 REGAN I never shall endure her. Dear my lord,
Be not familiar° with her.   *intimate*
EDMUND   Fear° me not.   *Doubt*
She and the duke her husband!
          Enter, with drum and colors, ALBANY, GONERIL, *and*
          soldiers
GONERIL (*aside*) I had rather lose the battle than that sister
Should loosen° him and me.   *disunite*
20 ALBANY Our very loving sister, well be-met.
Sir, this I hear: the king is come to his daughter,
With others whom the rigor° of our state°   *harshness / government*
Forced to cry out. Where I could not be honest,°   *honorable*
I never yet was valiant. For this business,
25 It toucheth° us, as France invades our land,   *concerns*
Not bolds the king, with others, whom, I fear,
Most just and heavy causes make oppose.[6]
EDMUND Sir, you speak nobly.
REGAN   Why is this reasoned?[7]
GONERIL Combine together 'gainst the enemy;
30 For these domestic and particular broils°   *minor details*
Are not the question here.
ALBANY   Let's then determine
With the ancient° of war on our proceeding.   *experienced officer*
EDMUND I shall attend you presently° at your tent.   *in a moment*
REGAN Sister, you'll go with us?[8]
35 GONERIL No.
REGAN 'Tis most convenient;° pray you, go with us.   *suitable*
GONERIL (*aside*) O, ho, I know the riddle.°—I will go.   *disguised meaning*
          As they are going out, enter EDGAR *disguised*

5.1 Location: The British camp near Dover.
1. If his previous intention (to wage war) remains firm.
2. Since then anything has persuaded him.
3. Has surely come to grief by some accident.
4. Forbidden (to Edmund, because it is adulterous).
5. In total intimacy; all the way.
6. *It . . . oppose:* This is of concern to us because France

lands on our soil, not because it emboldens the King and
others, who, I am afraid, have been provoked for good
and solid reasons.
7. What is the point of this kind of speech?
8. Regan wants Goneril to go with Albany and her, rather
than with Edmund.

EDGAR   If e'er your grace had speech with man so poor,
Hear me one word.
ALBANY   I'll overtake you. Speak.
                              Exeunt all but ALBANY *and* EDGAR
40   EDGAR   Before you fight the battle, ope this letter.
If you have victory, let the trumpet sound
For him that brought it. Wretched though I seem,
I can produce a champion that will prove°   defend
What is avouched° there. If you miscarry,°   maintained / perish
45   Your business of the world hath so an end,
And machination° ceases. Fortune love you!   plotting
ALBANY   Stay till I have read the letter.
EDGAR   I was forbid it.
When time shall serve, let but the herald cry,
And I'll appear again.
50   ALBANY   Why, fare thee well. I will o'erlook thy paper.
                                             Exit EDGAR
        Re-enter EDMUND
EDMUND   The enemy 's in view; draw up your powers.°   troops
Here is the guess° of their true strength and forces   estimate
By diligent discovery;° but your haste   spying
Is now urged on you.
ALBANY   We will greet the time.[9]   *Exit*
55   EDMUND   To both these sisters have I sworn my love;
Each jealous° of the other, as the stung   suspicious
Are of the adder. Which of them shall I take?
Both? one? or neither? Neither can be enjoyed,
If both remain alive. To take the widow
60   Exasperates, makes mad her sister Goneril;
And hardly° shall I carry out my side,°   with difficulty / plan
Her husband being alive. Now then we'll use
His countenance[1] for the battle; which being done,
Let her who would be rid of him devise
65   His speedy taking off. As for the mercy
Which he intends to Lear and to Cordelia,
The battle done, and they within our power,
Shall° never see his pardon; for my state°   They shall / condition
Stands on° me to defend, not to debate.   *Exit*   Obliges

5.2

        Alarum within.[1] *Enter, with drum and colors,* LEAR, COR-
        DELIA, *and soldiers, over the stage; and exeunt*
        Enter EDGAR *and* GLOUCESTER
EDGAR   Here, father,[2] take the shadow of this tree
For your good host;° pray that the right may thrive: shelter
If ever I return to you again,
I'll bring you comfort.
GLOUCESTER   Grace go with you, sir!   *Exit* EDGAR
        Alarum and retreat° within. Re-enter EDGAR   trumpet signal
5   EDGAR   Away, old man! give me thy hand! away!

---

9. We will be ready to meet the occasion.
1. Authority or backing; also suggesting "face," to be used
like a mask for Edmund's ambition.
5.2 Location: The rest of the play takes place near the

battlefield.
1. Trumpet call to battle (backstage).
2. See note to 4.6.214.

King Lear hath lost, he and his daughter ta'en.
Give me thy hand! come on!
GLOUCESTER   No farther, sir; a man may rot even° here.   *right*
EDGAR   What, in ill thoughts again? Men must endure
10   Their going hence, even as their coming hither;
Ripeness is all.[3] Come on!
GLOUCESTER   And that's true, too.   *Exeunt*

5.3

Enter, in conquest, with drum and colors, EDMUND;
LEAR *and* CORDELIA, *prisoners;* CAPTAIN, *soldiers,* & C.
EDMUND   Some officers take them away. Good guard,
Until their greater pleasures[1] first be known
That are to censure° them.   *judge*
CORDELIA   We are not the first
Who, with best meaning,° have incurred the worst.   *intention*
5   For thee, oppresséd king, am I cast down;°   *(into unhappiness)*
Myself could else out-frown false Fortune's frown.[2]
Shall we not see these daughters and these sisters?
LEAR   No, no, no, no! Come, let's away to prison.
We two alone will sing like birds i' the cage.
10   When thou dost ask me blessing, I'll kneel down,
And ask of thee forgiveness. So we'll live,
And pray, and sing, and tell old tales, and laugh
At gilded butterflies,[3] and hear poor rogues
Talk of court news; and we'll talk with them too,
15   Who loses and who wins; who 's in, and who 's out;
And take upon 's the mystery of things,
As if we were Gods' spies; and we'll wear out,°   *outlast*
In a walled prison, packs and sects of great ones,
That ebb and flow by the moon.[4]
EDMUND   Take them away.
20   LEAR   Upon such sacrifices,[5] my Cordelia,
The gods themselves throw incense. Have I caught thee?
He that parts us shall bring a brand from heavens,
And fire us hence like foxes.[6] Wipe thine eyes;
The good-years shall devour them, flesh and fell,[7]
25   Ere they shall make us weep! We'll see 'em starved first.
Come.   *Exeunt* LEAR *and* CORDELIA, *guarded*
EDMUND   Come hither, captain; hark.
Take thou this note (*giving a paper*). Go follow them to prison:
One step I have advanced° thee. If thou dost   *promoted*
30   As this instructs thee, thou dost make thy way
To noble fortunes. Know thou this, that men
Are as the time is. To be tender-minded
Does not become a sword.° Thy great employment   *befit a swordsman*

---

3. To await the destined time is the most important thing, as fruit falls only when ripe (playing on Gloucester's "rot," line 8); readiness for death is our only duty (compare *Hamlet* 5.2.160, "The readiness is all").
5.3
1. *Good . . . pleasures:* Guard them well until the desires of those greater persons.
2. Otherwise, I could be defiant in the face of bad fortune.
3. Gaudy and ephemeral courtiers; trivial matters.

4. *packs . . . moon:* followers and factions of important people whose positions at court vary as the tide.
5. Upon such sacrifices as we are, or as you have made.
6. *shall . . . foxes:* must have divine aid to do so. The image is of using a torch to smoke foxes out of their holes, or, in the case of Lear and Cordelia, prison cells.
7. *flesh and fell:* meat and skin; entirely. The precise meaning of "good-years" has not been explained; it may signify simply the passage of time or may suggest some ominous, destructive power.

Will not bear question.° Either say thou'lt do 't,   *discussion*
Or thrive by other means.
35 CAPTAIN   I'll do 't, my lord.
EDMUND   About it; and write happy when thou hast done.[8]
    Mark, I say, instantly; and carry it° so   *carry it out*
    As I have set it down.
CAPTAIN   I cannot draw a cart, nor eat dried oats;°   *(like a horse)*
40   If it be a man's work, I'll do it.   *Exit*
       Flourish. Enter ALBANY, GONERIL, REGAN, *another* CAP-
       TAIN, *and soldiers*
ALBANY   Sir, you have showed today your valiant strain,°   *qualities; birth*
    And fortune led you well. You have the captives
    That were the opposites° of this day's strife.   *opponents*
    I do require them of you, so to use° them   *treat*
45   As we shall find their merits and our safety
    May equally determine.
EDMUND   Sir, I thought it fit
    To send the old and miserable king
    To some retention° and appointed guard;   *confinement*
    Whose° age has charms in it, whose title more,   *(Lear's)*
50   To pluck the common bosom[9] on his side,
    And turn our impressed lances° in our eyes   *conscripted lancers*
    Which[1] do command them. With him I sent the queen;
    My reason all the same; and they are ready
    Tomorrow, or at further space,° t' appear   *at a future point*
55   Where you shall hold your session.° At this time   *court of judgment*
    We sweat and bleed; the friend hath lost his friend;
    And the best quarrels, in the heat, are cursed
    By those that feel their sharpness.[2]
    The question of Cordelia and her father
    Requires a fitter place.
60 ALBANY   Sir, by your patience,
    I hold you but a subject of° this war,   *in waging*
    Not as a brother.
REGAN   That's as we list° to grace him.   *like*
    Methinks our pleasure might have been demanded,[3]
    Ere you had spoken so far. He led our powers;°   *armies*
65   Bore the commission of my place and person;
    The which immediacy° may well stand up,   *close connection*
    And call itself your brother.
GONERIL   Not so hot!°   *Not so fast*
    In his own grace° he doth exalt himself,   *merit*
    More than in your addition.[4]
REGAN   In my rights,
70   By me invested, he compeers° the best.   *equals*
GONERIL   That were the most,[5] if he should husband you.
REGAN   Jesters do oft prove prophets.
GONERIL   Holla, holla!
    That eye that told you so looked but a-squint.[6]

---

8. Go to it, and call yourself happy when you are done.
9. To garner the affection of the populace.
1. *in our eyes / Which:* in the eyes of us who.
2. *And . . . sharpness:* And in the heat of battle, even the most just wars are cursed by those who must suffer the fighting.

3. I think you should have inquired into my wishes.
4. In the honors you confer upon him.
5. That investiture would be complete.
6. Squinting was a proverbial effect of jealousy, because of the tendency to look suspiciously at potential rivals.

REGAN   Lady, I am not well; else I should answer

75   From a full-flowing stomach.° General,   *anger*
      Take thou my soldiers, prisoners, patrimony:
      Dispose of them, of me; the walls° are thine.   *fortress of my heart*
      Witness the world, that I create thee here
      My lord and master.
GONERIL   Mean you to enjoy him?
80 ALBANY   The let-alone° lies not in your good will.   *veto*
EDMUND   Nor in thine, lord.
ALBANY   Half-blooded° fellow, yes.   *Bastard*
REGAN (*to* EDMUND)   Let the drum strike,[7] and prove my title thine.
ALBANY   Stay yet; hear reason. Edmund, I arrest thee
      On capital treason; and, in thine attaint,[8]
      This gilded serpent (*pointing to* GONERIL). For your claim, fair
85   sister,°   *sister-in-law*
      I bar it in the interest of my wife;
      'Tis she is sub-contracted to this lord,
      And I, her husband, contradict your banes.°   *announcement of marriage*
      If you will marry, make your loves to me,
      My lady is bespoke.
90 GONERIL   An interlude!°   *A farce*
ALBANY   Thou art armed, Gloucester. Let the trumpet sound.
      If none appear to prove upon thy head
      Thy heinous, manifest, and many treasons,
      There is my pledge (*throwing down a glove*); I'll prove it on thy heart,
95   Ere I taste bread, thou art in nothing less°   *in no way less guilty*
      Than I have proclaimed thee.
REGAN   Sick, O, sick!
GONERIL (*aside*)   If not, I'll ne'er trust medicine.°   *poison (euphemistic)*
EDMUND   There 's my exchange (*throwing down a glove*). What°   *Whoever*
          in the world he is
      That names me traitor, villain-like he lies.
100   Call by thy trumpet. He that dares approach,
      On him, on you, who not? I will maintain
      My truth and honor firmly.
ALBANY   A herald, ho!
EDMUND   A herald, ho, a herald!
ALBANY   Trust to thy single virtue;° for thy soldiers,   *your unassisted power*
105   All levied in my name, have in my name
      Took their discharge.
REGAN   My sickness grows upon me.
ALBANY   She is not well; convey her to my tent.   *Exit* REGAN, *led*
                Enter a HERALD
      Come hither, herald—Let the trumpet sound—
      And read out this.
CAPTAIN   Sound, trumpet! (*A trumpet sounds*)
110 HERALD [*reads*]   "If any man of quality or degree within the lists
      of the army will maintain upon Edmund, supposed Earl of
      Gloucester, that he is a manifold traitor, let him appear by the
      third sound of the trumpet. He is bold in his defense."
EDMUND   Sound! (*First trumpet*)
115 HERALD   Again! (*Second trumpet*)

---

7. Perhaps to announce the betrothal, or a challenge.
8. And in order to accuse you; and as one who shares your corruption or crime.

HERALD Again! (*Third trumpet*)
Trumpet answers within
Enter EDGAR, *at the third sound, armed, with a trumpet*
before him
ALBANY Ask him his purposes, why he appears
Upon this call o' the trumpet.
HERALD   What° are you?   *Who*
Your name, your quality?° and why you answer   *degree, rank*
This present summons?
120 EDGAR   Know, my name is lost;
By treason's tooth bare-gnawn and canker-bit.°   *worm-eaten*
Yet am I noble as the adversary
I come to cope.°   *to encounter*
ALBANY   Which is that adversary?
EDGAR What's he that speaks for Edmund Earl of Gloucester?
EDMUND Himself. What say'st thou to him?
125 EDGAR   Draw thy sword,
That,° if my speech offend a noble heart,   *So that*
Thy arm may do thee justice. Here is mine.
Behold, it is the privilege of mine honors,
My oath, and my profession. I protest,
130 Maugre° thy strength, youth, place, and eminence,   *Despite*
Despite thy victor sword and fire-new° fortune,   *newly minted*
Thy valor and thy heart,° thou art a traitor;   *courage*
False to thy gods, thy brother, and thy father;
Conspirant 'gainst this high-illustrious prince;
135 And, from the extremest upward° of thy head   *top*
To the descent° and dust below thy foot,   *lowest part; sole*
A most toad-spotted⁹ traitor. Say thou "No,"
This sword, this arm, and my best spirits, are bent°   *ready*
To prove upon thy heart, whereto I speak,
Thou liest.
140 EDMUND   In wisdom I should ask thy name;
But, since thy outside looks so fair and warlike
And that thy tongue some say of breeding breathes,
What safe and nicely I might well delay
By rule of knighthood, I disdain and spurn.¹
145 Back do I toss these treasons to thy head;
With the hell-hated° lie o'erwhelm thy heart;   *hated as much as hell*
Which, for° they yet glance by and scarcely bruise,   *since*
This sword of mine shall give them instant way,°   *access*
Where they shall rest for ever. Trumpets, speak!
Alarums. They fight. EDMUND *falls*
ALBANY Save° him, save him!   *Spare*
150 GONERIL   This is practice,° Gloucester: *trickery*
By the law of arms thou wast not bound to answer
An unknown opposite.° Thou art not vanquished,   *opponent*
But cozened and beguiled.°   *cheated and deceived*
ALBANY   Shut your mouth, dame,
Or with this paper shall I stople° it.   *plug*
155 Thou worse than any name, read thine own evil.
No tearing, lady! I perceive you know it.

---

9. Venomous, like a toad; spotted with disgrace.
1. *And . . . spurn:* And since your speech may suggest high birth, I will not stick safely and meticulously to the rules of knighthood by refusing to fight you.

Gives the letter to EDMUND

GONERIL Say, if I do, the laws are mine, not thine.
　Who can arraign° me for 't?　　　　　　　　　　　　　*prosecute*
ALBANY　　　　　　　　Most monstrous! oh!
　Know'st thou this paper?
GONERIL　　　　　　　Ask me not what I know.　　*Exit*
160　ALBANY　Go after her: she's desperate; govern° her.　　　*restrain*
EDMUND　What you have charged me with, that have I done;
　And more, much more; the time will bring it out.
　'Tis past, and so am I. But what art thou
　That hast this fortune on me?[2] If thou 'rt noble,
　I do forgive thee.
165　EDGAR　　　　　　Let's exchange charity.°　　　　*forgiveness*
　I am no less in blood than thou art, Edmund;
　If more, the more thou hast wronged me.
　My name is Edgar, and thy father's son.
　The gods are just, and of our pleasant vices
170　Make instruments to plague us.
　The dark and vicious place where thee he got[3]
　Cost him his eyes.
EDMUND　　　　　　Thou hast spoken right, 'tis true;
　The wheel° is come full circle! I am here.[4]　　　*Fortune's wheel*
ALBANY　Methought thy very gait did prophesy
175　A royal nobleness. I must embrace thee.
　Let sorrow split my heart, if ever I
　Did hate thee or thy father!
EDGAR　　　　　　　　　Worthy prince. I know 't.
ALBANY　Where have you hid yourself?
　How have you known the miseries of your father?
180　EDGAR　By nursing them, my lord. List° a brief tale;　　*Listen to*
　And when 'tis told, O, that my heart would burst!
　The bloody proclamation to escape,[5]
　That followed me so near—O, our lives' sweetness!
　That we the pain of death would hourly die
185　Rather than die at once![6]—taught me to shift
　Into a madman's rags; to assume a semblance
　That very° dogs disdained; and in this habit　　　　　*even*
　Met I my father with his bleeding rings,°　　　　　*sockets*
　Their precious stones° new lost; became his guide,　　*eyes*
190　Led him, begged for him, saved him from despair;
　Never—O fault!—revealed myself unto him,
　Until some half-hour past, when I was armed:
　Not sure, though hoping, of this good success,°　　*conclusion*
　I asked his blessing, and from first to last
195　Told him my pilgrimage. But his flawed° heart—　　*cracked*
　Alack, too weak the conflict to support!—
　'Twixt two extremes of passion, joy and grief,
　Burst smilingly.
EDMUND　　　　　　This speech of yours hath moved me,
　And shall perchance do good; but speak you on;
200　You look as you had something more to say.

---

2. Who have this good fortune at my expense.　　　　5. In order to escape the sentence of death.
3. The adulterous bed in which you were born; or, possi-　6. *our . . . once:* how sweet must life be that we prefer the
bly, the vagina. *got:* begot.　　　　　　　　　　constant pain of dying to death itself.
4. Back at the lowest point.

ALBANY   If there be more, more woeful, hold it in;
　　For I am almost ready to dissolve,°   *melt into tears*
　　Hearing of this.
EDGAR　　　　　　This would have seemed a period°   *conclusion*
　　To such as love not sorrow; but another,
205　　To amplify° too much would make much more,   *enlarge, extend*
　　And top extremity.
　　Whilst I was big in clamor° came there in a man,   *lamenting loudly*
　　Who, having seen me in my worst estate,
　　Shunned my abhorred society; but then, finding
210　　Who 'twas that so endured, with his strong arms
　　He fastened on my neck, and bellowed out
　　As he'd burst heaven; threw him on my father;
　　Told the most piteous tale of Lear and him°   *himself*
　　That ever ear received; which in recounting
215　　His grief grew puissant,° and the strings of life   *powerful*
　　Began to crack. Twice then the trumpets sounded,
　　And there I left him tranced.
ALBANY　　　　　　　　　　But who was this?
EDGAR   Kent, sir, the banished Kent; who in disguise
　　Followed his enemy king,[7] and did him service
220　　Improper° for a slave.   *Unfit even*
　　　　　　Enter a GENTLEMAN, *with a bloody knife*
GENTLEMAN   Help, help, O, help!
EDGAR　　　　　　　　　　What kind of help?
ALBANY　　　　　　　　　　　　　Speak, man.
EDGAR   What means that bloody knife?
GENTLEMAN　　　　　　　　　　'Tis hot, it smokes,
　　It came even from the heart of—O, she's dead!
ALBANY   Who dead? speak, man.
225　GENTLEMAN   Your lady, sir, your lady! and her sister
　　By her is poisoned; she hath confessed it.
EDMUND   I was contracted to them both. All three
　　Now marry° in an instant.   *unite (in death)*
　　　　　　Enter KENT
EDGAR　　　　　　　　　　Here comes Kent.
ALBANY   Produce their bodies, be they alive or dead:
230　　This judgment of the heavens, that makes us tremble,
　　Touches us not with pity.　　　　　　*Exit* GENTLEMAN
　　　　　　　　　　O, is this he?
　　The time will not allow the compliment
　　Which very manners urges.[8]
KENT　　　　　　　　　I am come
　　To bid my king and master aye° good night.   *forever*
　　Is he not here?
235　ALBANY　　　　　　Great thing of° us forgot!   *by*
　　Speak, Edmund, where's the king? and where's Cordelia?
　　See'st thou this object,° Kent?   *spectacle*
　　　　　　The bodies of GONERIL *and* REGAN *are brought in*
KENT   Alack, why thus?
EDMUND　　　　　　　Yet° Edmund was beloved.   *Despite all*

---

7. Because Lear had previously banished him. *enemy:*　　8. *the compliment . . . urges:* the ceremony that barest
hostile.　　　　　　　　　　　　　　　　　　　　　　　custom demands.

The one the other poisoned for my sake,
240 And after slew herself.
ALBANY   Even so. Cover their faces.
EDMUND   I pant for life. Some good I mean to do,
Despite of mine own nature. Quickly send,
Be brief° in it, to the castle; for my writ[9]   *speedy*
245 Is on the life of Lear and on Cordelia:
Nay, send in time.
ALBANY   Run, run, O, run!
EDGAR   To who, my lord? Who hath the office?° send   *commission*
Thy token of reprieve.
EDMUND   Well thought on. Take my sword,
Give it the° captain.   *to the*
250 ALBANY   Haste thee for thy life.   *Exit* EDGAR
EDMUND   He hath commission from thy wife and me
To hang Cordelia in the prison, and
To lay the blame upon her own despair,
That she fordid herself.[1]
255 ALBANY   The gods defend her! Bear him hence awhile.
                                EDMUND *is borne off*
Re-enter LEAR, *with* CORDELIA *dead in his arms;* EDGAR,
     CAPTAIN, *and others following*
LEAR   Howl, howl, howl, howl! O, you are men of stones:
Had I your tongues and eyes, I'd use them so
That heaven's vault should crack. She's gone forever!
I know when one is dead, and when one lives;
260 She's dead as earth. Lend me a looking-glass;
If that her breath will mist or stain the stone,[2]
Why, then she lives.
KENT   Is this the promised end?[3]
EDGAR   Or image of that horror?
ALBANY   Fall, and cease![4]
LEAR   This feather stirs; she lives! If it be so,
265 It is a chance which does redeem all sorrows
That ever I have felt.
KENT (*kneeling*)[5]   O my good master!
LEAR   Prithee, away.
EDGAR   'Tis noble Kent, your friend.
LEAR   A plague upon you, murderers, traitors all!
I might have saved her; now she's gone for ever!
270 Cordelia, Cordelia! stay a little. Ha!
What is 't thou say'st? Her voice was ever soft,
Gentle, and low, an excellent thing in woman.
I killed the slave that was a-hanging thee.
CAPTAIN   'Tis true, my lords, he did.
LEAR   Did I not, fellow?
275 I have seen the day, with my good biting falchion°   *light sword*
I would have made them skip: I am old now,

9. Order of execution.
1. Destroyed herself. In most of Shakespeare's source texts for the play, Cordelia does in fact kill herself after reigning for some years.
2. Mica, or stone polished to a mirror finish.
3. Doomsday; expected end of the play. In no version of the story previous to Shakespeare's does Cordelia die at this point.
4. Let the world collapse and end.
5. Lear probably kneels over Cordelia's body during most of the scene, and Kent kneels here partly in submission, partly to catch Lear's attention.

And these same crosses spoil me.[6] Who are you?
Mine eyes are not o' the best. I'll tell you straight.°   *recognize you soon*
KENT   If fortune brag of two she loved and hated,
280   One of them we behold.[7]
LEAR   This is a dull sight.[8] Are you not Kent?
KENT   The same,
Your servant Kent. Where is your servant Caius?°   *(Kent's pseudonym)*
LEAR   He's a good fellow, I can tell you that;
He'll strike, and quickly too. He's dead and rotten.
285   KENT   No, my good lord; I am the very man—
LEAR   I'll see that straight.[9]
KENT   That, from your first of difference and decay,[1]
Have followed your sad steps.
LEAR   You are welcome hither.
KENT   Nor no man else.[2] All's cheerless, dark, and deadly.°   *deathly*
290   Your eldest daughters have fordone° themselves,   *destroyed*
And desperately° are dead.   *in despair*
LEAR   Aye, so I think.
ALBANY   He knows not what he says; and vain° it is   *in vain*
That we present us to him.
EDGAR   Very bootless.°   *futile*
      Enter a CAPTAIN
CAPTAIN   Edmund is dead, my lord.
ALBANY   That's but a trifle here.
295   You lords and noble friends, know our intent.
What comfort to this great decay° may come   *ruin, destruction*
Shall be applied. For us, we will resign,
During the life of this old majesty,
To him our absolute power; (*to* EDGAR *and* KENT) you, to your
rights;
300   With boot,° and such addition° as your honors   *reward / distinction*
Have more than merited. All friends shall taste
The wages of their virtue, and all foes
The cup of their deserving. O, see, see!
LEAR   And my poor fool[3] is hanged! No, no, no life!
305   Why should a dog, a horse, a rat, have life,
And thou no breath at all? Thou'lt come no more,
Never, never, never, never, never!
Pray you, undo this button. Thank you, sir.
Do you see this? Look on her, look, her lips,
Look there, look there!   *Dies*
310   EDGAR   He faints! My lord, my lord!
KENT   Break, heart; I prithee, break!
EDGAR   Look up, my lord.
KENT   Vex not his ghost.[4] O, let him pass! He hates him much
That would upon the rack[5] of this tough world
Stretch him out longer.
EDGAR   He is gone, indeed.

---

6. And these recent adversities have weakened me; and these parries I could once match would now destroy me.
7. *If . . . behold:* If there were only two supreme examples in the world of Fortune's ability to raise up and cast down, Lear would be one; alternatively, we are each of us one (Lear and Kent are here looking at each other).
8. This is a sad sight; my vision is failing.
9. I'll attend to that shortly; I'll comprehend that in a moment.
1. Who from the beginning of your alteration and deterioration.
2. No, neither I nor anyone else is welcome; that is, this is not a welcoming sight.
3. A term of endearment, here used for Cordelia.
4. Do not disturb his departing soul.
5. Instrument of torture, used to stretch its victims.

315 KENT   The wonder is, he hath endured so long.
       He but usurped his life.[6]
    ALBANY   Bear them from hence. Our present business
       Is general woe. (*To* KENT *and* EDGAR) Friends of my soul, you twain
       Rule in this realm, and the gored° state sustain.   *wounded; bloody*
320 KENT   I have a journey, sir, shortly to go;
       My master calls me, I must not say no.
    EDGAR   The weight of this sad time we must obey;
       Speak what we feel, not what we ought to say.
       The oldest hath borne most; we that are young
325   Shall never see so much, nor live so long.
                              Exeunt, with dead march

---

6. From death, which already had a claim on it.

Macbeth

On November 4, 1605, the night before King James I was due to appear in person to open a new session of Parliament, officers of the crown apprehended Guy Fawkes in a cellar that extended beneath the Parliament House. The cellar was filled with barrels of gunpowder and iron bars, concealed by a load of lumber and coal. Carrying a watch and devices to light fuses, Fawkes intended to carry out a desperate plot devised by a small group of conspirators, embittered by what they perceived as James's unwillingness to extend toleration to Roman Catholics. Under torture, Fawkes revealed the names of those who had conspired with him to blow up the entire government. Among those hunted down, arrested, and brought to trial for the Gunpowder Plot was Father Henry Garnet, head of the clandestine Jesuit mission in England. Garnet, against whom there was very little hard evidence, pleaded innocent, but the government prosecutors made much of the fact that he was the author of A *Treatise of Equivocation*, a book showing how to give misleading or ambiguous answers under oath. Garnet, Fawkes, and the others were all found guilty and executed, their severed heads displayed on pikes.

Eighteen months before these momentous events, a company of London actors experienced what was for them an important change in their legal status. On May 19, 1603, a scant two months after the death of Queen Elizabeth and the accession to the English throne of the Scottish King James, Shakespeare's company, the Lord Chamberlain's Men, was formally declared to be the King's Men. The players had every reason to be grateful to their royal master and attentive to his pleasure and interest. It has long been argued that one of the most striking signs of this gratitude is *Macbeth*, based on a story from Scottish history particularly apt for a monarch who traced his line back to Banquo, the noble thane whose murder Macbeth orders after he has killed King Duncan.

In Shakespeare's principal historical source, Raphael Holinshed's *Chronicles of England, Scotland, and Ireland* (1587), Banquo aids Macbeth in the murder of the King. Shakespeare suppresses this complicity. The witches (or "weird sisters") who tell Macbeth that he would be king tell Banquo that he will be the father of kings, but Banquo seems determined not to be drawn into any conspiratorial attempt to realize these prophecies. When, just before Duncan's assassination, Macbeth indirectly asks for his support, Banquo speaks of keeping his "allegiance clear" (2.1.27). Macbeth's only co-conspirator, then, is his wife. Innocent of the crime against Duncan, Banquo is killed because Macbeth fears and envies him and because he wishes to keep the crown he has seized from passing, as the witches had prophesied, to Banquo's heirs. Other significant changes Shakespeare made in his source materials further intensify Macbeth's isolation and his evil: in Holinshed's *Chronicles*, Duncan is a relatively young and feeble ruler, and Macbeth, having dispatched him, goes on to reign brilliantly for ten years. As Shakespeare staged the story, Duncan is a mature and virtuous king, and Scotland under the tyrant Macbeth is in the grip of a nightmare from which it will eventually awaken into the happy rule of Banquo's descendants.

As so often with Shakespeare, we do not have a secure date for either the composition or the first performance of *Macbeth*. The first printed text is in the 1623 First Folio, but the play is usually dated 1606, principally because of a joke made by a minor character that must have provoked a ripple of shuddering laughter among the original audiences. The joke comes at a strange moment: in the immediate wake of one of the most harrowing scenes of dread and soul sickness that Shakespeare ever wrote. Macbeth has just treacherously murdered the sleeping King Duncan, a guest in his castle. Deeply shaken by his deed and gripped by fear and remorse, he and his ambitious wife are exchanging anxious words when they hear a knocking at the castle gate. The knocking is a simple device, but in performance it almost always has a thrilling effect, an effect subtly anticipated by Macbeth's horrified sense before the murder that the very image of what he is about to do makes "my seated heart knock at my ribs" (1.3.135). As the insistent knocking continues, the conspirators exit to wash the blood off their hands and to change into their nightgowns. Lady Macbeth is—or strives to seem—icily calm, calculating, and confident: "A little water clears us of this deed" (2.2.65). Not so the appalled Macbeth: "Wake Duncan with thy knocking. I would thou couldst" (2.2.72), he declares in horror or despair, longing or bitter irony. (Here, as elsewhere in these great roles, the actors have a remarkable range of interpretive options.) At this point, a porter, roused by the noise but still half drunk from the evening's revelry, appears. As he grumblingly goes to unlock the gate, he imagines that he is the gatekeeper in hell, opening the door to new arrivals. "Here's an equivocator," he says of one of these imaginary sinners, "that could swear in both the scales against either scale, who committed treason enough for God's sake, yet could not equivocate to heaven. O, come in, equivocator" (2.3.8–11). This treasonous equivocator knocking on hell's gate is almost certainly an allusion to the recently executed Henry Garnet.

Of Shakespeare's great tragedies, *Macbeth* has always seemed the most topical, cannily alert not only to contemporary events but to King James's political beliefs and personal obsessions. Not surprising for someone whose mother and father had both been killed, James had a horror of assassination and a powerful conviction that a king was a sacred figure, God's own representative on earth. Regicide, in this political theology, was close to the ultimate crime, a demonic assault not simply on an individual and a community but on the fundamental order of the universe. James, who had written a learned book on witchcraft, suspected the hand of the devil in any plot against an anointed king, believed that witches had at various points in his own life conspired to harm him, and feared the existence of occult, invisible forces bent on bringing all things to ruin.

In several of his earlier plays, most notably in *Richard II*, Shakespeare's characters give

Henri IV of France (1553–1610) administers the royal touch, thought to cure scrofula. An etching by Pierre Firens (no date). See *Macbeth* 4.3.142–60.

voice to the theory that the king is God's deputy on earth and consequently that attacks upon him are evil, but kingship's claim to sacred authority is exceptionally powerful in *Macbeth* (not in Scotland alone, but also in neighboring England, where, as Malcolm tells Macduff, the touch of the pious King Edward cures disease). Exceptionally powerful too in this play is the metaphysical horror of regicide. The murder of Duncan is marked in the natural world with dreadful signs and portents and in the human world with an over-powering sense of devastation ironically given its most eloquent expression by the murderer Macbeth:

> Renown and grace is dead.
> The wine of life is drawn, and the mere lees
> Is left this vault to brag of.
>
> (2.3.90–92)

Macbeth is speaking hypocritically—"look like the innocent flower," his wife had earlier counseled him, "but be the serpent under't" (1.5.63–64)—and yet, at least in one interpre-tation of the part, he is saying what he himself knows to be the grim truth. Far more than any other of Shakespeare's villains, more than the homicidal Richard III, the treacherous Claudius in *Hamlet,* and the cold-hearted Iago in *Othello,* Macbeth is fully aware of the wickedness of his deeds and is tormented by this awareness. Endowed with a clear-eyed grasp of the difference between good and evil, he chooses evil, even though the choice horrifies and sickens him.

Before he has taken the irrevocable step, Macbeth tries to recover his moral bearings. The deed he is contemplating, he begins by telling himself, would work only if he could control all consequences, so that his blow "might be the be-all and the end-all" (1.7.5). But he grasps that there is no possibility of such complete control and therefore no hope of practical success. His thoughts then turn to the overwhelming ethical arguments against the murder: he is not only the King's kinsman and subject but also his host, "who should against his murderer shut the door, / Not bear the knife myself" (1.7.15–16). And from these considerations, practical and ethical, Macbeth's restless, brooding mind rises higher, imagining that the murdered Duncan's virtues will plead like angels against the "deep damnation of his taking-off,"

> And pity, like a naked new-born babe,
> Striding the blast, or heaven's cherubin, horsed
> Upon the sightless couriers of the air,
> Shall blow the horrid deed in every eye
> That tears shall drown the wind.
>
> (1.7.20–25)

No one else in the play has a moral sensibility so intense or so visionary, no one else imagines so vividly the forces that lie beyond the ordinary and familiar horizon of human experience. Macbeth understands exactly what is at stake and what he must do: "We will," he tells his wife decisively, "proceed no further in this business" (1.7.31).

Why, then, does he change his mind and commit a crime he cannot even contemplate without horror? A significant part of the answer lies in the instigation of his remarkable wife. When we first glimpse Lady Macbeth, she is reading a letter. (Reading was by no means a universal achievement for women of the early seventeenth century, let alone the eleventh, when the play's events are set, but Shakespeare frequently represents it in his plays in a variety of contexts.) The letter makes her burn with visions of the "golden round" that "fate and metaphysical aid" (1.5.26–27) seem to have conferred upon her husband. But though she speaks of the crown as if it were already on Macbeth's head, she fears that he is too full of the "milk of human kindness" (1.5.15) to seize what has been promised him. She resolves then to "chastise" her husband, to urge him, in a phrase taken from archery, to screw his courage to the sticking place. Lady Macbeth manipulates him in two principal ways. The first is through sexual taunting:

> Art thou afeard
> To be the same in thine own act and valour
> As thou art in desire?
>
> ·
>
> When you durst do it, then you were a man
> (1.7.39–41, 49)

And the second is through the terrible force of her determination:

> I have given suck, and know
> How tender 'tis to love the babe that milks me.
> I would, while it was smiling in my face,
> Have plucked my nipple from his boneless gums
> And dashed the brains out, had I so sworn
> As you have done to this.
>
> (1.7.54–59)

These words, and the gestures that viscerally intensify them onstage, cannot by themselves account for Macbeth's decision. He counters his wife's sexual terrorism with a clear sense of the proper boundaries of his identity as a male and as a human being: "I dare do all that may become a man; / Who dares do more is none" (1.7.46–47). As for Lady Macbeth's fantasy of murdering her infant, it might have served rather to deter Macbeth from his unnatural crime than to spur him toward it. Virtually everyone is subject to terrible dreams and lawless fantasies—"Merciful powers," Banquo prays, "restrain in me the cursèd thoughts that nature / Gives way to in repose" (2.1.7–9)—but not everyone gives way to them in waking reality. Macbeth, who is fully aware that "wicked dreams abuse / The curtained sleep" (2.1.50–51), nonetheless crosses the fatal line from criminal desire to criminal act.

That he does so without adequate motivation, that he murders a man toward whom he should be grateful and protective, deepens the mystery, linking it to a long current of theological and philosophical brooding on the nature of evil. For St. Augustine, the great fourth-century Church Father, evil in its most radical form is gratuitous, and this notion of gratuitousness haunts subsequent thinkers, including those far from Christian orthodoxy. Thus the Florentine Niccolò Machiavelli, notorious in the sixteenth century for freethinking, writes in Chapter 37 of his *Discourses* that "when men are no longer obliged to fight from necessity, they fight from ambition, which passion is so powerful in the hearts of men that it never leaves them, no matter to what height they may rise." The reason for this, Machiavelli proposes, is that "nature has created men so that they desire everything, but are unable to attain it; desire being thus always greater than the faculty of acquiring, discontent with what they have and dissatisfaction with themselves result from it."

Macbeth and Lady Macbeth act on ambition, restless desire, and a will to power normally kept in check by the pragmatic, ethical, and religious considerations to which the wavering Macbeth initially gives voice. Lady Macbeth in effect works to liberate that will to power in her husband, freeing him from his "sickly" fears of damnation so that he can act with a ruthless blend of murderous violence and cunning. In her radically disenchanted, coolly skeptical view, the murder of the King can be undertaken without fear of guilty conscience, vengeful ghosts, or divine judgment: "The sleeping and the dead," she tells her shaken husband, "are but as pictures. 'Tis the eye of childhood / That fears a painted devil" (2.2.51–53).

This reassurance, Shakespeare's tragedy shows, is hopelessly shallow. As the spectral dagger, the ghost sitting in Macbeth's chair, and the indelible bloodstains on Lady Macbeth's hands all chillingly demonstrate, the secure distinction between representation and reality, the dead and the living, repeatedly breaks down, not simply for the characters but for the spectators as well. In most productions, the dagger and the blood are visible only to the diseased minds of the murderers, but Banquo's ghost is almost always palpably present onstage, visible to the audience as well as to the unhinged Macbeth, though invisible to everyone around him. Moreover, the dream of a "clean" regicide proves psychologically untenable: the seizure of the crown leads to feverish sleeplessness, brooding anxiety about security, and an overwhelming sense of defilement. Macbeth and Lady Macbeth are equally devastated, but the psychological trajectory in the wake of the crime is not the same for the two conspirators. Initially frozen in moral numbness, Lady Macbeth experiences a gradual decomposition, a growing horror that breaks forth unforgettably in the sleep-walking scene with her compulsive attempts to free herself of the smell and stain of blood: "all the perfumes of Arabia will not sweeten this little hand" (5.1.42–43). Initially gripped by a heightened sensitivity to fear, a dread that threatens inward decomposition, Macbeth experiences a gradual numbing or deadening of the self until he reaches a state of absolute spiritual emptiness:

> Tomorrow, and tomorrow, and tomorrow
> Creeps in this petty pace from day to day
> To the last syllable of recorded time.
> (5.5.18–20)

The assassination also proves, as Macbeth had foreseen, politically untenable. There is always someone who escapes the murderer's net, someone who poses a threat or seeks to redress an injury or simply remembers what it felt like to be free and unafraid. It is impossible to trammel up the consequence, to break the chain of action and reaction, to reach a stable resting place. There are no clean murders. One crime leads to another and then to another, without bringing the criminal any closer to the security or contentment that each desperate act is meant to achieve. Macbeth cannot stop the bloody acts; instead he must multiply and extend them. Where Lady Macbeth had only fantasized the murder of children, Macbeth actually undertakes that and other crimes until he dreams, in his half-crazed words to the "secret, black, and midnight hags" (4.1.64), of universal destruction.

It is Macbeth's first encounter with these hags—the weird (or, in the original spelling, "weyward" or "weyard") sisters—that seems to initiate his descent toward murder and tyranny. But what kind of power do these malevolent bearded women have over Macbeth? Are they responsible, by magical influence or by planting the idea in his mind, for his decision to kill Duncan? Are they somehow privy to a predestined fate, as if they have seen the script of the tragedy before it is performed? Or, alternatively, are they uncanny emblems of Macbeth's psychological condition, a kind of screen onto which he projects

Macbeth and Banquo encounter the weird sisters (1.3). From Raphael Holinshed, *The First Volume of the Chronicles of England, Scotlande and Irelande* (1577).

his "horrible imaginings" (1.3.137)? The word "weird," in one of its etymologies, derives from the Old English word for "fate," but do the women Shakespeare depicts, trafficking in ambiguous prophecies, fretting over village squabbles, mumbling charms, actually control destiny (or, what amounts to the same thing, the tragedy's plot)? What is the nature of these strange creatures that "look not like th'inhabitants o'th' earth," as Banquo observes, "and yet are on't" (1.3.39–40)?

Actors' responses to these questions have ranged wildly, though virtually all productions have recognized that the witches' scenes are among the most theatrically powerful and compelling in the play and that it matters a great deal whether they are made up to look grotesque or stately, perversely comical or terrifying. Scholarly responses have been complicated by the high probability that not all of the witchcraft scenes are by Shakespeare himself: it appears that 3.5 and part of 4.1, the scenes featuring the goddess Hecate, were added to the play some time after its first performance and incorporate songs derived from Thomas Middleton's play *The Witch*. (The Folio text of *Macbeth* cites only the first words of these songs, which are given in full in this edition.) But even if we set aside the problems raised by these interpolated scenes, the status of the witches in Shakespeare's play remains ambiguous and seems to be so by design. "What are you?" asks Macbeth when he first encounters the bearded hags, and he receives in reply his own name: "All hail, Macbeth" (1.3.45–46). Banquo urgently renews the inquiry, asking the creatures before his eyes if they truly exist or are only figments of his imagination; but his question too remains unanswered. When Macbeth and Banquo demand to know more, the witches vanish: "what seemed corporal / Melted as breath into the wind" (1.3.79–80). "As breath into the wind"—*Macbeth* is a tragedy of meltings, category confusions, and liminal states.

Much of the play transpires on the border between fantasy and reality, a sickening betwixt-and-between where a "horrid image" in the mind has the uncanny power to produce bodily effects "against the use of nature" (1.3.136), where one mind is present to the innermost fantasies of another, where manhood threatens to vanish and murdered men walk and blood cannot be washed off. If these effects could be unequivocally attributed to the agency of the witches, the audience would at least have the security of a defined and focused fear. Alternatively, if the witches could be definitively dismissed as fantasy or fraud, the audience would at least have the clear-eyed certainty of witnessing human causes in an altogether secular world. But instead, Shakespeare achieves the remarkable effect of a nebulous infection, a bleeding of the demonic into the secular and the secular into the demonic.

The most famous instance of this effect is Lady Macbeth's great invocation of the "spirits / That tend on mortal thoughts" (1.5.38–39) to unsex her, fill her with cruelty, make thick her blood, and exchange her milk for gall. The speech appears to be a conjuration of demonic powers, an act of witchcraft in which the "murdering ministers" are directed to bring about a set of changes in her body. She calls these ministers "sightless substances" (1.5.47): though invisible, they are—as she conceives them—not figures of speech or projections of her mind, but objective, substantial beings or forces. (Macbeth similarly seems to imagine invisible but objective forces when he speaks of "the sightless couriers of the air," 1.7.23.) But the fact that the spirits she invokes are "sightless" already moves this passage away from the literal existence of the weird sisters and toward the metaphorical use of "spirits" in her speech of a few moments earlier: "Hie thee hither, / That I may pour my spirits in thine ear" (1.5.23–24). The spirits she speaks of here are manifestly figurative—they refer to the bold words, the undaunted mettle, and the sexual taunts with which she intends to incite Macbeth to murder Duncan—but, like all of her expressions of will and passion, they strain toward bodily realization, even as they convey a psychic and hence invisible inwardness. That is, there is something uncannily literal about Lady Macbeth's influence on her husband, as if marital intimacy were akin to demonic possession, as if she had contrived to inhabit his mind, as if, in other words, she had literally poured her spirits in his ear. Conversely, there is something uncannily figurative about the "sightless substances" she invokes, as if the spirit world, the realm of "fate and metaphysical aid,"

Witchcraft in Scotland. From *Newes from Scotland* (1591).

were only a metaphor for her blind and murderous desires, as if the weird sisters were condensations of her own breath.

In Shakespeare's plays, as in those of his contemporaries, evildoers may wreak havoc for a time, but in the final restoration of order and justice, they and their principal accomplices are almost inevitably punished. Thus, at the close of *Macbeth*, not only are Macbeth and Lady Macbeth dead, but the victorious Malcolm also speaks of settling scores with "the cruel ministers / Of this dead butcher and his fiend-like queen" (5.11.34–35). Yet though the play has deeply implicated the witches in Macbeth's monstrous assault on the fabric of civilized life, there is no gesture toward punishing them, no sign that the victors are even aware of their existence. This omission is the more striking if we recall that at the time Shakespeare wrote his play, the authorities in England and Scotland were still bringing women to trial on charges of witchcraft and executing them. The theatrical power of *Macbeth* seems bound up with its refusal to resolve the questions raised by the witches. At once marginal and central to the play, they are only briefly and intermittently onstage, but they are still suggestively present when we cannot see them, when the threats they embody are absorbed in the ordinary relations of everyday life.

"There's no art / To find the mind's construction in the face" (1.4.11–12), says the baffled Duncan about a man who had betrayed his trust, but Macbeth confronts a deeper perplexity, an appalling mystery within himself:

> My thought, whose murder yet is but fantastical,
> Shakes so my single state of man that function
> Is smothered in surmise, and nothing is
> But what is not.
>
> (1.3.138–41)

The witches have something to do with this inner torment, but what that something is remains as elusive as the dagger that Macbeth sees before him, handle toward his hand. Scotland is sick, "almost afraid to know itself" (4.3.166). But the sickness cannot be isolated in a conspiracy of witches. If violence stirs in the hinterlands, where marauding armies struggle, it breeds more murderously still in the inmost circles of the state: "This castle hath a pleasant seat," says Duncan, going unwittingly to his death:

> The air
> Nimbly and sweetly recommends itself
> Unto our gentle senses.
>
> (1.6.1–3)

If the mind is subject to "supernatural soliciting" (1.3.129) from some bizarre place, it is gripped still more terribly and irresistibly by "horrible imaginings" (1.3.137) from within. If there is sexual disturbance out on the heath, where the bearded hags stir the ingredients of their hideous caldron, there is deeper sexual disturbance at home, in the murderous intimacy of the marriage bond: "When you durst do it, then you were a man." If you are worried about losing your manhood, it is not enough to hunt for witches; look to your wife. If you are anxious about your future, scrutinize your best friends: "He was a gentleman on whom I built / An absolute trust" (1.4.13–14). If you are worried about interior temptation, fear your own dreams:

> Merciful powers,
> Restrain in me the cursèd thoughts that nature
> Gives way to in repose.
>
> (2.1.7–9)

And if you fear spiritual desolation, turn your eyes on the contents not only of the hideous caldron but of your skull: "O, full of scorpions is my mind, dear wife!" (3.2.37).

The point of the persecution of witches in Shakespeare's age was to achieve clarity, to compel full confessions, to pass judgment, and to escape from the terror of the inexplicable, the unforeseen, the aimlessly malignant. In *Macbeth*, the audience is given something better than confession, for it has visible proof of the demonic in action, but this visibility turns out to be as maddeningly equivocal as the witches' riddling words. The "wayward" witches appear and disappear, the language of the play subverts the illusory certainties of sight, and the forces of renewed order, Malcolm and Macduff, are themselves strange, strained, and insecure. The ambiguities of demonic agency are never resolved, and its horror spreads like a mist through a murky landscape. "What is't you do?" Macbeth asks the weird sisters. "A deed without a name" (4.1.65).

By the play's close, Macbeth has begun "to doubt th'equivocation of the fiend, / That lies like truth" (5.5.41–42). Equivocations are lies with mental reservations, words with double meanings, puns, twists of emphasis, and plays on false interpretations (such as the meaning of the phrase "not of woman born"). Like the witches, language in *Macbeth* is a boundary stalker, neither a trustworthy guide nor a manifest illusion. Words sit dangerously in a middle ground; they must be brought under control, but they always threaten to slide into lies or magic charms or riddles or sheer emptiness. It is this emptiness with which Macbeth seems haunted at the end, with his vision of life as

> a tale
> Told by an idiot, full of sound and fury,
> Signifying nothing.
>
> (5.5.25–27)

If the closing moments of the play invite us to recoil from this black hole—after all, the tyrant is killed—they invite us to recoil from too confident and simple a celebration of the triumph of grace. For somewhere beyond the immediate circle of order restored, the witches are dancing around the caldron, and, the play seems to imply, the caldron is in every one of us.

Stephen Greenblatt

TEXTUAL NOTE

The only authoritative text of *Macbeth* is the First Folio (1623), which consequently serves as the control text in this edition. Scholars generally agree that the Folio version (F) was based on a promptbook, a transcript derived, in all likelihood, from Shakespeare's rough draft of the play. F appears to be a fairly reliable record of its manuscript source, the promptbook.

There are, however, signs that this source was itself an abbreviated version of the play as first written and performed, for the text in F is considerably shorter than that of any of the other major tragedies. Moreover, the Folio's *Macbeth* appears to be a version of the play revised, sometime after Shakespeare had ceased to be active with the King's Men, for a court performance in the presence of King James. Scholars have long suspected that it contains material not by Shakespeare. In particular, the two songs referred to in 3.5 and 4.1 of F only by their opening phrases ("Come away, come away, &c.," "Blacke Spirits, &c.") are very likely by the playwright Thomas Middleton. Songs with the same opening phrases appear in a manuscript of Middleton's unsuccessful play *The Witch* (c. 1613) and are restored in full in this edition of *Macbeth*.

Middleton may have been personally responsible for the revision of *Macbeth* reflected in the Folio text. He could, in addition to the songs, have added all of 3.5 (which seems to diverge stylistically from the rest of the play) as well as parts of 4.1, particularly Hecate's speeches.

SELECTED BIBLIOGRAPHY

Adelman, Janet. " 'Born of Woman': Fantasies of Maternal Power in *Macbeth*." *Cannibals, Witches, and Divorce: Estranging the Renaissance.* Ed. Marjorie Garber. Baltimore: Johns Hopkins University Press, 1987. 90–121.

Booth, Stephen. *"King Lear," "Macbeth," Indefinition, and Tragedy.* New Haven: Yale University Press, 1983. 79–118.

Bradley, A. C. *Shakespearean Tragedy: Lectures on "Hamlet," "King Lear," "Macbeth."* London: Macmillan, 1905.

Brown, John Russell, ed. *Focus on "Macbeth."* London: Routledge and Kegan Paul, 1982.

Calderwood. James L. *If It Were Done: "Macbeth" and Tragic Action.* Amherst: University of Massachusetts Press, 1986.

Greenblatt, Stephen. "Shakespeare Bewitched." *New Historical Literary Study: Essays on Reproducing Texts, Representing History.* Ed. Jeffrey N. Cox and Larry J. Reynolds. Princeton: Princeton University Press, 1993. 108–35.

Mullaney, Steven. "Lying Like Truth: Riddle, Representation, and Treason." *The Place of the Stage: License, Play, and Power in Renaissance England.* Chicago: University of Chicago Press, 1988. 116–34.

Norbrook, David. "*Macbeth* and the Politics of Historiography." *Politics of Discourse: The Literature and History of Seventeenth-Century England.* Ed. Kevin Sharpe and Steven Zwicker. Berkeley: University of California Press, 1987. 78–116.

Rosenberg, Marvin. *The Masks of "Macbeth."* Berkeley: University of California Press, 1978.

Sinfield, Alan. "*Macbeth*: History, Ideology and Intellectuals." *Critical Quarterly* 28 (1986): 63–77.

The Tragedy of Macbeth

The Persons of the Play

KING DUNCAN of Scotland
MALCOLM ⎫
DONALBAIN ⎭ his sons
A CAPTAIN in Duncan's army
MACBETH, Thane of Glamis, later Thane of Cawdor, then King of Scotland
A PORTER at Macbeth's castle
Three MURDERERS attending on Macbeth
SEYTON, servant of Macbeth
LADY MACBETH, Macbeth's wife
A DOCTOR of Physic ⎫
A Waiting-GENTLEWOMAN ⎭ attending on Lady Macbeth
BANQUO, a Scottish thane
FLEANCE, his son
MACDUFF, Thane of Fife
LADY MACDUFF, his wife
MACDUFF'S SON
LENNOX ⎫
ROSS ⎪
ANGUS ⎬ Scottish Thanes
CAITHNESS ⎪
MENTEITH ⎭
SIWARD, Earl of Northumberland
YOUNG SIWARD, his son
An English DOCTOR
HECATE, Queen of the Witches
Six WITCHES
Three APPARITIONS, one an armed head, one a bloody child, one a child crowned
A SPIRIT LIKE A CAT
Other SPIRITS
An OLD MAN
A MESSENGER
MURDERERS
SERVANTS
A show of eight kings; Lords and Thanes, attendants, soldiers, drummers

1.1

Thunder and lightning. Enter three WITCHES
FIRST WITCH   When shall we three meet again?
   In thunder, lightning, or in rain?[1]
SECOND WITCH   When the hurly-burly's° done,   °*tumult is*
   When the battle's lost and won.
5   THIRD WITCH   That will be ere the set of sun.

1.1 Location: An open place.

1. Witches were thought to be able to cause bad weather.

FIRST WITCH   Where the place?
SECOND WITCH   Upon the heath.
THIRD WITCH   There to meet with Macbeth.
FIRST WITCH   I come, Grimalkin.
SECOND WITCH   Paddock² calls.
THIRD WITCH   Anon.°   *At once*
10 ALL   Fair is foul, and foul is fair,
      Hover through the fog and filthy air.   *Exeunt*

                              1.2
      Alarum within. Enter KING [DUNCAN], MALCOLM, DON-
      ALBAIN, LENNOX, *with attendants, meeting a bleeding*
      CAPTAIN°   *staff officer*
      KING DUNCAN   What bloody man is that? He can report,
      As seemeth by his plight, of the revolt
      The newest state.
      MALCOLM   This is the sergeant
      Who like a good and hardy soldier fought
5   'Gainst my captivity. Hail, brave friend.
      Say to the King the knowledge of the broil°   *battle*
      As thou didst leave it.
      CAPTAIN   Doubtful it stood,
      As two spent° swimmers that do cling together   *exhausted*
      And choke their art.¹ The merciless Macdonald—
10   Worthy to be a rebel, for to that°   *that end*
      The multiplying villainies of nature²
      Do swarm upon him—from the Western Isles°   *Hebrides and Ireland*
      Of kerns and galloglasses³ is supplied,
      And fortune on his damnèd quarry⁴ smiling
15   Showed° like a rebel's whore. But all's too weak,   *Appeared*
      For brave Macbeth—well he deserves that name!°—   *epithet*
      Disdaining fortune, with his brandished steel
      Which smoked with bloody execution,
      Like valour's minion°   *favorite*
20   Carved out his passage till he faced the slave,°   *(Macdonald)*
      Which° ne'er shook hands nor bade farewell to him   *Who*
      Till he unseamed him from the nave° to th' chops,°   *navel / jaws*
      And fixed his head upon our battlements.
      KING DUNCAN   O valiant cousin,° worthy gentleman!   *kinsman*
25   CAPTAIN   As whence the sun 'gins his reflection⁵
      Shipwrecking storms and direful thunders break,
      So from that spring° whence comfort seemed to come   *source; (season)*
      Discomfort swells.° Mark, King of Scotland, mark.   *wells up*
      No sooner justice had, with valour armed,
30   Compelled these skipping° kerns to trust their heels   *mobile; fleeing*
      But the Norwegian lord, surveying vantage,°   *seeing his chance*
      With furbished° arms and new supplies of men   *polished*
      Began a fresh assault.
      KING DUNCAN   Dismayed not this our captains, Macbeth and Banquo?

---

2. Paddock, a toad, and Grimalkin, a gray cat, are the
witches' familiars, or attendant evil spirits.
1.2 Location: A camp near the battlefield.
1. And confound their skill in swimming.
2. The evil aspects of his own nature; the villainous progeny of nature (the mercenaries).
3. *kerns:* lightly armed Irish foot soldiers. *galloglasses:*
axe-wielding horsemen.
4. Its condemned victim. Fortune smiled temporarily on
Macdonald, although it had already marked him for
destruction. Many editions emend "quarry" to "quarrel."
5. Begins its return after the spring equinox, thought to
cause turbulent weather.

35 CAPTAIN Yes, as sparrows eagles, or the hare the lion!
If I say sooth I must report they were
As cannons overcharged with double cracks,[6]
So they doubly redoubled strokes upon the foe.
Except° they meant to bathe in reeking wounds   *Unless*
40 Or memorize another Golgotha,[7]
I cannot tell—
But I am faint. My gashes cry for help.
KING DUNCAN So well thy words become thee as thy wounds:
They smack of honour both.—Go get him surgeons.
      [*Exit* CAPTAIN *with attendants*]
    Enter ROSS *and* ANGUS
Who comes here?
45 MALCOLM   The worthy Thane[8] of Ross.
LENNOX What haste looks through his eyes! So should he look
That seems to° speak things strange.   *seems about to*
ROSS   God save the King.
KING DUNCAN Whence cam'st thou, worthy thane?
ROSS   From Fife, great King,
Where the Norwegian banners flout° the sky   *mock*
50 And fan our people cold.°   *cold with fear*
Norway° himself, with terrible numbers,   *The King of Norway*
Assisted by that most disloyal traitor
The Thane of Cawdor, began a dismal° conflict,   *an ominous*
Till that° Bellona's bridegroom,[9] lapped in proof,[1]   *Until*
55 Confronted him with self-comparisons,°   *comparable deeds*
Point° against point, rebellious arm 'gainst arm,   *Swordpoint*
Curbing his lavish° spirit; and to conclude,   *wild*
The victory fell on us—
KING DUNCAN   Great happiness.
ROSS   That now
Sweno, the Norways'° king, craves composition;°   *Norwegians' / a truce*
60 Nor would we deign him burial of his men
Till he disbursèd at Saint Colum's inch[2]
Ten thousand dollars[3] to our general use.
KING DUNCAN No more that Thane of Cawdor shall deceive
Our bosom interest.[4] Go pronounce his present° death,   *immediate*
65 And with his former title greet Macbeth.
ROSS I'll see it done.
KING DUNCAN What he hath lost, noble Macbeth hath won.
      Exeunt severally°   *separately*

1.3

Thunder. Enter the three WITCHES
FIRST WITCH Where hast thou been, sister?
SECOND WITCH Killing swine.
THIRD WITCH   Sister, where thou?
FIRST WITCH A sailor's wife had chestnuts in her lap,
And munched, and munched, and munched. 'Give me,' quoth I.

6. Overloaded with double charges of gunpowder.
7. Or make the battlefield as memorable as Golgotha, the "place of skulls" where Jesus was crucified.
8. Title of Scottish nobility.
9. Macbeth, imagined as husband to Bellona, the Roman goddess of war.
1. Clad in tested armor.

2. Incholm, the island of St. Columba in the Firth of Forth.
3. German and Spanish coins (first minted in the sixteenth century, five hundred years after the events of the play).
4. Our closest concerns.
1.3 Location: An open place.

5 'Aroint thee,° witch,' the rump-fed runnion¹ cries.   *Begone*
   Her husband's to Aleppo gone, master o'th' Tiger.
   But in a sieve I'll thither sail,
   And like a rat without a tail
   I'll do, I'll do, and I'll do.
10 SECOND WITCH   I'll give thee a wind.
   FIRST WITCH   Thou'rt kind.
   THIRD WITCH   And I another.
   FIRST WITCH   I myself have all the other,°   *others*
   And the very ports they blow,°   *blow from*
15 All the quarters° that they know   *directions*
   I'th' shipman's card.°   *compass card*
   I'll drain him dry as hay.
   Sleep shall neither night nor day
   Hang upon his penthouse lid.²
20 He shall live a man forbid.°   *cursed*
   Weary sennights° nine times nine   *weeks*
   Shall he dwindle, peak,° and pine.   *waste away*
   Though his barque cannot be lost,
   Yet it shall be tempest-tossed.
   Look what I have.
25 SECOND WITCH   Show me, show me.
   FIRST WITCH   Here I have a pilot's thumb,
   Wrecked as homeward he did come.
                Drum within
   THIRD WITCH   A drum, a drum—
   Macbeth doth come.
30 ALL [*dancing in a ring*]   The weird³ sisters hand in hand,
   Posters° of the sea and land,   *Swift travelers*
   Thus do go about, about,
   Thrice to thine, and thrice to mine,
   And thrice again to make up nine.
35 Peace! The charm's wound up.
                Enter MACBETH *and* BANQUO
   MACBETH   So foul and fair a day I have not seen.
   BANQUO   How far is't called° to Forres?—What are these,   *said to be*
   So withered, and so wild in their attire,
   That look not like th'inhabitants o'th' earth
40 And yet are on't?—Live you, or are you aught
   That man may question?° You seem to understand me   *converse with*
   By each at once her choppy° finger laying   *chapped*
   Upon her skinny lips. You should be women,
   And yet your beards forbid me to interpret
   That you are so.
45 MACBETH [*to the* WITCHES]   Speak, if you can. What are you?
   FIRST WITCH   All hail, Macbeth! Hail to thee, Thane of Glamis.
   SECOND WITCH   All hail, Macbeth! Hail to thee, Thane of Cawdor.
   THIRD WITCH   All hail, Macbeth, that shalt be king hereafter!
   BANQUO   Good sir, why do you start and seem to fear
50 Things that do sound so fair? [*To the* WITCHES] I'th' name of truth,
   Are ye fantastical° or that indeed   *imaginary*

1. The fat-bottomed scabbed woman.   3. F: "weyward," from the Old English "wyrd," meaning
2. Eyelid, which projects out over the eye like the sloping   "fate."
roof of a penthouse.

Which outwardly ye show? My noble partner
You greet with present grace° and great prediction   title
Of noble having° and of royal hope,   estate
55   That he seems rapt withal.⁴ To me you speak not.
If you can look into the seeds of time
And say which grain will grow and which will not,
Speak then to me, who neither beg nor fear
Your favours nor your hate.
60 FIRST WITCH   Hail!
SECOND WITCH   Hail!
THIRD WITCH   Hail!
FIRST WITCH   Lesser than Macbeth, and greater.
SECOND WITCH   Not so happy,° yet much happier.   fortunate
65 THIRD WITCH   Thou shalt get° kings, though thou be none.   beget
So all hail, Macbeth and Banquo!
FIRST WITCH   Banquo and Macbeth, all hail!
MACBETH   Stay, you imperfect° speakers, tell me more.   incomplete
By Sinel's° death I know I am Thane of Glamis,   Macbeth's father
70   But how of Cawdor? The Thane of Cawdor lives,
A prosperous gentleman, and to be king
Stands not within the prospect of belief,
No more than to be Cawdor. Say from whence
You owe° this strange intelligence,° or why   possess / information
75   Upon this blasted° heath you stop our way   blighted
With such prophetic greeting. Speak, I charge you.
           [*The*] WITCHES *vanish*
BANQUO   The earth hath bubbles, as the water has,
And these are of them. Whither are they vanished?
MACBETH   Into the air, and what seemed corporal°   corporeal
80   Melted as breath into the wind. Would they had stayed.
BANQUO   Were such things here as we do speak about,
Or have we eaten on the insane root⁵
That takes the reason prisoner?
MACBETH   Your children shall be kings.
BANQUO   You shall be king.
85 MACBETH   And Thane of Cawdor too. Went it not so?
BANQUO   To th' self-same tune and words. Who's here?
           Enter ROSS *and* ANGUS
ROSS   The King hath happily received, Macbeth,
The news of thy success, and when he reads°   considers
Thy personal venture° in the rebels' sight   exploits
90   His wonders and his praises do contend
Which should be thine or his; silenced with that,⁶
In viewing o'er the rest o'th' self-same day
He finds thee in the stout Norwegian ranks,
Nothing° afeard of what thyself didst make,   Not at all
95   Strange images° of death. As thick as hail   forms
Came post° with post, and every one did bear   messenger
Thy praises in his kingdom's great defence,
And poured them down before him.
ANGUS [*to* MACBETH]   We are sent

4. He seems entranced by these predictions.   to speak of his astonishment or his admiration, and so is
5. Of the root causing insanity, possibly hemlock.   silent.
6. *His wonders . . . that:* Duncan does not know whether

To give thee from our royal master thanks;
100 Only to herald thee into his sight,
Not pay thee.
ROSS   And, for an earnest° of a greater honour,   *a pledge*
He bade me from him call thee Thane of Cawdor,
In which addition,° hail, most worthy thane,   *title*
For it is thine.
105 BANQUO   What, can the devil speak true?
MACBETH   The Thane of Cawdor lives. Why do you dress me
In borrowed robes?
ANGUS   Who was the thane lives yet,
But under heavy judgement bears that life
Which he deserves to lose. Whether he was combined°   *allied*
110 With those of Norway, or did line the rebel°   *support Macdonald*
With hidden help and vantage,° or that with both   *benefit*
He laboured in his country's wrack,[7] I know not;
But treasons capital, confessed, and proved
Have overthrown him.
MACBETH [*aside*]   Glamis, and Thane of Cawdor.
115 The greatest is behind.° [*To* ROSS *and* ANGUS] Thanks for your pains.   *to come*
[*To* BANQUO] Do you not hope your children shall be kings
When those that gave the thane of Cawdor to me
Promised no less to them?
BANQUO   That, trusted home,°   *completely*
Might yet enkindle° you unto the crown,   *encourage*
120 Besides the thane of Cawdor. But 'tis strange,
And oftentimes to win us to our harm
The instruments of darkness tell us truths,
Win us with honest trifles to betray's°   *betray us*
In deepest consequence.
125 [*To* ROSS *and* ANGUS] Cousins, a word, I pray you.
MACBETH [*aside*]   Two truths are told
As happy prologues to the swelling act[8]
Of the imperial theme. [*To* ROSS *and* ANGUS]   I thank you, gentlemen.
[*Aside*] This supernatural soliciting°   *temptation*
130 Cannot be ill, cannot be good. If ill,
Why hath it given me earnest of success
Commencing in a truth? I am Thane of Cawdor.
If good, why do I yield to that suggestion
Whose horrid image doth unfix my hair
135 And make my seated heart knock at my ribs
Against the use° of nature? Present fears   *custom*
Are less than horrible imaginings.
My thought, whose murder yet is but fantastical,[9]
Shakes so my single state of man[1] that function°   *capacity to act*
140 Is smothered in surmise,° and nothing is   *speculation*
But what is not.
BANQUO [*to* ROSS *and* ANGUS]
                     Look how our partner's rapt.
MACBETH [*aside*]   If chance will have me king, why, chance may crown me
Without my stir.°   *effort*

7. He worked to bring about his country's ruin.   9. In which murder is so far only a fantasy.
8. To the developing action, or climactic dramatic   1. My undivided self. Macbeth feels that his wholeness is
action.   coming apart under the pressure of his criminal thought.

BANQUO [to ROSS and ANGUS]
              New honours come upon him,
  Like our strange° garments, cleave not to their mould°   *new / wearer's form*
  But with the aid of use.
145 MACBETH [aside]   Come what come may,
  Time and the hour runs through the roughest day.[2]
BANQUO   Worthy Macbeth, we stay° upon your leisure.   *wait; attend*
MACBETH   Give me your favour.° My dull brain was wrought°   *pardon / agitated*
  With things forgotten. [To ROSS and ANGUS] Kind gentlemen,
    your pains
150 Are registered° where every day I turn   *recorded (in my memory)*
  The leaf to read them. Let us toward the King.
  [Aside to BANQUO] Think upon what hath chanced, and at
    more time,
  The interim having weighed it, let us speak
  Our free hearts° each to other.   *unconcealed thoughts*
155 BANQUO   Very gladly.
MACBETH   Till then, enough. [To ROSS and ANGUS] Come, friends.
                           Exeunt

1.4

Flourish. Enter KING [DUNCAN], LENNOX, MALCOLM,
DONALBAIN, *and attendants*
KING DUNCAN   Is execution done on Cawdor? Are not
  Those in commission[1] yet returned?
MALCOLM   My liege,
  They are not yet come back. But I have spoke
  With one that saw him die, who did report
5   That very frankly he confessed his treasons,
  Implored your highness' pardon, and set forth
  A deep repentance. Nothing in his life
  Became him like the leaving it. He died
  As one that had been studied° in his death   *practiced*
10   To throw away the dearest thing he owed°   *owned*
  As 'twere a careless° trifle.   *an uncared-for*
KING DUNCAN   There's no art
  To find the mind's construction in the face.
  He was a gentleman on whom I built
  An absolute trust.
        Enter MACBETH, BANQUO, ROSS, *and* ANGUS
  [To MACBETH]   O worthiest cousin,
15   The sin of my ingratitude even now
  Was heavy on me! Thou art so far before°   *ahead*
  That swiftest wing of recompense is slow
  To overtake thee. Would thou hadst less deserved,
  That the proportion both of thanks and payment
20   Might have been mine.[2] Only I have left to say,
  'More is thy due than more than all can pay'.
MACBETH   The service and the loyalty I owe,
  In doing it, pays itself. Your highness' part
  Is to receive our duties, and our duties

---

2. *Come . . . day*: What must happen will happen one
way or another.
1.4 Location: A camp near the battlefield.

1. Those charged to execute Cawdor.
2. *That . . . mine*: That the rewards would be generously
proportional to Macbeth's desert.

25 Are to your throne and state children and servants
Which do but what they should by doing everything
Safe toward° your love and honour.   *To safeguard*
KING DUNCAN   Welcome hither.
I have begun to plant thee, and will labour
To make thee full of growing.—Noble Banquo,
30 That hast no less deserved, nor must be known
No less to have done so, let me enfold thee
And hold thee to my heart.
BANQUO   There if I grow
The harvest is your own.
KING DUNCAN   My plenteous joys,
Wanton° in fullness, seek to hide themselves   *Unrestrained*
35 In drops of sorrow. Sons, kinsmen, thanes,
And you whose places are the nearest,° know   *nearest to the throne*
We will establish our estate³ upon
Our eldest, Malcolm, whom we name hereafter
The Prince of Cumberland;⁴ which honour must
40 Not unaccompanied invest him only,⁵
But signs of nobleness, like stars, shall shine
On all deservers. [*To* MACBETH] From hence to Inverness,°   *Macbeth's estate*
And bind us further to you.⁶
MACBETH   The rest is labour which is not used for you.⁷
45 I'll be myself the harbinger,⁸ and make joyful
The hearing of my wife with your approach;
So humbly take my leave.
KING DUNCAN   My worthy Cawdor.
MACBETH [*aside*]   The Prince of Cumberland—that is a step
On which I must fall down or else o'erleap,
50 For in my way it lies. Stars, hide your fires,
Let not light see my black and deep desires;
The eye wink at the hand;⁹ yet let that be°   *be done*
Which the eye fears, when it is done, to see.   *Exit*
KING DUNCAN   True, worthy Banquo, he is full so valiant,¹
55 And in his commendations I am fed.
It is a banquet to me. Let's after him,
Whose care is gone before to bid us welcome.
It is a peerless kinsman.   *Flourish. Exeunt*

1.5

Enter [LADY MACBETH,] *with a letter*
LADY MACBETH [*reading*]   'They met me in the day of success,
and I have learned by the perfect'st° report they have more in   *most accurate*
them than mortal knowledge. When I burned in desire to ques-
tion them further, they made themselves air, into which they
5 vanished. Whiles I stood rapt in the wonder of it came missives°   *messengers*
from the King, who all-hailed me "Thane of Cawdor", by
which title before these weird sisters saluted me, and referred
me to the coming on of time with "Hail, King that shalt be!"

3. We will settle the succession of the kingdom. At the time, the Scottish crown was not hereditary.
4. Title of the Scottish heir apparent.
5. *which . . . only:* honors will not be bestowed on Malcolm alone.
6. And make me further indebted to you by your hospitality.

7. Even repose seems wearisome when it is not dedicated to your purposes.
8. Forerunner; messenger sent ahead to arrange royal lodgings.
9. Let the eye deliberately ignore what the hand does.
1. As valiant as you say.

This have I thought good to deliver° thee, my dearest partner   *inform*
10   of greatness, that thou mightst not lose the dues of rejoicing by
being ignorant of what greatness is promised thee. Lay it to thy
heart, and farewell.'
Glamis thou art, and Cawdor, and shalt be
What thou art promised. Yet do I fear° thy nature.   *doubt*
15   It is too full o'th' milk of human kindness
To catch the nearest° way. Thou wouldst be great,   *most expedient*
Art not without ambition, but without
The illness° should attend it. What thou wouldst highly,   *wickedness (that)*
That wouldst thou holily; wouldst not play false,
20   And yet wouldst wrongly win. Thou'dst have, great Glamis,
That which cries 'Thus thou must do' if thou have it,
And that which rather thou dost fear to do
Than wishest should be undone. Hie° thee hither,   *Hasten*
That I may pour my spirits in thine ear
25   And chastise with the valour of my tongue
All that impedes thee from the golden round°   *crown*
Which fate and metaphysical° aid doth seem   *supernatural*
To have thee crowned withal.°   *with*

Enter [a SERVANT]

                       What is your tidings?
SERVANT   The King comes here tonight.
LADY MACBETH   Thou'rt mad to say it.
30   Is not thy master with him, who, were't so,
Would have informed for preparation?
SERVANT   So please you, it is true. Our thane is coming,
One of my fellows had the speed of° him,   *outdistanced*
Who, almost dead for breath, had scarcely more
Than would make up his message.
35   LADY MACBETH   Give him tending;
He brings great news.   *Exit* [SERVANT]
                The raven[1] himself is hoarse
That croaks the fatal entrance of Duncan
Under my battlements. Come, you spirits
That tend on mortal° thoughts, unsex me here,   *attend deadly*
40   And fill me from the crown to the toe top-full
Of direst cruelty. Make thick my blood,
Stop up th'access and passage to remorse,°   *pity*
That no compunctious visitings of nature
Shake my fell° purpose, nor keep peace° between   *cruel / intervene*
45   Th'effect and it.[2] Come to my woman's breasts,
And take my milk for° gall, you murd'ring ministers,°   *in exchange for / agents*
Wherever in your sightless° substances   *invisible*
You wait on° nature's mischief. Come, thick night,   *assist*
And pall° thee in the dunnest° smoke of hell,   *envelop / darkest*
50   That my keen knife see not the wound it makes,
Nor heaven peep through the blanket of the dark
To cry 'Hold, hold!'

Enter MACBETH

                Great Glamis, worthy Cawdor,
Greater than both by the all-hail hereafter,

1.5 Location: Inverness, Macbeth's castle.   2. My purpose and its accomplishment.
1. The raven was considered a bird of ill omen.

Thy letters have transported me beyond
55   This ignorant present, and I feel now
The future in the instant.

MACBETH   My dearest love,
Duncan comes here tonight.

LADY MACBETH   And when goes hence?

MACBETH   Tomorrow, as he purposes.

LADY MACBETH   O never
Shall sun that morrow see.
60   Your face, my thane, is as a book where men
May read strange matters. To beguile the time,
Look like the time;[3] bear welcome in your eye,
Your hand, your tongue; look like the innocent flower,
But be the serpent under't. He that's coming
65   Must be provided for; and you shall put
This night's great business into my dispatch,°   *management*
Which shall to all our nights and days to come
Give solely sovereign sway and masterdom.

MACBETH   We will speak further.

LADY MACBETH   Only look up clear.°   *appear innocent*
70   To alter favour[4] ever is to fear.
Leave all the rest to me.   *Exeunt*

1.6

Hautboys° and torches. Enter KING [DUNCAN], MAL-   *Oboes*
COLM, DONALBAIN, BANQUO, LENNOX, MACDUFF, ROSS,
ANGUS, *and attendants*

KING DUNCAN   This castle hath a pleasant seat.° The air   *location*
Nimbly and sweetly recommends itself
Unto our gentle senses.

BANQUO   This guest of summer,
The temple-haunting martlet,[1] does approve°   *prove*
5   By his loved mansionry° that the heavens' breath   *nest building*
Smells wooingly here. No jutty,° frieze,   *projection*
Buttress, nor coign of vantage° but this bird   *convenient corner*
Hath made his pendant bed and procreant° cradle;   *for breeding*
Where they most breed and haunt I have observed
The air is delicate.

Enter LADY [MACBETH]

10   KING DUNCAN   See, see, our honoured hostess!
The love that follows us sometime is our trouble,
Which still we thank as love.[2] Herein I teach you
How you shall bid God 'ield us for your pains,
And thank us for your trouble.[3]

LADY MACBETH   All our service
15   In every point twice done, and then done double,
Were° poor and single° business to contend   *Would be / small*
Against those honours deep and broad wherewith
Your majesty loads our house. For those of old,
And the late dignities heaped up to them,

---

3. *To . . . like the time:* To deceive the world, match your
expression to the occasion.
4. To alter your facial expression and thereby arouse suspicion.
1.6 Location: Outside Macbeth's castle.

1. A bird, the martin, that often built its nest in churches.
2. *The . . . love:* Love bestowed upon us sometimes causes
us inconvenience, but we are still grateful for it.
3. *How . . . trouble:* Ask God to reward ("yield") me for
the trouble I cause you.

We rest your hermits.[4]

20   KING DUNCAN   Where's the Thane of Cawdor?
We coursed him at the heels,° and had a purpose   *followed him closely*
To be his purveyor;[5] but he rides well,
And his great love, sharp as his spur, hath holp° him   *helped*
To his home before us. Fair and noble hostess,
We are your guest tonight.

25   LADY MACBETH   Your servants ever
Have theirs, themselves, and what is theirs in count°   *in trust*
To make their audit at your highness' pleasure,
Still to return your own.[6]

  KING DUNCAN   Give me your hand.
Conduct me to mine host. We love him highly,
30   And shall continue our graces towards him.
By your leave,[7] hostess.   *Exeunt*

1.7

Hautboys. Torches. Enter a sewer° and divers servants   *butler*
with dishes and service over the stage. Then enter MACBETH

  MACBETH   If it were done when 'tis done, then 'twere well
It were done quickly. If th'assassination
Could trammel up the consequence, and catch
With his surcease success:[1] that but this blow
5   Might be the be-all and the end-all, here,°   *in this world*
But here upon this bank and shoal[2] of time,
We'd jump° the life to come. But in these cases   *risk*
We still have judgement[3] here, that° we but teach   *in that*
Bloody instructions which, being taught, return
10   To plague th'inventor. This even-handed° justice   *impartial*
Commends th'ingredience° of our poisoned chalice   *contents*
To our own lips. He's here in double trust:
First, as I am his kinsman and his subject,
Strong both against the deed; then, as his host,
15   Who should against his murderer shut the door,
Not bear the knife myself. Besides, this Duncan
Hath borne his faculties° so meek, hath been   *authority*
So clear° in his great office, that his virtues   *blameless*
Will plead like angels, trumpet-tongued against
20   The deep damnation of his taking-off,°   *murder*
And pity, like a naked new-born babe,
Striding the blast,[4] or heaven's cherubin, horsed
Upon the sightless couriers[5] of the air,
Shall blow the horrid deed in every eye

4. We remain your beadsmen (monks hired to pray for their employers).
5. Attendant who preceded the king when he traveled and procured foodstuffs for the royal party.
6. *Your servants . . . own:* Your servants hold all that they have in trust from you, and they are always ready to settle accounts and return to you what is yours.
7. By your permission. A request for permission to leave or perhaps for a formal kiss.
1.7 Location: A courtyard or anteroom in Macbeth's castle.
1. *If th'assassination . . . success:* If only I could gain suc-

cess with Duncan's death; if only the assassination were the end of the matter. *trammel up the consequence:* restrain the subsequent sequence of events, as in a trammel, or net.
2. Sandbar. The mortal span is seen as a narrow piece of land in the river of time. F has "Schoole," and "bank" may also mean "bench," suggesting that life is a time of instruction and probation.
3. We are invariably punished.
4. Astride the storm provoked by Duncan's death.
5. The invisible runners, the winds.

25 That tears shall drown the wind.[6] I have no spur
To prick the sides of my intent, but only
Vaulting ambition which o'erleaps itself
And falls on th'other.[7]

Enter LADY [MACBETH]

How now? What news?

LADY MACBETH   He has almost supped. Why have you left the chamber?

MACBETH   Hath he asked for me?

30 LADY MACBETH   Know you not he has?

MACBETH   We will proceed no further in this business.
He hath honoured me of late, and I have bought°   *won*
Golden opinions from all sorts of people,
Which would be worn now in their newest gloss,
Not cast aside so soon.

35 LADY MACBETH   Was the hope drunk
Wherein you dressed yourself? Hath it slept since?
And wakes it now to look so green° and pale   *sickly*
At what it did so freely? From this time
Such I account thy love. Art thou afeard

40 To be the same in thine own act and valour
As thou art in desire? Wouldst thou have that°   *(the crown)*
Which thou esteem'st the ornament of life,
And live a coward in thine own esteem,
Letting 'I dare not' wait upon 'I would',
Like the poor cat i'th' adage?[8]

45 MACBETH   Prithee, peace.
I dare do all that may become a man;
Who dares do more is none.

LADY MACBETH   What beast was't then
That made you break° this enterprise to me?   *broach*
When you durst do it, then you were a man;

50 And to be more than what you were, you would
Be so much more the man. Nor time nor place
Did then adhere,° and yet you would make both.   *agree*
They have made themselves, and that their fitness now
Does unmake you. I have given suck, and know
How tender 'tis to love the babe that milks me.

55 I would, while it was smiling in my face,
Have plucked my nipple from his boneless gums
And dashed the brains out, had I so sworn
As you have done to this.

MACBETH   If we should fail?

LADY MACBETH   We fail![9]

60 But screw your courage to the sticking-place[1]
And we'll not fail. When Duncan is asleep—
Whereto the rather shall his day's hard journey
Soundly invite him—his two chamberlains°   *bedroom attendants*
Will I with wine and wassail° so convince°   *carousing / overpower*
That memory, the warder° of the brain,   *guard*
65 Shall be a fume, and the receipt° of reason   *receptacle*

---

6. Tears will fall like heavy rain, which was believed to still the wind.
7. The other side. The image is of a rider vaulting over his horse instead of into his saddle, or of a horseman who clears a high obstacle but falls on the other side.
8. Proverbial: "The cat wanted fish but would not wet her feet."
9. F: "faile?"
1. The notch on a crossbow that holds the string, which is cranked or screwed taut.

A limbeck² only. When in swinish sleep
Their drenchèd° natures lies as in a death,   *sodden*
What cannot you and I perform upon
70   Th'unguarded Duncan? What not put upon
His spongy officers, who shall bear the guilt
Of our great quell?°   *murder*
MACBETH   Bring forth men-children only,
For thy undaunted mettle° should compose   *substance*
Nothing but males. Will it not be received,°   *believed*
75   When we have marked with blood those sleepy two
Of his own chamber and used their very daggers,
That they have done't?
LADY MACBETH   Who dares receive it other,
As we shall make our griefs and clamour roar
Upon his death?
MACBETH   I am settled, and bend up
80   Each corporal° agent to this terrible feat.   *bodily*
Away, and mock° the time with fairest show.   *deceive*
False face must hide what the false heart doth know.

                               Exeunt

2.1

Enter BANQUO *and* FLEANCE, *with a torch
before him*
BANQUO   How goes the night, boy?
FLEANCE   The moon is down. I have not heard the clock.
BANQUO   And she goes down at twelve.
FLEANCE   I take't 'tis later, sir.
BANQUO [*giving* FLEANCE *his sword*]   Hold, take my sword.
There's husbandry° in heaven,   *thrift*
5   Their candles are all out. Take thee that,¹ too.
A heavy summons° lies like lead upon me,   *summons to sleep*
And yet I would not sleep. Merciful powers,²
Restrain in me the cursèd thoughts that nature
Gives way to in repose.
        Enter MACBETH, *and a servant with a torch*
               Give me my sword. Who's there?
10   MACBETH   A friend.
BANQUO   What, sir, not yet at rest? The King's a-bed.
He hath been in unusual pleasure, and
Sent forth great largesse° to your offices.³   *gifts*
This diamond he greets your wife withal
15   By the name of most kind hostess, and shut up°   *concluded*
In measureless content.
MACBETH   Being unprepared
Our will became the servant to defect,
Which else should free have wrought.⁴
BANQUO   All's well.
I dreamt last night of the three weird sisters.
To you they have showed some truth.

---

2. Alembic, the upper part of a still to which fumes rise.
The wine will make the memory a fume that will fill and
cloud the brain, the "receptacle of reason."
2.1 Location: The courtyard of Macbeth's castle.
1. Some article of clothing or armor.

2. Angels invoked as protection against demons.
3. Household departments.
4. *Being . . . wrought:* Our desire to entertain the King
liberally was constrained by the fact that we were unprepared. *defect:* deficiency. *free:* freely.

20 MACBETH   I think not of them;
    Yet, when we can entreat an hour to serve,
    We would spend it in some words upon that business
    If you would grant the time.
    BANQUO   At your kind'st leisure.
    MACBETH If you shall cleave to my consent when 'tis,[5]
    It shall make honour for you.
25 BANQUO   So° I lose none   *Provided*
    In seeking to augment it, but still keep
    My bosom franchised° and allegiance clear,°   *guiltless / unstained*
    I shall be counselled.°   *receptive*
    MACBETH   Good repose the while.
30 BANQUO   Thanks, sir. The like to you.
                        Exeunt BANQUO [*and* FLEANCE]
    MACBETH [*to the Servant*]   Go bid thy mistress, when my drink is ready,
    She strike upon the bell. Get thee to bed.   *Exit* [*Servant*]
    Is this a dagger which I see before me,
    The handle toward my hand? Come, let me clutch thee.
35 I have thee not, and yet I see thee still.
    Art thou not, fatal vision, sensible°   *perceptible*
    To feeling as to sight? Or art thou but
    A dagger of the mind, a false creation
    Proceeding from the heat-oppressèd° brain?   *fevered*
40 I see thee yet, in form as palpable
    As this which now I draw.
    Thou marshall'st° me the way that I was going,   *guide*
    And such an instrument I was to use.
    Mine eyes are made the fools o'th' other senses,
45 Or else worth all the rest. I see thee still,
    And on thy blade and dudgeon gouts° of blood,   *and handle drops*
    Which was not so before. There's no such thing.
    It is the bloody business which informs°   *creates shapes*
    Thus to mine eyes. Now o'er the one half-world
50 Nature seems dead, and wicked dreams abuse°   *deceive*
    The curtained sleep. Witchcraft celebrates
    Pale Hecate's offerings,[6] and withered murder,
    Alarumed° by his sentinel the wolf,   *Roused*
    Whose howl's his watch,° thus with his stealthy pace,   *watchword*
55 With Tarquin's[7] ravishing strides, towards his design°   *prey*
    Moves like a ghost. Thou sure and firm-set earth,
    Hear not my steps which way they walk, for fear
    Thy very stones prate of my whereabout,
    And take the present horror° from the time,   *terrible stillness*
60 Which now suits with it. Whiles I threat, he lives.
    Words to the heat of deeds too cold breath gives.
            A bell rings
    I go, and it is done. The bell invites me.
    Hear it not, Duncan; for it is a knell
    That summons thee to heaven or to hell.   *Exit*

---

5. If you will support my opinion or my cause when the time comes.
6. Sacrificial rites offered to Hecate, goddess of witchcraft and of the moon.
7. A Roman prince who ravished the chaste matron Lucrece. Shakespeare tells the story in *The Rape of Lucrece*.

2.2

Enter LADY [MACBETH]

LADY MACBETH That which hath made them drunk hath made me bold.
What hath quenched them hath given me fire. Hark, peace!—
It was the owl that shrieked, the fatal bellman°   *night watchman*
Which gives the stern'st good-night.¹ He is about it.
5   The doors are open, and the surfeited grooms°   *attendants*
Do mock their charge° with snores. I have drugged their   *duty*
       possets°   *mulled milk and wine*
That death and nature do contend about them
Whether they live or die.

Enter MACBETH [*above*]

MACBETH   Who's there? What ho?   [*Exit*]
LADY MACBETH Alack, I am afraid they have awaked,
10   And 'tis not done. Th'attempt and not the deed
Confounds° us. Hark!—I laid their daggers ready;   *Ruins*
He could not miss 'em. Had he not resembled
My father as he slept, I had done't.

[*Enter* MACBETH *below*]

                         My husband!

MACBETH I have done the deed. Didst thou not hear a noise?
15   LADY MACBETH I heard the owl scream and the crickets cry.
Did not you speak?
MACBETH   When?
LADY MACBETH   Now.
MACBETH   As I descended?
LADY MACBETH Ay.
MACBETH   Hark!—Who lies i'th' second chamber?
LADY MACBETH Donalbain.
MACBETH [*looking at his hands*] This is a sorry sight.
LADY MACBETH A foolish thought, to say a sorry sight.
20   MACBETH There's one did laugh in's sleep, and one cried 'Murder!'
That they did wake each other. I stood and heard them.
But they did say their prayers and addressed them°   *settled themselves*
Again to sleep.
LADY MACBETH   There are two lodged together.
MACBETH One cried 'God bless us' and 'Amen' the other,
25   As° they had seen me with these hangman's² hands.   *As if*
List'ning their fear I could not say 'Amen'
When they did say 'God bless us.'
LADY MACBETH Consider it not so deeply.
MACBETH But wherefore could not I pronounce 'Amen'?
30   I had most need of blessing, and 'Amen'
Stuck in my throat.
LADY MACBETH   These deeds must not be thought°   *thought on*
After these ways. So, it will make us mad.
MACBETH Methought I heard a voice cry 'Sleep no more,
Macbeth does murder sleep'—the innocent sleep,
35   Sleep that knits up the ravelled sleave° of care,   *tangled skein*
The death of each day's life, sore labour's bath,

2.2 Location: Scene continues with only a brief pause.
1. A bell was rung outside the cells of condemned prisoners the night before they were to be executed.

2. Bloodstained. The hangman had to disembowel and
quarter his victims.

Balm of hurt minds, great nature's second course,[3]
Chief nourisher in life's feast—
LADY MACBETH   What do you mean?
MACBETH   Still it cried 'Sleep no more' to all the house,
40   'Glamis hath murdered sleep, and therefore Cawdor
Shall sleep no more, Macbeth shall sleep no more.'
LADY MACBETH   Who was it that thus cried? Why, worthy thane,
You do unbend° your noble strength to think   *slacken*
So brain-sickly of things. Go get some water
45   And wash this filthy witness° from your hand.   *evidence*
Why did you bring these daggers from the place?
They must lie there. Go, carry them, and smear
The sleepy grooms with blood.
MACBETH   I'll go no more.
I am afraid to think what I have done,
Look on't again I dare not.
50   LADY MACBETH   Infirm of purpose!
Give me the daggers. The sleeping and the dead
Are but as pictures. 'Tis the eye of childhood
That fears a painted devil. If he do bleed
I'll gild[4] the faces of the grooms withal,
For it must seem their guilt.   *Exit*
        Knock within
55   MACBETH   Whence is that knocking?—
How is't with me when every noise appals me?
What hands are here! Ha, they pluck out mine eyes.
Will all great Neptune's ocean wash this blood
Clean from my hand? No, this my hand will rather
60   The multitudinous seas incarnadine,°   *turn red*
Making the green one red.[5]
        Enter LADY [MACBETH]
LADY MACBETH   My hands are of your colour, but I shame
To wear a heart so white.
        Knock [within]
                    I hear a knocking
At the south entry. Retire we to our chamber.
65   A little water clears us of this deed.
How easy is it then! Your constancy
Hath left you unattended.[6]
        Knock [within]
                    Hark, more knocking.
Get on your nightgown, lest occasion call us
And show us to be watchers.[7] Be not lost
70   So poorly in your thoughts.
MACBETH   To know my deed 'twere best not know myself.[8]
        Knock [within]
Wake Duncan with thy knocking. I would thou couldst.
        Exeunt

---

3. Second, and most nourishing, course of a meal; second or alternative habit, or practice.
4. Coat as if with gold leaf. Gold was often called red; compare 2.3.109.
5. *one red:* entirely red.

6. *Your . . . unattended:* Your resolve has deserted you.
7. Those who have stayed awake.
8. It is better that I lose consciousness altogether than face my deed.

2.3

Enter a PORTER. *Knocking within*

PORTER Here's a knocking indeed! If a man were porter of hell-
gate he should have old° turning the key.   *plenty of*

Knock [within]

Knock, knock, knock. Who's there, i'th' name of Beelzebub?°   *name of a devil*
Here's a farmer that hanged himself on th'expectation of
5   plenty.[1] Come in time![2] Have napkins° enough about you; here   *handkerchiefs*
you'll sweat for't.

Knock [within]

Knock, knock. Who's there, in th'other devil's name? Faith,
here's an equivocator[3] that could swear in both the scales
against either scale, who committed treason enough for God's
10 sake, yet could not equivocate to heaven. O, come in, equivocator.

Knock [within]

Knock, knock, knock. Who's there? 'Faith, here's an English
tailor come hither for stealing out of a French hose.[4] Come in,
tailor. Here you may roast your goose.[5]

Knock [within]

15 Knock, knock. Never at quiet. What are you?—But this place
is too cold for hell. I'll devil-porter it no further. I had thought
to have let in some of all professions that go the primrose way
to th'everlasting bonfire.

Knock [within]

Anon, anon!

[He opens the gate]

20 I pray you remember the porter.

Enter MACDUFF *and* LENNOX

MACDUFF Was it so late, friend, ere you went to bed
That you do lie so late?

PORTER Faith, sir, we were carousing till the second cock,° and   *3:00 A.M.*
drink, sir, is a great provoker of three things.

25 MACDUFF What three things does drink especially provoke?

PORTER Marry,° sir, nose-painting,[6] sleep, and urine. Lechery,   *Indeed*
sir, it provokes and unprovokes: it provokes the desire but it
takes away the performance. Therefore much drink may be
said to be an equivocator with lechery: it makes him and it
30 mars him; it sets him on and it takes him off; it persuades him
and disheartens him, makes him stand to° and not stand to; in   *maintain an erection*
conclusion, equivocates him in a sleep,[7] and, giving him the
lie,[8] leaves him.

MACDUFF I believe drink gave thee the lie last night.

35 PORTER That it did, sir, i'the very throat on me;[9] but I requited

2.3 Location: Scene continues, perhaps after a short pause.
1. *Here's . . . plenty:* A farmer had hoarded grain to sell at high prices but was ruined by a crop surplus that forced prices down.
2. Good timing.
3. One who speaks ambiguously. An allusion to the Jesuit doctrine that a seemingly false statement was not a lie (and therefore not repugnant to God) if the speaker had in mind a different meaning in which the utterance was true. Possibly an allusion to the 1606 trial of the Jesuit Henry Garnet for involvement in the Gunpowder Plot to blow up the Houses of Parliament; Father Garnet had written a treatise defending equivocation for Catholics

being persecuted for their beliefs.
4. Tight-fitting breeches, which would easily reveal the tailor's attempt to skimp on the cloth supplied him for their manufacture. He had apparently been able to do so undetected when loose-fitting breeches were in fashion.
5. Heat your smoothing iron. Also, a swelling ("goose") caused by venereal disease.
6. Reddening of the nose through drink.
7. Gives him an erotic experience in dreams only.
8. An elaborate pun: calling him a liar; laying him out flat; making him urinate ("lye," or urine).
9. *i'the . . . me:* provoking a duel by insulting me with a deliberate lie.

him for his lie, and, I think, being too strong for him, though
he took up my legs sometime, yet I made a shift to cast him.[1]
MACDUFF   Is thy master stirring?

Enter MACBETH

Our knocking has awaked him: here he comes.   [*Exit* PORTER]
LENNOX [*to* MACBETH]   Good morrow, noble sir.
40 MACBETH   Good morrow, both.
MACDUFF   Is the King stirring, worthy thane?
MACBETH   Not yet.
MACDUFF   He did command me to call timely° on him.   *early*
    I have almost slipped the hour.
MACBETH   I'll bring you to him.
MACDUFF   I know this is a joyful trouble to you,
45   But yet 'tis one.
MACBETH   The labour we delight in physics pain.[2]
    This is the door.
MACDUFF   I'll make so bold to call,
    For 'tis my limited° service.   *Exit* MACDUFF   *appointed*
LENNOX   Goes the King hence today?
MACBETH   He does; he did appoint so.
50 LENNOX   The night has been unruly. Where we lay
    Our chimneys were blown down, and, as they say,
    Lamentings heard i'th' air, strange screams of death,
    And prophesying with accents terrible
    Of dire combustion° and confused events   *tumult*
55   New-hatched to th' woeful time. The obscure bird[3]
    Clamoured the livelong night. Some say the earth
    Was feverous and did shake.
MACBETH   'Twas a rough night.
LENNOX   My young remembrance cannot parallel
    A fellow to it.

Enter MACDUFF

MACDUFF   O horror, horror, horror!
60   Tongue nor heart cannot conceive nor name thee.
MACBETH *and* LENNOX   What's the matter?
MACDUFF   Confusion° now hath made his masterpiece.   *Ruin*
    Most sacrilegious murder hath broke ope
    The Lord's anointed temple° and stole thence   *(the King's body)*
65   The life o'th' building.
MACBETH   What is't you say—the life?
LENNOX   Mean you his majesty?
MACDUFF   Approach the chamber and destroy your sight
    With a new Gorgon.[4] Do not bid me speak.
    See, and then speak yourselves. *Exeunt* MACBETH *and* LENNOX
70   Awake, awake!
    Ring the alarum bell. Murder and treason!
    Banquo and Donalbain, Malcolm, awake!
    Shake off this downy sleep, death's counterfeit,
    And look on death itself. Up, up, and see
75   The great doom's image.° Malcolm, Banquo,   *replica of Doomsday*
    As from your graves rise up, and walk like sprites

---

1. *being . . . cast him*: the effects of drunkenness are   3. The owl, bird of darkness.
described in the language of a wrestling match. *cast*:   4. A mythical monster with a woman's figure and snakes
throw off; vomit.   for hair, the sight of whose face turned beholders to stone.
2. Pleasure in labor mitigates its laboriousness.   Medusa was one of the three Gorgons.

To countenance° this horror.   *suit; behold*
   Bell rings. Enter LADY [MACBETH]
LADY MACBETH   What's the business,
 That such a hideous trumpet calls to parley
 The sleepers of the house? Speak, speak.
MACDUFF   O gentle lady,
80 'Tis not for you to hear what I can speak.
 The repetition° in a woman's ear   *report*
 Would murder as it fell.
    Enter BANQUO
       O Banquo, Banquo,
 Our royal master's murdered!
LADY MACBETH   Woe, alas—
 What, in our house?
BANQUO   Too cruel anywhere.
85 Dear Duff, I prithee contradict thyself,
 And say it is not so.
    Enter MACBETH, LENNOX, *and* ROSS
MACBETH   Had I but died an hour before this chance°   *occurrence*
 I had lived a blessèd time, for from this instant
 There's nothing serious in mortality.°   *worth living for*
90 All is but toys.° Renown and grace is dead.   *trifles*
 The wine of life is drawn, and the mere lees
 Is left this vault° to brag of.   *wine vault; world*
    Enter MALCOLM *and* DONALBAIN
DONALBAIN   What is amiss?
MACBETH   You are, and do not know't.
95 The spring, the head, the fountain of your blood
 Is stopped, the very source of it is stopped.
MACDUFF   Your royal father's murdered.
MALCOLM   O, by whom?
LENNOX   Those of his chamber, as it seemed, had done't.
 Their hands and faces were all badged° with blood,   *marked*
100 So were their daggers, which, unwiped, we found
 Upon their pillows. They stared and were distracted.
 No man's life was to be trusted with them.
MACBETH   O, yet I do repent me of my fury
 That I did kill them.
MACDUFF   Wherefore did you so?
105 MACBETH   Who can be wise, amazed, temp'rate and furious,
 Loyal and neutral in a moment? No man.
 Th'expedition° of my violent love   *haste*
 Outran the pauser,° reason. Here lay Duncan,   *delayer*
 His silver skin laced with his golden blood,
110 And his gashed stabs looked like a breach in nature
 For ruin's wasteful° entrance; there the murderers,   *destructive*
 Steeped in the colours of their trade, their daggers
 Unmannerly breeched⁵ with gore. Who could refrain,
 That had a heart to love, and in that heart
 Courage to make 's love known?
115 LADY MACBETH   Help me hence, ho!
 MACDUFF   Look to the lady.
 MALCOLM [*aside to* DONALBAIN] Why do we hold our tongues,

---

5. Covered—as if with breeches—with blood.

That most may claim this argument° for ours?   *subject*
DONALBAIN [*aside to* MALCOLM]   What should be spoken here,
        where our fate,
    Hid in an auger-hole,° may rush and seize us?   *in a cranny; in ambush*
    Let's away. Our tears are not yet brewed.
120 MALCOLM [*aside to* DONALBAIN]   Nor our strong sorrow
    Upon the foot of motion.[6]
    BANQUO   Look to the lady;
                        [*Exit* LADY MACBETH, *attended*]
    And when we have our naked frailties hid,°   *clothed*
    That suffer in exposure, let us meet
    And question° this most bloody piece of work,   *discuss*
125 To know it further. Fears and scruples° shake us.   *doubts*
    In the great hand of God I stand, and thence
    Against the undivulged pretence I fight
    Of treasonous malice.[7]
    MACDUFF   And so do I.
    ALL   So all.
    MACBETH   Let's briefly° put on manly readiness,°   *quickly / clothes; resolve*
    And meet i'th' hall together.
130 ALL   Well contented.
                    Exeunt [all but MALCOLM *and* DONALBAIN]
    MALCOLM   What will you do? Let's not consort with them.
    To show an unfelt sorrow is an office
    Which the false man does easy. I'll to England.
    DONALBAIN   To Ireland, I. Our separated fortune
135 Shall keep us both the safer. Where we are
    There's daggers in men's smiles. The nea'er in blood,
    The nearer bloody.[8]
    MALCOLM   This murderous shaft that's shot
    Hath not yet lighted,° and our safest way   *fallen*
    Is to avoid the aim. Therefore to horse,
140 And let us not be dainty of° leave-taking,   *polite about*
    But shift° away. There's warrant° in that theft   *slip / justification*
    Which steals itself[9] when there's no mercy left.   *Exeunt*

2.4

Enter ROSS *with an* OLD MAN
    OLD MAN   Threescore and ten I can remember well,
    Within the volume of which time I have seen
    Hours dreadful and things strange, but this sore night
    Hath trifled former knowings.[1]
    ROSS   Ha, good father,
5   Thou seest the heavens, as troubled with man's act,
    Threatens his bloody stage. By th' clock 'tis day,
    And yet dark night strangles the travelling lamp.°   *sun*
    Is't night's predominance° or the day's shame   *ascendancy*
    That darkness does the face of earth entomb
    When living light should kiss it?
10 OLD MAN   'Tis unnatural,

---

6. *Nor . . . motion:* Nor has our strong sorrow yet begun
to express itself.
7. *Against . . . malice:* I will fight against the hidden purposes behind this treasonous act.
8. *The nea'er . . . bloody:* The closer the kinship, the

nearer the danger of murder.
9. *Which steals itself:* Malcolm alludes to the fact that he
and Donalbain intend to "steal" away from the castle.
2.4 Location: Not far from Macbeth's castle.
1. Has made previous experiences seem trifling.

Even like the deed that's done. On Tuesday last
A falcon, tow'ring in her pride of place,[2]
Was by a mousing owl[3] hawked at and killed.

ROSS   And Duncan's horses— a thing most strange and certain—

15   Beauteous and swift, the minions° of their race,   *darlings*
Turned wild in nature, broke their stalls, flung out,
Contending 'gainst obedience, as° they would   *as if*
Make war with mankind.

OLD MAN   'Tis said they ate each other.

ROSS   They did so, to th'amazement of mine eyes
That looked upon't.

Enter MACDUFF

20   Here comes the good Macduff.
How goes the world, sir, now?

MACDUFF   Why, see you not?

ROSS   Is't known who did this more than bloody deed?

MACDUFF   Those that Macbeth hath slain.

ROSS   Alas the day,
What good could they pretend?[4]

MACDUFF   They were suborned.°   *bribed*

25   Malcolm and Donalbain, the King's two sons,
Are stol'n away and fled, which puts upon them
Suspicion of the deed.

ROSS   'Gainst nature still.
Thriftless ambition, that will raven up°   *devour*
Thine own life's means! Then 'tis most like

30   The sovereignty will fall upon Macbeth.

MACDUFF   He is already named and gone to Scone[5]
To be invested.

ROSS   Where is Duncan's body?

MACDUFF   Carried to Colmekill,[6]

35   The sacred storehouse of his predecessors,
And guardian of their bones.

ROSS   Will you to Scone?

MACDUFF   No, cousin, I'll to Fife.[7]

ROSS   Well, I will thither.

MACDUFF   Well, may you see things well done there. Adieu,
Lest our old robes sit easier than our new.

40   ROSS   Farewell, father.

OLD MAN   God's benison° go with you, and with those   *blessing*
That would make good of bad, and friends of foes.

                                        Exeunt severally

3.1

Enter BANQUO

BANQUO   Thou hast it now: King, Cawdor, Glamis, all
As the weird women promised; and I fear
Thou played'st most foully for't. Yet it was said
It should not stand in thy posterity,[1]

5   But that myself should be the root and father

---

2. Mounting to her highest point in the sky before stooping.
3. An owl that usually feeds on mice.
4. What good to themselves could they expect to gain from the murder?

5. Ancient royal city where Scottish kings were crowned.
6. Iona, the burial place of Scottish kings.
7. Macduff is the Thane of Fife.
3.1 Location: The royal palace at Forres.
1. It should not pass to your descendants.

Of many kings. If there come truth from them—
As upon thee, Macbeth, their speeches shine°—   *are brilliantly fulfilled*
Why by the verities on thee made good
May they not be my oracles as well,
10   And set me up in hope? But hush, no more.
                Sennet° sounded. Enter MACBETH *as King,* LADY MAC-   *Trumpet call*
                BETH *as Queen,* LENNOX, ROSS, *lords, and attendants*
MACBETH   Here's our chief guest.
LADY MACBETH   If he had been forgotten
        It had been as a gap in our great feast,
        And all-thing° unbecoming.   *entirely*
MACBETH [*to* BANQUO]   Tonight we hold a solemn° supper, sir,   *formal*
        And I'll request your presence.
15 BANQUO   Let your highness
        Command upon me, to the which my duties
        Are with a most indissoluble tie
        For ever knit.
MACBETH   Ride you this afternoon?
20 BANQUO   Ay, my good lord.
MACBETH   We should have else desired your good advice,
        Which still° hath been both grave° and prosperous,   *always / weighty*
        In this day's council; but we'll talk tomorrow.
        Is't far you ride?
25 BANQUO   As far, my lord, as will fill up the time
        'Twixt this and supper. Go not my horse the better,[2]
        I must become a borrower of the night
        For a dark hour or twain.
MACBETH   Fail not our feast.
30 BANQUO   My lord, I will not.
MACBETH   We hear our bloody cousins are bestowed°   *lodged*
        In England and in Ireland, not confessing
        Their cruel parricide, filling their hearers
        With strange invention.° But of that tomorrow,   *falsehood*
35   When therewithal we shall have cause of state
        Craving us jointly.[3] Hie you to horse. Adieu,
        Till you return at night. Goes Fleance with you?
BANQUO   Ay, my good lord. Our time does call upon 's.
MACBETH   I wish your horses swift and sure of foot,
40   And so I do commend° you to their backs.   *entrust*
        Farewell.   *Exit* BANQUO
        Let every man be master of his time
        Till seven at night. To make society
        The sweeter welcome, we will keep ourself
45   Till supper-time alone. While° then, God be with you.   *Till*
                Exeunt [all but MACBETH *and a* SERVANT]
        Sirrah, a word with you. Attend those men
        Our pleasure?
SERVANT   They are, my lord, without° the palace gate.   *outside*
MACBETH   Bring them before us.   *Exit* SERVANT
                                To be thus is nothing
50   But to be safely thus.[4] Our fears in° Banquo   *of*

---

2. If my horse does not go faster than I expect.
3. *cause . . . jointly*: state business demanding our joint
attention.

4. *To be thus . . . thus*: To be a king is no good unless one
can reign in safety ("thus" refers to "king").

Stick° deep, and in his royalty of nature°   *Prick / natural nobility*
Reigns that which would be feared. 'Tis much he dares,
And to° that dauntless temper of his mind   *added to*
He hath a wisdom that doth guide his valour
55   To act in safety. There is none but he
Whose being I do fear, and under him
My genius° is rebuked as, it is said,[5]   *tutelary spirit*
Mark Antony's was by Caesar.° He chid the sisters   *Octavius Caesar*
When first they put the name of king upon me,
60   And bade them speak to him. Then, prophet-like,
They hailed him father to a line of kings.
Upon my head they placed a fruitless crown,
And put a barren sceptre in my grip,
Thence to be wrenched with° an unlineal hand,   *by*
65   No son of mine succeeding. If't be so,
For Banquo's issue have I filed° my mind,   *defiled*
For them the gracious° Duncan have I murdered,   *full of grace*
Put rancours° in the vessel of my peace   *bitterness*
Only for them, and mine eternal jewel°   *soul*
70   Given to the common enemy of man°   *(the devil)*
To make them kings, the seeds of Banquo kings.
Rather than so, come fate into the list°   *arena*
And champion me to th'utterance.[6] Who's there?
        Enter Servant and two MURDERERS
[*To the Servant*] Now go to the door, and stay there till we call.
                                                                         Exit Servant
75   Was it not yesterday we spoke together?
MURDERERS   It was, so please your highness.
MACBETH   Well then, now
Have you considered of my speeches? Know
That it was he in the times past which held you
So under° fortune, which you thought had been   *out of favor with*
80   Our innocent self. This I made good to you
In our last conference, passed in probation° with you   *reviewed the proof*
How you were borne in hand,° how crossed,° the instruments,[7]   *deceived / thwarted*
Who wrought with them, and all things else that might
To half a soul, and to a notion crazed,[8]
Say 'Thus did Banquo'.
85   FIRST MURDERER   You made it known to us.
MACBETH   I did so, and went further, which is now
Our point of second meeting. Do you find
Your patience so predominant in your nature
That you can let this go? Are you so gospelled[9]
90   To pray for this good man and for his issue,
Whose heavy hand hath bowed you to the grave
And beggared yours° for ever?   *your family*
FIRST MURDERER   We are men, my liege.
MACBETH   Ay, in the catalogue ye go for men,
As hounds and greyhounds, mongrels, spaniels, curs,
95   Shoughs, water-rugs, and demi-wolves[1] are clept°   *called*

5. Said by Plutarch. Shakespeare paraphrases him in   8. Even to a half-wit or to a crazed mind.
Antony and Cleopatra (2.3).   9. Imbued with the gospel spirit.
6. And fight with me in single combat to the death.   1. Shaggy lapdogs, water dogs (for fowling), and cross-
7. Agents.   breeds between wolf and dog.

All by the name of dogs. The valued file²
Distinguishes the swift, the slow, the subtle,
The housekeeper,° the hunter, every one   *watchdog*
According to the gift which bounteous nature
100   Hath in him closed;° whereby he does receive   *enclosed*
Particular addition from the bill
That writes them all alike.³ And so of men.
Now, if you have a station° in the file,   *position*
Not i'th' worst rank of manhood, say't,
105   And I will put that business in your bosoms
Whose execution takes your enemy off,
Grapples you to the heart and love of us,
Who wear our health but sickly in his life,
Which in his death were perfect.
SECOND MURDERER   I am one, my liege,
110   Whom the vile blows and buffets of the world
Hath so incensed that I am reckless what
I do to spite the world.
FIRST MURDERER   And I another,
So weary with disasters, tugged with° fortune,   *mauled by*
That I would set° my life on any chance   *risk*
To mend it or be rid on't.
115   MACBETH   Both of you
Know Banquo was your enemy.
MURDERERS   True, my lord.
MACBETH   So is he mine, and in such bloody distance°   *enmity*
That every minute of his being thrusts
Against my near'st of life;⁴ and though I could
120   With barefaced power sweep him from my sight
And bid my will avouch° it, yet I must not,   *warrant*
For° certain friends that are both his and mine,   *Because of*
Whose loves I may not drop, but wail° his fall   *must bewail*
Who I myself struck down. And thence it is
125   That I to your assistance do make love,°   *I solicit your aid*
Masking the business from the common eye
For sundry weighty reasons.
SECOND MURDERER   We shall, my lord,
Perform what you command us.
FIRST MURDERER   Though our lives—
MACBETH   Your spirits shine through you. Within this hour at most
130   I will advise you where to plant yourselves,
Acquaint you with the perfect spy o'th' time,
The moment on't;⁵ for't must be done tonight,
And something° from the palace; always thought°   *at some distance / remember*
That I require a clearness;⁶ and with him,
135   To leave no rubs° nor botches in the work,   *flaws*
Fleance, his son, that keeps him company—
Whose absence is no less material to me
Than is his father's—must embrace the fate
Of that dark hour. Resolve yourselves apart.⁷
I'll come to you anon.

---

2. List specifying the value of the catalogued items.
3. *Particular . . . alike:* Distinction apart from a catalogue
that lists them indiscriminately.
4. My most vital part, the heart.

5. *Acquaint . . . on't:* I will give you full and precise
instructions as to when it is to be done.
6. A clearance (from suspicion).
7. Make up your minds privately.

140 MURDERERS   We are resolved, my lord.
     MACBETH   I'll call upon you straight. Abide within.
                                     [*Exeunt* MURDERERS]
         It is concluded. Banquo, thy soul's flight,
         If it find heaven, must find it out tonight.   *Exit*

                                  3.2
                  Enter LADY [MACBETH] *and a* SERVANT
     LADY MACBETH   Is Banquo gone from court?
     SERVANT   Ay, madam, but returns again tonight.
     LADY MACBETH   Say to the King I would attend his leisure
         For a few words.
5   SERVANT   Madam, I will.   *Exit*
     LADY MACBETH   Naught's had, all's spent,
         Where our desire is got without content.°   *happiness*
         'Tis safer to be that which we destroy
         Than by destruction dwell in doubtful joy.
                  Enter MACBETH
10   How now, my lord, why do you keep alone,
         Of sorriest° fancies your companions making,   *most wretched*
         Using° those thoughts which should indeed have died   *Entertaining*
         With them they think on? Things without all remedy
         Should be without regard.° What's done is done.   *not considered*
15   MACBETH   We have scorched° the snake, not killed it.   *slashed*
         She'll close° and be herself, whilst our poor malice   *heal*
         Remains in danger of her former tooth.[1]
         But let the frame of things disjoint, both the worlds suffer,[2]
         Ere we will eat our meal in fear, and sleep
20   In the affliction of these terrible dreams
         That shake us nightly. Better be with the dead,
         Whom we to gain our peace have sent to peace,
         Than on the torture° of the mind to lie   *rack*
         In restless ecstasy.° Duncan is in his grave.   *frenzy*
25   After life's fitful fever he sleeps well.
         Treason has done his worst. Nor steel nor poison,
         Malice domestic, foreign levy,[3] nothing
         Can touch him further.
     LADY MACBETH   Come on, gentle my lord,
         Sleek o'er your rugged looks, be bright and jovial
         Among your guests tonight.
30   MACBETH   So shall I, love,
         And so I pray be you. Let your remembrance
         Apply° to Banquo. Present him eminence°   *Be given / favor*
         Both with eye and tongue; unsafe the while that we
         Must lave our honours in these flattering streams[4]
35   And make our faces visors° to our hearts,   *masks*
         Disguising what they are.
     LADY MACBETH   You must leave this.
     MACBETH   O, full of scorpions is my mind, dear wife!
         Thou know'st that Banquo and his Fleance lives.

3.2 Location: The palace.
1. *our . . . tooth:* we remain in danger of her fangs, which
are as dangerous as they were before she was slashed. *poor
malice:* weak enmity.
2. Let the universe fall apart, and heaven and earth suffer

destruction.
3. An army levied abroad against Scotland.
4. *unsafe . . . streams:* we are unsafe at present, so we
must make our reputations look clean by flattering others;
we are unsafe as long as we must flatter.

LADY MACBETH   But in them nature's copy's[5] not eterne.°   *everlasting*
40   MACBETH   There's comfort yet, they are assailable.
      Then be thou jocund. Ere the bat hath flown
      His cloistered° flight, ere to black Hecate's summons   *restricted*
      The shard-borne[6] beetle with his drowsy hums
      Hath rung night's yawning peal,[7] there shall be done
45   A deed of dreadful note.
      LADY MACBETH   What's to be done?
      MACBETH   Be innocent of the knowledge, dearest chuck,[8]
      Till thou applaud the deed.—Come, seeling[9] night,
      Scarf up° the tender eye of pitiful day,   *Blindfold*
      And with thy bloody and invisible hand
50   Cancel and tear to pieces that great bond°   *Banquo's lease on life*
      Which keeps me pale. Light thickens, and the crow
      Makes wing to th' rooky° wood.   *full of rooks*
      Good things of day begin to droop and drowse,
      Whiles night's black agents to their preys do rouse.
55   Thou marvell'st at my words; but hold thee still.
      Things bad begun make strong themselves by ill.
      So prithee go with me.   *Exeunt*

3.3

                    Enter three MURDERERS
FIRST MURDERER [*to* THIRD MURDERER]   But who did bid thee
         join with us?
THIRD MURDERER   Macbeth.
SECOND MURDERER [*to* FIRST MURDERER]   He needs not our mis-
         trust, since he delivers
      Our offices and what we have to do
      To the direction just.[1]
FIRST MURDERER [*to* THIRD MURDERER]   Then stand with us.
5   The west yet glimmers with some streaks of day.
      Now spurs the lated° traveller apace   *belated*
      To gain the timely inn, and near approaches
      The subject of our watch.
THIRD MURDERER   Hark, I hear horses.
BANQUO (*within*)   Give us a light there, ho!
SECOND MURDERER   Then 'tis he. The rest
10   That are within the note of expectation°   *list of expected guests*
      Already are i'th' court.
FIRST MURDERER   His horses go about.[2]
THIRD MURDERER   Almost a mile; but he does usually,
      So all men do, from hence to th' palace gate
      Make it their walk.
                    Enter BANQUO *and* FLEANCE *with a torch*
SECOND MURDERER [*aside*]   A light, a light.
THIRD MURDERER [*aside*]   'Tis he.
15   FIRST MURDERER [*aside*]   Stand to't.

---

5. Lease on life (a copyhold lease was subject to cancellation and therefore "not eterne"); the individual human cast from nature's mold.
6. Carried on scaly wings; born in dung ("shards").
7. Macbeth likens the beetle's humming to a muffled, yawn-inducing peal of bells.
8. Chick (term of endearment).

9. Eye-closing. Falcons' eyelids were sewn shut ("seeled") as part of their training.
3.3 Location: Near the palace.
1. *He . . . just:* We need not mistrust this man, since he knows perfectly Macbeth's instructions to us.
2. Can be heard as servants take them to the stables.

BANQUO   It will be rain tonight.
FIRST MURDERER   Let it come down.
    [FIRST MURDERER *strikes out the torch. The others attack*
    BANQUO]
BANQUO   O, treachery! Fly, good Fleance, fly, fly, fly!
    Thou mayst revenge.—O slave!   [*He dies. Exit* FLEANCE]
THIRD MURDERER   Who did strike out the light?
20 FIRST MURDERER   Was't not the way?°   *proper thing*
THIRD MURDERER   There's but one down. The son is fled.
SECOND MURDERER   We have lost best half of our affair.
FIRST MURDERER   Well, let's away and say how much is done.
                              Exeunt [*with Banquo's body*]

3.4

Banquet prepared. Enter MACBETH [*as King*], LADY [MAC-
BETH *as Queen*], ROSS, LENNOX, *Lords, and attendants.*
    [LADY MACBETH *sits*]
MACBETH   You know your own degrees;° sit down. At first and last[1]   *ranks; places*
    The hearty welcome.
LORDS   Thanks to your majesty.
    [*They sit*]
MACBETH   Ourself will mingle with society
    And play the humble host. Our hostess keeps her state,°   *chair of state*
5   But in best time we will require° her welcome.   *request*
LADY MACBETH   Pronounce it for me, sir, to all our friends,
    For my heart speaks they are welcome.
    Enter FIRST MURDERER [*to the door*]
MACBETH   See, they encounter° thee with their hearts' thanks.   *answer*
    Both sides are even. Here I'll sit, i'th' midst.
10   Be large° in mirth. Anon we'll drink a measure   *unrestrained*
    The table round. [*To* FIRST MURDERER] There's blood upon thy face.
FIRST MURDERER [*aside to* MACBETH]   'Tis Banquo's, then.
MACBETH   'Tis better thee without than he within.[2]
    Is he dispatched?
15   FIRST MURDERER   My lord, his throat is cut. That I did for him.
MACBETH   Thou art the best o'th' cut-throats. Yet he's good
    That did the like for Fleance. If thou didst it,
    Thou art the nonpareil.°   *paragon (without equal)*
FIRST MURDERER   Most royal sir,
    Fleance is scaped.
20   MACBETH   Then comes my fit again; I had else been perfect,
    Whole as the marble, founded° as the rock,   *immovable*
    As broad and general° as the casing° air,   *unconstrained / surrounding*
    But now I am cabined, cribbed,° confined, bound in   *confined*
    To saucy° doubts and fears. But Banquo's safe?   *importunate*
25   FIRST MURDERER   Ay, my good lord. Safe in a ditch he bides,
    With twenty trenchèd gashes on his head,
    The least a death to nature.
MACBETH   Thanks for that.
    There the grown serpent lies. The worm° that's fled   *young serpent*
    Hath nature that in time will venom breed,

3.4 Location: The palace.   2. Better on you than inside him.
1. Once and for all.

30 No teeth for th' present. Get thee gone. Tomorrow
    We'll hear ourselves° again.   *Exit* [FIRST] MURDERER   *confer*
LADY MACBETH   My royal lord,
    You do not give the cheer.° The feast is sold   *entertain*
    That is not often vouched, while 'tis a-making,
    'Tis given with welcome.³ To feed° were best at home.   *Mere eating*
35 From thence° the sauce to meat is ceremony,   *Away from home*
    Meeting were° bare without it.   *Company would be*
        Enter the Ghost of Banquo, and sits in Macbeth's place
MACBETH   Sweet remembrancer.°   *reminder*
    Now good digestion wait on appetite,
    And health on both.
LENNOX   May't please your highness sit?
MACBETH   Here had we now our country's honour roofed⁴
40 Were the graced person of our Banquo present,
    Who may I rather challenge for° unkindness   *accuse of*
    Than pity for mischance.
ROSS   His absence, sir,
    Lays blame upon his promise. Please't your highness
    To grace us with your royal company?
MACBETH   The table's full.
45 LENNOX   Here is a place reserved, sir.
MACBETH   Where?
LENNOX   Here, my good lord. What is't that moves your highness?
MACBETH   Which of you have done this?
LORDS   What, my good lord?
MACBETH [*to the Ghost*]   Thou canst not say I did it. Never shake
50 Thy gory locks at me.
ROSS [*rising*]   Gentlemen, rise. His highness is not well.
LADY MACBETH [*rising*]   Sit, worthy friends. My lord is often thus,
    And hath been from his youth. Pray you, keep seat.
    The fit is momentary. Upon a thought°   *In a moment*
55 He will again be well. If much you note him
    You shall offend him, and extend his passion.°   *prolong his suffering*
    Feed, and regard him not.
        [*She speaks apart with* MACBETH]
                          Are you a man?
MACBETH   Ay, and a bold one, that dare look on that
    Which might appal the devil.
LADY MACBETH   O proper stuff!°   *mere nonsense*
60 This is the very painting of your fear;
    This is the air-drawn dagger⁵ which you said
    Led you to Duncan. O, these flaws° and starts,   *outbursts*
    Impostors to° true fear, would well become   *Compared with*
    A woman's story at a winter's fire
65 Authorized by her grandam. Shame itself,
    Why do you make such faces? When all's done
    You look but on a stool.
MACBETH   Prithee see there. Behold, look, lo—how say you?
    Why, what care I? If thou canst nod, speak, too!
70 If charnel-houses and our graves must send

---

3. *The . . . welcome:* A feast is like a purchased meal if the
guests are not assured often that they are welcome.

4. All the Scottish nobility under one roof.
5. The dagger made of, or carried on, the air.

Those that we bury back, our monuments
Shall be the maws of kites.[6]   [*Exit Ghost*]
LADY MACBETH   What, quite unmanned in folly?
MACBETH   If I stand here, I saw him.
LADY MACBETH   Fie, for shame!
MACBETH   Blood hath been shed ere now, i'th' olden time,
75   Ere human statute purged the gentle weal;[7]
          Ay, and since, too, murders have been performed
          Too terrible for the ear. The time has been
          That, when the brains were out, the man would die,
          And there an end. But now they rise again
80   With twenty mortal murders° on their crowns,°   *deadly wounds / heads*
          And push us from our stools. This is more strange
          Than such a murder is.
LADY MACBETH [*aloud*]   My worthy lord,
          Your noble friends do lack you.
MACBETH   I do forget.
          Do not muse° at me, my most worthy friends.   *wonder*
85   I have a strange infirmity which is nothing
          To those that know me. Come, love and health to all,
          Then I'll sit down.
To an [*attendant*]   Give me some wine. Fill full.
              Enter Ghost
          I drink to th' general joy of th'whole table,
          And to our dear friend Banquo, whom we miss.
90   Would he were here. To all and him we thirst,°   *drink*
          And all to all.[8]
LORDS   Our duties, and the pledge.°   *toast*
              [*They drink*]
MACBETH [*seeing the Ghost*]   Avaunt, and quit my sight! Let the
              earth hide thee.
          Thy bones are marrowless, thy blood is cold.
          Thou hast no speculation° in those eyes   *sight*
          Which thou dost glare with.
95   LADY MACBETH   Think of this, good peers,
          But as a thing of custom. 'Tis no other;
          Only it spoils the pleasure of the time.
MACBETH   What man dare, I dare.
          Approach thou like the ruggèd Russian bear,
100   The armed° rhinoceros, or th'Hyrcan[9] tiger;   *armored*
          Take any shape but that,° and my firm nerves°   *(Banquo's) / sinews*
          Shall never tremble. Or be alive again,
          And dare me to the desert° with thy sword.   *deserted place*
          If trembling I inhabit then,[1] protest me
105   The baby of a girl.[2] Hence, horrible shadow,
          Unreal mock'ry, hence!   [*Exit Ghost*]
                         Why so, being gone,
          I am a man again. Pray you sit still.
LADY MACBETH   You have displaced the mirth, broke the good meeting
          With most admired° disorder.   *wondered at*

---

6. *If . . . kites:* If the dead return from their graves, nothing will prevent them from being consumed by birds of
prey, and there is no point in burying them.
7. Before human or humane (Elizabethans did not spell
the two words differently) law cleansed the commonwealth and made it peaceable.
8. All good wishes to everyone.
9. From Hyrcania, a region near the Caspian Sea.
1. If then I tremble; if, trembling, I stay indoors.
2. A baby girl; a girl's doll.

MACBETH   Can such things be

110   And overcome° us like a summer's cloud,   *pass over*

     Without our special wonder? You make me strange

     Even to the disposition that I owe,[3]

     When now I think you can behold such sights

     And keep the natural ruby of your cheeks

     When mine is blanched with fear.

115 ROSS   What sights, my lord?

LADY MACBETH   I pray you, speak not. He grows worse and worse.

     Question enrages° him. At once, good night.   *Talk aggravates*

     Stand not upon the order of your going,

     But go at once.[4]

LENNOX   Good night, and better health

     Attend his majesty.

120 LADY MACBETH   A kind good-night to all.   *Exeunt Lords*

MACBETH   It will have blood, they say. Blood will have blood.

     Stones have been known to move, and trees to speak,

     Augurs° and understood relations[5] have   *Auguries*

     By maggot-pies and choughs and rooks[6] brought forth°   *revealed*

125   The secret'st man of blood.° What is the night?   *murderer*

LADY MACBETH   Almost at odds with morning, which is which.

MACBETH   How sayst thou[7] that Macduff denies his person

     At our great bidding?

LADY MACBETH   Did you send to him, sir?

MACBETH   I hear it by the way,° but I will send.   *indirectly*

130   There's not a one of them but in his house

     I keep a servant fee'd.° I will tomorrow,   *paid to spy*

     And betimes° I will, to the weird sisters.   *early*

     More shall they speak, for now I am bent° to know   *determined*

     By the worst means the worst. For mine own good

135   All causes° shall give way. I am in blood   *other concerns*

     Stepped in so far that, should I° wade no more,°   *were I to / farther*

     Returning were° as tedious as go° o'er.   *would be / going*

     Strange things I have in head that will to hand,

     Which must be acted ere they may be scanned.[8]

140 LADY MACBETH   You lack the season° of all natures, sleep.   *preservative*

MACBETH   Come, we'll to sleep. My strange and self-abuse°   *self-delusion*

     Is the initiate fear that wants hard use.[9]

     We are yet but young in deed.°   *Exeunt*   *crime*

3.5

Thunder. Enter the three WITCHES *meeting* HECATE

FIRST WITCH   Why, how now, Hecate? You look angerly.

HECATE   Have I not reason, beldams° as you are?   *hags*

     Saucy and over-bold, how did you dare

     To trade and traffic with Macbeth

5   In riddles and affairs of death,

     And I, the mistress of your charms,

     The close° contriver of all harms,   *secret*

---

3. *You . . . owe:* You make me a stranger to my own nature, which I had supposed brave.
4. *Stand . . . once:* Do not follow the order of precedence in departing, but all go at once.
5. Formerly hidden, now revealed relationships between causes and effects.
6. Magpies, traditionally sacrificed by augurers, and birds (choughs and rooks) of the crow family.
7. What do you think of the fact that.
8. *ere . . . scanned:* at once, before they can be considered.
9. Is the fear of a novice who lacks toughening experience.
3.5 Location: An open place.

Was never called to bear my part
Or show the glory of our art?—
10   And, which is worse, all you have done
Hath been but for a wayward son,
Spiteful and wrathful, who, as others do,
Loves for his own ends, not for you.
But make amends now. Get you gone,
15   And at the pit of Acheron°   *river in hell*
Meet me i'th' morning. Thither he
Will come to know his destiny.
Your vessels and your spells provide,
Your charms and everything beside.
20   I am for th'air. This night I'll spend
Unto a dismal and a fatal end.[1]
Great business must be wrought ere noon.
Upon the corner of the moon
There hangs a vap'rous drop profound.[2]
25   I'll catch it ere it come to ground,
And that, distilled by magic sleights,
Shall raise such artificial sprites[3]
As by the strength of their illusion
Shall draw him on to his confusion.
30   He shall spurn fate, scorn death, and bear
His hopes 'bove wisdom, grace, and fear;
And you all know security°   *overconfidence*
Is mortals' chiefest enemy.
SPIRITS [*singing dispersedly within*]°   Come away, come away.   *offstage*
35   Hecate, Hecate, come away.
HECATE   Hark, I am called! My little spirit, see,
Sits in a foggy cloud and stays for me.
                              [*The Song*]
SPIRITS [*within*]   Come away, come away,
                Hecate, Hecate, come away.
40   HECATE   I come, I come, I come, I come,
                With all the speed I may,
                With all the speed I may.
                Where's Stadlin?
SPIRIT [*within*]   Here.
HECATE   Where's Puckle?
ANOTHER SPIRIT [*within*]   Here.
OTHER SPIRITS [*within*] And Hoppo, too, and Hellwain, too,
45   We lack but you, we lack but you.
                Come away, make up the count.
HECATE   I will but 'noint,[4] and then I mount.
            [*Spirits appear above. A* SPIRIT LIKE A CAT *descends*]
SPIRITS [*above*]   There's one comes down to fetch his dues,
                A kiss, a coll,° a sip of blood,   *an embrace*
50   And why thou stay'st so long I muse,° I muse,   *wonder*
                Since the air's so sweet and good.
HECATE   O, art thou come? What news, what news?

---

1. Working toward a disastrous and fateful end.
2. Of deep or hidden significance; ready to fall.
3. Spirits produced by magic art.

4. Anoint myself, perhaps with an ointment to enable flying.

SPIRIT LIKE A CAT   All goes still to our delight.
    Either come, or else refuse, refuse.
55 HECATE   Now I am furnishedº for the flight.   *provided*
    [*She ascends with the* SPIRIT *and sings*]
    Now I go, now I fly,
    Malkin my sweet spirit and I.
SPIRITS *and* HECATE   O what a dainty pleasure 'tis
    To ride in the air
60   When the moon shines fair,
    And sing, and dance, and toy,º and kiss.   *play amorously*
    Over woods, high rocks and mountains,
    Over seas and misty fountains,
    Over steeples, towers and turrets,
65   We fly by night 'mongst troops of spirits.
    No ring of bells to our ears sounds,
    No howls of wolves, no yelps of hounds.
    No, not the noise of waters-breachº   *breaking waves*
    Or cannons' throat our height can reach.
70 SPIRITS [*above*]   No ring of bells to our ears sounds,
    No howls of wolves, no yelps of hounds.
    No, not the noise of waters-breach
    Or cannons' throat our height can reach.
    [*Exeunt into the heavens the*
    SPIRIT LIKE A CAT *and* HECATE]
FIRST WITCH   Come, let's make haste. She'll soon be back again.
                                  Exeunt

3.6

Enter LENNOX *and another* LORD
LENNOX   My former speeches have but hit your thoughts,
    Which can interpret farther.[1] Only I say
    Things have been strangely borne.º The gracious Duncan   *carried on*
    Was pitied of Macbeth: marry, he was dead;[2]
5   And the right valiant Banquo walked too late,
    Whom you may say, if't please you, Fleance killed,
    For Fleance fled: men must not walk too late.
    Who cannot want the thoughtº how monstrous   *can help thinking*
    It was for Malcolm and for Donalbain
10   To kill their gracious father? Damnèd fact,º   *deed*
    How it did grieve Macbeth! Did he not straight
    In piousº rage the two delinquents tear,   *loyal*
    That were the slaves of drink, and thrallsº of sleep?   *slaves*
    Was not that nobly done? Ay, and wisely too,
15   For 'twould have angered any heart alive
    To hear the men deny't. So that I say
    He has borne all things well, and I do think
    That had he Duncan's sons under his key—
    As, an'tº please heaven, he shall not—they should find   *if it*
20   What 'twere to kill a father. So should Fleance.
    But peace, for from broad words,[3] and 'cause he failed
    His presence at the tyrant's feast, I hear

3.6 Location: Somewhere in Scotland.
1. *My . . . farther:* What I have said has coincided with your thoughts. I need not say more; you can draw your own further conclusions.

2. *The . . . dead:* Macbeth pitied Duncan after he was dead, but not before. *of:* by.
3. As a result of his plain speaking.

Macduff lives in disgrace. Sir, can you tell
Where he bestows himself?°   *lodges*
LORD   The son of Duncan
25   From whom this tyrant holds° the due of birth°   *withholds / birthright*
Lives in the English court, and is received
Of the most pious Edward[4] with such grace
That the malevolence of fortune nothing
Takes from his high respect.[5] Thither Macduff
30   Is gone to pray the holy King upon his aid°   *in aid of Malcolm*
To wake Northumberland and warlike Siward,
That by the help of these—with Him above
To ratify the work—we may again
Give to our tables meat,° sleep to our nights,   *Hold our usual feasts*
35   Free from our feasts and banquets bloody knives,[6]
Do faithful homage, and receive free[7] honours,
All which we pine for now. And this report
Hath so exasperate their king° that he   *exasperated (Macbeth)*
Prepares for some attempt of war.
40 LENNOX   Sent he to Macduff?
LORD   He did, and with° an absolute 'Sir, not I,'   *on receiving*
The cloudy messenger turns me his back
And hums, as who should say 'You'll rue the time
That clogs me with this answer.'[8]
LENNOX   And that well might
45   Advise him to a caution t'hold what distance
His wisdom can provide.[9] Some holy angel
Fly to the court of England and unfold
His message ere he come, that a swift blessing
May soon return to this our suffering country
Under a hand accursed.[1]
50 LORD   I'll send my prayers with him.
                                                             Exeunt

4.1

[*A Cauldron.*] *Thunder. Enter the three* WITCHES
FIRST WITCH   Thrice the brinded° cat hath mewed.   *brindled*
SECOND WITCH   Thrice, and once the hedge-pig° whined.   *hedgehog*
THIRD WITCH   Harpier° cries ''Tis time, 'tis time.'   *(her familiar)*
FIRST WITCH   Round about the cauldron go,
5   In the poisoned entrails throw.
Toad that under cold stone
Days and nights has thirty-one
Sweltered venom sleeping got,[1]
Boil thou first i'th' charmèd pot.
10 ALL   Double, double, toil and trouble,
Fire burn, and cauldron bubble.

---

4. *received . . . Edward:* received by the saintly King
Edward (Edward the Confessor, reigned 1042–1066).
5. Does not deprive Malcolm of respect.
6. Free our feasts from bloody knives.
7. Freely given; enjoyed in freedom.
8. *He did . . . answer:* Macduff says, "Sir, not I." The
scowling ("cloudy") messenger from Macbeth turns his
back and hums. His rudeness seems to say ominously,
"You'll rue the time that burdens ('clogs') me with this

answer."
9. *And . . . provide:* Warn Macduff to keep as far from
Macbeth as he can.
1. *country . . . accursed:* country suffering under an
accursed hand.
4.1 Location: A cave with a boiling caldron.
1. *has . . . got:* has for thirty-one days and nights exuded
poison formed during sleep.

SECOND WITCH   Fillet° of a fenny° snake,   *Slice / from the swamps*
     In the cauldron boil and bake.
     Eye of newt and toe of frog,
15   Wool of bat and tongue of dog,
     Adder's fork° and blind-worm's sting,   *forked tongue*
     Lizard's leg and owlet's wing,
     For a charm of powerful trouble,
     Like a hell-broth boil and bubble.
20 ALL   Double, double, toil and trouble,
     Fire burn, and cauldron bubble.
     THIRD WITCH   Scale of dragon, tooth of wolf,
     Witches' mummy,° maw and gulf²   *mummified flesh*
     Of the ravined° salt-sea shark,   *ravenous, glutted*
25   Root of hemlock digged i'th' dark,
     Liver of blaspheming Jew,
     Gall of goat, and slips of yew
     Slivered° in the moon's eclipse,   *Cut off*
     Nose of Turk, and Tartar's³ lips,
30   Finger of birth-strangled babe
     Ditch-delivered by a drab,°   *whore*
     Make the gruel thick and slab.°   *viscous*
     Add thereto a tiger's chaudron°   *entrails*
     For th'ingredience of our cauldron.
35 ALL   Double, double, toil and trouble,
     Fire burn, and cauldron bubble.
     SECOND WITCH   Cool it with a baboon's blood,
     Then the charm is firm and good.
             Enter HECATE *and the other three* WITCHES
     HECATE   O, well done! I commend your pains,
40   And everyone shall share i'th' gains.
     And now about the cauldron sing
     Like elves and fairies in a ring,
     Enchanting all that you put in.
             Music and a song
     HECATE   Black spirits and white, red spirits and grey,
45   Mingle, mingle, mingle, you that mingle may.
     FOURTH WITCH   Titty,⁴ Tiffin, keep it stiff in;
             Firedrake, Puckey, make it lucky;
                 Liard, Robin, you must bob in.
     ALL   Round, around, around, about, about,
50   All ill come running in, all good keep out.
     FOURTH WITCH   Here's the blood of a bat.
     HECATE   Put in that, O put in that!
     FIFTH WITCH   Here's leopard's bane.
     HECATE   Put in a grain.
55 FOURTH WITCH   The juice of toad, the oil of adder.
     FIFTH WITCH   Those will make the younker° madder.   *fashionable young man*
     HECATE   Put in, there's all, and rid the stench.
     A WITCH   Nay, here's three ounces of a red-haired wench.
     ALL   Round, around, around, about, about,
60   All ill come running in, all good keep out.

2. Stomach and gullet.   4. The proper names are the names of spirits.
3. Both thought of as cruel pagans.

SECOND WITCH   By the pricking of my thumbs,
    Something wicked this way comes.
    [*Knock within*]
    Open, locks, whoever knocks.
    Enter MACBETH
MACBETH   How now, you secret, black, and midnight hags,
    What is't you do?
65   ALL THE WITCHES   A deed without a name.
MACBETH   I conjure you by that which you profess,°   *the black arts*
    Howe'er you come to know it, answer me.
    Though you untie the winds and let them fight
    Against the churches, though the yeasty° waves   *foamy*
70   Confound° and swallow navigation up,   *Defeat*
    Though bladed corn° be lodged° and trees blown down,   *ripe wheat / beaten down*
    Though castles topple on their warders' heads,
    Though palaces and pyramids do slope°   *bend*
    Their heads to their foundations, though the treasure
75   Of nature's germens[5] tumble all together
    Even till destruction sicken,° answer me   *be surfeited*
    To what I ask you.
FIRST WITCH   Speak.
SECOND WITCH   Demand.
THIRD WITCH   We'll answer.
FIRST WITCH   Say if thou'dst rather hear it from our mouths
    Or from our masters.
MACBETH   Call 'em, let me see 'em.
80   FIRST WITCH   Pour in sow's blood that hath eaten
    Her nine farrow;° grease that's sweaten°   *litter of nine / sweated*
    From the murderer's gibbet° throw   *gallows*
    Into the flame.
ALL THE WITCHES   Come high or low,
    Thyself and office° deftly show.   *function*
    Thunder. FIRST APPARITION: *an armed head*[6]
MACBETH   Tell me, thou unknown power—
85   FIRST WITCH   He knows thy thought.
    Hear his speech, but say thou naught.
FIRST APPARITION   Macbeth, Macbeth, Macbeth, beware Macduff,
    Beware the Thane of Fife. Dismiss me. Enough.
        [APPARITION] *descends*
MACBETH   Whate'er thou art, for thy good caution thanks.
90   Thou hast harped° my fear aright. But one word more—   *guessed*
FIRST WITCH   He will not be commanded. Here's another,
    More potent than the first.
        Thunder. SECOND APPARITION: *a bloody child*[7]
SECOND APPARITION   Macbeth, Macbeth, Macbeth.
MACBETH   Had I three ears I'd hear thee.
95   SECOND APPARITION   Be bloody, bold, and resolute. Laugh to scorn
    The power of man, for none of woman born
    Shall harm Macbeth.
        [APPARITION] *descends*
MACBETH   Then live, Macduff—what need I fear of thee?
    But yet I'll make assurance double sure,

5. Seeds from which all nature grows. If they were tumbled together, they would become barren or produce only monsters.
6. Perhaps symbolizing Macduff's rebellion or Macbeth's fate.
7. Perhaps symbolizing Macduff ripped from his mother's womb (5.10.15–16).

100 And take a bond of fate thou shalt not live,[8]
That I may tell pale-hearted fear it lies,
And sleep in spite of thunder.
          Thunder. THIRD APPARITION: *a child crowned, with a*
          tree in his hand[9]
                              What is this
That rises like the issue of a king,
And wears upon his baby-brow the round
And top° of sovereignty?   *crown*
105 ALL THE WITCHES   Listen, but speak not to't.
THIRD APPARITION   Be lion-mettled, proud, and take no care
Who chafes, who frets, or where conspirers are.
Macbeth shall never vanquished be until
Great Birnam Wood to high Dunsinane Hill
Shall come against him.
          [APPARITION] *descends*
110 MACBETH   That will never be.
Who can impress° the forest, bid the tree   *force into service*
Unfix his earth-bound root? Sweet bodements,° good!   *omens*
Rebellious dead,[1] rise never till the wood
Of Birnam rise, and on's high place Macbeth
115 Shall live the lease of nature,° pay his breath   *natural life span*
To time and mortal custom.[2] Yet my heart
Throbs to know one thing. Tell me, if your art
Can tell so much, shall Banquo's issue ever
Reign in this kingdom?
ALL THE WITCHES   Seek to know no more.
120 MACBETH   I will be satisfied. Deny me this,
And an eternal curse fall on you! Let me know.
          [*The cauldron sinks.*] *Hautboys*
Why sinks that cauldron? And what noise° is this?   *music*
FIRST WITCH   Show.
SECOND WITCH   Show.
125 THIRD WITCH   Show.
ALL THE WITCHES   Show his eyes and grieve his heart,
          Come like shadows, so depart.
          A show of eight kings, [the] *last with a glass° in his*   *mirror*
          hand; and BANQUO
MACBETH   Thou[3] art too like the spirit of Banquo. Down!
Thy crown does sear mine eyeballs. And thy hair,
130 Thou other gold-bound brow, is like the first.
A third is like the former. Filthy hags,
Why do you show me this?—A fourth? Start,° eyes!   *Bulge out*
What, will the line stretch out to th' crack of doom?
Another yet? A seventh? I'll see no more—
135 And yet the eighth appears, who bears a glass
Which shows me many more; and some I see
That twofold balls and treble sceptres[4] carry.

---

8. By killing Macduff, Macbeth hopes to bind fate to its
promise that no man of woman born shall harm Macbeth.
9. Signifying Malcolm. The tree anticipates 5.5.31 ff.
1. Perhaps Banquo. Some editors emend to "Rebellious
head" or "Rebellion's head," where "head" means
"army."
2. The custom of mortality; natural death.

3. The image of Banquo that appears in the caldron.
4. James I was crowned twice, once as King of Scotland
and later as King of England. He carried one orb at each
coronation. "Treble sceptres" refers to the fact that he
held two scepters in the English coronation and one in
the Scottish, or perhaps to his claim to be King of Britain,
France, and Ireland.

Horrible sight! Now I see 'tis true,
For the blood-baltered[5] Banquo smiles upon me,
And points at them for his.[6]

                      [Exeunt kings and BANQUO]

140   What, is this so?

HECATE   Ay, sir, all this is so. But why
    Stands Macbeth thus amazedly?°   *entranced*
    Come, sisters, cheer we up his sprites,°   *spirits*
    And show the best of our delights.
145   I'll charm the air to give a sound
    While you perform your antic round,°   *fantastic dance*
    That this great king may kindly say
    Our duties did his welcome pay.[7]

            Music. The WITCHES *dance, and vanish*

MACBETH   Where are they? Gone? Let this pernicious hour
150   Stand aye accursèd in the calendar.
    Come in, without there.

            Enter LENNOX

LENNOX   What's your grace's will?
MACBETH   Saw you the weird sisters?
LENNOX   No, my lord.
MACBETH   Came they not by you?
LENNOX   No, indeed, my lord.
MACBETH   Infected be the air whereon they ride,
155   And damned all those that trust them. I did hear
    The galloping of horse. Who was't came by?
LENNOX   'Tis two or three, my lord, that bring you word
    Macduff is fled to England.
MACBETH   Fled to England?
LENNOX   Ay, my good lord.
160 MACBETH [*aside*]   Time, thou anticipat'st° my dread exploits.   *forestall*
    The flighty purpose never is o'ertook
    Unless the deed go with it.[8] From this moment
    The very firstlings° of my heart shall be   *first notions*
    The firstlings° of my hand. And even now,   *first acts*
165   To crown my thoughts with acts, be it thought and done:
    The castle of Macduff I will surprise,
    Seize upon Fife, give to th'edge o'th' sword
    His wife, his babes, and all unfortunate souls
    That trace him in his line. No boasting like a fool;
170   This deed I'll do before this purpose cool.
    But no more sights! [*To* LENNOX] Where are these gentlemen?
    Come bring me where they are.   *Exeunt*

4.2

    Enter MACDUFF'S WIFE, *her* SON, *and* ROSS

LADY MACDUFF   What had he done to make him fly the land?
ROSS   You must have patience, madam.
LADY MACDUFF   He had none.

---

5. Having hair matted with blood.
6. Banquo was the legendary founder of the Stuart dynasty.
7. Our service repaid the welcome he gave us.

8. *The flighty . . . it:* The fleeting intention is never realized unless the deed is done immediately.
4.2 Location: Macduff's castle in Fife.

His flight was madness. When our actions do not,
Our fears do make us traitors.[1]
ROSS   You know not
5   Whether it was his wisdom or his fear.
LADY MACDUFF   Wisdom—to leave his wife, to leave his babes,
His mansion, and his titles° in a place   *estates*
From whence himself does fly? He loves us not,
He wants° the natural touch,° for the poor wren,   *lacks / affection*
10 The most diminutive of birds, will fight,
Her young ones in her nest, against the owl.
All is the fear and nothing is the love;
As little is the wisdom, where the flight
So runs against all reason.
ROSS   My dearest coz,°   *kinswoman*
15 I pray you school° yourself. But for your husband,   *control*
He is noble, wise, judicious, and best knows
The fits o'th' season.[2] I dare not speak much further,
But cruel are the times when we are traitors
And do not know ourselves;[3] when we hold rumour
20 From what we fear, yet know not what we fear,[4]
But float upon a wild and violent sea
Each way and none.[5] I take my leave of you;
Shall° not be long but° I'll be here again.   *It shall / before*
Things at the worst will cease, or else climb upward
25 To what they were before. My pretty cousin,
Blessing upon you!
LADY MACDUFF   Fathered he is, and yet he's fatherless.
ROSS   I am so much a fool, should I stay longer
It would be my disgrace and your discomfort.[6]
I take my leave at once.   *Exit*
30 LADY MACDUFF   Sirrah, your father's dead,
And what will you do now? How will you live?
MACDUFF'S SON   As birds do, mother.
LADY MACDUFF   What, with worms and flies?
MACDUFF'S SON   With what I get, I mean, and so do they.
LADY MACDUFF   Poor° bird, thou'dst never fear the net nor lime,[7] *Pitiful*
35 The pitfall nor the gin.°   *snare*
MACDUFF'S SON   Why should I, mother? Poor° birds they are not *Worthless*
     set for.
My father is not dead, for all your saying.
LADY MACDUFF   Yes, he is dead. How wilt thou do for a father?
MACDUFF'S SON   Nay, how will you do for a husband?
40 LADY MACDUFF   Why, I can buy me twenty at any market.
MACDUFF'S SON   Then you'll buy 'em to sell again.
LADY MACDUFF   Thou speak'st with all thy wit, and yet, i'faith,
with wit enough for thee.
MACDUFF'S SON   Was my father a traitor, mother?
45 LADY MACDUFF   Ay, that he was.

---

1. *When . . . traitors:* Even when we have committed no treason, our fear of suspicion makes us behave as though we are guilty.
2. The violent convulsions of the present time; what befits the time.
3. *we . . . ourselves:* we are denounced as traitors but do not know why.

4. *when . . . fear:* when we believe rumors inspired by our fears, but those fears are themselves vague.
5. In every direction, and so finally in none.
6. I would disgrace myself and embarrass you by weeping.
7. Birdlime, a sticky substance smeared on twigs to catch small birds.

MACDUFF'S SON   What is a traitor?

LADY MACDUFF   Why, one that swears and lies.[8]

MACDUFF'S SON   And be all traitors that do so?

LADY MACDUFF   Everyone that does so is a traitor, and must be
50   hanged.

MACDUFF'S SON   And must they all be hanged that swear° and   *speak profanely*
lie?

LADY MACDUFF   Every one.

MACDUFF'S SON   Who must hang them?

55   LADY MACDUFF   Why, the honest men.

MACDUFF'S SON   Then the liars and swearers are fools, for there
are liars and swearers enough to beat the honest men and hang
up them.

LADY MACDUFF   Now God help thee, poor monkey! But how wilt
60   thou do for a father?

MACDUFF'S SON   If he were dead you'd weep for him. If you
would not, it were a good sign that I should quickly have a new
father.

LADY MACDUFF   Poor prattler, how thou talk'st!
        Enter a MESSENGER

65   MESSENGER   Bless you, fair dame. I am not to you known,
Though in your state of honour I am perfect.[9]
I doubt° some danger does approach you nearly.   *fear*
If you will take a homely° man's advice,   *plain*
Be not found here. Hence with your little ones!
70   To fright you thus methinks I am too savage,
To do worse to you were fell cruelty,[1]
Which is too nigh your person.[2] Heaven preserve you.
I dare abide no longer.   *Exit* MESSENGER

LADY MACDUFF   Whither should I fly?
I have done no harm. But I remember now
75   I am in this earthly world, where to do harm
Is often laudable, to do good sometime
Accounted dangerous folly. Why then, alas,
Do I put up that womanly defence
To say I have done no harm?
        Enter MURDERERS
                                    What are these faces?

80   A MURDERER   Where is your husband?

LADY MACDUFF   I hope in no place so unsanctified
Where such as thou mayst find him.

A MURDERER   He's a traitor.

MACDUFF'S SON   Thou liest, thou shag-haired villain.

A MURDERER [*stabbing him*]   What, you egg!
Young fry° of treachery!   *spawn*

MACDUFF'S SON   He has killed me, mother.
85   Run away, I pray you.
        [*He dies.*] *Exit* [MACDUFF'S WIFE] *crying 'Murder!'*
        [*followed by* MURDERERS *with the Son's body*]

---

8. Takes an oath and breaks it.
9. Though I know perfectly well your high rank (an apology for bursting in).
1. *To fright . . . cruelty:* Even to frighten you by speaking

of such danger is savage; actually to harm you would be brutal ("fell") cruelty.
2. Such cruelty is already too near you.

4.3

Enter MALCOLM *and* MACDUFF

MALCOLM   Let us seek out some desolate shade, and there
    Weep our sad bosoms empty.

MACDUFF   Let us rather
    Hold fast the mortal° sword, and like good men   *deadly*
    Bestride our downfall birthdom.[1] Each new morn
5   New widows howl, new orphans cry, new sorrows
    Strike heaven on the face that° it resounds   *so that*
    As if it felt with Scotland and yelled out
    Like syllable of dolour.°   *A similar cry of pain*

MALCOLM   What I believe I'll wail,
    What know believe; and what I can redress,
10   As I shall find the time to friend,° I will.   *favorable*
    What you have spoke it may be so, perchance.
    This tyrant, whose sole° name blisters our tongues,   *mere*
    Was once thought honest. You have loved him well.
    He hath not touched° you yet. I am young, but something   *injured*
15 You may discern of him through me:[2] and wisdom°   *it's prudent*
    To offer up a weak poor innocent lamb
    T'appease an angry god.

MACDUFF   I am not treacherous.

MALCOLM   But Macbeth is.
20 A good and virtuous nature may recoil
    In an imperial charge.[3] But I shall crave your pardon.
    That which you are my thoughts cannot transpose.°   *transform*
    Angels are bright still, though the brightest° fell.   *(Lucifer)*
    Though all things foul would wear the brows of grace,
    Yet grace must still look so.[4]

25 MACDUFF   I have lost my hopes.[5]

MALCOLM   Perchance even there where I did find my doubts.[6]
    Why in that rawness° left you wife and child,   *unprotected condition*
    Those precious motives,° those strong knots of love,   *inducements to devotion*
    Without leave-taking? I pray you,
30 Let not my jealousies° be your dishonours,   *suspicions*
    But mine own safeties.° You may be rightly just,   *safeguards*
    Whatever I shall think.

MACDUFF   Bleed, bleed, poor country!
    Great tyranny, lay thou thy basis° sure,   *foundation*
    For goodness dare not check thee. Wear thou thy wrongs;°   *wrongful gains*
35 The title is affeered.° Fare thee well, lord.   *confirmed*
    I would not be the villain that thou think'st
    For the whole space that's in the tyrant's grasp,
    And the rich east to boot.°   *as well*

MALCOLM   Be not offended.
    I speak not as in absolute fear° of you.   *complete distrust*
40 I think our country sinks beneath the yoke.
    It weeps, it bleeds, and each new day a gash
    Is added to her wounds. I think withal°   *nonetheless*

4.3 Location: England, before King Edward's palace.
1. Stand in defense over our downtrodden native land.
2. *I . . . me:* I am inexperienced, but you might gain favor
with Macbeth by betraying me. Many editions emend
"discern" to "deserve."
3. *recoil . . . charge:* give way to a royal command.

4. *Though . . . so:* Though everything evil disguises itself
as virtue, virtue still looks like itself.
5. Hopes of Malcolm's help in a campaign against Macbeth.
6. Doubts of Macduff's loyalty, because he has left his
wife and children.

There would be hands uplifted in my right,
And here from gracious England° have I offer   the King of England
45   Of goodly thousands. But for all this,
When I shall tread upon the tyrant's head,
Or wear it on my sword, yet my poor country
Shall have more vices than it had before,
More suffer, and more sundry° ways, than ever,   in more various
By him that shall succeed.
50   MACDUFF   What° should he be?   Who
MALCOLM   It is myself I mean, in whom I know
All the particulars° of vice so grafted   varieties
That when they shall be opened° black Macbeth   disclosed
Will seem as pure as snow, and the poor state
55   Esteem him as a lamb, being compared
With my confineless° harms.   infinite
MACDUFF   Not in the legions
Of horrid hell can come a devil more damned
In evils to top Macbeth.
MALCOLM   I grant him bloody,
Luxurious,° avaricious, false, deceitful,   Lecherous
60   Sudden,° malicious, smacking of every sin   Violent
That has a name. But there's no bottom, none,
In my voluptuousness. Your wives, your daughters,
Your matrons, and your maids could not fill up
The cistern of my lust, and my desire
65   All continent° impediments would o'erbear   restraining; chaste
That did oppose my will. Better Macbeth
Than such an one to reign.
MACDUFF   Boundless intemperance
In nature° is a tyranny. It hath been   human nature
Th'untimely emptying of the happy throne,
70   And fall of many kings. But fear not yet°   nevertheless
To take upon you what is yours. You may
Convey° your pleasures in a spacious plenty   Manage secretly
And yet seem cold.° The time° you may so hoodwink.°   indifferent / age / deceive
We have willing dames enough. There cannot be
75   That vulture in you to devour so many
As will to greatness dedicate themselves,
Finding it so inclined.
MALCOLM   With this there grows
In my most ill-composed affection° such   character
A staunchless° avarice that were I king   An insatiable
80   I should cut off the nobles for their lands,
Desire his jewels and this other's house,
And my more having would be as a sauce
To make me hunger more, that I should forge
Quarrels unjust against the good and loyal,
Destroying them for wealth.
85   MACDUFF   This avarice
Sticks deeper, grows with more pernicious root
Than summer-seeming⁷ lust, and it hath been
The sword° of our slain kings. Yet do not fear.   undoing
Scotland hath foisons° to fill up your will   plenty

7. Appropriate to youth ("summer") but passing with age, unlike avarice; summerlike.

90   Of your mere own.[8] All these are portable,°   *bearable*
     With other graces weighed.
  MALCOLM   But I have none. The king-becoming graces,
     As justice, verity, temp'rance, stableness,
     Bounty, perseverance, mercy, lowliness,°   *humility*
95   Devotion, patience, courage, fortitude,
     I have no relish° of them, but abound   *trace*
     In the division° of each several° crime,   *variations / separate*
     Acting it many ways. Nay, had I power I should
     Pour the sweet milk of concord into hell,
100   Uproar the universal peace, confound
     All unity on earth.
  MACDUFF   O Scotland, Scotland!
  MALCOLM   If such a one be fit to govern, speak.
     I am as I have spoken.
  MACDUFF   Fit to govern?
     No, not to live. O nation miserable,
105   With an untitled° tyrant bloody-sceptered,   *a usurping*
     When shalt thou see thy wholesome days again,
     Since that the truest issue of thy throne
     By his own interdiction° stands accursed   *declaration of unfitness*
     And does blaspheme his breed?° Thy royal father   *disgrace his heritage*
110   Was a most sainted king. The Queen that bore thee,
     Oft'ner upon her knees than on her feet,
     Died[9] every day she lived. Fare thee well.
     These evils thou repeat'st upon thyself
     Hath banished me from Scotland. O, my breast—
     Thy hope ends here!
115 MALCOLM   Macduff, this noble passion,
     Child of integrity, hath from my soul
     Wiped the black scruples,° reconciled my thoughts   *dark suspicions*
     To thy good truth and honour. Devilish Macbeth
     By many of these trains° hath sought to win me   *stratagems*
120   Into his power, and modest wisdom° plucks me   *prudent moderation*
     From over-credulous haste; but God above
     Deal between thee and me, for even now
     I put myself to thy direction and
     Unspeak° mine own detraction, here abjure   *Retract*
125   The taints and blames I laid upon myself
     For° strangers to my nature. I am yet   *As*
     Unknown to woman, never was forsworn,
     Scarcely have coveted what was mine own,
     At no time broke my faith, would not betray
130   The devil to his fellow, and delight
     No less in truth than life. My first false-speaking
     Was this upon myself. What I am truly
     Is thine and my poor country's to command,
     Whither indeed, before thy here-approach,
135   Old Siward with ten thousand warlike men,
     Already at a point,° was setting forth.   *prepared*
     Now we'll together; and the chance of goodness

---

8. *Scotland . . . own:* Scotland is bountiful enough to satisfy your greed with your own royal property alone.

9. Dead to the world. ("By our rejoicing which I have in
Christ Jesus our Lord, I die daily," I Corinthians 15:31).

Be like our warranted quarrel![1]—Why are you silent?

MACDUFF   Such welcome and unwelcome things at once
140   'Tis hard to reconcile.
                    Enter a DOCTOR

MALCOLM   Well, more anon. [*To the* DOCTOR] Comes the King
         forth, I pray you?

DOCTOR   Ay, sir. There are a crew of wretched souls
         That stay° his cure. Their malady convinces   await
         The great essay of art,[2] but at his touch,
145   Such sanctity hath Heaven given his hand,
         They presently amend.°   heal

MALCOLM   I thank you, doctor.   *Exit* [DOCTOR]

MACDUFF   What's the disease he means?

MALCOLM   'Tis called the evil[3]—
         A most miraculous work in this good King,
         Which often since my here-remain in England
150   I have seen him do. How he solicits° heaven   moves by entreaty
         Himself best knows, but strangely visited° people,   afflicted
         All swoll'n and ulcerous, pitiful to the eye,
         The mere° despair of surgery, he cures,   utter
         Hanging a golden stamp° about their necks,   coin
155   Put on with holy prayers; and 'tis spoken,
         To the succeeding royalty he leaves
         The healing benediction. With this strange virtue°   power
         He hath a heavenly gift of prophecy,
         And sundry blessings hang about his throne
         That speak him full of grace.°   divine grace
                    Enter ROSS
160   MACDUFF   See who comes here.

MALCOLM   My countryman, but yet I know° him not.   recognize

MACDUFF   My ever gentle cousin, welcome hither.

MALCOLM   I know him now. Good God betimes° remove   quickly
         The means that makes us strangers!

ROSS   Sir, amen.

MACDUFF   Stands Scotland where it did?
165   ROSS   Alas, poor country,
         Almost afraid to know itself. It cannot
         Be called our mother, but our grave, where nothing
         But who knows nothing is once seen to smile;[4]
         Where sighs and groans and shrieks that rend the air
170   Are made, not marked;° where violent sorrow seems   noticed
         A modern ecstasy.° The dead man's knell   commonplace emotion
         Is there scarce asked for who,[5] and good men's lives
         Expire before the flowers in their caps,
         Dying or ere° they sicken.   before

MACDUFF   O relation°   report
         Too nice° and yet too true!   detailed
175   MALCOLM   What's the newest grief?

ROSS   That of an hour's age doth hiss the speaker;[6]
         Each minute teems° a new one.   yields

---

1. *the . . . quarrel:* may the chance of success be equal to the justice of our cause.
2. *convinces . . . art:* defeats the best efforts of medical skill.
3. "The king's evil," scrofula, thought to be cured by the royal touch.
4. No one smiles except he who knows nothing.
5. Scarcely anyone asks for whom it is rung.
6. Cause the speaker to be hissed for telling old news.

MACDUFF   How does my wife?
ROSS   Why, well.
MACDUFF   And all my children?
ROSS   Well, too.
MACDUFF   The tyrant has not battered at their peace?
180   ROSS   No, they were well at peace when I did leave 'em.
MACDUFF   Be not a niggard of your speech. How goes't?
ROSS   When I came hither to transport the tidings
   Which I have heavily° borne, there ran a rumour   *gravely*
   Of many worthy fellows that were out,°   *in arms*
185   Which was to my belief witnessed the rather°   *made more credible*
   For that I saw the tyrant's power° afoot.   *army*
   Now is the time of° help. [*To* MALCOLM] Your eye in Scotland   *moment for*
   Would create soldiers, make our women fight
   To doff° their dire distresses.   *remove*
MALCOLM   Be't their comfort
190   We are coming thither. Gracious England hath
   Lent us good Siward and ten thousand men;
   An older and a better soldier none°   *there is none*
   That Christendom gives out.°   *proclaims; provides*
ROSS   Would I could answer
   This comfort with the like. But I have words
195   That would be howled out in the desert air
   Where hearing should not latch° them.   *catch*
MACDUFF   What concern they—
   The general cause, or is it a fee-grief°   *private woe*
   Due to° some single breast?   *Owned by*
ROSS   No mind that's honest
   But in it shares some woe, though the main part
   Pertains to you alone.
200   MACDUFF   If it be mine,
   Keep it not from me; quickly let me have it.
ROSS   Let not your ears despise my tongue for ever,
   Which shall possess them with the heaviest sound
   That ever yet they heard.
MACDUFF   H'm, I guess at it.
205   ROSS   Your castle is surprised, your wife and babes
   Savagely slaughtered. To relate the manner
   Were on the quarry[7] of these murdered deer
   To add the death of you.
MALCOLM   Merciful heaven!
   [*To* MACDUFF] What, man, ne'er pull your hat upon your
       brows.°   *conceal your grief*
210   Give sorrow words. The grief that does not speak
   Whispers the o'erfraught° heart and bids it break.   *overburdened*
MACDUFF   My children too?
ROSS   Wife, children, servants, all
   That could be found.
MACDUFF   And I must be° from thence!   *had to be*
   My wife killed too?
ROSS   I have said.
MALCOLM   Be comforted.

---

7. Heap of slaughtered game.

215   Let's make us medicines of our great revenge
    To cure this deadly grief.
    MACDUFF   He has no children. All my pretty ones?
    Did you say all? O hell-kite! All?
    What, all my pretty chickens and their dam
220   At one fell swoop?
    MALCOLM   Dispute° it like a man.   *Fight*
    MACDUFF   I shall do so,
    But I must also feel it as a man.
    I cannot but remember such things were
225   That were most precious to me. Did heaven look on
    And would not take their part? Sinful Macduff,
    They were all struck for° thee. Naught° that I am,   *on account of / Wicked*
    Not for their own demerits but for mine
    Fell slaughter on their souls. Heaven rest them now.
230   MALCOLM   Be this the whetstone of your sword. Let grief
    Convert° to anger: blunt not the heart, enrage it.   *Be changed*
    MACDUFF   O, I could play the woman with mine eyes
    And braggart with my tongue! But gentle heavens
    Cut short all intermission.° Front to front°   *delay / Face-to-face*
235   Bring thou this fiend of Scotland and myself.
    Within my sword's length set him. If he scape,
    Heaven forgive him too.
    MALCOLM   This tune goes manly.
    Come, go we to the King. Our power° is ready;   *army*
    Our lack is nothing but our leave.[8] Macbeth
240   Is ripe for shaking, and the powers above
    Put on their instruments.[9] Receive what cheer you may:
    The night is long that never finds the day.   *Exeunt*

5.1

Enter a DOCTOR *of Physic and a Waiting-*
GENTLEWOMAN

DOCTOR   I have two nights watched with you, but can perceive
no truth in your report. When was it she last walked?
GENTLEWOMAN   Since his majesty went into the field° I have   *battlefield*
    seen her rise from her bed, throw her nightgown upon her,
5   unlock her closet,° take forth paper, fold it, write upon't, read   *chest*
    it, afterwards seal it, and again return to bed, yet all this while
    in a most fast sleep.
DOCTOR   A great perturbation in nature, to receive at once the
    benefit of sleep and do the effects of watching°. In this slum-   *act as if awake*
10   bery agitation° besides her walking and other actual° perfor-   *movement / active*
    mances, what at any time have you heard her say?
GENTLEWOMAN   That, sir, which I will not report after her.
DOCTOR   You may to me; and 'tis most meet° you should.   *proper*
GENTLEWOMAN   Neither to you nor anyone, having no witness to
15   confirm my speech.
    Enter LADY [MACBETH] *with a taper*
    Lo you, here she comes. This is her very guise,° and, upon my   *exact habit*
    life, fast asleep. Observe her. Stand close.°   *concealed*

---

8. We have only to take leave of the King.   5.1 Location: Macbeth's castle in Dunsinane.
9. Arm themselves; set us to work as their agents.

DOCTOR   How came she by that light?

GENTLEWOMAN   Why, it stood by her. She has light by her con-
20 tinually. 'Tis her command.

DOCTOR   You see her eyes are open.

GENTLEWOMAN   Ay, but their sense are shut.

DOCTOR   What is it she does now? Look how she rubs her hands.

GENTLEWOMAN   It is an accustomed action with her, to seem
25 thus washing her hands. I have known her continue in this a
quarter of an hour.

LADY MACBETH   Yet here's a spot.

DOCTOR   Hark, she speaks. I will set down what comes from her
to satisfy° my remembrance the more strongly.   *support*

30 LADY MACBETH   Out, damned spot; out, I say. One, two,—why,
then 'tis time to do't. Hell is murky. Fie, my lord, fie, a soldier
and afeard? What need we fear who knows it when none can
call our power to account? Yet who would have thought the
old man to have had so much blood in him?

35 DOCTOR   Do you mark that?

LADY MACBETH   The Thane of Fife had a wife. Where is she
now? What, will these hands ne'er be clean? No more o' that,
my lord, no more o' that. You mar all with this starting.°   *startled movement*
                                                                (expression of reproof)
DOCTOR   Go to, go to.° You have known what you should not.

40 GENTLEWOMAN   She has spoke what she should not, I am sure of
that. Heaven knows what she has known.

LADY MACBETH   Here's the smell of the blood still. All the perfumes of Arabia will not sweeten this little hand. O, O, O!

DOCTOR   What a sigh is there! The heart is sorely charged.°   *burdened*

45 GENTLEWOMAN   I would not have such a heart in my bosom for
the dignity° of the whole body.   *worth*

DOCTOR   Well, well, well.

GENTLEWOMAN   Pray God it be, sir.

DOCTOR   This disease is beyond my practice.° Yet I have known   *skill*
50 those which have walked in their sleep who have died holily in
their beds.

LADY MACBETH   Wash your hands, put on your nightgown, look
not so pale. I tell you yet again, Banquo's buried. He cannot
come out on's° grave.   *of his*

55 DOCTOR   Even so?

LADY MACBETH   To bed, to bed. There's knocking at the gate.
Come, come, come, come, give me your hand. What's done
cannot be undone. To bed, to bed, to bed.   *Exit*

DOCTOR   Will she go now to bed?

60 GENTLEWOMAN   Directly.

DOCTOR   Foul whisp'rings are abroad. Unnatural deeds
Do breed unnatural troubles; infected minds
To their deaf pillows will discharge their secrets.
More needs she the divine° than the physician.   *priest*
65 God, God forgive us all! Look after her.
Remove from her the means of all annoyance,°   *self-injury*
And still keep eyes upon her. So, good night.
My mind she has mated,° and amazed my sight.   *bewildered*
I think, but dare not speak.

GENTLEWOMAN   Good night, good doctor.   *Exeunt*

5.2

Enter MENTEITH, CAITHNESS, ANGUS, LENNOX, *soldiers,*
[*with a drummer*] *and colours*

MENTEITH   The English power is near, led on by Malcolm,
His uncle Siward, and the good Macduff.
Revenges burn in them, for their dear causes
Would to the bleeding° and the grim alarm°   bloody / call to battle
Excite° the mortified° man.   Rouse / insensible; dead

5 ANGUS   Near Birnam Wood
Shall we well° meet them. That way are they coming.   doubtless
CAITHNESS   Who knows if Donalbain be with his brother?
LENNOX   For certain, sir, he is not. I have a file°   roster
Of all the gentry. There is Siward's son,
10 And many unrough° youths that even now   beardless
Protest their first of manhood.¹
MENTEITH   What does the tyrant?
CAITHNESS   Great Dunsinane he strongly fortifies.
Some say he's mad, others that lesser hate him
Do call it valiant fury; but for certain
15 He cannot buckle his distempered° cause   disease-swollen
Within the belt of rule.°   restraint
ANGUS   Now does he feel
His secret murders sticking on his hands.
Now minutely° revolts upbraid his faith-breach.   every minute
Those he commands move only in command,°   under constraint
20 Nothing in love. Now does he feel his title
Hang loose about him, like a giant's robe
Upon a dwarfish thief.
MENTEITH   Who then shall blame
His pestered° senses to recoil and start   tormented
When all that is within him does condemn
Itself for being there?
25 CAITHNESS   Well, march we on
To give obedience where 'tis truly owed.
Meet we the medicine° of the sickly weal,°   (Malcolm) / state
And with him pour we in our country's purge,
Each drop of us.
LENNOX   Or so much as it needs
30 To dew° the sovereign° flower and drown the weeds.   bedew / royal; curative
Make we our march towards Birnam.   *Exeunt, marching*

5.3

Enter MACBETH, [*the*] DOCTOR [*of Physic*], *and attendants*

MACBETH   Bring me no more reports. Let them fly all.°   Let all thanes desert
Till Birnam Wood remove to Dunsinane
I cannot taint° with fear. What's the boy Malcolm?   be infected
Was he not born of woman? The spirits that know
5 All mortal consequences° have pronounced me thus: human destinies
'Fear not, Macbeth. No man that's born of woman
Shall e'er have power upon thee.' Then fly, false thanes,
And mingle with the English epicures.¹
The mind I sway° by and the heart I bear   rule myself

5.2 Location: The country near Dunsinane.   5.3 Location: Macbeth's castle in Dunsinane.
1. Declare for the first time that they are men.   1. Lovers of easy, luxurious living.

10 Shall never sag with doubt nor shake with fear.
          Enter SERVANT
    The devil damn thee black, thou cream-faced loon!°   *rogue*
    Where gott'st thou that goose look?
SERVANT   There is ten thousand—
MACBETH   Geese, villain?
SERVANT   Soldiers, sir.
15 MACBETH   Go prick thy face and over-red thy fear,²
    Thou lily-livered³ boy. What soldiers, patch?°   *fool*
    Death of° thy soul, those linen cheeks of thine   *on*
    Are counsellors to fear.° What soldiers, whey-face?   *Teach others to fear*
SERVANT   The English force, so please you.
MACBETH   Take thy face hence.   [*Exit* SERVANT]
20   Seyton!—I am sick at heart
    When I behold—Seyton, I say!—This push°   *crisis*
    Will cheer⁴ me ever or disseat° me now.   *dethrone*
    I have lived long enough. My way of life
    Is fall'n into the sere,° the yellow leaf,   *withered state*
25 And that which should accompany old age,
    As° honour, love, obedience, troops of friends,   *Such as*
    I must not look to have, but in their stead
    Curses, not loud but deep, mouth-honour,° breath   *lip service*
    Which the poor heart would fain deny and dare not.
30 Seyton!
          Enter SEYTON
SEYTON   What's your gracious pleasure?
MACBETH   What news more?
SEYTON   All is confirmed, my lord, which was reported.
MACBETH   I'll fight till from my bones my flesh be hacked.
    Give me my armour.
35 SEYTON   'Tis not needed yet.
MACBETH   I'll put it on.
    Send out more horses. Skirr° the country round.   *Scour*
    Hang those that talk of fear. Give me mine armour.
    How does your patient, doctor?
DOCTOR   Not so sick, my lord,
40 As she is troubled with thick-coming fancies
    That keep her from her rest.
MACBETH   Cure her of that.
    Canst thou not minister to a mind diseased,
    Pluck from the memory a rooted sorrow,
    Raze out the written troubles of⁵ the brain,
45 And with some sweet oblivious° antidote   *causing forgetfulness*
    Cleanse the fraught bosom of that perilous stuff
    Which weighs upon the heart?
DOCTOR   Therein the patient
    Must minister to himself.
MACBETH   Throw physic° to the dogs; I'll none of it.   *medicine*
50 [*To an attendant*] Come, put mine armour on. Give me my staff.°   *lance*
    Seyton, send out. Doctor, the thanes fly from me.

---

2. Redden your fearful pallor.
3. Lacking blood in your liver (thought to be the seat of courage); cowardly.
4. Comfort; enthrone or establish (punning on "cheer/chair").
5. Erase the troubles engraved in.

[*To an attendant*] Come, sir, dispatch.°—If thou couldst, doctor, cast   *hurry*
    The water[6] of my land, find her disease,
    And purge it to a sound and pristine health,
55   I would applaud thee to the very echo,
    That should applaud again. [*To an attendant*] Pull't off, I say.[7]
    [*To the* DOCTOR] What rhubarb, cyme,° or what purgative drug   *senna*
    Would scour° these English hence? Hear'st thou of them?   *purge*
DOCTOR   Ay, my good lord. Your royal preparation
    Makes us hear something.
60 MACBETH [*to an attendant*]   Bring it[8] after me.
    I will not be afraid of death and bane°   *destruction*
    Till Birnam Forest come to Dunsinane.
DOCTOR [*aside*]   Were I from Dunsinane away and clear,
    Profit again should hardly draw me here.[9]   *Exeunt*

5.4

Enter MALCOLM, SIWARD, MACDUFF, SIWARD'S SON, MEN-
TEITH, CAITHNESS, ANGUS, *and* SOLDIERS, *marching,*
[*with a drummer*] *and colours*

MALCOLM   Cousins, I hope the days are near at hand
    That chambers° will be safe.   *bedrooms*
MENTEITH   We doubt it nothing.°   *not at all*
SIWARD   What wood is this before us?
MENTEITH   The wood of Birnam.
MALCOLM   Let every soldier hew him down a bough
5   And bear't before him. Thereby shall we shadow°   *conceal*
    The numbers of our host, and make discovery°   *reconnaissance*
    Err in report of us.
A SOLDIER   It shall be done.
SIWARD   We learn no other but the confident tyrant
    Keeps still in Dunsinane, and will endure
    Our setting down before°'t.   *laying siege to*
10 MALCOLM   'Tis his main hope,
    For where there is advantage° to be gone,   *opportunity*
    Both more and less° have given him the revolt,   *great and lowly*
    And none serve with him but constrainèd things,
    Whose hearts are absent too.
MACDUFF   Let our just censures
15   Attend the true event,[1] and put we on
    Industrious soldiership.
SIWARD   The time approaches
    That will with due decision make us know
    What we shall say we have, and what we owe.°   *own*
    Thoughts speculative their unsure hopes relate,
20   But certain issue strokes must arbitrate;[2]
    Towards which, advance the war.   *Exeunt, marching*

---

6. *cast / The water*: analyze the urine as a method of diag-
nosis.
7. A piece of armor is not properly fitted; Macbeth orders
the attendant to take it off.
8. The armor not yet on Macbeth.
9. No large fees could lure me back.

5.4 Location: The country near Birnam Wood.
1. *Let . . . event*: Let our judgments await the actual outcome.
2. *Thoughts . . . arbitrate*: Speculation produces hopes
and unconfirmed optimism, but the issue will only be
decided by action.

5.5

Enter MACBETH, SEYTON, *and soldiers, with* [*a drummer*]
and colours

MACBETH   Hang out our banners on the outward walls.
The cry is still 'They come.' Our castle's strength
Will laugh a siege to scorn. Here let them lie
Till famine and the ague eat them up.
5   Were they not forced° with those that should be ours   reinforced
We might have met them dareful,° beard to beard,   boldly
And beat them backward home.
            A cry within of women
                                        What is that noise?
SEYTON   It is the cry of women, my good lord.   [*Exit*]
MACBETH   I have almost forgot the taste of fears.
10   The time has been my senses would have cooled°   been chilled with terror
To hear a night-shriek, and my fell of hair°   hair on my skin
Would at a dismal treatise° rouse and stir   story
As life were in't. I have supped full with horrors.
Direness, familiar to my slaughterous thoughts,
Cannot once start° me.   startle
            [*Enter* SEYTON]
15   Wherefore was that cry?
SEYTON   The Queen, my lord, is dead.
MACBETH   She should have died hereafter.[1]
There would have been a time for such a word.
Tomorrow, and tomorrow, and tomorrow
Creeps in this petty pace from day to day
20   To the last syllable of recorded time,
And all our yesterdays have lighted fools
The way to dusty death. Out, out, brief candle.
Life's but a walking shadow, a poor player
That struts and frets his hour upon the stage,
25   And then is heard no more. It is a tale
Told by an idiot, full of sound and fury,
Signifying nothing.
            Enter a MESSENGER
                                        Thou com'st to use
Thy tongue: thy story quickly.
MESSENGER   Gracious my lord,
I should report that which I say I saw,
But know not how to do't.
30   MACBETH   Well, say, sir.
MESSENGER   As I did stand my watch upon the hill
I looked toward Birnam, and anon methought
The wood began to move.
MACBETH   Liar and slave!
MESSENGER   Let me endure your wrath if't be not so.
35   Within this three mile may you see it coming.
I say, a moving grove.
MACBETH   If thou speak'st false
Upon the next tree shall thou hang alive
Till famine cling° thee. If thy speech be sooth,°   wither / truth

5.5 Location: Macbeth's castle.
1. She would certainly have died someday; she should have died at another, more peaceful time.

I care not if thou dost for me as much.

40 I pall° in resolution, and begin   *fail*

To doubt th'equivocation of the fiend,
That lies like truth. 'Fear not till Birnam Wood
Do come to Dunsinane'—and now a wood
Comes toward Dunsinane. Arm, arm, and out.

45 If this which he avouches does appear
There is nor flying hence nor tarrying here.
I 'gin to be aweary of the sun,
And wish th'estate° o'th' world were now undone.   *ordered structure*
Ring the alarum bell. [*Alarums*] Blow wind, come wrack,°   *ruin*

50 At least we'll die with harness° on our back.   *Exeunt*   *armor*

<h3 style="text-align:center">5.6</h3>

Enter MALCOLM, SIWARD, MACDUFF, *and their army with*
boughs, [with a drummer] and colours

MALCOLM   Now near enough. Your leafy screens throw down,
And show° like those you are.   *appear*
[*They throw down the boughs*]
                            You, worthy uncle,
Shall with my cousin, your right noble son,
Lead our first battle.° Worthy Macduff and we   *battalion*

5 Shall take upon's what else remains to do
According to our order.°   *battle plan*

SIWARD   Fare you well.
Do we but find the tyrant's power° tonight,   *army*
Let us be beaten if we cannot fight.

MACDUFF   Make all our trumpets speak, give them all breath,

10 Those clamorous harbingers of blood and death.
                         Exeunt. Alarums continued

<h3 style="text-align:center">5.7</h3>

Enter MACBETH

MACBETH   They have tied me to a stake. I cannot fly,
But bear-like I must fight the course.[1] What's he
That was not born of woman? Such a one
Am I to fear, or none.
Enter YOUNG SIWARD

5 YOUNG SIWARD   What is thy name?

MACBETH   Thou'lt be afraid to hear it.

YOUNG SIWARD   No, though thou call'st thyself a hotter name
Than any is in hell.

MACBETH   My name's Macbeth.

YOUNG SIWARD   The devil himself could not pronounce a title
More hateful to mine ear.

10 MACBETH   No, nor more fearful.

YOUNG SIWARD   Thou liest, abhorrèd tyrant. With my sword
I'll prove the lie thou speak'st.
              [*They*] *fight, and* YOUNG SIWARD [*is*] *slain*

MACBETH   Thou wast born of woman,

5.6 Location: As before.
5.7 Location: As before.
1. Referring to the practice of bearbaiting, in which a   bear was tied to a stake and set upon by dogs. *course:*
round of bearbaiting.

But swords I smile at, weapons laugh to scorn,
Brandished by man that's of a woman born.

Exit [with the body]

5.8

Alarums. Enter MACDUFF

MACDUFF That way the noise is. Tyrant, show thy face!
If thou beest slain and with° no stroke of mine,   *by*
My wife and children's ghosts will haunt me still.°   *always*
I cannot strike at wretched kerns, whose arms
5 Are hired to bear their staves.° Either thou, Macbeth,   *spears*
Or else my sword with an unbattered edge
I sheathe again undeeded.[1] There thou shouldst be;
By this great clatter one of greatest note
Seems bruited.° Let me find him, fortune,   *announced*
10 And more I beg not.   *Exit. Alarums*

5.9

Enter MALCOLM *and* SIWARD

SIWARD This way, my lord. The castle's gently rendered.°   *surrendered*
The tyrant's people on both sides do fight.
The noble thanes do bravely in the war.
The day almost itself professes yours,
And little is to do.
5 MALCOLM   We have met with foes
That strike beside us.[1]
SIWARD   Enter, sir, the castle.   *Exeunt. Alarum*

5.10

Enter MACBETH

MACBETH Why should I play the Roman fool,° and die   *the suicide*
On mine own sword? Whiles I see lives, the gashes
Do better upon them.

Enter MACDUFF

MACDUFF   Turn, hell-hound, turn.
MACBETH Of all men else I have avoided thee.
5 But get thee back. My soul is too much charged
With blood of thine already.
MACDUFF   I have no words;
My voice is in my sword, thou bloodier villain
Than terms can give thee out.°   *words can describe*
[They] fight; alarum
MACBETH   Thou losest labour.°   *waste effort*
As easy mayst thou the intrenchant° air   *incapable of being cut*
10 With thy keen sword impress° as make me bleed.   *mark*
Let fall thy blade on vulnerable crests;
I bear a charmèd life, which must not yield
To one of woman born.
MACDUFF   Despair° thy charm,   *Despair of*
And let the angel° whom thou still hast served   *evil spirit*

5.8 Location: Before Macbeth's castle; the battle continues.
1. Having accomplished no deeds.

5.9 Location: Before Macbeth's castle.
1. Fight on our side; deliberately miss us.
5.10 Location: Scene continues.

15   Tell thee Macduff was from his mother's womb
        Untimely° ripped.   *Prematurely*

MACBETH   Accursèd be that tongue that tells me so,
      For it hath cowed° my better part of man;   *intimidated*
      And be these juggling fiends no more believed,

20   That palter° with us in a double sense,   *equivocate*
      That keep the word of promise to our ear
      And break it to our hope. I'll not fight with thee.

MACDUFF   Then yield thee, coward,
      And live to be the show and gaze° o'th' time.   *spectacle*

25   We'll have thee as our rarer monsters° are,   *prodigies*
      Painted upon a pole,[1] and underwrit
      'Here may you see the tyrant.'

MACBETH   I will not yield
      To kiss the ground before young Malcolm's feet,
      And to be baited° with the rabble's curse.   *harassed*

30   Though Birnam Wood be come to Dunsinane,
      And thou opposed being of no woman born,
      Yet I will try the last.° Before my body   *the last resort*
      I throw my warlike shield. Lay on, Macduff,
      And damned be him that first cries 'Hold, enough!'

                                Exeunt fighting. Alarums
      [They] enter fighting, and MACBETH *[is] slain. [Exit MAC-*
      DUFF *with Macbeth's body]*

5.11

      Retreat[1] *and flourish. Enter with [a drummer] and col-*
      ours MALCOLM, SIWARD, ROSS, *thanes, and soldiers*

MALCOLM   I would° the friends we miss were safe arrived.   *wish*

SIWARD   Some must go off;° and yet by these[2] I see   *die*
      So great a day as this is cheaply bought.

MALCOLM   Macduff is missing, and your noble son.

5   ROSS *[to* SIWARD*]*   Your son, my lord, has paid a soldier's debt.
      He only lived but till he was a man,
      The which no sooner had his prowess confirmed
      In the unshrinking station[3] where he fought,
      But like a man he died.

SIWARD   Then he is dead?

10   ROSS   Ay, and brought off the field. Your cause of sorrow
      Must not be measured by his worth, for then
      It hath no end.

SIWARD   Had he his hurts before?°   *on his front*

ROSS   Ay, on the front.

SIWARD   Why then, God's soldier be he.
      Had I as many sons as I have hairs

15   I would not wish them to a fairer death;
      And so his knell is knolled.

MALCOLM   He's worth more sorrow,
      And that I'll spend for him.

SIWARD   He's worth no more.

---

1. Painted on a cloth or board supported by a pole as a
form of advertisement.
5.11 Location: Within the castle.

1. A trumpet call signaling the end of the battle.
2. To judge from those who are present.
3. Post from which he did not shrink.

They say he parted° well and paid his score,   *departed*
And so God be with him. Here comes newer comfort.
   Enter MACDUFF *with Macbeth's head*
20 MACDUFF [*to* MALCOLM] Hail, King, for so thou art. Behold where stands[4]
 Th'usurper's cursèd head. The time is free.°   *free from tyranny*
 I see thee compassed with thy kingdom's pearl,[5]
 That speak my salutation in their minds,
 Whose voices I desire aloud with mine:
 Hail, King of Scotland!
25 ALL BUT MALCOLM   Hail, King of Scotland!
   Flourish
 MALCOLM We shall not spend a large expense of time
 Before we reckon with° your several loves   *make an accounting of*
 And make us even with you.° My thanes and kinsmen, *reward your loyalty*
 Henceforth be earls, the first that ever Scotland
30 In such an honour named. What's more to do
 Which would be planted newly with the time,[6]
 As calling home our exiled friends abroad,
 That fled the snares of watchful tyranny,
 Producing forth[7] the cruel ministers°   *agents*
35 Of this dead butcher and his fiend-like queen—
 Who, as 'tis thought, by self and violent hands° *her own violent hands*
 Took off her life—this and what needful else
 That calls upon us, by the grace of grace
 We will perform in measure, time, and place.[8]
40 So thanks to all at once, and to each one,
 Whom we invite to see us crowned at Scone.
    Flourish. Exeunt Omnes°   *all*

TEXTUAL VARIANTS

Control text: F

F: The Folio of 1623
Fa, Fb: Successive states of F incorporating various print-shop corrections and changes

s.p. FIRST WITCH, SECOND WITCH, THIRD WITCH [F's use of *1, 2,* and *3* has been
 standardized throughout.]
s.p. KING DUNCAN [F's use of *King* has been standardized throughout.]
s.p. LADY MACBETH [F's use of *Lady* has been standardized throughout.]
s.p. FIRST MURDERER [F's use of *1 Murderer, 1,* and *Murderer* has been standardized
 throughout.]
s.p. SECOND MURDERER [F's use of *2 Murderer* and *2* has been standardized throughout.]
s.p. THIRD MURDERER [F's use of *3* has been standardized throughout.]
s.p. ALL THE WITCHES [F's use of *All.* has been standardized throughout.]
s.p. FIRST APPARITION, SECOND APPARITION, THIRD APPARITION [F's use of *1 Apparition,*
 2 Apparition, and *3 Apparition* has been standardized throughout.]
s.p. LADY MACDUFF [F's use of *Wife* has been standardized throughout.]

---

4. Presumably upon a pole or lance.
5. I see you surrounded by your nobles, here called the
"pearl" of the kingdom.
6. Which should be performed at the beginning of this
new era.
7. Bringing forward for trial.
8. In due order, at the proper time and place.

s.p. MACDUFF'S SON [F's use of *Son* has been standardized throughout.]
s.p. A MURDERER [F's use of *Murderer* has been standardized throughout.]
s.p. A SOLDIER [F's use of *Soldier* has been standardized throughout.]

1.1.9–11 s.p. SECOND WITCH Paddock calls. / THIRD WITCH Anon. / ALL Fair .. air. *All. Padock calls* anon: faire . . . ayre.
1.2.13 galloglasses Gallowgrosses 26 break [not in F] 31 Norwegian Norweyan 46 haste a haste 61 Colum's Colmes
1.3.30 weird weyward 37 Forres Soris 95 hail Tale 96 Came Can
1.4.1 Are Or
1.5.21 'Thus . . . do' [not in F] 29, 32 s.p. SERVANT *Mess.* 63 the innocent th'innocent
1.6.4 martlet Barlet 9 most must
1.7.6 shoal Schoole 47 do no
2.1.55 strides sides 56 sure sowre 57 way they they may
2.3.77 horror. horror. Ring the Bell. 108 Outran Out-run
3.1.2, 3.4.132, 4.1.152 weird weyard 23 talk take 76 s.p. MURDERERS [F uses *Murth.* three times in 3.1, and each time it would be appropriate for both to speak. See also 3.1.116 and 3.1.140.]
3.3.7 and end
3.4.77 time times 88 of o' 143 in deed indeed
3.5.34–35 s.p. SPIRITS . . . away. [not in F; see Textual Note] 38–73 s.p. SPIRITS . . . reach. [not in F; see Textual Note]
3.6.24 son Sonnes
4.1.44–60 s.p. HECATE . . . out. [not in F; see Textual Note] 75 germens Germaine 109 Dunsinane Dunsmane 114 on's high place our high plac'd
4.2.22 none moue 83 shag-haired shagge-ear'd
4.3.134 thy they 155 with [Fb] my with [Fa] 161 not nor 237 tune time
5.3.41 Cure her Cure 46 fraught stufft
5.4.11 gone giuen
5.5.40 pall pull
5.11.25 s.p. ALL BUT MALCOLM *All.*

Antony and Cleopatra

Antony and Cleopatra (1606–07) picks up where *Julius Caesar* leaves off. It presupposes familiarity not only with events dramatized in that play but also with earlier Roman con‑flicts. During the first century B.C., Rome, the overwhelming military power throughout the Mediterranean and beyond, entered into a protracted civil war that culminated in its transition from a republic (rule by a senatorial aristocracy) to an empire (monarchical power). As *Julius Caesar* opens, Caesar has already defeated his archrival Pompey the Great and governs Rome as dictator. The play recounts the republican assassination of him, led by Brutus and Cassius, and the assassins' subsequent defeat and death at the hands of Mark Antony (Caesar's lieutenant) and Octavius (Caesar's young grandnephew and adoptive son, who took the name of "Caesar" upon Julius Caesar's death and turned it to political use). *Antony and Cleopatra*, which covers the period from 40 to 30 B.C., completes the narrative of Roman civil war and the final destruction of the republic. Rome and its vast holdings are now ruled by the triumvirate of Lepidus, Octavius Caesar, and Mark Antony, who govern, respectively, the Mediterranean portions of Africa, Europe, and Asia. Yet Shakespeare's tragedy shifts the focus from the struggle over Rome's internal political system to Rome's external imperial domination of the East (the present-day Mid‑dle East) and to affairs of the heart. Mark Antony and Octavius Caesar contend for political supremacy, but the love between Antony and Cleopatra occupies center stage.

Much of the play's fascination arises from this intertwining of empire and sexuality. The issue is already present in Thomas North's translation of *Plutarch's Lives of the Noble Grecians and Romanes*—Shakespeare's favorite source, with the exception of Raphael Hol‑inshed's *Chronicles of England, Scotland, and Ireland*, and one that he follows closely here. Plutarch and other writers of Greek and Latin antiquity were preoccupied with the opposition between the conquering West, often thought by them to stand for political and moral virtue, and the older civilizations it subjugated in the East, frequently supposed to represent luxury and decadent, feminized sexuality. This particular understanding of empire reemerged in the Renaissance during a new era of Western expansion, as Europe entered the path to genuine global domination armed with an increasingly racialized and still sexualized view of the peoples it sought to subdue. *Antony and Cleopatra* is one response to European expansion, and the play's subsequent fortunes testify to its connec‑tion with the imperial enterprise of the West.

Long supplanted onstage by John Dryden's *All for Love* (1677), a rewriting of Shake‑speare's story as a tragedy of private life, Shakespeare's version came into its own only after 1800, when England became the world's leading power. During the last two centuries, both Cleopatra and the East with which she is identified have seemed female, dark, colo‑nized, available, animalistic, exotic, and excitingly dangerous. Comments on the text or on its performance have stressed the play's "strange pervasive influence of Oriental luxury and vice," its "effect of Oriental repose," Cleopatra's "corrupt and half-barbarous Oriental court." "Just as Antony's ruin results from his connection with Cleopatra," one critic argued, "so does the fall of the Roman Republic result from the contact of the simple hardihood of the West, with the luxury of the East." Actresses playing Cleopatra recall "an Indian dancer" and "Asiatic undulations of form." They bring to mind a "panther," a "sensuous tigress," "a wicked monkey," and a creature full of "feline cunning."

Not all of these responses chauvinistically assume Western superiority, and *Antony and Cleopatra* itself seems designed to elicit complicated judgments. Rome is contrasted to Egypt, West to East, the conquerors to the conquered; rapid shifts of scene across enor‑mous distances accentuate this division. A sober, masculine military ethos opposes a comi-

Octavius Caesar, later known as Augustus, as on this medal. From G. du Choul, *Discours de la Religion des Anciens Romains* (1567).

cally frivolous, pleasure-loving, feminized, emasculated, and sexualized court. Antony must decide between Octavius Caesar and Cleopatra, Octavius's sister Octavia and Cleopatra, the world and the flesh. Political opportunism drives Antony's marriage to Octavia, love and sexual desire his relationship with Cleopatra; he chooses between fidelity to a chaste, white wife and adultery with a promiscuous, "tawny," "black" seductress (1.1.6, 1.5.28). Where Caesar employs a rational self-interest (he is the "universal landlord," 3.13.72), Antony revels in an impetuous, extravagant generosity and challenges Caesar to one-on-one combat. Young Caesar is a bureaucrat of the future, old Antony a warrior of the past. Caesar's concerns are public and political, Antony's private and personal. Whereas Antony's brother and his previous wife, Fulvia, attack Caesar, Caesar promises that "the time of universal peace is near" (4.6.4). This assertion anticipates the *pax Romana* (Roman peace) instituted by Caesar throughout the empire. It also links the empire to Christianity by evoking the birth of Christ, which occurred in a Roman province during Caesar's long rule.

Through these conflicts, the play investigates the possibility of heroic action in a post-heroic world. It offers an epic view of the political arena, but deprives that arena of heroic significance. In this diminished environment, the protagonists' flaws are writ large. *Antony and Cleopatra* then asks whether heroic meaning can be transplanted to the private terrain of love. Throughout, Shakespeare maintains a studied ambivalence: critics disagree about whether the protagonists' concluding suicides are fruitless or redemptive. Following a series of tragedies—*Hamlet, Othello, King Lear,* and *Macbeth*—in which the protagonist's psychology is consistently probed, *Antony and Cleopatra* almost completely avoids soliloquy and thus inaugurates a final phase in Shakespeare's career, in which individual tragic intensity is sacrificed in favor of more broadly social representation. As a result, Antony's and Cleopatra's motives remain opaque to audiences and readers, to other characters in the play, to each other, and, arguably, even to themselves. Though we are invited to guess, we never definitively learn why Cleopatra flees at Actium, why she negotiates with Caesar in the last two acts, or why Antony thinks marriage to Octavia will solve his political problems. Instead of self-revelation, the play offers contradictory framing commentary by minor figures. These external perspectives help impart an epic feel, as do the geographical and scenic shifts, which also produce a loose, fragmentary, and capacious structure alien to classically inspired notions of proper dramatic form. Furthermore, like the other Roman plays based on Plutarch—*Julius Caesar* and *Coriolanus*—*Antony and Cleopatra* relies heavily on blank verse while almost entirely avoiding rhyme: Shakespeare may have been following the Earl of Surrey's sixteenth-century blank verse translation of part of the *Aeneid* (19 B.C.), Virgil's enormously influential epic of the founding of Rome. The Roman Empire would thus seem the obvious stage for heroic performance.

Yet this proves not to be the case, partly because the play's structuring dichotomies are unstable. It is as if *Antony and Cleopatra* created distinctions only to undermine them. For instance, the antitheses between Caesar and Antony and between Rome and Egypt lack political resonance. *Julius Caesar's* struggle between republic and empire arises only peripherally in *Antony and Cleopatra*, where it is voiced by Pompey:

what
Made the all-honoured, honest Roman Brutus,
With the armed rest, courtiers of beauteous freedom,
To drench the Capitol but that they would
Have one man but a man?

(2.6.15–19)

Pompey's rebellion is bought off by Caesar, Antony, and Lepidus. Pompey is then attacked by Lepidus and by Caesar (who later disposes of Lepidus) and is subsequently murdered by one of Antony's men, who may or may not have been acting on his master's orders. Although Antony supposedly "wept / When at Philippi he found Brutus slain" (3.2.56–57), he asserts that " 'twas I / That the mad Brutus ended" (3.11.37–38). The republic is thus already dead when *Antony and Cleopatra* opens. Caesar astutely conforms to the style of a republic, whereas Antony offends traditional Roman sensibilities by ostentatiously taking on the trappings of monarchy (3.6.1–19). Nonetheless, their political conflict concerns not rival systems of government but simply the desires of two ambitious men, each of whom wants absolute power. The independence of Egypt is at stake, although this occurs to no one except Cleopatra and then only belatedly and perhaps duplicitously. The end of civil war is also important, but it is hard either to celebrate the victory of the ruthless Caesar or to lament the defeat of the incompetent Antony.

Other apparent distinctions between the rivals also conceal basic similarities. Antony boasts of his valor at Philippi, while Caesar "alone / Dealt on lieutenantry" (battled exclusively through his officers; 3.11.38–39). Earlier, however, Antony's "officer" Ventidius, whom Plutarch calls "the only man that ever triumphed of the Parthians until this present day," remarks, "Caesar and Antony have ever won / More in their officer than person" (3.1.16–17). In addition, Caesar's promise of "universal peace" is anticipated in a version of Christ's Last Supper that Antony shares with his followers.

Tend me tonight.
Maybe it is the period of your duty.
Haply you shall not see me more; or if,
A mangled shadow. Perchance tomorrow
You'll serve another master.

(4.2.24–28)

Appropriately, Antony is criticized for moving his friends to tears by Enobarbus, a Judas-figure soon to betray Antony by defecting to Caesar and destined to die shortly thereafter, his heart broken by Antony's generosity.

Even the geographical contrast of the play partly dissolves into parallelisms and connections: Egyptian love is militarized, Roman war eroticized. Shakespeare does give Cleopatra a smaller political role than she has in Plutarch, to accentuate the basic conflict and perhaps also to reduce the threat of a powerful woman. But the external representation of the lovers' relationship, the absence of scenes of them alone, and their pride in exhibiting their affair intensify the feeling that love and war influence each other, that there is no distinction between public and private because nothing is private. Further, love is on both sides of the divide. Antony is preceded in suicide by his aptly named servant Eros (love), a figure from Plutarch. But the play opens with a criticism of "this dotage of our General's" by Philo (also "love"; 1.1.1), a figure invented by Shakespeare.

Antony and Cleopatra also renders problematic the object of desire. Presumably that object is Cleopatra. Loved by Antony, she elicits powerful responses from Enobarbus and Dolabella and had been the lover of "great Pompey" and "broad-fronted Caesar" (1.5.31, 29). Though this list may indicate the power of the Eastern femme fatale, the roll call of Romans in love has no Egyptian equivalent. It is unclear what they literally see in Cleopatra. Enobarbus's description of her initial meeting with Antony at Cydnus (2.2.192–232) elicits enthusiastic responses from Agrippa—"Rare Egyptian!" and "Royal wench!" (224, 232). But when Enobarbus says that "her own person . . . beggared all description" (203–04), he draws the logical inference, almost renouncing "all description":

> She did lie
> In her pavilion—cloth of gold, of tissue—
> O'er-picturing that Venus where we see
> The fancy outwork nature.
> (2.2.204–07)

All we know of Cleopatra's appearance is that she was reclining.

This absence of the seductress points in the same direction as the list of Roman lovers—toward the feelings of Roman men and away from any inherent attractiveness of an Egyptian woman. Some of these feelings are directed toward Antony. The Pompey and Caesar of *Antony and Cleopatra* at times act almost as if they were the sons—rather than the younger brother (Pompey) and grandnephew and adopted son (Caesar)—of Cleopatra's former lovers, whose paternal roles Antony has now assumed. In lines whose erotic charge goes beyond the intended objects (Antony and Cleopatra) to include the speaker himself, Pompey expresses pleasure that Antony takes him seriously (2.1.35–38). And Caesar is disgusted by Antony and Cleopatra's theatrical coronation:

> At the feet sat
> Caesarion, whom they call my father's son,
> And all the unlawful issue that their lust
> Since then hath made between them.
> (3.6.5–8)

Here, there is a possible confusion between Antony and the older Caesar and a definite one between Caesarion and the younger Caesar, both of whom are "my father's son." This is not the only intense familial feeling Caesar has for Antony. When he weeps at Antony's death, Maecenas sees a noble narcissism: "When such a spacious mirror's set before him / He needs must see himself" (5.1.34–35). Caesar himself recalls Antony movingly:

> thou, my brother, my competitor
> In top of all design, my mate in empire,
> Friend and companion in the front of war,
> The arm of mine own body, and the heart
> Where mine his thoughts did kindle.
> (5.1.42–46)

This outpouring of emotion, however calculated, leads in contradictory directions. By calling Antony his "mate" and invoking a meeting of "heart" and mind, Caesar on the one hand suggests an intimacy between the two men that recalls Renaissance celebrations of close male friendship but that also borders on the erotic. On the other hand, he neutralizes any filial anxiety he may feel by describing Antony as "my brother" and then as a subordinate, "the arm of mine own body."

Though Caesar betrays various kinds of emotional intensity, that is not what he consciously espouses. His ideal Antony is not the lover who "o'erflows the measure" (1.1.2) but the soldier who exercised heroic self-deprivation (1.4.58–61). He certainly does not emulate the older Caesar, whose sexual and military conquests were completely intertwined (3.13.82–85). Thus Octavius Caesar represents not the preservation but the diminution of traditional Roman values, a constriction of a heroic culture of which Antony is the last survivor. The jaundiced view of political power that emerges could be construed as an implicit critique of the centralizing monarchs of Shakespeare's own time. In any case, the play insists that one can no longer have it both ways, that politics and sex (or any kind of grandeur) are irrevocably sundered.

Antony and Cleopatra must exercise their peculiar brand of paradoxical hyperbole in this new and smaller world. Antony's heart "is become the bellows and the fan / To cool a gipsy's lust": his heart is a fan that cools Cleopatra's lust by satisfying it, but in so doing he rekindles her passion, as if his heart were also a bellows (1.1.9–10). Similarly, when Cleopatra meets Antony, "pretty dimpled boys" (2.2.208) attend her

> With divers-coloured fans whose wind did seem
> To glow the delicate cheeks which they did cool,
> And what they undid did.
>
> (2.2.209–11)

And when told that marriage to Octavia will force Antony to abandon Cleopatra, Enobarbus demurs in perhaps the play's most famous lines:

> Never. He will not.
> Age cannot wither her, nor custom stale
> Her infinite variety. Other women cloy
> The appetites they feed, but she makes hungry
> Where most she satisfies.
>
> (2.2.239–43)

But the protagonists' inexhaustibility and their "infinite variety" do not fare well until the final scene. Though Shakespeare makes Antony and Cleopatra more sympathetic than they are in Plutarch, they remain maddeningly self-absorbed and self-destructive—ignoring urgent business, acting impulsively, bullying underlings, reveling in vulgarity, lying, apparently betraying each other.

Moreover, except for the first Battle of Alexandria, in which the couple briefly synthesize military and amorous arms, the fighting scenes testify to their belatedness, their irrelevance. Shakespeare's uncharacteristic decision to follow the practice of classical theater and keep all fighting offstage leaves only a feeling of being let down, as helpless observers report on the debacle. Thus, Enobarbus laments at Actium:

> Naught, naught, all naught! I can behold no longer.
> Th'*Antoniad*, the Egyptian admiral,
> With all their sixty, fly and turn the rudder.
>
> (3.10.1–3)

At the last battle of the play, it is Antony's turn:

> All is lost.
> This foul Egyptian hath betrayèd me.
> My fleet hath yielded to the foe, and yonder
> They cast their caps up, and carouse together
> Like friends long lost.
>
> (4.13.9–13)

Beginning with Act 4, however, the restlessness of the play diminishes as Antony and Cleopatra's sphere of activity is reduced to Alexandria. The manipulative report of her death that Cleopatra sends Antony, his botched suicide in response, and her refusal to leave her monument to attend him as he lies dying convert Antony's presumably climactic death into a mere false ending and shift the weight of significance to the final scene. Instead, Egypt and Cleopatra are what matter. Both have been associated throughout with the overflowing that Antony is faulted for at the outset. Antony declares his love for Cleopatra by rejecting the state he rules: "Let Rome in Tiber melt, and the wide arch / Of the ranged empire fall" (1.1.35–36). Upon hearing of Antony's marriage to Octavia, Cleopatra prays, "Melt Egypt into Nile, and kindly creatures / Turn all to serpents!" (2.5.78–79). This apocalyptic imagery, which dissolves all distinction, anticipates Antony's loss of self when he thinks Cleopatra has betrayed him. His body seems to him as "indistinct / As water is in water" (4.15.10–11).

The language of liquefaction is also connected to the confusion of gender identity. Antony

> is not more manlike
> Than Cleopatra, nor the queen of Ptolemy
> More womanly than he.
>
> (1.4.5–7)

The Nile delta, showing the northern end of the river as it flows into the Mediterranean Sea. Alexandria is visible near the upper left-hand corner. From a map by Sebastian Münster (1550).

And Cleopatra reports, "I . . . put my tires and mantles on him whilst / I wore his sword Philippan" (2.5.21–23). Depending on one's perspective, this behavior either dangerously confuses gender roles, thereby leading to Antony's ignominious flight at Actium, or overcomes a destructive opposition. Furthermore, the language of inundation recalls not only the rise of the Nile, which fertilizes the surrounding plain, but Cleopatra herself, who is identified with Egypt throughout the play. The conclusion seeks this regenerative property in her. Shakespeare's probable recourse to Plutarch's *Of Isis and Osiris* apparently inspires the repeated invocation of the goddess Isis, the sister-wife of Osiris, whom she restores after he is pursued to his death by his brother-rival, Typhon. When Caesar complains of Antony's monarchical behavior, he finds Cleopatra's divine impersonation "of the goddess Isis" even more galling (3.6.17).

Cleopatra's suicide makes good on these imagistic patterns, retrospectively justifying Antony's decision to die for her. Unlike the protagonists' deaths in Shakespeare's earlier tragedies, this outcome is desired by readers and audiences. The ending also evokes the synthesis precluded by the play's dichotomies but implied by its more subtle patterns. Cleopatra dies a death that might be associated with a Roman man:

> My resolution's placed, and I have nothing
> Of woman in me. Now from head to foot
> I am marble-constant. Now the fleeting moon
> No planet is of mine.
> (5.2.234–37)

But in rejecting the inconstancy of the moon, of which Isis was goddess, arguably she also dies the death of a faithful Roman wife.

> methinks I hear
> Antony call. I see him rouse himself
> To praise my noble act. . . .
> . . . .
> . . . Husband, I come.
> Now to that name my courage prove my title.
> (5.2.274–79)

And in taking the poisonous asp to her breast, she may become a Roman matron as well:

> Peace, peace.
> Dost thou not see my baby at my breast,
> That sucks the nurse asleep? . . .
> As sweet as balm, as soft as air, as gentle.
> O Antony!
> [*She puts another aspic to her arm*]
> Nay, I will take thee too.
> (5.2.299–303)

Since the Folio lacks the stage direction included here, perhaps the final line can mean that she takes Antony to her breast, like a mother comforting her infant son.

But "O Antony" is also a cry of orgasm that looks back to Cleopatra's earlier sexual assertions, "I am again for Cydnus / To meet Mark Antony" and "Husband, I come," and forward to Charmian's orgasmic dying words, which Shakespeare added to his source: "Ah, soldier!" (5.2.224–25, 319). Furthermore, Cleopatra's manner of death is clearly Egyptian. The asp recalls Antony's description of her as "my serpent of old Nile" (1.5.25). Thus Rome and Egypt, Antony and Cleopatra, martial valor and sexual ecstasy, are united in death as they cannot be in life. "Dido and her Aeneas" (4.15.53), in Antony's vision soon to be eclipsed by himself and Cleopatra, wander together through the afterlife of the play. But the two legendary lovers remain bitterly unreconciled in the *Aeneid*, Shakespeare's source for the characters. With full awareness of the complexities and ironies at stake,

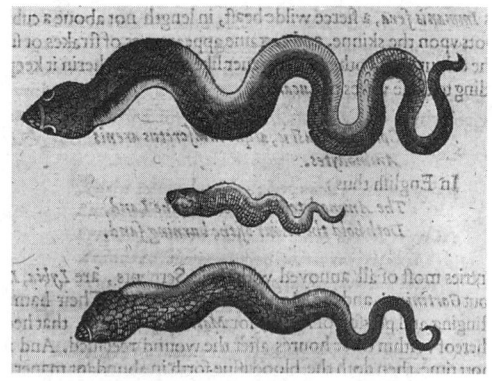

The Clown wishes Cleopatra "joy o'th' worm" (5.2.270) as she prepares to commit suicide. From Edward Topsell's *History of Serpents* (1608).

Virgil narrates Aeneas's abandonment of Dido, who is associated with Eastern sensuality, in the name of a higher cause, Roman civic virtue. *Antony and Cleopatra* thus answers the *Aeneid*, ambivalently distancing itself from Roman and, by extension, Renaissance imperialism. It seems to be saying that you *can* have it both ways. East and West, conquered and conquerer are affirmed in a final synthesis.

Yet countercurrents trouble even the metaphorical validation of Cleopatra's "immortal longings" (5.2.272). She resolves on suicide not when she learns that Antony killed himself for her but when she becomes certain that Caesar plans to lead her in a humiliating triumph in Rome. This explains her pleasure in imagining that Antony will "mock / The luck of Caesar," that the asp will "call great Caesar ass / Unpolicied" (5.2.276–77, 298–99). The concluding triumphant rhetoric thus cleans up earlier dubious behavior and puts the best face on defeat. Heroic aristocratic individualism can act in the world only by leaving it. Moreover, the domestic Cleopatra of the conclusion can be seen as the reduction to a conventional gender role of a woman who challenged sexual hierarchy. At her death, Cleopatra "lies / A lass unparalleled" (5.2.305–06), or has the play instead presented "lies alas unparalleled"?

How *Antony and Cleopatra* should be interpreted depends on the relationship one sees between the ending and the partly incompatible material that has preceded it. Most, though not all, critics have found the conclusion affirmative on balance. But the work registers ambivalence to the last. This duality is captured in Cleopatra's account of the response she expects in Rome:

> The quick comedians
> Extemporally will stage us, and present
> Our Alexandrian revels. Antony
> Shall be brought drunken forth, and I shall see
> Some squeaking Cleopatra boy my greatness
> I'th' posture of a whore.
>
> (5.2.212–17)

Cleopatra shudders at the absurdity of a boy actor badly impersonating her, yet the part of Cleopatra in *Antony and Cleopatra* was originally performed by a boy. This reminder punctures the dramatic illusion just when it would seem most essential. Arguably, we are being asked to recognize that a boy in the role of an extremely seductive woman can establish the same emotional intensity with the men in the audience that sometimes seems to exist between the male characters in that play. These lines certainly look back to Cleopatra's deliberate blurring of gender division. And they emphasize the artifice of Cleopatra herself, a veteran actress in her final performance. Shakespeare is here flaunting the power of his medium. But if it is impossible to "boy" Cleopatra's "greatness," to represent her adequately, perhaps that is merely an invitation to look beyond what can be shown, to take seriously her "immortal longings."

WALTER COHEN

TEXTUAL NOTE

The Tragedie of Anthonie, and Cleopatra was published in the First Folio of 1623 (F), which also gives the forms *Anthony and Cleopater* in other references to the title of the play. "Anthony & Cleopatra" was entered on May 20, 1608, in the Stationers' Register, a listing of books intended for legal publication. As it happened, the play went unpublished; this entry may have been designed to prevent someone else from printing it. Both stylistic tests and probable verbal echoes in other plays suggest a date of late 1606 or possibly early 1607. The Folio version is ultimately based on an authorial manuscript, but perhaps by way of a transcript of Shakespeare's "foul papers" (rough draft). There is no evidence of the revisions necessary for theatrical performance. Thus the stage directions list characters who have no role in the scene or even the entire play (characters excluded from the present edition); are insufficient at various points, especially in the closing scenes at Cleopatra's monument; and (like the speech prefixes) contain some authorial errors.

The play presents problems in modernizing proper names and in verse lineation. In addition, but less problematically, it has no act or scene divisions after an initial "Actus Primus. Scœna Prima." The ones supplied here follow editorial practice standard since the eighteenth century, except in starting a new scene after 4.7.3 (because the stage is cleared). This decision, of course, changes the scene numbering for the remainder of the act.

SELECTED BIBLIOGRAPHY

Adelman, Janet. *Suffocating Mothers: Fantasies of Maternal Origin in Shakespeare's Plays, "Hamlet" to "The Tempest."* New York: Routledge, 1992. 174–92.

Barton, Anne. *Essays, Mainly Shakespearean.* Cambridge: Cambridge University Press, 1994. 113–35.

Brown, John Russell, ed. *Shakespeare: "Antony and Cleopatra," A Casebook.* Revised edition. London: Macmillan, 1991.

Cantor, Paul A. *Shakespeare's Rome: Republic and Empire.* Ithaca, N.Y.: Cornell University Press, 1976. 127–208.

Colie, Rosalie L. *Shakespeare's Living Art.* Princeton: Princeton University Press, 1974. 168–207.

Drakakis, John, ed. *"Antony and Cleopatra": William Shakespeare.* New Casebooks. New York: St. Martin's, 1994.

Flesch, William. *Generosity and the Limits of Authority: Shakespeare, Herbert, Milton.* Ithaca, N.Y.: Cornell University Press, 1992. 189–222.

Harris, Jonathan Gil. " 'Narcissus in thy face': Roman Desire and the Difference It Fakes in *Antony and Cleopatra.*" *Shakespeare Quarterly* 45 (1994): 408–25.

Rose, Mark, ed. *Twentieth Century Interpretations of "Antony and Cleopatra."* Englewood Cliffs, N.J.: Prentice-Hall, 1977.

Sprengnether, Madelon. "The Boy Actor and Femininity in *Antony and Cleopatra.*" *Shakespeare's Personality.* Ed. Norman N. Holland, Sidney Homan, and Bernard J. Paris. Berkeley: University of California Press, 1989. 191–205.

The Tragedy of Antony and Cleopatra

The Persons of the Play

MARK ANTONY (Marcus Antonius), triumvir of Rome

DEMETRIUS ⎫
PHILO
Domitius ENOBARBUS
VENTIDIUS
SILIUS ⎬ friends and followers of Antony
EROS
CAMIDIUS
SCARUS
DECRETAS ⎭

Octavius CAESAR, triumvir of Rome
OCTAVIA, his sister

MAECENAS ⎫
AGRIPPA
TAURUS
DOLABELLA ⎬ friends and followers of Caesar
THIDIAS
GALLUS
PROCULEIUS ⎭

LEPIDUS, triumvir of Rome
Sextus POMPEY (Pompeius)

MENECRATES ⎫
MENAS ⎬ friends of Pompey
VARRIUS ⎭

CLEOPATRA, Queen of Egypt

CHARMIAN ⎫
IRAS
ALEXAS
MARDIAN, a eunuch ⎬ attending on Cleopatra
DIOMED
SELEUCUS ⎭

A SOOTHSAYER
An AMBASSADOR
MESSENGERS
A BOY who sings
A SENTRY and men of his WATCH
Men of the GUARD
An EGYPTIAN
A CLOWN
SERVANTS
SOLDIERS
Eunuchs, attendants, captains, soldiers, servants

1.1

Enter DEMETRIUS *and* PHILO

PHILO   Nay, but this dotage° of our General's   *absurd infatuation*
    O'erflows the measure.[1] Those his goodly eyes,
    That o'er the files and musters° of the war   *lines of troops*
    Have glowed like plated° Mars, now bend, now turn   *armored*
5   The office° and devotion of their view   *duty*
    Upon a tawny front.[2] His captain's heart,
    Which in the scuffles of great fights hath burst
    The buckles on his breast, reneges all temper,[3]
    And is become the bellows and the fan
    To cool a gipsy's° lust.   *Egyptian's; hussy's*

    Flourish. Enter ANTONY, CLEOPATRA, *her ladies, the*
    train, with eunuchs fanning her
10   Look where they come.
    Take but good note, and you shall see in him
    The triple pillar of the world[4] transformed
    Into a strumpet's fool. Behold and see.

CLEOPATRA *[to* ANTONY]   If it be love indeed, tell me how much.
15 ANTONY   There's beggary° in the love that can be reckoned.   *little value*
CLEOPATRA   I'll set a bourn° how far to be beloved.   *boundary*
ANTONY   Then must thou needs find out new heaven, new earth.[5]

    Enter a MESSENGER

MESSENGER   News, my good lord, from Rome.
ANTONY   Grates° me: the sum.°   *Irks / summary*
20 CLEOPATRA   Nay, hear them, Antony.
    Fulvia° perchance is angry; or who knows   *Antony's wife*
    If the scarce-bearded Caesar[6] have not sent
    His powerful mandate to you: 'Do this, or this,
    Take in° that kingdom and enfranchise° that.   *Annex / liberate*
25   Perform't, or else we damn thee.'
ANTONY   How,° my love?   *What*
CLEOPATRA   Perchance? Nay, and most like.[7]
    You must not stay here longer. Your dismission°   *marching orders*
    Is come from Caesar, therefore hear it, Antony.
30   Where's Fulvia's process°—Caesar's, I would say—both?   *summons*
    Call in the messengers. As I am Egypt's queen,
    Thou blushest, Antony, and that blood of thine
    Is Caesar's homager;° else so thy cheek pays shame   *Pays Caesar homage*
    When shrill-tongued Fulvia scolds. The messengers!
35 ANTONY   Let Rome in Tiber melt, and the wide arch
    Of the ranged° empire fall. Here is my space.   *orderly; extensive*
    Kingdoms are clay. Our dungy° earth alike   *made of manure*
    Feeds beast as man. The nobleness of life
    Is to do thus;° when such a mutual pair   *act as we do; embrace*
40   And such a twain can do't—in which I bind

1.1 Location: Cleopatra's palace, Alexandria.
1. Goes beyond suitable bounds.
2. A face or forehead of dark complexion (referring to Cleopatra; see the Introduction); military "front," or battle line.
3. Abandons all temperance ("temper" is also the hardness of tempered steel).
4. Antony, Octavius Caesar, and Lepidus were the three triumvirs ruling the Roman Empire (most of the known world, for Romans).

5. Alluding anachronistically to Revelation 21:1 ("I saw a new heaven, and a new earth") and to the discovery of the New World. This second meaning may connect to the imperial theme of the play—its sense of geographical expansiveness and European geographical expansion.
6. The opening of the play is set in 40 B.C., when Octavius Caesar was twenty-three; Antony was almost twenty years his senior.
7. It is most likely, rather than merely possible, that Fulvia is angry.

On pain of punishment the world to weet°—   *recognize*
We stand up peerless.
CLEOPATRA [*aside*]   Excellent falsehood!
Why did he marry Fulvia and not love her?
I'll seem the fool I am not. [*To* ANTONY] Antony
Will be himself.[8]
45 ANTONY   But stirred[9] by Cleopatra.
Now, for the love of Love and her soft hours
Let's not confound° the time with conference° harsh.   *ruin / conversation*
There's not a minute of our lives should stretch
Without some pleasure now. What sport° tonight?   *entertainment*
CLEOPATRA Hear the ambassadors.
50 ANTONY   Fie, wrangling queen,
Whom everything becomes—to chide, to laugh,
To weep; how every passion fully strives
To make itself, in thee, fair and admired!
No messenger but thine;[1] and all alone
55 Tonight we'll wander through the streets and note
The qualities of people. Come, my queen.
Last night you did desire it. [*To the* MESSENGER] Speak not to us.
              Exeunt [ANTONY *and* CLEOPATRA] *with the train*
                     [*and by another door the* MESSENGER]
DEMETRIUS Is Caesar with° Antonius prized° so slight?   *by / esteemed*
PHILO Sir, sometimes when he is not Antony
60 He comes too short of that great property°   *unique characteristic*
Which still° should go with Antony.   *always*
DEMETRIUS   I am full sorry
That he approves° the common liar who   *proves correct*
Thus speaks of him at Rome; but I will hope
Of better deeds tomorrow. Rest you happy.   *Exeunt*

1.2

       Enter ENOBARBUS, *a* SOOTHSAYER, CHARMIAN, IRAS, MAR-
          DIAN *the eunuch*, ALEXAS [*and attendants*]
CHARMIAN Lord Alexas, sweet Alexas, most anything Alexas,
almost most absolute° Alexas, where's the soothsayer that you   *perfect*
praised so to th' Queen?
O that I knew this husband, which you say
Must charge his horns[1] with garlands!
5 ALEXAS   Soothsayer!
SOOTHSAYER Your will?
CHARMIAN Is this the man? Is't you, sir, that know things?
SOOTHSAYER In nature's infinite book of secrecy
A little I can read.
10 ALEXAS [*to* CHARMIAN] Show him your hand.
ENOBARBUS [*calling*] Bring in the banquet° quickly,   *light meal; dessert*
Wine enough Cleopatra's health to drink.
         [*Enter servants with food and wine, and exeunt*]
CHARMIAN [*to* SOOTHSAYER] Good sir, give me good fortune.
SOOTHSAYER I make not, but foresee.

---

8. *I'll . . . himself*: I'll appear to believe Antony's false-   9. Aroused; motivated; disturbed.
hood, although I am really not so credulous; he will con-   1. I will hear only what you have to say.
tinue in his folly. (But Antony construes the words he   1.2 Location: Scene continues.
hears as a compliment. It is also possible that Antony   1. Must adorn his (proverbial) cuckold's horns.
hears Cleopatra's entire speech.)

CHARMIAN   Pray then, foresee me one.

15   SOOTHSAYER   You shall be yet
     Far fairer than you are.

CHARMIAN   He means in flesh.°   *(by getting fatter)*

IRAS   No, you shall paint° when you are old.   *use cosmetics*

CHARMIAN   Wrinkles forbid!

ALEXAS   Vex not his prescience. Be attentive.

CHARMIAN   Hush!

SOOTHSAYER   You shall be more beloving than beloved.

20   CHARMIAN   I had rather heat my liver with drinking.[2]

ALEXAS   Nay, hear him.

CHARMIAN   Good now,° some excellent fortune! Let me be mar-   *Please; fine; begin*
     ried to three kings in a forenoon and widow them all. Let me
     have a child at fifty to whom Herod of Jewry[3] may do homage.

25   Find° me to marry me with Octavius Caesar, and companion   *Find in my palm*
     me° with my mistress.   *make me equal*

SOOTHSAYER   You shall outlive the lady whom you serve.

CHARMIAN   O, excellent! I love long life better than figs.[4]

SOOTHSAYER   You have seen and proved° a fairer former fortune   *undergone*

30   Than that which is to approach.

CHARMIAN   Then belike° my children shall have no names.°   *likely / be bastards*
     Prithee, how many boys and wenches must I have?

SOOTHSAYER   If every of your wishes had a womb,
     And fertile every wish, a million.

35   CHARMIAN   Out, fool—I forgive thee for a witch.[5]

ALEXAS   You think none but your sheets are privy to your wishes.

CHARMIAN [*to the* SOOTHSAYER]   Nay, come, tell Iras hers.

ALEXAS   We'll know all our fortunes.

ENOBARBUS   Mine, and most of our fortunes, tonight shall be

40   drunk to bed.

IRAS [*showing her hand to the* SOOTHSAYER]   There's a palm pres-
     ages chastity,° if nothing else.   *(a dry palm)*

CHARMIAN   E'en as the o'erflowing Nilus presageth famine.[6]

IRAS   Go, you wild° bedfellow, you cannot soothsay.   *licentious*

45   CHARMIAN   Nay, if an oily palm° be not a fruitful prognostica-   *(sign of sensuality)*
     tion,° I cannot scratch mine ear. [*To the* SOOTHSAYER] Prithee,   *sign of fertility*
     tell her but a workaday° fortune.   *an everyday*

SOOTHSAYER   Your fortunes are alike.

IRAS   But how, but how? Give me particulars.

50   SOOTHSAYER   I have said.

IRAS   Am I not an inch of fortune better than she?

CHARMIAN   Well, if you were but an inch of fortune better than
     I, where would you choose it?

IRAS   Not in my husband's nose.°   *(sexual innuendo)*

55   CHARMIAN   Our worser° thoughts heavens mend! Alexas—come,   *lascivious*
     his fortune, his fortune. O, let him marry a woman that cannot
     go, sweet Isis,[7] I beseech thee, and let her die too, and give him

2. Both falling in love and excessive drinking were
thought to inflame the liver, the seat of the passions.
3. Anachronistic: Charmian wants homage to her child
even from Herod, Cleopatra's enemy, who was to become
proverbial for his brutality to children when he slaughtered the Holy Innocents in an effort to kill the infant
Jesus.
4. Genitalia (possibly proverbial); lines 27–28 also fore-
shadow 5.2.229–319.

5. Since you are a soothsayer, I will let you speak freely
and will not persecute you as a witch; I will forgive your
outlandish prognostications because they are unlikely to
come true.
6. Ironic: the silt brought down by the flooding Nile each
year gave Egypt its fertile soil.
7. Egyptian goddess of fertility, as well as of the earth and
moon. For the comparison of Cleopatra to Isis, see the
Introduction. go: come (sexual); bear children.

a worse, and let worse follow worse till the worst of all follow
him laughing to his grave, fiftyfold a cuckold. Good Isis, hear
60   me this prayer, though thou deny me a matter of more weight;
good Isis, I beseech thee.

IRAS   Amen, dear goddess, hear that prayer of the people. For as
it is a heart-breaking to see a handsome man loose-wived,° so it   *wedded to an adulteress*
is a deadly sorrow to behold a foul knave uncuckolded. There-
65   fore, dear Isis, keep decorum,° and fortune him accordingly.   *do the right thing*

CHARMIAN   Amen.

ALEXAS   Lo now, if it lay in their hands to make me a cuckold,
they would make themselves whores but they'd do't.[8]

Enter CLEOPATRA

ENOBARBUS   Hush, here comes Antony.

CHARMIAN   Not he, the Queen.

CLEOPATRA   Saw you my lord?

ENOBARBUS   No, lady.

70   CLEOPATRA   Was he not here?

CHARMIAN   No, madam.

CLEOPATRA   He was disposed to mirth, but on the sudden
A Roman° thought hath struck him. Enobarbus!   *of Rome; serious*

ENOBARBUS   Madam?

75   CLEOPATRA   Seek him, and bring him hither. Where's Alexas?

ALEXAS   Here at your service. My lord approaches.

Enter ANTONY *with a* MESSENGER

CLEOPATRA   We will not look upon him. Go with us.

Exeunt [all but ANTONY *and the* MESSENGER]

MESSENGER   Fulvia thy wife first came into the field.°   *battlefield*

ANTONY   Against my brother Lucius?[9]

80   MESSENGER   Ay, but soon that war had end, and the time's state°   *situation at the time*
Made friends of them, jointing their force 'gainst Caesar,
Whose better issue° in the war from Italy   *greater success*
Upon the first encounter drave them.°   *drove them out*

ANTONY   Well, what worst?

MESSENGER   The nature of bad news infects the teller.[1]

85   ANTONY   When it concerns the fool or coward. On.
Things that are past are done. With me 'tis thus:
Who tells me true, though in his tale lie death,
I hear him as° he flattered.   *as if*

MESSENGER   Labienus[2]—
This is stiff news—hath with his Parthian force

90   Extended° Asia; from Euphrates   *Seized*
His conquering banner shook, from Syria
To Lydia and to Ionia,
Whilst—

ANTONY   Antony, thou wouldst say—

MESSENGER   O, my lord!

ANTONY   Speak to me home.° Mince not the general tongue.[3]   *plainly*
95   Name Cleopatra as she is called in Rome.

---

8. *but they'd do't:* in order to do so.
9. Lucius Antonius, Roman consul.
1. Makes the teller hated by the hearer. For examples,
see 2.5 and 3.1.
2. Quintus Labienus, who was sent by Brutus and Cassius following their killing of Julius Caesar (see *Julius
Caesar*) to garner support from the Parthians, an Asian
people whose empire came to include much of Meso-

potamia (Iraq) and Persia (Iran) and who regularly warred
with Rome. After Brutus's and Cassius's defeat at Philippi
by Antony, Octavius Caesar, and Lepidus, Labienus
defected to take command of the Parthian army and
began a war against the Romans, conquering some of
their provinces in the Middle East (lines 90–92)—provinces Antony was supposed to protect.
3. Do not play down common opinion.

Rail thou in Fulvia's phrase,° and taunt my faults   *words*
With such full licence as both truth and malice
Have power to utter. O, then we bring forth weeds
When our quick winds lie still, and our ills told us
100   Is as our earing.⁴ Fare thee well a while.
MESSENGER   At your noble pleasure.   *Exit* MESSENGER
            Enter another MESSENGER
ANTONY   From Sicyon,⁵ ho, the news? Speak there.
SECOND MESSENGER   The man from Sicyon—
ANTONY   Is there such a one?
SECOND MESSENGER   He stays upon° your will.   *He attends*
ANTONY   Let him appear.
                    [*Exit* SECOND MESSENGER]
105   These strong Egyptian fetters I must break,
      Or lose myself in dotage.
                Enter another MESSENGER *with a letter*
                    What are you?
THIRD MESSENGER   Fulvia thy wife is dead.
ANTONY   Where died she?
THIRD MESSENGER   In Sicyon.
      Her length of sickness, with what else more serious
      Importeth thee° to know, this bears.   *Is important for you*
                [*He gives* ANTONY *the letter*]
110   ANTONY   Forbear° me.   *Leave*
                    [*Exit* THIRD MESSENGER]
      There's a great spirit gone. Thus did I desire it.
      What our contempts doth often hurl from us
      We wish it ours again. The present pleasure,
      By revolution low'ring,⁶ does become
115   The opposite of itself. She's° good being gone;   *Fulvia is*
      The hand could° pluck her back that shoved her on.   *would wish to*
      I must from this enchanting° queen break off.   *spellbinding*
      Ten thousand harms more than the ills I know
      My idleness doth hatch. How now, Enobarbus!
                Enter ENOBARBUS
ENOBARBUS   What's your pleasure, sir?
120   ANTONY   I must with haste from hence.
ENOBARBUS   Why, then we kill⁷ all our women. We see how
      mortal an unkindness is to them; if they suffer our departure,
      death's the word.
ANTONY   I must be gone.
125   ENOBARBUS   Under a compelling occasion let women die. It
      were pity to cast them away for nothing, though between them
      and a great cause they should be esteemed nothing. Cleopatra
      catching but the least noise of this dies instantly. I have seen
      her die twenty times upon far poorer moment.° I do think there   *for far less reason*
130   is mettle° in death, which commits some loving act upon her,   *(sexual) potency; courage*
      she hath such a celerity° in dying.   *speed*
ANTONY   She is cunning past man's thought.

4. O . . . *earing*: Antony compares his recent behavior to
an unplowed field: just as the field sprouts weeds when it
remains untilled (by hand or) by a "quick" (fertile) wind,
he falls into "ill" habits when he is not forced to face criticism (to undergo "earing," plowing).
5. City in Greece where Antony left Fulvia.

6. Growing lower by turning (as of a wheel, such as Fortune's).
7. Alluding to achieving an orgasm. Throughout the
scene "kill," "death," and "dying" all carry this bawdy resonance. "Nothing," which Enobarbus repeats, may refer
to the female genitals.

ENOBARBUS   Alack, sir, no. Her passions are made of nothing but
    the finest part of pure love. We cannot call her winds and
135   waters sighs and tears; they are greater storms and tempests than
    almanacs can report. This cannot be cunning in her; if it be,
    she makes a shower of rain as well as Jove.[8]

ANTONY   Would I had never seen her!

ENOBARBUS   O, sir, you had then left unseen a wonderful piece
140   of work,° which not to have been blessed withal° would have   *masterpiece / with*
    discredited your travel.[9]

ANTONY   Fulvia is dead.

ENOBARBUS   Sir.

ANTONY   Fulvia is dead.

145 ENOBARBUS   Fulvia?

ANTONY   Dead.

ENOBARBUS   Why, sir, give the gods a thankful sacrifice. When it
    pleaseth their deities to take the wife of a man from him, it
    shows to man the tailors of the earth; comforting therein that
150   when old robes° are worn out there are members[1] to make new.   *clothes; women*
    If there were no more women but Fulvia, then had you indeed
    a cut, and the case to be lamented. This grief is crowned with
    consolation; your old smock brings forth a new petticoat, and
    indeed the tears live in an onion that should water this sorrow.[2]

155 ANTONY   The business she hath broachèd in the state
    Cannot endure my absence.

ENOBARBUS   And the business you have broached here cannot
    be without you, especially that of Cleopatra's, which wholly
    depends on your abode.°   *staying on here*

160 ANTONY   No more light answers. Let our officers
    Have notice what we purpose. I shall break
    The cause of our expedience° to the Queen,   *haste*
    And get her leave to part; for not alone
    The death of Fulvia, with more urgent touches,°   *concerns*
165   Do strongly speak to us, but the letters too
    Of many our contriving friends[3] in Rome
    Petition us at home.° Sextus Pompeius   *to go home*
    Hath given the dare to Caesar and commands
    The empire of the sea.[4] Our slippery° people,   *inconstant*
170   Whose love is never linked to the deserver
    Till his deserts are past, begin to throw°   *ascribe (the title of)*
    Pompey the Great and all his dignities
    Upon his son, who—high in name and power,
    Higher than both in blood and life°—stands up   *vitality and energy*
175   For the main soldier;[5] whose quality, going on,
    The sides o'th' world may danger.[6] Much is breeding
    Which, like the courser's hair, hath yet but life,
    And not a serpent's poison.[7] Say our pleasure,

---

8. Jupiter; ruler of the gods: one of his duties was governing rain.
9. Would have cast doubt on your success as a traveler.
Travel also suggests travail, or work, as in "piece of work"
(lines 139–40).
1. Limbs; sexual organs. The sexual innuendo is continued in "cut" (line 152: severe blow; slash in a garment;
vagina, "case" (line 152: situation; set of clothes; vagina),
and "broachèd" (line 155, 157: opened or pricked).
2. *the tears . . . sorrow:* real tears are not called for.
3. Of many friends acting on our behalf.

4. Sextus Pompey was the younger son of Pompey the
Great, who was a foe of Julius Caesar (see *Julius Caesar*
1.1). Previously an outlaw, the Pompey of the play had
gained control of the shipping routes around Sicily.
5. *stands . . . soldier:* acts like the leading soldier.
6. *whose . . . danger:* whose accomplishments and character, should they continue to succeed, might endanger the
entire arrangement of the world.
7. A horse's ("courser's," line 177) hair was believed to
become a live snake if put in water.

To such whose place° is under us, requires   *rank*
Our quick remove from hence.
180 ENOBARBUS   I shall do't.   [*Exeunt severally*]

1.3

Enter CLEOPATRA, CHARMIAN, ALEXAS, *and* IRAS

CLEOPATRA   Where is he?
CHARMIAN   I did not see him since.°   *recently*
CLEOPATRA [*to* ALEXAS]   See where he is, who's with him, what he does.
   I did not send you.¹ If you find him sad,°   *serious*
   Say I am dancing; if in mirth, report
5   That I am sudden sick. Quick, and return.   [*Exit* ALEXAS]
CHARMIAN   Madam, methinks, if you did love him dearly,
   You do not hold the method° to enforce   *act appropriately*
   The like from him.
CLEOPATRA   What should I do I do not?°   *What else should I do*
CHARMIAN   In each thing give him way; cross him in nothing.
10 CLEOPATRA   Thou teachest like a fool, the way to lose him.
CHARMIAN   Tempt° him not so too far. Iwis,° forbear.   *Test / Indeed*
   In time we hate that which we often fear.

       Enter ANTONY

   But here comes Antony.
CLEOPATRA   I am sick and sullen.°   *dispirited*
ANTONY   I am sorry to give breathing° to my purpose.   *voice*
15 CLEOPATRA   Help me away, dear Charmian, I shall fall.
   It cannot be thus long—the sides of nature²
   Will not sustain it.
ANTONY   Now, my dearest queen.
CLEOPATRA   Pray you, stand farther from me.
ANTONY   What's the matter?
CLEOPATRA   I know by that same eye there's some good news.
20   What says the married woman°—you may go?   *(Fulvia)*
   Would she had never given you leave to come.
   Let her not say 'tis I that keep you here.
   I have no power upon you; hers you are.
ANTONY   The gods best know—
CLEOPATRA   O, never was there queen
25   So mightily betrayed! Yet at the first
   I saw the treasons planted.
ANTONY   Cleopatra—
CLEOPATRA   Why should I think you can be mine and true—
   Though you in swearing shake the thronèd gods³—
   Who have been false to Fulvia? Riotous madness,
30   To be entangled with those mouth-made° vows   *hypocritical*
   Which break themselves in swearing.°   *as they are made*
ANTONY   Most sweet queen—
CLEOPATRA   Nay, pray you, seek no colour° for your going,   *excuse*
   But bid farewell and go. When you sued staying,°   *entreated to remain*
   Then was the time for words; no going then.
35   Eternity was in our⁴ lips and eyes,
   Bliss in our brow's bent;° none our parts so poor   *curve*

1.3 Location: Scene continues.
1. Do not say I sent you.
2. This cannot go on much longer—the bodily frame.
3. When Jupiter swore an oath, Olympus was supposed
to shake.
4. My (royal plural); possibly also the conventional first-person plural.

But was a race of heaven.[5] They are so still,
Or thou, the greatest soldier of the world,
Art turned the greatest liar.
ANTONY   How now, lady!
40 CLEOPATRA   I would I had thy inches.° Thou shouldst know   *size; (phallic)*
There were a heart in Egypt.[6]
ANTONY   Hear me, Queen.
The strong necessity of time commands
Our services a while, but my full heart
Remains in use° with you. Our Italy   *in trust*
45 Shines o'er with civil swords.° Sextus Pompeius   *swords of civil war*
Makes his approaches to the port of Rome.[7]
Equality of two domestic powers
Breed scrupulous faction.° The hated, grown to strength,   *distrustful dissent*
Are newly grown to love.° The condemned° Pompey,   *popularity / banished*
50 Rich in his father's honour, creeps° apace   *insinuates himself*
Into the hearts of such as have not thrived
Upon the present state,° whose numbers threaten;   *government*
And quietness, grown sick of rest, would purge
By any desperate change.[8] My more particular,°   *personal motivation*
55 And that which most with you should safe° my going,   *sanction*
Is Fulvia's death.
CLEOPATRA   Though age from folly could not give me freedom,
It does from childishness. Can Fulvia die?
ANTONY   She's dead, my queen.
        [*He offers letters*]
60 Look here, and at thy sovereign leisure read
The garboils° she awaked. At the last, best,[9]   *upheavals*
See when and where she died.
CLEOPATRA   O most false love!
Where be the sacred vials[1] thou shouldst fill
With sorrowful water? Now I see, I see,
65 In Fulvia's death how mine received shall be.
ANTONY   Quarrel no more, but be prepared to know
The purposes I bear, which are° or cease   *continue*
As you shall give th'advice. By the fire°   *sun*
That quickens Nilus' slime,[2] I go from hence
70 Thy soldier-servant, making peace or war
As thou affects.°   *choose*
CLEOPATRA   Cut my lace,[3] Charmian, come.
But let it be. I am quickly ill and well;
So[4] Antony loves.
ANTONY   My precious queen, forbear,
And give true evidence° to his love, which stands   *be an honest witness*
An honourable trial.
75 CLEOPATRA   So Fulvia told me.

---

5. *none . . . heaven:* Even my poorest attributes were heavenly.
6. There were courage (to respond to such insults) in the country (Queen) of Egypt.
7. Ostia (sixteen miles from Rome).
8. *And . . . change:* And peace, made ill by inactivity, wishes to purge itself of impurities by a violently acting remedy.
9. The best news last; Fulvia was at her best at the end of her life.

1. Renaissance writers thought that the Romans filled small bottles with tears to place in graves; also, where are your sad and watery eyes ("vials")?
2. That causes plants to grow in the silt that the Nile deposits.
3. Cutting the strings would be quicker than untying the lace on her bodice to relieve her from her feigned fainting spell.
4. Thus (falsely); as long as.

I prithee turn aside and weep for her,
Then bid adieu to me, and say the tears
Belong to Egypt.° Good now, play one scene   *Cleopatra*
Of excellent dissembling, and let it look
Like perfect honour.
80   ANTONY   You'll heat my blood.° No more.   *make me angry*
CLEOPATRA   You can do better yet; but this is meetly.°   *fairly good (acting)*
ANTONY   Now by my sword—
CLEOPATRA   And target.⁵ Still he mends.°   *improves*
But this is not the best. Look, prithee, Charmian,
How this Herculean Roman does become
85   The carriage of his chafe.⁶
ANTONY   I'll leave you, lady.
CLEOPATRA   Courteous lord, one word.
Sir, you and I must part; but that's not it.
Sir, you and I have loved; but there's not it;
90   That you know well. Something it is I would—
O, my oblivion is a very Antony,
And I am all forgotten.⁷
ANTONY   But that your royalty
Holds idleness your subject, I should take you
For idleness itself.⁸
CLEOPATRA   'Tis sweating labour°   *hard work*
95   To bear such idleness° so near the heart   *flippancy; laziness*
As Cleopatra this. But sir, forgive me,
Since my becomings° kill me when they do not   *transformations; graces*
Eye° well to you. Your honour calls you hence,   *Look*
Therefore be deaf to my unpitied folly,
100 And all the gods go with you. Upon your sword
Sit laurel victory,⁹ and smooth success
Be strewed before your feet.
ANTONY   Let us go.
Come. Our separation so abides and flies¹
That thou residing here goes yet with me,
105 And I hence fleeting, here remain with thee.
Away.   *Exeunt [severally]*

1.4

Enter Octavius CAESAR *reading a letter,* LEPIDUS, *and*
their train
CAESAR   You may see, Lepidus, and henceforth know,
It is not Caesar's natural vice to hate
Our great competitor.° From Alexandria   *ally; rival*
This is the news: he fishes, drinks, and wastes
5   The lamps of night in revel; is not more manlike
Than Cleopatra, nor the queen of Ptolemy¹

5. Shield. Cleopatra parodies the blustering oaths of heroic drama.
6. *does . . . chafe*: emulates Hercules, his heroic ancestor, with his posture of rage.
7. *my . . . forgotten*: my memory has deserted me as you are doing, and I have forgotten everything (am totally forgotten—by Antony).
8. *But . . . itself*: If you were not queen over your flippancy and hence in full control of it, I would think that you were flippancy itself.

9. *Upon . . . victory*: May your military exploits receive the laurel wreath as the reward for victory.
1. Consists so much of both remaining together and being separated (in that we are united by the shared experience of it).
1.4 Location: Rome.
1. Julius Caesar had commanded Cleopatra to marry her half-brother Ptolemy XIV (acceptable within the Egyptian royal family); she was said to have had Ptolemy poisoned.

More womanly than he; hardly gave audience[2]
Or vouchsafed to think he had partners. You shall find there°   *(the letter); (Egypt)*
A man who is the abstract° of all faults   *paradigm*
That all men follow.
10   LEPIDUS   I must not think there are
Evils enough to darken all his goodness.
His faults in him seem as the spots of heaven,°   *stars*
More fiery by night's blackness; hereditary
Rather than purchased;° what he cannot change   *acquired*
15   Than° what he chooses.   *Rather than*
CAESAR   You are too indulgent. Let's grant it is not
Amiss to tumble on the bed of Ptolemy,
To give a kingdom for a mirth,° to sit   *joke*
And keep the turn of° tippling with a slave,   *take turns at*
20   To reel the streets at noon, and stand the buffet°   *come to blows*
With knaves that smells of sweat. Say° this becomes him—   *Even if*
As his composure° must be rare indeed   *And his character*
Whom these things cannot blemish—yet must Antony
No way excuse his foils° when we do bear   *faults*
25   So great weight in° his lightness. If he filled   *as a result of*
His vacancy° with his voluptuousness,   *leisure*
Full surfeits and the dryness of his bones[3]
Call on° him for't. But to confound° such time   *Afflict / waste*
That drums° him from his sport, and speaks as loud   *summons*
30   As his own state° and ours— 'tis to be chid   *public responsibility*
As we rate° boys who, being mature in knowledge,   *upbraid*
Pawn their experience to their present pleasure,
And so rebel to judgement.[4]
                    Enter a MESSENGER
LEPIDUS   Here's more news.
MESSENGER   Thy biddings have been done, and every hour,
35   Most noble Caesar, shalt thou have report
How 'tis abroad. Pompey is strong at sea,
And it appears he is beloved of those
That only have feared Caesar.[5] To the ports
The discontents° repair, and men's reports   *discontented people*
Give him° much wronged.   [*Exit*]   *Say he is*
40   CAESAR   I should have known no less.
It hath been taught us from the primal state[6]
That he which is was wished until he were,[7]
And the ebbed° man, ne'er loved till ne'er worth love,   *fallen*
Comes deared° by being lacked. This common body,°   *Is loved / The people*
45   Like to a vagabond flag° upon the stream,   *drifting reed*
Goes to, and back, lackeying° the varying tide,   *following slavishly*
To rot itself with motion.
                    [*Enter a* SECOND MESSENGER]
SECOND MESSENGER   Caesar, I bring thee word
Menecrates and Menas, famous pirates,°   *(allied with Pompey)*
Makes the sea serve them, which they ear° and wound   *plow*
50   With keels of every kind. Many hot inroads

---

2. Hardly listened (to Octavius's messengers, in 1.1).
3. *Full . . . bones:* Ill health caused by overeating and venereal disease.
4. *being . . . judgement:* old enough to know better, abandon their wisdom in favor of momentary pleasure, and

thus act against their better judgment.
5. That obeyed Caesar only out of fear.
6. Since the first society was organized.
7. That man who rules was supported until he began to rule.

They make in Italy. The borders maritime° *coastal territories*
Lack blood° to think on't, and flush° youth revolt. *Go pallid / spirited*
No vessel can peep forth but 'tis as soon
Taken as seen; for Pompey's name strikes more
Than could his war resisted.[8] [*Exit*]
55 CAESAR   Antony,
Leave thy lascivious wassails.° When thou once *drunken revels*
Was beaten from Modena,[9] where thou slew'st
Hirtius and Pansa, consuls, at thy heel
Did famine follow, whom thou fought'st against—
60 Though daintily brought up—with patience more
Than savages could suffer. Thou didst drink
The stale° of horses, and the gilded° puddle *urine / slime-covered*
Which beasts would cough at.° Thy palate then did deign° *refuse (to drink) / accept*
The roughest berry on the rudest hedge.
65 Yea, like the stag when snow the pasture sheets,° *covers*
The barks of trees thou browsed.° On the Alps *fed upon*
It is reported thou didst eat strange flesh,
Which some did die to look on; and all this—
It wounds thine honour that I speak it now—
70 Was borne so like a soldier that thy cheek
So much as lanked° not. *grew thin*
LEPIDUS 'Tis pity of him.
CAESAR Let his shames quickly
Drive him to Rome. 'Tis time we twain
75 Did show ourselves i'th' field; and to that end
Assemble we immediate council. Pompey
Thrives in our idleness.
LEPIDUS   Tomorrow, Caesar,
I shall be furnished to inform you rightly
Both what° by sea and land I can be able° *what forces / assemble*
To front° this present time. *To confront the enemy at*
80 CAESAR   Till which encounter
It is my business, too. Farewell.
LEPIDUS Farewell, my lord. What you shall know meantime
Of stirs° abroad I shall beseech you, sir, *incidents*
To let me be partaker.
85 CAESAR Doubt not, sir. I knew it for my bond.° *Exeunt* *responsibility*

1.5

Enter CLEOPATRA, CHARMIAN, IRAS, *and* MARDIAN
CLEOPATRA Charmian!
CHARMIAN Madam?
CLEOPATRA [*yawning*] Ha, ha. Give me to drink mandragora.[1]
CHARMIAN Why, madam?
5 CLEOPATRA That I might sleep out this great gap of time
My Antony is away.
CHARMIAN   You think of him too much.
CLEOPATRA O, 'tis treason!
CHARMIAN   Madam, I trust not so.
CLEOPATRA Thou, eunuch Mardian!

8. *Pompey's . . . resisted*: Pompey's name alone is more
powerful than his forces would be if confronted in battle.
9. Site of a battle in which Antony was defeated by the
combined armies of Octavius Caesar and the Roman Senate, at the instigation of Cicero.
1.5 Location: Alexandria.
1. A narcotic, made from the mandrake plant.

MARDIAN   What's your highness' pleasure?
CLEOPATRA   Not now to hear thee sing.[2] I take no pleasure
10   In aught[3] an eunuch has. 'Tis well for thee
    That, being unseminared,° thy freer thoughts   *castrated*
    May not fly forth of Egypt. Hast thou affections?°   *desires*
MARDIAN   Yes, gracious madam.
CLEOPATRA   Indeed?
15   MARDIAN   Not in deed, madam, for I can do° nothing   *(sexually)*
    But what indeed is honest° to be done.   *chaste; moral*
    Yet have I fierce affections, and think
    What Venus did with Mars.[4]
CLEOPATRA   O, Charmian,
    Where think'st thou he is now? Stands he or sits he?
20   Or does he walk? Or is he on his horse?
    O happy horse, to bear the weight of Antony!
    Do bravely, horse, for wot'st° thou whom thou mov'st?—   *know*
    The demi-Atlas[5] of this earth, the arm°   *champion*
    And burgonet° of men. He's speaking now,   *helmet; guardian*
25   Or murmuring 'Where's my serpent of old Nile?'[6]—
    For so he calls me. Now I feed myself
    With most delicious poison. Think on me,
    That am with Phoebus'° amorous pinches black,   *the sun god*
    And wrinkled deep in time. Broad-fronted° Caesar,°   *Broad-browed / (Julius)*
30   When thou wast here above the ground I was
    A morsel for a monarch, and great Pompey[7]
    Would stand and make his eyes grow in my brow.
    There would he anchor his aspect,° and die°   *gaze / (sexual)*
    With looking on his life.
          Enter ALEXAS
ALEXAS   Sovereign of Egypt, hail!
35   CLEOPATRA   How much unlike art thou Mark Antony!
    Yet, coming from him, that great medicine[8] hath
    With his tinct° gilded thee. How goes it   *power; color*
    With my brave° Mark Antony?   *magnificent*
ALEXAS   Last thing he did, dear Queen,
    He kissed—the last of many doubled kisses—
40   This orient[9] pearl. His speech sticks in my heart.
CLEOPATRA   Mine ear must pluck it thence.
ALEXAS   'Good friend,' quoth he,
    'Say the firm° Roman to great Egypt° sends   *loyal; resolute / Cleopatra*
    This treasure of an oyster; at whose foot,
    To mend° the petty present, I will piece°   *improve / add to*
45   Her opulent throne with kingdoms. All the East,
    Say thou, shall call her mistress.' So he nodded,
    And soberly did mount an arm-jaunced steed,[1]

---

2. Castrati were used in Italian music from the end of the sixteenth century, and Shakespeare associates singing eunuchs with the eastern Mediterranean in *Twelfth Night* and *A Midsummer Night's Dream*; they are not thought to have been used as singers in ancient Rome.
3. In anything; in the nothing. The eunuch has nothing instead of testicles.
4. Venus, goddess of love (married to Vulcan), and Mars, god of war, were lovers.
5. Octavius and Antony between them rule the world—Lepidus having conveniently been forgotten—as Atlas bore it on his shoulders.

6. See 2.7.25–26 for the superstition that snakes formed spontaneously in the Nile mud; the asp in particular was associated with Isis, with whom Cleopatra identifies herself.
7. Gnaeus Pompey, older brother of Sextus Pompey (the character in this play) and son of Pompey the Great. But Cleopatra's phrasing makes him sound like the father.
8. Elixir of life: sought by alchemists, it was thought able to turn base metals to gold and cure all disease.
9. From India (more lustrous than European pearls).
1. Steed jolted by one in armor (or by its own armor).

Who neighed so high that what I would have spoke
Was beastly dumbed° by him.   *drowned out*

CLEOPATRA   What, was he sad or merry?

50 ALEXAS   Like to the time o'th' year between the extremes
Of hot and cold, he was nor° sad nor merry.   *neither*

CLEOPATRA   O well divided° disposition! Note him,   *unwavering*
Note him, good Charmian, 'tis the man; but note him.
He was not sad, for he would shine on those

55 That make their looks by his;² he was not merry,
Which seemed to tell them his remembrance lay
In Egypt with his joy; but between both.
O heavenly mingle! Be'st thou sad or merry,
The violence of either thee becomes;

60 So does it no man else. Met'st thou my posts?°   *messengers*

ALEXAS   Ay, madam, twenty several° messengers.   *separate*
Why do you send so thick?

CLEOPATRA   Who's° born that day   *Whoever is*
When I forget to send to Antony
Shall die a beggar. Ink and paper, Charmian!

65 Welcome, my good Alexas. Did I, Charmian,
Ever love Caesar so?

CHARMIAN   O, that brave Caesar!

CLEOPATRA   Be choked with such another emphasis!
Say 'the brave Antony'.

CHARMIAN   The valiant Caesar.

CLEOPATRA   By Isis, I will give thee bloody teeth

70 If thou with Caesar paragon° again   *compare*
My man of men.

CHARMIAN   By your most gracious pardon,
I sing but after you.

CLEOPATRA   My salad days,
When I was green° in judgement, cold in blood,°   *immature / feeling*
To say as I said then. But come, away,

75 Get me ink and paper.
He shall have every day a several greeting,
Or I'll unpeople Egypt.³

                                        Exeunt

2.1

Enter POMPEY, MENECRATES, *and* MENAS, *in warlike*
manner

POMPEY   If the great gods be just, they shall assist
The deeds of justest men.

MENECRATES   Know, worthy Pompey,
That what they do delay they not deny.

POMPEY   Whiles we are suitors to their throne, decays
The thing we sue for.¹

5 MENECRATES   We, ignorant of ourselves,
Beg often our own harms, which the wise powers
Deny us for our° good; so find we profit   *our own*
By losing of our prayers.

POMPEY   I shall do well.

---

2. Who are dependent on his mood; who reflect his
appearance in their own.
3. If not, it will be only because I have run out of Egyptians to act as messengers (or, because I have killed all

Egyptians).
2.1 Location: Pompey's headquarters (in Sicily).
1. *Whiles . . . for:* While we are beseeching the gods, what
we request is losing its value.

The people love me, and the sea is mine.
10 My powers are crescent,° and my auguring° hope   *growing / prophesying*
Says it° will come to th' full.² Mark Antony   *(my military power)*
In Egypt sits at dinner, and will make
No wars without doors.³ Caesar gets money where
He loses hearts. Lepidus flatters both,
15 Of° both is flattered; but he neither loves,°   *By / loves neither*
Nor either cares for him.
MENAS   Caesar and Lepidus
Are in the field; a mighty strength they carry.
POMPEY   Where have you this? 'Tis false.
MENAS   From Silvius, sir.
POMPEY   He dreams. I know they are in Rome together,
20 Looking° for Antony. But all the charms° of love,   *Waiting / incantations*
Salt° Cleopatra, soften thy waned⁴ lip.   *Lecherous*
Let witchcraft join with beauty, lust with both
Tie up the libertine, in a field of feasts
Keep his brain fuming;° Epicurean⁵ cooks   *drunk*
25 Sharpen with cloyless sauce⁶ his appetite,
That sleep and feeding may prorogue° his honour   *postpone*
Even till a Lethe'd dullness⁷—
          Enter VARRIUS
                    How now, Varrius?
VARRIUS   This is most certain that I shall deliver:
Mark Antony is every hour in Rome
30 Expected. Since he went from Egypt, 'tis
A space for farther travel.⁸
POMPEY   I could have given less° matter   *less crucial*
A better ear. Menas, I did not think
This amorous surfeiter would have donned his helm°   *helmet*
For such a petty war. His soldiership
35 Is twice the other twain. But let us rear°   *elevate*
The higher our opinion,° that our stirring   *(of ourselves)*
Can from the lap of Egypt's widow⁹ pluck
The ne'er lust-wearied Antony.
MENAS   I cannot hope°   *suppose*
Caesar and Antony shall well greet together.
40 His wife that's dead did trespasses to° Caesar,   *offended against*
His brother warred upon him, although, I think,
Not moved° by Antony.   *prompted*
POMPEY   I know not, Menas,
How lesser enmities may give way to greater.
Were't not that we stand up against them all,
45 'Twere pregnant° they should square° between themselves,   *evident / argue*
For they have entertainèd° cause enough   *sustained*
To draw their swords. But how the fear of us
May cement their divisions,° and bind up   *unite them*

2. Like the "crescent" moon.
3. Outside doors. Antony is concerned only with the wars of love, conducted indoors.
4. Withered; decreased, like the moon, perhaps in implicit contrast to the "crescent" and potentially "full" moon of Pompey's "powers" (lines 10–11).
5. The philosopher Epicurus and his followers believed that the gods took no interest in men's actions and that the only aim of life was to seek pleasure.

6. Sauce that never wearies or disgusts.
7. Drinking the water of Lethe, one of the rivers bounding Hades, caused total loss of memory.
8. Sufficient time to have traveled even farther (than between Egypt and Rome).
9. Cleopatra had married one of her brothers, Ptolemy XIV, whom she later seems to have had murdered. See note to 1.4.6.

The petty difference, we yet not know.
50 Be't as our gods will have't; it only stands
Our lives upon to use¹ our strongest hands.
Come, Menas.   *Exeunt*

2.2

Enter ENOBARBUS *and* LEPIDUS

LEPIDUS   Good Enobarbus, 'tis a worthy deed,
And shall become you well, to entreat your captain
To soft and gentle speech.

ENOBARBUS   I shall entreat him
To answer like himself.¹ If Caesar move° him,   *angers*
5   Let Antony look over Caesar's head
And speak as loud as Mars. By Jupiter,
Were I the wearer of Antonio's beard
I would not shave't today.²

LEPIDUS   'Tis not a time
For private stomaching.°   *quarrels*

ENOBARBUS   Every time
10   Serves for the matter that is then born in't.

LEPIDUS   But small to greater matters must give way.

ENOBARBUS   Not if the small come first.

LEPIDUS   Your speech is passion.°   *not reasoned*
But pray you, stir no embers° up. Here comes   *old resentments*
The noble Antony.

Enter [at one door] ANTONY *and* VENTIDIUS

ENOBARBUS   And yonder Caesar.

Enter [at another door] CAESAR, MAECENAS, *and* AGRIPPA

15   ANTONY [*to* VENTIDIUS]   If we compose° well here, to Parthia.   *reach agreement*
Hark, Ventidius.

CAESAR   I do not know,
Maecenas; ask Agrippa.

LEPIDUS [*to* CAESAR *and* ANTONY]   Noble friends,
That which combined us was most great; and let not
A leaner° action rend us. What's amiss,   *less important*
20   May it be gently heard. When we debate
Our trivial difference loud,° we do commit   *loudly; violently*
Murder in° healing wounds. Then, noble partners,   *in the process of*
The rather for° I earnestly beseech,   *Especially because*
Touch you the sourest points with sweetest terms,
Nor curstness grow° to th' matter.   *Do not let ill temper add*

25   ANTONY   'Tis spoken well.
Were we° before our armies, and to° fight,   *If we were / about to*
I should do thus.³

[ANTONY *and* CAESAR *embrace.*] *Flourish*

CAESAR   Welcome to Rome.

ANTONY   Thank you.

30   CAESAR   Sit.

ANTONY   Sit, sir.

CAESAR   Nay then.

---

1. *it . . . use:* our lives depend entirely on the use of.
2.2 Location: Rome.
1. To answer in a manner appropriate to his character (greatness?; dissipation?).
2. Plucking a man's beard was an insult; Enobarbus wants

Antony to give Octavius the chance to insult him. Possibly, Enobarbus is suggesting not that Antony act heroically but that he merely look the part.
3. Formally embrace you, as I do now; possibly, speak as you request.

    [They sit]
ANTONY   I learn you take things ill which are not so,
  Or being,° concern you not.   *being ill*
CAESAR   I must be laughed at
35   If or° for nothing or a little I   *either*
  Should say myself offended, and with you
  Chiefly i'th'° world; more laughed at that I should   *Of all the*
  Once name you derogately,° when to sound your name   *censoriously*
  It not concernèd me.
40 ANTONY   My being in Egypt, Caesar, what was't to you?
CAESAR   No more than my residing here at Rome
  Might be to you in Egypt. Yet if you there
  Did practise on° my state, your being in Egypt   *scheme against*
  Might be my question.°   *concern*
ANTONY   How intend you 'practised'?
45 CAESAR   You may be pleased to catch at° mine intent   *grasp*
  By what did here befall me. Your wife and brother
  Made wars upon me, and their contestation
  Was theme for you. You were the word of war.[4]
ANTONY   You do mistake the business. My brother never
50   Did urge me in his act.[5] I did enquire° it,   *inquire into*
  And have my learning from some true reports°   *reliable sources*
  That drew their swords with you. Did he not rather
  Discredit my authority with yours,
  And make the wars alike against my stomach,°   *wish*
55   Having alike° your cause? Of this, my letters   *Since I shared*
  Before did satisfy you. If you'll patch a quarrel,
  As matter whole you have to make it with,[6]
  It must not be with this.
CAESAR   You praise yourself
  By laying defects of judgement to me, but
  You patched up your excuses.
60 ANTONY   Not so, not so.
  I know you could not lack, I am certain on't,
  Very necessity of this thought,[7] that I,
  Your partner in the cause 'gainst which he fought,
  Could not with graceful eyes attend[8] those wars
65   Which fronted° mine own peace. As for my wife,   *opposed*
  I would you had her spirit in such another.
  The third o'th' world is yours, which with a snaffle[9]
  You may pace° easy, but not such a wife.   *train to walk*
ENOBARBUS   Would we had all such wives, that the men might
70   go to wars with the women.
ANTONY   So much uncurbable,° her garboils,° Caesar,   *uncontrollable / tumults*
  Made out of her impatience—which not wanted°   *did not lack*
  Shrewdness of policy too—I grieving grant
  Did you too much disquiet, for that you must
  But° say I could not help it.   *Only*
75 CAESAR   I wrote to you

---

4. *contestation . . . war:* war was meant as an example for
you to follow (had you as its theme); Your name was the
war cry (war was waged in your name).
5. Claimed to be acting as my proxy.
6. *If . . . with:* If you'll patch together an old quarrel with
trivia, when you have enough material to make a new one

(or, possibly, as if you had enough material to make one).
7. *I know . . . thought:* I'm confident that you must have
been aware.
8. Could not look with approval on.
9. Bridle (one without a curb, for good-tempered horses).

When, rioting in Alexandria, you
Did pocket up my letters, and with taunts
Did gibe my missive out of audience.[1]

ANTONY   Sir, he fell upon° me ere admitted, then.   *broke in on*
80   Three kings I had newly feasted, and did want
Of what I was[2] i'th' morning; but next day
I told him of myself,° which was as much   *my situation*
As to have asked him pardon. Let this fellow
Be nothing° of our strife. If we contend,   *Be no part*
Out of our question° wipe him.   *dispute*
85 CAESAR   You have broken
The article° of your oath, which you shall never   *terms*
Have tongue to charge me with.

LEPIDUS   Soft, Caesar.

ANTONY   No, Lepidus, let him speak.
90   The honour is sacred which he talks on now,
Supposing that I lacked it.[3] But on, Caesar:
The article of my oath—

CAESAR   To lend me arms and aid when I required them,
The which you both denied.

ANTONY   Neglected, rather,
95   And then when poisoned hours had bound me up
From mine own knowledge.[4] As nearly as I may
I'll play the penitent to you, but mine honesty
Shall not make poor my greatness, nor my power
Work without it.[5] Truth is that Fulvia,
100   To have me out of Egypt, made wars here,
For which myself, the ignorant motive, do
So far ask pardon as befits mine honour°   *dignity*
To stoop in such a case.

LEPIDUS   'Tis noble spoken.

MAECENAS   If it might please you to enforce no further
105   The griefs° between ye; to forget them quite   *grievances*
Were to remember that the present need
Speaks to atone you.°   *Is to reconcile you*

LEPIDUS   Worthily spoken, Maecenas.

ENOBARBUS   Or if you borrow one another's love for the instant,
you may, when you hear no more words of Pompey, return it
110   again. You shall have time to wrangle in when you have nothing else to do.

ANTONY   Thou art a soldier only. Speak no more.

ENOBARBUS   That truth should be silent I had almost forgot.

ANTONY   You wrong this presence,° therefore speak no more.   *(noble) company*
115 ENOBARBUS   Go to, then; your considerate stone.[6]

CAESAR   I do not much dislike the matter,° but   *content*
The manner of his speech, for't cannot be
We shall remain in friendship, our conditions°   *dispositions*
So diff'ring in their acts. Yet if I knew
120   What hoop should hold us staunch,° from edge to edge   *watertight; bound*

---

1. Scoffed my messenger out of your (public) hearing (referring to 1.1).
2. *did . . . was:* was not myself.
3. *The honour . . . it:* What Caesar speaks of now is my sacred honor, which he assumes I lack (even assuming I lack it).

4. *bound . . . knowledge:* prevented me from realizing what I was doing.
5. *mine . . . it:* my honorable behavior (in admitting a fault) will not diminish my power, nor shall my power operate without honor.
6. Very well, then; still and silent, but capable of thought.

O'th' world I would pursue it.
AGRIPPA   Give me leave, Caesar.
CAESAR   Speak, Agrippa.
AGRIPPA   Thou hast a sister by the mother's side,
125   Admired Octavia. Great Mark Antony
Is now a widower.
CAESAR   Say not so, Agrippa.
If Cleopatra heard you, your reproof
Were well deserved of rashness.⁷
ANTONY   I am not married, Caesar. Let me hear
130   Agrippa further speak.
AGRIPPA   To hold you in perpetual amity,
To make you brothers, and to knit your hearts
With an unslipping knot, take Antony°   *let Antony take*
Octavia to° his wife; whose beauty claims   *for*
135   No worse a husband than the best of men;
Whose virtue and whose general graces speak
That which none else can utter.⁸ By this marriage
All little jealousies° which now seem great,   *mistrusts*
And all great fears which now import° their dangers,   *bring along*
140   Would then be nothing. Truths would be tales
Where now half-tales be truths.⁹ Her love to both
Would each to other and all loves to both
Draw after her. Pardon what I have spoke,
For 'tis a studied, not a present° thought,   *sudden*
By duty ruminated.
145   ANTONY   Will Caesar speak?
CAESAR   Not till he hears how Antony is touched°   *reacts*
With° what is spoke already.   *To*
ANTONY   What power is in Agrippa,
If I would say 'Agrippa, be it so',
To make this good?
150   CAESAR   The power of Caesar,
And his power unto Octavia.
ANTONY   May I never
To this good purpose, that so fairly shows,
Dream of impediment!¹ Let me have thy hand.
Further this act of grace, and from this hour
155   The heart of brothers govern in our loves
And sway our great designs.
CAESAR   There's my hand.
[ANTONY *and* CAESAR *clasp hands*]
A sister I bequeath° you whom no brother   *hand over to*
Did ever love so dearly. Let her live
To join our kingdoms and our hearts; and never
Fly off our loves again.²
160   LEPIDUS   Happily, amen.
ANTONY   I did not think to draw my sword 'gainst Pompey,
For he hath laid strange° courtesies and great   *uncommon*

7. *your . . . rashness:* the reproof you would receive would befit your rashness.
8. *speak . . . utter:* speak for themselves.
9. *Truths . . . truths:* True reports, even if they were disturbing, could be passed over, regarded as hearsay, where now incomplete rumors are accepted as truth.

1. *May . . . impediment:* alluding to the Anglican marriage service, as does sonnet 116: "Let me not to the marriage of true minds / Admit impediments." *so fairly shows:* appears so attractive.
2. *never . . . again:* may our love for each other never again desert us.

Of late upon me. I must thank him only,°   *at least*
Lest my remembrance° suffer ill report;   *gratitude*
At heel of° that, defy him.   *Right after*

165   LEPIDUS   Time calls upon's.
Of° us must Pompey presently° be sought,   *By / immediately*
Or else he seeks out us.

ANTONY   Where lies he?

CAESAR   About the Mount Misena.[3]

ANTONY   What is his strength
By land?

CAESAR   Great and increasing, but by sea
He is an absolute master.

170   ANTONY   So is the fame.°   *report*
Would we had spoke together.° Haste we for it;   *(earlier)*
Yet ere we put ourselves in arms, dispatch we
The business we have talked of.

CAESAR   With most gladness,
And do° invite you to my sister's view,   *I do*
Whither straight I'll lead you.

175   ANTONY   Let us, Lepidus,
Not lack your company.

LEPIDUS   Noble Antony,
Not sickness should detain me.

Flourish. Exeunt. Manent ENOBARBUS, AGRIPPA,
and MAECENAS

MAECENAS [*to* ENOBARBUS]   Welcome from Egypt, sir.

ENOBARBUS   Half the heart° of Caesar, worthy Maecenas! My   *Beloved friend*
180   honourable friend, Agrippa!

AGRIPPA   Good Enobarbus!

MAECENAS   We have cause to be glad that matters are so well
digested.° You stayed well by't[4] in Egypt.   *settled*

ENOBARBUS   Ay, sir, we did sleep day out of countenance,[5] and
185   made the night light° with drinking.   *bright; merry*

MAECENAS   Eight wild boars roasted whole at a breakfast and but
twelve persons there — is this true?

ENOBARBUS   This was but as a fly by° an eagle. We had much   *compared with*
more monstrous matter of feast, which worthily deserved noting.

190   MAECENAS   She's a most triumphant° lady, if report be square° to   *magnificent / fair*
her.

ENOBARBUS   When she first met Mark Antony, she pursed up his
heart upon the river of Cydnus.[6]

AGRIPPA   There she appeared indeed, or my reporter devised° well   *imagined*
195   for her.

ENOBARBUS   I will tell you.
The barge° she sat in, like a burnished throne   *oar-driven ship*
Burned on the water. The poop° was beaten gold;   *upper deck*
Purple° the sails, and so perfumèd that   *(royal dye)*
200   The winds were love-sick with them. The oars were silver,
Which to the tune of flutes kept stroke, and made
The water which they beat to follow faster,
As° amorous of their strokes. For° her own person,   *As if / As for*

---

3. Misenum, a hilly outcropping at the north end of the
Bay of Naples.
4. You hung in there; you had a high old time.
5. We disconcerted day by sleeping through it, and did

not see what it looked like.
6. She took possession of his heart on the Cydnus River
in Cilicia, Asia Minor (Turkey), on which the city of Tar-
sus stood.

It beggared all description. She did lie
205 In her pavilion—cloth of gold, of tissue[7]—
O'er-picturing that Venus where we see
The fancy outwork nature.[8] On each side her
Stood pretty dimpled boys, like smiling Cupids,
With divers-coloured fans whose wind did seem
210 To glow° the delicate cheeks which they did cool,   *make glow*
And what they undid did.

AGRIPPA   O, rare for Antony!

ENOBARBUS   Her gentlewomen, like the Nereides,°   *sea nymphs*
So many mermaids, tended her i'th' eyes,°   *under her watchful eyes*
And made their bends adornings.[9] At the helm
215 A seeming mermaid steers. The silken tackle°   *sails and ropes*
Swell with the touches of those flower-soft hands
That yarely frame° the office. From the barge   *artfully carry out*
A strange invisible perfume hits the sense
Of the adjacent wharfs.° The city cast   *banks*
220 Her people out upon° her, and Antony,   *toward*
Enthroned i'th' market-place, did sit alone,
Whistling to th'air, which but for vacancy[1]
Had° gone to gaze on Cleopatra too,   *Would have*
And made a gap in nature.

AGRIPPA   Rare Egyptian!

225 ENOBARBUS   Upon her landing Antony sent to her,
Invited her to supper. She replied
It should be better he became her guest,
Which she entreated. Our courteous Antony,
Whom ne'er the word of 'No' woman heard speak,
230 Being barbered ten times o'er, goes to the feast,
And for his ordinary° pays his heart   *public meal at an inn*
For what his eyes eat only.

AGRIPPA   Royal wench!
She made great Caesar° lay his sword to bed.   *(Julius)*
He ploughed her, and she cropped.[2]

ENOBARBUS   I saw her once
235 Hop forty paces through the public street,
And having lost her breath, she spoke and panted,
That° she did make defect° perfection,   *So that / her panting*
And breathless, pour breath forth.

MAECENAS   Now Antony
Must leave her utterly.

ENOBARBUS   Never. He will not.
240 Age cannot wither her, nor custom stale°   *familiarity diminish*
Her infinite variety. Other women cloy
The appetites they feed, but she makes hungry
Where most she satisfies. For vilest things
Become themselves° in her, that° the holy priests   *Are becoming / so that*
245 Bless her when she is riggish.°   *acts like a slut*

---

7. Fabric interwoven with gold thread.
8. *O'er-picturing . . . nature:* Outdoing even the picture of Venus in which the artist outdid nature.
9. Made their curtsies additions to the decoration.
1. Which if not for the fact that its absence would have left a vacuum (already in Shakespeare's time proverbially impossible in nature).
2. She bore Caesarion. After the assassination of Julius

Caesar in 44 B.C., Cleopatra returned from Rome, where she had accompanied him, to Egypt. There she reigned with their son, who became Ptolemy XV, after she ordered the death of her half-brother and previous coruler Ptolemy XIV. On Ptolemy XIV, see 1.4.6 with note and 2.1.37 with note. On Antony and Cleopatra's plans for Ptolemy XV, see 3.6.1–16. On Ptolemy XV's fate, see note to 5.2.352.

MAECENAS   If beauty, wisdom, modesty can settle
    The heart of Antony, Octavia is
    A blessèd lottery° to him.   *prize*
AGRIPPA   Let us go.
    Good Enobarbus, make yourself my guest
    Whilst you abide here.
250 ENOBARBUS   Humbly, sir, I thank you.   *Exeunt*

2.3

    Enter ANTONY [*and*] CAESAR; OCTAVIA *between them*
ANTONY   The world and my great office will sometimes
    Divide me from your bosom.
OCTAVIA   All which time,
    Before the gods my knee shall bow my prayers
    To them for you.
ANTONY   Good night, sir. My Octavia,
5   Read not my blemishes in the world's report.
    I have not kept my square,° but that° to come   *stayed in line / what's*
    Shall all be done by th' rule.[1] Good night, dear lady.
    Good night, sir.
CAESAR   Good night.   *Exeunt* [CAESAR *and* OCTAVIA]
    Enter SOOTHSAYER
10 ANTONY   Now, sirrah. You do wish yourself in Egypt?
SOOTHSAYER   Would I had never come from thence, nor you
    Gone thither.
ANTONY   If you can, your reason?
SOOTHSAYER   I see it in my motion,° have it not in my tongue.   *intuition*
    But yet hie° you to Egypt again.   *hurry*
ANTONY   Say to me
15   Whose fortunes shall rise higher: Caesar's or mine?
SOOTHSAYER   Caesar's. Therefore, O Antony, stay not by his side.
    Thy daemon, that thy spirit[2] which keeps thee, is
    Noble, courageous, high, unmatchable,
    Where Caesar's is not. But near him thy angel
20   Becomes afeard, as° being o'erpowered. Therefore   *as if*
    Make space enough between you.
ANTONY   Speak this no more.
SOOTHSAYER   To none but thee; no more but when[3] to thee.
    If thou dost play with him at any game
    Thou art sure to lose; and of° that natural luck   *by*
25   He beats thee 'gainst the odds. Thy lustre thickens°   *Your brightness dims*
    When he shines by. I say again, thy spirit
    Is all afraid to govern thee near him;
    But he away, 'tis noble.
ANTONY   Get thee gone.
    Say to Ventidius I would speak with him.   *Exit* [SOOTHSAYER]
30   He shall to Parthia; be it art or hap,°   *talent or luck*
    He° hath spoken true. The very dice obey him,°   *(the soothsayer) / (Caesar)*
    And in our sports my better cunning° faints   *capability*
    Under his chance.° If we draw lots, he speeds.°   *luck / succeeds*

2.3 Location: Rome.
1. Regulation; ruler, as unit of measure (picking up "square," line 6, a measuring tool).
2. *Thy daemon . . . spirit:* Your guardian angel, which is the spirit.
3. *no more but when:* only.

His cocks do win the battle still of° mine   *always against*
35 When it is all to nought, and his quails ever
Beat mine, inhooped, at odds.⁴ I will to Egypt;
And though I make this marriage for my peace,
I'th' East my pleasure lies.
  Enter VENTIDIUS
       O, come, Ventidius.
You must to Parthia, your commission's ready.
40 Follow me, and receive't.   *Exeunt*

2.4

  Enter LEPIDUS, MAECENAS, *and* AGRIPPA
LEPIDUS Trouble yourselves no further. Pray you, hasten
Your generals after.¹
AGRIPPA   Sir, Mark Antony
Will e'en but° kiss Octavia, and we'll follow.   *merely*
LEPIDUS Till I shall see you in your soldier's dress,
Which will become you both, farewell.
5 MAECENAS   We shall,
As I conceive the journey, be at the Mount°   *Mount Misenum*
Before you, Lepidus.
LEPIDUS   Your way is shorter.
My purposes do draw me° much about.   *force me to go*
You'll win two days upon me.
MAECENAS *and* AGRIPPA   Sir, good success.
10 LEPIDUS Farewell. *Exeunt* [MAECENAS *and* AGRIPPA *at one*
         door, LEPIDUS *at another*]

2.5

  Enter CLEOPATRA, CHARMIAN, IRAS, *and* ALEXAS
CLEOPATRA Give me some music—music, moody° food *melancholy*
Of us that trade in love.
CHARMIAN, IRAS, *and* ALEXAS The music, ho!
  Enter MARDIAN, *the eunuch*
CLEOPATRA Let it alone. Let's to billiards. Come, Charmian.
CHARMIAN My arm is sore. Best play with Mardian.
5 CLEOPATRA As well a woman with an eunuch played
As with a woman. Come, you'll play with me, sir?
MARDIAN As well as I can, madam.
CLEOPATRA And when good will is showed, though't come too
  short¹
The actor may plead pardon. I'll none now.°   *I won't play now*
10 Give me mine angle.° We'll to th' river. There,   *fishing rod*
My music playing far off, I will betray°   *catch*
Tawny-finned fishes. My bended hook shall pierce
Their slimy jaws, and as I draw them up
I'll think them every one an Antony,
And say 'Ah ha, you're caught!'
15 CHARMIAN   'Twas merry when
You wagered on your angling, when your diver

---

4. *When . . . odds:* When the odds completely favor me, and when our quails are placed in a round enclosure to make them fight, his always beat mine, against all odds.
2.4 Location: Rome.

1. *hasten . . . after:* follow your leaders.
2.5 Location: Alexandria.
1. Referring to Mardian's sexual incapacity.

Did hang a salt° fish on his hook, which he   *preserved*
With fervency drew up.
CLEOPATRA   That time—O times!—
I laughed him out of patience, and that night
20   I laughed him into patience, and next morn,
Ere the ninth hour, I drunk him to his bed,
Then put my tires and mantles° on him whilst   *headdresses and robes*
I wore his sword Philippan.[2]
       Enter a MESSENGER
                   O, from Italy.
Ram thou thy fruitful tidings in mine ears,
That long time have been barren.
25 MESSENGER   Madam, madam!
CLEOPATRA   Antonio's dead. If thou say so, villain,
Thou kill'st thy mistress; but well and free,
If thou so yield° him, there is gold, and here   *report*
My bluest veins to kiss—a hand that kings
Have lipped, and trembled kissing.
30 MESSENGER   First, madam, he is well.
CLEOPATRA   Why, there's more gold. But, sirrah, mark: we use
To say the dead are well. Bring it to that,
The gold I give thee will I melt and pour
Down thy ill-uttering throat.
35 MESSENGER   Good madam, hear me.
CLEOPATRA   Well, go to, I will.
But there's no goodness in thy face. If Antony
Be free and healthful, so tart a favour°   *so sour an expression*
To trumpet such good tidings! If not well,
40 Thou shouldst come like a Fury[3] crowned with snakes,
Not like a formal° man.   *Not in the shape of a*
MESSENGER   Will't please you hear me?
CLEOPATRA   I have a mind to strike thee ere thou speak'st.
Yet if thou say Antony lives, is well,
Or friends with Caesar, or not captive to him,
45 I'll set thee in a shower of gold, and hail
Rich pearls upon thee.
MESSENGER   Madam, he's well.
CLEOPATRA   Well said.
MESSENGER   And friends with Caesar.
CLEOPATRA   Thou'rt an honest man.
MESSENGER   Caesar and he are greater friends than ever.
CLEOPATRA   Make thee a fortune from me.
MESSENGER   But yet, madam—
50 CLEOPATRA   I do not like 'But yet'; it does allay°   *dissipate*
The good precedence.° Fie upon 'But yet'.   *preceding good news*
'But yet' is as a jailer to bring forth
Some monstrous malefactor. Prithee, friend,
Pour out the pack of matter to mine ear,°   *Give me all the news*
55 The good and bad together. He's friends with Caesar,
In state of health, thou sayst; and, thou sayst, free.
MESSENGER   Free, madam? No, I made no such report.
He's bound unto Octavia.

2. The sword with which Antony had beaten Brutus and   3. In Greek mythology, a female avenging spirit.
Cassius at Philippi.

CLEOPATRA	For what good turn?°	good deed
MESSENGER	For the best turn i'th' bed.	
CLEOPATRA	I am pale, Charmian.	
60 MESSENGER	Madam, he's married to Octavia.	
CLEOPATRA	The most infectious pestilence upon thee!	

      [She] strikes him down

MESSENGER	Good madam, patience!	
CLEOPATRA	What say you?	

      [She] strikes him

Hence, horrible villain, or I'll spurn° thine eyes   *kick*
Like balls before me. I'll unhair thy head,

      She hales° him up and down   *drags*

65 Thou shalt be whipped with wire and stewed in brine,
Smarting in ling'ring pickle.°   *saltwater*

MESSENGER	Gracious madam,

I that do bring the news made not the match.

CLEOPATRA   Say 'tis not so, a province I will give thee,
And make thy fortunes proud. The blow thou hadst
70 Shall make thy peace for moving me to rage,
And I will boot° thee with what° gift beside   *compensate / whatever*
Thy modesty can beg.

MESSENGER	He's married, madam.

CLEOPATRA   Rogue, thou hast lived too long.

      [She] draw[s] a knife

MESSENGER	Nay then, I'll run.

What mean you, madam? I have made no fault.   *Exit*

75 CHARMIAN   Good madam, keep yourself within yourself.°   *restrain yourself*
The man is innocent.

CLEOPATRA   Some innocents 'scape not the thunderbolt.
Melt Egypt into Nile, and kindly° creatures   *harmless*
Turn all to serpents! Call the slave again.
80 Though I am mad I will not bite him. Call!

CHARMIAN   He is afeard to come.

CLEOPATRA	I will not hurt him.

      [Exit CHARMIAN*]*

These hands do lack nobility that they strike
A meaner° than myself, since I myself   *One of lower rank*
Have given myself the cause.°   *(by loving Antony)*

      Enter the MESSENGER *again [with* CHARMIAN*]*

             Come hither, sir.
85 Though it be honest, it is never good
To bring bad news. Give to a gracious message
An host° of tongues, but let ill tidings tell   *A multitude*
Themselves when they be felt.⁴

MESSENGER	I have done my duty.

90 CLEOPATRA   Is he married?
I cannot hate thee worser than I do
If thou again say 'Yes'.

MESSENGER	He's married, madam.

CLEOPATRA   The gods confound° thee! Dost thou hold there still?   *destroy*

MESSENGER   Should I lie, madam?

CLEOPATRA	O, I would thou didst,

95 So° half my Egypt were submerged and made   *Even if*
A cistern° for scaled snakes. Go, get thee hence.   *reservoir; chamber pot*

---

4. *let . . . felt:* bad news is best revealed by letting the victim feel the effects.

Hadst thou Narcissus[5] in thy face, to me
Thou wouldst appear most ugly. He is married?
MESSENGER   I crave your highness' pardon.
CLEOPATRA   He is married?
100 MESSENGER   Take no offence that I would not° offend you.   *do not want to*
To punish me for what you make me do
Seems much unequal.° He's married to Octavia.   *most unfair*
CLEOPATRA   O that his fault should make a knave° of thee,   *villain*
That act not what thou'rt sure of![6] Get thee hence.
105 The merchandise which thou hast brought from Rome
Are all too dear for me. Lie they upon thy hand,[7]
And be undone° by 'em.   [*Exit* MESSENGER]   *ruined (financially)*
CHARMIAN   Good your highness, patience.
CLEOPATRA   In praising Antony I have dispraised Caesar.
CHARMIAN   Many times, madam.
110 CLEOPATRA   I am paid for't now. Lead me from hence.
I faint. O Iras, Charmian—'tis no matter.
Go to the fellow, good Alexas, bid him
Report the feature° of Octavia: her years,   *appearance*
Her inclination;° let him not leave out   *disposition*
115 The colour of her hair. Bring me word quickly.   [*Exit* ALEXAS]
Let him for ever go—let him not, Charmian;
Though he be painted one way like a Gorgon,
The other way's a Mars.[8] [*To* MARDIAN] Bid you Alexas
Bring me word how tall she is. Pity me, Charmian,
120 But do not speak to me. Lead me to my chamber.   *Exeunt*

2.6

Flourish. Enter POMPEY [*and*] MENAS *at one door, with*
[*a*] *drum*[*mer*] *and* [*a*] *trumpet*[*er*]; *at another,* CAESAR,
LEPIDUS, ANTONY, ENOBARBUS, MAECENAS, AGRIPPA, *with*
soldiers marching
POMPEY   Your hostages I have, so have you mine,
And we shall talk before we fight.
CAESAR   Most meet°   *fitting*
That first we come to words, and therefore have we
Our written purposes° before us sent,   *offers*
5 Which if thou hast considered, let us know
If 'twill tie up° thy discontented sword   *lead you to put aside*
And carry back to Sicily much tall° youth   *courageous*
That else must perish here.
POMPEY   To you all three,
The senators alone° of this great world,   *sole governors*
10 Chief factors° for the gods: I do not know   *agents*
Wherefore my father[1] should revengers want,°   *lack*

---

5. In Greek mythology, a surprisingly beautiful young
man.
6. Who do not commit the offense you know about; who
do not report the information you know.
7. Leave with your goods unsold.
8. Cleopatra imagines Antony as a figure in a perspective
painting: popular in Shakespeare's time, they showed different images according to the angle from which they
were viewed. In classical mythology, a Gorgon was one of
three female monsters with snakes for hair whose horrific
appearance could turn others to stone.
2.6 Location: Near Misenum, Italy.
1. Pompey the Great. The allusion in the following lines

is primarily to the events dramatized by Shakespeare in
Julius Caesar. After being defeated by Julius Caesar at
Pharsalia, Pompey the Great fled to Egypt and was there
assassinated by agents of Ptolemy, Cleopatra's half-brother
(prior to the events in *Julius Caesar*). Julius Caesar was
then himself assassinated by the Roman republican conspirators, who included Cassius and Brutus. The triumvirs Antony, Octavius, and Lepidus defeated and killed
Brutus and Cassius at Philippi in revenge (see note to
1.2.88). The younger Pompey thus believes that by making war on the triumvirate, he avenges his father's death
and the deaths of Brutus and Cassius (and therefore he
fights for the republic).

Having a son and friends, since Julius Caesar,
Who at Philippi the good Brutus ghosted,[2]
There saw you labouring for him.° What was't   *on his behalf*
15   That moved pale Cassius to conspire? And what
Made the all-honoured, honest° Roman Brutus,   *honorable*
With the armèd rest, courtiers° of beauteous freedom,   *seekers*
To drench° the Capitol but that they would   *(in blood)*
Have one man but a man?° And that is it   *(and not a king)*
20   Hath made me rig° my navy, at whose burden   *equip*
The angered ocean foams; with which I meant
To scourge th'ingratitude that despiteful Rome
Cast on my noble father.
CAESAR   Take your time.
ANTONY   Thou canst not fear° us, Pompey, with thy sails.   *intimidate*
25   We'll speak with° thee at sea. At land thou know'st   *engage*
How much we do o'ercount° thee.   *outnumber*
POMPEY   At land indeed
Thou dost o'ercount me of my father's house,[3]
But since the cuckoo builds not for himself,[4]
Remain in't as thou mayst.°   *as long as you can*
LEPIDUS   Be pleased to tell us—
30   For this is from the present°—how you take   *beside the point*
The offers we have sent you.
CAESAR   There's the point.
ANTONY   Which do not be entreated to,° but weigh   *convinced unfairly of*
What it is worth, embracèd.°   *if you consent*
CAESAR   And what may follow,
To try a larger fortune?[5]
POMPEY   You have made me offer
35   Of Sicily, Sardinia; and I must
Rid all the sea of pirates; then to send
Measures of wheat to Rome; this 'greed upon,
To part with unhacked edges,° and bear back   *unused swords*
Our targes undinted.°   *shields untouched*
CAESAR, ANTONY, *and* LEPIDUS   That's our offer.
POMPEY   Know, then,
40   I came before you here a man prepared
To take this offer. But Mark Antony
Put me to some impatience. Though I lose
The praise of it by telling, you must know,
When Caesar and your brother were at blows,
45   Your mother came to Sicily, and did find
Her welcome friendly.
ANTONY   I have heard it, Pompey,
And am well studied for° a liberal thanks   *intend to offer*
Which I do owe you.
POMPEY   Let me have your hand.
      [POMPEY *and* ANTONY *shake hands*]
I did not think, sir, to have met you here.

---

2. Caesar appeared as a ghost to Brutus at the Battle of Philippi.

3. Plutarch records that Antony agreed to buy the elder Pompey's house but ultimately refused to pay for it.

4. The cuckoo lays eggs in the nests of other birds rather than building a nest of its own.

5. If you try (by fighting us) for a still larger fortune than we have offered.

50 ANTONY   The beds i'th' East are soft; and thanks to you,
      That called me timelier° than my purpose° hither;   *earlier / intention*
      For I have gained by't.
   CAESAR [*to* POMPEY]   Since I saw you last
      There is a change upon you.
   POMPEY   Well, I know not
      What counts harsh fortune casts upon my face,⁶
55   But in my bosom shall she never come
      To make my heart her vassal.
   LEPIDUS   Well met here.
   POMPEY   I hope so, Lepidus. Thus we are agreed.
      I crave our composition° may be written   *pact*
      And sealed between us.
   CAESAR   That's the next to do.
60 POMPEY   We'll feast each other ere we part, and let's
      Draw lots who shall begin.°   *act as host*
   ANTONY   That will I, Pompey.
   POMPEY   No, Antony, take the lot.
      But, first or last, your fine Egyptian cookery
65   Shall have the fame. I have heard that Julius Caesar
      Grew fat with feasting there.
   ANTONY   You have heard much.
   POMPEY   I have fair° meanings, sir.   *amicable*
   ANTONY   And fair° words to them.   *(ironic)*
   POMPEY   Then so much have I heard,
70   And I have heard Apollodorus carried⁷ —
   ENOBARBUS   No more o' that, he did so.
   POMPEY   What, I pray you?
   ENOBARBUS   A certain queen to Caesar in a mattress.
   POMPEY   I know thee now. How far'st thou, soldier?
   ENOBARBUS   Well, and well am like to do, for I perceive
      Four feasts are toward.°   *to come*
75 POMPEY   Let me shake thy hand.
              [POMPEY *and* ENOBARBUS *shake hands*]
      I never hated thee. I have seen thee fight
      When I have envied thy behaviour.
   ENOBARBUS   Sir, I never loved you much, but I ha' praised ye
      When you have well deserved ten times as much
80   As I have said you did.
   POMPEY   Enjoy thy plainness.° It nothing ill becomes thee.   *matter-of-fact speech*
      Aboard my galley I invite you all.
      Will you lead, lords?
   CAESAR, ANTONY, *and* LEPIDUS   Show's the way, sir.
   POMPEY   Come.
              Exeunt. Manent ENOBARBUS *and* MENAS
   MENAS [*aside*]   Thy father, Pompey, would ne'er have made this treaty.
85   [*To* ENOBARBUS] You and I have known,° sir.   *met each other*
   ENOBARBUS   At sea, I think.
   MENAS   We have, sir.
   ENOBARBUS   You have done well by water.

---

6. What accounts cruel fortune calculates (by marking
notches, like wrinkles).
7. Alluding to the story that Cleopatra gained access to

her lover, Julius Caesar, by having herself rolled up in a
sleeping mat (told in Plutarch).

MENAS   And you by land.

90 ENOBARBUS   I will praise any man that will praise me, though it cannot be denied what I have done by land.

MENAS   Nor what I have done by water.

ENOBARBUS   Yes, something you can deny for your own safety. You have been a great thief by sea.

95 MENAS   And you by land.

ENOBARBUS   There I deny my land service; but give me your hand, Menas. If our eyes had authority,° here they might take two thieves kissing.[8]   *(to make an arrest)*

[*They shake hands*]

MENAS   All men's faces are true,° whatsome'er their hands are.   *honest*

100 ENOBARBUS   But there is never a fair woman has a true° face.   *(without makeup)*

MENAS   No slander;° they steal hearts.   *That's true*

ENOBARBUS   We came hither to fight with you.

MENAS   For my part, I am sorry it is turned to a drinking. Pompey doth this day laugh away his fortune.

105 ENOBARBUS   If he do, sure he cannot weep't back again.

MENAS   You've said,° sir. We looked not for Mark Antony here. Pray you, is he married to Cleopatra?   *spoken truly*

ENOBARBUS   Caesar's sister is called Octavia.

MENAS   True, sir. She was the wife of Caius Marcellus.

110 ENOBARBUS   But she is now the wife of Marcus Antonius.

MENAS   Pray ye, sir?

ENOBARBUS   'Tis true.

MENAS   Then is Caesar and he for ever knit together.

ENOBARBUS   If I were bound to divine° of this unity I would not   *make predictions*
115 prophesy so.

MENAS   I think the policy of that purpose made more[9] in the marriage than the love of the parties.

ENOBARBUS   I think so, too. But you shall find the band that seems to tie their friendship together will be the very strangler
120 of their amity. Octavia is of a holy, cold, and still conversation.°   *disposition*

MENAS   Who would not have his wife so?

ENOBARBUS   Not he that himself is not so, which is Mark Antony. He will to his Egyptian dish again; then shall the sighs of Octavia blow the fire up in Caesar, and, as I said before, that
125 which is the strength of their amity shall prove the immediate author° of their variance.° Antony will use his affection where   *cause / enmity*
it is. He married but his occasion here.[1]

MENAS   And thus it may be. Come, sir, will you aboard? I have a health for you.

130 ENOBARBUS   I shall take it, sir. We have used our throats in Egypt.

MENAS   Come, let's away.   *Exeunt*

---

8. Arrest two thieves embracing; catch two thieving hands in a handshake, plotting together.
9. I think the politics of that "unity" weighed more heavily.

1. *Antony . . . here:* Antony will act on his desire where it really is located (Egypt). He married out of self-interest here.

2.7

Music plays. Enter two or three SERVANTS *with a banquet*[1]

FIRST SERVANT   Here they'll be, man. Some o' their plants are ill rooted[2] already; the least wind i'th' world will blow them down.

SECOND SERVANT   Lepidus is high-coloured.

FIRST SERVANT   They have made him drink alms-drink.[3]

5   SECOND SERVANT   As they pinch one another by the disposition,[4] he cries out 'No more!'—reconciles them to his entreaty° and himself to th' drink.   *(to stop arguing)*

FIRST SERVANT   But it raises the greater war between him and his discretion.

10   SECOND SERVANT   Why, this it is to have a name° in great men's   *only a nominal place*
fellowship. I had as lief° have a reed that will do me no service   *just as soon*
as a partisan I could not heave.[5]

FIRST SERVANT   To be called into a huge sphere and not to be seen to move in't, are the holes where eyes should be which
15   pitifully disaster the cheeks.[6]

A sennet° *sounded. Enter* CAESAR, ANTONY, POMPEY, LEP-   *flourish of trumpets*
IDUS, AGRIPPA, MAECENAS, ENOBARBUS, [*and*] MENAS,
with other captains [*and a boy*]

ANTONY [*to* CAESAR]   Thus do they, sir: they take the flow° o'th'   *measure the depth*
Nile
By certain scales i'th'° pyramid. They know   *marks on the*
By th' height, the lowness, or the mean,° if dearth   *middle position*
Or foison° follow. The higher Nilus swells   *abundance*
20   The more it promises; as it ebbs, the seedsman
Upon the slime and ooze scatters his grain,
And shortly comes to harvest.

LEPIDUS   You've strange serpents there?

ANTONY   Ay, Lepidus.

25   LEPIDUS   Your serpent of Egypt is bred now of your mud by the operation of your sun; so is your crocodile.

ANTONY   They are so.

POMPEY   Sit, and some wine. A health to Lepidus!
[ANTONY, POMPEY, *and* LEPIDUS *sit*]

LEPIDUS   I am not so well as I should be, but I'll ne'er out.°   *leave; miss a round*
30   ENOBARBUS   Not till you have slept—I fear me you'll be in° till   *remain; be drunk*
then.

LEPIDUS   Nay, certainly, I have heard the Ptolemies' pyramises[7]
are very goodly things: without contradiction I have heard that.

MENAS [*aside to* POMPEY]   Pompey, a word.

POMPEY [*aside to* MENAS]   Say in mine ear; what is't?

35   MENAS [*aside to* POMPEY]   Forsake thy seat, I do beseech thee, captain,
And hear me speak a word.

POMPEY [*aside to* MENAS]   Forbear° me till anon.   *Wait for*
[*Aloud*] This wine for Lepidus!

2.7 Location: Pompey's galley, off Misenum.
1. One of the courses of the feast, possibly dessert.
2. *their . . . rooted:* the soles of the feet of the (drunken) leaders are unsteady; the alliance between Antony and Caesar is shaky.
3. Drink given out of charity; in this case, extra rounds given to reconcile the parties each time they quarrel; one too many.
4. As they irritate one another according to their natures.

5. As a spear I could not lift (position without power).
6. *To be . . . cheeks:* To be placed in high circles in which one is incapable of moving is like having, instead of eyes, empty eye sockets that disfigure one's face. (In Ptolemaic astronomy, a planet "moves" within its "sphere," one of a series of concentric circles of which the universe is formed, with the earth at the center. A planet's ill influence causes "disaster," which literally means "bad star.")
7. Pyramids (drunken speech).

[MENAS] *whispers in [Pompey's] ear*

LEPIDUS What manner o' thing is your crocodile?

ANTONY It is shaped, sir, like itself, and it is as broad as it hath
40   breadth. It is just so high as it is, and moves with it° own organs.   *its*
    It lives by that which nourisheth it, and the elements once out
    of it, it transmigrates.[8]

LEPIDUS What colour is it of?

ANTONY Of it own colour, too.

45 LEPIDUS 'Tis a strange serpent.

ANTONY 'Tis so, and the tears of it are wet.[9]

CAESAR [*to* ANTONY] Will this description satisfy him?

ANTONY With the health that Pompey gives him; else he is a
    very epicure.°   *an insatiable glutton*

50 POMPEY [*aside to* MENAS] Go hang, sir, hang! Tell me of that? Away,
    Do as I bid you. [*Aloud*] Where's this cup I called for?

MENAS [*aside to* POMPEY] If for the sake of merit° thou wilt hear me,   *past deeds*
    Rise from thy stool.

POMPEY [*rising*]   I think thou'rt mad. The matter?
        [MENAS *and* POMPEY *stand apart*]

MENAS I have ever held my cap off to° thy fortunes.   *ever served*

55 POMPEY Thou hast served me with much faith. What's else to say?
    Be jolly, lords.

ANTONY   These quicksands, Lepidus,
    Keep off them, for you sink.

MENAS Wilt thou be lord of all the world?

POMPEY   What sayst thou?

MENAS Wilt thou be lord of the whole world? That's twice.

POMPEY How should that be?

60 MENAS   But entertain° it   *consider*
    And, though thou think me poor, I am the man
    Will give thee all the world.

POMPEY   Hast thou drunk well?

MENAS No, Pompey, I have kept me from the cup.
    Thou art, if thou dar'st be, the earthly Jove.
65   Whate'er the ocean pales° or sky inclips°   *encloses / embraces*
    Is thine, if thou wilt ha't.

POMPEY   Show me which way!

MENAS These three world-sharers, these competitors,°   *allies; rivals*
    Are in thy vessel. Let me cut the cable;
    And when we are put off, fall to their throats.
    All there is thine.

70 POMPEY   Ah, this thou shouldst have done
    And not have spoke on't. In me 'tis villainy,
    In thee 't had been good service. Thou must know
    'Tis not my profit that does lead mine honour;
    Mine honour, it.[1] Repent that e'er thy tongue
75   Hath so betrayed thine act.[2] Being done unknown,
    I should have found it afterwards well done,
    But must condemn it now. Desist, and drink.

---

8. Passes into other forms of life: referring to Pythagoras's theory, apparently of Egyptian origin, that at death the soul moves into another newborn living thing.
9. Continuing the pattern of comically uninformative self-identity, this line may also refer to hypocritical crocodile tears and hence to Pompey, as his ensuing exchange

with Menas suggests. See also 3.2.54–60 and 5.1.26–49.
1. *'Tis . . . it:* It is my honor that precedes or is the basis of my profit.
2. Treacherously disclosed your intentions and so made it impossible to carry them out.

[*He returns to the others*]

MENAS [*aside*]   For this, I'll never follow thy palled° fortunes more.   *diminished*
    Who seeks and will not take when once 'tis offered,
    Shall never find it more.

80 POMPEY   This health to Lepidus!

ANTONY   Bear him ashore.—I'll pledge it° for him, Pompey.   *drink the toast*

ENOBARBUS   Here's to thee, Menas!

MENAS   Enobarbus, welcome.

POMPEY   Fill till the cup be hid.

    [*One lifts* LEPIDUS, *drunk, and carries him off*]

ENOBARBUS   There's a strong fellow, Menas.

MENAS   Why?

85 ENOBARBUS   A° bears the third part of the world, man; seest not?   *He*

MENAS   The third part then is drunk. Would it were all,
    That it might go on wheels.°   *easily; out of control*

ENOBARBUS   Drink thou, increase the reels.°   *revels; spinning*

MENAS   Come.

POMPEY   This is not yet an Alexandrian feast.

90 ANTONY   It ripens towards it. Strike the vessels,° ho!   *Open more casks*
    Here's to Caesar!

CAESAR   I could well forbear't.
    It's monstrous° labour when I wash my brain,   *unnatural*
    An° it grow fouler.   *If as a result*

ANTONY   Be a child o'th' time.

95 CAESAR   Possess it, I'll make answer.[3]
    But I had rather fast from all, four days,
    Than drink so much in one.

ENOBARBUS [*to* ANTONY]   Ha, my brave Emperor,
    Shall we dance now the Egyptian bacchanals,[4]
    And celebrate our drink?

100 POMPEY   Let's ha't, good soldier.

ANTONY   Come, let's all take hands
    Till that the conquering wine hath steeped our sense
    In soft and delicate Lethe.°   *oblivion*

ENOBARBUS   All take hands.
    Make battery to° our ears with the loud music.   *Besiege*
105   The while I'll place you, then the boy shall sing.
    The holding° every man shall beat° as loud   *refrain / beat out*
    As his strong sides can volley.°   *fire off*

    Music plays. ENOBARBUS *places them hand in hand*

BOY [*sings*]   Come, thou monarch of the vine,
        Plumpy Bacchus, with pink[5] eyne!
110   In thy vats our cares be drowned,
        With thy grapes our hairs be crowned!
        Cup us till the world go round,
        Cup us till the world go round!

CAESAR   What would you more? Pompey, good night.
    [*To* ANTONY]   Good-brother,°   *Brother-in-law*
115 Let me request you off.° Our graver business   *to come ashore*
    Frowns at this levity. Gentle lords, let's part.
    You see we have burnt° our cheeks. Strong Enobarb   *flushed*

---

3. Take it, and I'll drink too; be in command of the time,   and revelry.
I say.   5. Half-closed and red from drinking.
4. Wild, drunken revels in honor of Bacchus, god of wine

      Is weaker than the wine, and mine own tongue
      Splits° what it speaks. The wild disguise° hath almost   *Deforms / drunkenness*
120 Anticked us° all. What needs more words? Good night.   *Made us clowns*
      Good Antony, your hand.
POMPEY   I'll try you° on the shore.   *test your drinking*
ANTONY   And shall, sir. Give's your hand.
POMPEY   O Antony,
      You have my father's house. But what, we are friends!
      Come down into the boat.
                  [Exeunt all but ENOBARBUS *and* MENAS]
ENOBARBUS   Take heed you fall not, Menas.
125 MENAS   I'll not° on shore.   *not go*
      No, to my cabin. These drums, these trumpets, flutes, what!
      Let Neptune hear we bid a loud farewell
      To these great fellows. Sound and be hanged, sound out!
          Sound a flourish, with drums
ENOBARBUS *[throwing his cap in the air]*   Hoo, says a!° There's   *he*
      my cap.
MENAS   Ho, noble captain, come!   *Exeunt*

3.1

Enter VENTIDIUS *[with* SILIUS *and other Roman soldiers]*
as it were in triumph; the dead body of Pacorus borne
before him
VENTIDIUS   Now, darting Parthia,[1] art thou struck; and now
      Pleased fortune does of Marcus Crassus'[2] death
      Make me revenger. Bear the King's son's body
      Before our army. Thy° Pacorus, Orodes,   *Your son*
      Pays this for Marcus Crassus.
5 SILIUS   Noble Ventidius,
      Whilst yet with Parthian blood thy sword is warm,
      The fugitive Parthians follow.[3] Spur through Media,[4]
      Mesopotamia, and the shelters whither
      The routed fly. So thy grand captain, Antony,
10 Shall set thee on triumphant° chariots and   *triumphal*
      Put garlands on thy head.
VENTIDIUS   O Silius, Silius,
      I have done enough. A lower place,° note well,   *man of low rank*
      May make too great an act. For learn this, Silius:
      Better to leave undone than by our deed
15 Acquire too high a fame when him we serve's away.
      Caesar and Antony have ever won
      More in their officer than person.[5] Sossius,
      One of my place in Syria, his° lieutenant,   *(Antony's)*
      For quick accumulation of renown,
20 Which he achieved by th' minute,° lost his favour.   *more every minute*
      Who does i'th' wars more than his captain can
      Becomes his captain's captain; and ambition,

3.1 Location: Syria.
1. Parthian cavalry advanced flinging darts, then re-treated shooting arrows. "Parthia" here refers to both the nation and its king, Orodes.
2. A member, with Pompey the Great and Julius Caesar, of the first triumvirate, treacherously and cruelly killed in

defeat by Orodes in 53 B.C.
3. Chase the fleeing Parthians.
4. The land between Persia and Armenia, east of Meso-potamia—part of the Parthian empire.
5. Owing more to the skill of their officers than to their own skill.

The soldier's virtue, rather makes choice of loss
Than gain which darkens him.°   *eclipses his renown*
25 I could do more to do Antonius good,
But 'twould offend him, and in his offence
Should my performance perish.°   *lose its value*
SILIUS   Thou hast, Ventidius, that°   *(discretion)*
Without the which a soldier and his sword
Grants scarce° distinction. Thou wilt write to Antony?   *Scarcely admits of*
30 VENTIDIUS   I'll humbly signify what in his name,
That magical word of war, we have effected;
How, with his banners and his well-paid ranks,
The ne'er-yet-beaten horse° of Parthia   *cavalry*
We have jaded° out o'th' field.   *chased like tired nags*
SILIUS   Where is he now?
35 VENTIDIUS   He purposeth to Athens; whither, with what haste
The weight wc must convey with's will permit,
We shall appear before him.—On there; pass along.   *Exeunt*

3.2

Enter AGRIPPA *at one door,* ENOBARBUS *at another*
AGRIPPA   What, are the brothers parted?°   *brothers-in-law gone*
ENOBARBUS   They have dispatched° with Pompey; he is gone.   *finished the business*
The other three are sealing.° Octavia weeps   *signing their pact*
To part from Rome, Caesar is sad, and Lepidus
5   Since Pompey's feast, as Menas says, is troubled
With the green-sickness.[1]
AGRIPPA   'Tis a noble Lepidus.
ENOBARBUS   A very fine one. O, how he loves Caesar!
AGRIPPA   Nay, but how dearly he adores Mark Antony!
ENOBARBUS   Caesar? Why, he's the Jupiter of men.
10 AGRIPPA   What's Antony—the god of Jupiter?
ENOBARBUS   Spake you of Caesar? How, the nonpareil?°   *incomparable*
AGRIPPA   O Antony, O thou Arabian bird![2]
ENOBARBUS   Would you praise Caesar, say 'Caesar'; go no further.
AGRIPPA   Indeed, he plied them both with excellent praises.
15 ENOBARBUS   But he loves Caesar best; yet he loves Antony—
Hoo! Hearts, tongues, figures,° scribes, bards, poets, cannot   *(of speech); numbers*
Think, speak, cast,° write, sing, number°—hoo!—   *calculate / make verses*
His love to Antony. But as for Caesar—
Kneel down, kneel down, and wonder.
AGRIPPA   Both he loves.
ENOBARBUS   They are his shards,[3] and he their beetle.
    [*Trumpet within*]
20   So,
This is° to horse. Adieu, noble Agrippa.   *calls us*
AGRIPPA   Good fortune, worthy soldier, and farewell.
    Enter CAESAR, ANTONY, LEPIDUS, *and* OCTAVIA
ANTONY [*to* CAESAR]   No further, sir.

3.2 Location: Rome.
1. Anemia in adolescent, lovesick girls (hence, a feminiz-ing attribute): here, used humorously for Lepidus's hang-over and its effect, as well as ironically for his overblown affection for Caesar and Antony.
2. The phoenix, a legendary, self-resurrecting bird, only

one of which existed at a time. It was believed to live for several centuries, to die in flames, and to be reborn from its own ashes.
3. Dung patches (between which the beetle crawls to feed and breed); perhaps, wing cases (with which the bee-tle flies).

CAESAR You take from me a great part of myself.
25   Use me well in't. Sister, prove such a wife
        As my thoughts make thee, and as my farthest bond
        Shall pass on thy approof.[4] Most noble Antony,
        Let not the piece° of virtue which is set   paragon
        Betwixt us as the cement of our love
30   To keep it builded, be the ram to batter
        The fortress of it; for better might we
        Have loved without this mean° if on both parts   intermediary
        This be not cherished.
ANTONY   Make me not offended
        In° your distrust.   By
CAESAR   I have said.
ANTONY   You shall not find,
35   Though you be therein curious,° the least cause   overly probing
        For what you seem to fear. So, the gods keep you,
        And make the hearts of Romans serve your ends.
        We will here part.
CAESAR Farewell, my dearest sister, fare thee well.
40   The elements be kind to thee, and make
        Thy spirits all of comfort. Fare thee well.
OCTAVIA [weeping] My noble brother!
ANTONY The April's in her eyes;° it is love's spring,   She weeps
        And these the showers to bring it on. Be cheerful.
45 OCTAVIA Sir, look well to my husband's° house, and—   (Antony's)
CAESAR What, Octavia?
OCTAVIA   I'll tell you in your ear.
        [She whispers to CAESAR]
ANTONY Her tongue will not obey her heart, nor can
        Her heart inform her tongue—the swan's-down feather,
        That stands upon the swell at full of tide,
50   And neither way inclines.[5]
ENOBARBUS [aside to AGRIPPA] Will Caesar weep?
AGRIPPA [aside to ENOBARBUS] He has a cloud in's face.
ENOBARBUS [aside to AGRIPPA] He were the worse for that were he a horse;[6]
        So is he, being a man.
AGRIPPA [aside to ENOBARBUS] Why, Enobarbus,
55   When Antony found Julius Caesar dead
        He cried almost to roaring, and he wept
        When at Philippi he found Brutus slain.
ENOBARBUS [aside to AGRIPPA] That year indeed he was trou-
        bled with a rheum.°   flu; watery eyes
        What willingly he did confound° he wailed,°   destroy / mourned
        Believe't, till I wept too.
60 CAESAR   No, sweet Octavia,
        You shall hear from me still.° The time shall not   constantly
        Outgo[7] my thinking on° you.   of
ANTONY   Come, sir, come,
        I'll wrestle with you in my strength of love.

---

4. and as . . . approof: and (such a wife) as to make my
largest contractual commitment (also, my closest tie of
affection: here, Caesar's to Octavia) approved on the basis
of what you will prove to be.
5. the swan's-down . . . inclines: (she is like) the feather of

a swan's down that floats in still water, unmoving (just as
she can't speak) when the tide is on the turn.
6. A horse with a cloud—a dark rather than a white star
on its face—was supposedly ill-tempered.
7. The . . . / Outgo: Even time will not endure beyond.

Look, here I have you [*embracing* CAESAR]; thus I let you go,
And give you to the gods.
65 CAESAR   Adieu, be happy.
LEPIDUS   Let all the number of the stars give light
To thy fair way.
CAESAR   Farewell, farewell.
     [*He*] *kisses* OCTAVIA
ANTONY   Farewell.
     Trumpets sound. Exeunt [ANTONY, OCTAVIA, *and*
          ENOBARBUS *at one door,* CAESAR, LEPIDUS, *and*
                    AGRIPPA *at another*]

3.3
Enter CLEOPATRA, CHARMIAN, IRAS, *and* ALEXAS
CLEOPATRA   Where is the fellow?
ALEXAS   Half afeard to come.
CLEOPATRA   Go to, go to.
     Enter the MESSENGER *as before*
                    Come hither, sir.
ALEXAS   Good majesty,
Herod of Jewry¹ dare not look upon you
But when you are well pleased.
CLEOPATRA   That Herod's head
5 I'll have; but how, when Antony is gone,
Through whom I might command it?
     [*To the* MESSENGER]   Come thou near.
MESSENGER   Most gracious majesty!
CLEOPATRA   Didst thou behold
Octavia?
MESSENGER   Ay, dread Queen.
CLEOPATRA   Where?
MESSENGER   Madam, in Rome.
I looked her in the face, and saw her led
10 Between her brother and Mark Antony.
CLEOPATRA   Is she as tall as me?
MESSENGER   She is not, madam.
CLEOPATRA   Didst hear her speak? Is she shrill-tongued or low?
MESSENGER   Madam, I heard her speak. She is low-voiced.
CLEOPATRA   That's not so good.° He cannot like her long.   *favorable to Octavia*
15 CHARMIAN   Like her? O Isis, 'tis impossible!
CLEOPATRA   I think so, Charmian. Dull of tongue, and dwarfish.
What majesty is in her gait? Remember
If e'er thou looked'st on majesty.
MESSENGER   She creeps.
Her motion and her station° are as one.   *standing still*
20 She shows° a body rather than a life,   *seems to be*
A statue than° a breather.   *rather than*
CLEOPATRA   Is this certain?
MESSENGER   Or I have no observance.°   *powers of observation*
CHARMIAN   Three in Egypt
Cannot make better note.²
CLEOPATRA   He's very knowing,

3.3 Location: Alexandria.
1. Renowned for his irrational cruelty. See note to 1.2.24.
2. *Three . . . note:* There are not three better witnesses in all Egypt.

I do perceive't. There's nothing in her yet.
The fellow has good judgement.
25 CHARMIAN   Excellent.
CLEOPATRA [*to the* MESSENGER]   Guess at her years, I prithee.
MESSENGER   Madam,
   She was a widow—
CLEOPATRA   Widow? Charmian, hark.
MESSENGER   And I do think she's thirty.°   *(Cleopatra was 38)*
CLEOPATRA   Bear'st thou her face in mind? Is't long or round?
30 MESSENGER   Round, even to faultiness.
CLEOPATRA   For the most part, too, they are foolish that are so.
   Her hair—what colour?
MESSENGER   Brown, madam; and her forehead
   As low as she would wish it.[3]
CLEOPATRA [*giving money*]   There's gold for thee.
   Thou must not take my former sharpness ill.
35   I will employ thee back° again. I find thee   *to go back to Rome*
   Most fit for business. Go, make thee ready.
   Our letters are prepared.   [*Exit* MESSENGER]
CHARMIAN   A proper° man.   *An admirable*
CLEOPATRA   Indeed he is so. I repent me much
   That so I harried him. Why, methinks, by him,°   *by his account*
   This creature's no such thing.°   *nothing special*
40 CHARMIAN   Nothing, madam.
CLEOPATRA   The man hath seen some majesty, and should know.
CHARMIAN   Hath he seen majesty? Isis else defend,
   And serving you so long![4]
CLEOPATRA   I have one thing more to ask him yet, good Charmian.
45   But 'tis no matter. Thou shalt bring him to me
   Where I will write. All may be well enough.
CHARMIAN   I warrant you, madam.   *Exeunt*

3.4

Enter ANTONY *and* OCTAVIA
ANTONY   Nay, nay, Octavia, not only that,
   That were excusable, that and thousands more
   Of semblable° import; but he hath waged   *like*
   New wars 'gainst Pompey, made his will and read it
5   To public ear,[1] spoke scantly° of me;   *meanly*
   When perforce he could not
   But pay me terms of honour, cold and sickly
   He vented them, most narrow measure° lent me.   *little credit*
   When the best hint° was given him, he not took't,   *opportunity*
   Or did it from his teeth.°   *insincerely*
10 OCTAVIA   O my good lord,
   Believe not all, or if you must believe,
   Stomach° not all. A more unhappy lady,   *Resent*
   If this division chance, ne'er stood between,
   Praying for both parts.
15   The good gods will mock me presently,°   *at once*

---

3. So that she would wish it no lower: high foreheads were admired.
4. *Isis . . . long:* He surely has, considering how long he's served you. *else defend:* prohibit that it not be so. There may be a double irony in the lines, with Charmian appar-ently denying that anyone who has long served Cleopatra could recognize true majesty but not really meaning it.
3.4 Location: Athens.
1. Caesar's act implies promises to the public.

When I shall pray 'O, bless my lord and husband!',
Undo that prayer by crying out as loud
'O, bless my brother!' Husband win, win brother
Prays and destroys the prayer; no midway
'Twixt these extremes at all.

20 ANTONY   Gentle Octavia,
Let your best love draw to that point which seeks
Best to preserve it.[2] If I lose mine honour,
I lose myself. Better I were not yours
Than yours so branchless.° But, as you requested,   *amputated*
25 Yourself shall go between's. The meantime, lady,
I'll raise the preparation of a war
Shall stain your brother.° Make your soonest haste;   *hurt his reputation*
So° your desires are yours.   *In this way*

OCTAVIA   Thanks to my lord.
The Jove of power make me most weak, most weak,
30 Your reconciler! Wars 'twixt you twain would be
As if the world should cleave, and that slain men
Should solder° up the rift.   *close*

ANTONY   When it appears to you where this begins,°   *who started this*
Turn your displeasure that way, for our faults
35 Can never be so equal that your love
Can equally move with° them. Provide° your going,   *judge / Prepare for*
Choose your own company, and command what cost
Your heart has mind to.   *Exeunt*

3.5

Enter ENOBARBUS *and* EROS [*meeting*]

ENOBARBUS   How now, friend Eros?

EROS   There's strange news come, sir.

ENOBARBUS   What, man?

EROS   Caesar and Lepidus have made wars upon Pompey.

5 ENOBARBUS   This is old. What is the success?°   *outcome*

EROS   Caesar, having made use of him° in the wars 'gainst Pom-   *(Lepidus)*
pey, presently denied him rivality,° would not let him partake   *equal partnership*
in the glory of the action, and, not resting° here, accuses him   *stopping*
of letters he had formerly wrote to Pompey; upon his° own   *(Caesar's)*
10 appeal° seizes him; so the poor third is up,° till death enlarge   *accusation / imprisoned*
his confine.

ENOBARBUS   Then, world, thou hast a pair of chops,° no more,°   *jaws / (than two)*
And throw° between them all the food thou hast,   *if you should throw*
They'll grind the one the other. Where's Antony?

15 EROS   He's walking in the garden, thus, and spurns°   *kicks*
The rush° that lies before him, cries 'Fool Lepidus!'   *rushes*
And threats the throat of that his officer°   *that officer of his*
That murdered Pompey.[1]

ENOBARBUS   Our great navy's rigged.°   *prepared*

EROS   For Italy and Caesar. More,° Domitius: *There's more (to say)*
20 My lord desires you presently. My news
I might have told hereafter.

---

2. *Let . . . it*: Choose the one of us (Antony or Caesar)
who best strives to preserve your love.
3.5 Location: Athens.
1. Historically, though Shakespeare leaves Antony's re-

sponsibility for the killing unclear, Pompey was said to
have been murdered at the command of Antony, who
here regrets the death because Pompey might have been
a useful ally against Caesar.

ENOBARBUS   'Twill be naught.°   *of no consequence*
But let it be; bring me to Antony.
EROS   Come, sir.   *Exeunt*

3.6

Enter AGRIPPA, MAECENAS, *and* CAESAR

CAESAR   Contemning° Rome, he has done all this and more   *Despising*
In Alexandria. Here's the manner of't:
I'th' market place on a tribunal° silvered,   *platform*
Cleopatra and himself in chairs of gold
5   Were publicly enthroned. At the feet sat
Caesarion, whom they call my father's[1] son,
And all the unlawful issue that their lust
Since then hath made between them. Unto her
He gave the stablishment° of Egypt; made her   *full possession*
10 Of lower Syria, Cyprus, Lydia,[2]
Absolute queen.
MAECENAS   This in the public eye?
CAESAR   I'th' common showplace, where they exercise.[3]
His sons he there proclaimed the kings of kings;
Great Media, Parthia, and Armenia
15 He gave to Alexander. To Ptolemy he assigned
Syria, Cilicia, and Phoenicia. She
In th'habiliments° of the goddess Isis   *costume*
That day appeared, and oft before gave audience,
As 'tis reported, so.°   *in this costume*
MAECENAS   Let Rome be thus informed.
20 AGRIPPA   Who, queasy with° his insolence already,   *sick of*
Will their good thoughts call° from him.   *remove*
CAESAR   The people knows it,
And have now received his accusations.
AGRIPPA   Who does he accuse?
CAESAR   Caesar, and that having in Sicily
25 Sextus Pompeius spoiled,° we had not rated° him   *ransacked / allotted*
His part o'th' isle.° Then does he say he lent me   *Sicily*
Some shipping, unrestored.° Lastly, he frets   *not returned (by me)*
That Lepidus of the triumvirate
Should be deposed; and being,° that we detain   *being deposed*
All his revenue.
30 AGRIPPA   Sir, this should be answered.
CAESAR   'Tis done already, and the messenger gone.
I have told him Lepidus was grown too cruel,
That he his high authority abused
And did deserve his change. For° what I have conquered,   *As for*
35 I grant him part; but then in his Armenia,
And other of his conquered kingdoms,
I demand the like.
MAECENAS   He'll never yield to that.
CAESAR   Nor must not then be yielded to in this.

Enter OCTAVIA *with her train*

3.6 Location: Rome.
1. Julius Caesar (who adopted his grandnephew Octavius as his son). See 2.2.233–34 with note and note to 5.2.352.
2. District on the west coast of Asia Minor. Shakespeare

took the name from North's translation of Plutarch, but the original has Libya.
3. In the arena (theater), where they engage in sports (perform).

OCTAVIA Hail, Caesar, and my lord; hail, most dear Caesar!
40 CAESAR That ever I should call thee castaway!
OCTAVIA You have not called me so, nor have you cause.
CAESAR Why have you stol'n upon us thus? You come not
    Like Caesar's sister. The wife of Antony
    Should have an army for an usher, and
45   The neighs of horse to tell of her approach
    Long ere she did appear. The trees by th' way
    Should have borne men, and expectation fainted,
    Longing for what it had not. Nay, the dust
    Should have ascended to the roof of heaven,
50   Raised by your populous troops. But you are come
    A market maid to Rome, and have prevented°   *(by coming too early)*
    The ostentation° of our love; which, left unshown,   *public display*
    Is often left unloved.[4] We should have met you
    By sea and land, supplying every stage°   *(of the voyage)*
    With an augmented greeting.
55 OCTAVIA   Good my lord,
    To come thus was I not constrained, but did it
    On my free will. My lord, Mark Antony,
    Hearing that you prepared for war, acquainted
    My grievèd ear withal, whereon I begged
    His pardon for° return.   *permission to*
60 CAESAR   Which soon he granted,
    Being an obstruct 'tween his lust and him.
OCTAVIA Do not say so, my lord.
CAESAR   I have eyes upon him,
    And his affairs come to me on the wind.
    Where is he now?
OCTAVIA   My lord, in Athens.
65 CAESAR No, my most wrongèd sister. Cleopatra
    Hath nodded him to her. He hath given his empire
    Up to a whore; who° now are levying   *both of them*
    The kings o'th' earth for war. He hath assembled
    Bocchus, the King of Libya; Archelaus
70   Of Cappadocia; Philadelphos, King
    Of Paphlagonia; the Thracian King Adallas;
    King Malchus of Arabia; King of Pont;
    Herod of Jewry; Mithridates, King
    Of Comagene; Polemon and Amyntas,
75   The Kings of Mede and Lycaonia;[5]
    With a more larger° list of sceptres.   *yet longer*
OCTAVIA   Ay me most wretched,
    That have my heart parted betwixt two friends
    That does afflict each other!
CAESAR   Welcome hither.
    Your letters did withhold our° breaking forth   *restrain me from*
80   Till we perceived both how you were wrong° led   *wrongly*
    And we in negligent danger.° Cheer your heart.   *danger from negligence*
    Be you not troubled with the time,° which drives   *present business*
    O'er your content° these strong necessities;   *contentment*

4. Is often thought not to be love at all. Or, *which . . . un-*
loved: lack of opportunity to demonstrate love often leads
to its actual decline.
5. All kings from the East.

But let determined things to destiny
85   Hold unbewailed their way.⁶ Welcome to Rome;
Nothing more dear to me. You are abused
Beyond the mark° of thought, and the high gods,   *limits*
To do you justice, makes their ministers°   *agents*
Of us and those that love you. Best of comfort,
And ever welcome to us.
90   AGRIPPA   Welcome, lady.
MAECENAS   Welcome, dear madam.
Each heart in Rome does love and pity you.
Only th'adulterous Antony, most large°   *unlimited*
In his abominations, turns you off,
95   And gives his potent regiment° to a trull°   *powerful rule / whore*
That noises it° against us.   *cries out*
OCTAVIA   Is it so, sir?
CAESAR   Most certain. Sister, welcome. Pray you
Be ever known to patience. My dear'st sister!   *Exeunt*

3.7

Enter CLEOPATRA *and* ENOBARBUS
CLEOPATRA   I will be even with thee, doubt it not.
ENOBARBUS   But why, why, why?
CLEOPATRA   Thou hast forspoke° my being in these wars,   *opposed*
And sayst it is not fit.
ENOBARBUS   Well, is it, is it?
5   CLEOPATRA   Is't not denounced° against us? Why should not we   *Isn't war declared*
Be there in person?
ENOBARBUS [*aside*]   Well, I could reply
If we should serve with horse and mares together,
The horse were merely lost;¹ the mares would bear°   *seduce; carry*
A soldier and his horse.
CLEOPATRA   What is't you say?
10   ENOBARBUS   Your presence needs must puzzle° Antony,   *distract*
Take from his heart, take from his brain, from's time
What should not then be spared. He is already
Traduced° for levity; and 'tis said in Rome   *Slandered*
That Photinus, an eunuch, and your maids
Manage this war.
15   CLEOPATRA   Sink Rome,° and their tongues rot   *To hell with Rome*
That speak against us! A charge° we bear i'th' war,   *An expense; duty*
And as the president of my kingdom will
Appear there for° a man. Speak not against it.   *as if I were*
I will not stay behind.
Enter ANTONY *and* CAMIDIUS
ENOBARBUS   Nay, I have done.
Here comes the Emperor.
20   ANTONY   Is it not strange, Camidius,
That from Tarentum and Brundisium²
He could so quickly cut° the Ionian° Sea   *Cut across / Adriatic*
And take in° Toryne?°—You have heard on't, sweet?   *overrun / (near Actium)*

---

6. *let . . . way:* let predetermined events go to their destined conclusions without complaint.
3.7 Location: Antony's camp, near Actium, Greece.
1. *If . . . lost:* If we take both male and female horses

(whores) to the wars, the males would have no hope of
triumphing, because of the females ("merely" equals
"mare-ly").
2. Ports in southeast Italy.

CLEOPATRA Celerity is never more admired°   wondered at
    Than by the negligent.
25 ANTONY   A good rebuke,
    Which might have well becomed the best of men
    To taunt at slackness. Camidius, we
    Will fight with him by sea.
    CLEOPATRA   By sea—what else?
    CAMIDIUS Why will my lord do so?
    ANTONY   For that he dares us to't.
30 ENOBARBUS So hath my lord dared him to single fight.
    CAMIDIUS Ay, and to wage this battle at Pharsalia,°   (near Actium)
    Where Caesar fought with Pompey. But these offers
    Which serve not for his vantage, he shakes off,
    And so should you.
    ENOBARBUS   Your ships are not well manned,
35 Your mariners are muleters,° reapers, people   mule drivers
    Engrossed° by swift impress.° In Caesar's fleet   Amassed / conscription
    Are those that often have 'gainst Pompey fought.
    Their ships are yare,° yours heavy. No disgrace   smooth running
    Shall fall° you for refusing him at sea,   befall
    Being prepared for land.
40 ANTONY   By sea, by sea.
    ENOBARBUS Most worthy sir, you therein throw away
    The absolute soldiership you have by land;
    Distract° your army, which doth most consist   Divert
    Of war-marked footmen; leave unexecuted°   untapped
45 Your own renownèd knowledge; quite forgo
    The way which promises assurance,° and   victory
    Give up yourself merely° to chance and hazard   completely
    From firm security.
    ANTONY   I'll fight at sea.
    CLEOPATRA I have sixty sails, Caesar none better.
50 ANTONY Our overplus of shipping will we burn,[3]
    And with the rest full-manned, from th'head° of Actium   promontory
    Beat th'approaching Caesar. But if we fail,
    We then can do't at land.
                        Enter a MESSENGER
                            Thy business?
    MESSENGER The news is true, my lord. He is descried.°   He has been seen
55 Caesar has taken Toryne.
    ANTONY Can he be there in person? 'Tis impossible;
    Strange that his power° should be. Camidius,   his entire army
    Our nineteen legions thou shalt hold by land,
    And our twelve thousand horse. We'll to our ship.
    Away, my Thetis![4]
                        Enter a SOLDIER
60   How now, worthy soldier?
    SOLDIER O noble Emperor, do not fight by sea.
    Trust not to rotten planks. Do you misdoubt
    This sword and these my wounds? Let th'Egyptians

---

3. Antony seems to have burned his excess ("overplus")   taken by Octavius Caesar.
ships because he did not have enough sailors to man   4. Sea goddess, mother of the Greek hero Achilles.
them adequately and feared that they could easily be

And the Phoenicians go a-ducking;° we   *to sea*
65   Have used to conquer standing on the earth,
And fighting foot to foot.
ANTONY   Well, well; away!
Exeunt ANTONY, CLEOPATRA, *and* ENOBARBUS
SOLDIER   By Hercules, I think I am i'th' right.
CAMIDIUS   Soldier, thou art; but his whole action grows
Not in the power on't.[5] So our leader's led,
And we are women's men.
70   SOLDIER   You keep by land
The legions and the horse whole, do you not?
CAMIDIUS   Marcus Octavius, Marcus Justeius,
Publicola and Caelius are for sea,
But we keep whole° by land. This speed of Caesar's   *stay undivided*
Carries beyond° belief.   *Exceeds*
75   SOLDIER   While he was yet in Rome
His power went out in such distractions°   *separate detachments*
As beguiled all spies.
CAMIDIUS   Who's his lieutenant, hear you?
SOLDIER   They say, one Taurus.
CAMIDIUS   Well I know the man.
Enter a MESSENGER
MESSENGER   The Emperor calls Camidius.
80   CAMIDIUS   With news the time's in labour, and throws forth
Each minute some.[6]   *Exeunt*

3.8

Enter CAESAR *with his army, marching* [*and* TAURUS]
CAESAR   Taurus!
TAURUS   My lord?
CAESAR   Strike not by land. Keep whole.° Provoke not battle   *Stay in reserve*
Till we have done at sea. [*Giving a scroll*] Do not exceed
5   The prescript° of this scroll. Our fortune lies   *written orders*
Upon this jump.°   *ploy*
Exit [CAESAR *and his army at one door,* TAURUS *at another*]

3.9

Enter ANTONY *and* ENOBARBUS
ANTONY   Set we our squadrons on yon side o'th' hill
In eye° of Caesar's battle,° from which place   *view / battle line*
We may the number of the ships behold,
And so proceed accordingly.   *Exeunt*

3.10

CAMIDIUS *marcheth with his land army one way over the
stage, and* TAURUS, *the lieutenant of Caesar,* [*with his
army*] *the other way. After their going in is heard the
noise of a sea-fight. Alarum. Enter* ENOBARBUS
ENOBARBUS   Naught, naught, all naught! I can behold no longer.
Th'*Antoniad*, the Egyptian admiral,°   *flagship*
With all their sixty, fly and turn the rudder.

---

5. His entire plan is made without taking into account   **3.8** Location: Near Actium.
his resources.   **3.9** Location: Scene continues.
6. *throws . . . some*: each minute, more news is born.   **3.10** Location: Scene continues.

To see't mine eyes are blasted.°   *(as if by lightning)*
     Enter SCARUS
SCARUS   Gods and goddesses—
  All the whole synod° of them!   *assembly*
5 ENOBARBUS   What's° thy passion?   *What provokes*
SCARUS The greater cantle° of the world is lost   *corner; portion*
  With° very ignorance;° we have kissed away   *Through / idiocy*
  Kingdoms and provinces.
ENOBARBUS   How appears the fight?
SCARUS On our side like the tokened pestilence,[1]
10 Where death is sure. Yon riband-red[2] nag of Egypt—
  Whom leprosy o'ertake!—i'th' midst o'th' fight—
  When vantage like a pair of twins appeared,[3]
  Both as the same, or rather ours the elder°—   *ours likely the stronger*
  The breese upon her,[4] like a cow in June,
  Hoists sails and flies.
15 ENOBARBUS   That I beheld.
  Mine eyes did sicken at the sight, and could not
  Endure a further view.
SCARUS   She once being luffed,[5]
  The noble ruin° of her magic, Antony,   *casualty*
  Claps on his sea-wing° and, like a doting mallard,°   *sails / male duck*
20 Leaving the fight in° height, flies after her.   *at its*
  I never saw an action of such shame.
  Experience, manhood, honour, ne'er before
  Did violate so itself.
ENOBARBUS   Alack, alack!
     Enter CAMIDIUS
CAMIDIUS Our fortune on the sea is out of breath,
25 And sinks most lamentably. Had our general
  Been what he knew himself,° it had gone well.   *(to be)*
  O, he has given example for our flight
  Most grossly by his own.
ENOBARBUS Ay, are you thereabouts?° Why then, good night   *of the same mind*
  indeed!
30 CAMIDIUS Toward Peloponnesus are they fled.
SCARUS 'Tis easy to't,° and there I will attend   *to reach that place*
  What further comes.
CAMIDIUS   To Caesar will I render
  My legions and my horse. Six kings already
  Show me the way of yielding.
ENOBARBUS   I'll yet follow
35 The wounded chance° of Antony, though my reason   *fortune*
  Sits in the wind against me.°   [*Exeunt severally*]   *Opposes*

3.11

     Enter ANTONY *with Attendants*
ANTONY Hark, the land bids me tread no more upon't,
  It is ashamed to bear me. Friends, come hither.

---

1. Plague manifested in tokens (red spots presaging death).
2. Decked in red ribbons. This emendation of F's "ribau-dred"—a word of unclear meaning, if any—juxtaposes the image of Cleopatra bedecked like a horse or a whore with the red tokens of the plague.
3. When the fight could have gone either way.
4. Bitten by a gadfly; driven by a breeze.
5. Having prepared the ship's head to sail close to the wind (ready to leave).
3.11 Location: Alexandria.

I am so lated° in the world that I   *lost in the dark*
Have lost my way for ever. I have a ship
5 Laden with gold. Take that; divide it, fly,
And make your peace with Caesar.
ATTENDANTS   Fly? Not we.
ANTONY I have fled myself, and have instructed cowards
To run and show their shoulders.° Friends, be gone. *backs*
I have myself resolved upon a course
10 Which has no need of you. Be gone.
My treasure's in the harbour. Take it. O,
I followed that° I blush to look upon.   *that which*
My very hairs do mutiny, for the white
Reprove the brown for rashness, and they them° *they the others*
15 For fear and doting. Friends, be gone. You shall
Have letters from me to some friends that will
Sweep° your way for you. Pray you, look not sad, *Clear*
Nor make replies of loathness.° Take the hint° *reluctance / chance*
Which my despair proclaims. Let that be left
20 Which leaves° itself. To the seaside straightway! *ceases to be*
I will possess you of that ship and treasure.
Leave me, I pray, a little.° Pray you now, *for a brief time*
Nay, do so; for indeed I have lost command.° *authority*
Therefore I pray you; I'll see you by and by.
            [Exeunt attendants]
  [He] sits down.
  Enter CLEOPATRA *led by* CHARMIAN, [IRAS,] *and* EROS
25 EROS Nay, gentle madam, to him. Comfort him.
IRAS Do, most dear Queen.
CHARMIAN Do. Why, what else?
CLEOPATRA Let me sit down. O Juno!
  [She sits down]
ANTONY No, no, no, no, no.
30 EROS *[to* ANTONY] See you here, sir?
ANTONY O fie, fie, fie!
CHARMIAN Madam.
IRAS Madam. O good Empress!
EROS Sir, sir.
35 ANTONY Yes, my lord, yes. He° at Philippi kept *(Octavius)*
His sword e'en like a dancer,° while I struck *(for decoration only)*
The lean and wrinkled Cassius; and 'twas I
That the mad Brutus ended.° He alone   *defeated*
Dealt on lieutenantry,° and no practice had *Fought through others*
40 In the brave squares° of war. Yet now—no matter. *fine formations*
CLEOPATRA *[rising, to* CHARMIAN *and* IRAS] Ah, stand by.
EROS The Queen, my lord, the Queen.
IRAS Go to him, madam.
Speak to him. He's unqualitied°   *lost his sense of self*
With very shame.
45 CLEOPATRA   Well then, sustain me. O!
EROS Most noble sir, arise. The Queen approaches.
Her head's declined, and death will seize her but° *unless*
Your comfort makes the rescue.
ANTONY I have offended reputation;
A most unnoble swerving.°   *slippage*
50 EROS   Sir, the Queen.

ANTONY [*rising*]   O, whither hast thou led me, Egypt? See
How I convey° my shame out of thine eyes°   *steal back / sight*
By looking back° what I have left behind   *back on*
'Stroyed° in dishonour.   *Destroyed*
CLEOPATRA   O, my lord, my lord,
55   Forgive my fearful sails! I little thought
You would have followed.
ANTONY   Egypt, thou knew'st too well
My heart was to thy rudder tied by th' strings,
And thou shouldst tow me after. O'er my spirit
Thy full supremacy thou knew'st, and that
60   Thy beck° might from the bidding of the gods   *call*
Command me.
CLEOPATRA   O, my pardon!
ANTONY   Now I must
To the young man¹ send humble treaties,° dodge   *appeals*
And palter in the shifts of lowness,² who
With half the bulk o'th' world played as I pleased,
65   Making and marring fortunes. You did know
How much you were my conqueror, and that
My sword, made weak by my affection,° would   *desire*
Obey it on all cause.°   *for any reason*
CLEOPATRA   Pardon, pardon!
ANTONY   Fall° not a tear, I say. One of them rates°   *Weep / is worth*
70   All that is won and lost. Give me a kiss.
          [*He kisses her*]
Even this repays me. [*To an Attendant*]   We sent our school-
master;°   *tutor to our children*
Is a° come back? [*To* CLEOPATRA] Love, I am full of lead.   *he*
          [*Calling*] Some wine
Within there, and our viands!° Fortune knows   *food*
We scorn her most when most she offers blows.   *Exeunt*

3.12

Enter CAESAR, AGRIPPA, THIDIAS, *and* DOLABELLA, *with others*

CAESAR   Let him appear that's come from Antony.
Know you him?
DOLABELLA   Caesar, 'tis his schoolmaster;
An argument° that he is plucked, when hither   *A proof*
He sends so poor a pinion° of his wing,   *an outer feather*
5   Which° had superfluous kings for messengers   *He who*
Not many moons gone by.
          Enter AMBASSADOR *from Antony*
CAESAR   Approach and speak.
AMBASSADOR   Such as I am, I come from Antony.
I was of late as petty° to his ends   *inconsequential*
As is the morn-dew on the myrtle leaf
To his grand sea.¹
10   CAESAR   Be't so. Declare thine office.
AMBASSADOR   Lord of his fortunes he salutes thee, and

---

1. Octavius Caesar at this time (31 B.C.) was thirty-two, Antony fifty-one.
2. *dodge . . . lowness:* shuffle and play fast and loose in the shifty ways of a man brought low.
3.12 Location: Caesar's camp, Egypt.
1. In relation to the great sea that is Antony.

Requires° to live in Egypt; which not granted,   *Asks*
He lessens his requests, and to thee sues
To let him breathe between the heavens and earth,
15   A private man in Athens. This for him.
Next, Cleopatra does confess thy greatness,
Submits her to thy might, and of thee craves
The circle° of the Ptolemies for her heirs,   *crown*
Now hazarded to thy grace.°   *placed at your mercy*
CAESAR   For Antony,
20   I have no ears to his request. The Queen
Of audience nor desire shall fail, so² she
From Egypt drive her all-disgracèd friend,
Or take his life there. This if she perform
She shall not sue unheard. So to them both.
AMBASSADOR   Fortune pursue thee!
25   CAESAR   Bring° him through the bands.°   *Escort / ranks*
                                    [*Exit* AMBASSADOR, *attended*]
[*To* THIDIAS] To try thy eloquence now 'tis time. Dispatch.
From Antony win Cleopatra. Promise,
And in our name, what she requires. Add more
As thine invention° offers. Women are not   *imagination*
30   In° their best fortunes strong, but want will perjure   *While in*
The ne'er-touched vestal.³ Try thy cunning, Thidias.
Make thine own edict° for thy pains, which we   *Command your reward*
Will answer as a law.
THIDIAS   Caesar, I go.
CAESAR   Observe how Antony becomes his flaw,°   *reacts to his fall*
35   And what thou think'st his very action speaks
In every power that moves.⁴
THIDIAS   Caesar, I shall.
                    Exeunt [CAESAR *and his train at one door, and*
                                    THIDIAS *at another*]

3.13

Enter CLEOPATRA, ENOBARBUS, CHARMIAN, AND IRAS
CLEOPATRA   What shall we do, Enobarbus?
ENOBARBUS   Think,° and die.   *(about our misery)*
CLEOPATRA   Is Antony or we in fault for this?
ENOBARBUS   Antony only, that would make his will°   *lust*
Lord of his reason. What though° you fled   *What if*
5   From that great face of war, whose several ranges°   *battle lines*
Frighted each other? Why should he follow?
The itch of his affection should not then
Have nicked° his captainship, at such a point,   *bettered (gambling term)*
When half to half the world opposed, he being
10   The mooted° question. 'Twas a shame no less   *disputed*
Than was his loss, to course° your flying flags   *chase*
And leave his navy gazing.
CLEOPATRA   Prithee, peace.
Enter the AMBASSADOR *with* ANTONY

---

2. Shall not fail to receive either a hearing or fulfillment
of her wishes, as long as.
3. *want . . . vestal:* need will make the purest virgin break
her vows.

4. *his very . . . moves:* his actions themselves reveal in
every move he makes.
3.13 Location: Alexandria.

ANTONY   Is that his answer?
AMBASSADOR   Ay, my lord.
ANTONY   The Queen shall then have courtesy, so° she   *as long as*
   Will yield us up.
AMBASSADOR   He says so.
15 ANTONY   Let her know't.
   [*To* CLEOPATRA] To the boy Caesar send this grizzled head,
   And he will fill thy wishes to the brim
   With principalities.
CLEOPATRA   That head, my lord?
ANTONY [*to the* AMBASSADOR]   To him again. Tell him he wears the rose
20 Of youth upon him, from which the world should note
   Something particular.° His coin, ships, legions,   *A success of his own*
   May be a coward's, whose ministers° would prevail   *aides; underlings*
   Under the service of a child as soon°   *as well*
   As i'th' command of Caesar. I dare him therefore
25 To lay his gay caparisons° apart   *showy adornments*
   And answer me declined,[1] sword against sword,
   Ourselves alone. I'll write it. Follow me.
                        [*Exeunt* ANTONY *and* AMBASSADOR]
ENOBARBUS [*aside*]   Yes, like enough, high-battled° Caesar will   *with many troops*
   Unstate° his happiness and be staged to th' show[2]   *Overthrow*
30 Against a sworder! I see men's judgements are
   A parcel of° their fortunes, and things outward   *Consistent with*
   Do draw the inward quality after them
   To suffer all alike.° That he should dream,   *To decay together*
   Knowing all measures,[3] the full Caesar will
35 Answer° his emptiness! Caesar, thou hast subdued   *Fight; reply to*
   His judgement, too.
            Enter a SERVANT
SERVANT   A messenger from Caesar.
CLEOPATRA   What, no more ceremony? See, my women:
   Against the blown° rose may they stop their nose,   *decaying*
   That° kneeled unto the buds. Admit him, sir.   [*Exit* SERVANT]   *Who once*
40 ENOBARBUS [*aside*]   Mine honesty° and I begin to square.°   *honor / square off; argue*
   The loyalty well held° to fools does make   *given*
   Our faith mere° folly; yet he that can endure   *complete*
   To follow with allegiance a fall'n lord
   Does conquer him that did his master conquer,
   And earns a place i'th' story.
            Enter THIDIAS
45 CLEOPATRA   Caesar's will?
THIDIAS   Hear it apart.
CLEOPATRA   None but friends; say boldly.
THIDIAS   So haply° are they friends to Antony.   *possibly*
ENOBARBUS   He needs as many, sir, as Caesar has,
   Or needs not us.[4] If Caesar please, our master
50 Will leap to be his friend. For us, you know,
   Whose he is, we are: and that is Caesar's.

---

1. And meet me past my prime, in my misfortune.
2. Be displayed to the public gaze (as in the London theater or Roman gladiatorial combat).
3. Having known the best and worst of times ("all mea-

sures" of fortune, both "full[ness]" and "emptiness," line
35).
4. Or *needs not us:* If the situation is truly hopeless, he
doesn't even need our friendship.

THIDIAS   So. [*To* CLEOPATRA] Thus, then, thou most renowned:
    Caesar entreats
    Not to consider° in what case thou stand'st   *be concerned*
    Further than he is Caesar.[5]
CLEOPATRA   Go on; right royal.°   *most generous*
55   THIDIAS   He knows that you embraced not Antony
    As you did love, but as you fearèd him.
CLEOPATRA   O.
THIDIAS   The scars upon your honour therefore he
    Does pity as constrainèd° blemishes,   *involuntary*
    Not as deserved.
60   CLEOPATRA   He is a god, and knows
    What is most right. Mine honour was not yielded,
    But conquered merely.
ENOBARBUS [*aside*]   To be sure of that
    I will ask Antony. Sir, sir, thou art so leaky
    That we must leave thee to thy sinking, for
    Thy dearest quit thee.   *Exit*
65   THIDIAS   Shall I say to Caesar
    What you require° of him?—For he partly begs   *request*
    To be desired to give. It much would please him
    That of his fortunes you should make a staff
    To lean upon. But it would warm his spirits
70   To hear from me you had left Antony,
    And put your self under his shroud,°   *protection; burial sheet*
    The universal landlord.
CLEOPATRA   What's your name?
THIDIAS   My name is Thidias.
CLEOPATRA   Most kind messenger,
    Say to great Caesar this in deputation:°   *as my representative*
75   I kiss his conqu'ring hand. Tell him I am prompt
    To lay my crown at's feet, and there to kneel
    Till from his all-obeying° breath I hear   *which all obey*
    The doom of Egypt.[6]
THIDIAS   'Tis your noblest course.
    Wisdom and fortune combating together,
80   If that the former dare but what it can,[7]
    No chance may shake it. Give me grace to lay
    My duty on your hand.
        [*He kisses Cleopatra's hand*]
CLEOPATRA   Your Caesar's father oft,
    When he hath mused of taking kingdoms in,°   *subduing kingdoms*
    Bestowed his lips on that unworthy place,
    As° it rained kisses.   *As if*
        Enter ANTONY *and* ENOBARBUS
85   ANTONY   Favours, by Jove that thunders!
    What art thou, fellow?
THIDIAS   One that but performs
    The bidding of the fullest[8] man, and worthiest
    To have command obeyed.
ENOBARBUS   You will be whipped.

---

5. Beyond remembering that he is Caesar—and hence
nobly generous in forgiving insult and injury (but with a
more sinister undertone as well).

6. What he destines for Egypt and its Queen.
7. If the wise man confines his daring to what is possible.
8. Most complete; most successful.

ANTONY [*calling*]   Approach, there!—Ah, you kite!⁹ Now, gods and devils,
90   Authority melts from me of late. When I cried 'Ho!',
      Like boys unto a muss¹ kings would start forth,
      And cry 'Your will?'—Have you no ears? I am
      Antony yet.
              Enter servant[s]
                  Take hence this jack,° and whip him.   knave
ENOBARBUS [*aside to* THIDIAS]   'Tis better playing with a lion's whelp°   cub
      Than with an old one dying.
95 ANTONY   Moon and stars!
      Whip him! Were't twenty of the greatest tributaries
      That do acknowledge Caesar, should I find them
      So saucy with the hand of she here—what's her name
      Since she was Cleopatra?² Whip him, fellows,
100   Till like a boy you see him cringe° his face,   distort
      And whine aloud for mercy. Take him hence.
THIDIAS   Mark Antony—
ANTONY   Tug him away. Being whipped,
      Bring him again. This jack of Caesar's shall
      Bear us an errand to him.   *Exeunt [servants] with* THIDIAS
105   You were half blasted° ere I knew you. Ha,   decayed
      Have I my pillow left unpressed in Rome,
      Forborne the getting° of a lawful race,   begetting
      And by a gem of women, to be abused
      By one that looks on feeders?°   parasites; servants
110 CLEOPATRA   Good my lord—
ANTONY   You have been a boggler° ever.   fickle one
      But when we in our viciousness grow hard—
      O misery on't!—the wise gods seel³ our eyes,
      In our own filth drop our clear judgements, make us
115   Adore our errors, laugh at's while we strut
      To our confusion.
CLEOPATRA   O, is't come to this?
ANTONY   I found you as a morsel cold upon
      Dead Caesar's trencher;° nay, you were a fragment°   plate / leftover
      Of Gnaeus Pompey's,⁴ besides what hotter hours
120   Unregistered in vulgar fame° you have   base gossip
      Luxuriously° picked out. For I am sure,   Wantonly
      Though you can guess what temperance should be,
      You know not what it is.
CLEOPATRA   Wherefore is this?
ANTONY   To let a fellow that will take rewards
125   And say 'God quit° you' be familiar with   repay
      My playfellow your hand, this kingly seal
      And plighter° of high hearts! O that I were   pledger
      Upon the hill of Basan to outroar
      The hornèd herd!⁵ For I have savage cause,
130   And to proclaim it civilly were like
      A haltered° neck which does the hangman thank   in the noose

9. Predator or whore, addressed to either Cleopatra or
Thidias.
1. Game in which small items were tossed to the ground
for children to snatch and grab.
2. Antony's question suggests that since Cleopatra's behavior has changed, her name must have changed as well.
3. Blind: hawks' eyes were sealed (sewn up) to tame

them.
4. Older brother of the Pompey of the play and son of
Pompey the Great. See note to 1.5.31.
5. Alluding to the bulls of the hill of Basan in Psalms
68:15 and 22:12; Antony sees himself as a cuckold (a man
whose wife has committed adultery), conventionally imagined with horns.

For being yare° about him.   *swift*
        Enter a SERVANT *with* THIDIAS
                            Is he whipped?
SERVANT   Soundly, my lord.
ANTONY   Cried he, and begged a pardon?
135   SERVANT   He did ask favour.
ANTONY [*to* THIDIAS]   If that thy father live, let him repent
    Thou wast not made his daughter; and be thou sorry
    To follow Caesar in his triumph, since
    Thou hast been whipped for following him. Henceforth
140   The white hand of a lady fever thee,[6]
    Shake thou to look on't. Get thee back to Caesar;
    Tell him thy entertainment.° Look° thou say   *treatment / See that*
    He makes me angry with him, for he seems
    Proud and disdainful, harping on what I am,
145   Not what he knew I was. He makes me angry,
    And at this time most easy 'tis to do't,
    When my good stars that were my former guides
    Have empty left their orbs,° and shot their fires   *spheres*
    Into th'abyss of hell. If he mislike
150   My speech and what is done, tell him he has
    Hipparchus, my enfranchèd° bondman, whom   *emancipated*
    He may at pleasure whip, or hang, or torture,
    As he shall like, to quit° me. Urge it thou.   *requite*
    Hence, with thy stripes,° be gone!   *Exit* [SERVANT *with*] THIDIAS   *wounds*
155   CLEOPATRA   Have you done yet?
ANTONY   Alack, our terrene moon[7]
    Is now eclipsed, and it portends alone
    The fall of Antony.
CLEOPATRA [*aside*]   I must stay his time.[8]
ANTONY   To flatter Caesar would you mingle eyes
    With one that ties his points?[9]
160   CLEOPATRA   Not know me yet?
ANTONY   Cold-hearted toward me?
CLEOPATRA   Ah, dear, if I be so,
    From my cold heart let heaven engender hail,
    And poison it in the source, and the first stone
    Drop in my neck: as it determines,° so   *turns to liquid*
165   Dissolve my life! The next Caesarion smite,
    Till by degrees the memory of my womb,°   *my children*
    Together with my brave Egyptians all,
    By the discandying° of this pelleted storm   *dissolving*
    Lie graveless till the flies and gnats of Nile
    Have buried them for prey!
170   ANTONY   I am satisfied.
    Caesar sits down in° Alexandria, where   *besieges*
    I will oppose his fate.[1] Our force by land
    Hath nobly held; our severed navy too
    Have knit again, and fleet,° threat'ning most sea-like.   *are afloat*
175   Where hast thou been, my heart?° Dost thou hear, lady?   *bravery*
    If from the field I shall return once more

6. May the white hand of a lady make you feverish.
7. Terrestrial moon goddess—Cleopatra.
8. I must hold my tongue till he is over his rage.

9. *would . . . points*: would you flirt with one of his servants? *points*: laces (attaching stockings to other clothing).
1. I will resist his apparently destined victory.

To kiss these lips, I will appear in blood.°   *bloody; vigorous*
I and my sword will earn our chronicle.°   *historical reputation*
There's hope in't yet.
CLEOPATRA   That's my brave lord.
180 ANTONY   I will be treble-sinewed, hearted, breathed,
And fight maliciously;° for when mine hours   *furiously*
Were nice² and lucky, men did ransom° lives   *buy their*
Of° me for jests;° but now I'll set my teeth,   *From / trinkets*
And send to darkness all that stop me. Come,
185 Let's have one other gaudy° night. Call to me   *merry*
All my sad captains. Fill our bowls once more.
Let's mock the midnight bell.³
CLEOPATRA   It is my birthday.
I had thought to've held it poor,° but since my lord *modestly commemorated it*
Is Antony again, I will be Cleopatra.
190 ANTONY   We will yet do well.
CLEOPATRA   Call all his noble captains to my lord!
ANTONY   Do so. We'll speak to them, and tonight I'll force
The wine peep through their scars. Come on, my queen,
There's sap in't° yet. The next time I do fight   *vigor in (our cause)*
195 I'll make death love me, for I will contend°   *do battle*
Even with his pestilent° scythe.   *Exeunt [all but* ENOBARBUS] *plague-dealing*
ENOBARBUS   Now he'll outstare° the lightning. To be furious *stare down*
Is to be frighted out of fear, and in that mood
The dove will peck the estridge;° and I see still° *a kind of hawk / always*
200 A diminution in our captain's brain
Restores his heart. When valour preys on reason,
It eats the sword it fights with. I will seek
Some way to leave him.   *Exit*

4.1

Enter CAESAR, *reading a letter, with* AGRIPPA, MAECENAS,
   and his army
CAESAR   He calls me boy, and chides as° he had power   *as though*
To beat me out of Egypt. My messenger
He hath whipped with rods, dares me to personal combat,
Caesar to Antony. Let the old ruffian know
5 I have many other ways to die; meantime,
Laugh at° his challenge.   *Mock*
MAECENAS   Caesar must think,
When one so great begins to rage, he's hunted
Even to falling. Give him no breath,° but now   *time to catch breath*
Make boot° of his distraction.° Never anger   *Take advantage / fury*
Made good guard for itself.
10 CAESAR   Let our best heads°   *officers*
Know that tomorrow the last of many battles
We mean to fight. Within our files° there are,   *troops*
Of those that served Mark Antony but late,
Enough to fetch him in.° See it done,   *capture him*
15 And feast the army. We have store to do't,
And they have earned the waste.° Poor Antony! *Exeunt*   *expense*

---

2. *Were nice:* Permitted me to pick and choose, to act   the death knell that fate seems to ring for us.
with noble generosity; were lascivious; were pampered.   4.1 Location: Caesar's camp, before Alexandria.
3. Let's make a mockery of the hour by revelry; let's mock

4.2

Enter ANTONY, CLEOPATRA, ENOBARBUS, CHARMIAN,
IRAS, ALEXAS, *with others*

ANTONY He will not fight with me, Domitius?

ENOBARBUS   No.

ANTONY Why should he not?

ENOBARBUS He thinks, being twenty times of better fortune,
He is twenty men to one.

ANTONY   Tomorrow, soldier,
5   By sea and land I'll fight. Or° I will live   Either
Or bathe my dying honour in the blood
Shall make it live again. Woot thou° fight well?   Will you

ENOBARBUS I'll strike, and cry 'Take all!'°   Winner take all

ANTONY   Well said. Come on!
Call forth my household servants. Let's tonight
Be bounteous at our meal.

Enter SERVITORS
10   Give me thy hand.
Thou hast been rightly honest; so hast thou,
Thou, and thou, and thou; you have served me well,
And kings have been your fellows.°   companions

CLEOPATRA [*to* ENOBARBUS]   What means this?

ENOBARBUS [*to* CLEOPATRA]   'Tis one of those odd tricks which
sorrow shoots
Out of the mind.

15   ANTONY [*to a* SERVITOR]   And thou art honest too.
I wish I could be made° so many men,   split up into
And all of you clapped up together in
An Antony, that I might do you service
So good as you have done.

SERVITORS   The gods forbid!

20   ANTONY Well, my good fellows, wait on me tonight.
Scant not my cups, and make as much of me
As when mine empire was your fellow° too,   fellow servant
And suffered° my command.   obeyed

CLEOPATRA [*aside to* ENOBARBUS]   What does he mean?

ENOBARBUS [*aside to* CLEOPATRA]
To make his followers weep.

ANTONY   Tend me tonight.
25   Maybe it is the period° of your duty.   end
Haply° you shall not see me more; or if,°   Maybe / if you do
A mangled shadow.° Perchance tomorrow   phantom
You'll serve another master. I look on you
As one that takes his leave. Mine honest friends,
30   I turn you not away, but, like a master
Married to your good service, stay till death.
Tend me tonight two hours. I ask no more;
And the gods yield° you for't!   reward

ENOBARBUS   What mean you, sir,
To give them this discomfort? Look, they weep,
35   And I, an ass, am onion-eyed.° For shame,   weepy
Transform us not to women.

ANTONY   Ho, ho, ho,
     Now the witch take° me if I meant it thus!   *bewitch*
     Grace grow where those drops fall. My hearty friends,
     You take me in too dolorous a sense;
40   For I spake to you for your comfort, did desire you
     To burn this night with torches. Know, my hearts,
     I hope well of tomorrow, and will lead you
     Where rather I'll expect victorious life
     Than death and honour. Let's to supper, come,
45   And drown consideration.°   *Exeunt*   *serious thoughts*

4.3

Enter a company of SOLDIERS

FIRST SOLDIER   Brother, good night. Tomorrow is the day.
SECOND SOLDIER   It will determine one way. Fare you well.°   *Good luck*
     Heard you of nothing strange about° the streets?   *in*
FIRST SOLDIER   Nothing. What news?
5   SECOND SOLDIER   Belike° 'tis but a rumour. Good night to you.   *Most likely*
FIRST SOLDIER   Well, sir, good night.
     [Enter] other SOLDIERS, *meet[ing them]*
SECOND SOLDIER   Soldiers, have careful watch.
THIRD SOLDIER   And you. Good night, good night.
     They place themselves in every corner of the stage
SECOND SOLDIER   Here we; an if° tomorrow   *an if = if*
     Our navy thrive, I have an absolute hope
     Our landmen will stand up.°   *make a stand*
FIRST SOLDIER   'Tis a brave army,
     And full of purpose.
     Music of the hautboys° is under the stage   *oboe*
SECOND SOLDIER   Peace, what noise?
10   FIRST SOLDIER   List, list!
SECOND SOLDIER   Hark!
FIRST SOLDIER   Music i'th' air.
THIRD SOLDIER   Under the earth.
FOURTH SOLDIER   It signs° well, does it not?   *bodes*
THIRD SOLDIER   No.
FIRST SOLDIER   Peace, I say!
     What should this mean?
SECOND SOLDIER   'Tis the god Hercules, whom Antony loved,
     Now leaves him.
15   FIRST SOLDIER   Walk. Let's see if other watchmen
     Do hear what we do.
SECOND SOLDIER   How now, masters?°   *good sirs*
ALL *(speak[ing] together)*[1]   How now?
     How now? Do you hear this?
FIRST SOLDIER   Ay. Is't not strange?
THIRD SOLDIER   Do you hear, masters? Do you hear?
FIRST SOLDIER   Follow the noise so far as we have quarter.[2]
     Let's see how it will give off.°   *end*
20   ALL   Content. 'Tis strange.   *Exeunt*

4.3 Location: Outside Cleopatra's palace, Alexandria.
1. Individual soldiers probably address different questions and comments to one another rather than speaking in chorus.
2. As far as the limit of our watch.

4.4

Enter ANTONY *and* CLEOPATRA, *with* [CHARMIAN *and*]
others

ANTONY [*calling*]   Eros, mine armour, Eros!

CLEOPATRA   Sleep a little.

ANTONY   No, my chuck.° Eros, come, mine armour, Eros!   *my dear*

Enter EROS [*with armour*]

    Come, good fellow, put thine iron on.¹

    If fortune be not ours today, it is

    Because we brave° her. Come.   *dare*

5   CLEOPATRA   Nay, I'll help, too.

    What's this for?

ANTONY   Ah, let be, let be! Thou art

    The armourer of my heart. False, false!° This, this!   *wrong*

CLEOPATRA   Sooth, la, I'll help. Thus it must be.

    [*She helps* ANTONY *to arm*]

ANTONY   Well, well,

    We shall thrive now. Seest thou, my good fellow?

    Go put on thy defences.°   *armor*

10 EROS   Briefly,° sir.   *Soon*

CLEOPATRA   Is not this buckled well?

ANTONY   Rarely, rarely.

    He that unbuckles this, till we do please

    To doff't° for our repose, shall hear a storm.   *remove it*

    Thou fumblest, Eros, and my queen's a squire°   *an attendant to a knight*

15 More tight° at this than thou. Dispatch.° O love,   *able / Finish*

    That thou couldst see my wars today, and knew'st

    The royal occupation! Thou shouldst see

    A workman° in't.   *An expert*

Enter an armed SOLDIER

                Good morrow to thee. Welcome.

    Thou look'st like him that knows a warlike charge.°   *purpose*

20 To business that we love we rise betime,°   *early*

    And go to't with delight.

SOLDIER   A thousand, sir,

    Early though't be, have on their riveted trim,°   *armor*

    And at the port expect you.

Shout [*within*]. *Trumpets flourish. Enter* CAPTAINS *and*
SOLDIERS

CAPTAIN   The morn is fair. Good morrow, General.

SOLDIERS   Good morrow, General.

25 ANTONY   'Tis well blown,² lads.

    This morning, like the spirit of a youth

    That means to be of note, begins betimes.

    So, so. Come, give me that. This way. Well said.°   *Well done*

    Fare thee well, dame. Whate'er becomes of me,

    This is a soldier's kiss.

    [*He kisses* CLEOPATRA]

30   Rebukable

    And worthy shameful check° it were to stand   *reprimand*

    On more mechanic° compliment. I'll leave thee   *coarse*

    Now like a man of steel. You that will fight,

4.4 Location: Cleopatra's palace.   2. Well sounded (of the trumpet); well started (of the
1. Clad me in that piece of armor of mine that you have.   morning).

Follow me close. I'll bring you to't. Adieu.

Exeunt [all but CLEOPATRA *and* CHARMIAN]

CHARMIAN   Please you retire to your chamber?

35   CLEOPATRA   Lead me.
He goes forth gallantly. That he and Caesar might
Determine this great war in single fight!
Then, Antony—but now! Well, on.   *Exeunt*

4.5

Trumpets sound. Enter ANTONY *and* EROS [*meeting a*
SOLDIER]

SOLDIER   The gods make this a happy° day to Antony!   fortunate
ANTONY   Would thou and those thy scars had once° prevailed   earlier
To make me fight at land!
SOLDIER   Hadst thou done so,
The kings that have revolted,° and the soldier   deserted
5   That has this morning left thee, would have still
Followed thy heels.
ANTONY   Who's gone this morning?
SOLDIER   Who? One ever near thee. Call for Enobarbus,
He shall not hear thee, or from Caesar's camp
Say 'I am none of thine'.
ANTONY   What sayest thou?
SOLDIER   Sir, he is with Caesar.
10   EROS [*to* ANTONY]   Sir, his chests and treasure
He has not with him.
ANTONY   Is he gone?
SOLDIER   Most certain.
ANTONY   Go, Eros, send his treasure after. Do it.
Detain no jot, I charge thee. Write to him—
I will subscribe°—gentle adieus and greetings.   sign my name
15   Say that I wish he never find more cause
To change a master. O, my fortunes have
Corrupted honest men! Dispatch. Enobarbus!   *Exeunt*

4.6

Flourish. Enter AGRIPPA, CAESAR, *with* ENOBARBUS *and*
DOLABELLA

CAESAR   Go forth, Agrippa, and begin the fight.
Our will is Antony be took alive.
Make it so known.
AGRIPPA   Caesar, I shall.   [*Exit*]
CAESAR   The time of universal peace is near.[1]
5   Prove this° a prosp'rous day, the three-nooked world[2]   If this proves
Shall bear the olive° freely.   sign of peace
         Enter a MESSENGER
MESSENGER   Antony
Is come into the field.
CAESAR   Go charge Agrippa

4.5 Location: Antony's camp, Alexandria.
4.6 Location: Caesar's camp, Alexandria.
1. Octavius Caesar, later the Emperor Augustus, was known for the *pax Romana*—Roman peace—of his reign; the phrase also alludes to the birth of Christ, which occurred while Augustus was emperor. See the Introduction.

2. Three-cornered world. Referring (in descending order of probability) to Europe, Asia, Africa (the triumvirate's holdings); the three races descended from Noah's sons (Japhet, Shem, Ham); earth, sea, sky. The three races of Noah can to an extent be superimposed on the three continents and may connect with the later religious connotations of the Roman Empire. See the previous note.

Plant those that have revolted in the van,°   *front lines*
That Antony may seem to spend his fury
10 Upon himself.°   *On his former troops*
      Exeunt [MESSENGER *at one door,* CAESAR *and*
            DOLABELLA *at another*]
ENOBARBUS Alexas did revolt, and went to Jewry on
 Affairs of Antony; there did dissuade°   *persuade*
 Great Herod to incline himself to Caesar
 And leave his master, Antony. For this pains,
15 Caesar hath hanged him. Camidius and the rest
 That fell away have entertainment° but   *employment*
 No honourable trust. I have done ill,
 Of which I do accuse myself so sorely
 That I will joy no more.
     Enter a SOLDIER *of Caesar's*
SOLDIER   Enobarbus, Antony
20 Hath after thee sent all thy treasure, with
 His bounty overplus. The messenger
 Came on my guard,° and at thy tent is now   *on my watch*
 Unloading of his mules.
ENOBARBUS I give it you.
25 SOLDIER Mock not, Enobarbus,
 I tell you true. Best you safed the bringer
 Out of the host.³ I must attend mine office,°   *look after my duties*
 Or would have done't myself. Your Emperor
 Continues still a Jove.   *Exit*
30 ENOBARBUS I am alone the° villain of the earth, *the single greatest*
 And feel I am so most.° O Antony,   *I feel it most*
 Thou mine of bounty, how wouldst thou have paid
 My better service, when my turpitude
 Thou dost so crown with gold! This blows° my heart. *swells; bursts*
35 If swift thought° break it not, a swifter mean° *regret / means (suicide)*
 Shall outstrike thought; but thought will do't, I feel.
 I fight against thee? No, I will go seek
 Some ditch wherein to die. The foul'st best fits
 My latter part of life.   *Exit*

4.7

 Alarum. Enter AGRIPPA [*with*] *drum*[*mer*]*s and trum-*
 pet[*er*]*s*
AGRIPPA Retire!° We have engaged our selves too far. *Sound the retreat*
 Caesar himself has work,° and our oppression *is sorely challenged*
 Exceeds what we expected.   *Exeunt*

4.8

 Alarums. Enter ANTONY, *and* SCARUS *wounded*
SCARUS O my brave Emperor, this is fought indeed!
 Had we done so at first, we had droven them home
 With clouts° about their heads.   *bandages; blows*
ANTONY   Thou bleed'st apace.

---

3. *Best . . . host:* It would be best if you ensured safe con- 4.7 Location: The battlefield, Alexandria.
duct through the lines for the messenger who brought the 4.8 Location: Scene continues.
treasure.

SCARUS I had a wound here that was like a T,
   But now 'tis made an H.¹
         [*Retreat sounded*] *far off*
5 ANTONY   They do retire.
SCARUS We'll beat 'em into bench-holes.° I have yet   latrine holes
   Room for six scotches° more.   gashes
         Enter EROS
EROS They are beaten, sir, and our advantage serves
   For a fair victory.
SCARUS   Let us score° their backs   slash
10 And snatch 'em up as° we take hares, behind.   in the same way as
   'Tis sport to maul a runner.°   coward
ANTONY [*to* EROS]   I will reward thee
   Once for thy sprightly° comfort, and tenfold   cheerful
   For thy good valour. Come thee on.
SCARUS   I'll halt° after.   *Exeunt*   limp

                    4.9
         Alarum. Enter ANTONY *again in a march;* [*drummers
         and trumpeters;*] SCARUS, *with others*
ANTONY We have beat him to his camp. Run one before,
   And let the Queen know of our gests.°   [*Exit a soldier*]   deeds
                              Tomorrow,
   Before the sun shall see's, we'll spill the blood
   That has today escaped. I thank you all,
5 For doughty-handed° are you, and have fought   brave
   Not as° you served the cause, but as't had been   as though
   Each man's like mine. You have shown all Hectors.¹
   Enter the city, clip° your wives, your friends,   embrace
   Tell them your feats whilst they with joyful tears
10 Wash the congealment from your wounds, and kiss
   The honoured gashes whole.
         Enter CLEOPATRA
[*To* SCARUS]   Give me thy hand.
   To this great fairy° I'll commend thy acts,   enchantress
   Make her thanks bless thee.
[*To* CLEOPATRA, *embracing her*]   O thou day° o'th' world,   light
   Chain mine armed neck; leap thou, attire and all,
15 Through proof of harness° to my heart, and there   armor of proven strength
   Ride on the pants° triumphing.   heartbeats
CLEOPATRA   Lord of lords!
   O infinite virtue,° com'st thou smiling from   valor
   The world's great snare uncaught?
ANTONY   My nightingale,
   We have beat them to their beds. What, girl, though grey
20 Do something° mingle with our younger brown, yet ha' we   somewhat
   A brain that nourishes our nerves,° and can   muscles
   Get goal for goal of youth.² Behold this man.
   Commend unto his lips thy favouring hand;
   Kiss it, my warrior.

---

1. *wound . . . H:* the wound was originally shaped like a T, but another gash across its bottom has made it look like an H turned sideways (punning on "ache," pronounced "aitch").
4.9 Location: Scene continues.

1. You have all fought like Hector (the greatest of the Trojan warriors).
2. Compete with any youth. Antony is clearly referring here to the "boy" Caesar, but also, possibly, to his own boyhood.

[SCARUS *kisses Cleopatra's hand*]
                     He hath fought today
25   As if a god, in hate of mankind, had
     Destroyed in such a shape.
     CLEOPATRA   I'll give thee, friend,
     An armour all of gold. It was a king's.
     ANTONY   He has deserved it, were it carbuncled°   *bejeweled*
     Like holy Phoebus' car.° Give me thy hand.   *the sun god's chariot*
30   Through Alexandria make a jolly march.
     Bear our hacked targets like° the men that owe° them.   *shields as befits / own*
     Had our great palace the capacity
     To camp° this host, we all would sup together   *put up*
     And drink carouses to the next day's fate,
35   Which promises royal° peril. Trumpeters,   *great*
     With brazen din blast you the city's ear;
     Make mingle with our rattling taborins,°   *small drums*
     That heaven and earth may strike their sounds together,
     Applauding our approach.   [*Trumpets sound.*] *Exeunt*

4.10

             Enter a SENTRY *and his company;* ENOBARBUS *follows*
     SENTRY   If we be not relieved within this hour
     We must return to th' court of guard.° The night   *guardroom*
     Is shiny,° and they say we shall embattle°   *bright / go to battle*
     By th' second hour i'th' morn.
     FIRST WATCH   This last day was
     A shrewd° one to's.   *bad*
5   ENOBARBUS   O bear me witness, night—
     SECOND WATCH   What man is this?
     FIRST WATCH   Stand close,° and list° him. *hidden / listen to*
     ENOBARBUS   Be witness to me, O thou blessèd moon,
     When men revolted° shall upon record   *deserters*
     Bear hateful memory, poor Enobarbus did
     Before thy face repent.
     SENTRY   Enobarbus?
10   SECOND WATCH   Peace; hark further.
     ENOBARBUS   O sovereign mistress of true melancholy,°   *(the moon)*
     The poisonous damp of night disponge° upon me,   *pour down*
     That life, a very rebel to my will,
     May hang no longer on me. Throw my heart
15   Against the flint and hardness of my fault,
     Which,° being dried with grief, will break to powder,   *(his heart)*
     And finish all foul thoughts. O Antony,
     Nobler than my revolt is infamous,
     Forgive me in thine own particular,[1]
20   But let the world rank me in register°   *its records*
     A master-leaver and a fugitive.°   *deserter*
     O Antony! O Antony!   [*He dies*][2]
     FIRST WATCH   Let's speak to him.

4.10 Location: Caesar's camp.
1. In whatever aspects of this business concern only you.
2. Depending on how this moment is played, Enobarbus's death may not be obvious either to those onstage or
to the audience.

SENTRY   Let's hear him, for the things he speaks
　　　May concern Caesar.
25　SECOND WATCH　　　　Let's do so. But he sleeps.
　　SENTRY   Swoons, rather; for so bad a prayer as his
　　　Was never yet for° sleep.　　　　　　　　　　　　　*in preparation for*
　　FIRST WATCH　　　　　Go we to him.
　　SECOND WATCH   Awake, sir, awake; speak to us.
　　FIRST WATCH　　　　　　　　Hear you, sir?
　　SENTRY   The hand of death hath raught° him.　　　　　*taken*
　　　　Drums afar off
　　　　　　　　　　　　Hark, the drums
30　Demurely° wake the sleepers. Let us bear him　　　*With subdued sound*
　　　To th' court of guard; he is of note. Our hour
　　　Is fully out.°　　　　　　　　　　　　　　　　　*expired*
　　SECOND WATCH   Come on, then. He may recover yet.
　　　　　　　　　　Exeunt [with the body]

4.11
　　　　Enter ANTONY and SCARUS with their army
　　ANTONY   Their preparation is today by sea;
　　　We please them not by land.
　　SCARUS　　　　　　　For both, my lord.
　　ANTONY   I would they'd fight i'th' fire or i'th' air;
　　　We'd fight there too.¹ But this it is: our foot°　　*foot soldiers*
5　Upon the hills adjoining to the city
　　　Shall stay with us. Order for sea is given.
　　　They have put forth° the haven—　　　　　　*departed from*
　　　Where their appointment° we may best discover,　*purpose; battle plan*
　　　And look on their endeavour.　　*Exeunt*

4.12
　　　　Enter CAESAR and his army
　　CAESAR   But being° charged, we will be still° by land—　*unless we're / inactive*
　　　Which, as I take't, we shall, for his best force
　　　Is forth to man his galleys. To the vales,°　　　　　*valleys*
　　　And hold our best advantage.°　　*Exeunt*　*take the best position*

4.13
　　　　Alarum afar off, as at a sea fight.
　　　　Enter ANTONY and SCARUS
　　ANTONY   Yet they are not joined.° Where yon pine does stand　*(in battle)*
　　　I shall discover all. I'll bring thee word
　　　Straight° how 'tis like° to go.　　*Exit*　*Promptly / likely*
　　SCARUS　　　　　　Swallows have built
　　　In Cleopatra's sails their nests. The augurs°　　　*soothsayers*
5　Say they know not, they cannot tell, look grimly,
　　　And dare not speak their knowledge. Antony
　　　Is valiant, and dejected, and by starts
　　　His fretted° fortunes give him hope and fear　　*diminished*
　　　Of what he has and has not.
　　　　Enter ANTONY

4.11 Location: This and the next two scenes take place　　1. As well as in the other elements, earth and water.
on the battlefield.

ANTONY   All is lost.
10   This foul Egyptian hath betrayèd me.
      My fleet hath yielded to the foe, and yonder
      They cast their caps up, and carouse together
      Like friends long lost. Triple-turned whore![1] 'Tis thou
      Hast sold me to this novice, and my heart
15   Makes only wars on thee. Bid them all fly;
      For when I am revenged upon my charm,°   sorceress
      I have done all. Bid them all fly. Be gone.   [Exit SCARUS]
      O sun, thy uprise shall I see no more.
      Fortune and Antony part here; even here
20   Do we shake hands.° All come to this? The hearts   (before parting)
      That spanieled° me at heels, to whom I gave   fawned upon
      Their wishes, do discandy,° melt their sweets   melt
      On blossoming Caesar; and this pine° is barked[2]   (Antony)
      That overtopped them all. Betrayed I am.
25   O this false soul of Egypt! This grave° charm,   deadly
      Whose eye becked° forth my wars and called them home,   beckoned
      Whose bosom was my crownet,° my chief end,°   coronet / reward
      Like a right° gipsy hath at fast and loose[3]   true
      Beguiled° me to the very heart of loss.°   cheated / ruin
      What, Eros, Eros!
                    Enter CLEOPATRA
30   Ah, thou spell! Avaunt.°   Leave me
CLEOPATRA   Why is my lord enraged against his love?
ANTONY   Vanish, or I shall give thee thy deserving
      And blemish Caesar's triumph.° Let him take thee   triumphal procession
      And hoist thee up to the shouting plebeians;
35   Follow his chariot, like the greatest spot°   taint
      Of all thy sex; most monster-like be shown
      For poor'st diminutives,[4] for dolts, and let
      Patient Octavia plough thy visage up
      With her preparèd° nails.   Exit CLEOPATRA   specially sharpened
                        'Tis well thou'rt gone,
40   If it be well to live. But better 'twere
      Thou fell'st into° my fury, for one death   a victim to
      Might have prevented many. Eros, ho!
      The shirt of Nessus[5] is upon me. Teach me,
      Alcides, thou mine ancestor, thy rage.
45   Let me lodge Lichas on the horns o'th' moon,
      And with those hands that grasped the heaviest club
      Subdue my worthiest self. The witch shall die.
      To the young Roman boy she hath sold me, and I fall
      Under this plot. She dies for't. Eros, ho!   Exit

4.13
1. Cleopatra is "triple-turned" because disloyal to three (Julius Caesar, Pompey, and Antony); alluding to her changing political allegiances.
2. Stripped of its bark (and so killed).
3. *fast and loose*: a cheating game played by gypsies.
4. For the benefit of (in place of) the lowest people (dwarfs).
5. Hercules, also known as Alcides (line 44), with whom Antony is repeatedly compared, fatally wounded the centaur Nessus for trying to rape his wife, Deianira. Nessus gave her some of his blood, falsely claiming that it would act as a love potion. Years later, she smeared some of the deadly blood on a shirt and sent it to Hercules. Blaming Lichas (line 45), who had brought the shirt, Hercules cast him into the sea. When she realized what she had done, Deianira killed herself.

4.14

Enter CLEOPATRA, CHARMIAN, IRAS, MARDIAN

CLEOPATRA Help me, my women! O, he's more mad
Than Telamon for his shield;[1] the boar of Thessaly[2]
Was never so embossed.[3]

CHARMIAN   To th' monument![4]
There lock yourself, and send him word you are dead.
5 The soul and body rive° not more in parting   *separate*
Than greatness going off.°   *leaving someone*

CLEOPATRA   To th' monument!
Mardian, go tell him I have slain myself.
Say that the last I spoke was 'Antony',
And word it, prithee, piteously. Hence, Mardian,
10 And bring me° how he takes my death. To th' monument!   *bring me word*

Exeunt

4.15

Enter ANTONY *and* EROS

ANTONY Eros, thou yet behold'st me?

EROS   Ay, noble lord.

ANTONY Sometime we see a cloud that's dragonish,°   *in a dragon's shape*
A vapour sometime like a bear or lion,
A towered citadel, a pendent° rock,   *hanging*
5 A forkèd mountain, or blue promontory
With trees upon't that nod unto the world
And mock our eyes with air. Thou hast seen these signs;
They are black vesper's pageants.[1]

EROS   Ay, my lord.

ANTONY That which is now a horse even with a thought
10 The rack distains,° and makes it indistinct   *cloud dims*
As water is in water.

EROS   It does, my lord.

ANTONY My good knave° Eros, now thy captain is   *boy*
Even such a body. Here I am Antony,
Yet cannot hold this visible shape, my knave.
15 I made these wars for Egypt, and the Queen—
Whose heart I thought I had, for she had mine,
Which whilst it was mine had annexed unto't
A million more, now lost—she, Eros, has
Packed cards° with Caesar, and false-played my glory   *Stacked the deck*
20 Unto an enemy's triumph.°   *victory; trump card*
Nay, weep not, gentle Eros. There is left us
Ourselves to end ourselves.

Enter MARDIAN

                            O thy vile lady,
She has robbed me of my sword!°   *valor; manhood*

MARDIAN   No, Antony,

4.14 Location: Alexandria.
1. Ajax, also known as Telemon, went mad and killed
himself after the capture of Troy when he was not
awarded Achilles' shield.
2. Sent by Diana to lay waste Calydon (killed by Mel-
eager).
3. Was never driven to such extremity (a hunting term).

4. The tomb Cleopatra had built forseeing her death.
4.15 Location: Alexandria.
1. Illusory spectacles heralding the approach of night—
with a probable allusion to funerals and death. (Pageants
were originally moving stages on which miracle plays
were presented.)

My mistress loved thee, and her fortunes mingled
With thine entirely.

25 ANTONY   Hence, saucy° eunuch, peace!   *disrespectful*
     She hath betrayed me, and shall die the death.
   MARDIAN   Death of one person can be paid but once,
     And that she has discharged. What thou wouldst do
     Is done unto thy hand.° The last she spake   *for you*
30   Was 'Antony, most noble Antony!'
     Then in the midst a tearing groan did break
     The name of Antony. It was divided
     Between her heart and lips.[2] She rendered° life,   *gave up*
     Thy name so buried in her.
   ANTONY   Dead, then?
   MARDIAN   Dead.
35 ANTONY   Unarm, Eros.[3] The long day's task is done,
     And we must sleep. [*To* MARDIAN] That thou depart'st hence safe
     Does pay thy labour richly. Go.   *Exit* MARDIAN
                     Off, pluck off.
     [EROS *helps* ANTONY *to unarm*]
     The seven-fold shield[4] of Ajax cannot keep
     The battery° from my heart. O, cleave, my sides!   *onslaught*
40   Heart, once be stronger than thy continent;°   *container*
     Crack thy frail case. Apace,° Eros, apace.   *Quickly*
     No more a soldier. Bruisèd pieces,° do;   *of armor*
     You have been nobly borne.—From me a while.   *Exit* EROS
     I will o'ertake thee, Cleopatra, and
45   Weep for my pardon. So it must be, for now
     All length° is torture. Since the torch° is out,   *longer life / (Cleopatra)*
     Lie down, and stray no farther. Now all labour
     Mars what it does; yea, very force entangles
     Itself with strength.[5] Seal,° then, and all is done.   *Finish the deed*
50   Eros!—I come, my queen.—Eros!—Stay for me.
     Where souls do couch on flowers[6] we'll hand in hand,
     And with our sprightly port° make the ghosts gaze.   *cheerful stance*
     Dido and her Aeneas shall want troops,[7]
     And all the haunt° be ours. Come, Eros, Eros!   *place; ghosts*
       Enter EROS
   EROS   What would my lord?
55 ANTONY   Since Cleopatra died
     I have lived in such dishonour that the gods
     Detest my baseness. I, that with my sword
     Quartered the world, and o'er green Neptune's back°   *on the sea*
     With ships made cities,[8] condemn myself to lack°   *for lacking*
60   The courage of a woman; less noble mind
     Than she which by her death our Caesar tells
     'I am conqueror of myself.' Thou art sworn, Eros,

---

2. *It . . . lips:* It was half-uttered.
3. Here and in the following lines, the symbolic appropriateness of this historical figure's name ("Eros" means "love") is stressed.
4. A shield made of brass lined with six thicknesses of oxhide.
5. *very . . . strength:* strength defeats itself by its own exertions.
6. Lie ("couch") in the Elysian fields of the blessed dead in the mythological underworld.

7. Shall lack followers. Dido, Queen of Carthage, commits suicide after being abandoned by her lover Aeneas, legendary Trojan founder of Rome, in Virgil's *Aeneid*; they are not reconciled in the underworld. Dido, who originally hailed from Phoenicia, is meant to recall Cleopatra. In leaving her, Aeneas places public responsibility above personal desire—unlike Antony but very much like Octavius Caesar, whom Virgil intended him to resemble.
8. Put so many ships to sea that the fleet resembled a city.

That when the exigent° should come, which now   *urgent need*
Is come indeed—when I should see behind me
65   Th'inevitable prosecution° of   *pursuit*
Disgrace and horror—that on my command
Thou then wouldst kill me. Do't. The time is come.
Thou strik'st not me; 'tis Caesar thou defeat'st.
Put colour in thy cheek.
EROS   The gods withhold me!°   *God forbid*
70   Shall I do that which all the Parthian darts,
Though enemy, lost aim and could not?
ANTONY   Eros,
Wouldst thou be windowed° in great Rome and see   *put in a window*
Thy master thus with pleached° arms, bending down   *tied*
His corrigible° neck, his face subdued   *submissive*
75   To penetrative° shame, whilst the wheeled seat°   *piercing / chariot*
Of fortunate Caesar, drawn before him, branded
His baseness that ensued?[9]
EROS   I would not see't.
ANTONY   Come then; for with a wound I must be cured.
Draw that thy honest° sword, which thou hast worn   *honorable*
Most useful for thy country.
80   EROS   O sir, pardon me!
ANTONY   When I did make thee free, swor'st thou not then
To do this when I bade thee? Do it at once,
Or thy precedent° services are all   *earlier*
But accidents unpurposed.° Draw, and come.   *But pointless events*
85   EROS   Turn from me then that noble countenance
Wherein the worship° of the whole world lies.   *esteem, worth*
ANTONY *[turning away]*   Lo thee!
EROS   My sword is drawn.
ANTONY   Then let it do at once
The thing why thou hast drawn it.
EROS   My dear master,
90   My captain, and my Emperor: let me say,
Before I strike this bloody stroke, farewell.
ANTONY   'Tis said, man; and farewell.
EROS   Farewell, great chief. Shall I strike now?
ANTONY   Now, Eros.
       [EROS stabs himself]
EROS   Why, there then, thus I do escape the sorrow
Of Antony's death.   *[He dies]*
95   ANTONY   Thrice nobler than myself,
Thou teachest me, O valiant Eros, what
I should and thou couldst not. My queen and Eros
Have by their brave instruction got upon° me   *gained ahead of*
A nobleness in record.° But I will be   *history*
100 A bridegroom in my death, and run into't
As to a lover's bed.[1] Come then, and, Eros,
Thy master dies thy scholar. To do thus
I learned of thee.

---

9. *branded . . . ensued:* indicated, as if by a criminal's brand, the humiliation of the man who followed.
1. *But . . . bed:* death is here treated as a form of erotic union or climax, with Antony as the bridegroom and death (and Cleopatra) the bride.

            [He stabs] himself
               How, not dead? Not dead?
  The guard, ho! O, dispatch° me!   *finish*
         Enter a GUARD *[and* DECRETAS]

FIRST GUARD   What's the noise?

105 ANTONY   I have done my work ill, friends. O, make an end
  Of what I have begun!

SECOND GUARD   The star is fall'n.

FIRST GUARD   And time is at his period.°   *its end*

ALL THE GUARDS   Alas
  And woe!

ANTONY   Let him that loves me strike me dead.

FIRST GUARD   Not I.

SECOND GUARD   Nor I.

THIRD GUARD   Nor anyone.   *Exeunt [the* GUARD]

110 DECRETAS   Thy death and fortunes bid thy followers fly.
        [He takes Antony's sword]
  This sword but shown to Caesar, with this tidings,
  Shall enter me° with him.   *gain me favor*
        Enter DIOMEDES

DIOMEDES   Where's Antony?

DECRETAS   There, Diomed, there.

DIOMEDES   Lives he? Wilt thou not answer, man?
                 [Exit DECRETAS]

ANTONY   Art thou there, Diomed? Draw thy sword, and give me
  Sufficing° strokes for death.   *Enough*

115 DIOMEDES   Most absolute lord,
  My mistress Cleopatra sent me to thee.

ANTONY   When did she send thee?

DIOMEDES   Now, my lord.

ANTONY   Where is she?

DIOMEDES   Locked in her monument. She had a prophesying fear
  Of what hath come to pass; for when she saw—

120 Which never shall be found°—you did suspect   *(to be true)*
  She had disposed° with Caesar, and that your rage *made an alliance*
  Would not be purged, she sent word she was dead;
  But fearing since how it might work, hath sent
  Me to proclaim the truth; and I am come,

125 I dread, too late.

ANTONY   Too late, good Diomed. Call my guard, I prithee.

DIOMEDES   What ho, the Emperor's guard! The guard, what ho!
  Come, your lord calls.
        Enter four or five of the GUARD *of Antony*

ANTONY   Bear me, good friends, where Cleopatra bides.°   *waits; dwells*

130 'Tis the last service that I shall command you.

FIRST GUARD   Woe, woe are we, sir, you may not live to wear
  All your true followers out.°   *outlive them*

ALL THE GUARDS   Most heavy day!

ANTONY   Nay, good my fellows, do not please sharp fate
  To grace° it with your sorrows. Bid that welcome   *By gracing*

135 Which comes to punish us, and we punish it,
  Seeming to bear it lightly. Take me up.
  I have led you oft; carry me now, good friends,
  And have my thanks for all.   *Exeunt bearing* ANTONY *[and* EROS]

4.16

Enter CLEOPATRA *and her maids aloft, with*
CHARMIAN *and* IRAS

CLEOPATRA   O Charmian, I will never go from hence.
CHARMIAN   Be comforted, dear madam.
CLEOPATRA   No, I will not.
  All strange and terrible events are welcome,
  But comforts we despise. Our size of sorrow,
5 Proportioned to our cause, must be as great
  As that which makes it.
             Enter DIOMEDES [*below*]
                How now? Is he dead?
DIOMEDES   His death's upon him, but not dead.
  Look out o'th' other side your monument.
  His guard have brought him thither.
        Enter [*below*] ANTONY, [*borne by*] *the guard*
CLEOPATRA   O sun,
10 Burn the great sphere thou mov'st in; darkling¹ stand
  The varying shore o'th' world! O Antony,
  Antony, Antony! Help, Charmian,
  Help, Iras, help, help, friends below!
  Let's draw him hither.
ANTONY   Peace. Not Caesar's valour
15 Hath o'erthrown Antony, but Antony's
  Hath triumphed on itself.
CLEOPATRA   So it should be,
  That none but Antony should conquer Antony.
  But woe 'tis so!
ANTONY   I am dying, Egypt, dying. Only
20 I here importune death° awhile until
  Of many thousand kisses the poor last
  I lay upon thy lips.
CLEOPATRA   I dare not,° dear,
  Dear, my lord, pardon. I dare not,
  Lest I be taken. Nor th'imperious show°
25 Of the full-fortuned Caesar ever shall
  Be brooched° with me, if knife, drugs, serpents, have
  Edge, sting, or operation.° I am safe.
  Your wife, Octavia, with her modest eyes
  And still conclusion,° shall acquire no honour
30 Demuring° upon me. But come, come, Antony. —
  Help me, my women. — We must draw thee up.
  Assist, good friends.
ANTONY   O quick, or I am gone!
CLEOPATRA   Here's sport indeed. How heavy weighs my lord!
  Our strength is all gone into heaviness,°
35 That makes the weight. Had I great Juno's power
  The strong-winged Mercury should fetch thee up
  And set thee by Jove's side. Yet come a little.
  Wishers were ever fools. O come, come, come!

ask death to wait	
dare not come down	
triumphal procession	
decorated	
power	
silent judgment	
Gazing solemnly	
sadness; weight	

4.16 Location: Cleopatra's monument, Alexandria.
1. O . . . *darkling:* for the spheres in which the sun, like
the planets and stars, was thought to move around the
earth, see note to 2.7.15. If the sun burned its sphere,
presumably it would move out of orbit, thus leaving the
earth in darkness ("darkling").

They heave ANTONY *aloft to* CLEOPATRA
And welcome, welcome! Die when thou hast lived,°   lived again
40   Quicken° with kissing. Had my lips that power,   Revive
Thus would I wear them out.
         [*They kiss*]
ALL THE LOOKERS-ON   A heavy sight.
ANTONY   I am dying, Egypt, dying.
Give me some wine, and let me speak a little.
45   CLEOPATRA   No, let me speak, and let me rail so high
That the false hussy Fortune break her wheel,
Provoked by my offence.°   insults
ANTONY   One word, sweet queen.
Of Caesar seek your honour, with your safety. O!
CLEOPATRA   They do not go together.
ANTONY   Gentle, hear me.
50   None about Caesar trust but Proculeius.
CLEOPATRA   My resolution and my hands I'll trust,
None about Caesar.
ANTONY   The miserable change now at my end
Lament° nor sorrow at, but please your thoughts   Neither lament
55   In feeding them with those my former fortunes,
Wherein I lived the greatest prince o'th' world,
The noblest; and do now not basely die,
Not cowardly put off my helmet to
My countryman; a Roman by a Roman
60   Valiantly vanquished. Now my spirit is going;
I can no more.
CLEOPATRA   Noblest of men, woot die?°   will you
Hast thou no care of me? Shall I abide
In this dull world, which in thy absence is
No better than a sty?
         [ANTONY *dies*]
                       O see, my women,
65   The crown o'th' earth doth melt. My lord!
O, withered is the garland° of the war.   crowning glory
The soldier's pole[2] is fall'n. Young boys and girls
Are level now with men. The odds° is gone,   distinction among humans
And there is nothing left remarkable
70   Beneath the visiting moon.
         [*She falls*]
CHARMIAN   O, quietness, lady!
IRAS   She's dead, too, our sovereign.
CHARMIAN   Lady!
IRAS   Madam!
CHARMIAN   O, madam, madam, madam!
IRAS   Royal Egypt, Empress!
CHARMIAN   Peace, peace, Iras!
CLEOPATRA [*recovering*]   No more but e'en° a woman, and   just (no longer Queen)
75   commanded
By such poor passion as the maid that milks
And does the meanest chores. It were for° me   would befit
To throw my sceptre at the injurious gods,

---

2. Polestar; military standard; phallus.

To tell them that this world did equal theirs
80 Till they had stol'n our jewel. All's but naught.
Patience is sottish,° and impatience does   *foolish*
Become a dog that's mad. Then is it sin
To rush into the secret house of death
Ere death dare come to us? How do you, women?
85 What, what, good cheer! Why, how now, Charmian?
My noble girls! Ah, women, women! Look,
Our lamp is spent, it's out. Good sirs,° take heart;   *(to the women)*
We'll bury him, and then what's brave,° what's noble,   *fine*
Let's do it after the high Roman fashion,
90 And make death proud to take us. Come, away.
This case of that huge spirit now is cold.
Ah, women, women! Come. We have no friend
But resolution, and the briefest° end.   *fastest*

Exeunt [those above] bearing off Antony's body

5.1

Enter CAESAR *with his council of war:* AGRIPPA, DOLA-
BELLA, [MAECENAS, GALLUS, PROCULEIUS]
CAESAR   Go to him, Dolabella, bid him yield.
Being so frustrate, tell him, he but mocks
The pauses that he makes.[1]
DOLABELLA   Caesar, I shall.   [*Exit*]

Enter DECRETAS *with the sword of Antony*
CAESAR   Wherefore is that? And what art thou that dar'st
Appear thus° to us?   *with a drawn weapon*
5 DECRETAS   I am called Decretas.
Mark Antony I served, who best was worthy
Best to be served. Whilst he stood up and spoke
He was my master, and I wore my life
To spend° upon his haters. If thou please   *expend*
10 To take me to thee, as I was to him
I'll be to Caesar; if thou pleasest not,
I yield thee up my life.
CAESAR   What is't thou sayst?
DECRETAS   I say, O Caesar, Antony is dead.
CAESAR   The breaking° of so great a thing should make   *end; telling*
15 A greater crack.° The rivèd° world   *noise; fracture / split*
Should have shook lions into civil° streets,   *city*
And citizens to their° dens. The death of Antony   *(the lions')*
Is not a single doom; in that name lay
A moiety° of the world.   *half*
DECRETAS   He is dead, Caesar,
20 Not by a public minister of justice,
Nor by a hirèd knife; but that self° hand   *same*
Which writ his honour in the acts it did
Hath, with the courage which the heart did lend it,
Splitted the heart. This is his sword;
25 I robbed his wound of it. Behold it stained
With his most noble blood.
CAESAR [*weeping*]   Look you, sad friends,

5.1 Location: Caesar's camp.   1. *he but . . . makes:* his delays are a mere mockery.

The gods rebuke me;° but it is a tidings   *(for his tears)*
To wash the eyes of kings.

AGRIPPA   And strange it is
That nature must compel us to lament
Our most persisted deeds.°   *What we persevered in*

30   MAECENAS   His taints and honours
Waged° equal with° him.   *Fought as if / in*

AGRIPPA   A rarer spirit never
Did steer humanity;° but you gods will give us   *govern (any) man*
Some faults to make us men. Caesar is touched.

MAECENAS   When such a spacious mirror's set before him
He needs must see himself.

35   CAESAR   O Antony,
I have followed° thee to this. But we do lance°   *pursued / wound to cure*
Diseases in our bodies. I must perforce
Have shown to thee such a declining day,[2]
Or look on thine. We could not stall° together   *live in peace*
40   In the whole world. But yet let me lament,
With tears as sovereign[3] as the blood of hearts,
That thou, my brother, my competitor°   *comrade; foe*
In top of all design,° my mate in empire,   *In the greatest ventures*
Friend and companion in the front of war,
45   The arm of mine own body, and the heart
Where mine his° thoughts did kindle—that our stars,   *its*
Unreconciliable, should divide
Our equalness° to this. Hear me, good friends—   *partnership*
        Enter an EGYPTIAN
But I will tell you at some meeter season.°   *fitter time*
50   The business of this man looks out of him;
We'll hear him what he says.—Whence are you?

EGYPTIAN   A poor Egyptian, yet the Queen my mistress,
Confined in all she has, her monument,
Of thy intents desires instruction,
55   That she preparèdly may frame herself
To th' way she's forced to.

CAESAR   Bid her have good heart.
She soon shall know of us, by some of ours,
How honourable and how kindly we
Determine for her. For Caesar cannot live
To be ungentle.

60   EGYPTIAN   So; the gods preserve thee!   *Exit*

CAESAR   Come hither, Proculeius. Go, and say
We purpose her no shame. Give her what comforts
The quality° of her passion° shall require,   *strength / grief*
Lest in her greatness, by some mortal stroke,
65   She do defeat us; for her life in Rome
Would be eternal in our triumph.[4] Go,
And with your speediest bring us what she says
And how you find of her.

PROCULEIUS   Caesar, I shall.   *Exit*

---

2. *I must . . . day:* I would have had to exhibit my demise   bloodletting).
to you. *perforce:* necessarily.   4. *her life . . . triumph:* her presence alive in Rome would
3. As efficacious (weeping seems to be paralleled with   bring eternal renown to my triumphal procession.

CAESAR   Gallus, go you along.   [*Exit* GALLUS]
                              Where's Dolabella,
   To second Proculeius?
70 ALL BUT CAESAR   Dolabella!
CAESAR   Let him alone; for I remember now
   How he's employed. He shall in time be ready.
   Go with me to my tent, where you shall see
   How hardly° I was drawn into this war,   *unwillingly*
75 How calm and gentle I proceeded still
   In all my writings.° Go with me, and see   *letters to Antony*
   What I can show in this.   *Exeunt*

5.2

Enter CLEOPATRA, CHARMIAN, IRAS, *and* MARDIAN

CLEOPATRA   My desolation does begin to make
   A better life. 'Tis paltry to be Caesar.
   Not being Fortune, he's but Fortune's knave,°   *servant*
   A minister of her will. And it is great
5 To do that thing° that ends all other deeds,   *(suicide)*
   Which shackles accidents and bolts up change,
   Which sleeps and never palates more the dung,
   The beggar's nurse, and Caesar's.[1]

Enter PROCULEIUS[2]

PROCULEIUS   Caesar sends greeting to the Queen of Egypt,
10 And bids thee study on° what fair demands   *give thought to*
   Thou mean'st to have him grant thee.
CLEOPATRA   What's thy name?
PROCULEIUS   My name is Proculeius.
CLEOPATRA   Antony
   Did tell me of you, bade me trust you; but
   I do not greatly care to be deceived,
15 That° have no use for trusting. If your master   *Because I*
   Would have a queen his beggar, you must tell him
   That majesty, to keep decorum, must
   No less beg than a kingdom. If he please
   To give me conquered Egypt for my son,
20 He gives me so much of mine own as° I   *that*
   Will kneel to him with thanks.
PROCULEIUS   Be of good cheer.
   You're fall'n into a princely hand; fear nothing.
   Make your full reference° freely to my lord,   *case*
   Who is so full of grace that it flows over
25 On all that need. Let me report to him
   Your sweet dependency,° and you shall find   *meek obeisance*
   A conqueror that will pray in aid for kindness,[3]
   Where he for grace is kneeled to.
CLEOPATRA   Pray you, tell him
   I am his fortune's vassal, and I send him
30 The greatness he has got.[4] I hourly learn

5.2 Location: Cleopatra's monument.
1. *Which sleeps . . . Caesar's:* Which brings a sleep in
which we no longer taste the produce of the earth (dung),
nourisher of all from beggar to emperor.
2. Cleopatra and her women are inside the monument,
the others outside it.

3. Who will beg help in finding new ways to be kind.
4. *I am . . . got:* I do homage to his good fortune, and
acknowledge the great position he has won. "Send him"
may suggest Cleopatra's sense of superiority in conferring
greatness upon Caesar.

A doctrine of obedience, and would gladly
Look him i'th' face.
PROCULEIUS   This I'll report, dear lady;
  Have comfort, for I know your plight is pitied
  Of° him that caused it.   *By*
          [*Enter Roman soldiers from behind*]
35 PROCULEIUS [*to the soldiers*] You see how easily she may be surprised.
  Guard her till Caesar come.
IRAS   Royal Queen—
CHARMIAN   O Cleopatra, thou art taken, Queen!
CLEOPATRA [*drawing a dagger*]   Quick, quick, good hands!
PROCULEIUS [*disarming* CLEOPATRA]   Hold,
      worthy lady, hold!
  Do not yourself such wrong, who are in this
  Relieved° but not betrayed.   *Rescued*
40 CLEOPATRA   What, of° death too,   *deprived of*
  That rids our dogs of languish?⁵
PROCULEIUS   Cleopatra,
  Do not abuse my master's bounty by
  Th'undoing of yourself. Let the world see
  His nobleness well acted, which your death
  Will never let come forth.°   *allow to be displayed*
45 CLEOPATRA   Where art thou, death?
  Come hither, come. Come, come, and take a queen
  Worth many babes and beggars.⁶
PROCULEIUS   O temperance, lady!
CLEOPATRA   Sir, I will eat no meat.° I'll not drink, sir.   *food*
  If idle talk will once be necessary,⁷
50 I'll not sleep, neither. This mortal house° I'll ruin,   *My body*
  Do Caesar what he can. Know, sir, that I
  Will not wait pinioned⁸ at your master's court,
  Nor once be chastised with the sober eye
  Of dull Octavia. Shall they hoist me up
55 And show me to the shouting varletry°   *rabble*
  Of censuring Rome? Rather a ditch in Egypt
  Be gentle grave unto me; rather on Nilus' mud
  Lay me stark naked, and let the waterflies
  Blow me into abhorring;⁹ rather make
60 My country's high pyramides my gibbet,°   *gallows*
  And hang me up in chains.
PROCULEIUS   You do extend
  These thoughts of horror further than you shall
  Find cause in Caesar.
          Enter DOLABELLA
DOLABELLA   Proculeius,
  What thou hast done thy master Caesar knows,
65 And he hath sent for thee. For the Queen,
  I'll take her to my guard.
PROCULEIUS   So, Dolabella,
  It shall content me best. Be gentle to her.

---

5. Which rids even our dogs of protracted demise.
6. *babes and beggars:* death's cheapest victims; those most
often "relieved" (line 39) by the great.
7. (Even) if useless words are at times needed (to keep
me awake); if I am forced to engage in pointless chatter.

8. Will not serve shackled (or, will not wait like a bird
with clipped wings).
9. Lay their eggs on me (thereby breeding maggots) so
that I become disgusting, abhorrent.

[*To* CLEOPATRA] To Caesar I will speak what° you shall please,　　　　*whatever*
　If you'll employ me to him.
CLEOPATRA　　　　　　Say I would die. *Exit* PROCULEIUS
70　DOLABELLA　Most noble Empress, you have heard of me.
CLEOPATRA　I cannot tell.
DOLABELLA　　　　　Assurèdly you know me.
CLEOPATRA　No matter, sir, what I have heard or known.
　You laugh when boys or women tell their dreams;
　Is't not your trick?°　　　　　　　　　　　　　　　*custom*
DOLABELLA　　　　　I understand not, madam.
75　CLEOPATRA　I dreamt there was an Emperor Antony.
　O, such another sleep, that I might see
　But such another man!
DOLABELLA　　　　　If it might please ye—
CLEOPATRA　His face was as the heav'ns, and therein stuck°　　*were stuck*
　A sun and moon, which kept their course and lighted
　The little O o'th' earth.
80　DOLABELLA　　　　　Most sovereign creature—
CLEOPATRA　His legs bestrid° the ocean; his reared arm　　　*straddled*
　Crested[1] the world. His voice was propertied
　As all the tunèd spheres,[2] and that to friends;
　But when he meant to quail° and shake the orb,°　　*awe / globe*
85　He was as rattling thunder. For his bounty,
　There was no winter in't; an autumn 'twas,
　That grew the more by reaping. His delights
　Were dolphin-like; they showed his back above°　　*they rose above*
　The element they lived in. In his livery°　　　　　*service*
90　Walked crowns and crownets.° Realms and islands were　　*kings and princes*
　As plates° dropped from his pocket.　　　　　　　　*silver coins*
DOLABELLA　　　　　Cleopatra—
CLEOPATRA　Think you there was, or might be, such a man
　As this I dreamt of?
DOLABELLA　　　　　Gentle madam, no.
CLEOPATRA　You lie, up to the hearing of the gods.
95　But if there be, or ever were one such,
　It's past the size of dreaming.[3] Nature wants stuff
　To vie strange forms with fancy; yet t'imagine
　An Antony were nature's piece 'gainst fancy,
　Condemning shadows quite.[4]
DOLABELLA　　　　　Hear me, good madam:
100　Your loss is as yourself, great, and you bear it
　As answering to[5] the weight. Would I might never
　O'ertake° pursued success but° I do feel,　　　*Achieve / unless*
　By the rebound° of yours, a grief that smites　　　*reflection*
　My very heart at root.
CLEOPATRA　　　　　I thank you, sir.
105　Know you what Caesar means to do with me?
DOLABELLA　I am loath to tell you what I would you knew.
CLEOPATRA　Nay, pray you, sir.

---

1. Formed a crest over (as in heraldry).
2. *was . . . spheres:* sounded like the music of the spheres, supposedly produced by the harmonious structure of the universe. See note to 2.7.15.
3. My vision of him surpasses what can be dreamed.
4. *Nature . . . quite:* Nature lacks material to compete

with the remarkable visions of the imagination in creating fantastic forms; but by imaging and creating Antony, nature has produced a masterpiece that outstrips even fancy and thus discredits imaginary conceptions.
5. *you . . . to:* you do justice to.

DOLABELLA   Though he be honourable—
CLEOPATRA   He'll lead me then in triumph.
DOLABELLA   Madam, he will, I know't.
    Flourish. Enter CAESAR, *[with]* PROCULEIUS, GALLUS,
      MAECENAS, *and others of his train*
ALL°   Make way, there! Caesar!   *(Caesar's train)*
CAESAR   Which is the Queen of Egypt?
DOLABELLA *[to* CLEOPATRA*]*
  It is the Emperor, madam.
    CLEOPATRA *kneels*
110 CAESAR   Arise! You shall not kneel.
  I pray you rise, rise, Egypt.
CLEOPATRA *[rising]*   Sir, the gods
  Will have it thus.° My master and my lord   *that I obey you*
  I must obey.
CAESAR   Take to you no hard thoughts.
  The record of what injuries you did us,
115 Though written in our flesh, we shall remember
  As things but done by chance.
CLEOPATRA   Sole sir° o'th' world,   *lord*
  I cannot project° mine own cause so well   *lay out*
  To make it clear,° but do confess I have   *innocent seeming*
  Been laden with like frailties which before
  Have often shamed our sex.
120 CAESAR   Cleopatra, know
  We will extenuate rather than enforce.°   *emphasize (faults)*
  If you apply yourself° to our intents,   *conform*
  Which towards you are most gentle, you shall find
  A benefit in this change; but if you seek
125 To lay on me a cruelty° by taking   *charge of cruelty*
  Antony's course, you shall bereave yourself
  Of my good purposes and put your children
  To that destruction which I'll guard them from,
  If thereon you rely. I'll take my leave.
130 CLEOPATRA   And may through all the world![6] 'Tis yours, and we,
  Your scutcheons° and your signs of conquest, shall   *captured shields*
  Hang in what place you please. *[Giving a paper]* Here, my good lord.
CAESAR   You shall advise me in all for° Cleopatra.   *concerning*
CLEOPATRA   This is the brief° of money, plate, and jewels   *summary*
135 I am possessed of. 'Tis exactly valued,
  Not petty things admitted.° Where's Seleucus?   *Except trivial things*
    [Enter SELEUCUS*]*
SELEUCUS   Here, madam.
CLEOPATRA *[to* CAESAR*]*   This is my treasurer. Let him speak, my lord,
  Upon his peril, that I have reserved
140 To myself nothing. Speak the truth, Seleucus.
SELEUCUS   Madam, I had rather seal° my lips   *sew up*
  Than to my peril speak that which is not.
CLEOPATRA   What have I kept back?
SELEUCUS   Enough to purchase what you have made known.
145 CAESAR   Nay, blush not, Cleopatra. I approve
  Your wisdom in the deed.
CLEOPATRA   See, Caesar! O, behold

---

6. As you may (take your leave and go) anywhere (as ruler of the world).

How pomp is followed!⁷ Mine° will now be yours,   *My followers*
And should we shift estates,° yours would be mine.   *change positions*
The ingratitude of this Seleucus does
150   Even make me wild.—O slave, of no more trust
Than love that's hired! What, goest thou back? Thou shalt
Go back, I warrant thee; but I'll catch thine eyes
Though° they had wings. Slave, soulless villain, dog!   *Even if*
O rarely° base!   *exceptionally*
    CAESAR   Good Queen, let us entreat you.
155   CLEOPATRA   O Caesar, what a wounding shame is this,
That thou vouchsafing° here to visit me,   *stooping to come*
Doing the honour of thy lordliness
To one so meek—that mine own servant should
Parcel° the sum of my disgraces by   *Particularize; add to*
160   Addition of his envy.° Say, good Caesar,   *spite*
That I some lady° trifles have reserved,   *ladylike*
Immoment toys,° things of such dignity   *Worthless trinkets*
As we greet modern° friends withal;° and say   *everday / with*
Some nobler token I have kept apart
165   For Livia° and Octavia, to induce   *Caesar's wife*
Their mediation—must I be unfolded
With° one that I have bred? The gods! It smites me   *Turned in by*
Beneath the fall I have. [*To* SELEUCUS] Prithee, go hence,
Or I shall show the cinders° of my spirits   *burning coals*
170   Through th'ashes of my chance.° Wert thou a man°   *fortune / (not a eunuch)*
Thou wouldst have mercy on me.
    CAESAR   Forbear, Seleucus.
                     [*Exit* SELEUCUS]
  CLEOPATRA   Be it known that we, the greatest, are misthought°   *misjudged*
For things that others do; and when we fall
We answer others' merits in our name,⁸
Are therefore to be pitied.
175   CAESAR   Cleopatra,
Not what you have reserved nor what acknowledged
Put we i'th' roll of conquest. Still be't yours.
Bestow° it at your pleasure, and believe   *Dispense*
Caesar's no merchant, to make prize° with you   *haggle*
180   Of things that merchants sold. Therefore be cheered.
Make not your thoughts your prisons.⁹ No, dear Queen;
For we intend so to dispose you as
Yourself shall give us counsel. Feed and sleep.
Our care and pity is so much upon you
185   That we remain your friend; and so adieu.
  CLEOPATRA   My master and my lord!
    CAESAR   Not so. Adieu.
            Flourish. Exeunt CAESAR *and his train*
  CLEOPATRA   He words me, girls, he words me, that I should not
Be noble to myself.¹ But hark thee, Charmian.
    [*She whispers to* CHARMIAN]

---

7. How the great are served.
8. We are responsible for the deeds committed by others
in our names.
9. Don't think yourself a prisoner; don't be imprisoned

by (or in) your thoughts.
1. *He words . . . myself:* He puts me off from committing
suicide with mere words.

IRAS   Finish, good lady. The bright day is done,
　　And we are for the dark.
190　CLEOPATRA [*to* CHARMIAN]   Hie thee again.°　　　　　　　　*Hurry back*
　　I have spoke already, and it is provided.
　　Go put it to the haste.°　　　　　　　　　　　　　　　*Do it quickly*
　　CHARMIAN　　　　　　　　Madam, I will.
　　　　　　Enter DOLABELLA
　　DOLABELLA　Where's the Queen?
　　CHARMIAN　　　　　　　　Behold, sir.　　　[*Exit*]
　　CLEOPATRA　　　　　　　　　　Dolabella!
　　DOLABELLA　Madam, as thereto sworn by your command—
195　Which my love makes religion° to obey—　　　　　　　*compels me*
　　I tell you this: Caesar through Syria
　　Intends his journey, and within three days
　　You with your children will he send before.
　　Make your best use of this. I have performed
　　Your pleasure, and my promise.
200　CLEOPATRA　　　　　　　Dolabella,
　　I shall remain your debtor.
　　DOLABELLA　　　　　　　I your servant.
　　Adieu, good Queen. I must attend on Caesar.
　　CLEOPATRA　Farewell, and thanks.　　　*Exit* [DOLABELLA]
　　　　　　　　　　Now, Iras, what think'st thou?
　　Thou, an Egyptian puppet shall be shown
205　In Rome, as well as I. Mechanic slaves°　　　　　　　*Laborers*
　　With greasy aprons, rules,° and hammers shall　　*measuring sticks*
　　Uplift us to the view. In their thick° breaths,　　　　*foul*
　　Rank° of gross diet,° shall we be enclouded,　*Stinking / coarse food*
　　And forced to drink° their vapour.　　　　　　　　　*inhale*
　　IRAS　　　　　　　　　The gods forbid!
210　CLEOPATRA　Nay, 'tis most certain, Iras. Saucy lictors°　*Insolent law officers*
　　Will catch at us like strumpets, and scald° rhymers　　*scurvy*
　　Ballad us out o' tune. The quick comedians
　　Extemporally° will stage us, and present　　　　*In improvised manner*
　　Our Alexandrian revels. Antony
215　Shall be brought drunken forth, and I shall see
　　Some squeaking Cleopatra boy[2] my greatness
　　I'th' posture of a whore.
　　IRAS　　　　　　　　O, the good gods!
　　CLEOPATRA　Nay, that's certain.
　　IRAS　I'll never see't! For I am sure my nails
　　Are stronger than mine eyes.
220　CLEOPATRA　　　　　　　Why, that's the way
　　To fool their preparation and to conquer
　　Their most absurd intents.
　　　　　　Enter CHARMIAN
　　　　　　　　Now, Charmian!
　　Show° me, my women, like a queen. Go fetch　　　　　*Dress*
　　My best attires. I am again for Cydnus
225　To meet Mark Antony.[3] Sirrah Iras, go.
　　Now, noble Charmian, we'll dispatch° indeed,　　　*hurry; finish*

2. Cleopatra's part will be played by a boy (as it was in　　3. See 2.2.192–232.
Shakespeare's day).

And when thou hast done this chore I'll give thee leave
To play till doomsday.—Bring our crown and all.   [*Exit* IRAS]
    A noise within
Wherefore's this noise?
    Enter a GUARDSMAN
GUARDSMAN   Here is a rural fellow
230   That will not be denied your highness' presence.
He brings you figs.
CLEOPATRA   Let him come in.   *Exit* GUARDSMAN
                What° poor an instrument   *How*
May do a noble deed! He brings me liberty.
My resolution's placed,° and I have nothing   *unwavering*
235   Of woman in me. Now from head to foot
I am marble-constant. Now the fleeting° moon   *changeable*
No planet is of mine.
    Enter GUARDSMAN, *and* CLOWN° [*with a basket*]   *rustic*
GUARDSMAN   This is the man.
CLEOPATRA   Avoid,° and leave him.   *Exit* GUARDSMAN   *Withdraw*
                Hast thou the pretty worm[4]
Of Nilus there, that kills and pains not?
240   CLOWN   Truly, I have him; but I would not be the party that
    should desire you to touch him, for his biting is immortal;[5]
    those that do die of it do seldom or never recover.
CLEOPATRA   Remember'st thou any that have died on't?
CLOWN   Very many, men, and women too. I heard of one of
245   them no longer than yesterday, a very honest° woman, but   *truthful; chaste*
    something given to lie,° as a woman should not do but in the   *fib; lie with men*
    way of honesty, how she died° of the biting of it, what pain she   *perished; had an orgasm*
    felt. Truly, she makes a very good report o'th' worm; but he
    that will believe all that they say shall never be saved by half
250   that they do;[6] but this is most falliable:° the worm's an odd   *(error for "infallible")*
    worm.
CLEOPATRA   Get thee hence, farewell.
CLOWN   I wish you all joy of the worm.
CLEOPATRA   Farewell.
255   CLOWN   You must think this, look you, that the worm will do his
    kind.°   *what's in its nature*
CLEOPATRA   Ay, ay; farewell.
CLOWN   Look you, the worm is not to be trusted but in the keep-
    ing of wise people; for indeed there is no goodness in the worm.
260   CLEOPATRA   Take thou no care; it shall be heeded.
CLOWN   Very good. Give it nothing, I pray you, for it is not worth
    the feeding.
CLEOPATRA   Will it eat me?
CLOWN   You must not think I am so simple but I know the devil
265   himself will not eat a woman; I know that a woman is a dish
    for the gods, if the devil dress° her not. But truly, these same   *prepare (food); clothe*
    whoreson° devils do the gods great harm in their women; for in   *accursed*
    every ten that they make, the devils mar five.

---

4. Snake or serpent. In the Clown's description (lines 244–51), the "worm" also suggests the penis.
5. Comic error: the Clown means the opposite, but as so often with such malapropisms in Shakespeare, the mistake reveals an unintended truth. See Cleopatra's "Immortal longings" (line 272).

6. Perhaps the point is that a woman "given to lie" (line 246) is not to be believed. If Cleopatra acts on this "good report o'th'worm," she will "never be saved" (lines 248–50): she will die and, in Christian terms, will lose hope of salvation by committing suicide.

CLEOPATRA   Well, get thee gone, farewell.

270 CLOWN   Yes, forsooth. I wish you joy o'th' worm.

Exit [leaving the basket]

[Enter IRAS *with a robe, crown, and other jewels]*

CLEOPATRA   Give me my robe. Put on my crown. I have
Immortal longings in me. Now no more
The juice of Egypt's grape shall moist this lip.

*[*CHARMIAN *and* IRAS *help her to dress]*

Yare,° yare, good Iras, quick—methinks I hear   *Briskly*
275 Antony call. I see him rouse himself
To praise my noble act. I hear him mock
The luck of Caesar, which the gods give men
To excuse their° after wrath. Husband, I come.   *(the gods')*
Now to that name my courage prove my title.
280 I am fire and air; my other elements
I give to baser life.⁷ So, have you done?
Come then, and take the last warmth of my lips.

[She kisses them]

Farewell, kind Charmian. Iras, long farewell.

*[*IRAS *falls and dies]*

Have I the aspic° in my lips? Dost fall?   *asp*
285 If thou and nature can so gently part,
The stroke of death is as a lover's pinch,
Which hurts and is desired. Dost thou lie still?
If thus thou vanishest, thou tell'st the world
It is not worth leave-taking.
290 CHARMIAN   Dissolve, thick cloud, and rain, that I may say
The gods themselves do weep.

CLEOPATRA   This proves me base.°   *ignoble*
If she first meet the curlèd° Antony   *curly-haired*
He'll make demand of° her, and spend that kiss   *question; (sexual)*
Which is my heaven to have.

*[She takes an aspic from the basket and puts it to her
breast]*

                            Come, thou mortal wretch,°   *deadly creature*
295 With thy sharp teeth this knot intrinsicate°   *intricate*
Of life at once untie. Poor venomous fool,
Be angry, and dispatch. O, couldst thou speak,
That I might hear thee call great Caesar ass
Unpolicied!°   *Outsmarted*
CHARMIAN   O eastern star!°   *Venus; Cleopatra*
CLEOPATRA   Peace, peace.
300 Dost thou not see my baby at my breast,
That sucks the nurse asleep?
CHARMIAN   O, break! O, break!
CLEOPATRA   As sweet as balm, as soft as air, as gentle.
O Antony!

[She puts another aspic to her arm]

            Nay, I will take thee too.
What° should I stay—   *[She] dies*   *Why*

---

7. *I am . . . life:* the "other elements" (line 280) are earth and water, the lower and heavier elements traditionally linked
to women and thought to explain their fickleness. Cleopatra is particularly associated with these elements through her
equation with (the mud of) Egypt. By asserting that she is only "fire and air," she is claiming to be manly (as in lines
234–35) and also referring to the separation of the soul from the body at death.

CHARMIAN	In this vile world? So, fare thee well.	
305	Now boast thee, death, in thy possession lies	
	A lass unparalleled. Downy windows,° close,	*eyelids*
	And golden Phoebus never be beheld	
	Of eyes again so royal. Your crown's awry.	
	I'll mend it, and then play—	

Enter the GUARD, *rustling° in*   *clattering*

FIRST GUARD Where's the Queen?
310

CHARMIAN Speak softly. Wake her not.

FIRST GUARD Caesar hath sent—

CHARMIAN   Too slow a messenger.
[*She applies an aspic*]
O come apace, dispatch! I partly feel thee.

FIRST GUARD Approach, ho! All's not well. Caesar's beguiled.°   *deceived*
315
SECOND GUARD There's Dolabella sent from Caesar. Call him.
[*Exit a* GUARDSMAN]

FIRST GUARD What work is here, Charmian? Is this well done?

CHARMIAN It is well done, and fitting for a princess
Descended of so many royal kings.
Ah, soldier!   CHARMIAN *dies*

Enter DOLABELLA

DOLABELLA How goes it here?

SECOND GUARD   All dead.
320
DOLABELLA   Caesar, thy thoughts
Touch their effects° in this. Thyself art coming   *Are realized*
To see performed the dreaded act which thou
So sought'st to hinder.

ALL   A way there, a way for Caesar!

Enter CAESAR *and all his train, marching*

DOLABELLA [*to* CAESAR] O sir, you are too sure an augurer.
That° you did fear is done.   *What*
325
CAESAR   Bravest at the last,
She levelled at° our purposes, and, being royal,   *discerned rightly*
Took her own way. The manner of their deaths?
I do not see them bleed.

DOLABELLA [*to a* GUARDSMAN] Who was last with them?

FIRST GUARD A simple countryman that brought her figs.
This was his basket.

CAESAR   Poisoned, then.
330
FIRST GUARD   O Caesar,
This Charmian lived but now; she stood and spake.
I found her trimming up the diadem
On her dead mistress; tremblingly she stood,
And on the sudden dropped.

CAESAR   O, noble weakness!
335
If they had swallowed poison, 'twould appear
By external swelling; but she looks like sleep,
As° she would catch another Antony   *As if*
In her strong toil° of grace.   *snare*

DOLABELLA   Here on her breast
There is a vent of blood, and something blown.°   *emitted; swollen*
The like is on her arm.
340
FIRST GUARD   This is an aspic's trail,
And these fig-leaves have slime upon them such
As th'aspic leaves upon the caves of Nile.

CAESAR   Most probable
That so she died; for her physician tells me
345   She hath pursued conclusions° infinite   *trial outcomes*
Of easy ways to die. Take up her bed,
And bear her women from the monument.
She shall be buried by her Antony.
No grave upon the earth shall clip° in it   *embrace*
350   A pair so famous. High events as these
Strike° those that make° them, and their story is   *Afflict / cause*
No less in pity than his glory⁸ which
Brought them to be lamented. Our army shall
In solemn show attend this funeral,
355   And then to Rome. Come, Dolabella, see
High order in this great solemnity.

> *Exeunt all* [*soldiers bearing* CLEOPATRA *on her
> bed,* CHARMIAN, *and* IRAS]

TEXTUAL VARIANTS

Control text: F

F: The Folio of 1623
Fa, Fb: Fa is the uncorrected version, Fb the corrected version of F

Title: Anthony & Cleopatra [Stationers' Register entry] *Anthony and Cleopater* [F table of contents] *The Tragedie of Anthonie, and Cleopatra* [F head title] *The Tragedie of Anthony and Cleopatra* [F running title]

s.p. SILIUS [F's use of *Romaine* in 3.1 (where Silius is referred to by name in dialogue) is standardized throughout.]

s.p. BOY [Not in F's speech prefixes or stage directions, although Enobarbus refers to the boy in dialogue. See 2.7.]

s.p. WATCH, GUARD, SERVANTS, SOLDIERS [F refers to these characters either by category (*Soldier, 3. Watch,* etc.) or by number (*1, 2,* etc.). This edition never uses numbers alone, preferring prefixes such as "First Servant," "Third Soldier," etc.]

1.1.52 how who
1.2.0 s.d. Enter . . . attendants *Enter Enobarbus, Lamprius, a Southsayer, Rannius, Lucillius, Charmian, Iras, Mardian the Eunuch, and Alexas.* [Rannius and Lucillius are ghost characters; so is Lamprius, unless he is the soothsayer. As these three are not mentioned again, their names are irrelevant and hence omitted.]   **5 charge** change   **34 fertile** fore- / tell   **55 Alexas—come** *Alexas. Come* [F attributes the rest of the speech, beginning with "Come," to Alexas, taking the name as a speech prefix rather than an address.]   **70 Saw you** *Saue you*   **102 ho** how   **103 s.p. SECOND MESSENGER The . . . Sicyon—** / **s.p. ANTHONY Is . . . one?** *1. Mes.* (First Messenger) *The Scicion,* / *Is . . . one?* [The First

---

8. *their . . . glory:* there is no less pity in their story than there is glory in the exploits of Caesar. The immodesty of these lines, in the guise of praise, recalls Caesar's ambiguous grief, his combination of calculation and sentiment, at the news of Antony's death in 5.1. The historical Octavius Caesar went on to order the murder of Ptolemy XV (Caesarion), Cleopatra's son with Julius Caesar. Since Julius Caesar was Octavius's great-uncle and adoptive father, this act, which ended the Ptolemaic dynasty, might be seen as fraticide. See 2.1.37 with note, 2.2.233–34 with note, and 3.6.1–16 with note to line 6. By contrast, after Antony and Cleopatra's deaths, the historical Octavia, over her brother Octavius's objections, raised Anthony's children by Fulvia and Cleopatra, as well as her own five children with Antony and a previous husband.

Messenger speaks the entire line in F.] **125 occasion** an occasion **163 leave** loue **168 Hath** Haue **177 hair** heire **179 place is under us, requires** places under us, require
1.3.11 Iwis I wish **82 my** [not in F]
1.4.3 Our One **8 vouchsafed** vouchsafe **9 the abstract** th'abstracts **44 deared** fear'd **46 lackeying** lacking **56 wassails** Vassailes **57 Modena** *Medena* **58 Pansa** Pausa **76 we** me **76 council** counsell
1.5.3 mandragora *Mandragoru* **47 arm-jaunced** Arme-gaunt **49 dumbed** dumbe **60 man** mans
2.1.2, 5, 16, 18, 38 s.p. MENECRATES . . . MENECRATES . . . MENAS . . . MENAS . . . MENAS *Mene⟨crates⟩.* [Menecrates throughout in F] **21 waned** wand **38 ne'er** neere **41 warred** wan'd
2.2.49 the your **126 not so, Agrippa** not, say *Agrippa* **127 reproof** proofe **210 glow** gloue **212 gentlewomen** Gentlewoman **238 breathless, pour breath** breathlesse powre breath
2.3.12 Gone thither thither **20 afeard** a feare **28 away,** alway
2.4.6 at the at **9 s.p. MAECENAS** *and* AGRIPPA *Both.*
2.5.2 s.p. CHARMIAN, IRAS, *and* ALEXAS *Omnes.* **12 finned** fine **43 is** 'tis **52 But** Bur **104 act** art
2.6.16 the [not in F] **19 is** his **39 s.p. CAESAR, ANTONY,** *and* LEPIDUS *Omnes.* **53 There is** ther's **67 meanings** meaning **71 o'** [not in F] **83 s.p. CAESAR, ANTONY,** *and* LEPIDUS *All.*
2.7.1–13 s.p. FIRST SERVANT . . . SECOND SERVANT . . . FIRST SERVANT *I . . . 2 . . . I* **86 part then is** part, then he is **108 s.p. BOY** [*sings*] The Song. **110 vats** Fattes **115 off** of **119 speaks. The** [Fa] speakest: he [Fb] **123 father's** Father **125 s.p. MENAS** [Not in F; Enobarbus continues speaking until the second half of 1.129, which is spoken by Menas in F, as in this edition.] **127 hear** [Fb] heare a [Fa] **a loud** aloud
3.1.5, 27, 34 s.p. SILIUS *Romaine.* [variously spelled] **14 to** [Fa] too [Fb] **37 there** [Fa] their [Fb]
3.2.3 are [Fb] art [Fa] **10 s.p. AGRIPPA** *Ant⟨ony⟩.* **16 figures** Figure **26 bond** Band **49 at** at the **full of** [Fa]; of full [Fb] **60 wept** weepe
3.3.17 gait? gate, **18 looked'st** look'st
3.4.8 them, then **9 took't** look't **24 yours** your **30 Your** You **38 has** he's
3.5.12 world, thou hast a pair of chops, would thou hadst a pair of chaps **14 one** the [not in F]
3.6.13 he there . . . kings of kings hither . . . King of Kings **61 obstruct** abstract **72 Malchus** *Mauchus* **74 Comagene; Polemon** Comageat, *Polemen* **75 Lycaonia** Licoania **88 their** his
3.7.4 it is is it it **5 Is't not** If not, **21 Brundisium** Brandusium **23 Toryne** Troine **51 Actium** Action **69 leader's** led Leaders leade **72 s.p. CAMIDIUS** *Ven⟨tidius⟩.* **78 Taurus** *Towrus* **80 in** with
3.10.10 riband-red ribaudred **14 June** Inne **27 he** his
3.11.6 s.p. ATTENDANTS *Omnes.* **19 that** them **47 seize** cease **58 tow** stowe **59 Thy** The
3.12.0 s.d. DOLABELLA *Dollabello* **13 lessens** Lessons **29 As** From
3.13.10 mooted meered **25 caparisons** Comparisons **54 Caesar** *Caesars* **55 embraced** embrace **74 deputation** disputation **76–77 kneel / Till** kneele. / Tell him, **103 This** the **149 abyss** Abisme **165 smite** smile **168 discandying** discandering **171 sits** sets **201 on** in
4.2.1 Domitius *Domitian* **19 s.p. SERVITORS** *Omnes.*
4.3.7 s.p. THIRD SOLDIER *I.*
4.4.5–6 too. / . . . for? s.p. ANTONY too, *Antony.* / . . . for? [In F, Cleopatra's speech includes lines 6–7 and thus continues uninterrupted from line 5 to line 8.] **13 doff't** daft **24 s.p. CAPTAIN** *Alex⟨as⟩.* **25 s.p. SOLDIERS** *All.*
4.5.1, 3, 7 s.p. SOLDIER *Eros.*
4.6.15 Camidius *Caminidius* **19 more** mote

4.8 [Most editions continue 4.7, even though the stage is cleared. The new scene affects the numbering of the remaining scenes in the act.]

4.9.2 gests guests   **18 My** Mine

4.13.4 augurs Auguries   **21 spanieled** pannelled

4.15.4 towered toward   **10 distains** dislimes   **19 Caesar** *Caesars*   **107, 132 s.p. ALL THE GUARDS** *All.*   **110 s.p. DECRETAS** *Dercetus.*   **122 sent word** sent you word

4.16.42 s.p. ALL THE LOOKERS-ON *All.*   **46 hussy** huswife   **75 e'en** in   **77 chores** chares   **89 do it** doo't

5.1.0 s.d. MAECENAS *Menas*   **2 but** [not in F]   **15 rivèd** round   **18 that** the   **27 a** [not in F]   **28, 31 s.p. AGRIPPA** *Dola⟨bella⟩.*   **36 lance** launch   **59 live** leaue   **70 s.p. ALL BUT CAESAR** *All.*

5.2.80 O [not in F]   **86 autumn 'twas** *Anthony* it was   **95 or** nor   **103 smites** suites   **212 Ballad** Ballads o' a   **219 my** mine   **224 Cydnus** *Cidrus*   **304 vile** wilde   **308 awry** away

Coriolanus

Hērōs, the Greek word for "hero," originally meant "warrior." By Homer's time, eight centuries before the birth of Christ, the term was already beginning to be applied by extension to other kinds of praiseworthy people, but even today the military connotations of the word remain strong. The Latin word for "virtue" has a similar history, as the historian Plutarch remarks in his biography of Coriolanus, Shakespeare's principal source for his play. "Now in those days valiantness was honored in Rome above all other virtues: which they call *virtūs*, by the name of virtue itself, as including in that general name, all other special virtues besides. So that *virtūs* in the Latin, was as much as valiantness."

Writing *Coriolanus* in 1608, Shakespeare considered the extent to which the slipperiness of terms like *hērōs* or *virtūs* is really justified. To what extent does excellence in battle translate into other forms of meritoriousness? Shakespeare both worked in and deviated from an ageless tradition of exalting great warriors: the mythically dauntless Hercules and Theseus, the fierce battle-chieftains of classical epic, the indomitable knights of medieval chivalric romance, the superheroes of modern films and comic books. Caius Martius Coriolanus performs astonishing, almost superhuman acts of strength and bravery on the battlefield, fighting on behalf of a society that, as Plutarch observes, seems to venerate war. His aggressiveness ought to mesh perfectly, one would think, with the needs of the community. By the logic that generalizes from successful belligerence to excellence per se, a preeminent soldier should be a candidate for Rome's highest honors and its most important leadership positions.

Of course, if the historical Coriolanus had effortlessly transferred his phenomenal energies from battlefield to senate house, Shakespeare would not have had the materials for tragedy. In fact, Coriolanus's career is disastrous. Despite his unparalleled military successes and despite Rome's esteem for warriors, Coriolanus barely escapes the death penalty: he is banished from the city and eventually killed while in the employ of Rome's enemies. The relationship between the supposedly exemplary individual and the culture from which he springs seems anything but straightforward; so does the connection between "valiantness" and other forms of virtue.

What goes wrong in *Coriolanus*? There are three ways of answering the question: by pondering the Roman society out of which Coriolanus springs, by contemplating Coriolanus himself, and by examining the moral and political assumptions upon which the notion of a war hero inexplicitly depends. All of these possible avenues of investigation turn out, unsurprisingly, to imply one another, but perhaps it is best to begin with the first issue, since the historical situation of ancient Rome is likely to be unfamiliar to a modern reader.

During Coriolanus's lifetime in the late fifth century B.C., Rome had already embarked on the expansionist course that would culminate in its domination of Europe, North Africa, and the Middle East four hundred years later, in the time of Julius Caesar, Marcus Brutus, and Marc Antony. But in these early years, dreams of world rule were still far in the future: Coriolanus's Rome was still battling the nearby Volscians. Roman bellicosity was a cultural tendency, not yet a clear pathway to empire. At home, Rome was struggling to devise a new form of government. In Coriolanus's youth, Lucius Junius Brutus and his allies had driven out King Tarquin and his family on the grounds that they had been abusing their power (an episode upon which Shakespeare based his narrative poem *The Rape of Lucrece*). In place of the monarchy, Brutus instituted a republic: government not by a king but by a senate composed of patricians (aristocrats). For military and civic matters requiring executive authority, the senate elected consuls for short terms. Soon, however, this system proved inadequate, as the large plebeian, or working, class clamored for a say in the city's rule. In the aftermath of the uprising depicted in *Coriolanus* 1.1, the plebeians were granted the right to elect their own representatives, called tribunes.

In its eventual form, therefore, the Roman Republic was a "mixed" form of government that attempted to distribute rather than to concentrate power, as well as to balance the rights and privileges of various constituencies. Inventing republican institutions entailed addressing important questions about the nature of the polity and of citizenship. Is the Roman state, as Menenius suggests, an impersonal force "whose course will on / The way it takes" (1.1.60–61) no matter what the majority of the city's residents desire? Or does the state merely express collective opinion, as the plebeians insist when they cry, "The people are the city" (3.1.200)? Ought the Roman state to concern itself mainly with managing affairs within the city walls, or should its military undertakings outside the city take political precedence? Who has a voice in the government of the city, and on what basis is suffrage granted: class status? personal merit? place of residence? Does citizenship, as Coriolanus argues, primarily entail duties such as military service? Or is citizenship, as the tribunes assume, a matter of entitlements: grain rations in times of famine, a voice in political and judicial affairs?

For Shakespeare and his contemporaries, these were not questions of merely antiquarian interest. Most premodern states, including classical republics and Shakespeare's England, consisted of a relatively small, property-owning, politically empowered class and a large subpolitical population that was supposed to submit to the laws, but that had no voting rights. But how small ought to be the privileged group, how large the disempowered group, and how distinct the differences between the two? These were matters of hot debate in Jacobean England. King James I and his son Charles, who liked to associate themselves with the imagery of imperial Rome, were attracted by absolutist models of government in which the monarch exercised virtually unlimited sway. By contrast, their opponents in Parliament often invoked the Roman Republic, which dispersed power over consuls, senate, and tribunes, as an analogue to the English commonwealth with its monarch, House of Lords, and House of Commons.

Such political debates were given an especially keen edge in the early seventeenth century by increasingly marked class differences. There were literary and artistic, as well as economic, ramifications to the widening gap between social classes. Whereas the large outdoor theaters on London's South Bank built in the 1580s and 1590s were designed for large, relatively heterogeneous audiences, by the early years of James I's reign the theater companies were targeting their audiences more precisely. In 1608, perhaps immediately before *Coriolanus*'s first performance, Shakespeare's company contracted for an indoor theater at Blackfriars designed to cater to customers from the gentry (upper middle class) and above. Since the company retained its ownership of its big open-air Globe Theater, and put on the same plays there, the distinction between popular and elite tastes could not have been strongly marked. Nonetheless, the differences in the acting space, in the conditions of performance, and in the nature of the audience must have led Shakespeare to reflect on the theatrical consequences of the increasingly strained relations among England's various social groups.

Given the contemporary resonances of his story, Shakespeare's extensive alterations of Plutarch's account are fascinating. *Coriolanus* opens, as already mentioned, with an uprising among Rome's common people. According to Plutarch, the plebeians revolted because the moneyed patricians had promised easier terms on loans if the plebeians would agree to fight the nearby Sabines. After the plebeians acquitted themselves bravely in battle, the patricians reneged on the agreement and sold into slavery those debtors—many of them war veterans—who were bankrupted by high interest rates. Shakespeare's plebeians, by contrast, make only fleeting references to usury. Their main complaint is simple hunger: a familiar grievance to an English audience in 1608. Barely a year before *Coriolanus*'s first performance, food shortages precipitated serious rioting by the rural poor in the Midland counties west of London, where Stratford-upon-Avon was located. The rioters accused the rich of hoarding foodstuffs in hopes of higher prices, and of having created a dearth by replacing the traditional cultivation of cereal grains with lucrative sheep farming. The rich countered that bad weather was to blame.

In updating the motives of his lower-class characters, Shakespeare translates Roman class conflicts into terms more immediate for his contemporaries. But his revision has other consequences too: it minimizes the plebeians' political sophistication, their military indispensability, and much of the justification for their outrage. The famine might well be a natural rather than a political calamity: there is no hint of any prior betrayed agreement and no suggestion of unrewarded plebeian military service. Unlike Plutarch's plebeians, Shakespeare's are mediocre soldiers or worse: in *Coriolanus*, valor in battle seems less a "Roman" than a distinctively aristocratic trait, exercised and uniquely cherished by the patrician class. Shakespeare's Rome fails to appreciate Coriolanus's *virtūs* simply because the society is not, as Plutarch had claimed it to be, fully a warrior culture at all.

Shakespeare is hard not only on the plebeians. He entirely omits Plutarch's descriptions of the historical Coriolanus's considerable political and military shrewdness. Plutarch's Coriolanus had already played several influential political roles before he made his bid for the consulship. He underwent without apparent compunction the traditional rituals required of all seekers after office; the plebeians later repudiated him on the grounds of a long political record that, in Shakespeare, does not exist. After his exile, Plutarch's Coriolanus cleverly exacerbates class strife in Rome by selectively refraining from burning patrician estates as he approaches the city with his Volscian army. Shakespeare's relentless but hotheaded character would hardly be capable of such a calculated act.

The effect of Shakespeare's changes is to open up a chasm that does not exist in his sources between patrician and plebeian values, and between military and civic ones. The general Cominius, praising Coriolanus in the senate house, seems superficially to be echoing Plutarch:

> It is held
> That valour is the chiefest virtue, and
> Most dignifies the haver. If it be,
> The man I speak of cannot in the world
> Be singly counterpoised.
>   (2.2.79–83)

But even in the process of making his argument, Cominius appears, in his evasive passive constructions and his conditional "if," to be partly disowning it. Coriolanus's initial lack of political ambitions, together with his hopeless awkwardness as a candidate, suggests that his military prowess is not merely irrelevant to peacetime employment but indeed renders him politically incompetent or even dangerous. Shakespeare's Coriolanus succeeds in battle by channeling overpowering anger into feats of extraordinary strength, by refusing to calculate possible harm to himself or to others, and by preferring action to words. In the political domain, by contrast, relative goods are often more important than absolutes, negotiated compromises preferable to flat conquest. The ability to control oneself in the interests of manipulating others is crucial; so is the capacity to predict the effects of one's own and other people's words and actions. Like most of Shakespeare's tragic heroes after Richard II, Coriolanus is trapped not so much by his vices as by his virtues. The traits that equip him so superbly for one enterprise cripple him for another.

Coriolanus's difficulty is not merely a matter of personal idiosyncrasy. It reflects a persistent problem, in both early modern England and in ancient Rome, in defining the male aristocrat's proper role. In medieval England, noblemen were feudally obliged to serve as battle captains over troops of their own vassals; the aristocrat's military function was his raison d'être, although proficiency in war was supposed to carry over into the management of civic affairs. In Shakespeare's time, the aristocrat's function was theoretically unchanged, but altered social circumstances placed it under increasing pressure. Just as the equation of "valiantness" and "virtue" could fail in early republican Rome, it could also be seen to be failing in early modern England. Throughout the late sixteenth and early seventeenth centuries, bureaucrats and policy makers like William Cecil, Robert Cecil, and Francis Bacon were sharply at odds with passionate militarists like Walter Ralegh, King James's son Prince Henry, and Shakespeare's erstwhile patron the earl of Essex. In these conflicts, the bureaucrats almost always had the advantage. Their skill at such tasks as overhauling the taxation system was hardly glamorous but proved indispensable for the newly powerful nation-state. By the early seventeenth century, the notion that the aristocrat rendered his most important service to his king on the battlefield seemed a remnant of a simpler age.

Coriolanus then, like Hotspur in Shakespeare's *1 Henry IV*, seems to embody a conception of aristocratic excellence whose historical moment, for better or worse, has already passed. Interestingly, a sense of the archaic quality of mighty warriors seems almost universal. Homer's epic heroes were already beginning to specialize their functions during the siege of Troy. For Plutarch, writing in the time of the Roman Empire, the original identification of aristocrat and warrior seems to have shattered in the long-ago days of the Roman Republic. Medieval writers locate both the flowering of knightly service and the beginning of its breakdown in the legendary fourth-century Arthurian court. Many Hollywood Westerns look back to a time in the nineteenth century when the older, rougher codes of the Indian fighter or nomadic frontiersman were being displaced by the values of permanent white settlers, including women and professional-caste men. From time immemorial, glorifying warriors has been tied up with nostalgia—not merely for the mighty soldier himself, but for a simpler, "manly" alternative to civilized complexities, an alternative always already lost.

In the tense dramatic milieu of *Coriolanus*, compounded from Shakespeare's own experience and what his sources provided him, the nature of his protagonist's heroism thus seems more intelligible and its failure less surprising. Since the heterogeneous Roman population has difficulty coming to any consensus about what it values, no single individual could possibly exemplify its ideals. Rather, Coriolanus possesses a narrow subset of traits more appealing to some groups (the patricians) than others (the plebeians) and more useful in some situations (war) than in others (peace). Coriolanus's mother, Volumnia, describing her son's education, suggests how his "heroism" has been developed by rigorously selecting for desired traits and just as sternly suppressing others.

> When yet he was but tenderbodied and the only son of my womb, when youth with comeliness plucked all gaze his way, when for a day of kings' entreaties a mother should not sell him an hour from her beholding, I, considering how honour would become such a person . . . was pleased to let him seek danger where he was like to find fame. To a cruel war I sent him, from whence he returned his brows bound with oak. I tell thee, daughter, I sprang not more in joy at first hearing he was a man-child than now in first seeing he had proved himself a man. (1.3.5–15)

Volumnia's own shrewdness and ferocity seems to belie the "naturalness" of a system that excludes women from politics and combat. Unlike Virgilia, Volumnia hardly seems content to stay home and do the sewing. But the incongruity between her personality and her prescribed social role does not render her skeptical of that role. Instead, she embraces her gendered destiny with characteristic zeal. In maternity she finds an improbable outlet for her own aggressiveness.

> The breasts of Hecuba
> When she did suckle Hector looked not lovelier
> Than Hector's forehead when it spit forth blood
> At Grecian sword, contemning.
>
> (1.3.37–40)

Symbolically equating milk and blood, the lactating mother with her wounded son, Volumnia both identifies vicariously with her war hero and wishes suffering upon him, delighting not merely in his triumphs but in his pain. Virgilia's conventionally feminine recoil from Volumnia's gory fantasies makes their aberrancy clear for the audience. In Volumnia, the discipline required to submit to rules of Roman womanliness seems to have generated a complicated sadomasochistic adaptation. She displaces her own forbidden bellicosity onto a dream of exaggerated masculinity and then attempts to realize that dream in her son.

Volumnia's ruthless mothering produces a man whose characteristic gesture is violently to resist whatever he perceives to be outside himself. Battle is Coriolanus's model for identity formation, and his ideal self is like an impermeably walled city. Overstated *differences*—between patrician and plebeian, between Roman and Volsce, between male and female, between man and boy—are the principles upon which Coriolanus has established his own sense of identity. Contempt and anger, like aggression, reinforce and clarify the boundaries of the self, marking it vividly off from those whom one hates, despises, or conquers. Coriolanus does not merely happen to be inflexible and narrow-minded; too much tolerance, too much sensitivity, would endanger him to the core. So would introspection, which might reveal an unwelcome complexity within. Coriolanus is hardly a taciturn character, but he is perhaps Shakespeare's most opaque tragic protagonist, for he is not inclined to reflect upon his own motives either in conversation or alone (indeed, he has only a single short soliloquy in the entire play). The great moments of Coriolanus's life are moments of embattled solitude: fighting by himself inside Corioles, standing alone for consul or separated from the Roman people after his exile, reflecting in an unaccompanied moment in Aufidius's hall, isolated in Corioles again at the end of the play, shouting at his old (and new) enemy: "Alone I did it" (5.6.117). He is thrilled by fantasies of absolute independence: "As if a man were author of himself / And knew no other kin" (5.3.36–37). With some justice, the hostile tribunes accuse him of wanting to be the only man left in Rome and of considering himself a god superior to ordinary mortals.

In his defiant self-sufficiency, however, Coriolanus is far needier than he acknowledges. When he allies himself with Aufidius, his former enemy, Aufidius's elated speech of welcome clarifies their shared dilemma.

> I loved the maid I married; never man
> Sighed truer breath. But that I see thee here,

Marcius Coriolanus and the attack on Corioli. Jost Amman, from *Icones Livianae* (1572).

> Thou noble thing, more dances my rapt heart
> Than when I first my wedded mistress saw
> Bestride my threshold. . . .
>
> . . . .
>   Thou hast beat me out
> Twelve several times, and I have nightly since
> Dreamt of encounters 'twixt thyself and me—
> We have been down together in my sleep,
> Unbuckling helms, fisting each other's throat—
> And waked half dead with nothing.
>   (4.5.113–25)

The combination of pain and pleasure to which Aufidius bears witness is strikingly reminiscent of Volumnia's maternal feelings, in which aggressiveness toward the beloved seems to loom so large. It is impossible here to distinguish hostility from attraction, competition from dependency, combat from homosexual embrace. The warrior loves his adversary because he needs a manly competitor against whom to establish his own identity. The striving for autonomy depends on the existence of something set off against, beside, or below it.

To distinguish oneself from other people, then, one must rely on them. "Thy valiantness was mine, thou suck'dst from me," Volumnia informs her son (3.2.129). Coriolanus wants to imagine his courage and honor as intrinsically his own, rather than conferred by others. But "our virtues," as Aufidius claims, "lie in th'interpretation of the time." (4.7.49–50). Roman merit, inextricable from social goals and needs, demands an admiring audience. Even while he professes to despise flattery, Coriolanus takes pride in such apparently trivial honorific gestures as the surname or the oaken garland conferred upon him by those who value his services. Insignificant in themselves, such symbols acquire meaning from the way in which they are regarded by the group. The exiled Coriolanus defiantly insists that "there is a world elsewhere" (3.3.139), but it is impossible for him to retire to a quiet corner of Italy and live out his life in obscurity. He needs to prove himself against an enemy, but now that enemy, Rome, is the place from which his life has drawn its meaning. Threatening to annihilate the community that bore him, he puts himself in a painfully contradictory position.

Thus the superior is always dependent on the inferior, the inside on the outside, the civilized on the barbarian, the patrician on the plebeian, the performer on the audience, the man on the woman and on the boy, even while the "upper" term prides itself on its difference from its subordinate. Moreover, just as important, the dependency works in both directions, as the action of *Coriolanus* shows. If Coriolanus depends on the Roman populace in ways he refuses to recognize, so does the populace depend on him. By imagining it can dispense with him and what he represents, it comes close to bringing destruction on its head.

Since we hear an unusual amount about Coriolanus's boyhood, it is easy to see his self-contradictory desire for autonomy in terms of his simultaneous flight from and dependence on Volumnia. But that is an oversimplification: Coriolanus is not merely the product of a uniquely bad upbringing. His anxieties about autonomy and dependence, competitiveness and cooperation, are shared, in some form, by almost everyone in the play: they are aspects of social and political dilemmas, not merely individual neuroses. Early in the first scene, the First Citizen notes—perhaps enviously but also accurately—that the patricians enjoy seeing the lower classes suffer, because that suffering enhances their sense of comparative privilege. Who depends on whom, how far ought that dependency to extend, what forms ought it to take?

These concerns are powerfully evoked in the imagery of *Coriolanus*. It was a cliché already old in Plutarch's time, and still current in Shakespeare's, that human communities were modeled on individual bodies. In the optimistic version of this analogy, the state is a collection of harmoniously interrelated organs, each selflessly performing its own distinctive function in the service of the whole. Interconnectedness is the apparent moral of Menenius's "pretty tale" (1.1.80) of the belly in the opening scene. But even in Menenius's version, the analogy veers toward grotesquerie, the body-state becoming an apparently headless entity equipped with an unnaturally smiling belly. Elsewhere in *Coriolanus*, the body is less a marvel of smooth interaction than a site of disintegration: Coriolanus imagines the plebeians as "fragments" and as "voices" (1.1.212, 2.3.115–20); Menenius rebukes a malcontent he calls "the great toe of this assembly" (1.1.144). The mutilations of the battlefield begin to seem corporeal equivalents for a profound crisis of the body politic. The shared needs of embodied, vulnerable human beings for food, shelter, and defense provide an obvious material basis for societies. But individual bodies tend to be selfish, unwilling to forgo their own urgent requirements in the interests of a collective good, reluctant to admit their reliance on one another lest that reliance be made a pretext for exploitation. Once again, dependence and autonomy seem simultaneously antithetical and inextricable.

Because the body in *Coriolanus* is so often imagined in negative terms—as starving, wounded, or cut to pieces—attempts to escape corporeal limitation seem understandable, even laudable. In fact, Coriolanus's battlefield heroism seems largely a matter of refusing to acknowledge physical constraints: he is inexhaustible, undaunted by wounds or by danger. Late in the play, Menenius describes him as a kind of robot: "when he walks, he moves like an engine, and the ground shrinks before his treading" (5.4.15–16). But within a few lines, Menenius is proven wrong: blood relationships, the ties of the body, prove impossible for Coriolanus to disown. Volumnia, Virgilia, and young Martius come to the Volscian camp to plead for their city and their people; and in a capitulation he knows to be virtually suicidal, Coriolanus grasps his mother's hand.

Coriolanus is not only the last of Shakespeare's tragedies but the last of a series of plays about ancient Rome. It seems to look back upon, and to anatomize, social and individual pathologies that in *Julius Caesar* and even *Antony and Cleopatra* were merely hinted at: the way "Roman" valor on the battlefield, for instance, becomes both a flight from and a replacement for heterosexuality; the way aggression and repression undergird the psyches of Roman men and women; the way both sexes deform their personalities in order to

Volumnia entreating Coriolanus. Jost Amman, from *Icones Livianae* (1572).

conform to highly restrictive patterns of masculinity or femininity. While in *Julius Caesar* class tensions serve mainly to exalt the patrician class, here the plebeians' grievances, and their different priorities, are understandable. Coriolanus's inability to comprehend the plebeians is a telling sign of both his personal rigidity and the alienation of rich from poor. *Coriolanus* has seemed to many audiences a relentlessly bleak play, and no wonder. Subjecting both its formidable but unpleasant hero and his society to intense critical scrutiny, *Coriolanus* implies that no political arrangement could possibly satisfy human needs, portrayed here as incorrigibly self-contradictory.

KATHARINE EISAMAN MAUS

TEXTUAL NOTE

The 1623 First Folio is the only authority for *Coriolanus*. Some believe that the compositors set the Folio text of this play directly from Shakespeare's manuscript, but the Oxford editors argue that the immediate source for F was more likely to have been a promptbook. Stage directions are unusually elaborate and give important performance clues: for instance, the act divisions were clearly marked (since intermissions were observed at "private" theaters like the Blackfriars), and the specifications for small musical instruments like cornets also suggest a more intimate performance space. The F compositors may have had trouble reading the handwriting in the manuscript (whether it was Shakespeare's or a member of the theater company's). There are some obvious errors requiring emendation and some confusion in setting verse lines. On the whole, however, *Coriolanus* is not one of the more textually vexing of Shakespeare's plays.

SELECTED BIBLIOGRAPHY

Adelman, Janet. " 'Anger's My Meat': Feeding, Dependency, and Aggression in *Coriolanus*." *Representing Shakespeare: New Psychoanalytic Essays*. Baltimore: Johns Hopkins University Press, 1980. 129–49.

Barton, Anne. "Livy, Machiavelli, and Shakespeare's *Coriolanus*." *Shakespeare Survey* 38 (1985): 115–29.

Bloom, Harold, ed. *William Shakespeare's "Coriolanus."* New York: Chelsea House, 1988.

Calderwood, James. "*Coriolanus*: Wordless Meanings and Meaningless Words." *Studies in English Literature* 6 (1966): 211–24.

Cantor, Paul. "Part One: *Coriolanus*." *Shakespeare's Rome: Republic and Empire*. Ithaca: Cornell University Press, 1976. 55–124.

Cavell, Stanley. "Who Does the Wolf Love?" *Disowning Knowledge in Six Plays by Shakespeare*. Cambridge: Cambridge University Press, 1987. 143–78.

Fish, Stanley. "How to Do Things with Austin and Searle: Speech-Act Theory and Literary Criticism." *Is There a Text in This Class?* Cambridge: Harvard University Press, 1980. 197–245.

Jorgenson, Paul. "Shakespeare's Coriolanus: Elizabethan Soldier." *PMLA* 64 (1949): 221–35.

Patterson, Annabel. *Shakespeare and the Popular Voice*. Oxford: Basil Blackwood, 1989.

Rabkin, Norman. *Shakespeare and the Common Understanding*. New York: Free Press, 1967. 120–49.

Wheeler, David, ed. *"Coriolanus": Critical Essays*. New York: Garland, 1995.

The Tragedy of Coriolanus

The Persons of the Play

CAIUS MARTIUS, later surnamed CORIOLANUS ⎱
MENENIUS Agrippa
Titus LARTIUS ⎱ generals ⎰ patricians of
COMINIUS ⎰ Rome
VOLUMNIA, Coriolanus' mother
VIRGILIA, his wife
YOUNG MARTIUS, his son
VALERIA, a chaste lady of Rome
SICINIUS Velutus ⎱ tribunes of the Roman people
Junius BRUTUS ⎰
CITIZENS of Rome
SOLDIERS in the Roman army
Tullus AUFIDIUS, general of the Volscian army
His LIEUTENANT
His SERVINGMEN
CONSPIRATORS with Aufidius
Volscian LORDS
Volscian CITIZENS
SOLDIERS in the Volscian army
ADRIAN, a Volscian
NICANOR, a Roman
A Roman HERALD
MESSENGERS
AEDILES
A gentlewoman, an usher, Roman and Volscian senators and
  nobles, captains in the Roman army, officers, lictors

1.1

Enter a Company of mutinous CITIZENS *with staves,
clubs, and other weapons*

FIRST CITIZEN Before we proceed any further, hear me speak.
ALL Speak, speak.
FIRST CITIZEN You are all resolved rather to die than to famish?
ALL Resolved, resolved.
5 FIRST CITIZEN First, you know Caius Martius is chief enemy to
  the people.
ALL We know't, we know't.
FIRST CITIZEN Let us kill him, and we'll have corn° at our own   *grain*
  price. Is't a verdict?°   *Do we agree*
10 ALL No more talking on't, let it be done. Away, away.
SECOND CITIZEN One word, good citizens.
FIRST CITIZEN We are accounted poor citizens, the patricians
  good.° What authority[1] surfeits on would relieve us. If they   *noble; well-off*
  would yield us but the superfluity° while it were wholesome°   *excess/still edible*
15 we might guess they relieved us humanely, but they think we

1.1 Location: A street in Rome.   1. The nobility.

are too dear.[2] The leanness that afflicts us, the object° of our   *visible fact*
misery, is as an inventory to particularize their abundance;[3] our
sufferance° is a gain to them. Let us revenge this with our pikes°   *distress/spears; pitch-*
ere we become rakes;[4] for the gods know I speak this in hunger   *forks*
20   for bread, not in thirst for revenge.
SECOND CITIZEN   Would you proceed especially against Caius
     Martius?
THIRD CITIZEN   Against him first.
FOURTH CITIZEN   He's a very dog to° the commonalty.[5]   *persecutor of*
25   SECOND CITIZEN   Consider you what services he has done for his
     country?
FIRST CITIZEN   Very well, and could be content to give him good
     report for't, but that he pays himself with being proud.
FIFTH CITIZEN   Nay, but speak not maliciously.
30   FIRST CITIZEN   I say unto you, what he hath done famously,° he   *that has won fame*
     did it to that end°—though soft-conscienced men can be con-   *(to advance his pride)*
     tent to say 'it was for his country', 'he did it to please his mother,
     and to be partly proud'°—which he is even to the altitude of   *partly out of pride*
     his virtue.[6]
35   SECOND CITIZEN   What he cannot help in his nature you ac-
     count a vice in him. You must in no way say he is covetous.
FIRST CITIZEN   If I must not, I need not be barren of accusations.
     He hath faults, with surplus, to tire in repetition.
          Shouts within
     What shouts are these? The other side o'th' city is risen. Why
40   stay we prating° here? To th' Capitol!   *chattering*
ALL   Come, come.
          Enter MENENIUS
FIRST CITIZEN   Soft,° who comes here?   *Wait*
SECOND CITIZEN   Worthy Menenius Agrippa, one that hath
     always loved the people.
45   FIRST CITIZEN   He's one honest enough. Would all the rest were
     so!
MENENIUS   What work's, my countrymen, in hand? Where go you
     With bats° and clubs? The matter. Speak, I pray you.   *cudgels*
FIRST CITIZEN   Our business is not unknown to th' senate. They
50   have had inkling this fortnight what we intend to do, which now
     we'll show 'em in deeds. They say poor suitors° have strong[7]   *petitioners*
     breaths; they shall know we have strong arms, too.
MENENIUS   Why, masters,° my good friends, mine honest neigh-   *(artisans' title)*
     bours,
     Will you undo° yourselves?   *destroy*
55   FIRST CITIZEN   We cannot, sir. We are undone already.
MENENIUS   I tell you, friends, most charitable care
     Have the patricians of you. For° your wants,   *As for*
     Your suffering in this dearth,° you may as well   *famine*
     Strike at the heaven with your staves as lift them
60   Against the Roman state, whose course will on
     The way it takes, cracking ten thousand curbs[8]
     Of more strong link asunder than can ever

---

2. We cost too much to preserve; we are too rich.
3. To make their prosperity stand out by comparison.
4. Rakes are proverbially thin; playing on "pikes".
5. Common people.

6. That is, his pride is equal to his valor.
7. Strong smelling, from eating onions, the food of the poor.
8. Chain bits used to restrain unruly horses.

Appear in your impediment.[9] For the dearth,
The gods, not the patricians, make it, and
65 Your knees to them, not arms, must help. Alack,
You are transported by calamity
Thither where more attends° you, and you slander   *awaits*
The helms° o'th' state, who care for you like fathers,   *helmsmen*
When you curse them as enemies.
70 FIRST CITIZEN   Care for us? True, indeed! They ne'er cared for
    us yet: suffer us to famish, and their storehouses crammed with
    grain; make edicts for usury[1] to support usurers; repeal daily
    any wholesome act established against the rich; and provide
    more piercing° statutes daily to chain up and restrain the poor.   *severe*
75 If the wars eat us not up, they will; and there's all the love they
    bear us.
    MENENIUS   Either you must
    Confess yourselves wondrous malicious
    Or be accused of folly. I shall tell you
80 A pretty tale. It may be you have heard it,
    But since it serves my purpose, I will venture
    To stale't a little more.°   *To make it more familiar*
    FIRST CITIZEN   Well, I'll hear it, sir. Yet you must not think to
    fob off our disgrace[2] with a tale. But an't° please you, deliver.   *if it*
85 MENENIUS   There was a time when all the body's members,
    Rebelled against the belly, thus accused it:
    That only like a gulf° it did remain   *abyss*
    I'th' midst o'th' body, idle and unactive,
    Still cupboarding the viand,[3] never bearing
90 Like° labour with the rest; where th'other instruments°   *Equal/organs*
    Did see and hear, devise, instruct, walk, feel,
    And, mutually participate,° did minister   *participating*
    Unto the appetite and affection° common   *desire*
    Of the whole body. The belly answered—
95 FIRST CITIZEN   Well, sir, what answer made the belly?
    MENENIUS   Sir, I shall tell you. With a kind of smile,
    Which ne'er came from the lungs,° but even thus—   *(organs of laughter)*
    For look you, I may make the belly smile
    As well as speak—it tauntingly replied
100 To th' discontented members, the mutinous parts
    That envied his receipt;° even so most fitly[4]   *what it received*
    As you malign our senators for that°   *because*
    They are not such as you.
    FIRST CITIZEN   Your belly's answer—what?
    The kingly crownèd head, the vigilant eye,
105 The counsellor heart, the arm our soldier,
    Our steed the leg, the tongue our trumpeter,
    With other muniments° and petty helps   *supports*
    In this our fabric,° if that they—   *body*
    MENENIUS   What then?
    Fore me,° this fellow speaks! What then? What then?   *(an oath)*
110 FIRST CITIZEN   Should by the cormorant° belly be restrained,   *rapacious*
    Who is the sink° o'th' body—   *cesspool*

---

9. *than . . . impediment:* than you can ever offer in opposition.
1. Permitting the lending of money at interest (widely
considered immoral, because it enriched wealthy lenders

at the expense of poor borrowers).
2. Dismiss our hardship.
3. Always hoarding the food.
4. In just the way.

MENENIUS   Well, what then?
FIRST CITIZEN   The former agents, if they did complain,
     What could the belly answer?
MENENIUS   I will tell you,
     If you'll bestow a small° of what you have little—   *small amount*
115 Patience—a while, you'st hear the belly's answer.
FIRST CITIZEN   You're long about it.
MENENIUS   Note me this, good friend:
     Your° most grave belly was deliberate,   *This*
     Not rash like his accusers, and thus answered:
     'True is it, my incorporate° friends,' quoth he,   *united in one body*
120 'That I receive the general food at first
     Which you do live upon, and fit it is,
     Because I am the storehouse and the shop
     Of the whole body. But, if you do remember,
     I send it through the rivers of your blood
125 Even to the court, the heart, to th' seat° o'th' brain;   *throne*
     And through the cranks and offices⁵ of man
     The strongest nerves° and small inferior veins   *muscles*
     From me receive that natural competency°   *sustenance*
     Whereby they live. And though that all at once'—
130 You my good friends, this says the belly, mark me—
FIRST CITIZEN   Ay, sir, well, well.
MENENIUS   'Though all at once cannot
     See what I do deliver out to each,
     Yet I can make my audit up⁶ that all
     From me do back receive the flour⁷ of all
135 And leave me but the bran.' What say you to't?
FIRST CITIZEN   It was an answer. How apply you this?
MENENIUS   The senators of Rome are this good belly,
     And you the mutinous members. For examine
     Their counsels and their cares, digest⁸ things rightly
140 Touching the weal o'th' common,⁹ you shall find
     No public benefit which you receive
     But it proceeds or comes from them to you,
     And no way from yourselves. What do you think,
     You, the great toe of this assembly?
145 FIRST CITIZEN   I the great toe? Why the great toe?
MENENIUS   For that, being one o'th' lowest, basest, poorest
     Of this most wise rebellion, thou goest foremost.
     Thou rascal, that art worst in blood¹ to run,
     Lead'st first to win some vantage.°   *benefit*
150 But make you ready your stiff bats and clubs.
     Rome and her rats are at the point of battle.
     The one side must have bale.°   *injury*
          Enter MARTIUS   Hail, noble Martius!
MARTIUS   Thanks.—What's the matter, you dissentious° rogues,   *rebelling*
     That, rubbing the poor itch of your opinion,
     Make yourselves scabs?
155 FIRST CITIZEN   We have ever your good word.
MARTIUS   He that will give good words to thee will flatter

---

5. Through the winding passages and workrooms.
6. Show on my balance sheet.
7. Nourishment (punning on "flower," or choicest part).
8. Interpret (playing on the belly's function).

9. Concerning the public good.
1. Most desperate; lowest born. *rascal:* wretch; inferior
deer or dog.

Beneath abhorring. What would you have, you curs
That like nor° peace nor war? The one affrights you,   *neither*
The other makes you proud.° He that trusts to you,   *rebellious*
160   Where he should find you lions finds you hares,
Where foxes, geese. You are no surer, no,
Than is the coal of fire upon the ice,
Or hailstone in the sun. Your virtue° is   *characteristic skill*
To make him worthy whose offence subdues him,²
165   And curse that justice did it. Who deserves greatness
Deserves° your hate, and your affections° are   *Incurs / propensities*
A sick man's appetite, who desires most that
Which would increase his evil.° He that depends   *illness*
Upon your favours swims with fins of lead,
170   And hews down oaks with rushes. Hang ye! Trust ye?
With every minute you do change a mind,
And call him noble that was now° your hate,   *just now*
Him vile that was your garland.³ What's the matter,
That in these several° places of the city   *various*
175   You cry against the noble senate, who,
Under the gods, keep you in awe, which else°   *who otherwise*
Would feed on one another?
[*To* MENENIUS]   What's their seeking?
MENENIUS   For corn at their own rates,° whereof they say   *prices*
The city is well stored.
MARTIUS   Hang 'em! They say?
180   They'll sit by th' fire and presume to know
What's done i'th' Capitol,⁴ who's like to rise,
Who thrives and who declines; side° factions and give out°   *side with / announce*
Conjectural marriages, making parties strong
And feebling such as stand not in their liking
185   Below their cobbled° shoes. They say there's grain enough!   *patched*
Would the nobility lay aside their ruth°   *compassion*
And let me use my sword, I'd make a quarry⁵
With thousands of these quartered⁶ slaves as high
As I could pitch my lance.
190   MENENIUS   Nay, these are all most thoroughly persuaded,°   *appeased*
For though abundantly they lack discretion,
Yet are they passing° cowardly. But I beseech you,   *exceedingly*
What says the other troop?
MARTIUS   They are dissolved. Hang 'em.
They said they were an-hungry,° sighed forth proverbs—   *very hungry*
195   That hunger broke stone walls, that dogs° must eat,   *(even dogs)*
That meat was made for mouths, that the gods sent not
Corn for the rich men only. With these shreds
They vented° their complainings, which being answered,   *spoke; excreted*
And a petition granted them—a strange one,
200   To break the heart of generosity°   *the nobility*
And make bold power look pale—they threw their caps
As they would hang them on the horns o'th' moon,
Shouting their emulation.⁷

2. To extol the man whose wrongdoing makes him liable   5. A pile of animals killed in hunting.
to punishment.   6. Hacked to pieces (a punishment for treason).
3. Hero (traditionally wreathed with laurel or oak leaves).   7. Rivalry (either to shout loudest, or to defy the nobility).
4. The temple of Jupiter and hub of the Roman state.

MENENIUS   What is granted them?
MARTIUS   Five tribunes° to defend their vulgar wisdoms,   *representatives*
205   Of their own choice. One's Junius Brutus,
         Sicinius Velutus, and I know not. 'Sdeath,°   *God's death (an oath)*
         The rabble should have first unroofed the city
         Ere so prevailed with me! It will in time
         Win upon power° and throw forth greater themes   *Prevail upon authority*
210   For insurrection's arguing.
MENENIUS   This is strange.
MARTIUS [*to the* CITIZENS]   Go get you home, you fragments.°   *scraps of uneaten food*
         Enter a MESSENGER *hastily*
MESSENGER   Where's Caius Martius?
MARTIUS   Here. What's the matter?
215 MESSENGER   The news is, sir, the Volsces are in arms.
MARTIUS   I am glad on't. Then we shall ha' means to vent
         Our musty superfluity.°   *moldy excess*
         Enter SICINIUS, BRUTUS, COMINIUS, LARTIUS, *with other*
              SENATORS
                           See, our best elders.
FIRST SENATOR   Martius, 'tis true that you have lately told us.
         The Volsces are in arms.
MARTIUS   They have a leader,
220   Tullus Aufidius, that will put you to't.°   *to the test*
         I sin in envying his nobility,
         And were I anything but what I am,
         I would wish me only he.
COMINIUS   You have fought together!
MARTIUS   Were half to half the world by th' ears[8] and he
225   Upon my party,° I'd revolt to make   *side*
         Only my wars with him. He is a lion
         That I am proud to hunt.
FIRST SENATOR   Then, worthy Martius,
         Attend upon° Cominius to these wars.   *Serve under*
COMINIUS [*to* MARTIUS]   It is your former promise.
MARTIUS   Sir, it is,
230   And I am constant. Titus Lartius, thou
         Shalt see me once more strike at Tullus' face.
         What, art thou stiff?[9] Stand'st out?
LARTIUS   No, Caius Martius.
         I'll lean upon one crutch and fight with th'other
         Ere stay behind this business.
MENENIUS   O true bred!
235 FIRST SENATOR   Your company to th' Capitol, where I know
         Our greatest friends attend us.
LARTIUS [*to* COMINIUS]   Lead you on.
         [*To* MARTIUS] Follow Cominius. We must follow you,
         Right worthy° your priority.   *Who well deserve*
COMINIUS   Noble Martius.
FIRST SENATOR [*to the* CITIZENS]   Hence to your homes, be
              gone.
MARTIUS   Nay, let them follow.
240   The Volsces have much corn. Take these rats thither

---

8. If one half of the world were fighting the other.   9. Obstinate (but Lartius understands "stiff with age").

To gnaw their garners.°   CITIZENS *steal away*   *storehouses*
             Worshipful mutineers,
Your valour puts well forth.[1] [*To the* SENATORS] Pray follow.
        Exeunt. Manent° SICINIUS *and* BRUTUS   *Remain onstage*

SICINIUS   Was ever man so proud as is this Martius?
BRUTUS   He has no equal.
245 SICINIUS   When we were chosen tribunes for the people—
BRUTUS   Marked you his lip and eyes?
SICINIUS   Nay, but his taunts.
BRUTUS   Being moved,° he will not spare to gird[2] the gods.   *angry*
SICINIUS   Bemock the modest moon.
BRUTUS   The present wars devour him! He is grown
    Too proud to be so valiant.
250 SICINIUS   Such a nature,
    Tickled° with good success, disdains the shadow   *Excited; flattered*
    Which he treads on at noon. But I do wonder
    His insolence can brook° to be commanded   *endure*
    Under Cominius.
BRUTUS   Fame, at the which he aims—
255   In whom already he's well graced—cannot
    Better be held nor more attained than by
    A place below the first; for what miscarries
    Shall be the general's fault, though he perform
    To th' utmost of a man, and giddy censure°   *rash opinion*
260   Will then cry out of Martius 'O, if he
    Had borne the business!'
SICINIUS   Besides, if things go well,
    Opinion, that so sticks on° Martius, shall   *clings to*
    Of his demerits° rob Cominius.   *Of Cominius's deserts*
BRUTUS   Come,
    Half all Cominius' honours are to Martius,
265   Though Martius earned them not; and all his faults
    To Martius shall be honours, though indeed
    In aught he merit not.
SICINIUS   Let's hence and hear
    How the dispatch is made,° and in what fashion,   *business is executed*
    More than his singularity,[3] he goes
    Upon this present action.
270 BRUTUS   Let's along.   *Exeunt*

1.2

Enter AUFIDIUS, *with* SENATORS *of Corioles*
FIRST SENATOR   So, your opinion is, Aufidius,
    That they of Rome are entered° in our counsels   *instructed*
    And know how we proceed.
AUFIDIUS   Is it not yours?
    What ever have been thought on in this state
5   That could be brought to bodily act ere Rome
    Had circumvention?° 'Tis not four days gone   *means to circumvent it*
    Since I heard thence.° These are the words. I think   *from there*
    I have the letter here—yes, here it is.
    [*He reads the letter*]

1. Promises well, like a budding plant (ironic).
2. He will not refrain from sneering at.
3. Apart from his idiosyncrasies.
1.2 Location: Corioles, chief city of the Volscians.

'They have pressed a power,° but it is not known   *conscripted an army*
10   Whether for east or west. The dearth is great,
The people mutinous, and it is rumoured
Cominius, Martius your old enemy,
Who is of Rome worse hated than of you,
And Titus Lartius, a most valiant Roman,
15   These three lead on this preparation
Whither 'tis bent.° Most likely 'tis for you.   *Wherever it is bound*
Consider of it.'
FIRST SENATOR   Our army's in the field.
We never yet made doubt but Rome was ready
To answer us.
AUFIDIUS   Nor did you think it folly
20   To keep your great pretences° veiled till when   *aims*
They needs must show themselves, which in the hatching,
It seemed, appeared° to Rome. By the discovery   *became known*
We shall be shortened in our aim,° which was   *have to lower our sights*
To take in° many towns ere, almost, Rome   *seize*
Should know we were afoot.
25   SECOND SENATOR   Noble Aufidius,
Take your commission, hie° you to your bands.°   *haste / troops*
Let us alone to guard Corioles.
If they set down° before's, for the remove°   *encamp / to raise the siege*
Bring up your army, but I think you'll find
They've not prepared for us.
30   AUFIDIUS   O, doubt not that.
I speak from certainties. Nay, more,
Some parcels° of their power are forth already,   *parts*
And only hitherward.° I leave your honours.   *marching toward us*
If we and Caius Martius chance to meet,
35   'Tis sworn between us we shall ever strike°   *keep fighting*
Till one can do no more.
ALL THE SENATORS   The gods assist you!
AUFIDIUS   And keep your honours safe.
FIRST SENATOR   Farewell.
SECOND SENATOR   Farewell.
ALL   Farewell.
                    Exeunt [AUFIDIUS *at one door,*
                    SENATORS *at another door*]

1.3

Enter VOLUMNIA *and* VIRGILIA, *mother and wife to Mar-*
tius. They set them down on two low stools and sew
VOLUMNIA   I pray you, daughter, sing, or express yourself in a
more comfortable sort.° If my son were my husband, I should   *cheerful manner*
freelier rejoice in that absence wherein he won honour than in
the embracements of his bed where he would show most love.
5   When yet he was but tenderbodied and the only son of my
womb, when youth with comeliness plucked all gaze his way,
when for a day of kings' entreaties a mother should not sell him
an hour from her beholding, I, considering how honour would
become such a person°—that it was no better than, picture-   *handsome figure*
10   like, to hang by th' wall if renown made it not stir[1]—was

---

1.3 Location: Caius Martius's house, in Rome.   1. If desire for fame did not move it to action.

pleased to let him seek danger where he was like to find fame.
To a cruel war I sent him, from whence he returned his brows
bound with oak.[2] I tell thee, daughter, I sprang not more in joy
at first hearing he was a man-child than now in first seeing he
had proved himself a man.

VIRGILIA But had he died in the business, madam, how then?

VOLUMNIA Then his good report should have been my son. I
therein would have found issue. Hear me profess sincerely: had
I a dozen sons, each in my love alike, and none less dear than
thine and my good Martius', I had rather had eleven die nobly
for their country than one voluptuously surfeit out of action.[3]

Enter a GENTLEWOMAN

GENTLEWOMAN Madam, the Lady Valeria is come to visit you.

VIRGILIA [*to* VOLUMNIA] Beseech you give me leave to retire
myself.°   *to go in*

VOLUMNIA Indeed you shall not.
Methinks I hear hither your husband's drum,
See him pluck Aufidius down by th' hair;
As children from a bear, the Volsces shunning° him.   *fleeing*
Methinks I see him stamp thus, and call thus:
'Come on, you cowards, you were got° in fear   *begotten*
Though you were born in Rome!' His bloody brow
With his mailed° hand then wiping, forth he goes,   *armored*
Like to a harvest-man that's tasked° to mow   *ordered*
Or° all or lose his hire.°   *Either / pay*

VIRGILIA His bloody brow? O Jupiter, no blood!

VOLUMNIA Away, you fool! It more becomes a man
Than gilt° his trophy. The breasts of Hecuba[4]   *gold leaf*
When she did suckle Hector[5] looked not lovelier
Than Hector's forehead when it spit forth blood
At Grecian sword, contemning.°   *expressing contempt*

[*To the* GENTLEWOMAN]   Tell Valeria
We are fit° to bid her welcome.   *Exit* GENTLEWOMAN   *ready*

VIRGILIA Heavens bless my lord from fell° Aufidius!   *fierce*

VOLUMNIA He'll beat Aufidius' head below his knee
And tread upon his neck.

Enter VALERIA, *with an usher and the* GENTLEWOMAN

VALERIA My ladies both, good day to you.

VOLUMNIA Sweet madam.

VIRGILIA I am glad to see your ladyship.

VALERIA How do you both? You are manifest housekeepers.[6]
What are you sewing here? A fine spot,° in good faith. How   *embroidered design*
does your little son?

VIRGILIA I thank your ladyship; well, good madam.

VOLUMNIA He had rather see the swords and hear a drum
than look upon his schoolmaster.

VALERIA O' my word, the father's son! I'll swear 'tis a very pretty
boy. O' my troth, I looked upon him o' Wednesday half an
hour together. He's such a confirmed° countenance! I saw him   *determined*
run after a gilded butterfly, and when he caught it he let it go
again, and after it again, and over and over° he comes, and up   *head over heels*

2. A garland of oak leaves (awarded to one who saved the
life of a Roman citizen in battle).
3. Indulge himself to excess away from the battlefield.
4. Trojan queen, mother of many sons.

5. The greatest Trojan warrior, killed by the Greek Achilles (see *Troilus and Cressida*).
6. You are clearly being stay-at-homes.

again, catched it again. Or whether his fall enraged him, or
60   how 'twas, he did so set° his teeth and tear it! O, I warrant, how   clench
he mammocked° it!   shredded
VOLUMNIA   One on's° father's moods.   of his
VALERIA   Indeed, la, 'tis a noble child.
VIRGILIA   A crack,° madam.   lively lad
65   VALERIA   Come, lay aside your stitchery. I must have you play
the idle housewife° with me this afternoon.   hussy
VIRGILIA   No, good madam, I will not out of doors.
VALERIA   Not out of doors?
VOLUMNIA   She shall, she shall.
70   VIRGILIA   Indeed, no, by your patience. I'll not over the thresh-
old till my lord return from the wars.
VALERIA   Fie, you confine yourself most unreasonably. Come,
you must go visit the good lady that lies in.°   is confined with child
VIRGILIA   I will wish her speedy strength, and visit her with my
75   prayers, but I cannot go thither.
VOLUMNIA   Why, I pray you?
VIRGILIA   'Tis not to save labour, nor that I want love.°   lack affection for her
VALERIA   You would be another Penelope.[7] Yet they say all the
yarn she spun in Ulysses' absence did but fill Ithaca full of
80   moths. Come, I would your cambric° were sensible° as your   fine white linen / sensitive
finger, that you might leave pricking it for pity. Come, you
shall go with us.
VIRGILIA   No, good madam, pardon me, indeed I will not forth.
VALERIA   In truth, la, go with me, and I'll tell you excellent news
85   of your husband.
VIRGILIA   O, good madam, there can be none yet.
VALERIA   Verily, I do not jest with you: there came news from
him last night.
VIRGILIA   Indeed, madam?
90   VALERIA   In earnest, it's true. I heard a senator speak it. Thus it
is: the Volsces have an army forth, against whom Cominius the
general is gone with one part of our Roman power. Your lord
and Titus Lartius are set down before their city Corioles. They
nothing doubt prevailing,[8] and to make it brief wars. This is
95   true, on mine honour; and so, I pray, go with us.
VIRGILIA   Give me excuse,° good madam, I will obey you in   Pardon me
everything hereafter.
VOLUMNIA [to VALERIA]   Let her alone, lady. As she is now she
will but disease° our better mirth.   trouble
100   VALERIA   In truth, I think she would. Fare you well, then. Come,
good sweet lady. Prithee, Virgilia, turn thy solemness out o'
door and go along with us.
VIRGILIA   No, at a word, madam. Indeed, I must not. I wish you
much mirth.
105   VALERIA   Well then, farewell.
                    Exeunt [VALERIA, VOLUMNIA, *and usher at one door,*
                        VIRGILIA *and* GENTLEWOMAN *at another door*]

7. In Homer's *Odyssey*, Ulysses' wife, Penelope, pretends   els each night.
during his protracted absence that she cannot remarry   8. They don't at all doubt that they will prevail.
until she finishes her weaving, which she secretly unrav-

1.4

Enter MARTIUS, LARTIUS *with* [*a trumpeter and*] *drum
and colors,*° *with captains and soldiers* [*carrying scaling*   drummer and flagbearer
ladders], *as before the city Corioles;*[1] *to them a* MES-
SENGER

MARTIUS	Yonder comes news. A wager they have met.	
LARTIUS	My horse to yours, no.	
MARTIUS	'Tis done.	
LARTIUS	Agreed.	

MARTIUS [*to the* MESSENGER]   Say, has our general met the enemy?
MESSENGER   They lie in view, but have not spoke° as yet.   *encountered*
LARTIUS   So, the good horse is mine.
5 MARTIUS   I'll buy him of you.
LARTIUS   No, I'll nor° sell nor give him. Lend you him I will,   *neither*
For half a hundred years.
     [*To the trumpeter*]   Summon the town.
MARTIUS [*to the* MESSENGER]   How far off lie these armies?
MESSENGER   Within
     this mile and half.
MARTIUS   Then shall we hear their 'larum,° and they ours.   *call to arms*
10 Now Mars,° I prithee, make us quick in work,   *Roman god of war*
That we with smoking° swords may march from hence   *steaming (with blood)*
To help our fielded friends.[2]
     [*To the trumpeter*]   Come, blow thy blast.
     They sound a parley.[3] *Enter two* SENATORS, *with others,
     on the walls of Corioles*
     [*To the* SENATORS] Tullus Aufidius, is he within your walls?
FIRST SENATOR   No, nor a man that fears you less than he:
That's lesser than a little.
     Drum afar off
15   [*To the Volscians*]   Hark, our drums
Are bringing forth our youth. We'll break our walls
Rather than they shall pound us up.° Our gates,   *confine us*
Which yet seem shut, we have but pinned with rushes.°   *hollow reeds*
They'll open of themselves.
     Alarum far off
     [*To the Romans*]   Hark you, far off
20 There is Aufidius. List what work he makes
Amongst your cloven° army.   *divided, cut to pieces*
                  [*Exeunt Volscians from the walls*]
MARTIUS   O, they are at it!
LARTIUS   Their noise be our instruction. Ladders, ho!
     [*They prepare to assault the walls.*]
     Enter the army of the Volsces [*from the gates*]
MARTIUS   They fear us not, but issue° forth their city.   *rush from*
Now put your shields before your hearts, and fight
25 With hearts more proof° than shields. Advance, brave Titus.   *impenetrable*
They do disdain us much beyond our thoughts,[4]
Which makes me sweat with wrath. Come on, my fellows.

1.4 Location: Before the walls of Corioles.
1. The rear of the stage represented the city walls, the
tiring-house door the gate, and the balcony the ramparts.

2. Our comrades in the battlefield.
3. Trumpet call for conference with the enemy.
4. More than we had imagined.

He that retires, I'll take him for a Volsce,
And he shall feel mine edge.°   *(sword edge)*
　　　Alarum. The Romans are beat back [and exeunt]
　　　to their trenches[, the Volsces following]

1.5

　　　Enter [Roman SOLDIERS, *in retreat, followed by]* MAR-
　　　TIUS, *cursing*
MARTIUS　All the contagion of the south¹ light on you,
　　　You shames of Rome! You herd of—boils and plagues
　　　Plaster you o'er, that you may be abhorred°   *(by your smell)*
　　　Farther than seen, and one infect another
5　　　Against the wind a mile!° You souls of geese   *Even a mile upwind*
　　　That bear the shapes of men, how have you run
　　　From slaves that apes would beat! Pluto° and hell: *god of the underworld*
　　　All hurt behind!² Backs red, and faces pale
　　　With flight and agued° fear! Mend and charge home,³   *shivering*
10　　　Or by the fires of heaven° I'll leave the foe   *the stars*
　　　And make my wars on you. Look to't. Come on.
　　　If you'll stand fast, we'll beat them to their wives,
　　　As they us to our trenches. Follow.
　　　　　[The Romans come forward towards the walls.]
　　　　　Another alarum, and [enter the army of the Volsces.]
　　　　　MARTIUS *[beats them back through] the gates*
　　　So, now the gates are ope. Now prove good seconds.°   *supporters*
15　　　'Tis for the followers fortune widens° them,   *opens*
　　　Not for the fliers. Mark me, and do the like.
　　　　　[He] enters the gates
FIRST SOLDIER　Foolhardiness! Not I.
SECOND SOLDIER　　　　　　　　　　　Nor I.
　　　　　*Alarum continues. [The gates close,] and [*MARTIUS*] is*
　　　　　shut in
FIRST SOLDIER　See, they have shut him in.
THIRD SOLDIER　　　　　　　　　　To th' pot,° I warrant him.   *cooking pot*
　　　Enter LARTIUS
LARTIUS　What is become of Martius?
FOURTH SOLDIER　　　　　　　　Slain, sir, doubtless.
20　FIRST SOLDIER　Following the fliers at the very heels,
　　　With them he enters, who upon the sudden
　　　Clapped-to° their gates. He is himself alone   *Shut*
　　　To answer° all the city.   *confront*
LARTIUS　　　　　　　　O noble fellow,
　　　Who sensibly° outdares his senseless sword   *though having sensation*
25　　　And, when it bows, stand'st up! Thou art lost, Martius.
　　　A carbuncle entire,° as big as thou art,   *flawless ruby*
　　　Were not so rich a jewel. Thou wast a soldier
　　　Even to Cato's⁴ wish, not fierce and terrible
　　　Only in strokes, but with thy grim looks and
30　　　The thunder-like percussion of thy sounds
　　　Thou mad'st thine enemies shake as if the world
　　　Were feverous and did tremble.

1.5　Scene continues.
1. South wind (thought to carry disease).
2. An injury taken in flight was a disgrace.

3. Charge to the heart of their defenses.
4. Cato the Censor, Roman general and moralist.

Enter MARTIUS, *bleeding, assaulted by the enemy*

FIRST SOLDIER   Look, sir.

LARTIUS   O, 'tis Martius!
Let's fetch him off, or make remain alike.⁵
    They fight, and all [exeunt] into the city

1.6

Enter certain ROMANS *with spoils*

FIRST ROMAN   This will I carry to Rome.

SECOND ROMAN   And I this.

THIRD ROMAN   A murrain° on't, I took this for silver.   plague
    [*He throws it away.*]
    Alarum continues still afar off. Enter MARTIUS, [*bleed-*
    ing,] *and* [LARTIUS] *with a trumpet[er]. Exeunt* [ROMANS
    with spoils]

MARTIUS   See here these movers¹ that do prize their honours
5   At a cracked drachma!° Cushions, leaden spoons,   Greek coin
       Irons of a doit,² doublets that hangmen would
       Bury with those that wore them,³ these base slaves,
       Ere yet the fight be done, pack up. Down with them!
       And hark what noise the general makes. To him.
10   There is the man of my soul's hate, Aufidius,
       Piercing our Romans. Then, valiant Titus, take
       Convenient numbers to make good° the city,   secure
       Whilst I, with those that have the spirit, will haste
       To help Cominius.

LARTIUS   Worthy sir, thou bleed'st.
15   Thy exercise hath been too violent
       For a second course° of fight.   bout

MARTIUS   Sir, praise me not.
       My work hath yet not warmed me. Fare you well.
       The blood I drop is rather physical⁴
       Than dangerous to me. To Aufidius thus
       I will appear and fight.

20 LARTIUS   Now the fair goddess fortune
       Fall deep in love with thee, and her great charms
       Misguide thy opposers' swords! Bold gentleman,
       Prosperity be thy page.°   Success attend you
                                                      (Prosperity)
MARTIUS   Thy friend° no less
       Than those she placeth highest. So farewell.

25 LARTIUS   Thou worthiest Martius!   [*Exit* MARTIUS]
       Go sound thy trumpet in the market-place.
       Call thither all the officers o'th' town,
       Where they shall know our mind. Away.   *Exeunt* [*severally*]

1.7

Enter COMINIUS, *as it were in retire, with soldiers*

COMINIUS   Breathe you,° my friends. Well fought. We are come   Get your breath back
       off¹

---

5. Let's rescue him, or share his fate.
1.6 Location: Corioles.
1. Active persons (ironic); plunderers.
2. Worthless swords (a "doit" was a very small coin). *doublets*: close-fitting jackets (common male attire in Jacobean England).

3. That is, even a hangman, whose wage is his victim's clothing, would spurn these garments.
4. Curative (bloodletting was a common medical practice).
1.7 Location: The battlefield.
1. We have retreated.

Like Romans, neither foolish in our stands
Nor cowardly in retire. Believe me, sirs,
We shall be charged again. Whiles we have struck,°   *we were fighting*
5   By interims and conveying gusts² we have heard
The charges of our friends. The Roman gods
Lead their successes as we wish our own,
That both our powers, with smiling fronts° encount'ring,   *faces; front ranks*
May give you° thankful sacrifice!   *(the gods)*
           Enter a MESSENGER
                           Thy news?
10 MESSENGER   The citizens of Corioles have issued,°   *(from the gates)*
And given to Lartius and to Martius battle.
I saw our party to their trenches driven,
And then I came away.
COMINIUS   Though thou speak'st truth,
Methinks thou speak'st not well. How long is't since?
15 MESSENGER   Above an hour, my lord.
COMINIUS   'Tis not a mile; briefly° we heard their drums.   *a short time ago*
How couldst thou in a mile confound° an hour,   *waste*
And bring thy news so late?
MESSENGER   Spies of the Volsces
Held me in chase, that I was forced to wheel°   *detour*
20 Three or four miles about; else had I, sir,
Half an hour since brought my report.   *[Exit]*
        Enter MARTIUS [*bloody*]
COMINIUS   Who's yonder,
That does appear as he were flayed? O gods!
He has the stamp° of Martius, and I have   *form*
Before-time° seen him thus.   *Previously*
MARTIUS   Come I too late?
25 COMINIUS   The shepherd knows not thunder from a tabor°   *small drum*
More than I know the sound of Martius' tongue
From every meaner° man.   *lesser*
MARTIUS   Come I too late?
COMINIUS   Ay, if you come not in the blood of others,
But mantled in your own.
MARTIUS   O, let me clip° ye   *clasp*
30 In arms as sound as when I wooed, in heart
As merry as when our nuptial day was done,
And tapers burnt to bedward!
        [They embrace]
COMINIUS   Flower of warriors! How is't with Titus Lartius?
MARTIUS   As with a man busied about decrees,
35 Condemning some to death and some to exile,
Ransoming him or pitying, threat'ning th'other;
Holding Corioles in the name of Rome
Even like a fawning greyhound in the leash,
To let him slip° at will.   *off the leash*
COMINIUS   Where is that slave
40 Which told me they had beat you to your trenches?
Where is he? Call him hither.
MARTIUS   Let him alone.
He did inform° the truth. But for our gentlemen,°   *report / (sarcastic)*
The common file°—a plague—tribunes for them?—   *sort*

---

2. At intervals, conveyed by the wind.

      The mouse ne'er shunned the cat as they did budge°   *flinch*
      From rascals worse than they.
45 COMINIUS   But how prevailed you?
    MARTIUS   Will the time serve to tell? I do not think.
      Where is the enemy? Are you lords o'th' field?
      If not, why cease you till you are so?
    COMINIUS   Martius, we have at disadvantage fought,
50   And did retire to win our purpose.°   *for tactical reasons*
    MARTIUS   How lies their battle?° Know you on which side   *army*
      They have placed their men of trust?
    COMINIUS   As I guess, Martius,
      Their bands i'th' vanguard are the Antiates,
      Of their best trust; o'er them Aufidius,
      Their very heart of hope.
55 MARTIUS   I do beseech you
      By all the battles wherein we have fought,
      By th' blood we have shed together, by th' vows we have made
      To endure° friends, that you directly set me   *remain*
      Against Aufidius and his Antiates,
60   And that you not delay the present,° but,   *matter at hand*
      Filling the air with swords advanced and darts,
      We prove° this very hour.   *try*
    COMINIUS   Though I could wish
      You were conducted to a gentle bath
      And balms applied to you, yet dare I never
65   Deny your asking. Take your choice of those
      That best can aid your action.
    MARTIUS   Those are they
      That most are willing. If any such be here—
      As it were sin to doubt—that love this painting°   *(blood)*
      Wherein you see me smeared; if any fear
70   Lesser his person than an ill report[3]
      If any think brave death outweighs bad life,
      And that his country's dearer than himself,
      Let him alone, or so many so minded,
          [*He waves his sword*]
      Wave thus to express his disposition,
75   And follow Martius.
          They all shout and wave their swords, [then some] take
          him up in their arms and [they] cast up their caps
      O' me alone, make you a sword of me?
      If these shows be not outward,° which of you   *superficial*
      But is four Volsces? None of you but is
      Able to bear against the great Aufidius
80   A shield as hard as his. A certain number—
      Though thanks to all—must I select from all.
      The rest shall bear the business in some other fight
      As cause will be obeyed.° Please you to march,   *the situation requires*
      And I shall quickly draw out my command,[4]
      Which men are best inclined.
85 COMINIUS   March on, my fellows.
      Make good this ostentation,° and you shall   *show of enthusiasm*
      Divide in all[5] with us.   *Exeunt [marching]*

---

3. Less for his body than for his reputation.   5. Share the honor and winnings.
4. Select those I will command.

1.8

Enter LARTIUS *[through the gates of] Corioles, with
drum and trumpet, a* LIEUTENANT, *other soldiers, and a
scout*

LARTIUS *[to the* LIEUTENANT] So, let the ports° be guarded. Keep your duties   *gates*
    As I have set them down. If I do send, dispatch
    Those centuries¹ to our aid. The rest will serve
    For a short holding.° If we lose the field   *brief occupation*
5   We cannot keep the town.
LIEUTENANT   Fear not our care, sir.
LARTIUS   Hence, and shut your gates upon's.   *[Exit* LIEUTENANT]
    [To the scout] Our guider, come; to th' Roman camp conduct us.
                Exeunt toward COMINIUS *and* MARTIUS

1.9

Alarum, as in battle. Enter MARTIUS, *[bloody,] and*
AUFIDIUS at several° doors   *separate*

MARTIUS   I'll fight with none but thee, for I do hate thee
    Worse than a promise-breaker.
AUFIDIUS   We hate alike.
    Not Afric owns° a serpent I abhor   *Africa doesn't contain*
    More than thy fame and envy.° Fix thy foot.   *enviable reputation*
5 MARTIUS   Let the first budger die the other's slave,
    And the gods doom him after.
AUFIDIUS   If I fly, Martius,
    Holla° me like a hare.   *Shout in pursuit of*
MARTIUS   Within these three hours, Tullus,
    Alone I fought in your Corioles' walls,
    And made what work I pleased. 'Tis not my blood
10   Wherein thou seest me masked. For thy revenge,
    Wrench up thy power to th' highest.
AUFIDIUS   Wert thou the Hector
    That was the whip of your bragged progeny,¹
    Thou shouldst not scape me here.
          Here they fight, and certain Volsces come in the aid of
          AUFIDIUS. MARTIUS *fights till [the Volsces] be driven in*
          breathless[, MARTIUS *following]*
    Officious° and not valiant, you have shamed me   *Meddling*
15   In your condemnèd seconds.²
                              Exit

1.10

Alarum. A retreat is sounded. Flourish.¹ Enter at one
door COMINIUS *with the Romans, at another door* MAR-
TIUS *with his arm in a scarf°*   *sling*

COMINIUS *[to* MARTIUS]   If I should tell thee o'er this thy day's work
    Thou'lt not believe thy deeds. But I'll report it
    Where senators shall mingle tears with smiles,
    Where great patricians shall attend and shrug,°   *(with incredulity)*
5   I'th' end admire;° where ladies shall be frighted   *marvel*

1.8 Location: The gates of Corioles.
1. Companies of a hundred men.
1.9 Location: The battlefield.
1. Romans claimed descent from the Trojans; Hector, the
finest Trojan soldier, was the scourge ("whip") of the

Greeks.
2. Contemptible assistance.
1.10 Location: The battlefield.
1. Trumpet call for the entry of the victorious Romans.
retreat: signal to cease pursuit.

And, gladly quaked,° hear more; where the dull° tribunes,   *made to tremble / sullen*
That with the fusty° plebeians hate thine honours,   *moldy; stinking*
Shall say against their hearts° 'We thank the gods   *despite themselves*
Our Rome hath such a soldier.'
10   Yet cam'st thou to a morsel of this feast,
Having fully dined before.[2]

Enter [LARTIUS,] *with his power,° from the pursuit*   *troops*

LARTIUS   O general,
Here is the steed, we the caparison.[3]
Hadst thou beheld—

MARTIUS   Pray now, no more. My mother,
Who has a charter° to extol her blood,°   *right / offspring*
15   When she does praise me grieves me. I have done
As you have done, that's what I can; induced
As you have been, that's for my country.
He that has but effected his good will[4]
Hath overta'en mine act.

COMINIUS   You shall not be
20   The grave of your deserving. Rome must know
The value of her own. 'Twere a concealment
Worse than a theft, no less than a traducement,°   *slander*
To hide your doings and to silence that
Which, to the spire and top of praises vouched,°   *declared*
25   Would seem but modest.° Therefore, I beseech you—   *inadequate*
In sign° of what you are, not to reward   *As a token*
What you have done—before our army hear me.

MARTIUS   I have some wounds upon me, and they smart
To hear themselves remembered.

COMINIUS   Should they not,
30   Well might they fester 'gainst ingratitude,
And tent[5] themselves with death. Of all the horses—
Whereof we have ta'en good, and good store[6]—of all
The treasure in this field achieved and city,
We render you the° tenth, to be ta'en forth   *one*
35   Before the common distribution
At your only° choice.   *sole*

MARTIUS   I thank you, general,
But cannot make my heart consent to take
A bribe to pay my sword. I do refuse it,
And stand° upon my common part with those   *insist*
40   That have upheld the doing.

A long flourish. They all cry 'Martius, Martius!' [and]
cast up their caps and lances. COMINIUS *and* LARTIUS
stand bare

May these same instruments which you profane
Never sound more. When drums and trumpets shall
I'th' field prove flatterers, let courts and cities be
Made all of false-faced soothing.[7] When steel grows
45   Soft as the parasite's° silk, let him be made   *flatterer's*

---

2. *Yet . . . before:* either "The feast of description is a morsel compared with the full dinner of your deeds," or "Your
final onslaught was a mere morsel in addition to your earlier fighting."
3. That is, here is he who really did the work (Coriolanus, the horse); we are only the horse's trappings ("capar-

ison").
4. Carried out his resolution.
5. Heal (a "tent" was a probe that cleansed a wound).
6. We have captured good quality and quantity.
7. Hypocritical compliments.

An overture for th' wars.[8] No more, I say.
For that I have not washed my nose that bled,
Or foiled some debile° wretch, which without note   *feeble*
Here's many else° have done, you shout me forth   *others*
50   In acclamations hyperbolical,°   *In exaggerated praise*
As if I loved my little[9] should be dieted°   *fattened*
In praises sauced with lies.
COMINIUS   Too modest are you,
More cruel to your good report than grateful
To us that give° you truly. By your patience,   *describe*
55   If 'gainst yourself you be incensed we'll put you,
Like one that means his proper harm,° in manacles,   *harm to himself*
Then reason safely with you. Therefore be it known,
As to us, to all the world, that Caius Martius
Wears this war's garland, in token of the which
60   My noble steed, known to the camp, I give him,
With all his trim belonging;° and from this time,   *fine trappings*
For what he did before Corioles, call him,
With all th'applause and clamour of the host,
Martius Caius Coriolanus. Bear th'addition°   *title*
65   Nobly ever!
        Flourish. Trumpets sound, and drums
ALL   Martius Caius Coriolanus!
CORIOLANUS [*to* COMINIUS]   I will go wash,
And when my face is fair° you shall perceive   *clean*
Whether I blush or no. Howbeit, I thank you.
70   I mean to stride your steed, and at all times
To undercrest° your good addition   *uphold*
To th' fairness° of my power.   *best*
COMINIUS   So, to our tent,
Where, ere we do repose us, we will write
To Rome of our success. You, Titus Lartius,
75   Must to Corioles back. Send us to Rome
The best,[1] with whom we may articulate°   *make terms*
For their own good and ours.
LARTIUS   I shall, my lord.
CORIOLANUS   The gods begin to mock me. I, that now
Refused most princely gifts, am bound to beg
Of my lord general.
80 COMINIUS   Take't, 'tis yours. What is't?
CORIOLANUS   I sometime lay here in Corioles,
And at a poor man's house. He used° me kindly.   *treated*
He cried° to me; I saw him prisoner;   *appealed*
But then Aufidius was within my view,
85   And wrath o'erwhelmed my pity. I request you
To give my poor host freedom.
COMINIUS   O, well begged!
Were he the butcher of my son he should
Be free as is the wind. Deliver° him, Titus.   *Free*
LARTIUS   Martius, his name?
CORIOLANUS   By Jupiter, forgot!
90   I am weary, yea, my memory is tired.
Have we no wine here?

---

8. *let . . . wars*: a debated and perhaps corrupt passage: 9. Small achievement.
perhaps "let the parasite call soldiers to war."   1. The most noble Volscians.

COMINIUS   Go we to our tent.
The blood upon your visage dries; 'tis time
It should be looked to. Come.   *Exeunt. A flourish [of] cornetts*

1.11

Enter AUFIDIUS, *bloody, with two or three* SOLDIERS
AUFIDIUS   The town is ta'en.
A SOLDIER   'Twill be delivered back on good condition.[1]
AUFIDIUS   Condition?
I would I were a Roman, for I cannot,
5   Being a Volsce, be that I am.° Condition?   *what I am (proud)*
What good condition can a treaty find
I'th' part that is at mercy?° Five times, Martius,   *For the conquered side*
I have fought with thee; so often hast thou beat me,
And wouldst do so, I think, should we encounter
10   As often as we eat. By th' elements,
If e'er again I meet him beard to beard,
He's mine, or I am his! Mine emulation°   *rivalry*
Hath not that honour in't it had, for where°   *whereas*
I thought to crush him in an equal force,
15   True sword to sword, I'll potch° at him some way   *thrust*
Or° wrath or craft may get him.   *Either*
A SOLDIER   He's the devil.
AUFIDIUS   Bolder, though not so subtle. My valour, poisoned
With only suff'ring stain° by him, for him   *disgrace*
Shall fly out of itself. Nor sleep nor sanctuary,[2]
20   Being naked, sick, nor fane° nor Capitol,   *temple*
The prayers of priests nor times of sacrifice—
Embargements° all of fury—shall lift up   *Impediments*
Their rotten° privilege and custom 'gainst   *worn-out*
My hate to Martius. Where I find him, were it
25   At home upon° my brother's guard,° even there,   *under / protection*
Against the hospitable canon,° would I   *rule of hospitality*
Wash my fierce hand in's heart. Go you to th' city.
Learn how 'tis held, and what they are that must
Be hostages for Rome.
A SOLDIER   Will not you go?
30   AUFIDIUS   I am attended° at the cypress grove. I pray you—   *expected*
'Tis south the city mills—bring me word thither
How the world goes, that to the pace of it[3]
I may spur on my journey.
A SOLDIER   I shall, sir.
                    *Exeunt [*AUFIDIUS *at one door,* SOLDIERS
                              at another door]

2.1

Enter MENENIUS *with the two tribunes of the people,*
      SICINIUS *and* BRUTUS
MENENIUS   The augurer[1] tells me we shall have news tonight.
BRUTUS   Good or bad?
MENENIUS   Not according to the prayer of the people, for they
love not Martius.

1.11 Location: Outside Corioles.
1. Terms (Aufidius takes the meaning "state of being").
2. In early modern England, those who sought sanctuary
in a church were protected from attack or legal prosecu-

tion. *fly out of itself:* deviate from its nature.
3. In accordance with the situation.
2.1 Location: Rome.
1. Religious official who interpreted omens.

5   SICINIUS   Nature teaches beasts to know their friends.
    MENENIUS   Pray you, who does the wolf love?
    SICINIUS   The lamb.
    MENENIUS   Ay, to devour him, as the hungry plebeians would
    the noble Martius.
10   BRUTUS   He's a lamb indeed that baas like a bear.
    MENENIUS   He's a bear indeed that lives like a lamb.[2] You two
    are old men. Tell me one thing that I shall ask you.
    SICINIUS *and* BRUTUS   Well, sir?
    MENENIUS   In what enormity is Martius poor in that you two
15   have not in abundance?
    BRUTUS   He's poor in no one fault, but stored° with all.   *well stocked*
    SICINIUS   Especially in pride.
    BRUTUS   And topping all others in boasting.
    MENENIUS   This is strange now. Do you two know how you are
20   censured° here in the city—I mean of us o'th' right-hand file.[3]   *judged*
    Do you?
    SICINIUS *and* BRUTUS   Why, how are we censured?
    MENENIUS   Because—you talk of pride now—will you not be
    angry?
25   SICINIUS *and* BRUTUS   Well, well, sir, well?
    MENENIUS   Why, 'tis no great matter, for a very little thief of
    occasion will rob you of a great deal of patience.[4] Give your
    dispositions the reins, and be angry at your pleasures—at the
    least, if you take it as a pleasure to you in being so. You blame
30   Martius for being proud?
    BRUTUS   We do it not alone, sir.
    MENENIUS   I know you can do very little alone, for your helps
    are many, or else your actions would grow wondrous single.°   *solitary; trivial*
    Your abilities are too infant-like for doing much alone. You talk
35   of pride. O that you could turn your eyes toward the napes of
    your necks, and make but an interior survey of your good
    selves! O that you could!
    SICINIUS *and* BRUTUS   What then, sir?
    MENENIUS   Why, then you should discover a brace° of unmer-   *pair*
40   iting, proud, violent, testy magistrates, alias fools, as any in
    Rome.
    SICINIUS   Menenius, you are known well enough too.
    MENENIUS   I am known to be a humorous° patrician, and one   *whimsical*
    that loves a cup of hot wine with not a drop of allaying Tiber°   *water*
45   in't; said to be something imperfect in favouring the first com-
    plaint,[5] hasty and tinder-like upon too trivial motion;° one that   *provocation*
    converses more with the buttock of the night than with the
    forehead of the morning.[6] What I think, I utter, and spend my
    malice in my breath. Meeting two such wealsmen° as you   *statesmen*
50   are—I cannot call you Lycurguses[7]—if the drink you give me
    touch my palate adversely, I make a crooked face at it. I cannot
    say your worships have delivered the matter well, when I find
    the ass in compound with the major part of your syllables.[8] And

---

2. That is, how can you accuse him of being a bear when he lives an innocent life?
3. Patrician class (who made up the right-hand "file," or line, in battle).
4. The least pretext will make you lose your temper.
5. *favouring the first complaint:* accepting the first version

of a dispute I hear before considering the other side.
6. That experiences more late nights than early mornings.
7. Lycurgus was a famous Spartan lawgiver.
8. I find stupidity mixed in most of what you say.

though I must be content to bear with those that say you are
55 reverend grave men, yet they lie deadly° that tell you have good   *extremely*
faces. If you see this in the map of my microcosm,⁹ follows it
that I am known well enough too? What harm can your bisson
conspectuities° glean out of this character,¹ if I be known well   *dim vision*
enough too?
60 BRUTUS   Come, sir, come, we know you well enough.
MENENIUS   You know neither me, yourselves, nor anything. You
are ambitious for poor knaves' caps and legs.² You wear out a
good wholesome forenoon in hearing a cause between an
orange-wife and a faucet-seller,³ and then rejourn° the contro-   *adjourn*
65 versy of threepence to a second day of audience.° When you   *hearing*
are hearing a matter between party and party, if you chance to
be pinched with the colic,° you make faces like mummers,⁴ set   *intestinal gas*
up the bloody flag° against all patience, and in roaring for a   *declare war*
chamber-pot, dismiss the controversy bleeding,° the more   *unhealed*
70 entangled by your hearing. All the peace you make in their
cause is calling both the parties knaves. You are a pair of
strange ones.
BRUTUS   Come, come, you are well understood to be a perfecter
giber for the table than a necessary bencher in the Capitol.⁵
75 MENENIUS   Our very priests must become mockers if they shall
encounter such ridiculous subjects° as you are. When you   *objects; citizens*
speak best unto the purpose it is not worth the wagging of your
beards, and your beards deserve not so honourable a grave as
to stuff a botcher's° cushion or to be entombed in an ass's pack-   *clothes mender*
80 saddle.⁶ Yet you must be saying 'Martius is proud', who, in a
cheap estimation,° is worth all your predecessors since Deucal-   *low estimate*
ion,⁷ though peradventure some of the best of 'em were heredi-
tary hangmen.⁸ Good e'en to your worships. More of your
conversation would infect my brain, being° the herdsmen of   *you two being*
85 the beastly plebeians. I will be bold to take my leave of you.
      [*He leaves*] BRUTUS *and* SICINIUS, [*who stand*] *aside.*
      Enter [*in haste*] VOLUMNIA, VIRGILIA, *and* VALERIA
How now, my as fair as noble ladies—and the moon,⁹ were she
earthly, no nobler—whither do you follow your eyes so fast?
VOLUMNIA   Honourable Menenius, my boy Martius approaches.
For the love of Juno, let's go.
90 MENENIUS   Ha, Martius coming home?
VOLUMNIA   Ay, worthy Menenius, and with most prosperous
approbation.¹
MENENIUS [*throwing up his cap*]   Take my cap, Jupiter, and I
thank thee! Hoo, Martius coming home?
95 VIRGILIA *and* VALERIA   Nay, 'tis true.
VOLUMNIA   Look, here's a letter from him. The state hath another, his wife another, and I think there's one at home for
you.

---

9. My face (thought to map the "little world" of the
human body).
1. Verbal description.
2. For deferentially doffed caps and bent legs.
3. Between a woman fruit vendor and someone who sells
taps for liquor barrels.
4. Dumb-show actors (who use exaggerated facial expressions).

5. *perfecter giber . . . Capitol*: better at dinner jests than at
serving in the senate.
6. Hair from cut beards was used as stuffing.
7. Deucalion and his wife were sole survivors of a great
flood; their son was the ancestor of the Greeks.
8. A very base occupation.
9. Diana, goddess of chastity.
1. Rich praise; happy success.

MENENIUS   I will make my very house reel tonight. A letter for
100   me?
VIRGILIA   Yes, certain, there's a letter for you; I saw't.
MENENIUS   A letter for me? It gives me an estate° of seven years'   *endowment; condition*
        health, in which time I will make a lip° at the physician. The   *sneer*
        most sovereign° prescription in Galen[2] is but empiricutic° and,   *effective / quackish*
105   to° this preservative, of no better report than a horse-drench.[3]   *compared with*
        Is he not wounded? He was wont° to come home wounded.   *accustomed*
VIRGILIA   O, no, no, no!
VOLUMNIA   O, he is wounded, I thank the gods for't!
MENENIUS   So do I, too, if it be not too much. Brings a° victory   *If he brings*
110   in his pocket, the wounds become him.
VOLUMNIA   On's brows, Menenius. He comes the third time
        home with the oaken garland.
MENENIUS   Has he disciplined Aufidius soundly?
VOLUMNIA   Titus Lartius writes they fought together, but Aufid-
115   ius got off.
MENENIUS   And 'twas time for him too, I'll warrant him that. An°   *If*
        he had stayed by him, I would not have been so fidiussed[4] for
        all the chests in Corioles and the gold that's in them. Is the
        senate possessed° of this?   *informed*
120 VOLUMNIA   Good ladies, let's go. Yes, yes, yes. The senate has
        letters from the general, wherein he gives my son the whole
        name° of the war. He hath in this action outdone his former   *credit*
        deeds doubly.
VALERIA   In truth, there's wondrous things spoke of him.
125 MENENIUS   Wondrous, ay, I warrant you; and not without his
        true purchasing.°   *truly earning it*
VIRGILIA   The gods grant them true.
VOLUMNIA   True? Pooh-whoo!
MENENIUS   True? I'll be sworn they are true. Where is he
130   wounded? [*To the tribunes*] God save your good worships. Mar-
        tius is coming home. He has more cause to be proud. [*To
        VOLUMNIA*] Where is he wounded?
VOLUMNIA   I'th' shoulder and i'th' left arm. There will be large
        cicatrices° to show the people when he shall stand for his   *scars*
135   place.[5] He received in the repulse of Tarquin[6] seven hurts
        i'th' body.
MENENIUS   One i'th' neck and two i'th' thigh — there's nine that
        I know.
VOLUMNIA   He had before this last expedition twenty-five wounds
140   upon him.
MENENIUS   Now it's twenty-seven. Every gash was an enemy's
        grave.
        A shout and flourish
        Hark, the trumpets.
VOLUMNIA   These are the ushers of Martius. Before him he car-
145   ries noise, and behind him he leaves tears.
        Death, that dark spirit, in's nervy° arm doth lie,   *muscular*
        Which being advanced, declines;° and then men die.   *being raised, descends*

---

2. Ancient medical authority still standard in the Renaissance (Galen actually lived six centuries after Coriolanus).
3. Horse medicine.
4. "Aufidiussed." Menenius's coinage for "beaten."

5. Will offer himself as a candidate for consul, republican Rome's highest office.
6. Martius's first military experience was in the war
against the former King Tarquin.

Trumpets sound a sennet.° Enter [in state] COMINIUS *the*   ceremonial flourish
general and LARTIUS, *between them* CORIOLANUS,
crowned with an oaken garland, with captains and sol-
diers and a HERALD

HERALD   Know, Rome, that all alone Martius did fight
Within Corioles' gates, where he hath won
150   With fame a name to° 'Martius Caius'; these   in addition to
In honour follows 'Coriolanus'.
Welcome to Rome, renownèd Coriolanus!
       A flourish sound[s]
ALL   Welcome to Rome, renownèd Coriolanus!
CORIOLANUS   No more of this, it does offend my heart.
Pray now, no more.
COMINIUS   Look, sir, your mother.
155   CORIOLANUS [*to* VOLUMNIA]   O,
You have, I know, petitioned all the gods
For my prosperity!°   success
       [*He] kneels*
VOLUMNIA   Nay, my good soldier, up,
My gentle Martius, worthy Caius,
       [*He rises*]
And, by deed-achieving honour newly named—
160   What is it?—'Coriolanus' must I call thee?
But O, thy wife!
CORIOLANUS [*to* VIRGILIA]   My gracious silence, hail.
Wouldst thou have laughed had I come coffined home,
That weep'st to see me triumph? Ah, my dear,
Such eyes the widows in Corioles wear,
And mothers that lack sons.
165   MENENIUS   Now the gods crown thee!
CORIOLANUS [*to* VALERIA]   And live you yet? O my sweet lady, pardon.
VOLUMNIA   I know not where to turn. O, welcome home!
And welcome, general, and you're welcome all!
MENENIUS   A hundred thousand welcomes! I could weep
170   And I could laugh, I am light and heavy.° Welcome!   (of heart)
A curse begnaw at very root on's heart
That is not glad to see thee. You are three
That Rome should dote on. Yet, by the faith of men,
We have some old crab-trees° here at home that will not   (gnarled, sour men)
175   Be grafted to your relish.° Yet welcome, warriors!   liking
We call a nettle but a nettle, and
The faults of fools but folly.
COMINIUS   Ever right.
CORIOLANUS   Menenius, ever, ever.
HERALD   Give way there, and go on.
180   CORIOLANUS [*to* VOLUMNIA *and* VIRGILIA]   Your hand, and yours.
Ere in our own house I do shade my head
The good patricians must be visited,
From whom I have received not only greetings,
But with them change of honours.°   a new set of honors
VOLUMNIA   I have lived
185   To see inherited° my very wishes,   realized
And the buildings of my fancy. Only
There's one thing wanting, which I doubt not but
Our Rome will cast upon thee.

CORIOLANUS   Know, good mother,
    I had rather be their servant in my way
    Than sway⁷ with them in theirs.
190 COMINIUS   On, to the Capitol.

        Flourish [of] cornetts. Exeunt in state, as before, [all
        but] BRUTUS *and* SICINIUS[*, who come forward*]

BRUTUS   All tongues speak of him, and the blearèd sights°   dim-sighted people
    Are spectacled to see him. Your prattling nurse
    Into a rapture° lets her baby cry   fit
    While she chats him;⁸ the kitchen malkin° pins   wench
195 Her richest lockram° 'bout her reechy° neck,   linen / filthy
    Clamb'ring the walls to eye him. Stalls, bulks,⁹ windows
    Are smothered up, leads filled and ridges horsed
    With variable complexions,¹ all agreeing
    In earnestness to see him. Seld-shown flamens°   Seldom-seen priests
200 Do press among the popular° throngs, and puff°   plebeian / pant
    To win a vulgar station.° Our veiled dames   a place in the crowd
    Commit the war of white and damask² in
    Their nicely³ guarded cheeks to th' wanton spoil
    Of Phoebus'° burning kisses. Such a pother°   the sun's / commotion
205 As if that whatsoever god who leads him°   (Coriolanus)
    Were slily crept into his human powers
    And gave him graceful posture.
SICINIUS   On the sudden°   At once
    I warrant him consul.
BRUTUS   Then our office may
    During his power° go sleep.   term of authority
210 SICINIUS   He cannot temp'rately transport° his honours   convey
    From where he should begin and end,° but will   to where he should end
    Lose those he hath won.
BRUTUS   In that there's comfort.
SICINIUS   Doubt not
    The commoners, for whom we stand, but they
    Upon their ancient malice⁴ will forget
215 With the least cause these his new honours, which°   (which cause)
    That he will give them make I as little question
    As⁵ he is proud to do't.
BRUTUS   I heard him swear,
    Were he to stand for consul, never would he
    Appear i'th' market-place nor on him put
220 The napless vesture° of humility,   threadbare garment
    Nor, showing, as the manner is, his wounds
    To th' people, beg their stinking breaths.°   votes
SICINIUS   'Tis right.
BRUTUS   It was his word. O, he would miss it° rather   forgo the consulship
    Than carry° it, but by the suit of the gentry to him,   go through with it
    And the desire of the nobles.
225 SICINIUS   I wish no better
    Than have him hold that purpose, and to put it
    In execution.

---

7. Rule; prevail; deviate from a straight course.
8. Discusses Coriolanus.
9. Framework projecting from shopfronts ("stalls").
1. *leads . . . complexions:* lead roofs filled and rooftops
bestridden by all types of people.

2. The conflict between white and pink in delicate skin
("damask" refers to the dark-pink damask rose).
3. Fastidiously (by the veils they usually wear).
4. Because of their long-standing hostility.
5. *I as . . . as:* I have as little doubt as that.

BRUTUS	'Tis most like he will.	
SICINIUS	It shall be to him then, as our good wills,°	*as our benefit requires*

A sure destruction.

BRUTUS   So it must fall out

230 To him, or our authority's for an end.
We must suggest° the people in what hatred   *insinuate to*
He still° hath held them; that to's power he would   *always*
Have made them mules, silenced their pleaders,°   *representatives*
And dispropertied° their freedoms, holding them   *taken away*
235 In human action and capacity
Of no more soul nor fitness for the world
Than camels in their war, who have their provand°   *food*
Only for bearing burdens, and sore blows
For sinking under them.

SICINIUS   This, as you say, suggested
240 At some time when his soaring insolence
Shall touch° the people—which time shall not want°   *kindle / be lacking*
If he be put upon't, and that's as easy
As to set dogs on sheep—will be his fire
To kindle their dry stubble,⁶ and their blaze
Shall darken him for ever.

Enter a MESSENGER

245 BRUTUS   What's the matter?

MESSENGER   You are sent for to the Capitol. 'Tis thought
That Martius shall be consul. I have seen
The dumb men throng to see him, and the blind
To hear him speak. Matrons flung gloves,
250 Ladies and maids their scarves and handkerchiefs,
Upon him as he passed. The nobles bended
As to Jove's statue, and the commons made
A shower and thunder with their caps and shouts.
I never saw the like.

BRUTUS   Let's to the Capitol,
255 And carry with us ears and eyes for th' time,°   *present occasion*
But hearts for the event.°   *outcome*

SICINIUS   Have with you.°   *Exeunt*   *Let's go, I'm with you.*

2.2

Enter two OFFICERS, *to lay cushions, as it were
in the Capitol*

FIRST OFFICER   Come, come, they are almost here. How many
stand for consulships?

SECOND OFFICER   Three, they say, but 'tis thought of everyone
Coriolanus will carry it.

5 FIRST OFFICER   That's a brave fellow, but he's vengeance° proud   *intensely*
and loves not the common people.

SECOND OFFICER   Faith, there hath been many great men that
have flattered the people who ne'er loved them; and there be
many that they° have loved they know not wherefore,° so that   *(the people) / why*
10 if they love they know not why, they hate upon no better a
ground. Therefore for Coriolanus neither to care whether they
love or hate him manifests the true knowledge he has in° their   *of*

6. That is, Coriolanus's fiery insolence will kindle the dry   2.2 Location: The Capitol, Rome.
fuel of the plebeians' resentment.

disposition, and out of his noble carelessness lets them plainly
see't.

15 FIRST OFFICER   If he did not care whether he had their love or
no he waved indifferently¹ 'twixt doing them neither good nor
harm; but he seeks their hate with greater devotion than they
can render it him, and leaves nothing undone that may fully
discover° him their opposite.° Now to seem to affect° the mal-   *reveal / adversary / desire*
20 ice and displeasure of the people is as bad as that which he
dislikes, to flatter them for their love.
SECOND OFFICER   He hath deserved worthily of his country, and
his ascent is not by such easy degrees as those who, having been
supple and courteous to the people, bonneted,² without any
25 further deed to have them at all into their estimation and
report.° But he hath so planted his honours in their eyes   *good opinion*
and his actions in their hearts that for their tongues to be silent
and not confess so much were a kind of ingrateful injury. To
report otherwise were a malice that, giving itself the lie,³ would
30 pluck reproof and rebuke from every ear that heard it.
FIRST OFFICER   No more of him. He's a worthy man. Make way,
they are coming.

> *A sennet. Enter the Patricians, and* [SICINIUS *and* BRU-
> TUS], *the tribunes of the people, lictors⁴ before them;*
> CORIOLANUS, MENENIUS, COMINIUS *the consul.* [*The*
> *Patricians take their places and sit.*] SICINIUS *and* BRU-
> TUS *take their places by themselves.* CORIOLANUS *stands*

MENENIUS   Having determined of° the Volsces, and   *made a decision about*
To send for Titus Lartius, it remains
35 As the main point of this our after-meeting
To gratify° his noble service that   *reward*
Hath thus stood for his country. Therefore please you,
Most reverend and grave elders, to desire
The present consul and last° general   *recent*
40 In our well-found° successes to report   *happily encountered*
A little of that worthy work performed
By Martius Caius Coriolanus, whom
We met here both to thank and to remember
With honours like° himself.   *befitting*
   [CORIOLANUS *sits*]
FIRST SENATOR   Speak, good Cominius.
45 Leave nothing out for° length, and make us think   *on account of*
Rather our state's defective for requital
Than we to stretch it out.⁵
   [*To the tribunes*]   Masters o'th' people,
We do request your kindest ears and, after,
Your loving motion toward° the common body   *persuasion of*
To yield° what passes here.   *agree to*
50 SICINIUS   We are convented°   *met together*
Upon a pleasing treaty,° and have hearts   *subject for discussion*
Inclinable to honour and advance
The theme of our assembly.
BRUTUS   Which the rather

---

1. He would waver without caring.
2. Put their bonnets back on (after doffing them as a gesture of respect).
3. Showing itself to be false.

4. Officers who attended upon magistrates.
5. *Rather our . . . out:* We lack resources for adequate
reward, rather than the will to reward him to the utmost.

We shall be blessed° to do if he remember   *happy*
55   A kinder value of the people than
He hath hereto prized them at.
MENENIUS   That's off, that's off.°   *irrelevant*
I would you rather had been silent. Please you
To hear Cominius speak?
BRUTUS   Most willingly,
But yet my caution was more pertinent
Than the rebuke you give it.
60   MENENIUS   He loves your people,
But tie him not to be their bedfellow.
Worthy Cominius, speak.
          CORIOLANUS *rises and offers*° *to go away*   *begins*
[*To* CORIOLANUS]   Nay, keep your place.
FIRST SENATOR   Sit, Coriolanus. Never shame to hear
What you have nobly done.
CORIOLANUS   Your honours' pardon,
65   I had rather have my wounds to heal again
Than hear say how I got them.
BRUTUS   Sir, I hope
My words disbenched° you not?   *unseated*
CORIOLANUS   No, sir, yet oft
When blows have made me stay I fled from words.
You soothed° not, therefore hurt not; but your people,   *flattered*
I love them as they weigh°—   *deserve*
70   MENENIUS   Pray now, sit down.
CORIOLANUS   I had rather have one scratch my head i'th' sun
When the alarum° were struck than idly sit   *battle summons*
To hear my nothings monstered.[6]   *Exit*
MENENIUS   Masters of the people,
Your multiplying spawn° how can he flatter—   *fast-breeding plebeians*
75   That's thousand to one good one—when you now see
He had rather venture all his limbs for honour
Than one on's° ears to hear it? Proceed, Cominius.   *of his*
COMINIUS   I shall lack voice; the deeds of Coriolanus
Should not be uttered feebly. It is held
80   That valour is the chiefest virtue, and
Most dignifies the haver. If it be,
The man I speak of cannot in the world
Be singly counterpoised.° At sixteen years,   *equaled by anyone*
When Tarquin made a head for° Rome, he fought   *raised an army against*
85   Beyond the mark° of others. Our then dictator,[7]   *reach*
Whom with all praise I point at, saw him fight
When with his Amazonian[8] chin he drove
The bristled lips° before him. He bestrid   *bearded soldiers*
An o'erpressed° Roman, and, i'th' consul's view,   *overwhelmed*
90   Slew three opposers. Tarquin's self he met,
And struck him on his knee. In that day's feats,
When he might act the woman in the scene,[9]
He proved best man i'th' field, and for his meed°   *reward*
Was brow-bound with the oak. His pupil age

6. My trivial actions treated as marvels.   8. Beardless (like a female Amazon warrior).
7. Roman magistrate with absolute authority, elected dur-   9. Might be expected to be cowardly (with an allusion to
ing emergencies.   boys acting women's parts in the theater).

95   Man-entered thus, he waxèd like a sea,
And in the brunt° of seventeen battles since   *violence*
He lurched° all swords of the garland. For this last   *cheated*
Before and in Corioles, let me say
I cannot speak him home.° He stopped the fliers,   *praise him enough*
100   And by his rare example made the coward
Turn terror into sport. As weeds before
A vessel under sail, so men obeyed
And fell below his stem.° His sword, death's stamp,   *prow*
Where it did mark, it took.[1] From face to foot
105   He was a thing of blood, whose every motion
Was timed[2] with dying cries. Alone he entered
The mortal° gate of th' city, which he, painted   *fatal*
With shunless destiny,[3] aidless came off,
And with a sudden reinforcement struck
110   Corioles like a planet.[4] Now all's his.
When by and by the din of war gan° pierce   *began to*
His ready° sense, then straight his doubled spirit   *alert*
Requickened° what in flesh was fatigate,°   *Reanimated / exhausted*
And to the battle came he, where he did
115   Run reeking[5] o'er the lives of men as if
'Twere a perpetual spoil;° and till we called   *slaughter*
Both field and city ours he never stood
To ease his breast with panting.
MENENIUS   Worthy man.
FIRST SENATOR   He cannot but with measure° fit the honours   *exactly*
Which we devise him.
120 COMINIUS   Our spoils he kicked at,°   *spurned*
And looked upon things precious as° they were   *as if*
The common muck of the world. He covets less
Than misery° itself would give, rewards   *poverty*
His deeds with doing them, and is content
To spend the time to° end it.   *merely in order to*
125 MENENIUS   He's right noble.
Let him be called for.
FIRST SENATOR   Call Coriolanus.
OFFICER   He doth appear.
        Enter CORIOLANUS
MENENIUS   The senate, Coriolanus, are well pleased
To make thee consul.
130 CORIOLANUS   I do owe them still°   *always*
My life and services.
MENENIUS   It then remains
That you do speak to the people.
CORIOLANUS   I do beseech you,
Let me o'erleap that custom, for I cannot
Put on the gown, stand naked,° and entreat them   *exposed*
135   For my wounds' sake to give their suffrage.
Please you that I may pass this doing.
SICINIUS   Sir, the people
Must have their voices,° neither will they bate°   *votes / forgo*

---

1. It made a clear imprint (of death).
2. Rhythmically accompanied.
3. *painted . . . destiny:* covered with the blood of his victims, unable to avoid their fate.

4. Planets were believed to have the power to afflict, or blast, people and places.
5. Steaming (with blood and sweat).

One jot of ceremony.

MENENIUS [*to* CORIOLANUS]   Put them not to't.°   *Do not defy them*
    Pray you, go fit you° to the custom and   *adapt yourself*
140   Take to you, as your predecessors have,
    Your honour with your form.°   *the custom prescribed you*

CORIOLANUS   It is a part
    That I shall blush in acting, and might well
    Be taken from the people.

BRUTUS [*to* SICINIUS]   Mark you that?

CORIOLANUS   To brag unto them 'Thus I did, and thus',
145   Show them th'unaching scars, which I should hide,
    As if I had received them for the hire
    Of their breath° only!   *voice*

MENENIUS   Do not stand° upon't. —   *insist*
    We recommend° to you, tribunes of the people,   *commit*
    Our purpose° to them; and to our noble consul   *proposal*
150   Wish we all joy and honour.

SENATORS   To Coriolanus come all joy and honour!
                Flourish [of] cornetts, then exeunt. Manent
                           SICINIUS *and* BRUTUS

BRUTUS   You see how he intends to use the people.

SICINIUS   May they perceive's intent! He will require° them   *ask from*
    As if he did contemn° what he requested   *scorn that*
    Should be in them to give.

155 BRUTUS   Come, we'll inform them
    Of our proceedings here. On th' market-place
    I know they do attend° us.   [*Exeunt*]   *await*

2.3

Enter seven or eight CITIZENS

FIRST CITIZEN   Once,° if he do require our voices we ought not   *In short*
    to deny him.

SECOND CITIZEN   We may, sir, if we will.

THIRD CITIZEN   We have power in ourselves to do it, but it is a
5   power that we have no power to do.° For if he show us his   *no justification to use*
    wounds and tell us his deeds, we are to put our tongues into
    those wounds[1] and speak for them; so if he tell us his noble
    deeds we must also tell him our noble acceptance of them.
    Ingratitude is monstrous, and for the multitude to be ingrateful
10   were to make a monster of the multitude, of the which we,
    being members, should bring ourselves to be monstrous mem-
    bers.

FIRST CITIZEN   And to make us no better thought of, a little help
    will serve;° for once we stood up about the corn, he himself   *it won't take much*
15   stuck° not to call us the many-headed multitude.   *hesitated*

THIRD CITIZEN   We have been called so of many, not that our
    heads are some brown, some black, some abram,° some bald,   *auburn*
    but that our wits are so diversely coloured; and truly I think if
    all our wits were to issue out of one skull, they would fly east,
20   west, north, south, and their consent of° one direct way should   *agreement to go*
    be at once to all the points o'th' compass.

SECOND CITIZEN   Think you so? Which way do you judge my
    wit would fly?

2.3 Location: The marketplace in Rome.   1. That is, let those wounds inspire our voices.

THIRD CITIZEN   Nay, your wit will not so soon out as another
25   man's will, 'tis strongly wedged up in a blockhead. But if it
were at liberty, 'twould sure southward.[2]
SECOND CITIZEN   Why that way?
THIRD CITIZEN   To lose itself in a fog where, being three parts
melted away with rotten° dews, the fourth would return for con-   unwholesome
30   science' sake, to help to get thee a wife.
SECOND CITIZEN   You are never without your tricks. You may,
you may.°   (have your joke)
THIRD CITIZEN   Are you all resolved to give your voices? But
that's no matter, the greater part carries it.° I say, if he would   majority decides
35   incline to° the people there was never a worthier man.   support

        Enter CORIOLANUS *in a gown of humility, with* MENENIUS
Here he comes, and in the gown of humility. Mark his behaviour. We are not to stay all together, but to come by him where
he stands by ones, by twos, and by threes. He's to make his
requests by particulars,° wherein every one of us has a single   to individuals
40   honour in giving him our own voices with our own tongues.
Therefore follow me, and I'll direct you how you shall go by
him.
ALL THE CITIZENS   Content, content.   [*Exeunt* CITIZENS]
MENENIUS   O sir, you are not right. Have you not known
The worthiest men have done't?
45   CORIOLANUS   What must I say?
'I pray, sir'? Plague upon't, I cannot bring
My tongue to such a pace. 'Look, sir, my wounds.
I got them in my country's service, when
Some certain of your brethren roared and ran
From th' noise of our own drums'?
50   MENENIUS   O me, the gods!
You must not speak of that, you must desire them
To think upon you.
CORIOLANUS   Think upon me? Hang 'em.
I would they would forget me like the virtues
Which our divines lose by 'em.[3]
MENENIUS   You'll mar all.
55   I'll leave you. Pray you, speak to 'em, I pray you,
In wholesome[4] manner.
CORIOLANUS   Bid them wash their faces
And keep their teeth clean.   *Exit* [MENENIUS]
        Enter three of the CITIZENS
                        So, here comes a brace.
You know the cause, sir, of my standing here.
THIRD CITIZEN   We do, sir. Tell us what hath brought you to't.
60   CORIOLANUS   Mine own desert.
SECOND CITIZEN   Your own desert?
CORIOLANUS   Ay, but not mine own desire.
THIRD CITIZEN   How not your own desire?
CORIOLANUS   No, sir, 'twas never my desire yet to trouble the
65   poor with begging.
THIRD CITIZEN   You must think if we give you anything we hope
to gain by you.

2. The south is associated with plague.   4. Proper (but Coriolanus takes it as "healthy").
3. Our priests vainly try to instill in them.

CORIOLANUS Well then, I pray, your price o'th' consulship?

FIRST CITIZEN The price is to ask it kindly.

70 CORIOLANUS Kindly, sir, I pray let me ha't. I have wounds to
show you which shall be yours° in private. [*To* SECOND CITIZEN]   *yours to see*
Your good voice, sir. What say you?

SECOND CITIZEN You shall ha't, worthy sir.

CORIOLANUS A match,° sir. There's in all two worthy voices   *agreement*
75 begged. I have your alms. Adieu.

THIRD CITIZEN [*to the other* CITIZENS] But this is something odd.

SECOND CITIZEN An° 'twere to give again—but 'tis no matter.   *If*

Exeunt [CITIZENS]

Enter two other CITIZENS

CORIOLANUS Pray you now, if it may stand° with the tune of your   *accord*
voices that I may be consul, I have here the customary gown.

80 FOURTH CITIZEN You have deserved nobly of your country, and
you have not deserved nobly.

CORIOLANUS Your enigma?

FOURTH CITIZEN You have been a scourge to her enemies, you
have been a rod to her friends. You have not, indeed, loved the
85 common people.

CORIOLANUS You should account me the more virtuous that I
have not been common° in my love. I will, sir, flatter my sworn   *indiscriminate*
brother the people to earn a dearer estimation of them. 'Tis° a   *(Flattery) is*
condition they account gentle.° And since the wisdom of their   *noble*
90 choice is rather to have my hat than my heart, I will practise
the insinuating nod and be off° to them most counterfeitly; that   *bareheaded*
is, sir, I will counterfeit the bewitchment° of some popular   *charisma*
man,° and give it bountiful to the desirers. Therefore, beseech   *demagogue*
you I may be consul.

95 FIFTH CITIZEN We hope to find you our friend, and therefore
give you our voices heartily.

FOURTH CITIZEN You have received many wounds for your
country.

CORIOLANUS I will not seal° your knowledge with showing them.   *confirm*
100 I will make much of your voices, and so trouble you no farther.

BOTH CITIZENS The gods give you joy, sir, heartily.

CORIOLANUS Most sweet voices.   [*Exeunt* CITIZENS]
Better it is to die, better to starve,
Than crave the hire which first we do deserve.[5]
105 Why in this womanish toge[6] should I stand here
To beg of Hob and Dick[7] that does appear
Their needless vouches?° Custom calls me to't.   *votes*
What custom wills, in all things should we do't,
The dust on antique time would lie unswept,
110 And mountainous error be too highly heaped
For truth to o'erpeer.[8] Rather than fool it° so,   *act the fool*
Let the high office and the honour go
To one that would do thus. I am half through.
The one part suffered, the other will I do.

Enter three CITIZENS *more*

115 Here come more voices.

---

5. Than beg for the wages we have already earned.
6. F has "woolvish toge"; some editors read "wolvish" or
"wool-less." The "toge" is the toga (gown of humility).

7. Any Tom, Dick, or Harry.
8. To look over the top.

Your voices! For your voices I have fought,
Watched° for your voices, for your voices bear   *Gone sleepless*
Of wounds two dozen odd; battles thrice six
I have seen and heard of for your voices, have
120   Done many things, some less, some more. Your voices!
Indeed I would be consul.
SIXTH CITIZEN   He has done nobly, and cannot go without any
honest man's voice.
SEVENTH CITIZEN   Therefore let him be consul. The gods give
125   him joy and make him good friend to the people!
ALL THE CITIZENS   Amen, amen. God save thee, noble consul!
CORIOLANUS   Worthy voices.   [*Exeunt* CITIZENS]
       Enter MENENIUS *with* BRUTUS *and* SICINIUS
MENENIUS   You have stood your limitation,° and the tribunes   *allotted time*
Endue° you with the people's voice. Remains   *Invest*
130   That in th' official marks° invested, you   *insignia*
Anon° do meet the senate.   *Immediately*
CORIOLANUS   Is this done?
SICINIUS   The custom of request° you have discharged.   *requesting votes*
The people do admit you, and are summoned
To meet anon upon your approbation.⁹
CORIOLANUS   Where, at the senate-house?
135   SICINIUS   There, Coriolanus.
CORIOLANUS   May I change these garments?
SICINIUS   You may, sir.
CORIOLANUS   That I'll straight do, and, knowing myself again,
Repair to th' senate-house.
MENENIUS   I'll keep you company. [*To the tribunes*] Will you along?
BRUTUS   We stay here for the people.
140   SICINIUS   Fare you well.
            Exeunt CORIOLANUS *and* MENENIUS
He has it now, and by his looks methinks
'Tis warm at's heart.¹
BRUTUS   With a proud heart he wore
His humble weeds.° Will you dismiss the people?   *garments*
       Enter the Plebeians
SICINIUS   How now, my masters, have you chose this man?
145   FIRST CITIZEN   He has our voices, sir.
BRUTUS   We pray the gods he may deserve your loves.
SECOND CITIZEN   Amen, sir. To my poor unworthy notice
He mocked us when he begged our voices.
THIRD CITIZEN   Certainly. He flouted us downright.
150   FIRST CITIZEN   No, 'tis his kind of speech. He did not mock us.
SECOND CITIZEN   Not one amongst us save yourself but says
He used us scornfully. He should have showed us
His marks of merit, wounds received for's country.
SICINIUS   Why, so he did, I am sure.
ALL THE CITIZENS   No, no; no man saw 'em.
155   THIRD CITIZEN   He said he had wounds which he could show in private,
And with his hat, thus waving it in scorn,
'I would be consul,' says he. 'Agèd custom
But by your voices will not so permit me.
Your voices therefore.' When we granted that,

---

9. For your ratification as consul.   1. That is, he's well pleased.

160   Here was 'I thank you for your voices, thank you.
    Your most sweet voices. Now you have left your voices
    I have no further° with you.' Was not this mockery?   *(to do)*
    SICINIUS   Why either were you ignorant° to see't,   *were you either unable*
    Or, seeing it, of such childish friendliness
    To yield your voices?
165   BRUTUS [*to the* CITIZENS]   Could you not have told him
    As you were lessoned: when he had no power
    But was a petty servant to the state,
    He was your enemy, ever spake against
    Your liberties and the charters that you bear
170   I'th' body of the weal;° and now arriving°   *state / reaching*
    A place of potency and sway o'th' state,
    If he should still malignantly remain
    Fast foe to th' plebeii, your voices might
    Be curses to yourselves. You should have said
175   That as his worthy deeds did claim no less
    Than what he stood for,° so his gracious nature   *the office he sought*
    Would think upon you for your voices and
    Translate° his malice towards you into love,   *Change*
    Standing your friendly lord.
    SICINIUS [*to the* CITIZENS]   Thus to have said
180   As you were fore-advised had touched° his spirit   *tested*
    And tried his inclination, from him plucked
    Either his gracious promise which you might,
    As cause had called you up, have held him to,
    Or else it would have galled his surly nature,
185   Which easily endures not article°   *stipulation*
    Tying him to aught. So putting him to rage,
    You should have ta'en th'advantage of his choler°   *wrath*
    And passed him unelected.
    BRUTUS [*to the* CITIZENS]   Did you perceive
    He did solicit you in free contempt
190   When he did need your loves, and do you think
    That his contempt shall not be bruising to you
    When he hath power to crush? Why, had your bodies
    No heart among you? Or had you tongues to cry
    Against the rectorship of judgement?°   *rule of common sense*
    SICINIUS [*to the* CITIZENS]   Have you
195   Ere now denied the asker, and now again,
    Of him that did not ask but mock, bestow
    Your sued-for tongues?
    THIRD CITIZEN   He's not confirmed, we may deny him yet.
    SECOND CITIZEN   And will deny him.
200   I'll have five hundred voices of that sound.
    FIRST CITIZEN   I twice five hundred, and their friends to piece° 'em.   *add to*
    BRUTUS   Get you hence instantly, and tell those friends
    They have chose a consul that will from them take
    Their liberties, make them of no more voice
205   Than dogs that are as often beat for barking,
    As therefor kept to do so.
    SICINIUS [*to the* CITIZENS]   Let them assemble,
    And on a safer° judgement all revoke   *sounder*
    Your ignorant election. Enforce° his pride   *Emphasize*
    And his old hate unto you. Besides, forget not

210 With what contempt he wore the humble weed,
How in his suit° he scorned you; but your loves,   *petition; apparel*
Thinking upon his services, took from you
Th'apprehension° of his present portance,°   *perception / demeanor*
Which most gibingly, ungravely he did fashion
After the inveterate hate he bears you.

215 BRUTUS [*to the* CITIZENS]   Lay
A fault on us your tribunes, that we laboured
No impediment between,[2] but that you must
Cast your election on him.

SICINIUS [*to the* CITIZENS]   Say you chose him
More after our commandment than as guided

220 By your own true affections, and that your minds,
Preoccupied with what you rather must do
Than what you should, made you against the grain
To voice him consul. Lay the fault on us.

BRUTUS [*to the* CITIZENS]   Ay, spare us not. Say we read lectures to you,

225 How youngly he began to serve his country,
How long continued, and what stock he springs of,
The noble house o'th' Martians, from whence came
That Ancus Martius, Numa's daughter's son,
Who after great Hostilius here was king;

230 Of the same house Publius and Quintus were,
That our best water brought by conduits hither;
And Censorinus that was so surnamed,[3]
And nobly named so, twice being censor,[4]
Was his great ancestor.

SICINIUS [*to the* CITIZENS]   One thus descended,

235 That hath beside well in his person wrought
To be set high in place, we did commend
To your remembrances, but you have found,
Scaling° his present bearing with his past,   *Weighing*
That he's your fixèd enemy, and revoke
Your sudden° approbation.   *hasty*

240 BRUTUS [*to the* CITIZENS]   Say you ne'er had done't—
Harp on that still—but by our putting on;°   *instigation*
And presently when you have drawn° your number,   *gathered*
Repair to th' Capitol.

A CITIZEN   We will so.

ANOTHER CITIZEN   Almost all
Repent in their election.   *Exeunt* [CITIZENS]

BRUTUS   Let them go on.

245 This mutiny were better put in hazard°   *risked*
Than stay,° past doubt, for greater.   *await*
If, as his nature is, he fall in rage
With their refusal, both observe and answer
The vantage of[5] his anger.

SICINIUS   To th' Capitol, come.

250 We will be there before the stream o'th' people,
And this shall seem, as partly 'tis, their own,
Which we have goaded onward.   *Exeunt*

---

2. *we . . . between:* we refused to allow anything to stand
in the way.
3. Line missing in F; reconstructed from Plutarch.
4. Roman magistrate who supervised public morals and

drew up the census.
5. *answer the vantage of:* seize the opportunity provided
by.

3.1

Cornetts. Enter CORIOLANUS, MENENIUS, *all the gentry;°*   *patricians*
COMINIUS, LARTIUS, *and other* SENATORS
CORIOLANUS   Tullus Aufidius then had made new head?°   *raised a new army*
LARTIUS   He had, my lord, and that it was which caused
   Our swifter composition.[1]
CORIOLANUS   So then the Volsces stand but as at first,
5   Ready when time shall prompt them to make raid
   Upon's again.
COMINIUS   They are worn,° lord consul, so   *exhausted*
   That we shall hardly in our ages see
   Their banners wave again.
CORIOLANUS *[to* LARTIUS*]*   Saw you Aufidius?
LARTIUS   On safeguard° he came to me, and did curse   *Under safe-conduct*
10   Against the Volsces for they had so vilely
   Yielded the town. He is retired to Antium.
CORIOLANUS   Spoke he of me?
LARTIUS   He did, my lord.
CORIOLANUS   How? What?
LARTIUS   How often he had met you sword to sword;
   That of all things upon the earth he hated
15   Your person most; that he would pawn his fortunes
   To hopeless restitution,[2] so he might
   Be called your vanquisher.
CORIOLANUS   At Antium lives he?
LARTIUS   At Antium.
20 CORIOLANUS   I wish I had a cause to seek him there,
   To oppose his hatred fully. Welcome home.
       Enter SICINIUS *and* BRUTUS
   Behold, these are the tribunes of the people,
   The tongues o'th' common mouth. I do despise them,
   For they do prank them° in authority   *adorn themselves*
25   Against all noble sufferance.[3]
SICINIUS   Pass no further.
CORIOLANUS   Ha, what is that?
BRUTUS   It will be dangerous to go on. No further.
CORIOLANUS   What makes this change?
30 MENENIUS   The matter?
COMINIUS   Hath he not passed° the noble and the common?   *been accepted by*
BRUTUS   Cominius, no.
CORIOLANUS   Have I had children's voices?
FIRST SENATOR   Tribunes, give way. He shall to th' market-place.
BRUTUS   The people are incensed against him.
SICINIUS   Stop,
   Or all will fall in broil.°   *turmoil*
35 CORIOLANUS   Are these your herd?
   Must these have voices, that can yield them now
   And straight° disclaim their tongues? What are your offices?   *immediately*
   You being their mouths, why rule you not their teeth?
   Have you not set them on?
MENENIUS   Be calm, be calm.
40 CORIOLANUS   It is a purposed° thing, and grows by plot   *deliberate*

3.1 Location: A street in Rome.   2. Without hope of recovery.
1. Agreement (about returning Corioles to the Volscians).   3. Beyond what the nobility can endure.

To curb the will of the nobility.
Suffer't, and live with such as cannot rule
Nor ever will be ruled.
BRUTUS   Call't not a plot.
The people cry you mocked them, and of late
45   When corn was given them gratis, you repined,
Scandalled° the suppliants for the people, called them   *Defamed*
Time-pleasers, flatterers, foes to nobleness.
CORIOLANUS   Why, this was known before.
BRUTUS   Not to them all.
CORIOLANUS   Have you informed them sithence?°   *since*
BRUTUS   How, I inform them?
50   CORIOLANUS   You are like to do such business.
BRUTUS   Not unlike
Each way to better yours.[4]
CORIOLANUS   Why then should I be consul? By yon clouds,
Let me deserve so ill as you, and make me
Your fellow tribune.
55   SICINIUS   You show too much of that°   *(quality)*
For which the people stir.° If you will pass   *are aroused*
To where you are bound,[5] you must enquire your way,
Which you are out of,° with a gentler spirit,   *strayed from*
Or never be so noble as a consul,
Nor yoke with him° for tribune.   *(Brutus)*
60   MENENIUS   Let's be calm.
COMINIUS   The people are abused, set on. This palt'ring°   *trifling*
Becomes not Rome, nor has Coriolanus
Deserved this so dishonoured rub,° laid falsely   *shameful obstruction*
I'th' plain way of his merit.
CORIOLANUS   Tell me of corn?
65   This was my speech, and I will speak't again.
MENENIUS   Not now, not now.
FIRST SENATOR   Not in this heat, sir, now.
CORIOLANUS   Now as I live,
I will. My nobler friends, I crave their pardons.
70   For the mutable rank-scented meinie,°   *multitude*
Let them regard me, as I do not flatter,
And therein behold themselves. I say again,
In soothing them we nourish 'gainst our Senate
The cockle° of rebellion, insolence, sedition,   *weed*
75   Which we ourselves have ploughed for, sowed, and scattered
By mingling them with us, the honoured number
Who lack not virtue, no, nor power, but that
Which they have given to beggars.
MENENIUS   Well, no more.
FIRST SENATOR   No more words, we beseech you.
CORIOLANUS   How, no more?
80   As for my country I have shed my blood,
Not fearing outward force, so shall my lungs
Coin words till their decay against those measles°   *skin eruptions*
Which we disdain should tetter° us, yet sought   *infect*
The very way to catch them.

---

4. *Not unlike . . . yours:* Not unlikely in every respect to   5. That is, the marketplace; the consulship.
do better than you.

85 BRUTUS   You speak o'th' people as if you were a god
To punish, not a man of their infirmity.°   *with the same frailty*
SICINIUS   'Twere well we let the people know't.
MENENIUS   What, what, his choler?
CORIOLANUS   Choler? Were I as patient as the midnight sleep,
By Jove, 'twould be my mind.°   *opinion*
SICINIUS   It is a mind
90 That shall remain a poison where it is,
Not poison any further.
CORIOLANUS   'Shall remain'?
Hear you this Triton[6] of the minnows? Mark you
His absolute 'shall'?
COMINIUS   'Twas from the canon.°   *out of order*
CORIOLANUS   'Shall'?
O good but most unwise patricians, why,
95 You grave but reckless senators, have you thus
Given Hydra[7] here to choose an officer
That, with his peremptory 'shall', being but
The horn and noise° o'th' monster's, wants not spirit   *noisy horn*
To say he'll turn your current° in a ditch   *stream of power*
100 And make your channel his? If he have power,
Then vail° your impotence; if none, awake°   *bow down / awake from*
Your dangerous lenity.° If you are learned,   *forbearance*
Be not as common fools; if you are not,
Let them have cushions by° you. You are plebeians   *senate seats beside*
105 If they be senators, and they are no less
When, both your voices blended, the great'st taste
Most palates theirs.[8] They choose their magistrate,
And such a one as he, who puts his 'shall',
His popular° 'shall', against a graver bench[9]   *plebeian*
110 Than ever frowned in Greece. By Jove himself,
It makes the consuls base, and my soul aches
To know, when two authorities are up,°   *established*
Neither supreme, how soon confusion°   *chaos*
May enter 'twixt the gap of both and take°   *overthrow*
The one by th' other.
115 COMINIUS   Well, on to th' market-place.
CORIOLANUS   Whoever gave that counsel to give forth
The corn o'th' storehouse gratis, as 'twas used
Sometime in Greece—
MENENIUS   Well, well, no more of that.
CORIOLANUS   Though there the people had more absolute power—
120 I say they nourished disobedience, fed
The ruin of the state.
BRUTUS   Why shall the people give
One that speaks thus their voice?
CORIOLANUS   I'll give my reasons,
More worthier than their voices. They know the corn
Was not our recompense,° resting well assured   *a payment from us*
125 They ne'er did service for't. Being pressed° to th' war,   *conscripted*
Even when the navel° of the state was touched,°   *center / threatened*

---

6. Neptune's trumpeter, a minor sea god.
7. Mythical many-headed snake, a common figure for
the multitude.

8. *the great'st . . . theirs:* the result tastes more like (or appeals more to) them than you.
9. A more respected body.

They would not thread° the gates. This kind of service   *go through*
Did not deserve corn gratis. Being i'th' war,
Their mutinies and revolts, wherein they showed
130 Most valour, spoke not° for them. Th'accusation   *did not speak well*
Which they have often made against the senate,
All cause unborn,° could never be the native°   *Without any cause / source*
Of our so frank° donation. Well, what then?   *liberal*
How shall this bosom multiplied[1] digest
135 The senate's courtesy? Let deeds express
What's like to be their words: 'We did request it,
We are the greater poll,° and in true fear   *number*
They gave us our demands.' Thus we debase
The nature of our seats,° and make the rabble   *senatorial positions*
140 Call our cares fears, which will in time
Break ope the locks o'th' senate, and bring in
The crows to peck the eagles.[2]

MENENIUS   Come, enough.
BRUTUS   Enough with over measure.
CORIOLANUS   No, take more.
What may be sworn by, both divine and human,
145 Seal what I end withal! This double worship,[3]   *Authorize*
Where one part does disdain with cause, the other
Insult° without all reason, where gentry, title, wisdom   *Behave insolently*
Cannot conclude but by the yea and no
Of general ignorance, it must omit   *neglect*
150 Real necessities, and give way the while
To unstable slightness.° Purpose° so barred, it follows   *Vitiating/Purpose...*
Nothing is done to purpose.° Therefore beseech you—   *my*
You that will be less fearful than discreet,   *fear*
That love the fundamental part of state
155 More than you doubt the change on't,[4] that prefer
A noble life before a long, and wish
To jump° a body with a dangerous physic
That's sure of death without it—at once pluck out
The multitudinous tongue;[5] let them not lick
160 The sweet which is their poison. Your dishonour
Mangles true judgement, and bereaves the state
Of that integrity which should become't,
Not having the power to do the good it would
For° th'ill which doth control't.[6]

BRUTUS   He's said enough.
165 SICINIUS   He's spoken like a traitor, and shall answer
As traitors do.
CORIOLANUS   Thou wretch, despite° o'erwhelm thee!
What should the people do with these bald° tribunes,
On whom depending, their obedience fails
To the greater bench? In a rebellion,
170 When what's not meet, but what must be, was law,[7]
Then were they chosen; in a better hour

1. Multifarious belly (of the many-headed multitude).
2. The eagle not only is associated with courage and nobility but is the symbol of Roman power.
3. Divided magistracy.
4. You fear changing it (by repudiating the tribunes).
5. The tongue of the
tribunes.
6. Overpower it.
7. When ... law:
prevailed. meet: ...

Let what is meet be said it must be meet,[8]
And throw their power i'th' dust.
BRUTUS   Manifest treason.
SICINIUS   This a consul? No.
BRUTUS   The aediles,° ho!   *tribune's officers*
          Enter an AEDILE
175   Let him be apprehended.
SICINIUS   Go call the people,   [*Exit* AEDILE]
          [*To* CORIOLANUS]   in whose name myself
          Attach° thee as a traitorous innovator,°   *Arrest/revolutionary*
          A foe to th' public weal. Obey, I charge thee,
          And follow to thine answer.°   *trial*
CORIOLANUS   Hence, old goat!
ALL THE PATRICIANS   We'll surety him.°   *ensure his compliance*
180 COMINIUS [*to* SICINIUS]   Aged sir, hands off.
CORIOLANUS [*to* SICINIUS]   Hence, rotten thing, or I shall shake thy bones
          Out of thy garments.
SICINIUS   Help, ye citizens!
          Enter a rabble of Plebeians, with the AEDILES
MENENIUS   On both sides more respect.
SICINIUS   Here's he
          That would take from you all your power.
BRUTUS   Seize him, aediles.
ALL THE CITIZENS   Down with him, down with him!
185 SECOND SENATOR   Weapons, weapons, weapons!
          They all bustle about CORIOLANUS
CITIZENS *and* PATRICIANS [*in dispersed cries*]   Tribunes! Patricians!
          Citizens! What ho!
          Sicinius! Brutus! Coriolanus! Citizens!
SOME CITIZENS *and* PATRICIANS   Peace, peace, peace! Stay! Hold! Peace!
MENENIUS   What is about to be? I am out of breath.
190 Confusion's° near; I cannot speak. You tribunes   *Chaos is*
          To th' people, Coriolanus, patience!
          Speak, good Sicinius.
SICINIUS   Hear me, people, peace.
ALL THE CITIZENS   Let's hear our tribune! Peace! Speak, speak, speak!
SICINIUS   You are at point° to lose your liberties.   *about*
195 Martius would have all from you—Martius
          Whom late you have named for consul.
MENENIUS   Fie, fie, fie,
          This is the way to kindle, not to quench.
FIRST SENATOR   To unbuild the city, and to lay all flat.
SICINIUS   What is the city but the people?
ALL THE CITIZENS   True,
          The people are the city.
200 BRUTUS   By the consent of all
          We were established the people's magistrates.
ALL THE CITIZENS   You so remain.
MENENIUS   And so are like to do.
CORIOLANUS   That is the way to lay the city flat,
          To bring the roof to the foundation,
205 And bury all which yet distinctly ranges[9]
          In heaps and piles of ruin.

8. Let what is proper be declared necessary.   9. Extends in orderly ranks.

SICINIUS   This deserves death.
BRUTUS   Or° let us stand to our authority,   *Either*
    Or let us lose it. We do here pronounce,
    Upon the part o'th' people in whose power
210   We were elected theirs, Martius is worthy
    Of present° death.   *immediate*
SICINIUS   Therefore lay hold of him,
    Bear him to th' rock Tarpeian;¹ and from thence
    Into destruction cast him.
BRUTUS   Aediles, seize him.
ALL THE CITIZENS   Yield, Martius, yield.
MENENIUS   Hear me one word.
215   Beseech you, tribunes, hear me but a word.
AEDILES   Peace, peace!
MENENIUS [*to the tribunes*]   Be that you seem, truly your country's friend,
    And temp'rately proceed to what you would
    Thus violently redress.
BRUTUS   Sir, those cold ways
220   That seem like prudent helps are very poisons
    Where the disease is violent. Lay hands upon him,
    And bear him to the rock.
                    CORIOLANUS *draws his sword*
CORIOLANUS   No, I'll die here.
    There's some among you have beheld me fighting.
    Come, try upon yourselves what you have seen me.
225   MENENIUS   Down with that sword. Tribunes, withdraw a while.
BRUTUS   Lay hands upon him.
MENENIUS   Help Martius, help!
    You that be noble, help him, young and old.
ALL THE CITIZENS   Down with him, down with him!
                    In this mutiny the tribunes, the AEDILES, *and the*
                    people are beat in
MENENIUS [*to* CORIOLANUS]   Go get you to your house. Be gone, away!
    All will be naught else.
230   SECOND SENATOR [*to* CORIOLANUS]   Get you gone.
CORIOLANUS   Stand fast; we have as many friends as enemies.
MENENIUS   Shall it be put to that?
FIRST SENATOR   The gods forbid!
    [*To* CORIOLANUS]   I prithee, noble friend, home to thy house.
    Leave us to cure this cause.°   *disease*
MENENIUS   For 'tis a sore upon us
235   You cannot tent° yourself. Be gone, beseech you.   *treat*
COMINIUS   Come, sir, along with us.
CORIOLANUS   I would they were barbarians, as they are,
    Though in Rome littered;° not Romans, as they are not,   *born (like animals)*
    Though calved i'th' porch o'th' Capitol.
MENENIUS   Be gone.
240   Put not your worthy° rage into your tongue.   *justifiable*
    One time will owe° another.   *occasion will compensate*
CORIOLANUS   On fair ground
    I could beat forty of them.
MENENIUS   I could myself
    Take up a brace o'th' best of them, yea, the two tribunes.

---

1. The cliff from which murderers and traitors were hurled to their deaths.

COMINIUS   But now 'tis odds beyond arithmetic,°   *calculation*
245   And manhood° is called foolery when it stands   *courage*
    Against a falling fabric.°   *building*
    [*To* CORIOLANUS]   Will you hence
    Before the tag° return, whose rage doth rend   *rabble*
    Like interrupted° waters, and o'erbear   *overflowing*
    What they are used to bear?²
MENENIUS [*to* CORIOLANUS]   Pray you be gone.
250   I'll try whether my old wit be in request
    With those that have but little. This must be patched
    With cloth of any colour.³
COMINIUS   Nay, come away. *Exeunt* CORIOLANUS *and* COMINIUS
A PATRICIAN   This man has marred his fortune.
255 MENENIUS   His nature is too noble for the world.
    He would not flatter Neptune for his trident
    Or Jove for's power to thunder. His heart's his mouth.
    What his breast forges, that his tongue must vent,
    And, being angry, does forget that ever
    He heard the name of death.
         A noise within
260   Here's goodly work.
A PATRICIAN   I would they were abed.
MENENIUS   I would they were in Tiber.
    What the vengeance, could he not speak 'em fair?°   *speak to them politely*
       Enter BRUTUS *and* SICINIUS, *with the rabble again*
SICINIUS   Where is this viper
    That would depopulate the city and
    Be every man himself?
265 MENENIUS   You worthy tribunes—
SICINIUS   He shall be thrown down the Tarpeian rock
    With rigorous hands. He hath resisted law,
    And therefore law shall scorn° him further trial   *deny*
    Than the severity of the public° power,   *commoners'*
    Which he so sets at naught.
270 FIRST CITIZEN   He shall well know
    The noble tribunes are the people's mouths,
    And we their hands.
ALL THE CITIZENS   He shall, sure on't.
MENENIUS   Sir, sir.
SICINIUS   Peace!
MENENIUS   Do not cry havoc⁴ where you should but hunt
    With modest warrant.
275 SICINIUS   Sir, how comes't that you
    Have holp to make this rescue?⁵
MENENIUS   Hear me speak.
    As I do know the consul's worthiness,
    So can I name his faults.
SICINIUS   Consul? What consul?
280 MENENIUS   The consul Coriolanus.
BRUTUS   He consul?
ALL THE CITIZENS   No, no, no, no, no!

2. *o'erbear . . . bear:* overpower that to which they ordinarily submit.
3. *patched . . . colour:* mended by whatever means possible.

4. "Havoc" was the signal to an army to pillage.
5. Have helped to remove this prisoner from custody
("make rescue" is a legal term).

MENENIUS If, by the tribunes' leave and yours, good people,
  I may be heard, I would crave a word or two,
285 The which shall turn° you to no further harm   *bring*
  Than so much loss of time.
SICINIUS   Speak briefly, then,
  For we are peremptory to dispatch
  This viperous traitor. To eject him hence
  Were but our danger, and to keep him here
290 Our certain death. Therefore it is decreed
  He dies tonight.
MENENIUS   Now the good gods forbid
  That our renownèd Rome, whose gratitude
  Towards her deservèd° children is enrolled   *deserving*
  In Jove's own book, like an unnatural dam°   *mother*
295 Should now eat up her own!
SICINIUS He's a disease that must be cut away.
MENENIUS O, he's a limb that has but a disease—
  Mortal to cut it off, to cure it easy.
  What has he done to Rome that's worthy death?
300 Killing our enemies, the blood he hath lost—
  Which I dare vouch is more than that he hath
  By many an ounce—he dropped it for his country;
  And what is left, to lose it by his country
  Were to us all that do't and suffer° it   *allow*
  A brand° to th' end o'th' world.   *stigma*
305 SICINIUS   This is clean cam.°   *completely perverse*
BRUTUS Merely° awry. When he did love his country   *Absolutely*
  It honoured him.
SICINIUS   The service of the foot,
  Being once gangrened, is not then respected
  For what before it was.
BRUTUS   We'll hear no more.
310 Pursue him to his house and pluck him thence,
  Lest his infection, being of catching nature,
  Spread further.
MENENIUS   One word more, one word!
  This tiger-footed rage, when it shall find
  The harm of unscanned° swiftness, will too late   *heedless*
315 Tie leaden pounds° to's heels. Proceed by process,° *weights/due process*
  Lest parties°—as he is beloved—break out   *factions*
  And sack great Rome with Romans.
BRUTUS If it were so?
SICINIUS [*to* MENENIUS] What do ye talk?
320 Have we not had a taste of his obedience:
  Our aediles smote, ourselves resisted? Come.
MENENIUS Consider this: he has been bred i'th' wars
  Since a could draw a sword, and is ill-schooled
  In bolted[6] language. Meal and bran° together   *Flour and husks*
325 He throws without distinction. Give me leave,
  I'll go to him and undertake to bring him
  Where he shall answer by a lawful form,
  In peace, to his utmost peril.[7]
FIRST SENATOR   Noble tribunes,

---

6. Sifted; that is, carefully considered.   7. Even at peril of his life.

It is the humane way. The other course
330 Will prove too bloody, and the end of it
Unknown to the beginning.
SICINIUS   Noble Menenius,
Be you then as the people's officer.
[*To the* CITIZENS]   Masters, lay down your weapons.
BRUTUS   Go not home.
SICINIUS   Meet on the market-place. [*To* MENENIUS]   We'll attend° you there,   *await*
335 Where if you bring not Martius, we'll proceed
In our first way.
MENENIUS   I'll bring him to you.
[*To the* SENATORS] Let me desire your company. He must come,
Or what is worst will follow.
FIRST SENATOR   Pray you, let's to him.
                        Exeunt [tribunes and CITIZENS *at one door,*
                                PATRICIANS at another door]

                                3.2
                Enter CORIOLANUS, *with Nobles*
CORIOLANUS   Let them pull all about mine ears, present me
Death on the wheel or at wild horses' heels,
Or pile ten hills on the Tarpeian rock,
That the precipitation° might down stretch   *steepness*
5 Below the beam of sight, yet will I still
Be thus to them.
                Enter VOLUMNIA
A PATRICIAN   You do the nobler.
CORIOLANUS   I muse° my mother   *wonder that*
Does not approve me further, who was wont
To call them woollen° vassals, things created   *coarsely clad*
To buy and sell with groats,° to show bare heads   *fourpenny pieces*
10 In congregations, to yawn, be still, and wonder,
When one but of my ordinance° stood up   *rank*
To speak of peace or war. [*To* VOLUMNIA] I talk of you.
Why did you wish me milder? Would you have me
False to my nature? Rather say I play
The man I am.
15 VOLUMNIA   O, sir, sir, sir,
I would have had you put your power well on
Before you had worn it out.
CORIOLANUS   Let go.°   *Stop*
VOLUMNIA   You might have been enough the man you are
With striving less to be so. Lesser had been
20 The taxings° of your dispositions if   *challenging*
You had not showed them how ye were disposed
Ere they lacked° power to cross you.   *Before they lost*
CORIOLANUS   Let them hang.
VOLUMNIA   Ay, and burn too.
                Enter MENENIUS *with the* SENATORS
MENENIUS [*to* CORIOLANUS]   Come, come, you have been too rough,
          something too rough.
You must return and mend it.
25 FIRST SENATOR   There's no remedy

3.2 Location: Coriolanus's house.

Unless, by not so doing, our good city
Cleave in the midst and perish.
VOLUMNIA [*to* CORIOLANUS]   Pray be counselled.
I have a heart as little apt as yours,
But yet a brain that leads my use of anger
To better vantage.
30 MENENIUS   Well said, noble woman.
Before he should thus stoop to th' herd, but that
The violent fit o'th' time craves it as physic°   *medicine*
For the whole state, I would put mine armour on,
Which I can scarcely bear.
35 CORIOLANUS What must I do?
MENENIUS Return to th' tribunes.
CORIOLANUS Well, what then, what then?
MENENIUS Repent what you have spoke.
CORIOLANUS For them? I cannot do it to the gods.
Must I then do't to them?
40 VOLUMNIA   You are too absolute,°   *inflexible*
Though therein you can never be too noble,
But when extremities° speak. I have heard you say,   *extreme situations*
Honour and policy,° like unsevered friends,   *tactical shrewdness*
I'th' war do grow together. Grant that, and tell me
45 In peace what each of them by th' other lose
That they combine not there.
CORIOLANUS   Tush, tush!
MENENIUS   A good demand.
VOLUMNIA If it be honour in your wars to seem
The same° you are not, which for your best ends   *That which*
You adopt your policy, how is it less or worse
50 That it° shall hold companionship in peace   *(dissimulation)*
With honour, as in war, since that to both
It stands in like request?°   *need*
CORIOLANUS   Why force° you this?   *urge*
VOLUMNIA Because that now it lies you on to speak to th' people,
Not by your own instruction,° nor by th' matter   *conviction*
55 Which your heart prompts you, but with such words
That are but roted° in your tongue, though but   *memorized*
Bastards and syllables of no allowance
To¹ your bosom's truth. Now this no more
Dishonours you at all than to take in°   *capture*
60 A town with gentle words, which else would put you
To your fortune² and the hazard of much blood.
I would dissemble with my nature where
My fortunes and my friends at stake required
I should do so in honour. I am in this°   *I speak in this for*
65 Your wife, your son, these senators, the nobles;
And you will rather show our general° louts   *common*
How you can frown than spend a fawn° upon 'em   *cringing courtesy*
For the inheritance° of their loves and safeguard   *acquisition*
Of what that want° might ruin.   *lack (of their loves)*
MENENIUS   Noble lady!
70 [*To* CORIOLANUS] Come, go with us, speak fair. You may salve° so,   *smooth over*

---

1. *Bastards . . . / To:* Illegitimate words not acknowledged by.
2. *put . . . fortune:* force you to take your chances (in battle).

Not what is dangerous present, but the loss
Of what is past.[3]
VOLUMNIA   I prithee now, my son,
     [*She takes his bonnet*]
Go to them with this bonnet° in thy hand,   hat
And thus far having stretched it—here be with them—
75   Thy knee bussing° the stones—for in such business   kissing
Action is eloquence, and the eyes of th' ignorant
More learnèd than the ears—waving° thy head,   repeatedly bowing
With often, thus, correcting thy stout heart,
Now humble[4] as the ripest mulberry
80   That will not hold the handling; or say to them
Thou art their soldier and, being bred in broils,°   tumults
Hast not the soft way which, thou dost confess,
Were fit for thee to use as they to claim,°   for them to expect
In asking their good loves; but thou wilt frame
85   Thyself, forsooth, hereafter theirs so far
As thou hast power and person.°   ability and authority
MENENIUS [*to* CORIOLANUS]   This but done
Even as she speaks, why, their hearts were yours;
For they have pardons, being asked, as free
As words to little purpose.
VOLUMNIA [*to* CORIOLANUS]   Prithee now,
90   Go, and be ruled, although I know thou hadst rather
Follow thine enemy in a fiery gulf
Than flatter him in a bower.°   arbor
          Enter COMINIUS
                              Here is Cominius.
COMINIUS   I have been i'th' market-place; and, sir, 'tis fit
You make strong party,° or defend yourself   gather strong support
95   By calmness or by absence. All's in anger.
MENENIUS   Only fair speech.
COMINIUS   I think 'twill serve, if he
Can thereto frame his spirit.
VOLUMNIA   He must, and will.
Prithee now, say you will, and go about it.
CORIOLANUS   Must I go show them my unbarbèd sconce?°   unhelmeted head
100 Must I with my base tongue give to my noble heart
A lie that it must bear? Well, I will do't.
Yet were there but this single plot° to lose,   (Coriolanus's body)
This mould° of Martius they to dust should grind it   form; earth
And throw't against the wind. To th' market-place.
105 You have put me now to such a part which never
I shall discharge to th' life. °   perform convincingly
COMINIUS   Come, come, we'll prompt you.
VOLUMNIA   I prithee now, sweet son, as thou hast said
My praises made thee first a soldier, so,
To have my praise for this, perform a part
Thou hast not done before.
110 CORIOLANUS   Well, I must do't.
Away, my disposition; and possess me
Some harlot's[5] spirit! My throat of war be turned,

3. *Not . . . past:* Not only the present danger, but what was lost before.
4. Malleable (or possibly a verb, "let droop").
5. Vagabond; buffoon; prostitute.

Which choired° with my drum, into a pipe   *harmonized*
Small as an eunuch or the virgin voice
115 That babies lull asleep! The smiles of knaves
Tent° in my cheeks, and schoolboys' tears take up   *Encamp*
The glasses° of my sight! A beggar's tongue   *windows*
Make motion through my lips, and my armed knees,
Who bowed but in my stirrup, bend like his
120 That hath received an alms! I will not do't,
Lest I surcease° to honour mine own truth,   *cease*
And by my body's action teach my mind
A most inherent° baseness.   *fixed*
VOLUMNIA   At thy choice, then.
To beg of thee it is my more dishonour
125 Than thou of them. Come all to ruin. Let
Thy mother rather feel° thy pride than fear   *suffer*
Thy dangerous stoutness,° for I mock at death   *stubbornness*
With as big heart as thou. Do as thou list.°   *wish*
Thy valiantness was mine, thou sucked'st it from me,
But owe° thy pride thyself.   *own*
130 CORIOLANUS   Pray be content.
Mother, I am going to the market-place.
Chide me no more. I'll mountebank⁶ their loves,
Cog° their hearts from them, and come home beloved   *Wheedle*
Of all the trades in Rome. Look, I am going.
135 Commend me to my wife. I'll return consul,
Or never trust to what my tongue can do
I'th' way of flattery further.
VOLUMNIA   Do your will.   *Exit* VOLUMNIA
COMINIUS   Away! The tribunes do attend you. Arm yourself
To answer mildly, for they are prepared
140 With accusations, as I hear, more strong
Than are upon you yet.
CORIOLANUS   The word is 'mildly'. Pray you let us go.
Let them accuse me by invention,° I   *with invented charges*
Will answer in mine honour.
145 MENENIUS   Ay, but mildly.
CORIOLANUS   Well, mildly be it, then—mildly.   *Exeunt*

3.3

Enter SICINIUS *and* BRUTUS
BRUTUS   In this point charge him home:¹ that he affects°   *desires*
Tyrannical power. If he evade us there,
Enforce° him with his envy° to the people,   *Urge against / malice*
And that the spoil got on° the Antiats   *booty taken from*
Was ne'er distributed.
        Enter an AEDILE
5   What, will he come?
AEDILE   He's coming.
BRUTUS   How accompanied?
AEDILE   With old Menenius, and those senators
That always favoured him.
SICINIUS   Have you a catalogue

---

6. Cajole (a mountebank was an itinerant quack who sold   3.3 Location: The marketplace.
his cures from an improvised platform).   1. Press charges against him forcefully.

Of all the voices° that we have procured,   *votes*
Set down by th' poll?°   *individually*

10 AEDILE   I have, 'tis ready.

SICINIUS   Have you collected them by tribes?[2]

AEDILE   I have.

SICINIUS   Assemble presently the people hither,
And when they hear me say 'It shall be so
I'th' right and strength o'th' commons', be it either
15 For death, for fine, or banishment, then let them,
If I say 'Fine', cry 'Fine!', if 'Death', cry 'Death!',
Insisting on the old prerogative
And power i'th' truth o'th' cause.[3]

AEDILE   I shall inform them.

BRUTUS   And when such time they have begun to cry,
20 Let them not cease, but with a din confused
Enforce the present execution[4]
Of what we chance to sentence.

AEDILE   Very well.

SICINIUS   Make them be strong, and ready for this hint
When we shall hap° to give't them.   *chance*

BRUTUS [*to the* AEDILE]   Go about it. [*Exit* AEDILE]
25 Put him to choler° straight. He hath been used   *anger at once*
Ever to conquer and to have his worth[5]
Of contradiction. Being once chafed,° he cannot   *excited*
Be reined again to temperance. Then he speaks
What's in his heart, and that is there which looks
30 With us[6] to break his neck.

        Enter CORIOLANUS, MENENIUS, *and* COMINIUS, *with*
        other [SENATORS *and* PATRICIANS]

SICINIUS   Well, here he comes.

MENENIUS [*to* CORIOLANUS]   Calmly, I do beseech you.

CORIOLANUS   Ay, as an hostler° that for th' poorest piece°   *stable keeper/coin*
Will bear the knave by th' volume.[7]—Th' honoured gods
35 Keep Rome in safety and the chairs of justice
Supplied with worthy men, plant love among's,
Throng our large temples with the shows° of peace,   *ceremonies*
And not our streets with war!

FIRST SENATOR   Amen, amen.

40 MENENIUS   A noble wish.

        Enter the AEDILE *with the* CITIZENS

SICINIUS   Draw near, ye people.

AEDILE   List to your tribunes. Audience!
Peace, I say.

CORIOLANUS   First, hear me speak.

SICINIUS *and* BRUTUS   Well, say.—Peace ho!

CORIOLANUS   Shall I be charged no further than this present?°   *at this present time*
Must all determine° here?   *be determined*

SICINIUS   I do demand
45 If you submit you to the people's voices,
Allow° their officers, and are content   *Acknowledge*

---

2. Romans voted by tribes (districts) or by social class; the former method favored the plebeians.
3. *old prerogative . . . cause:* traditional right to determine the truth of the case.

4. Insist upon the immediate performance.
5. Enjoy his fill; establish his reputation from.
6. *looks / With us:* promises with our help.
7. Will endure being called knave any number of times.

To suffer lawful censure for such faults
As shall be proved upon you.
CORIOLANUS   I am content.
MENENIUS   Lo, citizens, he says he is content.
50   The warlike service he has done, consider. Think
Upon the wounds his body bears, which show
Like graves i'th' holy churchyard.
CORIOLANUS   Scratches with briers,
Scars to move laughter only.
MENENIUS   Consider further
That when he speaks not like a citizen,
55   You find him like a soldier. Do not take
His rougher accents for malicious sounds,
But, as I say, such as become a soldier
Rather than envy° you.   *show hatred to*
COMINIUS   Well, well, no more.
60   CORIOLANUS   What is the matter
That, being passed for consul with full voice,
I am so dishonoured that the very hour
You take it off again?
SICINIUS   Answer to us.
65   CORIOLANUS   Say, then. 'Tis true I ought so.
SICINIUS   We charge you that you have contrived to take
From Rome all seasoned° office, and to wind°   *time-honored/insinuate*
Yourself into a power tyrannical,
For which you are a traitor to the people.
CORIOLANUS   How, traitor?
70   MENENIUS   Nay, temperately—your promise.
CORIOLANUS   The fires i'th' lowest hell fold in° the people!   *enfold*
Call me their traitor, thou injurious° tribune?   *insulting*
Within thine eyes sat twenty thousand deaths,
In thy hands clutched as many millions, in
75   Thy lying tongue both numbers, I would say
'Thou liest' unto thee with a voice as free
As I do pray the gods.
SICINIUS   Mark you this, people?
ALL THE CITIZENS   To th' rock, to th' rock with him!
80   SICINIUS   Peace!
We need not put new matter to his charge.
What you have seen him do and heard him speak,
Beating your officers, cursing yourselves,
Opposing laws with strokes, and here defying
85   Those whose great power must try him—
Even this, so criminal and in such capital kind,[8]
Deserves th'extremest death.
BRUTUS   But since he hath
Served well for Rome—
CORIOLANUS   What do you prate° of service?   *babble*
BRUTUS   I talk of that that know it.
CORIOLANUS   You?
90   MENENIUS   Is this the promise that you made your mother?
COMINIUS   Know, I pray you—

8. Important; deserving death.

CORIOLANUS   I'll know no further.
  Let them pronounce the steep Tarpeian death,
  Vagabond exile, flaying, pent° to linger   *imprisoned*
  But with a grain a day, I would not buy
95 Their mercy at the price of one fair word,
  Nor check my courage° for what they can give   *restrain my spirit*
  To have't with saying 'Good morrow'.
SICINIUS   For that he has,
  As much as in him lies, from time to time
  Inveighed against the people, seeking means
100 To pluck away their power, as now at last
  Given hostile strokes, and that not in the presence
  Of dreaded justice, but on the ministers
  That doth distribute it, in the name o'th' people,
  And in the power of us the tribunes, we
105 E'en from this instant banish him our city
  In peril of precipitation
  From off the rock Tarpeian, never more
  To enter our Rome gates. I'th' people's name
  I say it shall be so.
ALL THE CITIZENS   It shall be so,
110 It shall be so. Let him away. He's banished,
  And it shall be so.
COMINIUS   Hear me, my masters and my common friends.
SICINIUS   He's sentenced. No more hearing.
COMINIUS   Let me speak.
  I have been consul, and can show for Rome
115 Her enemies' marks upon me. I do love
  My country's good with a respect more tender,
  More holy and profound, than mine own life,
  My dear wife's estimate,° her womb's increase,   *reputation*
  And treasure of my loins.° Then if I would   *(that is, children)*
  Speak that—
120 SICINIUS   We know your drift. Speak what?
BRUTUS   There's no more to be said, but he is banished,
  As enemy to the people and his country.
  It shall be so.
ALL THE CITIZENS   It shall be so, it shall be so.
CORIOLANUS   You common cry° of curs, whose breath I hate   *yelping pack*
125 As reek° o'th' rotten fens,° whose loves I prize   *vapor/swamps*
  As the dead carcasses of unburied men
  That do corrupt my air: I banish you.
  And here remain with your uncertainty.
  Let every feeble rumour shake your hearts;
130 Your enemies, with nodding of their plumes,°   *(helmet plumes)*
  Fan you into despair! Have the power still
  To banish your defenders, till at length
  Your ignorance—which finds not till it feels[9]—
  Making but reservation of° yourselves,   *Seeking only to preserve*
135 Still your own foes, deliver you
  As most abated° captives to some nation   *debased*
  That won you without blows! Despising

---

9. Which does not learn until it undergoes.

For° you the city, thus I turn my back.   *On account of*
There is a world elsewhere.
      Exeunt CORIOLANUS, COMINIUS, *and* [MENENIUS],
      with [*the rest of the Patricians. The* CITIZENS] *all shout,*
      and throw up their caps

140 AEDILE The people's enemy is gone, is gone.
ALL THE CITIZENS Our enemy is banished, he is gone. Hoo-oo!
SICINIUS Go see him out at gates, and follow him
  As he hath followed you, with all despite.°   *contempt*
  Give him deserved vexation. Let a guard
145 Attend us through the city.
ALL THE CITIZENS Come, come, let's see him out at gates. Come.
  The gods preserve our noble tribunes! Come.   *Exeunt*

4.1

      Enter CORIOLANUS, VOLUMNIA, VIRGILIA, MENENIUS,
      [*and*] COMINIUS, *with the young nobility of Rome*
CORIOLANUS Come, leave your tears. A brief farewell. The beast
  With many heads butts me away. Nay, mother,
  Where is your ancient° courage? You were used   *former*
  To say extremities was the trier of spirits,
5 That common chances common men could bear,
  That when the sea was calm all boats alike
  Showed mastership in floating; fortune's blows
  When most struck home, being gentle wounded craves
  A noble cunning.[1] You were used to load me
10 With precepts that would make invincible
  The heart that conned° them.   *learned*
VIRGILIA O heavens, O heavens!
CORIOLANUS Nay, I prithee, woman—
VOLUMNIA Now the red pestilence[2] strike all trades in Rome,
  And occupations° perish!   *handicrafts*
15 CORIOLANUS   What, what, what?
  I shall be loved when I am lacked. Nay, mother,
  Resume that spirit when you were wont to say,
  If you had been the wife of Hercules[3]
  Six of his labours you'd have done, and saved
20 Your husband so much sweat. Cominius,
  Droop not. Adieu. Farewell, my wife, my mother.
  I'll do well yet. Thou old and true Menenius,
  Thy tears are salter than a younger man's,
  And venomous to thine eyes. My sometime[4] general,
25 I have seen thee stern, and thou hast oft beheld
  Heart-hard'ning spectacles. Tell these sad women
  'Tis fond° to wail inevitable strokes   *as foolish*
  As 'tis to laugh at 'em. My mother, you wot° well   *know*
  My hazards still° have been your solace, and—   *always*
30 Believe't not lightly—though I go alone,
  Like to a lonely dragon that his fen
  Makes feared° and talked of more than seen, your son   *fearful*

4.1 Location: Near the city gates of Rome.
1. *being . . . cunning:* to suffer nobly requires a gentle-man's skill.
2. Bubonic plague or typhoid.

3. Mythical hero of great strength who was assigned twelve near-impossible labors.
4. Former (addressing Cominius).

Will or° exceed the common° or be caught   *either/usual standard*
With cautelous° baits and practice.   *deceitful*
VOLUMNIA   My first son,
35   Whither will thou go? Take good Cominius
With thee a while. Determine on some course
More than a wild exposure to each chance
That starts° i'th' way before thee.   *leaps up*
VIRGILIA   O the gods!
COMINIUS   I'll follow thee a month, devise with thee
40   Where thou shalt rest, that thou mayst hear of us
And we of thee. So, if the time thrust forth
A cause for thy repeal,° we shall not send   *recall from banishment*
O'er the vast world to seek a single man,
And lose advantage,° which doth ever cool   *favorable occasion*
I'th' absence of the needer.
45 CORIOLANUS   Fare ye well.
Thou hast years upon thee, and thou art too full
Of the wars' surfeits to go rove with one
That's yet unbruised. Bring me but out at gate.
Come, my sweet wife, my dearest mother, and
50   My friends of noble touch.° When I am forth,   *proven nobility*
Bid me farewell, and smile. I pray you come.
While I remain above the ground you shall
Hear from me still, and never of me aught
But what is like me formerly.
MENENIUS   That's worthily
55   As any ear can hear. Come, let's not weep.
If I could shake off but one seven years
From these old arms and legs, by the good gods,
I'd with thee every foot.
CORIOLANUS   Give me thy hand. Come.   *Exeunt*

4.2

Enter the two tribunes, SICINIUS *and* BRUTUS, *with the*
AEDILE
SICINIUS [*to the* AEDILE]   Bid them all home. He's gone, and we'll no further.
The nobility are vexed, whom we see have sided
In his behalf.
BRUTUS   Now we have shown our power,
Let us seem humbler after it is done
Than when it was a-doing.
5 SICINIUS [*to the* AEDILE]   Bid them home.
Say their great enemy is gone, and they
Stand in their ancient strength.
BRUTUS   Dismiss them home.
                         Exit AEDILE
     Enter VOLUMNIA, VIRGILIA [*weeping*], *and* MENENIUS
Here comes his mother.
SICINIUS   Let's not meet her.
10 BRUTUS   Why?
SICINIUS   They say she's mad.
BRUTUS   They have ta'en note of us. Keep on your way.

4.2 Location: Near the city gates of Rome.

VOLUMNIA   O, you're well met! Th'hoarded plague o'th' gods
   Requite° your love!   *Repay*
MENENIUS   Peace, peace, be not so loud.
15 VOLUMNIA [*to the tribunes*]   If that I could for weeping, you should hear—
   Nay, and you shall hear some. Will you be gone?
VIRGILIA [*to the tribunes*]   You shall stay, too. I would I had the power
   To say so to my husband.
SICINIUS [*to* VOLUMNIA]   Are you mankind?[1]
VOLUMNIA   Ay, fool. Is that a shame? Note but this, fool:
20 Was not a man my father? Hadst thou foxship°   *slyness*
   To banish him that struck more blows for Rome
   Than thou hast spoken words?
SICINIUS   O blessèd heavens!
VOLUMNIA   More noble blows than ever thou wise words,
   And for Rome's good. I'll tell thee what—yet go.
25 Nay, but thou shalt stay too. I would my son
   Were in Arabia,[2] and thy tribe before him,
   His good sword in his hand.
SICINIUS   What then?
VIRGILIA   What then?
   He'd make an end of thy posterity.
VOLUMNIA   Bastards and all.
30 Good man, the wounds that he does bear for Rome!
MENENIUS   Come, come, peace.
SICINIUS   I would he had continued to his country
   As he began, and not unknit° himself   *untied*
   The noble knot he made.
BRUTUS   I would he had.
35 VOLUMNIA   'I would he had'! 'Twas you incensed the rabble—
   Cats that can judge as fitly of his worth
   As I can of those mysteries which heaven
   Will not have earth to know.
BRUTUS [*to* SICINIUS]   Pray, let's go.
40 VOLUMNIA   Now pray, sir, get you gone.
   You have done a brave deed. Ere you go, hear this:
   As far as doth the Capitol exceed
   The meanest house in Rome, so far my son—
   This lady's husband here, this, do you see?—
45 Whom you have banished does exceed you all.
BRUTUS   Well, well, we'll leave you.
SICINIUS   Why stay we to be baited
   With one that wants° her wits?   *Exeunt tribunes*   *lacks*
VOLUMNIA   Take my prayers with you.
   I would the gods had nothing else to do
   But to confirm my curses. Could I meet 'em
50 But once a day, it would unclog° my heart   *unburden*
   Of what lies heavy to't.
MENENIUS   You have told them home[3]
   And, by my troth, you have cause. You'll sup° with me?   *dine*
VOLUMNIA   Anger's my meat, I sup upon myself,
   And so shall starve with feeding.

---

1. Male (thus to speak in public); Volumnia takes the
word to mean "human."
2. That is, in a desert without political institutions or

places to hide.
3. Scolded them thoroughly.

[*To* VIRGILIA]   Come, let's go.
55   Leave this faint puling and lament as I do,
      In anger, Juno-like.⁴ Come, come, come.
                                     Exeunt VOLUMNIA *and* VIRGILIA
MENENIUS   Fie, fie, fie.   *Exit*

4.3

Enter [NICANOR,] *a Roman, and* [ADRIAN,] *a Volsce*
NICANOR   I know you well, sir, and you know me. Your name, I
      think, is Adrian.
ADRIAN   It is so, sir. Truly, I have forgot you.
NICANOR   I am a Roman, and my services are, as you are, against
5   'em.° Know you me yet?   *(the Romans)*
ADRIAN   Nicanor, no?
NICANOR   The same, sir.
ADRIAN   You had more beard when I last saw you, but your
      favour° is well approved° by your tongue. What's the news in   *face / attested*
10   Rome? I have a note° from the Volscian state to find you out   *instruction*
      there. You have well saved me a day's journey.
NICANOR   There hath been in Rome strange insurrections, the
      people against the senators, patricians, and nobles.
ADRIAN   Hath been?—is it ended then? Our state thinks not so.
15   They are in a most warlike preparation, and hope to come
      upon them in the heat of their division.
NICANOR   The main blaze of it is past, but a small thing would
      make it flame again, for the nobles receive so to heart the ban-
      ishment of that worthy Coriolanus that they are in a ripe apt-
20   ness to take all power from the people, and to pluck from them
      their tribunes for ever. This lies glowing,° I can tell you, and is   *smoldering*
      almost mature for the violent breaking out.
ADRIAN   Coriolanus banished?
NICANOR   Banished, sir.
25   ADRIAN   You will be welcome with this intelligence, Nicanor.
NICANOR   The day° serves well for them° now. I have heard it   *moment / (the Volscians)*
      said the fittest time to corrupt a man's wife is when she's fallen
      out with her husband. Your noble Tullus Aufidius will appear
      well in these wars, his great opposer Coriolanus being now in
30   no request of° his country.   *unvalued by*
ADRIAN   He cannot choose.° I am most fortunate thus acciden-   *He is bound to*
      tally to encounter you. You have ended my business, and I will
      merrily accompany you home.
NICANOR   I shall between this and supper tell you most strange
35   things from Rome, all tending to the good of their adversaries.
      Have you an army ready, say you?
ADRIAN   A most royal one—the centurions and their charges dis-
      tinctly billeted already in th'entertainment,¹ and to be on foot
      at an hour's warning.
40   NICANOR   I am joyful to hear of their readiness, and am the man,
      I think, that shall set them in present° action. So, sir, heartily   *immediate*
      well met, and most glad of your company.

---

4. Goddess of marriage and childbirth (and frequently
infuriated by the infidelities of her husband, Jupiter, king
of the gods).

4.3 Location: A road between Rome and Antium.
1. *their . . . entertainment:* the men under their command
already listed unit by unit on the payroll.

ADRIAN You take my part° from me, sir. I have the most cause to   *lines*
  be glad of yours.
45 NICANOR Well, let us go together.   *Exeunt*

4.4

Enter CORIOLANUS *in mean apparel, disguised*
and muffled
CORIOLANUS A goodly city is this Antium. City,
  'Tis I that made thy widows. Many an heir
  Of these fair edifices fore my wars°   *before my onslaught*
  Have I heard groan and drop. Then know me not,
5 Lest that thy wives with spits and boys with stones
  In puny battle slay me.
      Enter a CITIZEN
                Save° you, sir.   *God save*
CITIZEN And you.
CORIOLANUS   Direct me, if it be your will,
  Where great Aufidius lies. Is he in Antium?
CITIZEN He is, and feasts the nobles of the state
  At his house this night.
10 CORIOLANUS   Which is his house, beseech you?
CITIZEN This here before you.
CORIOLANUS   Thank you, sir. Farewell.
                        Exit CITIZEN
  O world, thy slippery turns! Friends now fast sworn,
  Whose double bosoms seem to wear one heart,
  Whose hours, whose bed, whose meal and exercise
15 Are still together, who twin as 'twere in love
  Unseparable, shall within this hour,
  On a dissension of a doit,° break out   *trivial quarrel*
  To bitterest enmity. So fellest foes,
  Whose passions and whose plots have broke their sleep
20 To take the one the other,[1] by some chance,
  Some trick° not worth an egg, shall grow dear friends   *trifle*
  And interjoin their issues.[2] So with me.
  My birthplace hate I, and my love's upon
  This enemy town. I'll enter. If he slay me,
25 He does fair justice; if he give me way,°   *allows me to proceed*
  I'll do his country service.   *Exit*

4.5

Music plays. Enter a SERVINGMAN
FIRST SERVINGMAN Wine, wine, wine! What service is here?
  I think our fellows° are asleep.   *[Exit]*   *fellow servants*
      Enter [a SECOND*]* SERVINGMAN
SECOND SERVINGMAN Where's Cotus? My master calls for him.
  Cotus!   *Exit*
      Enter CORIOLANUS *[as before]*
5 CORIOLANUS A goodly house. The feast
  Smells well, but I appear not like a guest.
      Enter the FIRST SERVINGMAN

4.4 Location: Before Aufidius's house in Antium.
1. Whose plots to capture one another have kept them
awake.

2. Unite their causes; marry their children to one another.
4.5 Location: Inside Aufidius's house.

FIRST SERVINGMAN What would you have, friend? Whence are you? Here's no place for you. Pray go to the door. *Exit*

CORIOLANUS I have deserved no better entertainment
10   In being Coriolanus.

Enter SECOND [SERVINGMAN]

SECOND SERVINGMAN Whence are you, sir? Has the porter his eyes in his head, that he gives entrance to such companions?°   low persons
Pray get you out.

CORIOLANUS Away!

15 SECOND SERVINGMAN Away? Get you away.

CORIOLANUS Now thou'rt troublesome.

SECOND SERVINGMAN Are you so brave?° I'll have you talked   insolent
with anon.°   right away

Enter THIRD SERVINGMAN. *The* FIRST *meets him*

THIRD SERVINGMAN What fellow's this?

20 FIRST SERVINGMAN A strange one as ever I looked on. I cannot get him out o'th' house. Prithee, call my master to him.

THIRD SERVINGMAN [*to* CORIOLANUS] What have you to do° here,   are you doing
fellow? Pray you, avoid° the house.   leave

CORIOLANUS Let me but stand. I will not hurt your hearth.

25 THIRD SERVINGMAN What are you?

CORIOLANUS A gentleman.

THIRD SERVINGMAN A marvellous poor one.

CORIOLANUS True, so I am.

THIRD SERVINGMAN Pray you, poor gentleman, take up some other
30   station.[1] Here's no place for you. Pray you, avoid. Come.

CORIOLANUS Follow your function.[2] Go and batten° on cold   gorge
bits.

[*He*] *pushes him away from him*

THIRD SERVINGMAN What, you will not? — Prithee tell my master what a strange guest he has here.

35 SECOND SERVINGMAN And I shall.   *Exit* SECOND SERVINGMAN

THIRD SERVINGMAN Where dwell'st thou?

CORIOLANUS Under the canopy.°   (*of the sky*)

THIRD SERVINGMAN Under the canopy?

CORIOLANUS Ay.

40 THIRD SERVINGMAN Where's that?

CORIOLANUS I'th' city of kites and crows.°   (*carrion birds*)

THIRD SERVINGMAN I'th' city of kites and crows? What an ass it is! Then thou dwell'st with daws,[3] too?

CORIOLANUS No, I serve not thy master.

45 THIRD SERVINGMAN How, sir? Do you meddle[4] with my master?

CORIOLANUS Ay, 'tis an honester service than to meddle with thy mistress. Thou prat'st and prat'st. Serve with thy trencher.°   wooden plate
Hence!

[*He*] *beats him away.*

Enter AUFIDIUS, *with the* [SECOND] SERVINGMAN

AUFIDIUS Where is this fellow?

50 SECOND SERVINGMAN Here, sir. I'd have beaten him like a dog but for disturbing the lords within.

[*The* SERVINGMEN *stand aside*]

---

1. Place to stand (punning on "social rank").
2. Perform your servant's tasks.
3. Jackdaws (proverbially foolish).

4. Busy yourself; but Coriolanus plays on the sense "have sexual intercourse."

AUFIDIUS   Whence com'st thou? What wouldst thou? Thy name?
 Why speak'st not? Speak, man. What's thy name?
CORIOLANUS [*unmuffling his head*]   If, Tullus,
 Not yet thou know'st me, and seeing me dost not
55 Think me for the man I am, necessity
 Commands me name myself.
AUFIDIUS   What is thy name?
CORIOLANUS   A name unmusical to the Volscians' ears
 And harsh in sound to thine.
AUFIDIUS   Say, what's thy name?
 Thou hast a grim appearance, and thy face
60 Bears a command in't. Though thy tackle's torn,
 Thou show'st° a noble vessel. What's thy name?   *appear to be*
CORIOLANUS   Prepare thy brow to frown. Know'st thou me yet?
AUFIDIUS   I know thee not. Thy name?
CORIOLANUS   My name is Caius Martius, who hath done
65 To thee particularly, and to all the Volsces,
 Great hurt and mischief. Thereto witness may
 My surname Coriolanus. The painful service,
 The extreme dangers, and the drops of blood
 Shed for my thankless country, are requited
70 But with that surname—a good memory°   *reminder*
 And witness of the malice and displeasure
 Which thou shouldst bear me. Only that name remains.
 The cruelty and envy of the people,
 Permitted by our dastard nobles, who
75 Have all forsook me, hath devoured the rest,
 And suffered me by th' voice of slaves to be
 Whooped out of Rome. Now this extremity
 Hath brought me to thy hearth. Not out of hope—
 Mistake me not—to save my life, for if
80 I had feared death, of all the men i'th' world
 I would have 'voided thee, but in mere° spite   *utter*
 To be full quit of° those my banishers   *revenged upon; rid of*
 Stand I before thee here. Then if thou hast
 A heart of wreak° in thee, that wilt revenge   *vengeance*
85 Thine own particular wrongs and stop those maims
 Of shame seen through thy country, speed° thee straight,   *hasten*
 And make my misery serve thy turn. So use it
 That my revengeful services may prove
 As benefits to thee; for I will fight
90 Against my cankered° country with the spleen°   *infected/wrath*
 Of all the under-fiends.° But if so be   *underworld fiends*
 Thou dar'st not this, and that to prove° more fortunes   *try*
 Thou'rt tired, then, in a word, I also am
 Longer to live most weary, and present
95 My throat to thee and to thy ancient° malice,   *long-standing*
 Which not to cut would show thee but a fool,
 Since I have ever followed thee with hate,
 Drawn tuns° of blood out of thy country's breast,   *huge casks*
 And cannot live but to thy shame unless
 It be to do thee service.
100 AUFIDIUS   O Martius, Martius!
 Each word thou hast spoke hath weeded from my heart
 A root of ancient envy. If Jupiter

Should from yon cloud speak divine things
And say ' 'Tis true', I'd not believe them more
105 Than thee, all-noble Martius. Let me twine
Mine arms about that body whereagainst
My grainèd ash[5] an hundred times hath broke,
And scarred the moon with splinters.
          [*He embraces* CORIOLANUS]
                              Here I clip°   *embrace*
The anvil[6] of my sword, and do contest
110 As hotly and as nobly with thy love
As ever in ambitious strength I did
Contend against thy valour. Know thou first,
I loved the maid I married; never man
Sighed truer breath. But that I see thee here,
115 Thou noble thing, more dances my rapt heart
Than when I first my wedded mistress saw
Bestride my threshold. Why, thou Mars, I tell thee
We have a power on foot,° and I had purpose   *army in the field*
Once more to hew thy target° from thy brawn,°   *shield / arm*
120 Or lose mine arm for't. Thou hast beat me out°   *outright*
Twelve several° times, and I have nightly since   *separate*
Dreamt of encounters 'twixt thyself and me—
We have been down° together in my sleep,   *(on the ground)*
Unbuckling helms, fisting° each other's throat—   *clutching*
125 And waked half dead with nothing. Worthy Martius,
Had we no other quarrel else to Rome but that
Thou art thence banished, we would muster all°   *enlist everyone*
From twelve to seventy,° and, pouring war   *(years old)*
Into the bowels of ungrateful Rome,
130 Like a bold flood o'erbear't. O, come, go in,
And take our friendly senators by th' hands
Who now are here taking their leaves of me,
Who am prepared against your territories,
Though not for Rome itself.
CORIOLANUS   You bless me, gods.
135 AUFIDIUS Therefore, most absolute° sir, if thou wilt have   *perfect*
The leading of thine own revenges, take
Th'one half of my commission° and set down°—   *force / determine*
As best thou art experienced, since thou know'st
Thy country's strength and weakness—thine own ways:
140 Whether to knock against the gates of Rome,
Or rudely visit° them in parts remote   *afflict*
To fright them ere destroy. But come in.
Let me commend thee first to those that shall
Say yea to thy desires. A thousand welcomes!
145 And more a friend than ere an enemy;
Yet, Martius, that was much. Your hand. Most welcome!
                                        Exeunt
          [*The*] *two* SERVINGMEN [*come forward*]
FIRST SERVINGMAN Here's a strange alteration!
SECOND SERVINGMAN By my hand, I had thought to have strucken

---

5. Close-grained ashwood spear.
6. Coriolanus's body, on which Aufidius has beaten his sword.

him with a cudgel, and yet my mind gave° me his clothes made   *suggested to*
150 a false report of him.
FIRST SERVINGMAN   What an arm he has! He turned me about
with his finger and his thumb as one would set up a top.
SECOND SERVINGMAN   Nay, I knew by his face that there was
something in him. He had, sir, a kind of face, methought—I
155 cannot tell how to term it.
FIRST SERVINGMAN   He had so, looking, as it were—would I were
hanged but I thought there was more in him than I could
think.
SECOND SERVINGMAN   So did I, I'll be sworn. He is simply the
160 rarest man i'th' world.
FIRST SERVINGMAN   I think he is yet a greater soldier than he you
wot on.°   *know of*
SECOND SERVINGMAN   Who, my master?
FIRST SERVINGMAN   Nay, it's no matter for° that.   *no doubt about*
165 SECOND SERVINGMAN   Worth six on him.
FIRST SERVINGMAN   Nay, not so, neither; but I take him to be the
greater soldier.
SECOND SERVINGMAN   Faith, look you, one cannot tell how to
say[7] that. For the defence of a town our general is excellent.
170 FIRST SERVINGMAN   Ay, and for an assault too.
            Enter the THIRD SERVINGMAN
THIRD SERVINGMAN   O, slaves, I can tell you news—news, you
rascals!
FIRST *and* SECOND SERVINGMEN   What, what, what? Let's partake.
THIRD SERVINGMAN   I would not be a Roman of all nations. I had
175 as lief° be a condemned man.   *gladly*
FIRST *and* SECOND SERVINGMEN   Wherefore? Wherefore?
THIRD SERVINGMAN   Why, here's he that was wont to thwack our
general, Caius Martius.
FIRST SERVINGMAN   Why do you say 'thwack our general'?
180 THIRD SERVINGMAN   I do not say 'thwack our general'; but he was
always good enough for him.
SECOND SERVINGMAN   Come, we are fellows and friends. He was
ever too hard for him. I have heard him say so himself.
FIRST SERVINGMAN   He was too hard for him directly.° To say the   *simply*
185 truth on't, before Corioles he scotched° him and notched him   *scored*
like a carbonado.[8]
SECOND SERVINGMAN   An° he had been cannibally given, he   *If*
might have broiled and eaten him too.
FIRST SERVINGMAN   But more of thy news!
190 THIRD SERVINGMAN   Why, he is so made on° here within as if he   *made so much of*
were son and heir to Mars; set at upper end o'th' table, no
question asked him by any of the senators but they stand bald°   *hatless*
before him. Our general himself makes a mistress of° him,   *woos*
sanctifies himself with's hand,[9] and turns up the white o'th'
195 eye° to his discourse. But the bottom° of the news is, our gen-   *(in pious devotion)/gist*
eral is cut i'th' middle, and but one half of what he was yester-
day, for the other° has half by the entreaty and grant of the   *(Coriolanus)*
whole table. He'll go, he says, and sowl° the porter of Rome   *drag*

---

7. There's no basis for saying.   9. Treats the touch of his hand as holy.
8. Piece of meat for broiling.

gates by th' ears. He will mow all down before him, and leave
200 his passage polled.°   *stripped*
SECOND SERVINGMAN   And he's as like to do't as any man I can
    imagine.
THIRD SERVINGMAN   Do't? He will do't; for look you, sir, he has
    as many friends as enemies; which friends, sir, as it were durst
205 not—look you, sir—show themselves, as we term it, his friends
    whilst he's in dejectitude.°   *disgraced*
FIRST SERVINGMAN   Dejectitude? What's that?
THIRD SERVINGMAN   But when they shall see, sir, his crest up
    again and the man in blood,[1] they will out of their burrows like
210 conies° after rain, and revel all with him.   *rabbits*
FIRST SERVINGMAN   But when goes this forward?
THIRD SERVINGMAN   Tomorrow, today, presently.° You shall have   *at once*
    the drum struck up this afternoon. 'Tis as it were a parcel° of   *part*
    their feast, and to be executed ere they wipe their lips.
215 SECOND SERVINGMAN   Why, then we shall have a stirring° world   *busy*
    again. This peace is nothing but to rust iron, increase tailors,
    and breed ballad-makers.[2]
FIRST SERVINGMAN   Let me have war, say I. It exceeds peace as
    far as day does night. It's sprightly walking, audible and full of
220 vent.[3] Peace is a very apoplexy, lethargy; mulled,° deaf, sleepy,   *stupefied*
    insensible; a getter of more bastard children than war's a
    destroyer of men.
SECOND SERVINGMAN   'Tis so, and as war in some sort may be
    said to be a ravisher, so it cannot be denied but peace is a great
225 maker of cuckolds.
FIRST SERVINGMAN   Ay, and it makes men hate one another.
THIRD SERVINGMAN   Reason; because they then less need one an-
    other. The wars for my money. I hope to see Romans as cheap
    as Volscians.
        [*A sound within*]
230 They are rising, they are rising.°   *(from dinner)*
FIRST *and* SECOND SERVINGMEN   In, in, in, in.   *Exeunt*

4.6

Enter the two tribunes, SICINIUS *and* BRUTUS
SICINIUS   We hear not of him, neither need we fear him.
    His remedies are tame[1]—the present peace
    And quietness of the people, which before
    Were in wild hurry.° Here do we make his friends   *tumult*
5   Blush that the world goes well, who rather had,
    Though they themselves did suffer by't, behold
    Dissentious numbers pest'ring° streets than see   *obstructing*
    Our tradesmen singing in their shops and going
    About their functions friendly.
        Enter MENENIUS
10 BRUTUS   We stood to't° in good time. Is this Menenius?   *acted resolutely*
SICINIUS   'Tis he, 'tis he. O, he is grown most kind of late.
    Hail, sir.

---

1. In full vigor (usually refers to hounds).
2. Fashionable dress and idle songs flourish in peacetime.
3. *audible . . . vent*: either loud and full of action, or quick
of hearing and scent (like a hunting dog).

4.6 Location: A public place in Rome.
1. Those who favor him are unable to act; curing ourselves of him is without violent effects.

MENENIUS   Hail to you both.

SICINIUS   Your Coriolanus is not much missed

15   But with° his friends. The commonwealth doth stand,   *by*
      And so would do were he more angry at it.

MENENIUS   All's well, and might have been much better if
      He could have temporized.

SICINIUS   Where is he, hear you?

20   MENENIUS   Nay, I hear nothing.
      His mother and his wife hear nothing from him.

Enter three or four CITIZENS

ALL THE CITIZENS [*to the tribunes*]   The gods preserve you both.

SICINIUS   Good e'en, our
          neighbours.

BRUTUS   Good e'en to you all, good e'en to you all.

FIRST CITIZEN   Ourselves, our wives and children, on our knees
      Are bound to pray for you both.

25   SICINIUS   Live and thrive.

BRUTUS   Farewell, kind neighbours.
      We wished Coriolanus had loved you as we did.

ALL THE CITIZENS   Now the gods keep you!

SICINIUS *and* BRUTUS   Farewell, farewell.

Exeunt CITIZENS

SICINIUS   This is a happier and more comely time

30   Than when these fellows ran about the streets
      Crying confusion.

BRUTUS   Caius Martius was
      A worthy officer i'th' war, but insolent,
      O'ercome with pride, ambitious past all thinking,°   *beyond imagination*
      Self-loving—

SICINIUS   And affecting one sole throne°   *aspiring to rule alone*
      Without assistance.

35   MENENIUS   I think not so.

SICINIUS   We should by this,° to all our lamentation,   *now*
      If he had gone forth consul found it so.

BRUTUS   The gods have well prevented it, and Rome
      Sits safe and still without him.

Enter an AEDILE

AEDILE   Worthy tribunes,

40   There is a slave whom we have put in prison
      Reports the Volsces, with two several powers,°   *separate armies*
      Are entered in the Roman territories,
      And with the deepest malice of the war
      Destroy what lies before 'em.

MENENIUS   'Tis Aufidius,

45   Who, hearing of our Martius' banishment,
      Thrusts forth his horns again into the world,
      Which were inshelled when Martius stood for Rome,
      And durst not once peep out.

SICINIUS   Come, what talk you of Martius?

BRUTUS [*to the* AEDILE]   Go see this rumourer whipped. It cannot be
      The Volsces dare break° with us.   *(their treaty)*

50   MENENIUS   Cannot be?
      We have record that very well it can,
      And three examples of the like hath been
      Within my age. But reason° with the fellow,   *discuss*

Before you punish him, where he heard this,
55   Lest you shall chance to whip your information
And beat the messenger who bids beware
Of what is to be dreaded.
SICINIUS   Tell not me.
I know this cannot be.
BRUTUS   Not possible.

Enter a MESSENGER

MESSENGER   The nobles in great earnestness are going
60   All to the senate-house. Some news is come
That turns° their countenances.   *changes*
SICINIUS   'Tis this slave.
[*To the* AEDILE]   Go whip him fore the people's eyes.—His raising,°   *incitement*
Nothing but his report.   *Exit* AEDILE
MESSENGER   Yes, worthy sir,
The slave's report is seconded, and more,
More fearful, is delivered.
65 SICINIUS   What more fearful?
MESSENGER   It is spoke freely out of many mouths—
How probable I do not know—that Martius,
Joined with Aufidius, leads a power 'gainst Rome,
And vows revenge as spacious as between
The young'st and oldest thing.
70 SICINIUS   This is most likely!°   *(sarcastic)*
BRUTUS   Raised only that the weaker sort may wish
Good Martius home again.
SICINIUS   The very trick on't.°   *Exactly*
MENENIUS   This is unlikely.
75   He and Aufidius can no more atone°   *reconcile*
Than violent'st contrariety.

Enter [*another*] MESSENGER

SECOND MESSENGER   You are sent for to the senate.
A fearful army, led by Caius Martius
Associated with Aufidius, rages
80   Upon our territories, and have already
O'erborne their way, consumed with fire and took
What lay before them.

Enter COMINIUS

COMINIUS   O, you have made good work!
MENENIUS   What news? What news?
85 COMINIUS   You have holp° to ravish your own daughters and   *helped*
To melt the city leads° upon your pates,°   *roof lead/heads*
To see your wives dishonoured to° your noses.   *in front of*
MENENIUS   What's the news? What's the news?
COMINIUS   Your temples burnèd in their cement,° and   *to their foundations*
90   Your franchises,° whereon you stood,° confined   *freedoms/insisted*
Into an auger's bore.²
MENENIUS   Pray now, your news?
[*To the tribunes*] You have made fair work, I fear me.
[*To* COMINIUS]   Pray, your news.
If Martius should be joined wi'th' Volscians—
COMINIUS   If? He is their god. He leads them like a thing
95   Made by some other deity than nature,

2. A drill hole (that is, a narrow space).

That shapes man better, and they follow him
Against us brats° with no less confidence   *mere children*
Than boys pursuing summer butterflies,
Or butchers killing flies.
MENENIUS [*to the tribunes*]   You have made good work,
100   You and your apron-men,° you that stood so much   *(artisans wore aprons)*
Upon the voice of occupation° and   *opinion of tradesmen*
The breath of garlic-eaters!
COMINIUS [*to the tribunes*]   He'll shake your Rome about your ears.
MENENIUS   As Hercules did shake down mellow fruit.³
105   [*To the tribunes*] You have made fair work.
BRUTUS   But is this true, sir?
COMINIUS   Ay, and you'll look pale
Before you find it other.° All the regions   *otherwise*
Do smilingly° revolt, and who resists   *happily*
110   Are mocked for valiant° ignorance,   *steadfast*
And perish constant° fools. Who is't can blame him?   *obstinate*
Your enemies° and his⁴ find something in him.   *(the patricians)*
MENENIUS   We are all undone unless
The noble man have mercy.
COMINIUS   Who shall ask it?
115   The tribunes cannot do't, for shame; the people
Deserve such pity of° him as the wolf   *from*
Does of the shepherds. For his best friends, if they
Should say 'Be good to Rome', they charged° him even   *would direct*
As those should do that had deserved his hate,
And therein showed° like enemies.   *would behave*
120   MENENIUS   'Tis true.
If he were putting to my house the brand°   *fire*
That should consume it, I have not the face°   *shamelessness*
To say 'Beseech you, cease.'
[*To the tribunes*]   You have made fair hands,°   *done well*
You and your crafts! You have crafted fair!
COMINIUS [*to the tribunes*]   You have brought
125   A trembling upon Rome such as was never
S'incapable of help.
SICINIUS *and* BRUTUS   Say not we brought it.
MENENIUS   How? Was't we?
We loved him, but like beasts and cowardly nobles
130   Gave way unto your clusters,° who did hoot   *crowds*
Him out o'th' city.
COMINIUS   But I fear
They'll roar° him in again. Tullus Aufidius,   *(in fear)*
The second name of men,⁵ obeys his points°   *directions*
As if he were his officer. Desperation
135   Is all the policy, strength, and defence
That Rome can make against them.
        Enter a troop of CITIZENS
MENENIUS   Here come the clusters.
[*To the* CITIZENS] And is Aufidius with him? You are they
That made the air unwholesome when you cast

3. Hercules' twelfth labor was to gather the apples of the   4. The Volscians.
Hesperides.   5. The second in reputation only to Coriolanus.

Your stinking greasy caps in hooting at
140 Coriolanus' exile. Now he's coming,
And not a hair upon a soldier's head
Which will not prove a whip. As many coxcombs°   fools
As you threw caps up will he tumble down,
And pay you for your voices. 'Tis no matter.
145 If he could burn us all into one coal,
We have deserved it.
ALL THE CITIZENS   Faith, we hear fearful news.
FIRST CITIZEN   For mine own part,
When I said 'banish him' I said 'twas pity.
150 SECOND CITIZEN   And so did I.
THIRD CITIZEN   And so did I, and to say the truth so did very
    many of us. That° we did, we did for the best, and though we   What
    willingly consented to his banishment, yet it was against our
    will.
COMINIUS   You're goodly things, you voices.
155 MENENIUS   You have made good work,
You and your cry. Shall's to the Capitol?
COMINIUS   O, ay, what else?   Exeunt [MENENIUS and COMINIUS]
SICINIUS   Go, masters, get you home. Be not dismayed.
These are a side° that would be glad to have   faction
160 This true which they so seem to fear. Go home,
And show no sign of fear.
FIRST CITIZEN   The gods be good to us! Come, masters, let's home.
I ever said we were i'th' wrong when we banished him.
SECOND CITIZEN   So did we all. But come, let's home.
                                                           Exeunt CITIZENS
BRUTUS   I do not like this news.
165 SICINIUS   Nor I.
BRUTUS   Let's to the Capitol. Would half my wealth
Would buy this for a lie.
SICINIUS   Pray let's go.   Exeunt

4.7

Enter AUFIDIUS *with his* LIEUTENANT
AUFIDIUS   Do they still fly to th' Roman?
LIEUTENANT   I do not know what witchcraft's in him, but
Your soldiers use him as the grace fore meat,
Their talk at table, and their thanks at end,
5 And you are darkened° in this action, sir,   overshadowed
Even by your own.°   (followers)
AUFIDIUS   I cannot help it now,
Unless by using means° I lame the foot   stratagems
Of our design. He bears himself more proudlier,
Even to my person, than I thought he would
10 When first I did embrace him. Yet his nature
In that's no changeling,° and I must excuse   waverer
What cannot be amended.
LIEUTENANT   Yet I wish, sir—
I mean for your particular°—you had not   own sake
Joined in commission° with him, but either   command
15 Have borne the action of yourself or else
To him had left it solely.
AUFIDIUS   I understand thee well, and be thou sure,

When he shall come to his account,[1] he knows not
What I can urge against him. Although it seems—
20 And so he thinks, and is no less apparent
To th' vulgar eye—that he bears all things fairly
And shows good husbandry for the Volscian state,
Fights dragon-like, and does achieve as soon
As draw his sword, yet he hath left undone
25 That which shall break his neck or hazard mine
Whene'er we come to our account.
LIEUTENANT   Sir, I beseech you, think you he'll carry° Rome?   *defeat*
AUFIDIUS   All places yields to him ere he sits down,°   *lays siege*
And the nobility of Rome are his.
30 The senators and patricians love him too.
The tribunes are no soldiers, and their people
Will be as rash in the repeal° as hasty   *recall from exile*
To expel him thence. I think he'll be to Rome
As is the osprey to the fish, who takes it
35 By sovereignty of nature.[2] First he was
A noble servant to them, but he could not
Carry his honours even.° Whether 'twas pride,   *equably*
Which out of daily fortune[3] ever taints
The happy° man; whether defect of judgement,   *fortunate*
40 To fail in the disposing of those chances
Which he was lord of; or whether nature,
Not to be other than one thing, not moving
From th' casque° to th' cushion,° but commanding peace   *helmet/senate seat*
Even with the same austerity and garb°   *stern demeanor*
45 As he controlled the war: but one of these—
As he hath spices° of them all—not all,   *touches*
For I dare so far free him—made him feared,
So hated, and so banished. But he has a merit
To choke it in the utt'rance.[4] So our virtues
50 Lie in th'interpretation of the time,°   *contemporary observers*
And power, unto itself most commendable,
Hath not a tomb so evident as a chair
T'extol what it hath done.[5]
One fire drives out one fire, one nail one nail;
55 Rights by rights falter, strengths by strengths do fail.
Come, let's away. When, Caius, Rome is thine,
Thou art poor'st of all; then shortly art thou mine.   *Exeunt*

5.1

Enter MENENIUS, COMINIUS, SICINIUS, BRUTUS, *the two*
tribunes, with others
MENENIUS   No, I'll not go. You hear what he hath said
Which was sometime his general,° who loved him   *(Cominius)*
In a most dear particular.° He called me father,   *affectionate regard*
But what o' that? [*To the tribunes*] Go, you that banished him.
5 A mile before his tent fall down, and knee°   *crawl*

4.7 Location: The Volscian camp near Rome.
1. That is, with the Volscian state.
2. Fish were imagined to surrender to ospreys without a struggle.
3. As a result of repeated successes.
4. *he has . . . utt'rance*: his merit is so great that it overwhelms the recital of his faults; alternatively, his merit is

of a kind that impedes attempts to praise it.
5. *Hath not . . . done*: a confusing passage, perhaps meaning, Will fall into certain oblivion unless it receives praise from the public rostrum; alternatively, is clearly ruined by public praise. In the first case, power requires reputation; in the second, reputation threatens power.
5.1 Location: A public place in Rome.

The way into his mercy. Nay, if he coyed°   *pretended not*
To hear Cominius speak, I'll keep at home.
COMINIUS   He would not seem° to know me.   *was reluctant*
MENENIUS [*to the tribunes*]   Do you hear?
COMINIUS   Yet one time he did call me by my name.
10   I urged our old acquaintance and the drops
That we have bled together. 'Coriolanus'
He would not answer to, forbade all names.
He was a kind of nothing, titleless,
Till he had forged himself a name o'th' fire
Of burning Rome.
MENENIUS [*to the tribunes*]
15   Why, so! You have made good work.
A pair of tribunes that have wracked° fair Rome   *destroyed*
To make coals cheap—a noble memory!°   *memorial*
COMINIUS   I minded him how royal 'twas to pardon
When it was less expected. He replied
20   It was a bare° petition of a state   *worthless; barefaced*
To one whom they had punished.
MENENIUS   Very well.
Could he say less?
COMINIUS   I offered° to awaken his regard   *tried*
For's private friends. His answer to me was
25   He could not stay to pick them in° a pile   *pick them out from*
Of noisome, musty chaff. He said 'twas folly,
For one poor grain or two, to leave unburnt
And still to nose° th'offence.   *smell*
MENENIUS   For one poor grain or two?
I am one of those. His mother, wife, his child,
30   And this brave fellow too—we are the grains.
[*To the tribunes*] You are the musty chaff, and you are smelt
Above the moon. We must be burnt for you.
SICINIUS   Nay, pray be patient. If you refuse your aid
In this so never-needed help, yet do not
35   Upbraid's with our distress. But sure, if you
Would be your country's pleader, your good tongue,
More than the instant army we can make,[1]
Might stop our countryman.
MENENIUS   No, I'll not meddle.
SICINIUS   Pray you go to him.
MENENIUS   What should I do?
40 BRUTUS   Only make trial what your love can do
For Rome towards Martius.
MENENIUS   Well, and say that Martius return me,
As Cominius is returned, unheard—what then?
But as a discontented friend, grief-shot°   *grief-stricken*
With his unkindness? Say't be so?
45 SICINIUS   Yet your good will
Must have that thanks from Rome after the measure
As° you intended well.   *To the extent that*
MENENIUS   I'll undertake't.
I think he'll hear me. Yet to bite his lip°   *(in anger)*
And 'hmh' at good Cominius much unhearts me.

---

1. The army we can raise right now.

50   He was not taken well,[2] he had not dined.
    The veins unfilled, our blood is cold, and then
    We pout upon the morning, are unapt
    To give or to forgive; but when we have stuffed
    These pipes and these conveyances° of our blood   *channels*
55   With wine and feeding, we have suppler souls
    Than in our priest-like fasts. Therefore I'll watch him
    Till he be dieted° to my request,   *made amenable by food*
    And then I'll set upon him.
BRUTUS You know the very road into his kindness,
    And cannot lose your way.
60 MENENIUS   Good faith, I'll prove° him.   *try*
    Speed° how it will, I shall ere long have knowledge   *Turn out*
    Of my success.°   *Exit*   *whether I succeed*
COMINIUS   He'll never hear him.
SICINIUS   Not?
COMINIUS I tell you, he does sit in gold, his eye
    Red as 'twould burn Rome, and his injury[3]
65   The jailer to his pity. I kneeled before him;
    'Twas very faintly he said 'Rise', dismissed me
    Thus with his speechless hand. What he would do
    He sent in writing after me, what he would not,
    Bound with an oath to hold to his conditions.
70   So that all hope is vain unless his noble mother
    And his wife, who as I hear mean to solicit him
    For mercy to his country. Therefore let's hence,
    And with our fair entreaties haste them on.   *Exeunt*

5.2

Enter MENENIUS *to the* Watch *or guard*

FIRST WATCHMAN Stay. Whence are you?
SECOND WATCHMAN Stand, and go back.
MENENIUS You guard like men; 'tis well.
    But, by your leave, I am an officer
5   Of state, and come to speak with Coriolanus.
FIRST WATCHMAN From whence?
MENENIUS From Rome.
FIRST WATCHMAN   You may not pass, you must return.
    Our general will no more hear from thence.
SECOND WATCHMAN You'll see your Rome embraced with fire before
    You'll speak with Coriolanus.
10 MENENIUS   Good my friends,
    If you have heard your general talk of Rome
    And of his friends there, it is lots to blanks°   *the odds are*
    My name hath touched your ears. It is Menenius.
FIRST WATCHMAN Be it so; go back. The virtue° of your name   *power*
    Is not here passable.[1]
15 MENENIUS   I tell thee, fellow,
    Thy general is my lover.° I have been   *friend*
    The book° of his good acts, whence men have read   *recorder*
    His fame unparalleled happily amplified;

---

2. Not tackled at the right time.
3. The wrong inflicted on him.

5.2 Location: The Volscian camp near Rome.
1. Current (like a coin); effective (as a password).

For I have ever verified² my friends,

20 Of whom he's chief, with all the size° that verity   *amplitude*

Would without lapsing suffer.° Nay, sometimes,   *erring allow*

Like to a bowl upon a subtle° ground,   *misleading*

I have tumbled past the throw,³ and in his praise

Have almost stamped the leasing.⁴ Therefore, fellow,

25 I must have leave to pass.

FIRST WATCHMAN   Faith, sir, if you had told as many lies in his behalf as you have uttered words in your own, you should not pass here, no, though it were as virtuous to lie as to live chastely.⁵ Therefore go back.

30 MENENIUS   Prithee, fellow, remember my name is Menenius, always factionary on° the party of your general.   *adherent to*

SECOND WATCHMAN   Howsoever you have been his liar, as you say you have, I am one that, telling true under him, must say you cannot pass. Therefore go back.

35 MENENIUS   Has he dined, canst thou tell? For I would not speak with him till after dinner.

FIRST WATCHMAN   You are a Roman, are you?

MENENIUS   I am as thy general is.

FIRST WATCHMAN   Then you should hate Rome as he does. Can

40 you, when you have pushed out your gates the very defender of them, and in a violent popular ignorance given your enemy your shield, think to front° his revenges with the easy⁶ groans   *confront* of old women, the virginal palms of your daughters, or with the palsied intercession of such a decayed dotant° as you seem to   *old fool*

45 be? Can you think to blow out the intended fire your city is ready to flame in with such weak breath as this? No, you are deceived, therefore back to Rome, and prepare for your execution. You are condemned, our general has sworn you out of reprieve and pardon.

50 MENENIUS   Sirrah, if thy captain knew I were here, he would use me with estimation.°   *esteem*

FIRST WATCHMAN   Come, my captain knows you not.

MENENIUS   I mean thy general.

FIRST WATCHMAN   My general cares not for you. Back, I say, go,

55 lest I let forth your half pint of blood. Back. That's the utmost of your having.° Back.   *the most you'll get*

MENENIUS   Nay, but fellow, fellow—

Enter CORIOLANUS *with* AUFIDIUS

CORIOLANUS   What's the matter?

MENENIUS [*to* FIRST WATCHMAN]   Now, you companion,° I'll say   *knave*

60 an errand° for you. You shall know now that I am in estimation.   *deliver a message* You shall perceive that a jack guardant° cannot office⁷ me from   *uncouth guard* my son Coriolanus. Guess but by my entertainment with him if thou stand'st not i'th' state of hanging, or of some death more long in spectatorship and crueller in suffering. Behold now

65 presently, and swoon for what's to come upon thee. [*To* CORIO- LANUS] The glorious gods sit in hourly synod° about thy particu-   *council* lar prosperity, and love thee no worse than thy old father Menenius does! [*Weeping*] O, my son, my son, thou art prepar-

---

2. Testified to the character of.
3. Overshot the mark (from the game of bowls).
4. Authenticated falsehood.

5. Honestly (but playing on "lies with a sexual partner").
6. Easily obtained; insignificant.
7. Officiously keep.

ing fire for us. Look thee, here's water to quench it. I was
hardly° moved to come to thee, but being assured none but   *with difficulty*
myself could move thee, I have been blown out of our gates
with sighs, and conjure thee to pardon Rome and thy petition-
ary° countrymen. The good gods assuage thy wrath and turn   *suppliant*
the dregs of it upon this varlet here, this, who like a block° hath *blockhead; obstruction*
denied my access to thee!
CORIOLANUS Away!
MENENIUS How? Away?
CORIOLANUS Wife, mother, child, I know not. My affairs
Are servanted° to others. Though I owe   *subjected*
My revenge properly,⁸ my remission° lies   *forgiveness*
In Volscian breasts. That we have been familiar,
Ingrate forgetfulness shall poison rather
Than pity note how much.⁹ Therefore be gone.
Mine ears against your suits are stronger than
Your gates against my force. Yet, for° I loved thee,   *because*
    [*He gives him a letter*]
Take this along. I writ it for thy sake,
And would have sent it. Another word, Menenius,
I will not hear thee speak.—This man, Aufidius,
Was my beloved in Rome; yet thou behold'st.
AUFIDIUS You keep a constant temper.
                              Exeunt [CORIOLANUS *and* AUFIDIUS]
FIRST WATCHMAN Now, sir, is your name Menenius?
SECOND WATCHMAN 'Tis a spell, you see, of much power. You
know the way home again.
FIRST WATCHMAN Do you hear how we are shent° for keeping   *scolded*
your greatness back?
SECOND WATCHMAN What cause do you think I have to swoon?
MENENIUS I neither care for th' world nor your general. For
such things as you, I can scarce think there's any, you're so
slight. He that hath a will to die by himself° fears it not from   *at his own hand*
another. Let your general do his worst. For you, be that you are
long, and your misery increase with your age. I say to you as I
was said to, 'Away!'   *Exit*
FIRST WATCHMAN A noble fellow, I warrant him.
SECOND WATCHMAN The worthy fellow is our general. He's the
rock, the oak, not to be wind-shaken.   *Exeunt*

5.3

Enter CORIOLANUS *and* AUFIDIUS [*with Volscian soldiers.*
CORIOLANUS *and* AUFIDIUS *sit*]
CORIOLANUS We will before the walls of Rome tomorrow
Set down our host.° My partner in this action,   *Lay siege with our forces*
You must report to th' Volscian lords how plainly
I have borne this business.
AUFIDIUS   Only their ends
You have respected, stopped your ears against
The general suit of Rome, never admitted

---

8. *owe . . . properly*: possess my own power of revenge.
9. *That we . . . much*: The memory of our friendship shall
be poisoned by Rome's (alternatively, my own) ungrateful
forgetfulness, rather than compassion be awakened by my
awareness of how intimate we were.
5.3 Location: The Volscian camp.

A private whisper, no, not with such friends
That thought them sure of you.
CORIOLANUS   This last old man,
    Whom with a cracked heart I have sent to Rome,
10   Loved me above the measure of a father,
    Nay, godded° me indeed. Their latest refuge°   *deified / last hope*
    Was to send him, for whose old love I have—
    Though I showed sourly to him—once more offered
    The first conditions, which they did refuse
15   And cannot now accept, to grace him only
    That thought he could do more. A very little
    I have yielded to. Fresh embassies and suits,
    Nor from the state nor private friends, hereafter
    Will I lend ear to.
           Shout within
                  Ha, what shout is this?
20   Shall I be tempted to infringe my vow
    In the same time 'tis made? I will not.
          Enter VIRGILIA, VOLUMNIA, VALERIA, YOUNG MARTIUS,
          with attendants
    My wife comes foremost, then the honoured mould
    Wherein this trunk° was framed, and in her hand   *body*
    The grandchild to her blood. But out, affection!
25   All bond and privilege of nature break;
    Let it be virtuous to be obstinate.
          [VIRGILIA *curtsies*]
    What is that curtsy worth? Or those dove's eyes
    Which can make gods forsworn? I melt, and am not
    Of stronger earth than others.
          [VOLUMNIA *bows*]
                  My mother bows,
30   As if Olympus to a molehill should
    In supplication nod; and my young boy
    Hath an aspect of intercession° which   *pleading look*
    Great nature cries 'Deny not'.—Let the Volsces
    Plough Rome and harrow Italy! I'll never
35   Be such a gosling° to obey instinct, but stand   *(foolish) baby goose*
    As if a man were author of himself
    And knew no other kin.
VIRGILIA   My lord and husband.
CORIOLANUS   These eyes are not the same I wore in Rome.
VIRGILIA   The sorrow that delivers° us thus changed   *presents*
    Makes you think so.
40 CORIOLANUS   Like a dull actor now
    I have forgot my part, and I am out°   *at a loss*
    Even to a full disgrace. [*Rising*] Best of my flesh,
    Forgive my tyranny, but do not say
    For that 'Forgive our Romans'.
          [VIRGILIA *kisses him*]
                  O, a kiss
45   Long as my exile, sweet as my revenge!
    Now, by the jealous queen of heaven,[1] that kiss
    I carried from thee, dear, and my true lip

---

1. Juno, queen of the gods and guardian of marriage.

Hath virgined it e'er since. You gods, I prate,
And the most noble mother of the world
50 Leave unsaluted! Sink, my knee, i'th' earth.
    [*He*] *kneels*
Of thy deep duty more impression° show   *indentation; effect*
Than that of common sons.
VOLUMNIA   O, stand up blest,
    [CORIOLANUS *rises*]
Whilst with no softer cushion than the flint
I kneel before thee, and unproperly°   *against propriety*
55 Show duty as mistaken all this while
Between the child and parent.
    [*She kneels*]
CORIOLANUS   What's this?
Your knees to me? To your corrected² son?
    [*He raises her*]
Then let the pebbles on the hungry beach
Fillip° the stars; then let the mutinous winds   *Strike against*
60 Strike the proud cedars 'gainst the fiery sun,
Murd'ring³ impossibility to make
What cannot be slight work.⁴
VOLUMNIA   Thou art my warrior.
I holp to frame° thee. Do you know this lady?   *helped to make*
CORIOLANUS   The noble sister of Publicola,
65 The moon° of Rome, chaste as the icicle   *(emblem of chastity)*
That's candied° by the frost from purest snow   *crystallized*
And hangs on Dian's⁵ temple—dear Valeria!
VOLUMNIA [*showing* CORIOLANUS *his son*]   This is a poor epitome°   *abridgement*
    of yours,
Which by th' interpretation of full time⁶
May show like all yourself.
70 CORIOLANUS [*to* YOUNG MARTIUS]   The god of soldiers,
With the consent of supreme Jove, inform
Thy thoughts with nobleness, that thou mayst prove
To shame unvulnerable, and stick° i'th' wars   *stand firm*
Like a great sea-mark standing every flaw⁷
75 And saving those that eye thee!
VOLUMNIA [*to* YOUNG MARTIUS]   Your knee, sirrah.
    [YOUNG MARTIUS *kneels*]
CORIOLANUS   That's my brave boy.
VOLUMNIA   Even he, your wife, this lady, and myself
Are suitors to you.
CORIOLANUS   I beseech you, peace.
80 Or if you'd ask, remember this before:
The things I have forsworn to grant may never
Be held by you denials.⁸ Do not bid me
Dismiss my soldiers, or capitulate°   *come to terms*
Again with Rome's mechanics.° Tell me not   *workmen*
85 Wherein I seem unnatural. Desire not t'allay
My rages and revenges with your colder reasons.
VOLUMNIA   O, no more, no more!

2. Rebuked (by Volumnia's irony).
3. Putting an end to the idea of.
4. An easy task of what cannot be.
5. Goddess of the moon and of chastity.

6. When time has clarified its full meaning.
7. Like a landmark at sea, withstanding every gust.
8. Be regarded by you as refusals.

You have said you will not grant us anything—
For we have nothing else to ask but that
90 Which you deny already. Yet we will ask,
That, if you fail in our request, the blame
May hang upon your hardness. Therefore hear us.
CORIOLANUS   Aufidius and you Volsces, mark, for we'll
Hear naught from Rome in private.
    [*He sits*]
                                        Your request?
95 VOLUMNIA   Should we be silent and not speak, our raiment
And state of bodies would bewray° what life   *divulge*
We have led since thy exile. Think with thyself
How more unfortunate than all living women
Are we come hither, since that thy sight, which should
100 Make our eyes flow with joy, hearts dance with comforts,
Constrains them weep and shake with fear and sorrow,
Making the mother, wife, and child to see
The son, the husband, and the father tearing
His country's bowels out; and to poor we
105 Thine enmity's most capital.° Thou barr'st us   *fatal*
Our prayers to the gods, which is a comfort
That all but we enjoy. For how can we,
Alas, how can we for our country pray,
Whereto we are bound, together with thy victory,
110 Whereto we are bound? Alack, or° we must lose   *either*
The country, our dear nurse, or else thy person,
Our comfort in the country. We must find
An evident° calamity, though we had   *A certain*
Our wish which side should win. For either thou
115 Must as a foreign recreant° be led   *traitor*
With manacles thorough our streets, or else
Triumphantly tread on thy country's ruin,
And bear the palm for having bravely shed
Thy wife and children's blood. For myself, son,
120 I purpose not to wait on fortune till
These wars determine.° If I cannot persuade thee   *conclude*
Rather to show a noble grace to both parts°   *sides*
Than seek the end of one, thou shalt no sooner
March to assault thy country than to tread—
125 Trust to't, thou shalt not—on thy mother's womb
That brought thee to this world.
VIRGILIA   Ay, and mine,
That brought you forth this boy to keep your name
Living to time.
YOUNG MARTIUS   A° shall not tread on me.   *He*
I'll run away till I am bigger, but then I'll fight.
130 CORIOLANUS   Not of a woman's tenderness to be
Requires nor child nor woman's face to see.[9]
I have sat too long.
    [*He rises and turns away*]
VOLUMNIA   Nay, go not from us thus.
If it were so that our request did tend
To save the Romans, thereby to destroy

9. *Not . . . see*: To avoid having a woman's tenderness, a man must not see a child's or woman's face.

135   The Volsces whom you serve, you might condemn us
        As poisonous of your honour. No, our suit
        Is that you reconcile them: while the Volsces
        May say 'This mercy we have showed', the Romans
        'This we received', and each in either side
140   Give the all-hail to thee and cry 'Be blest
        For making up this peace!' Thou know'st, great son,
        The end of war's uncertain; but this certain,
        That if thou conquer Rome, the benefit
        Which thou shalt thereby reap is such a name
145   Whose repetition will be dogged with curses,
        Whose chronicle thus writ:[1] 'The man was noble,
        But with his last attempt he wiped it out,
        Destroyed his country, and his name remains
        To th' ensuing age abhorred.' Speak to me, son.
150   Thou hast affected° the fine strains° of honour,   *cherished/qualities*
        To imitate the graces of the gods,
        To tear with thunder the wide cheeks o'th' air,
        And yet to charge thy sulphur[2] with a bolt
        That should but rive[3] an oak. Why dost not speak?
155   Think'st thou it honourable for a noble man
        Still° to remember wrongs? Daughter, speak you,   *Perpetually*
        He cares not for your weeping. Speak thou, boy.
        Perhaps thy childishness will move him more
        Than can our reasons. There's no man in the world
160   More bound to's mother, yet here he lets me prate
        Like one i'th' stocks.[4] Thou hast never in thy life
        Showed thy dear mother any courtesy,
        When she, poor hen, fond of° no second brood,   *desiring*
        Has clucked thee to the wars and safely home,
165   Loaden with honour. Say my request's unjust,
        And spurn me back. But if it be not so,
        Thou art not honest, and the gods will plague thee
        That thou restrain'st° from me the duty which   *withhold'st*
        To a mother's part belongs.—He turns away.
170   Down, ladies. Let us shame him with our knees.
        To his surname 'Coriolanus' 'longs° more pride   *belongs*
        Than pity to our prayers.[5] Down! An end.
        This is the last.
                [*The ladies and* YOUNG MARTIUS *kneel*]
                  So we will home to Rome,
        And die among our neighbours.—Nay, behold's.
175   This boy, that cannot tell what he would have,
        But kneels and holds up hands for fellowship,
        Does reason our petition with more strength
        Than thou hast to deny't.—Come, let us go.
        This fellow had a Volscian to his mother.
180   His wife is in Corioles, and this child
        Like him by chance.—Yet give us our dispatch.[6]

1. Whose biography will thus be written.
2. To discharge thy thunder (like Jove, king of the gods, whose tree was the oak).
3. Tear (destroy a tree, not human beings).
4. *prate . . . stocks:* rail pointlessly like a prisoner sentenced to public humiliation in the stocks.
5. Volumnia reinterprets the name as a sign of allegiance to Corioles.
6. Dismissal (with wordplay on "deathblow").

I am hushed until our city be afire,
And then I'll speak a little.
       [*He*] *holds her by the hand, silent*
CORIOLANUS   O mother, mother!
What have you done? Behold, the heavens do ope,
185   The gods look down, and this unnatural scene
They laugh at. O my mother, mother, O!
You have won a happy victory to Rome;
But for your son, believe it, O believe it,
Most dangerously you have with him prevailed,
190   If not most mortal to him. But let it come.
      [*The ladies and* YOUNG MARTIUS *rise*]
Aufidius, though I cannot make true° wars,   *(as I vowed)*
I'll frame convenient° peace. Now, good Aufidius,   *suitable*
Were you in my stead would you have heard
A mother less, or granted less, Aufidius?
AUFIDIUS   I was moved withal.°   *as well*
195 CORIOLANUS   I dare be sworn you were.
And, sir, it is no little thing to make
Mine eyes to sweat compassion. But, good sir,
What peace you'll make, advise me. For my part,
I'll not to Rome; I'll back with you, and pray you
200   Stand to° me in this cause. —O mother! Wife!   *by*
AUFIDIUS [*aside*]   I am glad thou hast set thy mercy and thy honour
At difference in thee. Out of that I'll work
Myself a former fortune.[7]
CORIOLANUS [*to* VOLUMNIA *and* VIRGILIA]   Ay, by and by.
But we will drink together, and you shall bear
205   A better witness back than words, which we
On like conditions will have counter-sealed.
Come, enter with us. Ladies, you deserve
To have a temple built you. All the swords
In Italy, and her confederate arms,
210   Could not have made this peace.   *Exeunt*

5.4

Enter MENENIUS *and* SICINIUS
MENENIUS   See you yon coign° o'th' Capitol, yon cornerstone?   *corner*
SICINIUS   Why, what of that?
MENENIUS   If it be possible for you to displace it with your little
finger, there is some hope the ladies of Rome, especially his
5   mother, may prevail with him. But I say there is no hope in't,
our throats are sentenced and stay upon° execution.   *wait for*
SICINIUS   Is't possible that so short a time can alter the condition°   *character*
of a man?
MENENIUS   There is differency between a grub and a butterfly,
10   yet your butterfly was a grub. This Martius is grown from man
to dragon. He has wings, he's more than a creeping thing.
SICINIUS   He loved his mother dearly.
MENENIUS   So did he me, and he no more remembers his
mother now than° an eight-year old horse. The tartness of his   *than does*
15   face sours ripe grapes. When he walks, he moves like an
engine,° and the ground shrinks before his treading. He is able   *war machine*

---

7. *work . . . fortune:* regain my former preeminence.   **5.4** Location: A public place in Rome.

to pierce a corslet° with his eye, talks like a knell, and his 'hmh!'   *armored shirt*
is a battery.° He sits in his state as a thing made for Alexander.¹   *bombardment*
What he bids be done is finished with his bidding. He wants°   *lacks*
20   nothing of a god but eternity and a heaven to throne in.
SICINIUS   Yes: mercy, if you report him truly.
MENENIUS   I paint him in the character.° Mark what mercy his   *as he is*
mother shall bring from him. There is no more mercy in him
than there is milk in a male tiger. That shall our poor city find;
25   and all this is 'long° of you.   *on account*
SICINIUS   The gods be good unto us!
MENENIUS   No, in such a case the gods will not be good unto us.
When we banished him we respected not them, and, he
returning to break our necks, they respect not us.
        Enter a MESSENGER
30   MESSENGER [*to* SICINIUS]   Sir, if you'd save your life, fly to your house.
The plebeians have got your fellow tribune
And hale° him up and down, all swearing if   *drag*
The Roman ladies bring not comfort home
They'll give him death by inches.°   *little by little*
        Enter another MESSENGER
SICINIUS   What's the news?
35   SECOND MESSENGER   Good news, good news. The ladies have prevailed,
The Volscians are dislodged,° and Martius gone.   *broken*
A merrier day did never yet greet Rome,
No, not th'expulsion of the Tarquins.
SICINIUS   Friend,
Art thou certain this is true? Is't most certain?
40   SECOND MESSENGER   As certain as I know the sun is fire.
Where have you lurked that you make doubt of it?
Ne'er through an arch so hurried the blown° tide   *swollen*
As the recomforted° through th' gates.   *reinvigorated*
        Trumpets, hautboys,° drums, beat all together   *oboes*
                                Why, hark you,
The trumpets, sackbuts, psalteries,° and fifes,   *trobones, zithers*
45   Tabors° and cymbals and the shouting Romans   *Drums*
Make the sun dance.
        A shout within
                        Hark you!
MENENIUS   This is good news.
I will go meet the ladies. This Volumnia
Is worth of consuls, senators, patricians,
A city full; of tribunes such as you,
50   A sea and land full. You have prayed well today.
This morning for ten thousand of your throats
I'd not have given a doit.°   *small coin*
        [*Music*] *sound[s] still with the shouts*
                        Hark how they joy!
SICINIUS [*to the* MESSENGER]   First, the gods bless you for your tidings. Next,
[*Giving money*] Accept my thankfulness.
55   SECOND MESSENGER   Sir, we have all great cause to give great thanks.
SICINIUS   They are near the city.

---

1. Sits on his throne like a statue of Alexander the Great (who actually postdated Coriolanus).

SECOND MESSENGER   Almost at point to enter.
SICINIUS   We'll meet them, and help the joy.   *Exeunt*

5.5

Enter [at one door] Lords [and CITIZENS; at another
door] two SENATORS with [the] ladies [VOLUMNIA, VIR-
GILIA, and VALERIA,] passing over the stage
A SENATOR   Behold our patroness, the life of Rome!
    Call all your tribes together, praise the gods,
    And make triumphant fires.° Strew flowers before them.   *(of sacrifice)*
    Unshout the noise that banished Martius,
5   Repeal¹ him with the welcome of his mother.
    Cry 'Welcome, ladies, welcome!'
ALL   Welcome, ladies, welcome!
A flourish with drums and trumpets. Exeunt

5.6

Enter Tullus AUFIDIUS with attendants
AUFIDIUS   Go tell the lords o'th' city I am here.
    Deliver them this paper. Having read it,
    Bid them repair to th' market-place, where I,
    Even in theirs and in the commons' ears,
5   Will vouch the truth of it. Him I accuse
    The city ports° by this° hath entered, and   *gates / this time*
    Intends t'appear before the people, hoping
    To purge himself with words. Dispatch.   *[Exeunt attendants]*
      Enter three or four CONSPIRATORS of Aufidius' faction
                 Most welcome.
FIRST CONSPIRATOR   How is it with our general?
AUFIDIUS   Even so
10   As with a man by his own alms impoisoned,
    And with his charity slain.
SECOND CONSPIRATOR   Most noble sir,
    If you do hold the same intent wherein
    You wished us parties,° we'll deliver you   *allies*
    Of° your great danger.   *From*
AUFIDIUS   Sir, I cannot tell.
15   We must proceed as we do find the people.
THIRD CONSPIRATOR   The people will remain uncertain whilst
    'Twixt you there's difference,° but the fall of either   *disagreement*
    Makes the survivor heir of all.
AUFIDIUS   I know it,
    And my pretext to strike at him admits
20   A good construction.° I raised him, and I pawned   *interpretation*
    Mine honour for his truth; who being so heightened,
    He watered his new plants¹ with dews of flattery,
    Seducing so my friends; and to this end
    He bowed his nature, never known before
25   But to be rough, unswayable, and free.
THIRD CONSPIRATOR   Sir, his stoutness°   *stubbornness*
    When he did stand for consul, which he lost
    By lack of stooping—

5.5 Location: Near the city gates of Rome.
1. Recall him from banishment.

5.6 Location: Corioles.
1. Followers (formerly Aufidius's adherents).

AUFIDIUS   That I would have spoke of.
  Being banished for't, he came unto my hearth,
30 Presented to my knife his throat. I took him,
  Made him joint-servant° with me, gave him way   *partner*
  In all his own desires; nay, let him choose
  Out of my files,° his projects to accomplish,   *troops*
  My best and freshest men; served his designments°   *plans*
35 In mine own person, holp to reap the fame
  Which he did end all his,[2] and took some pride
  To do myself this wrong, till at the last
  I seemed his follower, not partner, and
  He waged° me with his countenance° as if   *paid/appearance*
  I had been mercenary.
40 FIRST CONSPIRATOR   So he did, my lord.
  The army marvelled at it, and in the last,
  When he had carried° Rome and that we looked   *was about to vanquish*
  For no less spoil than glory—
AUFIDIUS   There was it,
  For which my sinews shall be stretched upon him.
45 At a few drops of women's rheum,° which are   *tears*
  As cheap as lies, he sold the blood and labour
  Of our great action; therefore shall he die,
  And I'll renew me in his fall.
       Drums and trumpets sound, with great shouts of the
       people
                    But hark.
FIRST CONSPIRATOR Your native town you entered like a post,[3]
50 And had no welcomes home; but he returns
  Splitting the air with noise.
SECOND CONSPIRATOR   And patient fools,
  Whose children he hath slain, their base throats tear
  With giving him glory.
THIRD CONSPIRATOR   Therefore, at your vantage,°   *best opportunity*
  Ere he express himself or move the people
55 With what he would say, let him feel your sword,
  Which we will second. When he lies along,°   *prostrate*
  After your way° his tale pronounced shall bury   *In your version*
  His reasons with his body.
       Enter the LORDS *of the city*
AUFIDIUS   Say no more.
  Here come the lords.
60 ALL THE LORDS You are most welcome home.
AUFIDIUS I have not deserved it.
  But, worthy lords, have you with heed perused
  What I have written to you?
ALL THE LORDS   We have.
FIRST LORD   And grieve to hear't.
  What faults he made before the last, I think
65 Might have found easy fines.° But there to end   *light penalties*
  Where he was to begin, and give away
  The benefit of our levies,° answering us   *levied troops*

---

2. Which he did conclude was (or did finally make) en-   3. Messenger (bearing news of Coriolanus).
tirely his own.

With our own charge,[4] making a treaty where
There was a yielding—this admits no excuse.

70 AUFIDIUS He approaches. You shall hear him.
            Enter CORIOLANUS *marching with drum and colors, the*
            Commoners being with him
   CORIOLANUS Hail, lords! I am returned your soldier,
   No more infected with my country's love
   Than when I parted hence, but still subsisting
   Under your great command. You are to know
75 That prosperously[5] I have attempted, and
   With bloody passage led your wars even to
   The gates of Rome. Our spoils we have brought home
   Doth more than counterpoise a full third part[6]
   The charges of the action. We have made peace
80 With no less honour to the Antiates
   Than shame to th' Romans. And we here deliver,
   Subscribed by th' consuls and patricians,
   Together with the seal o'th' senate, what
   We have compounded° on.   agreed
            He gives the LORDS *a paper*
   AUFIDIUS   Read it not, noble lords,
85 But tell the traitor in the highest degree
   He hath abused your powers.
   CORIOLANUS Traitor? How now?
   AUFIDIUS Ay, traitor, Martius.
   CORIOLANUS Martius?
90 AUFIDIUS Ay, Martius, Caius Martius. Dost thou think
   I'll grace thee with that robbery, thy stol'n name,
   'Coriolanus', in Corioles?
   You lords and heads o'th' state, perfidiously
   He has betrayed your business, and given up,
95 For certain drops of salt,° your city, Rome—   (tears)
   I say your city—to his wife and mother,
   Breaking his oath and resolution like
   A twist° of rotten silk, never admitting   thread
   Counsel o'th' war.[7] But at his nurse's tears
100 He whined and roared away your victory,
   That pages[8] blushed at him, and men of heart°   courage
   Looked wond'ring each at others.
   CORIOLANUS   Hear'st thou, Mars?
   AUFIDIUS Name not the god, thou boy of tears.
   CORIOLANUS   Ha?
   AUFIDIUS   No more.
   CORIOLANUS Measureless liar, thou hast made my heart
105 Too great for what contains it. 'Boy'? O slave!—
   Pardon me, lords, 'tis the first time that ever
   I was forced to scold. Your judgements, my grave lords,
   Must give this cur the lie, and his own notion°—   awareness of the truth
   Who wears my stripes° impressed upon him, that   wounds

---

4. *answering . . . charge*: rewarding us with our own costs
(of mounting the campaign); answering accusations by
saying that he acted on our authority.
5. Successfully; with gain of wealth.

6. Outweighs by more than a third.
7. *admitting . . . war*: taking any advice about the war.
8. Youthful servants.

110 Must bear my beating to his grave—shall join
To thrust° the lie unto him.   *turn the accusation of*
FIRST LORD   Peace both, and hear me speak.
CORIOLANUS   Cut me to pieces, Volsces. Men and lads,
Stain all your edges° on me. 'Boy'! False hound,   *sword blades*
If you have writ your annals true, 'tis there
115 That, like an eagle in a dove-cote,° I   *pigeon house*
Fluttered your Volscians in Corioles.
Alone I did it. 'Boy'!
AUFIDIUS   Why, noble lords,
Will you be put in mind of his blind⁹ fortune,
Which was your shame, by this unholy braggart,
Fore your own eyes and ears?
120 ALL THE CONSPIRATORS   Let him die for't.
ALL THE PEOPLE [*shouting dispersedly*]   Tear him to pieces! Do
it presently!°   *immediately*
He killed my son! My daughter! He killed my cousin
Marcus! He killed my father!
SECOND LORD   Peace, ho! No outrage,° peace.   *violence*
The man is noble, and his fame folds in°   *envelops*
125 This orb o'th' earth. His last offences to us
Shall have judicious hearing. Stand,° Aufidius,   *Hold off*
And trouble not the peace.
CORIOLANUS [*drawing his sword*]   O that I had him with six Aufidiuses,
Or more, his tribe, to use my lawful sword!
AUFIDIUS [*drawing his sword*]   Insolent villain!
130 ALL THE CONSPIRATORS   Kill, kill, kill, kill, kill him!
            [*Two*] CONSPIRATORS *draw and kill* MARTIUS, *who falls.*
            AUFIDIUS [*and* CONSPIRATORS] *stand on him*
LORDS   Hold, hold, hold, hold!
AUFIDIUS   My noble masters, hear me speak.
FIRST LORD   O Tullus!
SECOND LORD [*to* AUFIDIUS]   Thou hast done a deed whereat
Valour will weep.
THIRD LORD [*to* AUFIDIUS *and the* CONSPIRATORS]
                       Tread not upon him, masters.
All be quiet. Put up your swords.
135 AUFIDIUS   My lords,
When you shall know—as in this rage
Provoked by him you cannot—the great danger
Which this man's life did owe° you, you'll rejoice   *hold in store for*
That he is thus cut off. Please it your honours
140 To call me to your senate, I'll deliver°   *show*
Myself your loyal servant, or endure
Your heaviest censure.
FIRST LORD   Bear from hence his body,
And mourn you for him. Let him be regarded
As the most noble corpse that ever herald
Did follow to his urn.
145 SECOND LORD   His own impatience
Takes from Aufidius a great part of blame.
Let's make the best of it.
AUFIDIUS   My rage is gone,

---

9. Random (fortune was commonly personified as blind).

And I am struck with sorrow. Take him up.
Help three o'th' chiefest soldiers; I'll be one.
150 Beat thou the drum, that it speak mournfully.
Trail your steel pikes. Though in this city he
Hath widowed and unchilded many a one,
Which to this hour bewail the injury,
Yet he shall have a noble memory.° Assist.   *memorial*

*A dead march sounded. Exeunt
bearing the body of Martius*

TEXTUAL VARIANTS

Control text: F

F: The Folio of 1623

s.p. NICANOR *Roman.*
s.p. ADRIAN *Vol⟨scian⟩.*

1.1.23–24 s.p. THIRD CITIZEN Against . . . first. / s.p. FOURTH CITIZEN He's . . . commonalty. *All.* Against . . . comonality. 29 s.p. FIFTH CITIZEN *All.* 49 s.p. FIRST CITIZEN 2
Cit⟨izen⟩; likewise for the remainder of 1.1. 82 stale't scale't 99 tauntingly taint-
ingly 161 geese. You are no Geese you are: No 190 all most almost 205 Junius
Annius 207 unroofed vnroo'st 230 Lartius *Lucius* 232, 236 s.p. LARTIUS *Tit⟨us⟩.*
1.3.33 that's that 40 Grecian sword, contemning. Tell Grecian sword. *Contenning,*
tell 77 s.p. VIRGILIA *Vlug.* 79 Ithaca *Athica*
1.5.13 trenches. Follow Trenches followes 18 s.p. THIRD SOLDIER *All.* 19 s.p. LARTIUS
Tit⟨us⟩. s.p. FOURTH SOLDIER *All.* 25 art lost, art left, 28 Cato's *Calues*
1.6.4 honours hours
1.7.53 Antiates Antients 70 Lesser Lessen 76 O' Oh 84 I foure
1.10.40 upheld beheld 67, 78, 81 s.p. CORIOLANUS *Martius.* 82 And at At 89 s.p. CORI-
OLANUS *Martius.*
1.11.17 valour, poisoned *valors poison'd*
2.1.16 with all withall 22 how are ho ware 51 cannot can 95 s.p. VIRGILIA *and* VALERIA
2. Ladies. 151 Coriolanus *Martius Caius Coriolanus* 166 s.p. CORIOLANUS *Com⟨in-
ius⟩.* 171 begnaw at begin at 172 You Yon 203 guarded gawded 241 touch teach
2.2.63, 119, 127 s.p. FIRST SENATOR *Senat⟨or⟩.*
2.3.47 tongue tougne 62 but not but 80, 83 s.p. FOURTH CITIZEN 1. 95 s.p. FIFTH
CITIZEN 2. 97 s.p. FOURTH CITIZEN 1. 104 hire higher 105 womanish toge Wooluish
tongue 108 do't doo't? 122 s.p. SIXTH CITIZEN 1. *Cit⟨izen⟩.* 232 And . . . surnamed
[not in F] 243 s.p. A CITIZEN We . . . s.p. ANOTHER CITIZEN Almost *All.* We . . . almost
3.1.33 s.p. FIRST SENATOR *Senat.* 50 s.p. CORIOLANUS *Com⟨inius⟩.* 61 abused, set
on. abus': set on, 94 good God! 101 impotence Ignorance 146 Where one
Whereon 180 s.p. ALL THE PATRICIANS *All.* 185 s.p. ALL THE CITIZENS *All.* 186 s.p.
CITIZENS AND PATRICIANS [not in F] 193, 199 s.p. ALL THE CITIZENS *All.* 198 s.p.
FIRST SENATOR *Sena⟨tor⟩.* 203 s.p. CORIOLANUS *Com⟨inius⟩.* 220 poisons poyso-
nous 228 s.p. ALL THE CITIZENS *All.* 229 your our 231 s.p. CORIOLANUS *Com⟨in-
ius⟩.* 236 s.p. COMINIUS *Corio⟨lanus⟩.* 237 s.p. CORIOLANUS *Mene⟨nius⟩.* 239 s.p.
MENENIUS Be Be 272, 282 s.p. ALL THE CITIZENS All. 289 our one 307 s.p. SICINIUS
Menen⟨ius⟩. 326 bring him bring him in peace
3.2.20 taxings things 25 s.p. FIRST SENATOR *Sen.* 31 herd heart 78 With Which 101
bear? Well beare well? 102 plot to lose, Plot, to loose

3.3.33 for th' fourth   **37 Throng** Through   **56 accents** Actions   **99 Inveighed** Enui'd   **114 for** from   **143 despite.** despight

4.1.38 s.p. VIRGILIA Corio⟨lanus⟩.

4.3.9 approved appear'd

4.4.13 seem seems   **23 hate** haue

4.5.130 o'erbear't o're-beate   **161 is yet** is: but   **188 broiled** boyld   **206, 207 dejectitude** Directitude   **220 sleepy** sleepe   **221 war's** Warres

4.6.36 lamentation Lamention   **60 come** comming   **145 one** oue

4.7.37 'twas 'was   **39 defect** detect   **49 virtues** Vertue,   **55 falter** fouler

5.1.16 fair for   **69 hold to his** yeeld to his

5.2.62 but by but   **71 our** your

5.3.48 prate pray   **63 holp** hope   **66 candied** curdied   **81 things** thing   **116 thorough** through   **150 fine** fiue   **153 charge** change   **170 him with** him with him with   **180 this** his

5.6.116 Fluttered Flatter'd

APPENDICES

APPENDICES

The Shakespearean Stage
by
ANDREW GURR

Publication by Performance

The curt exchange between the sentries in the first six lines of *Hamlet* tells us that it is very late at night (" 'Tis now struck twelve") and that " 'tis bitter cold." This opening was staged originally at the Globe in London in broad daylight, at 2 o'clock probably on a hot summer's afternoon. The words required the audience, half of them standing on three sides of the stage platform and all of them as visible to one another as the players were, to imagine themselves watching a scene quite the opposite of what they could see and feel around them. The original mode of staging for a Shakespearean play was utterly different from the cinematic realism we are used to now, where the screen gives us close-ups on a simulacrum of reality, an even more privileged view of the actors' facial twitches than we get in ordinary life. Eloquence then was in words, not facial expressions.

The playgoers of Shakespeare's own time knew the plays in forms at which we can only now guess. It is a severe loss. Shakespeare's own primary concept of his plays was as stories "personated" onstage, not as words on a page. He himself never bothered to get his playscripts into print, and more than half of them were not published until seven years after his death, in the First Folio of his plays published as a memorial to him in 1623. His fellow playwright Francis Beaumont called the printing of plays "a second publication"; the first was their showing onstage. Print recorded a set of scripts, written for the original players to teach them what they should speak in the ensemble of the play in production. The only technology then available to record the performances was the written word. If video recordings had existed at that time, our understanding of Shakespeare would be vastly different from what it is today.

Since the texts were composed only to be a record of the words the players were to memorize, we now have to infer how the plays were originally staged largely by guesswork. Shakespeare was himself a player and shareholder in his acting company, and he expected to be present at rehearsals. Consequently, the stage directions in his scripts are distinctly skimpy compared with some of those provided by his fellow playwrights. He was cursory even in noting entrances and exits, let alone how he expected his company to stage the more complex spectacles, such as heaving Antony up to Cleopatra on her monument. There are sometimes hints in the stage directions and more frequently in the words used to describe some of the actions, and knowing what the design of the theater was like is a help as well. Knowing more about how Shakespeare expected his plays to be staged can transform how we think about them. But gaining such knowledge is no easy matter. One of the few certainties is that Shakespeare's plays in modern performance are even more different from the originals than modern printed editions are from the first much-thumbed manuscripts.

The Shakespearean Mindset

The general mindset of the original playgoers, the patterns of thinking and expectation that Tudor culture imposed on Shakespeare's audiences, is not really difficult to identify. It is less easy, though, to pin it down in the sort of detail that tells us what the original concept of staging the plays would have been like. We know that all the original playgoers paid for the privilege of attending the plays and committed themselves willingly to suspend their disbelief in what they were to see. They knew as we do that they were paying to be entertained by fictions. Beyond that, we need reminding today that going to open-air performances in daylight in Shakespeare's time meant being constantly aware that one was in a theater, a place designed to offer illusions. On the one hand, this consciousness of oneself and where one was meant that the players had to do more to hold attention than is needed now, when audiences have nothing but the stage to look at and armchairs to sit in. On the other hand, it made everyone more receptive to extratheatrical tricks, such as Hamlet's reference to "this distracted globe," or Polonius's claim in the same play to have taken the part of Julius Caesar at the university and been killed by Brutus. The regular playgoers at the Globe who recognized Polonius as the man who had played Caesar in Shakespeare's play of the year before, and who recognized Hamlet as the man who had played Brutus, would laugh at this theatrical in-joke. But two scenes later, when Hamlet kills Polonius, they would think of it again, in a different light.

Features of the original mindset such as these are quite readily identifiable. For others, though, we need to look further, into the design of the theaters and into the staging traditions that they housed and that Shakespeare exploited. Invisibility has a part to play in A Midsummer Night's Dream that we can easily underrate, for instance. Invisibility onstage is a theatrical in-joke, an obvious privileging of the audience, which is allowed to see what the characters onstage can't. The impresario Philip Henslowe's inventory of costumes used at the Rose theater in 1597, which lists "a robe for to go invisible," indicates a fictional device that openly expects the willing suspension of the audience's disbelief. In A Midsummer Night's Dream, the ostensible invisibility of all the visible fairies emphasizes the theatricality of the whole presentation while pandering to the audience's self-indulgent superiority, the feeling that it knows what is going on better than any character, whether he be Bottom or even Duke Theseus. That prepares us for the mockery of stage realism we get later, in the mechanicals' play in Act 5, and even for the doubt we as willing audience might feel over Theseus's own skepticism about the dangers of imagination that he voices in his speech at the beginning of Act 5.

More to the point, though, it throws into question our readiness to be an audience, since we have ourselves been indulging in just the games of suspending disbelief that the play staged by the mechanicals enters into so unsuccessfully. When Theseus disputes with Hippolyta about the credibility of the lovers' story, he voices the very skepticism—about the lover, the lunatic, and the poet—that any sensible realist in the audience would have been feeling for most of the previous three acts in the forest. The play starts and ends at the court in broad daylight, while the scenes of midsummer madness take place at night in a forest. At the early amphitheaters, all the plays were staged in broad daylight, between 2 and 5 o'clock in the afternoon, and without any persuasive scenery: the two stage posts served as trees onstage. So the play, moving as it does from daylight realism to nocturnal fantasy and back again, with a last challenge to credulity in the mechanicals' burlesque of how to stage a play, has already thoroughly challenged the willing suspension of the viewers' disbelief. A Midsummer Night's Dream is a play about nocturnal dreams and fictions that are accepted as truths in broad daylight. It was only a small extension of this game to have the women's parts played by boys, as well as plots in which the girls dressed as boys, to the point where in As You Like It Rosalind was played by a boy playing a girl pretending to be a boy playing a girl.

The Shakespeare plays were written for a new and unique kind of playhouse, the Elizabethan amphitheater, which had a distinctive design quite different from modern theaters. Elizabethans knew what the standard features in their theaters stood for, and Shakespeare drew on that knowledge for the staging of his plays. The physical features of the playhouses were a potent element in the ways that the plays were designed for the Elizabethan mindset. When Richard III, the archdeceiver and playactor, appears "aloft between two Bishops" to claim the crown in Richard III 3.7, his placing on the stage balcony literally above the crowd on the stage would, even without the accompanying priests, have signified his ironic claim to a social and moral superiority that ought to have matched his elevation. When Richard II comes down from the wall of Flint Castle to the "base court" in *Richard II* 3.3, Elizabethans would have seen his descent as a withdrawal from power and status. These theaters were still new when Shakespeare started to write for them, and their novelty meant that the plays were written more tightly to fit their specific design than the plays of later years, when theatergoing had become a more routine social activity and different kinds of theater were available.

London Playgoing and the Law

This heightened sense of theatricality, or "metatheater," in Shakespearean audiences was far from the only difference in their mindset from that of all modern audiences. Regular playgoing in London only started in the 1570s, and through Shakespeare's earlier years it was always a perilous and precarious activity. The Lord Mayor of London and the mayors of most of England's larger towns hated playgoing and tried to suppress it whencver and wherever it appeared. Playgoing was exciting not only because it was new but because it was dangerous. The hostility of so many authorities to plays meant that they were seen almost automatically as subversive of authority. Paradoxically, the first London companies were only able to establish themselves in London through the active support of Queen Elizabeth and her Privy Council, which tried hard, in the face of constant complaints from the lord mayor, to ensure that the best companies would be on hand every Christmas to entertain the queen's leisure hours. Popular support for playgoing depended on royal protection for the leading companies.

London was by far the largest city in England. Within a few years of Shakespeare's death, it became the largest in Europe. It was generally an orderly place to live, especially in the city itself. Even in the suburbs, where the poorer people had to live, there were not many of the riots and other disorders that preachers always associated with the brothels, animal-baiting arenas, and playhouses clustering there. The reputation that the playhouses gained for promoting riots was not well justified. Any crowd of people was seen by the authorities as a potential riot, and playhouses regularly drew some of the largest crowds that London had yet seen. The city's government was not designed to control large crowds of people. There was no paid police force, and the lord mayor was held responsible by the Privy Council, the queen's governing committee, for any disorders that did occur. So the city authorities found that playgoing challenged their control over their people.

The rapid growth of London did not help the situation. Officially, the city was governed by the lord mayor and his council. But he had authority only inside the city, and London now spread through a large suburban area in the adjacent counties of Middlesex to the north and Surrey across the river to the south. Because the court and the national government were housed in London, the Privy Council often intervened in city affairs in its own interests, as well as when orders were needed that covered broader zones than the city itself. The periodic outbreaks of bubonic plague were one clear instance of such a need, because the plague took no notice of parish or city boundaries. The intrusion of the professional companies to play in London provided another. In the early years, they were chronic travelers and London was simply one of many stopovers. But the queen enjoyed seeing plays at Christmas, and her council accordingly supported the best companies so that they could perform for her. It protected the playing companies against the hatred of successive lord mayors, except when a national emergency such as a plague epidemic erupted. The Privy Council took control then by ordering the 126 parishes in and around London to list all deaths from plague separately from ordinary deaths. Each Thursday, the parish totals were added together. When the total number of deaths from plague in these lists rose above thirty in any one week, the Privy Council closed all places of public assembly. This meant especially the playhouses, which created by far the largest gatherings. When the theaters were closed, the playing companies had to revert to their traditional practice of going on tour to play in the towns through the country, provided that the news of plague did not precede them.

Plague was not the only reason for the government to lay its controlling hand on the companies. From the time the post was inaugurated in 1578, the Master of the Revels controlled all playing. He was executive officer to the lord chamberlain, the Privy Council officer responsible for the annual season of royal entertainment and thus by extension for the professional playing companies. The Master of the Revels licensed each company and censored its plays. He was expected to cut out any references to religion or affairs of state, and he tried to prevent other offenses by banning the depiction of any living person on-stage. After 1594, he issued licenses to the approved London playhouses too. Later still, the printing of any playbook was allowed only if he gave authority for it. The companies had to accept this tight control because the government was its only protector against the hostile municipal authorities, who included not only the Lord Mayor of London but also the mayors of most of the major towns in the country.

Most mayors had the commercial interest of keeping local employees at work to justify their hostility to playgoing. But across the country, the hostility went much deeper. A large proportion of the population disliked the very idea of playacting. Their reasons, ostensibly religious, were that for actors to pretend to be characters they were unlike in life was a deception and that for boys to dress as women was contrary to what the Bible said. Some-where beneath this was a more basic fear of pretense and deceit, of people not acting honestly. It put actors into the same category as con men, cheats, and thieves. That was probably one reason why companies of boys acting men's parts were thought rather more tolerable than men pretending to be other kinds of men. The deception involved in boys playing men was more transparent than when men played characters other than them-selves. There was also a strong Puritan suspicion about shows of any kind, which looked too much like the Catholic ceremonial that the new Church of England had renounced. Playgoing found much better favor on the Catholic side of English society than on the Puritan side. Different preachers took different positions over the new phenomenon of playgoing. But few would speak in its favor, and most of them openly disapproved of it. Playgoing was an idle pastime, and the devil finds work for idle hands.

In the 1590s, when *Romeo and Juliet* and Shakespeare's histories and early comedies were exciting audiences, only two playhouses and two companies were officially approved by the queen's Privy Council for the entertainment of London's citizens. The other main forms of paid entertainment were bear- and bullbaiting, which were much harder on the performers than was playing and so could be staged less frequently. The hostility to plays meant that the right to perform was confined to only a few of the most outstanding compa-nies. These few companies were in competition with one another, and this led to a rapid growth in the quality of their offerings. But playacting was always a marginal activity. Paying to enter a specially built theater in order to see professional companies perform plays was still a new phenomenon, and it still met with great opposition from the London authorities. The open-air theaters like the Globe were built out in the suburbs. London as a city had no centrally located playhouses until after the civil war and the restoration of the monarchy, in 1661. And even playing in the city's suburbs, where they were free from the lord mayor's control, the companies had to work under the control of the Privy Coun-cil. All the great amphitheaters were built either in Middlesex, to the north of the city walls, or in Surrey across the river from the city, on the south bank of the Thames. At the height of their success, in the years after Shakespeare's death, the Privy Council never licensed more than four or five playhouses in London.

Playgoing in London was viewed even by the playgoers as an idle occupation. The largest numbers who went to the Globe were apprentices and artisans taking time off work, often surreptitiously, and law students from the Inns of Court doing the same. These fugitives were linked with the wealthier kind of idler, "gallants" or rich gentlemen and other men of property, along with soldiers and sailors on leave from the wars, people visiting London from the country on business or pleasure (usually both), and above all the women of London. Women were not expected to be literate, but one did not need to be able to read and write to enjoy hearing and seeing a play. A respectable woman had to make sure she was escorted by a man. He might be a husband or a friend, or her page if she was rich, or her husband's apprentice if she was a middle-class citizen. She might have

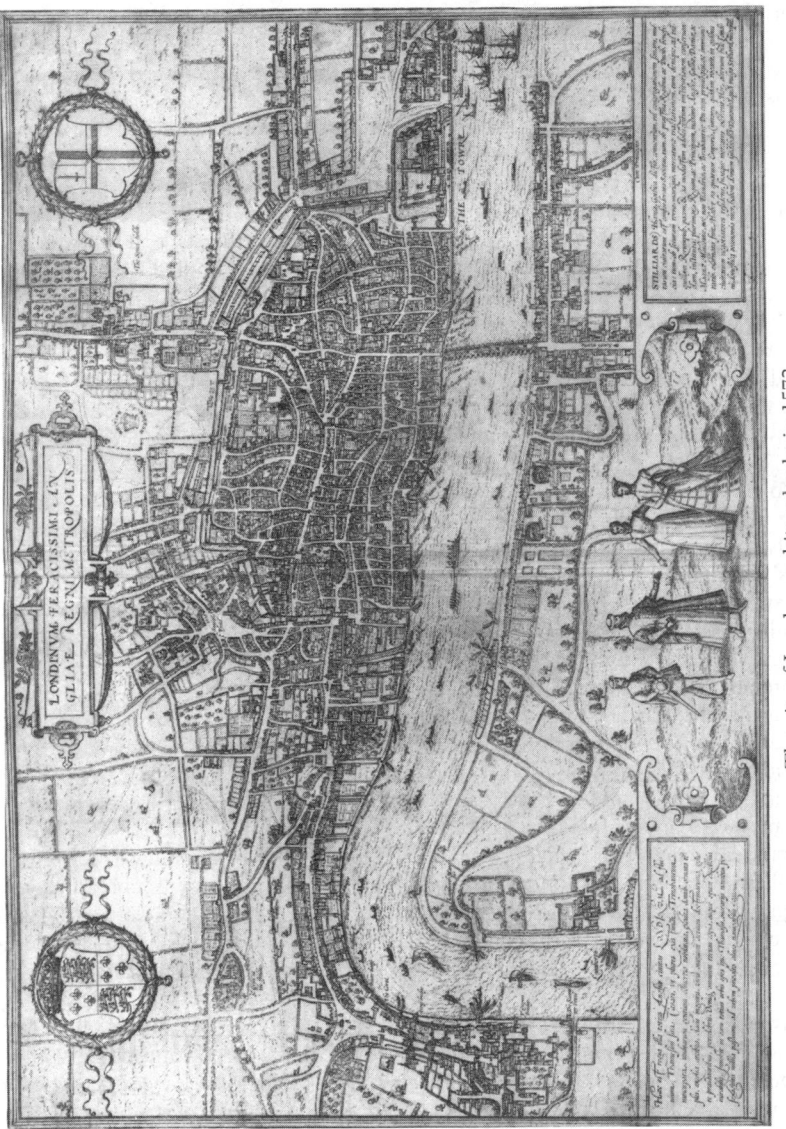

The city of London and its suburbs in 1572.

a mask on, part of standard women's wear outdoors to protect the face against the weather and to assert modesty, and perhaps anonymity. Market women (applewives and fishwives) went to plays in groups. Whores were expected to be there looking for business, especially from the gallants, but they usually had male escorts too.

The social range of playgoers at the two playhouses approved for use in 1594 was almost complete, stretching from the aristocracy to the poorest workmen and boys. Many people disapproved of plays, but at peak times up to 25,000 a week flocked to see the variety of plays being offered. Prices for playgoing remained much the same throughout the decades up to 1642, when the parliamentary government that was fighting the king closed all the theaters for eighteen years. Until then, one could get standing room at an amphitheater for one penny (¹⁄₂₄₀th of a modern pound, roughly one cent), or a seat on a bench in the roofed galleries for twopence. A seat in a lord's room cost sixpence, which was not much less than a day's wage for a skilled artisan in 1600. The smaller roofed theaters that opened in 1599 were much more expensive. They were called "private" theaters to distinguish them from the "public" open-air amphitheaters, though the claim to privacy was mainly a convenient fiction to escape the controls imposed on the "public" theaters. At the Blackfriars hall theater, sixpence only gained you a seat in the topmost gallery, while a seat in the pit near the stage cost three times that amount and a seat in a box five times, or half a skilled worker's weekly wage.

It was not only the plays and players that were the sights at the playhouses. The richest lords and gallants went to be seen as much as they went to see. At the Globe, the costliest rooms were positioned alongside the balcony "above," over the stage. They were called "lords' rooms," and the playgoers who chose to sit there had a limited view of what went on beneath them. They saw no "discoveries," for instance, such as Portia's three caskets in *The Merchant of Venice*, which were uncovered underneath them inside the alcove in the center of the *frons scenae*, nor anything other than the backs of the players when they entered. But as audience they were themselves highly visible, and that was what they paid for. In the hall, or "private," playhouses, with much higher admission prices than at the Globe, there were boxes flanking the stage for the gentry, which gave them a better view of the "discoveries." But at these "select" (because costlier) hall playhouses, where unlike the Globe everyone had a seat, some of the most colorful and exhibitionistic gallants could go one better. Up to fifteen gallants could pay for a stool to sit and watch the play on the stage itself, sitting in front of the boxes that flanked the stage. Each would enter from the players' dressing room (the "tiring-house") with his stool in hand before the play started. This gave them the best possible view of the play and easily the most conspicuous place in the audience's eye. Playgoing was a public occasion in which the visibility of audience members allowed them to play almost as large a part as the players.

Through the 1590s, the only permanent and custom-made playhouses were the large open-air theaters. Paying sixpence for a ferry across the river, as the richer playgoers did, or walking across London Bridge to the Rose or the Globe, or else trudging north through the mud of Shoreditch and Finsbury Fields or Clerkenwell to the Theatre or the Fortune in order to see a play, did not have great appeal when it was raining. Consequently, the companies were always trying to secure roofed halls nearer the city center. Up to 1594, they could use city inns, especially in winter, but the lord mayor's hostility to playing never made them reliable places for performing. Two constant problems troubled the players throughout these first years of professional theater in London: the city officials' chronic hatred of plays and the periodic visitations of the plague, which always led the government to close the theaters as soon as the number of plague deaths rose to dangerously high levels.

Playgoing was not firmly established in London until the Privy Council chose to protect it in 1594 and to approve specific playhouses for the two companies that it officially sanctioned. By then, Shakespeare had already made his mark. He became a player, a shareholder, and the resident playwright for one of these two companies. That status gained him a privileged place in the rapidly growing new world of playgoing. From then on, although his theater was still located only in the suburbs of the city, his work had the law behind it. That status was amply confirmed in 1603, when the new king made himself the company's patron. The King's Men held their status until the king himself lost power in 1642.

The Design of the Globe

The Globe was Shakespeare's principal playhouse. He put up part of the money for its construction and designed his best plays for it. It was built on the south side of the Thames in 1599, fashioned out of the framing timbers of an older theater. Essentially, it was a polygonal scaffold of twenty bays or sections, nearly one hundred feet in outside diameter, making a circle of three levels of galleries that rose to more than thirty feet high, with

The second Globe, from Wenceslas Hollar's engraving of the "Long View" of London (1647).

wooden bench seating and cushions for those who could afford them. This surrounded an open "yard," into which the stage projected.

The yard was over seventy feet in diameter. Nearly half the audience stood on their feet to watch the play from inside this yard, closest to the stage platform. The stage extended out nearly to the middle of the yard, so the actors could stand in the center of the crowd. The uncertain privilege of having standing room in the open air around the stage platform could be bought with the minimal price for admission, one penny (about a cent). It had the advantage of proximity to the stage and the players; its disadvantage was keeping you on your feet for the two or three hours of the play, as well as leaving you subject to the weather. If you wanted a seat, or if it rained and you wanted shelter, you paid twice as much to sit in the three ranks of roofed galleries that circled behind the crowd standing in the yard. With some squeezing, the theater could hold over three thousand people. It was an open-air theater because that gave it a larger capacity than a roofed hall. The drawback of its being open to the weather was more than outweighed by the gain in daylight that shone on stage and spectators alike.

The stage was a great square platform as much as forty feet wide. It had over it a canopied roof, or "heavens," to protect the players and their expensive costumes from rain. This canopy was held up by two pillars rising through the stage. The stage platform was about five feet high, and without any protective rails, so that the eyes of the audience in the yard were at the level of the players' feet. At the back of the stage, a wall, or *frons scenae*, stretched across the front of the players' tiring-house, the attiring or dressing room. It had a door on each flank and a wider curtained space in the center, which was used for major entrances and occasionally for set-piece scenes. Above these entry doors was a gallery or balcony, most of which was partitioned into rooms for the wealthiest spectators. A central room "above" was sometimes used in staging: for example, as Juliet's balcony, as the place for Richard III to stand between the bishops, as the wall of Flint Castle in *Richard II*, and as the wall over the city gates of Harfleur in *Henry V*. After 1608, when Shakespeare's company acquired the Blackfriars consort of musicians, this central gallery room

A photograph of the interior framework of the "new" Globe on the south bank of the Thames in London, showing the general dimensions of the yard and the surrounding galleries.

was turned into a curtained-off music room that could double as an "above" when required. Fewer than half of Shakespeare's plays need an "above."

The Original Staging Techniques

Shakespearean staging was emblematic. The "heavens" that covered the stage was the colorful feature from which gods descended to the earth of the stage platform. When Jupiter made his appearance in *Cymbeline*, in clouds of "sulphurous breath" provided by fireworks, he was mounted on an eagle being lowered through a trapdoor in the heavens. The other trapdoor, set in the stage platform itself, symbolized the opposite, a gateway to hell. The large stage trap was the place where the Gravedigger came to work at the beginning of Act 5 of *Hamlet*. It was the cell where Malvolio was imprisoned in *Twelfth Night*. The Shakespearean mindset accepted such conventions automatically.

Shakespeare inherited from Marlowe a tradition of using the stage trap as the dreaded hell's mouth. Barabbas plunges into it in *The Jew of Malta*, and the demons drag the screaming Faustus down it at the end of *Dr. Faustus*. Hell was not a fiction taken lightly by Elizabethans. Edward Alleyn, by far the most famous player of Faustus in the 1590s, wore a cross on his breast while he played the part, as insurance—just in case the fiction turned serious. Tracking the Elizabethan mindset about the stage trapdoor can give us a few warnings of what we might overlook when we come fresh to the plays today.

In the original staging of *Hamlet* at the Globe, the stage trap had two functions. Besides serving as Ophelia's grave, it was the distinctive entry point, not used by any other character, for the Ghost in Act 1. When he tells his son that he is "for the day confined to fast in fires," the first audiences would have already taken the point that he had come up from the underworld. His voice comes from under the stage, telling the soldiers to swear the oath of secrecy that Hamlet lays upon them. The connection between that original entry by the Ghost through the trap and the trap's later use for Ophelia is one we might easily miss. At the start of Act 5, the macabre discussion between the Gravediggers about whether

The Globe as reconstructed in Southwark near the original site in London.

she committed suicide and is therefore consigned to hell gets its sharpest edge from the association of the trap, here the grave being dug for her, with the Ghost's purgatorial fires. More to the point, though, Hamlet, as he eavesdrops on the curtailed burial ceremony, makes the same connection when he discovers that it is the body of Ophelia being so neglectfully interred. He remembers the other apparition that came up through the trap

The *frons scenae* of the new Globe.

A gesture using the language of hats, as shown by the man attending the brothers Browne.

and springs forward in a grotesque parody of the Ghost, crying, "This is I, Hamlet the Dane!" It is a melodramatic claim to be acting a new role, that of his father the dead King. The first audiences would have remembered the ghost of dead King Hamlet using the stage trap at this point more readily than we do now. Hamlet's private knowledge of the Ghost and the trapdoor sets him, as so often in the play, at odds with his audience. Consequently, centuries of editors, like the characters onstage, have misread this claim as a declaration that young Hamlet ought to be king.

Since his own name is Hamlet, and since he alone could have made the connection between the Ghost and the trapdoor, he was all too likely to be misunderstood. In the next scene, Osric certainly shows that he understands Hamlet's graveside claim that he is his father's ghost to be a claim that he should now be King of Denmark. That explains why Osric insists on keeping his hat in his hand when he comes to invite Hamlet to duel with Laertes. With equals, an Elizabethan gentleman would doff his hat in greeting and then put it back on. Only in the presence of your master, or as a courtier in the presence of the king, did you keep it in your hand. Osric is trying tactfully to acknowledge what he thinks is Hamlet's lunatic claim to be king. He missed the private connection that Hamlet had made with the trapdoor and his father's ghost. Tudor body language, with its wordless gestures and signals that defined human relations, was an aspect of social life so widely understood that it needed no stage direction. The language of hats was a part of the Shakespearean mindset that we now have to register in footnotes.

Other signifiers are necessarily more elusive. We might take heart from the range of the comments made in *Much Ado About Nothing* 4.1 when Hero is accused and is seen to go red. Each of the viewers—Claudio, Leonato, and Friar Francis—gives a different reading (or "noting") of her blush. Different mindsets lead to visual indicators being read in different ways. Each reading tells as much about the observer as about the thing observed. We might add that since the blush is commented on so extensively, Shakespeare must have been concerned to save the boy playing Hero from the necessity of holding his breath long enough to produce the right visual effect.

Costume was a vital element in the plays, a mute and instant signifier of the scene. If a character entered carrying a candle and dressed in a gown with a nightcap on his head, he had evidently just been roused from bed. Characters who entered wearing cloaks and riding boots and possibly holding a whip had just ended a long journey. York, entering in *Richard II* with a gorget (a metal neck plate, the "signs of war about his agèd neck" [2.2.74]), was preparing for battle. Even the women's wigs that the boys wore could be used to indicate the wearer's state of mind. Hair worn loose and unbound meant madness, whether in *Hamlet*'s Ophelia or *Troilus*'s Cassandra.

Comparable audience expectations could be roused by other visual features. Charac-

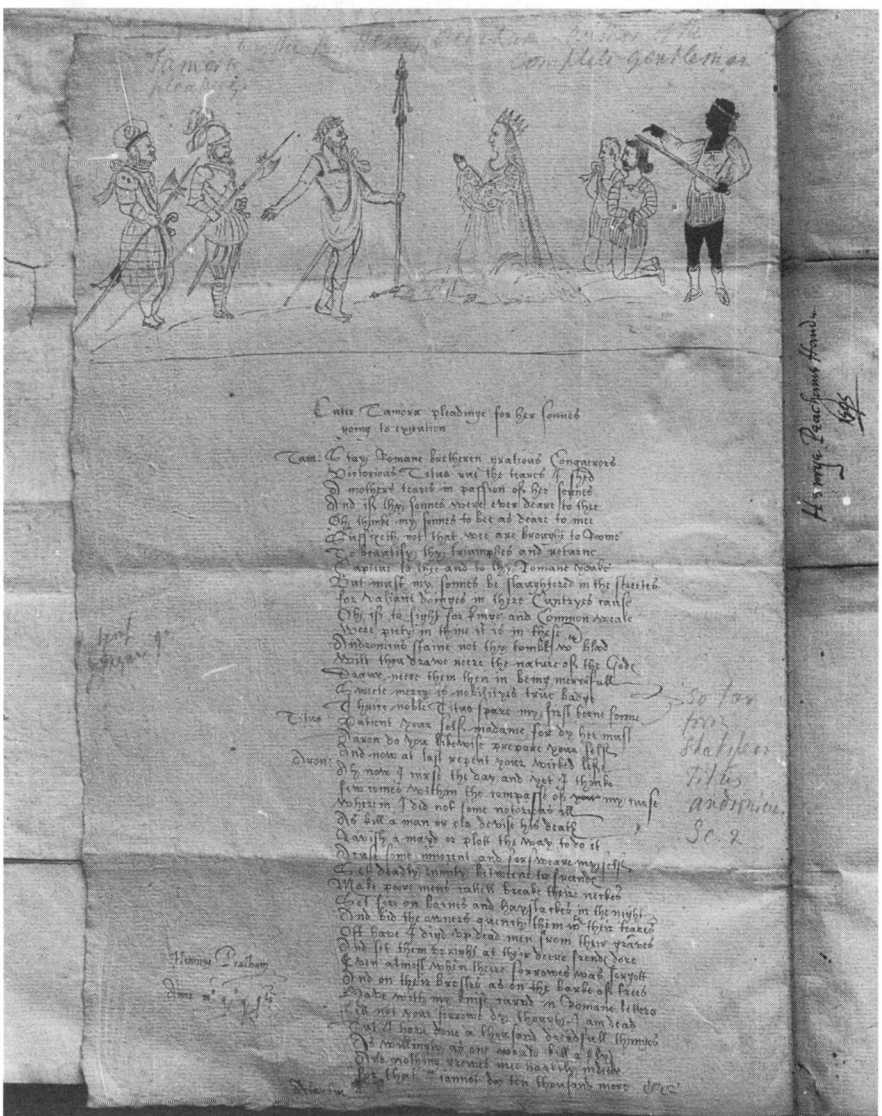

A sketch by Henry Peacham of an early staging of *Titus Andronicus* by Shakespeare's company (1595). Note the attempt at Roman costume for Titus but not for his soldiers, who carry Tudor halberds, and note Aaron's makeup and wig.

ters with faces blackened and wigs of curly black wool were recognized as Moors, alien and dangerous non-Christians. Aaron the Moor in *Titus Andronicus* and the Prince of Morocco in *The Merchant of Venice* acquire that character as soon as they come in view. Othello, by Iago's report and by his own first appearance, takes on the same stereotype. By contrast, Iago is dressed like a simple and honest soldier. Only in the course of Act 1 does it become apparent that it is Othello who is the honest soldier, Iago the un-Christian alien. The play neatly reverses the visual stereotypes of Elizabethan staging. Twentieth-century playgoers miss most of these signals and the ways that the original players used them to

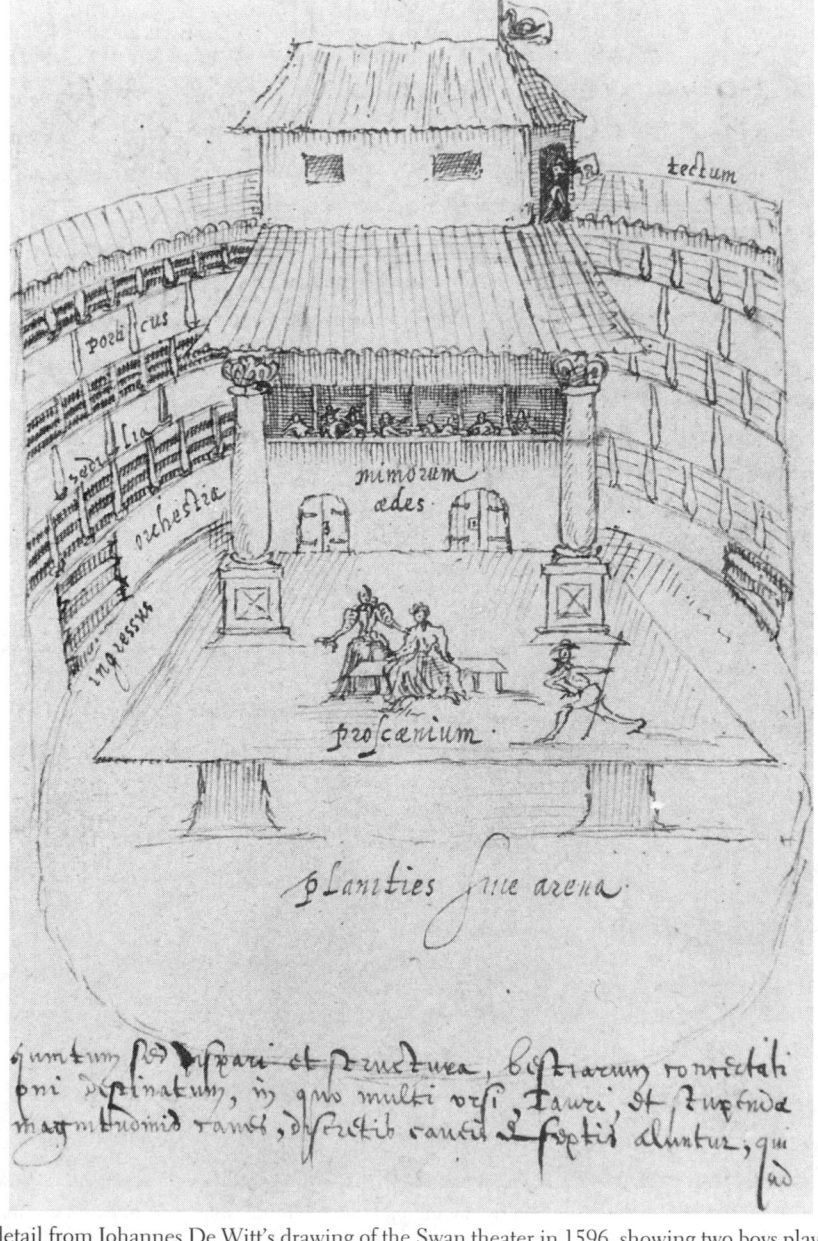

A detail from Johannes De Witt's drawing of the Swan theater in 1596, showing two boys playing women greeted by a chamberlain.

show the discrepancy between outward appearance and inner person. As King Lear said, robes and furred gowns hide all.

For *The Merchant of Venice*, Shylock wore his "Jewish gabardine" and may also have put on a false nose, as Alleyn was said to have done for the title role in *The Jew of Malta*. Other national characteristics were noted by features of dress, such as the Irish "strait strossers" (tight trousers) that Macmorris would have worn in *Henry V*. The dress of the women in the plays, who were usually played by boys with unbroken voices, was always a special expense. The records kept by Philip Henslowe, owner of the Rose playhouse and impresario for the rival company to Shakespeare's, show that he paid the author less for the script of *A Woman Killed with Kindness* than he paid the costumer for the heroine's gown.

Women's clothing and the decorums and signals that women's costume contained were very different from those of men and men's clothing. Men frequently used their hats, doffing them to signal friendship and holding them in their hands while speaking to anyone in authority over them. Women's hats were fixed to their heads and were rarely if ever taken off in public. The forms and the language of women's clothes reflected the silent modesty and the quiet voices that men thought proper for women. Women had other devices to signal with, including handkerchiefs, fans, and face masks, and the boys playing the women's parts in the theaters exploited such accessories to the full. A lady out of doors commonly wore a mask to protect her complexion. When Othello is quizzing Emilia in 4.2 about his wife's behavior while she spoke to Cassio, he asks Emilia, who should have been chaperoning her mistress, whether Desdemona had not sent her away "to fetch her fan, her gloves, her mask nor nothing?" There is little doubt that the boys would have routinely worn masks when they played gentlewomen onstage, and not just at the masked balls in *Romeo and Juliet*, *Love's Labour's Lost*, and *Much Ado About Nothing*.

Other features of the original staging stemmed from the actor–audience relationship, which differs radically in daylight, when both parties can see one another, from what we are used to in modern, darkened, theaters. An eavesdropping scene onstage, for instance, works rather on the same basis as the "invisible" fairies in *A Midsummer Night's Dream*, where the audience agrees to share the pretence. At the Globe, it also entailed adopting the eavesdropper's perspective. In *Much Ado*, the two games of eavesdropping played on Benedict and Beatrice are chiefly done around the two stage posts. In these scenes, the posts that held up the stage cover, or "heavens," near what we now think of as the front of the stage were round, like the whole auditorium, and their function was to allow things to be seen equally by all of the audience, wherever people might be standing or sitting. Members of the audience, sitting in the surrounding galleries or standing around the stage itself at the Globe or its predecessors, had the two tall painted pillars in their sight all the time, wherever they were in the playhouse. And since the audience was in a complete circle all around the stage, if the stage posts were used for concealment there was always a large proportion of the audience who could see the player trying to hide behind a post. It was a three-dimensional game in which the audience might find itself behind any of the game players, victims or eavesdroppers, complicit in either role.

The first of *Much Ado*'s eavesdropping scenes, 2.3, starts as usual in Shakespeare with a verbal indication of the locality. Benedict tells his boy, "Bring it hither to me in the orchard." So we don't need stage trees to tell us where we are supposed to be. He later hides "in the arbour" to listen to what Don Pedro and the others have set for him; this means concealing himself behind a stage post, closer to the audience than the playactors who are talking about him. Don Pedro asks, "See you where Benedict hath hid himself?," a self-contradiction that confirms the game. When it is Beatrice's turn in her arbor scene, 3.1, she slips into a "bower" behind "this alley," which again signals a retreat behind the prominent stage post. These games are played with both of the eavesdroppers hiding behind the post at the stage edge, while the others do their talking at center stage between the two posts.

Such games of eavesdropping, using the same bits of the stage structure, make a strong visual contrast with all that goes on at what we two-dimensional thinkers, used to the pictorial staging of the cinema, call the "back" of the stage, or upstage—where, for instance, the Friar starts the broken-off wedding and where Claudio and Don Pedro later figure at Leonato's monument. These events are more distant from the audience, less obviously comic and intimate. The close proximity of players to audience in such activities as eavesdropping strongly influenced the audience's feeling of kinship with the different groupings of players.

A multitude of other staging differences can be identified. Quite apart from the fact that the language idioms were more familiar to the playgoers at the original Globe than they are now, all playgoers in 1600, many of them illiterate, were practiced listeners. The speed of speech, even in blank verse, was markedly higher then than the recitation of Shakespeare is today. The original performances of Hamlet, if the Folio version reflects what was usually acted, would have run for not much more than two and a half hours (the time quoted by Ben Jonson for a play as long as Hamlet), compared with the more than four hours that the full Folio or 1605 Quarto text with at least one intermission would take today. Quicker speaking, quicker stage action, no intermissions, and the audience's ability to grasp the language more quickly meant that the plays galloped along. The story, not the verse, carried the thrust of the action. Occasional set speeches, like Hamlet's soliloquies or Gaunt's "sceptred isle" speech in Richard II, would be heard, familiar as they already were to many in the audience, like a solo aria in a modern opera. In theory if not in practice, the business of hearing, as "audience" (from the Latin audire, "to hear"), was more important than the business of seeing, as "spectators" (from the Latin spectare, "to see"). The visual aspects of acting, like scenic staging, are inherently two-dimensional and do not work well when the audience completely surrounds the actors. Most of Shakespeare's fellow writers, notably Jonson, understandably set a higher priority on the audience's hearing their verse than on their seeing what the players did with the lines. The poets wanted listeners, although the players did try to cater to the viewers. Yet for all the games with magic tricks and devils spouting fireworks that were part of the Shakespearean staging tradition, spectacle was a limited resource on the scene-free Elizabethan stage. Shakespeare in this was a poet more than a player. Even in his last and most richly staged plays, Cymbeline, The Winter's Tale, and The Tempest, he made notably less use of such "spectacles" than did his contemporaries.

One piece of internal evidence about the original staging is Hamlet's advice to the visiting players. In 3.2, before they stage the Mousetrap play that he has rewritten for them, he lectures them on what a noble student of the theater then considered to be good acting. He objects first to overacting and second to the clown who ad libs with his own jokes and does not keep to the script. How far this may have been Shakespeare's own view it is impossible to say. Hamlet is an amateur lecturing professionals about how they should do their job. His views are what we would expect an amateur playwright with a liking for plays that are "caviar to the general" to hold. His objections to the clown are noteworthy, because once the original performances ended, the clown would conclude the afternoon's entertainment with a comic song-and-dance jig. Thomas Platter, a young German-speaking Swiss student, went to the Globe in 1599 to see Julius Caesar. He reported back home that

> on 21 September after lunch I and my party crossed the river, and there in the play-house with the thatched roof witnessed an excellent performance of the tragedy of the first emperor Julius Caesar with a cast of about fifteen people. When the play was over they danced marvellously and gracefully together as their custom is, two dressed as men and two as women.[1]

The script for one jig survives, probably played by Will Kemp, who was the Shakespeare company clown until he left just before Hamlet came to the Globe. Its story is a bawdy knockabout tale of different men trying to seduce a shopkeeper's wife in rhyming couplets, hiding in a chest from her husband, and beating one another up. There is nothing to say

---

1. Thomas Platter's Travels in England (1599), rendered into English from the German, and with introductory matter by Clare Williams (London: Cape, 1937), p. 166.

The hall screen in the Middle Temple Hall, built in 1574. Shakespeare's company staged *Twelfth Night* in this hall in February 1602.

what the audience reaction to such a jig might have been after they had seen a performance of *Julius Caesar* or *Hamlet*. It is possible that the Globe players stopped offering that kind of coda when they acquired the clown who played Feste in *Twelfth Night* in 1601. The song with which Feste ends that play might have become an alternative form of closure, replacing the traditional bawdy jig.

Vigorous and rapid staging was inevitable when the half of the audience closest to the stage had to stand throughout the performance. Shakespeare's plays were distinctive among the other plays of the time for their reliance on verbal sparkle over scenes of battle and physical movement, but even the soliloquies raced along. There was little occasion for long pauses and emoting. Dumb shows, like the players' prelude to the *Mousetrap* play in *Hamlet*, were the nearest that the players came to silent acting. There were no intermissions—apples, nuts, and drink were peddled in the auditorium throughout the performance—and the only "comfort stations" were, for the men, the nearest blank wall; for the women, whatever convenient pots or bottles they might be carrying under their long skirts.

Nor were there any pauses to change scenes. There was no static scenery apart from an emblematic candle to signify a night scene, a bed "thrust out" onto the stage, or the canopied chair of state on which the ruler or judge sat for court scenes. Usually any special locality would be signaled in the first words of a new scene, but unlocalized scenes were routine. Each scene ended when all the characters left the stage and another set entered. No act breaks appear in the plays before *The Tempest*. *Henry V* marked each act with a Chorus, but even he entered on the heels of the characters from the previous scene. Blue-coated stagehands were a visibly invisible presence onstage. They would draw back the central hangings on the *frons scenae* for a discovery scene, carry on the chair of state on its dais for courtroom scenes, or push out the bed with Desdemona on it for the last act of *Othello*. They served the stage like the house servants with whom the nobility peopled every room in their great houses, silent machines ready to spring into action when needed.

There has been a great deal of speculation about the tiring-house front at the rear of the stage platform: did it look more like an indoor set or an outdoor one, like the hall screen of a great house or palace or like a house front exterior? In fact, it could easily be either. The upper level of the *frons*, the balconied "above," might equally represent a musicians' gallery, like those in the main hall of a great house, or a city wall under which the central discovery space served as the city gates, as it did for York in *Richard Duke of York (3 Henry VI)* 4.8, or *Henry V*'s Harfleur (3.3.78). The "above" could equally be an indoor gallery or an outdoor balcony. The appearance of the stage was everything and nothing, depending on what the play required. Players and playwrights expected the audience members to use their imagination, as they had to with the opening lines of *Hamlet*, or, as the Prologue to *Henry V* put it, to "piece out our imperfections with your thoughts."

Shakespeare's Companies and Their Playhouses

Shakespeare's plays were written for a variety of staging conditions. Until 1594, when he joined a new company under the patronage of the lord chamberlain, the queen's officer responsible for licensing playing companies, poets had written their plays for any kind of playhouse. The Queen's Men, the largest and best company of the 1580s, is on record as playing at the Bell, the Bel Savage, and the Bull inns inside the city, and at the Theatre and the Curtain playhouses in the suburbs. Early in 1594, it completed this sweep of all the available London venues by playing at the Rose. But in that year, the system of playing changed. The lord mayor had always objected to players using the city's inns, and in May 1594 he succeeded in securing the lord chamberlain's agreement to a total ban. From then on, only the specially built playhouses in the suburbs were available for plays.

The Queen's Men had been set up in 1583, drawn from all the then-existing major companies with the best players. This larger and favored group at first monopolized playing in London. But it was in decline by the early 1590s, and the shortage of companies to perform for the queen at Christmas led the lord chamberlain and his son-in-law, the lord admiral, to set up two new companies in its place as a duopoly in May 1594. Shakespeare became a "sharer," or partner, in one of these companies. As part of the same new establishment, his company, the Lord Chamberlain's Men, was allocated the Theatre to perform in, while its partner company in the duopoly, the Lord Admiral's Men, was assigned to the Rose. This was the first time any playing company secured a playhouse officially authorized for its use alone.

The Theatre, originally built in 1576 by James Burbage, father of the leading player of the Lord Chamberlain's company, was in Shoreditch, a suburb to the north of the city. The Rose, built in 1587 by Philip Henslowe, father-in-law of the Lord Admiral's leading player, Edward Alleyn, was in the suburb of Southwark, on the south bank of the Thames. Henslowe's business papers, his accounts, some lists of costumes and other resources, and his "diary," a day-by-day listing of each day's takings and the plays that brought the money in, have survived for the period from 1592 until well into the next decade. Together they provide an invaluable record of how one of the two major companies of the later 1590s, the only rival to Shakespeare's company, operated through these years.[2] Some of Shakespeare's earlier plays, written before he joined the Lord Chamberlain's Men, including *1 Henry VI* and *Titus Andronicus*, were performed at the Rose. After May 1594, the new company acquired all of his early plays; every Shakespeare play through the next three years was written for the Theatre. Its familiarity supplied one sort of resource to the playwright. But the repertory system laid heavy demands on the company.

Henslowe's papers give a remarkable record of the company repertory for these years. Each afternoon, the same team of fifteen or so players would stage a different play. With

---

2. See *Henslowe's Diary*, ed. R. A. Foakes and R. T. Rickert (Cambridge: Cambridge University Press, 1961).

only two companies operating in London, the demand was for constant change. No play at the Rose was staged more than four or five times in any month, and it was normal to stage a different play on each of the six afternoons of each week that they performed. A new play would be introduced roughly every three weeks—after three weeks of transcribing and learning the new parts; preparing the promptbook, costumes, and properties; and rehearsing in the mornings—while each afternoon, whichever of the established plays had been advertised around town on the playbills would be put on. The leading players had to memorize on average as many as eight hundred lines for each afternoon. Richard Burbage, who played the first Hamlet in 1601, probably had to play Richard III, Orlando in *As You Like It*, and Hamlet on successive afternoons while at the same time learning the part of Duke Orsino and rehearsing the new *Twelfth Night*—and still holding at least a dozen other parts in his head for the rest of the month's program. In the evenings, he might be called on to take the company to perform a different play at court, or at a nobleman's house in the Strand. The best companies made a lot of money, but not without constant effort.

The companies were formed rather like guilds, controlled by their leading "sharers." Each senior player shared the company's profits and losses equally with his fellows. Most of the plays have seven or eight major speaking parts for the men, plus two for the boys playing the women. A normal London company had eight or ten sharers, who collectively chose the repertory of plays to be performed, bought the playbooks from the poets, and put up the money for the main company resource of playbooks and costumes (not to mention the wagon and horses for touring when plague forced the London theaters to close). Shakespeare made most of his fortune from his "share," first in his company and later in its two playhouses.

As a playhouse landlord, Henslowe took half of the takings from the galleries each afternoon for his rent, while the players shared all the yard takings and the other half of the gallery money. From their takings, the sharers paid hired hands to take the walk-on parts and to work as stagehands, musicians, bookkeeper or prompter, and "gatherers" at the different entry gates. The leading players also kept the boys who played the women's parts, housing and feeding them as "apprentices" in an imitation of the London livery companies and trades, which ran apprenticeships to train boys to become skilled artisans, or "journeymen." City apprenticeships ran for seven years from the age of seventeen, but the boy players began much younger, because unbroken voices were needed. They graduated to become adult players at an age when the city apprentices were only beginning their training. Most of the "extras," apart from the playing boys, would be left in London whenever the company had to go on tour.

Because the professional companies of the kind that Shakespeare joined all started as traveling groups rather than as companies settled at a single playhouse in London, the years up to 1594 yielded plays that could be staged anywhere. The company might be summoned to play at court, at private houses, or at the halls of the Inns of Court as readily as at inns or innyards or the custom-built theaters themselves. They traveled the country with their plays, using the great halls of country houses, or town guildhalls and local inns, wherever the town they visited allowed them. Consequently, the plays could not demand elaborate resources for staging. In this highly mobile tradition of traveling companies, they were written in the expectation of the same basic but minimal features being available at each venue. Besides the stage platform itself, the basic features appear to have been two entry doors, usually a trap in the stage floor, a pair of stage pillars, sometimes a discovery space, and very occasionally a heavens with descent machinery. Apart from these fixtures, properties such as chairs and a table, a canopied throne on a dais, and sometimes a bed were also in regular use, though in a pinch these could be as mobile as the players themselves. The only essential traveling properties were players, playbooks, and costumes.

Once the two authorized companies settled permanently at the Theatre and the Rose in 1594, they slowly lost some of this mobility. The demands of versatility and readiness to make rapid changes now had to be switched from the venues to the plays themselves. A traveling company needed very few plays, since the locations and audiences were always changing. When the venues became fixed, it was the plays that had to keep changing. The Henslowe papers record that the Lord Admiral's Men staged an amazingly varied repertory of plays at the Rose. Shakespeare's company must have been equally versatile. The practice of giving popular plays long runs did not begin until the 1630s, by which time the number of London playhouses had grown to as many as five, all offering their plays each afternoon. Shakespeare's company in London had only the one peer from 1594 until 1600; and only two from then until 1608, aside from the once-weekly plays by the two boy companies, the "little eyases" mentioned in *Hamlet*, that started with the new century.

In the years from May 1594 to April 1597 at the Theatre, in addition to all his earlier plays that he brought to his new company, Shakespeare gave them possibly *Romeo and Juliet* and *King John*, and certainly *Richard II*, *A Midsummer Night's Dream*, *1 Henry IV*, and *The Merchant of Venice*. But then they ran into deep trouble, because they lost the Theatre. In April 1597, its original twenty-one-year lease expired, and the landlord, who disliked plays, refused to let them renew it. Anticipating this, the company's impresario James Burbage had built a new theater for them, a roofed place in the Blackfriars near St. Paul's Cathedral. The Blackfriars precinct was a "liberty," free from the lord mayor's jurisdiction. But the plan proved a disaster. The rich residents of Blackfriars objected, and the Privy Council stopped the theater from opening. From April 1597, Shakespeare's company had to rent the Curtain, an old neighbor of their now-silent Theatre, and it was there that the next four of Shakespeare's plays—*2 Henry IV*, *Much Ado About Nothing*, *The Merry Wives of Windsor*, and probably *Henry V*—were first staged.

In December 1598, losing hope of a new lease for the old Theatre, the Burbage sons had it pulled down and quietly transported its massive framing timbers across the Thames to make the scaffold for the Globe on the river's south bank, near the Rose. Most of their capital was sunk irretrievably into the Blackfriars theater, and they could afford only half the cost of rebuilding. So they raised money as best they could. Some of the company's more popular playbooks were sold to printers, including *Romeo and Juliet*, *Richard III*, *Richard II*, and *1 Henry IV*. More to the point, the Burbage brothers raised capital for the building by cutting in five of the leading players, including Shakespeare, and asking them to put up the other half of its cost. The Globe, its skeleton taken from the old Theatre, thus became the first playhouse to be owned by its players, and, within the limits set by the old frame, the first one built to their own design.

For this theater, one-eighth of which he personally owned, Shakespeare wrote his greatest plays: *Julius Caesar*, *As You Like It*, *Hamlet*, *Twelfth Night*, *Othello*, *All's Well That Ends Well*, *Measure for Measure*, *King Lear*, *Macbeth*, *Pericles*, *Antony and Cleopatra*, *Coriolanus*, *Cymbeline*, *The Winter's Tale*, and most likely *Troilus and Cressida* and *Timon of Athens*. As the first playhouse to be owned by the players who expected to use it, its fittings must have satisfied all the basic needs of Shakespearean staging. At one time or another, the company staged every one of Shakespeare's plays there.

In 1600, a company consisting entirely of boys started using the Blackfriars playhouse that Richard Burbage's father had tried to open four years before. Companies of boy players had a higher social status than the adult professionals, and, playing only in halls, they commanded a more affluent clientele. The boys performed only once a week, and the relative infrequency of their crowds, plus their skills as trained singers (they were choir-school children turned to making money for their choirmasters), proved less offensive to the local residents than a noisy adult company with its drums and trumpets. Leasing the Blackfriars to the boy company made a minor profit for the Burbages, who took the rent for eight years.

In the longer run, though, this arrangement provided a different means for the Burbage–Shakespeare company to advance its career. The boys' eight years of playing in their rented hall playhouse eventually made it possible for the company of adult players to renew Burbage's old plan of 1596. Shakespeare's company had been made the King's Men when James came to the throne in 1603, and their new patron gave them a status that made it impossible for the residents of Blackfriars to prevent them from implementing the original plan. During a lengthy closure of all the theaters because of a plague epidemic in

A section from Hollar's "Long View" of London. Drawn from a standpoint on the tower of the church that is now Southwark Cathedral, Hollar's view shows the roof of the great hall in which the Blackfriars playhouse was built. It can be seen as the long angled roof with a central turret, below and to the east of St. Bride's Church.

1608, the boys' manager surrendered his lease of the hall playhouse to the Burbages. They then took possession for their own company of the playhouse that their father had built for them twelve years before. They divided the new playhouse property among the leading players as they had done in 1599 with the Globe. They were the King's Men, the leading company in the country, and their status after ten years of playing at the Globe was matched by their wealth. By the time theaters reopened late in 1609, the company had established a new system of playing.

The King's Men now had two playhouses, a large open amphitheater and a much smaller roofed hall. Instead of selling or renting one out and using the other for themselves, they decided to use both in turn, for half of each year. It was a reversion to the old system with the city inns, where through the summer they played in the large open yards and in the winter played at inns with big indoor rooms. This time, though, the company owned both playhouses. Their affluence and their high status are signaled by the fact that they chose to keep one of their playhouses idle while they used the other, despite there now being a shortage of playhouses in London. That affluence was needed in 1613 when the Globe burned down at a performance of *All Is True (Henry VIII)*, and the company chose the much more expensive option of rebuilding it instead of reverting to the Blackfriars for both winter and summer. That decision, in its way, was the ultimate gesture of affection for their original playhouse. It was a costly gesture, but it meant that the Globe continued in use by the company until all the theaters were closed down by Parliament in 1642.

In 1609, when they reopened after the closure for plague, Shakespeare's company had made several changes in their procedures. The restart was at the Blackfriars, and although they offered the same kind of plays, they began to alter their style of staging. Along with the Blackfriars playhouse, they acquired a famous consort of musicians who played on strings and woodwinds in a music room set over the stage. The new consort was a distinct enhancement of the company's musical resources, which until then had been confined to song, the occasional use of recorders or hautboys, and military drums and trumpets for the scenes with soldiery. In 1608, a central room on the Globe's stage balcony was taken over to serve as a music room like the one at the Blackfriars. From this time on, the King's Men's performances began with a lengthy overture or concert of music before the play.

With that change, the plays themselves now had music to back their singers and provide other sorts of atmospheric effects. Some of the songs and music that appear in the plays not printed until the First Folio of 1623, such as the song that Mariana hears in *Measure for Measure* 4.1, may have been added after Shakespeare's time to make use of this new resource. Shakespeare did use songs, sometimes with string accompaniment, quite regularly in the early plays, but instrumental music hardly ever appears. The last play that he wrote alone, *The Tempest*, was the only one in which he made full use of this new resource.

All the plays containing soldiers and battles used the military drums that in war conveyed signals to infantry formations, as well as the trumpets that were used for signaling to cavalry. These were usually employed for offstage noises, sound effects made from "within" (inside the dressing room or tiring-house behind the stage). Soldiers marching in procession, as in the dead march at the close of *Hamlet*, would have the time marked by an onstage drum. Shakespeare never calls for guns to be fired onstage, though other writers did, but he did have other noises at his command. A small cannon or "chamber" might be used, fired from the gable-fronted heavens over the stage, as Claudius demands in *Hamlet* and as the Chorus to Act 3 of *Henry V* notes. It was wadding from a ceremonial cannon shot that set the gallery thatch alight at a performance of *All Is True* in July 1613 and burned the Globe to the ground. Stage battles such as Shrewsbury at the end of *1 Henry IV*, written for the Theatre, were accompanied by sword fights that were not the duels of *Hamlet*'s finale but exchanges with broadswords or "foxes" slammed against metal shields or "targets." That action guaranteed emphatic sound effects. The drums and trumpets, with clashes of swords and a great deal of to-ing and fro-ing onto and off the stage, were highlighted in between the shouted dialogue by some hard fighting between the protagonists. The leading players were practiced swordsmen, who knew they were being watched by experts. These were the scenes of "four or five most vile and ragged foils" that the fourth Chorus self-consciously derided in *Henry V* at the Curtain.

The second great reason for noise in the amphitheaters was to mark storm and tempest. Stagehands used the kind of device that Jonson mocked in the Prologue to *Every Man in His Humour*, written for its 1616 publication. His play, wrote Jonson, was free from choruses that wafted you over the seas, "nor rolled bullet heard / To say, it thunders; nor tempestuous drum / Rumbles, to tell you when the storm doth come." For centuries, lead balls rolling down a tin trough were a standard way of making thunder noises in English theaters. The tempest in Act 3 of *King Lear* is heralded several times in the text before a stage direction, "Storm and tempest" (Folio 2.2.450), tells us that it has at last arrived. In 2.2, Cornwall notes its coming twice (Folio 2.2.452, 473). Kent comments on the "Foul weather" in his first line in Act 3, prefaced by the entry stage direction for Act 3, "Storm still," which is repeated for 3.2. Such stage directions appear in both texts (Q has "Storm" for the equivalent Scenes 8, 9, and also at 11, F's 3.4, where F omits any further reference to these noises). These explicit signals indicate that the stagehands provided offstage noises, for all that Lear himself outstorms them with his violent speeches in 3.2.

The main question about the storm scenes in *King Lear* is this: with such consistent emphasis on storm in the language, what was the design behind the stage directions? In the centuries that *Lear* has been restaged, the tempest has been made to roar offstage in a wide variety of ways, often with so much effect that, in the face of complaints that the storm noises made it difficult for the audience to hear the words, some modern productions reduced the storm to solely visual effects, or even left Lear's own raging language to express it unsupported. But the two stage directions indicate that in the original performances the "storm in nature" was not left to Lear himself to convey. The two "Storm still" directions in the Folio suggest a constant rumbling, not the intermittent crashes that might allow Lear to conduct a dialogue with the occasional outbursts of storm noises, as some modern productions have done.

Shakespeare left regrettably few stage directions to indicate the special tricks or properties that he wanted. Curtained beds are called for in *Othello* 5.2 and *Cymbeline* 2.2, and there is the specification "Stocks brought out" in *King Lear* 2.2.132. Small and portable things like papers were a much more common device, from the letters in *The Two Gentlemen of Verona* 1.2.46, 1.3.44, and 2.1.95 to Lear's map at 1.1.35. Across the whole thirty-eight plays, though, there are very few such directions. Shakespeare's economy in preparing his scripts is a major impediment to the modern reader. He hardly ever bothered to note the standard physical gestures, such as kneeling or doffing a hat, and did little more to specify any special effects. Nonetheless, it is important not to imagine elaborate devices or actions where the text does not call for them. On the whole, the demands Shakespeare made of his fellows for staging his plays appear to have been remarkably modest. Since he was a company shareholder, his parsimony may have had a simple commercial motive. Stage properties cost the company money, and one had to be confident of a new play's popularity before investing much in its staging.

There may have been other reasons for avoiding extravagant staging spectacles. Shakespeare made little use of the discovery space until the last plays, for instance, for reasons that we can only guess at. The few definite discoveries in the plays include Portia's caskets in *The Merchant of Venice*, Falstaff sleeping off his sack in *1 Henry IV* 2.5.482, the body of Polonius in *Hamlet*, Hermione's statue in *The Winter's Tale* 5.3.20, and the lovers in *The Tempest* 5.1.173, who are found when discovered to be playing chess. The audience's shock when Hermione moves and comes out of the discovery space onto the main stage is rare in Shakespeare: in every other play, whether comedy or tragedy, the audience knows far more than the characters onstage about what is going on. Shakespeare matched this late innovation in *The Winter's Tale* with his last play, *The Tempest*. After the preliminary and soothing concert by the resident Blackfriars musicians, it opens with a storm at sea so realistic that it includes that peculiarly distinctive stage direction "Enter Mariners, wet" (1.1.46). That startling piece of stage realism turns out straightaway to be not real at all but a piece of stage magic.

Documents

This selection of documents provides a range of contemporary testimony about Shakespeare's character, his work, and the social and institutional conditions under which it was produced. In the absence of newspapers and reviewers, few references to the theater survive. The availability of such hints and fragments as are presented here serves as a mark of Shakespeare's distinction, for the theater was perceived by much of the literate population as ephemeral popular entertainment. The reports of spectators whose accounts we have are more like reviews than any other texts the period has to offer; hence the importance even of brief notes such as Nashe's or Platter's, and the particular value of extended accounts such as those of Simon Forman. The government documents included here offer a vivid glimpse of the institutional procedures by which the theater was regulated. The legal documents—a contract for the construction of a theater modeled on the Globe, and Shakespeare's will—provide the most detailed account available of the material conditions of his life and work. The poems, extracts from criticism, and other literary texts show the diversity of contemporary response to his art.

The source for each text is given at the end of the introductory headnote.

WS: E. K. Chambers, *William Shakespeare: A Study of Facts and Problems.* 2 vols. Oxford: Clarendon Press, 1930.
ES: E. K. Chambers, *The Elizabethan Stage.* 4 vols. Oxford: Clarendon Press, 1923.

Robert Greene on Shakespeare (1592)

[Robert Greene (1560–1592), a prolific author of plays, romances, and pamphlets, attacked Shakespeare in his *Greenes Groats-worth of Wit, bought with a million of Repentaunce*. Greene had studied at Cambridge, and his "M.A." was prominently displayed on his title pages. Shakespeare's lack of a university education is clearly one motive for the professional resentment of the following excerpt. Another is probably that Greene was poor and very ill and felt forsaken while writing the *Groats-worth of Wit*; the preface refers to it as his "Swanne-like song," and the narrative is framed as the repentance of a dying man. (Some scholars have held that the posthumously published work contains fabrications by a publisher attempting to capitalize on Greene's name.) The three colleagues Greene addresses are likely to be Christopher Marlowe, Thomas Nashe, and George Peele. The text is that of 1596, as printed in Alexander B. Grosart's edition of Greene's *Life and Complete Works*, vol. 12 (New York: Russell and Russell).]

To those Gentlemen his Quondam acquaintance,
that spend their wits in making Plaies, R. G.
wisheth a better exercise, and wisdome
to prevent his extremities. . . .

Base minded men al three of you, if by my miserie ye be not warned: for unto none of you (like me) fought those burres to cleave: those Puppits (I meane) that speake from our mouths, those Anticks garnisht in our colours. Is it not strange that I, to whom they al have beene beholding: is it not like that you, to whome they all have beene beholding, shall (were ye in that case that I am now) be both at once of them forsaken? Yes trust them not: for there is an upstart Crow, beautified with our feathers, that with his *Tygers heart wrapt in a Players hide,*[1] *supposes he is as well able to bumbast out a blanke verse as the best of you: and being an absolute Johannes fac totum,*[2] is in his owne conceit the onely Shake-scene in a countrie. O that I might intreate your rare wits to be imployed in more profitable courses: & let those Apes imitate your past excellence, and never more acquaint them with your admired inventions. I know the best husband[3] of you all will never prove an Usurer, and the kindest of them / all will never proove a kinde nurse: yet whilst you may, seeke you better Maisters; for it is pittie men of such rare wits, should be subject to the pleasures of such rude groomes.

Thomas Nashe on *1 Henry VI* (1592)

[Thomas Nashe (1567–1601), Greene's fellow playwright and pamphleteer, protests the attribution to himself of the *Groats-worth of Wit* in the preface to the 1592 edition of a pamphlet of his own, *Pierce Penilesse his Supplication to the Divell.* The satire of *Pierce Penilesse* is more general and political than that of the *Groats-worth,* attacking the manners of the middle class. The allusion to the Talbot scenes of *1 Henry VI* (4.2–7) comes in a section subtitled "The defence of Playes." Talbot is supposed to have been played by Richard Burbage, later the leading actor of the Lord Chamberlain's and King's Men. The text is from McKerrow's 1904 edition of Nashe's *Works,* vol. 1 (London: Bullen).]

How would it have joyed brave *Talbot* (the terror of the French) to thinke that after he had lyne two hundred yeares in his Tombe, hee should triumphe againe on the Stage, and have his bones newe embalmed with the teares of ten thousand spectators at least (at severall times), who, in the Tragedian that represents his person, imagine they behold him fresh bleeding.

Henry Chettle on Greene and Shakespeare (1592)

[Henry Chettle was involved in publishing Greene's *Groats-worth of Wit* and saw fit several months afterward to offer an apology for Greene's unfavorable treatment of Shakespeare. Chettle's willingness to serve as a kind of character witness for Shakespeare ("the other" playwright of whom he writes) may testify to Shakespeare's growing reputation. The first playwright Chettle mentions, of whom he writes more unfavorably, is Christopher Marlowe. The text is from Chettle's introductory epistle to a literary work of his own, entitled *Kind-Harts Dreame,* as reprinted in WS, vol. 2.]

About three moneths since died M. *Robert Greene,* leaving many papers in sundry Booke sellers hands, among other his Groatsworth of wit, in which a letter written to divers play-makers, is offensively by one or two of them taken; and because on the dead they cannot be avenged, they wilfully forge in their conceites[1] a living Author: and after tossing it to and fro, no remedy, but it must light on me. How I have all the time of my conversing in printing hindered the bitter inveying against schollers, it hath been very well knowne; and how in that I dealt, I can sufficiently proove. With neither of them that take offence was I acquainted, and with one of them I care not if I never be: The other, whome at that time I did not so much spare, as since I wish I had, for that as I have moderated the heate of living writers, and might have usde my owne discretion (especially in such a case) the Author beeing dead, that I did not, I

---

1. A parody of *Richard Duke of York (3 Henry VI)* 1.4.138: "O tiger's heart wrapped in a woman's hide!" This obvious allusion and the following pun on Shakespeare's name make it certain that Shakespeare is the

"crow" described here.
2. Jack-of-all-trades. *conceit:* imagination.
3. Steward.
1. Imaginations.

am as sory as if the originall fault had beene my fault, because my selfe have seene his demeanor no lesse civill than he exelent in the qualitie he professes: Besides, divers of worship[2] have reported his uprightnes of dealing, which argues his honesty, and his facetious grace in writting, that aprooves[3] his Art.

Gesta Grayorum on The Comedy of Errors (December 28, 1594)

[*Gesta Grayorum* is the title of an account of the holiday revels conducted by the law students of Gray's Inn. It was first published in 1688 (hence the modern spelling) from a manuscript that apparently had been handed down since the previous century. The subtitle of the book, "History of the High and mighty Prince, Henry Prince of Purpoole," alludes to the ceremonial ruler chosen for the occasion, the "Prince of State" referred to in the excerpt below. The performance of *The Comedy of Errors* was evidently part of the entertainment for the second night of revels. The text is from the 1968 reprint of Desmond Bland (Liverpool: Liverpool University Press).]

The next grand Night was intended to be upon *Innocents-Day* at Night; at which time there was a great Presence of Lords, Ladies, and worshipful Personages, that did expect some notable Performance at that time; which, indeed, had been effected, if the multitude of Beholders had not been so exceeding great, that thereby there was no convenient room for those that were Actors; by reason whereof, very good Inventions and Conceipts could not have opportunity to be applauded, which otherwise would have been great Contentation to the Beholders. Against which time, our Friend, the *Inner Temple*,[1] determined to send their Ambassador to our Prince of State, as sent from *Frederick Templarius*, their Emperor, who was then busied in his Wars against the Turk. The Ambassador came very gallantly appointed, and attended by a great number of brave Gentlemen, which arrived at our Court about Nine of the Clock at Night. . . . He was received very kindly of the Prince, and placed in a Chair besides His Highness, to the end that he might be Partaker of the Sports intended. . . .

When the Ambassador was placed, as aforesaid, and that there was something to be performed for the Delight of the Beholders, there arose such a disordered Tumult and Crowd upon the Stage, that there was no Opportunity to effect that which was intended: There came so great a number of worshipful Personages upon the Stage, that might not be displaced; and Gentlewomen, whose Sex did privilege them from Violence, that when the Prince and his Officers had in vain, a good while, expected and endeavoured a Reformation, at length there was no hope of Redress for that present. The Lord Ambassador and his Train thought that they were not so kindly entertained, as was before expected, and thereupon would not stay any longer at that time, but, in a sort,[2] discontented and displeased. After their Departure the Throngs and Tumults did somewhat cease, although so much of them continued, as was able to disorder and confound any good Inventions whatsoever. In regard whereof, as also for that the Sports intended were especially for the gracing of the *Templarians*, it was thought good not to offer any thing of Account, saving Dancing and Revelling with Gentlewomen; and after such Sports, a Comedy of Errors (like to *Plautus* his *Menechmus*) was played by the Players. So that Night was begun, and continued to the end, in nothing but Confusion and Errors; whereupon, it was ever afterwards called, *The Night of Errors*. . . .

The next Night upon this Occasion, we preferred Judgments thick and threefold, which were read publickly by the Clerk of the Crown, being all against a Sorcerer or Conjurer that was supposed to be the Cause of that confused Inconvenience. Therein

---

2. *divers of worship*: various men of rank. *qualitie he professes*: his vocation.
3. Demonstrates. *facetious*: polished, agreeable.

1. Another of the Inns of Court.
2. Departed.

was contained, How he had caused the Stage to be built, and Scaffolds to be reared to the top of the House, to increase Expectation. Also how he had caused divers Ladies and Gentlewomen, and others of good Condition, to be invited to our Sports; also our dearest Friend, the State of *Templaria*, to be disgraced, and disappointed of their kind Entertainment, deserved and intended. Also that he caused Throngs and Tumults, Crowds and Outrages, to disturb our whole Proceedings. And Lastly, that he had foisted a Company of base and common Fellows,[3] to make up our Disorders with a Play of Errors and Confusions; and that that Night had gained to us Discredit, and it self a Nickname of Errors. All which were against the Crown and Dignity of our Sovereign Lord, the Prince of *Purpoole*. . . .

The next grand Night was upon *Twelfth-day* at Night. . . . First, There came six Knights of the Helmet, with three that they led as Prisoners, and were attired like Monsters and Miscreants. The Knights gave the Prince to understand, that as they were returning from their Adventures out of *Russia*, wherein they aided the Emperor of *Russia*, against the *Tartars*, they surprized these three Persons, which were conspiring against His Highness and Dignity.[4] . . . Which being done, the Trumpets were commanded to sound, and then the King at Arms came in before the Prince, and told His Honour, that there was arrived an Ambassador from the mighty Emperor of *Russia* and *Moscovy*, that had some Matters of Weight to make known to His Highness. So the Prince willed that he should be admitted into his Presence; who came in Attire of *Russia*, accompanied with two of his own Country, in like Habit.

Francis Meres on Shakespeare (1598)

[Francis Meres (1565–1647) was educated at Cambridge and was active in London literary circles in 1597–98, after which he became a rector and schoolmaster in the country. The descriptions of Shakespeare are taken from a section on poetry in *Palladis Tamia*, *Wits Treasury*, a work largely consisting of translated classical quotations and *exempla*. Unlike the main body of the work, the subsections on poetry, painting, and music include comparisons of English artists to figures of antiquity. Meres goes on after the extract below to list Shakespeare among the best English writers for lyric, tragedy, comedy, elegy, and love poetry. The text is from D. C. Allen's 1933 edition of the section "Poetrie" (Urbana: University of Illinois).]

From XI

As the Greeke tongue is made famous and eloquent by *Homer, Hesiod, Euripedes, Aeschilus, Sophocles, Pindarus, Phocylides* and *Aristophanes*; and the Latine tongue by *Virgill, Ovid, Horace, Silius Italicus, Lucanus, Lucretius, Ausonius* and *Claudianus*: so the English tongue is mightily enriched, and gorgeouslie invested in rare ornaments and resplendent abiliments by Sir *Philip Sidney, Spencer, Daniel, Drayton, Warner, Shakespeare, Marlow* and *Chapman*.

From XIV

As the soule of *Euphorbus* was thought to live in *Pythagoras*: so the sweete wittie soule of Ovid lives in mellifluous & honytongued *Shakespeare*, witnes his *Venus* and *Adonis*, his *Lucrece*, his sugred Sonnets.

From XV

As *Plautus* and *Seneca* are accounted the best for Comedy and Tragedy among the Latines: so *Shakespeare* among yᵉ English is the most excellent in both kinds for

---

3. That is, the actors.
4. This last paragraph has been included because of the theory that this ostensible visit of the Russian ambassa-

dor to the court of the Prince of Purpoole provided a model for the masque of Muscovites in *Love's Labour's Lost* 5.2.

the stage; for Comedy, witnes his *Gētlemē of Verona*, his *Errors*, his *Love labors lost*, his *Love labours wonne*,[1] his *Midsummers night dreame*, & his *Merchant of Venice*: for Tragedy his *Richard the 2. Richard the 3. Henry the 4. King John, Titus Andronicus* and his *Romeo and Juliet*.

As *Epius Stolo* said, that the Muses would speake with *Plautus* tongue, if they would speak Latin: so I say that the Muses would speak with *Shakespeares* fine filed phrase, if they would speake English.

Parnassus Plays on Shakespeare (1598–1601)

[The three *Parnassus* plays, *The Pilgrimage to Parnassus* and *The Return from Parnassus*, *Parts 1* and *2*, were performed at Christmastime, probably in 1598, 1599, and 1601, by students of St. John's College, Cambridge. The references to Shakespeare and other contemporary writers are frequently ironic or equivocal. In the excerpts from *The Return, Part 1*, Ingenioso is an aspiring poet and Gullio a fop. In the second excerpt, Ingenioso is presenting the verses requested in the previous excerpt, having begun with examples in the vein or style of Chaucer and Spenser. Ingenioso returns in *Part 2* to discuss the merits of contemporary poets with Judicio (a critic). In the last two excerpts, Richard Burbage and Will Kempe, famous actors and colleagues of Shakespeare, turn up to try recruiting students as actors for their company "at a low rate" of pay. Burbage auditions one of them for the part of Richard III. The text is from J. B. Leishman's edition of 1949 (London: Nicholson and Watson).]

The Return from Parnassus, Part 1
ACT 3, SCENE 1

GULLIO   Suppose also that thou wert my M^ris, as somtime woodden statues represent the goddesses, thus I woulde looke amorously, thus I would pace, thus I woulde salute thee.

INGENIOSO   It will be my lucke to dye noe other death than by hearinge of his follies, I feare this speach thats a comminge will breede a deadly disease in my ears.

GULLIO   Pardon faire lady, thoughe sicke thoughted Gullio maks a maine unto thee, & like a bould faced sutore gins to woo thee.[1]

INGENIOSO   We shall have nothinge but pure Shakspeare, and shreds of poetrie that he hath gathered at the theators.

GULLIO   Pardon mee moy mittressa, ast am a gentleman the moone in comparison of thy bright hue[2] a meere slutt, Anthonies Cleopatra a blacke browde milkmaide, Hellen a dowdie.[3]

INGENIOSO   Marke Romeo and Juliet: o monstrous theft, I thinke he will runn throughe a whole booke of Samuell Daniells.[4]

GULLIO   Thrise fairer than my selfe, thus I began,
    The gods faire riches, sweete above compare,
    Staine to all Nimphes, [m]ore lovely the[n][5] a man,
    More white and red than doves and roses are:
    Nature that made thee, with herselfe had strife,
    Saith that the worlde hath ending with thy life.[6]

INGENIOSO   Sweete Mr Shakspeare.

GULLIO   As I am a scholler, these arms of mine are long and strong withall:
    Thus elms by vines are compast ere they falle.

---

1. The play—or at least the title—has not survived; a bookseller's record of the title does survive, however.
1. *sicke . . . thee:* compare *Venus and Adonis*, lines 5–6. Of the numerous quotations and allusions, only those referring to Shakespeare are identified.
2. Is. *ast:* as I.
3. *Anthonies . . . dowdie:* compare *Romeo and Juliet*

2.3.37.
4. Probably Samuel Daniel's sonnet sequence *Delia*.
5. *more lovely then:* correction is based on *Venus and Adonis*; other slight errors or misquotations are left uncorrected.
6. *Thrise . . . life:* compare *Venus and Adonis*, lines 7–12. *had strife:* the phrase in Shakespeare is "at strife."

INGENIOSO Faith gentleman, youre reading is wonderfull in our English poetts.

GULLIO Sweet M^{ris}, I vouchsafe to take some of there wordes and applie them to mine owne matters by a scholasticall imitation. Report thou upon thy credit, is not my vayne in courtinge gallant & honorable?

INGENIOSO Admirable sanes compare, never was soe mellifluous a witt joynet to so pure a phrase, such comly gesture, suche gentleman like behaviour.

GULLIO But stay, its verie true, good wittes have badd memories: I had almoste forgotten the cheife pointe I cald thee out for: new years day approcheth, and wheras other gallants bestowe Jewells upon there Mistrisses (as I have done whilome), I now count it base to do as the comon people doe; I will bestow upon them the precious stons of my witt, a diamonde of Invention, that shall be above all value & esteeme; therfore, sithens I am employed in some weightie affayrs of the courte, I will have thee, Ingenioso, to make them, and when thou hast done, I will peruse, pollish, and correcte them.

INGENIOSO My pen is youre bounden vassall to comande, but what vayne woulde it please you to have them in?

GULLIO Not in a vaine veine (prettie y faith): make mee them in two or three divers vayns, in Chaucers, Gowers and Spencers, and Mr Shakspeares. Marry I thinke I shall entertaine[7] those verses which run like these:

Even as the sunn with purple coloured face
Had tane his laste leave on the weeping morne,[8] etc.

O sweet Mr Shakspeare, Ile have his picture in my study at the courte.

INGENIOSO Take heede my maisters, hele kill you with tediousness ere I can ridd him of the stage.

ACT 4, SCENE 1

GULLIO Youe schollers are simple felowes, men that never came where Ladies growe; I that have spente my life amonge them knowes best what becometh my pen, and theire Ladishipps ears. Let mee heare Mr Shakspears veyne.

INGENIOSO Faire Venus, queene of beutie and of love,
Thy red doth stayne the blushinge of the morne,
Thy snowie neck shameth the milke white dove,
Thy presence doth this naked worlde adorne;
Gazinge on thee all other nymphes I scorne.
When ere thou dyest slowe shine that Satterday,
Beutie and grace muste sleepe with thee for aye.

GULLIO Noe more, I am one that can judge accordinge to the proverbe *bovem ex unguibus.*[9] Ey marry S^r, these have some life in them: let this duncified worlde esteeme of Spĕcer and Chaucer, Ile worshipp sweet Mr Shakspeare, and to honoure him will lay his *Venus and Adonis* under my pillowe, as wee reade of one[1] (I do not well remember his name, but I am sure he was a kinge) slept with Homer under his beds heade. Well, Ile bestowe a Frenche crowne in the faire writinge of them out, and then Ile instructe thee about the delivery of them. Meane while, Ile have thee make an elegant description of my M^{ris}; liken the worste part of her to Cynthia, make also a familiar Dialogue betwixt her and my selfe. Ile now in, and correct these verses.   *Exit.*

INGENIOSO Why, who coulde endure this post put into a sattin sute, this haberdasher of lyes, this Bracchidochio,[2] this Ladye munger, this meere rapier and dagger, this cringer, this foretopp, but a man thats ordayned to miserie?

---

7. Accept; prefer.
8. *Euen . . . morne:* compare *Venus and Adonis,* lines 1–2.
9. [One may know] the bull by his hoof: Gullio's cor-
ruption of the proverb *Leonem ex unguibus æstimare* (The lion is known by his claws).
1. Alexander the Great.
2. Braggart.

The Return from Parnassus, Part 2
ACT 1, SCENE 2

INGENIOSO *Benjamin Johnson.*
JUDICIO The wittiest fellow of a Bricklayer in England.
INGENIOSO A meere Empyrick, one that getts what he hath by observation, and makes onely nature privy to what he endites; so slow an Inventor, that he were better betake himselfe to his old trade of Bricklaying; a bould whorson, as confident now in making of a booke, as he was in times past in laying of a brick.

William Shakespeare.
JUDICIO Who loves not *Adons* love, or *Lucrece* rape?
His sweeter verse contaynes hart robbing lines,
Could but a graver subject him content,
Without loves foolish lazy languishment.

ACT 4, SCENE 3

KEMPE Few of the uniuersity [men] pen plaies well, they smell too much of that writer *Ovid*, and that writer *Metamorphoses*,[3] and talke too much of *Proserpina & Juppiter*. Why heres our fellow *Shakespeare* puts them all downe, I and *Ben Jonson* too. O that *Ben Jonson* is a pestilent fellow, he brought up *Horace* giving the Poets a pill, but our fellow *Shakespeare* hath given him a purge that made him beray his credit.[4]
BURBAGE Its a shrewd fellow indeed. I wonder these schollers stay so long, they appointed to be here presently that we might try them: oh here they come.

ACT 4, SCENE 4

BURBAGE I like your face and the proportion of your body for *Richard* the 3., I pray [you] M. *Philomusus* let me see you act a little of it.
PHILOMUSUS Now is the winter of our discontent
Made glorious summer by the sonne of Yorke, [&c.]
BURBAGE Very well I assure you.

Epilogue to the Queen, possibly by Shakespeare (1599)

[This epilogue was copied into a commonplace book by Henry Stanford, a retainer of the household of the Lord Chamberlain, who was also the official patron of Shakespeare's company. Shakespeare was the chief writer for the company, and the epilogue could have followed a court performance by the Lord Chamberlain's Men recorded for Shrove Tuesday, February 20, 1599, matching the year (1598 by the old calendar) and period (Shrovetide, the three days preceding Lent) specified in the heading and the text, respectively. The scholars who discovered the manuscript argue that the poem matches Shakespeare's style more closely than that of other potential authors. The text is taken from the article in which its discovery was first announced, in *Modern Philology* 70 (1972): 138–39.]

---

3. The title of a work by Ovid, not another "writer." The playwright here mocks the supposed ignorance of a mere player.
4. *he brought . . . credit:* this is a reference to the so-called War of the Theaters, a polemic involving Jonson against fellow playwrights John Marston and Thomas Dekker.

to ye Q. by ye players 1598.

As the diall hand tells ore /
  ye same howers yt had before
  still beginning in ye ending /
  circuler account still lending
  So most mightie Q. we pray /
  like ye diall day by day
  you may lead ye seasons on /
  making new when old are gon.
that the babe wch now is yong /
  & hathe yet no use of tongue
  many a shrovetyde here may bow /
  to ye empresse I doe now
  that the children of these lordes /
  sitting at your counsell bourdes
  may be grave & aeged seene /
  of her ye was ther father Quene
  once I wishe this wishe again /
  heaven subscribe yt wth amen.

John Weever on Shakespeare (1599)

[This sonnet, which follows the "Shakespearean" rhyme scheme, was published in a collection entitled *Epigrammes in the oldest Cut, and newest Fashion.* Like many of the other
references to Shakespeare's writings in this period, Weever's poem pays less attention to
the plays than to the narrative poems, which were of higher literary status and (to judge,
for example, from the *Parnassus* plays) popular among young men of fashion. Weever
(1576–1632) was himself a student at Cambridge not long before this poem was published.
The text is from WS, vol. 2.]

Ad Gulielmum Shakespeare.

Honie-tongued Shakespeare when I saw thine issue
I swore *Apollo* got them[1] and none other,
Their rosie-tainted features cloth'd in tissue,[2]
Some heaven born goddesse said to be their mother:
Rose-checkt[3] Adonis with his amber tresses,
Faire fire-hot *Venus* charming him to love her,
Chaste *Lucretia* virgine-like her dresses,
Prowd lust-stung *Tarquine* seeking still to prove[4] her:
Romea Richard; more whose names I know not,
Their sugred tongues, and power attractive beuty
Say they are Saints althogh that Sts they shew not
For thousands vowes to them subjective dutie:[5]
They burn in love thy children *Shakespear* het them,
Go, wo thy Muse more Nymphish brood beget them.[6]

1. *when . . . them:* Shakespeare's poetic productions
("issue") are so perfect they seem to have been created
(begotten) by the patron of poets, Apollo, himself. The
identification of Shakespeare's muse as goddess (line 4)
or nymph (line 14) continues the trope of divine inspiration.
2. Rich fabric. *tainted:* tinted.
3. Cheeked.
4. Attempt.
5. *Their . . . dutie:* Shakespeare's characters are so compelling that they have elicited the devotion ordinarily
given to saints. Their actions may not be saintly ("Sts
they show not"), but "thousands" have given to them
the devotion a subject gives a sovereign.
6. *They burn . . . them:* the antecedent for "they" is
"thousands" in line 12; with modern spelling and punctuation, the couplet might read: "They burn in love; thy
children, Shakespeare, het [heated] them. / Go woo thy
muse, more nymphish brood beget them."

Thomas Platter on *Julius Caesar* (September 21, 1599)

[Thomas Platter (b. 1574), a Swiss traveler, recorded his experience at the Globe playhouse in an account of his travels. The German text is printed in WS 2:322.]

Den 21 Septembris nach dem Imbissessen, etwan umb zwey vhren, bin ich mitt meiner geselschaft vber daz wasser gefahren, haben in dem streüwinen Dachhaus die Tragedy vom ersten Keyser Julio Caesare mitt ohngefahr 15 personen sehen gar artlich agieren; zu endt der Comedien dantzeten sie ihrem gebraucht nach gar vber-ausz zierlich, ye zwen in mannes vndt 2 in weiber kleideren angethan, wunderbahr-lich mitt einanderen.

On the 21st of September after lunch, about two o'clock, I crossed the water [the Thames] with my party, and we saw the tragedy of the first emperor Julius Caesar acted very prettily in the house with the thatched roof, with about fifteen characters; at the end of the comedy, according to their custom, they danced with exceeding elegance, two each in men's and two in women's clothes, wonderfully together.

[Translated by Noah Heringman]

Gabriel Harvey on *Hamlet, Venus and Adonis,* and *The Rape of Lucrece* (1598–1603)

[Gabriel Harvey (c. 1550–1631), a scholar perhaps best remembered as the particular friend of Spenser, gave the following account of Shakespeare and other contemporaries in a long manuscript note in his copy of Speght's 1598 edition of Chaucer. The date of the note is uncertain, but internal evidence makes it highly unlikely to be later than 1603. The references to Shakespeare are brief but suggestive, and the note is useful both in providing a context for the appreciation of Shakespeare and for its characteristically keen assessment of the state of modern literature. The text is from G. C. Moore Smith's edition of *Gabriel Harvey's Marginalia* (Stratford-upon-Avon: Shakespeare Head Press, 1913).]

And now translated Petrarch, Ariosto, Tasso, & Bartas himself deserve curious comparison with Chaucer, Lidgate, & owre best Inglish, auncient & moderne. Amongst which, the Countesse of Pembrokes Arcadia, & the Faerie Queene ar now freshest in request: & Astrophil, & Amyntas ar none of the idlest pastimes of sum fine humanists. The Earle of Essex much commendes Albions England:[1] and not unwor-thily for diverse notable pageants, before, & in the Chronicle. Sum Inglish, & other Histories nowhere more sensibly described, or more inwardly discovered. The Lord Mountjoy makes the like account of Daniels peece of the Chronicle,[2] touching the Usurpation of Henrie of Bullingbrooke, which in deede is a fine, sententious, & poli-tique peece of Poetrie: as proffitable, as pleasurable. The younger sort takes much delight in Shakespeares Venus, & Adonis: but his Lucrece, & his tragedie of Hamlet, Prince of Denmarke, have it in them, to please the wiser sort. Or such poets: or better: or none.

Vilia miretur vulgus: mihi flavus Apollo
Pocula Castaliæ plena ministret aquæ:[3]

quoth Sir Edward Dier, betwene jest, & earnest. Whose written devises farr excell most of the sonets, and cantos in print. His Amaryllis, & Sir Walter Raleighs Cynthia,

1. By William Warner (1586).
2. *The Civil Wars Between the Two Houses of Lancaster and York* (1595).
3. "Let what is cheap excite the marvel of the crowd; for me may golden Apollo minister full cups from the Castalian fount" (Ovid, *Amores* 1.15.35–36, Loeb trans-lation). These lines also appear on the title page of Shakespeare's *Venus and Adonis* (1593).

how fine & sweet inventions? Excellent matter of emulation for Spencer, Constable, France, Watson, Daniel, Warner, Chapman, Silvester, Shakespeare, & the rest of owr florishing metricians. I looke for much, aswell in verse, as in prose, from mie two Oxford frends, Doctor Gager, & M. Hackluit: both rarely furnished for the purpose: & I have a phansie to Owens new Epigrams, as pithie as elegant, as plesant as sharp, & sumtime as weightie as breife: & amongst so manie gentle, noble, & royall spirits meethinkes I see sum heroical thing in the clowdes: mie soveraine hope. Axiophilus[4] shall forgett himself, or will remember to leave sum memorials behinde him: & to make an use of so manie rhapsodies, cantos, hymnes, odes, epigrams, sonets, & discourses, as at idle howers, or at flowing fitts he hath compiled. God knowes what is good for the world, & fitting for this age.

Contract for the Building of the Fortune Theatre (1600)

[This contract was drawn up between Philip Henslowe and Edward Alleyn, partners in the venture, and Peter Street, the carpenter (or general contractor) in charge of the construction. In fact, Alleyn seems to have put up all the money, £440 for the work specified in the contract in addition to £80 for decoration and considerable sums to acquire the lot and surrounding properties. Alleyn faced opposition from residents of the neighborhood, but he had secured the favor of key supporters, so that he was able to proceed with the construction. As the new home of the Lord Admiral's Men, the Fortune did in fact become a center of disturbances, with complaints coming to the Middlesex Bench of assaults, petty thefts, and riotous behavior. Alleyn had been the leading actor of the Lord Admiral's Men, chief competitors of the Lord Chamberlain's Men, and the Fortune was conceived to compete with the Globe, meanwhile replacing the decaying and poorly situated Rose Theatre. The contract's descriptions and frequent references to the Globe, given this background, can be seen as providing some of our best evidence on the nature of the Globe itself. The text is reprinted in ES, vol. 2.]

'This Indenture made the Eighte daie of Januarye 1599,[1] and in the Twoe and Fortyth yeare of the Reigne of our sovereigne Ladie Elizabeth, by the grace of god Queene of Englande, Fraunce and Irelande, defender of the Faythe, &c. betwene Phillipp Henslowe and Edwarde Allen of the parishe of Ste Saviours in Southwark in the Countie of Surrey, gentlemen, on thone parte, and Peeter Streete, Cittizen and Carpenter of London, on thother parte witnesseth That whereas the saide Phillipp Henslowe & Edward Allen, the daie of the date hereof, have bargayned, compounded & agreed with the saide Peter Streete ffor the erectinge, buildinge & settinge upp of a new howse and Stadge for a Plaiehouse in and uppon a certeine plott or parcell of grounde appoynted oute for that purpose, scytuate and beinge nere Goldinge lane in the parishe of Ste Giles withoute Cripplegate of London,[2] to be by him the saide Peeter Streete or somme other sufficyent woorkmen of his provideinge and appoyntemente and att his propper costes & chardges, for the consideracion hereafter in theis presentes expressed, made, erected, builded and sett upp in manner & forme followinge (that is to saie); The frame of the saide howse to be sett square[3] and to conteine ffowerscore foote of lawfull assize everye waie square withoutt and fiftie five foote of like assize square everye waie within, with a good suer and stronge foundacion of pyles, brick, lyme and sand bothe without & within, to be wroughte one foote of assize att the leiste above the grounde; And the saide fframe to conteine three Stories in heighth, the first or lower Storie to conteine Twelve foote of lawfull assize in

4. Probably Harvey himself.
1. 1600 (New Style).
2. nere . . . London: an area then in the northwest suburbs, literally outside Cripplegate and, like the Globe across the water, outside the jurisdiction of a City Council often inimical to the theater.
3. This square shape was unusual; the outlines of comparable theaters of the period were round or polygonal (with more than four sides).

heighth, the second Storie Eleaven foote of lawfull assize in heigth, and the third or upper Storie to conteine Nyne foote of lawfull assize in heigth; All which Stories shall conteine Twelve foote and a halfe of lawfull assize in breadth througheoute, besides a juttey forwardes in either of the saide twoe upper Stories of Tenne ynches of lawfull assize, with ffower convenient divisions for gentlemens roomes,[4] and other sufficient and convenient divisions for Twoe pennie roomes, with necessarie seates to be placed and sett, aswell in those roomes as througheoute all the rest of the galleries of the saide howse, and with suchelike steares, conveyances & divisions withoute & within, as are made & contryved in and to the late erected Plaiehowse on the Banck in the saide parishe of Ste Saviours called the Globe; With a Stadge and Tyreinge howse[5] to be made, erected & settupp within the saide fframe, with a shadowe or cover[6] over the saide Stadge, which Stadge shalbe placed & sett, as alsoe the stearecases of the saide fframe, in suche sorte as is prefigured in a plott[7] thereof drawen, and which Stadge shall conteine in length Fortie and Three foote of lawfull assize and in breadth to extende to the middle of the yarde[8] of the saide howse; The same Stadge to be paled in belowe with good, stronge and sufficyent newe oken bourdes, and likewise the lower Storie of the saide fframe withinside, and the same lower storie to be alsoe laide over and fenced with stronge yron pykes; And the saide Stadge to be in all other proporcions contryved and fashioned like unto the Stadge of the saide Plaie howse called the Globe; With convenient windowes and lightes glazed to the saide Tyreinge howse; And the saide fframe, Stadge and Stearecases to be covered with Tyle, and to have a sufficient gutter of lead to carrie & convey the water frome the coveringe of the saide Stadge to fall backwardes; And also all the saide fframe and the Stairecases thereof to be sufficyently enclosed withoute with lathe, lyme & haire, and the gentlemens roomes and Twoe pennie roomes to be seeled[9] with lathe, lyme & haire, and all the fflowers of the saide Galleries, Stories and Stadge to be bourded with good & sufficyent newe deale bourdes of the whole thicknes, wheare need shalbe; And the saide howse and other thinges beforemencioned to be made & doen to be in all other contrivitions, conveyances, fashions, thinge and thinges effected, finished and doen accordinge to the manner and fashion of the saide howse called the Globe, saveinge only that all the princypall and maine postes of the saide fframe and Stadge forwarde shalbe square and wroughte palasterwise,[1] with carved proporcions called Satiers[2] to be placed & sett on the topp of every of the same postes, and saveinge alsoe that the said Peeter Streete shall not be chardged with anie manner of pay[ntin]ge in or aboute the saide fframe howse or Stadge or anie parte thereof, nor rendringe[3] the walls within, nor seeling anie more or other roomes then the gentlemens roomes, Twoe pennie roomes and Stadge before remembred. Nowe theiruppon the saide Peeter Streete dothe covenant, promise and graunte ffor himself, his executours and administratours, to and with the saide Phillipp Henslowe and Edward Allen and either of them, and thexecutours and administratours of them and either of them, by theis presentes in manner & forme followeinge (that is to saie); That he the saide Peeter Streete, his executours or assignes, shall & will att his or their owne propper costes & chardges well, woorkmanlike & substancyallie make, erect, sett upp and fully finishe in and by all thinges, accordinge to the true meaninge of theis presentes, with good, stronge and substancyall newe tymber and other necessarie stuff, all the saide fframe and other woorkes whatsoever in and uppon the saide plott or parcell of grounde (beinge not by anie aucthoretie restrayned, and haveinge ingres, egres & regres to doe the same) before the ffyve & twentith daie of Julie next commeinge after the date hereof; And

---

4. Something like the V.I.P. boxes of the present day.
5. "Attiring house," a dressing room and backstage area extending onto the rear of the stage.
6. A roof (known as "the heavens") partially covering the stage, supported by the pillars that also served as versatile pieces of scenery.
7. Plan.
8. *in breadth . . . yarde:* the stage would then extend

about twenty-seven feet into the yard, specified earlier as fifty-five feet square.
9. Coated both on the "ceiling" (a related word) and the walls.
1. Finished in the form of pilasters, ornamental columns in the classical style.
2. Satyrs. *proporcions:* figures.
3. Plastering.

shall alsoe at his or theire like costes and chardges provide and finde all manner of woorkmen, tymber, joystes, rafters, boordes, dores, boltes, hinges, brick, tyle, lathe, lyme, haire, sande, nailes, lade, iron, glasse, woorkmanshipp and other thinges whatsoever, which shalbe needefull, convenyent & necessarie for the saide fframe & woorkes & everie parte thereof; And shall alsoe make all the saide fframe in every poynte for Scantlinges[4] lardger and bigger in assize then the Scantlinges of the timber of the saide newe erected howse called the Globe; And alsoe that he the saide Peeter Streete shall furthwith, aswell by himself as by suche other and soemanie woorkmen as shalbe convenient & necessarie, enter into and uppon the saide buildinges and woorkes, and shall in reasonable manner proceede therein withoute anie wilfull detraccion untill the same shalbe fully effected and finished. In consideracion of all which buildinges and of all stuff & woorkemanshipp thereto belonginge, the saide Phillipp Henslowe & Edward Allen and either of them, ffor themselves, theire, and either of theire executours & administratours, doe joynctlie & severallie covenante & graunte to & with the saide Peeter Streete, his executours & administratours by theis presentes, that they the saide Phillipp Henslowe & Edward Allen or one of them, or the executours administratours or assignes of them or one of them, shall & will well & truelie paie or cawse to be paide unto the saide Peeter Streete, his executours or assignes, att the place aforesaid appoynted for the erectinge of the saide fframe, the full somme of Fower hundred & Fortie Poundes of lawfull money of Englande in manner & forme followeinge (that is to saie), att suche tyme and when as the Tymberwoork of the saide fframe shalbe rayzed & sett upp by the saide Peeter Streete his executours or assignes, or within seaven daies then next followeinge, Twoe hundred & Twentie poundes, and att suche time and when as the saide fframe & woorkes shalbe fullie effected & ffynished as is aforesaide, or within seaven daies then next followeinge, thother Twoe hundred and Twentie poundes, withoute fraude or coven.[5] Provided allwaies, and it is agreed betwene the saide parties, that whatsoever somme or sommes of money the saide Phillipp Henslowe & Edward Allen or either of them, or thexecutours or assignes of them or either of them, shall lend or deliver unto the saide Peter Streete his executours or assignes, or anie other by his appoyntemente or consent, ffor or concerninge the saide woorkes or anie parte thereof or anie stuff thereto belonginge, before the raizeinge & settinge upp of the saide fframe, shalbe reputed, accepted, taken & accoumpted in parte of the firste paymente aforesaid of the saide some of Fower hundred & Fortie poundes, and all suche somme & sommes of money, as they or anie of them shall as aforesaid lend or deliver betwene the razeinge of the saide fframe & finishinge thereof and of all the rest of the saide woorkes, shalbe reputed, accepted, taken & accoumpted in parte of the laste pamente aforesaid of the same somme of Fower hundred & Fortie poundes, anie thinge abovesaid to the contrary notwithstandinge. In witnes whereof the parties abovesaid to theis presente Indentures Interchaungeably have sett theire handes and seales. Geoven[6] the daie and yeare ffirste abovewritten.

P S

Sealed and delivered by the saide Peter Streete in the presence of me William Harris Pub[lic] Scr[ivener] And me Frauncis Smyth appr[entice] to the said Scr[ivener]
    [*Endorsed:*] Peater Streat ffor The Building of the Fortune.

Augustine Phillips, Francis Bacon, et al. on *Richard II* (1601)

[These extracts from testimony submitted at the Earl of Essex's trial for treason, and related documents, show that some of Essex's supporters had contracted with the Lord Chamberlain's Men to revive *Richard II*, apparently in order to provide a model for the justified deposition of a monarch and thus propitiate the coup in which Essex planned to depose

4. Prescribed dimensions of the beams.   6. Given.
5. Deceit.

Elizabeth. The play was performed on February 7, and "it was on the same day," according to E. K. Chambers, "that Essex received a summons to appear before the Privy Council. This interrupted his plans for securing possession of the Queen's person and arresting her ministers, and precipitated his futile outbreak of February 8." Augustine Phillips was one of Shakespeare's colleagues in the Lord Chamberlain's Men. Sir Edward Coke was, for a time, chief justice under King James. The last excerpt is a contemporary record of a conversation between the queen and her archivist several months after Essex was executed. The texts are from WS, vol. 2.]

From the Abstract of Evidence

The Erle of Essex is charged with high Treason, namely, That he plotted and practised with the Pope and king of Spaine for the disposing and settling to himself Aswell the Crowne of England, as of the kingdom of Ireland.

From the Examination of Augustine Phillips, February 18, 1601

The Examination of Augustyne Phillypps servant unto the L Chamberlyne and one of hys players taken the xviij[th] of Februarij 1600 upon hys oth

He sayeth that on Fryday last was sennyght or Thursday S[r] Charles Percy S[r] Josclyne Percy and the L. Montegle with some thre more spak to some of the players in the presans of thys examinate to have the play of the deposyng and kyllyng of Kyng Rychard the second to be played the Saterday next promysyng to gete them xls. more then their ordynary to play yt. Wher thys Examinate and hys fellowes were determyned to have played some other play, holdyng that play of Kyng Richard to be so old & so long out of use as that they shold have small or no Company at yt. But at their request this Examinate and his fellowes were Content to play yt the Saterday and had their xls. more then their ordynary for yt and so played yt accordyngly

Augustine Phillipps

From the speech of Sir Edward Coke at Essex's trial, February 19

I protest upon my soul and conscience I doe beleeve she should not have long lived after she had been in your power. Note but the precedents of former ages, how long lived Richard the Second after he was surprised in the same manner? The pretence was alike for the removing of certain counsellors, but yet shortly after it cost him his life.

From [Francis Bacon's] "A Declaration of the . . . Treasons . . . by Robert late Earle of Essex"

The afternoone before the rebellion, Merricke,[1] with a great company of others, that afterwards were all in the action, had procured to bee played before them, the play of deposing King Richard the second. Neither was it casuall, but a play bespoken by Merrick. And not so onely, but when it was told him by one of the players, that the play was olde, and they should have losse in playing it, because fewe would come to it: there was fourty shillings extraordinarie given to play it, and so thereupon playd it was. So earnest hee was to satisfie his eyes with the sight of that tragedie which hee thought soone after his lord should bring from the stage to the state, but that God turned it upon their owne heads.

From a Memorandum in the Lambard family manuscript, August 4

. . . so her Majestie fell upon[2] the reign of King Richard II. saying, 'I am Richard II. know ye not that?'

---

1. Sir Gilly Merrick, one of Essex's supporters, was later tried separately for treason.

2. Came across (in reading). The memorandum describes a scene in which the queen is reading over the

W.L. 'Such a wicked imagination was determined and attempted by a most unkind Gent. the most adorned creature that ever your Majestie made.'

Her Majestie. 'He that will forget God, will also forget his benefactors; this tragedy was played 40^{tie} times in open streets and houses.'

John Manningham on *Twelfth Night* and *Richard III* (1602)

[John Manningham (d. 1622) kept a diary during his time as a law student at the Middle Temple, recording the witticisms of his colleagues and a rich variety of anecdotes. The vibrant and boisterous life of the Inns of Court is also illustrated by the *Gesta Grayorum* (see above). The February entry describes the festivities organized for Candlemas Day at the Middle Temple, while the second recounts an anecdote related to Manningham by one Mr. Touse (this name is difficult to read in the manuscript). As with all the documents in this section, any date before March 25 is assigned to the following year according to our calendar, so that 1601 here becomes 1602 (New Style). The text is from the 1976 edition of Robert Sorlien (Hanover, N.H.: University Press of New England).]

Febr. 1601

2. At our feast wee had a play called "Twelve night, or what you will"; much like the commedy of errores, or Menechmi[1] in Plautus, but most like and neere to that in Italian called Inganni.[2] A good practise in it to make the steward beleeve his Lady widdowe[3] was in Love with him, by counterfayting a letter, as from his Lady, in generall termes, telling him what shee liked best in him, and prescribing his gesture in smiling, his apparraile, &c., and then when he came to practise, making him beleeve they tooke him to be mad.

Marche. 1601

13. . . . Upon a tyme when Burbidge played Rich[ard] 3. there was a Citizen grewe soe farr in liking with him, that before shee went from the play shee appointed him to come that night unto hir by the name of Ri[chard] the 3. Shakespeare, overhearing their conclusion, went before, was intertained, and at his game ere Burbidge came. Then message being brought that Richard the 3^d. was at the dore, Shakespeare caused returne to be made that William the Conquerour was before Rich[ard] the 3. Shakespeare's name William. (Mr. Touse.)

Letters Patent formalizing the adoption of the Lord Chamberlain's Men as the King's Men (May 19, 1603)

[James I issued the warrant ordering this patent shortly after his coronation, enhancing the status of Shakespeare's company. As retainers of the royal household with the title of Grooms of the Chamber, they performed at the court with increasing frequency (177 times between 1603 and 1616) and assisted occasionally with other court functions, but more important, they acted throughout the kingdom under the authority of the royal patent, whose scope the forceful wording below makes clear. The patent, bearing the Great Seal, was issued May 19 as ordered in the warrant of May 17. There is some evidence to suggest that James was particularly taken with Shakespeare's poetry, and the playwright's valorization of James's ancestry (as originating with Banquo) in *Macbeth* certainly suggests that Shakespeare cultivated his esteem. The text is from *ES*, vol. 2.]

---

archives that have been in the keeping of her interlocutor, William Lambard.

1. Source for *The Comedy of Errors.*
2. The two plays with this exact title (1562 and 1592) seem less likely to be "most like" *Twelfth Night* than another Italian play, *Ingannati* (1537), which has char-

acters named Fabio and Malevolti and makes reference to Twelfth Night (Epiphany).
3. Olivia is not a widow in the version of Shakespeare's play that has come down to us, though she is so described in one of Shakespeare's principal sources for the play.

Commissio specialis pro Laurencio Fletcher & Willelmo Shacke-speare et aliis[2]	James by the grace of god &c. To all Justices, Maiors, Sher-iffes, Constables, hedboroweses,[1] and other our Officers and lovinge Subjectes greetinge. Knowe yee that Wee of our spe-ciall grace, certeine knowledge, & mere motion[3] have

licenced and aucthorized and by theise presentes[4] doe licence and aucthorize theise our Servauntes Lawrence Fletcher, William Shakespeare, Richard Burbage, Augustyne Phillippes, John Heninges, Henrie Condell, William Sly, Robert Armyn, Richard Cowly, and the rest of theire Assosiates freely to use and exercise the Arte and faculty of playinge Comedies, Tragedies, histories, Enterludes, moralls,[5] pastoralls, Stageplaies, and Suche others like as theie have alreadie studied or hereafter shall use or studie, aswell for the recreation of our lovinge Subjectes, as for our Solace and pleasure when wee shall thincke good to see them, duringe our pleasure. And the said Commedies, tragedies, histories, Enterludes, Morralles, Pastoralls, Stageplayes, and suche like to shewe and exercise publiquely to theire best Commoditie,[6] when the infection of the plague shall decrease, aswell within theire nowe usual howse called the Globe within our County of Surrey, as alsoe within anie towne halls or Moute halls[7] or other conveniente places within the liberties and freedome of anie other Cittie, universitie, towne, or Boroughe whatsoever within our said Realmes and domynions. Willinge and Commaundinge you and everie of you, as you tender our pleasure, not onelie to permitt and suffer them herein without anie your lettes hin-drances or molestacions during our said pleasure, but alsoe to be aidinge and assistinge to them, yf anie wronge be to them offered, And to allowe them such former Curtesies as hath bene given to men of theire place and quallitie,[8] and alsoe what further favour you shall shewe to theise our Servauntes for our sake wee shall take kindlie at your handes. In wytnesse whereof &c. witnesse our selfe at Westminster the nyntenth day of May

per breve de privato sigillo[9] &c.

Master of the Wardrobe's Account (March 1604)

[This entry offers us a rare glimpse of the players in the entourage of King James, sporting festive regalia in their capacity as Grooms of the Chamber. The royal procession took place March 15, 1604. The text is from WS, vol. 2.]

Red Clothe bought of sondrie persons and given by his Majestie to diverse persons against[1] his Majesties sayd royall proceeding through the Citie of London, viz.:— . . .

The Chamber . . .	
Fawkeners[2] &c. &c.	Red cloth
William Shakespeare	iiii yardes di.
Augustine Phillipps	"
Lawrence Fletcher	"
John Hemminges	"
Richard Burbidge	"
William Slye	"
Robert Armyn	"
Henry Cundell	"
Richard Cowley	"

1. A parish officer similar to a petty constable.
2. *Commissio . . . aliis:* By special commission on behalf of . . . and others.
3. Inclination, desire.
4. The present document.
5. Morality plays.
6. Advantage.
7. Council chambers.

8. Profession.
9. In sum, from the privy seal.
1. For.
2. Obsolete form of "falconers," very likely the men who trained the falcons used for James's fowl-hunting expeditions. The falconers might owe their place in the retinue to James's well-known passion for hunting.

Henry Jackson on *Othello* (September 1610)

[Several excerpts from the letters of Henry Jackson (d. 1662) of Corpus Christi College, Oxford, were made, probably after Jackson's death, by William Fulman, Jackson's successor in the college living of Meysey Hampton. One of these letters reveals that the King's Men played at Oxford in 1610, probably in September when the letter was written (the specific days are not given). After expressing some shock at the "violation" of Holy Scripture occurring in Jonson's *The Alchemist,* also in the repertoire of the King's Men, Jackson proceeds in the excerpt below to a more favorable discussion of the company's "tragedies," singling out *Othello* for special praise. Geoffrey Tillotson reprinted Fulman's transcripts in the *Times Literary Supplement* for July 20, 1933. The original letters do not survive.]

Habuerunt et Tragœdias, quas decorè, et aptè agebant. In quibus non solùm, dicendo, sed etiam faciendo quædam lachrymas movebant.—

—At verò Desdemona illa apud nos a marito occisa, quanquam optimè semper causam egit, interfecta tamen magis movebat; cum in lecto decumbens spectantium misericordiam ipso vultu imploraret.—

Sept. 1610.

They also had some tragedies, which they performed beautifully and with propriety. Among those, a few aroused tears, not only through their words, but even their gestures.—

—But truly Desdemona, having been killed by her husband before our eyes, although she pleaded her cause superbly throughout, nevertheless she moved [us] more after she had been murdered, when, lying upon her bed, her face itself implored pity from the onlookers.

Simon Forman on *Macbeth, Cymbeline,* and *The Winter's Tale* (1611)

[Simon Forman (1552–1611) was a largely self-educated physician and astrologer who rose from humble beginnings to establish a successful London practice. A large parcel of his manuscripts, including scientific and autobiographical material as well as the diary from which this account of the plays is taken, has survived, making his life one of the best-documented Elizabethan lives. These manuscripts provide detailed information about Forman's many sidelines, such as the manufacture of talismans, alchemy, and necromancy, as well about his sex life. The text is from WS, vol. 2.]

The Bocke of Plaies and Notes therof per formane for Common Pollicie[1]

In Mackbeth at the Glob, 1610 ⟨1611⟩, the 20 of Aprill ♄ (Saturday), ther was to be observed, firste, howe Mackbeth and Bancko, 2 noble men of Scotland, Ridinge thorowe a wod, the ⟨r⟩ stode before them 3 women feiries or Nimphes, And saluted Mackbeth, sayinge, 3 tyms unto him, haille Mackbeth, king of Codon;[2] for thou shalt be a kinge, but shalt beget No kinges, &c. Then said Bancko, What all to Mackbeth And nothing to me. Yes, said the nimphes, haille to thee Bancko, thou shalt beget kinges, yet be no kinge. And so they departed & cam to the Courte of Scotland to Dunkin king of Scotes, and yt was in the dais of Edward the Confessor. And Dunkin bad them both kindly wellcome, And made Mackbeth forth with Prince of Northumberland,[3] and sent him hom to his own castell, and appointed Mackbeth to provid for

---

1. *Common Pollicie:* practical use. Forman's title for his notes on plays is not printed in Chambers, but interpolated here from G. Blakemore Evans's transcription in the *Riverside Shakespeare.*

2. Cawdor.
3. Probably Forman's error; Duncan gives Macbeth the title Thane of Cawdor. Duncan's son Malcolm is the Prince of Northumberland.

him, for he would sup with him the next dai at night, & did soe. And Mackebeth contrived to kill Dunkin, & thorowe the persuasion of his wife did that night Murder the kinge in his own Castell, beinge his guest. And ther were many prodigies seen that night & the dai before. And when Mack Beth had murdred the kinge, the blod on his handes could not be washed of by Any meanes, nor from his wives handes, which handled the bloddi daggers in hiding them, By which means they became both moch amazed & Affronted. The murder being knowen, Dunkins 2 sonns fled, the on to England, the ⟨other to⟩ Walles, to save them selves, they being fled, they were supposed guilty of the murder of their father, which was nothinge so. Then was Mackbeth crowned kinge, and then he for feare of Banko, his old companion, that he should beget kinges but be no kinge him selfe, he contrived the death of Banko, and caused him to be Murdred on the way as he Rode. The next night, beinge at supper with his noble men whom he had bid to a feaste to the which also Banco should have com, he began to speake of Noble Banco, and to wish that he wer ther. And as he thus did, standing up to drincke a Carouse to him, the ghoste of Banco came and sate down in his cheier behind him. And he turninge About to sit down Again sawe the goste of Banco, which fronted him so, that he fell into a great passion of fear and fury, Utterynge many wordes about his murder, by which, when they hard that Banco was Murdred they Suspected Mackbet.

Then MackDove fled to England to the kinges sonn, And soe they Raised an Army, And cam into Scotland, and at Dunston Anyse overthrue Mackbet. In the meantyme whille Macdovee was in England, Mackbet slewe Mackdoves wife & children, and after in the battelle Mackdove slewe Mackbet.

Observe Also howe Mackbetes quen did Rise in the night in her slepe, & walke and talked and confessed all, & the docter noted her wordes.

Of Cimbalin king of England.

Remember also the storri of Cymbalin king of England, in Lucius tyme, howe Lucius Cam from Octavus Cesar for Tribut, and being denied, after sent Lucius with a greate Arme of Souldiars who landed at Milford haven, and Affter wer vanquished by Cimbalin, and Lucius taken prisoner, and all by means of 3 outlawes, of the which 2 of them were the sonns of Cimbalim, stolen from him when they were but 2 yers old by an old man whom Cymbalin banished, and he kept them as his own sonns 20 yers with him in A cave. And howe ⟨one⟩ of them slewe Clotan, that was the quens sonn, goinge to Milford haven to sek the love of Innogen the kinges daughter, whom he had banished also for lovinge his daughter,[4] and howe the Italian that cam from her love conveied him selfe into A Cheste, and said yt was a chest of plate sent from her love & others, to be presented to the kinge. And in the depest of the night, she being aslepe, he opened the cheste, & cam forth of yt, And vewed her in her bed, and the markes of her body, & toke awai her braslet, & after Accused her of adultery to her love, &c. And in thend howe he came with the Romains into England & was taken prisoner, and after Reveled to Innogen, Who had turned her self into mans apparrell & fled to mete her love at Milford haven, & chanchsed to fall on the Cave in the wodes wher her 2 brothers were, & howe by eating a sleping Dram they thought she had bin deed, & laid her in the wodes, & the body of Cloten by her, in her loves apparrell that he left behind him, & howe she was found by Lucius, &c.

In the Winters Talle at the glob 1611 the 15 of maye ☿ ⟨Wednesday⟩.

Observe ther howe Lyontes the kinge of Cicillia was overcom with Jelosy of his wife with the kinge of Bohemia his frind that came to see him, and howe he contrived his death and wold have had his cup berer to have poisoned, who gave the king of Bohemia warning therof & fled with him to Bohemia.

Remember also howe he sent to the Orakell of Appollo & the Annswer of Apollo,

---

4. Morgan/Belarius is not banished in the version of the play that comes down to us.

that she was giltles and that the king was jelouse &c. and howe Except the child was found Again that was loste the kinge should die without yssue, for the child was caried into Bohemia & ther laid in a forrest & brought up by a sheppard And the kinge of Bohemia his sonn maried that wentch & howe they fled into Cicillia to Leontes, and the sheppard having showed the letter of the nobleman by whom Leontes sent a was ⟨away?⟩ that child and the jewells found about her, she was knowen to be Leontes daughter and was then 16 yers old.

Remember also the Rog[5] that cam in all tottered like coll pixci[6] and howe he feyned him sicke & to have bin Robbed of all that he had and howe he cosened the por man of all his money, and after cam to the shep sher[7] with a pedlers packe & ther cosened them Again of all their money And howe he changed apparrell with the kinge of Bomia his sonn, and then howe he turned Courtier &c. Beware of trusting feined beggars or fawninge fellouss.

Chamber Account of Performances by the King's Men (May 1613)

[The performances of Shakespeare's company at court are especially well documented, because there were established systems of record keeping for the activities of the royal household. The players, as the King's Men, were officially Grooms of the Chamber, and it was this division of the royal household, under the supervision of the Lord Chamberlain, that organized entertainments, along with many other aspects of the operation of the court. The most significant item to the Treasurer of the Chamber who prepared the accounts was naturally the sum paid to the company on each occasion. In some instances, the titles of the plays given are also preserved, and the list given for May 20, when the company received payment (in two installments) for twenty plays given over the previous weeks, is especially complete. This list indicates the full range of the company's repertoire, which included many plays not by Shakespeare. The amount paid for the first group of plays was 93 pounds, 6 shillings, 8 pence, and for the second, smaller, group, 60 pounds. The text is from the first column of the accounts as reproduced under the heading "Payees" in *ES*, vol. 4.]

'To him [Hemynges] more'; 'fowerteene severall playes, viz: one playe called ffi-laster, One other called the knott of ffooles, One other Much adoe aboute nothinge, The Mayeds Tragedy, The merye dyvell of Edmonton, The Tempest, A kinge and no kinge, The Twins Tragedie, The Winters Tale, Sir John ffalstaffe,[1] The Moore of Venice,[2] The Nobleman, Caesars Tragedye, And on other called Love lyes a blee-dinge'.

'the sayd John Heminges'; 'Sixe severall playes, viz: one play called a badd begininge makes a good endinge, One other called y[e] Capteyne, One other the Alcumist. One other Cardenno, One other the Hotspur,[3] And one other called Benedicte and Betteris'.[4]

Sir Henry Wotton on *All Is True (Henry VIII)* and the Burning of the Globe (1613)

[Sir Henry Wotton (1568–1639), a highly educated poet and essayist, distinguished diplomat, and finally provost of Eton College, wrote to his nephew Sir Edmund Bacon shortly

5. Rogue (Autolycus).
6. Probably "colt-pixie," a mischievous sprite or fairy.
7. Sheep shearing.
1. *1* or *2 Henry IV*, or possibly *The Merry Wives of*

Windsor.
2. *Othello.*
3. *1 Henry IV.*
4. *Much Ado About Nothing.*

after the burning of the Globe. Chambers includes several other accounts of this incident in *The Elizabethan Stage*, vol. 2, pp. 419ff. The event is also recorded in John Stow's chronicles and was lamented by poets, including (several years later) Ben Jonson, and held up by Puritan divines like Prynne as an intimation of God's wrath. The excerpt below is from the earliest extant text, *Letters of Sir Henry Wotton to Sir Edmund Bacon* (London, 1661), p. 29.]

Now, to let matters of State sleep, I will entertain you at the present with what hath happened this week at the banks side. The Kings Players had a new Play, called *All is true*, representing some principall pieces of the raign of *Henry* 8, which was set forth with many extraordinary circumstances of Pomp and Majesty, even to the matting of the stage; the Knights of the Order, with their Georges and Garter, the Guards with their embroidered Coats, and the like: sufficient in truth within a while to make greatness very familiar, if not ridiculous. Now, King *Henry* making a Masque at the Cardinal, *Wolsey*'s house, and certain Chambers[1] being shot off at his entry, some of the paper, or other stuff wherewith one of them was stopped, did light on the thatch, where being thought at first but an idle smoak, and their eyes more attentive to the show, it kindled inwardly, and ran round like a train, consuming within less then an hour the whole house to the very grounds.

This was the fatal period of that vertuous fabrique, wherein yet nothing did perish, but wood and straw, and a few forsaken cloaks; only one man had his breeches set on fire, that would perhaps have broyled him, if he had not by the benefit of a provident wit put it out with bottle Ale. The rest when we meet.

Ballad on the Burning of the Globe (June 30, 1613)

[The ballad reprinted here may be one of the ballads on the burning of the Globe entered in the Stationers' Register on June 30, 1613, the day after the fire occurred. It survives only in a nineteenth-century transcript. The fire was in any case a significant news item, and topical ballads were often turned out rapidly, as a means of disseminating news, and sold cheaply on the streets as single printed sheets, or broadsides. The burning of the Globe had the additional appeal of being a peculiarly literary topic. The text is from ES, vol. 2.]

A Sonnett upon the pittiful burneing of the Globe playhowse in London.

Now sitt the downe, Melpomene,[1]
  Wrapt in a sea-cole robe,
And tell the dolefull tragedie,
  That late was playd at Globe;
For noe man that can singe and saye
[But?] was scard on St. Peters daye.[2]
  Oh sorrow, pittifull sorrow, and yett all this is true.[3]

All yow that please to understand,
  Come listen to my storye,
To see Death with his rakeing brand[4]
  Mongst such an auditorye;
Regarding neither Cardinalls might,
Nor yett the rugged face of Henry the Eight.
  Oh sorrow, &c.

1. Small pieces of artillery, used for firing salutes.
1. The muse of tragedy. *the:* thee.
2. June 29, the day of the fire. *scard:* Chambers's emendation; some such word appears to be missing.

3. Reference to the title of the "tragedie" being performed onstage at the time of the fire.
4. Torch; but also, blade—hence the traditional scythe of Death.

This fearfull fire beganne above,
 A wonder strange and true,
And to the stage-howse did remove,
 As round as taylors clewe;[5]
And burnt downe both beame and snagg,
And did not spare the silken flagg.[6]
  Oh sorrow, &c.

Out runne the knightes, out runne the lordes,
 And there was great adoe;
Some lost their hattes, and some their swordes;
 Then out runne Burbidge too;
The reprobates, though druncke on Munday,
Prayd for the Foole and Henry Condye.
  Oh sorrow, &c.

The perrywigges and drumme-heades frye,
 Like to a butter firkin;
A wofull burneing did betide
 To many a good buffe jerkin.
Then with swolne eyes, like druncken Flemminges,
Distressed stood old stuttering Heminges.[7]
  Oh sorrow, &c.

No shower his raine did there downe force
 In all that Sunn-shine weather,
To save that great renowned howse;
 Nor thou, O ale-howse, neither.[8]
Had itt begunne belowe, sans doubte,
Their wives for feare had pissed itt out.
  Oh sorrow, &c.

Bee warned, yow stage-strutters all,
 Least yow againe be catched,
And such a burneing doe befall,
 As to them whose howse was thatched;
Forbeare your whoreing, breeding biles,[9]
And laye up that expence for tiles.[1]
  Oh sorrow, &c.

Goe drawe yow a petition,
 And doe yow not abhorr itt,
And gett, with low submission,
 A licence to begg for itt
In churches, sans churchwardens checkes,
In Surrey and in Midlesex.
  Oh sorrow, pittifull sorrow, and yett all this is true.

---

5. A tailor's ball of thread. Probably a reference to the name "Globe" as well as the shape of the Globe, though not quite round.
6. A flag flying from the top of the theater to indicate that a performance was in progress.
7. John Heminges, Richard Burbadge, and Henry Condell were colleagues of Shakespeare in the King's Men.

8. Another report on the fire indicates that a house adjoining the Globe burned down as well. This house may be the same as the "ale-howse."
9. Boils.
1. Roof tiles, in place of the more flammable thatched roof. The rebuilt Globe, which opened a year after the fire, did in fact have a tile roof.

Ben Jonson on *The Tempest* (and *Titus Andronicus*) (1614)

[This extract from *Bartholomew Fair* contains one of several allusions to Shakespeare in the plays of his associate and sometime rival. The first paragraph alludes to the fashion for revenge plays such as Shakespeare's *Titus Andronicus* and Kyd's *Spanish Tragedy*, at its height roughly twenty-five years before *Bartholomew Fair* was written. The second paragraph refers disapprovingly to *The Tempest* (1613), first produced shortly before *Bartholomew Fair*. The text is that reprinted in WS, vol. 2, from the 1631 edition of Jonson's play (from the play's Induction).]

Hee that will sweare, *Jeronimo*, or *Andronicus* are the best playes, yet, shall passe unexcepted at,[2] heere, as a man whose Judgement shewes it is constant, and hath stood still, these five and twentie, or thirtie yeeres. . . .

If there bee never a *Servant-monster* i' the Fayre; who can helpe it? he[3] sayes; nor a nest of Antiques?[4] Hee is loth to make Nature afraid[5] in his *Playes*, like those that beget *Tales*, *Tempests*, and such like *Drolleries*, to mixe his head with other mens heeles; let the concupisence of *Jigges* and *Dances*, raigne as strong as it will amongst you.[6]

Francis Beaumont (?) on Shakespeare (c. 1615)

[Chambers was the first to print this poem in full, and the attribution to Francis Beaumont, a lawyer (not the playwright) who died in 1616, remains conjectural, though plausible. Not much is known about Beaumont's precise relationship to Jonson, but he had previously written a well-known verse-epistle to the poet, and theatrical allusions in this poem suggest a taste for the theater. The excerpted passage is remarkable as a precursor of the long-dominant view of Shakespeare as an untutored genius whose artistic accomplishment was due to the force of nature's gifts alone. In the lines preceding the excerpt, Beaumont amplifies the claim to authenticity of the love he wishes to express in the epistle by abjuring all stylistic refinement. The text is from WS, vol. 2.]

To Mr. B.J.

heere I would let slippe
(If I had any in mee) schollershippe,
And from all Learninge keepe these lines as ⟨cl⟩eere[7]
as Shakespeares best are, which our heires shall heare
Preachers apte to their auditors to showe
how farr sometimes a mortall man may goe
by the dimme light of Nature.

Shakespeare's Will (March 25, 1616)

[Shakespeare probably dictated this will sometime around January 1616. The first draft seems to have been dated in January, and 1616 is the most likely inference for the year (see note 1). The final revision was certainly made on the date given, but no clean copy was prepared, so the manuscript contains a substantial number of insertions and deletions.

2. Uncriticized.
3. The author.
4. Variant spelling of "antics," grotesque or ludicrous representations, or the actors (such as the clowns in *The Tempest*) playing such parts.
5. Make nature afraid by inexact imitation or too much fantasy.

6. *concupisence . . . you:* a reference to the dance generally incorporated into theatrical performance (see, for example, Platter's account above). Jonson suggests he is refusing to cater to the vulgar taste for more dancing in plays.
7. Chambers's emendation. The manuscript reads "deere," probably a scribal error.

The text here has been silently emended to assist in ease of reading. Deleted passages have been eliminated; the most significant of these is reproduced in the notes, where significant interlineations are also identified. Most of the altered passages, as Chambers writes, simply "correct slips, make the legal terminology more precise, or incorporate afterthoughts." The revision of the will was occasioned chiefly by the February marriage of Shakespeare's daughter Judith. Our text is adapted from E. A. J. Honigmann and Susan Brock, *Playhouse Wills, 1558–1642*. For a facsimile and thorough discussion of the will, see WS 2:169–80.]

Testamentum willelmij Shackspeare
Vicesimo Quinto die martij Anno Regni Domini nostri Jacobi nunc Regis Anglie &c decimo quarto & Scotie xlixo Annoque domini 1616[1]
In the name of god Amen I William Shackspeare of Stratford upon Avon in the countie of warrwick gentleman in perfect health & memorie god be praysed doe make & Ordayne this my last will & testament in manner & forme followeing That ys to saye ffirst I Comend my Soule into the handes of god my Creator hoping & assuredlie beleeving through thonelie merittes of Jesus Christe my Saviour to be made partaker of lyfe everlastinge And my bodye to the Earth whereof yt ys made Item I Gyve & bequeath unto my Daughter Judyth One Hundred & ffyftie poundes of law-full English money to be paied unto her in manner & forme followeing That ys to saye One Hundred Poundes in discharge of her marriage porcion[2] within one yeare after my Deceas with consideracion[3] after the Rate of twoe shillinges in the pound for soe long tyme as the same shalbe unpaied unto her after my deceas & the ffyftie poundes Residewe thereof upon her Surrendring of or gyving of such sufficient securi-tie as the overseers of this my Will shall like of to Surrender or graunnte All her[4] estate & Right that shall discend or come unto her after my deceas or that shee nowe hath of in or to one Copiehold tenemente with thappurtenaunces lyeing & being in Stratford upon Avon aforesaied in the saied countie of warrwick being parcell or holden of the mannour of Rowington unto my Daughter Susanna Hall & her heires for ever Item I Gyve & bequeath unto my saied Daughter Judith One Hundred & ffyftie Poundes more if shee or Anie issue of her bodie be Lyvinge att thend of three Yeares next ensueing the daie of the Date of this my Will during which tyme my executours to paie her consideracion from my deceas according to the Rate afore saied And if she dye within the saied terme without issue of her bodye then my will ys & I doe gyve & bequeath One Hundred Poundes thereof to my Neece Elizabeth Hall & the ffiftie Poundes to be sett fourth by my executours during the lief of my Sister Johane Harte & the use & proffitt thereof Cominge shalbe payed to my saied Sister Jone & after her deceas the saied l li[5] shall Remaine Amongst the children of my saied Sister Equallie to be Devided Amongst them But if my saied Daughter Judith be lyving att thend of the saied three Yeares or anie yssue of her bodye then my Will ys & soe I devise & bequeath the saied Hundred & ffyftie poundes to be sett out by my executours & overseers for the best benefitt of her & her issue & the stock[6] not to be paied unto her soe long as she shalbe marryed & Covert Baron[7] but my will ys that she shall have the consideracon yearelie paied unto her during her lief & after her deceas the saied stock and consideracion to bee paied to her children if she have Anie & if not to her executours or assignes she lyving the saied terme after my deceas Provided that if such husbond as she shall att thend of the saied three Yeares be marryed unto or attaine after doe sufficientle Assure unto her & thissue of her bodie landes Awnswereable to the porcion by this my will gyven unto her & to be adjudged

1. *Testamentum . . . 1616*: The Will of William Shake-speare (marginal heading). On the twenty-fifth day of March, in the fourteenth year of the reign of our lord James now King of England, etc., and of Scotland the forty-ninth, in the year of our Lord 1616. (The abbrevia-tion for "January" is crossed out in the manuscript, "March" having been substituted at the time the will was revised.)

2. The phrase "in discharge of her marriage porcion" was inserted during the course of revision.
3. Compensation, or interest.
4. Susanna Hall's. (The preceding "All" marks the beginning of a new sentence.)
5. *l li*: fifty pounds.
6. Principal.
7. *Covert Baron*: under the protection of a husband.

soe by my executours & overseers then my will ys that the saied Cl li[8] shalbe paied to such husbond as shall make such assurance to his owne use Item I gyve & bequeath unto my saied sister Jone xx li & all my wearing Apparrell to be paied & Delivered within one yeare after my deceas And I doe Will & devise unto her the house with thappurtenaunces in Stratford wherein she dwelleth for her naturall lief under the yearelie Rent of xii d. Itm I gyve & bequeath unto her three sonns William Harte[9] hart & Michaell Harte ffyve poundes A peece to be payed within one Yeare after my deceas[1] Item I gyve & bequeath unto her the saied Elizabeth Hall All my Plate (except my brod silver & gilt bole)[2] that I nowe have att the Date of this my Will Itm I gyve & bequeath unto the Poore of Stratford aforesaied tenn poundes to mr Thomas Combe my Sword to Thomas Russell Esquier ffyve poundes & to ffrauncis Collins of the Borough of Warrwick in the countie of Warrwick gentleman thirteene poundes Sixe shillinges & Eight pence to be paied within one Yeare after my Deceas Itm I gyve & bequeath to Hamlett Sadler xxvi s viii d[3] to buy him A Ringe to William Raynoldes gentleman xxvi s viii d to buy him A Ringe to my godson William Walker xx s in gold to Anthonye Nashe gentleman xxvi s viii d & to mr John Nashe xx vi s viii d & to my fellows John Hemynnges Richard Burbage & Henry Cundell xxvi s viii d A peece to buy them Ringes[4] Item I Gyve Will bequeath & Devise unto my Daughter Susanna Hall for better enabling of her to performe this my will & towardes the performans thereof All that Capitall messuage or tenemente[5] with thappurtenaunces in Stratford aforesaied Called the newe place Wherein I nowe Dwell & twoe mes-suages or tenementes with thappurtenaunces scituat lyeing & being in Henley streete within the borough of Stratford aforesaied And all my barnes stables Orchardes gar-dens landes tenementes & hereditamentes[6] Whatsoever scituat lyeing & being or to be had Receyved perceyved or taken within the townes Hamlettes villages ffieldes & groundes of Stratford upon Avon Oldstratford Bushopton & Welcombe or in anie of them in the saied countie of warrwick And alsoe All that Messuage or tenemente with thappurtenaunces wherein one John Robinson dwelleth scituat lyeing & being in the blackfriers in London nere the Wardrobe & all other my landes tenementes & hereditamentes Whatsoever To Have & to hold All & singuler the saied premisses with their Appurtenaunces unto the saied Susanna Hall for & During the terme of her naturall lief & after her Deceas to the first sonne of her bodie lawfullie Issueing & to the heires males of the bodie of the saied first Sonne lawfullie Issueinge & for defalt of such issue to the second Sonne of her bodie lawfullie issueinge & to the heires males of the bodie of the saied Second Sonne lawfullie issueinge & for defalt of such heries to the third Sonne of the bodie of the saied Susanna Lawfullie issueing & of the heires males of the bodie of the saied third sonne lawfullie issueing And for defalt of such issue the same soe to be & Remaine to the ffourth ffyfth sixte & Seaventh sonnes of her bodie lawfullie issueing one after Another & to the heires[7] Males of the bodies of the saied ffourth fifth Sixte & Seaventh sonnes lawfullie issueing in such manner as yt ys before Lymitted to be & Remaine to the first second & third Sonns of her bodie & to their heires males And for defalt of such issue the saied premisses to

---

8. *Cl li:* One hundred fifty pounds.
9. A blank in the manuscript. Shakespeare appears to have forgotten the name of one of his nephews, Thomas.
1. *unto . . . deceas:* this passage was inserted at the top of the second page, probably when the will was revised. The following lines, with which the page originally began, are crossed out in the original: "to be sett out for her within one Yeare after my Deceas by my executours with thadvise & direccions of my overseers for her best proffitt untill her Marriage & then the same with the increase thereof to be paied unto her." These lines evi-dently referred to Judith Shakespeare as unmarried.
2. This parenthetical clause is an insertion, and has sparked some debate about Shakespeare's opinion of

Judith's marriage.
3. The "s" stands for "shillings," the "d" for "pence."
4. *to my fellows . . . Ringes:* Shakespeare's "fellows," or colleagues, Heminges, Burbage, and Condell, had worked with him in the Lord Chamberlain's Men and King's Men for many years. Many other wills and docu-ments of the period provide evidence of the practice of wearing mourning rings alluded to here.
5. Residence. *messuage:* dwelling house with its out-buildings or adjoining lands.
6. Heritable property.
7. In addition to the signature near the end, Shake-speare signed the will here, in the bottom right-hand corner of the second page.

be & Remaine to my sayed Neece Hall[8] & the heires Males of her bodie Lawfullie yssueing for Defalt of such issue to my Daughter Judith & the heires Males of her bodie lawfullie issueinge And for Defalt of such issue to the Right heires of me the saied William Shackspere for ever Itm I gyve unto my wief my second best bed[9] with the furniture Item I gyve & bequeath to my saied Daughter Judith my broad silver gilt bole All the Rest of my goodes Chattelles Leases plate Jewels & household stuffe Whatsoever after my dettes and Legasies paied & my funerall expences discharged I gyve Devise & bequeath to my Sonne in Lawe John Hall gentleman & my Daughter Susanna his wief Whom I ordaine & make executours of this my Last Will & testament And I doe intreat & Appoint the saied Thomas Russell Esquier & ffrauncis Collins gentleman to be overseers hereof And doe Revoke All former wills & publishe this to be my last Will & testament In Witnes Whereof I have here unto put my hand the Daie & Yeare first above Written. / By me William Shakespeare witnes to the publishing hereof Fra: Collyns Julyus Shawe John Robinson Hamnet Sadler Robert Whattcott[1]

William Basse's Elegy for Shakespeare (1616–23)

[This highly literary elegy was written sometime between 1616 and 1623 by William Basse (c. 1583–c. 1653), of whom Chambers reports that he "was an Oxford student and a retainer of Lord Wenman of Thame." In numerous manuscript sources, the poem is ascribed to Basse, and in the 1640 *Poems: Written by Wil. Shake-speare, Gent.*, it is subscribed "W. B.," but it was also published in the 1633 edition of John Donne's poetry. In one source, "comedian" is substituted for the "Tragœdian" of line 12. The text is from WS, vol. 2.]

On Mr. Wm. Shakespeare
he dyed in Aprill 1616.

Renowned Spencer, lye a thought more nye
To learned Chaucer, and rare Beaumont lye
A little neerer Spenser to make roome
For Shakespeare in your threefold fowerfold Tombe.
To lodge all fowre in one bed make a shift
Untill Doomesdaye, for hardly will a fift
Betwixt this day and that by Fate be slayne
For whom your Curtaines may be drawn againe.
If your precedency in death doth barre
A fourth place in your sacred sepulcher,
Under this carved marble of thine owne
Sleep rare Tragœdian Shakespeare, sleep alone,
Thy unmolested peace, unshared Cave,
Possesse as Lord not Tenant of thy Grave,
 That unto us and others it may be
 Honor hereafter to be layde by thee.

Wm. Basse

8. Susanna Hall's daughter Elizabeth, actually Shakespeare's granddaughter (the sense of "niece" is less restricted in early modern usage). Elizabeth proved to be Susanna's only surviving child, and since Susanna was already thirty-three in 1616, the hypothetical series of seven sons preceding this mention of Elizabeth is doubly remarkable.
9. This bequest to Shakespeare's wife, Anne, was inserted in the course of his revision of the will. She is not mentioned elsewhere in the will at least partly because, as Shakespeare's widow, she would be guaranteed a certain portion of the estate by law. The appearance of this inserted bequest is nevertheless strange enough to have evoked much speculation.
1. After Shakespeare's death, the will was endorsed here at the bottom of the third page with a Latin inscription indicating that the will had gone to probate before a magistrate on June 22, 1616.

Nicholas Richardson on *Romeo and Juliet* (1620)

[The following passage from *Romeo and Juliet*, together with the note describing its spiritual application, is recorded in an early seventeenth-century commonplace book. The recorder had evidently heard the sermons in which Richardson, a Church of England clergyman, used the passage (slightly misquoted here) from Shakespeare, and was impressed by them. Of Richardson it is known that he became a fellow of Magdalen College, Oxford, in 1614. The text is from WS, vol. 2.]

> 'Tis almost morning I would have thee gone
> And yet no farther then a wantons bird,
> That lets it hop a little from his hand,
> Like a poore prisoner, in his twisted gyves,
> Then with a silken thread plucks it back againe
> So jealous loving of his liberty. Tragedy of
> Romeo and Juliet. 40: pag. 84:
> Said by Juliet: pro eadem.[1]

this Mr Richard^son Coll. Magd: inserted hence into his Sermon, preached it twice a^t St Maries 1620. 1621. applying it to gods love to his Saints either hurt with sinne, or adversity never forsaking thè.[2]

Front Matter from the First Folio of Shakespeare's Plays (1623)

[John Heminges and Henry Condell, friends and colleagues of Shakespeare, organized this first publication of his collected (thirty-six) plays. Eighteen of the plays had not appeared in print before, and for these the First Folio is the sole surviving source. Only *Pericles*, *The Two Noble Kinsmen*, and *Sir Thomas More* are not included in the volume. The first twelve (printed) pages of the Folio are reproduced below in reduced facsimile, with a minimum of explanatory notes. This "front matter" includes Droeshout's portrait of Shakespeare, Jonson's brief address "To the Reader" along with four other commendatory poems, two epistles by Heminges and Condell, a table of contents, and a list of actors, followed by the first page of text from *The Tempest*.]

---

1. On her own behalf.   2. Them.

To the Reader.

This Figure, that thou here feeſt put,
    It was for gentle Shakeſpeare cut;
Wherein the Grauer had a ſtrife
    with Nature, to out-doo the life :
O, could he but haue drawne his wit
    As well in braſſe, as he hath hit
His face ; the Print would then ſurpaſſe
    All, that was euer writ in braſſe.
But, ſince he cannot, Reader, looke
    Not on his Picture, but his Booke.

                                    B. I.

Mr. WILLIAM
SHAKESPEARES

COMEDIES,
HISTORIES, &
TRAGEDIES.

Publiſhed according to the True Originall Copies.

Martin Droeshout ſculpſit London.

LONDON
Printed by Iſaac Iaggard, and Ed. Blount. 1623.

TO THE MOST NOBLE
And
INCOMPARABLE PAIRE
OF BRETHREN.

William
Earle of Pembroke, &c. Lord Chamberlaine to the
Kings most Excellent Maiesty.

AND

Philip
Earle of Montgomery, &c. Gentleman of his Maiesties
Bed-Chamber. Both Knights of the most Noble Order
of the Garter, and our singular good
LORDS.

Right Honourable,

 *Hilst we studie to be thankful in our particular, for
the many fauors we haue receiued from your L.L
we are falne vpon the ill fortune, to mingle
two the most diuerse things that can bee, feare,
and rashnesse; rashnesse in the enterprize, and
feare of the successe.* For, when we valew the places your H.H.
sustaine, we cannot but know their dignity greater, then to descend to
the reading of these trifles: and, vvhile we name them trifles, we haue
depriu'd our selues of the defence of our Dedication. But since your
L.L. haue beene pleas'd to thinke these trifles some-thing, heereto-
fore; and haue prosequuted both them, and their Authour liuing,
vvith so much fauour: we hope, that (they out-liuing him, and he not
hauing the fate, common with some, to be exequutor to his owne writings) you will vse the like indulgence toward them, you haue done
$A2$ unto

Line 2. *L.L.*: Lordships.
Line 6. *places*: rank(s), status. *H.H.*: Highnesses.

Line 11. *prosequuted*: pursued.

The Epiſtle Dedicatorie.

vnto their parent. There is a great difference, vvhether any Booke choose his Patrones, or finde them : This hath done both. For, ſo much were your L L. likings of the ſeuerall parts, vvhen they were acted, as before they vvere publiſhed, the Volume ask'd to be yours. We haue but collected them, and done an office to the dead, to procure his Orphanes, Guardians; vvithout ambition either of ſelfe-profit, or fame: onely to keepe the memory of ſo worthy a Friend, & Fellow aliue, as was our SHAKESPEARE, *by humble offer of his playes, to your moſt noble patronage. Wherein, as we haue iuſtly obſerued, no man to come neere your L.L. but vvith a kind of religious addreſſe; it hath bin the height of our care, vvho are the Preſenters, to make the preſent worthy of your H.H. by the perfection. But, there we muſt alſo craue our abilities to be conſiderd, my Lords. We cannot go beyond our owne powers. Country hands reach foorth milke, creame, fruites, or what they haue : and many Nations (we haue heard) that had not gummes & incenſe, obtained their requeſts with a leauened Cake. It vvas no fault to approch their Gods, by what meanes they could: And the moſt, though meaneſt, of things are made more precious, when they are dedicated to Temples. In that name therefore, we moſt humbly conſecrate to your H.H. theſe remaines of your ſeruant* Shakeſpeare; *that what delight is in them, may be euer your L.L. the reputation his, & the faults ours, if any be committed, by a payre ſo carefull to ſhew their gratitude both to the liuing, and the dead, as is*

Your Lordſhippes moſt bounden,

IOHN HEMINGE.
HENRY CONDELL.

To the great Variety of Readers.

Rom the moſt able,to him that can but ſpell: There you are number'd.We had rather you were weighd. Eſpecially, when the fate of all Bookes depends vpon your capacities : and not of your heads alone, but of your purſes. Well ! It is now publique, & you wil ſtand for your priuiledges wee know : to read, and cenſure. Do ſo,but buy it firſt. That doth beſt commend a Booke, the Stationer ſaies. Then,how odde ſoeuer your braines be, or your wiſedomes, make your licence the ſame,and ſpare not. Iudge your ſixe-pen'orth, your ſhillings worth, your fiue ſhillings worth at a time, or higher, ſo you riſe to the iuſt rates, and welcome. But, what euer you do, Buy. Cenſure will not driue a Trade, or make the Iacke go. And though you be a Magiſtrate of wit, and ſit on the Stage at *Black-Friers*, or the *Cock-pit*, to arraigne Playes dailie, know, theſe Playes haue had their triall alreadie, and ſtood out all Appeales ; and do now come forth quitted rather by a Decree of Court, then any purchas'd Letters of commendation.

It had bene a thing, we confeſſe, worthie to haue bene wiſhed,that the Author himſelfe had liu'd to haue ſet forth, and ouerſeen his owne writings ; But ſince it hath bin ordain'd otherwiſe,and he by death departed from that right,we pray you do not envie his Friends,the office of their care, and paine, to haue collected & publiſh'd them ; and ſo to haue publiſh'd them, as where (before) you were abuſ'd with diuerſe ſtolne, and ſurreptitious copies, maimed,and deformed by the frauds and ſtealthes of iniurious impoſtors, that expoſ'd them : euen thoſe, are now offer'd to your view cur'd, and perfect of their limbes; and all the reſt, abſolute in their numbers, as he conceiued thē.Who,as he was a happie imitator of Nature,was a moſt gentle expreſſer of it.His mind and hand went together: And what he thought, he vttered with that eaſineſſe, that wee haue ſcarſe receiued from him a blot in his papers. But it is not our prouince,who onely gather his works, and giue them you, to praiſe him. It is yours that reade him. And there we hope,to your diuers capacities, you will finde enough, both to draw, and hold you : for his wit can no more lie hid, then it could be loſt. Reade him, therefore ; and againe, and againe : And if then you doe not like him, ſurely you are in ſome manifeſt danger, not to vnderſtand him. And ſo we leaue you to other of his Friends, whom if you need,can bee your guides : if you neede them not, you can leade your ſelues,and others. And ſuch Readers we wiſh him.

A 3   *Iohn Heminge.*
     Henrie Condell.

Line 8. *Stationer:* bookseller.
Line 13. *Iacke:* machine.
Lines 13–14. *And though . . . dailie:* addressed in particular to men of fashion who occupied seats onstage so they could be seen while watching the play.
Lines 15–17. *these Playes . . . commendation:* the legal puns that began with "Magistrate of wit" (fashionable playgoer) in line 13 continue here. The "purchas'd Letters of commendation" refer to escaping the conse-
quences of a crime by means of bribery or other undue influence; Shakespeare's plays, by contrast, have been acquitted after a proper and rigorous trial (approved by theater audiences and not insinuated into the public favor by some outside influence).
Line 27. *absolute in their numbers:* correct in their versification. *the:* them.
Line 28. *a happie:* an apt; a successful.

To the memory of my beloued,
The AVTHOR
Mr. WILLIAM SHAKESPEARE:
AND
what he hath left vs.

T O draw no enuy (Shakespeare) on thy name,
    Am I thus ample to thy Booke, and Fame:
While I confesse thy writings to be such,
As neither Man, nor Muse, can praise too much.
'Tis true, and all mens suffrage. But these wayes
    Were not the paths I meant vnto thy praise:
For seeliest Ignorance on these may light,
    Which, when it sounds at best, but eccho's right;
Or blinde Affection, which doth ne're aduance
    The truth, but gropes, and vrgeth all by chance;
Or crafty Malice, might pretend this praise,
    And thinke to ruine, where it seem'd to raise.
These are, as some infamous Baud, or whore,
    Should praise a Matron. What could hurt her more?
But thou art proofe against them, and indeed
    Aboue th'ill fortune of them, or the need.
I, therefore will begin. Soule of the Age!
    The applause! delight! the wonder of our Stage!
My Shakespeare, rise; I will not lodge thee by
    Chaucer, *or* Spenser, *or bid* Beaumont *lye*
A little further, to make thee a roome:
    Thou art a Moniment, without a tombe,
And art aliue still, while thy Booke doth liue,
    And we haue wits to read, and praise to giue.
That I not mixe thee so, my braine excuses;
    I meane with great, but disproportion'd Muses:
For, if I thought my iudgement were of yeeres,
    I should commit thee surely with thy peeres,
And tell, how farre thou didst our Lily *out-shine,*
    Or sporting Kid, *or* Marlowes *mighty line.*
And though thou hadst small Latine, *and lesse* Greeke,
    From thence to honour thee, I would not seeke
For names; but call forth thund'ring Æschilus,
    Euripides, *and* Sophocles *to vs,*
Paccuuius, Accius, *him of* Cordoua *dead,*
    To life againe, to heare thy Buskin tread,
And shake a Stage: Or, when thy Sockes were on,
    Leaue thee alone, for the comparison

Of

Of all, that insolent Greece, *or haughtie* Rome
 sent forth, or since did from their ashes come.
Triumph, my Britaine, *thou hast one to showe,*
 To whom all Scenes of Europe *homage owe.*
He was not of an age, but for all time !
 And all the Muses *still were in their prime,*
when like Apollo *he came forth to warme*
 Our eares, or like a Mercury *to charme !*
Nature her selfe was proud of his designes,
 And ioy'd to weare the dressing of his lines !
which were so richly spun, and wouen so fit,
 As since, she will vouchsafe no other Wit.
The merry Greeke, *tart* Aristophanes,
 Neat Terence, *witty* Plautus, *now not please;*
But antiquated, and deserted lye
 As they were not of Natures family.
Yet must I not giue Nature all : Thy Art,
 My gentle Shakespeare, *must enioy a part.*
For though the Poets *matter, Nature be,*
 His Art doth giue the fashion. And, that he,
Who casts to write a liuing line, must sweat,
 (such as thine are) and strike the second heat
Vpon the Muses *anuile : turne the same,*
 (And himselfe with it) that he thinkes to frame;
Or for the lawrell, he may gaine a scorne,
 For a good Poet's *made, as well as borne.*
And such wert thou. Looke how the fathers face
 Liues in his issue, euen so, the race
Of Shakespeares *minde, and manners brightly shines*
 In his well torned, and true-filed lines :
In each of which, he seemes to shake a Lance,
 As brandish't at the eyes of Ignorance.
Sweet Swan of Auon! *what a sight it were*
 To see thee in our waters yet appeare,
And make those flights vpon the bankes of Thames,
 That so did take Eliza, *and our* Iames !
But stay, I see thee in the Hemisphere
 Aduanc'd, and made a Constellation there !
Shine forth, thou Starre of Poets, *and with rage,*
 Or influence, chide, or cheere the drooping Stage;
Which, since thy flight frō hence, hath mourn'd like night,
 And despaires day, but for thy Volumes light.

BEN: IONSON.

Vpon the Lines and Life of the Famous
Scenicke Poet, Mafter WILLIAM
SHAKESPEARE.

Hofe hands, which you fo clapt, go now, and wring
You *Britaines* braue; for done are *Shakefpeares* dayes :
His dayes are done, that made the dainty Playes,
Which made the Globe of heau'n and earth to ring.
Dry'de is that veine, dry'd is the *Thefpian* Spring,
Turn'd all to teares, and *Phœbus* clouds his rayes :
That corp's, that coffin now befticke thofe bayes,
Which crown'd him *Poet* firft, then *Poets* King.
If *Tragedies* might any *Prologue* haue,
All thofe he made, would fcarfe make one to this :
Where *Fame*, now that he gone is to the graue
(Deaths publique tyring-houfe) the *Nuncius* is.
 For though his line of life went foone about,
 The life yet of his lines fhall neuer out.

    HVGH HOLLAND.

Line 5. *Thespian:* the Greek poet Thespis was regarded as the originator of tragedy.
Line 6. *Phoebus:* Apollo; the sun.
Line 7. *besticke:* cover; infest. *bayes:* a crown of bay leaves was the traditional prize for the victors of Greek poetry contests.

Line 10. *All those.* All those tragedies. *this:* the great tragedy of Shakespeare's death.
Line 12. *publique tyring-house:* the tiring-house was the actors' dressing room; the grave is a public tiring-house because there every mortal prepares for Judgment Day.
Line 12. *Nuncius:* messenger.

A CATALOGVE

of the feuerall Comedies, Histories, and Tragedies contained in this Volume.

TO THE MEMORIE

of the deceafed Authour Maifter
W. SHAKESPEARE.

Hake-fpeare, *at length thy pious fellowes giue*
The world thy Workes: thy Workes,by which,out·liue
Thy Tombe, thy name muft· when that ftone is rent,
And Time diffolues thy Stratford *Moniment,*
Here we aliue fhall view thee ftill. This Booke,
When Braffe and Marble fade,fhall make thee looke
Frefh to all Ages: when Pofteritie
Shall loath what's new,thinke all is prodegie
That is not Shake-fpeares ; *eu'ry Line,each Verfe*
Here fhall reuiue,redeeme thee from thy Herfe.
Nor Fire,nor cankring Age,as Nafo *faid,*
Of his,thy wit-fraught Booke fhall once inuade.
Nor fhall I e're beleeue, or thinke thee dead
(Though mift)vntill our bankrout Stage be fped
(Impofsible) with fome new ftraine t'out-do
Pafsions of Iuliet,*and her* Romeo ;
Or till I heare a Scene more nobly take,
Then when thy half-Sword parlying Romans *fpake.*
Till thefe,till any of thy Volumes reft
Shall with more fire,more feeling be expreft,
Be fure,our Shake-fpeare, *thou canft neuer dye,*
But crown'd with Lawrell,liue eternally.

L. Digges.

To the memorie of M. *W.Shake-fpeare.*

VVE E *wondred* (Shake-fpeare) *that thou went'ft fo foone*
From the Worlds-Stage,to the Graues-Tyring-roome.
Wee thought thee dead, but this thy printed worth,
Tels thy Spectators,that thou went'ft but forth
To enter with applaufe. An Actors Art,
Can dye,and liue,to acte a fecond part.
That's but an Exit *of Mortalitie ;*
This, a Re-entrance to a Plaudite.

I. M.

Digges
Line 8. *prodegie:* freakish, deformed.
Line 11. *cankring age:* meddlesome or critical period of history. Naso is the Roman poet Ovid.
Line 14. *mist:* missed. *sped:* provided.

Line 15. *straine:* song or verse.
I. M.
Line 2. *Graves-Tyring-roome:* see note to Holland poem, line 12.
Line 8. *Plaudite:* accolade, applause.

The Workes of William Shakeſpeare,

containing all his Comedies, Hiſtories, and
Tragedies : Truely ſet forth, according to their firſt
ORIGINALL.

The Names of the Principall Actors
in all theſe Playes.

Illiam Shakeſpeare.	Samuel Gilburne.
Richard Burbadge.	Robert Armin.
John Hemmings.	William Oſtler.
Auguſtine Phillips.	Nathan Field.
William Kempt.	John Underwood.
Thomas Poope.	Nicholas Tooley.
George Bryan.	William Eccleſtone.
Henry Condell.	Joſeph Taylor.
William Slye.	Robert Benfield.
Richard Cowly.	Robert Goughe.
John Lowine.	Richard Robinſon.
Samuell Croſſe.	Iohn Shancke.
Alexander Cooke.	Iohn Rice.

I

THE TEMPEST.

Actus primus, Scena prima.

A tempestuous noise of Thunder and Lightning heard: Enter a Ship-master, and a Botefwaine.

Master.

Ote-swaine.

Botef. Heere Master: What cheere?

Maft. Good: Speake to th'Mariners: fall too't, yarely, or we run our felues a ground, beftirre, beftirre. *Exit.*

Enter Mariners.

Botef. Heigh my hearts, cheerely, cheerely my harts: yare, yare: Take in the toppe-fale: Tend to th'Mafters whiftle: Blow till thou burft thy winde, if roome enough.

Enter Alonfo, Sebaftian, Anthonio, Ferdinando, Gonzalo, and others.

Alon. Good Botefwaine haue care: where's the Mafter? Play the men.

Botef. I pray now keepe below.

Anth. Where is the Mafter, Bofon?

Botef. Do you not heare him? you marre our labour, Keepe your Cabines: you do afsift the ftorme.

Gonz. Nay, good be patient.

Botef. When the Sea is: hence, what cares thefe roarers for the name of King? to Cabine; filence: trouble vs not.

Gon. Good, yet remember whom thou haft aboord.

Botef. None that I more loue then my felfe. You are a Counfellor, if you can command thefe Elements to filence, and worke the peace of the prefent, wee will not hand a rope more, vfe your authoritie: If you cannot, giue thankes you haue liu'd fo long, and make your felfe readie in your Cabine for the mifchance of the houre, if it fo hap. Cheerely good hearts: out of our way I fay. *Exit.*

Gon. I haue great comfort from this fellow:methinks he hath no drowning marke vpon him, his complexion is perfect Gallowes: ftand faft good Fate to his hanging, make the rope of his deftiny our cable, for our owne doth little aduantage: If he be not borne to bee hang'd, our cafe is miferable. *Exit.*

Enter Botefwaine.

Botef. Downe with the top-Maft: yare, lower, lower, bring her to Try with Maine-courfe. A plague——

A cry within. *Enter Sebaftian, Anthonio & Gonzalo.*

vpon this howling: they are lowder then the weather, or our office: yet againe? What do you heere? Shal we giue ore and drowne, haue you a minde to finke?

Sebaf. A poxe o'your throat, you bawling, blafphemous incharitable Dog.

Botef. Worke you then.

Anth. Hang cur, hang, you whorefon infolent Noyfemaker, we are leffe afraid to be drownde, then thou art.

Gonz. I'le warrant him for drowning, though the Ship were no ftronger then a Nutt-fhell, and as leaky as an vnftanched wench.

Botef. Lay her a hold, a hold, fet her two courfes off to Sea againe, lay her off.

Enter Mariners wet.

Mari. All loft, to prayers, to prayers, all loft.

Botef. What muft our mouths be cold?

Gonz. The King, and Prince, at prayers, let's affift them, for our cafe is as theirs.

Sebaf. I'am out of patience.

An. We are meerly cheated of our liues by drunkards, This wide-chopt-rafcall, would thou mightft lye drowning the wafhing of ten Tides.

Gonz. Hee'l be hang'd yet, Though euery drop of water fweare againft it, And gape at widft to glut him. *A confufed noyfe within.* Mercy on vs.

We fplit, we fplit, Farewell my wife, and children, Farewell brother: we fplit, we fplit, we fplit.

Anth. Let's all finke with' King

Seb. Let's take leaue of him. *Exit.*

Gonz. Now would I giue a thoufand furlongs of Sea, for an Acre of barren ground: Long heath, Browne firrs, any thing; the wills aboue be done, but I would faine dye a dry death. *Exit.*

Scena Secunda.

Enter Profpero and Miranda.

Mira. If by your Art (my deereft father) you haue Put the wild waters in this Rote; alay them: The fkye it feemes would powre down ftinking pitch, But that the Sea, mounting to th' welkins cheeke, Dafhes the fire out. Oh! I haue fuffered With thofe that I faw fuffer: A braue veffell

A (Who

Leonard Digges on Shakespeare (1623–35)

[Leonard Digges (1588–1635) was a scholar apparently associated for most of his adult life with University College, Oxford. According to Chambers, he is remembered primarily as a translator, and G. Blakemore Evans adds that he was a scholar, traveler, and poet. It is impossible to date the following poem exactly, for Digges had been dead five years when it was printed as one of two commendatory poems in the opening pages of a 1640 edition of Shakespeare, *Poems: Written by Wil. Shake-speare, Gent.* He had written a shorter commendatory poem for the First Folio of 1623 (see above). The first forty lines of praise are quite conventional, but the discussion of specific plays and their impact on audiences is almost unique among such records of Shakespeare. The text is from the first edition (1640).]

Upon Master William Shakespeare, the Deceased Authour, and his Poems

Poets are borne not made,[1] when I would prove
This truth, the glad rememberance I must love
Of never dying *Shakespeare*, who alone
Is argument enough to make that one.
First, that he was a Poet none would doubt,
That heard th'applause of what he sees set out
Imprinted; where thou hast (I will not say
Reader his Workes for to contrive a Play:
To him twas none) the patterne of all wit,
Art without Art unparaleld as yet.
Next Nature onely helpt him, for looke thorow
This whole Booke, thou shalt find he doth not borrow,
One phrase from Greekes, nor Latines imitate,
Nor once from vulgar Languages Translate,
Nor Plagiari-like from others gleane,
Nor begges he from each witty friend a Scene
To peece his Acts with, all that he doth write,
Is pure his owne,[2] plot, language exquisite,
But oh! what praise more powerfull can we give
The dead, then that by him the Kings men live,
His Players, which should they but have shar'd the Fate,
All else expir'd within the short Termes date;
How could the Globe have prospered, since through want
Of change, the Plaies and Poems had growne scant.
But happy Verse thou shall be sung and heard,
When hungry quills shall be such honour bard,
Then vanish upstart Writers to each Stage,
You needy Poetasters of this Age,
Where *Shakespeare* liv'd or spake, Vermine forbeare,
Least with your froth you spot them, come not neere;
But if you needs must write, if poverty
So pinch, that otherwise you starve and die,
On Gods name may the Bull or Cockpit[3] have
Your lame blancke Verse, to keepe you from the grave
Or let new Fortunes younger brethren see,

1. A commonplace of the period, based on an anonymous Latin saying.
2. *Art without Art . . . owne:* another, more exaggerated view of Shakespeare's untutored genius and originality (compare Beaumont's poem, above).
3. The Red Bull, the Cockpit, and the Fortune (below) were other public theaters. The Fortune was rebuilt in 1623 after being destroyed by fire.

What they can picke from your leane industry.
I doe not wonder when you offer at
Blacke-Friers,[4] that you suffer; tis the fate
Of richer veines, prime judgements that have far'd
The worse, with this deceased man compar'd.
So have I seene, when Cesar would appeare,
And on the Stage at halfe-sword parley were,
Brutus and Cassius:[5] oh how the Audience,
Were ravish'd, with what wonder they went thence,
When some new day they would not brooke a line,
Of tedious (though well laboured) Catalines;
Sejanus[6] too was irkesome, they priz'de more
Honest Iago, or the jealous Moore.[7]
And though the Fox and subtill alchimist,[8]
Long intermitted could not quite be mist,
Though these have sham'd all the Ancients, and might raise,
Their Authours merit with a crowne of Bayes.
Yet these sometimes, even at a friends desire
Acted, have scarce defrai'd the Seacoale fire
And doore-keepers: when let but Falstaffe come,
Hall, Poines,[9] the rest you scarce shall have a roome
All is so pester'd: let but Beatrice
And Benedicke[1] be seene, loe in a trice
The Cockpit Galleries,[2] Boxes, all are full
To heare Malvoglio[3] that crosse garter'd Gull.
Briefe, there is nothing in his wit fraught Booke,
Whose sound we would not heare, on whose worth looke
Like old coynd gold, whose lines, in every page,
Shall passe true currant to succeeding age.
But why do I dread Shakespeares praise recite,
Some second Shakespeare must of Shakespeare write;
For me tis needlesse, since an host of men,
Will pay to clap his praise, to free my Pen.

Richard James on Falstaff (c. 1625)

[The following is one of several surviving discussions of Shakespeare's great comic character and his resemblance to the two actual personages for whom he was successively named,
Sir John Oldcastle and Sir John Falstaff. Richard James studied at Oxford and served as
librarian to Sir Robert Cotton. The text is an excerpt from the *Epistle* to Sir Harry Bour-
chier, as printed in WS, vol. 2.]

A young Gentle Lady of your acquaintance, having read ye works of Shakespeare,
made me this question. How Sr John Falstaffe, or Fastolf, as he is written in ye Statute
book of Maudlin[1] Colledge in Oxford, where everye day that society were bound to
make memorie of his soul, could be dead in ye time of Harrie ye Fift and again live in
ye time of Harrie ye Sixt to be banished for cowardice: Whereto I made answear that

4. The indoor, "private" theater acquired by the King's
Men in 1608 and used afterward along with the Globe.
5. See *Julius Caesar* 4.3.
6. Ben Jonson's two poorly received tragedies.
7. In *Othello*.
8. Jonson's comedies *Volpone* and *The Alchemist*.

9. Characters in *1* and *2 Henry IV*.
1. Characters in *Much Ado About Nothing*.
2. Standing room around the stage, more often known
simply as "the pit."
3. Character in *Twelfth Night*.
1. Magdalen.

it was one of those humours[2] and mistakes for which Plato banisht all poets out of his commonwealth.[3] That S[r] John Falstaffe was in those times a noble valiant souldier, as apeeres by a book in y[e] Heralds Office dedicated unto him by a Herald who had binne with him, if I well remember, for the space of 25 yeeres in y[e] French wars; that he seems also to have binne a man of learning, because, in a Library of Oxford, I find a book of dedicating Churches sent from him for a present unto Bishop Wainflete, and inscribed with his own hand. That in Shakespeares first shew of Harrie the fift, the person with which he undertook to playe a buffone was not Falstaffe, but Sir Jhon Oldcastle, and that offence beinge worthily taken by Personages descended from his title (as peradventure by many others allso whoe ought to have him in honourable memorie) the poet was putt to make an ignorant shifte of abusing Sir Jhon Falstophe, a man not inferior of Vertue, though not so famous in pietie as the other, who gave witnesse unto the truth of our reformation with a constant and resolute Martyrdom, unto which he was pursued by the Priests, Bishops, Moncks, and Friers of those days.

Milton on Shakespeare (1630)

[John Milton (1608–1674) was born in London and as a boy might conceivably have seen Shakespeare's company act. This poem first appeared prefixed to the Second Folio of Shakespeare's works in 1632, and again in the 1640 *Poems* of Shakespeare. The text is from the 1645 edition of Milton's *Poems*, as reprinted in WS, vol. 2, but the title given is from the Second Folio version.]

An Epitaph on the admirable Dramaticke Poet, W. Shakespeare

> What needs my *Shakespear* for his honour'd Bones,
> The labour of an age in piled Stones,
> Or that his hallow'd reliques should be hid
> Under a star-ypointing[1] *Pyramid?*
> Dear son of memory, great heir of Fame,
> What need'st thou such weak witnes of thy name?
> Thou in our wonder and astonishment
> Hast built thy self a live-long Monument.
> For whilst toth' shame of slow-endeavouring art,
> They easie numbers flow, and that each heart
> Hath from the leaves of thy unvalu'd[2] Book,
> Those Delphick[3] lines with deep impression took,
> Then thou our fancy of itself bereaving,[4]
> Dost make us Marble with too much conceaving;
> And so Sepulcher'd in such pomp dost lie,
> That Kings for such a Tomb would wish to die.

Ben Jonson on Shakespeare (1623–37)

[In addition to numerous allusions to Shakespeare in his plays, Ben Jonson (1573–1637) writes explicitly about his friend, colleague, and rival in a number of places, most significantly in the two commendatory poems prefixed to the First Folio (see above) and in the

---

2. Whims.
3. See the *Republic*, Books 2–3.
1. Pointing to the stars.
2. Invaluable.
3. Reference to Apollo, god of poetry, whose most

famous shrine was at Delphi.
4. *our ... bereaving:* "our imaginations are rapt 'out of ourselves,' leaving behind our soulless bodies like statues"—Isabel MacCaffrey.

published extracts from his notebooks entitled *Timber: or, Discoveries; Made upon Men and Matter*, first published in his *Works* of 1640. It is impossible to date the original entries precisely; Chambers's conjecture is that the following entry on Shakespeare was made after 1630. The text is from the authoritative edition of Herford and Simpson, vol. 8 (Oxford: Clarendon Press, 1952).]

Indeed, the multitude commend Writers, as they doe Fencers, or Wrastlers; who if they come in robustiously, and put for it, with a deale of violence, are received for the *braver-fellowes*: when many times their owne rudenesse is a cause of their disgrace; and a slight touch of their Adversary, gives all that boisterous force the foyle. But in these things, the unskilfull are naturally deceiv'd, and judging wholly by the bulke, thinke rude things greater then polish'd; and scatter'd more numerous, then compos'd: Nor thinke this only to be true in the sordid multitude, but the neater sort of our *Gallants*: for all are the multitude; only they differ in cloaths, not in judgement or understanding.

I remember, the Players have often mentioned it as an honour to *Shakespeare*, that in his writing, (whatsoever he penn'd) hee never blotted out line.[1] My answer hath beene, Would he had blotted a thousand. Which they thought a malevolent speech. [I had not told posterity this,] but for their ignorance, who choose that circumstance to commend their friend by, wherein he most faulted. And to justifie mine owne candor, (for I lov'd the man, and doe honour his memory (on this side Idolatry) as much as any.) Hee was (indeed) honest, and of an open, and free nature: had an excellent *Phantsie*[2]; brave notions, and gentle expressions: wherein hee flow'd with that facility, that sometime it was necessary he should be stop'd: *Sufflaminandus erat;*[3] as *Augustus* said of *Haterius*.[4] His wit was in his owne power; would the rule of it had beene so too. Many times hee fell into those things, could not escape laughter: As when hee said in the person of *Cæsar*, one speaking to him; *Cæsar, thou dost me wrong*. Hee replyed: *Cæsar did never wrong, but with just cause*[5]: and such like; which were ridiculous. But hee redeemed his vices, with his vertues. There was ever more in him to be praysed, then to be pardoned.

John Aubrey on Shakespeare (1681)

[What Chambers calls "the Shakespeare-mythos" was already well under way by the time John Aubrey (1626–1697) collected these anecdotes for the biographies in his *Brief Lives*, first anthologized in 1692. Aubrey's chief sources were prominent figures of the Restoration stage, which had seen increasingly popular revivals and adaptations of *Hamlet, The Tempest*, and many other plays of Shakespeare. Numerous actors and critics in the latter part of the seventeenth century helped to "rehabilitate" Shakespeare; if at the time of the Restoration his plays had seemed terribly musty and old-fashioned, by the 1680s his reputation as an author of lasting value was well established, thanks to the enthusiasm of Restoration playgoers. Aubrey's first source, Christopher Beeston, was the son of a one-time member of Shakespeare's company. William Davenant was a formidable entrepreneur as well as a dramatist, and Thomas Shadwell a prolific playwright perhaps best remembered as Dryden's King of Dullness. The text is from Chambers's transcription (WS, vol. 2), with a few silent emendations for ease of reading. Some of the material is from the published version of *Brief Lives*, and some of it from manuscript notes apparently used in writing the *Lives*.]

1. Compare Heminges and Condell's address to the reader in the First Folio: "And what he thought, he uttered with that easinesse, that wee have scarce received from him a blot in his papers."
2. Imagination.

3. "He needed the drag-chain" (adapted from Marcus Seneca's *Controversiae* 4, Preface).
4. Quintus Haterius, Roman rhetorician (d. A.D. 26).
5. See *Julius Caesar* 3.1.47.

the more to be admired q[uia][1] he was not a company keeper[2]
lived in Shoreditch, wouldnt be debauched, & if invited to
writ; he was in paine.[3]

W. Shakespeare.

M[r]. William Shakespear. [*bay-wreath in margin*] was borne at Stratford upon
Avon, in the County of Warwick; his father was a Butcher, & I have been told hereto-
fore by some of the neighbours, that when he was a boy he exercised his father's
Trade, but when he kill'd a Calfe, he would doe it in a *high style*, & make a Speech.
There was at that time another Butcher's son in this Towne, that was held not at all
inferior to him for a naturall witt, his acquaintance & coetanean,[4] but dyed young.
This Wm. being inclined naturally to Poetry and acting, came to London I guesse
about 18. and was an Actor at one of the Play-houses and did act exceedingly well:
now B. Johnson was never a good Actor, but an excellent Instructor. He began early
to make essayes at Dramatique Poetry, which at that time was very lowe; and his
Playes tooke well: He was a handsome well shap't man: very good company, and of
a very readie and pleasant smooth Witt. The Humour[5] of . . . the Constable in a
Midsomersnight's Dreame, he happened to take at Grendon [*In margin*, 'I thinke it
was Midsomer night that he happened to lye there'.] in Bucks[6] which is the roade
from London to Stratford, and there was living that Constable about 1642 when I first
came to Oxon.[7] M[r]. Jos. Howe is of that parish and knew him. Ben Johnson and he
did gather Humours of men dayly where ever they came. One time as he was at the
Tavern at Stratford super[8] Avon, one Combes an old rich Usurer was to be buryed,
he makes there this extemporary[9] Epitaph

> Ten in the Hundred[1] the Devill allowes
> But *Combes* will have twelve, he sweares & vowes:
> If any one askes who lies in this Tombe:
> Hoh! quoth the Devill, 'Tis my John o' Combe.

He was wont to goe to his native Country once a yeare. I thinke I have been told that
he left 2 or 300[li] per annum[2] there and therabout: to a sister. [*In margin*, 'V.[3] his
Epitaph in Dugdales Warwickshire'.] I have heard S[r] Wm. Davenant and M[r]. Thomas
Shadwell (who is counted the best Comœdian we have now) say, that he had a most
prodigious Witt, and did admire his naturall parts beyond all other Dramaticall writers. He was wont to say, That he never blotted out a line in his life: sayd Ben: Johnson,
I wish he had blotted out a thousand. [*In margin*, 'B. Johnsons Underwoods'.] His
Comœdies will remaine witt, as long as the English tongue is understood; for that he
handles mores hominum;[4] now our present writers reflect so much upon particular
persons, and coxcombeities, that 20 yeares hence, they will not be understood.
Though as Ben: Johnson sayes of him, that he had but little Latine and lesse Greek,
He understood Latine pretty well: for he had been in his younger yeares a Schoolmas-
ter in the Countrey. [*In margin*, 'from M[r] —— Beeston'.]

S[r] William Davenant Knight Poet Laureate was borne in ____ street in the City of
Oxford, at the Crowne Tavern. His father was John Davenant a Vintner there, a very

---

1. Because.
2. "Company keeper" can mean "libertine" or "rev-
eler"; the general sense of the passage is that Shakespeare is "the more to be admired" for his temperance
and modesty.
3. The embarrassment ("paine") at being asked to write
is presumably due to the same alleged modesty.
4. Contemporary.
5. Character, personality.
6. Buckinghamshire.

7. Oxford.
8. Upon.
9. Extemporaneous.
1. 10 percent interest. (Combe is damned because he
charges 12 percent on his loans, 2 percent above the
maximum allowed for usury not to be a mortal sin.)
2. 300 pounds a year.
3. See.
4. *for that . . . hominum:* because he treats of (general)
human manners or customs.

grave and discreet Citizen: his mother was a very beautifull woman, & of a very good witt and of conversation extremely agreable. . . . Mr William Shakespeare was wont to goe into Warwickshire once a yeare, and did commonly in his journey lye at this house in Oxon: where he was exceedingly respected. I have heard parson Robert D[avenant] say that here Mr W. Shakespeare here gave him a hundred kisses. Now S^r Wm. would sometimes when he was pleasant over a glasse of wine with his most intimate friends e.g. Sam: Butler (author of Hudibras) &c. say, that it seemed to him that he writt with the very spirit that Shakespeare,[5] and seemed contented enough to be thought his Son: he would tell them the story as above. in which way his mother had a very light report, whereby she was called a whore.

5. A word such as "had" seems to be missing.

A Shakespearean Chronicle
1558–1616

Entries marked by ● are from John Stow's *Abridgement of the English Chronicle* (1618). Stow, a member of the Merchant Tailor's Guild, published his first chronicle in 1565 and offered continued, expanded, and abridged versions constantly thereafter, sometimes as often as every year; after his death in 1605, the work was continued by Edmund Howes. Stow's chronicles give us a sense of how "history" was actually experienced from day to day by the citizens of London. Major political events share the page with developments in civic government and portentous signs of all kinds; Stow does not record the date of distant events like the Battle of Lepanto (1571), but he tells us when the news arrived in London and how the citizens responded.

Following Stow, marked by ■, are additional cultural and political details, and then, marked by ♦, information about (probable) first performances of Shakespeare's and others' works, Shakespeare's life and career, and stage history. While some years include all of the categories, most do not. Plays are listed under the year of their first performance; dates in parentheses are (probable) dates of composition, and those in brackets are dates of publication (in the case of Shakespeare's plays, quarto publication).

1558

● The 17 of November 1558 came certain news unto the Parliament house of the death of Queen Mary, whereat many rejoiced, and many lamented, and forthwith her death being generally known, they proclaimed the Lady Elizabeth second daughter to King Henry the eighth Queen of England, France, and Ireland, defender of the faith, &c.

♦ *Translation of Euripides'* Iphigenia in Aulis *by Jane Lumley.*

Mary I (1553–58), by John Master (fl. 1544–45).

1559

● The 20 of January began a Parliament . . . the Queen granted license for a free disputation to be held in Westminster Church, concerning some different points in Religion, but it came to no effect.

The 24 of June the Book of Common Prayer was established, and the Mass clean suppressed in all Churches.

In August following all ancient Church relics and new made Images in Queen Mary's reign, were beaten down and burned in the open streets.

■ **Acts of Uniformity and Supremacy passed. Elizabeth rejects a reluctant offer of marriage from Philip II of Spain.**

♦ *First account of Lord Robert Dudley's Men (later known as the Earl of Leicester's Men).*

Sources: Bentley, *Shakespeare: A Biographical Handbook*; Bullough, *Narrative and Dramatic Sources of Shakespeare*; Chambers, *The Elizabethan Stage* and *William Shakespeare: A Study of Facts and Problems*; Harbage, Schoenbaum, and Wagonheim, eds., *Annals of English Drama, 975–1700.*

1560

- In April the Lord Gray entered Scotland with ten thousand men, and besieged Leith, where between the French and the English were many hot skirmishes, and many slain on either part.

  The 5 of July through shooting of a Gun in a house in crooked lane, a barrel of powder was set on fire, which blew up four houses, shattered divers others, slew twenty persons outright, and hurt as many, besides great damage to houses and goods.

  This year the Queen by consent of her council, made Proclamation for the utter abolishing and suppression of all manner of base copper monies, which until this time had been current through out the Realm in divers Kings' reigns, and after this publication there was not any base metal coined in England.

- **Treaty of Edinburgh: French withdraw from Scotland. Presbyterianism established in Scotland. Publication of the Geneva Bible.**

- *Translation of Seneca's* Thyestes *by Jasper Heywood.*

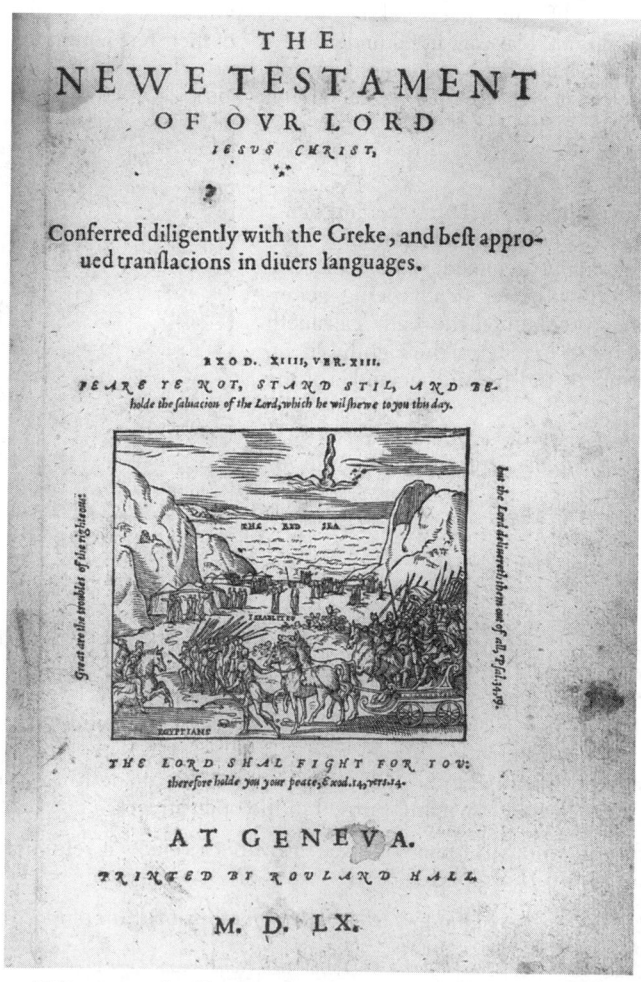

Title page to the New Testament of the Geneva Bible (1560).

1561

- The 21st of March, the wardens and assistants of the Merchant-Tailors in London, founded the famous free school in the Parish of St. Lawrence Pountenay.

  The 10 of April W. Geffrey was whipped from the Marshalsea unto Bedlam, for publishing that one John Moore was Jesus Christ, which said John Moore after he had been well whipped, confessed himself a cozening knave.

  The 4 of June between 4 and 5 a clock in the afternoon, there chanced a terrible tempest of thunder and lightning, and chiefly about London, where amongst many harms, it fired the lofty spire of Paul's steeple.

- **Silver coinage reformed. Tulips brought to Europe. Rebellion in Ireland.**

- ◆ *Translation of pseudo-Seneca's* Hercules Oetaeus *by Elizabeth I.*

1562

- The 14 of May a man child was borne at Chichester in Sussex, the head, arms, and legs whereof, were like an Anatomy, the breast and belly big, from the navel a long string hanging about the neck, a collar of flesh like the ruff of a neckerchief, coming up about the ears.

- **French civil wars begin. Elizabeth sends an English force to occupy Le Havre. First slave-trading voyage of John Hawkins.**

- ◆ *Thomas Norton and Thomas Sackville,* The Tragedy of Gorboduc *[1565], the first English play in blank verse; shows strong influence of Seneca.*

1563

- The plague of pestilence being in the town of Newhaven [Le Havre], through the number of soldiers that returned into England, the infection thereof spread into divers parts of this realm, but especially the City of London.

  There was no term kept Michaelmas.

  An earthquake in the month of September, specially in Lincoln and Northhampton shires.

- **Church of England adopts the Thirty-Nine Articles.**

1564

- Peace proclaimed between England and France.

  The second of October was an obsequy at Pauls for Ferdinando late Emperor.

  The seventh of October at night all the North parts of the Element seemed to be covered with flames of fire, proceeding from the Northeast and Northwest toward the midst of the firmament, and descended West.

- ◆ *Birth of William, John Shakespeare's eldest son (christened April 26). John Shakespeare listed as a "capital burgess" of Stratford and contributes toward the relief of local plague victims.*

1565

- The third day of February, Henry Stuart Lord Darnley . . . took his journey toward Scotland, and in summer following married Mary Queen of Scotland.

✦ *John Shakespeare is made an alderman of Stratford.*

1566

- The 31 of August the Queen's Majesty in her Progress came to the University of Oxford, and was of all the Students honorably received.

  Charles James, the first of that name, son to Henry Stuart Lord Darnley and Mary, King and Queen of Scots, was born in Edinburgh Castle. . . . The Queen's Majesty of England was the Godmother, who gave a font of gold curiously wrought and enamelled, weighing 333 ounces.

■ **Tobacco brought from the New World around this time.**

✦ *Ariosto's Il Suppositi, translated by George Gascoigne [1573]; first English comedy with significant amount of prose.*

1567

- The 10 of February in the morning, H. Stuart Lord of Darnley, before named King of Scots, was traitorously murdered, the revenge whereof remaineth in the mighty hands of God.

  Within the space of ten months last past, died seven Aldermen in London.

  The 29 of July Charles James the young Prince of Scotland, after a sermon made by John Knox, was crowned King of Scots [James VI] at Sterling Church, and at that time the Queen of Scots was prisoner at Loughleven.

■ **Revolt against Spanish rule in the Netherlands. The Irish leader Shane O'Neill defeated by Lord Deputy Sir Henry Sidney and later murdered by "certain wild Scots."**

1568

- The 16 of May, Mary Q. of Scots after her escape made out of Loughleven, where she had been long imprisoned, arrived at Werkington in England . . . where she was stayed, and conveyed to Carlisle, and from thence to Bolton castle.

  The eleventh of October were taken in Suffolk at Downham Bridge, 17 monstrous fishes, some of them 27 foot in length, 2 miles from Ipswich.

  The 22 of December was the first day that the Marchants left their meeting in Lombard street, and came into the Burse in Cornhill, builded for that purpose.

■ **Publication of the Bishops' Bible. Foundation of English College at Douai, to train Jesuits.**

✦ *John Shakespeare elected Bailiff of Stratford, the town's highest office. The Queen's Players and Earl of Worcester's Men perform at Stratford.*

1569

- The 27 of January a Frenchman & two Englishmen were drawn from Newgate to Tiburne, and there hanged, the French man quartered, who had coined gold counterfeit, the Englishmen, the one had clipped silver, the other cast testons of tin.

The 17 of August, an Ambassador from Muscovy, landed at Tower-wharf, and was there received by the Lord Mayor of London.

The 11 of October, Thomas Duke of Norfolk was brought to the Tower prisoner.

The 24 of November the Queen's Majesty caused the Earls of Northumberland and Westmerland, who rebelled in the north, to be proclaimed traitors, and forthwith prepared an Army for their suppression.

Two swordsmen. From "The Norfolke Gentleman," *Roxburghe Ballads.*

1570

- The fourth and fifth of January did suffer [for their part in the Northern Rebellion] at Durham to the number of sixty six Constables and other, amongst whom an Alderman of the towne, and a Priest called Parson Plomtree.

  The Lord Scrope Warden of the West Marches, entered Scotland the 18 of April, burnt and spoiled almost the Dumfries, took many prisoners, and returned safely. . . . There were razed and overthrown and burnt in this journey, above fifty strong Castles and piles, and above 3 thousand towns and villages.

- **Elizabeth excommunicated by Pope Pius V.**

1571

- The 16 of July Rebecca Chambers of Heriettesham, for poisoning T. Chambers her husband, was burnt at Maidstone in Kent.

  The 9 of November great rejoicing was made in London, for the late come news of a marvelous victory obtained against the Turks [The Battle of Lepanto].

1572

- It was enacted that all persons above the age of fourteen years, being taken, vagrant, and wandering misorderly, should be apprehended, whipped, and burnt through the right ear with a hot iron for the first time so taken, the second time to be hanged. [The order includes actors not under the protection of a patron.]

This year 1572, was the [St. Bartholomew's Day] Massacre in Paris.

The 2 of June Thomas Duke of Norfolk was beheaded on Tower Hill.

The 18 of November was seen a star Northward, very bright and clear in the constellation of Cassiopeia, which with three chief fixed stars of the said constellation made a Geometrical figure lozengewise, of the learned men called Rombus. . . . The same star was found to be in place celestial, far above the Moon, otherwise than ever any comet hath been seen, or naturally can appear: therefore it is supposed, that the signification thereof is directed purposely, and specially to some matter not natural but celestial, or rather supercelestial, so strange, as from the beginning of the world never was the like.

✦ *The Earl of Leicester's Men perform at Stratford.*

1573

• The 18 of January William Lord Herbert Earl of Worcester, began his journey toward France, to the christening of the King's daughter there, in stead of the Queen's majesty of England. The said Earl with many of his company, were robbed upon the sea of much of their baggage, and three or four of their men slain.

1574

• The 7 of August, a solemn Obsequy was held in Paul's Church in London, for Charles the 9 King of France.

The 15 of August, being Sunday, Agnes Bridges, a maid about the age of 20 years, and Rachel Pinder, a wench about 12 years old, who both of them had counterfeited to be possessed by the devil, stood at Paul's Cross, where they acknowledged their hypocritical counterfeiting, requiring forgiveness of God, & the world: for they had made the people believe many things.

✦ *The Earl of Warwick's and Earl of Worcester's Men perform at Stratford. The Earl of Leicester's men are issued a patent by Queen Elizabeth permitting them to act in London and the provinces.*

1575

• The 16 of February, between four and five of the clock in the afternoon, great Earthquakes happened in the City of York, Worcester, Gloucester, Bristol, Hereford, and the Countries about, which caused the people to run out of their houses, for fear they should have fallen upon their heads.

On Easter day, the third of April, was disclosed a Congregation of Anabaptists, Dutchmen, in a house without the bars of Algate, at London, whereof 17 were taken, and sent to prison, and four of them bearing faggots, recanted at Paul's cross, on the 15 of May. [The rest were later banished or burned.]

✦ *Gascoigne (?) and Sir Henry Lee (?), The Queen's Entertainment at Woodstock.*

1576

- The 11 of February Anne Averies widow, forswearing herself for a little money, that she should have paid for six pounds of tow [rope] at a Shop in Woodstreet in London, fell immediately down speechless, casting up at her mouth, the same matter, which by Nature's course, should have been voided downwards, till she died.

- **Spanish sack Antwerp. Dutch provinces unite against Spain (Treaty of Ghent). Martin Frobisher makes his first voyage in search of the Northwest Passage to Asia.**
- ♦ *James Burbage (father of Richard, the leading actor in Shakespeare's company) builds The Theatre (located in Shoreditch), London's first regular playhouse.*

Burning city under siege. From Raphael Holinshed, *Chronicles of England, Scotland, and Ireland* (1587).

1577

- The 31 of May, Martin Frobisher, with one Ship and two Barks, furnished for that purpose, sailed from Harwich, in Essex, towards Cathay, by the Northwest Seas, and entered his straits, beyond Queen Elizabeth's foreland, about thirty leagues, where he went on shore, and finding store of gold Ore (as he had been informed) fraught his Ship and Bark, caught a man, woman and child of that country, and then on the twenty four of August, returning, arrived at Milford haven on the twentieth of September.

    The stone tower of London Bridge, being decayed, was taken down, and a new foundation drawn.

- **Sir Francis Drake begins his voyage around the world.**

- ♦ *Around this time, John Shakespeare begins his decline into debt.*
    The Curtain Theatre (Shoreditch) opens.

1578

- The 3 of February, John Nelson, for denying the Queen's supremacy, was drawn to Tyburn, and there hanged and quartered.

♦ *Mary Shakespeare pawns her estate, Asbyes at Wilmcote, and her lands at Snitterfield. Lord Strange's Men and Lord Essex's Men perform at Stratford. (Performances in Stratford continue at the rate of at least one a year.)*

1579

- This year Mark Scaliot, Blacksmith of London, for trial of his workmanship made one hanging lock of Iron, steel and brass of eleven several pieces, and a pipe key, all clean wrought, which weighed but one grain of gold. He also at the same time made a chain of gold of forty-three links, to which chain the lock and key being fastened and put about a fleas neck, she drew the same with ease. All which lock, key, chain, and flea, weighed but one grain and a half: a thing most incredible, but that I myself have seen it.
  This year John Fox of Woodbridge, William Wicnor, Robert Moore Englishmen, having been prisoners in Turkey about the space of thirteen years, with more than 260 other Christians of divers nations, by killing of their keeper, marvelously escaped, and returned to their native countries.

- **Protestant northern provinces of Holland unite (Union of Utrecht). John Stubbs loses his right hand for attacking Elizabeth's proposed marriage to the Duke of Alençon.**

1580

- About the 18 of July, the Lord Gray took his voyage towards Ireland, as Lord Deputy thereof, after whom were sent divers bands of lusty soldiers, both horsemen and footmen, under the leading of expert captains. [In November, Gray massacred several hundred Spanish and Italian mercenaries at Smerwick.]
  The 23 of September at Fennistanton in Huntingtonshire, one Agnes, wife to William Linsey, was delivered of an ugly and strange monster, with a face black, mouth and eyes like a Lion, and both male and female.

- **Jesuit mission established in England. Return of Sir Francis Drake.**

♦ *John Shakespeare unable to redeem Mary Shakespeare's pawned property.*

1581

- About the 11 of January proclamation was published at London, for revocation of sundry of the Queen's Majesty's subjects remaining beyond the seas under color of study, and yet living contrary to the laws of the Realm. And also against the retaining of Jesuits and massing Priests, sowers of sedition, and other treasonable attempts, &c.
  The first of November Monsieur the French King's brother Duke of Anjou, and other Nobles of France having lately arrived in Kent, came to London, and were honorably received and retained at the Court with great banqueting.
  The first of December, Edmund Campion Jesuit, Ralph Sherwin, and Alexander Brian Seminary Priests, having been arraigned and condemned for high treason, were drawn from the tower of London to Tyburn, and there hanged and quartered.

♦ *A new patent is issued to the Master of the Revels authorizing him to "reform, authorize and put down, as shall be thought meet or unmeet unto himself" any play to be performed in England.*

1582

- This year was first founded a public lecture in Surgery, to begin to be read in the College of Physicians in London.

    Peter Morris free denizen, conveyed Thames water in pipes of Lead . . . up to the Northwest corner of Leaden Hall (the highest ground of London) . . . plentifully serving to the commodity of the inhabitants near adjoining in their houses, and also cleansing the kennels of the street towards Bishops gate, Algate, the Bridge, and the Stocks market. But now no such matter, private commodity being preferred, common commodity is neglected, and not reformed as was promised.

- **Alençon departs from England. Plague in London. Pope Gregory XIII reforms calendar; Protestant countries retain old calendar.**

◆ *Shakespeare marries Anne Hathaway (license issued November 27).*

1583

- This year 1583, William Prince of Orange was slain by John Jowrigny a Walloon Soldier, who notwithstanding sundry extreme torments inflicted upon his body and limbs in prison, as also having his flesh plucked off with hot pincers upon an open stage, yet he neither shrunk, nor craved any favor, neither repented him of the fact, but feared he had not slain him. [In fact, William was assassinated in 1584.]

    This year 1583, the Queen being at Barne Elmes, at the earnest suit of Sir Francis Walsingham, she entertained twelve Players into her service, and allowed them wages and liveries, as Grooms of the Chamber, and until then she had none of her own, but divers Lords had Players [Queen Elizabeth's Men].

- **Galileo discovers the principle governing the motion of the pendulum.**

◆ *Birth of Shakespeare's older daughter, Susanna.*
  Queen Elizabeth's Men established by royal order.

1584

- On the 10 of January, William Carter was arraigned and condemned of high treason, for printing a seditious and traitorous book, entitled, A Treatise of Schism, and was for the same on the next morrow, drawn from Newgate to Tyburn, and there hanged, boweled and quartered, and forthwith a book was published, entitled, A Declaration of the favorable dealing of her Majesty's Commissioners, &c.

- **Failure of Sir Walter Ralegh's Virginia colony.**

Indians gathering food in their Virginia village. From Thomas Hariot, *A Briefe and True Report of the New Found Land of Virginia* (1590).

1585

- The 26 of June, arrived at London, Deputies for the States of the Netherlands, who were lodged about the Tower street, and had their diet worshipfully appointed at the charges of her Majesty, in the Clothworkers hall. Those on the 29 of June, repaired to the Court then at Greenwich, where they presented to her Majesty the sovereignty of those countries.

- **Elizabeth declines sovereignty of the Netherlands but sends an army to the Low Countries under the Earl of Leicester.**

- ◆ *Birth of Shakespeare's twin son and daughter, Hamnet and Judith. John Shakespeare fined for not going to church.*

1586

- A Commission was erected from her Majesty, tending to the ratifying of a firm League of amity, between her Majesty and James King of Scots [confirmed July 1].
  In the month of July, divers traitorous persons were apprehended, and detected of most wicked conspiracy against her Majesty [the Babington Plot], and also of minding to have stirred up a general rebellion throughout the whole Realm. For joy of whose apprehension, the Citizens of London on the 15 of the same month at night, and on the next morrow caused the Bells to be rung, and bonfires to be made, and also banqueted every man according to his ability, some in their houses, some in the streets.

- **Mary, Queen of Scots is implicated in the Babington Plot and sentenced to death. Sir Philip Sidney dies from wounds received at the Battle of Zutphen. Leicester is recalled to England.**

- ◆ *Shakespeare may leave Stratford at about this time. A contemporary reports that he became a country schoolmaster. It is certain only that he is in London by 1592.*

1587

- The 8 of February being Wednesday according to sentence lately given by the nobility, Mary Stuart Queen of Scots, about ten of the Clock before noon, was executed and suffered death, by beheading. . . .
  This year was a late spring, and a cold Summer, so that at Midsummer Peas in the cods were sold at London for 8 pence the peck, yet after were plenty, no cherries ripe til Saint James's-tide or Lammas, and then such plenty that they were sold for a penny the pound.

- **Drake defeats Spanish fleet at Cadiz.**

- ◆ *Thomas Kyd, The Spanish Tragedy [c. 1592]. Christopher Marlowe, 1 Tamburlaine the Great [1590].*
  John Shakespeare loses his position as an alderman.
  The Rose Theatre (located at Bankside, on the Thames) built by Philip Henslowe.

1588

- Great provision was made this year both by Land and Sea, for withstanding the invasion by the Spanish Armada against the Realm.

The 19 of July, intelligence was brought to the Lord Admiral by a pirate Pinnace, whose captain was Thomas Fleming, that the Spanish Fleet was seen in the sea.

The 20 of July, the Lord Admiral made toward the Sea, and the same day had sight of the Spanish fleet, in number by estimation 158 sails. The Lord Admiral cast about toward the land to interrupt them from approaching, & having got the wind of them, prosecuted them all that night, and so continually, from place to place, until the second of August, in which space by the power of GOD having wonderfully overcome them, he returned to Margate in Kent.

▪ **Death of Leicester. Puritan "Martin Marprelate" tracts ridicule the prelacy. African Company receives charter.**

◆ *John Lyly*, Endymion, the Man in the Moon.

Naval battle. From Raphael Holinshed, *Chronicles of England, Scotland, and Ireland* (1587).

1589

● The first of February two soldiers were set on the Pillory at the Leadenhall, whereon they stood by the space of three hours, the one had his ear nailed, the other his tongue pierced with an awl, which awl remained in his tongue till he was taken from the Pillory, for abusing their captains and Governors with bad speeches.

In the month of September, the Citizens of London furnished 1000 men to be sent over into France, to the aiding of Henry late King of Navarre, then challenging the Crown of France.

This year 1589, was devised and perfected, the Art of knitting, or weaving of silk stockings, Wastcotes, Coverlets, and divers other things by engines, or steel Looms, by William Lee, sometime master of St. John's College in Cambridge: and sixteen years after this, he went into France, and taught it to the French, because he was not regarded in England.

▪ **Henry III of France assassinated by a friar.**

Medal of Henry III of France. From the
Shirburn Ballads, no. 46.

✦ *Robert Greene,* Friar Bacon and Friar Bungay.
Thomas Kyd, Hamlet *(1582–89, not extant;
likely source of Shakespeare's* Hamlet*). John
Lyly,* Midas *[1592]. Christopher Marlowe,* The
Jew of Malta. *Anonymous,* The Taming of a
Shrew *(c. 1588–93) [1594]; may be a "bad
quarto" of Shakespeare's play.*

*Shakespeare is probably affiliated with the
amalgamated Lord Strange's and Lord Admiral's Men from about this time until 1594.*

*Master of the Revels obtains authority to
censor and license all plays.*

1590

• The 21 of September, being the Feast of Saint Matthew in the afternoon, was a great
stir at Lincoln's Inn, by Prentices, and others, against young Gentlemen students at
Law there, for some rude demeanors, late before by them done, against the inhabitants of Chancery Lane, which had like to have grown to great mischief, had not the
same been by wise Magistrates soon appeased: for the uproar grew great and violent,
suddenly.

▪ James VI returns to Scotland with his bride, Anne of Denmark. Beginning of
witchcraft trials in Scotland.

✦ *Translation of Garnier's* Tragedy of Antonius *by Mary Herbert, Countess of Pembroke.
Anonymous,* Edward III *(the "Countess scenes" in this play have been attributed to
Shakespeare). Anonymous,* The True Chronicle History of King Leir, and His Three
Daughters.

1591

• The 16 of July, Edmund Coppinger,
and Henry Arthington, Gentlemen,
came into Cheap, and there in a car,
proclaimed news from heaven, (as they
said) to wit, that one William Hacket
Yeoman, represented Christ, by partak-
ing his glorified body, by his principal
spirit, and that they were two Prophets,
the one of mercy, the other of Judgment, called and sent of God, to assist
him in his great work, &c. [Hacket

Three old witches with familiars. From *The
Wonderful Discoverie of the Witchcrafts of Margaret and Phillip Flower* (1619).

was hanged and quartered; Coppinger starved himself to death in prison; Arthington repented and was set free.]

■ **Robert Devereux, Earl of Essex, leads expedition to France in aid of Henry IV. Tea is first drunk in England.**

◆ 2 Henry VI *(1591)*; *quarto*, The First Part of the Contention of the Two Famous Houses of York and Lancaster *[1594]*. 3 Henry VI *(1591)*; *octavo*, The True Tragedy of Richard Duke of York and the Good King Henry the Sixth *[1595]*.

  Acting is restricted on Sundays and Thursdays to provide for sufficient turnout at bearbaitings.

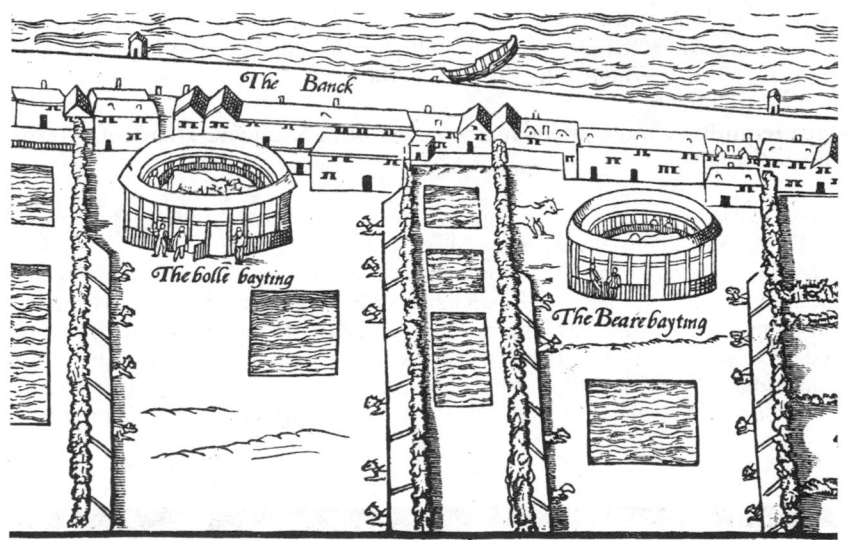

The bull- and bearbaiting arenas. Detail of *Civitas Londinum*, by Ralph Agas.

1592

• The 13 of December, a certain gentlewoman by the Council's commandment was whipped through the City of London, for affirming her self to be the daughter of Philip king of Spain, as she had been persuaded (by some accounted Soothsayers, after proved liars) for she was known to be a Butcher's daughter in Eastcheap.

■ **Plague hits London.**

◆ 1 Henry VI *(1592)*. Richard III *(1592–93) [1597]*. Venus and Adonis *(1592–93) [1593]*. The Comedy of Errors *(1592–94)*.

  Marlowe, The Tragical History of Dr. Faustus *and* The Troublesome Reign and Lamentable Death of Edward II.

  Robert Greene attacks Shakespeare in his Groats-worth of Wit, *the earliest reference to Shakespeare's career in the theater.*

  Philip Henslowe's records show a total of 105 performances between February 19 and June 22, 1592, in London by Lord Strange's Men, probably in the Rose Theatre. Of the plays listed, two are possibly by Shakespeare: Harey the vj *(1 Henry VI, 15 performances) and* Titus & Vespacia *(Titus Andronicus?, 7 performances). Other plays include Greene's* Friar Bacon and Friar Bungay *and Marlowe's* Jew of Malta.

Henslowe begins his diary (continued until 1604), an important source on the theater. From June 1592 until June 1594, London theaters are shut down because of the plague, and acting companies take to the provinces.

1593

- This year was no Bartholomew fair kept at London, for the avoiding of concourse of people, whereby the infection of the pestilence might have increased.

  The whole number this year buried within the City of London, the suburbs and other places adjoining, as well of the plague, as of the other diseases, from the 29 of December in the year 1592, until the 20 of December, 1593 was as followeth. Within the walls of all diseases, 8598, whereof the plague, 5390, without the walls & in the liberties, 9295, the plague 5285. So that within the City and Liberties, of all diseases 17863 *[sic]*. Whereof the Plague was 10675.

- **Decree requiring church attendance on pain of banishment. Henry of Navarre becomes Catholic.**

- *Sonnets (1593–1603) [1609]. The Rape of Lucrece (1593–94) [1594]. Titus Andronicus (1592) [1594]. The Taming of the Shrew (1592).*

  Henslowe's records show 29 performances for December 29, 1592, to February 1, 1593, again including 1 Henry VI and Titus Andronicus. Lord Strange's Men are led at this time by Edward Alleyn (from the associated Lord Admiral's Men), and also include Will Kempe and John Hemings, Shakespeare's eventual colleagues in the Lord Chamberlain's Men. (There is no mention of Shakespeare himself, who may have traveled with another company or may not have acted at all during the plague years of 1592–94.)

Woodcut showing the plague in London.

1594

- The last of February, Roderigo Lopez a Portugal (as it was said) professing Physic, was arraigned in the Guild-hall of London, found guilty, and had judgment of high Treason, for conspiring her majesty's destruction by poison.

  The 16 of April Ferdinando Earl of Derby deceased at Latham, in a very strange manner.

- **Henry of Navarre crowned Henry IV of France. Birth of James VI's first son, Henry.**

- ◆ *Shakespeare dedicates* The Rape of Lucrece *to Henry Wriothesley, Earl of Southampton.* The Two Gentlemen of Verona *(1590–91).* Love's Labour's Lost *(1594–95) [1598].* Sir Thomas More *(1592–93; parts revised by Shakespeare, 1603–4).*

  Francis Bacon, Thomas Campion, et al., Gesta Grayorum *(1594–95; contains the first surviving formal masque).*

  Henslowe's record for the early part of this winter includes one play probably by Shakespeare, listed as Titus & Ondronicous, *suggesting a possible revision of the previous season's* Titus *play. On June 11,* The Tamynge of a Shrowe *enters the London record; this could be an early version of* The Taming of the Shrew, *similar to the bad quarto of this year bearing the same title. The repertoire of the united Lord Admiral's and Lord Chamberlain's Men at this time also includes* Hamlet *(the "Ur-Hamlet," not Shakespeare's), as well as* The Jew of Malta, Titus Andronicus, *and other plays. After June 15, however, the Lord Chamberlain's company re-forms as a separate entity, no longer involving Edward Alleyn.*

1595

- This year by means of the late transportation of grain into foreign Countries, the same was here grown to an excessive price, as in some parts of this Realm, from fourteen shillings to four marks the quarter.

  On the 29 of June being Sunday in the afternoon, a number of unruly youths on the Tower hill, being blamed by the Warders of Towerstreet-ward to sever themselves and depart from thence, threw at them stones, and drave them back into Tower street, and were heartened thereunto by a late Soldier, sounding of a trumpet, but the trumpeter and many other of them being taken by the sheriffs of London, and committed to prison.

  The two & twenty of July, in presence of the Earl of Essex, and other sent from the Queen, were arraigned in the Guild-hall of London, five of those unruly youths that were on the Tower hill apprehended, they were condemned, and had judgment to be drawn, hanged and quartered.

- **Hugh O'Neill, Earl of Tyrone, rebels in Ireland. Sir Walter Ralegh sails to Guiana. Robert Southwell, Jesuit poet, is executed.**

- ◆ Richard II *(1595) [1597].* Romeo and Juliet *(1595) [1599; "bad quarto," 1597].* A Midsummer Night's Dream *(1594–96) [1600].*

  Shakespeare living in St. Helen's Parish, Bishopsgate, in London. He apparently becomes a sharer in (provides capital for) the newly re-formed Lord Chamberlain's Men.

  Evidence of the activity of the Lord Chamberlain's Men from 1595 to 1599, no longer reflected in Henslowe's records, is scanty. Records of payments in Cambridge and Ipswich indicate at least one provincial tour. Internal evidence suggests that A Midsummer Night's Dream *was the play performed at the court wedding of the Earl of Derby and Lady Elizabeth Vere on January 26, 1595.*

  Swan Theatre (Bankside) built.

1596

- On the 11 of April being Easter day about ten of the clock came a new charge, so that all men being in the parish Churches ready to have received the Communion, the Aldermen, their deputies, and Constables, were fain to close up the Church-doors, till they had pressed so many to be soldiers, that by 12 of the Clock, they had in the whole City 1000 men, and they were forthwith furnished of armor and weapons &c. And they were for the most part that night and the rest on the next morning sent away, to Dover, as the like out of other parts of the Realm, but returned again about a week after, for the French had lost Calais, &c. [The Spanish held Calais until 1598.]

     This year, like as in the months of August, September, October, and November, fell great rains, whereupon high waters followed: wheat in meal was sold at London for ten shillings the bushel, Rye six shillings, and Oatmeal eight shillings.

- ■ "League of amity" between England and France.

- ◆ King John (1596). The Merchant of Venice (1596–97) [1600]. 1 Henry IV (1596–97) [1598].

John Shakespeare is granted a coat of arms, hence the title of "gentleman." William Shakespeare's son Hamnet dies.

Court records list payments to the Lord Chamberlain's Men for several performances in the winter of 1596 and again a year later. Provincial records indicate extensive touring in 1596–97. Payments during this tour average about 20 shillings.

The Shakespeare coat of arms, drafted October 20, 1596.

1597

- This summer arrived here an Ambassador from the King of Polonia, and had audience the twenty five of July, whose Oration was presently answered by her Majesty in Latin.

     A Parliament began at Westminster, on the 24 of October: on the which day divers people were smuldered and crushed to death, pressing between White-hall, and the College Church, to have seen her Majesty, and Nobility riding in their Robes to the said Parliament.

- ◆ The Merry Wives of Windsor (1597–98) [1602].

     James Burbage builds Second Blackfriars Theatre. Restraint on playing in London forces the Lord Chamberlain's Men to tour the provinces. They perform at the Curtain Theatre from late 1597 to 1599 while the Globe is under construction. The scene showing the deposition of Richard is cut from the First Quarto of Richard II, as Elizabeth perceives an analogy between Richard and herself.

1598

- On the third of April, Twiford Town in Devonshire was burnt by casualty of fire, beginning in a poor cottage, a woman there frying pancakes with straw, the same fired the house, and so to the Town, about one of the clock in the afternoon.
  The third of September, died Philip the second of that name, King of Spain.
  In the month of December, great frosts, the Thames nigh over-frozen at London.

- **Edict of Nantes ends French civil wars, granting toleration to Protestants.**

- ◆ 2 Henry IV *(1597–98) [1600]*. Much Ado About Nothing *(1598) [1600]*.
  Jonson, Every Man in His Humor.
  Shakespeare's name is first on the list of "principal Comedians" for Every Man in His Humor.
  Court records of 1598 and 1599 again show payments to the Lord Chamberlain's Men in late December, early January, and late February, specifying Shakespeare's colleagues "Thomas Pope and John Heminges servants to the Lord Chamberlain" as recipients.
  Materials from the demolished Theatre (at Shoreditch) are transported across the river and used in building the Globe as the "public," outdoor theater to replace it.

1599

- The 27 of March, about two of the clock in the afternoon, Robert Devereux, Earl of Essex, Lieutenant General, Lord High Marshal, &c. departed from his house in Seding lane, through Fenchurch street, Grace-street, Cornhill, Cheap, &c. toward Iseldone, High-gate, and rode that night to Saint Albans, towards Ireland.
  The City and Citizens kept unusual watch and ward, and all sorts of people were much amazed and frighted, as well by reason of preparation for wars, not knowing any cause, as also by the sudden strange, and terrible rumors and reports of the Spaniards fierce approach.
  On Michaelmas even, Robert, Earl of Essex, Lieutenant General for Ireland, having secretly returned into England, came to the Court at Nonsuch, & spake with the Queen, and on the second of October, was for contempt, &c. committed to the Lord Keeper.

- **Satires and other offensive books called in and burned by ecclesiastical order. Thomas Nashe and Gabriel Harvey forbidden to publish.**

- ◆ Henry V *(1598–99) [1600]*. Julius Caesar *(1599)*. As You Like It *(1599–1600)*.
  Drayton et al., The First Part of the True and Honorable History of the Life of Sir John Oldcastle, the Good Lord Cobham *(response to Shakespeare's treatment of Oldcastle-Falstaff in the* Henry IV *plays; falsely attributed to Shakespeare).*
  Globe playhouse opens as home of the Lord Chamberlain's Men. Will Kempe, the most famous comedian of his day, leaves the Lord Chamberlain's Men around the same time that he performs his famous dance from London to Norwich.

1600

- The fifth of June, the Earl of Essex was called before the Lords of the Council, at the Lord Keepers, where for matters laid to his charge, he was supended from use of divers offices, till her Majesty's pleasure to the contrary, to keep his house, as before: whereat the people still murmured.
  The 8 of August, 1600, came Ambassadors from Abdela Wayhetanow, King of

Barbary. . . . They were very bountifully entertained at the Queen's charges, during their five months abode, they were very subtle and unthankful, they abhorred to give any manner of Alms unto any poor Christians, they sold their broken meat unto those who would give most for it, they killed all their own meat in the Ambassador's house, as Lambs, and all kinds of Pullen, &c. which they usually killed, turning their faces toward the East, they used to wash their own feet twice or thrice a day, and sometimes to wash their bodies: they use beads, and pray to Turkish Saints: they diligently observed the manner of our weights and measures, and all things else that might avail their native Merchants, and prejudice the English Nation.

■ **Birth of James VI's second son, Charles. Founding of East India Company.**

◆ Hamlet *(1600–1) [1604; "bad quarto," 1603].*
    Jonson, Cynthia's Revels.
    A letter of Rowland Whyte to Sir Robert Sidney describes a command performance of one of the Falstaff plays arranged by the lord chamberlain (Lord Hunsdon) to entertain a foreign dignitary on March 6: "Upon Thursday my Lord Chamberlain feasted him, and made him very great, and a delicate Dinner, and there in the Afternoon his Players acted, before Vereiken, Sir John Oldcastle [Falstaff], to his great Contentment."
    Edward Alleyn and Philip Henslowe build the Fortune Theatre for the Lord Admiral's Men, competing with the Globe.

Engraving of the Earl of Essex as Lord General.

1601

- Sunday the eight of February, about ten of the clock before noon, Robert Devereux Earl of Essex, assisted by sundry Noblemen and Gentlemen in warlike manner entered the City of London at the Temple Bar, crying for the Queen. [The rising failed, and Essex yielded to arrest the same day.]

  Ash Wednesday, the five and twenty of February, the Earl of Essex was beheaded in the Tower. . . . The Hangman was beaten as he returned thence, so that the Sheriffs of London were sent for, to assist and rescue him from such as would have murdered him.

  The 15 of March, in the night, a new Scaffold was carried from Leaden Hall in London to the Tower hill, and there set up by Torchlight.

  Lightning and thunder often before Christmas, and in the holy days, and an Earthquake at London on Christmas even at noon.

The execution of the Earl of Essex. From the *Shirburn Ballads*, no. 79.

- **New Poor Law places responsibility for relief for the poor on the local parish.**

- ♦ *"The Phoenix and Turtle" (1601) published in Robert Chester's* Loves Martyr. Twelfth Night *(1601).*

  Shakespeare's father, John, dies.

  Essex's followers arrange a staging of Richard II *at the Globe, to incite rebellion. Culmination of the War of the Theaters, with Ben Jonson in opposition to John Marston and Thomas Dekker.*

1602

- In the month of January news came out of Ireland, that on Christmas day the Spaniards and Irish were overcome and slain in great numbers, and the Englishmen were victors.

  The last of June, Atkenson a customer of Hull, was set on the Pillory in Cheap, and with him three other, who had been brought thither on horse back, with their faces toward the horses' tails, and papers on their heads. They were there whipped on the Pillory, and lost their ears by judgment of the Star-Chamber, for slanderous words by them spoken, against the Council.

✦ Troilus and Cressida *(1602) [1609].*
> *Anonymous,* Timon *(its relationship to Shakespeare's* Timon of Athens *is unclear).*
> *Shakespeare receives a conveyance of land in Old Stratford (127 acres) for £320 and copyhold for a cottage in Stratford.*
> *Salmon Pavy, a boy player referred to as "the stage's jewel" in his epitaph written by Ben Jonson, dies at the age of thirteen.*
> *Opening of the Bodleian Library.*

Sketch by George Vertue (1737) of Shakespeare's house in Stratford.

1603

• In the month of March, the Queen lying at Richmond, dangerously sick, straight watches were kept in London with warding at the gates, lanthorns with lights hanged out all night, at which news the people were sore perplexed.

> Thursday the four and twenty of March, about two of the clock in the morning, deceased Queen Elizabeth. . . .

> [James VI of Scotland declared King James I of England.] This change was very plausible, and well pleasing to the nobility and the Gentry, and generally to all the Commons of the Realm, among whom the name of a King was then so strange, as few could remember, or had seen a King before, except they were aged persons, considering that the government of the Realm had continued near the space of 50 years under the reign of two Queens, which is the far greater part of an old man's age.

> Against this time of Coronation, the citizens had made wondrous great provision; but through the terrible increase of pestilence in the City and the Suburbs, their sumptuous Pageants, and other triumphant entertainments, stood like ruins, being not yet finished, and the King constrained to omit his former determination in riding through London, as Kings have accustomed, and all Londoners prohibited by Proclamation from coming at Court: there died that week of all diseases, eleven hundred and three: the twenty five of July being Monday, and the feast of St. James the Apostle, King James the first of that name, King of England, and the most noble Lady Queen Anne his wife, were both crowned and anointed at Westminster.

▪ **Hugh O'Neill surrenders in Ireland.**

✦ *Shakespeare's name appears for the last time in Jonson's actors' lists, as a "principal Tragedian" in* Sejanus.
> *The average take during a provincial tour of this year by Shakespeare's company,*

*now the King's Men, seems to increase relative to earlier tours, approaching 30 shillings.
A letter described by Lady Herbert in 1865 but never subsequently found alludes to a
performance of* As You Like It *that may have taken place in the fall 1603: "We have a
letter, never printed, from Lady Pembroke to her son, telling him to bring James I from
Salisbury to see* As You Like It; *'we have the man Shakespeare with us.'"*

Theaters closed again on account of the plague from mid-1603 until April 1604.

The coronation of Macbeth. From Raphael Holinshed, *Chronicles of England, Scotland, and
Ireland* (1587).

1604

- The 5 of March was Proclamation made, for the authorizing the Book of Common
Prayer.

    In October, the Customs of Merchandise were raised both inward and outward,
and then let to farm.

■ **Peace with Spain. Tax on tobacco.**

◆ Measure for Measure *(1603).* Othello *(1603–4) [1622].*

    The Malcontent *(possible source for Gloucester's suicide attempt in* King Lear*).
Anonymous,* The London Prodigal *(possibly influenced Edgar's use of dialect in* King
Lear*).*

    *Shakespeare's status as a member of the King's Men is recognized in an allowance
of four yards of red cloth to wear as a participant in James's coronation procession
through London.*

    *A nobleman's letter of January 15, 1604, states: "On New years night we had a
play of Robin goodfellow," probably* A Midsummer Night's Dream. *Records of eight
performances at court during the winter season reflect the growing prominence of the
King's Men. The first entry in the Revels Accounts, kept under the auspices of Edmund
Tilney, for the 1604–5 season reads: "Hallowmas Day being the first of November A
Play in the Banqueting house at Whitehall Called The Moor of Venice [Othello]." The*
Merry Wives of Windsor *is performed on November 4. Shakespeare is listed several
times under the category "the poets which made the plays," though in the unusual
spelling "Shaxberd"; he is credited for the performance of* Measure for Measure *on
December 26 and of* The Comedy of Errors *two days later.*

1605

- The twenty first of February was a Lion whelped in the Tower, which whelp was taken from the Dam, and brought up by hand, as the King had commanded.

  Upon May day last, Richard Haydocke, a Physician, asked forgiveness of the Lord Archbishop of Canterbury, for deluding the King and many others, under pretense of being inspired, and to preach in his sleep by night with which deceit he had so strongly possessed the vulgar, as it was hard to remove them, although he confessed the abuse.

  [Discovery of Gunpowder Plot] to undermine and blow up the Parliament House, at the instant when the King, Queen, Prince, Peers, and Commons were all assembled. [Guido ("Guy") Fawkes arrested.] The same day in the afternoon, the manner of the treason was by Proclamation made known unto the people, for joy whereof, there was that night as many bonfires as the streets could permit.

- All's Well That Ends Well *(1604–5)*. King Lear *(1604–5) [1608]*.

  Ben Jonson writes his first masque for the court.

  The Revels Accounts continue into the new year, listing Love's Labour's Lost *for early January,* Henry V *for January 7, and* The Merchant of Venice *for February 10. The Merchant of Venice is evidently a hit; the entry for February 12 states, "On Shrove Tuesday A play Called the Merchant of Venice Again Commanded By the Kings Majesty." The company also performs three plays not by Shakespeare, including Jonson's* Every Man in His Humour *(February 2).*

  Red Bull Theatre built.

1606

- A very great Whale came within eight miles of London whose length was divers times seen above the water, and the same was judged to be a great deal longer than the longest ship in the river.

  Friday the 28 of March 1606 in the Guildhall in London was arraigned and condemned Henry Garnet Provincial of the Jesuits in England, for being acquainted with the Gunpowder plot, and concealing the same, for the which he was adjudged to be drawn, hanged & quartered, and his head to be set upon London bridge. [The chief conspirators in the plot had been executed in January.]

  The 15 of July the wife of Richard Homwood of East Grimsted in Sussex without any known cause murdered her own three children, and threw them into a pit, and then cut her own throat likewise.

- **London and Plymouth Companies receive charters to colonize Virginia.**

- Macbeth *(1606)*. Antony and Cleopatra *(1606)*.

  Jonson, Volpone, *or* The Fox. *Anonymous,* The Revenger's Tragedy.

  Provincial performances of the King's Men continue along with regular London engagements.

  Parliament passes "An Act to Restrain Abuses of Players" in order to purify the language in plays.

1607

- About the middle of May, certain common persons assembled themselves in Northamptonshire, Warwickshire, and Leicestershire: they cut and brake down hedges, filled up ditches, and laid open all such enclosures of commons and other grounds, which of ancient time had been open, and employed to tillage.

About the beginning of September, there fled out of Ireland into the parts beyond the Seas, Hugh Earl of Tyrone, Tyrconnel, Hugh Baron of Dongannon . . . with divers others their servants and followers.

■ **Captain John Smith settles Jamestown, Virginia.**

♦ Timon of Athens *(1607–8)*. Pericles *(1607–8) [1609]*.
   Shakespeare's daughter Susanna married to John Hall. Shakespeare's brother Edmund (described as a player) dies.

1608

• From Sunday the tenth of January, until the fifteenth of the same, the frost grew extreme, so as the Ice [on the Thames] became firm, and removed not, & then all sorts of men, women, and children, went boldly upon the Ice in most parts; some shot at pricks, others bowled and danced, with other variable pastimes; by reason of which concourse of people, there were many that set up booths and standings upon the Ice, as Fruit sellers, Victuallers, that sold beer and wine, Shoemakers, & a Barber's tent, &c. Every of them had fire near their beings.

All the Hartichokes in gardens about London were killed with this frost.

♦ Coriolanus *(1608)*.
   William Rowley, The Birth of Merlin *(Shakespeare mistakenly named as a collaborator on the title page). Documents mention performances in London of* Pericles.
   Birth of Shakespeare's granddaughter and death of his mother. Shakespeare obtains a one-seventh share in the Second Blackfriars Theatre.
   Hamlet *and* Richard II *(not performed by the King's Men) serve as entertainment on board an East India vessel, the* Dragon, *off the coast of Sierra Leone. On March 31, Captain Keeling records in his journal: "I invited Captain Hawkins to a fish dinner, and had* Hamlet *acted aboard me: which I permit to keep my people from idleness and unlawful games, or sleep."*
   The King's Men lease the Second Blackfriars as a second venue, for private indoor performances.

1609

• The last year, and this spring, according to his Majesty's express order, upon apparent reason and great likelihood of future good & utility to the common subjects of this land, there were many thousands of young Mulberry trees brought hither out of France . . . which were likewise by order sent into divers shires, and there planted for the feeding of Silkworms to make silk, like as it is made in France.

The first, second and third of June, the king in person royal heard the differences between the ecclesiastical and the temporal Judges argued, touching prohibitions out of the King's Bench, and Common Pleas.

■ **Moors expelled from Spain.**

♦ *Publication of the Sonnets.* Cymbeline *(1609–10).* A Lover's Complaint *(1609).*

1610

- Thursday the 3 of May, the French Queen, with all solemnity was crowned in Paris, having been ten years before married to the king: and the next day after the King was murdered in his coach as he rode through Paris by a base villain that stabbed him in the body with a long knife twice, that he died instantly, and his body was carried to the Louvre.

  The Triumphs, Trophies, and pleasant devices at this time, in honor of the Lord Mayor and City of London, were extraordinary great, being in a manner twice so much as hath been usual within the City, and so likewise were the stately shows and ingenious devices upon the water, at the charges of the Company of Merchant-Tailors.

- Henry is made Prince of Wales. James dissolves Parliament.

- The Winter's Tale *(1609)*.
  Jonson, The Alchemist.
  Shakespeare probably returns to Stratford and settles there.
  Documents mention performances in London of Othello *(Globe, April 30, 1610).*
  There are also records of five provincial performances.

1611

- The 6 of June the King by Proclamation straightly commanded the oath of Allegiance to be ministered unto all sorts of people, and a true certificate to be made thereof unto the great Lords of the Council.

  At this time was concluded a double match between the young French King and the King of Spain's daughter, and the Prince of Spain and the French King's sister.

- Plantation of Ulster. Publication of the Authorized (King James) Version of the Bible.

Inigo Jones's design for Oberon's palace in Ben Jonson's masque *Oberon, the Fairy Prince* (1611).

◆ *The Revels Accounts are again available for 1611–12. Two of Shakespeare's last plays are given:* The Tempest *(November 1) and "ye winters nightes Tayle" (November 5). The series also includes Francis Beaumont and John Fletcher's* A King and No King.

1612

● Barthelmew Legat an obstinate Arian Heretic was burned in Smithfield. . . . Edward Wightman, an other perverse Heretic, having refused more favor than he could either desire or deserve, was burned at Lichfield, this Heretic would fain have made the people believe, that he himself was the Holy Ghost and immortal, with sundry other most vile opinions, not fit to be mentioned among Christians.

At this time the corpse of Queen Mary late Queen of Scotland, was translated from Peterborough to Westminster . . . and there placed in a vault, upon the South-side whereof the King had made a Royal Tomb for her, where she now resteth.

Friday the sixth of October [actually November] died the most Noble and hopeful Prince Henry Prince of Wales.

■ **Execution of Lancashire Witches.**

◆ Cardenio, *with Fletcher (1612–13, lost).*

John Webster, The White Devil *(1609–12). Anonymous,* Thorney Abbey, *or* The London Maid *(1606–14; influenced by* Macbeth*).*

Henry, Prince of Wales (1610–11), by Isaac Oliver.

1613

● The 17 of April 1613 at Alington in Lancashire was born a maiden child, having four Legs, four Arms, two Bellies joined to one back, one head with two faces, the one before and the other behind, and this year likewise was great Shipwrack, by violent tempests, there happened also sundry Inundations, and strange accidents, and much damage done by fire in divers places, and upon Saint Peter's day the Globe on the bankside was burned.

■ **Princess Elizabeth married to Frederick, Elector Palatine.**

✦ All Is True (Henry VIII), *probably with John Fletcher (1613)*. The Two Noble Kinsmen, *with Fletcher (1613–14) [1634]*.
 Shakespeare purchases Blackfriars Gatehouse.
 The Chamber Accounts for 1612–13 indicate that the King's Men had given a total of twenty plays at court by May 20, including revivals of Much Ado About Nothing, 1 *and* 2 Henry IV, Othello, *and* Julius Caesar, *taking in £60. A further payment is recorded in compensation of a performance before a foreign dignitary in June.*

1614

● In September there was a general muster of horse and foot throughout the Land, and therewithal training of soliders, but chiefly in the City of London by the citizens themselves, many whereof by their former voluntary exercise of Armes and Military discipline, were now so ready and expert that they taught others.

■ "Addled" Parliament is summoned and dissolved.

✦ *Jonson,* Bartholomew Fair. *Webster,* The Duchess of Malfi.
 Philip Henslowe and Jacob Meade build the Hope Theatre (Bankside), a combination theater and bear garden. The Globe reopens.

1615

● At this time proclamation was made again, not only to stay, all further increase of buildings, which were daily erected in and about London, contrary to sundry former Edicts, and thereupon this Proclamation ratified and confirmed all former Proclamations, and straightly charged all Commissioners in that behalf, to look and search in to the depth of such offenders, and offenses, and to punish them accordingly. This Proclamation was dated the 16 of July 1615. And yet for all this, there was wondrous new increase of buildings round about London.

✦ *Lady Elizabeth's players draw up a series of articles of grievance against Philip Henslowe, concerning their considerable debt to him. The Privy Council orders the eight leading members of four London companies, including Richard Burbage and Christopher Beeston, to come before them for performing during Lent against the orders of the Master of the Revels.*

1616

● This Summer, and harvest was so dry, that passengers were annoyed with dust in the highways the 20 of November.

■ William Harvey describes the circulation of blood.

✦ *Marriage of Shakespeare's daughter Judith. Shakespeare makes his will on March 25; he dies April 23.*
 Ben Jonson, The Works of Benjamin Jonson, *the first collection of plays by an English author. His* Masque of Christmas *presented at court.*
 Christopher Beeston builds the Phoenix Theatre.

James I (1603–25), by Simon de Passe.

1616–23

♦ The First Folio of Shakespeare's plays is published by members of the King's Men in 1623.

Records for the years immediately following Shakespeare's death show the continued popularity of Twelfth Night and A Winter's Tale, among other plays. Both are performed at court by the King's Men in April 1618; a performance at court of A Winter's Tale is recorded for 1619–20 and of Twelfth Night for Candlemas (February 2), 1623. A letter of May 20, 1619, written by Sir Gerrard Herbert describes the entertainment of a visiting French nobleman: "In the kinges greate Chamber they went to see the play of

Pirrocles, Prince of Tyre, which lasted till 2 aclocke. After two actes, the players ceased till the French all refreshed them with sweetmeates brought on Chinay voiders, & wyne & ale in bottells, after the players begann anewe." The new Master of the Revels, Sir Henry Herbert, notes on August 19, 1623: "For the king's players. An olde playe called *Winter's Tale,* formerly allowed of by Sir George Bucke, and likewise by mee on Mr Hemminges his worde that there was nothing profane added or reformed, thogh the allowed booke was missinge; and therefore I returned it without a fee."

General Bibliography

There is a huge and ever-expanding scholarly literature about Shakespeare and his culture. This general list and the ten-item lists accompanying the individual plays and poems in this volume are only a small sampling of the available resources. Journals devoted to Shakespeare studies include *Shakespeare Bulletin*, *Shakespeare Jahrbuch* (Germany), *Shakespeare Newsletter*, *Shakespeare Quarterly*, *Shakespeare Studies*, *Shakespeare Studies* (Tokyo), and *Shakespeare Survey* (England). The categories below are only approximate; many of the texts could properly belong in more than one category.

Shakespeare's World

Social, Political, and Economic History

Archer, Ian W. *The Pursuit of Stability: Social Relations in Elizabethan London*. Cambridge: Cambridge University Press, 1991.

Aries, Philippe, and Georges Duby, eds. A *History of Private Life: Passions of the Renaissance*. Vol. 3. Ed. Roger Chartier. Trans. Arthur Goldhammer. Cambridge: Belknap Press of Harvard University Press, 1989.

Barry, J., ed. *The Tudor and Stuart Town*. London: Longman, 1990.

Barry, Jonathan, and Christopher Brooks. *The Middling Sort of People*. New York: St. Martin's Press, 1994.

Barthelmey, Gerard. *Black Face, Maligned Race*. Baton Rouge: Louisiana State University Press, 1987.

Beier, A. L. *Masterless Men: The Vagrancy Problem in England, 1560–1640*. New York: Methuen, 1987.

——, and Roger Finlay, eds. *London 1500–1700: The Making of a Metropolis*. London: Longman, 1986.

Ben-Amos, Ilana Krausman. *Adolescence and Youth in Early Modern England*. New Haven: Yale University Press, 1994.

Bridenbaugh, Carl. *Vexed and Troubled Englishmen, 1590–1642*. New York: Oxford University Press, 1968.

Camden, Carroll. *The Elizabethan Woman*. Rev. ed. Mamaroneck, N.Y.: Appel, 1975.

Chew, Samuel. *The Crescent and the Rose*. New York: Octagon Books, 1965.

Clark, Alice. *Working Life of Women in the Seventeenth Century*. 1968. London: Routledge, 1992.

Clay, C. G. A. *Economic Expansion and Social Change*. 2 vols. Cambridge: Cambridge University Press, 1984.

Cruickshank, C. G. *Elizabeth's Army*. 2nd ed. Oxford: Clarendon Press, 1966.

Elliot, J. H. *The Old World and the New, 1492–1650*. Cambridge: Cambridge University Press, 1970.

Ellis, Steven G. *Tudor Ireland*. London: Longman, 1985.

Elton, G. R. *The Tudor Revolution in Government*. Cambridge: Cambridge University Press, 1959.

——. *England Under the Tudors*. London: Methuen, 1955.

Emmison, P. G. *Elizabethan Life: Disorder*. Chelmsford: Essex County Council, 1970.

Erickson, Amy Louise. *Women and Property in Early Modern England*. London: Routledge, 1993.

Finlay, Roger. *Population and Metropolis: The Demography of London, 1580–1650*. Cambridge: Cambridge University Press, 1979.

Fletcher, Anthony. *Gender, Sex, and Subordination in England, 1500–1800*. New Haven: Yale University Press, 1995.

——, and John Stevenson, eds. *Order and Disorder in Early Modern England*. Cambridge: Cambridge University Press, 1985.

Gittings, C. *Death, Burial and the Individual in Early Modern England*. London: Croom Helm, 1984.

Helgerson, Richard. *Forms of Nationhood: The Elizabethan Writing of England*. Chicago: University of Chicago Press, 1990.

Hirst, Derek. *Authority and Conflict: England, 1603–1658*. Cambridge: Harvard University Press, 1986.

Ingram, Martin. *Church Courts, Sex, and Marriage in England, 1570–1640*. Cambridge: Cambridge University Press, 1987.

James, Mervyn. *Society, Politics and Culture: Studies in Early Modern England*. Cambridge: Cambridge University Press, 1986.

Kantorowicz, E. H. *The King's Two Bodies*. Princeton: Princeton University Press, 1957.

King, J. N. *Tudor Royal Iconography*. Princeton: Princeton University Press, 1989.

Klein, Joan Larsen. *Daughters, Wives, and Widows: Writings by Men about Women and Marriage in England, 1500–1640*. Urbana: University of Illinois Press, 1992.

Laqueur, Thomas. *Making Sex: Body and Gender from the Greeks to Freud*. Cambridge: Harvard University Press, 1990.

Laslett, Peter. *The World We Have Lost: Further Explored*. 3rd ed. New York: Scribner, 1984.

Levin, Carole. *"The Heart and Stomach of a King": Elizabeth I and the Politics of Sex and Power*. Philadelphia: University of Pennsylvania Press, 1994.

Lockyer, Roger. *The Early Stuarts: A Political History of England*. London: Longman, 1989.

MacCaffrey, Wallace T. *Elizabeth I: War and Politics*. Princeton: Princeton University Press, 1992.

——. *The Shaping of the Elizabethan Regime*. Princeton: Princeton University Press, 1968.

Manning, Roger B. *Village Revolts: Social Protest and Popular Disturbances in England, 1509–1640*. Oxford: Clarendon Press, 1988.

Mattingly, Garrett. *The Armada*. Boston: Houghton Mifflin, 1959.

Mukerji, Chandra. *From Graven Images: Patterns of Modern Materialism*. New York: Columbia University Press, 1983.

Neale, J. E. *Queen Elizabeth I*. London: Cape, 1961.

Neale, John E. *Elizabeth I and Her Parliaments*. 2 vols. New York: St. Martin's Press, 1958.

Nichols, John, ed. *The Progresses and Public Processions of Queen Elizabeth*. 3 vols. London, 1823.

Notestein, Wallace. *The House of Commons, 1604–1610*. New Haven: Yale University Press, 1971.

Palliser, D. M. *The Age of Elizabeth*. 2nd ed. London: Longman, 1992.

Parry, G. *The Age of Reconnaissance: Discovery, Exploration, and Settlement, 1450–1650*. New York: Praeger, 1969.

Pearson, Lu Emily. *Elizabethans at Home*. Stanford: Stanford University Press, 1957.

Peck, Linda Levy. *Court Patronage and Corruption in Early Stuart England*. Boston: Unwin Hyman, 1990.

Pocock, J. G. A. *The Ancient Constitution and the Feudal Law*. Rev. ed. Cambridge: Cambridge University Press, 1987.

Quinn, David B. *The Elizabethans and the Irish*. Ithaca, N.Y.: Cornell University Press, 1966.

Scarisbrick, J. J. *Henry VIII*. Berkeley and Los Angeles: University of California Press, 1968.

Sharpe, J. A. *Crime in Seventeenth-Century England: A Country Study.* Cambridge: Cambridge University Press, 1983.

Slack, Paul. *The Impact of Plague in Tudor and Stuart England.* London: Routledge & Kegan Paul, 1985.

——, ed. *Rebellion, Popular Protest and the Social Order in Early Modern England.* Cambridge: Cambridge University Press, 1984.

Stone, Lawrence. *The Causes of the English Revolution, 1529–1642.* New York: Routledge & Kegan Paul, 1986.

——. *The Family, Sex and Marriage in England, 1500–1800.* New York: Harper & Row, 1977.

——. *The Crisis of the Aristocracy, 1558–1641.* Oxford: Clarendon Press, 1965.

Stow, John. *Survey of London.* Ed. C. L. Kingsford. Oxford: Clarendon Press, 1971.

Tawney, R. H. *Religion and the Rise of Capitalism.* 1926. New York: Peter Smith, 1962.

Thirsk, Joan. *Economic Policy and Projects: The Development of a Consumer Society in Early Modern England.* Oxford: Clarendon Press, 1978.

Thomas, Keith. *Religion and the Decline of Magic.* New York: Scribner, 1971.

Underdown, David. *Revel, Riot, and Rebellion: Popular Politics and Culture in England, 1603–1660.* Oxford: Clarendon Press, 1985.

Walvin, James. *The Black Presence: A Documentary History of the Negro in England, 1555–1860.* London: Orbach & Chambers, 1971.

Willson, David Harris. *King James VI & I.* 1956. London: Cape, 1972.

Wilson, F. P. *Elizabethan and Jacobean.* Oxford: Clarendon Press, 1945.

Yates, Frances. *Astraea: The Imperial Theme in the Sixteenth Century.* London: Routledge & Kegan Paul, 1975.

Zagorin, Perez. *Rebels and Rulers, 1500–1660.* 2 vols. Cambridge: Cambridge University Press, 1982.

——. *The Court and the Country: The Beginnings of the English Revolution.* New York: Atheneum, 1970.

Zeeveld, W. Gordon. *Foundations of Tudor Policy.* Cambridge: Harvard University Press, 1948.

Intellectual and Religious History

Baker, Herschel C. *The Race of Time: Three Lectures on Renaissance Historiography.* Toronto: University of Toronto Press, 1967.

Barkan, Leonard. *Nature's Work of Art: The Human Body as Image of the World.* New Haven: Yale University Press, 1975.

Bouwsma, William J. *John Calvin: A Sixteenth-Century Portrait.* New York: Oxford University Press, 1988.

Brower, Reuben A. *Hero and Saint: Shakespeare and the Graeco-Roman Tradition.* New York: Oxford University Press, 1971.

Cassirer, Ernst. *The Individual and the Cosmos in Renaissance Philosophy.* Trans. Mario Domandi. Philadelphia: University of Pennsylvania Press, 1972.

Collinson, Patrick. *The Elizabethan Puritan Movement.* New York: Oxford University Press, 1989.

——. *The Religion of Protestants: The Church in English Society, 1559–1625.* Oxford: Clarendon Press, 1982.

Dickens, A. G. *The English Reformation.* New York: Schocken Books, 1964.

Haydn, Hiram. *The Counter-Renaissance.* 1950. Gloucester, Mass.: P. Smith, 1966.

Hill, Christopher. *Society and Puritanism in Pre-Revolutionary England.* New York: Schocken Books, 1967.

Kelly, Henry Ansgar. *Divine Providence in the England of Shakespeare's Histories.* Cambridge: Harvard University Press, 1970.

Klaits, Joseph. *Servants of Satan: The Age of the Witch Hunts.* Bloomington: Indiana University Press, 1985.

Kocher, Paul. *Science and Religion in Elizabethan England.* 1953. New York: Octagon Books, 1969.

Kristeller, Paul Oskar. *Renaissance Thought: The Classic, Scholastic, and Humanistic Strains.* New York: Harper, 1961.

Levao, Ronald. *Renaissance Minds and Their Fictions.* Berkeley and Los Angeles: University of California Press, 1985.

Levin, Harry. *The Myth of the Golden Age in the Renaissance.* Bloomington: University of Indiana Press, 1969.

Levy, Fred J. *Tudor Historical Thought.* San Marino, Calif.: Huntington Library Press, 1967.

Lovejoy, A. O. *The Great Chain of Being: A Study of the History of an Idea.* Cambridge: Harvard University Press, 1936.

Mack, Peter, ed. *Renaissance Rhetoric.* New York: St. Martin's Press, 1994.

Popkin, Richard H. *The History of Skepticism from Erasmus to Spinoza.* Berkeley and Los Angeles: University of California Press, 1979.

Rossi, Paolo. *Francis Bacon: From Magic to Science.* London: Routledge & Kegan Paul, 1968.

Shuger, Debora Kuller. *Habits of Thought in the English Renaissance: Religion, Politics, and the Dominant Culture.* Berkeley and Los Angeles: University of California Press, 1990.

Sonnino, Lee A. *A Handbook to Sixteenth-Century Rhetoric.* London: Routledge & Kegan Paul, 1968.

Strong, Roy. *The Cult of Elizabeth.* London: Thames and Hudson, 1977.

——. *The English Icon: Elizabethan and Jacobean Portraiture.* London: Routledge & Kegan Paul, 1969.

Tillyard, E. M. W. *The Elizabethan World Picture.* London: Chatto & Windus, 1943.

Wind, Edgar. *Pagan Mysteries in the Renaissance.* 2nd ed. London: Faber, 1968.

Cultural History

Aers, David, Bob Hodge, and Gunther Kress. *Literature, Language and Society in England, 1589–1680.* Totowa, N.J.: Barnes & Noble, 1981.

Austern, Linda Phyllis. " 'Sing Againe Syren': The Female Musician and Sexual Enchantment in Elizabethan Life and Literature." *Renaissance Quarterly* 42 (1989): 420–48.

Bakhtin, Mikhail. *Rabelais and His World.* Cambridge: MIT Press, 1968.

Barkan, Leonard. *The Gods Made Flesh: Metamorphosis and the Pursuit of Paganism.* New Haven: Yale University Press, 1986.

Barker, Francis. *The Tremulous Private Body.* London: Methuen, 1994.

Beilin, Elaine V. *Redeeming Eve: Women Writers of the English Renaissance.* Princeton: Princeton University Press, 1987.

Bevington, David. *Tudor Drama and Politics: A Critical Approach to Topical Meaning.* Cambridge: Harvard University Press, 1968.

Bray, Alan. *Homosexuality in Renaissance England.* London: Gay Men's Press, 1982.

Briggs, K. M. *Pale Hecate's Team: An Examination of the Beliefs on Witchcraft and Magic among Shakespeare's Contemporaries and His Immediate Successors.* New York: Humanities Press, 1962.

——. *The Anatomy of Puck: An Examination of Fairy Beliefs among Shakespeare's Contemporaries and Successors.* London: Routledge & Kegan Paul, 1959.

Burke, Peter. *Popular Culture in Early Modern Europe.* New York: New York University Press, 1978.

Burt, Richard, and John Michael Archer, eds. *Enclosure Acts: Sexuality, Property, and Culture in Early Modern England.* Ithaca, N.Y.: Cornell University Press, 1994.

Buxton, John. *Elizabethan Taste.* London: Macmillan, 1963.

Caldwell, John. *The Oxford History of English Music.* Vol. 1. Oxford: Clarendon Press, 1991.

Cressy, David. *Literacy and the Social Order: Reading and Writing in Tudor and Stuart England*. Cambridge: Cambridge University Press, 1980.

Dolan, Frances. *Dangerous Familiars: Representations of Domestic Crime in England, 1550–1700*. Ithaca, N.Y.: Cornell University Press, 1994.

Eisenstein, Elizabeth. *The Printing Press as an Agent of Change*. 2 vols. Cambridge: Cambridge University Press, 1979.

Ferguson, Margaret W., Maureen Quilligan, and Nancy J. Vickers, eds. *Rewriting the Renaissance: The Discourses of Sexual Difference in Early Modern Europe*. Chicago: University of Chicago Press, 1986.

Fumerton, Patricia. *Cultural Aesthetics: Renaissance Literature and the Practice of Social Ornament*. Chicago: University of Chicago Press, 1991.

Garber, Marjorie, ed. *Cannibals, Witches, Divorce: Estranging the Renaissance*. Baltimore: Johns Hopkins University Press, 1987.

Gillies, John. *Shakespeare and the Geography of Difference*. New York: Cambridge University Press, 1994.

Goldberg, Jonathan. *Writing Matter: From the Hands of the English Renaissance*. Stanford: Stanford University Press, 1990.

———. *James I and the Politics of Literature: Jonson, Shakespeare, Donne and Their Contemporaries*. Baltimore: Johns Hopkins University Press, 1983.

———, ed. *Queering the Renaissance*. Durham, N.C.: Duke University Press, 1994.

Greenblatt, Stephen. *Learning to Curse: Essays in Early Modern Culture*. New York: Routledge, 1990.

———. *Renaissance Self-Fashioning: From More to Shakespeare*. Chicago: University of Chicago Press, 1980.

———, ed. *New World Encounters*. Berkeley and Los Angeles: University of California Press, 1993.

———, ed. *Representing the English Renaissance*. Berkeley and Los Angeles: University of California Press, 1988.

Grout, Donald Jay. *A Short History of Opera*. New York: Columbia University Press, 1988.

Hall, Kim F. *Things of Darkness: Economies of Race and Gender in Early Modern England*. Ithaca, N.Y.: Cornell University Press, 1996.

Haselkorn, Anne M., and Betty S. Travitsky, eds. *The Renaissance Englishwoman in Print: Counterbalancing the Canon*. Amherst: University of Massachusetts Press, 1990.

Henderson, Katherine Usher, and Barbara F. McManus. *Half Humankind: Contexts and Texts of the Controversy About Women in England, 1540–1640*. Urbana: University of Illinois Press, 1985.

Hendricks, Margo, and Patricia Parker, eds. *Women, "Race," and Writing in the Early Modern Period*. London: Routledge, 1994.

Hoeniger, F. David. *Medicine and Shakespeare in the English Renaissance*. Newark: University of Delaware Press, 1991.

Huizinga, Johan. *The Autumn of the Middle Ages*. Trans. Rodney J. Payton and Ulrich Mammitzsch. Chicago: University of Chicago Press, 1996.

Hull, Suzanne W. *Chaste, Silent and Obedient: English Books for Women, 1475–1640*. San Marino, Calif.: Huntington Library, 1982.

Jardine, Lisa. *Still Harping on Daughters: Women and Drama in the Age of Shakespeare*. 1983. 2nd ed. New York: Columbia University Press, 1989.

Javitch, Daniel. *Poetry and Courtliness in Renaissance England*. Princeton: Princeton University Press, 1978.

Jordan, Constance. *Renaissance Feminism: Literary Texts and Political Models*. Ithaca, N.Y.: Cornell University Press, 1990.

Kelso, Ruth. *Doctrine for the Lady of the Renaissance*. 1956. Urbana: University of Illinois Press, 1978.

———. *The Doctrine of the English Gentleman in the Sixteenth Century*. 1929. Gloucester, Mass.: P. Smith, 1964.

Manley, Lawrence. *Literature and Culture in Early Modern London.* Cambridge: Cambridge University Press, 1995.

Marcus, Leah. *The Politics of Mirth: Jonson, Herrick, Milton, Marvell, and the Defense of Old Holiday Pastimes.* Chicago: University of Chicago Press, 1986.

Miller, David Lee, Sharon O'Dair, and Harold Weber, eds. *The Production of English Renaissance Culture.* Ithaca, N.Y.: Cornell University Press, 1994.

Norbrook, David. *Poetry and Politics in the English Renaissance.* London: Routledge & Kegan Paul, 1984.

Orlin, Lena Cowen. *Private Matters and Public Culture in Post-Reformation England.* Ithaca, N.Y.: Cornell University Press, 1994.

Parry, G. *The Golden Age Restor'd: The Culture of the Stuart Court, 1603–1642.* Manchester: Manchester University Press, 1981.

Patterson, Annabel. *Censorship and Interpretation: The Conditions of Writing and Reading in Early Modern England.* Madison: University of Wisconsin Press, 1984.

Shapiro, James. *Shakespeare and the Jews.* New York: Columbia University Press, 1996.

Sharpe, K., and Lake, P., eds. *Culture and Politics in Early Stuart England,* Stanford: Stanford University Press, 1993.

Simon, Joan. *Education and Society in Tudor England.* Cambridge: Cambridge University Press, 1966.

Sinfield, Alan. *Literature in Protestant England, 1560–1660.* Totowa, N.J.: Barnes & Noble, 1983.

Smith, Bruce. *Homosexual Desire in Shakespeare's England.* Chicago: University of Chicago Press, 1991.

Spufford, Margaret. *Small Books and Pleasant Histories: Popular Fiction and Its Readership in Seventeenth-Century England.* Athens: University of Georgia Press, 1981.

Stallybrass, Peter, and Allon White. *The Politics and Poetics of Transgression.* Ithaca, N.Y.: Cornell University Press, 1986.

Turner, James Grantham, ed. *Sexuality and Gender in Early Modern Europe: Institutions, Texts, Images.* Cambridge: Cambridge University Press, 1993.

Whigham, Frank. *Ambition and Privilege: The Social Tropes of Elizabethan Courtesy Theory.* Berkeley and Los Angeles: University of California Press, 1984.

Woodbridge, Linda. *Women and the English Renaissance: Literature and the Nature of Womankind, 1540–1620.* Urbana: University of Illinois Press, 1986.

Wright, L. B. *Middle-Class Culture in Elizabethan England.* Chapel Hill: University of North Carolina Press, 1935.

Shakespeare's Literary and Theatrical Contexts

Agnew, Jean-Christophe. *Worlds Apart: The Market and the Theatre in Anglo-American Thought, 1550–1750.* Cambridge: Cambridge University Press, 1986.

Alpers, Paul. *What Is Pastoral?* Chicago: University of Chicago Press, 1996.

Altman, Joel. *The Tudor Play of Mind.* Berkeley and Los Angeles: University of California Press, 1978.

Barber, C. L. *Creating Elizabethan Tragedy: The Theater of Kyd and Marlowe.* Chicago: University of Chicago Press, 1988.

Barish, Jonas. *Ben Jonson and the Language of Prose Comedy.* Cambridge: Harvard University Press, 1960.

———. *The Antitheatrical Prejudice.* Berkeley and Los Angeles: University of California Press, 1981.

Bate, Jonathan. *Shakespeare and Ovid.* Oxford: Clarendon Press, 1993.

Bates, Catherine. *The Rhetoric of Courtship in Elizabethan Language and Literature.* Cambridge: Cambridge University Press, 1992.

Belsey, Catherine. *The Subject of Tragedy: Identity and Difference in Renaissance Drama.* London: Methuen, 1985.

Bentley, G. E. *The Profession of Player in Shakespeare's Time, 1590–1642.* Princeton: Princeton University Press, 1984.

———. *The Profession of Dramatist in Shakespeare's Time, 1590–1642.* Princeton: Princeton University Press, 1971.

———. *The Seventeenth-Century Stage: A Collection of Critical Essays.* Chicago: University of Chicago Press, 1968.

———. *The Jacobean and Caroline Stage.* 7 vols. Oxford: Clarendon Press, 1941–68.

Bevington, David. *From "Mankind" to Marlowe: Growth of Structure in the Popular Drama of Tudor England.* Cambridge: Harvard University Press, 1962.

Bowers, Fredson T. *Elizabethan Revenge Tragedy, 1587–1642.* Princeton: Princeton University Press, 1940.

Bradbrook, M. C. *The Rise of the Common Player: A Study of Actor and Society in Shakespeare's England.* London: Chatto & Windus, 1962.

Braden, Gordon. *Renaissance Tragedy and the Senecan Tradition.* New Haven: Yale University Press, 1985.

Briggs, Julia. *This Stage-Play World: English Literature and Its Background, 1580–1625.* Oxford: Oxford University Press, 1983.

Bristol, Michael D. *Carnival and Theater: Plebeian Culture and the Structure of Authority in Renaissance England.* New York: Methuen, 1985.

Bruster, Douglas. *Drama and the Market in the Age of Shakespeare.* Cambridge: Cambridge University Press, 1992.

Bullough, Geoffrey, ed. *Narrative and Dramatic Sources of Shakespeare.* 8 vols. New York: Columbia University Press, 1957–75.

Butler, Martin. *Theatre and Crisis, 1632–1642.* Cambridge: Cambridge University Press, 1984.

Clubb, Louise George. *Italian Drama in Shakespeare's Time.* New Haven: Yale University Press, 1989.

Cohen, Walter. *Drama of a Nation: Public Theater in Renaissance England and Spain.* Ithaca, N.Y.: Cornell University Press, 1985.

Dessen, Alan C. *Recovering Shakespeare's Theatrical Vocabulary.* Cambridge: Cambridge University Press, 1995.

———. *Elizabethan Stage Conventions and Modern Interpreters.* Cambridge: Cambridge University Press, 1984.

———. *Elizabethan Drama and the Viewer's Eye.* Chapel Hill: University of North Carolina Press, 1977.

Doran, Madeleine. *Endeavors of Art: A Study of Form in Elizabethan Drama.* Madison: University of Wisconsin Press, 1954.

Empson, William. *The Structure of Complex Words.* 1951. London: Chatto & Windus, 1970.

Farnham, Willard. *The Medieval Heritage of Elizabethan Tragedy.* 1936. New York: Barnes & Noble, 1956.

Foakes, R. A. *Illustrations of the English Stage, 1580–1642.* Stanford: Stanford University Press, 1985.

Gardiner, H. C. *Mysteries' End.* New Haven: Yale University Press, 1946.

Harbage, Alfred. *Shakespeare and the Rival Traditions.* 1952. New York: Barnes & Noble, 1968.

Hardison, O. B. Jr. *Christian Rite and Christian Drama in the Middle Ages.* Baltimore: Johns Hopkins University Press, 1965.

Hattaway, Michael. *Elizabethan Popular Theatre: Plays in Performance.* London: Routledge & Kegan Paul, 1982.

Heinemann, Margot. *Puritanism and Theatre: Thomas Middleton and Opposition Drama under the Early Stuarts.* Cambridge: Cambridge University Press, 1980.

Homan, Sidney, ed. *Shakespeare's "More Than Words Can Witness."* Lewisburg, Pa.: Bucknell University Press, 1980.

Hosley, Richard, ed. *Shakespeare's Holinshed: An Edition of Holinshed's Chronicles.* New York: Putnam, 1968.

Hunter, G. K. *John Lyly: The Humanist as Courtier.* Cambridge: Harvard University Press, 1962.

Jones, Emrys. *Scenic Form in Shakespeare.* Oxford: Clarendon Press, 1971.

Kernan, Alvin. *The Cankered Muse: Satire of the English Renaissance.* New Haven: Yale University Press, 1959.

Kolve, V. A. *The Play Called Corpus Christi.* Stanford: Stanford University Press, 1966.

Leggatt, Alexander. *Citizen Comedy in the Age of Shakespeare.* Toronto: University of Toronto Press, 1973.

Levin, Harry. *The Overreacher: A Study of Christopher Marlowe.* 1932. Cambridge: Harvard University Press, 1964.

Levin, Richard. *The Multiple Plot in English Renaissance Drama.* Chicago: University of Chicago Press, 1971.

Lomax, Marion. *Stage Images and Traditions: Shakespeare to Ford.* Cambridge: Cambridge University Press, 1987.

McLuskie, Kathleen. *Renaissance Dramatists.* New York: Harvester Wheatsheaf, 1989.

McMillin, Scott. *The Elizabethan Theatre and the Book of Sir Thomas More.* Ithaca, N.Y.: Cornell University Press, 1987.

Montrose, Louis. *The Purpose of Playing: Shakespeare and the Cultural Politics of the Elizabethan Theatre.* Chicago: University of Chicago Press, 1996.

Muir, Kenneth. *Shakespeare's Sources.* 2 vols. London, 1957.

Orgel, Stephen. *The Illusion of Power: Political Theater in the English Renaissance.* Berkeley and Los Angeles: University of California Press, 1975.

Rose, Mark. *Shakespearean Design.* Cambridge: Harvard University Press, 1972.

Rose, Mary Beth. *The Expense of Spirit: Love and Sexuality in English Renaissance Drama.* Ithaca, N.Y.: Cornell University Press, 1988.

Sanders, Wilbur. *The Dramatist and the Received Idea: Studies in the Plays of Marlowe and Shakespeare.* Cambridge: Cambridge University Press, 1968.

Spivack, Bernard. *Shakespeare and the Allegory of Evil.* New York: Columbia University Press, 1958.

Waith, Eugene. *The Herculean Hero in Marlowe, Chapman, Shakespeare, and Dryden.* New York: Columbia University Press, 1962.

Weimann, Robert. *Shakespeare and the Popular Tradition in the Theater: Studies in the Social Dimension of Dramatic Form and Function.* Ed. Robert Schwartz. Baltimore: Johns Hopkins University Press, 1978.

Woolf, Rosemary. *The English Mystery Plays.* Berkeley and Los Angeles: University of California Press, 1972.

The Playing Field: London Theaters and State Regulation

Astington, John H., ed. *The Development of Shakespeare's Theater.* New York: AMS Press, 1992.

Barrol, Leeds. *Politics, Plague, and Shakespeare's Theater: The Stuart Years.* Ithaca, N.Y.: Cornell University Press, 1991.

Beckerman, Bernard. *Shakespeare at the Globe, 1599–1609.* New York: Macmillan, 1962, 1967.

Berry, Herbert. *Shakespeare's Playhouses.* Illustrated by C. Walter Hodges. AMS Studies in the Renaissance 19. New York: AMS Press, 1987.

Chambers, E. K. *The Elizabethan Stage.* 4 vols. Oxford: Clarendon Press, 1923.

———. *The Medieval Stage.* 2 vols. Oxford: Clarendon Press, 1903.

Clare, Janet. *"Art Made Tongue-Tied by Authority": Elizabethan and Jacobean Dramatic Censorship*. New York: St. Martin's Press, 1990.

Cook, Ann Jennalie. *The Privileged Playgoers of Shakespeare's London: 1576–1642*. Princeton: Princeton University Press, 1981.

Gair, W. Reavley. *The Children of Paul's*. Cambridge: Cambridge University Press, 1982.

Gildersleeve, Virginia C. *Government Regulation of the Elizabethan Drama*. Westport, Conn.: Greenwood Press, 1975.

Greg, W. W., ed. *Dramatic Documents from the Elizabethan Playhouses: Stage Plots; Actor's Parts; Prompt Books*. 2 vols. 1931. Oxford: Clarendon Press, 1969.

Gurr, Andrew. *The Shakespearean Stage, 1574–1642*. 3rd ed. Cambridge: Cambridge University Press, 1992.

——. *Playgoing in Shakespeare's London*. Cambridge: Cambridge University Press, 1987.

——, and John Orrell. *Rebuilding Shakespeare's Globe*. London: Weidenfeld and Nicolson, 1989.

Harbage, Alfred. *Shakespeare's Audience*. New York: Columbia University Press, 1941.

Henslowe, Philip. *Henslowe's Diary*. Ed. R. A. Foakes and R. T. Rickert. Cambridge: Cambridge University Press, 1961.

Hodges, C. Walter. *The Globe Restored*. 1953. New York: Norton, 1968, 1973.

Ingram, William. *The Business of Playing: The Beginnings of Adult Professional Theater in Elizabethan London*. Ithaca, N.Y.: Cornell University Press, 1992.

Joseph, Bertram L. *Acting Shakespeare*. London: Routledge & Kegan Paul, 1960.

Kernodle, G. R. *From Art to Theatre: Form and Convention in the Renaissance*. 1944. Chicago: University of Chicago Press, 1965.

King, T. J. *Shakespearean Staging, 1599–1642*. Cambridge: Harvard University Press, 1971.

Knutson, Roslyn L. *The Repertory of Shakespeare's Company, 1594–1613*. Fayetteville: University of Arkansas Press, 1991.

Mullaney, Steven. *The Place of the Stage: License, Play and Power in Renaissance England*. Chicago: University of Chicago Press, 1987.

Orgel, Stephen. *Impersonations: The Performance of Gender in Shakespeare's England*. Cambridge: Cambridge UP, 1996.

Shapiro, Michael. *Children of the Revels: The Boy Companies of Shakespeare's Time and Their Plays*. New York: Columbia University Press, 1977.

Smith, Irwin. *Shakespeare's Blackfriars Playhouse*. New York: New York University Press, 1964.

——. *Shakespeare's Globe Playhouse*. New York: Scribner, 1956.

Wickham, Glynne. *Early English Stages: 1300 to 1660*. 4 vols. New York: Columbia University Press, 1959–81.

Shakespeare's Life

Alexander, Peter. *Shakespeare's Life and Art*. New ed. New York: New York University Press, 1961.

Baldwin, T. W. *William Shakspere's Small Latine and Lesse Greeke*. 2 vols. Urbana: University of Illinois Press, 1944.

Bentley, G. E. *Shakespeare: A Biographical Handbook*. New Haven: Yale University Press, 1961.

Bradbrook, Muriel. *Shakespeare: The Poet in His World*. London: Weidenfeld and Nicolson, 1978.

Burton, S. H. *Shakespeare's Life and Stage*. Edinburgh: W. & R. Chambers, 1989.

Chambers, E. K. *William Shakespeare: A Study of Facts and Problems*. 2 vols. Oxford: Clarendon Press, 1930.

Eccles, Mark. *Shakespeare in Warwickshire*. Madison: University of Wisconsin Press, 1961.

Fraser, Russell. *Shakespeare: The Later Years*. New York: Columbia University Press, 1992.

———. *Young Shakespeare.* New York: Columbia University Press, 1988.

Greer, Germaine. *Shakespeare.* New York: Oxford University Press, 1986.

Honigmann, E. A. J. *Shakespeare: The Lost Years.* Totowa, N.J.: Barnes & Noble, 1985.

———, ed. *Shakespeare and His Contemporaries: Essays in Comparison.* Manchester: Manchester University Press, 1986.

Hotson, Leslie. *Shakespeare Versus Shallow.* London: Nonesuch Press, 1931.

Levi, Peter. *The Life and Times of William Shakespeare.* New York: Holt, 1989.

Matus, Irvin Leigh. *Shakespeare: The Living Record.* New York: St. Martin's Press, 1991.

Reese, M. M. *Shakespeare: His World and His Work.* Rev. ed. New York: St. Martin's Press, 1980.

Rogers, Joyce. *The Second Best Bed: Shakespeare's Will in a New Light.* Westport, Conn.: Greenwood Press, 1993.

Sams, Eric. *The Real Shakespeare: Retrieving the Early Years, 1564–1594.* New Haven: Yale University Press, 1995.

Schmidgall, Gary. *Shakespeare and the Poet's Life.* Lexington: University Press of Kentucky, 1990.

Schoenbaum, Samuel. *Shakespeare's Lives.* New ed. New York: Oxford University Press, 1991.

———. *Shakespeare: His Life, His Language, His Theater.* New York: Signet, 1990.

———. *William Shakespeare: A Compact Documentary Life.* Rev. ed. Oxford: Oxford University Press, 1987.

Thomson, Peter. *Shakespeare's Professional Career.* Cambridge: Cambridge University Press, 1992.

Wells, Stanley. *Shakespeare: A Life in Drama.* New York: Norton, 1995.

Shakespearean Criticism

Founding Figures

Shakespeare: The Critical Heritage. Ed. Brian Vickers. Multiple volumes. London: Routledge & Kegan Paul, 1974–.

Coleridge, S. T. *Coleridge on Shakespeare: The Text of the Lectures of 1811–12.* Ed. R. A Foakes. Charlottesville: University of Virginia Press, 1971.

Coleridge, S. T. *Samuel Taylor Coleridge: Shakespearean Criticism.* 2 vols. 2nd ed. 1960. Ed. T. M. Raysor. Totowa, N.J.: Biblio Distribution Center, 1974, 1980.

Hazlitt, William. *Characters of Shakespear's Plays.* London, 1817.

Johnson, Samuel. *Johnson on Shakespeare.* Ed. Arthur Sherbo. Vol. 7 of The Yale Edition of the Works of Samuel Johnson. New Haven: Yale University Press, 1968.

Morgann, Maurice. *Shakespearean Criticism.* Ed. Daniel Fineman. Oxford: Clarendon Press, 1972.

Language and Style

Baxter, John. *Shakespeare's Poetic Styles.* London: Routledge & Kegan Paul, 1980.

Blake, N. F. *Shakespeare's Language: An Introduction.* New York: St. Martin's Press, 1983.

Cercignani, Fausto. *Shakespeare's Works and Elizabethan Pronunciation.* New York: Oxford University Press, 1981.

Clemen, Wolfgang. *The Development of Shakespeare's Imagery.* London: Methuen, 1951.

Danson, Lawrence. *Tragic Alphabet: Shakespeare's Drama of Language.* New Haven: Yale University Press, 1974.

Donawerth, Jane. *Shakespeare and the Sixteenth-Century Study of Language.* Urbana: University of Illinois Press, 1984.

Edwards, Philip, Inga-Stina Ewbank, and G. K. Hunter, eds. *Shakespeare's Styles*. Cambridge: Cambridge University Press, 1980.

Hussey, S. S. *The Literary Language of Shakespeare*. London: Longman, 1982.

Kökeritz, Helge. *Shakespeare's Pronunciation*. New Haven: Yale University Press, 1959.

Mahood, M. M. *Shakespeare's Wordplay*. London: Methuen, 1957.

Miriam Joseph, Sister. *Shakespeare's Use of the Arts of Language*. New York: Columbia University Press, 1947.

Parker, Patricia. *Shakespeare from the Margins: Language, Culture, Context*. Chicago: University of Chicago Press, 1996.

Partridge, Eric. *Shakespeare's Bawdy: A Literary and Psychological Essay and a Comprehensive Glossary*. 3rd ed. New York: Routledge, 1991.

Spurgeon, Caroline. *Shakespeare's Imagery and What It Tells Us*. 1935. Cambridge: Cambridge University Press, 1968.

Vickers, Brian. "Shakespeare's Use of Rhetoric." *A New Companion to Shakespeare Studies*. Ed. Kenneth Muir and S. Schoenbaum. Cambridge: Cambridge University Press, 1971. 83–98.

——. *The Artistry of Shakespeare's Prose*. London: Methuen, 1968.

Wright, George T. *Shakespeare's Metrical Art*. Berkeley and Los Angeles: University of California Press, 1988.

Critical Approaches

Adelman, Janet. *Suffocating Mothers: Fantasies of Maternal Origin in Shakespeare's Plays*. New York: Routledge, 1992.

Andrews, John F. *William Shakespeare: His World, His Work, His Influence*. 3 vols. New York: Scribner, 1985.

Bamber, Linda. *Comic Women, Tragic Men: A Study of Gender and Genre in Shakespeare*. Stanford: Stanford University Press, 1982.

Barber, C. L. *Shakespeare's Festive Comedy: A Study of Dramatic Form and Its Relation to Social Custom*. Princeton: Princeton University Press, 1959.

——, and Richard P. Wheeler. *The Whole Journey: Shakespeare's Power of Development*. Berkeley and Los Angeles: University of California Press, 1986.

Barker, Deborah E., and Ivo Kamps, eds. *Shakespeare and Gender: A History*. New York: Verso, 1995.

Barton, Anne. *Essays, Mainly Shakespearean*. Cambridge: Cambridge University Press, 1994.

Battenhouse, Roy, ed. *Shakespeare's Christian Dimension: An Anthology of Commentary*. Bloomington: Indiana University Press, 1994.

Berry, Ralph. *Shakespeare and Social Class*. Atlantic Highlands, N.J.: Humanities Press International, 1988.

——. *Shakespeare and the Awareness of the Audience*. New York: St. Martin's Press, 1985.

Boose, Lynda E. "The Father and the Bride in Shakespeare." *PMLA* 97 (1982): 325–47.

Booth, Stephen. *"King Lear," "Macbeth," Indefinition and Tragedy*. New Haven: Yale University Press, 1983.

Bradley, A. C. *Shakespearean Tragedy*. 1904. 3rd ed. New York: St. Martin's Press, 1992.

Bradshaw, Graham. *Misrepresentations: Shakespeare and the Materialists*. Ithaca, N.Y.: Cornell University Press, 1993.

——. *Shakespeare's Skepticism*. New York: St. Martin's Press, 1987.

Brissenden, Alan. *Shakespeare and the Dance*. Atlantic Highlands, N.J.: Humanities Press International, 1981.

Bristol, Michael. *Shakespeare's America, America's Shakespeare*. London: Routledge, 1990.

Burkhardt, Sigurd. *Shakespearean Meanings*. Princeton: Princeton University Press, 1968.

Calderwood, James. *Shakespeare and the Denial of Death*. Amherst: University of Massachusetts Press, 1987.

——. *Shakespearean Metadrama.* Minneapolis: University of Minnesota Press, 1971.

Callaghan, Dympna. *Woman and Gender in Renaissance Tragedy: A Study of "King Lear," "Othello," "The Duchess of Malfi," and "The White Devil."* Atlantic Highlands, N.J.: Humanities Press International, 1989.

Carroll, William C. *The Metamorphoses of Shakespearean Comedy.* Princeton: Princeton University Press, 1985.

Cavell, Stanley. *Disowning Knowledge in Six Plays of Shakespeare.* Cambridge: Cambridge University Press, 1987.

Charnes, Linda. *Notorious Identity: Materializing the Subject in Shakespeare.* Cambridge: Harvard University Press, 1993.

Clemen, Wolfgang H. *Shakespeare's Soliloquies.* Trans. Charity Scott Stokes. London: Methuen, 1987.

Cohen, Derek. *Shakespeare's Culture of Violence.* New York: St. Martin's Press, 1993.

Colie, Rosalie L. *Shakespeare's Living Art.* Princeton: Princeton University Press, 1974.

Colman, E. A. M. *The Dramatic Use of Bawdy in Shakespeare.* London: Longman, 1974.

Cox, John D. *Shakespeare and the Dramaturgy of Power.* Princeton: Princeton University Press, 1989.

Cunningham, J. V. *Woe or Wonder: The Emotional Effect of Shakespearean Tragedy.* Denver: University of Denver Press, 1951.

Dash, Irene. *Wooing, Wedding, and Power: Women in Shakespeare's Plays.* New York: Columbia University Press, 1981.

Dawson, Anthony. *Indirections: Shakespeare and the Art of Illusion.* Toronto: University of Toronto Press, 1978.

De Grazia, Margreta. "Homonyms before and after Lexical Standardization." *Deutsche Shakespeare Gesellschaft West (Jahrbuch).* Bochum, Germany, 1990. 143–56.

Dollimore, Jonathan, and Alan Sinfield, eds. *Political Shakespeare: Essays in Cultural Materialism.* 2nd ed. Manchester: Manchester University Press, 1994.

——. *Radical Tragedy: Religion, Ideology, and Power in the Drama of Shakespeare and His Contemporaries.* Durham, N.C.: Duke University Press, 1993.

Drakakis, John, ed. *Alternative Shakespeares.* London: Methuen, 1985.

Dubrow, Heather, and Richard Strier. *The Historical Renaissance.* Chicago: University of Chicago Press, 1988.

Dusinberre, Juliet. *Shakespeare and the Nature of Women.* 2nd ed. Houndsmill, Basingstoke: Macmillan, 1996.

Eagleton, Terry. *William Shakespeare.* Oxford: Blackwell, 1987.

Edwards, Philip. *Shakespeare: A Writer's Progress.* Oxford: Oxford University Press, 1986.

Eliot, T. S. "Shakespeare and the Stoicism of Seneca." *Selected Essays, 1917–1932.* 1932. New York: Harcourt Brace Jovanovich, 1950.

Engle, Lars. *Shakespearean Pragmatism: Market of His Time.* Chicago: University of Chicago Press, 1993.

Erickson, Peter. *Patriarchal Structures in Shakespeare's Drama.* Berkeley and Los Angeles: University of California Press, 1985.

——, and Coppèlia Kahn, eds. *Shakespeare's Rough Magic: Essays in Honor of C. L. Barber.* Newark: University of Delaware Press, 1985.

Evans, Malcolm. *Signifying Nothing: Truth's True Contents in Shakespeare's Text.* Athens: University of Georgia Press, 1986.

Farrell, Kirby. *Play, Death, and Heroism in Shakespeare.* Chapel Hill: University of North Carolina Press, 1989.

Felperin, Howard. *Shakespearean Romance.* Princeton: Princeton University Press, 1972.

Fiedler, Leslie. *The Stranger in Shakespeare.* New York: Stein & Day, 1972.

French, Marilyn. *Shakespeare's Division of Experience.* London: Cape, 1981.

Frye, Northrop. *Fools of Time: Studies in Shakespearean Tragedy.* Toronto: University of Toronto Press, 1967.

——. *A Natural Perspective: The Development of Shakespearean Comedy and Romance.* New York: Columbia University Press, 1965.

Garber, Marjorie. *Coming of Age in Shakespeare.* London: Methuen, 1981.

———. *Shakespeare's Ghost Writers: Literature as Uncanny Causality.* New York: Methuen, 1987.

Girard, Rene. *A Theater of Envy: William Shakespeare.* New York: Oxford University Press, 1991.

Goldberg, Jonathan. *Sodometries: Renaissance Texts, Modern Sexualities.* Stanford: Stanford University Press, 1992.

Goldman, Michael. *Shakespeare and the Energies of Drama.* Princeton: Princeton University Press, 1972.

Grady, Hugh. *The Modernist Shakespeare: Critical Texts in a Material World.* Oxford: Clarendon Press, 1991.

Greenblatt, Stephen. *Shakespearean Negotiations: The Circulation of Social Energy in Renaissance England.* Berkeley and Los Angeles: University of California Press, 1988.

Hapgood, Robert. *Shakespeare: The Theatre-Poet.* Oxford: Oxford University Press, 1988.

Hawkes, Terence. *Meaning by Shakespeare.* London: Routledge, 1992.

———. *That Shakespeherian Rag.* London: Methuen, 1986.

Hibbard, G. R. *The Making of Shakespeare's Dramatic Poetry.* Toronto: University of Toronto Press, 1981.

Holderness, Graham, ed. *Shakespeare's History Plays: "Richard II" to "Henry V."* New York: St. Martin's Press, 1992.

———, ed. *The Shakespeare Myth.* Manchester: Manchester University Press, 1988.

Holland, Norman. *Psychoanalysis and Shakespeare.* New York: McGraw-Hill, 1966.

———, et al., eds. *Shakespeare's Personality.* Berkeley and Los Angeles: University of California Press, 1989.

Honigmann, E. A. J. *Myriad-Minded Shakespeare: Essays, Chiefly on the Tragedies and Problem Plays.* New York: St. Martin's Press, 1989.

———, ed. *Shakespeare's Impact on His Contemporaries.* London: Macmillan, 1982.

Hope, Jonathan. *The Authorship of Shakespeare's Plays.* Cambridge: Cambridge University Press, 1994.

Houston, John Porter. *Shakespearean Sentences: A Study in Style and Syntax.* Baton Rouge: Louisiana State University Press, 1988.

Howard, Jean. *The Stage and Social Struggle in Early Modern England.* New York: Routledge, 1994.

———, and Marion F. O'Connor, eds. *Shakespeare Reproduced: The Text in History and Ideology.* New York: Methuen, 1987.

Hughes, Ted. *Shakespeare and the Goddess of Complete Being.* London: Faber, 1992.

Hunt, Maurice. *Shakespeare's Labored Art: Stir, Work, and the Late Plays.* New York: Peter Lang, 1995.

Jones, Emrys. *The Origins of Shakespeare.* Oxford: Clarendon Press, 1977.

Kahn, Coppèlia. *Man's Estate: Masculine Identity in Shakespeare.* Berkeley and Los Angeles: University of California Press, 1981.

Kamps, Ivo, ed. *Materialist Shakespeare: A History.* New York: Verso, 1995.

Kastan, David Scott. *Shakespeare and the Shapes of Time.* Hanover: University Press of New England, 1982.

Kermode, Frank, ed. *Four Centuries of Shakespearean Criticism.* 1965. New York: Avon, 1974.

Kernan, Alvin. *Shakespeare, the King's Playwright: Theater in the Stuart Court, 1603–1613.* New Haven: Yale University Press, 1995.

Kirsch, Arthur. *Shakespeare and the Experience of Love.* Cambridge: Cambridge University Press, 1981.

Knapp, Jeffrey. *An Empire Nowhere: England, America, and Literature from "Utopia" to "The Tempest."* Berkeley and Los Angeles: University of California Press, 1992.

Knapp, Robert S. *Shakespeare—The Theater and the Book.* Princeton: Princeton University Press, 1989.

Knight, G. Wilson. *The Wheel of Fire*. 1930. 5th rev. ed. Cleveland: World Publishing, 1962.

Kott, Jan. *Shakespeare Our Contemporary*. Trans. Boleslaw Taborski. Garden City, N.Y.: Doubleday Anchor, 1966.

Laroque, François. *Shakespeare's Festive World: Elizabethan Seasonal Entertainment and the Professional Stage*. Cambridge: Cambridge University Press, 1993.

Lenz, Carolyn Ruth Swift, Gayle Greene, and Carol Thomas Neely, eds. *The Woman's Part: Feminist Criticism of Shakespeare*. Urbana: University of Illinois Press, 1980.

Levin, Harry. *Shakespeare and the Revolution of the Times*. New York: Oxford University Press, 1976.

Levith, Murray J. *Shakespeare's Italian Settings and Plays*. New York: St. Martin's Press, 1989.

Loomba, Ania. *Gender, Race, Renaissance Drama*. Manchester: Manchester University Press, 1989.

Lukacher, Ned. *Daemonic Figures: Shakespeare and the Question of Conscience*. Ithaca, N.Y.: Cornell University Press, 1994.

Mack, Maynard. *Everybody's Shakespeare: Reflections Chiefly on the Tragedies*. Lincoln: University of Nebraska Press, 1993.

Mahon, John W., and Thomas A. Pendleton, eds. *"Fanned and Winnowed Opinion": Shakespearean Essays Presented to Harold Jenkins*. London: Methuen, 1987.

Mallin, Eric S. *Inscribing the Time: Shakespeare and the End of Elizabethan England*. Berkeley and Los Angeles: University of California Press, 1995.

Marcus, Leah S. *Puzzling Shakespeare: Local Reading and Its Discontents*. Berkeley and Los Angeles: University of California Press, 1988.

Maus, Katharine. *Inwardness and Theater in the English Renaissance*. Chicago: University of Chicago Press, 1995.

McDonald, Russ. *The Bedford Companion to Shakespeare: An Introduction with Documents*. Boston: Bedford Books, 1996.

McMullan, Gordon, and Jonathan Hope, eds. *The Politics of Tragicomedy: Shakespeare and After*. London: Routledge, 1992.

Miola, Robert. *Shakespeare's Rome*. Cambridge: Cambridge University Press, 1983.

Mooney, Michael E. *Shakespeare's Dramatic Transactions*. Durham, N.C.: Duke University Press, 1990.

Mowat, Barbara. *The Dramaturgy of Shakespeare's Romances*. Athens: University of Georgia Press, 1976.

Muir, Kenneth. *The Sources of Shakespeare's Plays*. London: Methuen, 1977.

Neely, Carol Thomas. *Broken Nuptials in Shakespeare's Plays*. New Haven: Yale University Press, 1985.

Nevo, Ruth. *Tragic Form in Shakespeare*. Princeton: Princeton University Press, 1972.

Newman, Karen. *Fashioning Femininity and English Renaissance Drama*. Chicago: University of Chicago Press, 1991.

Novy, Marianne. *Love's Argument: Gender Relations in Shakespeare*. Chapel Hill: University of North Carolina Press, 1984.

———, ed. *Women's Re-Visions of Shakespeare*. Urbana: University of Illinois Press, 1990.

O'Brien, Peggy, ed. *Shakespeare Set Free*. 3 vols. New York: Washington Square, 1993–95.

Orkin, Martin. *Shakespeare against Apartheid*. Craighall, South Africa: Ad. Donker, 1987.

Parker, Patricia, and Geoffrey Hartman, eds. *Shakespeare and the Question of Theory*. London: Routledge & Kegan Paul, 1985.

Paster, Gail Kern. *The Body Embarrassed: Drama and the Disciplines of Shame in Early Modern England*. Ithaca, N.Y.: Cornell University Press, 1993.

Patterson, Annabel. *Shakespeare and the Popular Voice*. Oxford: Blackwell, 1989.

Pechter, Edward. *What Was Shakespeare?: Renaissance Plays and Changing Critical Practice*. Ithaca, N.Y.: Cornell University Press, 1995.

Pitt, Angela. *Shakespeare's Women*. Totowa, N.J.: Barnes & Noble, 1981.

Rabkin, Norman. *Shakespeare and the Problem of Meaning.* Chicago: University of Chicago Press, 1981.
———. *Shakespeare and the Common Understanding.* New York: Free Press, 1967.
Rackin, Phyllis. *Stages of History: Shakespeare's English Chronicles.* Ithaca, N.Y.: Cornell University Press, 1990.
Ranald, Margaret Loftis. *Shakespeare and His Social Context: Essays in Osmotic Knowledge and Literary Interpretation.* New York: AMS Press, 1987.
Ryan, Kiernan. *Shakespeare.* 2nd ed. London: Prentice Hall, 1995.
Salingar, Leo. *Dramatic Form in Shakespeare and the Jacobeans.* Cambridge: Cambridge University Press, 1986.
———. *Shakespeare and the Traditions of Comedy.* London: Cambridge University Press, 1974.
Schwartz, Murray, and Coppélia Kahn, eds. *Representing Shakespeare: New Psychoanalytic Essays.* Baltimore: Johns Hopkins University Press, 1980.
Shapiro, Michael. *Gender in Play on the Shakespearean Stage: Boy Heroines and Female Pages.* Ann Arbor: University of Michigan Press, 1994.
Shepard, Simon. *Amazons and Warrior Women: Varieties of Feminism in Seventeenth-Century Drama.* N.Y.: St. Martin's Press, 1981.
Siemon, James. *Shakespearean Iconoclasm.* Berkeley and Los Angeles: University of California Press, 1985.
Skura, Meredith Anne. *Shakespeare the Actor and the Purposes of Playing.* Chicago: University of Chicago Press, 1993.
———. *The Literary Use of the Psychoanalytic Process.* New Haven: Yale University Press, 1981.
Snyder, Susan. *The Comic Matrix of Shakespeare's Tragedies.* Princeton: Princeton University Press, 1979.
Sprengnether, Madelon, and Shirley Nelson Garner, eds. *Shakespearean Tragedy and Gender.* Bloomington: Indiana University Press, 1996.
Stockholder, Kay. *Dream Works: Lovers and Families in Shakespeare's Plays.* Toronto: University of Toronto Press, 1987.
Summers, Joseph H. *Dreams of Love and Power: On Shakespeare's Plays.* Oxford: Clarendon Press, 1984.
Tennenhouse, Leonard. *Power on Display: The Politics of Shakespeare's Genres.* New York: Methuen, 1986.
Thomas, Vivian. *The Moral Universe of Shakespeare's Problem Plays.* New York: Routledge, 1991.
Traub, Valerie. *Desire and Anxiety: Circulations of Sexuality in Shakespearean Drama.* London: Routledge, 1992.
Trousdale, Marion. *Shakespeare and the Rhetoricians.* Chapel Hill: University of North Carolina Press, 1982.
Watson, Robert. *The Rest Is Silence: Death as Annihilation in the English Renaissance.* Berkeley and Los Angeles: University of California Press, 1994.
———. *Shakespeare and the Hazards of Ambition.* Cambridge: Harvard University Press, 1984.
Wells, Robin Headlam. *Shakespeare: Politics and the State.* London: Macmillan, 1986.
Wheeler, Richard P. *Shakespeare's Problem Comedies: Turn and Counter Turn.* Berkeley and Los Angeles: University of California Press, 1981.
Wilson, Richard. *Will Power: Essays on Shakespearean Authority.* Detroit: Wayne State University Press, 1993.
Woodbridge, Linda, and Edward Berry, eds. *True Rites and Maimed Rites: Ritual and Anti-Ritual in Shakespeare and His Age.* Urbana: University of Illinois Press, 1992.
Young, David. *The Action to the Word: Structure and Style in Shakespearean Tragedy.* New Haven: Yale University Press, 1990.
Zimmerman, Susan, ed. *Erotic Politics: Desire on the Renaissance Stage.* New York: Routledge, 1992.

The Dream of the Master Text

Allen, Michael J. B., and Kenneth Muir, eds. *Shakespeare's Plays in Quarto*. Berkeley and Los Angeles: University of California Press, 1981.

Blayney, Peter W. M. *The First Folio of Shakespeare*. Washington: Folger Library Publications, 1991.

——. *The Texts of "King Lear" and Their Origins*. Vol. 1: *Nicholas Okes and the First Quarto*. Cambridge: Cambridge University Press, 1982.

Bower, Fredson. *On Editing Shakespeare*. Charlottesville: University of Virginia Press, 1966.

Crewe, Jonathan. *Trials of Authorship: Anterior Forms and Poetic Reconstruction from Wyatt to Shakespeare*. Berkeley and Los Angeles: University of California Press, 1990.

De Grazia, Margreta. *Shakespeare Verbatim: The Reproduction of Authenticity and the 1790 Apparatus*. Oxford: Oxford University Press, 1991.

——, and Peter Stallybrass. "The Materiality of the Shakespearean Text." *Shakespeare Quarterly* 44 (1993): 255–83.

Franklin, Colin. *Shakespeare Domesticated: The Eighteenth-Century Editions*. Brookfield, Vt.: Scolar Press, 1991.

Greg, W. W., ed. *The Merry Wives of Windsor, 1602*. Oxford: Clarendon Press, 1910.

Hinman, Charlton. *The Norton Facsimile: The First Folio of Shakespeare*. 2nd ed. New York: Norton, 1996.

——. *The Printing and Proof-Reading of the First Folio of Shakespeare*. 2 vols. Oxford: Clarendon Press, 1963.

Honigmann, E. A. J. *The Stability of Shakespeare's Text*. London: E. Arnold, 1965.

Ioppolo, Grace. *Revising Shakespeare*. Cambridge: Harvard University Press, 1991.

Irace, Kathleen O. *Reforming the "Bad" Quartos: Performance and Provenance of Six Shakespearean First Editions*. Newark: University of Delaware Press, 1994.

Maguire, Laurie E. *Shakespeare's Suspect Texts: The "Bad" Quartos and Their Contexts*. Cambridge: Cambridge University Press, 1996.

McKerrow, R. B. *Prolegomena for the Oxford Shakespeare*. Oxford: Clarendon Press, 1939.

Mcleod, Randall, ed. *Crisis in Editing: Texts of the English Renaissance*. New York: AMS Press, 1994.

Pollard, A. W. *Shakespeare's Fight with the Pirates*. Cambridge: Cambridge University Press, 1920.

——. *Shakespeare's Folios and Quartos*. London: Methuen, 1909.

Seary, Peter. *Lewis Theobald and the Editing of Shakespeare*. Oxford: Clarendon Press, 1990.

Taylor, Gary, and Michael Warren, eds. *The Division of the Kingdoms*. Oxford: Clarendon Press, 1983.

Urkowitz, Steven. *Shakespeare's Revision of "King Lear."* Princeton: Princeton University Press, 1980.

Walker, Alice. *Textual Problems of the First Folio*. Cambridge: Cambridge University Press, 1953.

Wells, Stanley. *Re-Editing Shakespeare for the Modern Reader*. New York: Oxford University Press, 1984.

——, and Gary Taylor. *William Shakespeare: A Textual Companion*. Oxford: Clarendon Press, 1987.

——, and Gary Taylor. *Modernizing Shakespeare's Spelling*. Oxford: Clarendon Press, 1979.

Werstine, Paul. "Narratives About Printed Shakespeare Texts: 'Foul Papers' and 'Bad' Quartos." *Shakespeare Quarterly* 41 (1990): 65–86.

Williams, George Walton. *The Craft of Printing and the Publication of Shakespeare's Works*. Washington: Folger Books, 1985.

Wilson, J. Dover. *The Manuscript of Shakespeare's "Hamlet" and the Problems of Its Transmission.* 2 vols. Cambridge, Eng. 1934.

Shakespeare in Performance

Ball, Robert Hamilton. *Shakespeare on Silent Film.* New York: Theater Art Books, 1968.

Bartholomeusz, Dennis. *Macbeth and the Players.* Cambridge: Cambridge University Press, 1969.

Barton, John. *Playing Shakespeare.* London: Methuen, 1984.

Bate, Jonathan, and Russell Jackson, eds. *Shakespeare: An Illustrated Stage History.* New York: Oxford University Press, 1996.

Berger, Harry Jr. *Imaginary Audition: Shakespeare on Stage and Page.* Berkeley and Los Angeles: University of California Press, 1989.

Berry, Francis. *The Shakespeare Inset: Word and Picture.* London: Routledge & Kegan Paul, 1965.

Berry, Ralph. *Changing Styles in Shakespeare.* Boston: Allen & Unwin, 1981.

Bevington, David. *Action Is Eloquence: Shakespeare's Language of Gesture.* Cambridge: Harvard University Press, 1984.

Branam, George C. *Eighteenth-Century Adaptions of Shakespearean Tragedy.* Berkeley and Los Angeles: University of California Press, 1936, 1956, 1973.

Brennan, Anthony. *Onstage and Offstage Worlds in Shakespeare's Plays.* New York: Routledge, 1989.

———. *Shakespeare's Dramatic Structures.* Boston: Routledge & Kegan Paul, 1986.

Brockbank, Philip, ed. *Players of Shakespeare.* Cambridge: Cambridge University Press, 1985.

Brown, Ivor. *Shakespeare and the Actors.* London: Bodley Head, 1970.

Brown, John Russell. *Shakespeare's Dramatic Style.* London: Heineman, 1970.

———. *Shakespeare's Plays in Performance.* New York: St. Martin's Press, 1967.

Bulman, James C., and H. R. Coursen, eds. *Shakespeare on Television.* Hanover, N.H.: University Press of New England, 1988.

———, J. R. Mulryne, and Margaret Shewring. *Shakespeare in Performance Series.* Manchester: Manchester University Press, 1982.

Carlisle, Carol Jones. *Shakespeare from the Greenroom: Actors' Criticisms of Four Major Tragedies.* Chapel Hill, N.C.: University of North Carolina Press, 1969.

Cohn, Ruby. *Modern Shakespeare Offshoots.* Princeton: Princeton University Press, 1976.

Cook, Judith. *Shakespeare's Players.* London: Harrap, 1983.

Dawson, Anthony B. *Indirections—Shakespeare and the Art of Illusion.* Toronto: University of Toronto Press, 1978.

Dean, Winton. "Shakespeare in the Opera House." *Shakespeare Survey* 18 (1965): 75–93.

Donohue, Joseph W., Jr. *Dramatic Character in the English Romantic Age.* Princeton: Princeton University Press, 1970.

Downer, Alan S. *The Eminent Tragedian, William Charles Macready.* Cambridge: Harvard University Press, 1966.

Eckert, Charles W., ed. *Focus on Shakespearean Films.* Englewood Cliffs, N.J.: Prentice-Hall, 1972.

Goldman, Michael. *Acting and Action in Shakespearean Tragedy.* Princeton: Princeton University Press, 1985.

Hartwig, Joan. *Shakespeare's Analogical Scene: Parody as Structural Syntax.* Lincoln: University of Nebraska Press, 1983.

Hirsch, James F. *The Structures of Shakespearean Scenes.* New Haven: Yale University Press, 1981.

Hogan, Charles B., ed. *Shakespeare in the Theatre, 1701–1800.* 2 vols. Oxford: Clarendon Press, 1952–57.

Homan, Sidney, ed. *When the Theater Turns to Itself: The Aesthetic Metaphor in Shakespeare.* Lewiston, Pa.: Bucknell University Press, 1981.

——, ed. *Shakespeare's "More Than Words Can Witness": Essays on Visual and Nonverbal Enactment in the Plays.* Lewisburg, Pa.: Bucknell University Press, 1980.

Howard, Jean E. *Shakespeare's Art of Orchestration: Stage Technique and Audience Response.* Urbana: University of Illinois Press, 1984.

Jones, Emrys. *Scenic Form in Shakespeare.* Oxford: Clarendon Press, 1971.

Jorgens, Jack L. *Shakespeare on Film.* Bloomington: Indiana University Press, 1976.

Manvell, Roger. *Shakespeare and the Film.* London: Dent, 1971.

McGuire, Philip C. *Speechless Dialect: Shakespeare's Open Silences.* Berkeley and Los Angeles: University of California Press, 1983.

——, and David A. Samuelson. *Shakespeare: The Theatrical Dimension.* New York: AMS Press, 1979.

Odell, George C. D. *Shakespeare from Betterton to Irving.* 2 vols. New York: Scribner, 1920, 1966.

Poel, William. *Shakespeare in the Theatre.* 1913, 1968. New York: AMS Press, 1974.

Rosenberg, Marvin. *The Masks of Lear.* Berkeley and Los Angeles: University of California Press, 1972.

Rutter, Carol, et al. *Clamorous Voices: Shakespeare's Women Today.* London: Women's Press, 1988.

Shattuck, Charles H. *Shakespeare on the American Stage from the Hallams to Edwin Booth.* Washington, D.C.: Folger Shakespeare Library, 1976. . . . *from Booth and Barrett to Sothern and Marlowe.* Washington, D.C.: Folger Shakespeare Library, 1987.

——. *The Shakespeare Promptbooks: A Descriptive Catalogue.* Urbana: University of Illinois Press, 1965.

Slater, Ann Pasternak. *Shakespeare the Director.* Totowa, N.J.: Barnes & Noble, 1982.

Speaight, Robert. *Shakespeare on the Stage: An Illustrated History of Shakespearian Performance.* Boston: Little, Brown, 1973.

——. *William Poel and the Elizabethan Revival.* London: Heineman, 1954.

Spencer, Hazelton. *Shakespeare Improved: The Restoration Versions in Quarto and on the Stage.* Cambridge, Mass., 1927.

Sprague, Arthur Colby. *Shakespearian Players and Performances.* Cambridge: Harvard University Press, 1953.

——. *Shakespeare and the Actors.* Cambridge: Harvard University Press, 1944.

Styan, J. L. "Sight and Space: The Perception of Shakespeare on Stage and Screen." *Shakespeare, Pattern of Excelling Nature.* Ed. David Bevington and Jay L. Halio. Newark: University of Delaware Press, 1978.

——. *Shakespeare's Stagecraft.* Cambridge: Cambridge University Press, 1967.

Thaler, Alwin. *Shakespeare to Sheridan.* Cambridge, Mass.: Arno Press, 1922.

Thompson, Marvin and Ruth, eds. *Shakespeare and the Sense of Performance.* Newark: University of Delaware Press, 1989.

Trewin, J. C. *Shakespeare on the English Stage, 1900–1964.* London: Barrie & Rockliff, 1964.

Van den Berg, Kent. *Playhouse and Cosmos: Shakespearean Theater as Metaphor.* Newark: University of Delaware Press, 1985.

Wells, Stanley. *Royal Shakespeare: Four Major Productions at Stratford-upon-Avon.* Manchester: Manchester University Press, 1977.

Glossary

"Above" The gallery on the upper level of the *frons scenae*. In open-air theaters, such as the Globe, this space contained the lords' rooms. The central section of the gallery was sometimes used by the players for short scenes. Indoor theaters such as Blackfriars featured a curtained alcove for musicians above the stage.

"Aloft" See *"Above."*

Amphitheater An open-air theater, such as the Globe.

Arras See *Curtain.*

Cellerage See *Trap.*

Chorus In the works of Shakespeare and other Elizabethan playwrights, a single individual (not, as in Greek tragedy, a group) who speaks before the play (and often before each act), describing events not shown on stage as well as commenting on the action witnessed by the audience.

Curtain Curtains, or arras (hanging tapestries), covered a part of the *frons scenae*, thus concealing the discovery space, and may also have been draped around the edge of the stage to conceal the open area underneath.

Discovery space A central opening or alcove concealed behind a curtain in the center of the *frons scenae*. The curtain could be drawn aside to "discover" tableaux such as Portia's caskets, the body of Polonius, or the statue of Hermione. Shakespeare appears to have used this stage device only sparingly.

Doubling The common practice of having one actor play multiple roles, so that a play with a large cast of characters might be performed by a relatively small company.

Dumb shows Mimed scenes performed before a play (or before each act), summarizing or foreshadowing the plot. Dumb shows were popular in early Elizabethan drama, but although they already seemed old-fashioned in Shakespeare's time, they were employed by writers up to the 1640s.

Epilogue A brief speech or poem addressed to the audience by an actor after the play. In some cases, as in *2 Henry IV*, the epilogue could be combined with, or could merge into, the jig.

Forestage The front of the stage, closest to the audience.

Frons scenae The wall at the back of the stage, behind which lay the players' tiring-house. The *frons scenae* of the Globe featured two doors flanking the central discovery space, with a gallery "above."

Gallery Covered seating areas surrounding the open yard of the public amphitheaters. There were three levels of galleries at the Globe; admission to these seats cost an extra penny (in addition to the basic admission fee of one penny to the yard), and seating in the higher galleries another penny yet. In indoor theaters such as Blackfriars, where there was no standing room, gallery seating was less expensive than seating in the pit; indeed, seats nearest the stage were the most expensive.

Gatherers Persons employed by the playing company to take money at the entrances to the theater.

Groundlings Audience members who paid the minimum price of admission (one penny) to stand in the yard of the open-air theaters; also referred to as "understanders."

Heavens Canopied roof over the stage in the open-air theaters, protecting the players and their costumes from rain. The "heavens" would be brightly decorated with sun, moon, and stars, and perhaps the signs of the zodiac.

Hut A structure on the top of the cover over the stage, where stagehands produced the effects of thunder and lightning and operated the machinery by which gods, such as Jupiter in *Cymbeline*, descended through the trapdoor in the "heavens."

Jig A song-and-dance performance by the clown and other members of the company at the conclusion of a play. These performances were frequently bawdy and were officially banned in 1612.

Lords' rooms Partitioned sections of the gallery "above," where the most prestigious and expensive seats in the public playhouses were located. These rooms were designed not to provide the best view of the action on the stage below, but to make their privileged occupants conspicuous to the rest of the audience.

Open-air theaters Unroofed public playhouses in the suburbs of London, such as the Theatre, the Rose, and the Globe.

Part The character played by an actor. In Shakespeare's theater, actors were given a roll of paper called a "part" containing all of the speeches and all of the cues belonging to their character. The term "role," synonymous with "part," is derived from such rolls of paper.

Patrons Important nobles and members of the royal family under whose protection the theatrical companies of London operated; players not in the service of patrons were punishable as vagabonds. The companies were referred to as their patrons' "Men" or "Servants." Thus the name of the company to which Shakespeare belonged for most of his career was first the Lord Chamberlain's Men, then was changed to the King's Men in 1603, when James I became their patron.

Pillars The "heavens" were supported by two tall painted pillars or posts near the front of the stage. These occasionally played a role in stage action, allowing a character to "hide" while remaining in full view of the audience.

Pit The area in front of the stage in indoor theaters such as Blackfriars, where the most expensive and prestigious bench seating was to be had.

Posts See *Pillars*.

Proscenium The space of the transparent "fourth wall," which divides the actors from the orchestra and audience in the standard modern theater. The stages on which Shakespeare's plays were first performed had no proscenium.

Rearstage The back of the stage, farthest from the audience.

Repertory The stock of plays a company had ready for performance at a given time. Companies generally performed a different play each day, often more than a dozen plays in a month and more than thirty in the course of the season.

Role See *Part*.

Sharers   Senior actors holding shares in a joint-stock theatrical company; they paid for costumes, hired hands, and new plays, and they shared profits and losses equally. Shakespeare was not only a longtime "sharer" of the Lord Chamberlain's Men but, from 1599, a "housekeeper," the holder of a one-eighth share in the Globe playhouse.

Tiring-house   The players' dressing (attiring) room, a structure located at the back of the stage and connected to the stage by two or more doors in the *frons scenae*.

Trap   A trapdoor near the front of the stage that allowed access to the "cellarage" beneath and was frequently associated with hell's mouth. Another trapdoor in the "heavens" opened for the descent of gods to the stage below.

"Within"   The tiring-house, from which offstage sound effects such as shouts, drums, and trumpets were produced.

Yard   The central space in open-air theaters such as the Globe, into which the stage projected and in which audience members stood. Admission to the yard in the public theaters cost a penny, the cheapest admission available.

TEXTUAL TERMS

Aside   See *Stage direction.*

Autograph   Text written in the author's own hand. With the possible exception of a few pages of the collaborative play *Sir Thomas More*, no dramatic works or poems written in Shakespeare's hand are known to survive.

Canonical   Of an author, the writings generally accepted as authentic. In the case of Shakespeare's dramatic works, only two plays that are not among the thirty-six plays contained in the First Folio, *Pericles* and *The Two Noble Kinsmen*, have won widespread acceptance into the Shakespearean canon. (This sense of "canonical" should not be confused with the use of "the canon" to denote the entire body of literary works, including but not limited to Shakespeare's, that have traditionally been regarded as fit objects of admiration and study.)

Catchword   A word printed below the text at the bottom of a page, matching the first word on the following page. The catchword enabled the printer to keep the pages in their proper sequence. Where the catchword fails to match the word at the top of the next page, there is reason to suspect that something has been lost or misplaced.

Compositor   Person employed in a print shop to set type. To speed the printing process, most of Shakespeare's plays were set by more than one compositor. Compositors frequently followed their own standards in spelling and punctuation. They inevitably introduced some errors into the text, often by selecting the wrong piece from the type case or by setting the correct letter upside-down.

Conflation   A version of a play created by combining readings from more than one substantive edition. Since the early eighteenth century, for example, most versions of *King Lear* and of several other plays by Shakespeare have been conflations of quarto and First Folio texts.

Control text   The text upon which a modern edition is based.

Dramatis personae   A list of the characters appearing in the play. In the First Folio such lists were printed at the end of some but not all of the plays. The editor

Nicholas Rowe (1709) first provided lists of dramatis personae for all of Shakespeare's dramatic works.

Exeunt / Exit   See *Stage direction.*

Fair copy   A transcript of the "foul papers" made either by a scribe or by the playwright.

Folio   A book-making format in which each large sheet of paper is folded once, making two leaves (four pages front and back). This format produced large volumes, generally handsome and expensive. The First Folio of Shakespeare's plays was printed in 1623.

Foul papers   An author's first completed draft of a play, typically full of blotted-out passages and revisions. None of Shakespeare's foul papers is known to survive.

Licensing   By an order of 1581, new plays could not be performed until they had received a license from the Master of the Revels. A separate license, granted by the Court of High Commission, was required for publication, though in practice plays were often printed without license. From 1610, the Master of the Revels had the authority to license plays for publication as well as for performance.

Manent / Manet   See *Stage direction.*

Memorial reconstruction   The conjectured practice of reconstructing the text of a play from memory. Companies touring in the provinces without access to prompt-books may have resorted to memorial reconstruction. This practice also provides a plausible explanation for the existence of the so-called bad quartos.

Octavo   A book-making format in which each large sheet of paper is folded three times, making eight leaves (sixteen pages front and back). Only one of Shakespeare's plays, *Richard Duke of York* (3 *Henry VI,* 1595), was published in octavo format.

Playbook   See *Promptbook.*

Press variants   Minor textual variations among books of the same edition, resulting from corrections made in the course of printing or from damaged or slipped type.

Promptbook   A manuscript of a play (either foul papers or fair copy) annotated and adapted for performance by the theatrical company. The promptbook incorporated stage directions, notes on properties and special effects, and revisions, sometimes including those required by the Master of the Revels. Promptbooks are usually identifiable by the replacement of characters' names with actors' names.

Quarto   A book-making format in which each large sheet of paper is folded twice, making four leaves (eight pages front and back). Quarto volumes were smaller and less expensive than books printed in the folio format.

Scribal copy   A transcript of a play produced by a professional scribe (or "scrivener"). Scribes tended to employ their own preferred spellings and abbreviations and could be responsible for introducing a variety of errors.

Speech prefix (s.p.)   The indication of the identity of the speaker of the following line or lines. Early editions of Shakespeare's plays often use different prefixes at different points to designate the same person. On occasion, the name of the actor who was to play the role appears in place of the name of the character.

Stage direction (s.d.)   The part of the text that is not spoken by any character but that indicates actions to be performed onstage. Stage directions in the earliest editions of Shakespeare's plays are sparse and are sometimes grouped together at the beginning of a scene rather than next to the spoken lines they should precede, accompany, or follow. By convention, the most basic stage directions were written in Latin. "Exit" indicates the departure of a single actor from the stage, "exeunt" the departure of more than one. "Manet" indicates that a single actor remains onstage, "manent" that more than one remains. Lines accompanied by the stage direction "aside" are spoken so as not to be heard by the others on stage. This stage direction appeared in some early editions of Shakespeare plays, but other means were also used to indicate such speech (such as placing the words within parentheses), and sometimes no indication was provided.

Stationers' Register The account books of the Company of Stationers (of which all printers were legally required to be members), recording the fees paid for permission to print new works as well as the fines exacted for printing without permission. The Stationers' Register thus provides a valuable if incomplete record of publication in England.

Substantive text The text of an edition based upon access to a manuscript, as opposed to a derivative text based only on an earlier edition.

Variorum editions Comprehensive editions of a work or works in which the various views of previous editors and commentators are compiled.

ILLUSTRATION ACKNOWLEDGMENTS

General Introduction   Plague death bill: By permission of the Folger Shakespeare Library • Webbe: By permission of the British Library • Amman: Spencer Collection, The New York Public Library, Astor, Lenox and Tilden Foundation • *Swetnam* title page: By permission of The Huntington Library, San Marino, California • Pope as Antichrist: By permission of the Folger Shakespeare Library • de Heere: The National Museum of Wales • Armada portrait: By kind permission of Marquess of Tavistock and Trustees of the Bedford Estate • Boaistuau: By permission of The Huntington Library, San Marino, California • Mandeville: By permission of the Houghton Library, Harvard University • Funeral procession: Additional Ms. 35324, folio 37v. By permission of the British Library • Gheeraerts: By permission of the Trustees of Dulwich Picture Gallery • van den Broek: Fitzwilliam Museum, University of Cambridge • Swimming: Bodleian Library, University of Oxford, 4°G.17.Art • Panorama of London: By permission of the British Library • Tarleton: Harley 3885, folio 19. By permission of the British Library • Hanging: Pepys Library, Magdalene College, Cambridge • Syphilis victim: By permission of The Huntington Library, San Marino, California • *Spanish Tragedy* title page: By permission of the Folger Shakespeare Library • Stratford-upon-Avon: By permission of City of York Libraries • Cholmondeley sisters: Tate Gallery, London • Alleyn: By permission of the Trustees of Dulwich Picture Library • *If You Know Not Me* title page: By permission of The Huntington Library, San Marino, California • van der Straet: By permission of the Folger Shakespeare Library

Titus Andronicus   Tempesta: © British Museum • van der Noot: Reproduced by permission of The Huntington Library, San Marino, California

Romeo and Juliet   Wither: By permission of the Houghton Library, Harvard University • Speed: By permission of the Folger Shakespeare Library

Julius Caesar   Plutarch (Caesar and Marc Antony): By permission of the Folger Shakespeare Library • Whitney: By permission of the Folger Shakespeare Library

Hamlet   Clerke: By permission of the Houghton Library, Harvard University • von Landshut: © British Museum • Saviolo: By permission of the Folger Shakespeare Library

Othello   Moorish ambassador: Reproduced by permission of the Shakespeare Institute, University of Birmingham, UK • Knight: By permission of the Folger Shakespeare Library

Timon of Athens   Inigo Jones: Devonshire Collection, Chatsworth. Reproduced by permission of the Duke of Devonshire and the Chatsworth Settlement Trustees. Photo credit: The Courtauld Institute of Art • Wither: By permission of the Houghton Library, Harvard University

King Lear   Holinshed: By permission of the Houghton Library, Harvard University • Cypriano: By permission of the Houghton Library, Harvard University • Gheeraerts: Tom Durie by Marcus Gheeraerts the Younger, 1614. The Scottish National Portrait Gallery

Macbeth   Firens: Bibliothèque Nationale de France • Holinshed: By permission of the Houghton Library, Harvard University • Witchcraft: Courtesy of the Archbishop of Canterbury and the Trustees of Lambeth Palace Library

Antony and Cleopatra   du Choul: By permission of the Folger Shakespeare Library • Topsell: By permission of the Folger Shakespeare Library

Coriolanus   Amman (attack on Colioli; Volumnia entreating Coriolanus): Rare Books and Manuscripts Division, The New York Public Library, Astor, Lenox and Tilden Foundations

The Shakespearean Stage   Braun and Hogenburg: 8.Tab.c.4. Bk.1.pl.1. By permission of the British Library • Hollar: Guildhall Library, Corporation of London • Interior of the "new" Globe: Courtesy of The International Shakespeare Globe Center Ltd. Photo: John Tramper • Exterior of the "new" Globe: Courtesy of The International Shakespeare Globe Center Ltd. Photo: Richard Kalina • Frons scenae of the "new" Globe: Courtesy of The International Shakespeare Globe Center Ltd. Photo: Richard Kalina • Oliver: The Burghley House Collection. Photograph: Courtauld Institute of Art • Peacham: Reproduced by permission of the Marquess of Bath, Longleat House, Warminster, Wiltshire, Great Britain. Photograph: Courtauld Institute of Art • de Witt: University Library, Utrecht, MS 842, f.132r • Middle Temple Hall: The Benchers of the Honorable Society of the Middle Temple, London • Hollar: Guildhall Library, Corporation of London

Contemporary Documents

First Folio front matter: *The Norton Facsimile of the First Folio of Shakespeare*, 2nd ed. (1996)

A Shakespearean Chronicle, 1558–1616

Master John: By courtesy of the National Portrait Gallery, London • Geneva Bible page: Bodleian Library, University of Oxford, Bibl.Eng.1560 • Swordsmen: By permission of the Folger Shakespeare Library • Holinshed (burning city): By permission of the Houghton Library, Harvard University • Holinshed (naval battle): By permission of the Houghton Library, Harvard University • Henri III: By permission of the Folger Shakespeare Library • Witches: C.27.b.35. By permission of the British Library • Agas: Guildhall Library, Corporation of London • Plague woodcut: Ashley 617. By permission of the British Library • Coat of Arms: Shakespeare Drafts (Vincent 157, no. 23). By permission of the College of Arms • Earl of Essex: © British Museum • Execution of Essex: By permission of the Folger Shakespeare Library • Vertue sketch: Additional Ms. 70438, folio 18. By permission of the British Library • Holinshed (Macbeth's coronation): By permission of the Houghton Library, Harvard University • Inigo Jones: Devonshire Collection, Chatsworth. Reproduced by permission of the Duke of Devonshire and the Chatsworth Settlement Trustees. Photo credit: The Courtauld Institute of Art • Henry, Prince of Wales: Fitzwilliam Museum, University of Cambridge • van de Passe (James I): Bodleian Library, University of Oxford, E 14 Th.Seld